Romania under Commu

Communism has cast a long shadow over Romania. The passage of little over a quarter of a century since the overthrow in December 1989 of Romania's last Communist leader, Nicolae Ceauşescu, offers a symbolic standpoint from which to penetrate that shadow and to throw light upon the entire period of Communist rule in the country. An appropriate point of departure is the observation that Romania's trajectory as a Communist state within the Soviet bloc was unlike that of any other. That trajectory has its origins in the social structures, attitudes and policies in the pre-Communist period. The course of that trajectory is the subject of this inquiry.

Dennis Deletant is Visiting Ion Raţiu Professor of Romanian Studies in the School of Foreign Service at Georgetown University, Washington DC, and Emeritus Professor of Romanian Studies at University College, London.

Routledge Histories of Central and Eastern Europe

https://www.routledge.com/Routledge-Histories-of-Central-and-Eastern-Europe/book-series/CEE

1 Hungary since 1945

Árpád von Klimó, translated by Kevin McAleer

2 Romania under Communism

Denis Deletant

3 Bulgaria under Communism

Ivaylo Znepolski, Mihail Gruev, Momtchil Metodiev, Martin Ivanov, Daniel Vatchkov, Ivan Elenkov, Plamen Doynow

Romania under Communism

Paradox and Degeneration

Dennis Deletant

Routledge
Taylor & Francis Group
LONDON AND NEW YORK

First published 2019
by Routledge
2 Park Square, Milton Park, Abingdon, Oxon OX14 4RN

and by Routledge
52 Vanderbilt Avenue, New York, NY 10017

First issued in paperback 2020

Routledge is an imprint of the Taylor & Francis Group, an informa business

British Library Cataloguing-in-Publication Data
A catalogue record for this book is available from the British Library

Library of Congress Cataloging-in-Publication Data
A catalog record has been requested for this book

ISBN 13: 978-0-367-58557-0 (pbk)
ISBN 13: 978-1-138-70742-9 (hbk)

Typeset in Goudy
by Sunrise Setting Ltd, Brixham, UK

MIX
Paper from responsible sources
FSC™ C013985
FSC www.fsc.org

Printed in the United Kingdom
by Henry Ling Limited

For Andrea, with gratitude for her support and her patience

Contents

Acknowledgements

Without the assistance of numerous friends and several institutions this study would not have been completed. Among the latter I wish to acknowledge the support given to me through the award of travel grants by The School of Slavonic and East European Studies of University College, London, where I taught between 1969 and 2011, the University of Amsterdam, to which I was seconded for several semesters between 2003 and 2010, and my present academic home, Georgetown University, where since August 2011 I have the honour of being the Ion Raţiu Visiting Professor of Romanian Studies. Indeed, the completion of this study was greatly facilitated by the generosity of the Raţiu Family Foundation and the encouragement of Nicolae Raţiu.

Among my many friends in Romania I wish to thank first and foremost George Cipăianu and his brother Enea. They are my invaluable anchor in Cluj-Napoca, extending a warm welcome in their home and providing me with countless opportunities to review the progress of my study with them and their colleagues at the Babeş-Bolyai University, Ioan Piso, Liviu Ţîrău, Ioan Ciupea, Marius Bucur, Gheorghe Mândrescu, and Ştefan Matei and Ottmar Traşca of the Romanian Academy 'Gheorghe Bariţiu' Institute of History in Cluj-Napoca. Virgiliu Ţârău, Professor of History at Babeş-Bolyai and Vice President of the National Council for the Study of the *Securitate* Archives (CNSAS) deserves special recognition for facilitating access to the files of Romania's Communist security police. Virgiliu has extended down the years the warm hand of friendship which transcends the bounds of formal contact. Claudiu Secaşiu, at the same institution, has played an invaluable role in identifying sources for me, and I remain especially indebted to him and to the archival staff of the CNSAS.

In Bucharest, family friends Mihaela, Ana and the late Sandu Hodoş, deserve particular mention. Without their decades-long hospitality and stimulating conversation on all matters Romanian I would not have gained those insights which are necessary for a sensitive understanding of the country's past. Ana Blandiana, the late Romulus Rusan and Ioana Boca, the heart and soul and backbone of the Sighet Memorial and of the Civic Academy Foundation, through their generosity of spirit, enabled me to know and draw upon the experience of many victims of the Communist regime. I have derived enormous benefit from the discussion of my research with Şerban Papacostea and Andrei Pippidi, both of whom I am honoured to count as close personal friends, while Ioan Chiper, Viorel Achim and Cristian Vasile have all enriched my knowledge of particular aspects of Communist rule in Romania. Armand Goşu, Stejărel Olaru, Andrei Muraru, Dragoş Petrescu, Ştefan Bosomitu, Marius Stan and Dumitru Lăcătuş helped me to identity and access secondary Romanian literature and relevant journal publications. Marius Oprea merits special thanks. Our shared experiences in challenging a Communist mentality with regard to access to research materials in the 1990s forged a close bond of friendship between us and Marius's intrepidness allowed me to broaden my knowledge and understanding of the activity of the *Securitate*.

In London, Dan Brett, Irina Marin, Trevor Thomas, Martyn Rady, Radu Cinpoeş, Alex Boican and Alex Drace-Francis (on his visits from Amsterdam) provided invaluable intellectual stimulation. In Washington DC, my wife and I were especially privileged to form a firm friendship with Mircea Răceanu and his wife Mioara. Mircea was generous in sharing with me his intimate experience of the activity of the Romanian Foreign Ministry over a thirty-year period from 1959, thereby enriched my understanding of Ceauşescu's foreign policy which I trust that I have brought to this study. I was also fortunate to receive precious insights into Communist Romania from Vladimir Tismăneanu to whom I am especially grateful. Discussion with my friends Ernest Latham, Radu Ioanid and the late Andrei Brezianu has given me fresh perspectives on the policies of Ceauşescu. Grant Harris at the Library of Congress identified a number of relevant sources which otherwise would have escaped me. Ruth Sulynn Taylor in Charles Town, West Virginia and Mick and Irene Schubert in Mount Vernon have been gracious and affectionate hosts to my wife and to me. Angela Stent, the Director of the Center for Eurasian, Russian and East European Studies at Georgetown University, Benjamin Loring, her deputy, and Cristina Watts and Sarah Radomsky, the Center's administrative officers, have leavened the invaluable support which they have given to my academic endeavours with charm and good humour, while I have always been able to count upon the perceptive insights of Charles King to fine-tune my understanding of Romania's relations with its neighbours in south-eastern and eastern Europe.

My greatest intellectual debt is owed to Maurice Pearton. His acute appreciation of twentieth-century economic and political history saved me from a number of misguided judgements. I regard it as an honour to be counted among his friends and record here my gratitude for his unstinting assistance and respect for his invaluable guidance in my research over the last forty years.

For my wife Andrea I reserve my most profound admiration for her good-humoured understanding and forbearance during frequent periods of self-imposed quarantine in my study whilst giving substance and shape to this book.

July 2017

Biographies of key figures

Gheorghiu-Dej and Nicolae Ceauşescu play a dominant role in this study and are naturally omnipresent in its pages

Gheorghe Apostol (Tudor Vladimirescu, Galaţi, 16 May, 1913; Bucharest, 21 August 2010) is believed to have joined the Communist Party in 1934. In 1937, he was sentenced to three years' jail for membership of the outlawed party and held in Târgu-Jiu prison until his escape in August 1944. He was made head of the Communist trade unions association after 1944 and appointed a member of the Politburo. In 1954, he was named First Secretary of the Romanian Workers' Party with the approval of Gheorghiu-Dej for a year after the fallout from Stalin's death, and then first vice prime minister when Gheorghiu-Dej resumed his leadership of the party. His close association with Gheorghiu-Dej led him to consider himself the latter's successor but his ambition was thwarted by Ion Gheorghe Maurer who engineered the appointment of Nicolae Ceauşescu. Apostol's resentment was translated into periodic critical memoranda addressed to the latter. Following an attack on him by Constantin Dăscălescu at the RCP's Tenth Congress in 1969, Apostol was removed from the Politburo. Between 1977 and 1988, he served successively as Romanian ambassador to Argentina, Uruguay and Brazil. He was the principal author of the "Letter of the Six" broadcast by the international media in March 1989. For further details of Apostol see chapter ten.

Alexandru Bârlădeanu (Comrat, Bessarabia, 25 January 1911; Bucharest, 13 November 1997). Bârlădeanu completed his secondary schooling at Iaşi and in 1932 was taken on as a lecturer in political economics at the University of Iaşi. He appears to have been active in the National Peasant Party at this time since Corneliu Coposu, its youth leader, recalls that Bârlădeanu was presented to him during a visit he made to the town (C. Coposu, *Dialoguri*, p.67). Bârlădeanu admitted to being a Communist from his student days and having flirted with the NPP, but he left the latter after its handling of the Griviţa strikes in 1933. The Soviet annexation of Bessarabia caught him there on holiday at his mother's house and he remained in the province. He worked at an economics institute in Chişinău until the outbreak of war in 1941, when he was evacuated to Kazakhstan. Poor eyesight saved him from conscription and he was sent down a coal mine in Karaganda for several months before persuading a local Party boss to assign him to a secondary school in the town teaching mathematics. In 1943, he was sent to Moscow for doctoral studies and returned to Romania in 1946. Bârlădeanu's unusually long stay in the Soviet Union led to rumours that he was in fact a Russian and a member of the Soviet Communist Party, but he denied these, claiming that he joined the Romanian Communist Party in 1946 (Lavinia Betea, *Maurer şi lumea de ieri*, pp.289–90).

Emil Bodnăraş (Colomea, 10 February 1904; Bucharest, 24 January 1976). There are many questions marks over Bodnăraş's real loyalties. According to his party file he was born in Colomea (now in the Ukraine) on 10 February 1904 of Ukrainian-German parentage. (I am grateful to Claudiu Secaşiu for this information). Bodnăraş studied law at Iaşi University where, according to his official obituary, he first came into contact with Marxist groups. He then joined the officers' academy in Timişoara where he completed his training in 1927 (*Anale de istorie*, vol.22, 1976, no.1, p.189). His obituary says nothing about the following seven years until his arrest and his sentencing in 1934 to ten years hard labour. The gap has been filled from other sources. In 1927, he was posted to Craiova with the rank of lieutenant and later transferred to a barracks at Sadagura in northern Romania only thirty kilometres from the river Dniester and the border with the Soviet Union. From there he defected to the Soviet Union on the night of 16–17 February 1932 (Stelian Tănase, *Clienţii lu' Tanti Varvara*, Bucharest: Humanitas, 2005, p.175. Two questions arise at this point. Why should Bodnăraş, with his Ukrainian background, be posted so close to the Soviet frontier? Was he, perhaps, recruited by Romanian military intelligence and his defection planned? Information from the KGB archives suggests answers to these questions. It claims that it was as the military intelligence officer of the 12th artillery regiment based in Sadagura that Bodnăraş was sent into the Soviet Union. He was turned, however, by the Soviets and was trained as an agent at school in the town of Astrakhan (G. Iavorschi, "Pentru cine a lucrat 'inginerul Ceauşu'?", *Magazin Istoric*, vol.28, no.9 (September 1994), p.18). Bodnăraş admitted as much in a meeting of the Politburo held on 13–14 March 1961: "Towards the end of 1933 [Vyacheslav] Menzhinsky was still alive [and] he headed the special agency where I worked [...] my contact was one of the deputy heads of this service". Menzhinsky was the head of the OGPU (Soviet Security Service) from 1926 until his death in May 1934, when he was succeeded by his first deputy, Genrikh Yagoda, who may have been the deputy to whom Bodnăraş was referring. Bodnăraş fondly reminisced about his treatment by the Soviets:

> The Soviet secret services were particularly considerate towards me and took care to brief me, giving me access to books and papers so that I didn't get cut off from events in Romania. I also received the daily *Universul*. When the strike at the Griviţa yards took place (February 1933), the Soviets brought me from my lodgings to their headquarters where I spent several days following the information that they received from their secret services who were noting what was happening.

'Stenogram of the RWP Politburo meeting of 13–14 March 1961'—my thanks to Marius Oprea for passing onto me a copy of this document. The stenogram is cited in Tănase with the reference Arhiva CC al PCR [Archive of the Central Committee of the Romanian Communist Party], Biroul Politic, MTG, 12–14 March, 1961 (S.Tănase, *Clienţii lu' Tanti Varvara*, p.185). This archive is held in the National Central Historical Archives (ANIC) in Bucharest. A number of Romanian intelligence officers who served during and immediately after the Second World War have stated that Bodnăraş's fluent knowledge of German allowed him to be used on various espionage missions by the NKVD in Poland and the Baltic republics before being sent to Bulgaria in 1934. At the end of July, en route through Romania, he was recognized in the Gara de Nord station in Bucharest and arrested. He was tried for desertion, for stealing documents, and for crimes against the country's security by a military tribunal in Iaşi two months later and found guilty. His sentence was confirmed on 19 February 1935: 10 years' imprisonment (S.Tănase, *Clienţii lu' Tanti Varvara*, p.184). Other questions arise. Why was he sent by his Soviet masters to Bulgaria by train through Romania, with all the risks of recognition that the journey entailed, when he could have travelled direct by boat from Odessa to Burgas? Was he sent deliberately by train in the hope that he would be caught by the Romanians as a Soviet spy and imprisoned with the Romanian Communists whom he could infiltrate on behalf of the NKVD? Was he, in fact, a double agent? His mission from the Soviets may well have been to evaluate Gheorghiu-Dej because the latter, unlike other leading figures in the RCP, had not studied in the Soviet Union. Serghei Nikonov, the Soviet-trained head of the SSI (the Romanian Intelligence Service) from 1946 to 1951, expressed the conviction in a conversation in 1988 with Titu Simon, a former officer in Romanian military intelligence, that Bodnăraş had been recruited in the 1920s by an officer in the SSI named Florin Becescu (cover name Georgescu) to penetrate the NKVD and that this was the purpose of his mission to the Soviet Union. In 1947, information was passed to Bodnăraş by the Soviets that Georgescu had worked as a double agent, for both the Romanians and the Soviets, and Bodnăraş gave orders for his liquidation, before Nikonov could investigate the charges. The reason for Bodnăraş's haste, Nikonov believed, was to prevent the emergence of any details of his recruitment by Becescu (T. Simon, *Pacepa: Quo Vadis*, Bucharest: Odeon, 1992, pp.77–78). Simon's account of Bodnăraş's hand in Becescu's death is corroborated by Traian Borcescu, head of the counter-intelligence section of the SSI between 1941 and 1944. Becescu joined the Communist Party after 23 August 1944 and was appointed head of counter-intelligence in the SSI (he had held this post until 1941). However, he released information about Ana Pauker's private life as a young woman and lost the confidence of Bodnăraş. It was for this indiscretion that Bodnăraş, according to Borcescu, ordered Becescu's removal. While travelling to attend a meeting in Sinaia on the orders of Bodnăraş, Becescu's car was ambushed and he was shot dead by Communist agents (author's interview with Traian Borcescu, 8 March 1995). Bodnăraş served his sentence for desertion at Doftana, Aiud, Galaţi and Braşov, according to the official obituary. He was also held at Caransebeş jail, for he was seen there by a fellow inmate Mircea Oprişan, in 1942 (letter to the author from M. Oprişan, 29 August 1994). In Doftana Bodnăraş formed a close friendship with Gheorghiu-Dej and became a member of the Communist Party. He was released from prison on 7 November 1942 at the suggestion of the SSI (the Romanian Intelligence Service) and settled in the town of Brăila near the mouth of the Danube. It was here that, in return for payments made to Rânzescu, the local inspector of police who was a friend of SSI head Eugen Cristescu, he was able to wander freely around the town and its outskirts and consequently to pick up instructions dropped by Soviet planes on the outskirts of town. Using the cover of a commercial representative for a small company based in Brăila and the name of 'engineer Ceauşu', Bodnăraş travelled freely, albeit under the surveillance of the *Siguranţa* (security service), and he was a frequent visitor to Bucharest. There Bodnăraş collected information from an agent named Kendler, a timber merchant who on instructions from Bodnăraş, paid a sum of 30,000 lei monthly in 1943 to Colonel Enache Borcescu, a member of the Romanian General Staff, for information about Romanian and German troop movements. Kendler's regular meeting place with Borcescu was a Greco-Catholic church in Bucharest (author's interview with Traian Borcescu, 8 March 1995). Bodnăraş was also a frequent visitor to Târgu-Jiu where, by suborning Colonel Şerban Lioveanu, the commandant of the internment camp, he was able to consult Gheorghiu-Dej on several occasions. Drawing on secret Communist Party funds, Bodnăraş bought weapons from German soldiers based in Romania in order to arm Communist detachments which he formed in Bucharest in the early summer of 1944. This activity did not escape the attention of the Gestapo who requested his arrest but Colonel Traian Borcescu, the head of counter-intelligence in the SSI refused, in the belief that Bodnăraş "could be of use in Romania's exit from the war" (interview with T. Borcescu; see also G. Iavorschi, "Pentru cine a lucrat 'inginerul Ceauşu'?" p.19). Bodnăraş gave his own account of his actions between the time of his release from prison in early November 1942 (he dates this to 2 November) and the removal of Foriş from the Party leadership on 4 April 1944 in discussions with Valter Roman, Gheorghe Zaharia and Ada Grigorian on 18 and 20 January 1960 (see Dennis Deletant, *Communist Terror in Romania, Gheorghiu-Dej and the Police State, 1948-1965*, London: Hurst and Co., 1999, appendix 1, pp.297–308). After the establishment of the Groza government in March 1945, Bodnăraş was appointed secretary-general to the prime minister and in the following month he was given control of the intelligence service, the SSI. As a faithful servant of Moscow, he played a key role in consolidating Communist rule and eliminating potential opposition to it. This brought Borcescu onto Bodnăraş's radar. He was arrested on 26 March 1945 at the latter's home after accepting an invitation from Bodnăraş to lunch there. Bodnăraş proposed to Borcescu that he work with the Soviets, represented at the meal by Colonel Timofteiv, the NKVD adviser in Bucharest. When he refused, he was given blacked-out glasses and taken by car to an airfield and flown to Moscow where he was interrogated about his wartime activity by Viktor Abamukov, Beria's deputy. After two weeks, he was returned to Bucharest and taken into custody on Bodnăraş's orders and held, first in Jilava prison and then in Malmaison, where he was interrogated on several occasions by Bodnăraş. He was released on 23 December 1945 but rearrested on 26 May 1949, tried for his role under the Antonescu regime, and sentenced to hard labour for life. In January 1963, his sentence was reduced to 25 years and he was amnestied on 13 April 1964 (author's interview with Traian Borcescu, 8 March 1995). Bodnăraş became a member of the Central Committee in 1945, a position he retained until his death in 1976, and a member of the Politburo (1948–1965), Minister of the Armed Forces (1947–1956), and Vice President of the Council of Ministers (1954–1965). According to Khrushchev's memoirs it was Bodnăraş who, as Minister of War, first raised the question of the withdrawal of Soviet troops from Romania during Khrushchev's visit to Romania in August 1955. Khrushchev was convinced that the matter had already been discussed by the Romanian Party leadership and Gheorghiu-Dej chose Bodnăraş to broach the subject because of his impeccable credentials. These were his past services to the Soviet Union, the confidence and respect which Khrushchev acknowledged he enjoyed amongst the Soviet leaders; and his senior position—he was one of the three deputy prime ministers. Khrushchev records that Bodnăraş justified the subject by pointing out that there was little threat to Soviet security interests because Romania was hemmed in by other socialist countries and that there was "nobody across the Black Sea from us except the Turks". The international situation in 1955 did not permit the Soviet leader to act on the suggestion straightaway but the idea of withdrawal had been planted in his mind and he used it three years later at a time he regarded as more appropriate. Bodnăraş was appointed a vice premier and remained close to Gheorghiu-Dej until the latter's death in 1965. Upon his elevation to the Party leadership that year, Ceauşescu offered Bodnăraş the position of vice president of the state council in return for his total obedience. Bodnăraş honoured the agreement, leading a largely withdrawn life—he was divorced—until his death in 1976. In conformity with his will, his body was not buried near Gheorghiu-Dej's in the Heroes' Monument in Bucharest but in the churchyard in Iaslovăţ in northern Moldavia.

Traian Borcescu (22 November 1899, Cireşanu, Prahova county, 22 November 1899; Bucharest, 1997?) was head of Romanian counter-intelligence from 1942 until the 23 August *coup* of 1944. He was arrested on 26 March 1945 at the home of Emil Bodnăraş, who after 23 August 1944 effectively became head of the Romanian security service. Bodnăraş, had invited him to lunch there. After turning down a proposal from the latter that he work with the Soviets, represented at the meal by Colonel Timofteiv, the NKVD adviser in Bucharest, he was given blacked-out glasses and taken by car to an airfield and flown to Moscow where he was interrogated about his wartime activity by Viktor Abamukov, Beria's deputy. After two weeks he was returned to Bucharest and taken into custody on Bodnăraş's orders and held, first in Jilava prison and then in Malmaison, where he was interrogated on several occasions by Bodnăraş,. He was released on 23 December 1945 but rearrested on 26 May 1949, tried for his role under the Antonescu regime, and sentenced to hard labour for life. In January1963 his sentence was reduced to 25 years and he was amnestied on 13 April 1964 (author's interview with Traian Borcescu, 8 March 1995).

Petre Borilă, pseudonym of Iordan Dragan Rusev (Silistra, 13 February 1906; Bucharest, 2 January 1973). He joined the outlawed Communist Party in 1934 and served in the International brigades during the Spanish Civil War. During the Second World War, he worked alongside Georgi Dimitrov and Dmitri Manuilsky in the Comintern and joined the so-called Moscow group of the Communist Party of Romania formed by Ana Pauker, Vasile Luca, Leonte Răutu and Valter Roman. As a member of the Politburo (1952–1965), he was deeply involved in the purges carried out by Gheorghiu-Dej (see Vladimir Tismăneanu, *Stalinism for All Seasons*, p.257).

Constantin (Dinu) Brătianu (Ştefăneşti, Argeş, 13 January 1866; Sighet prison, 23 August, 1953?). Second son of Ion C. Brătianu (1821–1891), appointed leader of the National Liberal Party in 1934. Constantin (Dinu) Brătianu was arrested by the Communist authorities during the night of 5/6 May 1950 and imprisoned at Sighet without trial, The date of his death is unclear, one source giving 20 August 1950, another 23 August 1953 (see Florian Tănăsescu, Nicolae Tănăsescu, *Constantin (Bebe) I.C. Brătianu – Istoria P.N.L. la interogatoriu*, Bucharest: Editura Paralela 45, 2005, p.179.)

Elena Ceauşescu (Petreşti, Dâmboviţa, 7 January 1919; Târgovişte, 25 December 1989). She joined the Communist Party as a textile factory worker in 1939 and married Nicolae Ceauşescu in December 1947. After being awarded a degree in chemical engineering from Bucharest Polytechnic in 1957, she was given a doctorate from the Institute of Chemistry in Iaşi in 1967 although there is anecdotal evidence that her thesis was written by a university professor since she had only a rudimentary knowledge of the discipline. Director General of Central Institute of Chemistry in Bucharest between 1972 and 1980, she enjoyed a rapid political rise, becoming a member of the party central committee in 1973 and a member of the politburo in January 1977. She was the key architect in the promotion of the Ceauşescu personality cult in the wake of her husband's 'election' to the new post of President of the Republic in March 1974. Its extension to Elena—the second most important figure in the Party and state after her appointment as First Deputy Prime Minister in March 1980—absorbed more and more of the *Securitate*'s resources. Disbursements were made from special hard currency accounts to pay foreign publishers to publish hagiographies of Nicolae and the ghostwritten studies on chemistry attributed to his wife, "the scholar of world-renown". Bucharest sources allege that the occasion for one *Securitate* agent's defection in Vienna in January 1989 was his assignment to pay a Western publisher the reputed sum of $30,000 for publication of one of Elena's 'studies'. Furtherance of the cult was assumed by Elena who, from 1985, took especial interest in it and regularly browbeat the successive Central Committee propaganda secretaries to ensure that public meetings were festooned with photographs of the happy couple. She became increasingly protective of her husband as his diabetes seemed to be accelerating both his ageing and his irascibility, and it was for this reason that she frustrated the attempts of Major General Emil Macri, the head of the Economic Directorate, to discuss with the President the true state of the country's disastrous economic plight.

Nicu Ceauşescu (Bucharest, 1 September 1951; Vienna, 26 September, 1996). Son of Nicolae and Elena, he studied physics at Bucharest University and in 1982 was 'elected' to the Party Central Committee in 1982 whilst first secretary of the Communist Youth Movement. In 1987, he was appointed head of the local Party organization in the Transylvanian town of Sibiu. His notorious drinking bouts and alleged maltreatment of young women led him to flee the town on the arrest of his parents but he was caught and charged in 1990 with "instigation of aggravated murder" relating to the deaths of some 100 persons during the revolution in Sibiu. Found guilty and sentenced to twenty years in prison, the charge was modified in November 1992 to illegal possession of firearms and his sentence was reduced to five years. He was released on medical grounds suffering from hepatitis and cirrhosis of the liver, and died in Vienna.

Iosif Chişinevski (Roitman) (Chişinău, Bessarabia, 1905; Bucharest, 1963) Chişinevski is believed to have studied at the Communist Party academy in Moscow during the late 1920s. He was arrested in 1941 as the head of a Communist cell and sent to Caransebeş jail. He was spared deportation to Transnistria because only Jews with sentences under 10 years were sent to the province while those with heavier sentences, like Chişinevski, Simion Zeiger and Radu Mănescu, remained in Caransebeş until their release on 23 August 1944. The RCP's principal ideologue and a close associate of Gheorghiu-Dej between 1944 until 1957 when his criticism of the latter led to his exclusion from the politburo and the end of his political career (see Vladimir Tismăneanu, *Stalinism for All Seasons,* p.259).

Miron Constantinescu (Chişinău, 13 December 1917; Bucharest, 18 July 1974) was a significant figure in the history of Romanian Communism, in particular in the first decade following the imposition of the Romanian People's Republic. He joined the Communist movement out of conviction as a student at Bucharest University where he attended the sociology seminar of Dimitrie Gusti. Arrested in 1941 for clandestine activity, he was sentenced in February 1941 to ten years' hard labour. The *coup* of 23 August led to his release two days later and shortly afterwards he was appointed Director of the Party newspaper *Scânteia* and became a member of the Politburo, a position he held until 1957 when he was expelled together with Chişinevski for having criticized Gheorghiu-Dej and the *Securitate* following Khrushchev's secret speech of February 1956. Constantinescu's conflict with Gheorghiu-Dej, and his marginalization in 1957 gave him the opportunity to focus upon his intellectual gifts by working at a number of academic institutions in Bucharest. Gheorghiu-Dej's death and Nicolae Ceauşescu's aim to legitimize his own leadership by delegitimizing that of his predecessor paved the way for Constantinescu's rehabilitation.

Corneliu Coposu (Bobota Sălaj, 20 May 1914; Bucharest, 11 November 1995). A devout member of the Romanian Greek-Catholic (Uniate) church, he joined the Romanian National Party as a young man and after studying law at the University of Cluj (1930–1934), took up work as a lawyer. He became private secretary to Iuliu Maniu, the leader of the RNP and of its successor, the National Peasant Party. Coposu moved to Bucharest in summer 1940, after Northern Transylvania was ceded to Hungary. During the Second World War, Coposu played an important role in maintaining the NPP's clandestine links with the British by encrypting many of the telegrams sent by Maniu to the British Special Operations Executive. In August 1944, after King Michael's *coup* against the Ion Antonescu regime, Coposu became deputy secretary of the NPP and, after the reunion of Northern Transylvania, the party's delegate to the leadership of provisional administrative bodies. He was also active in organizing the party as the main opposition to the Communist Party and the Petru Groza government before the 1946 general election. As such he rapidly became a target of the Communist authorities and was arrested on 14 July 1947, together with the entire leadership of the NPP after several of its leading members attempted to flee the country in a private plane. He was imprisoned without trial for nine years. Charges were eventually brought against him in 1956 when he was sentenced to life imprisonment for "betrayal of the working class" and "crimes against social reforms". In April 1964, he was freed after fifteen years of imprisonment in a succession of jails and two years of forced residence in the village of Rubla in Brăila County. After his release, Coposu worked as an unskilled worker on various construction sites (given his status as a former prisoner, he was denied employment in any other field), and was subjected to *Securitate* surveillance and regular interrogation. His wife Arlette was also prosecuted in 1950 and jailed on a spurious charge of espionage. She died in 1965, shortly after her release from prison. On 22 December 1989, (on the day of Ceaușescu's flight from Bucharest), Coposu and Ion Rațiu proclaimed the reconstitution of the NPP under the name Christian-Democratic National Peasants' Party. Together with the National Liberal Party, the NPP represented the opposition to the neo-Communist National Salvation Front. But they proved to be shadows of their former selves. For over forty years the activities of these historic parties had been suspended. The severity of the Communist regime meant that it had been impossible to carry on even an underground existence or to enrol members of the new generation into these parties. Young Romanians did join the NPP, largely because of Coposu's reputation as a valiant symbol to Communist oppression. But the NPP, like the NLP, found that they no longer possessed the social and economic bases which had sustained them between the two world wars. The NPP's task in reconstituting itself was particularly difficult. The Communists had dealt ruthlessly with the party, which was widely felt to have won the general election held in 1946. Coposu took the initiative in reviving the NPP in late December 1989. The fact that he had spent seventeen years in jail, followed by another twenty-five years of tight restrictions upon his movements and activities, gave him prestige amongst those Romanian voters which none of the other political leaders could claim. His links with Maniu, who was widely respected for his high ethical standards and for having played a key role in uniting Transylvania with Romania, lent stature to Coposu, whose dignity, simplicity of manner and clarity of expression proved appealing to younger people searching for a moral lead in confused political times. But Coposu was one of the few assets the party possessed in the task of reconstruction. Its links with the countryside, its main reservoir of support until 1947, had been severed. After 1990, the NPP found that little advantage was to be gained from stressing its involvement in politics before 1947. The recovery of the NPP was blocked by the fact that large elements of the population seemed to have an interest in the perpetuation of a modified version of Communist Romanian society. Opinion polls after 1990 showed that Romanian citizens possessed a strongly egalitarian outlook. More than 70% of the population believed that income levels should be almost equal. The low level of support which the NPP had in the countryside showed how collectivization had turned many peasants away from the private ownership of land advocated by the NPP. Coposu was a moderating influence within the party. He denounced the anti-Semitic sentiments expressed in the Party newspaper *Dreptatea* in the early months of 1990. He tried to make a distinction between Communism and Communists, realizing that the electoral slogan of the NPP "Down with the Communists" was a clear threat to the millions of Romanians who had joined the party out of convenience rather than conviction. It was thanks to Coposu that the NPP, unlike the NLP, was not worn down by internal rivalries, although with his passing it did not escape this fate. Coposu was one of the few senior politicians untainted by the endemic corruption of the post-Communist years. Without him, Romanian political life lost its symbol of rectitude, probity and consistency.

Ştefan Foriş (Tărlungeni, Braşov, 9 May 1892; Bucharest, 1946). After completing a degree in physics and mathematics at Budapest University, he returned to Braşov in September 1919 and joined the Hungarian language socialist newspaper *Munkas* (Worker) as an editor. He joined the Communist party in 1921 and in the following year moved to Bucharest where, after the proscription of the party, he worked underground as an agitator. In 1926, he became secretary of *Ajutorul Roşu* (Red Aid), the Romanian section of the Comintern-controlled International Organization for Aiding the Fighters of the Revolution, known by its Russian initials MOPR (*Mezhdunarodnaia organizatsiia pomoshchi bortsam revoliutsii*). The MOPR provided food and legal aid to activists in prison. In 1927, Foriş was co-opted as a member of the Central Committee and took part in the fourth party congress in the following year. He was arrested in July 1928 but a rapid deterioration in his health led to his release and he was able to make his way to Moscow. At the end of 1930 he returned to Romania and was arrested once again on 26 August 1931. Freed in 1935, he was appointed in 1938 to the secretariat of the Central Committee, and in February 1940 he was summoned by the Comintern to Moscow from where he returned in December as general secretary of the party. He was arrested by the Communist *Siguranţa* on 9 June 1945 and beaten to death with an iron bar in summer 1946 (N.I. Florea, 'Ştefan Foriş', *Analele de Istorie*, vol.18 (1972), no.3, pp.150–53). The report of the Party commission, charged by Nicolae Ceauşescu in 1967 with investigating the circumstances of Foriş's death, concluded that "Foriş's execution was carried out by [*Siguranţa* chief] Gheorghe Pintilie, aided by his chauffeur Dumitru Necin [also known as Dimitrie Mitea], through blows administered with an iron bar". The body was thrown into a specially prepared pit in the grounds of the building in which he was murdered [Communist Party HQ on Aleea Alexandru] (Stenogram of Gheorghe Pintilie's deposition before the commission in Deletant, *Communist Terror*, pp.316–317; see also 'Statement by Gheorghe Pintilie, former Head of the *Securitate,* dated 15 May 1967 and Presented to the Party Commission Charged with Investigating the Death of Ştefan Foriş', (*ibid.*, pp.314–18), and A.G. Savu, "Ştefan Foriş. Schiţă pentru o viitoare biografie", *Magazin Istoric*, no.7, 1968, pp.53–58). This issue of the review was withdrawn from circulation by the authorities shortly after its appearance because of this article on Foriş. (I am grateful to Marian Ştefan for providing me with a copy.)

Teohari Georgescu (Bucharest, 31 January 1908; Bucharest, 31 December 1976). After four years of elementary school he became a printer's apprentice and in 1923 entered the printing plant of *Cartea Românească.* In 1928, he joined the printers' union and helped to organize a strike. His role in the strike brought him to the attention of the *Siguranţa* who placed him under surveillance. In the following year, he joined the Communist Party. In November 1933, he was arrested for distributing Communist manifestoes and detained for several months before being released on grounds of "insufficient proof". He was rearrested in June 1934 for Communist activity but released on bail. He was arrested once again in Ploieşti in January 1935 for failing to appear at his trial, and held for several months before being released until the trial date was fixed. His trial was postponed on more than ten occasions between 1937 and 1940 when he was finally sentenced to two months imprisonment. From 1937 to 1938 he worked as a printer for the daily *Adevărul* and the National Printing Office. In August 1940 on orders from Georgi Dimitrov, secretary of the Comintern, he was sent to Moscow to receive instruction from the NKVD on how to code messages and to use a special technique of writing them on glass. He was arrested in April 1941 as part of the Bucharest Party cell led by Iosif Chişinevschi (Roitman) and sentenced in May to ten years in jail. The first part of his sentence was executed at Caransebeş jail. In April 1942, he was moved to Văcăreşti prison to work in the printing press and returned to Caransebeş at the end of August where he stayed until his release at the end of August 1944. He served as Minister of Internal Affairs from 6 March 1945 until 28 May 1952 when he was accused at the Communist Party plenary meeting alongside Ana Pauker and Vasile Luca of "rightist deviation" and purged from the politburo. He was arrested and held until April 1956. He was appointed by Gheorghiu-Dej director of the *13 December* (formerly *Cartea Românească)* printing press, the same press at which he had obtained his first job in 1923. He was rehabilitated in April 1968.

Ion Iliescu (Oltenița, 3 March, 1930). A member of the Communist Youth Movement at the age of nineteen, he was among a group of Romanian students who studied fluid mechanics at the energy institute of Moscow State University. In 1960, he was appointed to the Central Committee of the Party, and in 1965 chief of the section for Agitation and Propaganda. In the presentation of his 'July theses' of 1971, Ceaușescu criticized Iliescu, then culture secretary of the CC, and the latter was removed from his position and sent to Timișoara as secretary for propaganda for Timiș County. This was followed by promotion as first secretary of the party in Iași before his appointment in 1982 as head of the State Committee for Water. In 1984, he was moved to direct the Scientific Publishing House (*Editura Științifică*) in Bucharest, in which capacity the outbreak of the 1989 Revolution found him. Acknowledged as head of the National Salvation Front on 22 December, he led this provisional government until May 1990 when he was elected President of Romania. In 1992, he won a second four-year term but was defeated in the 1996 election by Emil Constantinescu. In December 2000, he was elected for a third time as President.

Vasile Luca (Cătălina, Covasna, 8 June 1898; Aiud prison, 23 July 1963) was the Romanianized name of Laszlo Luca, a Hungarian born in the commune of Catalina in the county of Covasna in Transylvania on 8 June 1898. He lost his parents at the age of seven and was placed in an orphanage in Sibiu. When he was thirteen he became apprentice to a local padlock maker. In 1915, he secured a job in the railway yards in Brașov but at the end of the year was called up into the Austro-Hungarian army and sent to the front. In 1919, as a conscript in the Romanian army, he took part in the campaign against Bela Kun's Soviet Republic. He resumed his railway job at the end of the year when he also joined the trade union movement. In 1924, he became regional secretary of the Communist Party in Brașov. Arrested in the same year for membership of an illegal organization, he spent three years in jail. In 1928, he was elected to the Party Central Committee. As a result of the internal struggles within the Party he was sent to do basic Party work in Moldavia. In 1933, he was arrested for organizing trade union activity, tried and imprisoned for five years. After his release from jail he was co-opted into the Party Central Committee and delegated to present a report to the Comintern about the Party's activity. On 4 April 1940, he was caught while trying to cross the frontier into the Soviet Union and detained in Cernăuți in northern Bukovina. He was released from custody following the Soviet occupation of the province at the end of June ('Documentarul referitor la procesul privind pe Vasile Luca', *Arhivele Naționale Istorice Centrale (The National Central Historical Archives,* henceforth abbreviated to ANIC), *Arhiva Comitetului Executiv al CC al PCR (Archive of the Executive Committee of the Central Committee of the Romanian Communist Party),* No.264/19, 18.02.1972. I am grateful to Marius Oprea for locating this document.) By virtue of his presence on Soviet territory, Luca was offered the right to claim Soviet citizenship which he exercised. He spent the following four years in Moscow, working for the Romanian section of Radio Moscow and for the Comintern-backed Romanian radio station *România liberă* (Ionescu, *Communism in Rumania*, p.353; see also G. Buzatu, "Cominterniştii români se pregătescţ", *Magazin Istoric,* vol.28, no.2 (February 1994), pp.41–42).

Iuliu Maniu (Şimleu Silvaniei, 8 January, 1873; Sighet prison, 5 February, 1953). Maniu attended elementary school in Blaj and secondary school in Zalău, and went on to study in Vienna and Budapest where he took a degree in law. On his return to Transylvania he became a professor of law at the Greek-Catholic seminary in Blaj and legal adviser to the metropolitan bishop. He joined the Romanian National Party of Transylvania whose programme focused on the establishment of Transylvanian autonomy and the assertion of Romanian rights commensurate with the Romanian demographic majority in the province. In 1909, he was elected a deputy in the Hungarian parliament where he was a powerful advocate of Romanian aspirations. After being called up into the Austro-Hungarian army in 1915 he emerged from military academy with the rank of second lieutenant and was despatched, first to the Russian front, and then to Italy. As a member of the National Committee of the Romanian National Party he was one of the principal figures that organized the Grand National Assembly of 1 December 1918 which proclaimed the union of Transylvania with Romania. Maniu elected President of the Directory Council which administered Transylvania from 2 December 1918 until 4 April 1920 when the government of the province was handed over to Bucharest. On 9 August 1919, Maniu was elected President of the National Party—as it was known after the Union—and in October 1926, on its merger with the Peasant Party, he became President of the National Peasant Party. In November 1928, he led the party to victory in the general election and served as Prime Minister until June 1930 when Prince Carol returned to Romania. Maniu had supported the return of the prince on condition that he renounced Lupescu, but Carol's unwillingness to do so prompted him to resign on 7 June. His place was taken by Gheorghe Mironescu who annulled the act excluding Carol from the throne and then resigned himself. After a period of confusion Maniu was recalled on 13 June after Carol gave an undertaking to be crowned with his wife Helen in September. On learning of Lupescu's return to Romania Maniu submitted his resignation once more on 6 October 1930. In October 1932, Carol turned to Maniu at the height of a grave economic crisis to head the National Peasant Party government following the resignation of Alexandru Vaida-Voievod. Maniu once again set the conditions of June 1930 for his acceptance, namely Carol's re-marriage to Queen Helen. He also demanded that the King rule in the spirit of the 1923 constitution and dismiss his influential clique of advisers, the 'camarilla'. Although Carol agreed to the conditions it soon became clear that he had no intention of abiding by them. The result was that Maniu broke off personal relations with the King and resigned in January 1933. At the same time, he stood down as President of the National Peasant Party and ostensibly withdrew from politics. However, the increasingly dictatorial stance of the King led the NPP to call upon Maniu in November 1937 as the champion of constitutional government and he returned to lead the party. His desire to thwart Carol's moves to install a royal dictatorship led him to sign an electoral pact with Corneliu Codreanu, head of the Iron Guard, in the same month, which had the desired effect of defeating the Tătărescu government. However, Carol dissolved the newly elected parliament and instituted a government of his own choice under Octavian Goga. With Carol's suspension of the constitution in February 1938 Maniu's fear of the institution of a royal dictatorship was confirmed. On 30 March, a decree dissolving all political parties was issued and a strict regime of political censorship applied. Maniu's protests to Carol went unheeded and he thus began what was to be a six-year period as head of the democratic opposition in Romania. His attempts to reconcile his pro-Allied sympathies with his contempt for totalitarian rule and mistrust of the Soviet Union gave the British, with whom he was in contact throughout the war, the impression of vacillation and indecision. His refusal to participate in the government appointed by King Michael on 23 August 1944 proved in retrospect to be a major tactical error for the National Peasant Party was more easily relegated to the sidelines as the Soviet Union imposed its will with increasing force on Romania. The suppression of the democratic process required the elimination of the 'historical' parties. The arrest of senior figures in the National Peasant Party while trying to flee the country on 14 July 1947 provided the Communist-led government with a pretext for arresting Maniu and his deputy Ion Mihalache on 25 July, on the grounds of plotting to overthrow the state. They and several other prominent members of the National Party were tried, found guilty and given life sentences on 11 November. After four years in Galaţi prison (14 November 1947–14 August 1951) Maniu was transferred to Sighet jail where he died on 5 February 1953 (Andrea Dobeş, Ilie Lazăr, Cluj-Napoca: Argonaut, 2006, p.176.)

Ion Gheorghe Maurer (Bucharest, 23 September 1902; Bucharest, 8 February, 2000). His mother was Romanian while his father was from Alsace and was employed as French tutor to Prince Carol (later King Carol II). After studying law at Bucharest University, he practised at the bar. He developed Marxist sympathies and appeared for the defence of Ana Pauker, Alexandru Drăghici and Alexandru Moghioroş at their trial in Craiova in 1936. According to his own testimony, he joined the Party "somewhat before 1936"; see Lavinia Betea, *Maurer şi lumea de ieri* (Arad: Fundaţia Culturală Ion Slavici, 1995), p.13. Sidelined by Pauker after 1944, he re-emerged on the political scene as Foreign Minister in 1957 and served as Prime Minister between 1961 and 29 March 1974 when he withdrew from political life. He played a key role in the appointment of Ceauşescu as Gheorghiu-Dej's successor.

Michael I, King of Romania (25 October, 1921, Foişor Castle, Romania, the son of Carol II of Romania (then Crown Prince of Romania) and Princess Elena of Greece). When Carol eloped with his mistress Elena 'Magda' Lupescu and renounced 'temporarily' his rights to the throne in December 1925, Michael succeeded to the throne upon King Ferdinand's death in July 1927. Michael was king of Romania from 20 July 1927 to 8 June 1930 and again from 6 September 1940 to 30 December 1947. He was forced to abdicate in 1947 by the government controlled by the Communist Party of Romania. As a great-great-grandson of Queen Victoria of the United Kingdom through both of his parents he is a third cousin of: Queen Margrethe II of Denmark, King Harald V of Norway, King Juan Carlos I of Spain, King Carl XVI Gustaf of Sweden and Queen Elizabeth II of the United Kingdom.

Ana Pauker (Codăeşti, 13 December 1893; Bucharest, 3 June 1960). Born Ana Rabinsohn into a middle-class family. Her father was a *haham*, a Jewish butcher and teacher of Hebrew at the local school. At the turn of the century, the Rabinsohns moved to Bucharest. Details of Ana's youth and education are sketchy and largely anecdotal, and the first mention of any professional activity concerns her employment as a teacher of Hebrew at the *Brotherhood of Zion* primary school in Bucharest. Shortly afterwards, in September 1915, she joined the socialist movement. According to an autobiographical pamphlet published in 1951, Ana helped to distribute literature produced by the Romanian Social Democratic Party. She was more forthcoming about her activity during this period to Corneliu Coposu, the private secretary of National Peasant Party leader Iuliu Maniu, whom she encountered at Cluj prison in the mid-1930s. There, she revealed that after leaving her post as a schoolteacher, she found a position as a secretarial assistant at the newspaper *Dimineața* where she had responsibility for the library. It was while working here that in 1921 she met the son of one of the major shareholders of the newspaper, Marcel Pauker, who was three years her junior and had just returned from Paris where he had taken a doctorate in law (C. Coposu, *Dialoguri*, p.63). The two took part in the foundation congress of the RCP in May 1921, but the arrest of its leading members prompted them to flee to Zurich where they were married on 1 June. Marcel enrolled as a student of engineering at *L'École Polytéchnique Federale* while Ana began a course in medicine. A few months after the wedding, Ana returned to Bucharest to give birth to her first child, a daughter called Tania, who died of dysentery before she was one year old. At the second RCP congress, held at Ploieşti in October 1922, both Marcel and Ana were elected to the Central Committee of the Party. After the proscription of the party and the suppression of its newspaper *Socialismul* in April 1924, Ana was given the task of publishing underground propaganda, thereby becoming a target of the *Siguranța*, the security police. She was arrested with four female colleagues and held in Văcăreşti prison. At Ana's instigation the four went on hunger strike and were beaten, after which they, and Ana, were released until the date of their trial, fixed for July 1925 (M. Mircu, *Dosar Ana Pauker*, p.43. The defendants absconded and Ana Pauker was sentenced *in absentia* to ten years' imprisonment. The Paukers managed to flee abroad in 1926, staying in Berlin, Paris and Prague, and in the same year Ana gave birth to a son, Vlad, in Vienna. From there they went to Moscow where Ana attended the Comintern training school in order to become an instructor. In Moscow Ana produced a second daughter, named Tatiana, in 1928. Her husband returned to Romania clandestinely in the spring of 1929, only to be arrested on 4 May, but he was to benefit from an amnesty of which he took advantage to work underground for two years before returning to Moscow. In December 1932, he was again sent by the Comintern to Romania, this time to organize Communist activity in Transylvania, and in the following year he was recalled to the Soviet capital. Ana, too, was given a mission by the Comintern. She was attached, in turn, to the Czechoslovak, German and French Communist Parties (from 1931 to 1932) as an instructor, with the cover name of Marina. It was in Paris that she had an affair with Albert Fried (Clément), a fellow instructor for the French Communist Party, as a result of which she gave birth to a daughter, Maria, in Moscow in December 1932. Marcel was similarly wayward in his affections at this time. He had an affair in Bessarabia with an RCP activist, Rosa Elbert, who bore a son named Iacov in 1931 (author's interview with Tatiana Brătescu, 30 July 1994). In March 1934, she was sent back by the Comintern to Romania in the company of other comrades in an attempt to revive clandestine activity which had been severely curtailed following the Griviţa strike. She was eventually arrested in Bucharest in the early hours of 13 July 1935. Her trial, and that of eighteen other Communists who included Alexandru Moghioroş, his future wife Stela (Esther Radoshovetsky), Alexandru Drăghici and Liuba Chişinevski Roitman, was scheduled to be held in the capital but street demonstrations in support of the defendants led the authorities to move it to Craiova. Proceedings opened on 5 June 1936 and were attended by several foreign press correspondents and observers. Among the twenty-four lawyers for the defence were Lucreţiu Pătrăşcanu and Ion Gheorghe Maurer, as well as personalities from the Bucharest bar. Ana Pauker was found guilty of being a leading member of an outlawed organization and sentenced on 7 July to ten years imprisonment. She spent five years in the prisons of Dumbrăveni, Râmnicu-Sărat and Caransebeş before being exchanged on 3 May 1941 for Ion Codreanu, a sixty-two-year old Romanian from Bessarabia who had been arrested for "anti-Soviet agitation" in the previous July following the Soviet annexation of the province. While Ana was in prison, her husband was arrested in Moscow in 1937 together with other senior members of the RCP for "Trotskyist" sympathies: Alexandru Dobrogeanu-Gherea, Ecaterina Arbore, Pavel Tcacenko, Elek Köblös and David Fabian. All became victims of Stalin's purges and were executed without trial in 1937. For Pauker's career after her return to Romania in September 1944, and her purge by Gheorghiu-Dej in summer 1952 see Chapters Five and Six.

Constantin Pârvulescu (Olăneşti, Vâlcea, 10 November 1895; Bucharest, 11 July 1992). A railway mechanic by training, he found his way to Ukraine during the civil war in Russia and is credited with being a founding member of the Communist Party in Romania. Between 1921 and 1926 he appears to have attended the Party school in Moscow and worked as a mechanic in the Soviet capital. Between 1929 and 1931 he was secretary of the outlawed Romanian party in Chişinău in Bessarabia. Arrested in 1934, he escaped to the Soviet Union where he remained until the outbreak of the Second World War. Having returned to Romania he was one of the leaders of the underground party and between April and September 1944 was designated its general secretary. A member of the Politburo from 1948 to 1960, he was removed from this position because of his association with the discredited Chişinevski and Constantinescu. At the Twelfth Party Congress in 1979, he protested, as a veteran Communist—he was eighty-four—at not being allowed to speak and when permission was granted he took the unprecedented step of criticising Ceauşescu for subordinating the country's interests to those of his own. A period of political isolation followed until he re-emerged into the public arena as one of the signatories of the "Letter of the Six" in March 1989.

Lucreţiu Pătrăşcanu (Bacău, 4 November 1900; Bucharest, 17 April 1954). See Chapters Five And Six.

Titel Petrescu (Craiova, 5 February, 1888; Bucharest, 2 September, 1957). Leader of the Social Democratic Party, Petrescu's fate was emblematic of that of opposition leaders. He was arrested on 6 May 1948, held in the security police headquarters in Bucharest, sent to Jilava prison and finally tried *in camera* in January 1952 for crimes against the state. He was sentenced to life imprisonment and served three years in Sighet jail before being transferred to the Calea Rahovei headquarters of the *Securitate* in Bucharest in December 1954 where he was told by the Minister of the Interior, Alexandru Drăghici, that a number of his colleagues in the former SDP would be released from prison if he signed a letter giving his support to the regime for publication in the Party daily *Scînteia*. He refused and in August 1955 was sent to Râmnicu Sărat jail where he learned from fellow prisoners of the death in prison of numerous socialists. He agreed to sign a text on 13 September on condition that all leading SDP members were released and he himself was freed but kept under virtual house arrest. The letter appeared in *Scînteia* on 18 December 1955 but only a small number of SDP colleagues were released (see *Cartea Albă a Securităţii*, Bucharest: SRI, 1994, vol.II, doc. 237, pp. 527–29). Petrescu complained to Petru Groza, the President of the Grand National Assembly, after which further releases were announced.

Grigore Ion Răceanu (Cojocna, Cluj, 1 October 1906; Bucharest, September 1996). An engine driver at Cluj, he joined the railwaymen's union, becoming one of the leaders of the Cluj railway strikes of 1929 and 1933. His trade union activities led him to be sent as a delegate to the World Conference of Trade Unions held in Paris in 1929. On his return from Paris, during which he travelled on carriage buffers, he was arrested by the Romanian authorities for several weeks. In 1936, he joined the Communist Party of Romania. In 1938 he moved to Braşov and worked in the aircraft factory IAR (*Industria Aeronautică Română*). He played a major role in the organization of a mass demonstration in Braşov on 1 September 1940 against the Vienna Award of 30 August, as a result of which he was arrested and jailed. In February 1942, he moved to Bucharest and worked directly with Foriş, living clandestinely in a one-bedroom apartment close to the police headquarters in Bucharest. He soon fell out with Foriş over the latter's continued support for the

Comintern line over the issue of Bessarabia and northern Bukovina (see Chapter One), for the annexation of both territories by the Soviet Union in June 1940, and over Foriş's reluctance to sanction organized Communist resistance to the Antonescu regime. In autumn 1942, Foriş ordered Răceanu to put his objections to the party line in a memorandum in autumn 1942, and on the basis of this Răceanu was expelled from the party He was readmitted in 1945 and appointed director of a tobacco factory in Cluj where he remained until 1949 when he moved to Bucharest. In the period 1951–1953, he was head of the accounting office of the Ministry of Food Production until he was removed after the party verification process. Chişinevski informed Grigore's wife that her husband had been declared "a class enemy", "an enemy of the Comintern" and of "comrade Stalin"—Chişinevski cited Răceanu's memorandum of 1942. After a few years without employment, Răceanu returned to work for the railway in Bucharest. Grigore was unemployed from 1960 to 1963 when he began work at the printing press at the Central Press Office *Casa Scânteі*. He remained there until 1968, the year in which he was rehabilitated and readmitted to the party following the plenary meeting of 22–25 April. He retired in the same year. In October 1988, he was contacted by Gheorghe Apostol through Mircea (Apostol, having served as Romanian ambassador in Argentina at the end of the 1970s frequently dropped into the Foreign Ministry for a coffee and on this occasion sought out Mircea). Apostol worked with Grigore on "The Letter of the Six". Grigore was arrested in March 1989, interrogated at Rahova prison and then sent to his birthplace at Cojocna where he remained under house arrest until the downfall of Ceauşescu. Although he responded to the appeal of the National Salvation Front for assistance and presented himself in Bucharest at its headquarters, he was overlooked and ignored. He passed away in September 1996. (I owe these and other biographical details about Grigore, his wife Ileana and his stepson Mircea, to the latter who has shared his authoritative experience as a Romanian diplomat between 1959 and 1989 with me. I record here my thanks for his generosity of spirit).

Mircea Răceanu (Văcăreşti jail, Bucharest, 17 October 1935). Mircea Răceanu was born Mircea Bernat. His mother, Ileana Pop (Ilonka Papp), had worked in a sweet factory in Arad, and joined the Communist Party at an early age. His father, Andrei Bernat, was a carpenter from Târgu-Mureş. Both were arrested in 1935 for clandestine activity on behalf of the outlawed Communist Party in Romania and sentenced to prison terms. Upon her release, Mircea's mother took him to Moscow in 1938, shortly after King Carol declared a royal dictatorship in February 1938. He spent two years at a boarding school at the *Interdom*, a special boarding school for foreigners located in the city of Ivanovo situated some 300 km northeast of the Soviet capital. Andrei Bernat was sentenced to ten years' imprisonment and after the outbreak of hostilities between Romania and the Soviet Union in June 1941, was moved to a jail in Râbniţa in Transnistria. On the instructions of the Comintern Ileana returned to Romania in 1942 and worked clandestinely as an administrative secretary for the Communist Party. Andrei was murdered by retreating German troops in Râbniţa on 18/19 March 1944. In September 1944,

Ileana went to Moscow and brought Mircea back to Bucharest. She married Grigore Răceanu who helped to raise Mircea as his own son. Mircea Răceanu continued his education in Bucharest, studying at the 'Ion Luca Caragiale' high school and in 1954 was sent to Moscow to study at the State Institute of International Relations. He graduated in 1960, after having spent six months of that year on practical assignment at the Romanian embassy in Washington DC, and joined the Romanian Foreign Ministry. Between 1969 and 1978 he served at the Romanian embassy in Washington DC, rising to become Counsellor. It was during his period at the embassy that his trial documents allege that he was recruited, in 1975, by the CIA. After a two-day trial Mircea was sentenced to death by a military tribunal on 21 July for "treachery through the transmission of secret documents" to the CIA (ACNSAS, Mircea Răceanu, Rechizitoriu, P 011564, vol.5). The severity of the sentence may have been explained by Răceanu's background as the son of parents who had been veteran Party activists from the time of its prohibition in the interwar years, and that Ceauşescu regarded Mircea's action as a personal betrayal. His appeal was rejected on 28 August. Only the intervention of President George H. Bush, formerly Director of the CIA (1976–77) in a personal letter to Ceauşescu delivered to him by the US chargé in Bucharest at the beginning of September 1989, led the dictator to commute Raceanu's sentence on 19 September to twenty years' imprisonment. (Mircea Răceanu, *Infern '89,* pp.378–79, 545). He was released from jail on 23 December 1989. His disillusionment with the neo-Communist character of the ruling National Salvation Front led him to give vocal support to the anti-Communist demonstrators who had gathered in Bucharest's University Square during the election campaign of May 1990. After Răceanu had addressed the protesters, Silviu Brucan, a leading member of the NSF, went to the US embassy to "resolve the Răceanu case" (*ibid.,* p.289). He told the US chargé, Larry Napper, that Răceanu was an obstacle to relations between Romania and the United States because of his activity with the CIA and suggested that Răceanu leave the country. On the following day, Napper invited Răceanu to his residence and informed him of Brucan's proposal, suggesting that Răceanu might like to leave Romania with his family for the United States. Răceanu flatly refused, stating that he had not risked his life in order to leave his homeland but in order to see an open and democratic society established there. However, after two attempts to run him down by car in Bucharest, he decided to leave (*ibid.,* p.291). He flew out of the country on 20 May with his wife and two children. On 16 January 1991, Răceanu was received by CIA director William Webster, to whom he expressed his thanks for the support from the US government in escaping the consequences of his death sentence (details communicated to this author by Mircea Răceanu to whom I express my thanks); see also ANIC, Comitetul Central al PCR, Secţia Cadre, dosar R648).

Nicolae Rădescu (Călimăneşti, 30 March, 1874; New York, 16 May, 1953) won the Order of Michael the Brave, the highest Romanian military decoration, during the First World War. From April 1926 to July 1928 he served as Romanian military attaché in London. Upon his return to Romania, he became a member of the military household of the royal palace. In 1930 he was discharged from the army on the grounds of age. In November 1941, he was interned on Antonescu's orders for writing a defiant letter to Baron Killinger, Hitler's envoy, in reply to disparaging remarks made by the Baron about Romania. On 15 October 1944, he was appointed Chief of General Staff and held this position until the beginning of December. On 6 December, he was appointed Prime Minister and Minister of the Interior. Under pressure from the Soviet emissary to Romania, Andrei Vishinski, Rădescu offered his resignation on 28 February 1945 to King Michael who reluctantly accepted it. Rădescu was taken under British protection and lived in the legation building for nine weeks (6 March–7 May 1945) until an agreement was reached between the British and Soviet governments assuring the former that Rădescu would not be harmed on returning home. On 11 November, he received orders from the Ministry of the Interior to stay at home, from which he did not move until the spring of 1946 when the police provided him with a car, a driver and a detective. An incident on 13 May 1946 persuaded him to leave Romania as soon as possible. That day, while attending a function at the Athenaeum in Bucharest, he was attacked by a group of men armed with clubs, and he and his detective were injured. His escape was arranged by his secretary, Barbu Niculescu. On 15 June, Rădescu, together with his secretary and four other persons, including a Romanian airman, took off from Cotroceni airfield and flew to Cyprus. He settled in New York in 1947 where he helped to found the anti-Communist Romanian National Committee under the patronage of King Michael. Its work was financed by several million dollars secreted out of Romania between 1945 and 1946. In February 1950, Rădescu requested that this money be publicly accountable but other committee members disagreed and he resigned. He died in New York on 16 May 1953. The Committee, whose chairmanship was taken over by Constantin Vişoianu, remained active until 1975.

Valter Roman, pseudonym of Ernest Neuländer (Oradea, 9 October 1913; Bucharest, 11 November 1983). A Hungarian-speaking Romanian Communist activist who served in the International Brigades in the Spanish Civil War and was considered by some fellow Communists to be an NKVD officer (author's interview with Eduard Mezincescu, 7 April 1993). Mezincescu told this author that Roman was exfiltrated from southern France after the Spanish Civil War by the Soviet embassy in Paris, taken to Le Havre and given passage to Leningrad on a Soviet vessel. The other Romanian Communist combatants made their way to Marseilles from where they eventually found their way back to their homeland. Roman held the position of Head of the Political Directorate of the Romanian army (1947–1951). While working during the Second World War for the Comintern radio station *România liberă* in Moscow, Roman got to know Imre Nagy, the Hungarian Prime Minister, during the Hungarian uprising of autumn 1956, and for this reason he was chosen by the KGB to participate in the interrogation of Nagy in Bucharest after the latter's kidnap from Budapest in November. Between 1954 and 1983 he was director of *Editura Politică,* the principal political publishing house in Romania.

Abbreviations

AMAE	Arhiva Ministerului Afacerilor Externe (Archive of the Ministry of Foreign Affairs, Bucharest).
AMAN	Arhiva Ministerului Apărării Naţionale (Archive of the Ministry of National Defence, Piteşti)
AMSSR	Autonomous Moldavian Soviet Socialist Republic
ANIC	Arhivele Naţionale Istorice Centrale (The Central Historical National Archives, (formerly the State Archives) Bucharest)
APC	Armoured Personnel Carrier
ASRI	Archive of the Romanian Information Service [the Romanian Security Service]
BRCE	Romanian Bank for Foreign Trade
CIA	The Central Intelligence Agency
CIE	Centrul de Informaţii Externe [Romanian Foreign Intelligence Service, October 1978–December 1989]
CMEA/ Comecon	Council for Mutual Economic Assistance
CNSAS	Consiliul National pentru Studierea Arhivelor fostei Securităţi (National Council for the Study of the Archives of the former Securitate).
Comintern	Communist International
CSCE	Conference on Security and Cooperation in Europe
DGC	Canal Directorate
DGIE	Direcţia Generală de Informaţii Externe [Romanian Foreign Intelligence Service, 1963–72, March 1978–October 1978]
DGSP	Direcţia Generală a Securităţii Poporului [Romanian Security Service, 1948–51]
DGSS	Direcţia Generală a Securităţii Statului [Romanian Security Service, 1951–56]
DIE	Direcţia de Informaţii Externe [Romanian Foreign Intelligence Service, 1972–March 1978]
DS	Departamentul Securităţii [Romanian Security Service, 1956–78]
FBIS	Foreign Broadcast Information Service

FDSN	Frontul Democrat al Salvării Naţionale
FO	Foreign Office
GATT	General Agreement on Trade and Tariffs
GRU	Main Intelligence Directorate of the General Staff of the Armed Forces of the Soviet Union
HAR	Hungarian Autonomous Region
HDF	Hungarian Democratic Forum
IAR	Romanian Aeronautic Industry *(Industria Aeronautică Română)*
IPU	Inter-Parliamentary Union
KGB	Soviet Security Service, 1954–91
MGB	Soviet Security Service, 1946–54
MI5	British Security Service
MI6	British Intelligence Service
MOPR	International Organization for Aiding the Fighters of the Revolution *(Mezhdunarodnaia organizatsiia pomoshchi bortsam revoliutsii)*
NARA	National Archives and Records Administration
NDB	National Democratic Bloc
NDF	National Democratic Front
NKGB	People's Commissariat of State Security, 1943–6 [Soviet Security Service]
NKVD	People's Commissariat for Internal Affairs, 1934–43 [Ministry of Internal Affairs]
NPT	Nuclear Non-Proliferation Treaty
NSF	National Salvation Front
OGPU	Soviet Security service
OSS	Office of Strategic Services
PDSR	Partidul Social Democrat din România
RGANI	Russian State Archive of Contemporary History (*Rossiiskii Gosudarstvennyi Arkhiv Noveishei Istorii)*
RCP	Romanian Communist Party
SDP	Social Democratic Party
Siguranţa	Romanian secret police
SIS	Secret Intelligence Service
SLOMR	Free Trade Union of the Working People of Romania
Smersh	Soviet military counter-intelligence
SOE	Special Operations Executive
SRI	Serviciul Român de Informaţii [Romanian Security Service, 1990–]
SSI	Serviciul Special de Informaţii [Romanian Intelligence Service, 1940–1944, 1945–1951]
TNA	The National Archives, Kew, London
VPK	Military Industrial Commission

Extent of Romania
1914
1919
1985
USSR
HUNGARY
YUGOSLAVIA
BULGARIA
MOLDAVIAN SSR
BLACK SEA
BUKOVINA
MARAMUREŞ
CRIŞANA
MOLDAVIA
BANAT
MUNTENIA
WALLACHIA
OLTENIA
DOBROGEA
Czernowitz (Cernauţi)
Sighet
Suceava
Cîmpulung
Iasi
Kishinev (Chişinău)
Odessa (Cdesa)
Akerman (Cetatea Alba)
Roman
Bistriţa
Oradea Mare
Cluj
Sărmăşel
Tîrgu Mureş
Curtici
Arad
Alba Iulia
Sibiu
Timişoara
Hunedoara
Petroşani
Reşiţa
Oraviţa
Orşova
Turnu Severin
Belgrade
Craiova
Braşov
Predeal
Sinaia
Focşani
Galaţi
Reni
Ismail
Brăila
Tulcea
Sulina
St Gheorghe
Ploieşti
Snagov
Slobozia
Bucharest
Cernavoda
Constanta
Giurgiu
Russe (Rusciue)
R. Dnister
R. Prut
R. Sêret
R. Mureş
R. Jiul
R. Dimbroviţa
R. Ialomiţa
R. Argeş
R. Danube
Land over 2000 feet
0
100 km

Introduction

It is tempting to approach Communism solely in terms of its repressive nature and its gross denial of human rights. Indeed, the manner in which the political experiment, represented by the ideology and practised by its Soviet masters, was imposed upon the countries of Central Europe exemplified its coercive character, and is discussed in this study. Communism was not elected to power. But once established, its agent, the Communist Party, skilfully employed strategies to maintain itself in power. An examination of those strategies is essential for an understanding of the longevity of Communism in the Soviet Union and its satellite states.

For that reason, a cogent study of Communism must be multifaceted and interdisciplinary. It should consider the cost-benefit analysis that citizens made in choosing to tolerate the regime—in Romania's case—to demonstrate support for it and Ceauşescu. When considering Romania's experience in the aftermath of the Second World War, the words of the British socialist Richard Crossman come to mind. Writing in 1949, he argued that

> no one who has not wrestled with Communism as a political philosophy, and Communists as political opponents can really understand the values of Western Democracy. The Devil once lived in Heaven, and those who have not met him are unlikely to recognize an angel when they see one.[1]

Life went on under dictatorship, even if it was largely mapped out for the individual by the regime. How did the citizen negotiate the challenges placed in his or her path by the state? To what degree was the moral compass of the person deflected? What role were intellectuals called upon to play in 'validating' the regime? Why did utopia descend into dystopia under Ceauşescu? What was the ideological inspiration for his policy of "village systematization"? In what forms was the personality cult manifested? These are some of the questions addressed in this analysis.

Several laudable studies have appeared on aspects of Communist rule under Ceauşescu, notably by Adam Burakowski, Mary Ellen Fischer and J.F. Brown.[2] Vladimir Tismăneanu has given us an admirable analysis of the history of the Romanian Communist Party (*Stalinism for All Seasons. A Political History of*

Romanian Communism (Los Angeles, 2003)) which places a focus on the struggle for dominance in the party. Gheorghiu-Dej, has received less attention.[3] Yet Gheorghiu-Dej made the regime of Nicolae Ceauşescu possible. It is the aim of this book to chart that development and to focus on the descent of Ceauşescu into "the demonic obsessiveness of a man possessed and blinded by a crazed sense of himself and his mission".[4]

While drawing upon these aforementioned studies, I have also relied upon my own extensive research into primary sources on these topics which has resulted in the publication of three monographs: *Ceauşescu and the Securitate: Coercion and Dissent in Communist Romania, 1965–89 (London, New York: Hurst and M.E. Sharpe, 1995); Romania under Communist Rule (Bucharest: Civic Alliance Press, 1997);* and *Gheorghiu-Dej and the Police State, 1948–1965 (London, New York: Hurst and St Martin's Press, 1999).* In the intervening years, however, a considerable number of secondary works have appeared in Romanian, consultation of which permits a more nuanced analysis of Communist rule.

My involvement in Romanian studies began in the mid-1960s with language and literature and has, by natural progression, come to extend to history and culture as a whole. Detailed study over many years has interacted with experience. My research draws not only upon primary sources but also on my contacts with dissidents, especially poets and critics, who emerged in the later stages of the Ceauşescu regime. Not surprisingly, I became *persona non grata* to the regime in late 1988. After the Revolution of 1989, this moral identification with the society—in the broadest sense—opened to me doors which were closed to most indigenous as well as 'Western' inquirers.

My research into the security apparatus and its connections with the political leadership reflect these experiences. The three volumes mentioned above are based not only upon the state archives but also on the oral evidence of leading political and security figures, and of their victims. These volumes form part of a corpus of published and unpublished research which provides the 'building blocks' of this study. Hitherto, attention has tended to concentrate either on Romania's leadership or upon its economic development, both considered from the point of view of social sciences. This present study offers a detailed *vue d'ensemble* of Romania under Communism.

My characterization of that period is one of paradox and degeneration. The paradox is evident in the several iterations of Communist rule. Whereas in 1956 Romania under Gheorghiu-Dej showed itself to be the Soviet Union's most active ally in the suppression of the Hungarian uprising, within two years the same Gheorghiu-Dej had persuaded Nikita Khrushchev to withdraw Soviet troops from his country. Whereas Gheorghiu-Dej's successor, Nicolae Ceauşescu, could, in the late 1960s, present himself to the outside world as a young, dynamic reformer in contrast to the ageing Leonid Brezhnev, so after the accession of Mikhail Gorbachev to the Soviet leadership in March 1985 the images were reversed: Ceauşescu now assumed the *persona* of a fossilized Brezhnev. The paradox is most marked in a comparison of Ceauşescu's domestic and foreign policies. In foreign policy, he demonstrated the same skill, sensitivity and resourcefulness that had been displayed by Gheorghiu-Dej in taking Romania on its autonomous course. It was Ceauşescu who put Romania firmly on the map of international relations; the fact that he made three state visits to the United States, an honour unprecedented for the leader of a Warsaw Pact member, shows the importance attached by successive US administrations to cultivating this maverick ruler. In contrast, in domestic policy, Ceauşescu displayed a doctrinaire obstinacy, degenerating into an inflexible, single-minded despot, insensitive to the needs of the population, and attentive only to his domineering wife Elena.

Visitors to Romania today will still find plenty of physical evidence of the legacy of the Ceauşescu regime, notably the monumental *Casa Republicii* (House of the Republic) in the centre of Bucharest, the largest building in Europe, and the abandoned plants of his countrywide industrialization drive. Less visible are the psychological scars which his repressive rule left on his people. This book seeks to provide a radiography of it.

Dennis Deletant
June 2017

Notes

1 Richard Crossman (ed.), *The God that Failed* by Andre Gide, Richard Wright, Ignazio Silone, Stephen Spender, Arthur Koestler, Louis Fischer (New York: Harper, 1950), p.10.
2 Adam Burakowski, *Dictatura lui Nicolae Ceauşescu, 1965–1989, Geniul Carpaţilor* (Iaşi: Polirom, 2011); Mary Ellen Fischer, *Nicolae Ceauşescu. A Study in Political Leadership* (Boulder, Colorado: Lynne Rienner Publishers, 1989); J.F. Brown, *Surge to Freedom: The End of Communist Rule in Eastern Europe* (London: Adamantine Press, 1991).
3 His period of leadership of the Party is discussed by Ghita Ionescu, *Communism in Rumania, 1944–1962* (London, RIIA: Oxford University Press, 1964), and by Tismăneanu in *Stalinism for All Seasons*.
4 Brown, *Surge to Freedom*, p.202.

1 The early years of the Romanian Communist Party (1921–1944)

The Romania in which the Communist Party operated was radically different from the Romania in which socialism first appeared. As a result of its participation in the First World War, the country more than doubled in area and increased in population from 7.5 million to more than 17 million. The enlarged Romania included areas formerly ruled by Russia, Hungary and Bulgaria—which left it with two neighbours unwilling to accept their losses and bent on revision of the treaties which legalized them; and one, the Soviet Union, refusing to recognize the loss of Bessarabia. By these additions of territory, the new Romania had minorities amounting to 29% of the population, which the centralizing policies of governments in the 1920s did little or nothing to reconcile to their new status. Both before and after the war, there were the Jews, largely concentrated in Moldavia, whose arrival, often under duress, from Russia and the Ukraine, nevertheless made them widely regarded, especially among peasants, as 'Russians'. Sephardic immigrants from the south, largely settled in Wallachia, were not so much resented, and indeed were much more integrated, especially in finance and industry.

Industrial development was confined to an east-west axis from Timişoara to Braşov in Transylvania, and a north-south axis from Sighişoara in Transylvania to Ploieşti and Bucharest in Wallachia. This left the country a prominently agricultural one, with great discrepancies between town and country. According to the 1930 census, 80% of the population of 18 million lived on the land in villages that were poorly served by transport and communications while according to one source there were 819,422 people employed in industry.[1] Few villages had piped water or electricity, health services were primitive, especially in the more backward regions of Moldavia and Bessarabia, and in such conditions it is hardly surprising that infant mortality was amongst the highest levels in Eastern Europe.

These problems were of a complexity which would have taxed the most far-sighted government and the most thoroughgoing cadres of administration. In the interwar period, Romania had neither. The greatest discrepancy, from a Western point of view, lay in the gulf between word and deed. Behind the facade of political institutions copied from the West the practice of government was subject to patronage and to narrow sectional interests. Under the constitution of 1923 the king had the power to dissolve parliament and to appoint a new government. That government was charged with seeking a popular mandate by organizing elections whose conduct was entrusted to the county prefects. Invariably the new government appointed new prefects to secure the desired result. By general consensus the only elections deemed to have been relatively free of such gerrymandering were those of 1928. Institutionalized corruption was matched by a personal variety. The exploitative rule of foreign princes in Wallachia and Moldavia in the eighteenth and early nineteenth century had helped to create a culture amongst the dominant élite in which rapacity was regarded as proof of dexterity and cunning, and therefore corruption of principles had become widespread. This culture had been assimilated by the small, bureaucratic middle class who expected to rely on unofficial remuneration in the form of bribes to supplement their meagre salaries. There was no native economic middle class to act as a check upon the élite since commerce had fallen mostly into the hands of the largely disenfranchised Jews who were barred from public service.

Idealism was scorned and those who searched for it, the young, were driven to the sole parties which seemed to have any on offer, those of the Right. Although a radical land reform was introduced soon after the war, many peasants were unable to afford the loans necessary to buy agricultural machinery. The economic recession of the 1930s ushered in a decade of instability in which the xenophobia of the impoverished peasantry was exploited by right-wing movements, principally by the Iron Guard, and directed against the Jews.[2] Disillusion with the failure of parliamentary government to solve economic problems fuelled support for the Guard, with its promise of spiritual regeneration and its programme of combatting 'Jewish Bolshevism'.

Until the end of the Second World War, the Romanian Communist Party was on the fringes of Romanian politics. The Party's identification with the doctrines of Communism, and the threat posed by the Soviet Union as a hostile neighbour, deprived it of any popular support.[3] The interventions of the Moscow-based Communist International (Comintern) in the Party's affairs were invariably disastrous and further marginalized the Party since it was considered subservient to Soviet interests. Two Comintern policies gave particular offence: the demand for the return of Bessarabia to the Soviet Union, and for self-determination for the minorities in Romania. This view of the Party as 'alien' and as a tool of the Soviet Union led the Romanian government to ban it on 11 April 1924. The ban remained for 20 years and crippled the Party's activity. The faithful were obliged to work clandestinely and they were liable to be caught by the *Siguranţa*, the secret police. Jail was therefore a common experience of party activists in the interwar period. Prison crystallized their beliefs and convinced many of them of the righteousness of their cause. In these circumstances, the Party became more like a sect, its members deprived of any check on their convictions which overt participation in politics might promote.

Some of the problems which the Party faced were not unique. The parties of the left in general exerted little influence on political life in the interwar years. Romania, being a predominantly agricultural country, lacked a powerful indigenous working class upon which these parties might have formed a base, whilst the electoral strength of the National Peasant Party (formed in 1926 from the union of the Peasant Party and the National Party of Transylvania) demonstrated its attractiveness to the peasantry with its programme of peasant control of the means of production in agriculture, and of devolution of government administration in the village. In the 1926 general elections, the NPP won 727,000 votes (28% of the votes cast), in 1928, 2,209,000 (78%), in 1932, 1,204,000 (40%), and in 1937, 627,000 (20%).

The Social Democratic Party (SDP), the principal democratic party of the left, had been rent by dissension during the First World War and emerged from it split into two factions dubbed 'maximalists' and 'minimalists'. The former paralleled the Bolsheviks by advocating the immediate dictatorship of the proletariat through revolution and was led by Alexandru Dobrogeanu-Gherea, Boris Ştefanov and Alecu Constantinescu. Among the younger members of this group were Marcel Pauker and his future wife, Ana Rabinsohn.[4] Their differences with the minimalists were more of emphasis rather than substance, with the minimalists taking a more cautious line on the need for violent change. Further fragmentation occurred with the emergence of a third faction, the 'centrists', who supported affiliation to the Comintern, provided that it did not vitiate Romania's independence.

The creation of the Comintern in March 1919 profoundly changed the course of the socialist movement in Romania for it exerted an irresistible attraction to those in the SDP who sought change by revolution. The maximalists argued for immediate affiliation with the Comintern but were thwarted by the minimalists who, at a SDP congress held in May, persuaded the participants to adopt a programme of democratic socialism; the transfer of all means of production from the private sector to state control but within the existing political system. The conflict between the two factions was brought out into the open again in November 1920, when a six-member delegation of maximalists and minimalists was sent to Moscow to negotiate Comintern affiliation. When Bukharin and Zinoviev criticized the SDP for its unwillingness to adopt a revolutionary programme, the minimalists responded by complaining about Comintern interference with the composition of the SDP's leadership.

Upon the delegation's return from Moscow in January 1921, its members put a motion to the party's general council recommending affiliation. The vote highlighted the divisions within the party, with the proposal receiving the endorsement of the maximalists and the centrists, who together formed a majority. The minimalists, who opposed affiliation, decided to leave the party. The council decided to convene a party congress in May where the principal item on the agenda was to be affiliation to the Comintern. This became what is regarded as the first congress of the Romanian Communist Party which opened in Bucharest on 8 May 1921. It was scheduled to run for five days, but police raids and arrests forced the abandonment of the congress on 12 May, the day after it voted to declare affiliation to the Comintern. According to C. Titel Petrescu, a leading socialist in the interwar period, three of the most fervent advocates of affiliation were police agents who aimed thereby to provide justification for the arrests.[5] The unfinished business, which included the adoption of a programme and the election of senior officials, was continued at a second congress, held in Ploieşti on 3–4 October 1922, when those participating took the name of the 'Communist Party of Romania, section of the Communist International'. This is indeed how the Party is styled in the records of the Comintern. Gheorghe Cristescu was elected general secretary.[6]

Membership of the Comintern gave the kiss of death to the fortunes of the Romanian Communists during the interwar period. By the time of the second congress of the Party, held in Ploieşti in 1922, the impact of affiliation to the Comintern had become clear. At the insistence of Moscow the 'centrists' were expelled in early 1922; Comintern sources indicated that whereas the SDP had over 45,000 members before the split, the Romanian Communist Party retained only 2,000 members in 1922.[7] On 11 April 1924, shortly after negotiations for resuming diplomatic relations between Romania and the Soviet Union collapsed over the Russian refusal to accept any formula which might be interpreted as an acknowledgement of Romanian sovereignty over Bessarabia, the Romanian government issued an order banning the RCP.

Henceforth, the Party was forced to conduct its activities underground or through surrogate organizations. Both means were impediments to recruitment and to the exercise of the democratic conduct of Party affairs. Even though it was reduced to a marginalized heap, the Party was required to behave by the Comintern as a 'proper' Communist Party by holding congresses and implementing a party line. Congresses were duly held, but in secret and outside Romania—the third in Vienna (August, 1924), the fourth in Kharkov (1928), and the fifth and final pre-war congress in Moscow (1931).

Most damaging to the RCP's hopes of winning new recruits were Comintern directives which constituted an attack on Romania's national integrity. These were diametrically opposed to the sentiments of the vast majority of Romanians, including those in the industrial working class. The directives also provoked divisions within the RCP. Cristescu, a Romanian by birth, recognized that the adoption of such a policy by the Party could lead to proscription, while the Transylvanian Hungarians Elek Köblös and Sandor Kőrősi-Krizsán were in favour. To resolve the conflict, Alexandru Dobrogeanu-Gherea proposed the despatch of an RCP delegation to Moscow to discuss the issue with the Comintern executive. The visit in September 1923 resulted in defeat for Cristescu.

Typical of the directives was the call from the fifth Comintern congress, held in June and July 1924, for "the political separation of oppressed peoples from Poland, Romania, Czechoslovakia, Yugoslavia, and Greece", the demand that Bessarabia, northern Bukovina and the Western Ukraine be united with the Soviet Union, and that Transylvania and the Dobrogea be made independent states. With the RCP now outlawed, there was nothing to be lost by adopting this position and, as if to emphasize its anti-Romanian character, the Party installed Köblös as general secretary at the third RCP congress held in Vienna.[8]

The delegates accepted a resolution proclaiming the right of the minorities to secede from the newly enlarged Romania, a stance which it was to reiterate at its fourth and fifth congresses. The resolution effectively endorsed Soviet claims to Bessarabia by declaring that the hope of "workers and peasants of Bessarabia that their national revolution would unite them with the USSR".[9] The Romanian parliament responded in December by passing a law making Communist activity an offence. As a result, over "eight hundred members of the Party were arrested and an entirely new party apparatus had to be erected", according to Comintern reports.[10]

The Party's policy of self-determination for the minorities inevitably drew members of these groups to the Party's ranks in disproportionate numbers and this, in turn, reinforced its 'alien' image.[11] That image was underlined both by the fact that between the late summer of 1924 and the spring of 1944, its general secretaries were not ethnic Romanians, and by the staging of its fourth and fifth Congresses in the Soviet Union. At the former, Vitali Holostenko, a one-time member of the Ukrainian Communist Party, was elected general secretary to replace Köblös, but the party continued to be rent by factional disputes generated by personality clashes rather than ideological conflict. Holostenko's authority was challenged by Marcel Pauker who, under his conspiratorial name of Luximin, claimed to represent the party. He was supported by Alexandru Dobrogeanu-Gherea, Boris Ştefanov, and László Luka (Vasile Luca), a Transylvanian Hungarian worker who, at the Kharkov Congress, had been elected to the party's Central Committee. With the party paralysed by this confusion, the Comintern intervened to convene the fifth congress in Moscow in 1931, imposing yet another non-Romanian, Alexandru Stefanski (Gorn), as general secretary. Stefanski was a member of the Polish Communist Party and served as leader of the RCP from his base in Berlin for three years before Eugen Iacobovici took his place. In June 1936, the Bulgarian Ştefanov took over and held office until December 1940 when the Transylvanian Hungarian Ştefan Foriş was appointed by the Comintern.[12]

The ethnic composition of the party's leadership made it particularly vulnerable in the ultranationalist arena of Romanian politics in the 1930s, when the myth of 'Judeo-Bolshevism' was propagated by Corneliu Codreanu's Iron Guard and other movements of the extreme right such as the National Christian Party led by Octavian Goga and Alexandru C. Cuza. In an effort to present a more indigenous image, some Jewish party members took Romanian cover names, among them Iosif Chişinevski (Iosif Roitman), Leonte Răutu (Lev Oigenstein), and Valter Roman (Ernst Neuländer). Those that did not, for example, Ana and Marcel Pauker, Bela Brainer and Remus Koffler, confirmed suspicions in the public mind about their real loyalties. Their presence, coupled with that of Transylvanian Hungarians such as Köblös and Foriş, and the Bulgarians Gheorghe Crosneff and Dimitar Colev (Dumitriu Coliu), invited the conclusion that the use of 'Romanian' in the title of the party was a fiction. Most Romanians ignored the fact that the majority of Jews in Romania did not belong to the RCP, and that a number of these leaders, such as Dobrogeanu-Gherea and Marcel Pauker, were victims of Stalin's purges in the Soviet Union.

Membership of the party remained small. In 1922, the party had 2,000 members but according to Comintern figures, the figure fell in 1925 to 1,661 members. In 1927, the number collapsed dramatically to barely 300, probably because the party's stance on Bessarabia had become well known, but membership was to rise slowly throughout the 1930s, reaching its highest point in 1937 with 1,635 activists.[13] The minorities provided a disproportionately large percentage. An analysis of membership for the 1930s shows that the Hungarians, who constituted less than eight per cent of the country's population, made up some 26 per cent of the RCP; the analogous figures for Jews were four per cent of the population and 18 per cent, for Russians and Ukrainians, three per cent and 10 per cent, and for Bulgarians, two per cent and ten per cent. Romanians, by contrast, constituted 72 per cent of the population and yet only 23 per cent of party members.[14]

The party, despite its proscription, responded to the difficult economic conditions by being active on the labour front. It organized a number of strikes, one of which was to bring to the fore a railway worker who, after the imposition of Communist rule in Romania, became Romania's leader. Gheorghe Gheorghiu was something of a rarity amongst RCP members, being at once an ethnic Romanian and from a working-class background (his father was a manual worker). His lack of a formal education marked him out from the intellectuals in the party, such as the Paukers and Lucreţiu Pătrăşcanu, and even from his later close friend, Emil Bodnăraş, who had passed out from a Romanian officers' school.[15] Gheorghiu was born in Bârlad in Moldavia on 8 November 1901. At the age of 11 his parents, Tănase and Ana, sent him to work as a porter in the Danube port of Galaţi. He managed to complete three years of secondary education in a trade school, qualifying as an electrician. According to one source, he took a series of jobs in a timber mill, a textile mill, and then in coopers' yards in Piatra Neamţ and Moineşti. From 1919 to 1921, he worked as an electrician in the town of Câmpina, after which he returned to Galaţi where he signed on as an electrician in a railway yard. Accusations of 'Communist agitation' led Gheorghiu to be transferred from the railway yards in Galaţi to Dej on 15 August 1931 and it was his association with the town which led the suffix Dej to be attached to his name.[16]

Various dates have been given for Gheorghiu-Dej's initiation into the Communist Party; 1928, 1930 and 1932. As state employees, railway workers were denied the right to strike, and this merely added to their disaffection. Gheorghiu-Dej took up his colleagues' grievances and on 20 March 1932 attended a national meeting of railwaymen in Bucharest where he was elected to the Central Action Committee. On 2 February 1933, the railway workers at the Griviţa yards in Bucharest went on strike after the government withdrew from earlier agreements on working conditions with the men. The strike spread to railwaymen in Cluj and Iaşi. Gheorghiu-Dej and other members of the committee were arrested on 14 February and on the following day there were violent clashes at the yards between workers and police which left several railwaymen dead. Although in jail during these disturbances, Gheorghiu-Dej was put on trial as one of the instigators alongside Constantin Doncea, Chivu Stoica, Dumitru Petrescu, Ilie Pintilie, Gheorghe Vasilichi and over one hundred other 'agitators'. Sentenced on 19 August 1933 to twelve years' hard labour, [17] Gheorghiu-Dej was sent to the Doftana prison near Câmpina where in 1936 he was joined by all the other jailed Communists following a decision by the authorities to place all of them together. If the aim was to supervise them more effectively, it was a patent failure, as a police report from September 1936 indicated:

> At Doftana the Communists, although isolated in their cells, carry on political work...hold daily conferences and...discuss subjects of communist agitation... The prisoners are organized in a collective which includes all communist prisoners... In addition, there is a communist group...which leads the collective.[18]

Imprisonment at Doftana, like the Griviţa strike and the *coup* of 23 August 1944, was accorded a sacred place in Gheorghiu-Dej's career by post-war Communist historiography. It continued to enjoy mythical status in the annals of the Communist movement compiled under Nicolae Ceauşescu, who also served a two-year sentence there for Communist agitation between 1936 and 1938. The prison experience of the Communists in Doftana was presented as an integral part of the class struggle between the proletariat and an alliance of the bourgeoisie and landowners in which the latter, faced with the prospect of defeat, resorted to the use of legislation "of a repressive nature" in order to stifle the growth of "the revolutionary movement of the proletariat". The conditions in which the Communists were held in Doftana, one Party historian claimed, revealed "the premeditated aim of destroying them physically and morally through the use of pressure, solitary confinement, beatings and starvation".[19]

So sweeping a condemnation is not supported by reliable evidence. While isolation cells were occasionally used in which the prisoners were kept in total darkness and solitary confinement, prisoners in ordinary adjacent cells could communicate with each other. The Doftana prisoners were allowed visitors, food parcels, money and reading matter.[20] Even correspondence was smuggled in, and this allowed Gheorghiu-Dej to keep in touch with the party leadership, for he was co-opted to its Central Committee *in absentia* in 1935.[21] In terms of his ethnic and social background he was, as a CC member, unique apart from Ilie Pintilie, a railwayman from Iaşi. Unlike Constantin Pârvulescu, Iosif Chişinevski, Petre Borilă and Gheorghe Stoica from among the Romanian Communists, or Klement Gottwald, Ernő Gerő, Boleslaw Bierut or Iosip Broz Tito from among the other East European Communist Parties, Gheorghiu-Dej did not study at the Comintern school in Moscow.

In Doftana the young Communists looked to Gheorghiu-Dej for leadership and he provided it. He cultivated an avuncular image, being addressed as 'the old man', even though he was only in his mid-thirties. Amongst their number were Gheorghe Apostol, Nicolae Ceauşescu, Alexandru Drăghici and Alexandru Moghioroş, all of whom were, after 1944, to be promoted to senior party and state positions as Gheorghiu-Dej's trusted lieutenants. Alongside this group of young activists he attracted a parallel set of friends who were all Soviet agents: Pintilie Bodnarenko, Vasile Bucikov, Pyotr Goncearuc, Serghei Nikonov and Misha Posteucă. It was from the latter that Gheorghiu-Dej learned his halting Russian.[22]

Nevertheless, prison was hardly a place from which Gheorghiu-Dej could translate his authority into effective action. It also cut him off from the Comintern and meant that he did not pass through the hands of its instructors, either in Moscow or elsewhere. This marked him out from those in the Communist Party in Romania who did and made him an unknown quantity to Stalin.

The opposite was true of the figure who was to become Gheorghiu-Dej's main rival after 1944. Ana Pauker was born on 13 December 1893 in the village of Codăeşti in Moldavia into a middle-class family called Rabinsohn. Her father was a *haham*, a Jewish butcher and teacher of Hebrew at the local school. At the turn of the century, the Rabinsohns moved to Bucharest. Details of Ana's youth and education are sketchy and largely anecdotal, and the first mention of any professional activity concerns her employment as a teacher of Hebrew at the *Brotherhood of Zion* primary school in Bucharest.[23] Shortly afterwards, in September 1915, she joined the socialist movement. According to an autobiographical pamphlet published in 1951, Ana helped to distribute literature produced by the Romanian SDP. She was more forthcoming about her activity during this period to Corneliu Coposu, private secretary to National Peasant Party leader Iuliu Maniu, who she encountered at Cluj prison in the mid-1930s. There she revealed that after leaving her post as a schoolteacher, she found a position as a secretarial assistant at the newspaper *Dimineaţa* where she had responsibility for the library. It was while working here that in 1921 she met the son of one of the major shareholders of the newspaper, Marcel Pauker, who was three years her junior and had just returned from Paris where he had taken a doctorate in law.[24]

The two took part in the foundation congress of the RCP in May 1921, but the arrest of its leading members prompted them to flee to Zurich where they were married on 1 June. Marcel enrolled as a student of engineering at *L'École Polytéchnique Federale* while Ana began a course in medicine. A few months after the wedding, Ana returned to Bucharest to give birth to her first child, a daughter called Tania, who died of dysentery before she was one year old. At the second RCP congress, held at Ploieşti in October 1922, both Marcel and Ana were elected to the Central Committee of the Party. After the proscription of the party and the suppression of its newspaper *Socialismul* in April 1924, Ana was given the task of publishing underground propaganda, thereby becoming a target of the *Siguranţa*, the security police. She was arrested with four female colleagues and held in Văcăreşti prison. At Ana's instigation the four went on hunger strike and were beaten, after which they and Ana were released until the date of their trial, fixed for July 1925.[25]

The defendants absconded and Ana Pauker was sentenced *in absentia* to ten years imprisonment. The Paukers managed to flee abroad in 1926, staying in Berlin, Paris and Prague, and in the same year Ana gave birth to a son, Vlad, in Vienna. From there they went to Moscow where Ana attended the Comintern training school in order to become an instructor. In Moscow, Ana produced a second daughter, named Tatiana, in 1928. Her husband returned to Romania clandestinely in the spring of 1929, only to be arrested on 4 May, but he was to benefit from an amnesty of which he took advantage to work underground for two years before returning to Moscow. In December 1932, he was again sent by the Comintern to Romania, this time to organize Communist activity in Transylvania, and in the following year he was recalled to the Soviet capital.

Ana, too, was given a mission by the Comintern. She was attached, in turn, to the Czechoslovak, German and French Communist Parties (from 1931 to 1932) as an instructor, with the cover name of Marina. In March 1934, she was sent back by the Comintern to Romania in the company of other comrades in an attempt to revive clandestine activity which had been severely curtailed following the Griviţa strike. She was eventually arrested in Bucharest in the early hours of 13 July 1935. Her trial, and that of 18 other Communists—who included Alexandru Moghioroş, his future wife Stela (Esther Radoshovetsky), Alexandru Drăghici and Liuba Chişinevski Roitman—was scheduled to be held in the capital but street demonstrations in support of the defendants led the authorities to move it to Craiova. Proceedings opened on 5 June 1936, and were attended by several foreign press correspondents and observers. Among the 24 lawyers for the defence were Lucreţiu Pătrăşcanu and Ion Gheorghe Maurer, as well as personalities from the Bucharest bar.[26]

Ana Pauker was found guilty of being a leading member of an outlawed organization and sentenced on 7 July to ten years' imprisonment. She spent five in the prisons of Dumbrăveni, Râmnicu-Sărat and Caransebeş before being exchanged on 3 May 1941 for Ion Codreanu, a 62-year old Romanian from Bessarabia who had been arrested for 'anti-Soviet agitation' in the previous July following the Soviet annexation of the province.[27] Whilst Ana was in prison, her husband was arrested in Moscow in 1937 for 'Trotskyist' sympathies, together with other senior members of the RCP: Alexandru Dobrogeanu-Gherea, Ecaterina Arbore, Pavel Tcacenko, Elek Köblös and David Fabian.[28] All became victims of Stalin's purges and were executed without trial in 1937.

These blows to the RCP did not prevent it from mounting a successful operation to recruit volunteers for the International Brigades during the Spanish Civil War. Volunteers were also raised by the National Peasant Party and the Social Democratic Party. 'Committees in Support of Republican Spain' were set up by all three parties to help provide food and clothing for the front. The Liberal Government espoused a policy of non-intervention and instructed the passport authorities not to issue passports to volunteers, but many volunteers left without them. More than five hundred Romanian Communists fought on the republican side, and their passage to Spain was organized by a network covering Romania, Czechoslovakia, Austria, Switzerland and France. Among those who fought were Petre Borilă, Mihai Burcă, Constantin Doncea, Mihail Florescu, Valter Roman and Gheorghe Stoica. After the republican defeat in the Civil War, a number of the Romanian volunteers were interned in the south of France but some, such as Mihail Florescu and Mihai Patriciu, escaped and fought in the French resistance until 1944, after which they found their way back to Romania.[29]

Internment in France, imprisonment in Romania and liquidation by Stalin all dealt crushing blows to the RCP. The Party's financial position was also disastrous. From a report compiled by Scevortzov, described as one of the Party leaders, which reached the Executive Committee of the Comintern in January 1940, it emerged that members' contributions were totally insufficient to cover the costs of the Party's activities in Romania. According to the report, in 1939 there were only 26 paid activists, seven of whom worked in Bucharest and the rest in regional branches. The financial support required to maintain the remnants of the Party came from the Comintern which used different channels to filter the funds through. One of these was France. From Moscow the money was sent to the Romanian Communists in France who then despatched it to Romania. At the beginning of 1939, Boris Ştefanov, the general secretary of the RCP living in Moscow, wrote to the Comintern secretary Gheorgi Dimitrov alerting him to the fact that two Party members, Bela Brainer and Gheorghe Vasilichi, based in France, had complained to him about a shortage of money. Dimitrov approved the despatch of 1,000 dollars to be shared by the two men. On 4 August 1939, Vasilichi informed Ştefanov that he was sending a man to Romania to pass on the latter's instructions.[30]

Until the summer of 1939, the Comintern, whose principal executives were the Bulgarian Gheorgi Dimitrov and Dmitri Manuilsky, a member of the Central Committee of the Soviet Communist Party, had conducted a crusade against Hitler and fascism as the main enemy of peace and of socialism in Europe, and in the context of this crusade the RCP had launched a slogan calling for 'defence of the frontiers'. But no sooner had Molotov and Ribbentrop signed the Nazi-Soviet Pact in August 1939, than the Comintern changed its line. Hitler and fascism were no longer the enemy; instead, Britain and France were to be blamed for the Second World War. A Comintern manifesto published in October 1939 avoided any attack on the Nazi dictatorship and echoed Molotov's and Ribbentrop's call for a negotiated peace. An article published in December 1939 in the *Communist International* by Ştefanov accused Britain and France of attempting to drag Romania into the imperialist war. He maintained that Romania's interests required a treaty of mutual assistance with the Soviet Union and directed the RCP to work for the right of self-determination in the annexed provinces of Bessarabia, Bukovina, Transylvania and Dobrogea, even if this meant their separation from Romania. Few Romanians believed the statement released later by the Soviet Foreign Ministry in which it denied that Ştefanov represented the views of the Soviet government, most Romanians being convinced that the article revealed a Soviet interest in Romania that went beyond the recovery of Bessarabia.[31]

The territorial losses suffered by Romania in the summer of 1940 almost eradicated the Party. Stalin, through his annexation of Bessarabia in June 1940, and Hitler, through his award of Northern Transylvania to Hungary in August, reduced Romania's total area and population by almost a third. The cession of these provinces was catastrophic for the RCP's membership since it removed areas where RCP loyalty was strong. According to Comintern figures, the RCP's membership of 4,210 dropped to about 1,000 as a result of the Soviet annexation of Bessarabia and northern Bukovina and the partition of Transylvania and the Dobrogea.[32]

The desire of Dimitrov to ensure that the RCP remained a slave to the Comintern's bidding led him to request in early 1940 that the party send two delegates to Moscow to report on its activity. Vasile Luca and Zighelboim Ştrul were chosen as representatives and left in April only to be arrested while attempting to cross the Romanian frontier with the Soviet Union illegally. At a meeting during the following month chaired by Ştefan Foriş and attended by Teohari Georgescu, Iosif Chişinevski and Gavrilă Birtaş, the decision was taken to send Foriş and Georgescu to Moscow for consultation with Comintern officials and they crossed secretly into newly-occupied Bessarabia to receive instructions and appear to have reached the Russian capital in August 1940.[33] Foriş was appointed general secretary of the party[34] and Georgescu allegedly designated Foriş's successor should anything befall him.[35]

The annexation of Bessarabia had other consequences for individual RCP members. Leonte Răutu[36] and Alexandru Bârlădeanu, who were both from the province, were accorded Soviet nationality and instructed to go to Moscow.[37] There they joined Valter Roman and Vasile Luca[38], the latter arrested as a Communist activist in Cernăuţi (Czernowitz) in 1940 but released after the Soviet occupation of northern Bukovina.[39] With the arrival of Ana Pauker in May 1941, this group constituted the so-called 'Moscow bureau' of the RCP. All were contributors to the Comintern-backed Romanian radio station *România liberă.* In 1943, Pauker was given the task of assisting in the recruitment of the *Tudor Vladimirescu* division of the Red Army, formed from Romanian prisoners of war, and together with Vasile Luca and two captured officers, Colonel Captaru and Colonel Nicolae Cambrea, she visited prison camps to attract volunteers.[40]

Romania's participation under her wartime pro-Nazi leader Ion Antonescu in the German attack on the Soviet Union in June 1941 perpetuated the divisions within the RCP. From this date, jailed Communists, as their prison sentences expired, were transferred from Caransebeş to the internment camp in Târgu Jiu, which had been established in autumn 1939 for Polish refugees.[41] Among them was Teohari Georgescu, who was caught by the police and jailed in Caransebeş in early 1941. These Communists were thus held, legally speaking, no longer as prisoners but as 'internees'. Gheorghiu-Dej emerged as the leader of this second group, the 'prison group' as it is sometimes known.[42] Despite internment they were able, by bribing the camp authorities, to maintain contact with the remnants of the party who had avoided arrest. The principal figures in this third group, the rump of the party, were Ştefan Foriş, who was confirmed as secretary general of the RCP by the Comintern in 1940; his deputy, Remus Koffler; Constantin Agiu; Lucreţiu Pătrăşcanu; Petre Gheorghe, head of the Bucharest party committee; Constantin Pârvulescu and Iosif Rangheţ. Yet Foriş's passivity in the face of Romania's participation in Operation *Barbarossa*, in particular the lack of significant partisan activity, attracted criticism from Gheorghiu-Dej which was shared by Rangheţ and Pârvulescu.[43] After his release from jail in November 1942, Bodnăraş allied himself with the latter in their opposition to Foriş. Their anger was fuelled following the arrest in May 1942 of Petre Gheorghe and an associate Nicolae Atanasoff by the Romanian Secret Service on a charge of espionage in favour of the Soviet

Union.[44] Foriş, whose relations with Gheorghe were strained, was alleged by colleagues to have refused to give any legal aid to Gheorghe and Atanasoff. At a summary trial in Ploieşti lasting only a single day—6 August—both were found guilty and sentenced to death. After a delay of several months both were executed by firing squad on 8 February 1943.

At Târgu Jiu discipline was even less strict than in the prisons.[45] Gustav Corbu, a British subject of Romanian origin interned at the camp between October 1941 and November 1943, distinguished three groups of internees: those who could afford to pay for their keep (the equivalent of £8 per month at 1945 prices); needy intellectuals who could only meet part of the costs; and the destitute and Communists who were made to work. Until 1942, the camp commandant was Colonel Zlătescu, who was alleged to have made a fortune while in charge. Those who could pay fully lived in clean and comfortable huts, and were given good food. However, they had to pay Zlătescu for the smallest service.[46] Newspapers and books approved by the censor were allowed into the camp, but no radios.[47]

On 8 September 1942, almost all the Jews among the Communists interned in Târgu Jiu were deported to Transnistria, the Romanian-administered territory between the Dniester and the Bug which had been overrun by German and Romanian armies in the autumn of 1941. The Jews were gathered in the camp at Vapniarka in the county of Jugastru.[48] A total of 1,312 Communists and Socialists from all over Romania were assembled in this camp.[49] The poor diet, which included a type of pea used for feeding cattle, caused permanent paralysis of the lower limbs in 117 detainees.

On 16 March 1944, General Constantin Vasiliu, the head of the gendarmerie, informed the Romanian Army Chief of Staff, that Antonescu had given orders for the repatriation of all Jews deported to Transnistria. Those deported from Bessarabia would be settled in Bălţi and Hotin counties, those from Bukovina in the city of Cernăuţi and in the districts of Cernăuţi and Storojineţ. Those from the Regat would be returned to their homes and the Jews interned in Grosulovo camp and those imprisoned in Râbniţa jail would be transferred to the Târgu Jiu camp.[50] Most of the Communists among the prisoners in Râbniţa never saw Romania again. Three categories of prisoner were distinguished by the Romanian authorities in Râbniţa: 1) Communists brought from prisons in Romania; 2) Communist partisans of both sexes who were Soviet citizens, and captured Soviet parachutists; and 3) common law offenders sentenced by the local court in Râbniţa.[51] Although the Ministry of Internal Affairs gave the order on 16 March to the gendarmerie in Râbniţa to evacuate the jail, the respective telegram never arrived because the post office in the town had been closed down. On the evening of 18 March, some 60 of the prisoners—apparently common law offenders—were removed from the prison under escort on the order of the local gendarmerie commander. Shortly afterwards, some of the partisans were also led away. The chief jailer, Văluţă Pintilie, in the absence of the prison governor who was on sick leave, handed over control of the prison and its inmates—215 in number according to the transfer document—to a German officer named Uresan Zozi.[52] The officer, identified as a captain in some witness statements, told the jailer Pintilie, to identify the principal

Communists and the two of them, accompanied by a Kalmuk soldier, went from cell to cell as the soldier shot each prisoner dead in the back of the neck.[53] The leader of the Communist youth movement, Andrei Bernard, was among the victims. Fifty-two prisoners were murdered, among them the female partisans.[54] The remainder survived the war and several of them, including Simion Bughici and Aurel Rottenberg (Ştefan Voicu), went on to occupy ministerial positions in the Communist government.

Following the battle of Stalingrad and the advance of the Soviet armies, the rules were relaxed for the Communist detainees in Târgu Jiu. At the same time, labour shortages meant that construction teams made up of Communists were sent to do repair work in the vicinity of the camp, and it was during such tasks that the Communists outside the camp were able to pass messages to those on labour detachment. Among those who did electrical repairs in homes near the camp was Nicolae Ceauşescu.

It was in the Târgu Jiu camp that the 'prison faction' under Gheorghiu-Dej took a decision to remove Foriş as General Secretary of the Party in April 1944. The circumstances in which this decision was taken are not entirely clear, for the mists of politically engineered distortion still linger over the matter. According to the official version propagated subsequently, a meeting was held on 4 April in the camp hospital involving Gheorghiu-Dej, Bodnăraş, Pârvulescu, Rangheţ and Chivu Stoica at which Gheorghiu-Dej demanded the removal of Foriş on the grounds that he was a police informer.[55] In his place a provisional secretariat of Bodnăraş, Pârvulescu and Rangheţ was appointed by those present. It is unclear as to whether Gheorghiu-Dej and his associates acted on their own initiative or upon instructions from Moscow, channelled to them by the Soviet agent Bodnăraş.

Contact between Foriş and the Comintern had been assured via Soviet agents in Sofia who travelled to Bucharest but this link was broken after Romania's entry into the war against the Soviet Union in June 1941. Instead, messages were relayed from Moscow to Foriş through Petre Gheorghe, the secretary of the Party in Bucharest, who had been sent for training to Moscow in the mid-1930s as an NKVD agent.[56] Relations between Foriş and Gheorghe became strained when the latter, apparently on the orders of the Comintern, instructed Foriş to organize sabotage actions behind the Romanian lines. Foriş refused, arguing that such a request was unrealistic in view of the fact that most of the Party members were either interned or under house arrest.[57] It was Foriş's inaction in this regard which appears to have driven Bodnăraş, Rangheţ and Pârvulescu to organize—with Gheorghiu-Dej's agreement—the abduction of Foriş on 4 April 1944 to a party safe house in the Bucharest district of *Vatra Luminoasă*.[58]

Much use of was made of Foriş's behaviour—whether justifiably or not is impossible to determine—by Gheorghiu-Dej and his associates in Târgu Jiu in plotting his removal. Bodnăraş gave his own account of his actions between the time of his release from prison in early November 1942 and his part in the removal of Foriş from the Party leadership on 4 April 1944 in discussions with Valter Roman, Gheorghe Zaharia and Ada Grigorian on 18 and 20 January 1960.[59] This group had been charged by Gheorghiu-Dej with examining the background to the

23 August *coup* in the light of the publication in the West of a book by General Hans Friessner, former commander of the German forces in Romania during the war, which had been partially serialized in a Soviet journal. Gheorghiu-Dej had also been stung by criticism in Soviet publications of Romania's part in the war against the Soviet Union and the RCP's alleged 'inactivity'.[60]

The removal of Foriş in April 1944 and his subsequent brutal murder on the orders of Gheorghiu-Dej, symbolize, as Vladimir Tismăneanu has noted, "the essentially repressive, anti-democratic character of Romanian Communism".[61] Gheorghiu-Dej's actions were characteristic of the inability of the Romanian Communists to follow any democratic procedures in implementing a change in leadership. Rumour and whispered denunciation were preferred to reasoned dialogue with Foriş, and Gheorghiu-Dej's *post factum* attempt to engineer a justification for his actions through the Pătrăşcanu-Koffler trial in April 1954 represented the height of cynicism. Foriş's removal was to herald a decade-long mafia-like struggle for power in the Party.

Notes

1 Vladimir Tismăneanu, *Stalinism for All Seasons. A Political History of Romanian Communism* (Berkeley, Los Angeles, London: University of California Press, 2003), p.39.

2 Two basic studies on the Iron Guard are Francisco Veiga, *La Mistica del Ultranacionalismo. Historia de la Guardia de Hierro* (Barcelona: Universitat Autonoma de Barcelona, Bellaterra, 1989), translated into Romanian as *Istoria Gărzii de Fier, 1919–1941. Mistica Ultranaţionalismului* [*The History of the Iron Guard, 1919–1941. The Mystique of Ultranationalism*] (Bucharest: Humanitas, 1993), and Armin Heinen, *Die Legion 'Erzengel Michael' in Rumänien Soziale Bewegung und Politische Organisation* (Munich: R. Oldenbourg Verlag, 1986); see also A. Heinen and O. J. Schmitt (eds.), *Inszenierte Gegenmacht von rechts. Die "Legion Erzengel Michael" in Rumänien 1918–1938* (Munich: R. Oldenbourg Verlag, 2013); Constantin Iordachi, *Charisma, Politics and Violence: The Legion of the "Archangel Michael" in Inter-war Romania* (Trondheim Studies on East European Cultures and Societies, no.15. Trondheim, Norway, 2004); Roland Clark, *Holy Legionary Youth. Fascist Activism in Interwar Romania* (Ithaca, New York: Cornell University Press), 2015, and Raul Cârstocea, "Uneasy Twins? The Entangled Histories of Jewish Emancipation and Anti-Semitism in Romania and Hungary, 1866–1913," *Slovo* 21(2009): 64–85.

3 Until it was legalized on 23 August 1944, the Romanian Communist Party was known by its Comintern designation of 'The Communist Party of Romania'. For the early history of the Party see: Tismăneanu, *Stalinism for All Seasons*, pp.37–84; also Ghita Ionescu, *Communism in Rumania, 1944–1962* (London: Royal Institute of International Affairs: Oxford University Press, 1964), pp.1–28, Robert R. King, *History of the Romanian Communist Party* (Stanford: Hoover Institution Press, 1980), pp.9–38, and Michael Shafir, *Romania. Politics, Economics and Society* (London: Frances Pinter, 1985), pp.9–28.

4 Marcel Pauker's son-in-law, Gheorghe Brătescu, selected material from the Russian Centre for the Preservation and Study of Documents of Contemporary History in Moscow relating to Pauker and published it in *Lichidarea lui Marcel Pauker*, ed. by G. Brătescu (Bucharest: Univers Enciclopedic, 1995). They include 400 pages of autobiographical material written in October and November 1937 in Pauker's own hand while he was under arrest in Moscow.

5 Ionescu, Communism in Romania, p.19.
6 Shafir, Romania. Politics, Economics and Society, pp.22–23.
7 Mary Ellen Fischer, *Nicolae Ceauşescu. A Study in Political Leadership* (Boulder: Lynne Rienner, 1989), p.20. For the sake of consistency I refer to the Party throughout this period as the Romanian Communist Party.
8 Tismăneanu, *Stalinism for all Seasons*, p.284, note 72.
9 Shafir, Romania, Politics, Economics and Society, p.24.
10 Mary Ellen Fischer, *Nicolae Ceauşescu*, p.16 quoting from G.D. Jackson, *Comintern and Peasant in Eastern Europe, 1919–1930* (New York: Columbia University Press, 1966), p.254.
11 Even key party documents were written, not in Romanian, but in German or Russian e.g. Marcel Pauker's 'self-criticism' addressed to the party's Central Committee in May 1932; see *Lichidarea lui Marcel Pauker*, pp.304–306.
12 For a biographical note on Ştefanov see Dennis Deletant, *Communist Terror in Romania. Gheorghiu-Dej and the Police State, 1948–1965* (London: Hurst and Co., 1999), p.2, note 3.
13 Membership of the RCP from 1925 to 1937 was as follows:

1925 1,661
1926 1,500
1927 300
1928 500
1929 461
1930 700
1936 1,083
1937 1,635

The breakdown of membership on ethnic affiliation for the year 1933 was: Hungarians 440, Romanians 375, Jews 300, Bulgarians 140, Russians 100, Moldavians 70, Ukrainians 70, Others 170 (Comintern files in RGASPI *Rossiiskii Gosudarstvennyi Arkhiv Sotsial'noi I Politicheskoi Istorii* [Russian State Archive of Social and Political History] formerly RTsKhIDNI [Russian Centre for the Preservation and Study of Documents on Contemporary History], fond 495, opis, 25, dos.744; I am grateful to Prof. Ioan Chiper of the 'Nicolae Iorga' Institute of History for this information).
14 Shafir, Romania, Politics, Economics and Society p.26.
15 See the biographical notes.
16 Gheorghiu-Dej's personal life, given his years of imprisonment, was fraught with problems. In 1927, he married Maria Alexe, a local girl whose father was a trader. The couple had two daughters, Vasilica (Lica), born in Galaţi on 28 August 1928 and died in Bucharest on 15 March 1987, and Constantina (Tanţi), born in Galaţi on 23 April 1931 who is believed to have died in 2000. In 1933, Maria divorced him and later remarried. In November 1938, Gheorghiu-Dej according to a police report, asked the party for permission to marry Elena Sârbu, a Communist activist, but he later withdrew this request (J. Enache, 'Căsătorii, divorţuri, iubiri, copii şi nepoţii', *Dosarele Istoriei*, vol.3, no.3 (1997), p.11). Maria was allegedly a heavy drinker and after his release from internment Dej took custody of his daughters. He did not remarry. Lica Gheorghiu made a name for herself as an actress, starring in a number of Romanian films in the early 1960s. She was married twice, first to Marcel Popescu whom Gheorghiu-Dej made minister for foreign trade (19 March 1957–17 August 1959). After Dej's death, he was vice-president of the Chamber of Commerce. He died in 1979. Lica and Marcel had two children: Sanda, born in 1950, and Camilia, born in 1955. In the late 1950s, Lica began a relationship with a doctor, Gheorghe Plăcinţeanu. Their affair infuriated Dej and he ordered Alexandru Drăghici, the minister of the interior, to 'remove' the doctor. Trumped-up charges of sedition were brought against the doctor and he was

found guilty and sentenced to ten years imprisonment. After developing tuberculosis, he was denied treatment in jail and died, it is believed, on 30 April 1961. Lica divorced Popescu and married Gheorghe Rădoi, who at the time was a director of the *Red Flag* tractor plant in Braşov. Tanţi, the younger daughter, trained as an engineer and became a lecturer at Bucharest Polytechnic. In 1953, she met a popular singer called Cezar Grigoriu. Dej frowned upon this liaison as well and in 1956 ordered Grigoriu's arrest. The singer was interrogated and beaten by Isidor Hollinger, head of the counter-intelligence directorate of the *Securitate*, and accused of being an Anglo-American agent. He was released after 24 hours and told by Hollinger to attribute his disappearance to drunkenness. Tanţi later married Stamate Popescu, a sculptor by whom she had a daughter (M. Oprea, 'Lica şi Tanţi Dej se iubeau cu doi burgheji', *Cuvîntul* (25–31 May 1992)).

17 His wife divorced him in the previous year and married a policeman. Mircea Chiriţoiu, 'Radiografia unui stalinist', *Dosarele Istoriei*, vol.3, no.3 (1997), pp.4–5 and Fischer, *Nicolae Ceauşescu*, p.23.

18 Fischer, *Nicolae Ceauşescu*, p.23.

19 Olimpia Matichescu, *Doftana. Simbol al Eroismului Revoluţionar* (Bucharest: Editura Politică, 1979), pp.12–13.

20 Author's interview with Gheorghe Apostol, 7 May 1990.

21 Mircea Bălănescu, an assistant to Ştefan Foriş, related how Foriş kept in touch with Gheorghiu-Dej by using couriers, known as *tehnicele*. These were young women to whom letters from Foriş were passed on by Bălănescu for delivery to Iosif Şraier, Dej's legal representative, who took them to his client in Doftana (Bălănescu interview, Romanian TV 1, 28 July 1994).

22 Letter from Mircea Oprişan to the author, 3 January 1996. Oprişan, who knew Gheorghiu-Dej from his time in Caransebeş, wrote that the latter also learned some Yiddish from Simion Zeigler, a lawyer who became a close friend and served as Gheorghiu-Dej's personal secretary when he became a government minister.

23 For this largely anecdotal account of Ana's background see Marius Mircu, *Dosar Ana Pauker* (Bucharest: Editura Gutenberg, 1991), pp.12–23. Another source places her in the northern Moldavian town of Buhuşi as a schoolteacher (Corneliu Coposu, *Dialoguri cu Vartan Arachelian* (Bucharest: Editura Anastasia, 1992), p.63). An authoritative biographical note on Pauker is given by Tismăneanu, *Stalinism for All Seasons*, pp.264–65.

24 Coposu, *Dialoguri*, p.63.

25 Mircu, *Dosar Ana Pauker*, p.43.

26 Ion Gheorghe Maurer (1902–2000) was born in Bucharest. His mother was Romanian but his father was from Alsace and was employed as French tutor to Prince Carol (later King Carol II). After studying law at Bucharest University, he practised at the bar. He developed Marxist sympathies and often appeared for the defence of Communists. According to his own testimony, he joined the Party 'somewhat before 1936'; see Lavinia Betea, *Maurer şi lumea de ieri* (Arad: Fundaţia Culturală Ion Slavici, 1995), p.13. For a more detailed bibliography see Tismăneanu, *Stalinism for All Seasons*, pp.262–63.

27 Details related by Codreanu to Archibald Gibson, Kemsley Newspapers correspondent, in 1945 and recorded in Gibson's private papers (seen by this author, courtesy of his widow).

28 Dobrogeanu-Gherea was executed on 4 December 1937 at the Lubianka prison in Moscow. For a biography of Fabian see *Anale de istorie*, vol.16, 1970, no.6, p.174.

29 *Voluntari români în Spania, 1936–1936,* ed. Gheorghe Adorian et al. (Bucharest: Editura Politică, 1971). I am grateful to Mihail Florescu for giving me a copy of this volume. Roman allegedly travelled from the south of France to Paris from where the Soviet embassy arranged his passage to Leningrad via Le Havre; author's interview with Eduard Mezincescu, 16 June 1994.

30 Details of this correspondence and of relations between the Comintern and the Communist Party in Romania in this period are to be found in T.A. Pokivailova, "1939–1940. 'Cominternul şi Partidul Comunist din România'", *Magazin Istoric*, vol.31, no.3 (March 1997), pp.45–48.

31 Henry L. Roberts, *Rumania: Political Problems of an Agrarian State* (New Haven: Yale University Press, 1951), p.258.

32 Comintern files in RGASPI *Rossiiskii Gosudarstvennyi Arkhiv Sotsial'noi I Politicheskoi Istorii* [Russian State Archive of Social and Political History] formerly RTsKhIDNI [Russian Centre for the Preservation and Study of Documents on Contemporary History], fond 495, opis, 25, dos.744; I am grateful to Prof. Ioan Chiper of the 'Nicolae Iorga' Institute of History for this information.

33 'Transcript of the Interrogation of Teohari Georgescu regarding the Departure and Activity of the Delegation of the Communist Party in Romania (Şt. Foriş, T. Georgescu) in the Soviet Union in 1940' in Dan Cătănuş, Ioan Chiper, *Cazul Ştefan Foriş* (Bucharest: Editura Vremea, 1999), pp.160–61. Georgescu was born on 31 January 1908 in Bucharest. After four years of elementary school, he became a printer's apprentice and in 1923 entered the printing plant of *Cartea Românească.* In 1928, he joined the printers' union and helped to organize a strike. His role in the strike brought him to the attention of the *Siguranţa* who placed him under surveillance. In the following year, he joined the Communist Party. In November 1933, he was arrested for distributing Communist manifestos and detained for several months before being released on grounds of 'insufficient proof'. He was rearrested in June 1934 for Communist activity but released on bail. He was arrested once again in Ploieşti in January 1935 for failing to appear at his trial, and held for several months before being released until the trial date was fixed. His trial was postponed on more than ten occasions between 1937 and 1940 when he was finally sentenced to two months' imprisonment. From 1937 to 1938 he worked as a printer for the daily *Adevărul* and the National Printing Office. In August 1940, he was sent to Moscow to receive instruction from the NKVD on orders from Georgi Dimitrov, secretary of the Comintern, on how to code messages and to use a special technique of writing them on glass. He was arrested in April 1941 as part of the Bucharest Party cell led by Iosif Chişinevski (Roitman) and sentenced in May to ten years in jail. The first part of his sentence was executed at Caransebeş jail. In April 1942, he was moved to Văcăreşti prison to work in the printing press and returned to Caransebeş at the end of August where he stayed until his release at the end of August 1944 (*Archive of the Romanian Security Service* (henceforth abbreviated to ASRI), fond Y, dosar 40009, vol.21, pp.111–37). This archive has been transferred to the Archive of the National Council for the Study of the Archives of the *Securitate* (ACNSAS) and is in the process of being re-catalogued. For this reason I have retained the original call-marks. For Georgescu see also Andrei Şiperco (ed.), *Confesiunile elitei comuniste. România 1944–1965). Arhiva Alexandru Şiperco*, vol. 2 (Bucharest: Institutul Naţional pentru Studiul Totalitarismului, 2015), pp.337–412.

34 Foriş was born on 9 May 1892 in the village of Tărlungeni near Braşov in Transylvania, which at that time was under Hungarian rule. After completing a degree in physics and mathematics at Budapest University, he returned to Braşov in September 1919 and joined the Hungarian language socialist newspaper *Munkas* (Worker) as an editor. He joined the Communist Party in 1921 and in the following year moved to Bucharest where, after the proscription of the party, he worked underground as an agitator. In 1926, he became secretary of *Ajutorul Roşu* (Red Aid), the Romanian section of the Comintern-controlled International Organization for Aiding the Fighters of the Revolution, known by its Russian initials MOPR (*Mezhdunarodnaia organizatsiia pomoshchi bortsam revoliutsii*). The MOPR provided food and legal aid to activists in prison. In 1927, Foriş was *co-opted* as a member of the Central Committee and took part in the fourth party congress in the following year. He was arrested in July 1928 but a

rapid deterioration in his health led to his release and he was able to make his way to Moscow. At the end of 1930 he returned to Romania and was arrested once again on 26 August 1931. Freed in 1935, he was appointed in 1938 to the secretariat of the Central Committee, and in February 1940 he was summoned by the Comintern to Moscow from where he returned in December as general secretary of the party (A.G.Savu, 'Ştefan Foriş. Schiţă pentru o viitoare biografie', *Magazin Istoric*, no.7 (1968), pp.53–58). This issue of the review was withdrawn from circulation by the authorities shortly after its appearance because of this article on Foriş. I am grateful to Marian Ştefan for providing me with a copy; see also N.I. Florea, 'Ştefan Foriş', *Analele de Istorie*, vol.18, no.3 (1972), pp.150–53.

35 An appraisal of Georgescu, made by the British political mission in 1946, shed some interesting light on his family background: "Several responsible reports claim, although baptized Orthodox, Georgescu is of Jewish origin and his actual name is Burah Tescovici. Married for second time to Jewess, Eugenia Samoila, a former dressmaker. He has one daughter. His family furnishes an interesting example of nepotism. He is the brother-in-law of General Nicolae Pârvulescu, Under-Secretary of Supplies, who through Georgescu entered into contact with the Communists. He has a brother who is the police chief of 31st Bucharest district. His wife has two brothers, one of whom was a press chief of the People's Court during war criminal trials, while the second on returning from Russia started in January 1946 a police information bureau under the name of 'Documentary Bureau'". (The National Archives, Kew (henceforth TNA), FO 371/59190/R7847/6181/37). General Pârvulescu was appointed Secretary General of Police in the Ministry of the Interior by Georgescu on 6 March 1945. Dissatisfied with this post, he was made Under-Secretary at the Ministry of Supplies in summer 1945.

36 For a biography of Răutu see Tismăneanu, *Stalinism for All Seasons*, pp.267–68.

37 Bârlădeanu was born at Comrat in Bessarabia in 1911. He completed his secondary schooling at Iaşi and in 1932 was taken on as a lecturer in political economics at the University of Iaşi. He appears to have been active in the National Peasant Party at this time since Corneliu Coposu, its youth leader, recalls Bârlădeanu being presented to him during a visit he made to the town (Coposu, *Dialoguri*, p.67). Bârlădeanu admitted to being a Communist from his student days and having flirted with the NPP but he left the latter after its handling of the Griviţa strikes. The Soviet annexation of Bessarabia caught him there on holiday at his mother's house and he remained in the province. He worked at an economics institute in Chişinău until the outbreak of war in 1941, when he was evacuated to Kazakhstan. Poor eyesight saved him from conscription and he was sent down a coal mine in Karaganda for several months before persuading a local Party boss to assign him to a secondary school in the town teaching mathematics. In 1943, he was sent to Moscow for doctoral studies and returned to Romania in 1946. Bârlădeanu's unusually long stay in the Soviet Union led to rumours that he was in fact a Russian and a member of the Soviet Communist Party, but he denied these, claiming that he joined the Romanian Communist Party in 1946 (Betea, *Maurer şi lumea de ieri*, pp.289–90).

38 Vasile Luca was the Romanianized name of László Luca, a Hungarian born in the commune of Cătălina in Covasna County in Transylvania on 8 June 1898. He lost his parents at the age of seven and was placed in an orphanage in Sibiu. When he was 13 he became apprentice to a local padlock maker. In 1915, he secured a job in the railway yards in Braşov but at the end of the year was called up into the Austro-Hungarian army and sent to the front. In 1919, as a conscript in the Romanian army, he took part in the campaign against Bela Kun's Soviet Republic. He resumed his railway job at the end of the year when he also joined the trade union movement. In 1924, he became regional secretary of the Communist Party in Braşov. Arrested in the same year for membership of an illegal organization, he spent three years in jail. In 1928, he was elected to the Party Central Committee. As a result of the internal struggles within the Party he was

sent to do basic Party work in Moldavia. In 1933 he was arrested for organizing trade union activity, tried and imprisoned for five years. After his release from jail he was *co-opted* into the Party Central Committee and delegated to present a report to the Comintern about the Party's activity. On 4 April 1940, he was caught while trying to cross the frontier into the Soviet Union and detained in Cernăuţi in northern Bukovina. He was released from custody following the Soviet occupation of the province at the end of June ('Documentarul referitor la procesul privind pe Vasile Luca', *Arhivele Naţionale Istorice Centrale (The National Central Historical Archives,* henceforth abbreviated to ANIC), *Arhiva Comitetului Executiv al CC al PCR (Archive of the Executive Committee of the Central Committee of the Romanian Communist Party),* No.264/19, 18.02.1972. I am grateful to Marius Oprea for locating this document.)

39 By virtue of his presence on Soviet territory, Luca was offered the right to claim Soviet citizenship which he exercised. He spent the next four years in Moscow, working for the Romanian section of Radio Moscow and for the Comintern-backed Romanian radio station *România liberă* (Ionescu, *Communism in Romania*, p.353); see also Gheorghe Buzatu ('Cominterniştii români se pregătesc', *Magazin Istoric*, vol.28, no.2 (February 1994), pp.41–42), who in Moscow consulted a register belonging to Ana Pauker with the names of 185 Romanian Communists who sought refuge in the Soviet Union during the war.

40 The first camp Pauker visited was at Oranki in July 1943; see: N. Fuiorea, *Divizia Stalinistă 'Tudor Vladimirescu' în Umbra Steagului Roşu* (Bucharest: Pan-Arcadia, 1992), p.17. Two army divisions, named 'Tudor Vladimirescu' and 'Horia Cloşca and Crişan', were formed respectively in October 1943 and April 1945 from Romanian prisoners of war in the Soviet Union. They were organized on the Soviet model in which political allegiance to the Communist Party was paramount. This was ensured by a political command which, in the 'Tudor Vladimirescu' division was composed as follows: Major Ştefan Iordanov, political officer for the division; Major Dumitru Petrescu, head of the section for education and culture; Captain Mihai Burcă, political officer for the 1st Infantry Regiment; Captain Dumitru Coliu, political officer for the 2nd Infantry Regiment; Captain Gheorghe Stoica, political officer for the 3rd Infantry Regiment; Captain Petre Borilă, political officer for 1st Artillery Regiment; Captain Sergiu Sevcenko, political officer for the anti-tank battalion; Alexandru Paraschiv, political officer of the reconnaissance section; Ştefan Rab, political officer for the signals company. They were Communists who had been given military rank. Petrescu and Stoica had taken part, alongside Ana Pauker, in the conference held on 3 and 4 September 1943 at Krasnogorsk, where a series of measures designed "to improve anti-Fascist activity" in the prisoner-of-war camps was taken. The most important took the form of the creation, in the following month, of the 'Tudor Vladmirescu' division from prisoners from various camps. They were encouraged to join at the instigation of Ana Pauker, Vasile Luca and other Romanian Communists living in the Soviet Union. Colonel Nicolae Cambrea, one of the prisoners, was appointed the division's commander. The Soviet High Command decided to prepare the division for action on 29 March 1944, and on that day General Kovalenko and General Melnikov visited the division. They resolved that the division should swear its oath on 30 March. This included the promise to "faithfully respect the brotherhood of arms with the Soviet Union" and "to fight for a lasting peace with the Soviet Union which has given me the power to fight with a weapon in my hand for the destruction of the common enemy, Nazi Germany". (A.D. Duţu, 'Politizarea armatei române', *Dosarele Istoriei*, vol.1, no.4 (1996), p.30.) However, sensitivity over the delicate problem of avoiding contact with Romanian units led the Soviets to keep the division away from the front line. It was moved to Vapniarka in Transnistria and on 9 May was visited once more by Ana Pauker and Vasile Luca. The 23 August *coup* removed the danger of a direct confrontation between the division and Romanian forces and it was ordered to move straight to Bucharest. To this end, it was provided with 150

Lorries, and on 30 August the advance units of the division entered Bucharest. Major Dumitru Petrescu immediately contacted Gheorghiu-Dej and other Communist leaders. The division went on to fight, as part of the Red Army, in Transylvania, Hungary and Slovakia. After being placed in the reserve on 20 March 1945, it was withdrawn from operations and sent back by train to Bucharest where it was received by Gheorghiu-Dej. Almost 1,000 officers and men were selected from the division and given training by Party activists. On 26 April, they were incorporated into the Romanian army, promoted and decorated. At the beginning of May, 986 of them were sent to units at the front where they were given the newly created posts of political officers. On 8 May 1945, the new command to which they were responsible, namely the Higher Directorate for Education, Culture and Propaganda of the Army, was established. This was the instrument by which the Communist Party imposed its policy on the army. The second division of Romanian volunteers, the 'Horia, Cloşca and Crişan' division, was formed at Kotovsk in the Soviet Union on 12 April 1945 by order of Stalin. Its commander was General Mihail Lascăr, who had been taken prisoner at Stalingrad. A Soviet counsellor was appointed to the division, in the person of Colonel Novikov Stepanovici, who was given the task of "helping the volunteers to familiarize themselves with Soviet weaponry". The political officer was Lt. Col. Dumitru Petrescu (who had fulfilled the same function with the 'Tudor Vladimirescu' division), while the head of the education and cultural section was Major Valter Roman. The division's mission was, in the words of Lascăr, "to be a model for the organization of the entire Romanian army for the purpose of building a new army, with a new spirit, the Romanian Democratic Army..." (A.D. Duţu, 'Politizarea', p.3). It was formally integrated into the Romanian army, together with the 'Tudor Vladimirescu' division on 15 August 1945.

41 Jailed Communists had been moved to Caransebeş in November 1940 after the destruction of Doftana jail in an earthquake. Some 26,000 Polish citizens—15,000 of whom were civilians—were, according to Romanian archival sources, interned in a number of localities in Romania, including Târgu Jiu, following their exodus from their homeland as a consequence of Stalin's attack of 17 September without a formal declaration of war (see *Refugiaţii polonezi în România 1939–1947). Documente din Arhivele Naţionale ale României. Polscy uchodżcy w Rumunii 1939–1947. Dokumenty z Narodowych archiwów Rumunii* [The Polish refugees in Romania, Documents from the Romanian National Archives], 2 vols. Warsaw-Bucharest: Arhivele Naţionale ale României, Institutul Memoriei Naţionale—Comisia pentru Condamnarea Crimelor Împotriva Naţiunii Poloneze, 2013.

42 It included Gheorghe Apostol, Nicolae Ceauşescu, Iosif Chişinevski, Miron Constantinescu, Alexandru Drăghici, Teohari Georgescu and Alexandru Moghioroş. Gheorghiu-Dej's leadership of the imprisoned Communists was initially contested. Pavel Câmpeanu, a young Communist jailed at Caransebeş, recalled how three fellow prisoners, Ion Meţiu, Tănase Bratosin and Virgil Fulgescu, who were also railwaymen, tried unsuccessfully to take over from Dej as leader of the Communist faction in the jail (Pavel Câmpeanu, 'Note asupra PCR în anii 40–50', *Sfera Politicii*, vol.1, no.2 (January 1993), p.18).

43 Antonescu had given the order in summer 1941 that if any act of sabotage was carried out by Communists, 20 Jewish Communists should be shot, and five non-Jewish Communists. There were occasional arrests of persons distributing Communist propaganda against the Antonescu regime. In a report of 18 August 1942, the head of the Bucharest police, General Pălăngeanu, reported that five printers had been arrested in January 1942 for printing and distributing a Communist pamphlet deriding the Romanian government. The ringleader had been sentenced to death. At a later date a further eight printers had been arrested for printing and distributing a speech of Stalin. Two received the death sentence (Arhivele Naţionale Istorice Centrale (henceforth ANIC), Ministerul Afacerilor Interne, Trial of Ion Antonescu, file 40010, vol.8, p.103).

44 Born on 19 March 1907 in Dobrici in Bulgarian Dobrogea, Gheorghe joined in 1927 the Bulgarian Revolutionary Organization, part of the wider Communist movement in the Balkans. In 1940, he became a member of the Dobrogea committee of the Communist Party in Romania and in 1941, secretary of the Ilfov district just north of Bucharest. He was arrested on 19 May 1942. The charge levelled against him at his trial was "crime against the security of the state" which police reports show to have been based on evidence that he had received instructions from the Soviet consulate in Varna through the intermediary of Soviet agents to carry out industrial sabotage at sites in Bucharest (see Mihai Burcea, 'Judecarea comuniştilor în timpul războiului. Procesul lui Petre Gheorghe', in Adrian Cioroianu (ed.), *Comuniştii înainte de Comunism. Procese şi Condamnări* (Bucharest: Editura Universităţii din Bucureşti, 2014), p.370.

45 While in Caransebeş, Gheorghiu-Dej had managed to get on the right side of the governor, Constantin Dobrian, who allowed him to listen to the radio, thereby following the progress of the war (letter to the author from Mircea Oprişan, 3 January 1996).

46 His tariffs were fixed on a sliding scale, the equivalent of £15 (at 1945 prices) being charged for five or six days 'leave' in Bucharest or a telephone call to the capital, £5 for permission to receive a visitor or for permission to go into Târgu Jiu, and £3 for sending a letter by private messenger. Corbu had been educated at Glasgow High School and University, had worked in a Scottish shipyard as an engineer, had lived in Britain for 29 years and had married an Englishwoman. He failed to leave Romania before the outbreak of war between Britain and Romania in December 1941 and was interned.

47 After a quarrel with Zlătescu, Corbu was sent to do hard labour on the Târgu Jiu-Petroşani railway. He was quartered, with 50 others, in a hut three metres by ten, and helped to hew eight tunnels through solid rock. A Lieutenant Trepăduş, who was in charge of the gangs, was said by Corbu to have been brutal to Jewish Communists. Corbu saw a Jew tied to a cross and left on it for 24 hours in the bitter cold, and also witnessed beatings administered to Jews, some of whom died. (Recorded in the private papers of Archibald Gibson, *The Times* correspondent in Romania from 1928 to 1940.) Zlătescu's malpractices came to the notice of the Ministry of the Interior and he was dismissed, being replaced by Colonel Serban Leoveanu who, nevertheless, is said by other internees to have continued them. A People's Tribunal sentenced Zlătescu and Trepăduş on 22 May 1945 to death and life imprisonment respectively. Zlătescu's sentence was commuted a few days later to life imprisonment.

48 An exception was Iosif Chişinevski (Roitman) who remained in Caransebeş. Born in 1905 in Bessarabia, Chişinevski is believed to have studied at the Communist Party academy in Moscow during the late 1920s. He was arrested in 1941 as the head of a Communist cell and sent to Caransebeş jail. He was spared deportation to Transnistria because only Jews with sentences under ten years were sent to the province while those with heavier sentences, like Chişinevski, Simion Zeiger and Radu Mănescu, remained in Caransebeş until their release on 23 August 1944; see Pavel Câmpeanu, 'Pe marginea unei recenzii. Mistere şi pseudo-mistere din istoria PCR', *22*, no.34 (23–30 August 1995), p.12.

49 The number of persons held in Vapniarka on 5 May 1943 was 1,312, of whom 1,092 were Jewish internees and 198 Christian internees. The remaining 22 were classified as criminals and were Christians. Of the Jews, 835 were males, 136 females, and five children (*Archive of the Romanian Ministry of the Interior*, packet 91, file 569, p.445).

50 Evreii din România între anii 1940–1944, vol.IV, 1943–1944: Bilanţul Tragediei – Renaşterea Speranţei, ed. Ion Şerbănescu (Bucharest: Editura Hasefer, 1998), pp.356–57.

51 Court testimony of Major Ştefan Mihăilescu, commander of the Legion of Gendarmes in Râbniţa, given in March 1945, *United States Holocaust Memorial Museum* (henceforth USHMM), RG.25.004M, reel 30, file 40013, vol.6, p.340.

52 United States Holocaust Memorial Museum (USHMM), RG.25.004M, reel 30, file 40013, vol.6, p.428).
53 Court testimony of Walter Isac, one of the survivors of the massacre (USHMM, RG.25.004M, reel 30, file 40013, vol.6, p.379); see also *Evreii din România între anii 1940–1944, vol.IV, 1943–1944: Bilanţul Tragediei – Renaşterea Speranţei*, ed. Ion Şerbănescu (Bucharest: Editura Hasefer, 1998), pp.299–300.
54 Dora Litani, *Transnistria* (Tel Aviv, 1981), p.77 (in Romanian); *Evreii din România între anii 1940–1944, Vol.IV*, pp.299–300.
55 Gheorghiu-Dej always spoke with great animosity about Foriş as he regarded him as a *Siguranţa* agent. He formed this view after an experience he had in Doftana jail in 1940 when, according to Alexandru Bârlădeanu, Gheorghiu-Dej told his lawyer, Ion Gheorghe Maurer, that he wanted to escape from the prison. Maurer relayed Gheorghiu-Dej's wishes to no one but Foriş. Gheorghiu-Dej was summoned a few days later by the prison commandant who told him that he had heard that Gheorghiu-Dej wanted to escape. (Author's interview with Alexandru Bârlădeanu, 8 August 1996.) Under cross-examination at his trial with Pătrăşcanu in April 1954, Koffler stated that the man behind the arrest of more than 60 Communist activists in 1942 was a certain Melinte who was secretary of the Ilfov party organization. After serving a six-month sentence in 1941, Melinte was re-appointed to his position, even though, Koffler claimed, he was known to be a police informer: see *Principiul Bumerangului. Documente ale Procesului Lucreţiu Pătrăşcanu* (Bucharest: Editura Vremea, 1996), p.576.
56 Author's interview with Eduard Mezincescu, 16 June 1994.
57 Mezincescu, 'Polemici', p.2.
58 Foriş was held responsible by Gheorghiu-Dej for a string of arrests which had debilitated its activity since 1940 (Mezincescu, 'Polemici', p.2). On the face of it, there was little to link Foriş and his deputy, Remus Koffler, with any of them, the arrests being the result either of the diligence of the *Siguranţa*, or of the ineptitude of the activists themselves, or of information received from informers within the Party itself. Nevertheless, at the trial of Koffler and Pătrăşcanu in April 1954, Koffler, Pătrăşcanu and Foriş were all blamed for keeping known police informers in positions of responsibility in the Party who betrayed much of its activity to the *Siguranţa* (Deletant, *Communist Terror*, p.32.)
59 See the biographical note on Bodnăraş in Deletant, *Communist Terror in Romania*, appendix 1. 'Account by Emil Bodnăraş of his actions between November 1942 and April 1944', pp.297–308. Foriş was held until January 1945. He was arrested by the Communist *Siguranţa* on 9 June 1945 and beaten to death with an iron bar in summer 1946 (N.I. Florea, 'Ştefan Foriş', *Analele de Istorie*, vol.18, no.3 (1972), p.153). The report of the Party commission, charged by Nicolae Ceauşescu in 1967 with investigating the circumstances of Foriş's death, concluded that 'Foriş's execution was carried out by [*Siguranţa* chief] Gheorghe Pintilie, aided by his chauffeur Dumitru Necin [also known as Dimitrie Mitea], through blows administered with an iron bar. The body was thrown into a specially-prepared pit in the grounds of the building in which he was murdered' [Communist Party HQ on Aleea Alexandru] (Stenogram of Gheorghe Pintilie's deposition before the commission in Deletant, *Communist Terror*, pp.316–17); see also 'Statement by Gheorghe Pintilie, former Head of the *Securitate*, dated 15 May 1967 and Presented to the Party Commission Charged with Investigating the Death of Ştefan Foriş', (*ibid.*, pp.314–18).
60 Deletant, *Communist Terror*, p.32.
61 V. Tismăneanu, *Arheologia Terorii* (Bucharest: Editura Eminescu, 1992), p.106.

2 The *coup* of 23 August 1944 and the path to power of the Romanian Communist Party

The *coup* of 23 August transformed the status of the Communist Party in Romania.[1] At the beginning of 1944, after twenty-three years' existence, the party was a small faction-ridden political group with little or no effective resonance in Romania, its leadership scattered over three main centres and constrained to respond to policies decided in Moscow that were relevant to Stalin's political strategies rather than Romanian political conditions. By the autumn of that year, the Communist Party had become a major factor in the Romanian political scene. By the end of 1944, it had been thrust into the forefront of events by the occupying Soviet power, its factional rivalry blurred by the need to prepare itself for the role assigned to it by Stalin in Romania's future.

The seeds of the *coup* of 23 August 1944 were sown by the Axis defeat at Stalingrad in January 1943. In the course of the Soviet counter-offensive two German armies, two Romanian armies and one Italian army were decimated. The Romanian losses in the period from 19 November 1942 to 7 January 1943 were put at 155,010 dead, wounded and missing, most of the latter being taken prisoner.[2] This represented over a quarter of all Romanian troops engaged on the Eastern Front. Hitler lost the initiative in the war against the Soviet Union and his forces now began to be thrown back across Europe. The consequences of Stalingrad were equally momentous for Antonescu. He now realized that Hitler could no longer win the war. On the advice of his Chief of Staff, General Ilie Şteflea, he had wisely not committed all of his forces to the campaigns in the Soviet Union, holding half of them in reserve to protect his country's sovereignty.

As the military situation steadily deteriorated after the Soviet victory at Stalingrad in January 1943, Marshal Antonescu's mind began to turn to consideration of an understanding with the Allies. His thoughts were shared by Mihai Antonescu, Vice-President of the Council of Ministers and Foreign Minister, who took the lead in taking soundings of the Italians. The Marshal tolerated the emission of such peace feelers, both from within his own government and from the opposition leader Iuliu Maniu, the leader of the National Peasant Party, but all these soundings foundered on the Anglo-American insistence upon "unconditional surrender" announced by Roosevelt and accepted by Churchill at the Casablanca Conference in January 1943.

Mihai Antonescu, gave some indication of his own change of heart in January 1943 to Bova-Scoppa, the Italian minister in Bucharest. Bova-Scoppa went to Rome to present a report of his conversation with Antonescu to Galeazzo Ciano, the Italian Foreign Minister, who had already anticipated the new mood of the Romanian leaders. In his diary entry for 10 January Ciano noted:

> I think the Germans would do well to watch the Romanians. I see an about-face in the attitude and words of Mihai Antonescu. The sudden will for conciliation with Hungary is suspicious to me. If the Russian offensive had not been so successful I doubt that all this would have taken place.[3]

Mihai Antonescu's proposal elicited some sympathy from Ciano who recorded on 19 January:

> Bova-Scoppa has made a report on his long conference with young Antonescu who has returned from German headquarters. The latter was very explicit about the tragic condition of Germany and foresees the need for Romania and Italy to contact the Allies in order to establish a defence against the bolshevization of Europe. I shall take the report to the Duce and shall make it the subject of a conversation which I have been planning for some time. Let us not bandage our heads before they are broken, but let us look at the situation realistically and remember that charity begins at home.[4]
> Mussolini, however, was not swayed by Ciano's argument:
> Taking my cue from Bova's report I told the Duce what I thought. The Duce began by replying that 'he was sure that the Germans would hold tenaciously'. Then he listened to me attentively. He naturally refused Antonescu's offer, saying that 'the Danube is not the way we must follow'. But he did not react when at a certain point I said openly that we too should try to make some direct contact.[5]
> The Duce reiterated his view the following day, 21 January:
> As I anticipated Mussolini wanted to reread the Bova report. He described Antonescu's language as oversubtle and he reaffirmed in terms much stronger than those of yesterday his decision to march with Germany to the end.[6]

This rebuff prompted Mihai Antonescu to attempt direct contact with the diplomatic representatives of the Allies in neutral countries with a view to concluding a separate peace. He himself raised the matter with Andrea Cassulo, the Papal Nuncio in Bucharest, while the Romanian minister in Berne was instructed to make contact with the Papal Nuncio there. In March, the Romanian minister in

Madrid asked his Portuguese and Argentinian counterparts to let the American ambassador Carlton Hayes know of Romania's desire to conclude a peace with the Allies. Similarly, Victor Cadere, the Romanian minister in Lisbon, took soundings in October of President Salazar and of the British Ambassador. In December, the Romanian Chargé in Stockholm, George Duca, contacted the British and American ministers in the name of Maniu and Brătianu.

When questioned by the writer Alexandru Brătescu-Voineşti, in an interview published on 5 March 1943 in the pro-regime *Porunca Vremii* (The Command of the Times), as to why, having sided with the Axis, he did not maintain links with the Allies in case they emerged victorious, Antonescu retorted,

> how, in the first instance, could such a stance be hidden from our own allies? And then, our major virtue, admired without reservation by our own great allies, is, alongside the bravery of our army, our loyalty, sincerity and lack of duplicity. This loyalty will represent one of the most precious possessions when peace is concluded.[7]

These peace feelers were not unknown to Hitler. At their meeting at Klessheim castle in Salzburg on 12 April 1943 the Führer confronted Antonescu with the information he had about them from German intelligence about the approaches made in Madrid and asked him "to analyse them" from the point of view of their impact on the international community. "He did not expect an immediate answer from Antonescu" to this unexpected problem. "He would fully understand, even if Antonescu did not give him a reply." Antonescu replied on the spot: "He could assure Hitler that the entire Romanian nation supported him now, more than ever, and that he would not allow anyone to carry out a policy other than that which he (Antonescu) considered the best one, in the interests of Romania and of Europe". He promised the Führer that,

> Romania would continue alongside Germany until the end of the war... The policy of the opposition, especially Maniu, did not count... However, he (Antonescu) could not touch Maniu, since he (Antonescu) knew his people and did not want, through measures taken against Maniu, to make a martyr of this man who was advanced in years and who had negative ideas, thereby granting him what he had long wished to obtain.

He told Hitler that he would never take an initiative without informing him and undertook to investigate the action of the Romanian minister in Madrid. At the same time he defended Mihai Antonescu: "It was inconceivable that Mihai would have tried to conclude peace or to request assistance from the Americans or other states, since he (the Marshal) would not have anyone alongside him who would be disloyal to Germany." Hitler accepted this declaration of loyalty.[8]

Nevertheless, Hitler returned to the subject the next day. He was concerned that the approaches made in March by the Romanian minister in Madrid gave the impression to the foreign (Portuguese and Argentinian) diplomats that Romania and Germany were ready to conclude a peace with the Allies. The Führer stated that "the important problem was that the main enemies of the Axis had formed a completely erroneous impression about the position of Germany and Italy and that was due solely to the action of Mihai Antonescu". He asked the Marshal to ensure that such a thing never happened in future. The latter replied that he was grateful that they had discussed this problem, "but the truth was totally the reverse of what Germany knew".[9]

Antonescu was less than honest with the Führer in this matter. He was aware of the approaches made by his Foreign Minister and did nothing to stop further soundings of all three Allies made by Mihai Antonescu and Maniu through different channels over the following twelve months. In their turn, the Western Allies, led by the British, sought to maintain regular contact with King Michael. On 2 December 1943, a figure arrived at the British embassy in Ankara and presented himself as Mr Stephen House, an ex-British journalist.[10] According to his story he was a representative of Allied Newspapers in Denmark. When Denmark was invaded by the Germans, House/Ujhazy was interned, but had managed to escape and reach Budapest. The French authorities helped him to obtain a French travel certificate in the name of Etienne Langlois with which he travelled to Bucharest. There the French Minister Henri Spitzmuller, who remained in Romania after the fall of France to serve the Allied interest,[11] befriended him and introduced him into Romanian political circles, eventually securing for him an interview on 26 November with King Michael, the results of which were described by Spitzmuller in a letter to Knatchbull-Hugessen.[12]

Spitzmuller's letter offers a rare contemporary first-hand account of Michael's predicament and his relations with Antonescu, which shows them to have been severely strained. The King told House/Ujhazy, not to

> forget to explain that consideration for my country's future does not blind me to the fact that the Allies' policy is based on cooperation between the three Powers and I therefore understand that Russia and Romania must come to some kind of agreement.
>
> Mr House then remarked that the Allies had repeated most recently that unconditional surrender remained the essential condition of any armistice. 'I know', the King replied, 'but it is not because of this formula that I would refuse to negotiate if the occasion arose. Without underestimating its importance, I consider and hope that even the framework of this formula would permit interpretations which would allow me to accept it.'
>
> The conversation then concentrated on the possibility of a *putsch* linked to an approach by the King to the Allies. The King and all those present explained to Mr House that such a move would result in the complete and immediate occupation of the country by the Germans, who would then have all the resources of Romania at their disposal. The King and his

> counsellors again explained to Mr House that the situation in Romania at that moment was unique in the sense that Marshal Antonescu's government represented only a tiny minority which, having taken power and maintained it with the support of the Germans, had imposed and continued to impose on the country a policy which was contrary to its wishes and its interests. A new government which would truly represent the people's wishes could only come to power through a *putsch*, which was impossible at the present moment with close cooperation with the Allies.
> 'If the Allies made a landing in the Balkans', the King said, 'everything would be simpler. The peninsula is practically undefended, but if Romania were to be occupied by the Germans the situation would immediately become less favourable.'[13]

The acceptance of unconditional surrender by the Romanians, whether Maniu or Antonescu, was the stumbling-block in all subsequent negotiations held between Maniu's representatives and the Allies in Cairo in the spring of 1944.[14] Yet approaches made in December 1943 by Soviet officials to Romanian diplomats in Stockholm suggested that their government wished to set up independent contacts with Antonescu and Maniu and was prepared to accept less than unconditional surrender. A curious situation thus emerged in which both the Romanian government and opposition were seeking to obtain the best possible terms for an armistice in parallel negotiations, one in Cairo with the Allies collectively, and the other in Stockholm with the Russians separately. Not surprisingly, both Antonescu and Maniu believed that they were in a position to bargain over unconditional surrender, hence the misunderstanding that arose between the Allies and Maniu, and the increasing British irritation with the latter. Maniu wanted some assurance as to what conditions he could get before making any plans to overthrow Antonescu and was particularly anxious to prevent Soviet occupation of Romania. The Russians, on the other hand, doubtless took the pragmatic view that it was more realistic to treat with Antonescu since he controlled the army and an about-turn by the latter against the Germans would preclude the need for a *coup* by the opposition which the Communists did not control.

Antonescu's own position on the desirability of an armistice is evident from a memorandum of what appears to have been a meeting between the Marshal and Iuliu Maniu dated 21 January 1944.[15] Antonescu argued that it was very difficult for Romania to withdraw from the war, given the importance of Romania's oil to Germany. Maniu said that "realistic solutions should be found to change our military and diplomatic position". The memorandum continued:

> What are these solutions? Marshal Antonescu asked that they should be put to him in practical terms, but you [Maniu] were unable to do this. Mr Maniu thinks, however, that Marshal Antonescu has a mission

> and that he can take the country out of the war immediately. What would this mission be? Mr Maniu must be explicit. Over the last three years he has been floating the same theoretical ideas, which seem deceptive.
> But Mr Maniu avoids and hestitates to ask himself, and in particular, to show how Romania's withdrawal from the war could carried out in practical terms – a withdrawal which is the wish of the Marshal and of the entire population – [and] whether the allies and the Germans would guarantee our borders and future. Yet neither side is giving us these guarantees, nor will they, or – what is more to the point – can they give them, guarantees which we have been seeking for three years.
> In these circumstances, who can attempt capitulation or a laying down of arms especially when – in either case – Romania will be forced, like Italy, to tolerate fighting on its own territory by both sides.[16]

Hitler was made aware of the continuing Romanian overtures to the Allies and ordered plans to be drawn up for the occupation of the country. Similar plans had already been prepared for the occupation in March 1944 of Hungary, whose reliance as an ally had been long shown to be wanting. Before taking action against the Marshal, the Führer decided to give him one last chance. The two leaders met at Klessheim on 23–24 March 1944 where Hitler railed against the duplicity of the Hungarians, declaring to Antonescu that he had irrefutable evidence of their intention to withdraw from the war.[17] Unaware that his future hung in the balance Antonescu pledged continued loyalty to Hitler. Not for the first time, Hitler was impressed by Antonescu's sincerity and decided not to remove his friend.[18] His faith in his Romanian ally was borne out by Antonescu's obstinate refusal to turn against Germany by accepting armistice conditions laid down by the Allies.

We can only speculate on the consequences of a decision by Hitler to occupy Romania; there is no doubt that King Michael would have had the support of most of his generals in ordering his army—half of which was held in reserve in Romania to defend the country—to take up arms against the Germans, and that the ensuing hostilities, by crippling German resistance, would have accelerated the Soviet advance westwards in Moldavia. Of one thing, however, we can be certain; German occupation would have the same monstrous impact on Romania's surviving Jews of Wallachia, Moldavia and Wallachia as it did on the Jews of Hungary. After the German occupation of that country on 19 March 1944, Jews were rounded up in ghettos with the collaboration of the Hungarian gendarmerie and sent to Auschwitz.

Antonescu, aware of the fragility of Romania's territorial integrity in the face of the Soviet advance, continued to hold out for armistice terms which would guarantee Romania's independence of Soviet authority. Yet the more he delayed, the closer the Red Army moved and the greater the threat of occupation. On 29 March, the Red Army took Cernăuţi in Northern Bukovina. Odessa, the Crimea's main port, fell on 10 April, putting Romania's occupation of Transnistria effectively at an end, while the evacuation of the Crimea was completed on 13 May.

Only King Michael and his advisors seemed to grasp the fact that Stalin would be tempted to withhold his assent to armistice conditions if he manoeuvred himself into a position to impose them through military might. Antonescu refused to accept what he considered to be unsatisfactory terms from the Allies; furthermore, he was adamant about not abandoning his German ally who was now on the defensive. At a Council of Ministers' meeting on 6 May 1944, the Marshal mad his position clear in this regard:

> So, gentlemen, [we should have] a perfectly correct attitude in our relations with the Germans: in 1940 we bent down before them, are we now to hit them when they are beaten and faced with destruction. We cannot do that, gentlemen. I was not a Germanophile and will never be. I told Hitler so. You cannot ask the Romanian people to love the German people. When we lost all [those] territories as a result of the political and military actions of the Germans, you cannot ask the Romanian people to love you. The Romanian people marches alongside the German people out of self-interest, and when you are in a position to help it [the Romanian people] win its rights, it will show its gratitude to you. We must behave correctly towards the Germans.[19]

Antonescu gave these same reasons for remaining loyal to his German ally at his trial in May 1946. When questioned about his meeting with Hitler on 6 August [it took place, in fact, on 5 August], Antonescu replied:

> Before 6 August I wanted to go to Germany on my own initiative—I had never been before on my own initiative, but now in 1944 I wanted to—to raise the matter of the Romanian army's withdrawal from the war. As a soldier, I have been throughout my life a man of honour and loyal, and I did not want to break with Germany, because Germany was and can be a great power, and Romania, being a small power, must think of that. And so, I wanted to break with Germany in a decent way and to warn her: you did not keep your word to guarantee Romania's frontiers, there are not sufficient forces to meet a concerted Russian attack, and so Romania runs the risk of being totally overrun and destroyed, therefore I am withdrawing from the war. I was advised not to do this by everyone; they were all terrified of what would happen in Romania if I told Hitler and gave him advance warning. Think of it, a war between us and the Germans on our territory, which would cause the damage that it did, and besides that, I was not a partisan, I could not and would not, even if I lived a million years, stab a comrade who had been alongside me in an action in the back.[20]

This stubbornness of Antonescu determined the King, in concert with the opposition leaders, to plot his overthrow.[21]

Following the disaster to Romanian troops at Stalingrad, King Michael, in his 1943 New Year broadcast to his people, called for peace and for Romania to discontinue the war alongside Hitler. Marshal Antonescu was furious, as was the German minister in Bucharest who protested violently. Irritated by what he considered to be the indecisiveness of the opposition led by Maniu and Constantin (Dinu) Brătianu, head of the National Liberal Party, the young King declared later that he had been ready to take Romania out of the war against the Allies in February 1944 but that "whenever plans appeared to be maturing he was prevented from taking action by objections raised by the opposition".[22] The King's impatience was doubtless a sign of his youth (he was only twenty-two), and the elderly Maniu advised more prudently against a *coup* at that time on the grounds that there were too many German troops in the country. Nevertheless, the King could turn to the wise counsel of his mother, Queen Helen, of General Sănătescu, the head of the military household, and of Grigore Niculescu-Buzeşti, the head of the cypher and communication section of the Foreign Ministry.

At this time Maniu was in regular radio contact with the British via a radio operator called Nicolae Ţurcanu (code-named 'Reginald') who had been sent into Romania in June 1943 by the Special Operations Executive.[23] At the end of October 1943, Maniu had expressed a desire to leave Romania in order to contact the Russians with British assistance. In response the Foreign Office told Maniu that any approaches from Romania, be they from individuals or from the government, should be addressed to all three Allies and that they should take the form of an offer by a duly authorized emissary to sign an unconditional surrender to the three principal Allies.[24] The Foreign Office told the Soviet government about Maniu's request. At the end of December 1943, the Romanian Counsellor in Stockholm, George Duca, contacted the British and American ministers in the name of Maniu about peace terms, unaware that his own minister, Frederick Nanu, had been approached, on 26 December, by what Nanu took to be an NKVD officer, with an offer to deal with the Romanian government.[25] Clandestine contact was maintained for several months. Nanu was told that the Russians would keep the Western Allies informed and that strict secrecy should be maintained. On 13 April 1944, armistice terms agreed by the representatives of the American, British and Soviet governments in Cairo were transmitted to the Marshal and to Maniu. They called for a Romanian volte-face against the Germans, the payment of reparations to the Russians, the confirmation of Bessarabia and Northern Bukovina as Soviet territory, the restoration of Northern Transylvania to Romania, and the granting to Soviet troops of unrestricted movement, although not occupation, throughout Romania during the period of the armistice.[26]

The receipt of the terms seems to have caused a breach to open up between the Marshal and Maniu. In a letter he wrote in mid-April, Maniu stated that Antonescu "wished to continue the war at the side of the Germans", while Maniu accepted the terms and said that once he was certain that Antonescu could not be moved, he would act in conjunction with the King.[27] An appeal to Antonescu to cease hostilities against the Allies was submitted under the signature of sixty-nine university teachers in April. Overtly pro-Soviet in sentiment, it reflected political reality as regards the key role that the Soviet Union would play in determining Romania's fate, accepting at face value the promises of the Kremlin:

> At this crucial time for the existence of the Romanian people, the Soviet Government, in agreement with the governments of

> Great Britain and the United States, states before the whole world that it does not intend to destroy the Romanian state, nor to annex territories beyond the frontiers of 1941, nor to change the existing social system of the country.....
> The Romanian people, exhausted by a war too long for its resources, cannot fight any longer. Step out into the streets and ask the passers-by, go into the villages and towns, listen to the voice of the people. Everywhere you will see despair in their eyes and [hear] the same reply: NO.
> Why should we continue to fight? The vital interests of the state and of our people require the immediate cessation of war, however difficult this step might be. The sacrifices which Romania should make will be incomparably smaller and less painful than the continuation of the war.[28]

On 5 May 1944, Eden saw the Soviet ambassador to London, Feodor Gusev, and 'casually' mentioned the possibility of some sort of understanding on the problems of Greece and Romania, as Eden put it later,

> agreeing between ourselves as a practical matter that Rumanian affairs would be in the main the concern of the Soviet government while Greek affairs would be in the main our concern, each government giving the other help in the respective countries.[29]

The suspicion that the Western Allies, and in particular Britain, had abandoned Romania to the Russians, troubled Maniu who used the Romanian emissary to Cairo, Constantin Vişoianu, to voice these concerns to Christopher Steel, the British representative, at the end of May. This provoked Antony Eden, the Foreign Secretary, to instruct Steel to tell Vişoianu that there was no use in his trying to obtain assurances about British policy "as distinct from that of the Soviet government".[30] But there was no rebuke from Eden when Steel, in answer to a further question from Vişoianu as to whether Maniu should form "a democratic coalition embracing the Romanian Communist Party", replied that in his own view a broad national union of this kind would be "warmly welcomed by Allied public opinion".[31]

This cautious advice probably confirmed for Maniu his view that it would be good politics to bring the Communists into a coalition and when Vişoianu asked Daniel Semionovici Selod, the assistant to Nikolai Novikov, the Soviet representative in Cairo, to suggest a name, Selod is said to have replied "Lucreţiu Pătrăşcanu".[32] Although held under house arrest throughout 1943 and early 1944 at a mountain village called Poiana Ţapului near Sinaia, the King's summer residence, Pătrăşcanu was kept informed of plans to take Romania out of the war by his brother-in-law Colonel Octav Ulea, Master of Ceremonies at the palace.[33] In April 1944, Pătrăşcanu negotiated an agreement with Titel Petrescu, the leader of the Social Democrats, to set up a United Workers' Front, thus giving the Communist Party greater authority. Both men took part in the secret preparations for the *coup* under the King's chairmanship. Pătrăşcanu was brought into meetings of a sub-committee under Colonel Dumitru Dămăceanu which prepared plans for the defence of Bucharest and at the beginning of June he suggested that the Communist Party's military representative, Emil Bodnăraş (code-named Engineer Ceauşu), should attend since he could organize small bands of armed workers who could assist in a volte-face.

Bodnăraş was no ordinary official of the Communist Party: he was also an NKVD officer whose role in the preparations for the *coup* remains shadowy and has consequently fomented speculation, including the suggestion that he was used by Marshal Antonescu as a clandestine conduit to the Soviet authorities.[34] After the Axis defeat at Stalingrad, it was clear to Antonescu that it would be prudent to establish closer links with the Russians, and Bodnăraş was an obvious channel. Unlike his colleagues Gheorghiu-Dej, Apostol, Chişinevski and Georgescu, he had been exempted from internment at the Târgu-Jiu prison camp, after being released from Caransebeş prison in December 1942, on the grounds of having been an officer in the Romanian army. Bodnăraş made his first appearance at one of the meetings to prepare the *coup* at a house on Calea Moşilor on the night of 13 June.[35] Even members of the King's circle were impressed by Bodnăraş's dedication and the latter, in his turn, was sufficiently convinced by the thoroughness of the plans to be able to satisfy his Communist colleagues that the Romanian Communist Party only stood to enhance its position by joining the National Peasant, National Liberal and Social Democratic parties in the formation of the National Democratic Bloc (NDB) on 20 June 1944.[36]

A week later, the Allied representatives in Cairo received the plan drawn up by the King and the NDB for the *coup*. To be successful, Maniu argued, the *coup* had to be accompanied by three Allied actions. First, there should be a major Soviet offensive on the Romanian front within twenty-four hours of the volte-face; second, three airborne brigades, either Anglo-American or Soviet, with an additional 2,000 parachute troops should be dropped at the time of the *coup*; third, there should be a heavy bombardment of communications with Hungary and Bulgaria. The plan met a favourable response from both the British and American representatives, yet when the American suggested a tripartite meeting to discuss it, the Soviet representative Nikolai Novikov said that this would be premature.

Novikov waited in vain for instructions from Moscow. The Russians had nothing to lose by pinning their hopes on a bilateral deal with Marshal Antonescu; this had the double advantage for them of dealing directly with Romania's military leader thereby obviating the need to negotiate with Maniu, and of giving them time in view of the Marshal's hesitancy, to prepare for their military occupation of Romania. Indeed, at the beginning of June, Madame Alexandra Kollontay, a veteran revolutionary and the Soviet minister in Stockholm, had offered improved armistice conditions to Nanu which, in addition to an unconditional promise to return Transylvania, pledged to allow 'free areas' where the Romanian government would be sovereign and where no foreign troops would be allowed to enter, to show leniency over reparations, and to allow 15 days between the signing of an armistice and a Romanian declaration of war on Germany.[37]

At the Marshal's request Hitler received him at his headquarters at Rastenburg in East Prussia on 5 August. The *Führer,* according to a Romanian officer present, used the meeting, lasting some six hours, to deliver a rant against all who had betrayed him, especially the German people, who had showed no gratitude for the heights to which he had raised them.[38] To Antonescu's complete surprise, Hitler posed the leading question as to whether Romania intended to fight on; the Marshal temporized by saying that this depended upon Germany's commitment to assist Romania in stemming the Russian advance, and upon the attitude of Hungary and Bulgaria.[39] He returned to Bucharest in a deep depression and did nothing about the Soviet terms. In the meantime, Maniu was desperately seeking a reply from Cairo to the *coup* plan sent on 27 June. On 7 July, the King and his advisors, including the opposition leaders, fixed 15 August as the date for action, hoping to synchronize their action with a Soviet offensive. The longer the *coup* was delayed, the greater the chance that the Red Army would push forward, occupying more Romanian territory and giving Moscow a reason for preferring a straightforward military conquest of the country without any help from the King and the opposition. Moreover, the increasingly frequent Anglo-American air raids on the oilfields around Ploieşti and on Bucharest were a reminder to the Romanians of the cost of the alliance with Germany.[40] Still Maniu heard nothing from Cairo, and the *coup* was postponed. Finally, on 20 August the long-awaited Soviet offensive came, prompting Maniu to inform Cairo that the King and his group had decided to take action.

On that date the Soviet generals Malinovsky and Tolbukhin successfully launched a massive assault confided to two armies of almost one million troops and 1,500 tanks against the combined German and Romanian forces straddling the Prut. The northern offensive, aimed at Focşani, Bucharest and Turnu Severin, breached the front south of Iaşi and the King rushed from Sinaia to Bucharest to consult with his advisors.[41] The representatives of the political parties could not be located. The King asked Colonel Dămăceanu how long he needed to get his part of the plan, namely to seize the telephone exhange and the radio station, ready, and was told 'five days'. The *coup* was therefore fixed for 26 August at 1 pm. The Marshal and Mihai Antonescu would be invited to lunch, after which there would be an audience to discuss the course to be adopted. If the Marshal refused negotiation with the Allies, the King would dismiss him and appoint a new government to be drawn from the opposition parties. This government would invite the Germans to evacuate Romania and empower its emissaries in Cairo, Barbu Ştirbey and Constantin Vişoianu, to sign an armistice.

On the following evening, 21 August, the plans agreed by the King and his advisors the day before were approved by the members of the NDB at their last full meeting before the *coup*. It was attended by the King, Maniu, Brătianu, Pătrăşcanu, Titel Petrescu, Grigore Niculescu-Buzeşti, the head of Foreign Ministry communications, Ion Mocsony-Styrcea, the Marshal of the King's Household,[42] General Constantin Sănătescu, and Mircea Ionniţiu, the King's private secretary.[43] Pătrăşcanu came with a draft proclamation for the King's approval and argued, with Petrescu's backing, for a government of national unity led by Maniu. Maniu refused and pressed for a government of technicians, headed by a soldier, to handle the armistice conditions and the presence of the Red Army. The matter was left in the hands of Maniu and Pătrăşcanu who were to draw up a list of ministers by 23 August. It was agreed that the politicians should disperse until the projected day of action, 26 August.

Yet once again, unforseen circumstances intervened in the timing of the *coup*. Antonescu, dismayed by the rapid advance of the Soviet forces, was moving back and forth between the front in southern Moldavia and Bucharest and decided to return to the front on 23 August. This meant that he would be absent from the capital on the day fixed for the *coup*. The news, which had been picked up fortuitously by Styrcea whilst he was at the Marshal's villa in Snagov,[44] was quickly transmitted to the King who was able to get word to Maniu that the *coup* should be brought forward to the 23 August. Mihai Antonescu, the Prime Minister, was unnerved by the deteriorating military situation and decided, on his own initiative, to negotiate an armistice with the Allies. He told the Marshal on the evening of 22 August and the latter raised no objections. That same evening the Marshal told the German minister Clodius that he would make one last effort to halt the Russians, and that in the event of failure, he reserved the right to act as he saw fit. After the meeting with Clodius, Mihai Antonescu sent a courrier to Stockholm instructing Nanu to tell Madame Kollontay of the Romanian government's willingness to conclude an armistice. In the event the courier arrived on 24 August, the day after the *coup*.[45]

Early in the morning of 23 August, Mihai Antonescu and Madame Antonescu tried to persuade the Marshal to see the King and agree to an armistice. Although the Marshal refused to commit himself, Mihai telephoned the King's office and spoke to Ionniţiu who woke the King. Michael agreed to see them both at 3 pm. In a last-ditch effort to get the Marshal to conclude an armistice, Maniu and Constantin Brătianu asked the historian Gheorghe Brătianu, the Liberal leader's nephew, to use the respect he enjoyed with the Romanian leader to persuade him to see the King that afternoon. The Marshal listened to Brătianu's arguments and apparently agreed to go to the palace, but on condition that Maniu and Gheorghe Brătianu send him a letter by 3 pm confirming that they stood behind him in signing an armistice.[46]

The King now convened his advisors and decided that the showdown with the Marshal should take place at his audience that afternoon. Niculescu-Buzeşti and Styrcea left the palace to warn Maniu and Pătrăşcanu respectively but Maniu was not at home and Pătrăşcanu's contact said that Pătrăşcanu and Titel Petrescu would come to the palace, but only after nightfall. Similarly, Gheorghe Brătianu could find neither his uncle nor Maniu and was therefore unable to meet the Marshal's condition that he should bring a letter from both by 3 pm. When Gheorghe Brătianu turned up to see the Marshal empty-handed the latter was furious and said that Mihai Antonescu could go to the palace alone and pass on the Marshal's apologies to the King.[47]

Mihai Antonescu arrived for his audience at the appointed time and was received by the King and General Sănătescu. He offered Marshal Antonescu's apologies, at which point Sănătescu left the room and telephoned the Marshal, saying that there was no point in snubbing the King at this critical time. The Marshal relented and agreed to come. He was escorted into the drawing room to meet the King who was with Mihai Antonescu and Sănătescu. The Marshal proceeded to give a detailed account of the situation at the front and said that he would only conclude an armistice after warning Hitler. The King replied that the military situation would brook no further delay; since Soviet troops were already in occupation of part of the country an armistice should be signed immediately. Asked by the King whether he would stand aside for someone who would contact the Allies the Marshal replied, "Never". After withdrawing briefly to his study to inform his advisors—Styrcea, Buzeşti, Ionniţiu and General Aurel Aldea—that the moment had now come for the Marshal's arrest, the King returned to the drawing room and told the Marshal that, in concordance with the wishes of the Romanian people as expressed through the four democratic parties, he was taking the country out of the war to save it from disaster. If the Marshal refused to implement the King's wish that an armistice be concluded, then he should consider himself dismissed.[48]

When the Marshal retorted he took orders from no one the King replied that, in that case, he was dismissed and he left the room. As he did so, Michael signalled to his aide, Colonel Emilian Ionescu, to arrest the Marshal and Mihai Antonescu. Ionescu summoned the four-man guard that had been prepared for such an eventuality and amid the protests of the Marshal the two Antonescus were escorted upstairs and locked in the King's strongroom.

Back in his study the King consulted with his advisors as to the immediate steps to be taken. The leaders of the political parties had to be informed of the arrests, the Allies had to be notified, the military plan for the *coup* had to be executed, but most important of all, a Prime Minister had to be named to replace Mihai Antonescu. In the absence of Maniu, it was decided to appoint General Sănătescu, who enjoyed the respect of the army. Ionniţiu typed out a decree to this effect, the King signed it, and the new Prime Minister set out for army headquarters to transmit the order for Romanian troops under Colonel Dămăceanu to take up positions at strategic points in Bucharest and to cease hostilities against the Soviet forces at the front. Proof that the army placed their loyalty to their supreme commander, the King, above that of Marshal Antonescu, was the fact that not a single senior officer disobeyed Sănătescu's orders and not one of them defected to the Marshal.

Since Maniu and Pătrăşcanu had failed to agree on a list of ministers and neither was at the palace, the new government had to be formed on the spot from the King's advisors. Niculescu-Buzeşti, a counsellor in the Foreign Ministry, was elevated to Foreign Minister, and General Aldea became Minister of the Interior, while the representatives of the four parties in the DNF—Maniu, Brătianu, Petrescu and Pătrăşcanu—were appointed Ministers of State without Portfolio. Ionniţiu was doubtless not alone in his feeling at the time that the politicians had, at this crucial moment, shown themselves to be "a pathetic bunch".[49]

The first of them to appear at the palace was Pătrăşcanu, who arrived shortly after 8 pm. He brought with him the King's proclamation, which was approved after amendments by Buzeşti and Sănătescu, and the texts of two decrees, previously agreed at meetings of the NDB, granting an amnesty to political prisoners and abolishing the internment camps in which many Communists and other political detainees had been held. At the same time, Pătrăşcanu asked the King for the post of Minister of Justice. Since none of the other political leaders had cabinet seats, the King did not want to risk an accusation of partiality, but given Pătrăşcanu's legal background, his diligence in producing the draft proclamation and the decrees, and that he was the first member of the NDB to appear at the palace, the King offered him a compromise, Minister of Justice *ad interim*. The fact that Pătrăşcanu, alone among the political representatives, secured this temporary position gave rise in accounts about the formation of this new government to the supposition that he was acting on orders from the Communist Party and this, in turn, helped to cement the fiction in Communist historiography of the dominant role of the Party in the *coup*. In the circumstances it was the most immediately plausible appointment for Pătrăşcanu, given the speed of events on the afternoon of 23 August and the lack of time in which to contact the leaders of the Communist Party.[50]

Pătrăşcanu was followed shortly afterwards by Titel Petrescu and then, an hour or so later, by Emil Bodnăraş who was presented to the King under the name of 'engineer Ceauşu' and head of a group of Communist-trained armed civilians known as the 'Patriotic Guards'. Mocsony-Styrcea and Buzeşti proposed that Antonescu and his colleagues be moved to a safe location under the charge of Bodnăraş and despite the opposition of Maniu, the King and Sănătescu agreed.[51] About an hour after the recording of the King's proclamation to the country announcing the *coup* and the immediate cessation of hostilities with the Allies was broadcast over the radio at 10.12 pm, Marshal Antonescu, who was still locked in the palace strongroom, asked for paper and made his will. Another hour passed before Bodnăraş and the group of armed workers took charge of the two Antonescus and drove them away to a safe house in the Bucharest district of Vatra Luminoasă.[52]

After the overthrow of Nicolae Ceauşescu, political opponents of the King joined admirers of Antonescu in seeking to make capital at the expense of the King over this transfer of the Marshal to the Communists, accusing the monarch of 'treachery'. The truth of the matter is that the first consideration for the King and the NDB had been, in planning the *coup*, to prevent the Marshal from reaching the German forces and thereby setting up a 'rebel' pro-German government. In this respect they were faced with a problem: they did not want to hand Antonescu over to the police, whom the Marshal had used to harass the opposition leaders, for fear that the police might release him. Pătrăşcanu proposed instead that a civilian guard, drawn from trusted persons from all four opposition parties, should take custody of Antonescu until the police force was purged. He was ready to offer volunteers from within the Communist Party and invited the other parties to do the same. This idea found favour with Maniu and Brătianu. At a subsequent meeting at the palace on 17 August, Maniu announced that he had a team of National Peasant Party volunteers ready to undertake this role. However, on the evening of the *coup* this team was not available, having been sent to Transylvania, according to Maniu, to assist in the fighting against the Germans.

Custody of the Marshal was therefore left in the hands of Bodnăraş whose group was the only one to appear at the palace.[53]

A few hours later Antonescu's fellow ministers were taken into custody: General Constantin Pantazi, Minister of Defence, General Constantin Vasiliu, Undersecretary of State at the Interior Ministry, and Colonel Mircea Elefterescu, head of Bucharest Police.[54] On 31 August, shortly after Soviet troops entered Bucharest, Lt-Gen. Tevcenkov, political chief of the Second Ukrainian Front, acting on Stalin's orders, went to the head of the Bucharest garrison, Iosif Teodorescu, to take Antonescu into Soviet custody.[55] Teodorescu invited General Aurel Aldea, the Minister of the Interior, and General Victor Dombrovski, mayor of Bucharest, to the garrison and they informed Tevcenkov that they were unaware of Antonescu's whereabouts. Tevcenkov insisted on finding out whereupon Teodorescu phoned the government and after a while a man in civilian clothes arrived. He introduced himself as Bodnăraş, a member of the Central Committee of the Romanian Communist Party. Asked by Tevcenkov for information about Antonescu, Bodnăraş replied that he was being held by the Communists.

Tevcenkov and General Nikolai Burenin, the commander of Soviet forces in Bucharest, accompanied by some forty Soviet officers and men, were then taken by Bodnăraş to the two-storey house where Antonescu and his colleagues were being held. The Marshal occupied a room on the second floor while Mihai Antonescu, Pantazi, Vasiliu and Elefterescu were kept on the ground floor. They were guarded inside the house by ten armed civilians. There was no guard on the outside. Tevcenkov told Bodnăraş that because of the poor security he proposed to take the prisoners into Soviet custody. Bodnăraş preferred to keep the captives where they were but under a guard reinforced by Soviet soldiers. Tevcenkov rejected this proposal, accepting instead the continued presence of some of the armed Romanian civilians around the prisoners. Bodnăraş added that "the [Romanian] government did not want Antonescu to end up in Moscow". At 5 pm on the same day—31 August—Antonescu and the others were taken to the headquarters of the Soviet 53rd Army.[56]

According to the memoirs of Constantin Pantazi, completed after his trial and that of Antonescu in May 1946, Antonescu and his colleagues were visited by General Aldea on 28 August and informed that they were to be taken to Russia.[57] They were transported in stages the following day to Iaşi by car and lorry, and on 2 September they continued by road to the station at Bălţi on the Soviet side of the frontier where they were put in a train for Moscow. After a three-day journey they reached the Soviet capital from where they were driven "in comfortable vehicles" to a hunting lodge at Galitsin some sixty kilometres to the south-east of Moscow. They were well treated.[58] Each member of the group had his own room and was allowed to walk in the park. During the period of their detention at Galitsin the group was questioned from time to time by officers from *Smersh*, Soviet military counter-intelligence, led by a Major Rodin.[59] Their translator was also a *Smersh* officer, Captain Grigore Carpovici Kalinin. Their conditions of detention remained relaxed for several months.

On 13 June 1945, they were moved to a *dacha* to the east of Moscow where Ion Antonescu was questioned by Victor Abamukov about the massacres of Jews at Odessa in October 1941.[60] On the following day, the Marshal tried to hang himself with a noose made from strips torn from his bedsheet.[61] Subsequently, a Soviet officer was billeted with the prisoners until they were transferred to the Lubyanka prison in Moscow on 17 June.[62] Here they were interrogated by *Smersh* officers until they were returned to Bucharest in the middle of April 1946. On 6 May, Ion Antonescu was brought from the cells in the basement of the Ministry of the Interior to stand trial for "bringing disaster upon the country" and "the crime of war". After proceedings lasting ten days, he and his associates were found guilty. On 17 May, he was sentenced to death, together with Mihai Antonescu, Constantin Vasiliu, Gheorghe Alexianu, Constantin Pantazi, Radu Lecca and Eugen Cristescu, head of the security service. The sentences of Pantazi, Lecca and Cristescu were subsequently commuted on appeal. The appeals of the other four accused were rejected and they were executed by firing squad shortly after 6 pm on 1 June.[63]

It is one of the many tragedies in the history of the Romanians that the principal architects of the *coup* of 23 August 1944, King Michael and the democratic leaders, overthrew a military dictatorship only to be virtually overthrown themselves within six months by another incipient totalitarian order. In the Soviet zone of Germany and Poland, where the ravages of war had removed all political structures, it was relatively simple for Stalin to bring his client Communist parties to power, but in Romania the imposition of the new order required the removal of surviving structures. King Michael's *coup* had pre-empted any Soviet move to seize immediate power, and when Soviet troops entered Bucharest eight days later they found a Romanian government without significant Communist representation ready to negotiate an armistice and hold elections.

With the entry of the Red Army, the advance units of which arrived in Bucharest on 31 August, the country came under Russian control. King Michael had gone to a mountain retreat in the Carpathians, having left the capital for fear that it might fall to the Germans in the early hours of 24 August. With or without the King's presence, at the time when the Antonescus were handed over to the Soviet authorities, the latter were in a position to impose their will without hindrance. Romania was now an occupied country and it is difficult to see how the King could have intervened against his new ally to prevent them taking a leader who had conducted hostilities against them during the previous three years. Those who argue that the King should have done so ignore the realities of the time.

What emerges from this description of the preparations for the *coup* and its implementation is that the Romanian Communists were but one of a number of players involved. Their part was defined by a number of considerations. As a party with little popular support within Romania, the Communists' importance in shaping the country's future depended on the influence their sponsor, Stalin, was able to wield in Romanian affairs. As the war progressed, that importance was magnified by the advance of the Red Army. The inclusion of representatives of the Romanian Communist Party in the NDB was therefore sound politics, being regarded by the King and the major opposition leaders as tactful in view of the impending entry of the Red Army onto Romanian soil and the lead that the Soviet Union would take in determining the conditions of an armistice. Having said that, the Communists were allowed to play a bigger part in the *coup* itself because of the lapses of the other parties which were compounded by the Communists' superior organization on the evening of the *coup*. Pătrăşcanu was the first party representative to appear at the palace on 23 August; Maniu and Brătianu could not be contacted, and Bodnăraş and his 'Patriotic Guards' were the only civilian militia to arrive to take charge of Antonescu. These facts were used by the Communists to underpin their exaggerated claim to have played the leading role in the *coup*.

The *coup* had a crucial impact upon the course charted by Stalin for the Romanian Communist Party. It was also responsible for bringing Gheorghiu-Dej into the forefront of political events, thereby launching him on the road to power. Since Gheorghiu-Dej emerged first as the leader of that wing of the party which was most closely involved with the *coup*—and he then went on to secure his domination of the entire party—the *coup* was accorded a sacred place in party history. Even before Gheorghiu-Dej achieved supremacy within the party and was able to control its historiography, his Communist colleagues sought to deny the credit gained by the King and the major democratic parties for the *coup* by assuming it exclusively for themselves, thereby claiming legitimacy for their rule. To this end, the role of the Romanian Communists in the *coup* was deliberately exaggerated by the party. King Michael was relegated to the position of a mere spectator. In this endeavour, Communist apologists were abetted by the suppression by the Communist authorities of any accounts of the *coup* which did not fit into their scenario of events. Therefore the accounts of key participants in the events, that is, of the King and members of his entourage who escaped to the West, describing the King's crucial act in ordering the arrest of Marshal Antonescu on 23 August 1944, were largely unknown in Romania before the overthrow of the Communist regime.[64]

An example of this distortion was Lucreţiu Pătrăşcanu's account of the preparations for the *coup*, published on its first anniversary in *România liberă*. Pătrăşcanu claimed that "three meetings were held at the palace with King Michael in the chair to prepare for the *coup* of 23 August" at which he (Pătrăşcanu) was "the only representative of the entire opposition".[65] This appears to be untrue. Preparations for the *coup* were discussed simultaneously at the palace where the King consulted with his personal advisers, and by the so-called National Democratic Bloc, formed on 20 June 1944 from representatives of the National Peasant, National Liberal, Social Democratic and Communist parties, who met at various houses. While it is true that even before the formation of the NDB, Pătrăşcanu and Titel Petrescu—the leader of the Social Democrats—were taking part in the secret preparations for the *coup* under the King's chairmanship, all the subsequent plans were discussed at meetings of the NDB, and the last meeting held before the *coup*, on 21 August, was attended by the King, his palace advisers, the leaders of the major opposition parties, and Pătrăşcanu.[66] Today, with the publication of eyewitness accounts of the *coup* and the disclosure by contemporaries of Pătrăşcanu and Gheorghiu-Dej of fresh information about the activities of the Romanian Communist Party during the war and its relationship to Moscow, the part played by the Communists in the *coup* can be determined with greater accuracy, and in the process the mystification perpetrated at Gheorghiu-Dej's behest can be dispelled.[67]

Notes

1 This a revised version of a chapter on the *coup* that appeared in my study *Communist Terror in Romania. Gheorghiu-Dej and the Police State, 1948–1965* (London: Hurst and Co., 1999), pp.34–52.

2 *România în anii celui de-al doilea război mondial*, Vol.1 (Bucharest: Editura Militară, 1989), p.489.

3 *The Ciano Diaries 1939–1943*, tr. and ed. by Hugh Gibson (Garden City, New York: Doubleday, 1946), p.568.

4 The Ciano Diaries 1939–1943, p.572.

5 *Ibid.*

6 The Ciano Diaries 1939–1943, p.573.

7 Lya Benjamin (ed.), Evreii din Romania intre anii 1940–1944. Vol.II. 1940–1944: Problema Evreiască în Stenogramele Consiliului de Miniştri (Bucharest: Hasefer, 1996), doc.160, p.501.

8 Vasile Arimia, Ion Ardeleanu, and Ştefan Lache (eds.), *Antonescu-Hitler. Corespondentă şi întîlniri inedite (1940–1944)*, vol.II, (Bucharest: Cozia, 1991), pp.68–73. See also Dinu Giurescu, *România în al doilea război mondial* (Bucharest: All, 1999), p.189–90.

9 Arimia et al., Antonescu-Hitler. Corespondentă..., p.80.

10 The British ambassador, Sir Hughe Knatchbull-Hugesson, explained in his report to the Foreign Office about House's visit, that the latter was of Hungarian origin and used the aliases Istvan Ujhazy and Etienne Langlois. "He appears an intelligent and observant man, but I am not altogether satisfied as to his bona fides or the explanations he has so far furnished of his journey through the Balkans. He has been interviewed by Hammond, visiting correspondent of the Allied Newspaper, who confirms that he was one of their correspondents in the early part of the war. Mr House wishes to proceed to the United Kingdom, but it is doubtful whether he will receive authority to do so. He is staying in Istanbul for the moment, on his temporary French travel document"; see despatch from Knatchbull-Hugesson, to FO, TNA (henceforth The National Archives), FO 371/37388, no date).

11 Spitzmuller joined the French legation in Bucharest as first secretary in April 1938. For several of his reports to Paris see Ottmar Traşca and Ana-Maria Stan, *Rebeliunea legionară în documente străine* (Bucharest: Albatros, 2002), passim.

12 Knatchbull-Hugesson, to FO, TNA (FO 371/37388, no date). Knatchbull-Hugessen goes on in his despatch to the Foreign Office to state that he was also apprised of Spitzmuller's report by the Romanian Minister to Ankara, Alexandru Creţianu, who had just returned from Bucharest and had brought the letter in his diplomatic bag. According to Creţianu, the appearance of House caused some bewilderment in Bucharest. "House made out that he was British and the more trusting Roumanians made him their confidant. Even the King seems to have spoken freely, no doubt accepting the French Minister's recommendation as proof of House's trustworthiness" (*ibid.*).

13 *Ibid.*; see also Gheorghe Buzatu, *Mareşalul Antonescu în faţa istoriei*, vol.1 (Iaşi, 1990), pp.388–91.

14 Antonescu gave his reasons for rejecting an armistice at his trial in May 1946: "In the first place I was afraid of losing the benefits of the Atlantic Charter and the benefit we

derived from the public declarations made in the British parliament by Mr Churchill and Mr Eden..." The Atlantic Charter stated categorically 'we will not recognize at the end of the war any change of frontier which has not been freely agreed'. Somewhat later—that was in August 1941—somewhat later Mr Eden repeated the same declaration in parliament and said: 'We will not recognize frontiers which have not been freely agreed'. ....Then the Russian armistice comes. What were the conditions laid out in this armistice? That we should accept the cession of Bessarabia and Bukovina. Acceptance would have meant the loss of the benefits of the Atlantic Charter and of Mr Eden's declarations. And so I, Marshal Antonescu, without any political party behind me, with only two plebiscites as political authority, could not assume the historical responsibility in the face of the present generation and in the face of past ones, that I had ceded Bessarabia......Both Mr Maniu and Mr Mihalache, and Mr Dinu Brătianu and all the other politicians asked me on several occasions to conclude an armistice and I said, 'I cannot conclude an armistice because of that problem, I cannot conclude an armistice because it requires me to turn my arms against Germany and I am a soldier and a man of honour and I cannot do that'.....I offered to turn over control of the state to them....I told His Majesty the King several times......I got a negative reply. All the time I was told that I must conclude the armistice. So I gave up [on offering to hand over power]...." (Marcel-Dumitru Ciucă (ed.), *Procesul Mareşalului Antonescu. Documente*, vol.1 (Bucharest: Editura Saeculum, Editura Europa Nova, 1995), pp.213–14).

15 The source of the memorandum is unclear. It is unsigned but bears the stamp of the Romanian Intelligence Service (SSI) certifying that it had been catalogued. In parts, it seems to be a verbatim record of a conversation between Antonescu and Maniu.

16 ANIC, Ministerul Afacerilor Interne (Ministry of Internal Affairs). Trial of Ion Antonescu, file 40010, vol.34, pp.140–43.

17 Arimia et al., Antonescu-Hitler. Corespondentă.., p.144.

18 The plan for the occupation of Hungary was code-named 'Margarethe I' and that of Romania 'Margarethe II'; see Klaus Schönherr, 'Die Auswirkungen der militärischen Situation 1944 auf die Deutsch-Rumänischen Beziehungen', *Revue roumaine d'histoire*, vol.38, nos.1–4 (1999), p.176, note 71.

19 Lya Benjamin (ed.), Evreii din Romania intre anii 1940–1944. Vol.II. 1940–1944: Problema Evreiască în Stenogramele Consiliului de Miniştri (Bucharest: Hasefer, 1996), doc.187, p.557.

20 Ciucă, *Procesul.*, p.211. Antonescu's assertion that he had never been to Germany before August 1944 on his own initiative overlooks his request to meet Hitler in January 1941 to express his concern about the Iron Guard's activities. He travelled to Obersalzburg to meet the Führer on 14 January 1941.

21 It should be emphasized that no one on the Romanian side, be it the Marshal, Mihai Antonescu or Maniu, was able to secure the joint agreement of the Americans, British and Russians to the conditional armistice proposals which it made between December 1943 and April 1944 in Stockholm (to the Russians) and in Cairo (to all three Allies). Eventually, agreement on armistice terms was reached with Britain and the US in Cairo in April 1944 and confirmed by the Russians through the Stockholm channel in June. However, no Romanian representative was empowered by Antonescu to sign them.

22 I. Ardeleanu, V. Arimia, and M. Muşat (eds.), 'Report of Lt. Col. A.G.G. de Chastelain on the "Autonomous" Mission, dated September 1944', in *23 August 1944. Documente*, vol.II (Bucharest: Editura Ştiinţifică şi Enciclopedică, 1984), p.802.

23 British contacts with the Romanian opposition are analyzed in Dennis Deletant, *British Clandestine Activities in Romania During the Second World War* (Basingstoke, UK: Palgrave Macmillian, 2016). Set up in July 1940 by Winston Churchill "in order to set Europe ablaze", SOE sent a second mission to Romania, code-named 'Autonomous', whose members were Lt-Col. Alfred Gardyne de Chastelain, Cpt. Ivor Porter and a Romanian radio operator, Silviu Meţianu. They were parachuted into southern

Romania at 00.30 hours on 22 December 1943. De Chastelain's task was to inform Maniu personally of Stalin's apparent change of heart in agreeing to a discussion of terms of "unconditional surrender" by the Romanians. The group was arrested shortly after landing by Romanian gendarmes and held in Bucharest by the Romanians until 23 August 1944 (see Ivor Porter, *Operation Autonomous: With S.O.E. in Wartime Romania* (London: Chatto and Windus, 1989)).

24 The National Archives of the United States (henceforth NARA), Washington DC, General Records of the Department of State (R.G. 59), European War, 74000119, EW 1939/2057. Reproduced in *23 August 1944. Documente*, vol.I, doc.456.

25 The Soviet official in question was a man named Spitchkine who the Special Operations Executive surmised was acting independently of his minister, Madame Alexandra Kollontay (Elisabeth Barker, *British Policy in South-East Europe in the Second World War* (London: Macmillan, 1976), p.229).

26 *Foreign Relations of the United States*, 1944, vol.IV (Washington, DC: US Department of State, 1966), p.170. The terms were also passed to the Romanian minister in Stockholm by the Soviet chargé who transmitted them on the same day (13 April) to Bucharest; see Buzatu, *Mareşalul Antonescu în faţa istoriei*, pp.418–20 and Ivor Porter, *Michael of Romania. The King and the Country* (London: Sutton, 2005), p.94.

27 Barker, *British Policy*, p.233.

28 Ion Scurtu et al. (eds.), *Culegere de documente şi materiale privind Istoria României (6 septembrie 1940–23 August 1944)* (Bucharest: University of Bucharest, 1978), pp.219–20 (I thank Viorel Achim for showing me this anthology).

29 Barker, *British Policy*, p.140.

30 *Ibid.*, p.237.

31 *Ibid.*, p.238.

32 Author's interview with Corneliu Coposu, 31 October 1991. In a paper presented at a symposium in Paris on 22 May 1994, Coposu disclosed, in his capacity as Maniu's secretary and the person responsible for enciphering and deciphering Maniu's telegrams in the British code sent via Ţurcanu to Cairo, that in response to Novikov's suggestion to Vişoianu that the Romanian opposition should involve the section of the Comintern in Romania, Novikov was told that the number of Communists in Romania identified by the SSI (Romanian Intelligence) was 845, of whom 720 were foreigners. In reply, Maniu was told that it was common knowledge that a section of the Comintern in Romania did not exist but that public opinion abroad had to have the impression of the existence of a homogeneous opposition embracing all social and political categories. Maniu said that, in that case, he had nothing against the enlargement of the opposition. However, none of the Communists contacted in Romania claimed to be the true representatives of the Romanian Communist Party. With some satisfaction, Maniu cabled Novikov for his direction as to who was official representative of the Comintern in Romania and Novikov replied: "Lucreţiu Pătrăşcanu" (Exilul Românesc: 'Identitate şi Conştiinţă istorică', *Lupta* (Paris), no.232 (7 octombrie 1994), p.5). According to Communist historiography, the meeting of 4 April in Târgu-Jiu is alleged to have instructed Pătrăşcanu, Bodnăraş, and Ion Gheorge Maurer to join the other political parties in an effort to extract Romania from the war with the Soviet Union. A few days later, Pătrăşcanu negotiated an agreement with Titel Petrescu, the leader of the Social Democratic Party, to set up a United Workers' Front. Bodnăraş made his first appearance at a sub-committee charged with the preparation of plans for the defence of Bucharest on 13 June, although according to one account the main purpose was to discuss future relations with Moscow (Ioan Hudiţa, 'Pagini de Jurnal', *Magazin Istoric*, vol.28, no.7 (July 1994), p.41).

33 Iosif Şraier, the Communist Party's legal representative, conducted negotiations with Iuliu Maniu and Prince Ştirbey in preparation for the 23 August *coup*. One source claims that he received full authority from Moscow in his conversations with Maniu

which initially he conducted alone. Later he acted as Lucreţiu Pătrăşcanu's liaison in the negotiations between the Communist Party and the other members of the National Democratic Bloc. Before the Groza cabinet was reorganized in January 1946 he hoped to become Minister of the Interior but with his political ambitions frustrated, he left Romania later that year. ('List of Roumanian Personalities, 1947', Report no.262, 3 November 1947, Public Record Office, London, FO/371/67272 B).

34 For his career see the Selected Biographies.

35 On 11 June 1941, the Minister of the Interior, General D. Popescu, transmitted Ion Antonescu's order to General E. Leoveanu, Director General of Police, that the gendarmerie should be prepared to arrest all Communists between 15 and 20 June (Ministerul Afacerilor Interne, file 40010, vol.11, p.87.)

36 Porter, Operation Autonomous, p.175.

37 Barker, *British Policy*, p.239.

38 Titus Gârbea; see Buzatu, *Mareşalul Antonescu*, p.487.

39 Vasile Arimia, Ion Ardeleanu, and Ştefan Lache (eds.), *Antonescu-Hitler. Corespondentă şi întîlniri inedite (1940–1944)*, vol.II (Bucharest: Cozia, 1991), p.173.

40 On 4 April 1944, 220 B-17 Fortresses and 93 B-24 Liberators of the 15th USAAF, escorted by 120 fighters, had dropped over 860 tons of bombs on railway yards at Chitila in the north-west part of Bucharest. Unknown to the raiders, trains carrying refugees from Moldovia were waiting in the yards. One report put the death-toll at over 3,000 (PRO, FO 371/44001).

41 The southern offensive was launched from Tiraspol and aimed at Izmail, Constanţa and Bulgaria.

42 Baron Ion de Mocsonyi-Styrcea was born at Cernăuţi on 16 May 1909. He graduated from Cambridge with a degree in modern languages in 1932 and joined the Romanian Foreign Ministry two years later. Between 1 April and 11 August 1942 he was private secretary to King Michael and head of the royal chancery, and from the latter date until 1 April 1944 served as acting Marshal of the Royal Court. On 23 August 1944, he was made Marshal of the Court, a position from which he resigned on 4 November 1944 for health reasons, but he remained on the roll of the Foreign Ministry until the purge of non-Communist employees on 6 March 1946. He spent much of the period between September 1947 and November 1962 in prison on charges fabricated by the Communists. He was allowed to leave Romania on 4 September 1964 and settled in Switzerland (letter from Mocsonyi-Styrcea to this author, 4 August 1984).

43 Porter, *Operation Autonomous*, pp.192–93.

44 Letter from Mocsonyi-Styrcea to this author, 4 August 1984; see also Porter, *Michael of Romania*, p.104.

45 See Nicholas Baciu, *Sell-Out to Stalin. The Tragic Errors of Churchill and Roosevelt* (New York: Vantage Press, 1984), p.147. The courier in question, Neagu Djuvara, made it quite clear to his audience at the fiftieth anniversary symposium on '23 August 1944 in the history of Romania', held in Bucharest on 8–9 October 1994 (to which King Michael had accepted an invitation but was refused entry to Romania by the authorities), that Mihai Antonescu, with the Marshal's approval, had merely told Nanu to approach Madame Kollontay to ask whether the earlier conditions given by the Russians were still valid or would have to be negotiated. At the same time, Djuvara revealed, Mihai Antonescu instructed Nanu not to tell the British and Americans of this approach to the Soviets. Mihai Antonescu did not, as Nanu later claimed, tell him that the Marshal was ready to withdraw from the war and had given Mihai a free hand to sign the armistice (F.C. Nano, 'The First Soviet Double-Cross: A Chapter in the Secret History of World War II', *Journal of Central European Affairs*, vol.12, no.3 (October 1952), 236–58). As Djuvara remarked, the events in the three-month period since the issue of the Russian conditions had rendered many of them irrelevant and the mere raising of the question as to whether they were still valid showed how out of touch with reality the two Antonescus were.

46 At his trial in May 1946 the Marshal recalled his meeting with Brătianu: "And I said then, to Mr Gheorghe Brătianu: 'Look here, Mr Brătianu, I have abandoned the idea of not concluding an armistice, I shall conclude it, but I need these letters of guarantee because I cannot assume the historical responsibility for destroying the Romanian people ..... So, commit yourselves, accept your responsibility in writing, not verbally in words which are forgotten and which can be denied tomorrow'. And then Mr Brătianu replied: 'I'll go and bring you the letters, both of them, from Mr [Dinu] Brătianu as well, at 3 pm.' He did not come at 3 pm, I went to the palace...." (Ciucă, *Procesul*, p.215).

47 This account of events on 23 August is taken from M. Ionniţiu, '23 August 1944. Amintiri şi reflecţiuni', *Revista istorică*, vol.2, nos.9–10 (1991), pp.557–75, and Porter, *Operation Autonomous*, pp.198–202.

48 Porter, *Michael of Romania*, p.109.

49 Ionniţiu, '23 August', p.570.

50 This is the view of Ionniţiu.

51 Ion Hudiţă, *Jurnal Politic*. 1 Ianuarie-24 August 1944 (Bucharest: Editura Roza Vânturilor, 1997), p.502.

52 On Strada Sighişoara. Among this group of armed civilians was Ştefan Mladin, who for a period after 23 August was one of those responsible for the bodyguard of Gheorghiu-Dej.

53 M. Ionniţiu, '23 August', p.574.

54 General Dumitru Popescu, Minister of the Interior, Eugen Cristescu and Radu Lecca were also arrested later.

55 The order was transmitted by General (later Marshal) Rodion Malinovski, Commander of the Second Ukrainian Front and therefore of Soviet operations in Romania, to his deputy Lt. Gen. Ivan Susaikov.

56 Details taken from a report addressed to Stalin by Malinovski and Susaikov on 2 September 1944; see Ciucă, *Procesul*, pp.18–19. In an unsigned handwritten note in the Romanian Intelligence Service files, an eyewitness reported that "on 31 August 1944, around 5 pm, as I was walking along Vatra Luminoasă street to catch the no. 26 tram, I was overtaken by a convoy of five vehicles. The first was an open-topped car and carried two civilians wearing the Romanian tricolor armband, and a Soviet officer. The second car had its roof up and had a Soviet soldier seated next to the driver. In the back sat Ion Antonescu and Mihai Antonescu. The third car carried General Pantazi, General Vasiliu and Colonel Elefterescu. The fourth car was open and had three Soviet officers. The fifth vehicle was a large lorry with Soviet troops armed with machine-guns. The convoy went off on Iancului street in the direction of Pantelimon" (ANIC, Ministerul Afacerilor Interne. Trial of Ion Antonescu, file 40010, vol.34, pp.219–20.)

57 Constantin Pantazi, Cu Mareşalul până la moarte. Memoriile Ministrului de Război al României în anii 1942–1944 (Bucharest: Publiferom, 1999), pp.318–24.

58 Pantazi, *Cu Mareşalul*, p.325; see also Ion Pantazi, 'O mărturie indirectă despre 23 august', *Apoziţia*, 1980–81, Munich, 20–30; see also the same author's *Am trecut prin iad* (I passed through hell) (Sibiu: Constant, 1992), pp.307–10.

59 *Smersh* is a conjunction of two Russian words: '*Smyert Shpionam*,' meaning 'Death to Spies'.

60 Victor Abamukov (1908–1954) In February 1943, he became chief of the Directorate of *Smersh*. In 1946, he was made the head of the Ministry for State Security (MGB). He was eventually tried after Stalin's death in 1953 for his role in the 'Leningrad Affair' of 1949 in which the Politburo members Nikolai Voznesensky and Aleksei Kuznetsov were executed. Found guilty, Abamukov was executed by order of Khrushchev for treason on 19 December.

61 Radu Ioanid, Lotul Antonescu în ancheta SMERŞ, Moscova, 1944–1946. Documente din arhiva FSB (Bucharest: Polirom, 2006), p.32.

62 Pantazi, *Cu Mareşalul*, p.339.

63 Dennis Deletant, *Hitler's Forgotten Ally. Ion Antonescu and his Regime, Romania 1940–1944* (Basingstoke, UK: Palgrave Macmillan, 2006), pp.250–59.

64 These included A. G. Lee, *Crown against Sickle* (London: Hutchinson, 1950); R.H. Markham, *Rumania under the Soviet Yoke* (Boston: Meador Publishing, 1949); R. Bishop and E.S. Crayfield, *Russia astride the Balkans* (London: Evans, 1949). The historiography of the *coup* is presented in R.R. King, *A History of the Romanian Communist Party* (Stanford: Hoover Institution Press, 1980), pp.40–43, and in M. Shafir, *Romania. Politics, Economics and Society* (London: Frances Pinter, 1985), pp.30–37.

65 In a conversation in December 1944 with V. Morev, the TASS correspondent in Romania, Pătrăşcanu claimed that "the first meeting in connection with the preparations for the *coup* took place with the King in May 1944. At the meeting, apart from the King, were generals Sănătescu, Mihail, Răşcanu and Aldea, Niculescu-Buzeşti, Styrcea, Pătrăşcanu and Bodnăraş. The latter two were the only representatives of a political party". (Foreign Policy Archive, Moscow, fond 0125, opis 33, file 6, folio 127, pp.128–34). I am grateful to the late Dr Florin Constantiniu for showing me this document. Niculescu-Buzeşti, however, is reported to have met Pătrăşcanu and Bodnăraş for the first time on 13 June; see Ioan Hudiţă, *Jurnal Politic, 1 ianuarie-24 august 1944* (Bucharest: Editura Roza Vânturilor, 1997), p.309.

66 The most lucid account of the *coup* and preparations for it is given by Porter, *Operation Autonomous*.

67 I. Ardeleanu, V. Arimia, and M. Muşat (eds.), 'Report of Lt. Col. A.G.G. de Chastelain on the "Autonomous" Mission, dated September 1944', in *23 August 1944. Documente*, vol. II, (Bucharest: Editura Ştiinţifică şi Enciclopedică, 1984), p.802.

3 The application of the totalitarian blueprint

Stalin used the Armistice Agreement, signed in Moscow on 12 September 1944[1] between Romania on the one hand, and the United Kingdom, the United States and the Soviet Union, on the other, to subvert the effects of the 23 August *coup* which had threatened to wrest the initiative in Romanian affairs from him. In order to regain that initiative the Soviet leader fashioned from the armistice a legal framework for securing a dominant political and economic interest in Romania. Since the Soviet Union had a monopoly of its interpretation, the Armistice Agreement became the mechanism for the takeover of Romania.[2] Soviet determination to have the main say in this matter was carried through in their armistice draft of 31 August which stated that the terms would be implemented "under the control of the Soviet High Command, hereinafter called Allied (Soviet) High Command, acting on behalf of the Allied powers". Stalin's policy in Romania was designed to exact retribution for the Romanian invasion of the Soviet Union and to provide for permanent military security—a notion implying not merely disarmament and treaty guarantees but also the abrogation of the political power of those who had launched the invasion.[3] Articles 13 and 14 provided for the arrest of war criminals and the dissolution of 'Fascist-type' organizations.

In practice, the Control Commission functioned under statutes drawn up by the Russians, under which, until Potsdam, American and British officers were treated as delegations to the Commission, not structurally part of it. Hence, rights formally granted to the Allies under the Armistice Agreement were defined and enforced by the Russians. Stalin, therefore, had two satisfactory instruments for pursuing his objectives in Romania: a Communist Party which was an acknowledged part of the country's political structure, and an agreement with his Allies giving the Red Army all the scope it needed.

The takeover of Romania resulted from the interaction between the two: while fighting was still in progress, the Red Army, as any army, required order behind the front, but in Romania the only order acceptable to the Russians was that guaranteed by the Romanian Communist Party. The Party, in August 1944, had less than 1,000 members, a figure, nevertheless, that should be interpreted in the context of the Party being outlawed.[4] The Party's role was to prevent the post-*coup* regime from establishing order on any other terms. That requirement implied, first, neutralizing the existing means of maintaining the social order, namely the army, judiciary and police and redesigning them to the Soviet model; second, creating mass support, which the RCP totally lacked, and which would provide the new regime with the necessary theoretical legitimation. Both activities involved reliance on fear, and both could be relied upon to destroy any vestiges of support for the monarchy and for 'Western' democracy. In terms of tactics, the RCP embarked upon an intense propaganda drive amongst the working class. That propaganda was produced in bilingual broadsheets in Transylvania—in Romanian and Hungarian—thus promoting an inclusive appeal and giving it a multi-ethnic dimension whereas the major democratic parties, the National Peasant and National Liberal, as their names suggest, emphasized their purely Romanian, yet exclusive from the minorities' standpoint, character with their monolingual electoral literature. This inclusive approach of the RCP appears to have attracted many sympathizers from amongst the minorities, although this observation should not blind the reader to the coercive aspect of the RCP's recruitment campaign and the part played by opportunism in attracting many of its new adherents.

British and American diplomats did not consider the armistice conditions unduly harsh. Nevertheless, Averell Harriman, US ambassador to Moscow, had serious doubts about Soviet intentions and predicted that the terms would "give the Soviet command unlimited control of Romania's economic life" and, more ominously, "police power for the period of the armistice".[5] Both the British and US governments endorsed the agreement without demur, indeed their acceptance of Moscow as the place of signature was a tacit admission that their Eastern partner, as the principal belligerent ally in Eastern Europe, had earned the right as victor to dictate its terms to the Romanians. That the Soviet Union should adopt this position was accepted as inevitable by Churchill in a speech to the House of Commons delivered on 26 September 1944. The Prime Minister admitted that:

> the armistice terms agreed upon for Finland and Romania bear, naturally, the imprint of the Soviet will - and here I must draw attention to the restraint which has characterized the Soviet treatment of these two countries, both of which marched blithely behind Hitler in his attempted destruction of Russia, and both of which added their quota of injuries to the immense volume of suffering which the Russian people have endured, have survived, and have triumphantly surmounted.[6]

Against Churchill's statement, made when the Red Army was still fighting its way across Eastern Europe, must be set the belief of King Michael and his ministers that his *coup* against Antonescu and the volte-face against the Germans had earned Romania the right to be treated not as a defeated enemy, but as a new co-belligerent. Such a view received no sympathy from Stalin, who was unwilling to forgive Romania for its contribution to Operation Barbarossa. Yet ironically, King Michael's action, by facilitating the Red Army's advance in the Balkans, was to seal his country's consignment to the Soviet sphere of influence and Stalin's domination. With Soviet troops pouring into Romania and Bulgaria,

Churchill was determined to save Greece and possibly Italy from a Communist takeover, and this spectre was to haunt Churchill's policy towards Romania.

By the time that Churchill decided to divide up responsibility in the Balkans with Stalin by talking to him personally, Britain had few cards to play. The Russians were already in occupation of much of Romania and Bulgaria and so Churchill, when he flew to Moscow at the beginning of October 1944, got straight down to business and proposed the now notorious 'percentages agreement', struck on the evening of 9 October.[7] Although Churchill maintained in his memoirs that "only immediate wartime arrangements" were under discussion, he knew that Stalin could not be dislodged by force from the position of influence which he had gained. Thus in proposing the deal, Churchill was merely being pragmatic; he was recognizing Soviet preponderance in the Balkans, one which was restricted only by the Red Army's own operational problems.[8] Stalin interpreted the 'percentages agreement' as he chose, and the absence of any Western forces, not just in Romania, but in the whole of Eastern Europe, ensured that the exercise of Soviet authority in the area remained unrestricted.

In the caretaker government of General Sănătescu (23 August–2 November 1944), set up to direct Romania's new war course, the majority of ministerial posts had gone to military officers, with only the Ministry of Justice being secured by the Communists in the person of Lucreţiu Pătrăşcanu. Both Maniu and Brătianu preferred not to participate in government, proposing other members of their parties instead. While several senior officers of the Intelligence Service, the SSI (*Serviciul Special de Informaţii*), were arrested in September 1944, the committee charged with screening the 600 personnel of the SSI employed nationally concluded, in a report of 20 October, that they could find only two officers against whom charges could be levelled and these were "abusive behaviour and unseemly conduct".[9] The personnel of the Ministry of the Interior and of the security police, the *Siguranţa*, remained largely unchanged.[10] It was the failure to replace these figures that provided a pretext for the Communists to set about torpedoing the Sănătescu government. At the same time the Soviet authorities set about weakening Romania's army and police force.

On 2 October, the Soviet High Command demanded the reduction of the police force from 18,000 to 12,000. On 6 October, it forced the resignation of General Gheorghe Mihail, the Chief of the Romanian General Staff, because of his opposition to the Soviet order that all Romanian units should be disarmed, except for the 12 divisions fighting alongside the Russians. Mihail's successor, General Nicolae Rădescu, consented under protest to the Soviet demand (26 October), that the Romanian army in the interior be reduced from 13 full-strength to three skeleton divisions with a total complement of 10,000, and that the numbers of frontier guards and gendarmerie be cut from 74,086 to 58,018. This process was continued over the next three years, leading to a fall in the strength of the Romanian Armed forces from 419,000 in May 1945 to 136,000 in December 1947.[11]

These actions by the Soviet authorities ensured that the Party could proceed without fundamental interference. Its first task was to broaden its bridgehead in government. That in itself demanded admission to crucial ministries—Interior and Defence as well as Justice—and the creation of mass support, which could be used to demand radical political change. On 2 October, the Communist Party and the Social Democratic Party joined forces to form the National Democratic Front (NDF). Members of the Front threatened workers at the major factories in Bucharest and elsewhere with arrest by the Soviet army if they refused to vote out the old works' committees and elect NDF representatives in their place. The new committees then took charge of the workers' canteens and the rationing procedures and soon the NDF had much of industry in its grip, forcing workers to accede to its will under pain of withdrawing rations and special ration cards.

In industry and elsewhere, the threats were given weight by the 'Guards of Patriotic Defence', enlarged from the nucleus of armed workers who took charge of Antonescu after his arrest. Enlargement, in September 1944, was supervised by the Soviet Security Service, the NKGB and placed under the command of Emil Bodnăraş. It provided the ideal cover for the training of agents and thugs who were to be infiltrated into the police and security forces when the Communists gained access to the Ministry of the Interior. The 'Guards' were used to root out 'Fascists' and encourage recalcitrants to see the error of opposition. When necessary, they enjoyed the logistic cooperation of the Russian command. Their recruits included jailbirds and former members of the Iron Guard, whose intimidatory skills had, of course, been honed in the late thirties.[12] On 15 January 1945, the Prime Minister, General Rădescu, ordered the Guards' disbandment, but Teohari Georgescu, the Deputy Minister of the Interior, and Bodnăraş simply ignored the instruction. With the truncated Romanian army absent or disarmed, the government had no countervailing power.

The Armistice Agreement had stipulated the dissolution of "all pro-Hitler organizations (of a Fascist type)" (Art.15). This, widely drawn, was liberally interpreted. In early September, the Foreign Minister, Niculescu-Buzeşti and Ion Mocsony-Styrcea, the Marshal of the Palace (both leading figures in the *coup* of 23 August), called for the immediate establishment of a tribunal for the trial of war criminals and of pro-Germans holding responsible positions. Maniu raised legalistic objections and the proposal was dropped.[13]

The liquidation of Fascism fell to the Russians and to their local minions. We should at this point recall that the war against the Axis still in progress was widely accepted as an 'anti-Fascist' crusade; that there were many in Romania who, in some sense or other, qualified as 'Fascist', and that the governments immediately after the *coup* appeared to be dilatory in dealing with them. So, an agitation to get rid of Fascists could count on some popular support. Events soon demonstrated that, in practice, 'Fascist' came to mean what the Communists said it was. And they could say it through 'spontaneous' demonstrations and through a press which was rapidly being brought under control.[14]

On 8 October the NDF organized its first mass meeting in Bucharest, at which some 60,000 demonstrators called for the resignation of the Sănătescu government for having failed to remove 'Fascists' from public life. On the following day General Vinogradov, the head of the Russian Military Mission, demanded that the government arrest 47 Romanians as war criminals, among them two cabinet ministers,

General Gheorghe Potopeanu, the Minister of the National Economy who had served for a brief period as Military Governor of Transnistria, and General Ion Boiteanu, the Minister of Education. The slowness with which Sănătescu acted against Antonescu's officials merely provided grist to the mill of the Communist Party and to the Soviet authorities. Both accused the Romanians of not respecting Articles 14 and 15 of the Armistice. In their defence Romanian officials argued that the bureaucracy would not be able to function if large-scale purges of the kind demanded by the Russians were implemented.[15] Confirmation of the Communists' charges came from an American OSS (Office of Strategic Services) report of February 1945 which stated that during the first six weeks after the August *coup* the Sănătescu government dismissed only eight Romanian officials.[16]

Demonstrations also focused on specific political figures who the Communists wanted removed. One such was the new Minister of the Interior, Nicolae Penescu, a member of the National Peasant Party, who was vehemently anti-Soviet. Mass demonstrations were organized to shout "Down with Penescu". At the end of November the NDF seized upon a suburban brawl as a pretext for demanding his resignation.[17] A group of drunken Romanian soldiers shot dead two trade unionists, for whom the NDF organized a huge funeral. The Communist press raged about "Hitlerist Fascist bullets from automatic rifles of the Fifth Column supported by leaders of the National Peasant Party". The Peasant Party ministers and their National Liberal colleagues withdrew from the cabinet of Sănătescu who they felt was too tolerant of the Communists' harassment. On 2 December, the King asked General Nicolae Rădescu, formerly Chief of the General Staff and a non-party figure, to form a cabinet.[18]

Rădescu received strong backing from King Michael, who on 4 December warned Andrei Vyshinsky, the Soviet Deputy Foreign Minister, that the Communists' activities threatened to throw the country into anarchy. Among these was an unremitting press campaign in the party newspaper *Scînteia* condemning the Romanians' alleged failure to fulfil the principal conditions of the armistice. *Scînteia* reprinted (6 December 1944) Soviet charges that the Romanian government had systematically shirked from honouring its direct debt and had openly supported the administration which sabotaged the Armistice Convention. The leaders of the so-called 'historical parties' in Romania—the National Peasant and National Liberal parties—who were widely represented in the Sănătescu government, were responsible. The conclusion was ominous:

> The Soviet Command in this part of the Soviet-German front is displaying the utmost patience which is being abused by those Romanian politicians who have transformed this region of the front into an area of intrigue which is undermining the mobilization of the forces of the Romanian people and basic order in the country...[19]

The King told Vyshinsky that if the Soviet Union continued to support the Communists in this way, he would find himself forced to abdicate and leave the country. Vyshinsky was said to have been surprised by the King's boldness and denied any Soviet responsibility. In the government reshuffle the Communist-dominated NDF had hoped to secure the Ministry of the Interior, but Rădescu reserved the post for himself. Thereupon the Party leaders, Ana Pauker and Vasile Luca, refused even to discuss NDF participation in the new government. However, under instructions from Vyshinsky, they now backed down.[20] Rădescu did, however, concede the position of Deputy Minister of the Interior to the Communists, appointing Teohari Georgescu, a member of the Party's Central Committee; his Communist colleagues in the cabinet were Pătrăşcanu, Minister of Justice and Gheorghiu-Dej, Minister of Communications and Public Works.

Vyshinsky's decision throws some light on Soviet intentions at this time. The short-term priority was to conclude the war against Germany as quickly as possible. Instability in Romania would compromise that aim. Furthermore, the Romanian Communist Party was still not strong enough to take over the administration of the country where the bulk of the population was hostile to Communism; therefore, should the King abdicate, the Russians were likely to have to assume part of the administration themselves. Such a move would raise questions about their motives in Britain and the United States. Consequently, Vyshinsky lowered the temperature in Romania. He left the country as he had come, without notice, on 8 December.[21]

So, for a brief period, NDF meetings and street demonstrations ceased, but Communist penetration of institutions continued unabated. Teohari Georgescu installed his own men in nine of the 16 prefectures in the provinces with strict orders to avoid government instructions and to do only his bidding. He also ignored an undertaking to Rădescu to disband the 10,000 strong Communist militia and introduced into the *Siguranţa* agents trained in the 'Patriotic Guards'. On 19 December, Maniu addressed a letter to his British friend De Chastelain drawing his attention to the "development of a new reign of terror in Roumania" and endeavouring to persuade him to return.[22] The truce ended with the publication of the NDF New Year's appeal to the people in which they condemned the Rădescu government for failing to fulfil the terms of the Armistice, and called for agrarian reform of all property exceeding an area of 50 hectares within six weeks.

It was soon evident that the RCP's moves were Soviet-orchestrated. On 4 January 1945, Stalin received Pauker, Gheorghiu-Dej and Gheorghe Apostol in his dacha outside Moscow. According to Gheorghi Dimitrov, the Bulgarian Communist Party leader who spent the war years in Moscow, Stalin advised the Romanian delegation to focus on agrarian reform and to use the Tudor Vladmirescu division as internal support for the NDF.[23] The actions of the NDF bore this claim out. The NDF attacked its National Liberal and National Peasant partners in the government, denouncing them as 'Fascists' who opposed the will of the people. On 29 January, the NDF published its government programme. It was clearly directed against its National Liberal and National Peasant partners in the government, denouncing them as 'reactionaries' who opposed the will of the people, and called for a new government, immediate agrarian reform and the democratization of the army.[24] When the Liberals and Peasants attempted to answer these charges, their newspapers ceased to appear owing to the refusal of the Communist-controlled printing union to produce them.

Acting on instructions from Vyshinsky, Gheorghiu-Dej approached the dissident Liberal leader Gheorghe Tătărescu with an invitation to enter the NDF in order to give it the appearance of a broader base. On 31 January, Gheorghiu-Dej told the NDF council of the talks which he had had with Tătărescu who said that he was ready to enter the NDF. "There are opinions", Gheorghiu-Dej stated, "in very competent places [i.e. Moscow], which indicate to us the need to bring Tătărescu close to us and not to reject him". Vasile Luca agreed; for him Tătărescu 'represented economic power'. Lothar Rădăceanu, however, was less enthusiastic. He criticised Tătărescu's tolerance of the Iron Guardists and the fact that "he was their greatest protector". Gheorghiu-Dej saw the attraction of Tătărescu not merely in the advantages he could bring to the NDF but also in terms of the damage he could do to Maniu: "Maniu wants to get rid of him [Tătărescu] as a dangerous adversary... Let us think seriously of breaking the National Peasant front", Gheorghiu-Dej concluded.[25]

The Communist press accused Rădescu of sabotaging the armistice by allegedly failing to cleanse Romanian public life of 'Fascism' but omitted to point out that it had failed to put its own house in order in the case of those ministries headed by Communists. Teohari Georgescu sent an open letter to the press accusing Rădescu of having hindered the 'decontamination' of the Ministry of the Interior. In a stormy cabinet meeting on 14 February, Rădescu requested Georgescu's resignation for acts of insubordination. Georgescu, supported by his Communist colleagues in the cabinet, refused to go and the Prime Minister responded by publishing on 16 February three circulars, dated 13 and 28 December 1944, and 20 January 1945, calling on the commission charged with compiling the list of officials liable for dismissal to complete its task. Rădescu was able to point out that the commission for purging the Ministry of the Interior, of which Teohari Georgescu himself was a member, had taken three months to examine 75 cases out of 300, and that following the general's intervention 137 cases had been dealt with in 12 days. In fact, under the Rădescu government 780 officers (i.e. employees of the Interior ministry) out of a total force estimated at 14,000, were purged.[26]

Aware of the power which Georgescu and Bodnăraş were amassing, Rădescu ordered the disbandment of the 'Patriotic Guards' on 15 January but the two Communists simply ignored his instruction. Still Georgescu refused to leave his post. He continued to go to his office and issued a telegram to prefects, informing them that "in compliance with the decision of the NDF council", he would remain in office. "I advise you most emphatically", he continued, "not to carry out orders directed against the people, given by General Rădescu, who has proved himself by his dictatorial action to be the enemy of our people".[27] In the meantime the Deputy Prime Minister Petru Groza, widely regarded as a tool of the Communists, was encouraging peasants to anticipate the land reform by seizing the land of the large estate owners, An article in *Scînteia* of 13 February 1945 reported the expropriation of estates by peasants in the counties of Prahova and Dâmboviţa. Two days later Rădescu accused Groza at a cabinet meeting of preparing civil war. Both Rădescu and King Michael feared that the Left was preparing a *coup* amidst reports that the Russians were sending NKGB troops to Bucharest.

The NDF staged demonstrations in several towns, among them Brăila, Constanţa, Craiova, Roman and Târgu-Mureş, calling for the resignation of the Rădescu government. Although many of the participants came of their own accord, the NDF also used blackmail to mobilize demonstrators. Workers who did not join trade unions were refused ration cards. A police report of 4 February stated that in many factories works' committees were paralleled by so-called 'sacrifice committees' composed of members of parties of the Left. These committees were set up to ensure that the workers followed the orders of the Communist Party and did not join any other parties or non-Communist organizations.[28]

Any hopes that the Romanian people might have had from the declaration on Liberated Europe, issued at the Yalta Conference, that "sovereign rights and self-government" would be restored "to those peoples who have been forcibly deprived of them" were soon dispelled. Organized thuggery was practised by the 'Patriotic Guards' in support of the NDF committees whose hold over several key factories in Bucharest was challenged by non-NDF workers. This particular campaign of Communist-inspired violence began at the ASAM defence works early in February and spread to the Official Gazette and Stella works where the NDF committees were thrown out. At the union elections at the ASAM shops only 14 of the 600 workers voted for the Communist candidates while 180 voted for the non-party list (the remainder abstained). On 6 February, 60 members of the 'Patriotic Guards' and two NKGB soldiers drove to the ASAM works, beat up those who had voted for the independent list, and took 11 of them away to the NKGB headquarters. On 19 February, 3,600 of the 5,500 employees at the Malaxa steel and armament works in Bucharest signed a resolution calling for the resignation of the NDF committee headed by Vasile Mauriciu, a former Iron Guardist. Voting on the resolution on the following day was interrupted when the NDF committee called on railwaymen and tramway employees to defend them at the factory. Fighting broke out between the Malaxa workers and the outsiders during which several workers were killed and the Communist labour leader Gheorghe Apostol was wounded. After the affray all those whose identity cards showed that they had voted were arrested and taken to NDF branches.[29]

Travesty was added to injury. *Scînteia* accused Rădescu of attempting to foment a civil war; its attacks were echoed by *Graiul Nou*, the Red Army newspaper in Romania, and Pravda. A. Pavlov, the Soviet political representative on the Allied Control Commission, followed the script by advising the chief American on the Commission that unless the Rădescu government "rid itself of... Fascist elements... the people themselves can be expected to take necessary corrective action".[30] Matters came to a head on 24 February. At the end of a large NDF demonstration, the crowd moved into the palace square in front of the Ministry of the Interior where Rădescu had his office. Shots were fired and several people were killed. On orders from Rădescu the Romanian troops guarding the building fired into the air to disperse the crowd. The American historian Henry Roberts:

> watched the procession and was in the crowd no more than 50 feet from the first shots. Yet at that time and since I have been

> unable to discover precisely what happened. I do know that government had kept Romanian troops off the streets that day to avoid inciting trouble. The crowd did move toward the Ministry of the Interior building, although it showed little signs of direction. The first shots were fired from a small piece and from somewhere in the crowd, but by whom and for what purpose I do not know.[31]

What was clearly established later by a joint Romanian-Russian commission of doctors was that the bullets extracted from the victims were not of a calibre used by the Romanian army, but these findings came too late for Rădescu. Unable to contain his anger at the provocation, the Prime Minister broadcast to the nation and denounced the Communist leaders, Ana Pauker and Vasile Luca, as "hyenas" and "foreigners without God or country", a reference to their non-Romanian origins and their atheism.[32] The Russians now intervened. Vyshinsky arrived unexpectedly in Bucharest on 27 February and went straight to the palace to demand that Rădescu be replaced. King Michael hesitated and told the Russian that constitutional procedures had to be respected. On the following afternoon Vyshinsky returned and demanded to know what action the King had taken. When Michael again announced that he was consulting political leaders, the Deputy Minister shouted his dissatisfaction and gave the King until six that evening to announce Rădescu's dismissal. The King was intimidated into consenting.

Michael turned to the British and American representatives for help and advice, but despite the lodging of Western protests in Bucharest and Moscow at Vyshinsky's behaviour, the Deputy Foreign Minister continued to force the pace:

> All the truly democratic forces in Romania must be represented in the government and such a government will be able to ensure order and peace in Romania, which is behind the front of the Red Army, whilst at the same time ensuring the honourable and conscientious fulfilment of the armistice conditions.[33]

Military pressure was soon added to political. On 28 February, Col. General Ivan Susaikov, the Deputy Commander of the Southern Group of Armies, replaced Lt. Gen. V. Vinogradov as Deputy Chairman of the Allied Control Commission.[34] Without consulting his British and American colleagues, he ordered some Romanian units stationed in and around Bucharest to the front and disbanded others. Their place was taken by Soviet tanks and troops who occupied the Prefecture of Police, the Central Post Office and the Romanian General Staff Headquarters. Two Romanian bomber groups and two fighter squadrons based in the capital were disbanded, and the rest of the Romanian air force was grounded. Hundreds of plain clothes and uniformed police were dismissed and Soviet troops patrolled the streets of Bucharest, checking the documents of pedestrians and of drivers and their vehicles, using this opportunity to commandeer even more Romanian vehicles.

On 1 March, Vyshinsky informed the King that Petru Groza, Rădescu's deputy and a trusted nominee of the Russians "was the Soviet choice". Michael reluctantly gave Groza the go-ahead to form a government but the Liberals and Peasants refused to join a government controlled by the NDF. Groza's first cabinet was rejected by the King. On 5 March, Vyshinsky informed Michael that unless a Groza government was accepted he "could not be responsible for the continuance of Romania as an independent state".[35] Fearing a *coup* the King acquiesced on the following afternoon. Thereafter, the Communist takeover of Romania proceeded rapidly.[36]

Susaikov later explained to the British and American representatives, respectively Air Vice Marshal Donald Stevenson and Brigadier General Cortland Van Resselaer Schuyler, that the Groza government was indeed imposed by force on the orders of Marshal Malinovsky who feared an uprising at the rear of his front. Susaikov had been sent to Bucharest to prevent a Romanian volte-face by disarming Romanian troops and bringing in Groza.[37] This argument is not entirely without substance. Soviet sensitivity to disorder behind the lines had been conveyed to Schulyer at the time by Pavlov, the Soviet political representative. At a meeting of the Allied Control Commission on 14 February 1945, Pavlov had told Schuyler that "no disorder can be permitted to occur in the rear of the Soviet armies ... nor can any Fascist activities within the state of Romania be permitted".[38]

From the archival evidence now available, there appears to have been some disagreement within the Communist Party leadership over the composition of the Groza government. The decisive voice in the matter appears to have been Vyshinsky. In a note dated 21 January 1945 to Serghei Dangulov, Senior Assistant to the Head of the Political Department of the Allied Control Commission, Vyshinsky told him "to maintain contacts and relations with Gheorghe Tătărescu", a former Prime Minister under King Carol and a dissident Liberal.[39] Vyshinsky's influence with Gheorghiu-Dej persuaded the latter to reject calls late in February from the National Liberal representative Constantin (Bebe) Brătianu for the Communists to continue to work with the National Liberals and National Peasants in government. Instead, Gheorghiu-Dej pressed for an alliance both with Tătărescu and with a dissident National Peasant faction led by Anton Alexandrescu. At an NDF council meeting held on 26 February, Gheorghiu-Dej made his position clear. He had told Brătianu that he did not have a mandate to hold discussions with him and told him bluntly that his proposal [for continued cooperation] was unacceptable. "We see no reason for the present government to carry on". Reviewing the current political situation, Gheorghiu-Dej said that although the NDF had consolidated its position in the government, it had not succeeded in resolving the political crisis.

> What we proposed was to enlarge our political base. The forces which today make up the NDF are not sufficient, new alliances must be found. We have found these in the progressive elements among the National Peasants [...] and secondly in the political grouping of Tătărescu. We can no longer make the same kinds of combinations with the representatives of the so-called 'historical' parties as we have made to date.[40]

Gheorghiu-Dej's views were not shared by other leading Communists. Vasile Luca, speaking at a meeting of the NDF council held on 5 March, insisted that despite the NDF's dislike of holding talks with the National Liberals and National Peasants, "we must do everything that is humanly possible to form a government in a constitutional manner in the interests and the country and in the current international context, [and] we must not, in our haste, destroy everything".[41] Ana Pauker was, according to Anton Alexandrescu, in favour of a new government formed in collaboration with Maniu and Brătianu and had allegedly received the backing of General Susaikov.[42]

The optimism felt in British and American quarters at the measure of agreement secured amongst the Allies at Yalta was largely dispelled by Soviet conduct after the conference, in particular in Romania. The imposition of the Groza government engendered a sense of hopelessness in Clark Kerr, British ambassador to Moscow, who in a paper on Soviet policy dated 27 March 1945, described Soviet policy in Romania as "the sheerest power politics, entirely out of harmony with the principles enshrined in the Crimea declaration". He went on to say that there had been

> no attempt to consult with us or with the Americans and we have been expected to condone and, indeed, to associate ourselves with the decisions imposed upon King Michael by M. Vyshinsky. When we quote the Yalta declaration to the Russians we meet with the reply that our arguments are not in accordance with the Statutes agreed upon for the Allied Control Commission. In other words, the Yalta declaration is being treated by the Soviet government as little more than a sedative which cannot be allowed to interfere with what is, in the eyes of the Russians, their established right, fully admitted by us, to do as they like in Roumania. When our protests become more urgent, no time is lost in starting a minor press campaign against General Plastiras and his administration in Greece, as if to remind us that Russian forbearance as regards that country is measured by ours in Roumania.[43]

The establishment of the Groza government brought with it the total subordination of the forces of order to the Communists. Citizens' committees were to assist the police, which had been reduced by Soviet order on 28 February and purged, and these arrogated to themselves the right to check people's documents in the street, to search homes for goods allegedly removed from the Soviet Union during the war or which had formerly belonged to Germans and Hungarians, and to inspect houses with a view to billeting refugees or Soviet officers. There was no legal supervision of these random intrusions into people's lives and the rapidity with which the police degenerated into a force of repression under Groza produced a widespread fear of authority.

In order to obtain the verdicts that he required Vyshinsky ordered Pătrăşcanu, the Minister of Justice, to dismiss more than 1,000 magistrates in April 1945 and replace them with pliant zealots.[44] It was not just the retributive aspect of these purges that was important but also the instrumental use of them. The two were linked: the threat of retribution was deployed to pressure people to become tools of the Communists. Groza himself told the British journalist Archie Gibson on 23 May 1945 that in the two months since he had taken office 90,000 Romanians had been arrested,[45] but there is no information to hand to confirm this figure. For some there were good grounds for arrest, as in the case of Nicolae Sturdza and Nelly Ostroveanu, two members of an Iron Guard group who were found to be housing 19 German soldiers living under assumed names in Bucharest and who were arrested in March. For others the opposite was true; 13 Poles were held in the internment camp at Caracal without being questioned. Persons convicted of atrocities during the Romanian administration of Transnistria were harshly punished. People's Tribunals were introduced by Pătrăşcanu to try alleged war criminals and on 22 May 29 officials, including Generals Nicolae Macici, Constantin Trestioreanu and Cornel Calotescu, were sentenced to death and eight to various terms of imprisonment.[46] The death sentences were commuted to life imprisonment on 5 June.[47] In August 1945, the discovery of two 'terrorist' plots led to the arrest of about 20 'hirelings of ex-Premier Rădescu', and of a second group of 17 people who had allegedly plotted 'againt the unity of the Romanian nation'. Both groups included National Peasants.

The young King was greatly unnerved by these developments and appealed to Britain and the United States for help, invoking the principles of the Atlantic Charter and the Yalta Declaration. On 2 August, at the end of the Potsdam Conference, both countries announced that they would sign peace treaties "only with recognized democratic governments", a stipulation which gave some hope to the King and the opposition leaders, Maniu and Brătianu.[48] The latter discussed plans to remove the Groza government and on 20 August the King asked for Groza's resignation but the Prime Minister, with the backing of General Susaikov, refused. King Michael, in retaliation, boycotted the government; he declined to see any of its ministers and to sign decrees.

The stalemate lasted for over four months. It was broken at the Moscow Conference of the Foreign Ministers of Britain, the United States and the Soviet Union, held between 16–26 December, where it was decided that a commission, composed of ambassadors Clark Kerr, Harriman and Deputy Foreign Minster Vyshinsky, should go to Bucharest to advise King Michael on the inclusion in the government of one representative each from the National Peasant and National Liberal parties. After this reorganization it was also agreed that free elections would be held "as soon as possible on the basis of universal suffrage and secret ballot".[49]

The Moscow Agreement was the final step for the Soviets in getting the West to recognize their dominance of Romania.[50] Had the agreement been respected to the letter, it would have represented a victory for King Michael's defiance, but as events were to prove, it merely allowed the Western Allies to disguise their impotence. Groza went through the motions of implementing the terms, accepting Emil Haţieganu of the Peasant Party and Mihai Romniceanu of the Liberals into his cabinet as ministers without Portfolio, and undertaking, on 8 January 1946, to hold early elections and to guarantee access to the radio and the media to all parties. On the basis of these assurances Britain and the United States expressed their willingness to recognize the Groza government at the beginning of February in the expectation that the elections would be held at the end of April or early May. In the event Groza procrastinated. On 27 May, both Britain and the United States protested to Groza at his failure to honour his pledges, and eventually his government produced an electoral law which was heavily weighted in its favour. All parties of the Left were to run on a common list, including the Social Democratic Party which the Communists had succeeded in splitting.

A new wave of arrests took place in May 1946. Among those detained was General Aldea, the Interior Minister in the first Sănătescu government, who was arrested on 27 May and charged with "plotting to destroy the unity of the Romanian state" on the grounds that "in the summer of 1945 he had brought together various subversive organizations under his own central command" in a "National Resistance Movement" (*Mişcarea Naţională de Rezistenţă*). Initially, these groups had acted independently, the most important of them being *Haiducii lui Avram Iancu* (The Outlaws of Avram Iancu), which had been set up in Transylvania on 1 December 1944 by leading figures of the National Peasant Party, among them Iuliu Maniu's nephew. An offshoot of this group was *Divizia Sumanele Negre* (The Black Greatcoats Division) which also had its centre of operations in Transylvania. In a declaration to the *Siguranţa* Aldea revealed that he had established links in autumn 1945 with these groups and brought them under his command. In fact, the National Resistance Movement was a paper tiger: its principal activities were the distribution of primitive anti-Communist propaganda. Its actions largely consisted of attacks on Hungarians by members of *Haiducii lui Avram Iancu* in revenge for murders of Romanians by Hungarian policemen during the period of Hungarian rule of Northern Transylvania and it was these which caused the greatest concern to the Soviet authorities for they raised the spectre of civil war in Transylvania. Aldea was tried along with 55 'accomplices' on the eve of the polls in November and sentenced on 18 November to hard labour for life.[51]

Opposition meetings were frequently interrupted during the election campaign by gangs of hooligans and when the American political representative in Bucharest, Burton Berry, protested, Groza told him that

> when the Anglo-Americans agreed to the Moscow decision they were thinking in terms of free elections such as were held in England or America, whereas the Russians were thinking in terms of free elections such as were held in Russia. In view of the presence of the Russian army in Romania, the coming elections would likely be held according to the Russian interpretation of free and unfettered.[52]

The results of the elections, held on 19 November, came as no surprise to the Foreign Office and to the State Department. The government bloc claimed almost five million votes (84%), while the National Peasants were awarded eight hundred thousand and the Liberals less than three hundred thousand. 414 deputies were elected to a single chamber parliament, of whom 348 represented government parties and 66 the opposition. In the view of Western diplomats and press correspondents the results were faked, and consequently Dean Acheson, the acting US Secretary of State, declared that his government would not recognize them. In the House of Commons Hector McNeil, the Under-Secretary for Foreign Affairs said that the elections were neither free nor fair. During the campaign the opposition parties were, he argued, denied full freedom of speech, and the arrangements on polling day were such as to permit wholesale fabrication of the results.[53] These assessments have been confirmed by documents from the Romanian Communist Party's own archives, published since the overthrow of Nicolae Ceauşescu.[54] Yet despite this condemnation of the results the British government, on advice from the Foreign Office, decided not to support an American protest to the Russians calling for new elections, on the feeble grounds that Moscow would simply prevaricate.

King Michael threatened to postpone the opening of parliament but Burton Berry, the American representative in Bucharest, to whom he appealed for support, was unable to give him any encouragement. Yet more arrests followed the signing of the Peace Treaty with Romania on 10 February 1947. Its political clauses were so lacking in definition that the Ministry of the Interior could interpret the phrases "organization of a Fascist type" and "war criminal" as arbitrarily as they wished. As one British observer pointed out, "there was no mention of a judiciary body to try the cases against such organizations and war criminals [and] this enabled the Groza government to make war on individual National Peasants and National Liberals as 'Fascists' and 'war criminals'".[55] On 20 March, 315 members of the opposition parties were arrested and on the night of 4 May, another six hundred. There was no legal basis for these arrests; those in May were made under the provisions of a top secret order of the Ministry of the Interior and the persons detained were sent to prisons in Gherla, Piteşti, Craiova and Miercurea Ciuc. Some of the 596 persons sent to Gherla were peasants who had opposed collectivization, others were teachers, doctors and priests who had campaigned on behalf of the opposition parties in November 1946. Many did not know why they had been arrested. Several managed to escape and most were released after six months but the Communist authorities had acheived their aim: to intimidate the population and to prepare the ground for the liquidation of the opposition parties.

Such was the atmosphere of fear that even Tătărescu, the Deputy Prime Minister, was moved in May to send a memorandum to the cabinet arguing that

> preventive arrests must cease so that the atmosphere of insecurity may be dispelled. The security police should be continually on the alert, but it should act only against offenders. The guilty persons should be punished without mercy, but only within the letter of the law. All illegally detained persons should be released.[56]

Tătărescu's argument fell on deaf ears, for the campaign to eliminate the opposition parties, approved by Stalin and coordinated by Vyshinsky, had entered its final stage. Instructions were given to Pintilie Bodnarenko, the head of the *Siguranţa,* to compromise the Peasant Party leadership. Bodnarenko did this by getting an *agent provocateur* to persuade Maniu's deputy Ion Mihalache to attempt to flee the country in a plane provided by him. The plan succeeded and on 14 July 1947 Mihalache and several prominent figures in the Peasant Party were arrested as they were about to leave for Turkey from Tămădău airfield, about 46 km from Bucharest. A few days later Maniu was detained and the whole leadership of the Party was put on trial on 30 October for plotting against the security of the state. Maniu and Mihalache were each sentenced to hard labour for life, commuted to life imprisonment and neither man was ever seen in public again.[57]

The final obstacle to complete Soviet domination of Romania was King Michael. Even in 1945 the continuation of the Romanian kingdom within the Soviet orbit appeared, in the circumstances, to be an anomaly. The young monarch had valiantly wrestled with the Soviet tentacles which were slowly throttling the country's independence, often with only half-hearted support from Britain and the United States, but the stage-managed trial of Maniu and the mockery of justice it represented were clear signs that his struggle was in vain. Nevertheless, the Romanian people clung to him as the last symbol of hope for a sane and settled future. In September 1947, Foreign Minister Tătărescu had been compelled to dismiss several hundred members of his ministry who were regarded as pro-Western, and on 7 November he and other Liberal cabinet members were removed from their posts at Groza's insistence. The King felt obliged to accept the Communists Ana Pauker and Vasile Luca as Foreign Minister and Minister of Finance respectively, while on 23 December Emil Bodnăraş became Minister of War. When the King went to London on 12 November with the Queen Mother for the marriage of Princess Elizabeth, Groza and Gheorghiu-Dej hoped that he would renounce the throne and not return. Indeed Michael asked for American advice on this subject and the US ambassador in London considered that his return 'would serve no useful purpose.'[58] Nevertheless, the King, who while abroad had announced his engagement to Princess Anne de Bourbon Parma, took the bold decision to return with the Queen Mother on 21 December. Nine days later the Communists acted. Groza and Gheorghiu-Dej asked the King to come to Bucharest from his mountain retreat at Sinaia and presented him with a ready-made abdication statement. When he refused the two men gave him half an hour to consider his position. In the meantime troops were brought in to surround the palace. Still the King declined to sign, whereupon Groza threatened civil war. Faced with the possibility of bloodshed Michael gave in. With his signature ended the Romanian kingdom and the country's possibilites of autonomous action. On that same day, 30 December 1947, the Romanian People's Republic was declared.

The threat of force used by the Communist leaders against the King was to typify the very nature of the People's Republic, one born not from the express will of the population, but from the dictates of a political group who were the puppets of a foreign master. Even the legality of the law establishing the Republic was suspect since the official record of the special session of the single chamber parliament, convened on the evening of 30 December, stated that it lasted only 45 minutes. In this time, the law was alleged to have been presented, a praesidium nominated and both measures voted upon by the casting of white balls by 295 deputies. In addition there are said to have been 19 ovations which interrupted the presentation. Doubts have been cast as to whether, in the first place, so many deputies could have been assembled so rapidly in Bucharest while parliament was in recess or the New Year, and secondly, whether the business could have been completed as rapidly as claimed.[59]

With the establishment of the Republic the foundations of the totalitarian state could be put in place.[60] The first step was to cement Romania into the Soviet bloc from a military point of view. This was done by the conclusion of a treaty of friendship, cooperation and mutual assistance between Romania and the Soviet Union which was signed on 4 February 1948.

The second step was the application of a fundamental principle of Marxist-Leninist ideology—the consolidation of the single mass party composed of an elite and a dedicated membership. This was achieved by dissolving the major opposition parties, the National Liberal and the National Peasant parties, in the summer of 1947, and by the merger of the Social Democrat Party with the Communist Party on 12 November 1947.[61] The SDP's veteran secretary, Titel Petrescu had seen his authority gradually eroded after the war by Communist infiltration. The Party Congress of 10 March 1946, at the insistence of two leading members Lothar Rădăceanu and Ştefan Voitec, voted for collaboration with the Communist Party. Petrescu walked out of the congress and led the rump of the SDP under the name of the Independent Social Democratic Party. The official SDP held its last congress on 5 October 1947, attended by Groza, Gheorghiu-Dej and Pauker, where a resolution on a merger with the Communist Party was passed by acclamation. According to figures presented at the congress the SDP at that time had some half a million members, only half of whom appear to have joined the newly-fused party which was known as the Romanian Workers' Party and had a combined membership of 1,060,000.[62]

The RWP held its First Congress on 21–23 February 1948 and Gheorghiu-Dej was re-elected secretary general and Pauker, Luca and Teohari Georgescu as the other three members of the secretariat. Emphasis was now given to the elite character of the Party and stricter membership requirements were introduced. No members of the 'former exploiting classes' were to be admitted, those applying for membership were to be carefully screened, and a period of 'candidate' or trial membership was made compulsory.

A warning of these measures against perceived opponents of the regime was given in Gheorghiu-Dej's report to the congress. Here he categorized "Iron Guardists, spies and diversionists" as "the enemies of Romanian democracy". Similarly, attacks on the Catholic clergy who used the church "as a means of propaganda directed against the democratic order", indicated what lay in store for them.[63] On 26 March, this category of 'hostile elements' was augmented by 'the saboteurs' who in Gheorghiu-Dej's view, "must be eradicated without mercy". Thus the Stalinist method of abstract accusation, followed by the physical liquidation of the accused, found its way into the practice of the Romanian Communist Party. Virtually all of Gheorghiu-Dej's speeches in 1948 were a continuous tirade of incitement to persecution of actual or anticipated opponents of the regime and, at the same time, they represented an authorization of Communist repression. They also gave the green light to informers and to thugs acting in the spirit of 'vigilance'.

The first step towards the legalization of repression was the amendment on 27 February 1948 of the Penal Code which had been in force since 2 March 1940. The revised code borrowed a series of concepts from Soviet legislation which were alien to Romanian law but useful for the consolidation of Communist political power. Novel notions such as 'counter-revolutionary sabotage', 'counter-revolutionary diversion', and 'counter-revolutionary agitation and propaganda' were introduced and were quickly applied to justify a round-up of Iron Guardists throughout the whole country during the night of 14–15 May 1948. By the end of the year, some 4,500 arrests had been made, while a further 1,162 Guardists were placed under surveillance. It should be pointed out that the raids led to the discovery of 6,000 cartridges of ammunition, 649 grenades, 32 machine guns, 27 machine-pistols and 128 pistols, but the arrests merely steeled the determination of those who were prepared to transform their opposition into armed resistance, and in furtherance of their aims they took to the mountains.[64]

A further step in the legalization of repression was a decree of 18 August which supplemented the Law on the Prosecution and Punishment of Those Guilty of War Crimes or of Crimes Against Peace and Security, introduced exactly one year earlier. Using this law, the Ministry of the Interior ordered the arrest of more than 1,000 officers of the SSI, the *Siguranţa* and the *Jandarmerie*. Their place was taken by Communist Party appointees. A verification campaign was undertaken as a result of a Central Committee resolution of November 1948 by what was called 'a non-party aktiv ' of some 200,000 investigators, a euphemism which covered the participation of the security police, the army and officials of the Ministry of Justice. The period of investigation lasted from November 1948 until May 1950 and was directed at the various waves of members who had been recruited into the Party. The process removed from the Communist Party 192,000 "exploiting and hostile elements" and their elimination could only but augment the sense of terror which permeated most of Romanian society. This purge, aimed at creating an elite, coincided with the Party's programme of revolutionizing agriculture, industrializing the economy and of transforming society.

The implementation of that programme required the institutionalization of the new Communist system and to this end a Party organization was created to supervise every aspect of endeavour. Central Committee sections were set up for women, youth, peasants, trade unions, transport, supply, industry and commerce, and these were paralleled at local level. Prime importance was attached to ideological training which not only helped to reinforce the sense of belonging to an elite, but also inculcated loyalty to the Party and cocooned the member from insidious external influences. The A.A. Zhdanov School was set up by the Party in October 1948 to prepare ideological cadres, and in July 1949 was transformed into a school of social sciences to train the teachers in the field, while the Ştefan

Gheorghiu Academy was established to prepare Party activists. The feeling of elitism and exclusivity, and the privileges by ranking, also served to increase coherence and unity within the Party.

A third step in the imposition of the Soviet totalitarian model upon Romania was the introduction of a Soviet-based judicial system and the adoption in April 1948 of the Constitution of the People's Republic. The purges initiated by Pătrăşcanu in April 1945 continued throughout his term of office.The trimming of the judicial system to suit the political ends of the Communist Party was confirmed on 24 November 1947 with the passage of a bill reorganizing the judiciary. It provided for the 'election' of magistrates, or 'people's assessors' who were Party nominees. These 'assessors' sat alongside the judges and outnumbered them by two to one, thus ensuring that the Party's will in all cases was paramount. In Pătrăşcanu's words: "by including elected representatives of the working class among the judges sitting in the courts, justice has indeed become people's justice".[65] Private legal practice was abolished by a decree of 31 March 1950.

The constitution, adopted on 13 April 1948 by the Grand National Assembly, followed the pattern of the 1936 Soviet constitution. The Grand National Assembly was a single chamber, described as "the supreme organ of state authority". A Praesidium, composed of a president, a secretary and 17 other members, acted on behalf of the Assembly when it was not in session, which was quite often, while the Council of Ministers was the supreme executive body. All these bodies were subject to the power of the Communist Party. Guarantees of civil liberties were generously provided but meaningless, as article 32 illustrated, "Citizens have the right to associate and organize themselves, as long as their purpose is not directed against the democratic order established by the constitution".[66] That democratic order was defined by the Communist Party and buttressed by the security police.

The Party moved swiftly to transform Romania following the Soviet model and employing Stalinist norms and practices. The nationalization in June 1948 of industrial, banking, insurance, mining and transport enterprises not only allowed the introduction of centralized quantitative planning but destroyed the economic basis of those stigmatized as class enemies. Confiscating private shareholdings and threatening their owners was relatively straightforward; agriculture posed more complex problems. On 2 March 1949, the ownership of land was completely removed from private hands. This permitted the liquidation of the remnants of the old landowning class and of the 'kulaks' (*chiaburi* in Romanian) a Soviet term defining those who owned land, hired labour or let out machinery, irrespective of the size of their holding. The land, livestock and equipment of landowners who possessed property up to the maximum of 50 hectares permitted under the 1945 land law was expropriated without compensation. Virtually overnight the militia moved in and evicted 17,000 families from their homes and moved them to resettlement areas. The confiscated land, totalling almost one million hectares, was either amassed to create state farms or was organized into collectives which were in theory collectively owned but in fact state run since the Ministry of Agriculture directed which crops were to be grown and fixed the prices. Members of the collective were allowed to keep small plots of land not exceeding just under half an acre.

The majority of peasants, ranging from the landless to 'kulaks' (*chiaburi*), were organized into state or collective farms. This required extensive coercion, despite Gheorghiu-Dej's assurance to villagers that "under no circumstances should the peasantry be forced into collectives".[67] Resistance to collectivization resulted in some 80,000 peasants being imprisoned for their opposition, 30,000 of them being tried in public.[68] Collectivization was completed in 1962 and its results put 60 per cent of the total area of 15 million hectares of agricultural land in collective farms, 30 per cent in state farms, and left nine per cent in private hands. The latter was upland whose inaccessibility made it impractical for collectivization.

The destruction of the opposition parties was followed by the liquidation of their press, as the media came under total state control. Libraries and bookshops were purged of politically incorrect titles, the activities of journalists, writers, artists and musicians were brought under the Agitprop (Agitation and Propaganda) section of the Central Committee of the Party. Nothing could be published or performed without approval. By the end of 1954, almost 13 million copies of the works of Stalin and Lenin had been printed in Romanian.

Education was similarly dealt with. In August 1948, the Law for Educational Reform closed down all foreign schools, including those run by religious orders. A purge was conducted of the teaching profession and of university students. Eminent professors were removed from the faculties of history and philosophy and their places taken by Stalinist indoctrinators, the most notorious of whom in the history field was the Agitprop activist Mihail Roller (1908–58). The Ministry of Education banned the use of certain didactic materials and authorized textbooks incorporating Marxist-Leninist precepts. Marxism-Leninism, in Stalin's interpretation, was made obligatory from secondary school upwards; the teaching of religion was totally banned.

The final major obstacle to the imposition of the Soviet model was the Church. The *Securitate* was called upon to remove it. Yet in tackling this problem the Romanian Communist Party did not follow to the letter the Soviet solution. Both the Romanian Orthodox Church and the Uniate or Greek Catholic Church in Transylvania had been vital in preserving a sense of national cohesion and identity during the eighteenth and nineteenth centuries, and both retained the allegiance of millions of Romanians. If both Churches could be manipulated to serve the regime's ends, then there was no point in destroying them. The Orthodox Church had been declared the dominant faith under the 1923 Constitution and had been given special privileges, such as the payment of its clergy's salaries by the state, and the Communist Party was to use this dependence to bring the Orthodox hierarchy under its control. The Uniate Church presented a different problem. It had been created at the beginning of the seventeenth century as a result of the conversion by Jesuits of many Orthodox Romanians in Transylvania to accept certain articles of the Catholic faith, among them the primacy of the Pope. As long as authority over the church resided in Rome, it would be difficult for the new regime to bring it to heel. Thus the Romanian Communist Party, while officially condemning religious worship, nevertheless tolerated it within certain bounds prescribed by law. In this respect it was more lenient than the Soviet regime. Tolerance of the recognized Churches required their subservience to the Party and their sonorous validation of the Party's policies, whether domestic or foreign.

The new limits imposed on the Church's freedom of action were laid out in the Law on Religious Confessions, enacted on 4 August 1948. Under the previous law of 1928, some 60 religious denominations had been recognized; under the new law this figure was reduced to 14. Control of the affairs of all churches in the country was vested in the Ministry of Religious Confessions (reorganized in 1957 as the Department of Religious Confessions). While asserting from the very outset a guarantee of "freedom of conscience and religion" (article 1), it severely circumscribed that freedom by qualifying it with the open-ended provision that the religion practised was in harmony with the constitution, internal security, public order and general morality (articles 6 and 7). Legal recognition of a denomination could be revoked at any time where considered justified (article 13). Similar restrictions were implicit in article 32 which stated that "ministers of religious faiths who express anti-democratic attitudes may be deprived temporarily or permanently of their salary, which is provided by the state". All confessions were required to submit for approval to the Ministry of Religious Confessions a statute regulating their activities in accordance with the laws of the state; in return, the ministry would pay the stipends of clergy from recognized confessions.

Even before the introduction of the law, steps were taken by the Ministry of Religious Confessions in the Groza government to purge the hierarchy of the Orthodox Church, the principal confession with some 10.5 million members, of those considered to be opponents of the regime. This was done under a pretence of legality. A law introduced in 1947 provided an upper age limit for all clergy of 70, and under its terms a number of incumbents of the five metropolitanates (Wallachia, Moldavia and Suceava, Transylvania, Crişana and Maramureş, Oltenia and Banat) and 12 bishoprics were replaced: Metropolitan Irineu of Moldavia, Metropolitan Nifon of Oltenia, Bishop Lucian of Roman, Bishop Cosma of the Lower Danube and Bishop Gheronte of Constanţa were all forced to resign. A second law from the same year ensured the regime's control of the election of bishops. Previously episcopal assemblies had been composed of delegates elected by parishioners for a period of three years; under the new law they had to include members of parliament and ministers belonging to the diocese, thus guaranteeing a majority for government approved nominees.[69]

In addition, the Orthodox Holy Synod and the National Church Council was stuffed with Communist Party members. Key positions in the Church were thus entrusted to tools of the regime who were completely unknown to the population. The death of Patriarch Nicodim on 27 February 1948 allowed the election of Justinian (lay name Ioan Marina), installed only in the previous December as Metropolitan of Moldavia, as his successor on 24 May 1948. Justinian owed his lightning ascendance to the favour of Gheorghiu-Dej which he had gained by sheltering him in his parish church at Râmnicul Vâlcea for a few days in the summer of 1944, and his sudden enrolment in the Party. In 1945 he was appointed episcopal vicar at Iaşi by Metropolitan Irineu of Moldavia, and after the enforced retirement of the latter in August 1947, Justinian was entrusted with the management of the archbishopric.

The new statute of the Orthodox Church, drawn up under the personal direction of Justinian, gave the Patriarch extensive control over the administration of the Church and allowed him to intervene in the internal affairs of dioceses with or without the approval of the bishops. Such powers were in marked contrast to previous practice, which had permitted the bishops wide discretion. This provision was characteristic of the statute as a whole, since it created a highly centralized form of administration which allowed the regime to manipulate the Church more easily.[70] As was the practice with Party and state fora, obedience to the official line, unanimity of views and conformity with decisions made by higher Party bodies, were demanded. The new statute received the approval of the Ministry of Religious Confessions and became law on 23 February 1949.

By stripping the Church of its assets, the regime removed its scope for independent action and made it reliant upon the favour of the state. Any Church contribution to the creation of a civil society was thus stifled at a stroke. All the estates and funds of the Orthodox Church were nationalized, and thus its dependence upon state support became vital. Under the education law of 3 August 1948, its teaching institutions were either taken over by the state or closed, in number 2,300 primary schools, 24 secondary schools, eight chapters' schools, 13 seminaries and one academy of church music. Two schools for priests were opened in Predeal in 1948, and in Bucharest in 1951, for students selected from Communist Youth organizations, and in January 1949 a theological institute was opened in Bucharest University. The spirit in which students were trained can be assessed from the pronouncement in the Party daily *Scînteia* on 22 February 1948 that

> the Romanian clergy has to follow the example of the Orthodox clergy in the Soviet Union, as the party of the working class cannot remain indifferent to the various prejudices and mystic views sowed in the ranks of the workers by the bourgeois landowning regime.[71]

Religious worship, then, was not to be outlawed by the Party, it was to be discouraged. Efforts made by the regime to inhibit religious practice included a ban on the conduct of baptisms and church weddings, and on the public celebration of Christmas and Easter. Party members were instructed not to attend church services, as were army officers and soldiers. Civil marriage ceremonies were the only ones recognized by the state, even after the ban on church weddings was removed. Denied religious education in schools, the family, whatever their faith, played a vital role in transmitting it.

Control by the Communist government of the Roman Catholic and Greek Catholic (Uniate) Churches met with greater resistance. This was partly because the close links they had with the West made them more resilient, but it is also the case that their bishops displayed remarkable dignity, courage and fidelity to their creed. There was, however, a major difference in the treatment of the two Churches at the hands of the regime: the Uniate Church was suppressed, the Roman Catholic was not, although it did not escape persecution. The explanation lies in the fact that most of the Roman Catholic faithful were Hungarians, and the Romanian regime was guided in policy towards the Church by the need to avoid actions which might be interpreted by its fraternal neighbour as directed specifically against the Hungarian minority. Consequently, the Communist Party's policy towards the Roman Catholic Church was not to abolish it, but to manipulate it by replacing control from the Vatican with control from Bucharest. It was only a partial success. Although the regime severed the Church's links with Rome, it was never able to impose its own authority on the Church. Throughout the Communist era the Roman Catholic Church was held in the ambiguous position of being tolerated, but unrecognized. Agreement was never reached with the Ministry of Religious Confessions over the Church's legal standing within the 1948 law on confessions and so the second largest surviving Church in Romania remained effectively illegal.

The status of the Roman Catholic Church was governed by the Concordat between the Romanian government and the Vatican which was concluded on 10 May 1927. Under it five dioceses were established: Alba Iulia, and Oradea-Satu Mare in Transylvania, which were largely Hungarian; Timişoara in the Banat, which was predominantly German; and Iaşi in Moldavia and Bucharest, which were mainly Romanian. Many of the Moldavian Catholics were Csangos, a people of mixed Hungarian and Romanian origin living near the town of Bacău. Of its estimated 1.3 million faithful, approximately 450,000 belonged to the Alba Iulia diocese, 200,000 to Oradea-Satu Mare, 300,000 to Timişoara, 200,000 to Iaşi, and 80,000 to Bucharest. The five bishops in 1948 were Monsignor Aron Marton of Alba Iulia, Monsignor Ianoş Scheffler of Oradea-Satu Mare, Monsignor Augustin Pacha of Timişoara, Monsignor Alexandru Cisar of Bucharest and Monsignor Anton Durcovici of Iaşi. In the early months of that year the Concordat came under violent attack from the press and Party leaders, with Dej denouncing it on 22 February 1948 as the sole obstacle to 'democracy'. The campaign culminated in the unilateral abrogation by the government of the Concordat on 17 July 1948. The Vatican's authority over the Church was removed under the Law on Religious Confessions, which was introduced on 4 August 1948. Article 41 stipulated that "foreign religious faiths may not exercise jurisdiction over faithful on the territory of the Romanian state", a provision that was to have grave implications for the Greek Catholics (Uniates) as well.[72] The government was able to reduce the number of Roman Catholic dioceses to two, Alba Iulia and Bucharest, by invoking article 22 of the law which stated quite arbitrarily that a diocese must have 750,000 faithful to warrant its existence. On this basis, three of the five bishops were deprived of their sees, with only Bishop Aron Marton of Alba Iulia and Bishop Alexandru Cisar of Bucharest remaining.

The law also required every denomination to present its own statute for the approval of the Ministry of Religious Confessions and the regime tried to draw the Catholic bishops into a compromise. Marton drew up an initial set of proposals but they were rejected by the government, and Marton was arrested in June 1949.[73] His fellow bishops shared the same fate. In March 1949, Bishop Scheffler of Satu Mare was detained and held in the Franciscan monastery at Baia de Criş before being moved to the notorious Sighet prison in 1950 where he died. The former Bishop of Bucharest, Alexandru Cisar, was arrested in June 1949, as was his successor Augustin Pacha, together with Aron Marton, Bishop of Alba Iulia and Anton Durcovici, Bishop of Iaşi. Pacha died shortly afterwards while Cisar was held in a monastery, Durcovici in the prisons of Gherla and Aiud, and Marton at the Ministry of the Interior in Bucharest; in 1950 all three were transferred to Sighet where Durcovici died on 10 December 1951. Cisar was allowed to return to Bucharest shortly before his death in 1954.[74]

Failure to reach a *modus vivendi* led to the arrest of large numbers from among the 800 Roman Catholic priests and 250 monks and nuns. Under the education reform of 3 August 1948, confessional schools were abolished and the Catholic seminaries closed. Roman Catholic newspapers and publications were suppressed, and by a decree of 29 July 1949 all Catholic orders and congregations were abolished. On 30 August 1949, an order was issued by which all monasteries and convents were to be completely evacuated before midnight, and *Securitate* officers were charged with the speedy execution of this order.

The Ministry of Religious Confessions now drafted a new 'Statute for the Organization, Direction, and Functioning of the Roman Catholic Confession in the Romanian People's Republic'. The document recognized the Pope as the supreme ecclesiastical authority of the Church in matters of faith and dogma, but in all other respects the Church was subject to the laws of the state. The right of the Holy See to appoint bishops was accepted but appointments were to be solely on the recommendation of the Catholic Church in Romania, and subject to the approval of the Romanian government. Communication with Rome was to be made exclusively through the Ministry of Religious Confessions and the Foreign Ministry, thus preventing any direct contact with the Vatican. Before these proposals were presented on 28 July 1950 by the Committee for Action to all Catholics for acceptance, the Pope instructed his nuncio bishop Gerald O'Hara to veto them, thus ruling out any chance of reaching the kind of compromise with the government that was to be secured in Poland.

After the arrest of the Roman Catholic bishops had begun the Pope instructed O'Hara to consecrate secret bishops. In the first six months of 1950, the nuncio appointed 20 apostolic administrators, drawing up a list of replacements to succeed each other if the predecessor was arrested. O'Hara consecrated Joseph Schubert as Bishop of Bucharest in the chapel of the Bucharest nunciature on 30 June 1950. Adalbert Boros was ordained as Bishop of Timişoara and Ion Duma as Bishop of Iaşi in a similar fashion. A week later O'Hara was ordered to leave Romania by the government. He had been accused of 'gathering military information' in a trial staged against his chaffeur, an accusation based on the fact that incidents of harassment of priests and faithful by Soviet troops based in Romania were reported to the nuncio who passed the information on to his American compatriots in the Allied Control Commission.[75] O'Hara, before his departure, also consecrated a number of Uniate bishops in secret but not one of them was ever able to officiate; all the Roman Catholic and Uniate bishops appointed in this way were under arrest by 1951. Bishop Duma, for example, was arrested on 5 December 1951 and held in the *Securitate* headquarters in Arad, and later in Cluj. He was then sent to Sighet prison where he served four years before being freed on 23 September 1955 into compulsory residence in the town of Târgu-Jiu.

The list of clergy arrested for refusing to serve the regime included Bishop Schubert of Bucharest and Bishop Boros of Timişoara, both detained on 17 February 1951. Other arrests followed in the same year.[76] Most of those arrested were brought before a military tribunal alongside Bishop Augustin Pacha in September 1951 in a show trial. Confessions were extorted from them and they were convicted of "spying in favour of the Vatican and of the United States, and of having attempted to set up a Christian Social Party in order to overthrow the present regime with the help of the Americans".[77] Pacha, although 80 years of age, Schubert and Boros, were sentenced to 18 years in prison; Father Gatti and Father Joseph Walther to 15 years, Father Ion Heber to 12 years, and Father Schiopa to ten years. To complete the mockery, Radio Bucharest transmitted a thirty-minute broadcast after the trial in which the accused repeated their confessions.

In a cynical attempt to deflect the embarassment of death in jail, the Ministry of the Interior occasionally ordered the release of prominent prelates who were judged to be especially frail; Bishop Pacha, who was 80 years of age when jailed, went blind in prison and was released in 1954 into compulsory residence in Timişoara. He died two years later. Others served almost their full term before the general amnesties of 1963–64 gave them their freedom, although in some cases it was hedged with restrictions. Bishop Schubert, for example, was released in July 1964 after 13 years in jail to the compulsory residence of the mountain village of Timişul de Sus, just south of Braşov. The Vatican gave little support to its imprisoned bishops. "The only attitude recognized in Rome is that of Monsignore Schubert", wrote Domenico Tardini (the Secretary for Extraordinary Affairs in the Secretariat of State) as late as 10 May 1951, to the doubtful Bucharest cathedral chapter, when Schubert had already been in prison for three months and no other Romanian bishop remained free. That 'attitude', honourable and obedient, of course also gave those in the West who spoke of "the silent church in the East with a pious shudder, an alibi for their own political sloth".[78]

The Uniates' fidelity to their Church resulted in a brutal campaign to destroy it. The last figures available before suppression indicated that there were one and a half million Uniates, with 1,725 churches served by 1,594 priests, 34 canons and 75 prelates. Under the terms of the Concordat of 1927 five dioceses were recognized: Alba Iulia-Făgăraş, with its see at Blaj, Gherla, which in 1931 moved its see from Gherla to Cluj, Oradea Mare, and Lugoj and Maramureş, with its see at Baia Mare. In 1948 the incumbents were Metropolitan Bishop Ion Suciu, apostolic administrator of the see of Blaj; Iuliu Hossu, Bishop of Cluj; Valeriu Traian Frenţiu, Bishop of Oradea Mare; Ioan Bălan, Bishop of Lugoj; and Bishop Alexandru Rusu of Baia Mare. There was also a vicar general at Bucharest, Bishop Vasile Aftenie, who in 1940 had been consecrated auxiliary bishop of Alba Iulia-Făgăraş while retaining his position in Bucharest. The Church had 143 religious houses, 377 educational institutes and 111 charitable and welfare institutions.[79]

The same political reasons which had led to the creation of the Uniate Church in 1699 were invoked by the Communists to force it back into the fold of the Orthodox Church. The union with Rome was branded in official publications throughout the Communist period as 'anti-national and anti-historical' since it had split the unity of the Romanian people. The campaign to woo Uniates back to the Orthodox Church was part and parcel of the drive against the Concordat which was launched in February 1948. On 31 March 1948, the Grand National Assembly (the Communist parliament) took the arbitrary decision to retire all priests over the age of 60, a measure that was not recognized either by the Roman Catholic or by the Uniate heirarchy. A particular appeal to Uniates to "return to the bosom of the Mother Church" was made on the occasion of the centenary of the meeting on the Field of Liberty near Blaj, where Transylvanian Romanians of both Orthodox and Uniate confessions had gathered on 15 May 1848 to demand recognition of their rights as a nation. Patriarch Justinian, the newly elected head of the Orthodox Church, echoed the appeal on 6 June in his address to the Uniate clergy:

> What separates us at this time? Nothing but the faithful submission you still give to Rome. Give back this loyalty to the Church of our nation, the Church of our forefathers and of yours [...] The widest prospects open before us and before our future activity, as soon as we no longer work in isolation.[80]

With the example before them of the Uniates in Galicia who in April 1946 had been dragooned into a merger with the Russian Orthodox Church, the authorities tried to infiltrate Communist Party members into Uniate diocesan councils. The ground was now prepared by the Ministry of Religious Confessions for the manipulated merger of the Uniate and Orthodox Churches. Blank proxy forms were distributed throughout Transylvania for Uniate clergy to sign. These were to designate two priests from each district, possibly unknown to the signatories, who were to represent them at a meeting to be convened in Cluj on 1 October. The purpose of the meeting, according to the form, was "the return of the Greek Catholic Church to the Orthodox Church".[81] An indication of the methods used to extract signatures was provided by nuncio O'Hara in a protest note handed to the Ministry of Foreign Affairs on 2 October:

> The priests were in many instances brought by force into the offices of the state security police, intimidated, threatened with imprisonment, with separation from their families, with deportation and even death. Those who resisted the initial acts of violence were thrown in underground cells, ill-treated, subjected to exhausting questioning, and finally set free only when, broken down by the inhuman treatment of their jailors, they consented to sign.[82]

Bishop O'Hara's protest note of 2 October was angrily rejected by the Romanian government two days later who considered it "an act of provocation against the Romanian state and people". The protest was "a step in line with the campaign carried on by imperialist circles and their agents against the democratic achievements of the Romanian People's Republic". On 21 October, the 'reintegration' of the Uniate Church was celebrated in the Uniate cathedral of the Holy Trinity in Alba Iulia which was henceforth renamed the "cathedral of the unification of the Romanian Church of Transylvania". Six days later, the persecution of those opposed to the merger began. Thus, during the nights of 27 and 28 October, Metropolitan Suciu and all of his fellow bishops, together with some 600 Uniate priests, were systematically rounded up. The callousness of the security forces was illustrated by the fatal shooting of Father Ieronim Susman. He was gunned down while attempting to flee the village of Asinip near Blaj where he had been officiating. All six bishops (Suciu, Hossu, Frenţiu, Bălan, Rusu and Aftenie) were first taken to the summer residence of the Orthodox Patriarch in the village of Dragoslavele near Câmpulung in Wallachia and placed under armed guard. Then on 27 February 1949, they were moved to the monastery of Căldăruşani north of Bucharest from where they could be more easily transferred to the Ministry of the Interior for interrogation. Just as the Vatican had acted in the circumstances of the arrested Roman Catholic bishops, so too in the case of the Uniates were instructions passed in 1950 to nuncio O'Hara to secretly consecrate six auxiliary bishops on the recommendation of the six arrested ones. The secret bishops, whose names were soon discovered by the Communist authorities, but not listed in the *Annuario Pontificio*, were Ioan Ploscaru, appointed to the diocese of Lugoj, Ioan Chertes for Cluj-Gherla, Alexandru Todea for Alba Iulia and Făgăraş, Ioan Dragomir for Maramureş, Iuliu Hirţea for Oradea and Liviu Chinezu for Bucharest.[83]

Chinezu and Chertes were consecrated by Bishop Frenţiu on 3 December 1949 while they were all being held in confinement at Căldăruşani monastery; Dragomir, Hirţea, and Ploscaru were consecrated on 28 March 1949 by nuncio O'Hara at the nunciature in Bucharest.[84] Todea was consecrated at the hands of the Roman Catholic bishop Joseph Schubert on 19 November 1950 in St Joseph's cathedral in Bucharest. Father Gheorghe Guţiu was the only witness.[85] After the ceremony Todea returned to Reghin and went underground. The *Securitate* located the house in which he was staying and after surrounding it on 30 January 1951, forced Todea to give himself up. He was taken to Târgu Mureş for interrogation, after which he transferred to the Ministry of the Interior in Bucharest and then to Jilava and Uranus, one of the interrogation centres of the SSI, the intelligence service. Accused of being an enemy of the state, he was put on trial in Bucharest on 15 February 1952 and sentenced to hard labour for life. He began his sentence at Sighet prison on 28 February 1952.[86] By 1951, all the auxiliary bishops were under arrest; Chinezu died in Sighet prison on 15 January 1955.

Uniate churches were handed over to the Orthodox Church while their convents and monasteries were closed. Only those Uniate priests who accepted Orthodoxy were paid a stipend by the state and the legal existence of the Church was finally terminated by decree no. 358 of the Grand National Assembly, issued on

1 December 1948, which abolished all dioceses and institutions of the Uniate Church and awarded all churches to the Orthodox Church. An effort was made by their *Securitate* interrogators to link Suciu, Aftenie and one of the clandestine bishops—Liviu Chinezu—with the groups of partisans who had set up centres of resistance to Communist authority in the Carpathian mountains in Transylvania. Aftenie was moved to Jilava jail where he shared a cell with Vasile Gârneţ. He told Gârneţ that he had been taken to the Ministry of the Interior for interrogation and from there to a villa in Sinaia to recuperate. While in Sinaia he was visited by Gheorghiu-Dej and Patriarch Justinian who tried to convince him to pass over to the Orthodox Church, allegedly offering as an inducement the metropolitan see of Iaşi. Aftenie reportedly replied to Justinian with the words *"nu am nici suflet, nici conştiinţă, nici credinţă, nici neam de vânzare"* (I have neither a soul, conscience, faith nor a people to sell). Aftenie was then taken back to Jilava and from there to the Ministry of the Interior where he was beaten so badly that he died on 10 May 1950. Details of his beating were passed on to Father Tertullian Langa by Father Johann Baltheiser, the parish priest of St Joseph's cathedral in Bucharest, who was ordered by two *Securitate* agents to officiate at a burial service in the capital's Bellu cemetery. Left for a few moments alone with the coffin at the cemetery, Baltheiser lifted the lid and saw that Aftenie had a badly beaten face and swollen eyes.[87]

Chinezu was transferred on 24 May 1950 to Sighet jail in Maramureş with Hossu, Rusu and Bălan; they were joined there in September by Suciu, and later by Frenţiu. The latter died on 11 July 1952 at the age of 77. Less than a year later, Suciu died at the age of 43 on 27 June 1953 and was buried near the jail, like Frenţiu. On 15 January 1955, Chinezu, who was in his late forties, died in prison of hypothermia. Of the six imprisoned Uniate bishops—Iuliu Hossu, Vasile Aftenie, Alexandru Rusu, Ioan Bălan, Ioan Suciu and Valeriu Traian Frenţiu—only Bălan, Hossu, and Rusu survived the five years of prison until their 'release' on the orders of Gheorghiu-Dej in 1955.[88] Rusu was transferred to the Cocoş monastery in Dobrogea on 2 February 1955 where he was placed under a form of house arrest,[89] only to be re-arrested at the end of December in the following year on a charge of high treason for sending petitions abroad regarding the status of the Uniate Church in Romania and pastoral letters to the Uniate faithful. He was found guilty and sentenced on 12 May 1957 to twenty-five years' hard labour. He died in Gherla jail on 9 May 1963.[90]

The freedom granted to the Uniate priests was short-lived for they were targeted in the waves of arrests which followed the Hungarian uprising. In October 1957, a group of priests, among them Alexandru Raţiu and Teofil Baliban, were tried in Bucharest on charges of 'plotting' to reinstitute the Uniate Church. After receiving sentences of 15 years hard labour, they were sent to Aiud jail and then transferred to Gherla. All were finally released in the general amnesty of 1964, as were the five surviving auxiliary bishops, Chertes, Dragomir, Hirţea Ploscaru and Todea. Todea had been transferred from Sighet in March 1955 to Râmnicu Sărat, and then in 1957 to Piteşti. On 5 June 1960, he was moved to the prison in the town of Dej, and then finally, in February 1963, to Gherla. As was customary with these transfers, Jilava was used as a holding point for the prisoners. On his release from Gherla in 1964, Todea returned to Reghin.[91]

The persecution of the Uniate Church was the Orthodox Church's gain. Adjustment to their privileged position led the Orthodox Church hierarchy to seek a justification of its position. Christianity's mission to defend the poor and needy provided the basis for Justinian's reconciliation of the Church's role with dialectal materialism:

> Some consider materialism hostile to Christianity. We, however, judge men according to their deeds and achievements. We judge doctrine according to the order of society it produces. Can we not see in the present social order the most sacred principles of the Gospel being put into practice? Is not the sharing of goods, thus excluding them from the use of exploiters, better? ....Let us therefore be loyal and recognize that the state leadership has brought peace to men by assuring them of an existence and by allowing them to live off the first-fruits of their own honourable labours.[92]

There was nothing in Justinian's pronouncements of this period about the peace denied by the Communist regime to men and women, nor about its deprival of an existence to the tens of thousands of Romanians held in prisons and labour camps, many of whom had been placed there simply for their fidelity to a particular religious faith. Instead, Justinian concentrated on preserving his own Church by giving its goals consistent with the Communist revolution. To this end he proposed in 1949 the reorganization of pastoral training, which would contain an emphasis on the education of villagers in new agricultural methods, assistance with the government's literacy programme, and a reform of monastic life, so that monks and nuns should be instructed in a useful trade. Justinian was anxious to point out that these "new forms of life", as he called them, did not diminish the primacy of prayer.

Justinian's public sympathies enabled the Orthodox Church to survive the early fifties relatively unscathed. To his supporters he was regarded as a major reformer, encouraging his clergy to take an interest in social work, a notable departure from Orthodox tradition. He improved theological training by requesting the professors of the two theological institutes to compile a number of manuals for use in seminaries throughout the country. As a result the Romanian clergy were, in the view of one Western observer, "the best trained in the Orthodox Church", and after 1964 a number were sent to study in Western Europe.[93] Justinian's most successful reform involved monastic life. There were, in Justinian's first and only public admission of their numbers on 9 October 1955, "more than two hundred monasteries".[94] His requirement of monks and nuns to learn a trade enabled him to defend the monasteries by enabling them to register in 1951 as cooperatives and to set up workshops for weaving and other rural arts whose proceeds generated a useful income. Other monasteries set up farming cooperatives and in the process made themselves a vital part of a village community, employing labour from amongst the local peasantry.

To Justinian's detractors, this 'success' was seen as a reward for subservience to the Communist regime. Many Uniates dismissed Justinian as a Communist stooge and an opportunist, particularly because of his exuberant reaction to the suppression of their Church and its absorption into the Orthodox Church. Yet his attitude was one which was rooted in a widespread belief which identified the unity of the Orthodox Church with the unity of the Romanian people. Such an attitude was easily exploited by the regime's propagandists who translated diversity as a threat to national integrity. Many of those who were imprisoned by the Communists pointed with bitterness to Justinian's exhortations to his clergy to participate in the construction of the new People's Republic, but it was clear from the Patriarch's writings, assembled in a series entitled *Apostolat* Social,[95] that he saw forms of socialism as an integral part of Christian belief. What Justinian failed to do was to question the methods used to build the new republic, and in doing so he was following his conviction that the Church should not engage in 'thoughtless' acts of opposition.[96]

Reconciliation of the Church's transcendental mission to save souls through faith in the teachings of Christ with its perceived obligations to serve the best interests of the People's Republic can only be attempted if one denies that a political system can influence this spiritual mission. And this is precisely what Justinian argued, ascribing to the Church a dual role as a spiritual body and a social institution. There is little evidence to suggest that many Orthodox faithful quibbled about this distinction, seeing in Justinian an effective leader and defender of their Church.

Individual Orthodox priests did feel the hand of repression under Communism. In a report for 1949 drawn up by that department of the *Securitate 's* First Directorate responsible for overseeing the activity of the Orthodox Church, the writers concluded that "the Orthodox problem has grown owing to the increase in the number of challenges to the regime which are the work of priests who own land". This was clearly a reference to resistance from priests to the Land Reform of March 1949. However, the report went on to emphasize that "the majority of the Orthodox clergy and faithful—there are 18,000 priests and monks—have elected to stand by the regime and to fight for peace".[97] Such compliance by the Orthodox did not spare their Church a measure of persecution. In a speech given on 12 May 1953, Justinian revealed that the Orthodox Church had "more than 10,000" monks and nuns in 1951, but that this number had fallen two years later to "almost 7,000". Roughly half of these, he pointed out, worked in the monastery cooperatives. This figure of almost 7,000 remained stable until the strictures placed on the monastic life of the Church were introduced in December 1958.[98]

Close supervision of Orthodox priests was among the string of drastic internal security measures adopted by Dej in order to preempt any anti-Communist agitation which he feared might arise after the withdrawal of Soviet troops from Romania in the summer of 1958, and to allay Khrushchev's fears that the withdrawal might undermine the Romanian Party's control, Dej adopted a string of drastic internal security measures. These included close supervision of Orthodox priests, several of whom had been associated with the Iron Guard. Indeed, the members of a number of informal discussion groups, which included Orthodox priests, were arrested in 1958 and 1959 on charges of belonging to "clandestine reactionary and mystico-legionary associations", tried and jailed.[99] The monasteries were also identified as a source of potential opposition. In a report of October 1958, signed by Alexandru Drăghici, Minister of the Interior, Patriarch Justinian himself was accused of "acting systematically since assuming the leadership of the Orthodox Church to remove progressive elements and to promote the most reactionary elements in the clergy, especially Iron Guardists". He therefore proposed "the removal from the monasteries of Iron Guardists[...]; the abolition of the monastic seminaries [...]; a 50 per cent reduction in the number of monasteries; and a minimum age-limit of 50 for entry into the monastic life".[100] A *Securitate* report of 2 April 1960 claimed that:

> During 1958, the Party and State leadership analysed the position of monks in our country and reached the conclusion that the number of monasteries and monks in the Romanian People's Republic was inordinately high and that they had become centres of counter-revolutionary activity and immorality. In fact, on 15 December 1958 there were 224 monasteries and 6,214 monks in our country. In view of this situation, the Department of Relgious Confessions persuaded the Synod of the Orthodox Church to take steps to restrict the number of monks and so, on 15 December 1958, the Synod decided to remove from the monasteries minors, those who had not completed elementary schooling, immoral persons and elements who were hostile to our regime.[101]

The report went on to say that according to this decision, 1,492 monks and nuns were to be dismissed from the monasteries, and that despite the opposition and machinations of some of the Orthodox Church leaders, 1,200 monks had been ejected by 1 November 1959. The main obstacle had been Patriarch Justinian Marina. Justinian's silence in the face of the persecution of the Roman Catholic Church, and his approbation of the Uniate Church's suppression in 1948, did not mean that he was prepared to stand aside when his own Church was under threat. The *Securitate* reported that the Patriarch

> showed his opposition in the session [of 15 December] of the Synod, and then took a series of measures designed to compromise the decision, namely: he openly stated his intention not to recognize the Synod's decision in the presence of other Church leaders, describing it as a government measure and not a Church one and as contravening canonical laws....[102]

Other prelates had shown solidarity with the Patriarch and their common stance led some dismissed monks to return to the monasteries, prompting the intervention of the security forces who were called upon to eject them. Since the number of monasteries and monks failed to fall sufficiently, the Grand National Assembly issued a decree on 28 October 1959 stipulating that only monks over the age of 55 and nuns above the age of 50 could remain in the monasteries and that they should give up their state pension if they received one. The three monastic seminaries were closed, thus halting the flow of novices. In preparation for the application of the decree, the Department of Religious Confessions carried out a survey of monasteries and their populations and established that there were 132 monasteries and 3,239 monks and nuns. Under the terms of the decree, 1,456 monks and nuns were given orders to abandon the monastic life.[103]

Thus, in the space of ten months, almost 3,000 monks and nuns were compelled to leave the religious life and 92 monasteries closed. But the authorities were still concerned about the large number of Orthodox priests. In a paper of 1962, the *Securitate* calculated that the Orthodox Church had "9,853 priests for 6,000 posts", the excess being used for proselytizing activity which was against the official atheist policy. One of the methods used for reducing the figure was to place restrictions on the number of students entering the theological institutes. In 1960, 701 priests were held in prison or under arrest; the majority were Orthodox accused of being former Iron Guardists.[104] In most cases their arrest had been prompted neither by any act of resistance to the regime, nor by their appartenance to the Orthodox faith, but because of the Communists' deep-seated fear of an extremist movement which had drawn deeply in the 1930s upon the Orthodox priesthood for its support and validation and which was seen as the most serious potential threat to their rule.

Throughout the period of Communist power in Romania, Justinian's leadership was judged in terms of his effectiveness in preserving the Church, in keeping Orthodox churches open as a sanctuary against the trials and torments of everyday existence, offering a place for private prayer and reflection for those deeply troubled by their ordeal under Communism. Ambiguity, as in other avenues of Romanian affairs, explains Justinian's achievement, for in harnessing the Church to the social revolution, he was able to maintain throughout the 29 years of his ministry—he died on 26 March 1977—a Church which provided a repository for the spiritual nourishment of his flock. Herein, the Orthodox will argue, lies the measure of his success.

Notes

1 *Conditions of an Armistice with Roumania*, Miscellaneous No.1 (1945) (London: HMSO, 1945, Cmd. 6585).

2 Maurice Pearton and Dennis Deletant, 'The Soviet Takeover in Romania, 1944–1948', in Dennis Deletant and Maurice Pearton (eds.), *Romania Observed* (Bucharest: Editura Enciclopedică, 1998), p.145.

3 Maurice Pearton, *Oil and the Romanian State* (London: Oxford University Press, 1971), pp.265–67.

4 According to RCP politburo member Iosif Rangheţ speaking in late April 1945: "[...] on 23 August, 1944, our party had, in Bucharest, 80 party members, no more, no less. And throughout the land our party had less than 1,000 party members, including our comrades in prisons and labour camps" (Radu Colt, 'Şi creştea într-o zi cât alţii într-un

an. Evoluţia numărului membrilor PCR în 1944–1945', *Magazin Istoric*, no.6 (June 1999), p.18.) This figure tallies with that given by Grigore Răceanu, a close associate of Foriş in the period 1941–44, who had responsibility for Party membership (author's conversation with Mircea Răceanu, 22 April, 2017).

5 Paul D. Quinlan, *Clash over Romania. British and American Policies Towards Romania: 1938–1947* (Los Angeles: American-Romanian Academy of Arts and Sciences, 1977), p.109.

6 Hansard, 5th series, vol.403, col.488.

7 Winston. S. Churchill, *The Second World War*, vol.VI. *Triumph and Tragedy* (London: Penguin, 1985), p.202. See also Elisabeth Barker, op.cit., p.145.

8 Pearton, *Oil and the Romanian State*, p.265. For the wider pressures on Churchill at the time see Maurice Pearton, 'Puzzles about Percentages', in Dennis Deletant and Maurice Pearton (eds.), *Romania Observed* (Bucharest: Editura Enciclopedică, 1998), pp.119–28.

9 *Cartea Albă a Securităţii*, vol.1 (Bucharest: SRI, 1995), p.92. The officers arrested were Eugen Cristescu, the head of the Intelligence Service (SSI), Gheorghe Cristescu and Nicolae Trohani, both department heads, Florin Begnescu, an officer in the counter-espionage section, and Eugen Haralamb.

10 The policing and public order duties were carried out by the Directorate General of the Police (to which the *Siguranţa* was subordinated), the Corps of Detectives and the General Inspectorate of the Gendarmes. The latter were responsible for public order in rural districts. All three bodies came under the aegis of the Ministry of the Interior.

11 A. Duţu, 'Comisia Aliată de Control Destructurează Armata Română (3)', *Revista de Istorie Militară*, no.5 (1992), p.221.

12 One of the advantages of a class theory of politics is that it legitimates casual murder. The Guards' victims, who were killed or later died of their injuries, have yet to be counted. Apart from their role as 'shock troops', the Guards (known in Romanian as *Formaţiunile de Luptă Patriotice*) also played an intelligence role and infiltrated the SSI and Romanian Military Intelligence (Section II of the Romanian General Staff). These FLP agents went on to occupy senior positions in the Communist *Securitate* and militia: see Claudiu Secaşiu, 'Serviciul de Informaţii al PCR; Secţia a II-a Informaţii şi Contrainformaţii din cadrul Comandamentului Formaţiunilor de Luptă Patriotice (FLP) -Penetrarea Serviciilor Oficiale de Informaţii (23 August 1944–6 Martie 1945)', *6 martie 1945. Inceputurile Comunizării României* (Bucharest: Editura Enciclopedică, 1995), pp.146–57.

13 See the digest of OSS reports in The National Archives, Kew, London (TNA), FO to Minister Resident, Cairo, No. 3251, 16.09.1944 (WO 201 1602).

14 Pearton and Deletant, 'The Soviet Takeover in Romania, 1944–1948', pp.142–63. The fate of *Viitorul*—the National Liberal organ—is instructive. Between the Armistice and February 1945, publication was frequently suspended by order of the Control Commission, in consequence of its exposure of official communiqués claiming the liberation by Russian troops of towns already freed by Romanian units and of its editorials attacking Communist leaders. Within the enterprise, from November a self-appointed Communist committee prevented printing of articles critical of the NDF. The workers capitulated, on the threatened withdrawal of their ration cards, and of possible deportation. The editor received death threats. Finally, the Control Commission ordered the paper's suppression on 15 February, when all non-Communist journals were closed down. One of the charges was that the paper was printing suspicious abbreviations. They turned out to be the distinctions of Air Vice Marshal Stevenson, head of the British Military Mission, his 'CBE, DSO, MC' being interpreted as a coded message.

15 The same argument was invoked 45 years later by former Communists in Romania in defending the retention of the Ceauşescu bureaucracy after the revolution of 1989.

16 Quinlan, *Clash Over Romania*, p.116, note 58.

17 James Marjoribanks, Assistant to the British political representative on the Allied Control Commission, sent a minute to the Foreign Office on 2 December 1944 describing a conversation with Penescu. "Penescu said that he had taken office with two aims: a) to ensure order in the country; b) to hold communal elections. The Communists had agreed to his appointment because they considered him an agrarian member of the National Peasant Party's left wing. Mr Penescu had positive evidence: a) that the shooting incident which was being used to discredit his ministry involved a man who was not a simple workman but a wealthy ex-legionary who had been shot because he was having an affair with someone else's wife; b) that ex-legionaries were encouraged to join the Communist Party (he said that he would send me a photostatic copy of the order to this effect); c) that a considerable quantity of arms—machine guns, rifles, grenades etc. of which he had the exact location and particulars—had been supplied to the Communist Guards by the Soviet Army" (The National Archives, FO 371/48547. R/95/28/37).

18 Rădescu (1874–1953) won the Order of Michael the Brave, the highest Romanian military decoration, during the First World War. From April 1926 to July 1928 he served as Romanian military attaché in London. Upon his return to Romania, he became a member of the military household of the royal palace. In 1930 he was discharged from the army on grounds of age. In November 1941 he was interned on Antonescu's orders for writing a defiant letter to Baron Killinger, Hitler's envoy, in reply to disparaging remarks made by the Baron about Romania. On 15 October 1944, he was appointed Chief of the General Staff and held this position until the beginning of December. On 6 December, he was appointed Prime Minister and Minister of the Interior.

19 'In Bucureşti acum 50 ani', *Magazin Istoric*, vol.28, no.12 (December 1994), pp.49–50.

20 Dinu C. Giurescu, *Romania's Communist Takeover: The Rădescu Government* (Boulder, Colorado: East European Monographs, 1994), p.135. Pătrăşcanu, in conversation with the Tass correspondent in late December 1944, considered that the Communist Party had made a mistake in provoking the fall of the Sănătescu government since the more energetic Rădescu had replaced him. "If before we had a prime minister whom the NDF had in its pocket, now we have a prime minister who is in someone else's pocket". When asked to explain what he meant by this, Pătrăşcanu declared that hostile internal and external forces were behind Rădescu. "He meant the British," the Tass correspondent told Moscow (F. Constantiniu, A, Duţu and M. Retegan, *România în război, 1941–1945* (Bucharest: Editura Militară, 1995), p.285).

21 Giurescu, Romania's Communist Takeover, p.137.

22 TNA, HS 186, p.26.

23 Gheorghi Dimitrov, *Dnevnik (9 marta 1933–6 februari 1949)* (Sofia: Universitetsko izdatelstvo 'Sv. Kliment Ohridski', 1997), p.458 quoted from Dan Cătănuş, Vasile Buga (eds), *Gh. Gheorghiu-Dej la Stalin. Stenograme, Note de Convorbire, Memorii, 1944–1952* (Bucharest: Institutul Naţional pentru Studiul Totalitarismului, 2012), pp.27–29. Apostol, in a memorandum addressed to Nicolae Ceauşescu and written in summer 1979 when he was Romanian ambassador to Argentina, recalled this visit to Moscow. The delegation, he stated, "left in secret between 20–25 December" in a Soviet aircraft from Băneasa airport. Their flight lasted eight hours and they were taken after their arrival to the Hotel Ararat. The need for the delegation's visit, he wrote, had arisen from the fact that there was disagreement in the provisional leadership of the RCP regarding the line the Party should adopt towards the other political parties. One group, led by Gheorghiu-Dej, argued for a strategy to reduce the influence of Maniu's National Peasant Party and Brătianu's National Liberals amongst the wealthier peasants and the middle class, and for cooperation with a Liberal faction led by Gheorghe Tătărescu, which had broken away from Brătianu, and with a Peasant Party splinter group under Anton Alexandru which had left Maniu. A second body of Communists, represented by Pauker, favoured a tightening of collaboration with Maniu and Brătianu. The delegation was received by Stalin in the Kremlin. He invited

both Gheorghiu-Dej and Pauker to express their viewpoint and came down on the side of the former, after describing Maniu and Brătianu as, according to Apostol, "enemies to the death of the Soviet Union and therefore of the RCP". He advised Gheorghiu-Dej to use Tătărescu "as a fellow comrade as long as he can be useful in your struggle for the democratization of the country, for the instalment of worker and peasant power in Romania" (Arhiva Consiliului Naţional pentru Studierea Arhivelor Fostei Securităţi (ACNSAS), Dosar Gheorghe Apostol, Fond D 008936, vol.III, ff.339–350).

24 'Programul de Guvernare al Frontului National Democrat', Ioan Scurtu et al. (eds.), *Viaţa politică în Documente* (Bucharest: Arhivele Statului, 1994), pp.93–96.

25 'Stenograma Şedinţei Consiliului FND', *Viaţa politică în Documente*, pp.97–119.

26 *Cartea Albă a Securităţii*, vol.1, pp.12, 92. The number of police officers remained virtually the same until the reorganization of the police according to the Soviet model in August 1948.

27 Text in the private papers of Ivor Porter, to whom I owe a sight of this document. A similar disregard for Rădescu had been shown one month earlier by Georgescu and Bodnăraş.

28 N. Tampa, 'Starea de spirit din România la începutul anului 1945 [The Atmosphere in Romania at the Beginning of 1945],' *6 martie 1945. Începuturile Comunizării României* (Bucharest: Editura Enciclopedică, 1995), pp.312–18.

29 A broadsheet issued by the workers at the Malaxa factory on 23 February read: "We protest most strongly at the terror tactics which irresponsible persons from outside the factory are employing at the Malaxa works in support of the committee of dishonourable agitators which has been kept in place against the workers' will. We protest at the violence of the armed mercenaries who were brought in by lorries under the direction of Gheorghiu-Dej, who has come to impose the will of a disparate minority which has even shot its own supporters. We denounce the hooligans who wish to halt with gun fire the free expression of the workers' will. We demand the arrest of the armed bands of NDF supporters, who have been brought in from outside and have no place amongst us. We demand the arrest of Gheorghiu-Dej and the other Trotskyist agitators. We want free elections and a secret ballot. We want trade unions based on professions and not politically manipulated hordes. We demand that the government ensure freedom and the secret ballot, and prevent the terror practised against us by irresponsible criminals. We want work and order. We want peace. Down with the terror in the trade unions!"

30 *Cartea Albă a Securităţii*, vol.1, p.122.

31 Henry L. Roberts, *Rumania: Political Problems of an Agrarian State* (New Haven: Yale University Press, 1951), p.263, note 29. Rear-Admiral L. Bogdenko, Vice-Chairman of the Allied Control Commission, wrote in a report sent to Moscow that "Romanian troops who were guarding the Ministry of the Interior opened fire. Some of the demonstrators responded with fire. Simultaneously, shooting started from the building of the prefecture in Bucharest". At 1700 hours Bogdenko demanded that Prime Minister Rădescu order all troops, gendarmes and police to cease firing from their side. The same ultimatum was given to the Romanian military commander as well as to the head of the gendarmerie. It was accepted (see T.A. Pokivailova, 'A.Y. Vyshinsky, first deputy Commissar for Foreign Affairs of the USSR and the Establishment of the Groza Government' in *6 martie 1945*, pp.53–54).

32 The text of the speech can be found in Ioan Scurtu et al. (eds.), *Viaţa politică în Documente* (Bucharest: Arhivele Statului, 1994), pp.149–50.

33 Photocopies Russia, packet XIII, document 5, p.21. Quoted in M. Ignat, 'The Implications of the Armistice Convention for Romanian Politics', in *6 martie 1945*, p.33.

34 The nominal Chairman, Marshal Rodion Malinovsky, as Commander of the Second Ukrainian Front, was preoccupied with hostilities in Hungary and Czechoslovakia.

35 Quinlan, *Clash Over Romania*, p.128.

36 Following his dismissal Rădescu was taken under British protection and lived in the legation building for nine weeks (6 March–7 May 1945) until an agreement was

reached between the British and Soviet governments assuring the former that Rădescu would not be harmed on returning home. On 11 November, he received orders from the Ministry of the Interior to stay at home, from which he did not move until the spring of 1946 when the police provided him with a car, a driver and a detective. An incident on 13 May 1946 persuaded him to leave Romania as soon as possible. That day, while attending a function at the Athenaeum in Bucharest, he was attacked by a group of men armed with clubs, and he and his detective were injured. His escape was arranged by his secretary, Barbu Niculescu. On 15 June, Rădescu, together with his secretary and four other persons, including a Romanian airman, took off from Cotroceni airfield and flew to Cyprus. He settled in New York in 1947 where he helped to found the anti-Communist Romanian National Committee under the patronage of King Michael. Its work was financed by several million dollars secreted out of Romania between 1945 and 1946. In February 1950, Rădescu requested that this money be publicly accountable but other committee members disagreed and he resigned. He died in New York on 16 May 1953. The Committee, whose chairmanship was taken over by Constantin Vişoianu, remained active until 1975 (Oana Ionel Demetriade and Alexandru Şerbănescu, *Generalul Nicolae Rădescu*). *Profilul unui Om de Stat în Imagine şi Documente* (Bucharest: Editura Oscar Print, 2015, passim).

37 Susaikov gave this explanation at the end of October 1945, asking Stevenson and Schuyler whether they would have done otherwise. They agreed that they would not, but thought that it was a pity that this had not been explained before (H. Hanak, 'The Politics of Impotence: The British Observe Romania, 6 March 1945 to 30 December 1947', in I. Agrigoroaie, Gh. Buzatu, and V. Cristian (eds.), *Românii în istoria universală*, vol.III/1 (Iaşi: no publisher, 1988), p.433). Soviet sensitivity to disorder behind their lines had been conveyed to Schuyler at the time by A. Pavlov, the Soviet political representative. At a meeting of the Allied Control Commission on 14 February 1945, Pavlov had told Schuyler that "no disorder can be permitted to occur in the rear of the Soviet armies...nor can any Fascist activities within the state of Romania be permitted" (Giurescu, *Romania's Communist Takeover: The Rădescu Government*, p.67). Soviet unease about the possibility of a Romanian uprising had been fuelled by the infiltration of German agents and German-held Romanian prisoners of war into Romanian units in order to instigate mutinies. Roland Gunne, an SD officer from Transylvania, had wormed his way onto the staff of the Romanian Fourth Army which was fighting in Hungary. The commander of the Fourth Army was General Gheorghe Avramescu who, before the 23 August *coup*, had fought against the Russians in the Crimea and whose son-in-law, Ilie Vlad Sturdza, was the son of the foreign minister of the Iron Guard government in exile set up in Vienna on 10 December 1944. Avramescu's anti-Russian sentiments made him a prime candidate for German manipulation and Gunne and Iron Guard sympathizers persuaded the general to defect with his forces to the German side in the event of a successful German counter-offensive (P. Biddiscombe, 'Prodding the Russian Bear: pro-German Resistance in Romania, 1944–5', *European History Quarterly*, vol.23, no.2 (April 1993), pp.205–12 and G. Klein, 'Începuturile rezistenţei antisovietice în România (23 august 1944–6 martie 1945)' in *6 martie 1945*, pp.295–311. On 3 March 1945, Avramescu and his chief-of-staff, General Nicolae Dragomir, were arrested at the command post of the Second Ukrainian Front at Divin in Czechoslovakia on the orders of Marshal Malinovski by Soviet counter-espionage officers. Avramescu's fate is unclear. According to a report presented to Stalin by Beria and his deputy Abamukov, he was killed in a German air attack on Budapest (Klein, 'Începuturile rezistenţei antisovietice în România (23 august 1944–6 martie 1945)', p.309). This is confirmed by a reply sent in summer 1963 by the USSR Supreme Court to a request from the Romanian Ministry of Justice for information about Avramescu's fate. The letter stated that the general had died on 3 March 1945 near the town of Iasbereni following a German air attack and was buried in Soshalom, a district of Budapest (A. Duţu and F. Dobre, 'S-a mai dezlegat o

enigmă în cazul Avramescu?',*Magazin Istoric*, vol.31, no.5 (May 1997), pp.7–8). No mention was ever made by the Soviet authorities of his arrest. His wife and daughter were arrested on the same day. The daughter committed suicide three days later, and Avramescu's wife spent 11 years in Soviet labour camps before being allowed to return to Romania (J. Urwich-Ferry, *Fără Paşaport prin URSS* (In the USSR without a Passport) (Munich: Iskra, 1977), vol.II, pp.51–57). Dragomir was taken straight to the Soviet Union where he was tried and sentenced to eight years' hard labour. After completing his sentence, he was sent on 4 April 1953 to work as a veterinary assistant on a state farm in the region of Kustanai. He requested repatriation to Romania and was returned on 10 January 1956. On 11 January 1957, he was re-arrested in Bucharest for no apparent reason. He appealed unsuccessfully against his arrest on numerous occasions and was held in various prisons until his release on 27 July 1964. He died in 1981 aged 83 (A. Duţu and F. Dobre, 'Opt ani muncă silnică pentru un post de felcer veterinar', *Magazin Istoric*, vol.30, no.6 (June 1996), pp.47–52).

38 Giurescu, Romania's Communist Takeover, p.67.

39 Pokivailova, 'A.Y. Vyshinsky, first deputy Commissar for Foreign Affairs of the USSR and the Establishment of the Groza Government', p.52.

40 'Meeting of the NDF Council, 26 February 1945', Central Archive of the Institute of Party History of the Central Committee of the Romanian Workers' Party, fond 80, inventory 1, file no.16, p.7–8, 11. Gheorghiu-Dej was to claim later, at a plenary meeting of the Central Committee held on 9–10 June 1958, that 'he alone worked' for a limited coalition with Tătărescu while Pauker, Pătrăşcanu and Soviet officials on the Allied Control Commission argued 'that we should continue with the National Peasants and the National Liberals' (R. Levy, 'Power Struggles in the Romanian Communist Party Leadership During the Period of the Formation of the Groza Regime', in *6 martie 1945. Începuturile Comunizării României*, p.88). Gheorghiu-Dej's words may have been a retrospective attempt to show that he had acted independently of the Soviet Union and the so-called 'Muscovite faction' of Pauker and Luca and in doing so omitted any mention of Vyshinsky's decisive role.

41 'Stenograma Şedinţei Consiliului Partidului Naţional Democrat' in *Viaţa politică în Documente*, pp.170–71.

42 'Piese Noi la "Dosarul Ana Pauker"', *Magazin Istoric*, no.10 (October), 1992, p.26; see also Robert Levy, 'Power Struggles in the Romanian Communist Party Leadership During the Period of the Formation of the Groza Regime', p.88.

43 G. Ross (ed.), The Foreign Office and the Kremlin. British Documents on Anglo-Soviet Relations, 1941–45 (Cambridge: Cambridge University Press, 1984), p.194.

44 Communist activists were appointed as public prosecutors in the Ministry of Justice in April 1945. They were Stroe Botez, Avram Bunaciu, Alexandru Drăghici, H. Leibovici, M. Mayo, C. Mocanu, M. Popilian, I. Pora, I. Raiciu, Ştefan Ralescu, Dumitru Săracu, Alexandru Sidorovici, V. Stoican, Camil Suciu, C. Vicol. Drăghici, who in 1952 became Minister of the Interior, acted as a public prosecutor in the trial of Ion Antonescu in May 1946. For a biography of Drăghici see Andrei Şiperco (ed.), *Confesiunile elitei comuniste. România 1944–1965). Arhiva Alexandru Şiperco*, vol.2 (Bucharest: Institutul Naţional pentru Studiul Totalitarismului, 2015), pp.183–204.

45 Unpublished Archibald Gibson MS.

46 Macici, Trestioreanu and Calotescu were charged with carrying out reprisals against the Jewish population of Odessa in October 1941. On 22 October 1941, a huge explosion destroyed the Romanian military headquarters in Odessa, killing 128 soldiers and civilians, including General Ioan Glogojanu, the town commander. Marshal Antonescu immediately gave the order for reprisals: for every Romanian and German officer killed, 200 Communists were to be hanged; for every soldier, 100 Communists. During the night of 22 October, the military authorities carried out the order and by daybreak 450 Jews, considered Communists, were left hanging on the streets of Odessa. In addition, about 50,000 Jews were force-marched to Dalnik, about eight

kilometres outside the city, to be executed. On the intervention of Odessa's mayor, Gherman Pântea and General Macici, the column was sent back to Odessa, but not before those Jews at the head of the column were herded into four large sheds and machine-gunned to death, after which the sheds were set on fire. How many Jews were killed in this way is not known exactly but a figure of 20,000 was mentioned at Macici's trial. (*Cotidianul. Arhiva*, vol.5, no.3 (22 March 1996), p.3).

47 *Universul*, 6 June 1945. Macici died in Aiud prison on 15 June 1950 of heart failure. *Cotidianul. Arhiva*, vol.5, no.3 (22 March 1996), p.7.

48 Quinlan, *Clash Over Romania*, p.140.

49 *Ibid.*, p.151.

50 *Ibid.*

51 Aldea died in Aiud jail on 17 October 1949 of heart failure. The groups *Haiducii lui Avram Iancu* and *Divizia Sumanelor Negre* took their name from a Transylvanian Romanian Avram Iancu and the bands of men (Cătanele Negre) who raised a revolt against the Hungarian authorities in the 1848 revolution. Reports on these opposition groups, together with examples of their manifestos, are preserved in Archive of the Romanian Security Service (ASRI), Fond 'D', file 9046, vols 1–4.

52 Quinlan, Clash over Romania, p.154.

53 The National Peasant Party may well have been able to increase its share of the vote had it been, in the words of one scholar, "more coherent, well-organized, able to spread propaganda and physically engage with politics on the ground" (Brett, Dan (2010), *Peasants and Politics: Agrarianism and Rural Transformation in Romania, 1918–1947.* Thesis submitted to the School of Slavonic and East European Studies, University College, London, December, 2010, p.314.)

54 These archives contained "Confidential reports on the true results of the parliamentary elections". The results in the counties of Cluj, Someş and Turda show a clear, but not overwhelming, victory for Maniu's National Peasant Party which obtained more than 40% of the votes. In Someş, for example, the Communists were officially credited with 67.9% of the votes, whereas in reality they polled only 22.8%. The National Peasant Party was awarded only 11.1% when it in fact won 51.6% (V. Târău, 'Campania electorală şi rezultatul real al alegerilor din 19 noiembrie 1946 în judeţele Cluj, Someş şi Turda', in Sorin Mitu and Florin Gogâltan (eds.), *Studii de Istorie a Transilvaniei* (Cluj: Asociaţia Istoricilor din Transilvania şi Banat, 1994), pp.204–12).

55 A. Gibson MS.

56 *Ibid.* No copy of the top secret order no. 50000 of 1947 under which the arrests were carried out has been found. The reasons for the arrests were manifold and have been reconstituted from local police reports by Dumitru Şandru in 'Detinuţii politici de la Gherla în 1947', *Anuarul Institutului de Istorie Cluj-Napoca*, vol.34, 1995, pp.271–82.

57 Maniu died in Sighet prison on 2 February 1953, and Mihalache at Râmnicu Sărat on 5 March 1963.

58 Quinlan, *Clash over Romania*, p.157.

59 E. Focşeneanu, 'O Descoperire Istorica', *România liberă*, 15 October 1991, p.4.

60 The imposition of the Soviet totalitarian model in Romania has been described in detail in Ionescu, *Communism in Rumania* and briefly in Deletant, *Ceauşescu and the Securitate*, pp.13–56.

61 Titel Petrescu's fate was emblematic of that of opposition leaders. He was arrested on 6 May 1948, held in the security police headquarters in Bucharest, sent to Jilava prison and finally tried *in camera* in January 1952 for crimes against the state. He was sentenced to life imprisonment and served three years in Sighet jail before being transferred to the Calea Rahovei headquarters of the *Securitate* in Bucharest in December 1954 where he was told by the Minister of the Interior, Alexandru Drăghici, that a number of his colleagues in the former SDP would be released from prison if he signed a letter giving his support to the regime for publication in the Party daily *Scînteia*. He refused and was sent in August to Râmnicu Sărat jail where he learned

from fellow prisoners of the death in prison of numerous socialists. He agreed to sign a text on 13 September on condition that all leading SDP members be released, and he himself was freed but kept under virtual house arrest. The letter appeared in *Scînteia* on 18 December 1955 (see also *Cartea Albă a Securităţii* (Bucharest: SRI, 1995), vol.II, doc. 237, pp.527–29, yet only a small number of SDP colleagues were released). Petrescu complained to Petru Groza, the President of the Grand National Assembly, after which further releases were announced. Petrescu died on 2 September 1957 in Bucharest.

62 R. R. King, *A History of the Romanian Communist Party* (Stanford: Hoover Institution Press, 1980), p.71.

63 *Cartea Albă a Securităţii*, vol.II, p.7. An analysis of the editorials in the Party newspaper *Scînteia* charts the evolution of the language used to categorize the "enemies of the state" during the years 1945 to 1953; see Liviu Ţîrău, 'Ziarul "Scânteia" şi războiul rece. Atitudine politică şi limbaj, 1945–1953', *Revista Istorică*, vol.4 nos.7–8 (1993), pp.725–41. Orthographic reforms in Romania in 1954 and 1965 meant that the noun *Scînteia* ('the Spark' was not spelt consistently, being replaced by the form *Scânteia*. For the sake of consistency I have used *Scînteia*.

64 Cartea Albă a Securităţii, vol.II, p.8.

65 M. Oprea, 'Cum a întinat Pătrăşcanu valorile comunismului', *Dilema*, no.177 (31 mai-6 iunie) 1996, p.9. Under article 65 of the Constitution of the People's Republic, enacted in 1952, the role of the judiciary was defined "to defend the regime of popular democracy and the conquests of the working people, to assure the respect of popular legality, of public property and of the rights of citizens". The courts, represented by the judges and assessors, also had the power to appoint defence attorneys whose role was largely limited to apologizing for the defendant's alleged offences.

66 http://www.constitutia.ro/const1948.htm. Accessed 19 April 2017.

67 *Scînteia*, 22 January 1949.

68 *Scînteia*, 7 December 1961, quoted from Ionescu, *Communism in Rumania*, p.201.

69 Raoul Bossy, 'Religious Persecutions in Captive Romania', *Journal of Central European Affairs*, vol.15, no.2 (July 1955), p.163.

70 Keith Hitchins, 'The Romanian Orthodox Church and the State', in B.R. Bociurkiw and J.W. Strong (eds.), assisted by J. K. Laux, *Religion and Atheism in the USSR and Eastern Europe* (Toronto: University of Toronto Press; London: Macmillan, 1975), p.317.

71 Bossy, 'Religious Persecutions', p.165.

72 Hansjakob Stehle, *Eastern Politics of the Vatican, 1917–1979*, tr. by Sandra Smith (Ohio: Ohio University Press, 1981), p.265.

73 Janice Broun, 'The Latin-Rite Roman Catholic Church of Romania', *Religion in Communist Lands*, vol.12, no.2 (Summer 1984), p.169.

74 Stehle, Eastern Politics of the Vatican, p.422, note 5.

75 *Ibid.*, p.264.

76 Fathers Waltner, Heber and Schwartz from Timişoara, in February; on 8 March, Father Clementi Gatti, parson of the Italian church in Bucharest; on 10 March, the curates Petz, Clofanda, Vamosin, Bachmeyer and Mihoc from the diocese of Iaşi; Maghiar and Borz from the Oradea diocese; Imre Sandar, Czumbel, Bela Gajdaczi from the Alba Iulia diocese; on 24 April, three nuns: Mother Superior Hildegarde and sisters Judith and Christina; on 11 May Father Baltheiser from Bucharest.

77 Procesul unui grup de spioni, trădători şi comploţişti în slujba Vaticanului şi a centrului de spionaj italian, Bucureşti, 10–17 septembrie 1951 (Bucharest: Editura de stat pentru literatura ştiinţifică, 1952), p.102.

78 Some Western Catholics were highly critical of what they saw as the Vatican's lack of action on behalf of their imprisoned clergy in Romania. According to Stehle, no attempt was made by the Vatican to free Schubert. He was received for the first and

last time by the Pope on 23 February 1969, just six weeks before his death in Munich on 4 April where he was buried, in the Frauenkirche. It was only in early 1969, when he was already fatally ill, that he was permitted to leave Romania, arriving in Rome on 8 February. Then he had to wait two weeks before Pope Paul VI embraced him. Stehle, who first met Schubert in 1965, says that the bishop died an embittered man, unhonoured by his Church.

79 Bossy, 'Religious Persecutions', p.167.

80 *Ibid.*, p.168.

81 *Ibid.*

82 *Ibid.*, p.169.

83 Stehle, Eastern Politics of the Vatican, p.422, note 4.

84 A. Ratiu and W. Virtue, *Stolen Church. Martyrdom in Communist Romania* (Huntington, Indiana: Our Sunday Visitor, 1978), p.169.

85 *Ibid.*

86 Cartea Albă a Securităţii, vol.II, August 1948-July 1958 (Bucharest: SRI, 1994), doc.110, p.226.

87 Author's interview with Father Langa, 31 May 1993.

88 Bălan was freed in January and Hossu and Rusu in June. For the fate of the Uniate bishops see Cristian Vasile, *Între Vatican şi Kremlin. Biserica Greco-Catolică în timpul Regimului Comunist* (Bucharest: Curtea Veche, 2003).

89 Domiciliul obligatoriu in Romanian.

90 Marius Bucur, Culpa de a fi Greco-Catolic. Procesul Episcopului Alexandru Rusu (1957) (Cluj: Argonaut, 2015), p.VII.

91 S.A. Prunduş and C. Plaianu, *Cardinalul Alexandru Todea* (Cluj: Ordinul Sfântul Vasile cel Mare, 1992), p.30.

92 Alan Scarfe, 'Patriarch Justinian of Romania: His Early Social Thought', *Religion in Communist Lands*, vol.5, no.3 (Autumn 1977), p.166. For a detailed examination of Justinian's alignment with the Communist regime see Lucian N. Leuştean, *Orthodoxy and the Cold War: Religion and Political Power in Romania, 1947–1965* (Basingstoke, England; New York: Palgrave Macmillan, 2009).

93 T. Beeson, *Discretion and Valour. Religious Conditions in Russia and Eastern Europe* (London: Fontana, 1974), p.311. In 1973 there were 8,185 parishes and 11,722 places of worship served by 8,564 priests and 78 deacons. In Bucharest alone there were almost 250 churches and 400 priests. The Church possessed two theological institutes of university standing, in Bucharest and Sibiu, with 496 and 780 students respectively in 1972–73. The majority of the clergy were trained in the seven cantors' schools and seminaries where 1,597 students were in residence over the same period (*Ibid.*, p.303).

94 Ioan Dură, *Monahismul românesc în anii 1948–1989* (Bucharest: Harisma, 1994), p.59.

95 *Social Apostolate* (10 vols, Bucharest, 1948–76).

96 Hitchins, 'The Romanian Orthodox Church and the State', p.322.

97 Archive of the SRI (ASRI), Fond D, dosar 9051, vol.2. I am grateful to Marius Oprea for this information.

98 Ioan Dură, *Monahismul românesc*, pp.56–57.

99 Amongst these groups was the so-called *Rugul aprins al Maicii Domnului* (The Burning Stake of the Virgin Mary) which was accused of seeking to attract students from the theological institutes in Bucharest and Iaşi. Those arrested included the theologians Dumitru Stăniloae, Alexandru Mironescu, Sandu Tudor, Anania Valeriu Bartolomeu, Ghius Benedict, Braga Roman and Antonie Plămădeală. (*Cartea Albă a Securităţii*, vol.III, 1958–1968 (Bucharest: SRI, 1995), p.56).

100 *Ibid.*

101 *Cartea Albă a Securităţii*, vol.III, 1958–1968 (SRI: Bucharest, 1996), doc. 74, p.243.

102 *Ibid.*

103 *Ibid.*

104 *Ibid.* The other priests were Uniates and Catholics. The last group of Uniate priests was arrested in February 1962 and they were all released two years later. In 1966, further strictures were placed on the monasteries with the introduction of a regulation stipulating that all nuns under the age of 40, and all lay brothers under the age of 50, must leave their monasteries and take up 'more socially useful' work. (Beeson, *Discretion and Valour*, p.303). Discouragement of the monastic life continued throughout the Ceauşescu period but, as in the general case of religious worship itself, toleration rather than suppression became the order of the day. On 25 June 1966, Justinian announced that there were "over 2,500 souls living in the monasteries" of whom "almost 2,000 were nuns". (Dură, *Monahismul românesc*, p.59). The effect of the measures taken against the monasteries can be gauged from the decrease in the number of over 200 monasteries with almost 7,000 monks and nuns in 1956, to 114 monastic houses and 2,068 religious (1,493 nuns and 575 monks) in 1972 (Beeson, *Discretion and Valour*, p.303).

4 The *Securitate* as an instrument of coercion

The security police, popularly known as the *Securitate,* was the blunt instrument of repression of the Communist Party. It was set up according to a Soviet blueprint and under Soviet direction.[1] Broadly speaking, the role assigned by the Soviet authorities to the *Siguranţa,* as the political police continued to be known until 1948, was similar to that played by the same body under King Carol's dictatorship and that of Antonescu, but with one major difference. Whereas the coercion between 1938 and 1944 was directed against one particular group in society, the Jews and against the small number of individual opponents of the Antonescu regime, it was after the *coup* extended to the whole of Romanian society. Even during the war the landowner, the peasant, the banker, the lawyer and the priest carried on with their lives largely without the intrusion of the political police; now, in the building of the People's Democracy, the security police were called upon to eradicate existing political institutions and social structures. Police coercion and intrusion became part of everyday life and a feature of existence which generated a pervasive fear, a state of mind which revolutionized not just society's structures, but also personal behaviour. The animated conversation gave way to the furtive whisper, or parable, suggestion replaced open discussion and the simplest of messages was wrapped in a code.

Soviet penetration of the secret service (the SSI), and the security police, was undertaken by infiltrating them in autumn 1944 with Emil Bodnăraş's 'Patriotic Guards' and with NKVD/NKGB agents.[2] Control of both organizations was secured after the installation of the Groza government in March 1945. On 27 April, Groza signed an order giving the secretary general control of the SSI.[3] The order stated that the SSI was constituted "from its own civilian personnel and from military personnel seconded from the Ministry of War on the recommendation of the secretary general".[4] A second Soviet agent, Serghei Nikonov (Sergiu Nicolău),[5] was appointed to be the actual director of the SSI, under the supervision of Bodnăraş. Soviet control was further illustrated by the composition in 1948 of Gheorghiu-Dej's immediate entourage. Nikonov's wife Nina worked as Gheorghiu-Dej's private secretary. The latter's *chef de cabinet* was Mikhail Gavrilovici, an NKGB agent and the head of his personal guard was Valerian Bucikov, also an NKGB agent.[6]

The SSI's remit covered "the gathering of general intelligence which met the higher interests of the state". It was organized in four sections, later renamed directorates and a secretariat. The first section was charged with "obtaining intelligence from abroad of a political, economic, social and military nature" and "control of all diplomatic offices abroad", and was subdivided into three departments, organized on a geographical basis, 'South', 'West' and 'North'. Section One also included the 'Office for Issuing Entry-Exit Visas and Passports to Romanian Citizens' which was to be used "as an auxiliary means of recruiting part-time informers".[7] Here, for the first time, we find a policy statement of a government agency in Romania making the issue of a passport conditional on collaboration with an organ of state security. It was a tactic that remained an integral part of the Communist regime's armoury of coercion until the overthrow of Ceauşescu.

Other sections of the SSI were responsible for obtaining intelligence from within the country and for mounting counter-espionage operations, both civilian and military. A Bessarabian-born Russian, Pyotr Goncearuc was named head of the counter-espionage section.[8] According to Eduard Mezincescu, a senior Foreign Ministry official, who met Goncearuc on several occasions in a professional capacity, the latter was a "cunning brute" who proved himself "very efficient" with his interrogation methods. These were displayed in his treatment of Lucreţiu Pătrăşcanu, a senior figure in the Communist Party who was arrested in April 1948.[9]

Eavesdropping and shadowing of targets was carried out by Section Four of the SSI in collaboration with a parallel directorate in the *Siguranţa*. Military intelligence remained the task of the Second Bureau of the Army General Staff but this was also subordinated to a Soviet master, the GRU. The subservience of the Romanian security and intelligence services to the interests of the Soviet Union was completed by making the security police, still known by its pre-war title of *Direcţia Poliţiei de Siguranţă* responsible in 1945 to Pantelimon Bodnarenko, a Ukrainian-born Soviet agent also known as Pantiusha who had been imprisoned for spying in Romania in the late 1930s. Bodnarenko's sadistic impulses were revealed in a drunken confession he once made at a party to Tatiana Brătescu, Ana Pauker's daughter, in the early 1950s. He told her that as a member of the Komsomol in Ukraine he had discovered a priest holding a service in a hollow on the edge of his village. He gathered other youths and together they pinned down the priest and buried him alive by piling earth over him with tractors.[10]

Bodnarenko assumed a Romanian name, Gheorghe Pintilie, as did a number of agents who later joined Bodnarenko at the apex of the *Siguranţă*, among them Boris Grunberg (who took the name of Alexandru Nicolski). Instructions were channelled to both Bodnăraş and Pintilie by Dmitri Georgievich Fedichkin, the chief Soviet advisor in Romania from 1944 to 1947 and principal representative of the Foreign Intelligence Division (INO) of the NKGB.[11]

Pintilie's promotion to membership of the Central Committee of the Romanian Workers' Party Central Committee in February 1948, and the status of his wife Ana Toma as an INO agent demonstrated the stranglehold which the Soviet Security Service had upon the Romanian leadership. Ana Toma's role was typical of that assigned by the NKGB/INO to its female agents who were often described in Romanian Party circles as 'amazons'. After being infiltrated into the Party before the war, she seems to have acted as much as a custodian of her partners as a wife. Her first marriage to a veteran Communist Sorin Toma disintegrated following the latter's exile to the Soviet Union and in 1942 she became the partner of Constantin Pârvulescu, another senior figure in the embryonic Party. Four years later, she married Pintilie who was a notorious drinker and over whom the NKGB/INO deemed it prudent to have total supervision in view of the position he was given.[12]

In August 1948, Pintilie was moved from his post as head of the political and administrative section of the Central Committee to head the newly reorganized *Siguranța*. It was renamed *Direcția Generală a Securității Poporului* (DGSP) or *Securitate* for short. The new name signalled a new mission for the security police. Formally, it remained a branch of the Ministry of the Interior. Its role, defined under its founding decree no. 221 of 30 August 1948, was "to defend the democratic conquests and to ensure the security of the Romanian People's Republic against the plotting of internal and external enemies".[13] Defence of the 'democratic conquests' meant the maintenance of the Romanian Workers Party in power and thus the new Romanian People's Republic officially certified itself a police state. Ninety per cent of the *Securitate* officers were Party members and Pintilie's membership of the Central Committee was an implicit indication of nominal Party control of the organization.[14]

Two weeks earlier, on 15 August, Lt. Gen. Gheorghe Pintilie had been appointed by decree the DGSP's director. Two assistant directors, with the rank of major general, were appointed on 1 September; they were Alexandru Nicolski, a Russian-speaking Bessarabian Jew and Vladimir Mazuru, a Ukrainian from Bessarabia (later Romanian ambassador to Poland).[15] All three were agents of the NKGB/MGB.

A body of Soviet counsellors from the MGB supervised the activity of the young DGSP. The MGB chief advisers in Bucharest were Serghei Savcenko (1947–1949) and Alexandr Mihailovici Saharovski (1949–1952), who in 1956 became head of the First Chief Directorate of the KGB.[16] The Soviet ambassador to Bucharest, Serghei Kavtaradze, appointed in 1948, came under the authority of the newly formed KI (foreign intelligence service), headed by Vyacheslav Molotov and his deputy Fedotov. In 1949, Molotov was succeeded as Foreign Minister and Chairman of the KI by Andrei Vyshinsky, a sycophant of Lavrenti Pavlovich Beria, head between 1939 and 1946 of the NKVD, the Soviet Ministry of Internal Affairs.

It was Beria who oversaw the creation of the security framework with the satellite states. Although Stalin had attempted to dilute his power, which had grown enormously as a result of the wartime expansion of the security network, by replacing him as head of the NKVD in 1946, Beria remained, through his position as Deputy Chairman of the Council of Ministers, and through the sycophancy shown to him by the new head of the MGB, Viktor Semyonovich Abakumov, the second most powerful figure in the Soviet Union. Abakumov's management style in the MGB was, like that of Beria, brutal, a feature characteristic of the men chosen by the NKGB/MGB to head Romania's security police.[17] The conduct of both Pintilie and Nicolski speaks for itself. The former, as head of the Political and Administrative Section of the Central Committee whose attributes included Party security, instructed his chauffeur to carry out the death sentence imposed on the former RCP general secretary Ştefan Foriş in 1946.[18] He then gave instructions for Foriş's mother to be murdered. She was drowned with millstones hung around her neck in the Criş river in Transylvania.[19]

Pintilie's philosophy was outlined in an address he gave to *Securitate* chiefs on 1 March 1950:

> There is no place in our country for comrades who believe in God... We need honest, dedicated party members so that we can carry out our tasks, there is no alternative. We are short on discipline. Why are we short on discipline? Because we consider ourselves the centre of things.[20]

It was this feeling of superiority which had led *Securitate* officers to be over-zealous in their beatings of the accused. Pintilie emphasized that prisoners should only be beaten on the orders and instructions of superior officers. Pintilie's manual background coloured his description of *Securitate* methods:

> Comrades, every craftsman, every doctor, everybody has an instrument and he looks after that instrument. In the *Securitate* what is our instrument? We, too, have an instrument. If the barber has his razor, if the carpenter has his lathe, I say that our informers are our instrument. Let us be conscious of our task and of our opponents. Just as the labourer takes care of his tools, so too must we take care of our informers. If the barber has his razor, we have people, and real people at that! That means that we have got to take care of them, give them instructions, indicate the Party line and not, just like that, to beat them till they are black and blue! If a carpenter destroys his lathe, what will he eat the next day? Is that what the Party teaches us?[21]

Yet Pintilie did not follow his own advice concerning self-centredness. He offered clear signs of megalomania after attending a concert given by the Ministry of the Interior choir and orchestra on 8 May 1949:

> I order the artists not to be so glum! An artist is an artist, irrespective of his feelings, and he should not forget that he is on the stage! And why is the symphony orchestra in the pit and the chorus on the stage? The orchestra should immediately mount the stage, because together with the chorus it forms an ensemble and they should support each other. Accordeons should be added forthwith to the symphony orchestra so that vigorous and mobilizatory marches can be played.[22]

The birth-name of Pintilie's deputy, Alexandru Nicolski, was Boris Grunberg.[23] After the imposition of the Groza government in March 1945, Nicolski was named deputy to the head of the Corps of Detectives of the police, Gheorghe Guţa Petrovici.[24] On 17 April 1947, he was appointed Inspector General of the *Siguranţa* and when the DGSP was established in the following year, he was made one of Pintilie's deputies. In 1953, he was given the post of secretary general of the Ministry of the Interior.

Despite the veil of secrecy which was cast over the personnel of the DGSP, Nicolski's reputation for brutality earned him the dubious distinction of becoming the first senior officer to achieve notoriety outside Romania. In a statement made in Paris in January 1949, Adriana Georgescu Cosmovici, a 28 year-old woman arrested in Bucharest in July 1945 on the grounds of having belonged to a resistance movement, recounted how the "communist secret police investigators" beat her repeatedly with a sand-filled leather hose, struck her head against a wall, and hit her face and chin until she was left with only six teeth in her lower jaw. She named three investigators as having threatened her with guns: Stroescu, Bulz and Nicolski.[25] Documents published after Nicolski's death on 16 April 1992 suggested that in July 1949 he ordered the murder of seven prisoners, allegedly leaders of an anti-communist resistance movement, in transit from Gherla jail.[26]

Consultation of rudimentary figures surviving in the Ministry of Interior archives relating to the strength of the DGSP indicates that the number of officers serving in the ten national directorates shortly after its constitution was 1,151 of whom 848 were listed as secretarial and manual staff (the latter all carried military rank, such as sergeant major, even if they were typists, chauffeurs, plumbers or waitresses). The 13 regional directorates employed 2,822 officers, roughly two-thirds of whom were manual or ancillary staff.[27] These figures may appear abnormally low, given the popular conception of the DGSP as a ubiquitous and all-pervasive instrument of coercion. But they do not include the network of informers who enabled the *Securitate* to function as efficiently as it did.

Soviet advisors were attached to each of the national directorates to supervise the training of the Romanian recruits and to monitor their activity, and communication was carried out through interpreters, many of whom were from Bessarabia. Emphasis was placed on trustworthy cadres. In the eyes of the Soviet advisors many educated Romanians were considered unreliable and compromised because of the Antonescu regime's alliance with Germany. A second reason for caution derived from the fact that very few Romanians had willingly shown any enthusiasm for the Romanian Communist Party before its propulsion to power, whereas conversely, some members of the ethnic minorities had. Against this background we should not be surprised to find several recruits for the senior positions in the DGSP drawn from two categories of person: from the ethnic minorities; and from unskilled manual workers.

Contrary to claims made by ultranationalists, the numbers drawn from ethnic minorities, although disproportionate, do not appear to be excessive. I stress 'appear' because it is clear from the DGSP's own listings of the ethnic identity of its senior officers that it wished to obscure the Russian provenance of its three principal commanders, Pintilie, Nicolski and Mazuru, by entering them as Romanians. However, there is no evidence to suggest the 'Romanianization' of officers of other ethnic origins. An examination of the ethnic and professional background of senior officers in the DGSP, (i.e. with the rank of major and above) shows a total of 60, of whom 38 were Romanians, 14 were Jews, three Hungarians, three Russians (Pintilie, Nicolski and Mazuru), one Czech and one Armenian. These figures hardly bear out the claim made in the extreme nationalist weekly *România Mare* of 25 October 1991 by its editor Corneliu Vadim Tudor, a notorious sycophant of Ceauşescu, that the DGSP was staffed largely by Hungarians and Russian-speaking Jews. Both the latter minorities were well represented in the DGSP, but not abnormally so. Of the total number of 3,973 employees listed in 1950, 247 were Hungarians and 338 were Jews. Most of the former were employed in those regional directorates which covered the major concentrations of Hungarian population such as Braşov (72 Hungarians), Cluj (51), Oradea (60), Sibiu (26), and Timişoara (27). This same observation is valid also for the Jews: of the 1,151 personnel in the central directorates based in Bucharest 148 were Jews. Regional directorates with the largest numbers of Jewish staff were Bucharest (16), Cluj (36), Iaşi (35), Oradea (34) and Suceava (34).[28]

As far as professional background is concerned, the information available limits us to the national directorates and the secretariat; among 25 persons appointed to senior officer rank, there were two electricians, two carpenters, a locksmith, a blacksmith, a lathe operator, a craftsman, a tailor, a chemist, a schoolteacher, a doctor, an accountant, a lawyer, one person without a higher education, five with degree studies and five whose background was not given.[29] Compared to the population of some 18 million, the number of *Securitate* officers seems very small and the evidence provided by consultation of DGSP files shows that they relied heavily for information upon the 42,187 informers who were used in 1948. In the local bureaux, where there were often no more than a handful of staff, the officers were overworked. Their principal brief was to identify and monitor the activities of former members of outlawed opposition parties and organizations, such as the Iron Guard, and to provide monthly reports to the directorates responsible for information and counter-sabotage in Bucharest. These reports represent an invaluable survey of political allegiances and their relation to social background in Romania of the early 1950s.[30]

A major task of the *Securitate* was "to unmask imperialist espionage activity". Its main opponents in the Gheorghiu-Dej era, judging from the *Securitate's* archives, were the American, British, Yugoslav and Israeli intelligence agencies. At the beginning of 1949, the Central Intelligence Agency, through its Office of Political Coordination under the direction of Frank Wisner,[31] began to recruit Romanians from refugee camps in southern Germany, Austria and Yugoslavia. Preference was shown for young men who knew those regions in which partisan activity had been reported. These men were trained for secret missions whose objectives were either to obtain information about Romania's defences, or to link up with the anti-Communist resistance groups in the mountains. The Yugoslavs either infiltrated their agents across the border or used Romanian citizens of Serbian nationality. To combat border infiltration, a counter-intelligence section of the frontier troops was set up and subordinated to the Ministry of the Interior. Israeli intelligence activities focused on the situation of the Jews in Romania. According to *Securitate* files, 45,299 persons were suspected of espionage in Romania in 1951. They were monitored by networks made up of 904 agents, of whom five were resident *Securitate* officers, 306 qualified informers and 593 unqualified informers. As a result of the information gathered, 267 persons were arrested for espionage.[32]

A second principal aim of the *Securitate* was to seek out and destroy any form of internal resistance to the regime. This was described in *Securitate* jargon as "subversive anti-democratic activity by enemies of the people". The main targets were former factory owners and landowners, members of the outlawed democratic parties and of the Iron Guard, priests, students and teachers, and retired army officers and policemen.[33] In 1951, 417,916 persons were kept under surveillance of whom 5,401 were arrested for "hostile activity".[34] Information on them, as in the case of those suspected of espionage, was gathered by informers working under the direction of a *Securitate* officer. Details were collated at the local bureaux and a daily bulletin on the situation in each area was transmitted by telephone to the regional offices between 5 p.m. and 5.30 p.m.

Eavesdropping and monitoring of suspects' movements were auxiliary means used by the *Securitate* to gather evidence against their targets. The latter was particularly labour-intensive and for this reason informers were often employed to supplement the shadowing carried out by the departments of the *Securitate* charged with surveillance. It was not only perceived enemies of the regime who received such attention; senior Party members were also targeted. Among those whose telephone calls were monitored from 1948 by what came to be called 'unit T' were Ana Pauker, Vasile Luca, Teohari Georgescu, Ion Gheorghe Maurer, Alexandru Bârlădeanu and Valter Roman. Between 1953 and 1961, further names were added to this list: Iosif Chişinevski and his wife Liuba, Constantin Doncea and Nicolae Ceauşescu. In 1963, Miron Constantinescu became a target, and in 1964 Gheorghe Pintilie, the former head of the *Securitate*. In charge of this eavesdropping was, until 1954, Alexandru Nicolski. Not even Gheorghiu-Dej was spared. Colonel Andrei Arghiropol, who worked in unit T, revealed in 1968 that his first job in 1949 was to intercept the telephone calls made by Gheorghiu-Dej. The only other persons who knew about this operation, which was carried out on orders from Moscow channelled through the Soviet counsellors, were Pintilie, Nicolski and Colonel Alexandru Neacşu, head of unit T.[35]

Securitate files indicate that more than 70,000 people were arrested in the decade from 1948 to 1958, of whom 60,428 were between 1948 and 1953. These figures must be treated with caution since on Gheorghiu-Dej's own admission in 1961, 80,000 peasants alone had been arrested to enforce collectivization of agriculture.[36] Many of the arrests were illegal for they were carried out by *Securitate* officers acting purely on telephoned instructions from their superiors without an arrest warrant issued by the prosecutor's office. Cases of mistaken identity often led to the arrest of the wrong person. In 1955, the Ministry of Interior gave instructions to officers to carry out arrests only on the basis of an arrest warrant yet in September 1958, Alexandru Drăghici, Minister of the Interior, was still complaining of cases in which arrests had been made "without foundation and prematurely".[37]

In the early years of the *Securitate's* existence emphasis was placed on the quantity of informers rather than upon their quality. Many were small-time crooks and delinquents and their number included the casual informants and busybodies which, as Walter Bacon has remarked, all totalitarian regimes produce in parasitic abundance.[38] These categories boosted the number of informers to the levels reported as being used at the close of 1951 by the Directorate of Counter-Sabotage and the Directorate of Internal Intelligence, namely 30,585 and 10,698 respectively.[39]

Informers were often blackmailed into collaborating with the *Securitate.* Charges against them for offences committed were dropped in return for collaboration. They were frequently subjected to rough treatment by their handlers, as Pintilie's speech quoted above shows, and threats were levelled at them. Documents reveal that at the regional *Securitate* headquarters in Cluj and Constanţa, informers were brought in wearing blacked-out spectacles so that they could not recognize the place and "thrown into a room".[40] The unreliability of many of them led to a major purge of 70% of their numbers in March 1956 with fresh informers being recruited from among intellectuals. Informers were also used by two other organs of internal security, both of which were established early in 1949. On 23 January, the militia (*Direcţia Generală a Miliţiei*) was set up to replace the police and gendarmerie (rural police), and on 7 February, the security troops (*trupele de securitate*) were created.[41] Both bodies were placed under the authority of the Ministry of the Interior and Lt Gen Pavel Cristescu, allegedly a Russian, was named as commander of the former.[42]

Among the militia's duties was that of issuing residence permits, one which facilitated its task of regulating the movement of population, of monitoring suspects and of preparing for deportations. The principal duties of the security troops were to maintain public order in the major industrial centres and to quell any resistance to government measures such as collectivization or appropriation of goods and property. Throughout the 1950s they were deployed to eradicate partisan resistance in mountain areas and, in a more passive role, were employed to guard the labour camps (*colonii de muncă*) which in 1950 had been placed under a special department of the Ministry of Interior known as *Direcţia Unităţilor de Muncă.*

A legal framework for the actions of the *Securitate*, the militia, and the security troops was provided by the introduction of new laws which made opposition to the regime a criminal offence. The death penalty for treason and economic sabotage was introduced on 12 January 1949, and a decree promulgated in the same year punishing acts "considered as dangerous to society", even if these were "not specifically provided for in the law as crimes". A law of 12 August 1950 imposed the death penalty for crimes against national independence and sovereignty, for negligence by workers "leading to public disaster", for theft and destruction of military equipment, and for plotting against the state, spying and economic sabotage. The death penalty was applicable for the betrayal of "state secrets" to a foreign power but the nature of these state secrets was not defined. "Plotting against the internal and external security of the RPR" also attracted the death penalty, but once gain 'plotting' was not defined. The open-endedness of this legislation permitted its arbitrary application by the authorities. The category of "counter-revolutionary crimes" made its appearance in decree no. 83 of 1949. This provided for punishments of up to 15 years hard labour for those who resisted the expropriation of land under the land reforms of 1945 and 1949.

The Party body charged with initiating arrests and criminal proceedings was an institution specific to Communist regimes known in Romanian as the *procuratura*. It was vested with "supreme supervisory power to ensure the observance of the law by the ministries and other central organs, by the local organs of state power and administration, as well as by officials and other citizens".[43] Like the *Securitate*, the *procuratura* relied heavily upon informers whose activities were encouraged and rewarded, in the spirit of the procedures laid down by the Soviet prosecutor general of the show trials of the 1930s, Andrei Vishinsky, who boasted that "thousands of informers ensure that the *procuratura* can react swiftly".[44]

An idea of the 'principles' adopted by the Communist authorities in determining the guilt of citizens was given by an interrogator to George Tomaziu, an artist arrested in 1949 on the charge of being a spy in the pay of France and Britain. To Tomaziu's affirmation that at university he had learned that it was preferable to let one guilty man go free rather than imprison ten innocent suspects, his interrogator replied,

> That was bourgeois justice and the reason why the bourgeois system collapsed. In the Communist case the reverse is true. To avoid the risk of letting one guilty person slip through our hands, it is preferable to imprison him along with the other nine suspects.[45]

In the political trials conducted after the imposition of the Groza government the defendant was often found guilty not because he or she had committed an offence, but because they stood accused.[46] And because they were accused, they had to be removed. This was the perversion of justice which Communism practised. It was not just the actions of the person which were on trial, but the person himself, his family and his background. This was most graphically illustrated by the public trials of alleged saboteurs of the Danube-Black Sea Canal project in 1952, but it was equally true of the trial *in camera* of Lucrețiu Pătrășcanu in 1954. Many of the trials between 1948 and 1964 had a preventive character, with the accused being held guilty of *potential* crimes. This principle had been feverishly applied by Andrei Vyshinsky as public prosecutor in the Moscow trials between 1936 and 1938, and it was under his supervision that it was introduced in Romania.

In the conduct of political trials particular importance was attached to confession.[47] The means of extracting this was torture, be it psychological, physical or both. The insistence upon confession and the use of torture to extract it were alien to the Romanian legal system and it is tempting to speculate what impression it left on the senior Romanian Communists who had experienced the less ruthless regime of interwar Romania. Some Romanians have argued that the rituals of liquidation imported from the Soviet Union after 1945 required the hand in their execution of Bessarabian or Ukrainian-born NKVD agents such as Nicolski and Gonceariuc, but this would be to overlook the brutality of a number of Romanian DGSP officers, for example, Ion Şoltuţiu, under whose directions Belu Zilber, Lucreţiu Pătrăşcanu and Remus Koffler were beaten.

Beatings were usually administered at the direction of senior officers of Directorate Five for Penal Investigation. It was this directorate in particular which gave the *Securitate* the character of a political police. Confidential instructions issued by the Ministry of the Interior empowered the *Securitate* to detain a person for 24 hours without the need of an arrest warrant from a prosecutor. During this period the detainee was asked to give a declaration.[48] Arrest warrants were issued for the *Securitate* by military prosecutors on instructions from the Ministry of Justice. After the issue of an arrest warrant, interrogation of the prisoner began in the presence of a stenographer. The Fifth Directorate's first head was Colonel Mişu Dulgheru who was himself arrested in November 1952 on the charge of having delayed the investigation into Pătrăşcanu's activities.[49] *Securitate* documents indicate that Dulgheru approved the use of beatings, threats, the falsification of prisoner statements, and extension of interrogation beyond the physical endurance of the prisoner. Even Alexandru Drăghici, appointed Minister of the Interior in May 1952, recognized that interrogation officers in this directorate "had a fairly low level of training and general knowledge", but that these shortcomings were compensated for by "their powerful revolutionary enthusiasm, their healthy [i.e. non-bourgeois] background, and their work capacity which was placed at the service of the proletarian revolution".[50]

The low level of knowledge was often illustrated by the interrogations recorded in the *Securitate* files. One officer was unaware that the National Peasant Party was outlawed by the Antonescu regime, a second was unable to write the figure 309, confusing it with 3,009, 30,009 and 300,009. To surmount these difficulties, the Soviet counsellors drew up a list of questions and the desired replies from the accused, and in order to extract them, the interrogators resorted to psychological or physical pressure, denying the prisoner cigarettes, cutting his or her food rations, or administering a beating. Some *Securitate* interrogators used severe beatings with truncheons, others threw water on the concrete floors of a cell so that the prisoner would freeze, or would force a prisoner to stand upright until he dropped unconscious. In October 1954, at a meeting at the headquarters of the Penal Investigation Directorate, Drăghici ordered a halt to the use of such pressure by officers except in cases where he personally gave approval. The cynical explanation given for the brutal treatment meted out to some prisoners was because the directorate "had not organized a meeting with all heads of penal investigative sections in the country where they could exchange information and be given precise instructions for action".[51] Nevertheless, a *Securitate* report of September 1958 admitted that some officers continued to beat prisoners, thereby "breaking the most elementary rules of interrogation".[52]

It is difficult to give precise figures for the numbers of persons arrested and jailed in the Gheorghiu-Dej era for the simple reason that the *Securitate's* own statistics are contradictory. One Ministry of the Interior report states the following: in the ten years from 1948 to 1958, 58,733 persons were convicted of a multitude of crimes, all of which were of a political nature: conspiring against social order, belonging to subversive or terrorist organizations—these included the former democratic political parties and the Iron Guard—"hostile instigation against the regime", illegally crossing the frontier, failing to report a crime against the state, crimes "against humanity and activity against the working class", treason, espionage, distributing forbidden leaflets, sabotage, and "hostile religious activity". Most of those convicted received sentences ranging from one to ten years' imprisonment. A total of 73,310 persons were sentenced to imprisonment in the period 1945 to 1964, of whom 335 received the death penalty (for several it was commuted). A further 24,905 were acquitted or had the cases against them dropped. In addition, 21,068 people were sent to labour camps in the same period. The numbers of those who died in detention is given as 3,847, of whom 2,851 died while serving their sentence, 203 under interrogation, 137 as a result of the execution of the death sentence, and 656 in the labour camps.[53]

Yet another set of statistics shows that in the period from 1950 to 31 March 1958, 75,808 persons were arrested, of whom 73,636 were convicted. In the same period, 23,023 persons were sent to labour camps and between 1949 and 1958, about 60,000 put under house arrest.[54] Independent sources have produced quite a different set of figures; an examination of court records of the period indicates that in the years 1949 to 1960, 134,150 trials took place involving at least 549,400 accused.[55]

The majority of those sent to labour camps were not tried or sentenced. They were sent there on the orders of the Ministry of the Interior which itself was acting on instructions from the Gheorghiu-Dej and the Soviet counsellors. The euphemism 'administratively sentenced' (*condamnat administrativ*), which disguised the illegality of their plight, was used to justify their detention. Not even this fiction was employed to justify the arrest between 1948 and 1950 of the ministers of the pre-Communist regime, the bishops of the Greek and Roman Catholic Churches, and former policemen. There was no offence in the penal code to cover their arrest and they were imprisoned on the basis of orders issued by the Ministry of the Interior. This was the fate of Dumitru Caracostea, Minister of Education in the Gigurtu government of July 1940, and several hundred others who had held ministerial office in the preCommunist period. Caracostea was arrested in September 1950 and taken overnight to Sighet jail. On his certificate of release, issued on 6 July 1955, there are blank spaces against the number of the arrest warrant and the reason for his detention, proof from the authorities themselves that there was no legal basis for his arrest or for the five years of his imprisonment. Many of those detained in the labour camps were peasants who resisted the land reform of 2 March 1949. Their fate offers a graphic example of the use of coercion by the *Securitate* to implement the Communist revolution.

The ideological premise upon which collectivization was based was contained in the Communist Party resolution of 3–5 March. The main and most difficult task in the construction of socialism, it claimed, was the solution of the peasant problem. According to the Party there were five categories of people on the land. The first was formed by the agricultural proletariat, that is, landless peasants who numbered some 265,000 families and worked for the kulak or rich peasant. Poor peasants made up the second category. They had holdings of up to five hectares, which represented over 57% of the total area held by individuals. The resolution considered their plots unproductive, being scattered in many places over more than one lot, and concluded that the poor peasants would prefer a different form of production. The middle peasants formed the third category and produced 60% of the country's agricultural production. They used only family labour, had holdings of between five and 20 hectares which represented 34 per cent of the total area of cultivated land, and were to provide the nucleus of the collective farms. The fourth category consisted of rich peasants or kulaks (*chiaburi*) who were so defined because they hired labour or charged rent for machinery, and not because of the size of their holdings. The fifth category had been what remained of the landowning class, whose estates had been broken up by the 1945 land reform and distributed to peasants.[56]

Outlining the task facing the Party in imposing collectivization, Gheorghiu-Dej identified the first as "the complete liquidation of kulak property in the village".[57] They were not to be admitted to the collective farms. The second objective was to persuade the poor and middle peasants to unite in the collectives. The emphasis was upon persuasion and not coercion and as a preliminary step tillage associations (*întovărăşiri*) were set up. Nevertheless, harsh penalties were introduced for failure to deliver mandatory cereal quotas to the state and it was opposition to these that the first incidents of peasant resistance were reported in May in the village of Roma in the county of Botoşani when *Securitate* troops fired on demonstrators.[58] Large-scale disturbances occurred in July in Bihor which resulted in the execution by the *Securitate* of 16 peasants and the deportation of a further two hundred. There was more violence in August, this time in Arad County where 12 peasants were shot by *Securitate* troops and more than one hundred arrested.

Fear of peasant discontent led Ana Pauker, who was charged with directing the Agrarian Commission which had been established with the express aim of supervising the creation of the collectives, to proceed cautiously. Her strategy was in direct contradiction to the views of Veretenicov, one of the Soviet advisors to the Commission.[59] At a meeting of the Commission on 1 September 1949, she approved only four out of 12 proposals to set up collectives; of the remaining eight, she postponed the inauguration of half of them until conditions were met, and she rejected the other half outright. She displayed similar reserve at a session of the Council of Ministers on 13 September, when the proposed expropriation of peasant property was discussed:

> Purely and simply, there are to be no expropriations from poor and middle peasants for several thousand lei, because they're

> going to drink away the money and afterwards won't have anything to work with. They must receive other land in return... It's great to have a new railway, but it's not at all great to have peasant discontent.[60]

Only 56 collectives were set up in 1949, with isolated resistance to their establishment from the peasantry. But in January 1950, the Party Central Committee replaced the Agrarian Commission with an Agrarian Section and gave it increased resources to step up the campaign of collectivization. Despite this, Pauker rejected 655 of the 900 proposals for collectivization that were submitted to the Section in April. Her prudence did not carry the day for long. In the summer, while Pauker was in Moscow receiving treatment for breast cancer, the pace of collectivization was suddenly stepped up and in July and August approval was given for the creation of 1,012 new collectives, regardless of the conditions in the areas concerned. As a consequence, resistance from the peasants was countrywide.

Coercion now became the order of the day. The *Securitate* and militia were brought in, often in the middle of the night, to force peasants to register in the collectives. They were threatened with forced labour, or the expulsion of their children from school. Those that refused were arrested and taken to the People's Council headquarters where they were beaten and tortured. In the Cluj region some were given the choice of either paying a huge fine and spending ten years in jail, or joining a collective. Many families were expelled from their homes when their land was absorbed into the collective and received either poor quality land elsewhere in compensation or no land at all.

In several regions, such as Arad, Argeş, Dolj, Bihor, the Apuseni mountains, Vlaşca, Hunedoara and Timişoara, the peasants, sometimes aided by 'partisan groups', were engaged in violent skirmishes with the *Securitate* troops and militia. Peasant opposition to the reform resulted. In some areas buildings on the newly created collective farms were set on fire. This was the case in the county of Arad where *Securitate* reports show that after a state farm had been destroyed on 31 July 1949, frontier troops were summoned from Radna and restored order on 3 August after arresting 98 persons and shooting 12 peasants from the villages of Apateu, Somoşches, Berechiu and Sepreuş on the spot. Reports signed by the head of the *Securitate* office in Timişoara, Colonel Coloman Ambruş and his deputy Major Aurel Moiş, give details of what they called 'this rebellion' and mentioned that two other peasants were shot dead "while trying to escape while under arrest".[61]

An open rebellion took place in the north of Vlaşca County at the beginning of July. Peasants from more than a dozen villages armed themselves with pitchforks and axes and ransacked the local Party offices, destroying photographs of the Party leaders and cutting the telephone lines. Communist officials were beaten and driven from the buildings. The security forces were called in and fired on the protesters, killing ten of them and wounding many more. These events were repeated in several areas across the country.[62]

The accelerated process of collectivization coincided with increased pressure applied to the kulaks. After the introduction of the land reform, the kulaks had been permitted by the Party to rid themselves of the stigma of their class by 'donating' land to the collectives. This practice contributed considerably to the consolidation of the farms since the poorer peasants had little or no land to give. But in the summer of 1950, the Agrarian Section was told by the Party leadership that henceforth "*guilty* [my italics] kulaks should be sent to trial and their land confiscated".[63] The authorities in some counties dispensed with even this fig-leaf of legality by confiscating the land and sending the kulaks and their families to the Danube-Black Sea Canal without trial. Thousands suffered this fate. As Gheorghiu-Dej later admitted, "in the name of the struggle against the kulaks more than 80,000 peasants were sent for trial, the majority of them hard-working peasants, and of them more than 30,000 were tried in public proceedings".[64]

Gheorghiu-Dej claimed that these arrests were made on the orders of Ana Pauker[65] but, as mentioned above, she was in Moscow for six weeks in June and the whole of July 1950 receiving medical treatment, and she returned there in September, being unable to resume work until December. In her place, Alexandru Moghioroş, a close associate of Gheorghiu-Dej, issued instructions to the Agrarian Section, including the order of the arrest of kulaks.[66] Furthermore, her statements to the Agrarian Section after she resumed her duties indicate clearly that she regarded her gradual approach to collectivization as the best one and the use of force against the peasantry as a grave error. In January 1951, she proposed that the Central Committee introduce the penalty of a trial for those who forced peasants into collectives, declaring that "those who acted in this fashion aren't humans". Shortly afterwards, she halted the consolidation of the state farms (GOSTATS), a process that was due to be completed, according to the land reform, by 1952.

Pauker recognized the error of the policy of coercion in collectivization in addressing the Agrarian Section of the Central Committee on 28 April 1951:

> Instead of continuing on this path [the gradual one], a path that proved to be the best one, a path where things went more slowly and carefully—instead of this path, we began to use methods of forcefully pressuring the peasants to enter the collective farms... Starting in last summer, we proceeded with actions that are absolutely opposed to the line of our party and absolutely opposed to any serious Communist thought. Only someone irresponsible, only an adventurer, only a person cut off from the masses and from our party, only a person who imagines himself as here today and gone tomorrow can think that it is possible to establish collective farms with people who are coerced, and that such collective farms can possibly be viable.[67]

An internal Party report makes it plain that Pauker halted the creation of new collective farms during the winter of 1950–1951. "Our first concern", she argued, "must be the existing collectives, to strengthen them and transform them into examples for the individual peasants". As a consequence, not one new collective farm was set up in 1951; the 62 that were officially established that year (as compared with 971 in 1950) had actually been created and consolidated during the summer and autumn of 1950, but had not yet been formally inaugurated.[68]

Gheorghiu-Dej, too, also showed himself critical of the abuses committed during collectivization. In a speech delivered on 11 May 1951, he criticized the "methods of constraint used" which, he said, "had led to flagrant deviations from the Party line". Some regional committees had organized competitions for the creation of the largest number of collectives, and this had resulted "in a forced rate of growth in the number of collectives".[69] But such displays of regret can only strike the reader as cynical, since the Central Committee archives show quite clearly that the Party leadership knew full well what 'methods of constraint' were being used and did nothing to put a stop to them when they were mercilessly applied.

Indeed, on 3 July 1952, Gheorghiu-Dej called for the intensification of the campaign against the kulaks, calling on the press "to mobilize the mass of the working peasantry in the unremitting struggle against the kulaks".[70] The kulaks continued to be arrested in their thousands, often for the most petty oversights such as failing to tie up their dogs. A *Securitate* report of 1953 reported that 34,738 peasants had been arrested in 1951 and 1952, of whom 22,000 were kulaks.[71] Nevertheless, peasant opposition slowed down the progress of collectivization. By 1955, only 26 per cent of arable land had been collectivized or made over to state farms. In January 1958, there were numerous incidents in the county of Galaţi involving peasants who demanded that they be allowed to withdraw from the collectives, while on 12 January 1958, none other than Nicolae Ceauşescu, as a Party secretary for agriculture, is alleged to have given the militia orders to open fire on the villagers of Răstoaca in Vrancea, Moldavia who were against collectivization.[72] Throughout the following year, collective farms in various districts in Moldavia were attacked by peasants demanding their dissolution, and these actions were repeated across the country over the next three years, right up to the eve of Gheorghiu-Dej's announcement to a plenary meeting of the Central Committee on 27 April 1962 that collectivization had been completed.

Its results put 60 per cent of the total area of 15 million hectares of agricultural land in collective farms, 30 per cent in state farms, and left nine per cent in private hands. This last was upland whose inaccessibility made it impractical to collectivize.[73] The small peasant plots allowed to members of the collectives under the 1949 law represented six per cent of the collectivized area, thus giving a total of 15 per cent of land in private ownership after 1962. The cost of collectivization in human lives and misery is impossible to calculate.

The machinery of terror used against the peasantry to force through collectivization was set in motion by the Party to carry out the mass deportations of Serbs and Germans living in the western area of the Banat.[74] These groups were considered a security risk when tension between Yugoslavia and Romania grew following the former's expulsion from the Cominform in June 1948. Stalin coined a new heresy—'Titoism'—and the satellite states were forced to conduct a witch-hunt of senior cadres who were purged as an example to those who were alleged to have placed loyalty to their country before fidelity to Moscow. Following the Soviet lead, Yugoslav diplomats were expelled from Romania and the other Cominform states in 1949, and in 1950 Bulgaria forbade Yugoslav citizens the use of any land of theirs in the frontier zone which was on Bulgarian soil. The Romanian government stopped all rail and postal links with Yugoslavia in January 1950 on the grounds that Yugoslav espionage was taking advantage of them, and in the summer of that year put on trial a group of 12 Romanians of Serbian family accused of being "in the service of the espionage of Tito's Fascist clique", among them two former employees of the Yugoslav embassy in Bucharest. Three of the defendants were sentenced to death and the others received prison terms ranging from three to 25 years.[75]

The deportations from the Banat region began in the summer of 1951. On 14 November 1950, the *Securitate* finalized the deportation plan under the title "Evacuation plan of the frontier zone with Yugoslavia over a belt of 25 kilometres of elements who present a danger through their presence in the area". The operation was expected "not to exceed three months".[76] 40,320 persons were targeted for deportation from the area of Timişoara, Sânnicolau Mare, Oraviţa, Moldova Nouă, Reşiţa, Almaş, Turnu Severin, Baia de Aramă, Strehaia, Vânju Mare and Pleniţa. The *Securitate* classified the deportees as follows: 1,330 foreign citizens, 8,477 Bessarabians, 3,557 Macedonians, 2,344 persons who had collaborated with the German army during the war, 257 Germans, 1,054 'Titoists'; 1,218 people with relatives who had fled abroad, 367 persons who had helped the 'anti-Communist resistance', 731 "enemies of the socialist order", 19,034 kulaks and innkeepers, 162 former landowners and industrialists, and 341 convicted criminals. Many of the adult males had been enrolled in the Communist Party but this did not spare them their fate. Included in the number of deportees were 590 persons who lived outside the frontier zones. Under the plan they were all to be moved to the regions of Ialomiţa in the Bărăgan and Galaţi, more specifically to the villages of Bâlga, Ciulniţa, Călăraşi, Mărculeşti, Feteşti, Andrăşeşti, Perieţi, Bucu, Cioara, Lunca Dunării, Vădeni, Frumuşiţa, Dudeşti and Urleasca.[77]

The deportations themselves began on 16 June 1951 and were carried out by 10,229 officers and men from the Frontier Guards Academy at Oradea and from the Firemen's Training School. The whole operation was carried out under the strict supervision of Major General Mihail Burcă, the Deputy Minister of the Interior, and Major General Eremia Popescu, the commander of the Ministry of Interior troops (*trupele de securitate*).[78] For transporting the deportees 2,656 railway carriages were used and 6,211 lorries. Rumour of the impending deportations led many people to attempt to cross the frontier secretly into Yugoslavia, while others placed their children with friends and relatives outside the designated zone.

The first trains left between 16 and 20 June 1951. The deportees were only allowed to take what belongings they could carry, the rest of their property being bought by specially constituted commissions who paid them only a fraction of the value of the possessions. A shortage of trains meant that many of the deportees had to wait in the burning heat for two or three days in the fields. The special trains were guarded by troops and avoided stops in the main railway stations to prevent any communication with ordinary citizens. Upon arrival the fortunate deportees were allocated makeshift clay-walled huts with straw roofs in special settlements, some of which had been given Soviet names, such as 'Iosif Clisitch' in the region of Galaţi where 859 people were placed. Others, even on the *Securitate's* admission, were literally "dumped in the middle of nowhere in the full glare of the sun without the necessary means of shelter".[79] The same reports talk of a lack of drinking water and irregular supplies of bread, and many cases of children suffering from over-exposure to the sun. Despite these problems the deportees used the industry and enterprise typical of the population of the Banat to create new settlements which became a feature of the area.

A task of the *Securitate* as equally vital as that of removing alleged opponents of the regime was that of "defending the achievements of socialism" in Romania. For the *Securitate* and the militia, May Day—like the other red-letter days in the Communist calendar—was not a holiday as it was for most other citizens. On such a hallowed day, the destruction of a placard or of a poster presented a great danger to the regime through the example it offered and was therefore regarded as a crime against the state. Consequently, the Party leadership charged the *Securitate* with keeping a close eye on the crowds and careful stage management of the parades. The first directive in this respect was issued in 1952 by Gheorghe Pintilie and was renewed with only minor modifications up until the overthrow of the regime in 1989.[80] The *Securitate* was required to "guarantee the personal security and the homes of leading members of the Party and to ensure the orderly and peaceful conduct of the festivities throughout the country". Precise measures included the supervision by Securitate officers of the construction of the official stands which were to be guarded day and night by the militia. Officers were ordered to make background checks on every person involved in the construction, and to inspect all the drains and sewers around the stands and on the route taken by the parade. Five days before May Day, all persons who had access to the stands and those instructed by the Party to be in charge of rows and columns of marchers-by were to be verified. Similar checks were made on those serving drinks in the stands and on those who prepared the floats. An officer disguised in overalls was to ride in each of the latter.

Major General Alexandru Drăghici, Deputy Minister of the Interior at the time and the head of the political directorate of the Ministry, issued instructions that festooning with flags, ribbons and banners should begin on 28 April and the decorations removed on 3 May. On official buildings flags were to be flown in the proportion of 75 per cent red, party flags, 25 per cent the national tricolore.[81] As national Communism took the place of Stalinism, so the proportion of national flags increased. The *Securitate* was also given the job of making sure that there were stalls selling fried sausages and soft drinks along the parade route, that bouquets of flowers were made up for handing to the Party leaders in the stands. May Day, the international day of labour, was celebrated in a different fashion in the labour camps and in the prisons. A directive of the Ministry of the Interior, dated 8 April 1953, ordered normal working and a doubling of the guard. The only change for the prisoners was that no food parcels or mail would be delivered.[82]

With the imposition of Communist rule Romania was forced to turn its back on the West and face eastwards. The most graphic feature of this new stance was the adoption by Gheorghiu-Dej's regime of the Stalinist practice of mass arrests and imprisonment without trial. The application of the Soviet model in the Romanian legal system brought with it the notorious show trial which allowed the regime to dispose of its opponents under a cover of spurious legality. This was in marked contrast to the pre-war judicial regime which, despite its many flaws, was not the instrument of a single political party. The pre-war Romanian governments did not seek the elimination of a political class, nor did they rely upon the principle of guilt by association. The methods used by Gheorghiu-Dej against the Romanian people were also used against party members—the most prominent being Pătrăşcanu, Pauker, Luca and Georgescu—to keep them in line, all the time. This involved the violation of party statutes. Gheorghiu-Dej's interest in following the results of the stage management of Pătrăşcanu's trial by listening to the proceedings on a tape recorder echoes Stalin's presence on the balcony overlooking the Moscow show trials in 1937. Both leaders embodied the intrusiveness of the police state.

Notes

1 The structure of the *Securitate* between 1948 and 1989 is laid out in Dennis Deletant, *Ceauşescu and the Securitate. Coercion and Dissent in Romania, 1965–1989* (London: Hurst & Co., 1995), pp.57–67, 103–6 and 377–80.

2 The NKVD (Ministry of Internal Affairs) oversaw the Soviet Security Service between 1934 and 1943. In 1943, the service was renamed the NKGB, a designation it bore until 1946 when it became the MGB (in the same year the NKVD became the MVD). The MGB was itself rechristened the KGB in 1954. One example of the senior role given to NKVD agents in the security police was the appointment of Andrei Gluvacov as head of the *Siguranţa* in Braşov in 1947. He was born in Arad on 26 May 1914 and was a locksmith by trade. Arrested for Communist activity in the 1930s and suspected by the *Siguranţa* of having been trained in the Soviet Union as an NKVD agent, he was sentenced to six months' imprisonment which, according to his party file, he did not serve. He joined the Ministry of the Interior on 1 October 1945 (*Cartea Albă a Securităţii*, vol.I (Bucharest: SRI, 1995), doc.170, p.338).

3 The SSI (*Serviciul Secret de Informaţii al Armatei Române*), the Secret Intelligence Service of the Romanian Army), acquired a distinct status within the army in 1922, one which was consolidated by the appointment of Mihail Moruzov as its head in 1924 (or in 1925 according to some sources). Known as *Diviziunea II*, then *Secţia II*, it was reorganized and expanded in 1928 under Moruzov's supervision and formally christened the SSI. (Cristian Troncotă, *Mihai Moruzov şi Serviciul Secret de Informaţii al Armatei Române, Bucharest: Editura Evenimentul Românesc,* 1997, pp.44–47). On 13 November 1940, it was renamed *Serviciul Special de Informaţii*, relabelled simply *Serviciul de Informaţii* on 15 September 1944, and reverted to *Serviciul Special de Informaţii* on 27 April 1945.

4 The SSI, which was responsible for foreign espionage and counter-espionage, worked in parallel with directorates I and IV of the DGSP between 1948 and 1951 when it was absorbed into the *Securitate*. Regional directorates were established to cover the capital Bucharest and the cities of Braşov, Cluj, Constanţa, Craiova, Galaţi, Iaşi, Oradea Mare, Piteşti, Ploieşti, Sibiu, Suceava and Timişoara, and each of these directorates had its own organization corresponding to that of the ten national directorates to which they were subordinated. Each regional directorate was further subdivided into

county offices which themselves encompassed town and communes bureaux (*birouri de securitate*).

5 Nikonov was born in Bessarabia on 22 September 1905. His career is illustrative of the methods used by the NKVD/NKGB to infiltrate their agents. Nikonov had been expelled from Iaşi University where he was a student of chemistry for participating in Communist meetings and was sent to Brussels to continue his studies. From there he was moved to Marseilles where he was co-opted into the local leadership of the French Communist Party. From here he was brought back to Romania to run an espionage network but was caught, tried and imprisoned, first in Doftana jail and then, after its destruction in the earthquake of November 1940, in Caransebeş where he joined Bodnăraş and Pantelimon Bodnarenko. Upon his release following the 23 August *coup*, he was reassigned duties by INO, the Foreign Intelligence Directorate of the NKGB, and these were institutionalized with his appointment as head of Romanian foreign intelligence (SSI) on 9 January 1947. He continued in that position in the renamed service (DGSS) from the beginning of April 1951 until 6 January 1953 (Florian Banu, *De la SSI la SIE. O istorie a spionajului românesc în timpul regimului comunist (1948–1989)* (Bucharest: Corint, 2016), p.125). Official sources place him in March 1954 at the head of the Second Bureau of Military Intelligence of the Romanian General Staff with the rank of Lieutenant General, a post he retained until November1960 when he became head of the control directorate of the Ministry of Armed Forces. In December 1963, he was moved into the reserve. Nikonov died in 1999 (Florica Dobre, *Securitatea. Structuri-cadre, Obiective si Metode* [*The Security Police. Cadres, Objectives and Methods*], vol.1. Consiliul National pentru Studierea Arhivelor Securitatii (Bucharest: Editura Enciclopedică, 2006). p.702.

6 Bucicov was born on 8 December 1909 at Salabant in the district of Cetatea Albă in Bessarabia, at that time under Russian rule. According to his party file, he was a Romanian citizen of Russian nationality and a carpenter by trade. A brief biography of him appeared in a daily newspaper in 1995. In 1931, he deserted from the Romanian army to the Soviet Union from where he returned after several months to carry out espionage. He was arrested in September 1931, tried and sentenced by court martial in Chişinău to 15 years hard labour. He served his sentence at Ocnele Mari, Doftana, Caransebeş and in the camp at Târgu Jiu, from where he was released on 23 August 1944. From 1948 until his retirement in 1963, he worked in the Romanian Ministry of the Interior (*Ziua*, 5 June 1995, p.3). Research by Claudiu Secaşiu, to whom I am grateful for these details about Bucicov's career, has shown that Bucicov was enrolled in the Communist Patriotic Guards after 23 August 1944. It is not clear exactly when he became head of Gheorghiu-Dej's bodyguard (Directorate Six); evidence points to the fact that he held this position in January 1949 (ANIC, Archive of the Central Committee of the RCP, fond 1, dos. 198/1944 [rola --106-1-79-80], fila 173, cadrul 237; dos. 205/1944 [rola --106-1-79-81], f.207/c.572).

7 *Organizarea şi funcţionarea Organelor Ministerului de Interne de la Infiinţare până în prezent* (Bucharest: Ministry of the Interior, 1978), p.87.

8 Born in 1911 in Chişinău, Goncearuc joined the Communist Youth Movement in Bessarabia and in 1932 was sent to Moscow. Three years later, he was infiltrated back into Romania across the Dniester with a mission but was quickly captured, tried and sentenced to ten years imprisonment. After his release from Caransebeş jail in August 1944, he was given a post in the Administrative and Political Section of the Romanian Communist Party and in April 1945 transferred to the SSI. The personnel files shed light on the social background and competence of the *Securitate*. The head of Directorate I was Colonel Gavril Birtaş. He was born in 1905 in Baia Mare and was a carpenter by trade. He joined the Ministry of the Interior in 1946 and in April 1948 was head of the *Siguranţa* in Oradea. A character reference in his party file noted "an occasional inability to link theory to practice" (*Cartea Albă a Securităţii* (Bucharest: SRI, 1994),

vol.I, doc.168, p.337). Major Nicolae Briceag, chief of the Someş county office in the Regional Directorate of Cluj, was born in Negreni in Olt County in 1916 into a peasant family. A tailor by trade, he joined the Ministry of the Interior in 1945 and in April 1948 is recorded as being head of the *Siguranţa* in Dej. A character reference in his party file describes him as being "of mediocre intelligence" (*Cartea Albă a Securităţii*, vol.I, doc.164, p.335). Lt. Col. Mauriciu Strul, head of the Regional Directorate of Galaţi, was born 1911 in the commune of Sarmoş in the county of Mureş. He had a doctorate in law and practised as a lawyer before the war. He joined the Ministry of the Interior in 1945 and in April 1948 his party file records him as being head of the *Siguranţa* in Târgu-Mureş (*Cartea Albă a Securităţii*, vol.I, doc.158, p.332). Lt. Col. Ludovic Czeller, head of the Regional Directorate of Oradea, was born on 24 July 1896 in Kismarja, Hungary. He was a lathe operator by trade and joined the Romanian Ministry of the Interior in May 1945. He was described in his party file as having "a short temper". (*Cartea Albă a Securităţii* (Bucharest: SRI, 1995), vol.I, doc.163, p.334).

9 Eduard Mezincescu, Ecouri la Cazul Pătrăşcanu', *Magazin Istoric*, no.7 (July 1992), p.34.

10 Author's interview with T. Brătescu, 30 July 1994.

11 Christopher Andrew and Oleg Gordievsky, *KGB. The Inside Story of its Foreign Operations from Lenin to Gorbachev* (London: Sceptre, 1991), p.362.

12 Ana Toma was a close associate of Ana Pauker. When Pauker became Foreign Minister in November 1947, Toma was made secretary general of the Foreign Ministry, and in 1950 she was appointed Pauker's deputy. Toma and Iosif Chişinevski worked closely together. In August 1951, Chişinevski instructed Toma to make the travel arrangements for a visit made by him, Gheorghiu-Dej and Miron Constantinescu to Moscow to obtain from Stalin backing for the purge of Pauker, Luca and Georgescu. Chişinevski ordered Toma not to tell Pauker a word about the trip; Robert Levy, 'Did Ana Pauker Prevent a "Rajk Trial" in Romania?', *East European Politics and Societies*, vol.9, no.1, December 1994, p.164, note 127. Pauker's son-in-law, Gheorghe Brătescu, accused Toma of betraying Pauker in 1952 and for this reason he never spoke to her from that date until her death in 1993 (author's interview with G. Brătescu, 30 July 1994).

13 *Cartea Albă a Securităţii,* vol.II (Bucharest: SRI, 1995), doc.33, p.157.

14 The DGSP was organized in ten national or central directorates as follows: Information (I); Counter-sabotage (II); Counter-espionage in the Prisons and Police (III); Counter-espionage in the Armed Forces (IV); Penal Investigation (V); Protection of Ministers (VI); Technical (VII); Cadres (VIII); Political (responsible for Party purity) (IX); Administration (X). Auxiliary departments dealt with interception of mail, surveillance and eavesdropping and further included a cipher section and a secretariat. Thirteen regional directorates, including that for the city of Bucharest, were established.

15 According to his party file, Mazuru had joined the Communist Party in 1944 after the 23 August *coup*. He was born in 1915 in Chişinău, then under Russian rule. By profession he was a medical instrument technician. He joined the Ministry of the Interior in 1947 when he was made director of cadres (personnel). A report on his character and work dated 26 April 1948 and signed by B. Fuchs as responsible for the personnel of the *Siguranţa*, described him as "attentive to the needs of his colleagues, energetic, combative, courageous, vigilant and harsh with his enemies... He is liked by his subordinates, is authoritarian, but at the same time friendly". *Cartea Albă a Securităţii*, vol.1, doc.170, p.338.

16 Nikita Petrov, *По сценарию Сталина. Роль органов НКВД-МГБ СССР в советизации стран Центральной и Восточной Европы. 1945–1953 гг* [Po scenariu Stalina: Rol organov NKVD-MGB SSSR v sovietizacii stran Centralnoy i Vostochnoy Evropi 1945–1953] *(According to Stalin's scenario. The role of the bodies NKVD-MGB of the USSR in the sovietization of Central and Eastern Europe. 1945–1953)* (Moscow: Rospen., 2011), p.336. Other Soviet advisors were Serghei Vasilievici Patrakeev (1919–1985)

(MGB), appointed in November 1949, Serghei Surenovici Spandarian (1909–1980) (MGB), June 1950-November 1951, and Vitalie Ghennadievici Cernaviki (1920–2005) (MVD, June-July 1953) (Petrov, *According to Stalin's Scenario*, pp.338–45).

17 Andrew and Gordievsky, *KGB*, p.349.

18 See chapter one, footnote 55; also Eduard Mezincescu, 'Polemici', *România literară*, no.27 (9–15 September 1992), p.2.

19 Paul Ştefănescu, *Istoria Serviciilor Secrete Româneşti* (Bucharest: Divers Press, 1994), p.250; see also Vladimir Tismăneanu, 'The Tragicomedy of Romanian Communism', *East European Politics and Societies*, vol.3, no.2 (Spring 1989), p.350, note 47.

20 M. Oprea, 'Zeii de lut ai Securităţii Române', *Dilema*, III, no.133, p.11. Pintilie was appointed a Deputy Minister of the Interior in 1950, a position he held until 1962.

21 *Ibid.*

22 *Ibid.*

23 He was born on 2 June 1915 in Chişinău. In 1932, he joined the Union of Communist Youth in his native town and in the following year was detained for two weeks by the *Siguranţa*. Between 1937 and 1939, he did his military service in a signals regiment in Iaşi and after being demobbed he obtained a position in the telephone exchange in Chişinău. In December 1940, six months after the Soviet annexation of Bessarabia, he was recruited by the NKVD and moved to Cernăuţi where he underwent training as an agent of the foreign intelligence directorate (INO) of the NKVD. Supplied with false Romanian identity papers in the name of Vasile Ştefănescu, he was sent across the frontier on 26 May 1941 to gather information on Romanian troop movements. Within two hours he was arrested by Romanian frontier guards. According to the record of his interrogation, his rudimentary knowledge of Romanian betrayed his foreign identity and he passed himself off as an ethnic Russian with the name of Alexandru Sergheevici Nicolski. He was tried for espionage in July 1941 and sentenced to forced labour for life. The first part of his sentenced was served in Ploieşti jail from where he was moved to Aiud to join other imprisoned Soviet spies, among them Vladimir Gribici, Simion Zeigner and Afanasie Şişman, all of whom stayed after their release in August 1944 in Romania. Nikolski died in Bucharest on 16 April 1992.

24 I am grateful to Claudiu Secaşiu for this information.

25 *Suppression of Human Rights in Romania* (Washington, DC: The Rumanian National Committee, 1949), p.65.

26 *Cuvântul*, no. 119 (May), 1992, p.6.

27 Deletant, *Ceauşescu and the Securitate*, p.63.

28 The Composition of the *Securitate* by ethnic background in 1948 was as follows:

Total number of personnel of all ranks of whom 3,973
Jews (J) 338
Hungarians (H) 247
Russians (Rus) 24
Germans (G) 5
Armenians (Ar) 3
Czechs (Cz) 5
Italians (It) 1
Bulgarians (B) 3
Yugoslavs (Y) 13
Romanians (R) 3334

For further details see Deletant, *Ceauşescu and the Securitate*, p.63.

29 The heavy recruitment of manual workers into the *Securitate* is mentioned in the annual report for 1949 of Section Three of the First Directorate which dealt with the Orthodox Church. Thirty-two per cent of its personnel was made up of factory workers

while only 40 per cent had some professional training or experience in security matters (Arhiva Serviciului Român de Informaţii (henceforth ASRI), fond D, file no. 9051, vol.2, p.10).

30 Some of these reports are reproduced in *Cartea Albă a Securităţii*, Vol.II.

31 Frank Gardiner Wisner (23 June, 1909, Laurel, Mississippi—29 October, 1965, Locust Hill Farm, Maryland). Wisner's experience in Romania alerted him to the insidious nature of Communist practice and with the support of George Kennan he was instrumental in the creation in 1948 of the Office of Special Projects. Wisner was appointed director. Shortly afterwards it was renamed the Office of Policy Coordination (OPC) and became the espionage and counter-intelligence branch of the CIA. Wisner became a legend in his own time for his work in covert operations during the Cold War but the stress associated with this work was the likely cause of his suicide, with his son's shotgun. In the opinion of Ernest Latham, the most complete account of Wisner's career is probably that given by Evan Thomas in *The Very Best Men: Four Who Dared: The Early Years of the CIA* (New York: Simon and Shuster, 1995); see E.H. Latham Jr., *Timeless and Transitory. 20th Century Relations Between Romania and the English-Speaking World* (Bucharest: Vremea, 2012), p.330, footnote 58.

32 ASRI, fond 'D', file no. 9189, p.7.

33 To ensure the obedience of the army it was purged and a People's Army created under the supervision of a Party controlled body called 'The Higher Political Directorate of the Army' (*Direcţia Superioară Politică a Armatei)*. The DSPA was set up on 28 March 1948 and was staffed by officers known as 'political educators'. It was organized in five directorates responsible for planning and organization, administration and accounting, education in the military schools and colleges, propaganda and cadres or personnel. In addition it managed the Army Central Club, the Centre for Physical Education, the Military Institute and Army publications. An indication of the importance attached by the regime to the DSPA was the elevation of the civilian designated to be its head in March 1950 to the post of Deputy Minister of the Armed Forces with the rank of Lieutenant General; the civilian in question was Nicolae Ceauşescu. The DSPA exercised Party control in all army units. At the level of the division it was organized through a political council composed of a Party secretary, and secretaries for propaganda, for organization, for culture and sport and for the Communist Youth Organization, the UTM, to which all conscripts belonged. All such secretaries held senior military rank, and virtually all army officers were Party members. At the regimental level there was a Party committee with secretaries corresponding to the divisional ones, while in the battalions there was usually a single 'political commander' who held the rank of major and was responsible for organizing regular lectures on Party. The political commander authorized the posting of wall newspapers (*gazete de perete*) which contained anonymous criticism and, sometimes, denunciation of troops and officers. Reciprocal spying was encouraged under the euphemism of 'revolutionary vigilance' and reports were passed on either to Section II for military intelligence of the General Staff, or to the Fourth Directorate of the DGSP which dealt with military counter-intelligence. Ever since the imposition of the Groza government in March 1945 the activity of Section II of the General Staff had been closely monitored by Soviet officers and in 1948 a number were formally attached as counsellors to train young pro-Soviet Romanian officers in the work of counter-espionage. On 15 February 1951 Section II of the General Staff was renamed the Directorate for Intelligence of the General Staff and on 2 April was transferred from the Ministry of National Defence to the Ministry of the Interior. Throughout the period of Communist rule control of the frontier guards (*trupele de grăniceri*) alternated between the Ministry of National Defence and the Ministry of the Interior.

34 *Cartea Albă a Securităţii* (Bucharest: SRI, 1995), vol.II, p.45.

35 The officers in charge of all surveillance were Alexandru Nicolski (until 1954), Tănase Evghenie (1954–57), Vasile Negrea (1957–65), and Cornel Onescu (1965–67). The heads of unit T were Alexandru Neacşu (1948–52), Nicolae Panaitescu (1952–53),

Alexandru Szacsko (1953–61), and Ovidiu Diaconescu (1961–89). (ASRI, Fond 9604, vol.IV) document published in *Sfera Politicii*, no.44 (1996), pp.44–45).

36 *Sfera Politicii*, no.44, p.44 and G. Ionescu, *Communism in Rumania, 1944–1962* (London: Oxford University Press, 1964), p.201.

37 *Cartea Albă a Securităţii*, Vol.II, p.64.

38 W. Bacon, 'Romanian Secret Police', in J.R. Adelman (ed.), *Terror and Communist Politics: The Role of the Secret Police* (Boulder and London: Westview Press, 1984), p.135.

39 *Cartea Albă a Securităţii*, vol.II, p.47.

40 Bacon, 'Romanian Secret Police', p.142.

41 The principal duties of the security troops were to maintain public order in the major industrial centres and to quell any resistance to government measures such as collectivization or appropriation of goods and property. In December 1951 the number of security troops stood at 2,000 officers, 3,000 non-commissioned officers, and 59,000 rank-and-file functionaries; see Dennis Deletant, 'Romania', in Krzysztof Persak and Lukasz Kaminski (eds.), *A Handbook of the Communist Security Apparatus in East Central Europe, 1944–1989* (Warsaw: Institute of National Remembrance, 2005), pp.285–328 [289].

42 Bacon, 'Romanian Secret Police', p.142.

43 Ionescu, *Communism in Rumania*, p.217. The *procuratura* was divided into 12 directorates whose powers included the direction of military, state security and criminal prosecutions, the supervision of court activities and of militia criminal investigations, the fixing of penal sentences and inspection of prisons.

44 V. Veniamin, 'The Judiciary', in *Captive Rumania. A Decade of Soviet Rule* (London: Atlantic Press, 1956), p.313.

45 G. Tomaziu, *Jurnalul unui Figurant* (Bucharest: Univers, 1995), p.173; see the same author's *The Witness*, edited and translated by Jane Reid, (London: Theed Street Publishing, 2015).

46 This view was implicit in the question put by Mircea Vulcănescu to the court, after studying the case brought against him in January 1948 as an alleged war criminal, was whether his accusers 'were seeking the punishment of a guilty man or the sacrifice of a victim' (M. Vulcănescu, *Ultimul Cuvânt*, Bucharest: Humanitas, 1992, p.23). Vulcănescu, a university teacher of sociology, served as Undersecretary of State in the Ministry of Finance (January 1941–August 1944) in the Antonescu government. Like all ministers who had served under Antonescu, irrespective of their portfolios, Vulcănescu was arrested under the Law for the Prosecution and Punishment of Those Guilty of War Crimes or Crimes against Peace or Humanity, gazetted on 18 August 1947. He was found guilty and sentenced to eight years' hard labour. He died in Aiud prison on 28 October 1952 at the age of 48.

47 The role of the confession in the Moscow trials is examined in *Ritual of Liquidation. The Case of the Moscow Trials* (Glencoe, Illinois: The Free Press, 1954), pp.81–276.

48 This was given the Orwellian term in Romanian of giving a declaration "in a state of freedom" (*în fază de libertate).*

49 Dulgheru was dismissed from the Ministry of the Interior on 5 May 1955.

50 *Cartea Albă a Securităţii*, Vol.II, p.57.

51 *Ibid.*, p.58.

52 *Ibid.*, p.60.

53 These figures were compiled by Service 'C' of the Ministry of the Interior and were communicated to me privately. I have no date for their compilation. The editors of the official history of the *Securitate*, *Cartea Albă a Securităţii*, appear not to be aware of these figures for they claim that a lack of documentation makes it impossible to give an exact figure for the numbers of persons who died while in the custody of the Securitate during the period of terror under Gheorghiu-Dej (vol.II, p.73). Corneliu Coposu, the secretary of Peasant Party leader Maniu and himself an inmate of Romanian prisons

for 17 years, put the number of those arrested after 1947 as 282,000, of whom he estimated 190,000 to have died in detention. (C. Coposu, *Dialoguri cu Vartan Arachelian* (Bucharest: Editura Anastasia, 1992), p.95). His figures appear to be exaggerated.

54 The use of house arrest in 1949 was illegal since there was no legislation in place to authorize it. The breakdown by year of the figure of 75,808 persons arrested is as follows:

1950: 6,636 1955: 3,332.
1951: 19,236 1956: 2,357
1952: 24,826 1957: 3,257
1953: 4,730 1958: 6,362
1954: 5,073

Cartea Albă a Securităţii, Vol.III (Bucharest: SRI, 1995), p.159.

55 M. Lupu, C. Nicoară, and G. Onişor, *Cu unanimitate de voturi* (Bucharest: Fundaţia Academia Civică, 1997), p.22.

56 O. Roske, 'Colectivizarea agriculturii în România, 1949–1962', *Arhivele Totalitarismului*, vol.1, no.1 (1993), p.151 and H.L. Roberts, *Rumania. Political Problems of an Agrarian State* (New Haven, Connecticut: Yale University Press, 1951), p.324.

57 A chronology of collectivization is to be found in O. Roske, *Colectivizarea*, pp.146–68.

58 *Ibid.*

59 The other Soviet advisors were listed as Sevcenco, Potimkin, Zubcov, Bobovnicov, Homeacov and Tomoshenco; see R. Levy, 'The "Right Deviation" of Ana Pauker', *Communist and Post-Communist Studies*, vol.28, no.2, June 1995, p.251, note 90. A study of Central Committee papers reveals that Pauker, contrary to popular belief generated by Gheorghiu-Dej and his acolytes, was not an ardent advocate of rapid collectivization and was indeed guilty of the charge levelled against her in 1952 after her purge, of "disregarding Soviet experience and the assistance given by Soviet advisors... and not taking measures that put their advice into practice". (See Levy, *The Right Deviation*, p.251).

60 Levy, *The Right Deviation*, p.242.

61 *România liberă*, 2 October 1993, p.16.

62 O. Roske, *Colectivizarea*, p.156.

63 Levy, *The Right Deviation*, p.244.

64 Gheorghe Gheorghiu-Dej, *Articole şi cuvîntări, iunie 1961-decembrie 1962* (Bucharest: Editura Politică,1962), p.206.

65 Ionescu, *Communism in Rumania*, p.201.

66 Levy, *The Right Deviation*, p.245.

67 *Ibid.*, p.246.

68 *Ibid.*, pp.246–47.

69 Roske, *Colectivizarea*, p.158.

70 *Ibid.*, p.160.

71 *Cartea Albă a Securităţii*, Vol.II, doc. 189, p.426.

72 *România liberă*, 22 April 1996, p.1.

73 In the upland region of Maramureş, for example, only Ieud commune and Săpânţa were collectivized by 1962. The kulaks in these two villages who resisted were arrested, tried and sent to prison.

74 A comparison of the fate of the population in the Romanian Banat with that in the Yugoslav Banat is made by Irina Marin in her *Contested Frontiers in the Balkans: Ottoman and Habsburg Rivalries in Eastern Europe* (London: I.B. Tauris, 2012), pp.147–50.

75 *Trial of the Group of Spies and Traitors in the Service of the Espionage of Tito's Fascist Clique* (Bucharest, 1950). It is not clear whether the death sentences were carried out.

76 A register of the numbers deported from the Banat and from which villages is contained in *Rusalii '51 Fragmente din deportarea în Bărăgan'* (Timişoara: Editura Marineasa, 1994), pp.217–31. See also *România liberă*, 2 July 1993, p.11.
77 *Rusalii '51*, p.228.
78 Burcă was a mechanic who had joined the Communist Party in his twenties and was one of a group of young Romanians who volunteered to fight in the Spanish Civil War. Like several of his colleagues, he was withdrawn to the Soviet Union after that war and interned for a period. He returned to Romania in October 1944. He died in Bucharest on 21 December 1994.
79 *România liberă*, 2 July 1993, p.11.
80 'Directiva în vederea măsurilor de ordine, pază şi securitate cu ocazia zilei de I MAI 1952', ASRI, Fond 'D', vol.9897, pp.416–27.
81 Order no. SO111713 of 18 April 1952.
82 Details of this directive were given to me by Marius Oprea.

5 Gheorghiu-Dej's path to dominance

If Gheorghiu-Dej had played his part in scenarios provided by Stalin since the imposition of Communist rule in Romania, from 1952 he was offered the opportunity to direct. This was amply demonstrated when the order came from Stalin to purge alleged Zionists.[1] Apart from its political impact the purge had a further significance, in that it continued the pattern of internecine struggles that characterized the history of the RCP; and in doing so it reinforced a culture of violence and fear that the anti-Semitic far-right Iron Guard had introduced to Romania in the interwar years. Indeed, Gheorghiu-Dej had conducted his own purge in the murder of Ştefan Foriş.[2]

It was precisely because of Gheorghiu-Dej's loyalty to Moscow that he was able to eclipse his rivals. His method was the show trial.[3] Over a period of ten years, Gheorghiu-Dej oversaw the removal of three comrades whom he regarded as potential rivals for power; the first, Ştefan Foriş, was murdered; the second, Lucreţiu Pătrăşcanu, was executed after a cursory trial; and the third, Ana Pauker, reduced to the state of a political corpse. That Gheorghiu-Dej should have reached this position was, in part, testimony to his own abilities, those of a patient tactician and consummate manipulator. But his consolidation of power depended on his avoidance of giving his Soviet master any reason to question his loyalty. His vulnerability to Stalin's suspicions was all the greater because he, alone, amongst the leading figures in the Romanian Communist Party, had not been schooled in Moscow and was therefore something of an unknown quantity, as Georgi Dimitrov, Comintern secretary, admitted to Ana Pauker in September 1944.[4] To correct this disadvantage Gheorghiu-Dej did two things: first, he surrounded himself with a number of NKVD agents who had been held in prison during the war, and appointed them to senior positions in the security services and the Ministry of the Interior, thereby offering Stalin a guarantee of his loyalty. Among them were Pantelimon Bodnarenko, Sergei Nikonov, Pyotr Goncearuc, Misha Postanski and Vania Didenko. The latter was one of Gheorghiu-Dej's closest friends and had escaped with him in August 1944 from Târgu Jiu.[5] Second, Gheorghiu-Dej used every opportunity to exploit the potential flaws in the actions of his rivals, thereby giving Stalin grounds for doubting their reliability, whilst at the same time reinforcing his own credentials as a faithful servant.

Although Gheorghiu-Dej was not directly involved in the planning of the *coup* on 23 August 1944, his victory in the contest for Party control secured for him the credit in Communist historiography of a leading role not only in the preparations, but also in the events of the day. After the arrest of Pătrăşcanu in 1948 there was, predictably, no mention of the latter's part as the representative of the Communist Party in the discussions of the National Democratic bloc preceding the *coup* until the early 1960s. Typical of the regime's version of the *coup* was the view, promoted by Gheorghiu-Dej in a speech in May 1960, that King Michael "was forced to accept the plan of action established by the Communist Party, the only genuine political force active in the toppling of Antonescu's government".[6] The magnification of Gheorghiu-Dej's part in the *coup* was facilitated by the fact that his rivals for the leadership, Ana Pauker and Vasile Luca, were still in the Soviet Union on 23 August 1944 and could therefore claim no credit at all.

The *coup*, and the use made of it by Gheorghiu-Dej, was but one of the two events from which we can trace the origins of the internal Party struggle for supremacy. The second, which also took place in the summer of 1944 before the entry of Soviet troops into Bucharest, was the decision to remove Ştefan Foriş as general secretary of the Party in April 1944. For this reason, Foriş's fate and the obfuscation surrounding it is essential to our understanding of Gheorghiu-Dej's claim to legitimacy as Party leader. According to the version propagated during the period of Gheorghiu-Dej's supremacy within the Party, a meeting was held on 4 April in the hospital of the Târgu Jiu internment camp involving Gheorghiu-Dej, Emil Bodnăraş, Constantin Pârvulescu, Iosif Ranghet and Chivu Stoica at which Dej demanded the removal of Foriş on the grounds that he was a police informer.[7] In his place a provisional secretariat of Bodnăraş, Pârvulescu and Ranghet was appointed by those present who also instructed Bodnăraş, Pătrăşcanu and Ion Gheorge Maurer to join the other political parties in an effort to extract Romania from the war with the Soviet Union. Both these decisions were instrumental in establishing the authority of Gheorghiu-Dej and his associates over the Party, and in presenting Stalin with an effective Party leadership which played a significant part in the overthrow of Antonescu and in the new government. The latter role provided the basis for the Party's claim for broader support within the country and Gheorghiu-Dej exploited this to the full in the Party's propaganda after 23 August 1944.

It is, however, important, in the light of the subsequent ascent of Gheorghiu-Dej, to remember that he was not appointed Party leader at this meeting. Nevertheless, in the course of time, Gheorghiu-Dej came to be portrayed in the Communist media as having been the architect of the decision to exclude Foriş, for it served both as a stick with which to beat rivals such as Pauker who had allegedly questioned his removal, and as a banner of Gheorghiu-Dej's defence of Romanian interests when the rift with Moscow occurred in the early 1960s.[8] Yet the merit to be gained from Foriş's removal depended on his being proved a 'traitor'. Without that proof his dismissal and, more importantly, his murder had no justification. Barely three years after Gheorghiu-Dej's death, the accusation of being a 'traitor' made against Foriş was dropped: in April 1968, at the Party Plenary Meeting, Nicolae Ceauşescu condemned Gheorghiu-Dej for the 'assassination' of Foriş, who was considered 'innocent' of being an enemy agent. Nevertheless, Foriş was still branded as guilty of 'grave shortcomings' in his work which had made his dismissal necessary.[9]

Throughout the Communist era, the responsibility for the decision to remove Foriş as Party secretary was attributed to Gheorghiu-Dej but the close involvement in its implementation of Bodnăraş and of Gheorghiu-Dej's closest friend, Vania Didenko, an NKVD agent, imprisoned for espionage in favour of the Soviet Union, has since led to a finger of suspicion being pointed also at Moscow.[10] After Foriş and his assistant Victoria Sârbu were taken into custody by Bodnăraş on 4 April and moved to a safe house, they were instructed by Bodnăraş to write material for the underground Party newspaper *România liberă*. This requirement lapsed within a month, causing Foriş and Sârbu to demand "clarification of their situation".[11] Eventually Bodnăraş and Didenko separated Foriş from Sârbu, taking the former away to another safe house until 24 December 1944 when he was reunited with his partner. At the beginning of January 1945, Bodnăraş and Didenko returned, telling the couple that they had been found innocent of the accusation that they had collaborated with the wartime *Siguranţa* and that they were free to go to Cluj where the Party had found work for them. But it seems that Foriş was not satisfied with this decision and he threatened to go to Hungary and serve the Communists there. This would explain why, according to Sârbu, two *Securitate* officers appeared on 23 March 1945 and took Foriş to the Ministry of the Interior where he was held for several days for questioning about his activities.[12]

Foriş seemed to sense his end was approaching for he made his will on 7 April.[13] At the end of that month, Sârbu gave birth to a daughter whom she named Vera-Victoria. During the following month, Foriş and Sârbu were able to spend a few days together. On 9 June, he went into town to buy food for a trip he intended to make to see one of Sârbu's brothers who lived in the country. That was last time that a member of Foriş's circle saw him. Later that summer, Foriş's mother came to see Eduard Mezincescu, head of the Patriotic Defence organization which provided food and money for former Communist detainees, with a request for help in tracing her son but he was unable to help.[14]

Just as the decision to remove Foriş was used as a political expedient, first by Gheorghiu-Dej and later by Nicolae Ceauşescu, so too was the order to murder him. Some historians have attributed the decision solely to Gheorghiu-Dej, others, basing themselves on Ceauşescu's account given at the April 1968 Central Committee plenum at which Foriş was rehabilitated, to a collective decision by Gheorghiu-Dej, Pauker, Luca and Teohari Georgescu.[15] It is difficult to believe that such a move would have been taken without at least the acquiescence of Stalin, especially as it required the liquidation of a former Party leader without trial. Once again, the fact that, according to documents produced at the Party Plenary Meeting of 22–25 April 1968, the murder was entrusted to Pintilie Bodnarenko (Gheorghe Pintilie), an NKVD agent, is not without significance. Bodnarenko, as head of the Political and Administrative Section of the Central Committee whose attributes included Party security, is alleged to have admitted carrying out the death sentence imposed on Foriş. The latter was seized in the street by Pintilie on Gheorghiu-Dej's orders and held in cells in the Ministry of the Interior. In the summer of 1946, he was taken by officers under the command of Petre Bulgaru to Party headquarters on Aleea Alexandru on the pretext of being questioned there. Upon arrival, he had a final discussion with Alexander Nicolski, who asked him about a notebook found in the safe house in which he had given details of his activity during the war. He was then taken to an annexe where he was bludgeoned to death with an iron bar by Gheorghe Pintilie and his chauffeur, Dumitru Mitea. His body was buried in the grounds of the building.[16]

Persistant enquiries from Foriş's mother about her son's whereabouts led Pintilie to summon her to his office in the summer of 1947. He failed to convince her that no one in the Party had any information about him. Pintilie then ordered Gavril Birtaş, head of the *Securitate* in Oradea, a town in western Transylvania, to take the old woman and "silence her". Pintilie persuaded Foriş's mother to get into Birtaş's car by saying that her son was in the Oradea area and that Birtaş knew exactly where. Asked later what he had done with her, Birtaş said that he had handed Foriş's mother over to two policemen in Oradea who had thrown her into the Criş river with a millstone hung around her neck.[17]

Gheorghiu-Dej's internment came to an end on 12 August 1944 when a group of Communists, under instructions from Ion Gheorghe Maurer, managed to extract both him and his close friend, Vania Didenko, from Târgu Jiu. They found shelter for several days with a series of sympathizers in Oltenia, among them an Orthodox priest, Ioan Marina, who put them up in his parish house in Râmnicul Vâlcea, from where they continued their journey to Bucharest.[18]

Although Gheorghiu-Dej was credited throughout the era of his dominance and the Ceauşescu period with being general secretary of the Party after the dismissal of Foriş, a study of the Party newspaper *Scânteia* reveals otherwise.[19] In its first non-clandestine issue of 21 September 1944, a communiqué signed by Constantin Pârvulescu was published. He was styled "general secretary of the Romanian Communist Party". The following day's edition printed his photograph with the same title. Over the next few weeks, Pârvulescu was given titular precedence in the paper when Party documents were reproduced, but two other ethnic Romanians, Gheorghiu-Dej and Pătrăşcanu, were given the most column inches.[20]

In the first few weeks after the 23 August *coup*, Pătrăşcanu overshadowed Gheorghiu-Dej as the most prominent Communist; his gradual eclipse from his leading position stemmed from Gheorghiu-Dej's resentment towards him. Pătrăşcanu had joined the Party well over a decade before Gheorghiu-Dej and came from a middle-class background quite removed from Gheorghiu-Dej's working-class origins. He was born in 1900 in the Moldavian town of Bacău in 1900; his father was a writer and professor and Pătrăşcanu himself achieved distinction in his academic studies, graduating in law at Bucharest University in 1922 and completing a doctorate at Leipzig on the agrarian reform of 1918–21 in Romania. He continued his studies in France and was one of five Communists elected to the Romanian parliament in 1931 although he never took his seat because the elections were declared invalid, and from the autumn of 1933 until the spring of 1934 was the permanent representative of the Romanian Communist Party to the Comintern. On his return to Romania, he worked in the propaganda section of Party in Iaşi. During this period he acted as defence counsel for a number of Communists and was himself arrested six times between 1924 and 1941, although the longest period he was held for questioning was two months.[21]

The contrast between Gheorghiu-Dej and Pătrăşcanu was highlighted even in their treatment by the authorities. While Gheorghiu-Dej and associates such as Gheorghe Apostol, Alexandru Moghioroş and Gheorghe Stoica were sentenced to long prison terms, Pătrăşcanu was simply placed under surveillance by the *Siguranţa* and his home frequently searched. This apparent leniency on the part of the police towards Pătrăşcanu was to be used later by Gheorghiu-Dej to support the accusation that he was a police informer, and after Pătrăşcanu's arrest in 1948 Gheorghiu-Dej instructed his interrogators to extract confessions from Pătrăşcanu's friends to this effect.[22] Pătrăşcanu's relatively gentle treatment at the hands of the Antonescu regime was exemplified by the fact that he was only briefly interned on two occasions during the war, for five months in 1940, and for eight months in Târgu Jiu in 1943,[23] and that for the rest of the time he was confined to the family villa at the mountain resort of Poiana Ţapului where he wrote two major political studies. In December 1943, he obtained permission to spend twenty days in the capital on medical grounds and extended his stay until May 1944. This he was able to do with the help of his cousins Colonel Ştefan Stoica, who worked at the Ministry of Military Procurement, and Colonel Octav Ulea, who was on the staff of the Marshal of the Palace. During his stay in the capital Pătrăşcanu was able to meet the King as well as opposition leaders. According to *Siguranţa* records, Pătrăşcanu was unable to get permission to remain in the capital after May and he therefore went into hiding, but this did not prevent him from continuing to negotiate on behalf of the Party with the other parties in the National Democratic bloc between April and August 1944. Pătrăşcanu's subsequent appointment as the only Communist minister in the Sănătescu government, and then as Minister of Justice from November 1944 until February 1948, enhanced his standing both within some circles in the Party and within the country.

Coupled with Gheorghiu-Dej's resentment of Pătrăşcanu's growing public stature was an envy of his intellectual powers. Gheorghiu-Dej, by contrast, had little formal education and published nothing. In 1944 and 1945, Pătrăşcanu authored two major political studies and was the author of several articles in *Scînteia* on industrialization in Romania. Pătrăşcanu's analytical publications on the interwar period had already given him prestige among the intellectuals of the Romanian Communist Party and Gheorghiu-Dej came to fear that Pătrăşcanu was seeking to capitalize upon this in order to make himself the centre of a popular movement rivalling the Gheorghiu-Dej leadership of the Party.[24] This attempt had become manifest in the propagation of the slogan 'Pătrăşcanu la putere' (Pătrăşcanu to power) which was chanted at several Communist-organized meeting held in September and October 1944. It has been suggested that Pătrăşcanu had the support of

> a small group of genuinely revolutionary intellectuals, mostly young and of Jewish extraction, who, like him, were already sickened by the ease with which opportunists, politicians and intellectuals alike, were given full rights in the Communist Party under the new leadership.[25]

A manifestation of Gheorghiu-Dej's displeasure at Pătrăşcanu's popularity was recalled by Gheorghe Pintilie who related that when a column of supporters shouted out Pătrăşcanu's name at a demonstration in early 1945, Gheorghiu-Dej tugged his arm and whispered 'Bugger that Pătrăşcanu.'[26]

But while Pătrăşcanu offered a reassuring face of the Party to the population, with his neatly groomed appearance and his suit and tie, the smoothness of his public image obscured a distrust which the Russians were beginning to feel about him. Pătrăşcanu had aroused the suspicion of the Russians at the armistice negotiations in September 1944 with his close questioning of Molotov over some of the conditions.[27] Bodnăraş, aware of these suspicions, had Pătrăşcanu placed under close surveillance following the latter's return from Moscow in September, as Pătrăşcanu revealed under interrogation in 1949.[28]

Soviet suspicions about Pătrăşcanu can only have been confirmed by comments made about him by Vasile Luca in a conversation with V. Morev, the TASS correspondent in Romania, in December 1944. Luca is reported to have said that Pătrăşcanu's words "did not always reflect the point of view of the Communist Party". Pătrăşcanu, Luca continued, "is not even a member of the Central Committee, he entered by chance into history, and found himself at the helm of events. He is not a consistent Communist".[29]

Moscow's knowledge of Pătrăşcanu's secret meetings with members of the National Peasant and National Liberal parties, with a view to finding a way out of the impasse created by King Michael's demand on 20 August 1945 for the Groza government's resignation, hardened those suspicions, as the Party enquiry into the Pătrăşcanu case reported in 1968. Although Pătrăşcanu later declared under interrogation that he had informed the Party about these discussions with Grigore Niculescu-Buzeşti, Victor Rădulescu-Pogoneanu, Constantin Vişoianu and Ion Mocsony-Styrcea—all confidants of the King—he admitted hiding from it the proposal made to him that he should become prime minister.[30] Their deliberations, in any case, were rendered pointless in the face of the Russians' firm rejection of Michael's demand and his eventual submission.[31]

Gheorghiu-Dej was to play on this Soviet distrust to block Pătrăşcanu's election to the Politburo at the first National Conference of the Party which opened on 17 October 1945.[32] While Pătrăşcanu was elected to the Central Committee, he did not find a seat on the seven-member Politburo, four of whom – Gheorghiu-Dej, Pauker, Luca and Georgescu—were declared secretaries. According to Dumitru Petrescu, the political head of the army and a fellow member of the Central

Committee—although his military position prevented this from being made public—Pauker supported Pătrăşcanu's inclusion in the Politburo over the objections of Gheorghiu-Dej and the matter was allegedly raised by all four secretaries with Stalin during a visit to Moscow.[33] Petrescu claimed that Stalin came down on the side of Pauker, which would explain why, according to the 1968 report of the Party Commission set up to look into the Pătrăşcanu case, the latter was coopted into the Politburo in July 1946.[34]

Yet there were those among the Soviets who were prepared to back Pătrăşcanu. The latter revealed under interrogation in 1949 that General Ivan Susaikov, the head of the Allied (Soviet) Control Commission, had appealed to him not to resign as Minister of Justice following an attack on him by Gheorghe Apostol, an ally of Gheorghiu-Dej, at the Communist Party Conference.[35] Such encouragement led Pătrăşcanu to feel that he was regarded as a key figure by the Soviets and that he could hope to continue to play a major role in Romania's future.[36]

At the same time, his reservations about Soviet intentions led him to see in the Americans and British a potential counterweight. Through his colleague Belu Zilber, he maintained close contact with American and British officials in Bucharest and confided in them. His most regular links were with officers of the Western Allies' intelligence services. The two Communists had their first meeting with officers of the American Office of Strategic Services on 21 October 1944 and opened an association which lasted until 1946. Both Pătrăşcanu and Zilber impressed the Americans with an honesty which the latter considered rare in Romanian political circles.[37] To one of his American contacts, the historian and OSS officer Henry Roberts, Pătrăşcanu explained that "the working class movement [in Romania] was just getting under way and represented a potential rather than actual strength". The Communists, therefore, should not seek power through force but should act as a loyal opposition during the period of economic reconstruction until such time that they could assume political authority through popularity.[38]

Until the return of Pauker and Luca from the Soviet Union in mid-September 1944, the leadership of the Romanian Communist Party was composed principally of ethnic Romanians who had spent the war years in Romania: Gheorghiu-Dej, Pătrăşcanu, Pârvulescu, Georgescu and Apostol. Included in this group was Bodnăraş, a Romanian of Ukrainian and German parents. But this group was, with the exception of Bodnăraş, unknown to the Soviets and it was precisely because Stalin and Dimitrov, the head of the post-1943 'frozen' Comintern, had little idea of what was happening amongst the Communists in Romania, that Dimitrov ordered Ana Pauker to assume the leadership of the Party.[39] During an interrogation by a Party commission in June 1956, Pauker said that she was ordered by Dimitrov to return to Romania in September 1944 with two radio-transmission specialists. Pauker was apparently reluctant to do this: "Comrade Dimitrov," she explained, "I am a woman, I haven't been in Romania during the war, I was in prison [in Romania] and I've no idea what the situation is; ten years have passed and it is a difficult thing you are asking me to do. I am a woman, a Jewess and an intellectual". She then claimed to have told Dimitrov that Gheorghiu-Dej should be the Party leader: "We don't know too much about him, I saw him for a couple of hours at Caransebeş [jail], but I knew that he was a very popular comrade, a railwayman and a tried and trusted figure". Dimitrov disagreed: "We haven't had any information for the last five years from Romania. We don't know any one, but you we do know".[40] Dimitrov also probably had in the back of his mind the fact that, unlike Pauker and indeed, Pătrăşcanu, Gheorghiu-Dej had not been exposed to the discipline of Comintern instructors, either in Moscow or elsewhere.

Thus the predominance of the Gheorghiu-Dej group in the RCP leadership changed with the arrival of Ana Pauker. She was flown to Bucharest on 16 September 1944 in a Soviet military aircraft with her daughter Tatiana and upon arrival at Popeşti-Leordeni airfield was whisked away to a safe house of the Romanian Communist Party. A day or so later, she was visited by Gheorghiu-Dej and immediately found herself at odds with him. In the very first meeting she attended of the provisional Party leadership, Pauker is said to have ridiculed Pârvulescu and to have given Gheorghiu-Dej, Bodnăraş and the others present the feeling that she had come from Moscow with precise instructions to reorganize the Party. "She waved around a piece of paper which she kept taking out and putting back in her handbag, to give us the impression that these were the orders which she had received", recalled Bodnăraş in a politburo meeting of March 1961.[41]

Pauker was particularly critical of the Party's involvement in the 23 August *coup*, leaving Gheorghiu-Dej perplexed. "Now I don't know what to believe. Comrade Ana might have discussed this matter with the Soviet comrades and if that is their view, that it would have been better for them to have entered Bucharest as a conquering army, thereby ridding themselves of the King and of the bourgeois parties, there might be something in that", Gheorghiu-Dej allegedly admitted to Silviu Brucan, a young journalist on *Scânteia*.[42] She expressed a similar view to Pătrăşcanu, saying that it would have been better if they [i.e. Pauker and the Soviets] had come and the Communists in Romania had not carried out the *coup*.[43] The convenience of collective leadership masked the struggle for control of the Party.

Pauker's deputy in taking over the leadership of the Party was Vasile Luca.[44] He returned to Romania in October 1944.[45] Within a month, Luca had joined Pauker and Gheorghiu-Dej to form the leading triumvirate of the Party, with the latter two appearing to have equal prominence with each other. However, according to Pauker's daughter and to Pătrăşcanu, Ana Pauker was, in effect, general secretary until the RCP National Conference of October 1945.[46] The issue of the Party leadership was allegedly raised in a meeting between Molotov and Pauker held in Moscow in early summer 1945.[47] According to Pauker's daughter Tatiana, her mother ruled herself out as leader on the grounds that she was Jewish, that she was a woman, that she was an intellectual and not a worker, and that she had spent the war years in Moscow. She herself recommended Gheorghiu-Dej. Molotov expressed pleasure with her answer, declaring her 'a clever woman', but her son-in-law suspected that Pauker secretly wished that Molotov had shown regret at her self-effacement.[48]

If Pauker and Gheorghiu-Dej shared the public stage as the principal figures in the Communist Party at this time, there is no doubt that behind the scenes Emil Bodnăraş was a pivotal figure. He was also an ambiguous one; even now it is far from clear where his ultimate loyalties lay. He commanded considerable authority as Moscow's most trusted agent and his credentials as an NKVD officer made him the obvious choice for the position of Secretary General to the prime minister Petru Groza to which he was appointed on 17 March 1945. On 27 April, Groza signed an order giving Bodnăraş control of the SSI, the Foreign Intelligence Service.[49]

Bodnăraş had developed a close personal bond with Gheorghiu-Dej, which went back to their days together in the prison of Doftana. This relationship served Gheorghiu-Dej well in offering his Soviet masters, through the person of Bodnăraş, a guarantee of his obedience, and helped to offset any claim that Pauker could advance because of a close relationship with the Kremlin. But Bodnăraş was a master of deviousness and was equally prepared to file negative reports on both Gheorghiu-Dej, as well as upon Pauker and Luca, to senior Soviet officials. In a written statement given immediately after being purged in 1953, Pauker declared that: "Between 1945 and 1946 comrade Bodnăraş submitted reports against Luca and me and emphasized the fact that reactionary circles were talking too often about us both as party leaders. It was then proposed that we should be removed from Romania".[50] The idea to remove Pauker and Luca, came, Pauker claimed later, from Andrei Vyshinsky.[51] Vyshinsky strongly disapproved of the formal pact made in August 1945 between Teohari Georgescu, acting for Pauker and Nicolae Pătraşcu, a leader of the Iron Guard, which admitted into the ranks of the Communist Party a considerable part of the membership of the Fascist organization.

Pauker revealed this on 18 June 1956 to a Party commission, set up to interrogate her, which was composed of Alexandru Moghioroş, Constantin Pârvulescu and Ion Vinţe.[52] Gheorghiu-Dej confirmed in a meeting of the Romanian Politburo on 29 November 1961 that the idea to remove Pauker was planted in his mind in January 1946 by Vyshinsky. At the Moscow Conference in December 1945, the United States proposed that the Groza government should be reorganized to include members of the opposition parties. Stalin made a limited concession in this respect in the agreement signed on 26 December, in which the three Allies recommended that the Groza government should include one member each of the National Peasant and Liberal parties. Vyshinsky, Harriman and Clark-Kerr arrived in Bucharest from Moscow in 31 December to oversee the implementation of the agreement. The opposition parties nominated Ion Mihalache and Dinu Brătianu. The Groza government rejected these nominations, and finally Emil Haţieganu and Mihail Romniceanu were included in the cabinet to represent the national Peasants and Liberals respectively.

The relevant passage in the Politburo minutes reads as follows. Gheorghiu-Dej is speaking:

> Vishinsky arrived on behalf of the Soviet Union, Harriman for the Americans and Clark for the British. Vyshinsky got in touch with us, explained the whole business and we consulted with Groza and Tătărescu and those responsible for these matters. We agreed to accept a representative from each of these parties, as well as the date proposed by them for the elections. We agreed amongst ourselves not to accept leading figures from these two parties but only second-rate

people. We then settled upon Romniceanu and Haţieganu, if you recall. Then Groza, who was in constant touch with Vyshinsky, told him of our position... In the evening we went to the theatre. I, Groza and Ana were there. There were many of us. Vyshinsky was there as well, if I'm not mistaken.

Comrade E. Bodnăraş. No, Vyskinsky wasn't there.

Comrade Gh. Gheorghiu-Dej. Towards the finale Ana got up and called me. She continued to play the role of leader, although I was the general secretary. She still pulled all the strings and summoned me and said: 'My dear Ghiţă, look, there's a problem. You've got to go to Groza and inform him that we have to substitute Bebe [Dinu] Brătianu for Romniceanu'. I asked, 'Why?' I think she gave the following reason: 'It will be easier, things will be understood more easily.' It seemed that this proposal was supposed to help Vyshinsky. From the way she spoke to me, I took it to be a suggestion. This was her way of doing things, these things emerged from somewhere. She was never precise about it, but the suggestion was that they came from the highest Soviet circles.

Comrade E. Bodnăraş: All the more because we knew that Susaikov was leaning towards Brătianu.

Comrade Gh. Gheorghiu-Dej: We didn't know that then. We found out afterwards. So I went to Groza after the theatre and told him: 'Look, here's the problem. You remember that we settled on Romniceanu and Haţieganu, but now there's a proposal that we change Romniceanu for Bebe Brătianu.' He gazed in surprise at me. Then I told him the same story that there would be heated discussions and that a solution must be found, and we should give Vyshinsky a helping hand. When he heard this he said: 'O.K.'

The next day, Groza told Vyskinsky what I had told him. Vyshinsky hit the roof when he heard. Vyskinsky, Susaikov and their translator went to Groza's house. When Vyshinsky heard the whole story he got very angry. Groza said afterwards that Vyshinsky was almost shouting: 'What is the meaning of this? Have I come here, sent by my government, with an easy task. Am I one to run away from problems? I don't understand you.' In other words, a pretty heated discussion. 'Why did you make this last-minute change?' Groza did not say at the outset that Gheorghiu-Dej had come to see him. Then he related how Gheorghiu-Dej had come to see him and what I had said.

And so Vyshinsky sent for me and I went to Groza's house. I realized that the atmosphere was glacial. There was me, Groza, Vyshinsky, Susaikov and the translator. Vysinsky then asked me: 'Comrade Gheorghiu-Dej, you came by last night. Listen to what Mr Groza has to say. Well, then? What happened? Why?' Again the temperature rose. I said: 'Look here, Comrade Vyshinsky, Ana went to the theatre last night and made a concrete proposal to ease the discussions with the two representatives of the US and Britain in terms that suggested that it came from the Soviets. I then came and informed Groza in the exact words used by Ana to me.'

Vyshinsky calmed down, but it was now the turn of Susaikov. The penny dropped later. I wondered why Ana had raised the matter of Romniceanu's replacement by Bebe Brătianu. Susaikov then put the question: 'But who is

> the general secretary?' In other words he was asking: 'Why have you come with this story involving Ana when you are the general secretary.' I then asked him:'But who really is the general secretary?' I knew that he and Ana were close, they visited each other and talked. This happened less frequently with me.
>
> Susaikov said nothing and Vyshinsky took me to one side and said: 'Comrade Gheorghiu-Dej'—the others heard, perhaps, because he wasn't speaking softly, but fairly loudly—'how is Ana of help to you?' I said, 'You can see for yourself what help she gives me, and if this was not the only example.' He thought for a little and said, 'Wouldn't it be better if she was removed?' Removed could be understood in the sense that she should be removed from the leadership or removed from Romania.
>
> I then said to Vyshinsky: 'Comrade Vyshinsky, such a thought never crossed my mind, but I shall think about it and reflect on what you have said.' And with that it was over.
>
> On a later occasion, Vyshinsky criticised Ana and Teohari Georgescu very harshly over the question of the Iron Guardists.[53]

In February 1947, Gheorghiu-Dej and Pauker were received by Stalin in Moscow. The Soviet leader asked Gheorghiu-Dej whether there were any grounds in reality for the rumours, which had reached him, about the existence of

> a faction in the Romanian Communist Party, which would want to have only Romanians as members of the party, i.e. specifically speaking, so that Ana Pauker and Luka, who are not Romanians by nationality, would not be able to occupy leading positions in the party. Comrade Stalin emphasizes that in this case, the party from a social and class-based party would turn into a party based on race. If it preserves its social and class character, it will develop and grow stronger; however, if it has a racist character—it will inevitably perish.[54]

Pauker could also take solace from Bodnăraş's servility as an agent of the Soviets. In a confrontation with Pauker, Luca and Bodnăraş in early summer 1947, Gheorghiu-Dej was accused by Bodnăraş of leaning too much towards the British and Americans. Bodnăraş repeated his complaint to General Susaikov, deputy head of the Allied Control Commission, adding that "radical steps should be taken". Susaikov communicated this denunciation on 10 June to Mikhail Suslov, secretary of the Soviet Party Central Committee, but added his own comments to the effect that its author was wide of the mark; Gheorghiu-Dej had made an appeal to the British and Americans for some economic assistance but only because he felt that the Soviet Union was itself experiencing economic difficulties.[55]

These divisions in the party leadership were echoed in a detailed report on the political situation in Romania compiled by a senior official in the Section for International Relations of the Soviet Communist Party. V. Lesakov visited

Romania from 7–20 August 1947 and six days after his return to Moscow submitted his findings to his chief, L.S. Baranov. He relayed General Susaikov's view that Gheorghiu-Dej was seeking to oust Pauker and Luca from the party leadership whilst at the same time intimating that all three were habituated to deviousness and opportunism.[56]

Ostensibly, collective leadership of the Party continued throughout the period from 1945 until 1948. At the first post-war National Party Conference of October 1945 no new general secretary was named by *Scânteia* and four of the seven-member Politburo, namely Gheorghiu-Dej, Pauker, Luca and Teohari Georgescu, were declared secretaries. Gheorghiu-Dej presented the political report to the Conference, while Pauker gave the report on the Party statutes, and the precedence given to these two in the Party newspaper, with Dej's name being listed first in alphabetical order, was maintained for the next three years.[57] Gheorghiu-Dej was appointed 'political' secretary, that is general secretary, by the secretariat[58] although a record of this meeting only recently entered the public domain after 1989.[59] His public role had been enhanced by his inclusion in November 1944 in the second Sănătescu government as Minister of Transport and Communications, and was consolidated in the Groza government of March 1945 when this portfolio of his was enlarged to include public works. Joining fellow Communists Gheorghiu-Dej and Pătrăşcanu in the government was Georgescu, who was promoted from Under Secretary to head the Ministry of the Interior. In November 1946, Gheorghiu-Dej took over as Minister of National Economy—renamed the following year as Industry and Trade—and in this capacity he ensured that Romania's economic obligations under the armistice agreement were met whilst at the same time taking stock of the national resources and wealth in preparation for nationalization. This particular ministerial responsibility required several visits to Moscow, which Gheorghiu-Dej doubtless used to impress upon the Soviet leadership his obedience.

Pauker's grand leap into the public arena came in 7 November 1947 when she was appointed foreign minister.[60] She was joined by Vasile Luca, who was named Minister of Finance on the same day. Ana's leading position within the Party was translated into a senior position of state, one which was guaranteed to bring her the greatest international exposure, albeit of a notorious kind.[61] With the establishment of the People's Republic on 30 December the foundations of the totalitarian state could be put in place. The first step was to cement Romania into the Soviet bloc from a military point of view and a top-level delegation led by Prime Minister Groza, Dej and Pauker left for Moscow on 4 February 1948. There they signed a Treaty of Friendship, Cooperation and Mutual Assistance. But the photograph of the delegation's departure from Moscow on 11 February, published in *Scânteia*, indicated the Soviet view of precedence in the RCP, even if the caption beneath it, entered in Bucharest, did not reflect this. The line-up for the photograph, dictated by the Soviet authorities, showed Groza, Molotov, Gheorghiu-Dej and Vishinsky in the front row. Pauker and Luca were relegated to the second row. Gheorghiu-Dej, second only to Prime Minister Groza in the Romanian delegation in the photograph, was identified as head of the RCP. However, because of her position on the far left of the photograph, Pauker was listed in the caption first, followed by Groza, Luca, Molotov, Gheorghiu-Dej and the others.[62]

Stalin's preference for Gheorghu-Dej was confirmed at the First Congress of the new Romanian Workers' Party, formed from the union of the RCP and the Social Democratic Party, and held on 21–23 February 1948. Gheorghiu-Dej was elected general secretary while Pauker and Luca were appointed to the Party secretariat and the Politburo. Gheorghiu-Dej's elevation to a position of *primus inter pares* in the Party was complemented by the final eclipse of his earlier rival Pătrăşcanu. Although the latter had been pictured in *Scânteia* only ten days earlier greeting the Romanian delegation upon its return from Moscow, he was suddenly accused in a speech given at the congress by Teohari Georgescu, the Minister of the Interior, on 22 February of "becoming an exponent of bourgeois ideology" and of "over-estimating the forces of the class-enemy, potentially helped by the Western imperialist powers".[63] Pătrăşcanu was not elected to any of the RWP bodies and shortly afterwards he was dismissed from the Ministry of Justice. The final sanction upon him came after a few weeks when he was banned from giving his lectures at the Bucharest law faculty.[64]

Pătrăşcanu's downfall cannot be attributed solely to Gheorghiu-Dej. While it is clear that he disliked Pătrăşcanu, and that the latter's behaviour had angered other senior Party members,[65] there is evidence to indicate that Moscow was the source of the order for his demise.[66] A catalogue of 'errors' had been committed, in Soviet eyes, by Pătrăşcanu since the *coup* of 23 August. Soviet distrust of Pătrăşcanu had been fuelled in particular by his display of patriotism in a speech delivered in Cluj on 13 June 1945 in which he announced the establishment of a People's Tribunal there for the trial of war criminals. Taking a line which contrasted sharply with the conciliatory approach of Groza, Pătrăşcanu denounced 'chauvinist elements' who were, he said, conducting a whispering campaign designed to convince the Hungarian population of Northern Transylvania that the return of this province to Romania was not final. After paying tribute to the Red Army's part in the liberation of this region, he appealed to the Hungarian population to accept the idea of a single Romanian state and of its national symbols. The appearance of the Soviet flag side by side with the Romanian had been hailed with enthusiasm, but the juxtaposition of Soviet and Hungarian colours had not always been made in good faith and at times it was intended as an incitement to chauvinism and Fascism. The official language of the whole country was Romanian and in all branches of the administration, including justice, the Romanian language alone was valid. In conclusion Pătrăşcanu stated that he was not prepared to consider as reactionary the opposition of a 'small part' of the Romanian population to the Groza government which was largely due to ignorance.[67]

Pătrăşcanu's comments provoked an animated debate within the Communist Party leadership and the speech was released for publication in the face of strong opposition from Luca and Moghioroş, both Hungarians and Iosif Chişinevski, a close ally of Gheorghiu-Dej and the Party's chief propagandist.[68] A year later almost to the day, Pătrăşcanu returned to Cluj in the wake of clashes between Hungarian and Romanian students in the city over the proposals in the Paris Peace

Treaty to ratify the return of Northern Transylvania to Romania. Speaking in the name of the government and the RCP Central Committee, Pătrăşcanu claimed that the tension in Northern Transylvania had been fuelled by Hungarians from the region who had left Romania before August 1940, the time of its award to Hungary, and had returned during the Hungarian occupation. Measures would be taken, he said, against Hungarians and Romanians alike who stirred up hatred and tried to disturb the peace in Transylvania.[69]

Although well received by pro-government and opposition newspapers, this speech had attracted the wrath of Gheorghiu-Dej who, in an address to the Central Committee on "the position of the RCP regarding chauvinist and revisionist trends" delivered on 7 July 1946, criticized Pătrăşcanu for allegedly not mentioning the role of the National Peasant and National Liberal parties in fomenting hatred amongst the Romanians of the Hungarian minority.[70] But in the back of Gheorghiu-Dej's mind was the forthcoming Peace Conference in Paris where charges of fomenting ethnic tension were the last thing Romania needed if her possession of Northern Transylvania was to be confirmed. Indeed, Pătrăşcanu's presence at the Conference in Paris was later exploited by his interrogators to bring accusations of attempting to foment a split in the RCP and of assisting Foreign Minister Constantin Vişoianu's flight to the United States.[71]

'Chauvinism', a cardinal sin in Stalin's catechism of the late 1940s, was served up in 1948 as a euphemism for the alleged anti-Soviet postures of Tito in Yugoslavia, Kostov in Bulgaria, Gomulka in Poland and Rajk in Hungary. In Pătrăşcanu's case it had been used by Gheorghiu-Dej in 1946 to refer to the latter's anti-Hungarian attitude. Gheorghiu-Dej had not been alone in the Party in his anger at Pătrăşcanu's intemperate pronouncements: Pauker, Luca, Rangheţ and other senior Central Committee members such as Iosif Chişinevski, the propaganda secretary, and Miron Constantinescu,[72] had all expressed criticism at Party gatherings over the summer and autumn of 1946 of Pătrăşcanu's 'self-importance' and his failure to follow an agreed Party line but it had not led to any sanction against him.[73]

Pătrăşcanu's vulnerability had been increased by Peasant Party leader Iuliu Maniu's arrest in July 1947. On 14 July, Ion Mihalache, Maniu's deputy, and several other prominent figures in the Peasant Party were arrested as they were about to leave for Turkey from Tămădau airfield, 46 km from Bucharest.[74] A few days later, Maniu was detained and the whole leadership of the party was put on trial on 30 October for plotting against the security of the state. Maniu and Mihalache were each sentenced to hard labour for life, commuted to life imprisonment. The arrest of Maniu and his associates in the National Peasant Party, among them Victor Rădulescu-Pogoneanu, doubtless unnerved Pătrăşcanu. He had reason to fear that Rădulescu-Pogoneanu might reveal their secret meetings in August and September 1945 over the King's demand for the Groza government's resignation, and that the Soviets might order his own arrest. It would be later alleged, at his trial in April 1954, that after the arrest of Maniu, Pătrăşcanu decided to flee the country. He was said to have instructed a trusted assistant, Nicolae Betea, to find a pilot who would fly them to Istanbul and Betea was put in touch with a captain Zaharia.

Unfortunately, Zaharia was also an SSI informer. When Betea told Pătrăşcanu the pilot's name, the latter recognized it and realized that his plans were compromised.[75] There is, however, no reliable independent evidence to back these claims.

The expulsion from the Party of Herbert (Belu) Zilber in March 1947 for not following the 'Party line' and on suspicion of being an 'Anglo-American spy' had provided a clear warning to Pătrăşcanu. Zilber was a close friend who had seconded in the talks conducted with the opposition parties to plan the 23 August *coup*. Abandoned now by his own friends and colleagues, Zilber was driven to pen a letter to Ana Pauker in November 1947 requesting his own arrest and interrogation so that his innocence be established. His request was granted, for on 6 February 1948 he was arrested by order of the Central Committee.[76]

Pătrăşcanu's concerns about his position drove him to seek advice from Serghei Ivanovici Kavtaradze, the Soviet ambassador to Romania. On 29 January 1948, the two men met at the embassy. The Soviet record of their discussion records that Pătrăşcanu wished to speak to the ambassador "who was a comrade with greater experience, in a very delicate matter related to his position in the Party". According to Kavtaradze, "Pătrăşcanu began with a brief reference to the fact that he had been a member of the RCP for 29 years, being alongside Ana Pauker one of its founders". Despite making a few mistakes during this period, he said, he had remained a disciplined Party member. During the war, he had played an important role in planning the 23 August *coup*, which had earned him some popularity. This had increased considerably after the *coup* but was looked upon with suspicion by some leading Party members and had led to various accusations being levelled against him, among them that of being a nationalist. This was based on two things: his speech on the question of Transylvania, given in Cluj in 1946, and his position over the return of Jewish property.[77]

Pătrăşcanu considered the charge to be unfounded. In his speech at Cluj, he argued, he had criticized the Hungarian prime minister for his "chauvinist stance towards Romania over the problem of Transylvania", not the Hungarian people. In the matter of Jewish property, Jews had been evicted from their property by a decree of Antonescu and he—Pătrăşcanu—had been unable, as Minister of Justice, to right that wrong because many of the apartments involved were now occupied by state officials upon whom the new Groza government relied for the smooth running of the country; Jews were to be given back their property, with the exception of those dwellings in which civil servants resided.

The hostility towards him, Pătrăşcanu claimed, emerged immediately after the arrival of Pauker and Luca in Bucharest in September 1944. It was then that the word was put around that he played no role in the Party. Moreover, in December 1944 and January 1945, *Scânteia*, the Party daily, received instructions that Pătrăşcanu's activity as a senior Party figure and the sole Communist minister in the government should receive no mention in its columns. What angered Pătrăşcanu most of all, he confessed to the ambassador, was the refusal of the Party to assign him any Party role, despite the numerous requests he had made over the previous eighteen months. He had discussed these problems with Gheorghiu-Dej and Pauker, but his talk with Pauker had not gone well. "He knows", Kavtaradze wrote, "that his main enemy in the Politburo is Ana Pauker, but he does not know the reasons behind this because up to now, no direct accusation has been brought against him".[78]

Pătrăşcanu repeatedly told the ambassador that he was not asking him to intervene on his behalf with the RCP, but sought only advice. He insisted upon the confidential nature of the discussion. Kavtaradze said that he could only give Pătrăşcanu one piece of advice: that the Politburo discuss his position and take a decision. "Pătrăşcanu", the ambassador concluded, "accepted this advice". On 19 February, he transmitted the following report on his talk with Pătrăşcanu to Moscow:

> For some years now, an atmosphere of only marginal trust and caution has surrounded the person of Pătrăşcanu. Matters have reached the point of suspicion that he is in contact with Anglo-American espionage. But firm, convincing evidence has not been produced [...] The discussion related above represents a mixture of tendentiousness, lies, and ambition. Pătrăşcanu gave me the impression of a man without a very clear conscience. Recently, the Ministry of the Interior, namely Teohari Georgescu, passed on secret information relayed to him from a reliable source. It is lethal to Pătrăşcanu.
>
> According to this information, Pătrăşcanu has adopted an anti-Communist and anti-Soviet position and has contacts with reactionary circles of émigrés who have asked him to join their organization. In view of the fact that Pătrăşcanu could become a member of the Romanian Workers' Party, and that its congress opens on 21 February 1948, I immediately placed the question of Pătrăşcanu before the secretariat of the Central Committee (Gheorghiu-Dej, Pauker and Georgescu), and proposed that light should be finally shed on this sombre affair and a decision taken. The secretariat was in total agreement with me and decided to resolve the Pătrăşcanu problem by the time the congress began. I shall inform you of what follows.'[79]

Pătrăşcanu's downfall may well have been sealed by plans to establish a Balkan federation embracing Yugoslavia, Bulgaria and Romania, and Stalin's reaction to them. On 17 January 1948, Georgi Dimitrov, the Bulgarian Communist leader, had hinted at the creation of a Balkan federation in a statement made in Bucharest. Both Gheorghiu-Dej and Pauker were careful to refrain from backing it. A month earlier Tito had visited the Romanian capital for the signing of a Yugoslav-

Romanian Treaty. Dimitrov was forced to retract his statement following a violent attack on him in *Pravda* on 28 January and on 10 February was summoned to Moscow by Stalin who instructed him to cease all talk about a federation; his death in Moscow shortly afterwards ensured just that. At the same time, Stalin is said to have told Ana Pauker, during the visit of the top-level Romanian delegation, to distance Romania from Tito and on 12 February the Romanian government ordered that all pictures of Marshal Tito be removed from shop windows. A further instruction then followed from Moscow: 'chauvinistic' elements were to be purged from the Party.[80]

Pătrăşcanu was the obvious victim. He had, moreover, been amongst those who had received Tito in the previous December and could easily be implicated in charges of a pro-Tito conspiracy. Failure to act promptly might invite a charge of 'chauvinism', this time with an anti-Russian meaning, against other Party leaders. In line with Soviet ambassador Kavtaradze's recommendation that a decision be taken on 'the Pătrăşcanu problem', Teohari Georgescu, as Minister of the Interior, was called upon by Gheorghiu-Dej, to make the public denunciation of Pătrăşcanu at the opening congress of the Romanian Workers' Party, which was held from 21–23 February.[81] With his target sitting close by, Georgescu named Pătrăşcanu as one of those who had become "exponents of bourgeois ideology in various respects, were breaking away from the masses, and were distancing themselves completely from the ideology and principles of the party of the working class".[82] Four months passed before the charges were made more explicit. In a resolution of the Central Committee plenary meeting of 10–11 June it was alleged that

> several weeks before March 1945, Pătrăşcanu, in complete contradiction to the party line, resuscitated the slogan of collaboration 'with the whole bourgeoisie or with an important part of it.' In 1946 he defended the thesis of an alliance with the 'whole' peasantry, therefore also with the exploiting elements hostile to the working peasantry... In his practical activity he followed the policy of appeasement towards the exponents of bourgeois-landlord reaction when the Party was fully engaged in the struggle against reaction. He followed the line of nationalist-chauvinist policy.[83]

Indications that a Soviet hand was behind these accusations was the claim that Pătrăşcanu wanted to work with "the whole peasantry, including the exploiting elements hostile to the working peasantry". This charge echoed one made at the same time by the Soviet Communist Party against the Yugoslav one, namely that the Yugoslav Communist Party failed to distinguish between kulaks and other peasants and that it had ceded the leading role in the country's affairs to the Yugoslav People's Front composed of "kulaks, merchants, small manufacturers, bourgeois intelligentsia, various political groups, including some bourgeois parties".[84] The link between the charges against Pătrăşcanu and the Soviet-Yugoslav crisis became clearer two weeks later when the Yugoslav CP sent a letter on 20 June announcing its decision not to attend the Cominform Conference, due to be held at the end of the month in Bucharest. In retaliation, the Cominform expelled the Yugoslav CP, making its decision public on 28 June, and moved its headquarters from Belgrade to the Romanian capital.

The chronology of the steps taken against Pătrăşcanu shows Gheorghiu-Dej's need to follow a scenario whose script was prepared in Moscow. The interval between Georgescu's attack on 23 February, Pătrăşcanu's detention on 28 April, the explicit charges on 10 June, and the fact that he was only formally arrested two months later, on 24 August, indicate that there was some hesitation as to how to procede against him. The delay can probably be attributed to two things: Pătrăşcanu's stubborn refusal to subscribe to all the charges against him, and Gheorghiu-Dej's need to await further instructions from Moscow.

The five month interval between Pătrăşcanu's arrest in August 1948 and his police, as opposed to Party, interrogation, in January 1949 probably resulted from Moscow's wish to coordinate his purge with the purges of Titoist heretics in other satellite states, which culminated in the trials and executions of Laszlo Rajk in Hungary and Traicho Kostov in Bulgaria in September and December 1949 respectively. In testimony given on 11 May 1967 before the Committee of Enquiry set up by the Party's Central Committee to prepare the rehabilitation of Pătrăşcanu, Foriş and others, Gheorghe Pintilie claimed that he had been ordered (he did not say by whom) in 1949 to contact three Soviet counsellors based in Bucharest over the Pătrăşcanu case. Pintilie could only recall the names of two of them, Aleksandr Mikhailovich Sakharovsky, and 'Patriki'.[85] From the latter Pintilie learned that all three had been involved in preparations for the trial of Rajk. Throughout 1949, both Pătrăşcanu and his wife Elena were interrogated at length in the DGSP (*Securitate*) headquarters on Calea Rahovei, and during this period the interrogation was guided by the Soviet counsellors in an unofficial capacity. They were assisted by a second secretary from the Soviet embassy who communicated information about the progress of the interrogation to Moscow. Later in the year, Sakharovsky was appointed chief MGB advisor to the Ministry of the Interior while the other two counsellors returned to Moscow.[86] Gheorghiu-Dej, Pauker, and Chişinevski were kept informed by Sakharovsky about the Pătrăşcanu case and occasionally Pintilie was summoned to Gheorghiu-Dej's home to discuss it with him and Chişinevski.[87]

Several stages can be established in the evolution of Pătrăşcanu's interrogation and that of his friends. In March 1948, the SSI arrested Nicolae Betea, Anton Raţiu, Constantin Pavel and Remus Micşa, all of whom were friends of Pătrăşcanu with posts in public institutions. In the following month, Pătrăşcanu and his wife were detained and questioned by members of the Party Central Committee. In June, Betea, Raţiu and Pavel were handed over to the *Securitate*. In August 1948, Alexandru Ştefanescu was arrested.[88] Between January and October 1949, Pătrăşcanu and his wife were interrogated by the *Securitate*. In October 1949, the SSI took over the interrogation of Pătrăşcanu and 25 other persons which lasted until May 1950. Then, in February 1951 another stage of the enquiry began, with the interrogation by the *Securitate* of the groups associated with Pătrăşcanu, Ştefănescu and with Remus Koffler, a veteran Party colleague of Foriş, and attempts to link them in a grand plot against the regime.[89]

On 28 April 1948, Pătrăşcanu was summoned by Gheorghiu-Dej to the Party headquarters and detained, that is, two months after his denunciation at the Party congress.[90] The lapse in time was perhaps due to a delay in the transmission of further instructions from Stalin as to how to procede with 'national chauvinists'. Pătrăşcanu was told by Gheorghiu-Dej in the presence of Alexandru Drăghici, head of the political and administrative section of the Party, that he would have to appear before a Party commission charged with investigating his activity during the period in which the Party was outlawed (i.e. 1924–44). He was escorted by Gheorghiu-Dej from the headquarters to a secret house for interrogation at Băneasa where a commission, composed of Teohari Georgescu, the Minister of the Interior, Iosif Rangheţ, deputy member of the Politburo and secretary responsible for the Party cadres, and Alexandru Drăghici, awaited him.

The commission began its enquiries by asking Pătrăşcanu about his alleged intention to flee the country, an intention which the former Minister of Justice resolutely denied. For several weeks its members sought to get Pătrăşcanu to admit to plotting against the Party leadership but its efforts were frustrated because Georgescu himself, or so Drăghici suspected, had advised Pătrăşcanu to keep his mouth shut.[91] The failure of the commission's investigations 'along Party line', as the Party jargon put it, to get the former Minister of Justice to admit to any 'mistakes' necessitated the adoption of more coercive measures. A warrant for Pătrăşcanu's arrest was issued on 24 August 1948. He was accused of being a police informer and an agent of British espionage who "carried out a criminal activity to paralyse the actions of the Romanian Communist Party and to destroy the Party from within, thereby contributing to the cause, maintenance and continuation of the war against the USSR".[92] After the issue of the warrant Pătrăşcanu was taken to his villa by Lake Snagov some 35 km to the north of Bucharest where he rejoined his wife Elena. Both were held in confinement there under armed guard for the following five months.[93]

On 19 January 1949, the next stage in their ordeal began. On that date they were visited by Gheorghe Pintilie, Col. Valerian Bucikov, a Soviet advisor to the Sixth Directorate, responsible for Gheorghiu-Dej's bodyguard,[94] and Iosif Rangheţ, a deputy member of the Politburo charged with counter-espionage in the Party, who brought them to the *Securitate*'s headquarters on Calea Rahovei in Bucharest where they were placed in separate cells in the basement.[95] They were not to see each other again. Their interrogation followed Beria's blueprint for the purges of 'Titoist heretics' which were being prepared in Hungary, Bulgaria and Czechoslovakia. Synchronization with these trials required that charges that Pătrăşcanu was a traitor and police informer be proved and that he was not working alone, but as the head of a group of conspirators with links to Tito and the 'Western imperialists'. To give the semblance of a plot, Remus Koffler, a long-standing friend of the murdered general secretary Ştefan Foriş, was arrested several months later, on 13 December 1949. Under torture a 'confession' was extracted from Koffler admitting that he and Foriş had been "agents of the bourgeois-landowning Fascist police", and that in 1941 they had recruited Pătrăşcanu. The latter, it was alleged, had given information to the police which had led to the arrest of a number of Communists, including Teohari Georgescu.[96]

The links to Tito and the imperialists were provided by the inclusion in the 'plot' of several representatives of Yugoslav minority organizations in Romania and of a number of Pătrăşcanu's friends; among them Herbert (Belu) Zilber; Ion Mocsonyi-Styrcea, former Marshal of the Royal Court;[97] Alexandru Ştefănescu, an industrialist; Jac Berman and Emil Calmanovici, both construction engineers; Victoria Sârbu; Harry Brauner, a musician and former director of the Institute of Folklore; Herant Torossian, a Romanian-born Armenian businessman who had served as consul in Paris;[98] and Lena Constante, an ikon painter.[99] The Yugoslav officials were portrayed as agents of Tito while Pătrăşcanu and his friends were alleged to have set up a spy network under orders from the British and American intelligence services.

These allegations against Pătrăşcanu mirrored the charges against Laszlo Rajk in Hungary. Rajk had served in the Spanish Civil War as a Communist 'volunteer' and was interned in the south of France when it ended. He was released from internment in 1941 with the help of Noel Haviland Field, an American NKVD agent working as a relief worker, and returned to Hungary, but Field's subsequent eccentric behaviour, which included contact with Allen Dulles, head of the Office of Strategic Services (the forerunner of the CIA) in Switzerland, aroused Soviet suspicions about his motives in helping with Rajk's release. In the summer of 1948 Matyas Rakosi, the Hungarian Party First Secretary, was summoned to Moscow to be informed that Rajk, his Minister of the Interior, was an American agent infiltrated into the leadership of the Hungarian Party. General Fyodor Belkin, chief Soviet advisor of the MGB for South-East Europe, sent two generals, Likhachov and Makarov, to Budapest, to supervise preparations for Rajk's arrest and show trial. Some 30 other MGB officers joined them later. On 30 May 1949, Rajk was arrested and his interrogation overseen by Belkin.[100] His trial, which opened on 16 September, implicated Pătrăşcanu. Lazar Brankov, one of Rajk's co-defendants, alleged that Pătrăşcanu supported Tito's plans to create a Balkan federation of 'bourgeois democratic states' which would include Romania.[101]

Shortly afterwards, in October 1949, Pătrăşcanu and his wife were handed over to the SSI, the foreign espionage and counter-espionage service, for questioning on the personal order of Gheorghiu-Dej acting on instructions from Soviet counsellor Sakharovsky. Lt. Gen. Serghei Nikonov (Sergiu Nicolău), the head of the SSI, explained that the reason for this was to establish Pătrăşcanu's connection with foreign espionage agencies through the intermediary of Lena Constante.[102] Charged with Pătrăşcanu's interrogation was Petre (Pyotr) Gonceariuc, the head of the counter-espionage directorate of the SSI. In a deposition made on 3 July 1967 to the Committee of Enquiry set up by the Party's Central Committee to prepare the rehabilitation of Pătrăşcanu, Foriş and others, Gonceariuc declared that in 1950 he had received verbal orders from Nikonov, the SSI head, to interrogate the Pătrăşcanus and that they were brought to him at the headquarters of the

SSI Second Directorate in Maxim Gorki street from a villa near Băneasa airport by Colonel Valerian Bucikov. Nicolău gave Gonceariuc a list of questions which needed clarification in the course of the interrogation and these included the following: Which of the enemy intelligence agencies had recruited Pătrăşcanu as an agent?; and what links did he and his wife Eva have with foreigners?

Gonceariuc's declaration gave nothing away about his conduct of the interrogation and he maintained that neither Pătrăşcanu nor his wife was tortured. He did admit, however, that after one session in which Pătrăşcanu's relations with the palace were raised, the latter tried to commit suicide by slashing his wrists with a razor blade. In order to prevent detection of the source of the razor blade Pătrăşcanu broke it into small pieces and then swallowed it. What Goncealuc did not add was that SSI officers were instructed to give laxatives to Pătrăşcanu in an effort to retrieve the fragments and to closely examine his bowel movements. Although they managed to piece together the object the gastric juices had removed any traces of finger prints.[103] After he recovered, Pătrăşcanu was moved to another building of the SSI where he took an overdose of sleeping tablets in another unsuccessful attempt at suicide.

According to Eduard Mezincescu, a senior official in the Romanian Foreign Ministry at the time and an acquaintance of Gonceariuc, the latter was a 'cunning brute' who proved himself 'very efficient' with his interrogation methods.[104] Questions were put to Pătrăşcanu about alleged hard currency dealings with Herant Torossian, a Romanian of Armenian background, but Goncealuc's main objective was to discover what links Pătrăşcanu was alleged to have had with the British Secret Intelligence Service which were maintained through the intermediary of Harry Brauner and his wife Lena Constante.[105] Goncealuc claimed that Brauner admitted that he had accepted the proposal of a foreign intelligence agency that he should flee the country in order to take up a post at the BBC dealing with folk music and he had decided to avail himself of the earliest opportunity to do so. Goncealuc was convinced that Brauner was a British spy but Brauner had given no information which could implicate Pătrăşcanu with British intelligence.[106] In 1952, after Goncealuc's transfer to the DGSP (*Direcţia Generală a Securităţii Poporului*), following its gradual absorption of the SSI, he passed on the Pătrăşcanu dossier, on Pintilie's orders, to Lt. Col. Ioan Şoltuţiu.[107]

In specific terms Pătrăşcanu was accused of working for British intelligence; the links with it were allegedly provided by Harry Brauner, Lena Constante, Koffler and Ştefănescu. The contacts which they had with British officials on the Allied Control Commission were now adduced as proof of Pătrăşcanu 's complicity in espionage, even though at the time the British were allies of the Soviets. At the same time as confessions were extracted through beatings from the accused to support these charges, the accusations of 'Titoist heresy' were not forgotten. An item in the official Yugoslav daily *Borba* on 4 March 1950 announced that Pătrăşcanu was shortly to be tried with a number of Yugoslav citizens for a pro-Tito conspiracy,[108] but for reasons that are still unclear Beria allegedly ordered a postponement. One explanation given is that in comparison with the Rajk and Kostov trials, which led to extensive government purges in Hungary and Bulgaria, the Pătrăşcanu version could only appear lame and therefore Beria demanded a wider and deeper purge.[109] The reason for its lameness was the failure to extract from Pătrăşcanu a confession to his 'crimes', and the absence of any corroborating evidence from his friends. Another possible reason for the delay in bringing Pătrăşcanu to trial was the opposition of Ana Pauker and Teohari Georgescu. It has been argued that Pauker and her protégé Georgescu resisted attempts to prosecute Pătrăşcanu on trumped-up charges and that their protection of him was a significant factor behind the accusation of 'right-wing deviationism' launched against them in May 1952.[110]

The difficulty in finding credible evidence against Pătrăşcanu was highlighted by Pintilie in his statement given on 11 May 1967 to the Committee of Enquiry into the Pătrăşcanu and Foriş cases. He admitted that it was only after persistent 'hard' questioning that the interrogators managed, in the first place, to link all the members of the so-called Pătrăşcanu group to the same charges. For two or three months after the Pătrăşcanus were handed over to the *Securitate* (in January 1949), the three Soviet counsellors, led by Sakharovsky, guided the lines of interrogation, although they had no official status. It was only later in the year that Sakharovsky was named principal counsellor to Teohari Georgescu. There was also a second secretary in the Soviet embassy who reported to Moscow on the progress of the interrogations. These Soviet officials kept Gheorghiu-Dej, Pauker and Chişinevski informed about the Pătrăşcanu case but Pintilie provided no evidence of any opposition from them to its conduct,[111] even though Gheorghiu-Dej's rebuke of Georgescu at the May 1952 plenary meeting of the Central Committee for not pursuing the Pătrăşcanu enquiry rigorously enough—revealed by the party commission—might have been interpreted as evidence of vacillation on the part of the Minister of the Interior.[112]

There is no evidence to ascribe the delay in bringing Pătrăşcanu to trial to deliberate obstruction by Gheorghiu-Dej.[113] Against such a claim one must set the atmosphere of terror that reigned in the satellite parties during and immediately after the show trials of 1949. Self-preservation would have dictated prudence and a respect for Soviet dictates. Gheorghiu-Dej followed instructions from Moscow, which probably originated from Beria who was now ably abetted by Vyshinsky (the latter had replaced Molotov as foreign minister in 1949). The master-servant relationship between Vyshinsky and Gheorghiu-Dej which had been forged in the prelude to the establishment of the Groza government was renewed in applying purge scenarios. These changed according to the prevailing political mood of Stalin. The leading role played by Soviet counsellors in establishing the thrust of the Pătrăşcanu group's interrogation between October 1949 and 1952 bears this out.

That Gheorghiu-Dej was anxious to do anything to remove any suspicions about his loyalty to Stalin and to follow Soviet instructions to the letter is clear from his address to the third Cominform Conference, held in Bucharest in November 1949.[114] He used the occasion to attack Tito's heresies and identified Rajk, Brankov, Kostov and Pătrăşcanu as agents of the Anglo-American imperialist espionage agencies alongside the Yugoslav leader.[115] Yet there was still no confession to back up this charge against Pătrăşcanu. Gheorghiu-Dej's address was, according to Khrushchev, prepared in Moscow by Pavel Iudin, Mihai Suslov and Georgi Malenkov.[116] At the same time, Gheorghiu-Dej's delivery of the address was confirmation of his seniority in the RCP.

The Stalinist script was clear: the proof of the "anti-state and anti-communist activities" of those under arrest was to be produced *after* official party judgement had been passed on them. But proof, in the form of a confession from Pătrăşcanu, could not be extracted from him. Renewed efforts were made by the interrogators to 'prove' the existence of a grand plot involving Pătrăşcanu, Koffler and Ştefănescu and linking them with Rajk, Kostov and others. These efforts were made on the instructions of Sakharovsky and his two Soviet colleagues who had examined the lack of progress in the case during the winter of 1950. They recommended the abolition of the SSI and the transfer of its officers to the DGSS (*Securitate*). The restructuring took place in January and February 1951 and Directorate G (Penal Investigation) was given responsibility for the Pătrăşcanu case.[117] Further evidence that their course was plotted by Moscow was an attack by Gheorghiu-Dej published in *Pravda* on 4 September 1951 under the title 'The Revolutionary Vigilence of the Peoples in the Struggle for Socialism' in which he listed Pătrăşcanu among those "inveterate traitors and paid provocateurs and agents of the bourgeois class like Rajk, Kostov, Koci, Dzodze and others who were led by the Belgrade agency of American espionage, the band of Tito and Rankovici".[118]

This second stage of the Pătrăşcanu investigation was initially entrusted to Colonel Mişu Dulgheru, the head of the penal investigation directorate, who received instructions from Sakharovsky and Tiganov, the Soviet counsellor for this directorate.[119] Still no satisfactory progress was made. The frustration of Gheorghiu-Dej, and no doubt of the Soviet counsellors, was translated into the decision to replace Teohari Georgescu as Minister of the Interior with his deputy Alexandru Drăghici at a plenary meeting of the Central Committee on 26 May 1952. Among the accusations levelled at Georgescu was that "even after four years he had failed to bring to a conclusion the investigation regarding the espionage and counter-revolutionary activity of Pătrăşcanu and Koffler".[120]

A fresh team of interrogators was constituted under Colonel Ioan Şoltuţiu who undertook to expedite matters.[121] To help him in his task he was sent to Prague where he sat in for a while on the Slansky trial. According to Victor Vânătoru, one of the interrogators, Şoltuţiu reported to Sakharovsky and Chişinevski and repeatedly urged the team to establish Pătrăşcanu's guilt as a traitor. Beatings were administered to Koffler, Calmanovici and Berman, but they consistently denied the allegations made against them. Gheorghiu-Dej followed this phase of the investigations closely, annotating the statements of the accused and offering advice on what direction the interrogations should take. The coordination proper of the interrogations was carried out by Sakharovsky and his subordinate, Tiganov, the Soviet counsellor of the Penal Investigation Directorate of the *Securitate*, thereby indicating the direct interest of Moscow in staging a sensational show trial in Romania to rival those elsewhere in the Eastern bloc. The frustration felt by Sakharovsky eventually led him to order the arrest on 26 November 1952 of Colonel Dulgheru on the grounds of having delayed the investigation.[122]

At the same time, increased psychological pressure and beatings were administered to the prisoners up until the time of their trial in April 1954 in order to extract confessions. These illegal methods were the subject, in 1967, of a voluminous secret report drawn up by the Central Committee which noted "the use of beatings, of torture, of the tearing out of hair, and of prolonged starvation of the prisoners".[123] These abuses forced the accused to tell lies, as Gheorghe Pintilie himself acknowledged in the report, and these lies were to lead to the murder, in April 1954, of Lucreţiu Pătrăşcanu and Remus Koffler.

The conduct of investigations against Pătrăşcanu between 1948 and 1952 confirm clearly the back-seat role to which Gheorghiu-Dej and others in the RCP leadership were confined by their Soviet masters in the conduct of Romania's affairs, and that Gheorghiu-Dej thought it prudent, and useful, to accept it. The interrogation of Pătrăşcanu and his associates lay firmly in the hands of Sakharovsky, the MGB advisor to Georgescu, the Minister of the Interior, and the sequence of different accusations levelled against Pătrăşcanu followed a scenario established in Moscow.[124] Gheorghiu-Dej's behaviour, and that of the Romanian Party leadership, during the interrogations indicate men and women anxious, not unnaturally, to protect themselves from the whims of Stalin and to demonstrate their fidelity to Moscow. Holding onto power required anticipation of Stalin's next move and preemptive action in accordance with one's instincts. This explains the caution with which Gheorghiu-Dej proceeded over Pătrăşcanu and why he was anxious to be kept informed at every stage of the progress, or lack of it, in respect of his interrogation. Either could be implicated as an imagined enemy in the absurd game of roulette which was played out in Stalin's mind. It was Gheorghiu-Dej who weighted the wheel in his own favour.

Notes

1 Gheorghiu-Dej's trajectory towards leadership of the Romanian Communist Party and his relations with his rivals are the subject of an illuminating volume *Spectrele lui Dej. Incursiuni în biografia şi regimul unui dictator*, edited by Ştefan Bosomitu and Mihai Burcea (Iaşi: Polirom, 2012).

2 See chapter one.

3 George Hodoş, Show Trials. Stalinist Purges in Eastern Europe, 1948–1954 (New York: Praeger, 1987).

4 Author's interview with Eduard Mezincescu, 16 June 1994. Mezincescu was a protégé of Ana Pauker and was brought into the Romanian Foreign Ministry by her in 1948. In his youth he joined the Communist Party and in 1936 was sent to Cluj to coordinate a network that helped volunteers pass into Czechoslovakia from where they travelled to France and ultimately to Spain to join the Republicans in the civil war. During World War II he was secretary of the Romanian section of the International Red Aid Organization, known from its Russian initials as MOPR. He rose to become Deputy Foreign Minister in the 1950s.

5 Some 50 NKVD agents served time in Romanian prisons during the war; interview with Eduard Mezincescu, 16 June 1994.

6 Gheorghe Gheorghiu-Dej, *Articole şi cuvîntări 1959–1961* (Bucharest: Editura Politică, 1961), pp.438–40; quoted from Michael Shafir, *Romania: Politics, Economics and Society* (London: Frances Pinter, 1985), p.32.

7 For a first-hand account of the removal of Foriş from the Party leadership on 4 April 1944 see that given by Emil Bodnăraş to Valter Roman, Gheorghe Zaharia and Ada Grigorian on 18 and 20 January 1960 (see Dennis Deletant, *Communist Terror in Romania, Gheorghiu-Dej and the Police State, 1948–1965* (London: Hurst and Co., 1999), appendix 1, pp.297–308).

8 Mary Ellen Fischer, *Nicolae Ceauşescu. A Study in Political Leadership* (Boulder: Lynne Rienner Publishers, 1989), pp.38 and 276, note 10. When Ana Pauker met Pătrăşcanu in Moscow at the time of the armistice negotiations in September 1944 she asked him why Foriş had been removed. Pătrăşcanu replied that he had little knowledge of the affair. Pauker is said to have put the same question to Gheorghiu-Dej when they met shortly after her arrival in Bucharest on 16 September 1944, being particularly anxious to know the reason because Foriş had been confirmed in his position by the Comintern in 1940 (author's interview with Eduard Mezincescu, 16 June 1994).

9 Fischer, *Nicolae Ceauşescu*, p.131.

10 Eduard Mezincescu, who had occasion later to discuss in detail the career of Bodnăraş with Serghei Nikonov (Sergiu Nicolău), appointed head of the SSI, the Intelligence Service, under Bodnăraş on 7 December 1946, learned from Nikonov that the replacement of Foriş had been first discussed in the prison hospital at Târgu Jiu in June 1943. Gheorghiu-Dej's view was that Foriş should simply be ousted (author's interview with Mezincescu, 16 June 1994). He was supported in this by Teohari Georgescu and Constantin Pârvulescu. It was Bodnăraş who moved against Foriş, placing the latter, Victoria Sârbu and Remus Koffler under house arrest on 4 April under the supervision of Pârvulescu. The whole operation, involving the detention of the three and the seizure of the party archive was carried out 'in three hours' according to a letter dated 16 April addressed by Bodnăraş to Gheorghiu-Dej and Georgescu (see Dan Cătănuş and Ioan Chiper, *Cazul Ştefan Foriş. Lupta pentru Putere în PCR de la Gheorghiu-Dej la Ceauşescu* (Bucharest: Editura Vremea, 1999), p.44. According to a declaration of Victoria Sârbu, given under interrogation on 7 February 1950, Bodnăraş handed Foriş a type-written note ordering him to surrender all Party materials and authorizing his house arrest. Bodnăraş told Foriş that the order had come from the Soviet Union (Robert Levy, 'Power Struggles in the Romanian Communist Party during the Formation of the Groza regime', in *6 Martie 1945. Inceputurile Comunizării României* (Bucharest: Editura Enciclopedică, 1995), p.79, note 3).

11 Levy, 'Power Struggles', p.79.

12 Author's interview with Mezincescu, 16 June 1994.

13 He expressed his pride in his achievements and those of the RCP whilst admitting also his mistakes and shortcomings. He left most of his modest possessions to Sârbu and his books in German to Remus Koffler. (L. Betea, 'Testamentul lui Foriş', *Magazin Istoric*, vol.31, no.4 (April 1997), p.44).

14 Author's interview with E. Mezincescu, 16 June 1994.

15 See the articles by E. Mezincescu and V. Tismăneanu in *România literară*, nos 21, 27 and 41, 1992 and Shafir, *Romania: Politics, Economics and Society*, p.34. Pauker's son-in-law, Gheorghe Brătescu, conceded that while his mother-in-law was a party to the order to arrest Foriş, she was not consulted about the decision to murder him which, he alleged, was taken one evening at a secret meeting of Gheorghiu-Dej, Bodnăraş and Pintilie. Indeed, after Pauker learned of Foriş's death, she told Gheorghiu-Dej that Foriş should have been put on trial. Gheorghiu-Dej replied that the Romanian courts were not competent to handle such a trial. Pauker then said that, in that case, Foriş should have been handed over to the Soviets (author's interview with G. Brătescu, 30 July 1994). Gheorghiu-Dej's apparent failure to consult Pauker over the decision to murder Foriş lends weight to the view that Gheorghiu-Dej, supported by Bodnăraş, had Stalin's authority for the move. In another explanation for the murder, the claim has been made that Foriş had Moscow's backing in autumn 1943 to conclude a deal with Antonescu which involved the sacrifice of the Commu-

nists in Romania (S. Fischer-Galaţi, *The New Rumania. From People's Democracy to Socialist Republic* (Cambridge, Massachusetts: MIT Press, 1967), p.21). With plenty of examples of Soviet cynicism from the interwar period to point to, Gheorghiu-Dej and his interned colleagues decided to preempt this move by removing Foriş and take over the Party before the arrival of the Red Army and the Moscow bureau, which of course included Pauker. The murder of Foriş may well have suited Stalin, for any public revelations about attempts to forge a deal with Antonescu, not to mention one made at the expense of the interned Communists, would have exposed them to charges of duplicity before the Romanian public, have severely embarrassed the Gheorghiu-Dej faction in the Party, and damaged Stalin's relations with the Western Allies.

16 Pintilie gave this account to Lt Gen Grigore Răduică, a senior *Securitate* officer, who had been ordered by Nicolae Ceauşescu to investigate Foriş's fate in 1967 (P. Ştefănescu, *Istoria Serviciilor Secrete Româneşti* (Bucharest: Divers Press, 1994), p.251). A Party obituary of Foriş dates his arrest to 9 June 1945 and his murder to the summer of 1946 (N.I. Florea, 'Ştefan Foriş', *Analele de Istorie*, vol.18, no.3 (1972), p.153). This chronology is corroborated by George Fotino, a private secretary to the Minister of the Interior, Teohari Georgescu. Georgescu himself described under interrogation in May 1953 how the decision was taken to get rid of Foriş: "In spring 1946 General Nicolski came to me and asked me 'What are we going to do with Foriş? He has been under arrest for some time.' I told him that I would make enquiries and let him know. A few days later, I went to the Party General Secretary and asked him, 'What are we going to do with Foriş. We've held him for a long time, shall we get rid of him?' Comrade Gheorghiu told me that he agreed with my proposal. After that I looked for Vasile Luca and Ana Pauker. I found them together in a room of Pauker's on the first floor. I asked them, 'What are we going to do with Foriş?' in the sense that we should get rid of him. Both were in agreement" (ASRI, Fond P, file 40009, vol.1, pp.230–40). Marius Oprea was kind enough to show me this document. Fotino recalled an attempt made by Foriş's mother to seek an unscheduled audience with Georgescu in the early summer of 1945 to ascertain the whereabouts of her son. When Fotino, who had never heard of Foriş, went into the minister's office to tell him that a certain 'Mrs Foriş' was in the ante-room and would like to see him, Georgescu went bright red and told him to tell her that he had been called away to a meeting, adding an instruction to Fotino that 'the woman was not to be allowed into the Ministry again' (author's interview with G. Fotino, 9 April 1994). Pintilie was coopted as a member of the RCP Central Committee at a plenary meeting on 10–11 June 1948 (*Scânteia*, 13 June 1948, p.1). Despite being attacked in the April 1968 Central Committee plenary meeting for his role in Foriş's murder, Pintilie was decorated by Ceauşescu in May 1971 on the fiftieth anniversary of the Party. Pintilie's chaffeur, Dimitrie Necin (Dumitru Mitea), had originally been sent to Romania as one of a three-man NKGB group parachuted in May 1944 into the area of Predeal with a radio transmitter to communicate to the Red Army information on German military activity (M. Mircu, *Dosar Ana Pauker* (Bucharest: Gutenberg, 1991), p.130, note 21). Pintilie consistently denied to Eduard Mezincescu that he had wielded the iron bar, claiming that the chauffeur Mitea struck the mortal blows (author's interview with E. Mezincescu, 16 June 1994).

17 Ştefănescu, *Istoria Serviciilor Secrete Româneşti*, p.250; see also L. Betea, 'Testamentul lui Foriş', p.45.

18 The officially sanctioned account of Gheorghiu-Dej's escape, written by one of the group instructed by Maurer, was published at the height of Gheorghiu-Dej's power within the Party in 1964; see M. Roşianu, 'Cum a fost organizata· evadarea tovarăşului Gheorghe Gheorghiu-Dej din lagărul de la Târgu Jiu în august 1944', *Scînteia*, 18 August 1964, pp.2–3. Marina's part earned him elevation, on Gheorghiu-Dej's recommendation, to the position of Patriarch of the Romanian Orthodox Church in May 1948. Another light is shed on the initiative for the escape by Eduard Mezincescu who told this author that although Bodnăraş, Pârvulescu

and Ranghet were all in favour of Gheorghiu-Dej's escape from the camp, Gheorghiu-Dej himself was reluctant to leave because he felt safer inside than out. He agreed to be released only on condition that Maurer make arrangements that would ensure that Gheorghiu-Dej would not be hurt during the escape. Maurer therefore contacted the lawyer Grigore Geamănu, a cousin of a senior official in the Inspectorate of Gendarmes in Bucharest, who paid a suitable sum of money to the official to persuade Colonel Şerban Lioveanu, the camp director, to relax security on the perimeter fence on the day planned for the escape.

19 As a result of an orthographic reform of 1954 *Scânteia* became *Scînteia*, only to revert to the earlier spelling in 1965 as a consequence of a further reform.

20 Pârvulescu's name continued to appear with this title. However, by July 1945 Scânteia styled him simply as a 'member of the Central Committee of the RCP' (H. Nestorescu-Bălceşti, 'Structura Conducerii Superioare a Partidului Comunist Român', *Arhivele Totalitarianismului*, vol.2, nos.1–2 (1994), p.334).

21 Fischer, *Nicolae Ceauşescu*, p.40. Pătrăşcanu's own account of these arrests was given in a signed declaration to the *Securitate* dated 7 February 1950; see *Cartea Albă a Securităţii* (Bucharest: SRI, 1994), vol.1, doc.89, pp.222–25.

22 In the report of the Party commission, set up in November 1965 to clarify the circumstances of Pătrăşcanu's arrest, interrogation and execution, this accusation was deemed to be without foundation: see 'Raportul Comisiei de partid, constituită în vederea clarificării situaţiei lui Lucreţiu Pătrăşcanu', *Cuvîntul*, no.35 (1–7 September 1992), p.9. The report was made public for the first time in September 1992.

23 Pătrăşcanu's release from Târgu Jiu in 1943 came as a result of the intervention of Colonel Magistrate V. Gelep, the secretary general of the Ministry of Internal Affairs, who had been paid a large sum of money by Pătrăşcanu's wife to secure her husband's release: see 'Raportul Comisiei de partid', p.6.

24 Personal communication to the author from Eduard Mezincescu, 30 Dec. 1992.

25 Ghita Ionescu, *Communism in Rumania, 1944–1962* (London: Oxford University Press, 1964), p.95.

26 Cristian Popişteanu, 'Cazul Grupului Pătrăşcanu (V)', *Magazin Istoric*, no.11 (November 1991), p.44. Silviu Brucan, a deputy editor of *Scânteia* at the time, also recalled how Pătrăşcanu was wont to remark to foreign diplomats at receptions that he should have been party leader. Reports of these remarks undoubtedly reached Gheorghiu-Dej's ears (conversation with S. Brucan, 15 June 1994). Pătrăşcanu's behaviour at a New Year's Eve party, thrown by Ana Pauker in 1944, shows how little he had in common with some of the Party leadership. Pătrăşcanu left before midnight, offering his apologies to Pauker and thanking her for the invitation. When Pauker said that his departure would not look good to Gheorghiu-Dej, Bodnăraş and others, Pătrăşcanu said that he preferred to see the New Year in with his students at the Faculty of Law (interview with Tatiana Brătescu, 30 July 1994). Several years later Pauker told her son-in-law, Gheorghe Brătescu, that she had a great admiration for Pătrăşcanu as a person but did not agree with his anti-Soviet views, and despite Stalin's mistakes the future lay with the Soviet Union (interview with G. Brătescu, 30 July 1994).

27 On his return from the armistice negotiations in Moscow on 14 September 1944, Pătrăşcanu told Corneliu Coposu, who had an office adjacent to his in the Council of Ministers (Coposu was secretary general of the Council), that an audience with Zhdanov on 11 September had depressed him and made him pessimistic about Romania's future. Zhdanov, whom Pătrăşcanu had known since he served as Romanian delegate to the Comintern, met him with the reproach: "What are you doing here Mr (i.e. not Comrade) Pătrăşcanu". "Well, we overturned the dictatorship and brought Romania onto the side of the Allies, and we've come to sign the armistice." To which Zhdanov replied: "You've done wrong, for you've upset all our plans". Coposu surmised that these plans were for the Soviets to capture Bucharest, overthrow Antonescu and to treat Romania as a conquered enemy, without the impediment of a Romanian

government to deal with ('Exilul Românesc: Identitate şi Conştiinţă istorică,' *Lupta*, no.232 (7 octombrie 1994), p.5).

28 "Immediately after my return from Moscow in September 1944, I discovered that... Emil Bodnăraş had ordered Comrade Vania Didenko to tail me by car at the time when I was minister without portfolio. I never discussed with Bodnăraş why he had taken this step, but I did, however, get an explanation from Bodnăraş himself who told me in a conversation at that very time that in two weeks, exactly the period which I had spent in Moscow, anyone can become a traitor or a spy. He then explained to me the step he had taken. In December 1944, Emil Bodnăraş summoned me to the Central Committee and took out a file—my file—and asked me a series of questions, from which it clearly emerged that I was under surveillance." (undated declaration of L. Pătrăşcanu, Arhiva Serviciului Român de Informaţii (ASRI), Fond Y, File 40002, vol.1, p.23, translated from Levy, 'Power Struggles', p.85).

29 AVPRF (The Foreign Policy Archive of the Russian Federation – Arkhiv Veshnii Politiki Rossiskoi Federatsii), fond 0125, opis 33, folio 127, file (box) 6, pp.128–34. I am grateful to Professor Florin Constantiniu for drawing my attention to this note. Copies of Morev's note, dated 10 January 1945, were sent in the following order: 1. Stalin, 2. Molotov, 3. Malenkov, 4. Beria, 5. Vyshinsky, 6. Dekanozov, 7. to the file. Vladimir Georgievich Dekanozov, a Georgian, was a close associate of Beria who brought him to Moscow in 1938 to serve as head of INO, the foreign intelligence department of the NKGB/NKVD. In 1940 he was appointed Soviet Minister to Berlin, and in 1941 became a Deputy People's Commissar for Foreign Affairs alongside Andrei Vyshinsky. He was arrested in July 1953 at the same time as Beria and executed alongside him in December.

30 'Raportul Comisiei de partid', p.6.

31 A. Şerbulescu [Belu Zilber], *Monarhia de Drept Dialectic* (Bucharest: Humanitas, 1991), p.68.

32 Ionescu, *Communism in Rumania*, p.118.

33 'Declaration of Dumitru Petrescu to the Party Commission of Enquiry into the Pătrăşcanu case, dated 2 November 1967', quoted in C. Popişteanu, 'Un epilog neaşteptat: Malenkov aprobă lichidarea lui Lucreţiu Pătrăşcanu', *Magazin Istoric*, no.3 (March 1992), p.38.

34 'Raportul Comisiei de partid', p.8. The first mention of Pătrăşcanu as a member of the Politburo of the RCP is in *Scînteia* in its edition of 24 July 1946, p.1; see H. Nestorescu-Bălceşti, 'Structura Conducerii Superioare a Partidului Comunist Român', p.357.

35 For a biographical note on Apostol see Vladimir Tismăneanu, *Stalinism for All Seasons. A Political History of Romanian Communism* (Berkeley, Los Angeles, London: University of California Press, 2003), pp.255–56.

36 Robert Levy, 'Power Struggles in the Romanian Communist Party during the Formation of the Groza regime', *6 Martie 1945. Inceputurile Comunizării României* (Bucharest: Editura Enciclopedică, 1995), p.87.

37 The views of Pătrăşcanu and Zilber about developments in Romania are recorded in Office of Strategic Services reports which have been analysed by Eduard Mark, 'The OSS in Romania, 1944–45: An Intelligence Operation of the Early Cold War,' *Intelligence and National Security*, vol.9, no.2 (April 1994), pp.320–44.

38 Both Pătrăşcanu and Zilber revealed themselves as true Marxists and as opponents to Soviet Communism. Their ideological opposition soon came to be bolstered by patriotic indignation: Soviet reparation demands were described by Zilber as "ridiculous and impossible". This anti-Russian feeling sometimes clouded their judgement. Zilber, for example, confidently predicted that Stalin would not back the Romanian Communists after Rădescu opened his attacks on them in February 1945 (Mark, 'The OSS in Romania', p.333).

39 Although the Comintern was officially dissolved at the beginning of June 1943, it continued to operate in a reorganized fashion until autumn 1945. Its central organization

and relations with the Communist parties was subordinated to the Section for International Information of the Central Committee of the Communist (Bolshevik) Party of the Soviet Union. Officially, its head was Sherbakov, candidate member of the politburo and secretary of the Central Committee, but in reality, it was directed by Georgi Dimitrov who, in June 1944, received the formal position of head. A resolution of the politburo confirmed the section's place in the organizational structure of the Central Committee of the Soviet Communist Party. Documents from the Central Committee and those of other Communist parties show that long-term objectives and current problems of the satellite Communist parties played an important part in the section's work. After the return at the end of the war of many of the activists who worked in the Section for International Information to their countries of origin (e.g. Dimitrov to Bulgaria), the section operated as a foreign policy arm of the Central Committee of the Soviet Communist Party under the direction of Mihail Suslov. It was an important instrument of supervision of the East European Communist parties and was responsible for drawing up and transmitting Soviet directives. To this end coded radio messages were sent, as well as meeting with party activists who regularly visited Moscow. Another means used were the frequent visits of section members to the East European countries. Those whose reported on Romania, apart from Suslov, included L. Baronov, M. Burtsev, A. Kuznetzov, and I. Medvedev (see L. Ghibianski, 'URSS şi câteva aspecte ale formării blocului sovietic în Europa Orientală', in *6 Martie 1945. Inceputurile Comunizării României* (Bucharest: Editura Enciclopedică, 1995), pp.254–61.

40 R. Levy, 'Power Struggles', pp.79–80. Levy quotes from a transcript of Pauker's interrogation by Alexandru Moghioroş, Constantin Pârvulescu and Ion Vinţe dated 18 June 1956. Pauker's cover was an order from the Political Directorate of the Red Army to join the 'Political Directorate of the Second Ukrainian Front' in Bucharest in order to supervise the publication of the Romanian-language Red Army newspaper Graiul Nou. (E. Mezincescu, 'Punct', *România literară*, no.9 (9–15 March 1994), p.14). In reality, she had two missions: the first, to assume leadership of the Party and second, to make regular reports to Moscow using the two radio operators about what was happening within it. Eduard Mezincescu torpedoes assertions that Pauker was met at the airport by Gheorghiu-Dej, on which occasion she allegedly berated him for removing Foriş. She had, in fact, been seen in the northern Moldavian town of Botoşani on 7 April 1944 with the advancing Soviet forces. She was dressed in Soviet military uniform and was a political officer of the Second Soviet Army. She took charge of the reorganization of the local authorities in which Communists were given the leading positions (Slomo Leibovici, 'Cum au apărut fruntaşii comunişti Ana Pauker şi Vasile Luca la Botoşani în preajma lui 23 August 1944', *Magazin Istoric*, vol.29, no.12 (December 1995), pp.26–27). Soviet agents worked in conjunction with a radio operator to communicate details to Moscow of German troop movements and political developments in Romania throughout the war. One such team, run by an agent called Lowin, was caught in the Vatra Luminoasă of Bucharest; its Russian radio operator shot himself (C. Troncota·, *Eugen Cristescu* (Bucharest: Roza Vanturilor, 1994), pp.438–39).

41 Stenogram of the Politburo meeting of 13–14 March 1961, p.158. I am grateful to Vladimir Tismăneanu, Robert Levy and Marius Oprea for a sight of this document.

42 Silviu Brucan, *Generaţia Irosită*, (Bucharest: Univers & Calistrat Hogaş, 1992), p.56.

43 Deposition of Elena Pătrăşcanu, Lucreţiu's wife, made in 1967 in preparation for the Plenum of April 1968 at which Lucreţiu was rehabilitated (Archive of the Executive Committee of the CC of the RCP, no.264/18.02.1972). My thanks to Marius Oprea for showing me this document.

44 See Tismăneanu, *Stalinism for All Seasons*, p.262, for a biographical note on Luca.

45 According to Luca's own testimony, given under interrogation in March 1954 (R. Levy, 'Power Struggles', p.81, note 1).

46 Author's interview with Tatiana Brătescu, 30 July 1994. Pătrăşcanu made the same claim in a declaration under interrogation dated 2 November 1949 (see R. Levy, 'Power Struggles', p.80, note 4).
47 Pauker's connection to Molotov was through her close friendship with his wife, Polyana Zhemchuzhina, who was later arrested in 1949 as part of Stalin's anti-Semitic witch-hunt and sent into internal exile.
48 M. Mircu, *Dosar Ana Pauker* (Bucharest: Gutenberg, 1991, p.141) and author's interview with Dr G. Brătescu, 30 July 1994.
49 See Appendix 1 to the book: Emil Bodnăraş.
50 Levy, 'Power Struggles', p.83.
51 *Ibid.*, p.83, note 3.
52 *Ibid.*
53 'Stenograma Şedinţei Biroului Politic al CC al PMR din ziua 29 noiembrie 1961' pp.12–13, reproduced in *Sfera Politicii*, no. 47, 1997, pp.36–37.
54 'Record of Conversation between I. V. Stalin and Romanian Leaders G. Gheorghiu-Dej and A.Pauker,' February 02, 1947, History and Public Policy Program Digital Archive, APRF, f. 45, op. 1, d. 361, l. 62–66. Published in G.P. Murashko, et al. (eds.), *Vostochnaia Evropa V dokumentakh Rossiiskikh arkhivov, 1944—1953,* vol.1 (Moscow/Novosibirsk: Sibirski Khronograf, 1997), pp.564–68. Translated for Cold War International History Project by Svetlana Savranskaya. http://digitalarchive.wilsoncenter.org/document/118460. Accessed 15 May 2017. See also Tatiana Pokivailova, 'Tragica greşeală a lui Lucreţiu Pătrăşcanu', *Magazin Istoric*, vol.30, no.8 (August 1996), p.49.
55 G. P. Muraschko, A.F. Noskowa, T.Wolokitina, 'Das Zentralkomitee der WKP(B) und das Ende der nationalen Wege zum Sozialismus', *Jahrbuch fur Historische Kommunismusforschung*, 1994, p.17.
56 RGASPI (Russian State Archive of Social and Political History) – Rossiiski Gosudarstvennyi Arkhiv Sotsial'noi I Politicheskoi Istorii) Fond 575 Opis 1 dosar 33 Signed by V. Lesakov on 26 August 1947. I am grateful to Prof Ioan Chiper of the 'N.Iorga' Institute of History for providing me with this source reference. The report is published in Deletant, *Communist Terror in Romania*, appendix 2, pp.309–13. See also Ioan Chiper, 'Raportul lui Lesakov', *Dosarele Istoriei*, vol.3, no.8 (1997), pp.61–63. The report highlights the insidious nature of relations among the Romanian party leadership, with Gheorghiu-Dej, Pauker and Bodnăraş seeking to curry Soviet favour by denouncing their colleagues. In this sense, a report by General Susaikov to Mihail Suslov, Secretary of the Central Committee of the Soviet Communist Party, dated 10 June 1947, containing a strong criticism by Bodnăraş of Gheorghe-Dej's alleged anti-Soviet attitude, is eloqent; see Dan Cătănuş and Vasile Buga (eds), *Gh. Gheorghiu-De la Stalin. Stenograme, note de convorbire, memorii, 1944–1952* (Bucharest: Institutul Naţtional pentru Studiul Totalitarismului, 2012), pp.210–18.
57 Fischer, *Nicolae Ceauşescu*, p.44.
58 Ionescu, *Communism in Rumania*, p.188.
59 Levy, *Power Struggles*, p.82, note 1.
60 Major changes of personnel had already taken place in the Romanian Foreign Ministry; see Deletant, *Communist Terror in Romania*, appendix 5, pp.322–23.
61 Since Pauker was Minister of Foreign Affairs she became better known to the West than her colleagues. The reactions were frequently unfavourable: in a lengthy article in *Time* (20 September 1948) she was described thus: "Now she is fat and ugly; but once she was slim and (her friends remember) beautiful. Once she was warmhearted, shy and full of pity for the oppressed, of whom she was one. Now she is cold as the frozen Danube, bold as a boyar on his rich land and pitiless as a scythe in the Moldavian grain". Her fidelity to Moscow attracted a number of jokes. In June 1952, when Pauker was purged, *Time* recounted one of them: "One sunny day in Bucharest, as the story goes, a friend stopped Ana Pauker in the street and asked: 'Ana, why are

you carrying an umbrella? It's not raining'. Replied Romania's no.1 Communist: 'It's raining in Moscow. I heard it on the radio'."

62 Fischer, Nicolae Ceauşescu, p.46.

63 Ionescu, *Communism in Rumania*, p.152.

64 Pressure was brought to bear on George Fotino, a private secretary to Georgescu, to 'unmask' Pătrăşcanu in front of the students but Fotino alerted Pătrăşcanu to this and as he entered the classroom the first words of his lecture were already on his lips, thereby denying Fotino the opportunity to denounce him (interview with G. Fotino, 9 April 1994).

65 Most importantly, Bodnăraş. In a memorandum addressed to Nicolae Ceauşescu, secretary general of the Communist Party, at the time when the latter had ordered an enquiry into the abuses committed by the *Securitate* (1967–68), Anton Raţiu, a former commander of the 'Patriotic Guards', claimed to have been present at a discussion at the beginning of November between Bodnăraş and Vania Didenko. Bodnăraş commented on the fact that, at a meeting on 7 November 1944 in the 'ANEF' stadium in Bucharest, the slogan 'Pătrăşcanu as Prime Minister' had been chanted. Bodnăraş remarked: "That man is getting too big for his boots. We've got to get something on him! Pantiusha, Serghei, Vania and Misha should tail him!" (Arhivele Naţionale Istorice Centrale (henceforth ANIC), Bucharest, Archive of the Central Committee of the Romanian Communist Party, fond 95, file 122.420, p.4.) I am grateful to Claudiu Secaşiu for this information. See also his paper 'Serviciul de Informaţii al PCR; Secţia a II-a informaţii şi contrainformaţii din cadrul Comandamentului formaţiunilor de luptă patriotică (FLP)', in *6 Martie 1945. Inceputurile Comunizării României* (Bucharest: Editura Enciclopedică, 1995), p.153. The four men designated by Bodnăraş were Pintilie Bodnarenko, known as Pantiusha (he later called himself Gheorghe Pintilie), Serghei Nikonov, Ivan/Vania Didenko (known later as Ioan Vidraşcu) and Misha Postanski (later Vasile Posteucă). They were among a group of about 40 NKVD agents who had been sent to Romania in the interwar period and captured. Their shared experience of prison with Gheorghiu-Dej made them his faithful servants and with Bodnăraş, they could vouch for Gheorghiu-Dej's bona fides to Moscow.

66 Charlotte Gruia, a senior official in the Party's Control Commission, and Eugen Szabo, a *Securitate* officer, both interviewed by Robert Levy, maintain that the Romanian politburo received orders from Stalin late in 1947 to link Pătrăşcanu with the arrested leaders of the National Peasant and National Liberal parties, Iuliu Maniu and Constantin Brătianu (see R. Levy, 'Did Ana Pauker prevent a "Rajk Trial" in Romania?', *East European Politics and Societies*, vol.9, no.1 (Winter 1995), p.153).

67 Despatch from I. Le Rougetel, British Political Representative in Bucharest, to Foreign Office, 22 June 1945, TNA, FO 371/48645/ XC 5498.

68 For a biographical note, see Tismăneanu, *Stalinism for All Seasons*, p.259.

69 Roumania: Annual Review for 1946, Mr A. Holman to Mr Bevin, 12 March 1947, TNA, FO 371/67233/114052. A text of Pătrăşcanu's speech was printed in *Scânteia* on 14 June 1946. Among the declarations made by Pătrăşcanu during his interrogation by the *Securitate* and written up by Lt. Maj. Simion Siegler on 7 January 1952 was an 'admission' that "he concealed a part of his Cluj speech from the Central Commitee because he feared that he would not receive the party's permission to use it since it addressed the problem of Northern Transylvania". It is not clear to which of the two Cluj speeches, that in June 1945 or that in June 1946, Siegler is referring. Pătrăşcanu is also alleged to have recognized that "his nationalist deviations and manifestions placed him in the position of a traitor, exacerbating the conflict between Hungarians and Romanians in his Cluj speeches of June 1945 and July (sic!) 1946" (Popişteanu, *Magazin Istoric*, no.11 (November) 1991, p.41).

70 Ionescu, *Communism in Rumania*, p.154 and *Scânteia*, 8 July 1946, p.3.

71 In a declaration signed whilst under interrogation on 11 June 1951 Pătrăşcanu stated that before his departure for Paris at the end of July 1946 Vişoianu had sought an

audience with him at the Ministry of Justice and passed on to him an invitation from Brigadier General Cortland Van Rensselaer Schuyler, the US military representative on the Allied Control Commission, to go to the United States "on whatever terms he wanted". Pătrăşcanu adamantly turned down the invitation. Because he failed to divulge this invitation to the Party Pătrăşcanu 'admitted' his complicity in Vişoianu's defection (Vişoianu left Romania secretly in an American aircraft in October 1946 and settled in the United States). Pătrăşcanu also admitted to having had a conversation with Richard Franassovici, a member of the Romanian delegation in Paris, who proposed to him that he set up a breakaway Communist Party, and that he had failed to disclose this to the Party (C. Popişteanu, 'Cazul' Grupului Pătrăşcanu, pp.40–41).

72 Miron Constantinescu (1917–1974) is the subject of a sensitive biography by Ştefan Bosomitu, *Miron Constantinescu. O biografie* (Bucharest: Humanitas, 2014). Constantinescu was a significant figure in the history of Romanian Communism, in particular in the first decade following the imposition of the Romanian People's Republic. He joined the Communist movement out of conviction as a student at Bucharest University where he attended the sociology seminar of Dimitrie Gusti. Arrested in 1941 for clandestine activity, he was sentenced in February 1941 to ten years' hard labour. The *coup* of 23 August led to his release two days later and shortly afterwards he was appointed Director of the Party newspaper Scânteia and became a member of the Politburo, a position he held until 1957 when he was expelled together with Chişinevski for having criticized Gheorghe-Dej and the *Securitate* following Khruschev's secret speech of February 1956. Constantinescu's conflict with Gheorghiu-Dej, and his marginalization in 1957 gave him the opportunity to focus on his intellectual gifts by working at a number of academic institutions in Bucharest. Gheorghiu- Dej's death and Nicolae Ceauşescu's aim to legitimize his own leadership by delegitimizing that of his predecessor paved the way for Constantinescu's rehabilitation.

73 Author's interview with E. Mezincescu, 30 December 1992.

74 Declarations made to the security police by those involved in the escape attempt are published in *Cartea Albă a Securităţii*, vol.1, Anexă, *Manifestaţia de la 8 Noiembrie 1945. Capcana de la Tămădău, 14 Iulie 1947* (Bucharest: SRI, 1995), pp.51–92.

75 Andrei Şerbulescu [Belu Zilber], *Monarhia de Drept Dialectic* (Bucharest: Humanitas, 1991), p.69. These details were confirmed by George Fotino in an interview with the author on 9 April 1994. However, the Party Commission of Enquiry set up to examine the Pătrăşcanu affair, concluded that "Pătrăşcanu did not intend to leave the country permanently, even though he had many opportunities to do so" ('Raportul Comisiei de partid', *Cuvântul*, no.43 (27 October–2 November), 1992, p.6.

76 Tatiana Pokivailova, 'Tragica greşeală a lui Lucreţiu Pătrăşcanu', *Magazin Istoric*, vol.30, no.8 (August 1996), p.46.

77 Tatiana Pokivailova, 'Tragica greşeală', p.49.

78 *Ibid.*, p.52.

79 *Ibid.*

80 Hodoş, *Show Trials*, p.96.

81 On 12 November 1947, the Social Democrat Party agreed to merge with the Communist Party, thereby creating the Romanian Workers' Party.

82 Congresul Partidului Muncitoresc Român. Bucureşti, 21–23 februarie 1948 (Bucharest: Editura PMR, 1948), p.156.

83 *Scânteia*, 21 June 1948, p.1. These charges are analyzed by Ghiţă Ionescu, *Communism in Rumania*, pp.152–54.

84 'Letter from the Central Committee of the Communist Party of the Soviet Union to the Central Committee of the Communist Party of Yugoslavia, 4 May 1948', in *The Soviet-Yugoslav Dispute* (London: Royal Institute of International Affairs, 1948), p.45.

85 Probably Serghei Vasilievici Patrakeev (MGB), appointed in November 1949 to the Soviet embassy in Bucharest. The MGB chief advisors in Bucharest were Serghei

Savcenko (1947–1949) and Alexandr Mihailovici Sakharovsky (1949–1952), who in 1956 became head of the First Chief Directorate of the KGB.

86 The MGB (Soviet Ministry of State Security) 1946–54 was the successor to the NKGB (People's Commissariat of State Security) 1941 and 1943–46. The NKVD (People's Commissariat for Internal Affairs) 1922–46 incorporated the OGPU (Soviet Security service) between 1922–23 and 1934–43. In 1946, the NKVD became the MVD (Soviet Ministry of Internal Affairs).

87 C. Popişteanu, 'Procesul lui Lucreţiu Pătrăşcanu', *Magazin Istoric*, no.11 (November 1991), p.43.

88 Alexandru Ştefănescu, born 1 November in Ploieşti, representative of British cotton companies in Romania. A frequent visitor to Ion Antonescu whilst he was held in detention at Bistriţa monastery in 1938, he put Iuliu Maniu in contact with the general. He was arrested and accused of espionage in favour of Britain as part of the Lucreţiu Pătrăşcanu group on 25 August 1948, tried and sentenced to life imprisonment on 14 April 1954 for high treason. He died in Aiud jail of heart failure on 15 February 1956.

89 C. Popişteanu, 'Procesul lui Lucreţiu Pătrăşcanu', *Magazin Istoric*, no.9 (September 1991), p.48.

90 The Report of the Party Commission on the Pătrăşcanu case stated that he was detained on this date on the basis of 'an instruction given by Gheorghiu-Dej', 'Raportul Comisiei de partid', p.8.

91 E. Mezincescu, 'Detenţie fără mandat de arestare', *Magazin Istoric*, no.6 (June 1992), p.58.

92 ANIC, Arhiva Comitetului Executiv al CC al PCR (Archive of the Executive Committee of the Central Committee of the Romanian Communist Party), No.264, vol.21, p.15.

93 Mezincescu, 'Detenţie fără mandat de arestare', p.58.

94 Bucicov also supervised the search of Ana Pauker's house after her arrest (author's interview with Tatiana Brătescu, 30 July 1994).

95 E. Mezincescu, 'Ecouri la "Cazul" Pătrăşcanu', *Magazin Istoric*, no.7 (July 1992), p.33.

96 Hodoş, *Show Trials*, p.99.

97 Baron Ion de Mocsonyi-Styrcea was born at Cernăuţi on 16 May 1909. He graduated from Cambridge with a degree in modern languages in 1932 and joined the Romanian Foreign Ministry two years later. Between 1 April and 11 August 1942 he was private secretary to King Michael and head of the royal chancery, and from the latter date until 1 April 1944 served as acting Marshal of the Royal Court. On 23 August 1944, he was made Marshal of the Court, a position from which he resigned on 4 November 1944 for health reasons, but he remained on the roll of the Foreign Ministry until the purge of non-Communist employees on 6 March 1946. He was arrested on his estate at Bulci in the Banat on 6 September 1947 and forced to become a prosecution witness in the trial of Maniu and others in which he was a co-defendant (29 October–11 November 1947). Sentenced to two years imprisonment for concealing the so-called Maniu 'plot' to overthrow the regime, he served his time in Craiova jail from 12 December 1947 until 22 October 1949. He was charged a month after his release with being 'a wartime profiteer' because of his ownership of large estates in the Banat, and although acquitted before a tribunal in Timişoara, continued to be held in custody, first in Timişoara jail (23 November 1949–25 September 1950), and then at Casa Verde, a former royal hunting lodge ten kilometres from the city (25 September 1950–16 May 1951). On 16 May 1951, he was taken, first to Timişoara *Securitate* headquarters for interrogation in connection with the Pătrăşcanu 'plot' and afterwards, to the Ministry of the Interior in Bucharest where he remained until 18 March 1952. He was then transferred to the SSI's interrogation centre at Malmaison on Calea Plevnei in Bucharest where he was held until the trial of Pătrăşcanu on 6 April 1954 in which he was also a defendant. He was sentenced on 14 April to fifteen years hard labour which he executed in a succes-

sion of jails – Aiud (8 April 1954–15 February 1955), Jilava prison (15 February–4 April 1955), Aiud (4 April 1955–13 August 1956), Jilava (13 August 1956–20 July 1957), and Piteşti (20 July 1957–1 June 1959). On 1 June 1959, he was transferred, together with other prisoners from the Pătrăşcanu trial, to Dej prison. On 18 October 1961, he was brought to Malmaison and was offered a deal by Drăghici: that he should write his eyewitness account of the 23 August *coup* on condition for his release from prison into house arrest. Styrcea accepted and on completion of his text, which he was forced to rewrite several times, he was sent to the town of Câmpulung-Muscel on 28 November 1962 to which he was confined until he was allowed to leave Romania on 4 September 1964. He settled in Switzerland (letter from Mocsonyi-Styrcea to the author, 4 August 1984).

98 Torosian was caught trying to leave Romania secretly in March 1948 in order to rejoin his wife in Paris who was ill. He was sentenced to five years in jail.

99 Constante gave an account of her ordeal in her book *The Silent Escape* (Berkeley: University of California Press, 1995). In this autobiography she recounts the three thousand days which she spent, between 1950 and 1957, in solitary confinement as a political prisoner in Romanian jails. Lena was first arrested in April 1948 and was accused of involvement in an espionage ring run by Pătrăşcanu. She was released six months later, re-arrested in January 1950 and finally brought to trial in April 1954 when she was sentenced to twelve years imprisonment. By the time of her conviction she had served more than four years in solitary confinement and she spent a further three and a half years in the same conditions before being moved, in October 1957, into a communal cell. With the dubious distinction of being the only woman in Romania to endure a total of eight years of total isolation, she was finally released in July 1961. Her link to Pătrăşcanu was through his wife Elena. Constante had studied fine arts and had a particular fondness for dolls, puppets and puppet theatre. In 1945, she joined Elena in a project to establish the first puppet theatre in Bucharest and as a result of this collaboration the Pătrăşcanus became firm friends of Constante and her partner, Harry Brauner, an ethnomusicologist (they eventually married after their release from prison). Both Constante and Brauner were, together with other friends of the Pătrăşcanus, to become scapegoats in the show trial of Pătrăşcanu.

The 'silent escape' of the title is Constante's flight into self-examination during incarceration. She combines this examination with a meticulous account of prison ritual and routine, and of the boredom which accompanies it. French is the original language of the memoir. Constante began writing it in Paris in 1977, during one of her visits to the French capital after she and her husband, Harry Brauner, were allowed to travel by the Romanian authorities. Publication in Ceauşescu's Romania was out of the question, while publication abroad would have led to exile. So she ended up, in her own words, "writing this book with no hope of ever seeing it published". (p.257).

100 C. Andrew and O. Gordievsky, KGB: The Inside Story of its Foreign Operations from Lenin to Gorbachev (London: Sceptre, 1991), pp.413–15.

101 Hodoş, *Show Trials*, p.63.

102 C. Popişteanu, 'Procesul lui Lucreţiu Pătrăşcanu', *Magazin Istoric*, no.12 (December 1991), p.72.

103 E. Mezincescu, 'Ecouri', p.35.

104 *Ibid.*

105 *Ibid.*

106 C. Popişteanu, 'Procesul lui Lucreţiu Pătrăşcanu', *Magazin Istoric*, no.1 (January 1992), p.86.

107 Gonceariuc explained that during his investigation of Pătrăşcanu the SSI was absorbed into the DGSP and he was made head of Directorate B for Counter-espionage with the rank of Colonel (Popişteanu, 'Cazul Grupului Pătrăşcanu (VII)', p.86). According to the records of the Ministry of the Interior, the SSI was absorbed into the Direcţia Generală a Securităţii Statului (under which title the Direcţia Generală a Securităţii Popor-

ului had been rechristened in 1949) on 2 April 1951. Preparations for the merger had been under way during the preceding months under the supervision of Sakharovsky which involved the transfer of staff from the SSI into the DGSS directorates and, in some cases, their allocation to other duties. Thus Sergei Nikonov (Sergiu Nicolău), who became head of Romanian foreign intelligence (SSI) on 9 January 1947 and at the beginning of April 1951, continued in that position in the renamed (April 1951) service (DGSS) until March 1954. On the latter date, he was appointed head of military intelligence (DIMSM). In 1960, he became head of the Control Directorate of the Ministry of Armed Forces. In November 1960, Nicolău was named head of the Control Office of the Ministry of the Armed Forces, a position he retained until December 1963 when he was moved into the reserve (F. Dobre, *Securitatea. Structuri-cadre, Obiective si Metode* [*The Security Police. Cadres, Objectives and Methods*], vol.1. Consiliul National pentru Studierea Arhivelor Securităţii (Bucharest: Editura Enciclopedică, 2006), p.702.

108 Ionescu, *Communism in Romania*, p.155.

109 Hodoş, *Show trials*, p.99.

110 This has been plausibly argued by Robert Levy *Ana Pauker. The Rise and Fall of a Jewish Communist* (Berkeley: The University of California Press, 2001). pp.143–78.

111 Popişteanu, *Magazin Istoric*, no.12 (December) 1991, p.72.

112 At the plenary meeting of the Central Committee held on 26 May 1952 Georgescu was removed from all his Party and government positions.

113 As maintained by Hodoş, *Show Trials*, p.100.

114 Gheorghiu-Dej's anxiety was well-founded. In April 1968, Colonel Andrei Arghiropol, a former member of the eavesdropping directorate of the *Securitate*, revealed to a Communist Party committee that his first assignment in 1949 had been to intercept Gheorghiu-Dej's telephone calls on the orders of Pintilie and Nicolski. The latter were obviously acting on orders from Moscow (ANIC, Archive of the Executive Committee of the Central Committee, 264, vol.23, p.45). My thanks to Marius Oprea for providing me with this reference.

115 *Scânteia,* 6 December 1949, p.1.

116 *Khrushchev Remembers. The Glasnost Tapes*, translated and edited by J.L. Schecter with V.V. Luchkov (Boston: Little, Brown and Co., 1990), p.103. I am grateful to Robert Levy for this reference. Iudin is more likely to have been consulted in Bucharest since he was the representative of the Comintern when it was based in Yugoslavia and moved with it when its headquarters were transferred to Bucharest in June 1948. Pavel Fedorovich Iudin (1899–1968) was a leading theorist of the Soviet Communist Party. Director of the Institute of Philosophy of the Soviet Academy of Sciences from 1938 to 1944, he was appointed editor-in-chief of the journal Sovetskaya kniga in 1946 and elected a member of the Central Committee at the Nineteenth and Twentieth Party Congresses. He was succeeded as Comintern representative in Bucharest by Mark Borisovich Mitin. Mikhail Andreevich Suslov was appointed secretary of the Central Committee of the Soviet Communist Party in 1947 and between 1947 and 1950 was editor-in-chief of Pravda. (see note 42). In 1950 he became a member of the Praesidium of the Supreme Soviet. Georgi Malenkov was a trusted servant of Stalin. In the 1930s he helped to evaluate intelligence provided by the NKVD for the Politburo and became a member of the five-man State Defence Committee in 1941. He briefly succeeded Stalin as First Secretary.

117 The *Securitate* documents optimistically refer to this period as 'the final stage in the enquiry' (C. Popişteanu, 'Procesul lui Lucreţiu Pătrăşcanu', *Magazin Istoric*, no.9 (September 1991), p.48).

118 Nestorescu-Bălceşti, 'Structura Conducerii Superioare a Partidului Comunist Român', p.361.

119 Mişu Dulbergher (Dulgheru) was born in Tecuci on 16 January 1909. He started his professional life as a bank clerk in Galaţi in 1927. Shortly afterwards he left to take up

positions as an accountant, first with his uncle's firm of wholesale cereals merchants, then at his cousin's shop. In 1938, he married and in the following year he and his wife opened a workshop for making men's underwear. Poor sales led them to seek other employment and in 1940 his wife Liza secured a post at the Soviet commercial legation in Bucharest. Through her intervention Mişu was taken on at the legation as a chauffeur. On the 22 June 1941, the day after Romania's attack on the Soviet Union, the Dulberghers were arrested and interned at Târgu Jiu where they were 'adopted' by the Communist internees. Mişu was sent out on work parties while Liza spent her time in a workshop in the camp wrapping soap in cellophane. After the 23 August 1944 *coup*, Mişu was assisted by fellow inmate Vania Didenko (Ion Vidraşcu), an NKVD agent who played a leading role in setting up a Communist secret police. After a brief period in the 'Patriotic Guards', the Communist paramilitary group run by Bodnăraş, Dulbergher was made an inspector in the *Siguranţa* on 15 March 1945. It was at this time that, in order to provide himself with a cover, he changed his name to Dulgheru. When the DGSS was established in 1948, he was made head of the Directorate for Penal Investigation.

In internal evaluations Dulgheru was praised for his 'vigilence'. Lena Constante, one of the political prisoners who encountered him (in 1951), described him as follows: "He was tall, about 40 to 50 years old, in a light grey suit. He received me in a spacious and elegant office. The furniture was upholstered in bright-red velvet... I sat down on a chair which had been placed for me some distance from his desk. He told me that if I told the truth he would give me some American cigarettes. He opened the door at the back of the office, which opened onto a sort of cupboard, took a packet of Chesterfield cigarettes, and gave me one. But I said nothing". (Marius Oprea, 'Micul funcţionar şi capcanele memoriei', *Dilema*, no.126 (9–15 June), 1995, p.9 and *Cartea Albă a Securităţii*, vol.I, doc.159, p.332.

120 Nestorescu-Bălceşti, 'Structura Conducerii Superioare a Partidului Comunist Român', p.362.

121 Şoltuţiu was a railwayman who became party secretary for Cluj county after the war and was recruited into the SSI in 1949 by Rangheţ. The rest of Şoltuţiu's team was composed of Maj. Toma Drăghici, Maj. Gheran Moraru, Maj. Victor Vânătoru, Maj. Teodor Staicu, Maj. Mircea Anghel, Maj. Teodor Micle, Gheorghe Rujan and Alexandru Gorun. Transcripts of some of the interrogations conducted in the marathon Pătrăşcanu investigation show the resilience and dignity of this veteran Communist whose resolve and commitment had been steeled in the prison camps of King Carol's governments and who was now forced to call upon those resources to withstand an immeasurably greater ordeal at the hands of those acting in the name of erstwhile colleagues and the party he had served. Here, by way of an example, is an extract from the transcript of the interrogation conducted by Lt. Col. Ioan Şoltuţiu between 0825 and 1300 hrs on 23 October 1952 which was countersigned as a correct record by Pătrăsăcanu:

Question: Why did you oppose the extension of the law regarding war criminals?

Answer: I opposed it because I considered that Romania had fulfilled her obligations under the Armistice Convention.

Question: What did the Party demand of you in connection with the extension of the law regarding war criminals?

Answer: The Party demanded nothing of me in this respect. In March or April 1947 the President of the Allied (Soviet) Control Commission sent a letter to the Romanian government presenting a series of cases requiring the extension of the law on war criminals. Since I considered these cases inconclusive, I maintained my initial point of view.

Question: Whose interests were you serving by adopting this point of view?

Answer: By not extending the law on war criminals I served the interests of the Romanian state.

Question: What discussions and with whom from Palace circles did you discuss the problem of the war criminals.

Answer: I discussed this problem with the former King Michael. King Michael was against the extension of this law. On this matter the King had the same view as I did.

Question: Do you admit that you sabotaged the extension of the law on war criminals?

Answer: I do not recognize this because it cannot be a question of sabotage

C. Popişteanu, 'Procesul lui Lucreţiu Pătrăşcanu', *Magazin Istoric*, no.1 (January 1992), p.86).

122 C. Popişteanu, 'Procesul lui Lucreţiu Pătrăşcanu', *Magazin Istoric*, no.12 (December 1991), p.74. Dulgheru was interrogated for two years and three months but no charges were brought against him and he was released. Unlike the victims of his directorate he was not tortured during his detention and was well fed, given medicines when he required them and clean clothing. In 1967, Dulgheru recounted details of his arrest and interrogation to the party commission on rehabilitation. On 26 November 1952, he was ordered by Pintilie to go to the *Securitate* detention centre on Strada Uranus in Bucharest to receive an important prisoner. Upon arrival there he was placed under arrest for carrying out 'an identified criminal activity'. His interrogators lacked experience, according to Dulgheru, but they received guidance from Sakharovsky and Tiganov, the counsellor of the directorate for penal investigation. "Various methods were used to destroy my morale, culminating in interrogation in shifts. I was taken for interrogation on Wednesday morning and held without food or sleep until 2 p.m. on Saturday, that is for eighty hours, while the interrogators were replaced every eight hours." After nine months he was handed over to interrogator Teodor Micle who repeatedly uttered threats against Dulgheru's life and that of his wife and children. Addressing the Party commission on rehabilitation in 1967 Dulgheru exclaimed:

Comrades, I do not want to be misunderstood. I maintain, however, that from 1941 until 1944, the period in which I was held in the Târgu Jiu internment camp, I did not experience by a long way such maltreatment as that applied to be by my own people....Sakharovsky showed a particular interest in my interrogation since he sought at any price to prove the guilt of Pătrăşcanu and of those arrested in connection with the Pătrăşcanu enquiry. I felt this personally during my own interrogation when he wanted to prove that I was a spy

(C. Popişteanu, 'Procesul lui Lucreţiu Pătrăşcanu'*Magazin Istoric*, no.12 (December 1991), p.74).

118. Sakharovsky's leading role was emphasized in Şoltuţiu's declaration to the Party committee in 1967:

> In 1952 the interrogation of the Pătrăşcanu group was under my direction, but this was a mere formality since the enquiry was directed by the two Soviet counsellors, Sakharovsky and Tiganov, and by comrade Minister Drăghici.
>
> ...
>
> The process of interrogation was as follows: one copy of all the declarations of Pătrăşcanu, or of others in the group which were of some importance in respect of Pătrăşcanu, was given to Sakharovsky, and another to Drăghici... After this I was summoned either to Sakharovsky's office, or to that of Drăghici, where I received instructions as to how to proceed...
>
> The declarations which I handed over to Drăghici were returned to me personally by him...and on them were notes in the margin written by Gheorghiu-Dej, while comrade Minister Drăghici told me how to carry on the interrogation. When these declarations were given back to me counsellor Sakharovsky, who was Drăghici's personal advisor, was in most cases present. Throughout the interrogations I realized that the counsellor was in permanent contact with Gheorghiu-Dej and Chişinevski.
>
> ...
>
> I recall a moment when, in the presence of either comrade Minister Pintilie, or of comrade Minister Drăghici, counsellor Sakharovsky said that all that the interrogation had established at that point were Pătrăşcanu's mistakes, but that here it was not a question of mistakes, but of hostile and treacherous actions on the part of Pătrăşcanu. We interrogators had to understand this, for they, the Soviets, have all the details in connection with the hostile and treacherous attitude of Pătrăşcanu right from the time when he was in Moscow as a representative of the Romanian Communist Party at the Comintern. I emphasize that the questions put by me to Pătrăşcanu were formulated by counsellor Sakharovsky on the basis of the material he had from the other interrogations

(C. Popişteanu, 'Procesul lui Lucreţiu Pătrăşcanu', *Magazin Istoric*, no.12 (December 1991), p.74).

Şoltuţiu also admitted that some of the Pătrăşcanu group had been beaten, namely Koffler, Calmanovici and Zilber, but disclaimed any knowledge of torture administered to Lena Constante. He alleged that Sakharovsky had suggested the use of force against the prisoners and denied that he had played any part in it. Two footnotes are worth providing to illustrate the cynicism of the regime in the Pătrăşcanu affair: Major Toma Drăghici, one of the interrogators, was given Pătrăşcanu's appartment on Strada Vasile Lascăr no.100; and Drăghici and his fellow *Securitate* interrogators Alexandru Gorun, Victor Vânătoru, Gheran Moraru, Teodor Micle, Gheorghe Rujan, Ludovic Weiss and Ioan Şoltuţiu, were all decorated "for their important contribution to the struggle for the defence of the fatherland and the working people" on 22 May 1954, 36 days after the execution of Pătrăşcanu (C. Popişteanu, 'Procesul lui Lucreţiu Pătrăşcanu', *Magazin Istoric*, no.12 (December 1991), p.75).

123 Arhivele Naţionale Istorice Centrale (ANIC), Archive of the Executive Committee of the Central Committee, 264, vol.20, pp.309–63. My thanks to Marius Oprea for sharing this report with me.

124 For this reason Gheorghiu-Dej and Pauker compiled questionnaires which were put to Belu Zilber by his SSI interrogator George Firescu (real name Filipescu) in the winter of 1949. Gheorghiu-Dej could not hide signs of an inferiority complex in the questions he had transmitted, being particularly insistent as to why Zilber had allegedly described him as a 'zombie' and uneducated. Pauker, on the other hand, was more interested in the 'capitalist' literature Zilber had read (Şerbulescu, *Monarhia de Drept Dialectic*, p.75).

6 Gheorghiu-Dej's consolidation of power

In 1952, Gheorghiu-Dej had two major rivals in the Romanian leadership—Ana Pauker and Vasile Luca—but even he could not simply have them removed. There had to be ostensibly doctrinal reasons. By 1950, Zionism had replaced Titoism as the heresy of the day and by this token Pauker fell into the suspect category. In May 1951, at the celebration of the thirtieth anniversary of the Romanian Communist Party, Gheorghiu-Dej recognized Pauker and Luca as the oldest serving members of the Party leadership but they acknowledged him as the sole leader. Barely four months later, Gheorghiu-Dej was in Moscow, accompanied by fellow Politburo members Iosif Chişinevski and Miron Constantinescu, seeking Stalin's approval for the purge of Ana Pauker, Vasile Luca and Teohari Georgescu. One reason for Gheorghiu-Dej's eagerness was the opposition shown by Pauker and Georgescu to the trial of Pătrăşcanu. It has been credibly argued that Pauker and Georgescu resisted attempts to prosecute Pătrăşcanu on trumped-up charges and that their protection of him was a significant factor in the delay in bringing him to trial. This obstruction contributed to the charge of 'right-wing deviationism' launched against them both in May 1952.[1]

The origins of Pauker's downfall are to be found in the 'verification' findings relating to party membership. This 'verification' had been based on a Central Committee decision of November 1948 aimed at eliminating 'careerist and opportunist' elements and the investigation had lasted until May 1950. It resulted in a purge which removed 192,000 "exploiting and hostile elements" from the party who had been granted membership following a formal pact made in August 1945 by Teohari Georgescu acting for Pauker and the leader of the Iron Guard. Andrei Vyshinsky, the Soviet deputy foreign minister, was particularly critical of Pauker in this regard and it was he who had first suggested to Gheorghiu-Dej in January 1946 that he remove Pauker.[2] On 23 June 1950, an article by Gheorghiu-Dej had appeared in the Cominform journal *For a Lasting Peace, for a People's Democracy* condemning this recruitment policy which had led to the admittance into the party of "careerists... Fascists, bourgeois nationalists, exploiters, etc.". [3] Pauker could be held to account for this failing.

In September 1951, the campaign was stepped up and in Moscow an article signed by Gheorghiu-Dej appeared in *Pravda* on 4 September which resumed the Soviet-inspired drive to put Pătrăşcanu on trial:

> In the spring of 1948, when Pătrăşcanu and his accomplices were unmasked, it was proved that they constituted a secret enemy conclave in the leadership of our party. The penetration of enemy agents into our party leadership is explained by the fact that during the war and immediately afterwards our vigilance was weak.[4]

The arrest of Rudolf Slánský, the secretary-general of the Czechoslovak Communist Party, on 24 November 1951 as part of a Zionist 'conspiracy', sent another signal to Pauker that despite her close relations with Stalin and Molotov she was not immune, and yet another to Gheorghiu-Dej that she was not untouchable. Gheorghiu-Dej acted upon the signal to remove his only serious rivals for power. At a Central Committee plenary meeting held on 29 February and 1 March 1952 attacks were launched against Luca, and by implication Pauker and Georgescu, which presaged their eventual purge.

Several interpretations of the purge have been offered and require discussion. First, the purge was not *simply* a manifestation of a struggle between a 'native' Gheorghiu-Dej faction and the Pauker 'Moscow' faction. We have only to point to the fact that Teohari Georgescu, who was an ethnic Romanian and had spent the war years with Gheorghiu-Dej, was included among the 'right-wing deviators'. Georgescu's inclusion may have resulted from Gheorghiu-Dej's fear that Stalin might use him against him since the Cominform had in 1940 suggested Georgescu as general secretary of the Party, an elevation that Georgescu is said to have refused.[5]

Second, the attack on Pauker should not be seen in itself as evidence of anti-Semitism. When the order came from Stalin to purge alleged Zionists throughout the Soviet bloc, Pauker's Jewishness was a fortunate accident for Gheorghiu-Dej; he used the opportunity to dismiss not just Pauker but the gentile Luca who was a Transylvanian Hungarian. Moreover, two of Gheorghiu-Dej's associates in his move to take advantage of Stalin's paranoid delusions about a Zionist 'conspiracy' were themselves Jews, namely Iosif Chişinevski, who became a leading figure in the party secretariat and Leonte Răutu, the head of the party propaganda body.[6]

Third, the purge should not be interpreted as the embryo of Gheorghiu-Dej's autonomous policies of the late 1950s. Gheorghiu-Dej had shown himself to be no less Stalinist than Pauker and Luca. It was Gheorghiu-Dej who carried out Stalin's brief of denouncing Tito at the Cominform conference in Bucharest in July 1949, and in the following year he ordered the deportation of the Serb minorities living on Romania's border with Yugoslavia to an area east of Bucharest.[7] While the signal for the purge came from Stalin, the identity of the victims suggested itself and Gheorghiu-Dej went ahead with advice from his Soviet advisors. The charges against the 'deviators', as Pauker, Luca and Georgescu were dubbed, were prepared by Constantinescu, Chişinevski and Alexandru Moghioroş under strict supervision from Soviet counsellors, the principal one of whom was Aleksandr Mihailovici Sakharovsky, the Soviet security advisor to the Ministry of the Interior. A second Soviet 'advisor' who is alleged to have been consulted was

Mark Borisovich Mitin, a member of the Central Committee of the CPSU and editor-in-chief of *For a Lasting Peace, for a People's Democracy*.[8]

Luca was vulnerable. Several months earlier, in September 1951, the *Securitate* had begun to report an increase in violent criticism of the government and of the Russians as a result of persistent rumours of a currency reform. These rumours regarding what would be, in effect, a second confiscation of people's savings—following on the currency reform of August 1947—had been reinforced by the issue of instructions by the Ministry of Finance and the State Bank to speed up tax collection. Popular dissatisfaction with the reform continued after its introduction and Gheorghiu-Dej called upon Luca, as Minister of Finance, to pay the price for it, even though the reform had been drawn up with the approval of the entire Politburo at the insistence of the relevant Soviet counsellors. In Gheorghiu-Dej's reckoning Luca had to go in order to create a breach in the Pauker group. Increasingly prey to fits of anger—he suffered from chronic asthma, chronic laryngitis and problems with his liver, which forced him to follow a special diet—Luca offered the easiest target. Furthermore, Luca had lost several of his friends because of his behaviour and was therefore less difficult to remove.

The attack was mounted at the Central Committee plenary meeting held on 29 February and 1 March 1952. Luca was criticized for allowing 'grave' mistakes and 'frauds' to be committed by the Finance Ministry and the National Bank when applying the currency reform of 28 January. In a meeting of the Politburo which preceded the plenary meeting, Pauker and Georgescu came to the defence of Luca but without success. They were to pay for their action. By taking a 'conciliatory line' and shielding Luca, they could be implicated in these errors.[9] On 9 March, the report of the party commission set up by the Central Committee to investigate the actions of Luca and his 'rightist deviation' denounced the activity of "a large number of hostile, contra-revolutionary elements, grouped around comrade V. Luca, who have extensively undermined the regime of the people's democracy". The report recommended Luca's dismissal as Minister of Finance, which was announced in *Scînteia* the same day. The charges were presented to the Central Committee at a meeting held on 13 March. They consisted of aiding "capitalist elements in the villages and towns" through fiscal measures and increasing prices of agricultural products, of undermining the progress of industrialization by 'putting a brake on investment', and betraying Party secrets in respect of the currency reform".[10]

The March report of the party commission into Luca's 'rightist deviation' concluded that he should be dismissed as Minister of Finance and should be sent for investigation by the Party Control Commission on the grounds of having sabotaged the currency reform and of undermining the development of collective farms.[11] It demanded, in addition, "the mobilization of the entire Party in the fight against opportunism and conciliatoriness and the unmasking of Vasile Luca's and T. Georgescu's waywardness".[12] The term 'waywardness' (*împăciuitorism*) was soon to be replaced in party accusations against both men by the more dreaded 'deviation' (*deviere*).

Luca's expulsion from the party followed at a second plenary meeting on 26–27 May. Pauker was strongly criticized at the same plenary meeting for having "helped and encouraged the rightist deviations of Luca and Georgescu", and was not re-elected to the Politburo, but since she had "acknowledged some of her errors" she was allowed to retain her post as foreign minister.[13] The next day, *Scînteia* reported that Georgescu, Minister of the Interior since November 1944, whose defence of Luca Gheorghiu-Dej had never forgiven, had been replaced by Alexandru Drăghici.[14]

Gheorghiu-Dej's pre-eminence in the Romanian Party was sealed by his appointment, on 2 June 1952, as president of the council of ministers (prime minister), a post which he combined with that of secretary-general of the party held since October 1945. He promptly intensified the attack on Luca, Pauker and Georgescu. In a speech delivered on 29 June, he blamed Luca for "retarding the development of heavy industry", for protecting thousands of kulaks by disguising them as middle peasants, and for encouraging capitalism and profiteering. Pauker was condemned for obstructing the organization of cooperative farms and Georgescu for allowing the abuses committed by Luca and Pauker to take place.[15]

Luca was arrested on 16 August 1952 and placed under interrogation. It lasted until the autumn 1954 when he was put on trial. Arrested alongside him were 28 persons. The interrogation of Luca and his associates was coordinated by the Soviet counsellors to the Ministry of the Interior. Colonel Francisc Butyka, charged with leading the interrogation of Luca later recalled:

> At that time we had Soviet counsellors who took the initiative from the very start. And as usual, as in other cases, nothing was done without their guidance. The entire strategy of the inquiry, including the questions, was translated into Russian and monitored by the counsellors.[16]

Butyka's contact with the Soviet counsellor in question, Tiganov, was through General Vladimir Mazuru, one of the deputies of Gheorghe Pintilie, head of the *Securitate*. Brute force, involving beatings with an iron rod, was also applied, as one of the interrogators himself admitted to the party enquiry in March 1968. Alexandru Jacob, one of the prisoners, told his interrogator: "If I am badly beaten with an iron rod, as has been threatened, I shall try to tell the truth, but if I cannot stand the beatings, I shall invent lies".[17] Ion Craiu, another prisoner in the Luca group, was "beaten and held 40 days and nights without sleep, being forced in this way to sign statements which did not contain what I had declared".[18]

Using these methods the *Securitate*, under Soviet supervision, extracted from the 29 prisoners one falsehood after another. These formed the charges upon which three were sent for trial along with Luca; 24 were released, and one died while in custody. The other three to be put on trial were Alexandru Jacob, the Deputy Finance Minister, Ivan Solymos and Dumitru Cernicica, both senior trade and finance officials. Jacob was sentenced to 20 years' hard labour, Solymos to 15 and

Cernicica to three. Whether this group was to be placed on trial with Pătrăşcanu remains a matter of speculation but any such plans were probably buried with Stalin's death.[19]

Pauker and Georgescu were initially spared arrest but the political assassination of the former proceeded rapidly. A rumour campaign was launched by the *Securitate* that she had contacts with Western intelligence agencies through her brother who lived in Israel, and that she had money deposited in a personal bank account in Switzerland. On 5 July 1952, she was dismissed as foreign minister but held on to her post as vice-premier of the council of ministers until 24 November when she was stripped of that as well. Her association with Stalin and Molotov may well explain why her gradual elimination from public life was gradual, in contrast to Luca's abrupt arrest. The manner of her exit from politics, as well as the fact that she was succeeded as foreign minister by Simion Bughici, also a Jew, shows that her demise had little to do with the anti-Semitic drive which was at its height at the time in the rest of Eastern Europe.

Pauker was arrested on 20 February 1953. Like Luca, she denied the accusations of 'rightist deviation.' She was interrogated about her activity in Moscow during the war and her contacts with the Comintern, but she was spared the tribulations of Luca and Georgescu. Stalin's death proved her salvation. As a result of several telephone calls from Molotov to Gheorghiu-Dej, she was released exactly two months after her arrest (on 20 April). She was effectively a political corpse; she lived a secluded existence in Bucharest until her death on 3 June 1960.

With the purge of Pauker, Gheorghiu-Dej had removed his most formidable political rival. Their rivalry was fuelled by intense personal dislike of each other, which Gheorghiu-Dej later tried to obscure in periodic bouts of nostalgia in Politburo meetings when he reminisced about his 'friendship' with 'our Ana'. What Pauker lacked in proletarian credentials, she more than made up with her experience in the Comintern and her contacts in Moscow. For Gheorghiu-Dej the position was reversed. Each played upon their respective strengths in their struggle for Stalin's favour. Pauker's views on Gheorghiu-Dej were reflected in her discussion with the Soviet emissary Lesakov in August 1947.[20] She often attempted to outmanoeuvre Gheorghiu-Dej by emphasizing her loyalty to Moscow while suggesting that Gheorghiu-Dej was inclined to look to the West. But such arguments proved unconvincing. Vyshinsky held her responsible for the admission of thousands of Iron Guardists into the RCP and it was ultimately this charge which provided Gheorghiu-Dej with a convenient pretext for her purge.

Georgescu and his deputy at the interior ministry, Marin Jianu, had been arrested two days before Pauker, on 18 February 1953.[21] The enquiry into Georgescu's activities lasted two and a half years and set itself two objectives: first, "the verification in detail of the entire activity of Teohari Georgescu up to 23 August 1944", and second, "to ascertain the nature of the counter-revolutionary activity of Teohari Georgescu during the time he was Minister of the Interior and of his hostile and anti-state activity alongside Vasile Luca and Ana Pauker".[22]

In the first matter, the *Securitate* investigators could find no reliable evidence that Georgescu had prejudiced the party in any way and they concluded that "we have no precise proof that Teohari Georgescu was an informer of the *Siguranța*, as some indirect evidence suggested".[23] Following the second line of enquiry, they found that "in the period in which Teohari Georgescu was Minister of the Interior, he conducted himself against the interests of the party and the state. Losing his sense of class, he formed relations with corrupt and hostile elements". These included former Iron Guardists for whom Georgescu was alleged, under the influence of Pauker, to have facilitated contacts between 1945 and 1947 with members of the democratic opposition in order to sabotage the regime. Georgescu was also found to have had extra-marital relations over a long period with a considerable number of woman—41 on his own admission—most of whom were 'dubious elements' belonging to the 'bourgeois class'. These relations were largely sexual favours demanded by Georgescu from the wives and daughters of political detainees in return for their release. He was also found to have accepted large sums of money and jewellery from businessmen seeking a passport to emigrate.[24] Jianu was accused of selling a passport, in one case, for a set of cutlery!

In spite of the evidence which had been amassed against them, neither Georgescu nor Jianu were brought to trial. In contrast to thousands of others, they passed through the hands of the *Securitate* and emerged shaken but relatively unscathed. After his release in 1956, Georgescu was sent to work as a proofreader at the 13 December printing press (formerly *Cartea Românească*) and in a sign of magnanimity from Gheorghiu-Dej was made director of this same press in which he had secured his first job in 1923 as a typesetter.[25]

Stalin's death on 5 March 1953, and the trial and execution of Beria in December of the same year, ushered in a power struggle in the Kremlin; it also removed the pressure on Gheorghiu-Dej for a major show trial. The struggle confused the party leaderships in the satellite states but did not affect the master-servant relationship. In internal and external policies Romania, like the other East European satellite states, continued to imitate the Soviet Union. Gheorghiu-Dej showed himself to be both cunning and cautious in handling the repercussions of the Soviet political succession. By continuing with the trials of 'spies' and 'terrorists' he could arm himself against possible criticism of relaxing 'vigilance' against 'imperialist' enemies and earn himself some time to see which way the wind was blowing in Moscow. It became clear that separation of power was to be the order of the day when Khrushchev became first secretary of the CPSU in September 1953 and Georgi Malenkov was made prime minister. Yet this very separation of power in the Soviet Union gave Gheorghiu-Dej more room to manoeuvre and weave and until April 1954, he resisted Soviet pressure to separate his own powers as general secretary and premier by introducing collective leadership. Before doing so he took perhaps the most cynical decision of a career littered with shameful deeds of repression. In order to eliminate a possible rival to his personal power who he anticipated might receive the support of the 'reformist' Soviet leadership, he ordered that Lucrețiu Pătrăşcanu, who had been held in custody since 1948, be brought to trial.[26] It was not staged as a Soviet initiative, but was, rather, a manoeuvre by Gheorghiu-Dej to hold on to power in the face of de-Stalinization. The absence of any proof of the 'guilt' of the defendant made a mockery of the principles of a fair trial and justice and showed that Gheorghiu-Dej was merely using the cover of legality to remove his most serious rival. This required a reprise of the previous six years, conducted in the categories of Communist social theory.

The charges against Pătrăşcanu had been presented on 22 February 1948 at the First Congress of the Romanian Workers' Party. Teohari Georgescu, the Minister of the Interior, had denounced Pătrăşcanu as "an exponent of bourgeois ideology" who had "overestimated the forces of the enemy, that is, of the class-enemy, potentially helped by the Western imperialist powers".[27] These accusations had been expanded in a resolution of the Central Committee plenary meeting of 10–11 June:

> Several weeks before March 1945 Pătrăşcanu, in complete contradiction to the party line, resuscitated the slogan of collaboration with the whole bourgeoisie or with an important part of it. In 1946 he defended the thesis of an alliance with the whole peasantry, including the exploiting elements hostile to the working peasantry... In his practical activity he followed the policy of appeasement towards the exponents of bourgeois-landlord reaction when the Party was fully engaged in the struggle against reaction. He followed the line of nationalist-chauvinist policy.[28]

Gheorghiu-Dej's decision to place Pătrăşcanu on trial was influenced by Malenkov's wish that Gheorghiu-Dej introduce collective leadership, and by Malenkov's recognition that while Pătrăşcanu continued to live Gheorghiu-Dej would be reluctant to take such a step. In November 1967, when the trial and execution of Pătrăşcanu were examined by a party commission, Dumitru Petrescu, a veteran Communist, recalled a visit made by a Romanian government delegation to Moscow in January 1954 composed of Gheorghiu-Dej, Miron Constantinescu, Alexandru Bârlădeanu and himself. During the visit Constantinescu confided to Petrescu that he was taking to Malenkov a fifty-page dossier in Russian containing charges to be brought against Pătrăşcanu and a demand for the death sentence. When asked by Constantinescu for his opinion Petrescu declined to give one; when Constantinescu returned from seeing Malenkov, Petrescu stated, "he told me he had solved the problem. In what sense he did not say, but I understood 'solved' to mean that the Soviets had given their agreement to Pătrăşcanu's execution".[29]

On 14 March 1954, it was announced that the Romanian Politburo had decided "that the trial of the group of spies headed by Pătrăşcanu should now go ahead".[30] It was held *in camera* between 6 and 13 April 1954. No word had been published of Pătrăşcanu's arrest or interrogation and nothing was revealed about the conduct of the trial. The only information disclosed concerned the charges—which were summarized under their legal headings as articles of the penal code but not defined—the findings of the military tribunal, and the executions of Pătrăşcanu and Remus Koffler which were reported in a communiqué published in *Scînteia* on 18 April. It was only after Ceauşescu's downfall in 1989 that fuller details of Pătrăşcanu's ordeal were made public.

Pătrăşcanu was tried with ten co-defendants, Remus Koffler, Herbert (Belu) Zilber, Ion Mocsonyi-Stârcea, Alexandru Ştefănescu, Jac Berman, Emil Calmanovici, Victoria Sârbu, Harry Brauner, Lena Constante and Herant Torossian. The list of their alleged crimes ran to 36 pages. Pătrăşcanu himself was charged with:

> a) crime against peace, in that he served as an agent of the Fascist and bourgeois-landowners' police, and of the British Secret Service in trying to break up the Communist Party from within and paralyse its actions in the fight against Fascism and the imperialist war, and had supported Antonescu and the war against the Soviet Union; b) the crime of high treason, in that as Minister of Justice he led a group of conspirators who, with the help of the Anglo-American imperialists and their intelligence agencies, worked for the violent overthrow of the democratic regime installed on 6 March 1945 with a view to destroy the independence of the Romanian state; and c) the crime of high treason, in that he passed to the British and American intelligence agencies after 23 August 1944 secret information regarding the security of the Romanian state.

The same three charges were levelled against Zilber and Ştefănescu, while Koffler, Berman, Calmanovici were accused of a) and c). Only one charge (a) was brought against Sârbu and Mocsonyi-Stârcea (b). Constante was accused of a) "high treason, in that she passed secret information to the British Secret Service regarding the security of the Romanian state", and b) "complicity in Pătrăşcanu's actions designed to destroy Romania's independence". Brauner and Torossian faced these same charges, except that the latter was alleged to have passed information to the CIA.[31] According to an eyewitness account published in Athens in May 1958, certain Communists were paraded for the prosecution, among them Ecaterina Borilă, wife of Gheorghiu-Dej's associate Petre Borilă, who testified that Pătrăşcanu was plotting to gain power, and Ana Toma, wife of DGSS chief Gheorghe Pintilie (Bodnarenko). Ilka Wassermann, director of the Russian-language publishing house *Cartea rusă* alleged that Pătrăşcanu had connections with Western agents, was a nationalist and anti-Semite, and that he had collaborated with the *Siguranţa*. No proof of the allegations was provided. If Pătrăşcanu listened with disgust at the fabrications of his former Communist colleagues, he found the use of Gheorghe Tătărescu, King Carol's prime minister and a Communist stooge, too much to stomach. Rising from his seat he protested:

> Such scum of history are brought to this trial as witnesses against me, whom am a Communist. If such an individual has to prove that I am not a Communist, it is only a proof of the low level of the

> Romanian Communist Party which needs such elements, as well as evidence of the total lack of proof in this odious trial, so that it has been necessary to resort to such a witness.[32]

Neither Borilă, Toma nor Wassermann figure in the list of the 87 witnesses to be called which was annexed to the charge sheet drawn up by Colonel Rudolf Rosman, deputy chief military procurator, on 30 March 1954.[33]

The nature of the charges against Pătrăşcanu—"crimes against peace", "having supported Antonescu and the war against the Soviet Union" and being "an agent of British espionage"—brought the trial within the competence of a military court according to Romanian law.[34] It was therefore conducted in front of a military tribunal made up of Colonel Ilie Moisescu, the chairman, Colonel Alexandru Demeter and Colonel Ion Ciulei. The prosecuting counsel were Colonel Aurel Ardealeanu, Colonel Grigore Râpeanu, Colonel Rudolf Rosman and Major Ioan Pohonţiu.[35] Details of the conduct of the trial were given by Moisescu to the party commission on 24 April 1967. The order in which the witnesses were to be called, and the examination of the accused to take place, was pre-arranged by Iosif Chişinevski, a member of the Central Committee secretariat, the chief interrogator Ioan Şoltuţiu, and Moisescu. Neither the defendants nor their counsel, who were appointed by the court, were given the opportunity to question the witnesses and the defendants' statements, with the exception of those of Pătrăşcanu and Ştefănescu who were said to have nothing to say in their defence, were all self-incriminating.[36] Pătrăşcanu, in a pre-trial interview with Moisescu, expressed doubts as to whether Moisescu and his colleagues were ready to serve the interests of justice and declared the trial to be a 'frame-up'. He considered the charges against him were not in the tribunal's competence and could only be heard by the party leadership. Moisescu informed Chişinevski of Pătrăşcanu's attitude but Şoltuţiu 'guaranteed' that Pătrăşcanu would talk at the trial. In the event the interrogator was wrong. Pătrăşcanu refused to recognize the tribunal and remained silent. During the trial Moisescu was constantly summoned to the telephone by Chişinevski who instructed him as to how to proceed; on one occasion Moisescu was told to keep his questions of the accused to a minimum. Even the sentences were prescribed by the party leadership and dictated to Moisescu by Chişinevski while Gheorghiu-Dej followed the results of this stage management by listening to the proceedings on a tape recorder.[37]

The court's findings, announced in *Scânteia*, were that between 1940 and 1944 "the accused Pătrăşcanu, Koffler and their accomplices, together with the spy Alexandru Ştefănescu and the *agents provocateurs* and spies Ştefan Foriş, H. Zilber, E. Calmanovoci and J. Berman, had sought to weaken the struggle of the democratic forces against Fascism..." Investigations had shown that since 1940 Pătrăşcanu had been in contact with the Iron Guard head of the *Siguranţa* Alexandru Ghica and that he had been one of its most unscrupulous agents. During the war these agents and spies had betrayed many anti-Fascist patriots. In 1943, the court maintained, Pătrăşcanu arranged with Piki Vasiliu, the under-secretary of State at the Ministry of the Interior, to be interned for several months in the camp at Târgu Jiu to avoid any suspicion of contact with the *Siguranța*. After 23 August 1944, Pătrăşcanu was said to have received instructions from "some imperialist powers" to keep his office at any cost so that he could work against the interests of Romania. The court argued that he had organized a plot against the state and that about 24 February 1945 he had transmitted to Rădescu, via the American spy L. Madison, his agreement for the organization of a *coup*.[38]

With the help of the American 'spies' Thomas Hall and William Hamilton, Pătrăşcanu and his group made contact with the 'conspiratorial' group of Iuliu Maniu, Victor Rădulescu-Pogoneanu, Grigore Niculescu-Buzeşti, Constantin Vişoianu, and Ion Mocsony-Stârcea in order to organize a *coup* against the 'people's state'. The linkman between the two groups was Zilber. Pătrăşcanu was entrusted with leadership of the *coup* and in February 1947 he made contact abroad with Vişoianu and Niculescu-Buzeşti who had fled the country (Pătrăşcanu travelled to Paris at this time for the signing of the Peace Treaty). In the event of the plot's failure, Pătrăşcanu was to be smuggled out of the country by Hall and Hamilton but the two American agents were forced to leave the country unexpectedly and Pătrăşcanu was therefore forced to make his own arrangements to flee.[39] Pătrăşcanu's disgust and contempt at the trial proceedings, and at the behaviour of his old friend, Zilber, overflowed in court. During Zilber's final statement, Pătrăşcanu continually interrupted him, accusing him of being 'a wretch' who defiled his (Pătrăşcanu's) name when he uttered it. He condemned the trial as an outrage. When invited by the judge to make his own final statement, Pătrăşcanu said that he had nothing to say "except to spit on the accusations made against him".[40]

On the morning of 14 April, after the capital sentence on Pătrăşcanu and Koffler had been decided upon *by unanimous vote in the Politburo*, the court's verdict was pronounced.[41] Pătrăşcanu and Koffler were sentenced to death, Zilber, Ştefănescu and Calmanovici to hard labour for life, Mocsony-Stârcea and Torosian to 15 years hard labour, H. Brauner and L. Constante to 12 years hard labour, J. Berman to ten years hard labour, and V. Sârbu to eight years.[42] Pătrăşcanu refused to request a pardon, unlike Koffler who was, nevertheless, denied one. Pătrăşcanu's execution took place at Jilava prison at 3 a.m. on 17 April 1954 by firing squad, more than six years after he had been arrested.[43] According to Ministry of the Interior records Koffler was executed on 17 April.

At the very same Politburo meeting that determined the fate of Pătrăşcanu, Gheorghiu-Dej demonstrated his conformity to the new Soviet model by introducing collective leadership. On the same day that *Scânteia* published the communiqué about the trial—18 April—it was announced that a plenary session of the Central Committee decided to abolish the post of secretary-general and replace it with a secretariat headed by a first secretary. Gheorghiu-Dej resigned as secretary-general of the party but remained president of the council of ministers. His friend Gheorghe Apostol was elected first secretary of the RWP while the other three secretaries were all new: Nicolae Ceauşescu, Mihai Dalea and Janos Fazekas. Ceauşescu and Drăghici were at the same time made candidate members of the Politburo, a sign that both were on their way up the Party hierarchy and that the dominance of one would require the removal of the other. The timing of Ceauşescu's promotion, coming as it did after the Pătrăşcanu trial and execution in which Drăghici as Minister of the Interior was deeply implicated, proved extremely convenient 14 years later when Ceauşescu could claim his innocence in the affair whilst proclaiming Drăghici's guilt.

By executing Pătrăşcanu Gheorghiu-Dej was able to pre-empt any Soviet attempt to impose a post-Stalinist restructuring of the party. Unlike Poland or Hungary where such victims of Stalinist terror as Gomulka and Nagy were elevated to the party leadership, Romania now lacked a living martyr. Moreover, Gheorghiu-Dej could argue that Stalinists had already been purged from the Romanian Party by pointing to the removal of Pauker and Luca. To underline his point he ordered the trial of Luca in October 1954. Unlike the Pătrăşcanu trial, foreign correspondents were admitted, but this time the defendant's replies were read into the record by the president of the tribunal in order to avoid the embarrassment caused in the Pătrăşcanu trial by the latter's outbursts.[44] Luca's trial lasted four days. He was found guilty of charges of sabotage of the economy and conspiracy, and sentenced to death on 10 October. After entering a plea for clemency, his sentence was commuted to forced labour for life.[45]

A trial of Ana Pauker was not to be excluded. Debates in October over her fate appear to have caused the postponement, for the second time, of the party congress. This was announced only two days before it was due to convene and followed more than two months of intense congress propaganda. The announcement said that the congress would be held "after the completion of necessary autumnal agricultural work" but, as the British minister to Bucharest reported, it was doubtful whether there could have been any sudden economic crisis of sufficient gravity to necessitate a last-minute postponement after so much advance publicity. The minister suggested a (more plausible) reason, derived from his Yugoslav colleagues; that in fact it was a political matter, concerning the "disposal of Ana Pauker who had not yet been tried"; that there were two factions, one led by Gheorghiu-Dej, the other by Bodnăraş, with the latter supporting Pauker's rehabilitation. Some colour was given to this theory, otherwise unsubstantiated, by the non-appearance of Bodnăraş at any official function for three months from early November. Nevertheless, the manner in which Gheorghiu-Dej was toasted by the Soviet ambassador at the November banquet marking the anniversary of the Bolshevik Revolution showed that he retained the confidence of the Kremlin.[46]

In fact, Gheorghiu-Dej had remained a convinced Stalinist. Stalin's death had had little impact on Romania's internal affairs: there had been no major change in the party leadership, no decentralization of the economy, and no stop to the collectivization of agriculture. It was in Romania's relations with the Soviet Union that Stalin's death had greater influence, one which with the advantage of hindsight proved emblematic. The Soviet leadership, with the lesson of popular unrest in East Germany in mid-June 1953 over the economic situation there uppermost in their thoughts, summoned Gheorghiu-Dej to Moscow in July 1953 and strongly advised him to carry out reforms in Romania. It is not unfanciful to suggest that their counsel planted the seed of economic autonomy in Gheorghiu-Dej's mind. Work on the Danube-Black Sea Canal was abandoned after Khrushchev failed to share Stalin's interest in the project. According to the Soviet leader the canal was superfluous, born out of the desirability to access the Black Sea without passing through the Danube Delta which was exposed to Soviet control. In the July meeting, Malenkov admitted that "the construction of the canal was a gross mistake, which we also pushed you to make".[47] Gheorghiu-Dej was able to present the cancellation of the scheme to the Romanian population as a victory over Soviet ambitions. The Soviet government dissolved the *Sovroms*, the joint-stock companies set up in the late 1940s to exploit Romania's natural resources, by selling its interest to the Romanians in 14 of the 16 enterprises in the summer of 1954. The two sole surviving companies, involved in oil and uranium exploration and mining, were sold in 1955 and 1956.

On the internal front, Gheorghiu-Dej did introduce a short-lived amnesty of political prisoners in 1955 and a slight relaxation in cultural policy. Yet a clear sign that there had been no concession to Khrushchev's sanitized socialism was Gheorghiu-Dej's assumption of the position of first secretary in December 1955 and the re-election to the Politburo of the same figures as had been chosen in May 1952 when the purge of Pauker and Luca had taken place.[48] Two new members were added, Ceauşescu and Drăghici, thus confirming the parallel rise of the two up the party ladder. It was not long, however, before Gheorghiu-Dej had to face the implications of another reappraisal of the Stalinist legacy by the new Soviet leader.

Until February 1956, to be known as a 'Stalinist' was the highest accolade in the Soviet Union and in its satellite states. Their leaders had all risen to power and had been confirmed in it through their declared loyalty to Stalin. Then, during the night of 25 February 1956, Nikita Khrushchev turned this ascription on its head. Khrushchev's speech in closed session at the Twentieth Congress of the Communist Party of the Soviet Union accused Stalin of often violating all norms of morality and Soviet laws, of mass arrests and deportations of many thousands of people, of execution without trial and without normal investigation, and of creating conditions of fear and despair. Although Khrushchev did not mention the satellites in his speech, he had nevertheless raised a problem for Stalin's placemen who enjoyed office at Stalin's direction or with his compliance.

The speech threw Gheorghiu-Dej completely off balance and it took him a month to regain his composure. While the Soviet triumvirate of Khrushchev, Malenkov and Molotov had criticized Stalin for his abuse of power and his cultivation of a personality cult at their meeting with Gheorghiu-Dej in July 1953, these judgements had been made privately.[49] Their revelation by Khrushchev, albeit in a closed session, of the Twentieth Congress, was bound to become public. Gheorghiu-Dej had led the Romanian delegation to the Congress—the other members were Iosif Chişinevski, Miron Constantinescu and Petre Borilă—but it was only on 23 March that his first comment on the Congress's conclusions was made in a report of the Romanian delegation to an enlarged plenum of the Romanian Central Committee and this was only published in abridged form in *Scînteia* six days later. Gheorghiu-Dej admitted merely that Stalin had soiled his reputation by indulging in the personality cult and by allowing the security police to use terror; he added that Stalin's "departure from the Marxist-Leninist concept of the role of the personality" had a "negative influence". Nothing was said about Khrushchev's secret speech.[50]

Gheorghiu-Dej tried in his report to anticipate and deflect criticism of his own allegiance to Stalinism by pointing to, although not naming, Pauker, Luca and Georgescu as the real Stalinists in the party. Since the dismissal of these leaders the party, he alleged, had taken decisive steps to democratize itself, citing the second party congress of December 1955 as the beginning of the new phase by which collective leadership and internal democracy had been reintroduced. In an allusion to the use of terror by the security police, he recognized that although the security forces had achieved great successes, especially in unmasking Western spies, they had gone beyond the bounds of legality during, it was implied, the period of Georgescu's office. The only way to counter this was to consolidate party control of the *Securitate*. Drăghici emerged unsullied but ironically the arguments marshalled by Ceauşescu in 1967 to denounce Drăghici and to call for a return to legality by the Ministry of the Interior were startlingly like those presented at this plenum by Gheorghiu-Dej.

Gheorghiu-Dej's vulnerability over the indictment of Stalin was exposed by the attack made on him during the plenum by two other delegation members, Constantinescu and Chişinevski, who accused him of following Stalinist principles and employing Stalinist methods. The convergence of their opposition to Gheorghiu-Dej brought the two together. Chişinevski was perhaps driven by his friendship with Ana Pauker upon whose shoulders Gheorghiu-Dej was attempting to place the burden of past mistakes. Chişinevski himself was heavily implicated in the Pătrăşcanu affair, as was Constantinescu according to the testimony of Dumitru Petrescu cited earlier. Constantinescu saw the Khrushchev speech as an opportunity for discussion on the need for liberalization in the Party and country, and as a means of removing Gheorghiu-Dej.[51] For Gheorghiu-Dej, on the other hand, the demolition of Stalin's personality cult was most unnerving in view of his pliancy in the hands of the Soviet dictator, and he did his best to play it down, reserving it, as a US source remarked, as "matter for party cabal and not for public discussion".[52]

Gheorghiu-Dej's caution in this respect is shown by his convocation of a secret meeting at the Floreasca sports' hall at the end of March 1956, only a few days after the Central Committee plenum. The audience of three thousand represented the Party elite. The meeting was chaired by Gheorghiu-Dej and it was announced that note taking was forbidden. Gheorghiu-Dej read out a shortened version of Khrushchev's secret speech to the Soviet Twentieth Congress, commenting that the speech had no relevance to the Romanian Party since "thanks to the consistent Marxist-Leninist policy of the Central Committee" the excesses of the personality cult had been eliminated in 1952. Gheorghe Apostol made a fawning speech in favour of Gheorghiu-Dej and in the others that followed, all made by minor figures in the party, only one showed a discordant tone, calling for an assessment of the party leaders' actions in the light of Khrushchev's criticisms. Gheorghiu-Dej's speech, as Georges Haupt has observed, fixed the party line for the next three years; it placed the RCP amongst the most hard line of the Communist camp. The meeting itself was of major significance. It was the only one in Romania in which Khrushchev's text was presented in public; it showed the resistance of the party leadership to the process of de-Stalinization; and finally, it highlighted the weakness of opposition to Gheorghiu-Dej within the Party.[53]

The absence of speeches at this meeting from major figures in the party except Apostol reflected the divisions in the Politburo over Gheorghiu-Dej's refusal to embark on de-Stalinization, and Constantinescu and Chişinevski renewed their attack on Gheorghiu-Dej in Politburo meetings held on 3, 4, 6 and 12 April. The minutes of these meetings show Gheorghiu-Dej on the defensive, faced with criticism from Constantinescu and Chişinevski over the abuses of the *Securitate* for which he was held ultimately responsible, and over the repression of the previous decade. Constantinescu went on to emphasize the need for a wide-ranging discussion of the consequences of the personality cult surrounding Gheorghiu-Dej which had led to a weakening of the role of the party. These views unleashed a fury in Gheorghiu-Dej which he confined himself to expressing in notes in the margins of the minutes. There Gheorghiu-Dej expressed his disgust of Constantinescu, whom he suspected of trying to take his place, and of Chişinevski, whom he accused of betrayal.

Constantinescu launched into his attack on Gheorghiu-Dej from the very opening of the meeting on 3 April. He claimed that despite the improvement in health in the party following the purge of Pauker, Luca and Georgescu in 1952, some worrying signs had appeared since then. Of particular concern were the 'abnormalities' in the activity of the Ministry of the Interior. Among these he highlighted the presence of *Securitate* officers in various ministries and institutions without the knowledge of ministers, especially when those ministers and heads of institutions were Politburo members. He listed a number of cases in which citizens had been beaten and blackmailed into working as informers, and some of these he had reported to Gheorghiu-Dej:

> I am not saying that the Ministry of the Interior encouraged these abuses, Constantinescu stated, but it allowed them to take place and tolerated them. The Ministry of the Interior does not, however, work independently; the Minister is in contact with comrade Gheorghiu-Dej. I ask myself: how was it possible for comrade Gheorghiu-Dej not to take steps once he had been informed of these abuses? Comrade Gheorghiu-Dej did not bring the Politburo in on overseeing the activity of the Ministry of the Interior...
>
> I think the work of the Ministry of the Interior and of the *Securitate* should be placed firmly under the control of the Politburo. Perhaps even the *Securitate* should be separated from the Ministry of the Interior and placed under the control of a committee. I believe that comrade Drăghici can be of great help to the Politburo since he is aware of many cases of abuse. There is no point in us hiding these things because they keep on appearing

> all the. I think time..... that the Ministry of the Interior has had a bad influence on comrade Gheorghiu-Dej. He spent hours on end reading the reports of the Ministry. Comrade Gheorghiu-Dej was in the habit of making notes in the margins and writing instructions on almost all the reports which he received... Some might say that I am bringing up irrelevant things about comrade Gheorghiu-Dej.
>
> However, no one in our Party is infallible and even if only part of what I say is true, it is still of assistance...Comrade Gheorghiu-Dej's merits are well-known to us. However, I want to highlight some of his negative traits. Comrade Gheorghiu-Dej is one of the party leaders but he is not the only one because there are also others. Comrade Gheorghiu-Dej often pays no heed to Politburo members and even goes so far as to mock their views.... Comrade Gheorghiu-Dej does not pay attention to how he behaves. In January 1956, en route to Moscow for a meeting on economic matters, comrade Gheorghiu-Dej spoke only in the first person when talking about the monetary reform to a comrade in the Central Committee.
>
> It was as though the party, the Central Committee and the Politburo did not exist.....Regarding myself, I have made numerous mistakes. I played an important part in spreading the personality cult, I embraced and supported the theory of intensifying the class war, I employed aggressive methods and on several occasions I have made ill-tempered outbursts.
>
> But my faults cannot cover the faults of others, nor those of comrade Gheorghiu-Dej. I have never criticised comrade Gheorghiu-Dej and that was wrong.....In conclusion, I propose that we discuss things openly and then we concentrate on the powers of the Politburo, of the secretariat, on the methods of working in the Politburo, and that the role of the control commission be strengthened.[54]

Drăghici was the first to respond. He put a number of questions to Constantinescu: did he know of the existence of prison camps? Had he not put pressure on the Ministry of the Interior in 1952 to evacuate citizens from the Jiu Valley in order to make way for the building of apartments for miners? Constantinescu gave unconvincing replies, arguing that he did not know of the existence of prison camps, only of labour camps and that he did not put pressure on Drăghici to evacuate people, but 'proposed' that the evacuation take place. Other Politburo members came to Gheorghiu-Dej's aid. Gheorghe Apostol, Chivu Stoica and Alexandru Moghioroş challenged Constantinescu's affirmations. Stoica asked Constantinescu why he had chosen this moment to launch his attack on Gheorghiu-Dej and reminded him that he had contributed to the personality cult. It was left to Apostol to give a sense to the meeting:

> At the opening of the Politburo meeting, Miron Constantinescu accused comrade Gheorghiu-Dej of not taking measures to ensure that the report of the

> delegation to the Twentieth Congress was compiled collectively, he alluded to the lack of collegiality in the Politburo's work, and criticised the method of taking decisions without consulting all the members of the Politburo. Why has comrade Miron seen and sees only the faults in our activity? I think that it is necessary for us to see the faults, but let us see in the first place the good results as well. Can it really be said that the activity of the Politburo has been slack compared with the period before the removal of the deviators [Pauker, Luca and Georgescu]? I do not think so. On the contrary.[55]

Gheorghiu-Dej, by refusing with the backing of the party cadres to embark on de-Stalinization, managed to reinforce his own control of the party and to bind it more closely to his person. His success in resisting attempts to 'liberalize' the party proved, ironically, to be a boon for Khrushchev later in the year in the midst of major challenges to Communist authority in Poland and Hungary.

The most fundamental implications of de-Stalinization concerned Poland. There, the entire Communist Party had been liquidated on Stalin's orders in 1938 as an agency of German espionage. De-Stalinization meant the rehabilitation of Stalin's victims and the evidence upon which the liquidation was carried was officially declared—on 19 February 1956 during the Twentieth Party Congress—to have been faked. A few days later, the Polish Party leader Boleslaw Bierut, a committed Stalinist, who headed his Party's delegation at the Congress, fell ill and died in Moscow. His funeral in Warsaw provoked an anti-Soviet demonstration. On 20 March, Khrushchev arrived in Warsaw to procure the election of Edward Ochab. Ochab began to implement a policy of moderate liberalization. Many of Stalin's victims were released from jail, among them a veteran Communist Władysław Gomułka. The Polish intelligentsia wanted more radical change, though within socialism. In June, Polish workers added their voice. In Poznan, the rumour that a delegation to Warsaw of metalworkers had been arrested led to a protest march by their colleagues. The protest turned into a riot which was put down by Polish security forces at a cost of 54 dead and 300 wounded. The Polish Party newspaper blamed 'enemy agents' for the riot, as did the Soviet leadership, for whom the event was a great shock. Khrushchev saw in it the beginning of the counter-revolution which the West, led by the United States, had organized in order to detach Poland and other satellite states from the Soviet bloc.

Public interest in Romania in the events in Poland was, according to a British legation report, 'intense', but Romania was able to insulate itself against what was happening in Poland; it was less able to do so against Hungary. Hungary was a neighbour, Hungarians formed the largest minority in Romania, and Romanian workers, students and intellectuals shared the same problems as their Hungarian counterparts. In Romania itself discontent was rising in the summer of 1956. The same British source reported that:

> It was already evident in August that the harvest would be a bad one; an anticipatory scarcity of food, with a consequent rise in prices, began to show itself long before the crops were in and it grew throughout the autumn. There was no sign of any appreciable amelioration of the appalling housing shortage and even though the gradual improvement in the availability of clothing and household equipment which Mr Macdermot had noted seemed to be continuing, prices were high and the majority of workers were too ill-paid to buy much. Food and housing continued to be the most important elements in the standard of living, which could therefore be said to have suffered at least a temporary decline. Discontent was evidently rising, and reports of trouble at Poznan encouraged it; the establishment of the Gomulka regime in Poland and the revolt in Hungary made it stronger.[56]

If Gheorghiu-Dej was dilatory in handling the economic discontent, as suggested by this report, his reaction to the political manifestations was swift and firm. The Hungarian uprising allowed Gheorghiu-Dej to amply demonstrate his fidelity to the Soviet Union. The repercussions of the revolt, which began with a massive popular demonstration in Budapest on 23 October 1956 during which the Stalin monument was destroyed and the national flag hoisted with the emblem of the People's Republic removed, were soon felt in Romania.

At the time of the outbreak of the revolt, Gheorghiu-Dej was in Yugoslavia, returning the visit which Tito had made to Romania during the summer. He did not leave immediately but remained in touch with Bucharest by telephone where Nicolae Ceauşescu responded at the other end of the line. The Romanian Politburo met on 24 October. It decided to place heavy censorship on news reporting from Budapest, to strengthen the guard at the frontier points with Hungary, to avoid measures which would antagonize the Hungarian and German minorities, and to "display tact and political judgement over arrests so as not to anger the population needlessly".[57] The initial public reaction of the regime in Romania was to play down the demonstrations in Budapest. The British legation reported on 27 October:

> The first brief news of the disturbances in Budapest was only given by the Romanian radio on the evening of October 24 and in the press the following morning, which rapidly sold out. The press attributed the trouble in Hungary to the work of

> subversive reactionary organizations incited by foreign reaction, explained that the Hungarian Government had asked for Soviet help and alleged that Hungarian workers who continued to support the Communist Party and friendship with the USSR were hostile to the revolt... Anyone dependent entirely on the Romanian press and radio for his news would get little idea of the nationalist and anti-Soviet nature of the developments.[58]

On 24 October, some 300 students from the Romanian 'Babeş' and the Hungarian 'Bolyai' universities in Cluj gathered at the Institute of Fine Arts to protest at the demanding timetable of classes, compulsory attendance at lectures and criteria for awarding student bursaries. The leaders of the protest were arrested on the following day. Two students, Baláys Imre and Aristid Târnovan, were accused of the crime of 'public agitation' and sentenced by a military tribunal to five years' imprisonment. On the following day, several students of the philology faculty in Bucharest were also arrested after discussing the situation in Hungary, among them Ştefan Negrea and Teodor Lupaş, who had submitted a letter for publication in the student Party newspaper criticizing the Communist Party leadership. Both were tried for 'public incitement' and received a three-year jail term.[59]

On 26 October, with Gheorghiu-Dej still absent, the Politburo met again. Aware that the food shortages could bring people out onto the streets, the party leaders approved a set of measures designed to improve food supply and to raise wages. However, these steps came too late. On the following day, there were student and workers' demonstrations in Bucharest, Cluj, Iaşi and Timişoara. The emphasis of the student protests was upon the abolition of the teaching of Russian in schools and universities. At the polytechnic in Timişoara a group of students—Caius Muţiu, Teodor Stanca, Aurel Baghiu and Ladislau Nagy, to name but a few—backed by a lecturer Gheorghe Pop, held a secret meeting on 28 October 1956 at which they decided to convene a general meeting of students from all the educational establishments in Timişoara to discuss the meagreness of food in the student canteens and shortcomings in the teaching. The meeting was arranged over the heads of the polytechnic administration and the party organization and took place at the Faculty of Mechanical Engineering on 30 October. Some estimates put the number of students present at around 3,000.[60] It was attended by senior party officials, headed by Petre Lupu and Ilie Verdeţ, who heard criticism of the presence of Soviet troops in Romania and calls for the abolition of compulsory classes in Russian.[61] The officials promised to convey the students' complaints to Bucharest but immediately after their departure army units were called in to seal off the polytechnic campus and more than 2,000 arrests were made. Of these, 30 were sent for trial where they were given sentences ranging from three months to eight years imprisonment.[62]

In the meantime, Gheorghiu-Dej had returned to Romania on 28 October. He had doubtless discussed the Hungarian crisis with Tito. A non-Communist

Hungary suited neither leader. Immediately after Gheorghiu-Dej's return Aurel Mălnăşan, the deputy foreign minister, and Valter Roman, a senior Romanian Communist Party official—who had got to know Imre Nagy, the newly-appointed Hungarian prime minister, in the early 1940s in Moscow when the latter worked for the Soviet-backed Romanian radio station—were sent to Budapest to provide on-the-spot reports to Gheorghiu-Dej and to the Soviet leadership.[63] Some foreign correspondents reported that on 29 October railwaymen at the Griviţa yards in Bucharest held a protest meeting calling for improved conditions of work while in Iaşi there were street demonstrations in support of better food supplies. An exceptionally poor harvest had drastically cut food production, and queues in Bucharest and the other main towns were commonplace.

To placate the workers the government announced on 29 October that the minimum wage would be raised, and special concessions were given to railwaymen in the form of free travel. On 30 October, the Timişoara, Oradea and Iaşi regions were placed under military rule as Soviet troops based in Romania were concentrated on the frontier with Hungary. Three days later, Gheorghe Apostol addressed a railwaymen's meeting and promised help. Gheorghiu-Dej, himself a railwayman, stayed away.[64]

Two medical students, Alexandru Ivasiuc and Mihai Victor Serdaru, tried to organize a protest in Bucharest's University Square on 5 November by distributing leaflets calling for the removal of Russian and Marxism-Leninism from the university curriculum, but the authorities swooped to arrest the ringleaders. The protests, however, made their mark. On the same day, Miron Constantinescu addressed a student meeting in Cluj and promised that the compulsory classes in Russian at universities would be abolished and living conditions raised. Two weeks later, Constantinescu was made Minister of Education. The appointment of one of the toughest men in the party, and number seven in the Politburo, to a post hitherto held by a comparatively undistinguished ex-professor, was a clear sign that Gheorghiu-Dej was not satisfied with his regime's grip on the country's youth and was determined that it should be tightened. Other potential sources of disaffection were brought into line. Mihai Beniuc, secretary of the Writers' Union, condemned "the bandit-like acts of the counter-revolutionary Fascist elements in Budapest", while writers of the Hungarian Autonomous Region addressed a letter to the Central Committee denouncing "the Horthy-Fascist savage forces in Hungary".

The anti-Soviet demonstrations were driven largely by students who had a predominantly student agenda focusing upon the removal of Russian as a compulsory subject of study. There is little evidence of workers rallying to their support. This lack of solidarity between students and workers enabled the regime to suppress any opposition rapidly and remove any threat to its stability. In the subsequent clampdown Romanians amnestied in 1955 were also re-arrested. Khrushchev himself alluded to the demonstrations in an address to the Moscow Komsomol on 8 November 1956 when he said that there were "some unhealthy moods" among students "in one of the educational establishments in Romania" and he congratulated the RCP on having dealt with them quickly and effectively.[65]

The Chinese played a significant role in Khrushchev's decision to use force to suppress the Hungarian uprising. A Chinese delegation travelled to Moscow at the invitation of Khrushchev and arrived on 23 October when its head, Liu Shaoqi, First Vice Chairman of the Chinese Communist Party and third most powerful man in China after Chairman Mao and Prime Minister Zhou Enlai, met the Soviet leader.[66] On the 29th, Khrushchev met once again with Liu to discuss how to solve the problems besetting relations between the Soviet Union and other Eastern European countries. Following Liu's transmission of Mao's advice that the Soviet Union should allow the other countries greater freedom in political, economic and military affairs, the Soviets agreed to draft a declaration on the equality of the Soviet Union and the East European countries, to be adopted the next day.[67]

The "Declaration by the Government of the USSR on the Principles of Development and Further Strengthening the Friendship and Cooperation between the Soviet Union and Other Socialist States" announced its readiness to reconsider its stationing of troops in the countries of the Warsaw Pact:

> For the purposes of assuring mutual security of the socialist countries, the Soviet Government is prepared to review with the other socialist countries which are members of the Warsaw Treaty the question of Soviet troops stationed on the territory of the above-mentioned countries. In so doing, the Soviet Government proceeds from the general principle that stationing the troops of one or another state which is a member of the Warsaw Treaty on the territory of another state of the treaty is done by agreement among all its members and only with the consent of the state on the territory of which and at the request of which these troops are stationed or it is planned to station them.[68]

Gheorghiu-Dej was not slow to seize the opportunity that the Declaration afforded him to reintroduce to Khrushchev the issue of the withdrawal of Soviet troops from Romania, first raised in 1955. In an emergency meeting convened on 31 October at 6 p.m. the Romanian Politburo agreed to put the matter to the next meeting of the Warsaw Pact whilst at the same time stressing their commitment to "strengthening the unity among socialist countries" and to "the unshakeable friendship" between Romania and the Soviet Union.[69]

Gheorghiu-Dej, however, was overtaken by events. It was the Chinese who, having influenced the Soviet decision to withdraw the Soviet troops from Budapest, also influenced the decision to send them back on the 31 October. The CPSU praesidium on 30 October wavered as to whether to use military force in Hungary. Mao swayed the decision. He saw the violence in Budapest, especially the murder of Communists, as a threat to the survival of socialism. The Chinese Communist Party, at a Politburo meeting held on 30 October, "had pointed to the danger of 'capitalist restoration' in Hungary and resolutely opposed the withdrawal of Soviet forces". Mao was the first to declare openly for armed intervention and his view informed the decision made by the CPSU praesidium on 31 October to resolve the crisis in Hungary by force.[70] This sudden about-turn by Khrushchev was communicated to Gheorghiu-Dej on the following day. Fearful of appearing over-enthusiastic in his desire to rid Romania of Soviet forces, Gheorghiu-Dej had the minutes of the Romanian Politburo meeting annulled.[71]

Convergence of interest with the Soviet Union and not just slavish obedience determined the stance adopted by Gheorghiu-Dej and his colleagues. They had two main concerns: a successful revolt in Budapest against Communist rule might spread to the two-million strong Hungarian community in Transylvania, thus sparking an anti-Communist rising in Romania; and a non-Communist Hungary might lay claim to parts of Transylvania. Their fears had been fuelled by the participation of Hungarian students and workers in demonstrations in Cluj, Timişoara and the Autonomous Magyar Region. On 30 October, an emergency 'General Command' was set up by the Romanian government with orders to "take all measures necessary in order to guarantee public order throughout the entire territory of the Romanian People's Republic". Among the command's attributes was "the coordination and extension of intelligence gathering in order to identify subversive action", "to ensure security at all Party and state buildings, at communications centres and on all road, rail, air and sea links", and "to put down any action which threatened the control of the state". The army and the interior ministry were placed under the command of this new body which was headed by Emil Bodnăraş. The other members of the command were Nicolae Ceauşescu, Alexandru Drăghici and Leontin Sălăjan, the latter being minister of the armed forces.[72]

Khrushchev, in the meantime, was holding a series of emergency meetings with Communist leaders, including a delegation from China, in which he told them that Moscow would use force if necessary to resolve the crisis. There were no objections, not even from Tito and Gomulka.[73] On 1 November, Khrushchev met Gheorghiu-Dej and Bodnăraş. The Romanian duo pushed for firm military intervention against Imre Nagy's government, indeed Soviet troops based in Romania had been among the first to cross the Hungarian border on 26 October to reinforce the Soviet presence. Bodnăraş was a key figure in the Romanian Party's support for Soviet intervention in Hungary. During the uprising he was appointed minister of transport and communications and in this capacity he supervised the widening of certain roads of strategic importance to Soviet troops for their transit through Romania.

Gheorghiu-Dej was as anxious as Khrushchev to bring the Hungarians back into the socialist fold; the two leaders agreed that a Romanian delegation, led by Gheorghiu-Dej, should travel to Budapest on 3 November to hold discussions with Imre Nagy. Nagy attempted to coordinate a plan whereby Gheorghiu-Dej would petition Khrushchev for a Soviet-Hungarian summit. On that very same day, however, the Soviet leadership was holding a meeting of a very different nature with János Kádár, the purpose of which was to coordinate the violent overthrow of the Nagy government.[74] At dawn on 4 November, Soviet troops regrouped around Budapest, and began to move in. Red Army tanks opened fire on the barricades erected by the rebels. A few hours earlier, the authorized representatives of the Nagy government, Generals Maléter and Kovacs, who had been invited to Soviet headquarters to continue negotiations begun on 1 November, were arrested. The Soviet intervention quickly overcame the rebels' resistance.

In deposing the Nagy government, Khrushchev invoked the Warsaw Treaty which, as the Soviet delegate in the UN Security Council underlined, empowered the Soviet Union "to protect Hungary against subversion". An appeal was made to the Soviets by Kádár, who on the morning of 4 November, announced his break with Nagy over the radio and the formation of a 'revolutionary workers' and peasants' government'.

The establishment of the Kádár government allowed Gheorghiu-Dej to follow up his rapprochement with Tito by establishing his position with the new Hungarian leadership. On 4 November, the Romanian Central Committee sent a message of greeting and congratulation to the Revolutionary Worker-Peasant government. This was followed by the visit, from 21 to 25 November, of a full Romanian delegation led by Gheorghiu-Dej. The main object of the visit was to demonstrate, like the Czechoslovak and East German governments before them, the Romanians' support for the Kádár regime. But there was another, significant purpose to it. The question of what to do with Nagy was nagging at the Soviets.

Nagy had taken refuge in the Yugoslav Embassy in Budapest on 4 November with several colleagues from his government. He was offered political asylum by the Yugoslavs and accepted it. Following negotiations between the Yugoslav and Hungarian governments, a convention was signed under which both governments agreed that Nagy, his colleagues and their families, could leave the Yugoslav embassy as free persons and return to their homes with a guarantee from the Hungarian government of their personal security. At 6 p.m. on 22 November a bus arrived, as agreed, at the Yugoslav embassy to take Nagy and his colleagues home. However, the Yugoslav military attaché was indignant at discovering that the bus driver was a Russian and that there were several other Russian 'passengers'. Nagy appealed to the Yugoslav ambassador to intervene and the latter ordered the first secretary of his embassy and the attaché to accompany Nagy in the bus to his home. The moment the bus set off, two Soviet armoured cars drove out and sandwiched the bus between them, escorting it to the Soviet military headquarters. There, the two Yugoslavs were sent away and Nagy and his group were placed under Soviet guard. The bus continued its journey to a military school where Nagy and the others were effectively prisoners. They were placed in separate rooms and forbidden to speak to each other.

At 10.30 on the same evening, Nagy was summoned out of his room with a message that Valter Roman wanted to talk to him. His discussions with Roman lasted almost two hours. Roman said that he had the authority of Gheorghiu-Dej and Kádár to transmit their joint request that he (Nagy) should go to Romania where he would be treated in the best possible manner until the political situation in Hungary returned to normal. This would take two to three months, after which Nagy could return to Hungary and take part in political life. Nagy's departure for Romania was advisable since his life was in danger if he remained in Hungary. Roman suggested to Nagy that he put in writing his intentions in order to pacify public opinion.

Nagy told Roman that "as a prisoner of the Soviet security authorities I am not prepared to declare anything since I am not in a position to act freely. As a

Hungarian citizen, in full possession of my freedom of action, I am happy to talk things over with fellow comrades". He went on: "I emphasized to Valter Roman my determination not to leave Hungary voluntarily. I said that they could remove me from Hungary by force, because they have sufficient power, but I would never agree to this". Roman said in reply to Nagy that he would not be removed against his will and with that he left.[75]

The following afternoon, Nagy and his colleagues were herded into two, windowless military buses. They were joined by György Lukács, Zoltán Szántó and Zoltán Vas together with their wives. This latter group had left the Yugoslav embassy three days before Nagy and his associates, accepting Kádár's promise that they were free to return to their homes. The buses took them to an airport where they boarded two Soviet planes, one of which was the aircraft which had brought Gheorghiu-Dej and his delegation to Bucharest. The pilots were Russian and their guard was made up of Soviet soldiers and KGB officers. They arrived at Bucharest after a two-hour flight and were met by Alexandru Moghioroş, a member of the Romanian Politburo. It was only on seeing Moghioroş that Nagy realized that he was in the Romanian capital.

To give a semblance of formality to Nagy's kidnapping, a memorandum was signed between Kádár and Gheorghiu-Dej bearing the title "The understanding via an exchange of letters between the government of the Romanian People's Republic and the government of the Hungarian People's Republic regarding the assistance given to Imre Nagy and persons in his group on the territory of the Romanian People's Republic". Although the understanding appeared to be a simple arrangement between Gheorghiu-Dej and Kádár, it was overseen by the Kremlin, in particular by a 'crisis team' composed of Malenkov, Suslov and Aristov, who acknowledged in a report compiled on 23 November the role played by Roman in keeping them informed of his efforts to persuade Nagy to leave Hungary voluntarily for Romania. Suslov instructed both Kádár and Gheorghiu-Dej over the wording of their memorandum.[76]

Nagy was held, along with other members of his government, in a *Securitate* safe house in a locality just north of Bucharest, where their interrogation was coordinated by Boris Shumilin, chief KGB advisor "for counter-revolutionary affairs".[77] They were not allowed the visits from UN officials promised by Grigore Preoteasa, the Romanian Foreign minister, to prove that he was not under duress. Shumilin allowed Bodnăraş and Roman to question Nagy and the others.[78]

During his visit with Gheorghiu-Dej to Budapest in late November, Bodnăraş also offered help with the reorganization of the Hungarian security service, the AVH, which had been decimated during the uprising as the result of the shooting by demonstrators of hundreds of its officers. Several *Securitate* officers of Transylvanian Hungarian background were sent to Budapest and Bodnăraş's extended stay in the Hungarian capital indicates that he was closely involved in this operation. A second Soviet officer in Romanian clothing who assisted Bodnăraş was Wilhelm Einhorn, a Hungarian Transylvanian who had been recruited by the NKVD, had fought as a volunteer in the international brigades in the Spanish Civil War and had been appointed director of the secretariat of the *Securitate* in autumn 1948 with the rank of major. It was as deputy director of Directorate I for Foreign Intelligence of the *Securitate* that Einhorn was sent to Budapest under the cover of counsellor of the Romanian embassy.[79]

Romania was the Soviet Union's most active ally during the Hungarian crisis. Its support of the Soviet Union went beyond the political arena into the domain of practical assistance and open encouragement. Gheorghiu-Dej's stance justified Stalin's faith in him as a loyal Communist. Gheorghiu-Dej and Bodnăraş were among the first foreign leaders to visit Budapest after the Soviet invasion and in their official communiqué they opined that the Soviet action "was necessary and correct".[80] The Romanian delegation congratulated Kádár on the steps taken to crush the uprising and on the use of Soviet troops for that purpose. Gheorghiu-Dej's fulsome praise was doubtless driven by relief that a repressive regime had been restored to power in Hungary instead of a government pledged to introduce liberal measures which might well have stimulated discontent and demands for similar treatment, at least among the Hungarian minority in Transylvania if not more widely in Romania.

Notes

1 Robert Levy, 'Did Ana Pauker prevent a "Rajk Trial" in Romania?', *East European Politics and Societies*, vol.9, no.1 (Winter 1995), p.153.
2 *Ibid.*, p.165.
3 Ghita Ionescu, *Communism in Rumania* (London: Oxford University Press, 1964), p.209.
4 *Ibid.* An epigram popular at the time in party circles echoed the ubiquity of Iron Guardists in the party:

Ţine minte trei cuvinte,
Camarade: 'Nu fi trist!'
Garda merge înainte
Prin Partidul Comunist

(Remember three words, comrade: 'Don't be sad!' The Guard goes forward via the Communist Party).

5 See Vladimir Tismăneanu, 'The Tragicomedy of Romanian Communism', *East European Politics and Societies*, vol.3, no.2 (Spring 1989), p.361.
6 Pauker may have contributed to her own downfall by her alleged support of Romanian Jews. This theory is advanced by Ion Calafeteanu, 'Schimbări în aparatul diplomatic românesc după 6 martie 1945', in *6 Martie 1945, Inceputurile Comunizării României* (Bucharest: Editura Enciclopedică, 1995), p.168.
7 G. Hodoş, *Show Trials. Stalinist Purges in Eastern Europe, 1948–1954* (New York: Praeger, 1987), p.101.
8 Tismăneanu, 'The Tragicomedy of Romanian Communism', p.382.
9 Ionescu, *Communism in Romania*, p.210.
10 ASRI, Fond 'P', file 40009, vol.32, pp.308–9.
11 A senior officer in the *Securitate* alleged that Luca was also accused by Gheorghiu-Dej of not honouring the reparations agreement with the Soviet Union by failing to hand over sufficient material confiscated from the Germans (Private information). Confiscated property was administered by an agency called *Casa Bunurilor Inamice*.
12 ASRI, Fond P, file 40009, vol.32, p.312. Information supplied by Marius Oprea.

13 Ionescu, *Communism in Rumania*, p.211.

14 Drăghici had served as Pintilie's deputy in the political and administrative section of the Central Committee. The section's duties included counter-espionage monitoring of CC members, and when Pintilie left to assume the direction of the DGSP in August 1948, Drăghici succeeded him. On 30 December 1950, Drăghici was named first deputy to Teohari Georgescu and head of the General Political Directorate of the Ministry of the Interior in place of Mihail Burcă. He was given the rank of Major General. On 20 September 1952, the DGSP, now renamed the DGSS, was separated from the Ministry of the Interior and incorporated within a new distinct body, the Ministry of State Security (*Ministerul Securității Statului*) of which Drăghici was made the head. On 2 October, Drăghici was given the rank of Lieutenant General. The DGSS structure remained unchanged, except for the addition of a general inspectorate and section K for counter-intelligence in the militia and prison service. This reorganization was short-lived; perhaps the conflict with Beria and his arrest in June 1953 warned the new Soviet leadership under Khrushchev of the dangers of giving a state security service too long a leash, and it was for this reason that instructions were given to the Soviet advisors in Bucharest to recommend the merger of the MSS with the Ministry of the Interior. On 7 September 1953, the amalgamation of the two bodies was decreed (*Organizarea și Funcționarea Organelor Ministerului de Interne de la Inființare pînă în prezent* (Bucharest: Ministry of the Interior, 1978), p.113).

15 Ionescu, *Communism in Rumania*, p.213.

16 ANIC, Archive of the Central Committee's Executive Committee, 264, vol.19, pp.90–95. Documents shown to me by Marius Oprea.

17 ANIC, Archive of the Central Committee's Executive Committee, 264, vol.19, p.74.

18 *Ibid.*

19 Hodoș, *Show Trials*, p.105.

20 See Appendix 2.

21 Arhiva Serviciului Român de Informații (ASRI), Fond 'P', file 40009, vol.21, p.112.

22 *Ibid.* Gheorghiu-Dej's report to the plenum of the Central Committee, held from 28 November to 5 December 1961, provided a gospel according to him of Party history. He sought to lay the blame for Stalinism in Romania on others, notably on Ana Pauker and Vasile Luca, the *émigrés* from Moscow. He claimed that it was the Pauker-Luca alliance who actually ran the party until their purge in 1952; see Eliș Neagoe-Pleșa, Liviu Pleșa (eds), *Dosarul Ana Pauker*, 2 vols (Bucharest: Nemira, 2006). On orders given by Pauker, "the organs of the Ministry of the Interior, which were not under the control of the Party leadership, began to put party and state cadres under surveillance, to wire-tap telephone conversations, measures from which not even the secretary-general of the party's Central Committee was excepted" (Ionescu, *Communism in Rumania*, p.334). Gheorghiu-Dej maintained that Pauker and Luca terrorized the senior party members, especially those who had fought with the International Brigade in Spain and in France in the resistance during the Second World War, and these accusations were borne out in 1950 by several such figures, among them Petre Borilă and Valter Roman, respectively chief of the Army Political Directorate and Minister of Posts and Telegraphs. While insisting on Pătrășcanu's crimes, these two alleged that without Gheorghiu-Dej's intervention, they too would have been arrested and placed on trial, and they praised Gheorghiu-Dej for having protected them and for saving their lives (Ionescu, *Communism in Rumania*, p.53, note 36). In the stage-managed context of the 1961 plenum a question mark hangs over the veracity of their statements, supportive as they are of Gheorghiu-Dej. It is true that Stalin saw 'potential Rajks' in all the former volunteers in Spain, but according to one veteran Romanian Communist, Stalin was principally concerned about those Communists who on his orders had moved to France after the Spanish Civil War and had worked in the French resistance (author's interview with Eduard Mezincescu, 7 April 1993).

23 Arhiva Serviciului Român de Informaţii (ASRI), Fond 'P', file 40009, vol.21, p.137.
24 After Georgescu's arrest his wife burnt the hard currency and threw the gold he had received into Lake Snagov (Arhiva Serviciului Român de Informaţii (ASRI), Fond 'P', file 40009, vol.21, pp.138–41,153).
25 He died in 1976.
26 The background to Gheorghiu-Dej's decision is presented by Lavinia Betea, *Lucreţiu Pătrăşcanu. Moartea unui lider comunist* (Bucharest: Curtea Veche, 2001).
27 Ionescu, *Communism in Rumania*, p.152.
28 *Ibid.*
29 C. Popişteanu, 'Un epilog neaşteptat: Malenkov aprobă lichidarea lui Lucreţiu Pătrăşcanu', *Magazin Istoric*, no.3 (March 1992), p.39.
30 *Scînteia*, 14 March 1954.
31 C. Popişteanu, 'Cazul Grupului Pătrăşcanu (I)', *Magazin Istoric*, no.7 (July 1991), pp.64–66.
32 Quoted from Ionescu, *Communism in Romania*, p.156, n.17.
33 Popişteanu, 'Cazul Grupului Pătrăşcanu (I)', p.66.
34 *Principiul Bumerangului. Documente ale Procesului Lucreţiu Pătrăşcanu* (Bucharest: Editura Vremea, 1996), pp.12, 846.
35 Popişteanu, 'Finalul Cazului Pătrăşcanu', *Magazin Istoric*, no.2 (February 1992), p.23.
36 Popişteanu, 'Cazul Grupului Pătrăşcanu (VII)', *Magazin Istoric*, no.1 (January 1992), p.89.
37 Popişteanu, 'Finalul Cazului Pătrăşcanu', p.23 and 'Un epilog neaşteptat', p.39.
38 *Scânteia*, 18 April 1954.
39 *Ibid.*
40 *Cartea Albă a Securităţii* (Bucharest: SRI, 1995), vol.II, 1994, docs. 202–3, pp.459–60.
41 As a member of the Politburo, Emil Bodnăraş raised his right hand in favour of Pătrăşcanu's execution. With the same hand he wrote an article in 1968, at the time of Pătrăşcanu's rehabilitation, in which he lamented the loss of a great personality and a good friend. He might have even decorated Pătrăşcanu's wife in 1971 on the occasion of the fiftieth anniversary of the RCP, had Mrs Pătrăşcanu not left the room where the medals were being handed out in disgust. It was at this same ceremony that General Pintilie was decorated by Nicolae Ceauşescu, despite having being named by the party investigative committee in 1968 as one of those responsible for the murder of Foriş (T. Chiper, 'De la ideal la idol. Convorbire cu o fostă ilegalistă,' *Dilema*, vol.II, no.72 (27 May–2 June 1994), p.16).
42 Calmanovici died of heart failure in Aiud prison on 12 March 1956, according to his death certificate (Sfatul popular, Aiud, no.39/1956). Family friends say that his death occurred after he went on a hunger strike to protest his innocence.
43 Popişteanu, 'Finalul Cazului Pătrăşcanu', p.26. Iosif Moldoveanu, an officer in the Directorate of Penal Investigation who had interrogated Pătrăşcanu, confessed in a suicide note, left after Pătrăşcanu's rehabilitation in 1968, to having shot Pătrăşcanu in the back of the neck on Gheorghiu-Dej's orders during the night of 16 April 1954 at Jilava. Gheorghiu-Dej was said to be fearful that Pătrăşcanu would divulge details at his execution of Gheorghiu-Dej's part in his demise. These details were given by Ion Pacepa, formerly deputy head of the Romanian Intelligence Service of the Department of State Security, after his defection in 1978 (*Moştenirea Kremlinului* (Bucharest: Editura Venus, 1993), pp.125–26). Unfortunately, there is no corroborating evidence for Pacepa's statement.
44 See the deposition of Vasile Varga, a deputy judge at Luca's trial, dated 23 March 1968, for the party commission set up to investigate the charges against Pătrăşcanu (copy in possession of the author).
45 Under the provisions of decree no.3 of 1963, the sentence was modified to 25 years hard labour. Luca was first imprisoned at Râmnicul Sărat where ironically he shared

his incarceration with, among others, Ion Mihalache and Corneliu Coposu, two of the leading figures in the National Peasant Party whom Luca's own party had jailed in November 1947 (Mihalache died in prison on 5 March 1963). Luca was later transferred to Aiud where he died of a heart attack on 23 July 1963. ('Documentar Referitor la Procesul Privind pe Vasile Luca', ANIC, Archive of the Executive Committee of the Central Committee of the RCP, no. 264/19. 18.02.1972, p.2). The draconian conditions of incarceration at this prison included a complete ban on talking amongst the prisoners, one imposed by the solitary confinement of prisoners to each cell. On 24 July 2015, Alexandru Vişinescu, the former commandant of Râmnicu Sărat in the period 1956–1963, was found guilty of the death of 12 political prisoners who were beaten, starved and denied medical treatment. He was sentenced, at the age of 90, to a 20 year jail term.

46 TNA, FO 371/116579. Annual Report for 1954.

47 Quoted from Mavrodin, *A Maverick in the Making: Romania's de-Satellization Process and the Global Cold War (1953–1963)*. Thesis submitted to the Department of International History of the London School of Economics for the Degree of Doctor of Philosophy, London, February, 2017, p.55 citing 'Minutes of the meeting between Gh. Gheorghe-Dej and comrades Malenkov, Molotov, Khrushchev, Mikoyan and Parhuvyn', ANIC, fond CC of the RWP, Foreign Relations, document 26/1953, p.1.

48 Mary Ellen Fischer, *Nicolae Ceauşescu: A Study in Political Leadership* (Boulder and London: Lynne Rienner, 1989), p.51.

49 Corina Mavrodin, *A Maverick in the Making*, pp.49–50 citing a 'Note regarding the conversations on 8–13 July 1953 between a delegation of the CC of the RWP and a delegation of the CC of the CPSU composed of Malenkov, Molotov, Khrushchev, Mikoyan, Perhuvyn and Lavrentiev regarding the economic situation and the social atmosphere in Romania, 14 July 1953', ANIC, fond CC of the RWP, Foreign Relations, document 27/1953, p.6.

50 Ionescu, *Communism in Romania*, p.259.

51 *Ibid.* For a sensitive biography of Constantinescu see Ştefan Bosomitu, *Miron Constantinescu. O Biografie* (Bucharest: Humanitas, 2014) see also V. Tismăneanu, 'Miron Constantinescu or the Impossible Heresy', *Survey*, vol.28 (Winter 1984), p.182. Constantinescu joined the Communist movement during World War II, being one of a number of intellectuals with leftist leanings. He studied at Bucharest University and attended the sociology seminar of Dimitrie Gusti but was arrested in 1941. Constantinescu's conflict with Gheorghiu-Dej, and his marginalization in 1957 alongside Chişinevski, gave him the opportunity to focus upon his intellectual gifts. Gheorghiu-Dej's death and Nicolae Ceauşescu's aim to legitimize his own leadership by delegitimizing that of his predecessor paved the way for Constantinescu's rehabilitation.

52 S. Verona, *Military Occupation and Diplomacy. Soviet Troops in Romania 1944–1958* (Durham and London: Duke University Press, 1992), p.88.

53 G. Haupt, 'La Genèse du Conflit Soviéto-Roumain', *Revue Française du Science Politique*, vol.18, no.4 (August 1968), p.676.

54 V. Tismăneanu, 'Arhivele secrete şi istoria comunismului românesc', *Sfera Politicii*, no.25 (February 1995), pp.16–18.

55 V. Tismăneanu, 'Arhivele secrete şi istoria comunismului românesc', *Sfera Politicii*, no.26 (March 1995), pp.12–13.

56 *Roumania: Annual Review for 1956*, TNA. FO 371/128892.

57 Mihai Retegan, 'Actul decizional în timpul revoluţiei ungare', *Dosarele Istoriei*, vol..3, no.8 (1997), p.45.

58 TNA, FO 371/122699.

59 V. Tismăneanu, D. Dobrincu, and C. Vasile (eds.), *Comisia prezidenţială pentru analiza dictaturii comuniste din România. Raport final* (Bucharest: Humanitas, 2007), pp.682–83.

60 *Ibid.*
61 The withdrawal of Soviet troops from Romania was also an issue raised by students in Timişoara, doubtless due to the presence of the large Soviet garrison there (almost 10,000 troops), close to the border with Yugoslavia and also within striking distance of Hungary; see Ioana Boca, '1956 în România', in Doina Jela and Vladimir Tismăneanu (eds.), *Ungaria 1956: Revolta Minţilor şi Sfârşitul Mitului Comunist* (Bucharest: Curtea Veche, 2006), pp.169–95 and Johanna Granville, 'Temporary Triumph in Timişoara: Unrest among Romanian Students in 1956', *History*, vol.93, no.1 (1 January 2008), pp.69–93.
62 *NU*, no.108 (6–13 May 1993), p.9.
63 A record of a verbal account of their experience in Budapest, given to the party leadership on 2 November 1956, has been published in *Sfera Politicii*, no.42, pp.29–31 and no.43, pp.32–34. Valter Roman (real name Ernest Neuländer), was a Hungarian-speaker from Oradea who had fought in the International Brigade in Spain and was believed by Nagy, and prominent figures in the Romanian Communist Party, to be an NKVD officer: see Nagy's own notes on his discussion with Bodnăraş and Roman on 26 November 1956 whilst in detention in Romania (*Dosarele Istoriei*, no.1, 1996, p.40).
64 Ionescu, *Communism in Romania*, p.269.
65 *Ibid.*, p.272.
66 Zhihua Shen and Yafeng Xia, 'New Evidence for China's Role in the Hungarian Crisis of October 1956: A Note', *The International History Review*, vol.31, no.3 (September 2009), pp.558–75.
67 Shen and Xia, 'New Evidence', p.567.
68 See document no.50 in Csaba Bekes, Malcolm Byrne, and M. Janos Rainer (eds.), *The 1956 Hungarian Revolution. A History in Documents* (Budapest: Central European University Press, 2002), pp.300–7.
69 Corina Mavrodin, *A Maverick in the Making: Romania's de-Satellization Process and the Global Cold War (1953–1963).* Thesis submitted to the Department of International History of the London School of Economics for the Degree of Doctor of Philosophy, London, February, 2017, p.104 citing 'Minutes of the Politburo of the CC of the RWP meeting on 31 October, 1956', ANIC, fond CC of the RWP, Chancellery, document 126/1956 (strictly secret).
70 Shen and Xia, 'New Evidence', p.575.
71 Mavrodin, *A Maverick in the Making*, p.104. Gheorghiu-Dej kept a secret, unsigned copy of the Romanian decision of 31 October in his private papers (*ibid.*).
72 *Sfera Politicii*, no.42, p.33.
73 Csaba Békés, 'The 1956 Revolution and World Politics', *Hungarian Quarterly*, vol.36 (summer 1995), p.112. Khrushchev and Malenkov were rumoured to have paid a secret visit to Bucharest on 1 November 1956 to discuss the Hungarian crisis with Romanian, Bulgarian and Czechoslovak leaders and according to one report, Khrushchev demanded that Romanian troops be used to crush the Budapest revolt. Gheorghiu-Dej and Bodnăraş allegedly replied that, owing to a significant Hungarian minority in the Romanian army and general sympathy for Hungary, the army could not be relied upon for such an operation (Richard Lowenthal, *The Observer*, 25 November 1956, quoted from Verona, *Military Occupation and Diplomacy. Soviet Troops in Romania 1944–1958*, p.103). The Khrushchev memoirs claim, by contrast, that offers of military assistance were received from the Romanian and Bulgarian leaders (Verona, *Military Occupation and Diplomacy. Soviet Troops in Romania 1944–1958*, p.103).
74 Békés, 'The 1956 Revolution', p.112.
75 I have taken this account from Nagy's own notes, published in Romanian translation with an introduction by Florica Dobre, in *Dosarele Istoriei*, no.1, 1996, pp.37–40.
76 Retegan, *Actul decizional*, p.46.

77 Andrew and Gordievsky, *KGB: The Inside Story of Its Foreign Operations from Lenin to Gorbachev* (London: Sceptre, 1991), p.435.
78 Judit Ember, *Menedekjog-1956* (Budapest: Szabad Ter Kiado, 1989), pp.146–48.
79 Ion Pacepa, *Red Horizons* (London: Heinemann, 1988), p.359.
80 Verona, *Military Occupation and Diplomacy*, p.103.

7 The Romanian Gulag

Senior members of the Communist Party in Romania were no strangers to jail. Alongside members of the extremist party of the right—the Iron Guard—the Communists had been the principal targets of the *Siguranţa*, the political police of the interwar years.[1] Gheorghiu-Dej himself had spent more than ten years in jail for political activity hostile to the regime. With this experience fresh in their minds, the Communists probably lost little sleep over the incarceration of those whom they regarded as their political enemies. Their victims were preordained: whether they were guilty of their alleged crimes was irrelevant: Communist theory said they had to be. The party system of 'law' was outside the formal legal system and the latter only served as the public explanation of the measures taken. The Communists abandoned pre-war Romanian penology and practice, which was largely of French inspiration, and introduced the Soviet system which depended on self-incrimination and in which, accordingly, defence pleas could only be for mitigation.

Gheorghiu-Dej was directly involved in the application of terror. His principal political instrument throughout his rule was Alexandru Drăghici. Born on 27 September 1913 in Tisău in Buzău County, Drăghici was Gheorghiu-Dej's junior by 12 years. He followed in Gheorghiu-Dej's footsteps first as a railway worker, being employed as a locksmith in the railway yards in Buzău and Bucharest, and then as a participant in the Griviţa strike in 1933. He joined the Communist Party in the following year. In 1936, he was sentenced to nine years and nine months—later reduced to seven years and five months—imprisonment as a 'notorious Communist' with Ana Pauker and others and served his time in Jilava, Doftana, Caransebeş and Văcăreşti. Released on 25 April 1944, he was then interned in Târgu-Jiu where he joined Gheorghiu-Dej.

After his release in August 1944, Drăghici, who had left school at the age of 11, became a public prosecutor. He took part in the trials of alleged war criminals in summer 1945, and in October 1945 was co-opted onto the Central Committee of the Party at its National Conference. In February 1948, he was promoted to full member. Two months later, he joined Teohari Georgescu and Iosif Rangheţ in the initial investigation of Pătrăşcanu. On 30 December 1950, he was appointed head of the political directorate of the Ministry of the Interior, replacing General Mihai

Burcă. His career ended abruptly in April 1968, when he was removed for 'crimes and abuses' from all his party and state positions and reduced from general to the ranks.

As one of Gheorghiu-Dej's most trusted associates, Drăghici thus became a senior figure in the Ministry of the Interior at the height of Soviet control. The Pătrăşcanu case became an obsession with Gheorghiu-Dej and the Soviet counsellors and Drăghici, on becoming minister of the interior in May 1952 in place of Teohari Georgescu, and then head of the newly created Ministry of State Security in September 1952, was ordered by the party secretary to provide him with a 'blow by blow' account of the progress in the interrogations. Gheorghiu-Dej's frustration at the lack of results boiled over in his comments—written in macabre red ink—in the margins of Drăghici's reports. Gheorghiu-Dej vented his spleen on Pătrăşcanu, aware that failure to deliver a 'traitor' into Stalin's hands, could possibly signal his own demise.

Drăghici, too, was conscious of the need to follow the Soviet blueprint of terror. A reasoned estimate would put the number of his victims, held in the 75 prisons and labour colonies used by the regime in the early years of the 1950s at about 100,000.[2] Corneliu Coposu, Maniu's private secretary and himself an inmate of Communist prisons for 17 years, put the number of those arrested after 1947 at 282,000. Of these, he estimated 190,000 to have died in detention[3] but the evidence to hand does not support such a figure. Tens of thousands were forcibly displaced. Defining 'victims' of the regime and computing their number awaits authoritative research. Certain prisons were earmarked for certain categories of prisoner. Sighet, in the northern province of Maramureş, was chosen as the centre for incarceration of what the regime considered to be its most dangerous opponents, the heads of the major democratic parties and former ministers and leading churchmen, because of its relative remoteness and proximity to the Soviet Union. Built as a jail in 1896–1897 by the Hungarian authorities when Transylvania was part of the Austro-Hungarian Empire, its first political prisoners entered the gates on 22 August 1948.[4] Between that date and 1956, its 72 cells held four former prime ministers, notably Iuliu Maniu, the head of the National Peasant Party, Constantin Brătianu, the leader of the National Liberal Party, and the bishops of the Roman Catholic and Greek Catholic Churches. About 180 members of Romania's pre-war ruling elite were held in the prison, more than two-thirds of them being over the age of 60, and several, as in Maniu's case, over the age of 70. Many of them had never been tried for any crime but had been merely been arrested on orders issued by the Ministry of the Interior and taken straight to Sighet. Such was the fate of Constantin Giurescu, professor of history at Bucharest University, who served as Minister of Propaganda in the Tătărescu government of May and June 1940.

Giurescu was arrested at his home on 6 May 1950 at 4 a.m. and driven straight to Sighet in a prison van with several other former members of the period.[5] He arrived at Sighet on the following evening. He was released on 5 July 1955 but given mandatory residence in a village near Brăila, close to the Danube delta. He was allowed to return to his family in Bucharest in November. During his period of mandatory domicile, he recalled his experiences in Sighet in a manuscript which his family kept carefully concealed until the fall of Communism.[6]

Prisoners were usually placed two in a cell and were required to carry out menial duties, such as chopping wood, cleaning the corridors, carrying tubs of food, collecting water from a hand-pump in the courtyard and carrying it to the higher levels, and taking containers of human waste from the cells to the toilet. The toilet was, in Giurescu's words, 'a hole cut in the dirty cement of the floor'. There was no running water. The cleaning of the toilet was done by prisoners.

The prisoners' duties, while not onerous in themselves, became so by reason of the ferocious discipline with which they were enforced. Prisoners were punished for the slightest deviation from prison rules, such as the ban on speaking during exercise. Transgressors were flogged and made to act as a 'horse' while jailers vaulted over them,[7] or placed in solitary confinement in the *neagră*, a cell without windows. Those who were punished in this way were put inside wearing only a shirt and underwear, or even completely naked. Shortly after his arrival, Giurescu got up to look at the prisoners in the yard, but he got down before a warder entered the cell unexpectedly. He asked Giurescu three times whether he wanted to look out of the window, promising that he would not punish him if he answered honestly. Giurescu admitted that he did and for that he was sent to the solitary confinement cell (*neagră*).[8]

A feature of incarceration was the permanent sensation of hunger. In the morning prisoners received a mug of water with a 'vague smell of lime'.

> From 8 May 1950 to 3 July 1953, barley was the main meal in prison, and there were periods, like between 20 December 1950 and 5 January 1951, when we were given it all the time for lunch and dinner. The dinner consisted of barley soup, in reality a sort of leftover dish water. [....] A half an hour after you finish your lunch, you are hungry again; this sensation becomes more and more intense and reaches its extreme at half past five in the evening when, usually, the bell for dinner rings. After the watery soup in the evening, you don't even have half an hour's respite as with lunch; you are hungry the moment you finish eating.[9]

Giurescu's experience was matched by that of the inmates of Romania's other jails—in Aiud (see Appendix 7), where former members of the Iron Guard were concentrated;[10] in Galaţi, the prison to which National Peasant Party members were sent; in Gherla, where many schoolteachers and lawyers ended up; and in Făgăraş, the jail chosen for the detention of former policemen.[11]

The nadir of deliberate degradation was practised in the prison at Piteşti, situated some 120 km north-west of Bucharest. It became notorious for an experiment of a grotesque originality which began there on 6 December 1949. Termed 're-education', the experiment employed techniques of psychiatric abuse designed not only to inculcate terror into opponents of the regime, but also to destroy the personality of the individual. The nature and enormity of this experiment, conducted by prison officers under the direction of Alexandru Nicolski of the *Securitate*, are still largely unknown in the West. The 're-education' experiment lasted until August 1952 and was conducted in other prisons as well, including Gherla, albeit on a smaller scale, but the process became synonymous with Piteşti.[12]

The programme was based on the theories of the Soviet sociologist and educationalist Anton Makarenko (1888–1939) regarding common law criminals. The offender is made conscious of being a misfit whose only salvation lies in winning the support of the Communist Party. The only way in which he can do this is by leading other offenders down the road of honesty and this he achieves through 're-education'. In Makarenko's view 're-education' was to be conducted through collective labour and this method was applied in Romania through the establishment of labour camps, but a new sinister form of 're-education' was introduced which involved the application of continual physical torture combined with 'brainwashing'.

Physical torture was commonly applied by the *Securitate* during interrogation in both its centres and in prisons, but in the process of 're-education' the prisoner, after interrogation, was placed in a cell with his torturer who was a fellow prisoner, and the torture continued. Charged with the implementation of this programme was Alexandru Nicolski, the assistant director of the *Securitate* with special responsibility for interrogation of prisoners, who used as his principal instrument Eugen Ţurcanu. Ţurcanu was himself a prisoner in Piteşti and was instructed by Nicolski in the autumn of 1949 to form a team of torturers from amongst his fellow prisoners.[13] The majority of these were students from the university centres of Bucharest, Iaşi and Cluj, a thousand of whom had been rounded up in 1948 on charges of belonging either to the Iron Guard, or to the National Peasant Party, or to the Zionist movement.

Piteşti was a maximum security prison, built at the beginning of the last century. Located on the periphery of town, it was well suited for torture since the cries of the tortured were unlikely to be heard. The students were divided into four groups. The first comprised those imprisoned without trial, which did not prevent them from serving six to seven years, the second those convicted of minor offences, such as aiding political opponents of the regime, with sentences of three to five years, and the third those accused of 'plotting against the social order', with sentences of eight to 15 years. Most of the inmates belonged to this category. The last group contained those sentenced from ten to 25 years hard labour; these were leaders of student associations. It was from this later group, considered the most resilient, that in the middle of November 1949 a group of 15 students, led by Sandu Angelescu, were moved into hospital ward no. 4 of the prison where they found Ţurcanu's group, also made up of 15 prisoners, already installed.

Befriending each other they confessed their intimate thoughts until 6 December when one of the wardens ordered Angelescu to give him his pullover. Angelescu was left in the unheated ward in midwinter in just his shirt and cursed the warder as he left. This prompted his best friend in the cell Ţurcanu to strike him without warning in the face and to chide Angelescu for cursing the warden. At this signal the other members of the Ţurcanu group pounced on their 'friends' and a general brawl ensued. It was broken up by the entrance of warders, the prison director Captain Dumitrescu, and the political officer Lieutenant Marina. Angelescu explained what had happened. Dumitrescu, pretending to be furious with Ţurcanu, demanded a reply. The latter then revealed that he was the head of the ODCC, the Organization of Prisoners with Communist Convictions, and that their attempts to persuade Angelescu's group to join them had resulted in their being attacked.

Things had obviously been pre-arranged. Angelescu was accused of resisting 're-education' and was ordered, together with his friends, to strip naked and to lie down on the bare concrete floor. Then they were beaten for half an hour by the wardens armed with iron bars and clubs and left with Ţurcanu and his colleagues. For several days afterwards the beatings were repeated, this time by Ţurcanu and his cronies. In between the beatings Ţurcanu applied the programme of 're-education'. It progressed in four stages. The first was known as 'external unmasking' by which the prisoner had to show his loyalty to the ODCC by revealing everything he had hidden from the *Securitate* interrogators. The results were written down by Ţurcanu, signed by the prisoner and forwarded to the Ministry of the Interior. In the second phase, called 'internal unmasking', the tortured student had to reveal the names of those who had behaved more kindly or leniently towards him in prison, be it fellow inmate or a member of the staff. The third and fourth stages had another purpose: the destruction of the prisoner's personality and moral fibre. Thus the third stage, known as 'public moral unmasking', required the student to denounce everything he held most dear, his family, his faith, his friends and finally, himself. Only when his moral collapse seemed to Ţurcanu to be complete, and when he was thus worthy of admittance into the ODCC, was the student subjected to the final stage, the one which guaranteed no return: the re-educated figure was forced to conduct the process of re-education of his best friend, torturing him with his own hands and thus becoming one of Ţurcanu's disciples.

The confessions were regularly interrupted by physical violence. Over a period of weeks the student was subjected to an exhausting programme of labour. Sometimes he was made to clean the floor of a cell with a rag clenched between his teeth and to goad him on one of the re-educated students would ride on his back. At night the students slept on pallets. Other students, who had already been through the experiment, sat at the foot of each pallet and at the moment when a student fell off into a deep sleep, the one at the end of the pallet was required to strike him hard on the soles of his bare feet with a rubber hose. Each night thus became a torment during which the student tried *not* to fall asleep. Weary, and in constant fear of pain, the student soon reached a state of helplessness and desperation.[14]

In this first stage of brainwashing the treatment required the victims to experience intense pain sensations when eating and drinking. Students were made to kneel on the floor with their hands behind their backs and lap up scalding-hot food from bowls as fast as they could. Their excrement was sometimes placed in these same bowls and they were forced to eat it. Eating thus became a source of humiliation as well as of pain, and the senses of taste, smell and touch were repeatedly associated with pain. Ţurcanu was particularly sadistic towards theology students.

Some were 'baptized' in the mornings by having their heads plunged into a bucket of urine while others chanted the baptism rites. One student had been tortured in this way so often that he 'baptized' himself automatically in this way every morning. On Easter morning 1950, a student was made to play the role of priest. He was dressed in an excrement-covered sheet and given a roll of DDT in the shape of a phallus which his colleagues had to kiss. Many doubtless contemplated escape by suicide but there were no means of committing it. Cutlery was only given to the re-educated and the students were watched permanently. One student succeeded: Şerban Gheorghe threw himself from the fifth floor of the prison into the stairwell.

Ţurcanu's special victim was Alexandru Bogdanovici, his former friend whom he held responsible for his own arrest. In March 1950, he subjected him to three days of uninterrupted torture by jumping on his stomach and chest until his internal organs were crushed. Bogdanovici went into a coma and died on Maundy Thursday.[15] During his interrogation at Piteşti on 4 April 1953, Ţurcanu said that he had killed Bogdanovici because he had been a member of the SSI (the Secret Intelligence Service) during the war against the Soviet Union.[16] At least 14 others died in Piteşti during the re-education process.[17]

Eventually, "tortured, starved, sleepless, terrified, trapped, alone, at the edge of death but not allowed to die, the student at last reached a point at which he would plead to give incriminating evidence against himself".[18] It was at this point, after six weeks of torment, that the 'unmasking' began. It took the form of a written confession of the student's 'crimes'. He was made to dwell on every misdeed he had ever done prior to his arrest, even things he intended to do. Ţurcanu and his assistants sought systematically to destroy everything that anchored the personality of the prisoner so that they could control him at will. Each student who was an active Christian had to deny his faith by blaspheming the Eucharist, and by singing hymns into which obscene words had been inserted. Each family member's past was distorted and invested with aberrant features. A father, for example, had to appear as a crook. As many of the students were from country areas and were sons of priests, they were forced to describe erotic deeds ascribed to their fathers, while their mothers were made out to be prostitutes.

Next, the student was made to deny his own identity (his mask) by writing a false autobiography for which he concocted a history of sexual deviance. This was meant to inculcate in him a sense of moral decadence and to destroy his value system. Through torture lies were turned into truth and truth into lies. The student, as Bacu writes,

> would see the world as a god with two faces; the first, which he had thought was real, had now become unreal; the second, fantastic and ugly beyond any previous imaginings, had now become real... The lie was accepted as a biological necessity for survival.'[19]

Stripped of his old *persona* the student was now dependent on Ţurcanu's lies and a slave to his commands. Crazed with fear and reduced to an infantile state of reliance, the student became Ţurcanu's puppet, ready to be jerked into action. As a final act of self-destruction he was ordered to prove his loyalty to his new master by inflicting on the next group of students the same treatment that he himself had undergone. If he was regarded as too lenient in the beatings he gave, or less than zealous in depriving his victims of sleep, he was seen as a failure and subjected a second time to the 'unmasking' process. When the students were forced to inflict torture on others, or simply to witness it, their imagination exaggerated the pain felt; this had a stronger psychological effect than if they themselves were being struck. One student described this to Bacu:

> Watching others being tortured, I had the impression that I had been bound and placed on a powder keg, and that a madman constantly circled the keg with a lighted candle. I expected the flame to touch the powder at any moment, and that the keg with me on it would be blown up. That could have happened at any time; in other words, if a re-educator suddenly took the notion that I had been given too light a punishment for my suspected guilt, he could have transferred me from 'spectator' to 'sufferer' on the spot—the equivalent of setting off the powder with the candle flame.[20]

Gaining the confidence of those to be subjected to the process was a prerequisite for the brainwashing. Those freshly re-educated befriended or renewed old friendships with their intended victims. Then, at a given signal, they would pull out concealed cudgels and ferociously beat them. As the programme was applied throughout 1950 and 1951 in Piteşti teams of re-educated students were unleashed and sent to other prisons, notably to Gherla and the Danube-Black Sea Canal labour camp at the peninsula colony. At the latter the students were responsible for seeing that each day's work norm was done, and they pushed many prisoners so hard they died of exhaustion. Re-education was carried out in huts 13 and 14, the group in the former being led by a Cluj medical student named Bogdănescu, and that in hut 14 by Enăchescu, a student of medicine at Bucharest.

It was Bogdănescu's manslaughter of an eminent doctor, Professor Simionescu, while undergoing re-education in hut 13 that precipitated the termination of the programme at the canal. Simionescu's beatings at the hands of Bogdănescu led him to throw himself on the barbed wire perimeter fence where he was shot by the camp guards. News of the doctor's death reached his wife who protested to the Ministry of the Interior, and foreign radio stations broadcasting in Romanian such as Voice of America, Radio Free Europe and the BBC. Their reports prompted a Ministry of the Interior enquiry at the peninsular camp. Here is a vivid illustration of the iniquity of the Communist regime's machinery of repression: the very body which, in the person of Nicolski, implemented the programme, on realizing that its details could no longer be kept secret, set up an enquiry to absolve itself of responsibility. As a result of the enquiry some ten 're-educators' were transferred from the canal camp, and its director Georgescu was replaced by a certain Lazăr. Conditions in the camp improved; better food was served to the prisoners and standards of hygiene raised. Such were the circumstances in which the programme was stopped at the canal.[21]

The selection of students sent to the canal camps had been made at Piteşti by Colonel Zeller, an officer in the penitentiary directorate of the Ministry of the Interior. In the winter of 1951, he also despatched a group of 30 to 40 re-educators, led by Ţurcanu and including the Livinski brothers and Ion Popescu, to Gherla, to test the programme on older victims. Another group was sent to the Ocnele Mari prison near Râmnicu Vâlcea, and a third one to the prison sanatorium for tuberculosis sufferers at Târgu Ocna in Moldavia where the programme was supervised by Nuţi Pătrăşcanu. It was at these last two institutions that the programme ran into difficulties. In the sanatorium the patients, being sick, could not be subjected to its full force. One patient, a student called Virgil Ionescu, tried to commit suicide and other students went on hunger strike. One Sunday, while a football match was being played on ground adjacent to the sanatorium, the patients screamed for help and word reached the town. The local *Securitate* bureau chief Captain Bălan ordered an enquiry. Not one of the re-educators was punished, but the programme was halted.[22] At Ocnele Mari the prison regime was less severe than at Piteşti since it also held common law criminals and it was easier for prisoners to communicate amongst each other. Some prisoners were ex-ministers and university professors who threatened mass suicide when attempts were made to apply the programme. Fears that word would get out about the programme led to its suspension there.

Threats of disclosure did not always work. Bacu relates a visit to Gherla made, it seems, by Nicolski during the re-education drive in the prison and mentions the complaints made by a prisoner to the assistant director of the *Securitate*. The prison commandant Gheorghiu denied any knowledge of the programme. Subsequently the prisoner was tortured by Ţurcanu who pulled out his toenails with a pair of pliers. Former prisoners at Gherla testified to Bacu about the direct involvement of the prison commandant, his political officer Avădanei and the prison doctor Bărbosu in the re-education process. Aristide Ionescu, a Gherla inmate and one of the few unsuccessful targets of re-education, recalls the names of some of Ţurcanu's assistants: the Livinski brothers, Mărtinuş and Popa Ţanu.[23] These, it will be remembered, had not been through the programme themselves. Other alleged torturers at Gherla were Paul Caravia, later an archivist at the architecture faculty of the University of Bucharest, Aristotel Popescu, Cornel Pop, Danil Dumitreasa, Morărescu and Măgirescu. Another Gherla torturer named by Bacu was Ludovic Rek, a Transylvanian Hungarian, who clubbed to death Ion Fluieraş, a leading member of the Social Democratic Party, with a sack of sand in 1953.

Gherla, it appears, was the last bastion of the re-education programme. It was here that the veteran re-educators were active until the summer of 1952 when they were told to pack their belongings. Ţurcanu, Popa Ţanu, Livinski and others were moved to Bucharest and the prisoners at Gherla could breathe a little more easily. There is no published record of what happened next to Ţurcanu and his colleagues; word of mouth testimony indicates that they were ordered to write a report on the programme, its methods and its effectiveness, for the *Securitate*. On its completion they were asked to make a declaration stating that the programme had been carried out without authority from the Party and even without that of the prison authorities. They then realized that a trap had been laid for them and refused. It was now their turn to be tortured.

The re-education experiment was brought to an end in 1952. Its termination was linked to the purge of Pauker, Luca and Georgescu, and was possibly part of Gheorghiu-Dej's strategy to demonstrate the validity of his claims to have ended a regime of terror initiated by the *troika*. The fact that Colonel Zeller, a friend of Pauker, shot himself shortly after her dismissal, supports this explanation. But just as Pauker's friendship with Stalin and Molotov spared her a trial, so Nicolski's connection with the NKGB ensured his immunity from prosecution. Marin Jianu, a deputy minister of the interior under Teohari Georgescu, directly implicated Nicolski in the re-education programme carried out in Gherla, during his interrogation shortly after Georgescu's arrest in May 1952.[24] Preparations for the trial of Ţurcanu and his accomplices lasted two years. In order to absolve the regime of any blame in the re-education programme the re-educators were to be portrayed as agents of Horia Sima, the former Iron Guard leader. This scenario required that all the torturers who had no Iron Guard connections be tried separately (i.e. Titus Leonida, Fuchs, Steiner, Bogdănescu, Dan Diaca and Cori Gherman). Thus only the former Guardists Ţurcanu, Popa Alexandru (Ţanu), Nuţi Pătrăşcanu, Livinski and 18 others stood trial together.

At the secret trial of Ţurcanu and his associates, which opened on 20 September 1954, it was alleged that Horia Sima, from his place of exile in Spain, had given Ţurcanu orders in 1949 to carry out a programme of torture in Piteşti in order to compromise the Communist regime.[25] The prosecution indictment stated that 22 prisoners led by Ţurcanu, were being sent for trial

> for the murder of over thirty prisoners, and the abuse and torture of over 780 prisoners, of whom 100 had been left with severe injuries. Some of them had committed suicide to avoid torture, while others had gone mad owing to the psychological and physical pressures to which they had been subjected.[26]

Nothing was said about the involvement of the Soviets, of Nicolski, or indeed of the ODCC but the collusion of certain prison staff in the actions of Ţurcanu's group was recognized. In the words of the indictment:

> At Suceava prison the Iron Guardist Eugen Ţurcanu worked with the governor Tiron and second lieutenant Marici in the re-education of the prisoners, and later he arranged with the latter his transfer to Bucharest jail to organize the so-called re-education there. Both the inspector general of prisons Farcaş and his political advisor Stanga were aware of this transfer.

In the case of Piteşti prison, the indictment accused the governor Alexandru Dumitrescu, the political advisor Marina, the inspector general Iosif Nemeş, and lieutenants Mihai Mircea and Nicolae, of helping Ţurcanu.[27]

The most senior figure in the Ministry of the Interior to be implicated in the experiment in evidence presented under interrogation by some of the accused was Marin Jianu, a deputy minister of the interior. He was alleged by Gheorghe Popescu to have told prison officials at Piteşti to "use beatings for intimidation... and then he chose five of us and told us that we would receive extra food if we administered the beatings as well".[28] But it was the smaller-fry in the ministry who were used as scapegoats. Colonel Tudor Sepeanu of the prison directorate of the Ministry of the Interior, Alexandru Dumitrescu, director of Piteşti prison and three officers who had worked at Gherla, Gheorghe Sucigan, Constantin Avădanei and Viorel Bărbosu were tried in April 1957 for "encouraging criminal acts of terror" to take place, code for their part in the re-education programme at Piteşti and Gherla. They were sentenced to terms of imprisonment ranging from five to eight years, to be calculated from the time of their detention for questioning in spring 1953.[29]

No distinction was made at the trial, presided over by Colonel Alexandru Petrescu, the same man who had officiated at the trial of Iuliu Maniu in 1947, between the two categories of accused: those who had not been subjected to the programme (Ţurcanu, Popa, Nuţi Pătrăşcanu, and Livinski), and those who had become torturers because they had (Gheorghe Popescu, Cornel Pop, Dan Dumitrescu and Octavian Voinea). On 10 November 1954, the Bucharest Military Tribunal found the accused guilty and sentenced them all to death.[30]

The end of the re-education experiment did not mean the end of the suffering for its victims. The marks of the brainwashing and torture scarred many lives. One young man, formerly a student of literature, told Dumitru Bacu of his experiences at Piteşti and Bacu noted the aftermath:

> When the young man finished his narrative—this was several years after the 'unmaskings'—an indescribable despair could be read on his face. Then he concluded: 'By an unimaginable fatality we become the gravediggers of our own aspirations, of our own souls. For never again will we be able to raise our heads. Christians once died happily for their faith. But we, also Christians, could not attain that happiness. We became the tools of the Communism that we heartily detested... It was as if Satan had grabbed us from the hands of God... I may seem to be whole, but in reality I am only the wreck of myself, discredited in the eyes of my friends, and despised by my enemies. And yet, in essence, we were guilty of nothing, really.'[31]

Nothing illustrated more graphically the coercive nature of the centralizing policies pursued by the Communist regime than its use of forced labour. Just as the Ministry of State Security (MVD) was, at Stalin's death in 1953, the second largest employer of labour in the Soviet Union, so too the Ministry of the Interior in Romania was effectively charged with managing part of the economy.

Cosmetically obscured by the euphemism 'temporary labour service', forced labour was used as an instrument of punishment for the thousands charged with economic sabotage and absenteeism. Included among their number were the tens of thousands of peasants who resisted the forced collectivization of agriculture. The list of others liable to be interned in the camps was compendious: those who spread "alarmist, tendentious and hostile rumours", who slandered the Romanian Workers' Party, its leaders, the Soviet Government and its leaders, and the other People's Democracies, Romanian citizens who frequented 'imperialist' embassies or who had contacts with the diplomats or families of such embassies, those who urged resistance to government policies, "elements with a well-known reactionary past", active members of the former democratic opposition parties and of the Iron Guard, members of the former SSI, the *Siguranța* and of the former police, those convicted of trying to cross the frontier illegally since 1945, convicted speculators and saboteurs, the father and adult sons of those who had fled the country after 1945, and of Iron Guardists who had fled before 1944.

Forced labour was officially introduced under the labour code of 8 June 1950 although it had been practised for more than a year in the construction of the Danube-Black Sea Canal. The labour camps themselves, initially known as 'labour units' (*unități de muncă*), were similarly legalized retrospectively on 13 January 1950 by a decree of the Grand National Assembly since they had been established for the canal project in May 1949. The decree stipulated the setting up of units for "the re-education through labour elements hostile to the RPR".[32] It placed the running of the camps under the authority of the Council of Ministers, an authority which was transferred to the Ministry of the Interior by a further decree of 10 March 1950. Persons liable to be interned in the camps were defined in an order issued on 3 April 1950 by Gheorghe Pintilie, head of the *Securitate*.[33]

On 22 August 1952, the Council of Ministers adopted Resolution 1554 by which the camps were renamed 'work colonies' (*colonii de muncă*). It was signed by Gheorghiu-Dej as President of the Council. Ten new categories of persons liable for internment were added to those in the order of April 1950. The resolution also introduced the penalty of fixed domicile, or internal exile, (*domiciliu obligatoriu*) which was aimed at those who had not been 're-educated' in prison or in the labour camps and were still deemed to represent a threat to state security. Within its remit also fell former landowners, bankers and wholesale merchants, the close female relatives of those who fled the country before 1944 (Iron Guardists) and those who left since 1945 and were opponents of the regime in exile. Exempted from these provisions were artists, sculptors, composers and academicians "who work honestly and are useful to society".[34]

Identifying those to be sent to the labour camps—and later, into internal exile—was entrusted to a commission of the Ministry of the Interior, set up on 25 August 1952, by Drăghici and put under the chairmanship of his deputy, Gheorghe Pintilie, who was also chief of the *Securitate*.[35] The numbers of inmates were swelled by the victims of mass deportations, carried out by the militia, from the major cities. These had begun in 1952 to make room for the workers drafted in to provide manpower for new urban-based factories created in the drive to industrialize.

Under a decree of 16 February 1952, several categories of person were to be removed from Bucharest. The families of war criminals, persons in prison and of those who had fled abroad, purged army officers, former judges, lawyers, industrialists and those who owned more than ten hectares of land, were to receive notice 12–24 hours before being deported, and were allowed to take with them 50 kilos of luggage. Many of them were in fact taken to the labour camps.

The largest concentration of labour camps—14 in all—was for construction work on the Danube-Black Sea Canal project. In them were packed prisoners from every walk of life. Members of the professional classes rubbed shoulders with dispossessed farmers, teachers with students, Orthodox and Uniate priests with Zionist leaders, Yugoslavs from the Banat with Saxons from Transylvania; all were victims of the denial of human rights which accompanied the Romanian regime's programme of political and economic revolution. The construction of the canal was undertaken on the initiative of Comecon and approved by the Politburo on 25 May 1949. Its official purpose, according to decree no. 75 of the Grand National Assembly of 23 March 1950, was to provide the cheapest and most direct means of transport by river to the Black Sea by building a canal cutting the Danube's passage to the sea by 260 km. Construction of the canal would also help to industrialize the south-eastern corner of the country, would improve the irrigation of the Dobrogea province, thereby increasing agricultural yields and would provide training in new engineering techniques to those involved in its construction.[36]

But the canal may also have had a broader economic purpose as well as a military significance: in respect of the former, it could have served as part of a wider Soviet scheme to create an 'Eastern Ruhr' for which Soviet iron ore was to be shipped through a double canal; Black Sea-Danube and Danube-Oder-Rhine; its military rationale lay in the ability it offered Stalin to send many small Soviet vessels up the Danube in the event of a deterioration of relations with Yugoslavia. Support for both scenarios was found in the Soviet decision to give financial backing to the project.

Work on the canal began at the end of summer 1949 on the basis of construction plans drawn up by a special Soviet-Romanian commission in May. The plans were approved by the Council of Ministers on 22 June under Resolution 613 and a board called the *Direcţia Generală a Lucrărilor Canalul Dunăre-Marea Neagră* (The General Directorate of the Danube-Black Sea Canal Works) was set up to run the project. In September, Gheorghe Hossu was appointed director and Mayer Grunberg first assistant director and chief engineer.[37] Before excavation proper could be undertaken, a great deal of preparatory work was necessary. This involved the erection of barrack-like wooden shacks to house workers, canteens, access roads to the sites, modifications to the railways, electrical generators, and, of particular importance, measures to remove the mosquitoes which infested the area. Medical care was to be provided by one doctor, a health worker, and two nurses for every 1,500 workers.

The workforce was to be supplied from three sources: volunteer paid labour, forced labour and army conscripts. On 29 June 1949, the Canal Directorate (DGC) requested all ministries to instruct every factory under their control to recruit manpower for the canal. There was an urgent need for surveyors, mechanical and building engineers and technicians. Administrative personnel such as managers and accountants, together with support staff such as typists were also required. Among the skilled labourers sought were welders, blacksmiths, carpenters, locksmiths, plumbers, car mechanics and bricklayers. Recruiting offices were set up in Bucharest and in the major towns. It was reported that by September 8,960 persons had been recruited.[38]

Both the planning and execution of the canal was supervised by Soviet counsellors. The whimpering tone of some of the requests sent by Gheorghe Hossu, the director general of the canal, to Shaposhnikov, the head of the Soviet commission for planning the canal, indicates that relations between the two parties were far from smooth, and to judge from a stenogram of a meeting in May 1952 between Hossu and another Soviet specialist called Vorobiov about the payment of bonuses, the latter considered himself to be a master rather than a partner.[39]

A special newspaper called *Canalul Dunăre-Marea Neagră* was printed to instil enthusiasm into the workforce. Initially, it appeared as an eight-page weekly, but later appeared two or three times a week. In its first edition of 3 September 1949, it took up a speech of Ana Pauker, given on the eve of 23 August, the national holiday, in which she saluted the plan for the canal which "we will build without the bourgeoisie and against it". In fact, this slogan was hung from a pole in front of the canteen on the site at Cernavodă. Pauker's threatening tones contrasted with the idyllic, exalted character of the other articles in this issue, one of which reported the ceremonial handing over of a library and a radio to the workers on the sites at Poarta Albă and Canara. The library, it said, numbered almost a thousand volumes, "many of which were works of Soviet literature". The festive occasion was crowned by the singing of the *Internationale* and the showing of a Soviet film.

Another article laid down the tasks of the 'agitator', as he was termed. These tasks were to read out loud the party newspaper *Scînteia* in the evening in the dormitory, to get the labourers to listen to the radio in a group, to concoct suitable slogans to inspire the workforce, to encourage workers in the surrounding villages to give support to the canal labourers, and last, but probably not least, to unmask saboteurs. The charge of sabotage against unfortunate scapegoats came to be used with increasing frequency in an attempt to cover up a lack of planning which became all too evident in most areas.

The canal files are revealing: insufficient on-site accommodation meant that many workers were forced to sleep either in or under carts; the unasphalted tracks exacted a heavy toll on lorry tyres which continually exploded and there was a shortage of facilities for repairing inner tubes, medical care was administered from peasant houses due to a lack of clinics. Feeding the huge force of voluntary workers not only posed logistical problems but placed an enormous strain on the resources of the Dobrogea region. A report from the Ministry of Industry dated 26 September 1949 expressed alarm that between 600 and 800 sheep were being slaughtered daily to feed the workers on the canal. These sheep were prized for their wool and the ministry recommended that sheep from other parts of the country who gave poorer quality wool be slaughtered in their place.[40]

The political prisoners exploited on this project were euphemistically termed *forţe MAI* (labour resources of the Ministry of the Interior) and were held in 14 camps. By spring 1952, their numbers had reached 19,000. In addition, 20,000 voluntary civilian workers were employed, together with 18,000 conscript soldiers.[41] Once they had arrived at the canal, the political prisoners were subjected to the process of 're-education through labour'. The methods used were described in an internal report of the military procurature, drawn up for the Ministry of the Interior on 27 February 1954:

> Many prisoners were beaten without justification with iron bars, shovels, spades and whips. Many died as a result of the blows received while others remained crippled for the rest of their lives. A number of prisoners were shot dead, others were denied medical treatment when sick and forced to work against medical advice and consequently several died. Prisoners were put naked or skimpily dressed in isolation cells in winter. Prisoners were punished by making them stand in frozen water until lunchtime. Prisoners were tied by the hands and exposed naked in the summer to be bitten by mosquitos.[42]

The camp officers most frequently mentioned by prisoners as perpetrators of these excesses were Ioan Pavel, the commandant of the Salcia camp, and his fellow officers Ion Popa, Petre Manciulea and Tudor Ilinca, and Liviu Borcea from the Capul Midia camp. On Drăghici's orders, the deaths of prisoners were covered up and not reported to the registrar of deaths. It is therefore impossible to calculate accurately how many prisoners died in the camps. A *Securitate* investigation in 1967 into deaths in the labour camps revealed that "no documents were drawn up for the deaths of 1,304 prisoners who had died in the camps, and the deaths were not notified to the local council registrars".[43]

Labour camp memoir literature offers much detail about the conditions in which the political prisoners toiled. Eloquent in this sense are the views of no less a figure than Gheorghe Cristescu, the general secretary of the outlawed Romanian Communist Party from 1921 to 1924, who spent periods in prison in the inter-war period as a member of an illegal organization. In 1949, he was re-arrested for 'rightist deviation'. Asked by a fellow prisoner at the Capul Midia penal colony—one of the 14 camps supplying labour for the Danube-Black Sea Canal—to compare the penal regime under King Carol with that under the Communists, Cristescu replied that treatment at the hands of the 'bourgeois' *Siguranţa* and their prisons was 'luxurious' in comparison with that meted out by his comrades.[44]

The fellow prisoner in question was Şerban Papacostea. In the spring of 1950, as part of its campaign to break contacts with the West, the regime clamped down on Romanians who frequented Western institutes and libraries. Many students were arrested, among them Papacostea, who was detained on 3 March for using the French library in Bucharest. After being taken to Jilava jail and then to a screening centre at Ghencea on the outskirts of Bucharest, he was transported by train to the

Capul Midia labour camp on the Black Sea. On arrival, the prisoners were lined up before the camp commandant who called out their name and assigned them their tasks. Papacostea noticed that the commandant had a file for each prisoner and that a coloured diagonal stripe on it indicated the regime to be applied to him. Although suffering from a muscular disability, Papacostea was put to the daily task of digging four cubic metres of earth a day and carting it up a mound with a wheelbarrow.[45] Unable to fulfil this norm he expected severe punishment, but in fact he was shielded by one of the guards, a lieutenant Filip, who often helped the prisoners.[46] Other prisoners were less fortunate; many were driven to exhaustion in their attempts to meet the daily quota of digging four cubic metres of earth and died of tuberculosis or heart failure. According to *Securitate* figures, in the month of January 1953 alone, 133 prisoners died at the canal.[47]

In the Capul Midia penal colony, which Papacostea estimated to house some 4,000 detainees—20 huts each containing about two hundred men—there was only one small hut designated as a 'medical centre'. It had no medicines and the only doctors available were those who were themselves prisoners. The terms of imprisonment for those held ranged from six months to two years. The detainees were not issued with fresh clothing and not being entitled to parcels of food or clothing sent from home, they remained in the same clothes in which they had been arrested and these soon become threadbare and tattered. They were awoken at 5 a.m., they washed perfunctorily from standpipes, then had a cup of chicory and a piece of bread or *mămăligă* (polenta), before being summoned to parade for the count before they left for the construction site. The counting of several thousand prisoners lasted more than an hour. The prisoners were ordered to march off and return to the construction site singing a Communist song so as not to appear downcast. A break for lunch was taken at 1 p.m. on the site. It consisted of a mug of water and bean mush. Labour continued until the early evening. Upon their return to the colony, the prisoners were again counted in and only after the count had been completed were they allowed to wash and have their evening meal which usually consisted of potato soup.

The conditions under which even the conscript soldiers were expected to work drove them to protest. Their low morale was the subject of a *Securitate* report dated 1 October 1949. They complained that they had no underwear, boots or trousers and these conditions had led them to coin the slogan: *Armata democrată, desculţă şi dezbrăcată* (A people's army [is one which is] unshod and undressed). Insufficient food and space in the military canteens, unfinished billets, no washing facilities or soap added to their misery. They therefore washed in the Danube.[48] A report of the following day registered workers' dissatisfaction that they had not received their wages. Other reports signalled soldiers' complaints about their officers who struck them when they criticized the working conditions.

The true reasons for the abandonment of the canal project were never made public but archival documents reveal that bad planning played a major part. Work began long before the plans were completed and when they finally arrived, it was discovered that the original estimates in scale and cost of the construction were 50 per cent below the true costs. The geological studies made by Soviet specialists were found to be inaccurate, and the machinery imported from the Soviet Union was either in poor condition or did not work at all since much of it was brought from the construction sites for the Volga-Don Canal and those linking the White Sea and the Caspian Sea. Facing huge losses and robbed of a major propaganda victory, Gheorghiu-Dej sought scapegoats and the *Securitate* was ordered to organize show trials of workers who were accused of sabotage.

In the summer of 1952, Colonel Mişu Dulgheru, head of the penal investigations directorate of the *Securitate*, was summoned to a meeting at the Ministry of the Interior. The principal persons present were the minister, Alexandru Drăghici, politburo member Iosif Chişinevski, *Securitate* generals Gheorghe Pintilie, Alexandru Nicolski, Vladimir Mazuru, a Soviet official Agop Garabedian, and the Soviet security counsellors, Alecsandr Sakharovsky, Tiganov and Maximov. Chişinevski ordered Dulgheru to organize a show trial of saboteurs at the canal and told him that 'comrade Gheorghiu-Dej wants this trial over quickly.'[49]

The first of these trials opened on 29 August 1952 in the workers' club at Poarta Albă, some 20 kilometres west of the port of Constanţa. Eight engineers and two mechanics were charged with carrying out premeditated acts designed to sabotage the construction of the canal. One of the charges was that they had neglected the maintenance of machinery, including locomotives, which had consequently broken down. The accused, having undergone long hours of interrogation, confessed to their 'crimes'. Thirty-one witnesses were produced for the prosecution and none for the defence. On 1 September, the military prosecutor, Major Ovidiu Teodorescu, read out the indictment. The proceedings had, he argued,

> removed the mask from the hideous face of the criminals in the dock; this small number of worthless individuals, the scum of society, aided by the British and Americans, those cavaliers of crime and the gun, those propagators of death and destruction, have shown here their true face.[50]

After the defendants expressed regret for their 'crimes' to the court, sentence was passed immediately: five received the death penalty and the other five were condemned to hard labour for periods ranging from 20 years to life. The party newspaper reported that "the working people greeted the just sentence with stormy applause". Upon appeal, two of the death sentences were commuted to hard labour for life; the other three were upheld. On 14 October 1952, Nicolae Vasilescu, Aurel Rozei-Rozemberg and Dumitru Nichita were executed by firing squad somewhere in the Dobrogea.

In a move that was apparently linked to the Politburo's decision of 14 March 1954 to put Lucreţiu Pătrăşcanu and his associates on trial, a review of all internees in labour camps was ordered by the Council of Ministers.[51] All former Iron Guardists, senior members of the opposition parties, and officers of the pre-Communist SSI and *Siguranţa* were to be interrogated, presumably in an attempt to glean fresh evidence against the Pătrăşcanu group. By the same resolution of the Council of Ministers, the release was ordered of most of the other internees, that is those categorized in Resolution 1554 of August 1952.

The deployment of conscript soldiers in the construction of the canal presented another dimension to the practice of forced labour. In effect, the Romanian soldier was used as a navvy on major construction projects throughout the entire period of Communist rule and his conditions of labour were often little better than those of the political detainees. In some cases, on security sensitive sites, these conditions posed major health risks, as in the uranium mines in the Apuseni Mountains. In the mine at Băiţa-Plai, some 20 km east of the town of Ştei, several thousand conscript soldiers—one source puts the number at 10,000—worked under the command of Soviet officers in the extraction of uranium ore. The ore was then crushed and the dust shipped in 50-kilo drums to Kharkov in the USSR. The Soviet officers lived in purpose-built blocks of flats with their families while the conscripts were quartered in wooden huts. Many of the soldiers working underground and in the opencast mines suffered hair loss because of the high levels of radioactivity and in 1956 the mine was allegedly closed and the Russians withdrew from the site.[52]

Under a resolution of the Council of Ministers in February 1958, the conditions under which forced labour was used as a punishment were extended to those who "endanger public order, even if they do not commit any crime". Persons were still sent into forced labour until 1963, by which time *Securitate* documents show that 25,735 people had been subjected to it since 1950.[53] This figure includes only those considered 'political detainees', for the common law offenders sent to the labour camps are listed separately in the archives of the militia. Even so, we must treat this figure with caution since the Party investigation into the abuses committed against former activists showed in 1968 that tens of thousands were sent to the labour camps without trial and without any record of their detention being compiled.

Here is what Ilie Bădică, former deputy director of the *Securitate* directorate for labour camps, had to say on the subject on 16 March 1968:

> The camp authorities had no means of knowing what each detainee had done since they had no arrest warrant. [...] Very many of the prisoners did not know the reason for their arrest, and some were released after a year or two without ever knowing why they had been arrested. [...]. At the Canal there were many prisoners who were held simply on the orders of the Ministry of the Interior, in breach of the constitution and of any law.[54]
>
> The arrests were made, in fact, on other criteria, as Bădică admitted:
>
> These detainees had been arrested to meet the labour required for the construction of the Danube-Black Sea canal. If they needed 5,000 men at the canal, comrade Hossu, the director-general there, telephoned comrade Teohari [Georgescu] and then Colonel Dulgheru's machinery, at the Penal Investigation Directorate [of the *Securitate*], went into action and established the numbers of people to be rounded up by each county.

This practice of the *Securitate* of arresting people at the whim of the Interior Ministry was confirmed by Pavel Ştefan, himself minister of the interior from 1952 to 1957,[55] in a declaration also given in March 1968:

> There was a lawyer called Calotă who helped us a great deal in 1945. They arrested him because he was a National Peasant Party member and they took his house. I asked him why he had been arrested, perhaps he had said something. He replied that he hadn't. Then I rang Pintilie and asked him, because he knew Calotă well. Pintilie retorted: 'How many are there whom we haven't arrested just because we needed their houses!'[56]

Pintilie's actions typified the regime's violation of human rights. This had given rise to vigorous protests by Western governments and the United Nations in 1949. On 3 November 1950, the General Assembly had passed a resolution condemning Romania, Hungary and Bulgaria for the disregard shown by their governments for the rights and liberties of the persons under their jurisdiction. The effect was nil. In 1954, however, the Soviet Union now sought international acceptance of its satellites by proposing their admittance to the United Nations. On 25 September 1954, the Romanian government submitted a request for UN membership to the General Assembly. Gheorghiu-Dej, aware of the sensitivity of the United States and Britain to his regime's human rights' record, gave the signal in the summer of the following year for the release of thousands of political prisoners, including many of the former ministers imprisoned without trial in Sighet. At the same time, in order to show that he was not turning his back on his faithful lieutenant, Gheorghiu-Dej promoted Drăghici to the rank of colonel general on 20 August 1955. Exactly one month later, all those who had received sentences of up to ten years' imprisonment were pardoned. Excluded from the pardon were ministers in the 'Fascist' governments in the period 6 September 1940 to 23 August 1944.

In a package deal of 14 December 1955, Romania, Hungary and Bulgaria were among 16 nations admitted to the United Nations. Italy, Spain and Finland were the most significant admissions gained by the West in this deal. Respect for the principles of the UN charter required the Communist satellites to release all political prisoners and Gheorghiu-Dej made further concessions in this respect by issuing a pardon to so-called 'Zionists', 'Titoists', 'saboteurs' and 'deviators' in 1956 and 1957. Among those released, on 26 May 1956, was Elena Pătrăşcanu, the wife of Gheorghiu-Dej's most notable victim.

This 'clean-up' of the regime's image also led to the arrest of several labour camp officers. On 10 June 1955, a military court sentenced 32 persons— 21 officers of the Ministry of the Interior and 12 prisoners in charge of work details—to prison terms ranging from five years to hard labour for life. But at the intervention of Drăghici, decrees were issued between August and November 1957 giving a pardon to more than 50 torturers, among them camp commandants. On top of this, Pintilie, Drăghici's deputy, sent them away to the ministry's rest homes for a month, after which they were reassigned to other duties in the ministry. An edifying example of this cynicism on the part of Drăghici was the case of Liviu Borcea who was arrested on 1 December 1954 and sentenced to 25 years' hard labour. Drăghici had him released within 18 months and he was assigned the post of a deputy commandant of Cluj jail.

The records show that those convicted were merely subordinates who had carried out orders from the party and from the Ministry of the Interior. By treating them in this way, Drăghici and Pintilie bought their silence, but not for long. The party enquiry of 1967 and 1968 into abuses against former activists uncovered their responsibility and led to Drăghici's removal from all positions of authority in 1968.

Notes

1 This is a revised version of chapter nine in my *Communist Terror in Romania. Gheorghiu-Dej and the Police State, 1948–1965* (London: Hurst and Co., 1999).

2 *Securitate* files show that more than 70,000 persons were arrested in the decade from 1948 to 1958. (*Cartea Albă a Securităţii* (Bucharest: SRI, 1994), vol.II, p.45). This figure must be treated with caution since, on Gheorghiu-Dej's own admission in 1961, 80,000 peasants alone had been arrested in the collectivization drive. Moreover, the number of detainees in the labour colonies on the Danube-Black Sea Canal project alone was more than 20,000 in 1951. Many of these had not been 'arrested' but merely rounded up and did not figure in *Securitate* figures. Alexandru Drăghici was transferred from the Ministry of the Interior on 20 September 1952 to head the new ministry. The Ministry of State Security was reincorporated into the Ministry of the Interior on 7 September 1953. Drăghici retained his status as the most senior party member responsible for state security by being made first vice president of the Council of Ministers on 20 August 1954. He resumed his former post as minister of the interior on 20 March 1957. The minister of the interior from September 1952 until March 1957 was Pavel Ştefan. For further details of Drăghici's career see Andrei Şiperco (ed.), *Confesiunile elitei comuniste. România 1945–1965. Arhiva Alexandru Şiperco*, vol.2 (Bucharest: Institutul Naţional pentru Studiul Totalitarismului, 2015), pp.183–204.

3 C. Coposu, *Dialoguri cu Vartan Arachelian* (Bucharest: Editura Anastasia, 1992), p.95.

4 For a description of the prison and the experience of prisoners held there after 1948 see Andrea Dobeş, *Reprimarea elitelor interbelice Colonia ,Dunărea' Sighet (1950–1955)* (Sighetu Marmaţiei: Editura Valea Verde, 2010).

5 Among them was Dumitru Caracostea, a member of the Romanian Academy, who was for a brief spell minister of education in the Gigurtu government of August 1940.

6 This manuscript was entrusted by Giurescu's son, Dinu, to the care of Paul Michelson, an American history professor in the 1980s and after Dinu was allowed to emigrate to the United States in 1988, Michelson sent him a photocopy of the MS, which was published in Romania in 1994 under Constantin Giurescu's name as *Cinci Ani şi Două Luni în Penitenciarul de la Sighet* (Bucharest: Editura Fundaţiei Culturale Române, 1994). An edition in English appeared in the same year as *Five Years and Two Months in the Sighet Penitentiary* (Boulder, Colorado: East European Monographs).

7 Details related by my mother-in-law, Dumitru Caracostea's own daughter-in-law.

8 Giurescu, Five years and Two Months, p.xv.

9 Giurescu, *Penitenciarul de la Sighet*, p.11. The prison was finally closed in 1974 ('Memoria şi istoria', *România liberă*, 22–23 May 1993).

10 Its commandants were Lt. Col. Mihai Dorobanţu (1950–51), Lt. Ludovic Czegledi (1952–53), Col. Ştefan Koller (1954–58), and Col. Gheorghe Crăciun (1958–64). (*Ministerul Justiţiei. Direcţia Generală a Penitenciarelor*, document no. 35.372, dated

19 February 1992) According to his party file, Crăciun was born on 24 July 1913 in the commune of Mintiul Gherlei in the county of Someş in Transylvania. He worked as a maintenance man on the railways and joined the Communist Party in 1945 when he was recruited into the Ministry of the Interior. By spring 1948, he had been given the rank of inspector in the *Siguranţa* in Sibiu (*Cartea Albă a Securităţii* (Bucharest: SRI, 1994), vol.I, doc.166, p.336).

11 The commandants of Galaţi were Lt. Maj. Tiberiu Lazăr (1948–51), Lt. Col. Nicolae Moromete (1952–53), Capt. Ioan Stănescu (1954–56), Col. Dumitru Vodă (1957–59), and Col. Marian Petrescu (1960–65); those of Făgăraş were Maj. Iosif Maraviov (1954) and Lt. Col. Aron Trâmbiţaş (1955–59).

12 The Piteşti experiment should be distinguished from the other programmes bearing the label 're-education'. Striving to impose conformity through coercive methods such as forced labour or abuse of drugs was also euphemistically termed 're-education' by the Ministry of the Interior throughout the period of Communist rule and therefore the word, with a different currency, continued to be used after Piteşti. Underground whispers about the Piteşti experiment circulated in Romania's prisons throughout the 1950s. Some of this fragmented oral history was presented in 1963 in a book compiled by Dumitru Bacu, himself a political prisoner, which was published in Romanian in the United States and later translated into English as *The Anti-Humans* (Monticello, Illinois: TLC, 1977). Virgil Ierunca's study *Piteşti* (Paris: Limite, 1981) draws heavily on Bacu's presentation and enabled Romanians to learn of the enormity of the programme since extracts from it were broadcast on Radio Free Europe shortly after publication. After Ceauşescu's overthrow more evidence of the re-education drive emerged in the form of memoir literature. The effects of the extension of the re-education programme to Gherla prison in Transylvania in autumn 1951 are described by Aristide Ionescu, a former prisoner there, in his memoir, *Dacă vine ora H pe cine putem conta* (Piteşti, 1992), pp.46–55.

13 Transcripts of Ţurcanu's interrogation and extracts from the proceedings of his and his associates' trial, which began on 20 September 1954, are reproduced in *Memorialul Ororii. Documente ale Procesului Reeducării din închisorile Piteşti, Gherla* (Bucharest: Editura Vremea, 1995). Despite its wealth of documents, this volume lacks a critical introduction and apparatus. The material is the *Securitate*'s version of the re-education experiment, therefore it is not surprising that there is no mention of Alexandru Nicolski's role. Neither does the volume refer to the books by Baciu and Ierunca.

14 A.Raţiu and W. Virtue, *Stolen Church: Martyrdom in Communist Romania* (Huntington, Indiana: Our Sunday Visitor, 1978), p.101.

15 Ierunca, *Pitesti*, p.46.

16 C. Aioanei and C. Troncotă, 'Arhipelagul Ororii (II)', *Magazin Istoric*, vol.27, no.4 (April 1993), p.11, note 1.

17 At the trial, the prosecution identified the following as victims and mentioned an unspecified number of others: Alexandru Bogdanovici, Corneliu Nita, Eugen Gavrilescu, Gheorghe Şerban and Gheorghe Vatajoiu. *Memorialul Ororii. Documente*, p.644.

18 Raţiu, *Stolen Church*, p.101.

19 D. Bacu, *The Anti-Humans* (Monticello, Illinois: TLC, 1977), p.104.

20 Ibid., p.106.

21 Ierunca, *Piteşti*, pp.70–71.

22 Ibid., p.59.

23 Ionescu, *Dacă vine H pe cine putem conta* (Piteşti, 1992), p.46.

24 The relevant part of the transcript of Jianu's interrogation reads:

> Question. How and in what circumstances were a number of self-denunciations made by the prisoners in the prisons?
> Answer. I know from Colonel Teodor Sepeanu, Colonel Dulgheru and General Nicolski that in the prisons, as a positive

result of the work of the newly-introduced department of inspections, the Iron Guardists held in prison began to make self-denunciations of their own accord, making fresh disclosures which had not emerged during their interrogation before trial. I asked Colonel Sepeanu how he achieved these results. He replied that by using the 'enlightenment methods' employed by the officers in this department and the information which they extracted, they succeeded in persuading the imprisoned Iron Guardists to denounce themselves. I was not told that other methods or physical pressures were used in this respect (Declaration of Marin Jianu, from *Dosarul de anchetă al lotului de la* Interne, Ministerul de Interne [Interrogation file of the group from the Ministry of the Interior], ASRI, dosar 40009, vol.26, f.141).

25 Ierunca, *Piteşti*, p.80.

26 Aioanei, 'Arhipelagul Ororii (II)', p.16.

27 *Ibid.*

28 *Ibid.*

29 Memorialul Ororii, pp.781–82.

30 The 22 were Eugen Ţurcanu, Alexandru Popa (Ţanu), Nuţi Pătrăşcanu, Mihai Livinski, Gheorghe Popescu, Cornel Pop, Dan Dumitrescu, Octavian Voinea, Vasile Puşcaşu, Vasile Păvăloaie, Ion Stoian, Grigore Romanescu, Aristotel Popescu, Maximilian Sobolevschi, Constantin Juberian, Cornel Popovici, Ion Voiu, Ion Cerbu, Cristian Paul Şerbănescu, Constantin Ionescu, Octavian Zrbanca and Nicolae Colibaş. The youngest was 25 and the oldest 34 (Ţurcanu was 29). Six of the condemned, Alexandru Popa, Nuţi Pătrăşcanu, Dan Dumitrescu, Octavian Voinea, Vasile Puşcaşu and Aristotel Popescu, were spared execution for they were to be tried on other charges connected with the programme. They benefitted from an amnesty in 1955 which commuted all death sentences into ones of forced labour for life. Ţurcanu and the 15 others were executed at Jilava by firing squad on 17 December 1954. (*Cartea Albă a Securităţii* (Bucharest: SRI, 1995), vol.II, doc.219, pp.487–88).

31 Bacu, *The Anti-Humans*, pp.93–94.

32 *Organizarea şi funcţionarea Organelor Ministerului de Interne de la Infiinţare pînă în prezent* (Bucharest: Ministry of the Interior, 1978 (mimeographed)), p.112. Article 1 of the decree of 13 January 1950 read: "Labour camps are to be established for the re-education of elements hostile to the Romanian People's Republic and for the preparation and integration of these elements into the social life of a People's democracy where socialism is being constructed". Persons liable to be sent to the camps were defined in article 2 as, a) "those who through their actions or attitudes, directly or indirectly, threaten or attempt to threaten the People's democracy, who hamper or try to hamper the construction of socialism in the RPR, as well as those who slander the state or its bodies, [even] if these deeds do not constitute, or cannot constitute by analogy, crimes".

b) "those convicted of crimes against the security of the RPR who, on the expiry of their sentence, show not to have been re-educated".

The re-education term was stipulated to be from six months to two years, but the same article 4 provided for its extension up to five years. Anyone leaving the camps without written authority was subject to imprisonment for a period from six months to five years.

33 They included "all those who launch or spread alarmist, tendentious or hostile rumours, or listen or spread the shameless propaganda of the imperialist radio stations: all those who slander the Romanian Workers' Party or its leaders, or the Soviet Union and its leaders; all those Romanian citizens who have frequented or frequent the libraries and

embassies of the capitalist powers in Romania", and those who instigated resistance to collectivization or conducted religious proselytization; see Cristian Troncotă, 'Colonia de muncă', *Arhivele Totalitarismului*, vol.1, no.1 (1993), p.170.

34 Resolution 1554 of 22 August 1952 of the Council of Ministers. The conditions under which internal exile was to be served were revised in March 1954 when the period of detention was fixed at between six months and five years. Certain localities in the Bărăgan plain to the west of Bucharest were designated for internal exile (Resolution 337 of 11 March 1954 of the Council of Ministers). The designated villages or communes were Drepia, Pelican, Ezerul, Olaru, Măzăreni, Zagna, Rubla, Schei, Bumbăcari, Brateş, Salcîmi, Valea Viilor, Răchitoasa, Movila Goidoului, Lădeşti, Fundata, Viişoara, Dolga Noua.

35 The six other members were Maj. Gen. Alexandru Nicolski, Col. Aurel Corin, Lt. Col. Iosif Erdei and Majors Francisc Butica, Marin Vintilă and Wilhelm Einhorn.

36 Doina Jela, Cazul Nichita Dumitru. Incercare de reconstituire a unui proces comunist (Bucharest: Humanitas, 1995), p.28.

37 Jela, Cazul Nichita Dumitru, p.26.

38 On 9 August 1949, the DGC sent in a request to the Ministry of Trade and Food for 28,500 kilos of salted bacon for the workforce. At the same time, a large number of Ziss lorries were ordered from the State Planning Committee.

39 Jela, Cazul Nichita Dumitru, p.31.

40 Ibid., p.38.

41 Ibid., pp.21, 148.

42 Cristian Troncota, Colonia de muncă', *Arhivele Totalitarismului*, vol.1, no.1 (1993), p.174.

43 Troncota, ‚Colonia de muncă', p.176. Not all camp commandants turned a blind eye to excesses. On 23 August 1950, a prisoner at the Poarta Albă camp on the canal was shot by a guard while trying to escape. Captain Domşa, the commandant, who was the son of a priest from the Banat, ordered the arrest of the guard. The latter was tried and sentenced to five years' detention in the same camp where the prisoners regularly beat him. (Communication from Alexandru Salca, Braşov, 30 March 1997).

44 Communication from Dr Şerban Papacostea, 5 March 1995.

45 Prisoners were expected to chant the refrain: '*La muncă, la muncă*
Veniţi voioşi la muncă
Roaba e plină
Alta să vină
Veniţi voioşi la muncă' ('To work, to work, come with a smile on your face to work, the wheelbarrow is full, bring along another one, come with a smile on your face to work') Interview with Dr Şerban Papacostea, 21 July 2016.

46 Interview with Dr Şerban Papacostea, 24 April 1996. The food at Capul Midia was, in Papacostea's opinion, more consistent than in Jilava jail where breakfast consisted of a cup of chicory, lunch a piece of bread and cabbage or beans, and the evening meal a pearl barley soup. After two months at the canal, Papacostea, together with other students, was brought back by train to Bucharest and released.

47 *Cartea Albă a Securităţii*, vol.II, Anexă, doc.22. This figure leads us to question the accuracy of a Ministry of Interior document when it states that the *total* number of deaths in *all* labour camps between 1945 and 1964 was 656.

48 *Cartea Albă a Securităţii*, vol.II, Anexă, doc.6, p.13.

49 *Cartea Albă a Securităţii*, vol.II, Anexă., doc.31, p.96.

50 Jela, Cazul Nichita Dumitru, p.193.

51 H. Nestorescu-Bălceşti, ‚Structura Conducerii Superioare a Partidului Comunist Român', *Arhivele Totalitarianismului*, vol.2, nos.1–2 (1994), p.363. The Council's resolution was dated 11 March.

52 See the interview given by Constantin Andrieş, who was posted to the mine in 1955, to Vasile Iancu under the title 'Un fost ofiţer aduce mărturii revelatoare', *România liberă*,

23 April 1996, p.4. According to Andrieş, there was another uranium mine under Soviet command at Ciudanoviţa, 20 km north of the town of Oraviţa, in the Banat.

53 Troncota·, 'Colonia de muncă', p.172.

54 *Ibid.*

55 Ştefan was appointed minister after responsibility for the *Securitate* was moved to the newly created Ministry of State Security in September 1952. Alexandru Drăghici was transferred from the Ministry of the Interior on 20 September 1952 to head the new ministry. The Ministry of State Security was reincorporated into the Ministry of the Interior on 7 September 1953. Drăghici retained his status as the most senior Party member directly responsible for state security by being made first vice president of the Council of Ministers on 20 August 1954. He resumed his former post as minister of the interior on 20 March 1957.

56 Troncotă·, 'Colonia de muncă', p.173.

8 Armed resistance

Overt challenges to Communist rule under Gheorghiu-Dej were uncommon and none threatened the grip that the regime had upon the country, but to accuse the Romanians, as many commentators did, of being 'weak' and 'timorous', showed an ignorance of internal realities in their country.[1] Such accusations were based on what *appeared* to be a complete absence of challenge to the Communist regime in Romania when compared with the riots in Poland and East Germany in the early 1950s, and the uprising in Hungary in 1956. The unchallenged acceptance of these accusations is precisely a measure of the success of the *Securitate* in preventing information about resistance to the regime from leaking out.[2] Virtually nothing was known in the West of the defiant struggle in the Carpathian Mountains of small bands of partisans, led by Gheorghe Arsenescu, Toma Arnăţoiu and Ion Gavrilă-Ogoreanu.

Armed opposition to the Communist role in the government surfaced in the winter of 1944 and had been coordinated by General Aurel Aldea (interior minister in the first Sănătescu government) in the summer of 1945. After Aldea's arrest in May 1946, this opposition crumbled. In fact, his so-called 'National Resistance Movement' (*Mişcarea Naţională de Rezistenţă*) posed little direct threat to the Groza government, its principal activities being the distribution of primitive anti-Communist propaganda, but the attacks it had carried out during the winter of 1944 on Hungarians in revenge for murders of Romanians by Hungarian policemen during the period of Hungarian rule of Northern Transylvania, had raised the spectre of civil strife in Transylvania behind the Soviet front line and showed that it offered a potential nucleus of armed resistance to Communist rule.[3]

A number of Aldea's supporters escaped arrest by taking to the mountains. They were nearly always on the defensive, fending off regular attempts by the security forces to round them up. A letter from J.E. Hartley, a British consular official in Cluj to the British legation in Bucharest, dated 1 May 1949, retold stories he had heard of partisan exploits and misadventures in the Carpathians. Although he discounted a good deal of them on the score of distortion and exaggeration, he was in no doubt that the partisans had come to stay. Their leader was General Cornel Drăgălina (1877–1949).[4] They were all Romanians, a point Hartley regarded as being in their favour should the question of Transylvania raise its head once more in the future. The partisans enjoyed the sympathy of the peasantry and appeared to have sufficient small arms and ammunition for their defensive tactics. They were not short of money either. He went on:

> I am told, however, that clothing and medicines are short and this is probably true as their numbers have been increased by a considerable proportion of women and children since the March 1st land expropriation. I have been given a figure as high as 20,000 as the number who have joined since the expropriation [...]. The increase in the number of women and children will create problems of survival next winter [...]. I am told now and again of lorries of army supplies going over to the partisans, sometimes by capture and sometimes by desertion, but I cannot say to what extent this is happening.[5]

Such was the number of similar tales in circulation that the legation in Bucharest commented that it was "fairly confident that there must be a growing number of men in the hills who are outside the law and in armed opposition to the established authority of Romania". The legation was cautious in attaching much importance to this resistance: "We doubt if it would be right to describe these dissidents as more than outlaws. Nor are they likely to be able to influence the course of events in any foreseeable circumstances".[6]

Partisan activity was sufficiently serious for the CIA to try to exploit it. At the beginning of 1949, the Office of Political Coordination under the direction of Frank Wisner, began to recruit Romanians from refugee camps in southern Germany, Austria and Yugoslavia.[7] Preference was shown for young men who knew those regions in which partisan activity had been reported. Gordon Mason, the CIA station chief in Bucharest from 1949 to 1951, revealed that these agents were instructed to contact the resistance groups and to deliver light weapons, ammunition, radio transmitters and medicines to them. The agents had three objectives. First, to encourage the partisans to carry out acts of sabotage on railways and factories; this would also offer proof of their existence and of their activity. Second, the agents were to monitor troop movements, especially those which might indicate preparations for an attack on Yugoslavia or on Western Europe. Finally, they were to encourage the partisans to harass Soviet troops should a war break out.[8]

The Office of Policy Coordination (OPC) set up training schools in France, Italy and Greece. Recruits were instructed in parachute drops and in the use of radio transmitters. Gratien Yatsevich, who directed CIA covert operations in the Balkans at the time, disclosed that in terms of resources allocated and agents recruited, the operations in Romania came second only to those in Albania. Among the Romanians recruited at the beginning of 1951 were Constantin Săplăcan, Wilhelm Spindler, Gheorghe Bârsan, Mathias Bohm and Ilie Puiu.[9] Under interrogation by the *Securitate* after their capture, the group alleged that they had been recruited in Italy by a former Romanian pilot, Tudorica Crâsnaru, and introduced to two American agents code-named 'Charles' and Gunter.[10] They were given their training in enciphering in September at the Frascatti Franciscan convent in Rome and were then taken by car via Switzerland, France and Belgium to the

Netherlands. Some ten kilometres before reaching the Dutch frontier they transferred to a US military jeep driven by a US sergeant and crossed the frontier with Dutch passports issued by the Dutch embassy in Rome which were then returned to 'Charles'. They were taken to a Dutch army barracks where they received operational instructions, such as how to use the US radio they were given, from three persons—one Dutch, a second British and the third a German. At the same time, they received details of their mission: to ascertain the number of Soviet troops in Romania, their location and armament; the extent of industrialization and the state of the roads and railways and whether the former could be used as landing strips for aircraft. They were then flown from Amsterdam to Frankfurt where they stayed three days in a villa before being taken by air in a US military plane to Munich where they received parachute training which consisted of three jumps from a platform over a period of six days at a US airbase. They were then flown back to Frankfurt where they were given parachute training at an American air base. After a six-day stay, they flew to Athens. After completing this, they were flown to Athens and driven to a house in Chefelaria, some 30 kilometres from the Greek capital. After receiving further parachute training and instruction in the use of small arms, they were given 50 gold coins (Romanian *cocoşei*) a large sum of Romanian banknotes, supplies of bread, sausage, cheese, chocolate and vitamins, as well as Romanian identity cards and work certificates.

On 13 October, the group took off from Athens in an unmarked two-engine Douglas aircraft with a four-person crew in civilian clothes. The pilot and co-pilot were described by Bohm as speaking English with an American accent. However, the plane developed a technical fault some 20 minutes after take-off and returned to the airfield. Five days later, the group left once again, at 9 p.m., in the same aircraft with three Bulgarians who, they were told, were to be dropped in Hungary after the Romanians. The Săplăcan team parachuted into the Negoiu mountains after a flight lasting three and a half hours at a pre-arranged spot illuminated by an 'L' formed from small lights. After three days, they reached Cabana Negoiului, a mountain refuge, which was empty where they set up their radio transmitter and sent a message announcing their safe arrival.

Yet the group's attempts to carry out its mission were vitiated by an unrealistic appreciation of the harsh physical environment into which they were dropped. Survival in the mountains during the winter without suitable shelter and a regular supply of provisions meant dependence upon the help of the local population which was naturally suspicious of strangers during this period of oppression. The group soon found their position untenable and, after burying their radio sets, split up. They were rounded up within two months. Bârsan committed suicide by taking a cyanide capsule issued in Athens to each member of the group; his body was discovered by a policeman in the loft of a barn in Sărata, in the district of Făgăraş in Sibiu county on 15 December.[11] Puiu was found sleeping on a bench near the town of Copşa Mică by two policemen, asked for his papers and arrested. He then swallowed his poison pill, collapsed, was taken to hospital and recovered.[12] Săplăcan, Spindler and Bohm, living from hand to mouth and emaciated, also fell into the hands of the police.

A protest note was delivered by the Romanian government to the Americans on the basis of an admission by the group members that they had been "sent to carry out acts of terrorism an espionage against the Romanian army". The US government denied any connection with the group, but former CIA officers have since admitted that the group were American agents.[13] All four survivors were accused of "treachery to the homeland and plotting against the external security of the Romanian People's Republic".[14] Their trial, by a military tribunal presided over by Major General Alexandru Petrescu, opened on 25 December 1951.[15] All four accused were found guilty and sentenced to death. Their appeals were rejected on 26 December and the condemned men were taken to Jilava prison in Bucharest and executed by firing squad at 4.30 p.m. on the same afternoon.[16]

After the overthrow of Ceauşescu details emerged of how several small bands of self-styled 'partisans' took to the Carpathian Mountains in the late 1940s and resisted arrest by the authorities.[17] The last member of the longest-surviving group was not rounded up until 1960. This 'armed anti-Communist resistance', as it has been called, was a spontaneous phenomenon and there were no links between the different groups, but they were driven by a common aim, namely not to submit themselves to consequences of communization of their country. The groups, composed on average of between 20 and 40 persons, did not pose a major threat to Communist power, but as long as they remained at liberty they undermined the regime's claim to have total control of the country.

The groups were formed in the villages in the mountain foothills and were composed of peasants, former army officers, lawyers, doctors and students. Ill equipped, they relied on an assortment of rifles, revolvers and machine pistols left over from the war and were always faced with an acute shortage of ammunition. They received support from villagers who brought them food and clothing and often gave them shelter. The Communist propaganda of the period dubbed these anti-Communist partisans 'legionaries', that is, members of the extreme right-wing movement known as the Iron Guard, and indeed many of them had been members of it. However, the partisans were by no means exclusively 'legionaries' or 'Iron Guardists', as the *Securitate*'s very own statistics show. A report of the *Direcţia Generală a Securităţii Poporului* of 1951 states that the political affiliation of 804 persons arrested for either belonging to, or aiding 17 *bande din munţi*, was as follows: 88 former members of Iuliu Maniu's National Peasant Party, 79 members of the Ploughmen's Front, 73 former legionaries, 42 former members of the Communist Party, 15 members of the National Liberal Party and others.[18] According to another *Securitate* report, this one dated September 1949, there were 'terrorist bands' active in the regions of Craiova, Braşov, Sibiu, Ploieşti, Suceava, Galaţi, Oradea, Cluj, Timişoara and Constanţa. None of these groups was more than 25 strong, and most of them had less than ten members.[19]

Most of the members of the partisan group led by Major Nicolae Dabija in the Apuseni Mountains in Transylvania between 1947 and 1949 were peasants who were not, as the Communist authorities claimed, *chiaburi* or owners of land.[20] Thirty-two persons were tried as members or sympathisers of the group at the end of September 1949 in Sibiu, and seven were sentenced to death and executed on

28 October. Their unmarked graves were identified in the Communal Cemetery of Sibiu in January 1994.[21] The memoirs of a former Iron Guardist show that caution is required in applying the label 'Guardist' indiscriminately to the resistance groups. Filon Verca acknowledges that one of two main partisan groups in the Banat mountains in 1948 was led by Spiru Blănaru, a former Guardist, but points out that one of the commanders of the second group was Colonel Ioan Uţă, a prefect of Lugoj county, who had acted against the Guardists in 1939.[22] Blănaru and the bulk of his small group were caught and executed near Timişoara on 16 July 1949. Uţă's band of 30 partisans fought off a company of *Securitate* troops near the village of Teregova on 22 February 1949, only to be caught on 8 March in a skirmish in which Uţă died.[23]

The longest-surviving group was the *Haiducii Muscelului* (Outlaws of Muscel). Elisabeta Rizea, the only surviving member of the group, has given us an account of the early months of its activity but her arrest shortly afterwards means that for the remainder of the story we are reliant upon the second-hand versions by relatives of the participants. Many of the dates and incidents are confirmed by the *Securitate* records but not surprisingly, the latter give a different interpretation to them. For example, these records allege that innocent civilians were murdered by the 'partisans' who are constantly vilified, being termed 'fascist terrorists'. What is reasonably clear from both sides is that the group, which at one time never numbered more than 30 or 40 persons, was formed by two ex-army officers, Gheorghe Arsenescu (1907–62) and Toma Arnăţoiu (1921–59), in their native district of Muscel in the foothills of the Carpathians.

According to *Securitate* records Arsenescu had hidden weapons at a hermitage in the village of Cetăţeni in the summer of 1947 and in the following spring had set up a 'terrorist group' comprising Gheorghe Hachenzelner, Petre Cojocaru, Longhin Predoiu, Ion Mică, and Ion and Gheorghe Purnichescu. Arsenescu spent the autumn and winter in Bucharest and it was there, at the end of 1948, that Toma Arnăţoiu contacted Arsenescu with a view to setting up a resistance group in the district around Nucşoara. From accounts given by contemporaries, Arsenescu seems to have put his faith in a general armed insurrection which was to be led by other former army officers in the west of the country but which never materialized. He agreed to provide Arnăţoiu with small arms and the latter then returned to Nucşoara with Nicolae Niţu and recruited his brother Petre Arnăţoiu, Ion Chirca and the village priest Ion Drăgoi. In March 1949, Arsenescu came to Nucşoara to join the group and in the ensuing months it expanded to include several more villagers.

The Ministry of the Interior was clearly worried that the symbol of resistance posed by the band might be contagious and it was for this reason that it poured troops and *Securitate* officers into the region. Helped by their local knowledge of the difficult mountain terrain and by several families in the commune of Nucşoara, notably Gheorghe and Elisabeta Rizea, Ion Săndoiu and Ion Sorescu, the group secured provisions and escaped arrest. On the night of 18 June 1949, members of the group were ambushed as they came to collect supplies and in the ensuing gunfight two *Securitate* officers, Constantin Apavaloaiei and Florea Lungu were killed. The group's escape under cover of darkness through a security cordon thrown around the area resulted in a massive search being carried out for them by two army battalions and units of the *Securitate* troops, and the arrest of families suspected of aiding them.[24]

Among those arrested was Elisabeta Rizea. She recounted how she was taken to the mayor's office in Nucşoara where she was beaten with a heavy stick by second lieutenant Constantinescu of the *Securitate*.[25] She was then held in the cellar of a peasant house for four days after which she was transported to the prison in Piteşti. Eighteen months passed before she was put on trial. In the meantime she was beaten on several occasions by warrant officers Zamfirescu and Mecu. She was finally tried and sentenced in December 1950 to seven years' imprisonment for helping the partisan group.[26]

After the ambush of 18–19 June 1949, Arsenescu decided to split his men into two bands, one under his command, the second under the leadership of Arnăţoiu. The first band, which included Ion Chirca, Titi Mămăligă, Benone Milea, Constantin Popescu and Nae Ciolan, based itself in the Râul Doamnei valley, and the Arnăţoiu band, made up of his brother Petre, Titu, Maria and Constantin Jubleanu, and Maria Plop, in the Vâlsan valley. Arsenescu's band did not survive for long. Milea was captured on 1 November 1949 and Popescu and Ciolan suffered the same fate three days later. Chirca disappeared without trace. Arsenescu and Mămăligă were caught in a trap by the security troops, the latter being wounded in a shoot-out while Arsenescu fled from the area, and led a hermit-like existence in the hills for ten years until he was finally caught in 1960. Mămăligă managed to make his way to the Arnăţoiu group.

Shortly afterwards, in the spring of 1950, this group, too, was forced to split up to avoid detection. One band, made up of the husband and wife Titu and Maria Jubleanu, their son Tică, and a young doctor Ion Marinescu, were tracked down and in the resulting gunfight Maria was shot dead. Titu Jubleanu was arrested but the two young men managed to escape, joining the second band, composed of the two Arnăţoiu brothers, Toma and Petre, Maria Plop and Mămăligă. Marinescu and Mămăligă were killed in skirmishes with the *Securitate* in 1952 and the remaining four hid out in a cave near the village of Poenărei for several years. On 20 May 1958, the brothers were deceived by a local man into drinking drugged spirits, and after falling into a comatose state were arrested. Plop, who two years earlier had given birth to a daughter, surrendered with the child, but Tică Jubleanu refused and shot himself.[27] A sweep of the surrounding villages in the district was made and scores of families detained for assisting the Arnăţoiu brothers. The two brothers and Maria Plop were taken to Piteşti jail. There, together with others who were rounded up and accused of aiding the group, there were interrogated over a period of 12 months.[28]

The trial of the brothers took place the following year. Toma and Petre Arnăţoiu were sentenced to death and executed at Jilava prison by firing squad, on 18 October 1959, as were the following persons accused of rendering them assistance: Nicolae Andreescu and Ion Constantinescu, Orthodox priests in Poenărei, Ion Drăgoi, the Orthodox priest of Nucşoara, Nicolae Băşoiu, Titu Jubleanu, Constantin Popescu,

Ion Săndoiu, Nicolae Sorescu and Gheorghe Tomeci, all peasant farmers, and the teachers Alexandru Moldoveanu, Nicolae Niţu and Gheorghe Popescu. Benone Milea was also sentenced to death and executed but Maria Plop received life imprisonment and died in jail.[29] Others also tried with this group were, according to the *Securitate* records, Ilie Dragomirescu and Ion Grigore, arrested on 22 June 1958, Nicolae Vasilescu, arrested on 4 July 1958, and Ion Dumitrescu, arrested on 6 February 1959. All received long jail terms.[30] Arsenescu was tracked down to a house in Câmpulung-Muscel where he was being sheltered by friends and he surrendered to a *Securitate* squad on 1 February 1960.[31] His trial took place in February 1962. He was sentenced to death and executed at Jilava on 29 May 1962. His wife Maria and his father Gheorghe were also tried for assisting him and were given prison terms of ten and 15 years respectively.[32]

A second notable resistance group was that led by Ion Gavrilă-Ogoreanu in the Făgăraş mountains.[33] Gavrilă-Ogoreanu, a 25-year old student at Cluj university with close ties to the former Iron Guard, formed his group of 11 from his university colleagues in 1948.[34] For seven years they tied up several companies of security troops before being captured and sentenced to death in 1957. Gavrilă-Ogoreanu was enterprising enough to escape arrest and with the help of friends escaped detection until June 1976, when he was finally picked up in Cluj.[35]

Unlike Arnăţoiu and Arsenescu, Gavrilă-Ogoreanu was spared the death penalty and survived the Communist era to offer a unique personal view in his autobiography of the reaction of the population to his small band of 'partisans':

> When we took to the mountains, we knew enough about that unknown part of [Romanian] history. We never fooled ourselves. We did not count on the fact that everyone in the district of Făgăraş would join us or understand us. When I said that the mountain villages might have risen up in 1949 and in 1950, or that we were received and helped by the local people, I was not referring to a particularly large number of people... There might have been a hundred, two hundred, maybe a thousand. But the rest of the inhabitants? Some did not come out of fear. And they have to be understood. Others were only concerned with their own interests. Any step you take in life is a calculated one. Regimes change, the profiteers remain. One side exits the scene, and that very same side returns. They never have principles or pangs of conscience. Regimes and ideologies cannot be changed as long as they are able to adapt themselves so quickly... You are then left with the great mass of the labourers, whose life is reduced to work and food, in an eternal cycle, and whose consciences do not rise above the bowl of food in front of their noses. They are so down-trodden and so well-conditioned to be down-trodden that they cannot, would not and do not think of looking beyond. Their eyes are those of a mole's. They hate anyone who wants to deliver them from their existence as slaves. With them the authorities can do what they want; in the first place, to do their thinking for them.[36]

This appraisal, coming from such a dedicated figure in the resistance to Communist rule as Gavrilă-Ogoreanu has a more convincing ring about the attitude of much of the local population to resistance groups than the tendency towards hyperbole which characterizes some of the writing about the 'armed resistance' which appeared after 1989. It is as though some authors feel embarrassment at the fact that challenges to Communist authority in Romania under Gheorghiu-Dej were not as widespread or as serious as in some of the other Soviet satellites and seek to overcompensate by exaggerating the scale of resistance in Romania. The publication of *memoir* literature and access to the *Securitate* files have dispelled the general impression that there was no opposition to Communist rule, but at the same time, they have revealed the true dimension of resistance. It was not widespread, as Gavrilă-Ogoreanu pointed out and therefore his activity, like that of Arnăţoiu and Arsenescu and others, appears all the more valiant and poignant.[37]

Notes

1 This is a revised version of chapter ten in my *Communist Terror in Romania. Gheorghiu-Dej and the Police State, 1948–1965* (London: Hurst and Co., 1999).

2 An authoritative study of anti-Communist armed resistance in Romania is to be found in Dorin Dobrincu, *Rezistenţa Armată Anti-Comunistă din România (1944-începutul anilor '60)*, PhD doctoral dissertation presented at the Faculty of History, University of Iaşi, April 2006. For a perceptive analysis of the *Securitate's* tactics in combatting the partisan groups see Andrei Miroiu, 'Wiping Out "The Bandits": Romanian Counter-insurgency Strategies in the Early Communist Period', *The Journal of Slavic Military Studies*, vol.23,no.4 (2010), pp.666–91, DOI:10.1080/13518046.2010.526021.

3 Dobrincu, *Rezistenţa armată*, pp.183–91.

4 Richard Cummings, a scholar of American clandestine radio broadcasting to Eastern Europe during the Cold War, writes as follows: "A clandestine or 'black' radio station known as 'Vocea Padurii' (Voice of the Forest) was broadcasting in Romanian in 1951. It is not known if this was an early experimental CIA clandestine radio station or a domestic Romania propaganda station operated by partisans in the mountains and forests, who were fighting the Communist regime. In September 1951, a Radio Free Europe interviewer of refugees from Romania in Turkey wrote this about clandestine radio transmitters in Rumania (Romania).

More and more news from inside Rumania shows that the mysterious radio broadcasting station called Vocea Padurii (Voice of the Forest) is very much listed to and is growing increasingly popular. The broadcasts are starting almost daily about 0200 hours (Rumanian time) and many people in Bucharest especially wake up to hear it. They are made in the name of General DRAGALINA, who achieved great popularity in 1949 as head of the first spontaneous marquis in Rumania. Since then contradictory news about his death reached the outside world, but refugees who listened very recently to the broadcasts claim to recognize his voice and his manner of speaking. The style of the broadcasts is extremely vindictive. Many traitors and collaborators are named in these broadcasts and are promised very quick vengeance. The broadcasts seem to be well informed especially on local affairs. The wavelength is 6,700 kilocycles or 49,60 kilocycles on the 41 meter band.

RFE's evaluator commented: 'Source: reliability unknown; Information: unknown, wait for confirmation. It should be mentioned that Western monitoring has not yet been able to locate this station and unless further confirmation could be obtained, accounts of this matter should be taken with a certain reserve'." http://coldwarradios.blogspot.com. Accessed 6 May 2016.

5 TNA, FO.371/78603 15584.
6 *Ibid.* An annotated collection of *Securitate* documents on the resistance groups supported by a copious bibliography of secondary studies is to be found in the volume *Bande, Bandiţi şi Eroi* (Bucharest: Editura enciclopedică, 2003) edited by a group of archivists at the ACNSAS led by Florica Dobre, with an introductory study by Florian Banu and Silviu B. Moldovan. See also the useful bibliography in Monica Ciobanu, 'Reconstructing the History of Early Communism and Armed Resistance in Romania', *Europe-Asia Studies*, vol.66, no.9 (2014), pp.1452–81.
7 Frank Gardiner Wisner (23 June, 1909, Laurel, Mississippi – 29 October, 1965, Locust Hill Farm, Maryland). Wisner's experience in Romania with the OSS alerted him to the insidious nature of Communist practice and with the support of George Kennan he was instrumental in the creation in 1948 of the Office of Special Projects. Wisner was appointed Director. Shortly afterwards it was renamed the Office of Policy Coordination (OPC) and became the espionage and counter-intelligence branch of the CIA. Wisner became a legend in his own time for his work in covert operations during the Cold War but the stress associated with this work was the likely cause of his suicide, with his son's shotgun. The most complete account of Wisner's career is that given by Evan Thomas in *The Very Best Men: Four Who Dared: The Early Years of the CIA* (New York: Simon and Shuster, 1995).
8 E.W. Hazard, Cold War Crucible: United States Foreign Policy and the Conflict in Romania, 1943–1953 (Boulder, Colorado: East European Monographs, 1996), p.207.
9 Constantin Săplăcan, born on 1 November 1922 in Ocna Dejului, Someş county; Wilhelm Spindler, a Transylvanian Saxon, born on 1 August 1928; Ilie Puiu (alias Adrian Ştefănescu), born on 2 June 1927 in Rusca Montană in Severin county; Mathias Bohm, a Transylvanian Saxon, born on 18 June 1922 in Bălaci, Târnava Mică county (Arhiva Consiliul National pentru Studierea Arhivelor fostei Securităţi (ACNSAS), Fond P, vol.8, p.1). Personal details of Gheorghe Bârsan, who committed suicide and escaped interrogation, are not listed in this volume. Marius Oprea has written a moving study of the Săplăcan mission in his *Şase feluri de a muri* (Bucharest: Polirom, 2009).
10 Interrogation of Constantin Săplăcan, ACNSAS, Fond P, vol.1, p.7.
11 ACNSAS, Fond P, dosar 10635, vol.1, p.511.
12 ACNSAS, Fond P, dosar 10635, vol.1, p.478.
13 E. Hazard, 'Războiul Rece a Inceput în România', *Magazin Istoric*, vol.30, no.8 (August 1996), pp.58–59.
14 ACNSAS, Fond P, dosar 10635, vol.8, p.9.
15 ACNSAS, Fond P, dosar 10635, p.12. Petrescu had presided over the trial of Iuliu Maniu, the leader of the National Peasant Party, and of his associates, in October 1947.
16 ACNSAS, Fond P, dosar 10635, p.41. The head of the *Securitate* in Sibiu County reported on 10 June 1952 that two days earlier "some of the equipment buried by the parachutists was recovered on Cioarecu mountain" (*Ibid.*, p.56).
17 First-hand accounts from survivors of partisan groups have appeared in the review *Memoria*, published by Fundaţia Culturală 'Memoria' since 1990. See also *Cartea Albă a Securităţii*, vol.II, August 1948-Iulie 1958 (Bucharest: SRI, 1995), passim. For an account of the partisan group, led by a forester Nicolae Pop, in the Ţibleş mountains in Maramureş see Ştefan Bellu, *Pădurea răzvrătită* (Baia Mare: Editura Gutinul, 1993), and for that of the anti-Communist groups in Bukovina between 1944 and 1958 Daniel Popa, *Povestea Familiei Motrescu din Vicovu de Jos* (Bucharest: Fundaţia Academica Civică, 2015).
18 Cartea Albă a Securităţii, vol.II, p.82.
19 *Cartea Albă a Securităţii*, vol.II, doc.75, pp.198–204.
20 Dobrincu, *Rezistenţa armată*, pp.441–43.
21 Ştefan Andreescu, 'A Little-Known Issue in the History of Romania: The Armed Anti-Communist Resistance', *Revue Roumaine d'Histoire*, vol.33, nos.1–2 (1994), p.191).

22 Filon Verca, Paraşutaţi în România vândută. Mişcarea de rezistenţă 1944–1948 (Timişoara: Editura Gordian, 1993).
23 *Cartea Albă a Securităţii*, vol.II, doc.58, pp.184–85ş see also *Bande, Bandiţi şi Eroi*, doc.7, pp.58–60.
24 A. Marinescu, 'Pagini din rezistenţa armată anticomunistă', *Memoria*, no.7 (1992), pp.47–51.
25 I had the privilege of talking to Mrs Rizea about her exploits in her home on 9 February 1992.
26 *Povestea Elisabetei Rizea din Nucşoara* (Bucharest: Humanitas, 1993), pp.118–25.
27 The *Securitate* report on the capture of the Arnătoiu group suggests that Jubleanu was killed in an exchange of fire with *Securitate* troops (*Bande, Bandiţi şi Eroi*, doc.49, p.302). Plop's daughter, Ioana Raluca, was taken into care and brought up in an orphanage in Câmpulung. She was only able to discover who her mother was after the overthrow of Ceauşescu.
28 A comprehensive record of Arnăţoiu's interrogation and trial was published by his daughter, Ioana Raluca, in *Luptătorii din munţi. Toma Arnăţoiu. Grupul de la Nucşoara. Documente ale anchetei, procesului, detenţiei* (Bucharest: Vremea, 1997). Toma Arnăţoiu was interrogated on 42 separate occasions; 21 of the sessions lasted from three to six hours, 11 from six to ten hours, and one from ten to 15 hours (five of the interrogation transcripts do not show their duration). His brother Petre faced 37 sessions, 11 of which lasted between ten to 15 hours. I am grateful to Ioana Raluca Voicu for passing on her compilation of these figures which are based on files in the Ministry of Justice.
29 A. Marinescu, ‚Pagini din rezistenţa', pp.57–58.
30 ASRI, Fond D, File 9585, UM 0336 Piteşti, pp.44–66.
31 Bande, Bandiţi şi Eroi, doc.51, p.316.
32 M. Arsenescu-Buduluca, 'Sunt soţia "teroristului" Gheorghe Arsenescu', *Memoria*, no.8 (1993), p.59. The unwillingness of the post-1989 Romanian authorities to recognize that opponents of the Communist regime were the victims of political execution is illustrated by the following case. In December 1951, Traian Murariu, a peasant from the commune of Pădureni in the county of Timiş, was sentenced to death for sheltering Nicolae Mazilu and Ion Mogoş, two members of the anti-Communist group in the Făgăraş mountains. He was executed a year later at Jilava jail for "plotting against the social order". In 1992, his daughter appealed to the Supreme Court for the sentence to be rescinded. After three years, the court informed her that the sentence was "well-founded and legal". (*Ziua*, 18 July 1995).
33 Dobrincu, *Rezistenţa armată*, pp.692–95.
34 The association of Gavrilă-Ogoreanu and many of the partisans with the Iron Guard is examined in William Totok and Elena-Irina Macovei, *Între mit şi bagatelizare. Despre reconsiderarea critică a trecutului. Ion Gavrilă-Ogoreanu şi rezistenţa armată anticomunistă din România* (Iaşi: Polirom, 2016).
35 Ion Gavrilă-Ogoreanu, *Brazii se frâng, dar nu se îndoiesc*, vol.2 (Timişoara: Editura Marineasa, 1995), p.264. Gavrilă-Ogoreanu's arrest in Cluj is tersely reported in a *Securitate* note of 30 June 1976 (*Cartea Albă a Securităţii*, vol.IV, doc. 136, p.372). Gavrilă-Ogoreanu recounts an episode in 1952 which illustrates the motivation of the resistance groups. In order to distract the pursuing forces of the *Securitate*, Gavrilă-Ogoreanu took part of his group to a tourist chalet near Lake Bâlea. After forcing the tourists from the chalet Gavrilă-Ogoreanu addressed them as follows: "Tell everyone that there is still a place in the kingdom of Romania which has not bowed to Communism. As long as our heads are on our shoulders, this corner of the country will be free. Tell the people not to lose faith, for the day will come when the whole of Romania will be free. Pray God for it, so help us God" (Gavrilă-Ogoreanu, *Brazii se frâng, dar nu se îndoiesc*, vol.1., p.304).

36 Gavrilă-Ogoreanu, *Brazii se frâng, dar nu se îndoiesc*, vol.1, pp.267–68.

37 Around midnight on 14 February, 1955, a group of five Romanians—Ion Chirilă, Stan Codrescu, Dumitru Ochiu and Tudor Ciochină—led by Ovidiu Beldeanu, who had been a member of a youth group associated with the Iron Guard, broke into the Romanian embassy in Berne, Switzerland and entered the embassy chauffeur's rooms. According to their own testimony, they were searching for secret documents in an attempt to draw international attention to the human rights violations of the Romanian government and to expose the espionage activities of the embassy in Switzerland. They were disturbed by Aurel Şeţu, the chauffeur, who was shot by Codrescu. Though badly wounded, Şeţu managed to flee and was later discovered under a tree. He was then transported to hospital where he died. The Swiss police were notified by the ambassador and surrounded the building, but without intervening, since the ambassador would not allow them entry to the property. The group demanded the release from jail in Romania of a number of prominent anti-Communist politicians, among them Dinu Brătianu. On the night of February 15/16, Dumitru Ochiu left the embassy, carrying with him a number of documents and was immediately arrested by the Swiss police. The rest of the group surrendered the next day. The police returned the stolen documents immediately to the Romanian ambassador; see Ştejărel Olaru, 'Cei cinci care au speriat Estul' ('The Five Who Frightened the East'), *Timpul*, no.9 (September, 2003), pp.12–13). The members of the group were tried in Berne. Beldeanu was sentenced to four years in prison, Codrescu and Chirilă to three and a half years and Ochiu to a year and four months. Beldeanu was released from prison in 1957, but was lured to West Berlin and abducted by Stasi and *Securitate* agents (Cristian Troncotă, *Istoria serviciilor secrete româneşti: de la Cuza la Ceauşescu* ('The History of the Romanian Secret Services: from Cuza to Ceauşescu') (Bucharest: Editura Ion Cristoiu, 1999), p.461. He was brought to Bucharest on 2 September 1958, placed on trial for the Berne attack, found guilty in November 1959 and sentenced to death. He was executed on 18 February, 1960.

9 Asserting autonomy, 1956–1965

Gheorghiu-Dej's quest for autonomy was based on a number of factors. Several of those factors are obscured by his apparently ambivalent foreign policy conducted within the context of the Cold War. Was Gheorghiu-Dej's strategy of detachment from the Soviet Union clearly established in his mind or was it based on improvisation, a series of responses by which, with consummate skill, he took advantage of the international environment? The evidence available at present admits only of conjecture in this regard. Recent research makes a cogent case for an argument that Gheorghiu-Dej's path to autonomy can be traced back to the mid-1950s rather than to the early 1960s.[1] This involves, on the one hand, a consideration of the impact of de-Stalinization, Khrushchev's secret speech of February 1956 and the Hungarian uprising, and on the other, Romania's evolving relationship with the leading countries of the non-aligned movement.[2] Gheorghiu-Dej's cultivation of relations with states outside the Warsaw Pact is used to explain how Romania's efforts to gain political influence or economic advantage enhanced its detachment strategy.[3]

A graphic example of how Gheorghiu-Dej sought to complement his drive for autonomy by using Romania's oil products and drilling expertise—unique amongst bloc countries—for economic advantage and political capital was his cultivation of relations with India. In 1955, the country's Minister of Natural Resources, Keshav Dev Malaviya, set up the Oil and Natural Gas Corporation. In June, Malaviya contacted Bucharest with his plan to nationalize oil extraction and a request for support. Although the only goods India could offer—cotton and textiles—had to be exported through ports under foreign control, Gheorghiu-Dej saw consideration of the Indian request in the context of the ideological struggle between capitalism and socialism. In the following summer, an Indian parliamentary delegation visited Romania and signed a deal for the delivery of an oil drill which was inaugurated in the foothills of the Himalayas in April 1957. In January 1958, Malaviya presented a list of equipment needed to develop the country's oil infrastructure. He added that he did 'not really care if you buy from the Soviets the products that you will provide [India] with.'[4] Bucharest thus became India's main channel for oil equipment and technology from the Soviet bloc and thereby a key actor in developing the country's oil industry.[5]

The Hungarian uprising and the impact of it in Romania, not only amongst Romanian citizens of Hungarian origin, but also among ethnic Romanians, had reminded Gheorghiu-Dej and the Soviet leadership how dependent he was on force and upon the Soviet Union as the source of his power. At the same time, the events of 1956 in Poland and Hungary had demonstrated that economic discontent had been a major contributor to opposition to the Soviet system. Accordingly, the Soviets were prepared to assist in alleviating Romania's economic difficulties. This soon became clear from the visit made by Prime Minister Chivu Stoica at the head of a Romanian delegation to Moscow from 26 November to 4 December 1956.[6] Economic cooperation was discussed by the two sides. But comparisons between the Polish-Soviet agreement reached only days before Stoica's visit, and the Romanian-Soviet text, showed that the Romanians had been treated less generously. The Poles won the concession that all Polish 'debts' arising from credits given between 1946 and 1953 should be considered settled, whereas in the case of the Romanians, the Soviet Union agreed only to postpone for four years the repayment of credits granted between 1949 and 1955. In the words of a British newspaper, the Soviet-Romanian communiqué gave "the appearance of having been signed between two equal partners but it is clear from its terms that the Romanians are less equal than the Poles".[7]

The Soviet leaders, for their part, had advanced two main arguments in confronting the crises in Poland and Hungary. The first was that the Poznan riots and the Budapest uprising were the work of the West, led by the United States, and were an attempt to wrest Poland and Hungary from the socialist bloc. The second was that Nagy's actions threatened Soviet gains from the Second World War, achieved at massive cost to the Red Army. It was essential, Khrushchev concluded, that extra precautionary measures be taken to cement members into the bloc and therefore new troop-stationing agreements were to be signed with his allies. Such an agreement was signed with Romania in April 1957, but the basis for it was decided during Stoica's visit to Moscow in late November 1956.

The presence of Soviet troops on Romanian territory had been regulated by the Soviet-Romanian Armistice Agreement of September 1944. The Peace Treaty of February 1947 with Romania had given the Russians the right to station troops there in order to ensure lines of communication with the Soviet forces in eastern Austria. A US army intelligence report of January 1950 estimated the Soviet presence in Romania at two divisions, totalling 30,000 troops, supplemented by a 2,000-strong security force.[8]

In a joint statement released by *Tass* on 3 December 1956, the two governments were of the view that the stationing of NATO forces near socialist countries presented a threat to the latter's' security. In these circumstances, "the temporary stationing of Soviet armed forces in the Romanian People's Republic" was deemed to be necessary and was "in conformity with international treaties and agreements".[9] From the Romanian point of view the agreement was wanting in several respects. No time limit was laid down for the stationing of Soviet troops, there was no provision for it to be terminated by one of the parties and it could only be amended with the consent of both sides. This meant that in practice the Soviet government would be able to keep its troops in Romania as long as it wished. Moreover, a provision exempting Soviet troops from Romanian jurisdiction enabled them, if they wished, to ignore Romanian law. The publication of the agreement, which was contrary to normal practice, demonstrated that Soviet troops were in Romania legally, and with the consent of the Romanian government, thereby countering Western claims that they were not.

The lesson for Gheorghiu-Dej provided by the Hungarian uprising—that the position of the Communist Party in Romania continued to be dependent on repression of all opposition—translated itself into new measures. The strength of the *Securitate* was increased: in August 1956, it had numbered 13,155 officers and men, and 5,649 civilian employees, and in March its forces were supplemented by the addition of 2,059 officers and 429 men.[10] But there were no immediate large-scale arrests; the number of arrests rose from 2,357 in 1956 to 3,257 in the following year.[11] At the same time, Gheorghiu-Dej used political credit which he had gained through his fidelity to Moscow during the Hungarian uprising to strengthen his personal hold on the Party and to take action against his remaining rivals. The grounds he used against them were that they were 'Stalinists'. The 'Stalinists' in question were Miron Constantinescu and Iosif Chişinevski, both of whom in March of the previous year had used the same charge of 'Stalinist' against Gheorghiu-Dej in the debate on the 20th Congress of the Soviet Party. On 4 July 1957, it was announced in *Scînteia* that Constantinescu and Chişinevski had been removed from their posts at a Central Committee plenum held on 28 and 29 June, and on 1 and 3 July. The plenum resolution published five days later, stated that both "members of the Politburo of the RWP have been responsible for grave anti- expression of opinion directed against the unity of the party and its leadership". The direction they supported in debates on the 20th Soviet Congress "would have produced confusion within the ranks of the party... and have undermined the policy of the party and the state". There was a lesson to be learned from Hungary in their actions: "The events in Hungary are most instructive in this connection". To add weight to the charge of treachery, Constantinescu and Chişinevski were linked to the "anti-party fractionist group of Luca and Pauker".

It is difficult to dismiss as a coincidence the disclosure of this Romanian purge and the announcement on the very same day, 4 July, in Moscow that the Soviet Central Committee in plenary session from 22 to 29 June had dismissed the 'anti-party' group of Malenkov, Kaganovich, Molotov and Shepilov from their posts. Yet only by having advance warning of the *Pravda* announcement could Gheorghiu-Dej have linked his own one. The charges of disloyalty to the Party may have been similar, but the reasons behind them were precisely the opposite. Malenkov was opposed to de-Stalinization whereas Constantinescu had advocated it. The conclusion of Ian Dudley, the British Minister to Bucharest, was that "although it is likely enough that the infringement of Party unity... was the essential reason for getting rid of Constantinescu and Chişinevski, nevertheless the decision to get rid of them for this reason was taken in Moscow rather than here".[12] Maurice Pearton has pointed out:

> Although they had been allied tactically the two men [Constantinescu and Chişinevski] had little in common. Chişinevski, as the indictment confirmed, was an *apparatchik* of long standing, whose mind and experience revolved exclusively around doctrine and tactics. He struck Mr Dudley as 'an evil, intelligent weasel.' Constantinescu, by contrast, could discuss with the British Minister 'the relative importance of culture and economics.' Constantinescu was a genuine intellectual in a party whose leadership was deficient in that category, and naturally appealed to all those members who disliked the anti-intellectual bias in the running of its affairs. [...] How far his personal enthusiasm for de-Stalinization went was and remains problematical—he told Togliatti that he thought Khrushchev's explanations of Stalin's behaviour as 'the cult of the personality' over-simplified—but within the Romanian leadership he did offer an alternative to Gheorghiu-Dej.[13]

In the unsettled situation in Moscow Gheorghiu-Dej could not be certain that he himself would not be thought indispensable. Furthermore, like Pătrăşcanu before him, Constantinescu represented a class of party member with whom Gheorghiu-Dej never felt comfortable.

However the decision had been reached and to whatever degree it had been coordinated with Khrushchev, Gheorghiu-Dej had removed yet more potential rivals to his leadership. Yet criticism of Gheorghiu-Dej should not be dismissed solely as a pretext for a lust for power. One fellow railwayman, Grigore Răceanu, who derived his authority in the party from their close involvement in trade union militancy against the governments of the interwar period, was driven by his disaffection with Gheorghiu-Dej, to send word in autumn 1957 to the Romanian leader via Ion Panait, a trusted friend of the Romanian leader who had taken part in the Griviţa strike of 1933, that there was a good deal of dissatisfaction amongst the population with the Party's policies.[14] Răceanu repeated his remarks at a New Year party in 1958 organized by railwaymen. One of the participants divulged this to Ion Vinţe, vice president of the Party Control Commission, who reported the matter to Gheorghiu-Dej. The latter ordered Vinţe to set up a commission of enquiry to look into Răceanu's behaviour.[15] The enquiry was led by Constantin Pârvulescu and Gheorghe Stoica. They questioned Răceanu and insisted that he put the criticisms in writing. Răceanu obliged, addressing a memorandum on 3 May 1958 to Gheorghiu-Dej in which he raised the following issues:

> The deportation to the Danube-Black Sea Canal of intellectuals, peasants, members of the opposition parties, that is, of those considered 'class enemies'. The use of Soviet methods in agriculture. The creation of a 'workers' aristocracy'. The failure to seize the opportunity of the events in Hungary in 1956 to escape Soviet control.[16]

Gheorghiu-Dej's reaction was swift; Răceanu and a number of his colleagues were castigated at the Central Committee plenary meeting of 9–13 June.[17] Fourteen charges were levelled at Răceanu, among them that he was "a class enemy and enemy of the people" and "an agent of a Western espionage service", and he was expelled from the party. Răceanu withdrew to his country retreat in his birthplace at Cojocna, close to Cluj. Within a few days, he was arrested and imprisoned, without trial, at Malmaison jail in Bucharest. He was questioned on multiple occasions by officials from the Ministry of the Interior in an attempt to extract from him a confession of his 'guilt' but to no avail. After several months, he was released without explanation and threatened with further arrest should he fail to toe the party line.[18]

From now on, Gheorghiu-Dej was to proceed unchallenged, with the party firmly united behind him, to distance Romania from the Soviet Union.[19] A foretaste of this came in the speech of Emil Bodnăraş on the 40th anniversary of the Russian Revolution, which emphasized the role played by the RCP in overthrowing Marshal Antonescu, thereby overshadowing the contribution of the Red Army which hitherto had been given prominence in official accounts of the 23 August *coup*. Bodnăraş boldly revised the official line:

> The party was the organiser and leader of the armed insurrection of 23 August 1944 which, under the favourable conditions created by the victories of the USSR... overthrew Fascist dictatorship and led to Romania's passing over to the side of the anti-Hitler coalition headed by the USSR.[20]

Impetus to the apparent distancing of Romania from the Soviet Union came with the unexpected announcement on 24 May 1958 at a meeting of the Warsaw Pact in Moscow that the Soviet Union was withdrawing its troops from Romania. The decision was implemented with remarkable speed, and by 25 July the last of the 35,000 soldiers had crossed the border.[21] What, then, prompted this volte-face? According to Khrushchev's memoirs it was Bodnăraş who, as Minister of War, first raised the question of the withdrawal of Soviet troops from Romania during Khrushchev's visit to Romania in August 1955.[22] The idea of withdrawal had been conceived by Gheorghiu-Dej who feared that Khrushchev might try to purge him as a Stalinist. Withdrawal was, therefore, a question of survival for Gheorghiu-Dej and was advanced out as much from personal considerations as from ideological ones.[23] Gheorghiu-Dej's timing was influenced by the signature of the Austrian treaty on 15 May 1955, which established Austria's neutrality and by which the Soviet Union agreed to withdraw its troops. Without the need to maintain lines of communication with its forces in Austria, the Soviet Union lost its justification for keeping troops on Romanian—not to mention Hungarian—territory.

Displaying his usual prudence and cunning, Gheorghiu-Dej chose Bodnăraş to broach the subject because of his impeccable credentials: his past services to the Soviet Union; the confidence and respect which Khrushchev acknowledged he enjoyed among the Soviet leaders; and his senior position—he was one of the first three deputy prime ministers. Khrushchev records that Bodnăraş asked him for his reaction to the idea of withdrawing the Soviet troops from Romania. The Soviet leader flew into a rage. Bodnăraş justified the subject by pointing out that there was little threat to Soviet security interests because Romania was hemmed in by other Communist countries and that there was "nobody across the Black Sea from us except the Turks".[24] Seeing that he was not making any impression, Bodnăraş went on:

> All right, if that's how you feel, we'll withdraw the question. We just didn't want you to think that we were standing firmly on a socialist position only because your troops are stationed on our territory. We just want you to know that we sincerely believe in the building of socialism and in following Marxist-Leninist policies, and our people recognize us as their leaders and support us completely.[25]

These comments made no impact upon Khrushchev who lectured Bodnăraş on his underestimation of the West's strength and determination. Gheorghiu-Dej, in his turn, showed his annoyance with Khrushchev by not going to Bucharest airport to see off the Soviet leader.[26] If Khrushchev judged the idea to be premature in the international context of 1955, he did not abandon it at the time he regarded most appropriate.

That judgement had to be made first, in the context of a wider scenario composed by Khrushchev in 1958 for his policy of a new opening towards the West, and second, with regard to the Romanian Party's ability to ensure internal security. The key foreign policy element was the unilateral Soviet move to withdraw a limited number of troops from Eastern Europe as a whole which, Khrushchev hoped, might prompt a similar response from NATO. In order to attract the maximum publicity and to demonstrate Moscow's peaceful intentions, the notice of withdrawal was timed on 24 May to coincide with the announcement of Warsaw Pact troop cuts of 119,000 men—this in addition to an earlier Soviet decision to trim 300,000 from the Red Army in 1958.[27] Romania's strategic position, flanked as it was by other Warsaw Pact states, made it a safer proposition for the Soviet Union on security grounds for a troop withdrawal, and any fears about Romania's reliability as an ally had been dispelled by its actions during the Hungarian uprising. By the same token, the precautionary measure of keeping a large number of Soviet troops in Hungary after the revolution allowed Khrushchev to partially offset any overall reduction of Soviet troops in the area.

For Romania, the most significant impact of Soviet withdrawal upon the Romanian leadership was its psychological one. While Romania was still firmly enmeshed within the Soviet bloc—Soviet divisions in southern Ukraine and across the Prut in the Moldavian Soviet Socialist Republic could descend at once in an emergency—Gheorghiu-Dej could present it as a concession wrought from the Soviets. Furthermore, the departure of Soviet troops relieved the Romanians of an economic burden and removed a source of irritation. With the confidence thus gained Gheorghiu-Dej could embark, albeit cautiously, on policies which placed Romanian above Soviet interests.

A signal of Gheorghiu-Dej's immediate priority was given in his speech at the investiture on 25 July of Soviet generals marking the departure of Soviet forces. After praising the "valiant Soviet armies who, by delivering crushing blows to the fascist hordes, freed Romania from the yoke of Hitlerist imperialism", honouring the memory of the Soviet soldiers who fell in that struggle and evoking the "atmosphere of warm friendship which accompanied the departure of Soviet troops from our country", Gheorghiu-Dej turned his attention to the internal situation:

> At the same time, we should not forget the wretched wrecks of the old exploitative classes, remnants of the former fascist reactionary groups, who still wallow in the hope that the march of history might be reversed, and that Romania might be returned to the state of slavery and backwardness which it experienced in the time of the bourgeois-landowners' regime. Let it be clear to all these lamentable ghosts of the past, to all those whom our people have thrown into the dustbin of history, that their dreams will remain empty, and that the hand of the working people and its people's democracy will not hesitate in the future as well to strike mercilessly against all those who attack the revolutionary conquests of the people.[28]

The violence of Gheorghiu-Dej's language foreshadowed that which was to be used against the imagined enemies of the regime. To compensate for the Soviet withdrawal, and to allay Soviet fears that it might demolish the underpinning of the Romanian regime Gheorghiu-Dej approved the immediate introduction of stringent internal security measures in order to maintain the Party's control.[29] Amendments were made to the penal code which were even more draconian in their remit than the provisions for the death penalty enacted in 1949. Under decree 318 of 21 July 1958 new crimes attracting the death penalty were defined. Article 9 of the code imposed the death penalty on any Romanians contacting foreigners to perpetrate an act "which could cause the Romanian state to become involved in a declaration of neutrality or in the declaration of war". This was clearly designed to deter those who might be tempted by the example of Imre Nagy in Hungary who, during the 1956 revolution, proclaimed his country's neutrality and thus, implicitly, its withdrawal from the Warsaw Pact. The definition of 'economic sabotage' in the code was expanded to include theft and bribery, as was that of so-called 'hooligan' offences committed by juveniles. By the autumn of 1958 the first death sentences for the new crimes were applied.[30]

In his desire to give Moscow a guarantee of his Marxist-Leninist orthodoxy, Gheorghiu-Dej launched a campaign of 'revolutionary vigilance', designed to expel from the Party and punish all those who were deemed to have strayed from the party line. These expulsions were accompanied by the arrest, and in some cases re-arrest, of political and cultural personalities from the pre-Communist period who were considered to pose a threat to the stability of the regime. This new wave of arrests began in July 1958. *Securitate* figures show that between 1 July and 8 August, 1,103 persons were detained, the majority of them on charges of "agitation of a hostile character" or "membership of a counter-revolutionary organization".[31] The arrests continued over the following months, producing a total for the whole year of 6,362 persons.[32]

Among those who fell victim were two groups of writers and scholars, who were arrested over twelve months from December 1958 and tried together on 24 February 1960 on a charge of "conspiring against the social order". They included the philosophers Constantin Noica, Nicu Steinhardt and Alexandru Paleologu, the celebrated epigrammist Alexandru 'Păstorel' Teodoreanu, and the literary critic Constantin Pillat. Their crime was having received works written by Emil Cioran and Mircea Eliade, who were both living in the West, and having discussed them in private together. Cioran and Eliade were branded by the authorities as Iron Guardists. Noica was alleged to have written works which were hostile to the Communist regime—he had written an unpublished study on Hegel—and to have organized with the co-accused meetings in which they "prepared the violent overthrow of the regime of people's democracy in the Romanian People's Republic". In statements extracted by their *Securitate* interrogators through beatings and threats, some of the accused 'confessed' to the charges but Noica steadfastly refused. In his declaration before the court he denied that he had given certain statements to his interrogators in which he was alleged to have used the terms 'hostile', 'illegal', and 'banned'. Noica was sentenced to 25 years hard labour, as was Pillat, while Paleologu received fourteen years and Teodoreanu seven.[33]

The flow of convicts sentenced to forced labour under the new measures was channelled into penal colonies established in the marsh areas of the Danube Delta, notably at Periprava, to channel the flow of convicts sentenced to forced labour under the new measures into the collection of reeds for the recently constructed cellulose plants at Maliuc-Mahmudia and at Chişcani near Brăila, financed jointly by Romania, Poland, Czechoslovakia and East Germany.[34] It was estimated that a labour force of 25,000 would be required to gather the reeds and this was supplied by transferring political and common law prisoners to join the newly sentenced convicts. An article in *Scînteia* of 5 February 1959 eulogized the achievements of the workers in the delta without mention of their status or of the appalling conditions in which they lived and worked. Although many intellectuals and peasants passed through these camps, the majority of labourers were young opponents of the regime between the ages of 16 and 25, large numbers of whom succumbed to the ravages of malaria and tuberculosis. In fact, the production figures from the camps were so disappointing that the regime was forced to recruit 'voluntary' labour whose working conditions were far better than those of the convicts and who received a wage.

A former detainee described the conditions in these penal colonies in an émigré journal in the early 1960s. The camps were located in four areas in the delta: the Balta Brăilei, north of Hârşova, where there were about ten camps; near the village of Feteşti, where there were a number of smaller camps; around the village of Periprava, where the largest numbers of camps were; and around Lake Dranov. The largest camps, like that of Salcia in the Balta Brăilei, housed up to 6,000 prisoners, and it was estimated that the total number in the delta approached 60,000. The convicts had to work exclusively with their hands, standing waist-deep in water and cutting the reeds with a scythe-blade attached to a pole. After gathering the reeds into sheaves weighing about 50 kilos, they were forced to carry them on their backs for over a kilometre without allowing the reeds to touch the ground. Specially trained dogs bit the men's heels if they wavered. The daily quota for each convict was fifteen sheaves and those who failed to fulfil it had their food ration reduced and were sometimes beaten on the soles of their feet. Prisoners who bore the letters CR, meaning 'counter-revolutionary', on the back of their hand were particularly maltreated. Food consisted of several slices of bread and jam, and a cup of coffee substitute in the morning, and a piece of cold polenta and soup at lunchtime and in the evenings.

The areas to be harvested were sealed off with barbed wire and electrified fences and patrolled by guards on horseback and by teams of digs with handlers. Machine-gun points and floodlights were set up around the perimeter fences. The convicts returned each day having worked in the water to unheated and uninsulated wooden huts, and not surprisingly regularly fell prey to illness, especially malaria. Medical care was virtually non-existent with a total absence in some camps of medicines and dressings. The death rate was high, inviting the charge that the authorities deliberately sought to liquidate the detainees but such motives are difficult to reconcile with need to fulfil production targets. Camp conditions were more testimony to a mentality which saw the convicts as expendable slaves, worthy only of the barest of essentials to ensure a work capacity but denied any care which might enhance it or indeed protect it.

The delta's colony population was increased at the beginning of 1959, as the example of the Stoieneşti camp in the Balta Brăilei showed. Some 2,000 'convict' students were brought to this camp, containing about 1,400 peasants opposed to collectivization, in February 1959. Many of the students had been caught trying to leave the country clandestinely. They were quartered in three outbuildings for sheep, each six metres wide and 80 metres long, with walls only a metre high. Poorly clothed for the extreme winter temperatures, lacking running water and adequate sanitation, many of the students developed dysentery and typhoid. Despite this, they were forced to build a dam in sub-zero temperatures. After three weeks more than 400 had to be moved to Galaţi for treatment of whom 40 died en route. A medical commission was ordered to the camp and more than 1,500 prisoners were found to be in need of hospital treatment, but instead of being sent to Galaţi, the prison authorities, the General Directorate of Prisons, moved them to the colony at Periprava where many died after a few days.[35] Their numbers were made good by more than a thousand prisoners transferred from Gherla prison at the beginning of April 1960. The latter were herded into railway wagons during the night of 2/3 April and spent four nights without adequate sanitation or food before reaching Periprava. Some did not survive the journey.

A further decree of 1958 signalled another wave of purges from government employment of former officers in the royal army, former landowners, persons with a record of 'political' crime, and children of all the above. On a much more petty scale, divulging the location of Romanian archives also attracted the death penalty.[36] At Gherla alone, the prison records show that 30 persons accused of belonging to anti-Communist partisan groups were executed in 1958.[37] In the prisons discipline became noticeably harsher. Annie Samuelli, a prisoner for almost twelve years between 1949 and 1961, remembered how the warders' behaviour worsened overnight. 'They suddenly had a free hand to apply regulations literally, and that included a fresh range of punishments, maliciously meted out.'[38]

The effects of the clampdown were felt also felt by Western missions. Those who employed Romanian staff saw a number of them arrested, and police surveillance of all staff was tightened. In September 1958, the authorities insisted that all British nationals should either take Romanian citizenship or leave the country; similar demands were made of other Western citizens. In his Annual Review for 1958, the British Head of Mission commented that the new repressive measures, coupled with the granting of exit permits to large numbers of Jews, "all seemed to flow from the same objective of eliminating alien and bourgeois influences".[39]

It was not just the exceptional severity of these new measures which sent a clear signal to the Romanian people that the regime of terror was not to be relaxed; the failure to publicize them in the press or on the radio (the provisions were merely printed in the *Monitorul Oficial*, the record of legislation) generated uncertainty about the legislation and so amplified the fear inculcated into the population. The apparent randomness in the legislation's application by the instruments of the police state served perfectly to enhance the regime's control by terror at, ironically, the moment when the most public Soviet symbol of power, the Red Army, was withdrawn.

Gheorghiu-Dej was making a distinction between the Soviet model and the Soviet Union. In opting for the former, he took his Party and the country on a new course of autonomy from his Soviet overlord. Gheorghiu-Dej's motives were initially economic and were manifested in his refusal to accept for Romania the role within Comecon of 'breadbasket' for the industrialized members such as East Germany and Czechoslovakia. There is also a paradox here: Gheorghiu-Dej's commitment to the Leninist-Stalinist values of industrialization turned him into a 'national Communist'.[40]

The rift with Moscow was produced gradually and unevenly, with fluctuations in its development.[41] The relaxation of the Soviet grip upon Romania, exemplified by the Soviet troop withdrawal of summer 1958, was confirmed by the recall of Soviet advisors proposed in a letter addressed by the Central Committee of the Communist Party of the Soviet Union to the CC of the Romanian Workers' Party of 9 September 1958. Whilst noting "with satisfaction the high appreciation of the Soviet experts' role, repeatedly expressed by you" and the fact that qualified cadres had been trained in Romania, who had gained great expertise in all domains of economy and culture, the CPSU, in these circumstances, considered that the further presence of the Soviet advisors and experts in Romania might hamper to some extent the development of Romania's own workforce. The letter continued:

> Hence, we would consider it useful to recall from the Romanian People's Republic all Soviet advisors and experts and, to examine

> together with you maximum reduction, in the future, of the number of Soviet experts providing technical aid. We also take into account the fact that, practically speaking, it is difficult for us to have in our field of vision the activity of each and every Soviet expert working in Romania. Having extensive skill and knowledge in their field of activity, some of our experts are not always conversant with matters related to the political situation and the national particularities of your country. Therefore, some misunderstandings might occur, which is not to the advantage of our fraternal relations.[42]

The Romanian Politburo's acceptance of the Soviet proposal was followed by Gheorghiu-Dej's decision to scale down the dispatch of young Romanian officials for training in the Soviet Union, including those destined for the diplomatic service who had been sent on a regular basis to the institutes of foreign relations in Moscow and Kiev. Indeed, the warning given to the unmarried trainee diplomats in 1954 that they should avoid taking a Russian wife might be seen as an early indication of Gheorghiu-Dej's intention to insulate his regime from Moscow.[43] After 1960, only two or three children of senior Romanian Party members were studying in the Soviet capital.

At the same time, whilst reducing his reliance on Soviet advisors, Gheorghiu-Dej, in his search for modern technology and the accompanying expertise, turned to the neutral Scandinavian countries—Sweden and Finland. By doing so, he was following the example of the Soviet Union whose own technological deficiencies had pushed it in this direction.[44] In August 1959, Romania signed a trade agreement with Sweden. In order to address compensation claims for the nationalization of Swedish assets in Romania after the Second World War, the agreement including a clause allowing for a certain percentage of Romanian annual exports to Sweden towards compensation payments.

This provided a model for later agreements of a similar nature with Britain and the United States.[45] From the Technical Academy in Stockholm, Romania acquired data on mineral extraction and chemical manufacturing, a key element in the Romanian economy. As the largest producer of wood fibre in the world, Sweden also provided training for Romanian specialists to work in automated factories, producing the parquet floors for the increasing number of apartment blocks which the regime was building for workers in the newly industrialized cities and towns across the country. Expertise in wood processing and paper manufacturing was also obtained from Finland following the visit of a trade delegation that Gheorghiu-Dej sent to the country in autumn 1960. As with Sweden, Romania traded oil and chemical products with Finland.[46]

The campaign to establish Romania's new course was at once active and reactive. It was not only in furtherance of Gheorghiu-Dej's aim to distance Romania from the Soviet Union, thereby gaining greater popularity for his Party, but it was also a reaction to two major developments that posed a threat to Romania's new course. The first was Khrushchev's plan, presented in Moscow on 3–5 August 1961 to members of the CMEA (Comecon), to give the body a supranational planning role which, if accepted by Romania, would have obliged it to remain a supplier of raw materials, and to abandon its programme of rapid industrialization, thus risking economic chaos at home. In fact, the CMEA had little power since majority voting within it was prohibited and therefore every country could block its proposals by dissenting. Khrushchev's move would have made Romania susceptible to further economic exploitation by the Soviet Union, which was precisely what Gheorghiu-Dej had sought to avoid by embarking on the policy of industrialization.

The second major development was the Sino-Soviet rift, which first emerged at the Eighth Congress of the Romanian Communist Party in June 1960.[47] Gheorghiu-Dej used the Chinese formula affirming the equality of all Socialist states to justify his own autonomous policies towards the Soviet Union, thereby receiving Chinese backing for his rejection of the CMEA plan. The rift between China and the Soviet Union was indispensable to Gheorghiu-Dej's challenge to Khrushchev, and the fallout from that challenge can be sensed in the minutes of the Romanian Politburo's meeting with Iurii Andropov on 3 April 1963. Andropov stated that he was in full agreement with Gheorghiu-Dej over the need to strengthen unity in the Socialist bloc but he emphasized that the Chinese Party also had to desire this.[48]

Personal tension between Gheorghiu-Dej and Khrushchev exacerbated Romanian-Soviet relations. It came to the surface during the latter's week long visit to Romania from 18–25 June 1962. A short way into their four-hour train ride on 23 June from Bucharest to Constanţa, where the Soviet leader was due to deliver a major speech, the two leaders argued once again over the optimum weight at which to slaughter a pig. Such was their disagreement that silence reigned during the remainder of their journey.[49] This frostiness is confirmed by the memoirs of Arkady Shevchenko, the Soviet under-secretary general of the United Nations who defected to the United States in April 1978. In September 1960, Khrushchev travelled by sea to New York to attend a session of the UN and was accompanied on the voyage by Gheorghiu-Dej, and the Hungarian and Bulgarian leaders, Janos Kadar and Todor Zhivkov. Describing the atmosphere during the trip, Shevchenko has this to say:

> The Romanians, on the other hand, kept themselves aloof and there was an obvious chill between them and the Soviet delegation. At his table in the dining room, Gheorghiu-Dej generally remained silent. Khrushchev was annoyed at this but did not display his feelings toward the Romanians publicly,except on one occasion when he lost control of himself before a small group of Soviets and declared that Gheorghiu-Dej was not a bad Communist in general, but that as a leader he had no force; he was too passive. He added that in Romania, and even in the ranks of its Communist Party, pernicious nationalistic and anti-Soviet attitudes were developing which must be cut off at the very root. 'A firm hand is required for that,' he declared. 'The *Mamalyzhniki* (a derogatory Russian nickname for Romanians, based on the Romanian noun *mămăligă* meaning 'polenta') are not a nation, but

> a whore.' Khrushchev stopped short, realizing he had gone too far. 'I am referring,' he added lamely, trying to extricate himself, 'to pre-revolutionary Romania.'[50]

The Cuban Missile Crisis of 1962 demonstrated Gheorghiu-Dej's determination to distance himself from Moscow.[51] Indications of how far the Romanian leadership was prepared to go have been provided by Raymond L. Garthoff. Garthoff, who worked with US Secretary of State Dean Rusk revealed that the Romanian foreign minister Corneliu Mănescu told Rusk during a meeting on 4 October 1963 that Romania had not been consulted over the Soviet decision to place nuclear missiles in Cuba, and was not therefore a party to the dispute. The Romanian government wanted the United States to understand that Romania would remain neutral in any conflict generated by such actions as the Soviet deployment of nuclear missiles in Cuba, and sought assurances that in the event of hostilities arising from such a situation, the United States would not strike Romania on the mistaken assumption that it would be allied with the Soviet Union.[52] Garthoff concluded that:

> This was a stunning, unilateral breach of the central obligation of Warsaw Pact alliance membership, which Romania nominally maintained until the very end, when the Pact dissolved in 1991.[53]

Yet it would be hazardous to suggest, on the basis of Mănescu's statement,[54] that Romania was preparing to go so far as to renounce its Pact obligations.[55] Gheorghiu-Dej and his colleagues Ion Gheorghe Maurer and Foreign Minister Corneliu Mănescu were certainly unnerved not only by Khrushchev's failure to inform and consult their Warsaw Pact allies about his introduction of missiles into Cuba, but even more so by his denial of the missiles' existence. Khrushchev's unpredictability and intemperate behaviour during the crisis had serious implications for Romania's national security since against her will she was being implicated in collective action by the Warsaw Pact against the United States.[56] The Cuban crisis served only to reinforce Gheorghiu-Dej's conviction that placing further distance between Romania and the Soviet Union was in the Romanian national interest. A further signal of detachment from the Soviet Union was the introduction in 1963 of a series of anti-Russian measures which involved closing the Russian Institute in Bucharest, eliminating Russian as a compulsory school subject, and replacing the names of streets and public buildings that commemorated Russians with Romanian ones.

It was against this background that, in the Sino-Soviet dispute, the Romanian Party was careful to preserve neutrality. This is evident from the minutes of the meeting on 4 July 1963 of the Politburo of the Central Committee of the Romanian Workers' Party (RWP) concerning the declaration made by the Central Committee of the Chinese Communist Party about future talks between fraternal parties. The Politburo's view was that it did not want to involve itself in the polemic. The fact that the RWP published both the Soviet and Chinese communiqués was proof of this.[57] In an effort to mediate the conflict a Romanian delegation visited Beijing in February 1964, but returned empty-handed and this led only to further arm-twisting by Khrushchev to bring the Romanians back into line. One source states that Khrushchev formally, but not publicly, raised the question of territorial revision in Transylvania during the Romanians' stopover in Moscow on their return from China, and even indicated a willingness to hold a plebiscite in Bessarabia as well as in Transylvania.[58] This linkage of the Transylvanian problem with the Sino-Soviet conflict unnerved the Romanians and pressure from Moscow was stepped up in the same month when a plan to create an economic region encompassing much of the Moldovan SSR, half of Romania and part of Bulgaria was launched in the Soviet capital. Known as the Valev Plan, after its author who was a professor of economics at Moscow University,[59] it met with a hostile response from the Romanian government, which publicly condemned it in the Romanian media.[60]

These signals from Khrushchev, coupled with the realization that the Chinese were unable to help the Romanians economically, drove the Romanians into a public declaration of their autonomy which, apart from pre-empting any move by the Kremlin, would also constitute a claim to Western political and economic support against Moscow. The Romanian policy was formally legitimized in the 'Statement on the Stand of the Romanian Workers' Party Concerning the Problems of the World Communist and Working Class Movement, endorsed by the Enlarged Plenum of the Central Committee of the Romanian Workers' Party that was published in *Scînteia* on 26 April 1964.[61] As Emil Bodnăraş explained, by issuing the *April 1964 Declaration*, the Romanian leadership preferred "that it should be rather us those who explained our position, rather than the others [the Soviets] do so in our name, adding commas and full stops where they are needed, but especially where they are not needed".[62] At the same time the Party's Central Committee authorized the publication of a manuscript by Karl Marx highly critical of Russia's annexation of Bessarabia in 1812.[63]

Khrushchev's removal on 14 October 1964 as Soviet leader offered Gheorghiu-Dej, it has been claimed, a further chance to consolidate his break with Moscow. Exploiting the change in the Soviet leadership, he summoned the Soviet ambassador on 21 October and requested him to withdraw the KGB counsellors from Romania. Moscow reacted quickly and furiously. On the following day, the Chairman of the KGB, Vladimir Yefimovici Semichastny, allegedly sent a telegram to Drăghici reminding him that Romania lived "under the Soviet protective umbrella" and that it would regret Gheorghiu-Dej's move. A similar telegram from General Aleksandr Sakharovsky, the head of the First Chief Directorate and former MGB advisor in Bucharest, landed on the desk of General Nicolae Doicaru, the head of the Foreign Intelligence Directorate of the *Securitate*. In November, Sakharovsky arrived unexpectedly at Bucharest, followed by Semichastny.[64]

Irritation over the presence of KGB counsellors in the Romanian Ministry of the Interior had surfaced in the spring of 1963 when the issue was raised at a meeting of the Politburo chaired in May by Gheorghiu-Dej; he informed his colleagues that the Soviet ambassador, Ivan Jegalin, had been to see him and had raised the matter of the counsellors. Gheorghiu-Dej reported to Jegalin Drăghici's view that "there was no point in the counsellors sitting around and just reading newspapers" and that nothing was served by the counsellors remaining since there were solid links between the Romanian and Soviet ministries of the interior. Drăghici himself told the Politburo that Jegalin had brought a letter to him from KGB chairman Semichastny, offering to withdraw the counsellors if Drăghici continued to question their usefulness. Drăghici told Jegalin that he did and Jegalin then asked when they could leave. Drăghici replied that they could go the very next day to which Jegalin responded that they would go if his government gave the word—in fact, the last Soviet counsellor appears not to have left until the end of the following year. Drăghici complained to the Politburo that there were times when the Soviet counsellors tried to do the *Securitate*'s work for them and that they had lost agents because of this. He derided the effectiveness of cooperation between the Romanian and Soviet services, complaining that the Soviets passed on information that was, in some cases, seven years old!

> Whatever you say to the counsellors, they still go their own way. In effect, we have no counsellors, the professional ones left in 1956. For the past year, all they have done is sit in the office and read the newspapers, occasionally fishing for information from the odd person. In Pintilie's time, they spent the whole day in his office and of course Pintilie kept them informed.[65]

The discussions between Gheorghiu-Dej and Leonid Brezhnev in connection with the withdrawal of KGB counsellors from Bucharest allegedly went on until the end of November and also involved Aleksandr Shelepin who, until December 1961, had been KGB chairman and had been moved to head the Committee of Party and State Control which oversaw the work of the KGB. Sakharovsky was particularly wounded, since he had nursed the *Securitate* into being in 1948, but eventually the Soviet leadership relented and between 1962 and in 1964 the counsellors were gradually withdrawn,[66] being allowed to take all the contents of the flats which they had requisitioned. Thus the Romanian security and intelligence services became the first such agencies of a Warsaw Pact country to rid themselves of its Soviet counsellors, and, as regards the Foreign Intelligence Directorate, the DGIE, the only foreign intelligence agency in the Eastern bloc to enjoy this privilege down to the collapse of Communism in 1989. This did not mean, of course, that it ceased to collaborate with the KGB.

A condition of the withdrawal of KGB counsellors was that the DGIE should continue to meet Romania's obligations under the Warsaw Pact to play its part in the espionage activities coordinated by the Soviet Union. Moscow established the defence field as the chief priority of intelligence gathering in the 1960s and emphasis was placed on scientific and technical espionage. Both the First Chief Directorate of the KGB, charged with foreign intelligence, and the GRU, Soviet military intelligence, set the agendas for their counterpart bodies in the Warsaw Pact states—in Romania's case, the DGIE and the *Departamentul de Informații al Armatei* (DIA).[67] Soviet activity in scientific and technical espionage was coordinated by the Military Industrial Commission (VPK) and the United States, West Germany, France and Britain chosen as the principal targets.

Collaboration between the KGB and the DGIE, on the one hand and the GRU and the DIA on the other, served a dual purpose for the Soviets; not only was the intelligence gathered for Soviet needs, but the Romanian officers concerned were not asked, in their operational activities in the 1960s, to distinguish a loyalty to Romania from one to the Soviet Union, since the intelligence of both countries coincided. Furthermore, the Soviet training of most of the Romanian intelligence and security officers, cemented an extra bond with the Soviet master. Indeed, the DGIE scored a number of notable successes on behalf of the KGB in the early 1960s. In 1962 Mihai Caraman, a DGIE officer in Paris, recruited François Rousilhe, a Frenchman who worked in the library of NATO headquarters, to provide him with hundreds of secret documents.[68] Caraman's catch was considered so important by the KGB that they decided to pay the Frenchman in gold coins which Caraman received from Moscow. In the following year, Caraman took over the running of a Turkish colonel, Nahit Imre, who had been recruited by the DGIE in Ankara and transferred to Paris as deputy financial director of NATO. In order to exploit to the full these two contacts, Caraman was summoned on several occasions to Moscow. In 1965, the KGB was so impressed by the amount of material coming from NATO via Caraman that they sent one of their own officers, Vladimir Arhipov, to work with Caraman. All went well until 1969 when Colonel Ion Iacobescu, Caraman's deputy in Paris, asked for political asylum in the United States. Shortly afterwards Rousilhe and Imre were arrested, and Caraman was withdrawn.[69]

The Romanian leadership showed little sign of bridging the rift with Moscow. Gheorghiu-Dej and his prime minister, Ion Gheorghe Maurer, boldly criticized the Soviet Union for its 'imperious' behaviour towards its Warsaw Pact allies. When the Pact's Political Consultative Committee reconvened in Warsaw on 20 January 1965, Poland's leader Władysław Gomułka retrospectively censured Khrushchev's habit of not consulting with members of the alliance. Khrushchev's successor Leonid I. Brezhnev admitted that "we need to give an expression to our unity and striving for more concerted work". However, Maurer countered that "we are for consultation but against the creation of any organs", such as a committee of foreign ministers obliged to hold regular meetings. Objecting to Moscow's practice of submitting to the Allies ready-made proposals at short notice in the expectation of quick approval, Gheorghiu-Dej further questioned Brezhnev's demand to respond to NATO's plans by military counter-measures rather than by promotion of détente.[70]

Gheorghiu-Dej's drive for autonomy, by striking the chord of deep anti-Russian sentiment felt by most Romanians, attracted support for his regime. Drawing on this sentiment offered Gheorghiu-Dej a simple way of increasing the regime's popularity while at the same time putting a distance between himself and his Soviet master. With these changes in Romania's relationship with the Soviet Union came a shift in the severity of repression. Gheorghiu-Dej authorized the opening of the political prisons in 1962 and according to official figures 1,304 prisoners were released. In the following year an additional 2,892 were freed, and in the first four months of 1964 the 'final' 464 were allowed out.[71] The number of persons sentenced to imprisonment for crimes 'against state security' stood in January 1960 at 17,613. The first notable decrease occurred between January and December 1962 when the number fell from 16,327 to 13,017 as nearly 5,000 peasants who had opposed collectivization and many former Iron Guardists were freed. In the next 12 months, following pardons decreed by Gheorghiu-Dej in 1963 (nos. 5 and 767), the figure fell to 9,333 and in 1964 (no.176 of April and no. 411 of July) most of the remainder were released.[72] Various estimates of the numbers of persons jailed or sent to labour camps in the period 1945 to 1964 for alleged 'political' offences range between 500,000 and 750,000; at the same time, the discretionary nature in many cases of punishment should not be overlooked. Most of the detainees in labour camps were never brought before a court, as was the case of peasants who opposed collectivization, but were simply assigned to camps by order of the Ministry of Internal Affairs.

The amnesty marked the end of an era of political terror which had cost the lives of several thousands of Romanians, ranging from the pre-Communist political, economic and cultural elite; but the instrument of that terror, the *Securitate*, remained intact, unreformed and ubiquitous while its powerful and ambitious head, Alexandru Drăghici, who had first been appointed Minister of the Interior in May 1952, remained a constant reminder of the past and a threat to the future.

Notes

1 Notably that of Corina Mavrodin, *A Maverick in the Making: Romania's de-Satellization Process and the Global Cold War (1953–1963)*. Thesis submitted to the Department of International History of the London School of Economics for the Degree of Doctor of Philosophy, London, February, 2017.
2 See chapter six of this study.
3 By Mavrodin.
4 Quoted from Mavrodin, *A Maverick in the Making*, p.210.
5 Mavrodin, A Maverick in the Making, p.217.
6 Chivu Stoica (8 August 1908–18 February 1975) was a railway colleague of Gheorghiu-Dej and had been arrested for his part in the Griviţa strike in February 1933. He was sentenced on 19 August of that year to 12 years' hard labour. Between 1955 and 1961 he served as Prime Minister and March 1965 became President of the Council of State after the election of Ceauşescu as Party First Secretary. In December 1967, he was removed from this position by Ceauşescu. On 18 February 1975, he committed suicide by shooting himself, according to Ceauşescu, because of family problems. It was perhaps for this reason that Ceauşescu did not give an address at Stoica's funeral two days later; see the transcript of the meeting of the Permanent Bureau of the RCP Politburo of 18 February in Mihnea Berindei, Dorin Dobrincu, and Armand Goşu (eds.), *Istoria Comunismului din România*. Vol.III. *Documente Nicolae Ceauşescu (1972–1975)* (Iaşi: Polirom, 2016), doc.78, pp.508–9.
7 *Manchester Guardian*, 4 December 1956. Quoted from Ghita Ionescu, *Communism in Rumania, 1944–1962* (London: Oxford University Press, 1964), pp.274–75.
8 Donald R. Falls, 'Soviet Decision-Making and the Withdrawal of Soviet Troops from Romania', *East European Quarterly*, vol.XXVII, no.4 (winter 1993), p.490.

9 Ioan Scurtu (ed.), *România. Retragerea Trupelor Sovietice, 1958* (Bucharest: Editura Didactică şi Pedagogică, 1996), p.240.
10 *Cartea Albă a Securităţii*, vol.II (Bucharest: SRI, 1995), p.21.
11 *Cartea Albă a Securităţii*, vol.III (Bucharest: SRI, 1996), p.159.
12 Quoted from an article by Maurice Pearton entitled, The Romanian Leadership and its Problems, 1956–1957–1958', in Maurice Pearton and Dennis Deletant, *Romania Observed*, (Bucharest: Editura Enciclopedică, 1998). p.257.
13 *Ibid.*, p.255.
14 Grigore Răceanu, 'O privire în interiorul Partidului Comunist Român', *Magazin Istoric*, January 1994, p.48.
15 Author's discussion with Mircea Răceanu, 22 May 2016.
16 For the text of this memorandum I am grateful to Mircea Răceanu; see also Grigore Răceanu, 'O privire...'p.48.
17 At this time pressure was put on his stepson Mircea by members of the Union of Communist Youth to revert to his father's surname Bernat. Mircea refused and reported this to politburo member Petre Borilă of whose son he was a close friend. Overnight the source of the pressure apologized for the 'mistake'. At the same time, Mircea's mother, Ileana, requested an audience with Gheorghiu-Dej and persuaded him to allow Mircea to return to his studies in Moscow at the State Institute of International Relations. In exchange, she agreed to criticize her husband during the 1958 plenum for personal character weaknesses (author's conversation with Mircea Răceanu, 22 May 2016).
18 Grigore Răceanu, 'O privire...'p.50.
19 Relations between Gheorghiu-Dej, Khrushchev and Tito during this period are discussed by Mihai Croitor and Sanda Borşa in *Triunghiul Suspiciunii*, vol.1. Gheorghiu-Dej, Hruşciov şi Tito (1954–1964) (Cluj-Napoca: Editura Mega, 2014).
20 Maurice Pearton,The Romanian Leadership and its Problems, 1956–1957–1958', p.261.
21 Falls, Soviet Decision-Making, p.491.
22 Sergiu Verona, *Military Occupation and Diplomacy. Soviet Troops in Romania 1944–1958* (Durham and London: Duke University Press, 1992), p.83.
23 Author's interview with Alexandru Bârlădeanu, 8 August 1996.
24 N.S. Khrushchev, *Khrushchev Remembers—The Last Testament*, trans. by Strobe Talbott (Boston: Little, Brown and Co., 1974), p.228, and Verona, *Military Occupation and Diplomacy*, p.83.
25 Quoted from Falls, *Soviet Decision-Making*, p.491.
26 Author's interview with Alexandru Bârlădeanu, 8 August 1996.
27 Falls, *Soviet Decision-Making*, p.497. The communiqué on the meeting was published in *Scînteia* on 27 May and reprinted in Scurtu, *România*, pp.280–83.
28 Scurtu, *România*, p.359.
29 Foreign diplomats noted an increase in domestic tension throughout 1957 and in the last few months of the year the British Head of Mission opined that "the government was behaving in a highly nervous manner which I thought must mean that they had solid reasons to anticipate trouble". (TNA FO 371/143326. XC15773). His impressions were justified in mid-January 1958 by the outbreak of serious peasant disturbances in southern Moldavia which were put down with bloodshed. The rapid crumbling of the demonstrations was due not only to the severity with which they were curbed, but also to a one-metre snowfall which covered the region when the trouble was at its height.
30 Ionescu, *Communism in Rumania, 1944–1962*, p.290.
31 Cartea Albă a Securităţii, vol.III, p.132.
32 *Ibid.*, p.159.
33 The interrogations and trial proceedings are published in Prigoana. Documente ale Procesului C. Noica, C. Pillat, N. Steinhardt, Al. Paleologu, A. Acterian, S. Al-George, Al. O. Teodoreanu etc.(Bucharest: Editura Vremea, 1996). All the accused were released in 1963 and 1964. Noica was released in 1964 and died in 1987.

34 See the description of one colony in Petru Dumitriu, *Incognito* (London: Collins, 1964), pp.384–90.
35 'Les Camps de la Mort du Delta du Danube', *La Nation Roumaine*, no.215 (Nov.1962–Jan.1963), p.6.
36 G. Ionescu, *Communism in Rumania, 1944–1962* (London: Oxford University Press, 1964), p.290.
37 Information provided by Dr Ioan Ciupea, head of the contemporary history department of the National History Museum of Transylvania. A memorial erected in 1995 by the Association of Former Political Prisoners in Romania in Gherla cemetery bears the names of 47 persons executed in the Cluj region between 1948 and 1958.
38 A. Samuelli, *The Wall Between* (Washington, DC: Robert B. Luce, 1967), p.187.
39 TNA, FO 371/143326. XC15773.
40 As pointed out by Michael Shafir, *Romania. Politics, Economics and Society* (London: Frances Pinter, 1985), p.48.
41 Gheorghiu-Dej's break with Moscow is charted and analysed by Vladimir Tismăneanu, *Gheorghiu-Dej and the Romanian Workers' Party: From De-Sovietization to the Emergence of National Communism* (Washington, DC: Woodrow Wilson International Center for Scholars, Cold War International History Project), Working Paper No. 37.
42 'Letter addressed by the CC of the CPSU to the CC of the RWP on the recall of Soviet advisors from Romania, September 09, 1958', *History and Public Policy Program Digital Archive, Central Historical National Archives*, Fund CC of the RCP—Foreign Relations Section File 6/1955, pp.719–720. Translated by Delia Răzdolescu. http://digitalarchive.wilsoncenter.org/document/110474. Accessed 7 April 2017.
43 Those trainees who did marry Soviet citizens were assigned, not to the Romanian Ministry of Foreign Affairs, but to less sensitive ministries such as culture or finance: author's conversation on 23 April 2016 with Mircea Răceanu, former senior Romanian diplomat who himself studied in Moscow between 1954 and 1959. In 1959, Răceanu was assigned as part of his training to the Romanian embassy in Washington DC for six months, after which he formally completed his Moscow studies in 1960.The new wave of recruits sent for training in Kiev (between 1950 and 1952) and Moscow (after 1952) raised the intellectual standard of officials in the foreign ministry who had little professional diplomatic training, even though they attended the Party academy, founded in March 1945, which was given the name *Ştefan Gheorghiu* the following year. After 1960, graduates of the academy were assigned in equal numbers to the Ministry of Foreign Affairs, to *Agerpres*, the state news agency and to the *Securitate.*
44 Mavrodin, A Maverick in the Making, p.176.
45 In 1960; see Mavrodin, *A Maverick in the Making*, p.177.
46 Mavrodin, *A Maverick in the Making*, pp.178–79.
47 Robert R. King, 'Rumania and the Sino-Soviet Conflict', *Studies in Comparative Communism* vol.4 (1972), pp.373–85 [375].
48 Dennis Deletant and Mihail E. Ionescu (eds.), *Romania and the Warsaw Pact, 1955–1989* (Bucharest: Politeia-SNSPA, 2004), p.107; see also Mihai Retegan, *Război politic în blocul communist* (Bucharest: RAO, 2002); *Cold War International History Project (CWIHP), Virtual Archive: Romania and the Warsaw Pact, 1955–89* (http://www.wilsoncenter.org/index.cfm) and the Parallel History Project (PHP) (http://www.isn.ethz.ch/php/collections.) The author assisted in the procurement for both projects of a number of these documents from the Romanian archives and in editing their translation into English.
49 Author's conversation in July 1993 with Alexandru Bârlădeanu, senior Romanian party member who acted as interpreter on the occasion; see also Mihai Croitoru, 'An Episode of the Romanian-Soviet Differences. "The Medium Body-Weight of Slaughtered Pigs in Romania"', *Studia Universitatis Babeş-Bolyai. Historia*, vol.56 (December 2011), pp.105–15. The two leaders had, according to Bârlădeanu, clashed on this subject during the dinner of welcome after the Soviet leader's arrival in Bucharest. Khrush-

chev upbraided Gheorghiu-Dej for allegedly having a policy of slaughtering pigs when they reached a weight of 25 kilos. "Perhaps you are thinking of sucklings", Gheorghiu-Dej suggested, "No", stormed Khrushchev. Gheorghiu-Dej explained that Romanian practice was to kill pigs at 100 kilos. Later that evening, in an attempt to have the last word on the subject, Khrushchev allegedly telephoned Gheorghiu-Dej to admit that the figure of 25 kilos was incorrect and claimed that the true one was 50 kilos.

50 Arkady N. Shevchenko, *Breaking with Moscow* (New York: Alfred A. Knopf, 1985), p.97.

51 See Larry Watts, 'Romania Security Policy and the Cuban Missile Crisis', *Cold War International History Project, e-dossier no.38* (April 17, 2013).

52 Raymond L. Garthoff, 'When and Why Romania Distanced Itself from the Warsaw Pact', *Cold War International History Project Bulletin*, no. 5 (Spring 1995), pp.111–12. Garthoff received this information from Dean Rusk himself.

53 Garthoff, 'When and Why', p.111.

54 A personal account of his role as head of the Romanian delegation to the UN General Assembly in New York in September and October 1962 is given by Mircea Maliţa, 'Small Players in Big Gambles', *Cadran Politic* (October 2003), pp.12–24.

55 See the discussion in Ionescu's introduction to Deletant and Ionescu, *Romania and the Warsaw Pact*, p.67.

56 See Mioara Anton, *Ieşirea din cerc. Politica externă a regimului Gheorghiu-Dej* (Bucharest: Institutul Naţional pentru Studiul Totalitarismului, 2007), p.153.

57 Deletant and Ionescu, *Romania and the Warsaw Pact*, pp.125–26.

58 Verona, Military Occupation and Diplomacy, p.101.

59 See Valev's article 'The problems of the economic development of the Danube rayons from Romania, Bulgaria and the USSR', which appeared in the Moscow University review *Vestnik Moskovskogo Universitata* and in E.B. Valev, 'Problemele dezvoltării economice a raioanelor dunărene din România, Bulgaria şi URSS', *Viaţa economică*, Anul II, vol.43, no.24 (1964), pp.7–43.

60 I. Alexandrescu, 'Obsesia protecţionismului', *Dosarele Istoriei*, no.3 (1997), p.38.

61 The Romanian original is to be found in Arhivele Naţionale Istorice Centrale (National Central Historical Archives, henceforth abbreviated to ANIC), Fond CC of the RWP, Chancellery Section, File 23/ 1964. For the complete text see also Alexandru Osca and Vasile Popa, *România. O fereastră deschisă în Cortina de Fier* (Focsani, 1997), annex 13, pp.279–30. Documents chronicling the Soviet-Romanian split have been published by Mihai Croitor, *În Umbra Kremlinului. Gheorghe Gheorghiu-Dej şi Geneza Declaraţiei din Aprilie 1964* (Cluj-Napoca: Editura Mega, 2012). See also Florian Banu and Liviu Ţăranu, *Aprilie 1964—"Primăvara de la Bucureşti": Cum a fost adoptată "Declaraţia de independenţă a Romaniei?"* (Bucharest: Editura Enciclopedică, 2004); Dan Cătănuş, *Intre Beijing şi Moscova: Romania şi conflictul Sovieto-Chinez* (Bucharest: Institutul Naţional pentru Studiul Totalitarismului, 2004), Deletant and Ionescu, *Romania and the Warsaw Pact, 1955–1989*, Cold War International History Project, Working Paper No. 43, Washington, DC, July 2002, p.69, http://www.wilsoncenter.org/sites/default/files/ACF368.pdf. Accessed 7 April 2017, and Dan Cătănus, *Tot mai departe de Moscova. Politica externă a României 1956–1965* (Bucharest: Institutul Naţional pentru Studiul Totalitarismului, 2011), p.323.

62 'Minutes of the 12 May 1966 talks between Emil Bodnăraş and Zhou Enlai, in Romulus Ioan Budura, (ed.), *Relatiile Romano-Chineze, 1954–1975* (Bucharest: Ministerul Afacerilor Externe, Arhivele Naţionale, 2008), p.281; see also Elena Dragomir, *Cold War Perceptions. Romania's Policy Change Towards the Soviet Union, 1960–1964* (Cambridge: Cambridge Scholars Publishing), p.191.

63 Karl Marx, *Insemnări despre Români* (Bucharest: Editura Academiei Republicii Populare Române, 1964). The publication of the Marx manuscript broke the taboo of speaking openly about the Soviet annexation of Bessarabia after 1945 and the Romanian identity of its population.

64 Ion Pacepa, *Moştenirea Kremlinului* (Bucharest: Editura Venus, 1993), p.253. Between 1972 and 1978, the year of his defection to the United States, Pacepa was deputy-director of the Foreign Intelligence Directorate of the *Securitate* (DGIE).

65 Scurtu, *România*, pp.391–92.

66 Larry L. Watts, 'Romanian Security Policy and the Cuban Crisis', *Cold War International History Project e-dossier no.38, February 2013*. [Documents 4, 5, 6, 7, 8, 9]. In his introduction Watts writes, "In regard to this latter contest, senior officers of other bloc state security services confirm that the Romanian-Soviet and Romanian-Warsaw Pact intelligence cooperation began breaking down in 1962 and became essentially non-existent by the end of that decade".

67 The DIA was the successor to the Second Section of the Romanian Army General Staff (*Secţia a II-a de pe lângă Marele Stat Major*) which was charged with gathering military intelligence. By 1 July 1945, all Romanian military attaches had been withdrawn from foreign countries and most of the officers in the section purged or arrested on Soviet orders. In 1948, the first postwar appointment of a military attaché was made by the Soviet-controlled Ministry of National Defence, to the Romanian embassy in Moscow. On 15 February 1951, the Second Section was transformed into the *Direcţia Informaţii a Marelui Stat Major* (The Directorate of Information of the General Staff) and at the same time military counter-espionage activity was transferred to the *Securitate*. The work of the DIMSM, which was subordinated to the Ministry of National Defence, was supervised by GRU counsellors who trained young Romanian officers. After the withdrawal of Soviet troops in 1958 the Soviet counsellors were withdrawn from the DIMSM. Contacts were strengthened with other armies but Drăghici's desire, as Minister of the Interior, to extend his power by adding military intelligence to the military counter-espionage activities which he already controlled, led to the subordination of the DIMSM to the Ministry of the Interior by an order signed by both Drăghici and the Minister of National Defence on 22 October 1962. This supervision by the Ministry of the Interior was removed on 18 October 1968.

68 Caraman was born on 11 November 1928 in Oancea commune, Galaţi County.

69 For Caraman see also chapter 11, note 47.

70 Vojtech Mastny, Learning from the Enemy: NATO as a Model for the Warsaw Pact, Zürcher Beiträge zur Sicherheitspolitik und Konfliktforschung Nr. 58, Forschungsstelle für Sicherheitspolitik und Konfliktanalyse der ETH Zürich (Zürich, 2001), pp.15–16.

71 Vlad Georgescu, *The Romanians: A History, Columbus* (Columbus: Ohio State University Press, 1991), p.246.

72 *Cartea Albă a Securităţii*, vol.III, p.33. According to official figures, in 1965 only 258 persons were arrested by the *Securitate* for "actions hostile to the state"; in the following year, 294 were arrested and in 1967, 312 (*ibid.*, p.95).

10 The ascent of Nicolae Ceauşescu

In late January 1965, Gheorghiu-Dej showed signs of serious illness. A London surgeon had visited Bucharest in the spring of the previous year to perform a prostate and bladder operation on him, but he was now treated for cancer of the lungs. Despite this Gheorghiu-Dej carried on working. On the advice of Maurer, he travelled to Poland to attend a meeting of the Warsaw Pact since Maurer did not relish the prospect of facing the Soviet leader Leonid Brezhnev alone, and the Romanian delegation left immediately after the conclusion of the proceedings. The cancer quickly spread to Gheorghiu-Dej's liver, and foreign doctors were called in, among them Dr Geraint Evans, a Harley Street chest specialist, and his wife, a liver specialist, who flew out on the weekend of 6 March. On his return to London, Dr Evans told officials at the Foreign Office that Gheorghiu-Dej was dying and that he had "gained the impression that the news would be made public in about a month, and that the choice of Gheorghiu-Dej's successor as head of state and first secretary of the party was at present under consideration".[1]

The Romanian public had already had an opportunity to see the deterioration in Gheorghiu-Dej's condition. On 5 March, Gheorghiu-Dej had recorded for television and radio what turned out to be his last speech, delivered two days before elections to the National Assembly. Paul Niculescu-Mizil, the senior party official who supervised the recording in Gheorghiu-Dej's villa on Lake Herăstrău, was alarmed by the faltering nature of his voice and was obliged to ask him to re-read his text.[2] In comparison with his usual speeches, the brevity of his message could not fail to provoke comment among foreign analysts, especially on Radio Free Europe which commented that Gheorghiu-Dej's performance "provided the most recent and most alarming indication of his state of health".[3]

Gheorghiu-Dej made his last public appearance on the evening of Election Day, 7 March, at a polling station. *Scînteia* published two photographs of him the following day, the first showing him casting his vote with a smile, and the second in the company of Maurer, Ceauşescu and other comrades. It was only on 18 March that the secrecy surrounding Gheorghiu-Dej's illness was lifted. A medical bulletin, signed by the minister of health and seven Romanian doctors, announced that Gheorghiu-Dej was suffering from a lung disease and liver complications. The news was enough to cause public expressions of alarm throughout the party. The Central Committee sent Gheorghiu-Dej an open letter expressing its affection and devotion. A second medical bulletin appeared the following day stating that Gheorghiu-Dej's condition was unchanged, together with a telegram of good wishes from Mao Tse-tung, and messages from every corner of the country. But the end came rapidly. Shortly after 4 p.m. on that same day, 19 March 1965, the party secretary lapsed into a coma and within two hours he was dead. The fact was announced on hour later on Romanian radio.[4] Three days later, on 22 March 1965, Nicolae Ceauşescu was 'elected' as first secretary of the Romanian Communist Party.

On paper Ceauşescu was but one of a number of senior party officials who could put a case for election to the leadership. Yet only he, Drăghici, Chivu Stoica and Gheorghe Apostol were not ruled out from the post by virtue of their ethnic background, the other Politburo members being of Bulgarian (Coliu), Ukrainian (Bodnăraş) or German (Maurer) origin).[5] The manoeuvres which enabled Ceauşescu to emerge as first secretary were not made public and it was only after 1989 that some light was shed upon them. Although Gheorghiu-Dej appears to have designated Apostol as his successor, Ion Gheorghe Maurer, who had been elected president of the Council of Ministers (prime minister) as recently as 12 March, proposed Ceauşescu as first secretary. Maurer gave the reasons for his choice in a number of interviews after Ceauşescu's overthrow, the principal one being that he regarded Ceauşescu as having the courage to stand up to the Russians; at the same time, Maurer let it be understood that he regretted his action.[6] Drăghici, as the long-serving Minister of Internal Affairs, was feared by everyone, Stoica was not considered up to the job, and Apostol was deemed too headstrong. According to one inside source, Ceauşescu did a deal with Maurer: Ceauşescu would nominate Maurer as prime minister (he did so on 12 March) and, in exchange, after Gheorghiu-Dej's death, Maurer would propose Ceauşescu as first secretary.[7] In this way Ceauşescu outmanoeuvred Apostol who allegedly was Gheorghiu-Dej's choice as successor. Stoica was bought off with the post of president of the Council of State.

Large crowds attended Gheorghiu-Dej's funeral on 24 March. They listened in silence as four members of the Politburo delivered eulogies. The rhetoric which had followed him for much of his life accompanied him in death. This was its final flowering. Chivu Stoica, who had been elected to the titular position of president of the Council of State on that same day by the Grand National Assembly, spoke first, followed by Gheorghe Apostol, Ion Gheorghe Maurer and Ceauşescu. All stressed Gheorghiu-Dej's dedication to the principles of Marxism-Leninism and his decisive role in the triumph of Communism in Romania, but at the same time they gave great weight to Gheorghiu-Dej's contribution to the 'people's happiness'. Ceauşescu described him as the "beloved leader of the party and the state" and lauded Gheorghiu-Dej's "life-long devotion to the happiness of the people" which "has earned you the unanimous esteem, trust and love of the party and of the entire population".[8]

The eulogists were right: Gheorghiu-Dej's role "in the triumph of Communism in Romania" *was* decisive. But it was Ion Gheorghe Maurer who came closest to the truth that day in the closing words of his speech. After praising Gheorghiu-Dej for the "lofty moral qualities" and the "permanent osmosis that existed between his thoughts and deeds... and those of the people", he concluded:

> As we follow with unswerving consistency his instruction and his stimulus, having ever present before us in our minds and in our hearts the lofty example of devotion to the cause of the people's happiness... we and those who come after us will forever feel as we step towards the future the presence alongside us of the man who was and will remain in our history the builder of socialist Romania: Gheorghe Gheorghiu-Dej.[9]

Maurer spoke better than he knew. Gheorghiu-Dej's presence was represented most enduringly by his leading role in the post-war economic revolution in Romania, marked by nationalization of property, the collectivization of agriculture and rapid industrialization. The latter policy was continued with fervour by Ceauşescu.

Gheorghiu-Dej's body was laid to rest in a hideous mausoleum built in the 'Park of Liberty' in the southern part of the capital. In 1968, barely three years after his funeral tribute in which he praised Gheorghiu-Dej as a "dear colleague" whose memory he would "cherish in his mind and in his heart", Gheorghe Apostol gave a very different appraisal of Gheorghiu-Dej and his rule. As a fellow railway worker who had joined the Communist Party at the age of 18, Apostol had been imprisoned alongside Gheorghiu-Dej in Târgu Jiu, and had served as first secretary of the party between April 1954 and October 1955; Apostol was thus well placed to pass judgement on the Gheorghiu-Dej era. On 30 April 1968, only days after the plenary meeting of the Central Committee which rehabilitated Foriş and Pătrăşcanu and removed Alexandru Drăghici from his party and government positions, Apostol sent an article to *Scînteia*. The covering note read:

> We send you this article with a request that you publish it in *Scînteia* after, of course, some stylistic fine-tuning. 'You' does not mean a group but a figure of respect since I imagine that comrade censorship does not know the difference.
> If, indeed, freedom of the press exists, let us see if you can publish articles with personal opinions.
> In Which Direction Are We Heading
> We are witnessing a toppling of idols which should have taken place a long time ago. Gheorghiu-Dej and other beloved leaders can be firmly placed in the category of assassins. But all the blame has fallen upon comrade Drăghici. Our view is that he was the most innocent since all he did was to apply the party line, and where there is a line there is no messing around. In fact, that can be seen from the fact that his speech [at the plenum of April 1968] has not been published. As is the case in civilized countries, the defence and not just the prosecution should have been heard. But he would probably have brought a whole chain of people down with him and that is not yet desirable. I would give a great deal to see his reply in print and even more to see it in manuscript. Certain measures should be taken,

however, since it is not only a question of Foriş and Pătrăşcanu but also of hundreds and thousands of unknown persons who, like them, finished up with a bullet in their back.

Let us also examine the reason for these notable murders. It seems that the struggle for power between different groups explains the case of Foriş. But there is another explanation for the Pătrăşcanu case. Here the reason is the very ideology [of Communism] itself which brings out the *petit bourgeois* in intellectuals. This occurred at the very time of the Russian revolution and it caught on well in our country. However, it is clear to everyone that a modern state cannot be run by shepherds and railwaymen. You need a wide vision and broad beliefs which only the highest education in at least law and history can give you. But what education did Gheorghiu-Dej and Chivu Stoica have when they seized power? How did they know how to run a country? And how do even the present leaders know? In fact, this is obvious from the measures and laws which change from one day to the next. Our view is that the real people behind the policy of assassination were the Soviet comrades. There must be a document somewhere which shows this more clearly, even though there is information about this in the papers of the plenum. Many Romanians, whose names we have now learned, were similarly killed in Russia without a trial. Let us not forget that the Russian army withdrew from Romania in 1957 [*sic!*] but that Pătrăşcanu was liquidated in 1954.

The only fault of the poor fellow was that he was more of a patriot than others, and more cultivated and intelligent. The policy of cutting off a head which thinks for itself was successfully applied by the Soviet Union in the Baltic States, Poland and Moldavia, so that perhaps Gheorghiu-Dej's guilt and that of Drăghici is not so great. In fact, the insinuations of thefts of documents and of escape abroad [levelled at Pătrăşcanu] confirm that there is still something fishy about it all. Let us see now what guarantees there are that similar deeds will not take place again. We regret to say that there is no guarantee. We only have to read comrade Ceauşescu's speech of 27 April 1968 to realize this; when we see in it how many mistakes it contains, since it was written very hastily, and how many errors it proclaims loud and clear. It is clearly the case that the law is one thing for members of the party, and another for those who are not members. As long as that is the case, it is obvious that discretion will rule unfettered. A senior member of the party will be able to trample over a non-member but the law will not be used against him until his colleagues allow it. Another problem is that a resolution of the Party has the force of a law. In such circumstances we ought to act according to what the newspapers say and not according to the constitution and codes of law etc. The law is what appears in the *Official Bulletin* after it has been passed by the Grand National Assembly. A Party resolution is an instruction for the drafting of a law but it does not take the place of a law and cannot anticipate it. Yet the Party's role is confused with that of the state. The Party is not the state and must not be ubiquitous. For this reason, the *Securitate* have the duty to monitor every person in the country and to report to the prime minister, not to the first secretary. Legislative, executive and judicial power form a perfect amalgam with the party. They should be completely separated from each other to prevent any influence of one upon the other. As it stands, if the President of the State Council falls out with someone, he passes a special law against him and in his capacity as first secretary instructs the courts how to conduct the trial so that the person found guilty can be buried alive. There have been, and there still are, so many patent abuses of the law that our leaders believe that only the more lowly are obliged to respect it. It is commonplace to recount them. We limit ourselves to showing that two accused men [Foriş and Pătrăşcanu] were thrown out like servants without showing the least respect for the legal formalities. At least in Drăghici's case these formalities were respected. It is with bitterness that we ask ourselves what to believe in and to whom we can express a positive opinion, if we have one. No one pays any attention to us, because no view has any value unless it is flattery. Public debate is a farce and all that is published of it is that which the censorship allows, and nothing against the line imposed by two or three imbeciles. Gentlemen, set up a press without censorship and you will see the result immediately. Do you think that it gives us any pleasure to see you arguing amongst yourselves for good jobs if you are not doing anything for the country. Enormous sums are being spent for extraordinarily little benefit. The reason? Because there is no free press to denounce the guilty.[10] As long as the biggest zero, a man who thinks his opinion is infallible, is there at the top, as long as the deputies in the assembly are robots who raise their hand and applaud, we will do nothing with pleasure, and what we do will be done with disgust and dissimulation. We will always be behind all other states in the world. Nothing can be done just with decrees and arbitrary measures, and without freedom.[11]

Gh. Apostol
30 April 1968

The article was not published.

Since Stalin had been the only person who could call Gheorghiu-Dej to account, the latter had been able to do what he wanted, subject to Stalin's agreement. As long as Stalin was alive, Gheorghiu-Dej behaved according to Soviet interests, regarding them as his own; but once Stalin's successors departed from Stalinism, Gheorghiu-Dej's thoughts took a different course. In the 1960s there was a partial return to the West. Credits from Western governments enabled Romania to develop new industries and to redirect some of its trade away from the Communist bloc, and at the same time there was a de-Stalinization of Romanian cultural policies. In a certain sense, these developments can be interpreted as the triumph of the culture of Romanian behaviour over the culture of Communism. But they were not allowed to pose a threat to Communist rule in Romania, and were accommodated within the principles of Marxism-Leninism.

It was Gheorghiu-Dej who created the conditions for the emergence of Nicolae Ceauşescu, as Romania's leader. Gheorghiu-Dej's removal of all his opponents impoverished the political landscape and perverted Romanian society. Imprisoned husbands divorced their wives—and vice versa—so that partners and children would not carry the stigma of a political detainee which was a bar to higher education and to employment, and led to dismissal from work. Most children of political prisoners were denied entry to higher education until 1963 and it was precisely many of these children who left Romania at the first opportunity in the 1970s with dire consequences for the formation of an opposition to Ceauşescu. Yet initially, Ceauşescu himself sought to attenuate the reliance upon Communist coercion that had marked Romania's immediate post-war history.

Born the third of ten children, on 26 January 1918, into a poor peasant family in the south-western district of Oltenia, Ceauşescu himself could point to a youth spent on the wrong side of authority. After leaving home at the age of 11 to find work in Bucharest, he joined the Communist Party as a teenager and went to prison on four separate occasions between 1933 and 1938 for his political convictions (since 1924, the Party had been outlawed). By 1936, he was a secretary of a regional committee of the Union of Communist Youth and two years later was promoted secretary of the UCY's Central Committee. In September 1939 he was tried *in absentia* and sentenced to three and half years in jail. He continued to work underground until July 1940, when he was finally caught.[12]

During the war Ceauşescu was held in various prisons until, in August 1943, he was moved to the internment camp at Târgu Jiu where he remained until the overthrow of Antonescu in August 1944. It was here that he met senior members of the Romanian Communist Party, among them Gheorghiu-Dej, Chivu Stoica, who became president of the Council of State when Ceauşescu was later elected first secretary, and Ion Gheorghe Maurer, who served as prime minister under both Gheorghiu-Dej and Ceauşescu. After release, Ceauşescu occupied a number of party posts before being made regional secretary for Oltenia in November 1946 in preparation for the general election due that month.

Ceauşescu's experience of local Party work undoubtedly made him particularly useful to Gheorghiu-Dej as the planks in the platform of Communization of Romania were put into place. When the programme for the collectivization of agriculture was announced in March 1949, Ceauşescu was moved to the Ministry of Agriculture as a deputy minister. In the following year, he was transferred to the same position in the Ministry of Armed Forces, with special responsibility for the 'Higher Political Directorate of the Army', the party body set up to bring into being a People's Army. In was in this capacity that Ceauşescu served an invaluable apprenticeship for ensuring his complete control of the armed forces when he later acquired dictatorial power. When Gheorghiu-Dej purged his major rivals in May 1952, he promoted Ceauşescu to full membership of the Central Committee, and after the execution of Pătrăşcanu in April 1954 he made both Ceauşescu and Drăghici candidate members of the Politburo, and full members in the following year. The growth in party membership that Gheorghiu-Dej called for at the 1955 Party Congress was supervised by Ceauşescu in his capacity as Central Committee secretary for organization and cadres. This control exerted by Ceauşescu over Party appointments for much of the following decade gave him a powerful base from which to seek election as party leader after the death, on 19 March 1965, of Dej and, subsequently, to consolidate his position.

Relaxation of coercion, instituted by Gheorghiu-Dej, characterized the early years of Ceauşescu's leadership. He continued those policies which had turned his predecessor into a national Communist: rapid industrialization accompanied by an autonomous line in foreign policy. In pursuing an autonomous foreign policy Ceauşescu was able not only to offer the West an opportunity to exploit an apparent breach in the Communist bloc, but also to draw on his people's dislike for their Soviet overlord. Autonomy led axiomatically to greater popularity and, inevitably, to a cultivation of national sentiment, appeals to which were made in addressing the situation of the Hungarian minority in Transylvania and in raising the issue of Bessarabia. Promotion of the national interest was the claim which underpinned Ceauşescu's autonomous policies vis-à-vis the Soviet Union, but his efforts to advance that claim upon gaining power in 1965 were compromised by the association of the Romanian Communist Party—to which title the Romanian Workers' Party reverted in June 1965—with the coercion of the previous two decades, and the presence of Alexandru Drăghici as Minister of the Interior was a constant reminder of that association. Furthermore, in the manoeuvring for the succession to Gheorghiu-Dej, Drăghici emerged as an opponent of Ceauşescu, being the sole abstainer in the vote taken in the Politburo to elect Ceauşescu as the new first secretary.[13] Removal of Drăghici from his position of power would not only enable Ceauşescu to consolidate his own position as undisputed leader of the party but would allow him to attenuate the regime's link with terror. The very fact that Ceauşescu sought as a prime objective to bring the Ministry of Internal Affairs and the *Securitate* [14] fully under party, and ultimately, his own control was an indication of his priorities.

A measure of judicial supervision was brought to the activities of both bodies through the application of the principle of 'socialist legality' which was embodied in the new constitution proposed in June 1965 that declared Romania to be a Socialist Republic in place of a People's Republic. More power was invested in the courts, and a 24-hour limit was placed on the time that a citizen could be held without being charged. Like most legislation, however, its application was arbitrary.

The second move was the replacement in July 1965 of Drăghici as Minister of Internal Affairs by his deputy Cornel Onescu, a Ceauşescu protégé who had studied at the Moscow Party School in the 1950s—Onescu was replaced in April 1972. Drăghici's removal was the result of a major change in the party statutes which was engineered by Ceauşescu at the Ninth Congress of the RCP held between 19 and 24 July 1965. Article 13 (b) of the statutes was revised to read: "A member of the party may only hold one position of political leadership which necessitates full-time activity, whether it is in the party organs or the state organs".[15] To comply with the article Drăghici was obliged to give up the Ministry of Internal Affairs, which he had directed since 1952, so that he could remain a member of the party secretariat. Although he continued to supervise security matters by sharing responsibility in the secretariat for military and security affairs with Vasile

Patilineţ, his departure from the Ministry of Internal Affairs denied him his power base and made it easier for Ceauşescu to denounce him and oust him from the party leadership in April 1968.

Drăghici's removal also signalled a firm intention on the part of Ceauşescu to bring the *Securitate* back fully under party control. The Ninth Congress marked the end of Pintilie's murderous career at the head of the various parts of the security apparatus for he failed to be re-elected to the Central Committee; he died in Bucharest on 11 August 1985 at the age of 83. Towards Drăghici Ceauşescu adopted caution, for his rival remained an influential figure and it was only two years later, in the summer of 1967, that he orchestrated the former interior minister's demise. It was suggested to Drăghici that he might like to take a holiday in the West and in his absence in June Ceauşescu called a Central Committee plenum. Its decisions were made public in the following month in a speech to party activists in the Ministry of Internal Affairs in which Ceauşescu stressed the leading role of the party and congratulated the ministry on its achievements, conceding that "in the first years after their inception the security bodies lacked experience and ability, sometimes [they] also got erroneous guidance".[16]

'Erroneous' was a euphemism for 'Soviet' and as he continued his address the party leader drew attention to the mistakes of the past, identifying many of them with the 'beginning', that is, the period of Soviet dominance:

> In the course of years, especially at the beginning, there was sometimes a lack of political discernment in the activity of the security bodies, no distinction being made between hostile activity, directed against revolutionary gains of the people and some manifestations linked to the natural process of transforming the people's conscience and mode of thinking.[17]
> This had led to 'abuses of socialist legality' which had also been committed against Party and state activists who, in certain circumstances, had different views concerning some aspects of the political line, or made mistakes in their activity. Instead of such problems being solved by discussions on a party line they were sometimes deferred to the security bodies, creating conditions for the latter's interference in party life, gravely prejudicing the authority and leading role of the party.[18]

Ceauşescu ruled such mistakes 'inadmissible' in the future and declared that the ministry could no longer act as a law unto itself, "avoiding Party control". Hammering home his attack he went on:

> It is clear that there is no kind of secret or matter of a conspirative character that could or can be a reason for an organ, and the more so for a security organ, to avoid party control, an organ which, owing to the specific nature of its work and attributions, must permanently be under the guidance and control of the party bodies.[19]

Emphasizing the primacy of the party over the *Securitate* he declared that "no citizen could be arrested without a grounded and proved reason" and, in particular, "no activist, and no party member generally should be investigated or arrested without the approval of the party bodies".[20]

In the same speech Ceauşescu announced a measure to prevent the accumulation of power within the Ministry of the Interior by a single person—and therefore an indirect criticism of Drăghici. He reported the Central Committee's decision at the same June plenum to reorganize the ministry and place the *Securitate* under the control of a new Council of State Security (*Consiliul Securităţii Statului*) which would answer to the Party and the government.[21] The CSS was formally set up under decree 710 of 22 July 1967; it was to be part of the Ministry of the Interior but it was given its own president with the rank of minister and the office of First Deputy Minister of Internal Affairs, and three vice presidents. In the same sequence of reform the *Securitate* was itself reorganized under Resolution 2306 of the Council of Ministers of 13 September 1967, the principal changes being the merging of the First (domestic intelligence) and Second (economic counter-espionage) Directorates into the *Direcţia Generală de Informaţii Interne* (General Directorate of Domestic Intelligence) and the combination of the Third (counter-espionage) and Fourth (military counter-espionage) Directorates into the *Direcţia Generală de Contraspionaj* (General Directorate of Counter-espionage).

This process of removing the *Securitate* from the control of the Ministry of the Interior continued with a further reform of the ministry within a year and was coordinated with Ceauşescu's move to remove Drăghici from all positions of authority. On 3 April 1968, the Council of State, of which Ceauşescu was now president, issued two decrees relating to the Ministry of the Interior and the Council of State Security.[22] The first reorganized the structure of the ministry, and the second separated the CSS from the ministry and gave it independent status. The CSS's attributes were defined as

> the defence of state security against acts of sabotage, diversion, undermining of the national economy, as well as against actions undertaken by foreign espionage services, the organization and implementation of military intelligence and counter-espionage, and the protection of government and Party leaders.[23]

Signs that the new era of 'legality', announced so frequently by Ceauşescu, was about to begin were given by the establishment within the CSS of a bureau to examine complaints about the *Securitate*'s alleged past abuses (its first head was Lt. Col. Constantin Apostol), and by the passage of a further decree limiting the circumstances under which private homes could be entered without a warrant from a prosecutor.[24] However, a vital measure in this sense, second in importance only to the constitution according to Ceauşescu, was the new penal code, published in draft form in April. Ceauşescu reiterated criticisms which had been addressed to the Ministry of the Interior the previous July:

> It is no secret for anybody that certain outrages have been committed over the years. The Penal Code must ensure the strict observance of socialist legality, so that nobody may infringe upon it in any way or commit abuses... The main responsibility for the application of the laws devolves on our Party.[25]

Ion Stănescu, a Ceauşescu placeman, was appointed to head the CSS—he became Minister of the Interior in April 1972 but held the post for less than a year—and Lt. Gen. Grigore Răduică, a *Securitate* officer, was made his deputy.[26] Modifications to the regional organization of the CSS followed from the reorganization of local administration which passed into law in February 1968. Romania's 16 regions were regrouped into 39 counties and so the former regional directorates (*direcţii regionale*) became county inspectorates (*inspectorate judeţene*). These changes did nothing to remove the bureaucracy of coercion but the measures taken to introduce some sort of legal constraint and judicial supervision, however superficial, to the activity of the *Securitate* marked the end of control by fear and substituted, as one analyst has put it, restrictive for prescriptive control.[27] However, the fear engendered by the *Securitate* over two decades sufficed to make restrictive control just as efficient as prescriptive control in containing dissent which remained muted following the general amnesty of 1964 and the popularity gained by Ceauşescu's defiance of the Soviet Union during the 1968 invasion of Czechoslovakia. The seal on the break with the coercion of the past came at the plenum of the Central Committee of the Party in April 1968.

The final item presented at the plenum was the report on the *Rehabilitation of Certain RCP Activists* which formed an integral part of Ceauşescu's aim to introduce 'socialist legality' into the activity of the Ministry of the Interior. A small commission of pre-war Party members, composed of Gheorghe Stoica, Vasile Patilineţ, Nicolae Guină and Ion Popescu-Puţuri, had been set up in November 1965 to investigate abuses committed against party activists with the particular task of looking into the case of Lucreţiu Pătrăşcanu. Their report revealed that Pătrăşcanu had been arrested on 28 April 1948 and that his activity was investigated for 17 months by a commission comprising Teohari Georgescu, Iosif Rangheţ and Alexandru Drăghici. On 6 December 1949 at a meeting of the Cominform "Gheorghiu-Dej described Pătrăşcanu as an agent of Anglo-American espionage and these accusations led the investigating authorities to fabricate proofs to confirm them by any means possible".[28] According to the report no reliable evidence was found against Pătrăşcanu. He was handed over to the *Securitate* for interrogation and still no proof of his alleged treachery was found. Indeed, one of the charges levelled by Gheorghiu-Dej at Teohari Georgescu at the plenum of the Central Committee in May 1952 was that "even after four years he had not completed the investigation of the counterrevolutionary and espionage activities of Pătrăşcanu and Koffler".[29]

The report went on to say that Drăghici, Georgescu's successor, set up a team "to get at any cost evidence to justify the assertion that Lucreţiu Pătrăşcanu had allegedly been an agent of the *Siguranţa* and an Anglo-American spy". Based on the information presented by Drăghici, the Political Bureau of the CC of the RWP decided on 18 March 1954 "to proceed to the trial of the group of spies head by Pătrăşcanu". The trial took place from 6 to 13 April 1954 "in violation of the most elementary procedural guarantees. The death sentence was pronounced on 14 April and on the night of 16/17 April 1954 Lucreţiu Pătrăşcanu was executed at the Jilava prison".[30]

Ceauşescu was able to deflect any criticism of his own implication in the decision to execute Pătrăşcanu by pointing out that he did not become a member of the Political Bureau or secretary of the Central Committee until 19 April. Conversely, he was able to implicate the members of the Political Bureau of the time in the decision, most importantly Drăghici, but also Gheorghe Apostol, Emil Bodnăraş and Chivu Stoica, who were the only possible challengers to his power. All four were held responsible for allowing Pătrăşcanu's trial to take place without ensuring themselves of the soundness of the accusations brought against him. The plenum resolution pointed out that Pătrăşcanu's execution had taken place after Stalin's death when, "in the USSR and other socialist countries there started a course towards the rehabilitation of some persons sentenced without justification". Disregard for party control had permitted the Ministry of the Interior to wrongfully expel and imprison party members. The plenum took a very grave view of the fact that differences of opinion within the party were regarded as a reason for penal investigation instead of being resolved by discussion and that during that period in party meetings and public speeches "currency was given to the idea, which today is shown to be false, that in Romania abuses and transgressions of socialist legality had not taken place and that, therefore, the problem of post-mortem rehabilitation does not arise".[31]

Gheorghiu-Dej was directly blamed for

> intervening in the enquiry [against Pătrăşcanu], making suggestions as to how it should be carried out, adding notes to the reports of the interrogations, establishing what evidence should be obtained from those under interrogation and who else should be arrested.

Iosif Chişinevski was attacked for his part in concocting "monstrous falsehoods and the breaking of the most elementary norms of justice" in stage-managing the trial. Drăghici was singled out for special condemnation because instead of trying to establish the truth "he sought to obtain at any price proofs of guilt so that Pătrăşcanu could be sentenced and executed". He had been able to do this "because the Ministry of the Interior had been removed from the control of the collective organs of the Central Committee, while the minister had removed himself from their control and refused to accept subordination to them".[32] These conclusions led the plenum to decide on the "posthumous political rehabilitation of Lucreţiu Pătrăşcanu", and to recommend that the others involved in his trial should also be rehabilitated.

The case of Ştefan Foriş was also taken up in the plenum resolution. It did not criticize his removal as general secretary which, it claimed had been necessary due to 'grave shortcomings' in his work, but dismissed as unfounded the accusation that he had been an informer of the *Siguranţa*. Consequently, Foriş's 'execution' in 1946 "on the basis of a decision taken by Gheorghe Gheorghiu-Dej, Teohari Georgescu, Ana Pauker, and Vasile Luca" was condemned and he was granted posthumous rehabilitation.[33] While the doubts persist about the reasons for Foriş's murder, there is room for belief that his rehabilitation was a move directed by Ceauşescu against Gheorghiu-Dej and his associates rather than one designed to establish the truth.

Gheorghe Pintilie (Bondarenko) is also said to have been attacked in the plenum for his role in Foriş's murder but Ceauşescu's disapproval was shallow enough to allow him to decorate Pintilie in May 1971 on the 50th anniversary of the founding of the party, alongside his wife Ana Toma who, allegedly had been one of the witnesses against Pătrăşcanu.[34] Rehabilitation was also extended in the Central Committee plenum resolution to a number of Romanian Communists who died in the Soviet Union between 1936 and 1938 during Stalin's purges, among them Marcel Pauker, the husband of Ana. In view of the catalogue of condemnation adduced, the plenum's final act was hardly surprising. It removed Drăghici from the three senior party bodies and recommended his dismissal as Vice-President of the Council of Ministers (announced on 27 April) because of his "particular and direct responsibility" in the 'impermissible' actions against Pătrăşcanu, his repressive measures against other party members, and his defiance during the 1968 meetings of the Praesidium, Executive Committee and the Central Committee.[35]

How Drăghici defended himself can be inferred from Ceauşescu's speech to the Bucharest Party delivered on 26 April. In it the latter expanded upon the decisions of the plenum, including those relating to the rehabilitations, in an emotive language, describing Pătrăşcanu's arrest and trial as "a foul frame-up", and his execution "a dastard assassination".[36] Foriş, too, was the victim of an 'assassination'. The charges brought against these two and against Vasile Luca, Ceauşescu continued, "accuse and condemn Alexandru Drăghici as the organizer and executor of these criminal actions against the party and state apparatus, [and] accuse and condemn Gheorghiu-Dej, who initiated and sponsored these actions". Instead of admitting his errors and expressing regret, Drăghici tried to justify his actions, "cynically declaring that in fact he regretted his not managing to secure sufficient proofs to justify the crimes",[37] blaming this on the inefficiency of his subordinates and therefore implying that Pătrăşcanu had been guilty.

Drăghici had defended the *Securitate*'s methods by claiming that the *Siguranţa* had acted in the same way towards Communists, an assertion that Ceauşescu called "an insult to our security organs" because "resorting to forgeries, to frame-ups, mystifications is not in line with the ethics of Communists". In the same speech to the plenum Drăghici had also tried to shirk responsibility for the "sentencing and assassination of Pătrăşcanu" by referring to the struggle waged by the *Securitate* against 'counterrevolutionary' elements. This, in Ceauşescu's view, was a distortion of the truth, for it exaggerated the role of the security police.

> In the course of years, attempts were made to accredit in the *Securitate* ranks the idea that in fact it was the one body that waged the struggle against the enemy. Already in 1956 we criticized this idea, emphasizing that it was not the *Securitate*, but the party that was the organizer and leader of the fight against the enemy.[38]

The reference to 1956 was an interesting one, for in the resolution of the Central Committee on Rehabilitation published in *Scînteia* on 26 April 1968 reference was made to a meeting of the Politburo held in April 1956 which condemned the Minister of the Interior, that is Drăghici, for the abuses committed by the *Securitate*, and for the removal of the Ministry of the Interior from party control. It considered the self-criticism made by Drăghici at the time to be inadequate and that he had minimized the gravity of his failings. A decision was taken in that same meeting that the *Securitate* should be placed under a Committee for State Security which would be separate from the Ministry of the Interior, but the decision was reversed later in circumstances which were not made clear. In this light the resolution's claim that "after the analysis conducted in April 1956 measures were taken to strengthen party control over the *Securitate*" had a hollow ring to it. This view is supported by a passage in Ceaușescu's speech to the Bucharest Party in which he goes even further by stating that at the April 1956 Politburo meeting a decision was taken to remove Drăghici from the Ministry of Internal Affairs on the grounds that "the Minister of Internal Affairs should no longer be a member of the Political Bureau, a fact which implied the immediate removal of Drăghici from office". Opposition from Gheorghiu-Dej and Drăghici prevented this measure from being implemented.[39]

Despite the failure to bring Drăghici to heel in 1956 Ceaușescu wanted, nevertheless, to present himself as an early critic of the Ministry of the Interior and at the same time to disassociate himself from its abuses. In an effort to give himself the credentials of a long-time supporter of party primacy over the ministry he quoted in his speech criticisms which he claimed to have made at the 1956 Political Bureau meeting:

> As far as the Ministry of Internal Affairs is concerned, party spirit is as slender as party control. Comrade Drăghici thinks that he can do anything, because he has relations with Gheorghiu-Dej and is not accountable to anybody else... Comrade Drăghici does not work with the cadres: he does not take people into account [and] a large number of party members are being dismissed from the security machinery, under different pretexts. The year 1954 alone saw the dismissal of some 900 Party members. For three years now, that is since Drăghici has been there, the Ministry of Internal Affairs has not had a united executive. This is the result of Drăghici's stand on the question of cadres. He likes to be surrounded by toadies. He poorly guides the security work.[40]

It is, however, most unlikely that Ceaușescu would have dared to express himself in these terms in 1956. Not only would he have incurred the displeasure of Drăghici, but also that of Gheorghiu-Dej and other members of the Politburo involved in the Pătrășcanu affair.[41] Although it is not known what other speakers at the April 1968 plenum, including Drăghici, said, it is clear from Ceaușescu's speech that Drăghici did not take all of this criticism lying down. In defending himself, however, he fell into the fatal trap of ascribing his actions to his introduction of the party line into the Ministry of the Interior. Ceaușescu retorted by asking:

> What line? For what had happened in that period at the Ministry of Internal Affairs, the abuses and illegalities committed, do in no way represent the line of our Party. Such an allegation by Drăghici slanders the party, its profoundly humanist policy, which sets out from solicitude for man.[42]

These attributes of the Party must have seemed, in the circumstances of the Politburo's involvement at the time, difficult to recognize.

Absolving the Party from blame was one of the conclusions reached by Ceaușescu in his analysis of Drăghici's crimes. In answer to his rhetorical question as to how such things could occur, Ceaușescu dismissed their cause as being "the general climate of suspicion and mistrust" and "the trials and sentences during those years in a number of socialist countries". Romanian conditions had produced these crimes, specifically, the "harsh factional struggle" throughout the RCP's history of which Pătrășcanu was but one victim, and the "personal traits of character of Dej and Drăghici". These crimes were not, Ceaușescu explained, a by-product of socialism, but sprang from "the concepts of the bourgeoisie... from the retrograde mentality of those who committed these abuses".[43] Individuals, therefore and not the party were to blame.

On the contrary, the party's very strength and prestige was enhanced "precisely because it is capable of analysing its own activity critically and self-critically". A repetition of these crimes could only be avoided, Ceaușescu maintained, if four conditions were met. First, the leading role of the party must be strengthened and the party exercise permanent control over the activity of the security services and the judiciary. Second, the Central Committee's role in the party should be advanced. Third, "the principal of collective work" in the party must be applied: "all the decisions must be the product of a broad, principled and thorough debate in the party bodies". Finally, "socialist democracy" had to be developed: "there can be no socialist democracy, one cannot speak of legality if the laws are disregarded and transgressed". "No one must be allowed to violate these laws" and

> we must ensure that never again should any citizen of this country, whether minister, party official or just an ordinary working man, fear that on going to his work place he may not return home—as had occurred during the period we refer to and which we have fortunately left behind long since'.[44]

Drăghici's record continued to be the subject of scrutiny after the April plenum by the party commission on past abuses against members and at one stage there seems to have been an intention to bring him to trial. This we can infer from the speech of Ion Gheorghe Maurer before the Politburo on 19 September 1968 when he posed the question "What would a trial mean?" Drăghici in his defence, he argued, would reveal a whole serious of shameful deeds committed by the party leadership at that time. The trial would assume the character not only of condemnation of the leadership, but of the state itself. The trial could therefore not be held in public, while if it was held in secret, the party would be accused of hiding the whole truth. The best thing, in Maurer's view, was to let the 15-year year statute of limitations, which was fast approaching, overtake the matter and therefore not put Drăghici on trial.[45] Ceauşescu accepted Maurer's reservations and had good reason to do so, in view of the hint of blackmail contained in a reply made by Drăghici to the party commission on 30 October 1968: "You wanted to expel me from the party; well then, expel me, but then you should expel those who carried out repressions in the district of Focşani, because there people and children were shot". Drăghici was evidently referring to Ceauşescu.[46]

Ceauşescu's denunciation of past *Securitate* abuses and the reforms of 1965–68 created an atmosphere of optimism and an expectation of a further degree of internal liberalization. This did not mean, however, the caustic mentality that characterized senior officers in the service had undergone a drastic change. This became clear when Ceauşescu's personal doctor, Abraham Schachter fell to his death from a balcony of Floreasca hospital in Bucharest on 14 March 1973 in suspicious circumstances. Ceauşescu himself was livid and vented his ire at the *Securitate* before Party members, stating that pressure had been put on Schachter to become an informer with methods "that were completely unacceptable" and constituted "a criminal, hostile action".[47] Stănescu was dismissed that very same day.

On the economic level, Romanians were beginning to enjoy a rise in living standards which the whole of Eastern Europe, except Albania, experienced in the late 1960s and the first half of the 1970s. Car ownership increased significantly as the Romanian version of the French-made Renault, christened Dacia, began to roll off the assembly lines at a newly built factory in Piteşti, opened on 20 August 1968.[48] The number of cars sold annually jumped from 9,000 in 1965 to 25,000 in 1970, and 45,000 in 1975. Sales of television sets, refrigerators and vacuum cleaners, most of them Romanian made, also soared.[49] Although caution must be exercised in accepting all of these figures at their face value—in view of the regime's manipulation of statistics for propaganda purposes[50] and the propensity of factories to inflate production figures—there is no doubt that Romanians experienced a rapid rise in their standard of living in the decade 1968–78, as indeed this author can testify from his own experience of the country. A relaxation of the ideological controls governing popular entertainment allowed Romanian television to show Western television serials and sagas, most notably 'The Saint' with its lead actor Roger Moore, which led to Bucharest streets being deserted between 8 p.m. and 9 p.m. on Saturday evenings. The opening of a *Pepsi-Cola* bottling plant in Constanţa in 1968 represented the ultimate symbol of concessions to Western 'capitalism'. Of even greater importance for the population's morale, given the severe shortage of accommodation for workers moved to the cities to provide the manpower for the new factories, was the regime's programme of apartment building and its toleration of private house constructions on rural plots. The number of dwellings built rose from 56,000 in 1955, to 133,000 in 1960, and 192,000 in 1965. In the period 1966–70, 648,000 apartments and houses were completed, and from 1971–75, 751,000.[51] Tens of thousands of families moved into new apartments, rented from the state or bought with loans from the state Savings Bank.

A relaxation of the restrictions on the issue of passports to Romanian citizens saw an increase in the number of Romanian citizens travelling to the West; from 43,676 in 1967 to 65,067 in 1968.[52] At the same time, the number of Western citizens who visited Romania grew from 590 in 1956, to some 215,000 in 1966, and to approximately 281,000 in 1967.[53] In 1973, passport applications from 528,628 Romanian citizens were reported to have been approved, an increase of 168,486 over the previous year. Of these, 276,581 were for tourism, 138,469 for visits to relatives and friends resident abroad, and 113,567 for official business.[54] The number of applications rejected was 41,712.[55]

A consequence of the massive drive to industrialize under Gheorghiu-Dej had been the creation of what might be termed a middle class of technicians, scientists and economic managers. The ability of the new class to articulate a group interest was linked to the degree to which the party leadership was prepared to relax its monopoly of central planning and to introduce a measure of managerial autonomy, as the New Economic Mechanism in Hungary was to show in 1968. However, any such reformist ideas that Ceauşescu may have had were abandoned by him in 1967.[56] The Central Committee's rigid control over central planning was maintained, thereby suffocating any collective voice that the technocrats might have found in influencing policy. Ceauşescu's failure to reform therefore prevented any move towards market socialism and the development of any political constituency within the party which a more pluralistic economic approach might have spawned.

Notes

1 Note by H.F.T. Smith, 12 March 1965, TNA, FO 371, 182734.

2 For a biographical note on Niculescu-Mizil see Viladimir Tismăneanu, *Stalinism for All Seasons, A Political History of Romanian Communism* (Berkeley and Los Angeles: University of California Press, 2003), pp.263–64.

3 Quoted from Pierre du Bois, 'Ultimele zile ale lui Gheorghiu-Dej', *Dosarele Istoriei*, no.3, 1997, p.49.

4 *Ibid.*

5 Mary Ellen Fischer, *Nicolae Ceauşescu, A Study in Political Leadership* (Boulder, Colorado: Lynne Rienner, 1989), p.66.

6 See the interviews with Apostol, Maurer and Alexandru Bârlădeanu in 'Cum a venit la putere Nicolae Ceauşescu', *Magazin Istoric*, vol.29, no.7 (July, 1995), pp.3–7.

7 E. Mezincescu, 'Din nou despre fantoma lui Dej', *România literară*, no.41 (16–22 December 1992), p.14.

8 *Scînteia*, 25 March 1965, p.3.

9 *Ibid.*

10 The sentence that follows is ungrammatical and unintelligible. It reads: "We do not have nuclear physics and electronics. And yet we have a commission. What a great discovery was made by our party secretary in that until now it was the garbage collectors who were responsible for these, and not the 'party' and the ministers".

11 Apostol was Ceauşescu's main rival and was bitter at his failure to win the backing of his colleagues in the Politburo as Gheorghiu-Dej's successor. The article was found in

the archive of the SRI and passed to me by a friend who requests anonymity. Apostol's jibe at the lack of education of Gheorghiu-Dej and Stoica is tantamount to the pot calling the kettle black, as is clear from the ungrammatical structure of this article. I have reflected some of this structure in my translation to give it a more authentic ring but not, I hope, at the expense of meaning. Text in square brackets has been added by me for the reader's elucidation.

12 For these biographical details I am indebted to Fischer, *Nicolae Ceauşescu*, pp.24–31, 47–65.

13 E. Mezincescu, 'Din nou despre fantoma lui Dej', *România literară*, no.41 (16–22 December 1992), p.14.

14 Known officially at the time as *Departamentul Securităţii*. The structure of the *Securitate* between 1948 and 1989 is laid out in Dennis Deletant, *Ceauşescu and the Securitate. Coercion and Dissent in Romania, 1965–1989* (London: Hurst & Co., 1995), pp.57–67, 103–6 and 377–80.

15 Fischer, *Nicolae Ceauşescu*, p.79.

16 'Speech at the Meeting of the Basic Active of the Ministry of Internal Affairs, 18 July 1967,' *Romania On the Way Of Completing Socialist Construction. Reports*, vol.2 (Bucharest: Meridiane Publishing House, 1969), p.374.

17 Romania On the Way Of Completing Socialist Construction. Reports, vol.2, p.375.

18 *Ibid.*

19 *Ibid.*, p.376.

20 *Ibid.*

21 *Ibid.*, p.383.

22 Fischer, *Nicolae Ceauşescu*, p.127.

23 Organizarea şi funcţionarea Organelor Ministerului de Interne de la Infiinţare până în prezent (Bucharest; Ministry of the Interior, 1978), p.124.

24 Organizarea şi funcţionarea, p.125.

25 Quoted from Fischer, *Nicolae Ceauşescu*, p.127.

26 Stănescu was born on 23 January 1929 in the southern county of Dolj, the stepbrother of Leontin Sălăjean, who became a member of the Politburo in 1965. He died on 5 June 2010.

27 W. Bacon, 'Romanian Secret Police', in J.R. Adelman (ed.), *Terror and Communist Politics: The Role of the Secret Police* (Boulder, Colorado and London: Westview Press, 1984), p.147.

28 'Resolution of the Central Committee Regarding the Rehabilitation of Certain Party Activists', *Scînteia*, 26 April 1968.

29 *Ibid.*

30 *Ibid.*; see also Fischer, *Nicolae Ceauşescu*, pp.130–31.

31 Fischer, *Nicolae Ceauşescu*, p.132.

32 *Scînteia*, 26 April 1968.

33 Fischer, *Nicolae Ceauşescu*, p.132.

34 V. Tismăneanu, 'Ceauşescu's Socialism', *Problems of Communism*, vol.34, no.1 (Jan–Feb 1985), p.58, note 44.

35 Fischer, *Nicolae Ceauşescu*, p.132.

36 Ceauşescu, *Romania on the Way*, vol.3, p.172.

37 *Ibid.*, p.173.

38 Ceauşescu, *Romania on the Way*, pp.174–75.

39 *Ibid.*, p.179.

40 *Ibid.*

41 Fischer, *Nicolae Ceauşescu*, p.134.

42 Ceauşescu, *Romania on the Way*, vol.3, p.172.

43 Ceauşescu, *Romania on the Way*, p.181.

44 *Ibid.*, pp.171, 183–84.

45 *Evenimentul Zilei*, 7 May 1993, p.3.

46 *Ibid.*

47 ANIC, fond CC al PCR, secția cancelarie, file 48/1973, ff.18–19 quoted from 'O biografie neromanțată a unui fost șef al Securității', *Evenimentul Zilei,* 13 June, 2010.

48 Dragoș Petrescu, 'Closely Watched Tourism: The *Securitate* as Warden of Transnational Encounters, 1967–1989', *Journal of Contemporary History*, vol.50, no.2 (2015), pp.337–53 [p.343].

49 The figures are: 1955 1960 1965 1970 1975
Washing machines 0 31,000 84,000 109,000 149,000
Refrigerators 0 7,000 117,000 144,000 260,000
TVs 0 25,000 159,000 242,000 395,000
(*Anuarul Statistic 1976* (Bucharest: Directia Centrală de Statistică, 1977), p.369.)

50 As was confirmed after the revolution by statisticians from the World Bank.

51 *Anuarul Statistic 1976* (Bucharest: Directia Centrală de Statistică), p.330.

52 Of these a relatively small percentage had 'forgotten to return', as a popular euphemism put it: in 1967, out of a total of 43,676 travelling to the West, 186 had not returned; the figures for 1968 were 644 out of 65,067, and in the first quarter of 1969, 239 out of 8,657 (Petrescu, 'Closely Watched Tourism', p.348).

53 Dragoș Petrescu, 'Closely Watched Tourism', p.339.

54 Tourism in this context meant travel to socialist states; it was rare for passports to be issued for tourism in Western countries.

55 Requests for emigration numbered 25,708, an increase of 5,964 over 1972. Of these, 14,401 were approved. Broken down by nationality: Germans, 6,348; Jews, 4,611; Romanians, 2,336; Hungarians, 723; others, 383. 11,307 applications were rejected on the grounds that the applicants were young professionals essential to the economy; see the transcript of the Politburo meeting of the Executive Committee of the RCP of 22 April 1974 in Mihnea Berindei, Dorin Dobrincu and Armand Goșu (eds.), *Istoria Comunismului din România.* Vol.III. *Documente Nicolae Ceaușescu (1972–1975)* (Iași: Polirom, 2016), pp.222–32 [226].

56 Fischer, *Nicolae Ceaușescu*, pp.109–13.

11 Ceauşescu's development of autonomy

On succeeding Gheorghiu-Dej Ceauşescu continued those policies that had earned his predecessor the description 'national communist': rapid industrialization accompanied by an autonomous line in foreign policy. Ceauşescu not only maintained Gheorghiu-Dej's neutrality between the Soviet Union and China in their frosty relationship, but he was able to offer the West an opportunity to exploit an apparent breach in the Communist Bloc.[1] Romania became the second country in the Warsaw Pact after the Soviet Union to establish diplomatic relations with West Germany when on 31 January 1967, the foreign minister Corneliu Mănescu agreed to an exchange of ambassadors between the Federal Republic and Romania, and it did not break diplomatic ties with Israel after the Six-Day War.[2] Autonomy led axiomatically to greater popularity and to a cultivation of national sentiment, appeals to which were made in addressing the situation of the Hungarian minority in Transylvania and in raising the issue of Bessarabia with the Soviet Union.

Bucharest's quest for nuclear technology helped to consolidate its position as a 'maverick', anchoring Romania into the arena of global politics.[3] Romania's communist leadership sought to persuade its international partners to grant the country dual-use nuclear technology.[4] Between 1963 and 1968, Romania engaged in negotiations for nuclear technology with both East and West, without making a firm commitment to any of the potential partners. Gheorghe Gaston Marin, the President of Romania's State Committee for Nuclear Energy, arrived in the US on 18 May 1964 to talk to Averill Harriman wartime US ambassador to Moscow, who had played a significant role in the post-World War II settlement regarding Romania. Gaston Marin touched on the issue of Romanian-Soviet nuclear cooperation, rightly thinking that the US would be worried about shipments of Romanian uranium to the Soviet Union. He pointed out that Romania had uranium which it preferred to put into "generating electric power rather than in fissionable material".[5] Some members of the Johnson administration took this statement at face value.

The view that Romania should be granted nuclear technology for its autonomous foreign policy was advanced by Secretary of State Dean Rusk. In August 1965, the Chairman of the Joint Atomic Energy Committee pointed out that the US should elicit an agreement from Romania that it would neither manufacture nor accept a nuclear weapon on its territory. Romania's position towards nuclear weapons and proliferation was ambivalent. On the one hand, it supported total disarmament, but on the other hand it objected to signing the Nuclear Non-Proliferation Treaty (NPT). Gheorghe identifies a fascinating piece of the jigsaw of Romanian policy by revealing that the Romanians disclosed their actual reasons for opposing the NPT only to their Soviet counterparts. Prime Minister Ion Gheorghe Maurer declared to the Soviet leader Leonid Brezhnev in March 1967 that by signing the NPT, Romania would tie its own hands, giving up the possibility of acquiring a nuclear weapon in the future.[6]

Despite these considerations it remained the case that US legislation restricted nuclear trade with Romania on national security grounds. The US Export Control Act of 1947 provided for the denial of a licence where "the President shall determine that such export makes a significant contribution to the military and economic potential of such nation or nations which would prove detrimental to the national security and welfare of the United States".[7] The main obstacle in this respect was Vietnam because Romania supported the North Vietnamese with substantial political, economic and military assistance. The Romanians condemned the US aggression against Vietnam in international fora such as the UN General Assembly, organized rallies in Bucharest to protest against US bombings in Vietnam, and tried to influence other countries to support North Vietnam's position. Supporting the North Vietnamese automatically put Romania on an embargo list regarding transfers of sensitive technology, including nuclear reactors. With the Vietnam issue in the way, Romania had little chance of success in its pursuit of Western nuclear technology.

The Romanians sensed, nevertheless, that an intermediary role they could play between the North Vietnamese and the Americans might get them enough support from the US executive branch to allow the Johnson administration to make an exception for Romania from the provisions of the Export Control Act.[8] The US had been probing Bucharest for clues on Vietnam since the autumn of 1965. On 14 October, Dean Rusk nudged his Romanian counterpart Corneliu Mănescu, towards the possibility of Romania mediating between the warring parties of the Vietnam War: "if anyone is entitled to thinking of a role which could peacefully solve the Vietnamese issue, then Romania may come to mind".[9] The country continued to supply North Vietnam with aid, to the displeasure of the Johnson administration, "which naturally avoided pushing the nuclear deal forward".[10] Recent evidence reveals, however, that Romania did play a mediating role during 1965–66 leading up to the January 1967 'Trinh Signal', in which North Vietnam officially accepted the possibility of negotiating with the United States, and that it was "far more significant, consistent and influential than previously thought".[11] The ambivalence of the Romanian stance on mediation is illustrated by Ceaușescu's support in autumn 1966 of the Soviet position on ending the war by urging the Vietnamese to negotiate while fighting.[12]

Cooperation on nuclear technology was the first topic addressed by Ceaușescu in his meeting with Richard Nixon in Bucharest in August 1969. The US president believed the Romanians were a useful channel in negotiations with both Hanoi and Beijing and therefore indulged the Romanians more than any other

US president had. After his visit, Nixon urged the Atomic Energy Commission to approve Romania's bid for a heavy water plant. Romania was able to acquire the licences for a heavy water plant, a 14 MW TRIGA II research reactor and hot cells for plutonium reprocessing. Using its political leverage, on 20 May 1970, the Soviet Union signed an agreement with Romania for the purchase of a 440 MW VVR plant on Olt River, with a delivery deadline agreed for 1978. However, after considering Canadian CANDU (Canada Deuterium Uranium) technology, Ceauşescu decided to adopt the latter in constructing a five-unit power plant at Cernavodă on the Danube.[13] Work on the first unit started in 1980.[14]

Romania's most forceful affirmation of autonomy from Soviet dictates was Ceauşescu's condemnation of the Warsaw Pact's intervention in Czechoslovakia in 1968.[15] The Romanian leader was not consulted by his Warsaw Pact allies about their intervention. As Ceauşescu complained on 25 August 1968

> if the Soviet comrades really were preoccupied with the alleged 'danger' in Czechoslovakia, it would have been normal for them to meet with our Party and government, and to present the facts of the matter in question just to make sure that no misunderstanding whatsoever exists.[16]

Ceauşescu had met Alexander Dubček on 17 August 1968 in Prague to express solidarity with the Czechoslovak position. Reporting to the Executive Committee of the Central Committee of the Romanian Communist Party on his visit,[17] Ceauşescu stated:

> We feel that, in general, the manner in which we held the discussions and acted in the public meetings was both a help to the Czechoslovak comrades and a contribution to the strengthening of the friendship between us, and, at the same time, made it possible for us to find ways of contributing to the elimination of disagreements, and to the strengthening of the unity of Socialist countries.[18]

In view of the Romanian Party's policy of "non-intervention in the domestic affairs of another state", propounded in 1964 in the course of its split with the Soviet Union, Ceauşescu's failure to join the other East European members of the Warsaw Pact in their invasion of Czechoslovakia on 21 August was hardly surprising; his denunciation of the invasion was an act of courage for which he and his country gained worldwide respect. He refused to let Bulgarian troops pass through Romania on their way to Czechoslovakia (they were airlifted to Ukraine instead). Furthermore, the invasion led to deeper cleavages elsewhere in the Warsaw Pact. Albania, which had been only a nominal member of the alliance since 1961, showed its opposition to the invasion by severing its last remaining ties with the Pact and aligning itself more closely with China.

In his speech from the balcony of the Central Committee headquarters of the Romanian Communist Party on 21 August, just hours after Soviet and Warsaw Pact troops had begun moving en masse into Czechoslovakia, Ceauşescu denounced the Soviet Union for having "flagrantly violated the freedom and independence of another state".[19] Addressing a huge crowd of ordinary citizens as well as party loyalists, he described the invasion as "a colossal error and a grave danger to peace in Europe and to the fate of socialism around the world". Ceauşescu promised that Romania would take all necessary steps to defend its own sovereignty and territorial integrity:

> It has been said that in Czechoslovakia there was a danger of counter-revolution. Perhaps tomorrow they will claim that our meeting here has reflected counter-revolutionary trends. If that should be the case, we warn all of them that the entire Romanian people will never permit anyone to violate the territory of our homeland.

Shortly after Ceauşescu finished his speech, the Romanian Communist Party (RCP) Central Committee and the Romanian government met in an emergency session and adopted a joint communiqué expressing 'great alarm' at the

> flagrant violation of the national sovereignty of a fraternal, socialist, free, and independent state, an action that contravenes all the principles on which relations between socialist countries are based as well as on universally recognized norms of international law.

The joint statement called for the immediate withdrawal of the Soviet and East European troops to "allow the Czechoslovak people to handle their internal affairs themselves, without any outside interference".[20]

Ceauşescu's outspoken opposition to the Soviet invasion raised fears in Bucharest that Romania might be the next target for Soviet troops. Faced by this threat, the Romanian leader mollified his language. While he was careful in his pronouncements not to appear to legitimize the invasion, his change of tone was evident throughout the last week of August. He ceased his criticism of the invasion, and even placed on the back burner the polemics over Bessarabia and Northern Bukovina. Yet the Romanian authorities never explicitly disavowed Ceauşescu's balcony speech and the Warsaw Pact intervention made Ceauşescu even more determined to pursue an autonomous military course, raising fears amongst the Soviets that Romania might leave the Pact.

A new framework for Soviet-East European relations became even more explicit in the weeks following the 1968 invasion of Czechoslovakia, when the Soviet Union proclaimed what became known in the West (though not in the USSR until 1989) as the 'Brezhnev Doctrine'.[21] One of the clearest Soviet statements of the rationale behind the Doctrine actually came two months before the invasion, in a speech given by Foreign Minister Andrei Gromyko to the Supreme Soviet. For the Soviet Union, Gromyko declared

> there is nothing more sacred in the field of foreign policy than the consolidation of the commonwealth of socialist countries. The defense of the gains and the

> cohesion of states belonging to the socialist commonwealth is our sacred duty, to which our country will be loyal despite all trials... Those who hope to break even a single link in the socialist commonwealth are planning in vain. The socialist commonwealth will never permit this.[22]

Brezhnev's determination to bring errant Warsaw Pact members to heel by the use of force left Ceaușescu in no doubt that Brezhnev might seek on some future occasion to put military pressure on Romania by undertaking Warsaw Pact exercises on Romanian soil. On 15 January 1969, the Romanian military attaché in Athens sent a report to Bucharest regarding a discussion with his West German counterpart. The report was immediately forwarded to Ceaușescu. It stated that, during the discussion, he was told that Western sources had suggested that "joint military exercises with Warsaw Pact troops [are] planned to take place in March-April". In such an event, the West German officer said that,

> if such exercises with troops belonging to countries of the Warsaw Pact took place on Romanian soil, the Soviet leadership will seek, as it did in Czechoslovakia, to maintain the presence of Soviet troops, and also [attempt to] replace several senior officials of the party and state who oppose in one way or another the Soviet line.[23]

At the same time, senior Soviet officers openly threatened their Romanian counterparts.[24] On 11 February 1970, Major General Florian Truță, the Romanian deputy chief of the Warsaw Pact Armed Forces' General Staff in Moscow reported home that, during his talks with the Soviet General M.S. Shtemenko on 9 February, Shtemenko had made some revealing remarks. When Truță spoke about the Romanian request for a convention on deploying the troops of the Pact on Romanian soil for exercises, Shtemenko replied:

> We know that you passed a law on 21 August 1968, in connection with the events in Czechoslovakia. In the Statute signed in March 1968 there are no provisions about concluding conventions as a basis for performing military exercises. Laws, laws, laws! But if troops were in the field, would they ask about laws? Dubček also had his laws, and who asked him about them?[25]

After the intervention in Czechoslovakia, Romania affirmed the right not to assent to military action by the Pact.[26] This is evident from a number of documents. For example, the meeting on 28 September 1968 between Marshal Jakubovskii, Supreme Commander of the Warsaw Pact Unified Armed Forces, Ceaușescu and Prime Minister Ion Gheorghe Maurer, provided an opportunity for Bucharest to state its position on the need to strive for the principle of unanimity in decision-making in the Pact.[27] By insisting in the spring of 1970 that Pact exercises take place only on the basis of a bilateral convention between Romania and the Soviet Union (no such conventions had existed hitherto) Ceaușescu sought to limit the

Soviet Union's military expectations regarding its junior Warsaw Pact partner whilst at the same time erecting a legal obstacle to any Soviet-led use of force against Bucharest. Ceauşescu's insistence on unanimity should also be seen as an attempt to avoid engaging in war against NATO for which a decision by majority might be taken. The Romanian position is clear from the letter dated 7 March 1970 of General Ion Ioniţă, Minister of the Armed Forces, to Nicolae Ceauşescu about planned Warsaw Pact exercises in April 1970:

> After Colonel General Ion Gheorghe briefed Marshal Iakubovskii, the Supreme Commander of the Warsaw Pact forces, on the main elements of the exercise, he went on to show that, in accordance with the laws of our country, for the exercise to take place the conclusion of bilateral conventions is necessary between the governments of the Socialist Republic of Romania and the Union of Soviet Socialist Republics, on the one hand, and between the governments of the Socialist Republic of Romania and the Bulgarian People's Republic, on the other; these agreements have to be ratified, on the Romanian side by the General Assembly of the Socialist Republic of Romania.[28]

Brezhnev also levelled reproaches at Ceauşescu. During talks between the two leaders in Moscow in May 1970, Ceauşescu reported to the Romanian Politburo that Brezhnev had accused him of intending to leave the Warsaw Pact and to align himself with the West.[29] Emil Bodnăraş, a Politburo member, declared later to the US ambassador in Romania, Harry G. Barnes, in 1974, that in August 1968 even the option for a separation from the Pact was taken into account

> but (the Politburo *my note*) concluded that it was better to stay inside the Pact's councils, without any influence in running the Pact's military affairs. Romania could at least ask questions and try to keep informed. He [Bodnăraş] recalled that Ceauşescu had berated Brezhnev for not consulting with him about intervening in Czechoslovakia. Brezhnev replied that he had not because he knew Ceauşescu would be opposed, to which Ceauşescu replied he would have told Brezhnev how reckless and harmful an adventure it was.[30]

In the same memorandum it was reported that

> Bodnăraş agreed with the ambassador that in both the Pact and CEMA the Soviets were pursuing a dialectical approach of increasing efforts to tighten up as a reaction to the challenge of détente. Bodnăraş was categoric that Romanian policy would continue to oppose Pact manoeuvres on Romanian soil except for map drills and air defence exercises over Romania. He said Romanian forces in the past had used Soviet test ranges for tactical missilery but now had their own range from Cape Midia to Sulina so no longer need Soviet help. Romania now manufactures some of its own military hardware, Bodnăraş noted. He said the GOR [Government of Romania] had proposed to

> the Soviets a joint fighter aircraft project, but when Moscow refused, Romania turned to the Yugoslavs and the British for cooperation in this field, which is now underway. At the same time, Romania was trying to cut down its own military expenditures somewhat, figuring it might profit a bit from détente.[31]

Ceauşescu's protest at the occupation of Czechoslovakia led him to discover that appeals to national sentiment could be an efficient mechanism of social control and personal dictatorship. It persuaded him of the rewards to be gained by lending emphasis to national symbols and to his own position in Romania. The huge rally in Bucharest on 21 August and its acclamation of Ceauşescu's denunciation of the occupation proved to be his finest hour, which whetted his appetite for the establishment of a personality cult. His reaction to the Soviet-led invasion of Czechoslovakia drew its political justification from the Romanian Central Committee declaration of 1964 which remained, throughout the period of Ceauşescu's rule, the fundamental premise upon which Romanian autonomy within the Warsaw Pact and the Council for Mutual Economic Assistance (CMEA) was based.[32] Romanian foreign policy under Ceauşescu thus showed a continuity after 1968 which, by contrast, domestic policy lacked.

How seriously the threat of a Warsaw Pact invasion was taken by Ceauşescu can be gauged from two decisions: his announcement on 21 August 1968 of the setting up of the Patriotic Guards, a workers' militia, in which the majority of adult men and women was mobilized, and his secret order at the same time that an escape plan for him be drawn up by the Council of State Security (CSS). Work on the plan started immediately in Directorate XI (Technical Directorate) of the Council for State Security and was completed in 1970. The main thrust of the plan, code-named *Rovine-IS-70*, was that in the event of an invasion, the CSS should organize armed resistance on a nationwide scale involving the whole population.[33] If this failed, then Ceauşescu would flee to a foreign country. Over the years the plan was continually modified, in particular when Ceauşescu was told by the Directorate of Foreign Intelligence (DIE) of the Soviet plot, code-named *Dnestr*, to replace him with a leader more sympathetic to Moscow.

In its updated form it was given the name 'plan Z' by the Romanian press which published details of the 1987 version of it in the summer of 1993 (the 1989 version was said to be in the hands of the SRI, *Serviciul Român de Informaţii*, as the security service became in 1990). Handwritten in order to ensure maximum security *Rovine-IS-70* was

> to be carried out if, following an act of aggression against our state, there exists the imminent threat of temporary occupation of the capital and part of our country, a fact which would make more difficult and even impossible the conduct of armed resistance by the entire population from the present headquarters.

The plan consisted "mainly in the clandestine and protected removal from the capital of the senior party leadership, their passage along previously established routes".[34]

The party leader's escape was to be effected by using the underground sewage and drainage tunnels which linked public buildings and residences with secret exit points. Safe houses were to be prepared for the temporary stay of the leader in case the escape routes were blocked. Protection of the leader was to be provided by the army, the *Securitate*, the militia and by the Patriotic Guards. Landing sites for helicopters and planes carrying the party leader were to be designated and places of refuge chosen in wooded, mountain areas so that access to an enemy would be difficult and protracted defence easier. The plan specified that preference should be given in choosing hideouts to "localities which have a particular historical connotation, where the population would be driven by powerful patriotic sentiments to provide shelter and protection to the leaders of the Party".[35] This latter stipulation said much about Ceauşescu's psychology and his belief that he had inherited the mantle of the country's defenders and national leaders. The very choice of Rovine as the name for the plan is eloquent in this sense, being the spot in Wallachia where in 1394 Prince Mircea the Old halted the advance of the Ottoman army under Sultan Baiazid.

Coordination of *Rovine-IS-70* was entrusted to the Council for State Security in respect of protection and radio communication, the Ministry of the Armed Forces for provision of ground, anti-aircraft and anti-missile defence, the Ministry of the Interior for traffic control on the ground, and the Ministry of Posts and Telecommunications to ensure the maintenance of radio and TV links. The escape was planned in two stages: the first from Bucharest itself, the second from the capital to a country area for which five different itineraries were prepared. For flight in an emergency from Bucharest four sites were selected within the capital to which the Ceauşescus could make their way either from the party headquarters or from their residence by means of underground drainage tunnels. An elaborate diagram of the network of those tunnels which 'could be used for clandestine escape' to the four sites was appended to the plan.[36] Each of these four possible routes to the outskirts of Bucharest was given a code name: *Luceafărul* for route 1, *Venus* for route 2, *Saturn* for route 3 and *Soarele* for route 4. Provision was also made for a decoy column of cars to take a false route.

For each stage of the journey charts were drawn up showing the responsibilities of each CSS and army officer assigned to the escape plan, the number of cars and helicopters needed, and the frequencies and wavelengths to be used for communication. Thus for *Luceafărul* (route 1) the CSS officer placed in charge in 1970 was Lt. Col Ion Vasilică and 25 CSS officers were designated as the party leader's bodyguard. Six cars and two helicopters were allocated for Ceauşescu and other senior figures, and 15 cars and five helicopters for his bodyguard. The provision for both helicopters and cars was made to cover the eventuality of departure by either means; in the event of escape by air, the helicopters were to take off from Piaţa Gheorghiu-Dej, the square in front of the Central Committee building.

The significance of these escape plans with regard to the events of the morning of 22 December 1989 is obvious. The withdrawal of the armoured cars from in front of the Central Committee building at 10.30 that morning effectively scuppered any chance of the helicopters taking off from the ground there but the

Ceauşescus were saved by Lt. Gen. Victor Stănculescu's decision to call in two helicopters to land on the roof of the Central Committee. Only one was able to do so, the second being prevented by the aerials on the building. The summoning of two helicopters, coupled with the fact that the Ceauşescus fled in the direction of Târgovişte, pointed to the implementation of the escape plan along itinerary 4.[37]

In 1976, the escape plan *Rovine-IS-70* was modified to take into account the possibility of an attempt within the country to overthrow Ceauşescu. At the beginning of this year, the DIE, the Foreign Intelligence Directorate of the Department of State Security, learned of the existence of a Soviet plan code-named *Dnestr* to replace Ceauşescu with a senior member of the RCP faithful to Moscow.[38] If that was the case, the KGB managed to keep *Dnestr* a secret for almost seven years, for the defector Ion Mihai Pacepa asserted that the operation had been set in motion in August 1969 on Brezhnev's orders after President Nixon's visit to Romania that month.[39] Yet judging from the documents available, the changes introduced into the plan involved purely the addition of itineraries for escape from Ceauşescu's holiday resorts at Snagov, Predeal, Neptun and Sinaia for which provision had not been made in *Rovine-IS-70*, and the reconnoitring of new routes in the area of Olăneşti and Horezu; there was nothing in them to suggest a strategy for protection of Ceauşescu different from that in the original plan. With the incorporation of these changes *Rovine-IS-70* was rechristened *Luceafărul* after the codename for escape route 1.[40]

Security considerations led to the regular updating of *Luceafărul*. In April 1979, senior officers from the Directorate of Organization and Mobilization (DOM) of the Ministry of the Interior and from the Fifth Directorate of the CSS recommended that *Luceafărul* be revised since "the contents of the plan were known to some persons who no longer worked in the Ministry of the Interior" (perhaps a reference to the defector Pacepa), that it include security arrangements for the 'presidential family' as well as the president, and that the documents referring to the plan drawn up between 1971 and 1976 be transferred from the DOM to the Fifth Directorate. This proposal, put forward by Colonel Florică Stoicescu on behalf of the DOM, and Colonel Ion Băjenaru for the head of the Fifth Directorate, was approved by Ion Homoştean, the Minister of the Interior.[41]

Romania's 'unreliability' as an ally after August 1968 led Brezhnev to order the targeting of the country by the GRU, the Soviet military intelligence agency. While Ceauşescu acted to keep his security forces content, granting employees of the Ministry of the Interior a 15 per cent pay rise in October 1969, he was acutely aware of the fact that all the senior commanders in the Romanian army had been trained in Moscow which made them vulnerable to approaches from the GRU. The allegation made by the Czech defector Jan Sejna that shortly after becoming Party secretary "Ceauşescu ordered all Romanian officers with Soviet wives either to divorce them and send them back to the USSR, or to resign from the army"[42] may well be true but if so, it was an order that was not fully obeyed for General Ion Ioniţă, who was appointed Minister of Defence in 1966, was reputedly married to a Russian. The best known example of GRU attempts to glean information about Romania's defence plans was the case of Lt. Gen.

Ioan Şerb, head of the Bucharest garrison. Born in 1926 in southern Romania, he trained as an apprentice locksmith before volunteering as an infantryman in October 1944 to fight with the army in the Hungarian and Czechoslovak campaigns. In 1946, he was sent to an officer school and rose to the rank of major. Five years later, he was selected to attend the 'Voroshilov' military academy in Moscow where he studied for two years and at the age of 29 became the youngest general in the Romanian army.

Şerb was alleged to have passed documents in a Bucharest restaurant about the city's defences to the Soviet military attaché Col. F.A. Musatov in September 1971.[43] In an interview published in 1993, Şerb claimed that no proof of his alleged treachery had ever been produced. He recounted how he was demoted on 30 September 1971 by a decree of the State Council from the rank of Lieutenant General to that of private, and arrested on 5 October while visiting his son at the officer school in Sibiu. On the same night he was taken to Bucharest to the headquarters of the penal investigation directorate of the Committee of State Security on Calea Rahovei. There he was held for three months but his interrogators were unable to furnish any proof of his treachery.[44] He was, nevertheless, court-martialled in secret and sentenced to seven years imprisonment, but released in August 1976 and sent to work as an accountant at a pig farm after Ceauşescu met Brezhnev in the Crimea.[45] The Western media carried reports in February 1972 that he had been executed, the result, defector Ion Pacepa claimed, of a deliberate ploy by Ceauşescu to convince the West that he regarded the Soviet Union as an unfriendly state yet for the Western public, given the fading of the spotlight cast on Romania by the media during 1968, the country became once again as remote as the dark side of the moon.

Şerb had been a target both of the *Securitate's* Fourth Directorate for Military Counter-espionage (UM 0632) and of a special unit of counter-intelligence targeting the socialist countries with the designation UM 0110. The latter's highly classified mission was to counter other Soviet bloc countries' intelligence operations, including attempts on Ceauşescu's life and pretexts for Warsaw Pact military intervention in Romania. It was unique in a Warsaw Pact member state. UM 0110 developed from a special unit within the Section for Armed Forces and Security of the Central Committee of the RCP, set up by Ceauşescu to monitor the loyalty of senior party members. The head of this section was Politburo member Vasile Patilineţ, and his deputy, General Grigore Răduică. In late August 1968, immediately after the Soviet invasion of Czechoslovakia, Ceauşescu ordered the expansion of this unit to secretly verify Romanians suspected of having links to the Soviet Union and other East European countries. Colonel Aurel Mircea was appointed to lead this new, still numberless, unit, which was subordinated only to Ceauşescu and Răduică. The expanded unit had approximately 100 operations officers, assisted by an administrative group for personnel, secretarial services, archives and finance. The unit was authorised to intercept all telephone communications of Warsaw Pact countries' embassies in Romania. It received from Ceauşescu personally fresh individual targets, most of them with longer party status than Ceauşescu and known to have personal reservations about his leadership.

In April 1972, Ceauşescu authorised that, for operational reasons only, the unit be covered under the call sign of the DIE, UM 0920. The new unit received the designation UM 0920/A. Lt. Col. Constantin Iosif was named its head. Following Pacepa's defection in August 1978, the designation of UM 0920/A was changed to UM 0110.[46]

It was only with the publication of Pacepa's memoir *Red Horizons* in 1987 that another alleged case of betrayal by a Romanian general came to light. General Nicolae Militaru, commander of the Bucharest military district from 1975 to 1978, was one of a number of senior generals who had studied in Moscow who were being shadowed by the *Securitate's* Fourth Directorate for Military Counter-espionage. Militaru was filmed meeting the Soviet military attaché in Bucharest in 1978 who requested a copy of the General Staff telephone book. Militaru apparently agreed and his contact was therefore reported to Ceauşescu who ordered his removal. However, Ceauşescu's displeasure was not so great as to deter him from making Militaru a Deputy Minister for Industrial Construction. Militaru's downward spiral nevertheless continued. He was replaced as Deputy Minister in February 1984, and nine months later at the thirteenth RCP Congress, he lost his seat on the Central Committee, of which he had been an alternate member since August 1969.[47]

Pacepa claimed that by the time of his defection in July 1978 six other generals in the army and *Securitate*, apart from Militaru, had been identified as being involved in the Soviet plan *Dnestr*. The only one named by him is Maj. Gen. Grigore Naum, whom he listed as head of the Fifth Directorate for Military Counter-espionage.[48] In fact, the Fifth Directorate was responsible for Ceauşescu's personal protection. Naum was placed in reserve, and like the other officers allegedly implicated in the Soviet plot, was spared any public humiliation. Apparently Ceauşescu, in order to avoid irritating the Kremlin, forbade even their interrogation, preferring to quietly neutralize them by moving them to insignificant posts. Such was the treatment of Major General (two-star general) Mihai Caraman, the officer who had recruited in 1962 a Frenchman working in the library of NATO headquarters to provide him with hundreds of secret documents and had risen to be head of the counter-intelligence unit of the DIE, who was allegedly 'reactivated' by the GRU in 1978. Pacepa did not include him among those implicated in the Soviet plot but talked simply of his renewed contacts with the GRU, proof of which was presented to Ceauşescu in Pacepa's presence by the head of the Third Directorate of Counter-espionage of the *Securitate*, Major General Gheorghe Moga. Caraman was said to have been quietly demoted to a position in the Bucharest *Securitate* inspectorate.[49]

Information about the activity during this period of another senior Romanian officer on behalf of the GRU and KGB surfaced in 1993. A report in the weekly *Tinerama* alleged that "a high-ranking officer who holds one of the most senior positions in Romania's defence establishment, had been a Soviet spy for decades". The officer in question had started his career in the 1960s in Romanian military intelligence, in the DIMSM and was given a diplomatic posting in Belgrade. At the beginning of the 1970s he was posted to Paris where he worked for almost a decade. After two or three years there he attracted the attention of the Romanian counter-espionage service, not because of his contacts with the Soviet military attaché which were to be expected, but due to his frequent meetings with undercover agents from the Soviet embassy which took place at the Paris consulate and in Marseilles. In 1976, he was reported to have had a 'confidential' meeting with Vladimir Rybcenko, and two years later had four meetings with Anatoly Beliatsev. He was also seen talking to Boris Filipov, Evgheny Ivanov and Mihail Soloviev.[50]

Any hopes that the denunciation of past *Securitate* abuses and the defiance of the Soviet Union over the invasion of Czechoslovakia by Ceauşescu might lead to even broader liberalization proved misplaced. The machinery of terror, set up in 1948, remained in place. Disillusionment gave way to dissent and the *Securitate* was quick to act. Despite amnesties in 1976 and 1977 freeing 28,000 people (mainly juvenile offenders or people arrested or sentenced for leaving or attempting to leave the country illegally), serious human rights violations continued. Dissenters were subjected to surveillance, harassment, intimidation and loss of jobs. Failing this, they were arrested and tried, often on what Amnesty International believed to be trumped-up charges of offences such as 'parasitism' (i.e. unemployment), 'homosexual relations', and 'embezzlement', and either sent to prison or psychiatric institutions, or forced labour camps.[51]

In 1965, psychiatric abuse had been effectively institutionalized under the provisions of Decree Law 12 'On the Medical Treatment of Dangerously Mentally Ill Persons'. Evidence gathered by Amnesty International showed that this law was used to obtain the commitment of political dissidents to psychiatric institutions, initially for a period of a few months, but from the beginning of the 1970s some dissidents were confined for periods lasting up to five years. In the early 1970s, special psychiatric hospitals, such as Poiana Mare in the county of Dolj, and Dr Petru Groza in Bihor, were created and a number of prisoners of conscience were sent here on the basis of article 114 of the 1968 Criminal Code. This article provided for the psychiatric treatment of criminal offenders who were 'mentally ill and a danger to society' and the number of dissidents confined in these institutions increased significantly after their establishment.[52]

Under decree 12 of 1965 the decision to commit a person to a psychiatric institution was made by the State Prosecutor or health authorities and any extension of the period of confinement was to be made by a court. In the cases known to Amnesty International dissidents had been sent to psychiatric institutions without any previous record of violent behaviour and, in many cases, without any psychiatric diagnosis or examination having taken place prior to arrest. The decision to release a person from compulsory psychiatric confinement was to be based on a psychiatrist's report at the institution where the subject was held but the recommendations made to the courts were made on political and not medical criteria.

The dissidents sent to psychiatric institutions under article 114 of the 1968 Criminal Code were charged with non-violent political offences such as 'anti-state propaganda' and 'attempting to leave the country illegally'. Both offences were defined in articles 166 and 245 of the same code. Article 166 stated:

> Propaganda of a Fascist nature and propaganda against the socialist state, committed by any means in public, is punished by a sentence of imprisonment of five to fifteen years and the forfeiture of certain rights. Propaganda or the undertaking of any action with the aim of changing the Socialist system or activities which could result in a threat to the security of the state will be punished by a sentence of imprisonment from five to fifteen years and the forfeiture of certain rights.
>
> Article 245 read:
>
> Entering or leaving the country through illegal crossing of the frontier will be punished by a sentence of imprisonment from six months to three years.

'Illegal crossing'' meant without possession of a passport. Since the issue of a passport was, in many cases, dependent upon fulfilling certain 'security' criteria, such as collaboration with the DIE, the foreign intelligence department of the *Securitate*, the dissidents' fidelity to their principles vitiated their chances of ever satisfying the criteria. Romanian courts ordered the commitment of several mentally healthy persons found guilty under the aforementioned article to psychiatric institutions on the basis of false diagnoses.[53]

Three types of institutions were used for confinement. Many of those ruled to be 'mentally ill' were sent to psychiatric hospitals as in-patients and kept in 'high-security wards' for between one and two months. Others, charged with criminal offences and subjected to psychiatric diagnosis, were held for seven to eight weeks pending trial, in the psychiatric wards of prison hospitals such as Jilava, some 12 km south of Bucharest. Dissidents who were found guilty of 'anti-state propaganda' and to be mentally ill were committed to special psychiatric hospitals for the criminally insane. Detention here lasted from two to three years.

Many dissidents subjected to psychiatric abuse were sent to the Dr Petru Groza hospital in the town of the same name in the county of Bihor. Between 1973 and 1977, the number of dissidents held here rose from 50 to 150. Men and women were housed in separate buildings in a complex surrounded by a six-foot high metallic fence surmounted with barbed wire. Around the fence were neon lights and inside it four watchtowers manned by armed policemen. Patrols of the fence were carried out at regular intervals with German shepherd dogs. The death rate in the hospital in the 1970s was reported to be relatively high. In January and February 1975, six persons (one woman and five men) died from heart attack, tuberculosis, progressive paralysis (syphilis) and jaundice, and all were said to be under the age of 30.[54] Dissidents formerly held in the hospital claimed that there were several causes of deaths: high doses of drugs administered to persons suffering from serious somatic and psychic diseases; poor levels of hygiene; and inadequate medical treatment.

Of the 400 prisoners confined between 1975 and 1977, Amnesty International concluded that 150 were dissidents and the remainder common criminals. Most of the dissidents were subjected to psychiatric treatment on a court order based on article 114. There were only a handful of psychiatrists working in the hospital and approximately 30 auxiliary medical staff, including 25 male and female nurses, and a laboratory technician. The hospital director was Dr Ioan Pricop, with Dr Mircea Tocuţiu in charge of the women's section, and Dr Horia Ardelean responsible for the men. The wards were said to be poorly equipped, blankets were not washed for months and sheets were changed irregularly. Meals were served regularly three times a day but dissidents alleged that they were often laced with drugs.

A second hospital to which dissidents were committed was the Poiana Mare psychiatric hospital in the county of Dolj, about 14 km south of the town of Calafat. The buildings were originally built as army barracks in the early 1950s but later a tuberculosis sanatorium was set up here; in 1972, the Ministry of Internal Affairs transformed some of the other buildings into a special psychiatric hospital. The hospital was divided into four pavilions or centres, two each for men and women, with a four-metre high perimeter fence around each. Each pavilion contained several rooms where inmates were held, up to 25 to a room, together with a dining room and a treatment room for the administration of drugs. Despite a Ministry of Health recommendation in 1973 that the hospital be closed for not meeting standards of hygiene or medical care, the Ministry of Internal Affairs took no action. All the hospital personnel were employees of the latter ministry, including the political director who, in 1978, was Dr Enache.[55] Each ward had eight nurses, four guards and three janitors. The number of inmates in 1977 was reported to be 400, evenly distributed among the four wards and equally divided amongst men and women. Of them some 120 were estimated to be dissidents. The right to outside exercise was given only to those detainees who had been subjected to heavy dosages of drugs and had been adjudged to respond the process of 're-education' by behaving in a friendly manner towards the staff.

Both the Poiana Mare and the Dr Petru Groza hospitals were used for long-term treatment of prisoners while the Jilava prison hospital had a rapid turnover of short-term detainees. The hospital was part of one of the country's maximum security prisons which was built as an underground fortress in 1895 to defend Bucharest. Water dripped from the ceilings and the damp walls of the cells, hence the name Jilava which literally means 'the damp place'. A description of it in the 1950s is given by Annie Samuelli who spent part of her 12-year sentence there:

> The prison had once been an underground fort. The roof was covered with meadows on which cattle and sheep grazed. Nobody could guess from the road that ran alongside it that underneath, about four thousand political prisoners were held either for trial or for transfer. The cells had vaulted ceilings, stone floors, shuttered windows looking out onto deeply dug yards enclosed by high earth cliffs. Shrubs, trees and grass plots gave them the aspect of ordinary gardens in order to bluff any aeroplane flying overhead.
> Water dripped down the walls, especially during the hot airless summers and nothing, not even shoes, could be left for long on the floor without getting mouldy. The place richly deserved its nickname.[56]

The prison hospital was built above ground and its fourth floor housed the psychiatric section. According to dissidents confined there in the 1970s, the smallest rooms of the section were less than four square metres and used for the punishment of inmates, who were sometimes kept there in straitjackets for periods in extreme cases of up to ten days. Political prisoners were quartered in rooms with common criminals, the largest rooms being approximately 30 metres square and accommodating up to 26 patients. The psychiatric section held 100 or more inmates at any one time and these included political and criminal prisoners with serious mental illnesses. Some inmates, however, were dissidents without psychiatric disorders.[57]

It was in Jilava that a clear pattern of abuse involving the injection of powerful neuroleptic drugs could be established from the testimony of former prisoners of conscience. Doses were given without any medical examination being carried out on the new patient. Therefore patients with certain medical conditions such as cardiovascular disease were susceptible to drastic side effects from the administration of such drugs. After two weeks, an electroencephalogram was taken and a 20-minute interview conducted with a doctor. Dissidents who took part in such interviews were then transferred to special psychiatric hospitals but before being sent on were asked to sign a statement that no drugs had been administered to them. Particularly stubborn prisoners, both political and criminal, were transferred to the hospital in Sighetul Marmaţiei in the county of Maramureş.

Yet another psychiatric hospital to which dissidents were confined was the Dr Marinescu hospital in Bucharest. They were placed in wards 6 and 7, which housed the incurably ill who often walked around naked. The supervision of dissidents was entrusted to a medical assistant (alleged to be an officer in the *Securitate*) who administered a daily dose of drugs by injection. Prisoners were usually sent to this hospital by the court for 'observation' and were held for four to eight weeks. Between 1975 and 1978 there were believed to be no more than five dissidents held in the hospital at any one time.

Former dissidents reported to Amnesty International that psychiatric treatment was used as a means of political re-education throughout the 1970s and 1980s of those sentenced under article 114 of the Criminal Code. A psychiatrist was often present at the interrogation carried out by officers from the Directorate of Penal Investigation of the *Securitate*. The political offender was asked to describe his attitudes towards Communism, towards the country's leaders and towards society at large, and on the basis of his responses a diagnosis made. The diagnosis was often fabricated by drawing on the prisoner's medical record or on his or her complaints about headaches or allergies. If the offender was certified by the court as insane he was committed to a psychiatric hospital and the process of re-education set in motion. Threats, injections and sometimes beatings were given if the prisoner refused to admit his or her guilt and recant. Admittance of guilt led to the termination of drug treatment and even early release, but the dissident was required to sign a statement promising not to reveal details of his treatment on pain of re-incarceration. Breaking the interdiction on conversation with fellow prisoners was punished with injections of drugs or beatings. Contact with relatives was severely restricted. In Jilava hospital inmates were allowed to receive and send one letter a month, while in the Dr Petru Groza and Poiana Mare hospitals they were sometimes not allowed any contact for several months. In the period of 'forensic observation' at the Dr Marinescu hospital no contact was permitted.

Drugs and electric shocks were used not only in hospitals. Several accounts by dissidents describe their administration during interrogation by penal investigation officers of the *Securitate* at their headquarters on Calea Rahovei in Bucharest in an effort to extract self-incriminating statements. Two workers from the *Steagul Roşu* tractor plant in Braşov, Gheorghe Rusu and Vasile Brancu, were arrested in 1974 after a fire was started at the plant and slogans for improved wages appeared on the walls. Both were subjected to electric shock and drug treatment and charged with economic subversion and anti-state propaganda. Rusu was sentenced to death in a trial at the plant on 12 May 1975 but the sentence was not carried out and he was sent to Aiud prison. Brancu was rumoured to have died at Calea Rahovei following psychiatric abuse which included electric shock treatment.[58]

The details of 16 cases of dissidents confined to psychiatric hospitals for various periods between 1969 and 1978 were published by Amnesty International in 1978.[59] Three of them, Paulina Cătănescu, Gheorghe Braşoveanu and Vasile Paraschiv, all expressed their solidarity with an open letter addressed by the writer Paul Goma and seven others on 8 February 1977 to the 35 participating states at the CSCE Belgrade Conference which had signed the Helsinki Final Act. Goma drew attention to human rights abuses in Romania, and the government's failure to respect its international undertakings in this domain. Cătănescu and Braşoveanu were re-arrested and placed in psychiatric hospitals, while Paraschiv was given a passport at the end of 1977. He went to France where he underwent an independent psychiatric examination which confirmed that he was not mentally ill, and returned to Romania in the summer of 1978.

Braşoveanu was again confined to a psychiatric hospital in March 1979. Two months earlier a group of 15 workers and a number of intellectuals from the city of Turnu Severin in the south-west of Romania established a 'Free Trade Union of the Working People of Romania' (SLOMR) which attracted a countrywide membership in towns such as Ploieşti and Constanţa, and involved Hungarian workers in Târgu Mureş and Timişoara. The dissident Orthodox priest Gheorghe Calciu offered to be a spiritual advisor. The group circulated a manifesto calling for the legalization of unofficial trade unions and observance of the right to free association. In an open letter to Ceauşescu in April, the union protested against the frequent arrests of its members, among them Ion Cană and Gheorghe Braşoveanu, who were arrested on 10 March, and Nicolae Dascălu, who succeeded them as chairman of the union, and who was in June sentenced to 18 months in prison for allegedly passing state secrets to Amnesty International. Another SLOMR member, Eugen Onescu, was committed to the Dr Marinescu hospital for three weeks, while Cană and Braşoveanu were sent to jail but released in 1980. In 1986, the latter was allowed to leave Romania.

On 21 February 1989, Dr Ion Vianu, a practising psychiatrist based in Switzerland who had left Romania in the 1970s, told a public hearing of the Political Affairs Committee of the European Parliament of the case of Nestor Popescu, a cinema scriptwriter. Popescu had become a Baptist in 1986 and in the following year had been dismissed from his job for disseminating Baptist literature. He was put on trial and declared to be suffering from 'paranoiac psychosis' for which he was sent to the Poiana Mare hospital where he had remained.[60]

Notes

1 Cezar Stanciu, 'Autonomy and Ideology: Brezhnev, Ceauşescu and the World Communist Movement', *Contemporary European History*, vol.23, no.1 (February 2014), pp.115–34.
2 The USSR established diplomatic relations with West Germany in September 1955.
3 One can draw parallels with Charles de Gaulle's 'maverick' stance towards NATO.
4 The term 'dual-use' is applied when fissile material, such as plutonium, produced by many types of nuclear reactor, is capable of being diverted to the development of a nuclear weapon. Whilst nuclear reactors are used for peaceful purposes, such as providing electricity or developing radiopharmaceuticals, some states have been accused of having nuclear weapons programmes based on dual-use technology, notably in more recent years, Iran and North Korea. The International Atomic Energy Agency attempts to monitor dual-use technology in countries which are signatories of the NPT, to make sure that fissile material is not diverted to military functions. In 1991, over a year after the fall of Ceauşescu, Romania reported previously undeclared nuclear activities by the former regime, and the International Atomic Energy Agency (IAEA) reported this non-compliance to the Security Council for information only.
5 Eliza Gheorghe, 'Atomic Maverick: Romania's negotiations for nuclear technology, 1964–1970', *Cold War History* vol.13, no.3 (August 2013), pp.373–92 [379].
6 *Ibid.*, p.381.
7 *Foreign Relations of the United States*, IX. Washington, DC, 1997, 'Report of the President's Task Force on Foreign Economic Policy', undated, p.473.
8 In his monograph on the Vietnam War, James Hershberg points out that Romania's mediation was an attempt to improve its ties with the West and Washington specifically, for political and economic reasons. James G. Hershberg, *Marigold. The Lost Chance for Peace in Vietnam* (Stanford CA, Stanford University Press, 2012), p.639.
9 Gheorghe, 'Atomic Maverick', p.382.
10 *Ibid.*, p.383.
11 Larry Watts, 'Mediating the Vietnam War: Romania and the First Trinh Signal, 1965–1966', Woodrow Wilson International Center for Scholars, *Cold War International History Project. Working Paper* no.81 (July 2016), p.110.
12 *Ibid.* In a meeting with the US ambassador to Bucharest on 31 January 1967, Ceauşescu pressed for closer economic ties between their two countries, pointing out that although the Vietnam War was an obstacle, Romania was working hard to solve the conflict. He told the American ambassador that Hanoi "does not wish to have intermediaries but would like to talk directly with you". Ceauşescu applied the 'mediator-in-denial' approach: he agreed to relay the message that Washington wanted to talk to the leadership in Hanoi, but then quickly added that doing so did not mean that Romania wanted to be a mediator between Hanoi and Washington. Ceauşescu was reluctant to officially accept the role of mediator between the Americans and the North Vietnamese because he did not have a mandate from the Vietnamese Workers' Party and because he was apprehensive about the reaction of the Chinese (Gheorghe, 'Atomic Maverick', p.383).

13 Canada Deuterium Uranium is a type of pressurized heavy water reactor which uses deuterium oxide (heavy water) as moderator and natural uranium fuel. This type of reactor was developed in the 1950s and 1960s by the Atomic Energy Canada Limited (AECL) in partnership with the Hydro-Electric Power Commission of Ontario, Canadian General Electric and a variety of other companies. Cernavodă was based on technology transfer from Canada (AECL), Italy and the USA, with Candu-6 heavy water reactors. Construction of units 2–5 began in 1982. In 1991 work on the latter four was suspended in order to focus on unit 1, responsibility for which was handed to an AECL-Ansaldo (Canadian-Italian) consortium. Unit 1 was connected to the grid in mid-1996 and entered commercial operation in December 1996.

14 After Ceauşescu's 1974 assertion that "no state need refrain from a weapons acquisition", US specialists concluded that "if Romania were to opt to produce nuclear weapons, it can acquire the necessary know-how and material over a reasonably short span of years, from Western suppliers, such as the Germans, British, or French or even Chinese". (Gheorghe, 'Atomic Maverick', p.391). The United States continued to supply Romania with highly enriched uranium (93% enrichment) for the TRIGA II reactor until the second half of the 1980s, even after Ceauşescu publicly declared that he possessed the ability to develop nuclear weapons. Throughout this period, the US Department of Energy provided Romania with 38 kg of highly enriched uranium (HEU), a quantity that the International Atomic Energy Agency (IAEA) deems sufficient for producing a nuclear bomb. Romania was, therefore, the only country in the Soviet bloc with CANDU nuclear energy technology and Western plutonium reprocessing technology (Gheorghe, 'Atomic Maverick', p.374).

15 A discussion of Romania's reaction to the Prague Spring and the Warsaw Pact invasion is provided by Mihai Retegan, *1968. Din Primăvară până în Toamnă* (Bucharest: Editura RAO, 2014).

16 Dennis Deletant and Mihail E. Ionescu, *Romania and the Warsaw Pact, 1955–1989*, Cold War International History Project, Working Paper No. 43 Woodrow Wilson Center, Washington, DC, July 2002, p.177.

17 The Romanian Workers' Party (RWP) changed its name to the Romanian Communist Party (RCP) in 1965.

18 Deletant and Ionescu, *Romania and the Warsaw Pact*, p.166.

19 I draw heavily in the next three paragraphs on Mark Kramer, 'Moldova, Romania and the Soviet Invasion of Czechoslovakia', *Cold War International History Project Bulletin*, no.12/13 (Fall/Winter 2001), p.327.

20 *Ibid.*

21 This phrasing is taken from Mark Kramer, *The Kremlin, the Prague Spring and the Brezhnev Doctrine*, www. Foia.cia.gov/Czechinvasion/7-Miscellaneous/2009-09-01.pdf. Accessed 7 April 2017.

22 Quoted from Kramer, *The Kremlin, the Prague Spring*, p.60.

23 Deletant and Ionescu, *Romania and the Warsaw Pact*, p.77.

24 The degree of pressure which the Soviet Union placed on Romania to toe its line in the Warsaw Pact and in the CMEA is chronicled and analysed by Larry L. Watts, *With Friends Like These. The Soviet Bloc's Clandestine War Against Romania* (Bucharest: Military Publishing House, 2010).

25 *Ibid.*

26 Romania's defiance on this score was first revealed by Colonel Ryszard Kukliński in 'Wojna z narodem widziana od środka', *Kultura* (Paris), vol.4, no.475 (April 1987), pp.52–55, esp. p.53; see Kramer, *The Kremlin, the Prague Spring*, p.58, note 193. Kukliński was a senior officer on the Polish General Staff who also was a spy for the US Central Intelligence Agency. He escaped to the West in November 1981.

27 Deletant and Ionescu, *Romania and the Warsaw Pact*, pp.190–95.

28 *Ibid.*, pp.217–18.

29 *Ibid.*, p.78.

30 *Cold War International History Project Digital Archive*, "Memorandum of Conversation between Emil Bodnăraş and Harry G. Barnes, US Ambassador to Romania," May 24, 1974, History and Public Policy Program Digital Archive, Selected US Documents on Sino-American and Romanian/Soviet Relations (1969–1974) obtained by Mircea Munteanu, Cold War International History Project, from the National Archives, College park, Nixon NSC Box 701/703, for the George Washington Cold War Conference on the Sino-American Opening and the Cold War (1969–1972), George Washington University, 8–9 February 2002. http://digitalarchive.wilsoncenter.org/document/110457, accessed 17 April 2017. 7 1974
31 *Ibid.*
32 The CMEA, also known as Comecon, was the trading bloc set up by the Soviet Union in 1949 to coordinate economic development among the Communist states of Eastern Europe. It was dissolved in 1991.
33 For a discussion of *Rovine-IS-70* see Richard Andrew Hall, 'Nicolae Ceauşescu, Evacuarea din CC-ul, Soarele, Tîrgoviste, şi Rezistenţa' at https://romanianrevolutionofdecember1989.com/nicolae-ceausescu-evacuarea-din-cc-ul-soarele-tirgoviste-si-rezistenta/. Accessed 25 May 2016.
34 *Evenimentul Zilei*, 7 July 1993, p.3. One of those routes would take Ceauşescu to his native county of Oltenia, from where he would direct resistance. Indeed, the helicopter which took Ceauşescu and his wife from their villa in Snagov north of the capital was headed in the direction of Oltenia when the pilot received orders from air force chief Ioan Rus to put down near Târgovişte on 22 December 1989
35 *Ibid.*
36 The diagram was reproduced in *Evenimentul Zilei*, 10 July 1993, p.3.
37 M. Curea, 'Planul "Z" a Funcţionat până la Deciderea Judecării Cuplului', *Evenimentul Zilei*, 9 July 1993, p.3.
38 *Ibid.*
39 Ion Pacepa, *Moştenirea Kremlinului* (Bucharest: Editura Venus, 1993), p.302.
40 Appended to *Luceafărul* were the names of those officers and their units involved in drawing up *Rovine-IS-70* together with the names of those put forward by the Minister of the Interior to work on the plan. In the former category were Major General Nicolae Pleşiţă, Deputy Minister of the Interior, Major General Paul Marinescu and Colonels Constantin Constantinescu, Vasile Ivaşcu and Constantin Picioruş from the Directorate of Organization and Mobilization (DOM) of the same ministry, Major General Mircea Oprescu, deputy head of Foreign Intelligence (DIE), Colonel Iuliu Plăpcianu, from special unit 'R' (radio) of the Council for State Security, Colonel Marin Dumitru from special unit 'F' (surveillance) of the CSS, Colonel Ion Staicu and Lieutenant Colonel Alexandru Aliman of the Fifth Directorate (Security and Protection of the Party leadership) of the CSS, and Lieutenant Colonel Ştefan Prisecaru of the Third Directorate (Counter-espionage) of the CSS. Delegated to work on the whole of Luceafărul were Major General Paul Marinescu and Colonels Mircea Marmandiu and Constantin Picioruş of the DOM, and Lieutenant Colonel Mihai Bucuci of the Fifth Directorate. Radio links were assigned to Colonels Iuliu Plăpcianu and Mihai Scatula from special unit 'R' (radio) of the Council for State Security, while protection and defence along the routes was the responsibility of Colonel Dumitru Penciuc of the Command of the Ministry of the Interior Troops (*trupele de Securitate*). Lieutenant General Vasile Milea, the head of the General Staff of the Patriotic Guards and a future Minister of Defence, was given the task of assisting defence of the place of refuge chosen for Ceauşescu, and Major General Ioan Geoană had responsibility for providing anti-aircraft defence (*Evenimentul Zilei*, 12 July 1993, p.3).
41 *Evenimentul Zilei*, 12 July 1993, p.3.
42 J. Sejna, *We Will Bury You* (London: Sidgwick and Jackson, 1982), p.67.
43 Ion Mihai Pacepa, *Red Horizons* (Washington, DC: Regnery Gateway; London: William Heinemann, 1988), p.195.

44 'Generalul Ioan Şerb nu a fost executat', *Evenimentul Zilei*, 3 March 1993, p.3.

45 Şerb was elected mayor of his native village in the county of Dâmboviţa in 1996. He died in 2004. Mihnea Berindei, Dorin Dobrincu, and Armand Goşu (eds.), *Istoria Comunismului din România.* Vol.III. *Documente Nicolae Ceauşescu (1972–1975)* (Iaşi: Polirom, 2016), p.68, footnote 27.

46 UM 0920 UM meant *unitate militară* (military unit), 0 signified a classified unit, and 920 was the code number of DIE. For UM 0110 see Appendix 9; also Dennis Deletant, 'Romania', in Krzysztof Persak and Lukasz Kaminski (eds.), *A Handbook of the Communist Security Apparatus in East-Central Europe 1944–1989* (Warsaw: Institute of National Remembrance, 2005), pp.285–328 and personal communication to this author from Ion Mihai Pacepa.

47 M. Shafir, 'The New Romanian Government', *Radio Free Europe. Report on Eastern Europe*, vol.1, no.2 (12 January 1990), p.36).

48 Pacepa, *Moştenirea Kremlinului*, p.303.

49 *Ibid.*, p.492. After the revolution, Caraman was reactivated on 18 January 1990 at the insistence of Silviu Brucan and prime minister Petre Roman and appointed head of the CIE (Foreign Intelligence Service) which became, under Law no.39 (13 December 1990), the SIE (author's interview with General Nicolae Militaru, 7 January, 1995). The SIE was subordinated to the prime minister's office until the adoption of the Law no.39 when it was placed under the Supreme Defence Council, headed by the President of Romania. In July 1990, Prime Minister Roman issued an invitation to Manfred Wörner, NATO secretary general, to visit Romania, an invitation taken up in July of the following year, although the irreconcilability of Caraman's past with his position as head the intelligence service of a country seeking NATO membership was made clear to Roman. On 22 April 1992, President Iliescu approved Caraman's 'request' to be retired whilst at the same time promoting him to the rank of four-star general.

50 Soloviev was expelled in 1983 by the French authorities together with 46 other KGB and GRU officers for "activities incompatible with his diplomatic status". In 1979, after it had been established that the Soviet contacts of the Romanian officer belonged to Directorate T of the First Chief Directorate (Foreign Intelligence) of the KGB, responsible for scientific and technological espionage, the Romanian officer was recalled to Bucharest but treated with the same tolerance as Militaru, being given a post first in the military academy, and then one in the port of Brăila. After Ceauşescu's flight on 22 December 1989, the officer is said to have turned up at the army divisional HQ in Brăila claiming to be the new Chief of the General Staff and ordered the arrest of the commandant, Colonel Rizea, appointing a Colonel Şora in his place. He ordered Şora to make contact with the Soviet military command in Reni, on the opposite bank of the Danube, and "to facilitate the entry of Soviet troops into Romania in support of the revolution". When Şora tried to give these orders he was arrested by subordinate officers and confusion reigned until the self-proclaimed Chief of the General Staff was ordered to Bucharest by Militaru on 26 December and appointed head of 'one of Romania's secret services'. After Militaru was relieved of his office as Minister of Defence in February 1990, the officer was appointed by President Iliescu to a post which involved the coordination of the work of all the Romanian secret services. The weekly did not name the officer but called for his resignation or for his dismissal ('Un Spion la Cotroceni', *Tinerama*, no.125 (23–29 April 1993).). Several weeks later it was reported that "well-informed sources at Cotroceni [the Presidential Palace] anticipate with certainty the imminent removal from office and placing in the reserve of Major General Nicolae Pancea, the secretary general of the Supreme Defence Council... The removal of the important general is due, according to the same sources in the presidential circle, to revelations in the press from which it would seem to be the case that this person might have worked for a foreign power while he held a diplomatic post" (*Cotidianul*, 1 June 1993.).

51 *Amnesty International Briefing, Romania* (London: Amnesty International, 1980), p.3.

52 *Romania. Forced Labor, Psychiatric Repression of Dissent, Persecution of Religious Believers, Ethnic Discrimination and Persecution, Law and the Suppression of Human Rights in Romania* (New York: Amnesty International USA, 1978), p.13.
53 *Ibid.*, p.14.
54 *Ibid.*, p.15.
55 *Ibid.*, p.17.
56 A. Samuelli, *The Wall Between* (Washington, DC: Robert B. Luce, 1967), pp.45–46.
57 *Romania. Forced Labor*, p.18.
58 *Ibid.*, p.22.
59 Their names were Paulina Cătănescu, Ştefan Toia, Haralamb Ionescu, Ştefan Gavrila, Vasile Paraschiv, Ştefan Tudor, Ilona Luca, Marian Neagu, Cezar Mititelu, Victor Murea, Julia Petrescu, Ion Dobre, Gheorghe Braşoveanu, Trusca (Christian name not known), Genevieva Sfatcu, and Cornel Iliescu (*Romania. Forced Labor*, pp.23–28).
60 *European Parliament, Info Memo 34* (21 February 1989), p.8.

12 The paradox of foreign policy

Soviet attempts to unnerve Ceauşescu made little impression upon him, in fact they appeared to have fortified his resolve to place what he regarded as Romania's interest above that of the Kremlin. Unlike other members of the Pact, Romania did not break diplomatic ties with Israel after the Six-Day War. Growing recognition of Romania's political usefulness as a thorn in the flesh of the Soviet Union prompted a period of increasing Western courtship of Ceauşescu, exemplified by President Nixon's visit in August 1969.[1] Nixon's decision to meet Ceauşescu provided "a textbook example of Nixon's policy of differentiation".[2] Not only did it mark a turning point in Washington's relations with Bucharest, but it also demonstrated to other members of the Socialist bloc that the United States was willing to be a partner. The Romanian leader returned the visit in October 1970 when, at Nixon's invitation, he made the first state visit of a Romanian president to the United States.[3] There followed a succession of economic favours. In 1971, Romania was admitted to GATT (General Agreement on Trade and Tariffs) and in 1972 it was accepted into the International Monetary Fund and the World Bank. Throughout the 1970s, Romania expanded its foreign trade relations with the West to a greater degree than any other country in the East European bloc. The country's trading position was enhanced when the country acquired preferential trading status with the European Community in 1973.[4]

The US Congress, in passing the Trade Act of 1974, permitted the president to extend Most Favoured Nation status to Communist countries.[5] Section 402 of this act, known as the Jackson-Vanik amendment, prohibited the extension of MFN to any country that denied its citizens the right to emigrate, but also allowed the president to waive this provision if he found that such a waiver would "substantially promote the objectives of freedom of emigration". The initial 18-month waiver could be renewed for 12-month periods by the president, but either house of Congress could reverse such a decision. It was in recognition of Ceauşescu's success in "tweaking the nose of the Russians"[6] that at the end of July 1975, President Ford granted Romania Most Favoured Nation tariff status.[7]

With its award the US Congress was able to hold Ceauşescu's feet to the fire over human rights issues in Romania, most notably the right or opportunity to emigrate. The annual review of Romania's performance on emigration was to prove a key factor in Romania's relations with the United States in the 1980s.

President Ford took the decision to grant Romania MFN status after receiving an oral 'assurance' from Ceauşescu that he would "contribute to the solution of humanitarian problems on the basis of mutual confidence and goodwill".[8] Quite apart from its considerable trade benefits to Romania—Romanian exports to the US almost doubled from $133 to $233 million between 1975 and 1977—which the award of MFN brought, of even greater value to Ceauşescu was the certificate of respectability that it implied not only for his emigration policies, but also for his treatment of wider human rights issues in Romania.

Ceauşescu visited the United States again in April 1978 for a third state visit, at the invitation of President Jimmy Carter.[9] He thus set an unprecedented record of such visits for the head of state of a Warsaw Pact country. Two months later, he was given an honour unprecedented to the head of a Warsaw Pact country—a state visit to the United Kingdom. The visit was arranged in the hope that it "may act as a stimulus to British companies to grasp the growing opportunities for selling to Romania".[10]

Internally, Ceauşescu consolidated his control over the country by creating the position of President of the Republic in 1974 and the ceremony of his swearing into office was more like a coronation than a presidential inauguration. His appointment as president marked the intensification of a personality cult which he fuelled with his foreign policy successes. These features of Ceauşescu's rule bring us to consider the great paradox of it, namely that his skilful conduct of foreign policy contrasted so starkly with his mismanagement of domestic affairs. In foreign policy, Ceauşescu demonstrated the same sensitivity and resourcefulness that had been displayed by Gheorghiu-Dej and Maurer in taking Romania on its autonomous course. In domestic policy, he showed the opposite, becoming tyrannical and insensitive to the needs of the population.

A fellow Communist who shared a cell with Ceauşescu before the war detected in him, even at this early age "an unlimited confidence in himself which was nurtured by his equally unlimited lack of confidence in everyone else and especially in those to whom he was professionally subordinated".[11] That lack of confidence became manifest in his refusal to accept advice, a refusal which meant that he would accept only sycophants around him and these appeared in increasing numbers throughout the 1970s and 1980s. His intolerance of others drew him closer to his wife, Elena, a woman of unbounded ambition and vindictiveness, who exploited her husband's growing paranoia, thereby encouraging him to give reign to his prejudices and pretensions. Her pernicious influence was most manifest in the preposterous personality cult which was generated around her husband. In summer 1971, Ceauşescu visited China and North Korea. The experience aroused in him an admiration for the cultural revolution and for the grandiose spectacles dedicated to the personality cult. The stage-managed adulation of Mao and Kim Il Sung, so meticulously choreographed, fired Ceauşescu's imagination and he demanded the same upon his return to Romania. Stubbornness and capriciousness became the hallmarks of Ceauşescu's rule. It not only humiliated the Romanians, but robbed them of their dignity in their everyday lives and reduced them in the 1980s to an animal state, concerned only with the problems of day-to-day survival.

At the beginning of the 1970s, Ceauşescu could still bask in the applause and respect which the international community had accorded to him in August 1968 and he exploited this to the full. Yet the Western cultivation of Ceauşescu produced a second paradox: it took place at the very time when he was lapsing into what one analyst has described as "neo-Stalinism without terror".[12] Whereas Romanians felt that Ceauşescu had been moving forward at the end of the 1960s, they regarded him in the early 1970s as moving backwards.

"1978 marked the apogee of Ceauşescu's acceptability in the West".[13] It was only after Ceauşescu's relevance on the world stage was undermined by the accession to power of Mikhail Gorbachev in March 1985 that Western support for him faded. In September 1983, the popular Western image of Ceauşescu as a benign figure was still being perpetuated by leaders such as Vice President George Bush who described him as "one of Europe's good Communists".[14] With the advent of Gorbachev, Ceauşescu's usefulness as a bridge between East and West rapidly evaporated, for a number of the very positions which the Romanian leader had adopted in his foreign policy, and which had gilded his autonomous image in the West, now became features of Soviet policy; withdrawal from Afghanistan, removal of short-range nuclear weapons from Europe, and reductions in nuclear arsenals. Once Ceauşescu's failure to adopt *perestroika* and *glasnost* had begun to draw criticism from the Soviet leadership some Western ambassadors, though by no means all, were instructed to make a point of inviting dissidents to official receptions.[15]

There was another major reason behind Ceauşescu's success in projecting a favourable image in the West, namely his treatment of the Jewish minority. Under Ceauşescu the status enjoyed by the Jewish community was unique in the whole of the Communist bloc. The Jews enjoyed what one scholar described as "possibly the greatest measure of autonomy among all denominations".[16] This he attributed to their contracting numbers, leaving a predominantly elderly community which posed no threat to the regime, to Ceauşescu's desire to promote a favourable image in the West, especially in the United States, and to the personality of Romanian Chief Rabbi Moses Rosen.

Many of the Jews of Romania had been victims of the Holocaust.[17] The Holocaust in Romania was unlike that in other parts of Europe and the Soviet Union. In the first place, the mass murder was carried out by the Romanian authorities under Ion Antonescu's military dictatorship, and Romania was a sovereign German ally. Second, the deaths of Jews at the hands of the Romanians were the result not only of systematic killing, but also of deportation and its consequences. The Romanian and German armies shot 12,000–20,000 Jews in Bessarabia and Bukovina during July and August 1941.[18] Romanian forces themselves put to death an estimated 15,000–20,000 Jews in Odessa in a similar manner that same October. Of the 147,000 Jews who were deported from Bukovina and Bessarabia between 1941 and 1943 to Transnistria at least 90,000 died, the majority of typhus and starvation.[19] During the same period, 130,000–170,000 local Ukrainian Jews are also estimated to have perished in the same province.[20] These figures—totalling almost 300,000 Jews—give the Antonescu regime the sinister distinction of being responsible for the largest number of deaths of Jews after Hitler's Germany—the deportation of 500,000 Jews from Hungary, including 151,000 from the formerly Romanian territory of Northern Transylvania, to the death camps in Poland was carried out after the German occupation of that country on 19 March 1944.[21] Third, Romania's 'Jewish policy' was independent of Germany in the sense that Antonescu acted of his own volition regarding the Jews, but in a context established by Nazi domination of continental Europe. For example, in the summer of 1942 Antonescu changed his mind about acceding to German requests that the remaining Jewish population of Romania—from the Banat, southern Transylvania, Wallachia and Moldavia—be deported to the death camps in Poland.

Religious practice by the Jews had been permitted under a statute published on 12 July 1949 which grouped Jewish communities in a Federation. Upon the recommendation of the Federation a Supreme Rabbinical Council of 12 was appointed by the Minister of Cults and in September 1949 Chief Rabbi Moses Rosen was named its president. Rosen's predecessor, Chief Rabbi Alexandru Şafran, fled to Switzerland in December 1947 after the dissolution of the Jewish Party. Rosen was prominent in the public attacks on Zionism and at the 1950 conference of the Democratic Jewish Committee he denounced as 'warmongers' the US Treasury Secretary Henry Morgenthau, President Truman's veteran counsellor Bernard Baruch, and the advisor to the State Department Benjamin Cohen.[22] Jewish emigration was permitted between late 1949 and 1952 —more than 100,000 Jews were issued exit visas—due primarily, it appears, to the intervention of Ana Pauker, even though she was not a Zionist, but with her fall from grace in June 1952 it dried up.[23]

Behind the resumption of emigration to Israel in 1959 lay hopes held by the Romanian authorities for trade with the West and a desire to allay the negative image that their ban on emigration was causing in the international arena.[24] A secret deal between Romania and Israel, described by Ion Pacepa in *Red Horizons*, is said to have been struck.[25] In 1958 a British businessman, Henry Jakober, who had been conducting trade with Romania for several years, contacted the Romanian foreign intelligence resident in London, Gheorghe Marcu, and told him that Mossad was willing to pay the Romanian government a sum of money for each Jew allowed to emigrate.[26] This arrangement was conditional upon it remaining a secret between the two intelligence services whose channels would be Jakober and Marcu.[27]

In 1961, 12,150 Jews were granted visas provided they gave as a cover for their eventual destination of Israel a West European or Latin American country, or Cyprus, and in return a number of Western firms were secretly paid by Mossad to construct livestock farms in Romania. By the end of 1964, the Ministry of the Interior, in Pacepa's words, had become the largest meat producer in the country, exporting frozen pork, beef, turkey and chicken exclusively to the West. The money earned from these exports was placed in a secret account controlled by the Directorate of Foreign Intelligence of the *Securitate*. They were supplemented by funds paid to the *Securitate* by the families abroad of those seeking to emigrate.[28]

It was not only Jews whose emigration was purchased in this way. Jakober also acted as the conduit for payment to Romanian intelligence of monies given by private individuals in the West for exit visas for their relatives in prison in Romania. The ransom demanded varied according to the status of the prisoner but was between $4,000 and $6,000. The procedure was as follows: Jakober was approached at his address at 55 Park Lane in London and given the name of the person to be ransomed. He then gave the name a reference number which was quoted in all correspondence and took the details to Bucharest. There a ransom fee was fixed by the Romanian intelligence directorate acting on Gheorghiu-Dej's orders and communicated to Jakober who, on his return to Britain gave instructions to those paying the ransom to deposit the sum into Jakober's account at the Credit Suisse Bank in Lucerne, Switzerland. The monies were only paid over to the Romanian authorities after the ransomed person had arrived in the West. In one such case, a ransom of $4,200 was paid in August 1962 by relatives and friends for the release from prison of Maria Golescu, the librarian of the British Information Office in Bucharest who was arrested in July 1949 for allegedly passing two letters to a member of the British legation from Ştefan Neniţescu, the former secretary to the Romanian Foreign Minister Nicolae Titulescu, and sentenced to 20 years in prison.[29] Under Ceauşescu the 'Jakober-Marcu' agreement continued, but the exchange was not for animal farms but for dollars. After Jakober's death from cancer the deputy director of Israeli intelligence in immigration matters, Dan Shaike Yesahayahu (alias Dan Yitzak Yesahanu) was alleged by Pacepa to have become the new partner in the agreement.[30] A sliding scale of cash payment from $2,000 upwards according to the age, education and profession of the individual seeking emigration was established and regular meetings took place between Marcu and Yesahanu at the Romanian embassies in Bonn, Vienna and Berne at which Marcu handed over large sums of money in return for the lists of Jews approved for emigration. This sale of Jews netted Ceauşescu hundreds of millions of dollars and its success prompted him to authorize a similar export of ethnic Germans from Transylvania and the Banat after Romania established diplomatic relations with West Germany in 1967.[31]

Jewish autonomy was institutionalized through the Federation of Jewish Communities, whose president was Rabbi Rosen. The Federation secured the religious, educational, cultural and medical needs of the community by maintaining synagogues in the principal centres of Jewish population, by running chains of *kosher* restaurants and offering a service of 'meals on wheels' for the elderly, by organizing schools for the teaching of Hebrew and the study of the Talmud, by providing medical and health care for Jews, and by managing homes for the elderly. A Jewish museum was set up in Bucharest at the end of the 1970s, and one a few years later in Iaşi, and a fortnightly cultural journal *Revista Cultului Mozaic* with articles in four languages was published, although much of the material was censored by the Department of Cults. A Jewish theatre and a Centre for Jewish Studies also functioned.

Ceauşescu's policy towards the Jews can be summed up in a few words: to let those who so wished to emigrate in order to facilitate the process of creating a homogeneous Romania based on the majority Romanian element.[32] Emigration also released places of work and homes to be filled by the young generation of technocrats and skilled workers. At the same time, Ceauşescu created for himself the image of an enlightened leader, one who alone respected human rights in the Eastern bloc by allowing Jews to emigrate to their ancestral homeland and giving those who remained the possibility of cultivating their traditional values. In assessing the favourable impact his policies towards the Jews had both in Israel and in the United States, it should be remembered that Ceauşescu's stance contrasted sharply with that of his colleagues in the rest of Eastern Europe, and especially in the Soviet Union where the struggle for the rights of Soviet Jewry, both as a minority and for the right to emigrate, was energetically pursued both in Israel and in the West.

Furthermore, Ceauşescu's opposition to the Brezhnev doctrine of intervention in a Warsaw Pact state every time a member was threatened by a 'counter-revolution', his criticism of the Soviet invasion of Afghanistan, his refusal to break off links with Israel after the Six-Day War in 1967, and his abstention from voting in the United Nations for the resolution equating Zionism with racism, all produced the image of an autonomous foreign policy which enabled him to play the Jewish card very effectively when seeking Most Favoured Nation status from the US administration and indeed the Romanian ambassador to Washington often received useful tactical advice in pursuing this goal from his Israeli counterpart.

It was not surprising that the 'give and take' which characterized Ceauşescu's relations with the international Jewish community should also typify those with Rabbi Rosen, although many Jews both inside and outside Romania felt that what he had 'given' to the Communist regime since 1948 amounted to 'collusion'. Their opprobrium had been voiced most stridently by Golda Meir. "The Romanian government should award you a special decoration for the services you have rendered them and for the speeches you have been making on their behalf. I don't believe a word you say", an angry Meir is reported to have told Rosen in New York in 1961.[33] Rosen made no attempt to deny his record of support for the regime or for Ceauşescu and justified it on the grounds of protecting Jewish interests. However, his critics felt that he had hidden behind this argument to justify his own acquiescence in Ceauşescu's policies instead of recognizing that the Romanian leader was influenced more by what he could gain from international Jewish goodwill rather than from compliance at home. In short, the price Rosen paid at home for Ceauşescu's concessions had already been met by the Jewish lobby abroad. That price was validation of Ceauşescu's policies.

A case in point is the permission which Ceauşescu gave for the Jewish Federation in Romania to receive assistance, both financial and material, from the Jewish agency *Joint*. Some will argue that it was Ceauşescu's dependence upon international Jewish goodwill which enabled Rabbi Rosen to extract Ceauşescu's assent, an assent which, once again, he alone amongst Communist rulers gave. Supporters of the Rabbi will claim that the permission was given in return for the latter's services to Ceauşescu. Yet there was also a further element of self-interest in Ceauşescu's decision. By accepting Jewish funds, he was saving monies which the Romanian state would otherwise have to provide. All three considerations probably influenced Ceauşescu. It should not be forgotten that Rosen was particularly effective in running a campaign to get the American administration to grant Romania Most Favoured Nation status, which it finally awarded in 1975. He travelled frequently to Washington in the early 1970s at the expense of the regime to lobby Congress by testifying to the religious tolerance enjoyed by Romanian Jews; his critics point to the fact that he stayed silent about the persecution of other religious groups, notably the Uniates and the Baptists.

On 31 January 1967, Romania became the second Warsaw Pact state after the Soviet Union to establish diplomatic relations with the Federal Republic of Germany, an action based on the Warsaw Pact's Bucharest Declaration of 1966 which included a statement affirming that a basic condition for European security was the establishment of normal relations between states "regardless of their social system".[34] In the forefront of Romania's relations with the Federal Republic of Germany stood the situation of the large Germany minority. The census of 1948 put the figure of the German population of Romania at 343,913 (2.2 per cent).[35] Limited emigration of Germans from Romania had been permitted in the 1950s and 1960s to both East and West Germany, largely to permit the reintegration of families displaced by the effects of the Second World War. The bulk of the 16,873 Germans who left Romania between 1950 and 1968 had gone to West Germany.[36]

Romanian sensitivity to the status of its German minority had grown as a consequence of the Polish government's decision to allow members of its own German minority to emigrate to West Germany after the signing of the non-aggression treaty between the two states on 7 December 1970.[37] The Polish decision prompted calls from the Germans in Romania to be allowed to emigrate in greater numbers than hitherto, to which the Romanian government responded by launching a press campaign highlighting the difficulties experienced by those who had already left. Ceauşescu himself spoke out against German emigration, stressing that there would never be "any agreement or understanding with anyone on the removal of the population of German or any other nationality",[38] while official spokesmen pointed to the advantage to the Romanian economy of the skilled German workers. No mention was made of the secret agreement reached in May 1962 by the head of the Romanian Foreign Intelligence Service (DIE), General Nicolae Doicaru, with Ewald Garlepp, a West German lawyer, for the payment in Deutsche marks to the Romanian authorities of a 'head tax' on certain Germans allowed to emigrate.[39] This agreement was followed by numerous others with various lawyers down the years until 1990.[40]

A central role in the 'sale' of Jews and Germans, as well as other persons whose emigration from Romania was sought, was played by Major General Gheorghe Marcu of the DIE/CIE,[41] whose cover name was Dorin Pavelescu. Marcu was appointed head of the Department of Special Hard Currency Operations (*Departamentul Operaţiuni Valutare Speciale* (OVS)) of the *Securitate* in 1975 although his nominal position was deputy director of the Institute of World Economy.[42] It was the OVS which handled the sale of emigrants. An OVS report dated 29 December 1975 refers to the agreements made respectively between Romania and Israel in February 1973, and Romania and West Germany in May of the same year, in which the Romanian authorities undertook to allow the emigration of 40,000 Germans over five years, and of 24,000 Jews over three years. The tariff per person was linked to their education and professional status. The Romanian side had not respected the first two years of the agreement since the number of emigrants was considerably lower than that stipulated. In the period July 1973–December 1973, only 14,908 Germans had emigrated while in respect of Jews, of the 24,000, only 10,077 had left. In both cases, the West German and Israeli authorities had completed the payment of the relevant head tax. Over the five years 1970 to 1975, Romania received a total of $54,470,306 from West Germany and Israel for the emigrants.[43]

In addition to the monies paid through West German and Israeli banks by the respective authorities through the channel of the OVS to the Romanian Bank for Foreign Trade, further sums were, in some cases, handed over by West German, Israeli, and other families through lawyers into the account of the Romanian Ministry of the Interior at the Romanian National Bank, or into certain accounts at the Romanian Bank for Foreign Trade. There are also many credible accounts of payments being made to *Securitate* officers in Bucharest or in Sibiu and Braşov, the regional centres of the counties with the most numerous German populations.[44] An idea of the sums involved in this 'commerce' can be gauged from the fact that between 1950 and 1989 some 282,240 Germans emigrated from Romania.[45]

In 1979, West Germany's Chancellor Helmut Schmidt visited Bucharest and extended credit guarantees of US$368 million in return for Romanian pledges to facilitate the reunification of ethnic German families. These guarantees were in addition to the individual tariffs levied by the Romanian authorities and paid through lawyers by families in West Germany for the emigration of family members. The issue resurfaced in 1983. After visits by Bavarian premier Franz Joseph Strauss and West German foreign minister Hans-Dietrich Genscher, an agreement was reached whereby the West German government would pay to the Romanian authorities the sum of US$5,263 for each German emigrant. According to press reports, the agreement remained in effect until 30 June 1988, and as a result led to the emigration of 13,000 to 15,000 Germans annually.[46] The West German publication *Die Welt* reported that in January 1989 a follow-up agreement had been reached by which Romania would continue to permit emigration at the previous rate.[47]

When addressing the fate of the Jewish and German minorities under Gheorghiu-Dej and Ceauşescu it is easy to overlook the situation of a third equally significant minority, the Roma. The first Roma groups are believed to have reached Europe from the East in the middle of the eleventh century. Many Roma were driven from Armenia after its invasion at this time by the Seljuk Turks. By the end of the fourteenth century the Roma were established widely throughout the Balkan Peninsula.

In Wallachia and Moldavia the Roma endured an ignominious fate, being systematically turned into slaves. It is already as slaves that the Roma are first attested in Wallachia in a grant of land made to the monastery of Tismana in 1385 by Dan I, Prince of Wallachia (1383–86). In both principalities the Roma had acquired an economic importance which led to their enslavement. They were valued as artisans who specialized in certain trades such as blacksmiths and locksmiths but since they were peripatetic, they could not be tied to one place. To prevent them from escaping they were turned into slaves of the boyars and of the Church, when the latter was established in the middle of the fourteenth century. Every Roma without a master was declared the property of the state.

Their plight had probably changed little by the early nineteenth century when we have this description of them from William Wilkinson, British consul in Bucharest from 1814 to 1818:

> Gypsies have no admissible claim to any country as their own and are distinguished from other races by physical and moral qualities peculiar to themselves [...]
> Wallachia and Moldavia contain about one hundred and fifty thousand gypsies, and make a more profitable use of them than other countries do, by keeping them in a state of regular slavery [...]
> They acknowledge no particular religion as their own; neither do they think of following the precepts of any, unless, acting as domestic slaves, they are ordered so to do by their masters.
> In both principalities the gypsies are divided into two distinct classes of slaves; the one is composed of those who are the property of the government, and the other, of those who belong to private individuals. No regular traffic of them is carried on in the country. Both sales and purchases are conducted in private.
> The number of gypsies belonging to the two governments altogether amounts to eighty thousand, including women and children. They are suffered to stroll about the country, provided they bind themselves never to leave it, and to pay an annual tribute of the value of forty piastres each man, above the age of fifteen.
> The chief occupation, both of the men and women leading this vagrant life, consists in making common iron tools, baskets, and other woodwork of the kind for sale. But their industry and gain are confined to what is absolutely necessary for procuring them the means of subsistence. They possess a natural facility and quickness in acquiring the knowledge of the arts; but a small number, however, devote themselves to any, and musical performance seems to be that to which they give the preference: those who profess it attend the wine-houses every day, for a trifling remuneration and from thence they are frequently called to the houses of the first boyars, on occasions when a band of music is requisite. Some few become masons, and receive one piastre for a whole day's work. They are always employed, with a number of their

> less experienced companions, in public buildings and they are then allowed no other reward but their daily food, and a proportionable reduction from their tribute.
> Notwithstanding that the gypsies form here so necessary a part of the community, they are held in the greatest contempt by the other inhabitants who indeed treat them little better than brutes; and the insulting epithet of 'thief' or any equivalent would sooner be put up with than that of 'gypsy'.[48]

In 1930, the Romas numbered 262,501. Like the Jews, the Roma were targeted for deportation to Transnistria by Antonescu in 1942.[49] More than 25,000, that is about 11 per cent of the estimated 1942 population, were victims. Many of the deported Roma died in Transnistria from hunger and illness. There were no organized executions of Roma by the Romanian authorities, as in the case of the Jews; there were, however, instances of Roma being shot by the Romanian gendarmerie. The total number of Roma who died in Transnistria is unknown. A gendarmerie assessment in May 1944 of the numbers who made their way back to Romania after the abandonment of the territory two months earlier found only 6,000 persons, but this census was made at a time of upheaval; areas of eastern Romania were already occupied by Soviet troops at a time when Roma were still drifting back, and were no longer accessible for the census. Some Roma who lived in tolerable conditions may well have remained in Transnistria. It is unclear, then, whether as many as 19,000 of the 25,000 Roma deported to Transnistria died, but it is almost certain that more than half did.

On the other hand, some simple arithmetic suggests that many Roma from Romania perished during the war. According to the census of 21 February 1956, the Roma population stood at only 104,216. In drawing comparisons with the 1930 census it should be remembered that Bessarabia, Northern Bucovina and Southern Dobrogea had been amputated from post-war Romania. Nevertheless, allowing for the removal from the calculation of the 11,400 Roma located in both northern and southern Dobrogea in 1930, and the 16,000 from Bessarabia and Bukovina—many of whom died in Transnistria—there is still a shortfall of almost 130,000 Roma. And this figure excludes population growth!

This discrepancy may be largely attributed to losses during the war. But it may also have been inflated by under reporting of the numbers of Roma in the 1956 census. A reluctance on the part of the Roma to declare themselves as such in the census and/or a to desire on the part of the authorities not to recognize a larger number of Roma—with consequent effects for the proportion of minorities in relation to the country's population—would explain this. Under reporting of numbers in 1956 would thus partly—although not entirely—explain the massive increase in the numbers of Roma recorded barely 20 years later. The census of February 1977 gave the figure of 227,398 declaring themselves Roma, an increase of more than 100 per cent over two decades.[50]

Under Communist rule the Roma remained Romania's most socially and economically disadvantaged minority, with high illiteracy levels. Education was mandatory for all children and parents were offered work in the newly created industries. To meet the Communist objective of creating full employment, those Roma who still led a nomadic life were forced to settle down. Many Roma were given dwellings vacated by emigrating Germans and Jews. The traditional type of Roma trade was eroded as many Roma began to adopt an urban lifestyle. But the deepening economic crisis of the 1980s slowed down this process of assimilation and led to a revival of traditional skills and trades as a means of survival.

In considering Ceauşescu's evolution in respect of his domestic policies, an obvious question springs to mind, namely why did Ceauşescu fail to live up to the promise he showed in the late 1960s? One explanation given is that it was part of a strategy of consolidation adopted by Ceauşescu.[51] By neutralizing the old guard of Alexandru Drăghici, Gheorghe Apostol (sent as ambassador to Argentina), and Chivu Stoica, (removed as President of the State Council in 1967), Ceauşescu was able to show he was a reformer. By the Tenth Party Congress in 1969, he had crammed the Executive Committee of the Party with his own supporters such as Manea Mănescu, Paul Niculescu-Mizil, Vasile Patilineţ, Virgil Trofin and Ilie Verdeţ. Only Emil Bodnăraş and Ion Gheorghe Maurer survived from the Gheorghiu-Dej leadership to accompany Ceauşescu in the Praesidium. Maurer retired from politics in March 1974, and Bodnăraş died in January 1976, leaving Ceauşescu surrounded only by 'yes-men' who he had promoted. Each one of these figures became a victim of their patron's capriciousness, as 'rotation of cadres' became a principal plank of Ceauşescu's political manoeuvring. By constantly shuffling his pack of pliant cardboard characters, the Party Secretary was able to prevent each one of them from establishing a serious party clientele and a position in the public eye, thereby eliminating any possible opposition. His patronage naturally extended to the Ministry of the Interior and to the *Securitate* who maintained complete loyalty to the supreme leader until his downfall in December 1989.[52]

To a certain degree, Ceauşescu became a victim of the regime's economic achievements of the 1960s. Expectations of an ever-brighter economic future were raised by the increasing availability of consumer goods in the late 1960s and when cutbacks became the order of the day in the late 1970s and 1980s, these hopes were rudely shattered. In the light of Ceausescu's admiration for Stalin, it is not surprising that economic policy should have been characterized by the former's obsession with industrialization and total opposition to any form of private ownership. He was, therefore, all the more irritated that the champion of economic reforms in the Eastern bloc in 1985 should be the new Soviet leader, Mikhail Gorbachev, and his implacable opposition to change was expressed at the November 1985 Central Committee meeting of the Romanian Communist Party.[53] Ceauşescu had turned to the West for loans but the country's creditworthiness had been assessed on over-optimistic estimates of its ability to repay through exports, for these proved to be of poor quality. In turning to the West for markets, Romanian enterprises found that what passed as satisfactory for a finished product by Soviet standards was far from meeting Western ones. The problem was exacerbated by a political culture in management which prioritized Party service over professional competence. Not only did exports fail to generate the anticipated income, but the energy-intensive heavy industry plants became increasingly voracious due to inefficient running. In the mid-1970s, Ceausescu expanded Romania's oil-refining capacity in excess of the country's own domestic output and in 1976 was forced to begin the import of crude oil. When the price of oil soared on the international market in 1978 Romania was caught out and soon faced a major trade deficit. Her problem was exacerbated by the revolution in Iran, a chief supplier to Romania of oil, which put a halt to deliveries.

The Soviet Union granted all Council of Mutual Economic Assistance (CMEA) countries except Romania substantial rouble trade credits during 1975–84.[54] It sold relatively underpriced oil to Bulgaria, Czechoslovakia, East Germany, Hungary and Poland. Romania repeatedly tried to secure some preferentially priced Soviet oil after 1973–74 as the country became a net importer of oil in 1975, yet the Soviet Union steadfastly refused to sell preferentially priced oil to Romania and at most consented to barter, for example, 2.7 million metric tons in 1981 of crude oil valued in hard currency at world market prices for Romanian exports of food and certain raw materials, also valued in hard currency at those same prices. A connection between Ceausescu's autonomous foreign policy and Soviet unwillingness to provide Romania with the trade advantages offered to other East European countries seems, is highly plausible.[55]

An example of this link occurred in 1984. Romania received from the Soviet Union 1.5 million metric tons of crude oil, 300 million cubic metres of natural gas, and two million metric tons of processed oil. These deliveries were not included in the annual trade protocol, therefore Romania did not receive the preferential terms that were applied to other CMEA members. Rather, Romania paid in terms of hard currency plus food and raw materials valued in hard currency at world market prices. The widespread speculation surrounding these negotiations postulated that Romania would have boycotted the 1984 Summer Olympics in Los Angeles if the Soviet Union had exported oil to Romania on preferential terms.[56]

In absolute terms, Romania received the smallest amount of subsidies from the Soviet Union.[57] In fact, Romania paid modest trade taxes to the Soviet Union during 1960–69 but received minor subsidies during the 1970s. Subsidies to Romania, though still low, jumped in 1980 and stayed at approximately that level during 1981–84. It was really only the second world oil price shock (1979) which produced adjustment policies in Romania. This increase in oil prices occurred simultaneously with the depletion of Romania's key domestic resource: energy, especially petroleum. "Having failed to adjust earlier, large-scale energy-intensive industry—and indeed the economy as a whole—found itself dependent to a much greater degree on foreign sources of fuel, manufactured goods and increasingly, financing."[58]

Romania's foreign trade response to this economic crisis was also consistent with the above-mentioned speculation. Romanian trade overall began to shift from West to East. In two years (1980–82) Romanian imports from OECD countries were halved;

> by 1983 Romania was the least active importer of Western goods. As exports to the capitalist states remained stable—though lower—the hard currency trade surplus grew. At the same time, the Romanians began making overtures to the Soviet Union and its CMEA partners indicating their desire to 'improve cooperation' in the areas of raw material and energy trade.[59]

Romania's purchases of Soviet oil—at world market prices in hard currency—amounted to some $700 million in 1981. Though the Romanians' desire for more favourable terms was rejected, trade with CMEA nevertheless increased. CMEA trade, which had accounted for 33 per cent of Romanian total trade turnover in 1980, accounted for 53 per cent in 1983.[60]

Nature, however, was against the regime. A severe earthquake of 1977, followed by floods in 1980 and 1981, disrupted industrial production and reduced the exports of foodstuffs which Ceauşescu now looked to in order to pay off the foreign debt incurred through industrialization. In late 1981, the country's foreign debt rose to $10.4 billion—in 1976 it stood at only $0.5 billion—and Ceausescu requested its rescheduling.[61] On the recommendation of the International Monetary Fund imports were reduced and exports, especially of machinery, equipment and petroleum products, increased. The implications of this reduction of imports were not fully appreciated by foreign analysts at the time; since 1981 Romania had been a net importer of food from the West—food imports from the West in that year totalled $644 million and exports $158 million. In the same year, Soviet statistics show that Romania exported 106,000 tons of frozen meat to the Soviet Union. Cutting back on food imports, while at the same time continuing to export meat to the Soviet Union, forced Ceausescu to introduce meat rationing.[62]

More importantly, the very act of having to accept conditions from the Western banks was a great blow to the Romanian leader's inflated pride. On its heels came political isolation which made him less dependent on the support of foreign governments that might have exercised some influence in persuading him to moderate his policies towards his people. He declared defiantly in December 1982 that he would pay off the foreign debt by 1990—a target in fact reached in April 1989 according to the Romanian press—and to achieve this introduced a series of austerity measures unparalleled even in the bleak history of East-Central European Communist regimes. Rationing of bread, flour, sugar and milk was introduced in some provincial towns in early 1982, and in 1983 it was extended to most of the country, with the exception of the capital. The monthly personal rations were progressively reduced to the point where, on the eve of the 1989 revolution, they were in some regions of the country one kilo of sugar, one kilo of flour, a 500-gram pack of margarine and five eggs. At the same time, heavy industry was also called upon to contribute to the export drive, but because its energy needs outstripped the country's generating capacity drastic energy saving measures were introduced in 1981, which included a petrol ration of 30 litres (about 7 gallons) per month for private car owners. Other strictures stipulated a maximum temperature of 14 degrees centigrade (57 F) in offices and periods of provision of hot water (normally one day a week in flats). In the winter of 1983, these restrictions were extended, causing the interruption of the electricity supply in major cities and reduction of gas pressure during the day so that meals could only be cooked at night. During the severe winter of 1984–85 it was calculated from medical sources in the capital's hospitals that over 30 children had died as a result of unannounced power cuts affecting incubators.

The thesis that Romania's dissent in the CMEA was 'the principal cause of all the problems in the CMEA' obscures any analysis of the real causes of failure of CMEA projects. Such failures were above all

> the consequence of the peculiar composition of the CMEA community, consisting of a motley amalgamation of a superpower with hegemonic aspirations, and other industrially developed countries with different structures, as well as underdeveloped and developing countries. But they are also a consequence of the fact that planned economies do not have adequate contact mechanisms owing to their underdeveloped economic infrastructure, and are basically introverted.[63]

The signature of the Romanian state leadership was present on all important CMEA documents—the Basic Principles for the International Division of Labor, the decisions of the Ninth Council meeting in 1958 on price-forming practices, the agreement on multilateral clearing in transferable rubbles, and many others. Whilst it is true that Romania opposed the creation of supranational decision-making bodies in the CMEA, so too did other countries, such as Poland and Hungary, albeit more discreetly.[64]

Emil Bodnăraş, a Romanian Politburo member, in a discussion with the US ambassador in Romania, Harry G. Barnes in 1974, offered an insight into Romania's view of the CMEA. He explained Romania's concept of CMEA's 'openness', which he defined as the right of member states to cooperate only selectively according to their national economic interests and a receptivity to other states to join in the organization. He stressed that

> the Soviets really mean 'diktat' or 'subordination' when they say 'integration' as the Bulgarian and Hungarian experience showed. He averred that although the Romanians had agreed as a compromise to inclusion of the word 'integration' in the title of the 1971 CMEA complex programme, they had been able to keep the concept out of the text itself except in terms acceptable to them. Romania does not accept, for example, the overall unified plan approach of the Soviets.[65]

The Western share in Romania's total exports was 32.3 per cent in 1970, 35 per cent in 1975 and 36.9 per cent in 1980. The discrepancy between imports and exports from the West led to a dramatic rise in debt to Western banks of 1.6 billion dollars in 1970, 3.1 billion dollars in 1975, 9.3 billion dollars in 1980, and 9.7 billion dollars in 1981.[66] In 1982, Romania was compelled to stop its payments and apply for a postponement of the credits that had fallen due. Romania was not dependent on Soviet oil deliveries. Hence insofar as the country was dependent on imports for its refining capacities, which had in the meantime been expanded to far beyond its possibilities of supply, it did not experience the oil shock, like the other Eastern countries, in its relations with the Soviet Union, but in its relations with third countries as a supplier of crude oil and to the industrial states of the West as an importer of petroleum products. The terms of trade deteriorated, especially in trade with third countries. A drastic turn also took place in trade with the West. The Western share decreased to 28.2 per cent in 1981, 19.9 per cent in 1982, and to 16.2 per cent in 1983.[67] Western imports decreased by 45.5 per cent in one single year, 1982 and in the next year they decreased by another 25.1 per cent compared with 1982. Western imports began to rise again in 1984, but only by 7.3 per cent compared with the preceding year. In 1985 they remained at the 1984 level.

These drastic measures enabled Romania to reduce its debt to Western banks to 6.7 billion dollars in mid-1986, but with stark economic consequences.[68]

> The energy supply to the population was reduced drastically and power plants were placed under military control. Because of the low grain harvest, which was 2.3 per cent lower than in 1984, and low sugar-beet harvest, which had fallen by 27.5 per cent compared with 1984, the supply of the population with basic foods deteriorated drastically.[69]

Notes

1 Ceauşescu had been sole Warsaw Pact leader to receive Nixon in 1967 when he was preparing his run for the US presidency.
2 Paschalis Pechlivanis, 'Between Détente and Differentiation: Nixon's visit to Bucharest in August 1969', *Cold War History*, p.18. DOI:10.1080/14682745.2016.1267144, 2017.
3 Mircea Răceanu, *Cronologie comentată a relaţiilor româno-americane* (Bucharest: Silex, 2005), p.213.
4 Ceauşescu made his second state visit to the US at President Nixon's invitation from 4–7 December 1973.
5 It was signed by President Gerald Ford on 3 January 1975.
6 The phrase used by Corneliu Bogdan, one-time Romanian ambassador to Washington, is describing one of the reasons for President Nixon's visit to Bucharest in August 1969, and borrowed by J.F. Harrington and B.J. Courtney for the title of their book *Tweaking the Nose of the Russians: Fifty Years of American-Romanian Relations, 1940–1990* (Boulder: East European Monographs, 1991); see also Dennis Deletant, *New Evidence on Romania and the Warsaw Pact, 1955–1989*, http://www.wilsoncenter.org/publication/e-dossier-no-6-new-evidence-romania-and-the-warsaw-pact-1955-1989. Accessed 7 April 2017.
7 Mircea Răceanu, *Istoria Naţiunii Celei mai Favorizate în relaţiile româno-americane* (Bucharest: Institutul Naţional pentru Memoria Exilului Românesc, 2005), p.116.
8 Roger Kirk and Mircea Răceanu, *Romania versus the United States. Diplomacy of the Absurd, 1985–1989* (New York: St Martin's Press, 1994), p.5.
9 Răceanu, Cronologie comentată, p.241.
10 State Visit of the President of the Socialist Republic of Romania and Madame Ceauşescu, 13–16 June 1978, Background Note (London: Foreign and Commonwealth Office, June 1978).

11 Pavel Câmpeanu, 'Pe marginea unei recenzii. Mistere şi pseudo-mistere din istoria PCR', vol.22, no.34 (23–30 August), 1995, p.12: 'Chiar la 20 de ani, când, deţinut fiind, nu avea nici o putere, încrederea lui [Ceauşescu] nelimitată în sine se hrănea din neîncrederea la fel de nelimitată în toţi ceilalţi şi mai ales în cei cărora le era ierarhic subordonat'.

12 J.F. Brown, *Eastern Europe and Communist Rule* (Durham and London: Duke University Press, 1988), p.275.

13 M. Almond, The Rise and Fall of Nicolae and Elena Ceauşescu (London: Chapmans, 1992), p.100.

14 V. Georgescu, 'Romania in the 1980s: The Legacy of Dynastic Socialism,' *East European Politics and Societies*, vol.2, no.1 (1988), p.69.

15 The US and, within the European Community, the British, Dutch, French and West German governments took the lead. The Greek and Italian governments, in contrast, were less enthusiastic.

16 Michael Shafir, *Romania, Politics, Economics and Society* (London: Frances Pinter, 1985), p.157.

17 By *holocaust* I mean the systematic mass murder of Jews. The Jewish population of Romania, as recorded in censuses taken in the period 1930–1956, numbered as follows: 728,115 (1930), 356,237 (without ceded Bessarabia and Northern Bukovina) (April 1941), 138,795 (1948), 146,264 (1956) *Populaţia după etnie la recensămintele din perioada 1930–2002* (Bucharest: Institutul Naţional de Statistică, no date) http://www.insse.ro/cms/files/RPL2002INS/vol4/tabele/t1.pdf. Accessed 5 May 2017.

18 Radu Ioanid, *The Holocaust in Romania. The Destruction of Jews and Gypsies under Antonescu Regime, 1940–1944* (Chicago: Ivan R. Dee, 2000). Published in association with the United States Holocaust Memorial Museum), p.108. In his *Evreii sub regimul Antonescu* (Bucharest: Hasefer, 1998, pp.124–47) Ioanid estimates the number of Jews murdered by Romanian and German (Einsatzgruppe D) units in the first weeks of the war as 23,513. Of these 6,348 were victims of the Einsatzgruppe D. Dinu Giurescu, in an analysis of Ioanid's figures, argues that of the number of victims attributed to the Romanian army—that is, 16,805—5,841 were murdered by soldiers from identified units of the Romanian army whose deeds are documented in archives or memoir literature, and 10,964 are "persons murdered without supporting documentary evidence" (D. Giurescu, *România în al doilea război mondial* (Bucharest: All, 1999), p.156).

19 These figures are based on the reports sent to Antonescu by the governors of Bessarabia, Bukovina and Transnistria. They are the numbers of Jews deported and surviving in Transnistria on 15 November 1943; see USHMM. Archive of the Romanian Ministry of Foreign Affairs, RG 25.006m, reel 10, file 21, 133–35; reel 11, file 21, 589. Radu Ioanid estimates a similar death toll in *The Holocaust in Romania. The Destruction of Jews and Gypsies under Antonescu Regime, 1940–1944* (Chicago: Ivan R. Dee, 2000). Published in association with the United States Holocaust Memorial Museum), p.174. D. Bancoş gives a similar figure of 149,000 for the number of Jews deported to Transnistria by Antonescu and puts the total number of victims amongst the Jewish community in Romania at the hands of the Antonescu regime at 119,000 in his study *Social şi naţional în politica guvernului Ion Antonescu* (Bucharest: Editura Eminescu, 2000), p.173. If we add the estimate of between 130,000 and 170,000 local Ukrainian Jews who perished in Transnistria under Romanian administration we have a total figure of between 250,000 and 290,000 Jewish dead. In a report to Antonescu dated 9 December 1941, General Constantin Z. Vasiliu, Inspector-General of the Gendarmerie, stated that 'the evacuation' (sic!) of Jews from Bukovina and Bessarabia has finished. The evacuated Jews have been settled in the areas shown on the attached sketch. Their total numbers are 108,002 (ANIC, Ministerul Afacerilor Interne, Trial of Ion Antonescu, file 40010, vol.8, p.104.

20 A reflection of the callousness of the Romanian authorities in Transnistria towards the local Ukrainian Jews is the often cavalier attitude with which names and numbers were

recorded. This makes an accurate calculation of the numbers of Ukrainian Jews who perished difficult. Furthermore, there is no reliable figure of the numbers of Ukrainian Jews who left Transnistria with the Soviet forces in the summer and autumn of 1941. Consequently, the researcher is thrown back on an educated estimate. Of the 300,000 Jews recorded in the 1939 Soviet census of the region it is estimated that between 100,000 and 150,000 stayed behind in the territory when the Soviet forces withdrew (Ioanid, *The Holocaust in Romania*, p.177). Estimates of Ukrainian Jewish victims in the period from September 1941 to November 1943 range from 130,000 (see Ioanid, *The Holocaust in Romania*, p.289) to "at least 170,000" (see Jean Ancel, *Transnistria*, vol.III (Bucharest: Atlas, 1998), pp.300–1: "Between September 1941 and November 1943 at least 170,000 Ukrainian Jews were killed—the majority by the Romanians—or were handed over to the local German settlers, who butchered them (especially in the county of Berezovka)". As regards the provinces of Bessarabia and Bukovina, Radu Ioanid concludes that a total of 124,000 Jews—81,000 from Bessarabia and 43,000 from Bukovina—withdrew from these provinces with the Soviets in July 1941, leaving approximately 190,000 to face the Romanian and German advances (R. Ioanid, *The Holocaust in Romania*, p.172).

21 Jewish victims of the Holocaust in Hungary numbered 564,000. 63,000 were murdered before German occupation. The 501,000 murdered afterwards included 132,000 Jews from Hungarian-annexed Northern Transylvania; see Randolph L. Braham, 'Northern Transylvania', in *Encyclopedia of the Holocaust*, vol.4 (New York and London: Macmillan, 1990), pp.1476–78 and *Martiriul Evreilor din România, 1940–1944. Documente şi Mărturii* (Bucharest: Editura Hasefer, 1991), doc. 143, p.264 where a report of the Federation of Jewish Communities in Romania (undated) gives the number of Jews in Northern Transylvania before deportation in May 1944 as 165,061, the number deported: 151,180, the number in compulsory labour brigades between 1942 and 1944: 14,881, the number of survivors returning to Transylvania in September 1945: 15,769 (9.4%), the number of survivors in other countries: 10,000 (6.1%) and the number murdered in the death camps: 130,000. In a separate report by the Romanian section of the World Jewish Congress, published in Bucharest in 1945, the following details were presented about the fate of the Jews from Northern Transylvania under Hungarian occupation: the Jewish population of Northern Transylvania according to the Hungarian census of 31 January 1941 totalled 151,125 persons. The numbers surviving at 1 September 1945 were put at 29,405. Between May and June 1944, 137,486 Jews were deported from the region by the Hungarian and German authorities to labour and death camps in Poland and Germany. Of these 15,769 had been repatriated to Northern Transylvania by 1 September 1945. 13,636 Jews from Northern Transylvania escaped deportation, either by working for the auxiliary services of the Hungarian army, or by hiding (*La population juivre de la Transylvanie du Nord*, Section de Roumanie du Congrès Juif Mondial, Bucharest, 1945).

22 Ghita Ionescu, *Communism in Romania, 1944–1962* (London: Oxford University Press, 1964), p.184.

23 For an authoritative examination of the role of Pauker and that of her brother, Zalman Robinson, in the emigration of Romania's Jews at this time see Radu Ioanid, *The Ransom of the Jews* (Chicago: Ivan Dee, 2005), pp.56–62.

24 Ioanid, The Ransom of the Jews, p.76.

25 Pacepa, *Red Horizons* (London: Heinemann, 1988), p.73.

26 Born in 1900 in Munkacevo, Jakober had fled the rising tide of anti-Semitism in Hungary to Britain in 1938 (Ioanid, *The Ransom of the Jews*, p.84).

27 Pacepa, *Red Horizons*, p.73.

28 Ioanid, *The Ransom of the Jews*, pp.131–34.

29 Dennis Deletant, *Ceauşescu and the Securitate. Coercion and Dissent in Romania, 1965–89* (London: Hurst & Co.; New York: M.E. Sharpe, 1995), pp.208–9.

30 Pacepa, *Red Horizons*, p.75.

31 See later in this chapter.

32 Y. Govrim, 'Organizarea Comunităţilor Evreieşti din România în timpul lui Ceauşescu', p.7 (paper presented at a Conference on the History of the Jews in Romania at Tel Aviv University on 17 December 1991).
33 G. Galloway and B. Wylie, *Downfall: The Ceauşescus and the Romanian Revolution* (London: Futura, 1991), p.77.
34 Claudiu Florian, Dumitru Preda, and Ottmar Traşcă, *România-Republica Federală Germania, vol.1. Începutul Relaţiilor Diplomatice, 1966–1967* (Bucharest: Editura Enciclopedică, 2009), p.xxxvii.
35 http://en.wikipedia.org/wiki/Demographics of Romania. The number of Romanians was given as 13,597,613 (85.7%). Accessed 7 April 2017.
36 Florica Dobre, Luminiţa Banu, Florian Banu, and Laura Stancu (eds.), *Acţiunea "Recuperarea". Securitatea şi Emigrarea Germanilor din România (1962–1989)* (Bucharest: Editura Enciclopedică, 2011), p.lxxix, footnote 262.
37 Limited emigration of Germans from Romania had been permitted in the 1950s and 1960s to East Germany but the bulk of the 17,290 Germans who had left since 1950 had gone to West Germany after the opening of diplomatic relations between Romania and West Germany in 1967.
38 Robert King, Minorities under Communism. Nationalities as a Source of Tension among Balkan Communist States (Cambridge, Massachusetts: Harvard University Press, 1973), p.166.
39 *Acţiunea "Recuperarea"*, doc.2, pp.36–38.
40 This model was used for agreements made by the DIE with lawyers and intermediaries in other countries (e.g. the United Kingdom, Switzerland) for the issue of a permanent exit visa (in Romanian *o viză de plecare definitivă*).
41 See above.
42 It had the call sign UM 0107.
43 The tariffs by category were as follows: graduates (Jews) $3,000, (Germans) DM 11,000; students (Jews) $1,700, (Germans) DM 7,000; workers (Jews) $600, DM 2,900; unqualified (Jews) $500, (Germans) DM 1,800; see Radu Ioanid (ed.), *Securitatea şi vânzarea evreilor. Istoria acordurilor secrete dintre România şi Israel* (Iaşi: Polirom), 2015, pp.439–41. Erwin Wickert, the West German ambassador to Bucharest in the period 1971–1976, listed in his memoirs different tariff levels for Germans to emigrate to West Germany: 1,800 DM ($650) for a person without university education; 5,500 DM ($1,964) for a student; 7,000 DM ($2,500) for a student in their final year; 11,000 DM ($3,298) for a graduate, and 2,900 DM ($1,035) for a skilled worker (Erwin Wickert, *Die Glücklichen Augen. Geschichten aus meinem Leben* (Stuttgart-München, Deutsche Verlagsanstalt, 2001), p.54).
44 Author's conversations with family members who emigrated from Romania to West Germany.
45 Calculated from figures in *Acţiunea "Recuperarea"* p.lxxix, footnote 262.
46 *Ibid.*
47 http://countrystudies.us/romania/77.htm. Accessed 19 January 2017.
48 William Wilkinson, *An Account of the Principalities of Wallachia and Moldavia* (London: Longman, Hurst, Rees, Orme, and Brown, 1820), pp.168–76. Wilkinson was among the first to put a figure on the numbers of Roma in the principalities. They were not emancipated until 1856.
49 Viorel Achim, 'Deportarea ţiganilor în Transnistria', *Anuarul IRIR 2002*, Bucharest, 2003, p.129.
50 *Populaţia după etnie la recensămintele din perioada 1930–2002* (Bucharest: Institutul Naţional de Statistică, no date), http://www.insse.ro/cms/files/RPL2002INS/vol4/tabele/t1.pdf. Accessed 5 May 2017. In the 1992 census, the Roma population was recorded as 401,087 persons.
51 Michael Shafir, *Romania. Politics, Economics and Society* (London: Frances Pinter, 1985), pp.70–76.

52 The *Securitate*'s obsessive concern with Ceauşescu's well-being led it to attempt to recruit his doctor Abraham Schachter as an informer and to place such pressure upon him that under that the latter committed suicide on 14 March 1973. Ceauşescu reacted by denouncing the *Securitate*'s methods at a meeting of the Executive Committee of the Central Committee of RCP on 14 March 1973 and by dismissing the Minister of Internal Affairs, Ion Stănescu. Schachter (born in 1916), was the personal physician of both Nicolae and Elena Ceauşescu and of former Interior Minister Alexandru Drăghici and his wife Marta; see Mihnea Berindei, Dorin Dobrincu, and Armand Goşu (eds.), *Istoria Comunismului din România.* Vol.III. *Documente Nicolae Ceauşescu (1972–1975)* (Iaşi: Polirom, 2016), p.141, footnote 15.
53 *Scînteia*, 21 November 1985.
54 Michael Marrese, 'CMEA: Effective but Cumbersome Political Economy', *International Organization*, vol.40, no.2 (Spring 1986), pp.287–327 [p.305].
55 *Ibid.*, p.306.
56 *Ibid.*, p.307.
57 *Ibid.*, p.302.
58 Ronald H. Linden, 'Socialist Patrimonialism and the Global Economy, the Case of Romania' (Paper prepared for the Conference on Foreign Economic Strategies of Eastern Europe, University of California, Berkeley, 1–2 February 1985), p.14, quoted from Marrese, 'CMEA', p.315.
59 Marrese, 'CMEA', p.315.
60 *Ibid.*
61 Cornel Ban, 'Sovereign Debt, Austerity and Regime Change', *East European Politics and Societies and Cultures*, vol.26, no.4 (November 2012), pp.743–76 [p.758].
62 A.H. Smith, 'The Romanian Enterprise', in I. Jeffries (ed.), *Industrial Reform in Socialist Countries* (London: Edward Elgar, 1992), p.204.
63 Adam Zwass, The Council for Mutual Economic Assistance. The Thorny Path from Political to Economic Integration (New York: M.E. Sharpe, 1989), p.47.
64 *Ibid.*, p.196.
65 *Cold War International History Project Digital Archive*, 'Memorandum of Conversation between Emil Bodnăraş and Harry G. Barnes, US Ambassador to Romania', 24 May 1974, History and Public Policy Program Digital Archive, Selected US Documents on Sino-American and Romanian/Soviet Relations (1969–1974) obtained by Mircea Munteanu, Cold War International History Project, from the National Archives, College park, Nixon NSC Box 701/703, for the George Washington Cold War Conference on the Sino-American Opening and the Cold War (1969–1972), George Washington University, 8–9 February 2002. http://digitalarchive.wilsoncenter.org/document/110457, accessed 17 April 2017.
66 Zwass, *The Council*, pp.261–62.
67 *Ibid.*
68 "The produced national product increased by 3.8%, 7.7% and 5.9% in 1983, 1984 and 1985 respectively compared with the preceding year in each case. Growth in the machinery construction industry and the consumer goods industry was above average, 7.9% in 1985, but oil production decreased by 6.6% and gas extraction by 3.2%. Coal production was 46.6 million tons, short of the plan target of 64 million tons. Crude oil production was 10.7 million tons compared with a plan target of 12.6 million tons, and natural gas extraction was 27 million cubic meters, compared with a plan target of 32.8 million cubic meters" (*Ibid.*).
69 All these economic indicators are taken from Zwass, *The Council*, p.200.

13 Promoting national identity: Transylvania and Bessarabia

Just as Gheorghiu-Dej had gained internal legitimacy by distancing himself from the Soviet Union, an achievement marked by the withdrawal of Soviet troops in July 1958, so Ceauşescu appealed to national sentiment to consolidate his own rule.[1] Among his instruments were the issues of Transylvania and Bessarabia (at that time the Moldovan Soviet Socialist Republic). Both were used as a counterbalance to each other in the triangular relationship between Romania, Hungary and the Soviet Union. Moscow used the Transylvanian question both to put pressure on Romania and to encourage Hungary's loyalty. Ceauşescu responded by reminding Moscow that veiled irredentism was a game that two could play and stoked the Bessarabian controversy.

Romanian and Hungarian sensitivities over Transylvania stem from the fact that the province is regarded by both Romanians and Hungarians as an integral part of their ancestral homeland and in the minds of both peoples their own survival as a nation is linked to the fate of Transylvania. The latter region was conquered by the Roman Emperor Trajan in a campaign lasting from 105 to 107 AD and renamed Dacia. Intermarriage between Romans and the indigenous Dacians created the Daco-Roman population, one which pre-dated the arrival of the Magyars in the province at the end of the ninth century AD. 'Romanian primacy' in Dacia was a political tool designed to give historical legitimacy to Ceauşescu; the so-called 'independent centralized Dacian state' which, it was argued, was created under the Dacian king Burebista circa 80 BC, was presented as the archetype of the modern Romanian state ruled by Burebista's present-day counterpart. By extension, Ceauşescu was presented in official literature as the latest in a line of Romanian heroes who are seen as defenders of Romanian national identity and unity.[2] These include Stephen the Great, Prince of Moldavia (1457–1504), who for a while fought off Turkish and Polish attempts to subjugate his people, and Michael the Brave, who succeeded briefly in bringing the principalities of Moldavia, Wallachia and Transylvania together under his rule at the beginning of the seventeenth century, and, admitted to this band more recently, Alexandru Ioan Cuza, whose election as Prince in both Moldavia and Wallachia in 1859 effectively brought about their union.

Under Ceauşescu, the regime's efforts to strengthen Romanian national consciousness were accompanied by playing down the significance in the history of

Transylvania of the role of the minority Hungarian and German communities. In the teaching of history at secondary school level the principal Hungarian and German figures of Transylvanian history received no mention whatsoever judging from the guidelines laid down by the Ministry of Education.[3] Such insensitivity to both peoples' historical heritage, while fuelling their simmering resentment of the regime, confirmed the role which Romanian national historiography was called upon to play, namely that of promoting the primacy of Ceauşescu and of the Romanians in Romania.

For the Hungarians, Transylvania remains part of the homeland which was unjustly amputated at the Paris Peace Settlement after the First World War and they understandably show a natural concern for the fate of their 1.2 million minority in the province. Yet complaints about the treatment of the minority are, again understandably, equated by the Romanians with territorial ambitions on the part of Hungary to detach the province from Romania. It is this contiguity of Hungary, coupled with the size of the Hungarian minority, which made and continues to make, the treatment of the Hungarian minority such a sensitive issue for both states, and distinguished it from the problem of other minorities, such as the German one.

When Transylvania was transferred from Hungarian to Romanian rule its inhabitants, Romanian, Hungarian and German, had been promised some form of federal or devolved association with the new polity. This promise was ignored, in favour of centralized rule from Bucharest. This ruled out a possible accommodation between the government and those of its citizens who now found themselves a minority.

In the Communist period, integration or, as Ceauşescu often termed it, 'homogenization', was an extension of the strategy of consolidation of the newly enlarged state pursued by Romanian governments in the interwar period. The process had been accelerated by the drive for industrialization undertaken by the Communist regime after 1948. It increased the urbanization of the population as a whole and led to massive migrations of workers, usually from Romanian areas into those of Hungarian population.[4] Moreover, the emphasis in industrialization on *equal* regional development and modernization reflected the Romanian view about the relationship between individual and group rights, an understanding of which is also fundamental to an analysis of the Romanian perception of minorities.

After the Second World War, Soviet hegemony over both Hungary and Romania damped down jurisdictional conflict between the two. The Hungarian population (26% in 1945) received, and exercised, certain rights, mainly cultural. Additionally, two Hungarians Vasile Luca and Alexandru Moghioroş were members of the Politburo. The purge of Luca in 1952 was no more instigated by anti-Hungarian sentiment than that of Pauker was by anti-Semitic feeling. Equalization, the professed driving force behind the Party's revolutionary reform programme, brought for the peoples of Romania, irrespective of their ethnic identity, an equality in suffering. Just as Hungarians joined the Romanian Communist Party in 1945 in large numbers and provided their share of officers for the *Securitate*, so many were victims of the new regime. But the Hungarians' contribution to the forces of coercion was not disproportionate to the size of their community. An examination of the ethnic background of senior officers in the *Securitate* in 1948 shows that of a total of 60 only three were Hungarian. If we take the total number of staff listed in the records of the time, we find that of the 3,973 personnel recorded only 247 were Hungarians and most of these were employed in those regional directorates which covered the major concentrations of Hungarian population such as Braşov, Cluj, Oradea, Sibiu and Timişoara.[5]

As victims of Communist oppression Hungarians were affected by the persecution of the Roman Catholic Church which had in 1948 1.3 million faithful, most of whom were Hungarians and Germans. More than 700,000 Hungarians belonged to the Reformed or Calvinist Church, and 70,000 to the Unitarian Church. Control by the Communist government of the Roman Catholic Church met with great resistance from the priests and their congregations.

The first indication from the Romanian regime that special recognition might be given to the Hungarian minority was the announcement in the constitution of 1952, published on 18 July, of the formation of a Hungarian Autonomous Region (*Regiunea Autonomă Maghiară)*.[6] The regional capital was located in the city of Târgu-Mureş. There was no doubt about the region's Hungarian character, for according to the census of 21 February 1956 it had a population of 731,361, of whom 567,509 were Hungarians and 145,718 Romanians, but the fact that it embraced only a third of the Hungarians living in Romania gave rise to accusations that its boundaries were drawn to make the area "as small as possible" and "as far as possible from the Hungarian border".[7] A counter-argument could be that none of the other areas of Transylvania with a large Hungarian population was predominantly Hungarian. On ethnic criteria another autonomous region for Hungarians could have been set up along the Hungarian border.[8] Yet this would have posed security problems for Romania and have invited Hungarian claims for territorial adjustment in her favour. Establishing the Hungarian Autonomous Region (HAR) in eastern Transylvania posed no such security problems since it was far from the border and enclosed by areas with a majority Romanian population.

The creation of this region was the only example—with the exception of Yugoslavia—of integrative minority policy in post-war Communist East-Central Europe, and represented an attempt to solve a deeply rooted national question by giving administrative 'autonomy' to a predominantly Hungarian area of Transylvania.[9] The ideological underpinning of the region, dictated to the Romanian Party by Soviet leadership in 1952, followed the Bolshevik pattern of territorial autonomy elaborated by Lenin and Stalin in the early 1920s. The Hungarians of the region became a 'titular nationality' and were accorded significant cultural rights. However, the Romanian leadership also used the region as an instrument of political and social integration of the Hungarian minority into the communist state. The ideological framework into which the Romanian Communist Party attempted to set the creation of the HAR did not obscure the tensions between the Hungarian and Romanian populations of the area, on the contrary, the use of the term 'autonomy' in official public discourse merely served to exacerbate them. The borders of the area historically designated Szeklerland (*Székelyföld*), which for centuries until 1918, and again between 1940 and 1944, had formed part of Hungary, were radically modified. The entire area had been divided in 1950 under a national territorial reorganization into two regions which took the place of the previous four Szekler counties: the Braşov (renamed Stalin in 1950) region, taking its name from the eponymous capital, and the Mureş region, with its principal centre Târgu-Mureş (Marosvásárhely), a town which had at that time a population of about 47,000 (35,000 Hungarians, 11,000 Romanians and about 1,000 Jews). The Mureş region had a Hungarian majority (52%), though it also included Romanian districts such as Târnăveni and Luduş.

The division of the Szeklerland was justified on economic grounds by a Party commission headed by the Minister of the Interior, Teohari Georgescu. The backwardness of Szeklerland was attributed by the commission to both the lack of a modern industrial network and links to major transport junctions. To address this it was proposed that economic contacts between the industrialized city of Braşov and its hinterland be developed. The population of the HAR was promised investment which would put an end to large-scale massive migration to more developed parts of Transylvania and to Bucharest.

To the population of Romania at large the RCP's position was that the establishment of the HAR "corresponded to the fundamental interests of the Romanian working people", and went on to warn Hungarians that comrade Stalin said "autonomy does not mean independence", on the contrary, regional autonomy was "the most concrete form of unity".[10] Official propaganda did not describe the region as an exclusively Hungarian region but as an integrative structure, where every nationality could feel at home.

The question that arose from creation of the HAR is what administrative and territorial autonomy actually meant. In the assessment of one scholar, the establishment of HAR provoked quite a paradoxical situation.

> On the one hand the center kept political and repressive power and control in its hands. On the other hand, the Party itself was aware of the fact that the word 'autonomy' had not lost its meaning for the Transylvanian Hungarians, neither as a consequence of the trauma of World War II nor resulting from the internationalist rhetoric of Communism. In view of the fact that officially taboo subjects such as nationality rights and autonomy were publicly raised, the propaganda campaign involuntarily became a catalyst of national conflicts in an area where rivalry between Romanians and Hungarians—more exactly a mutually exclusive nation-building—had deep, historical traditions.[11]

The word 'autonomy' seemed to produce a conditioned reflex in some Hungarians who thought it was a move towards reannexation by Hungary, the memory of which—in 1940—was very much alive in the collective consciousness, while the Romanian population (whether they were born there or settlers) feared that they would once again become "foreigners in their own land".[12]

Obvious though the Hungarian character of the region was, its autonomy was spurious for its status differed in no way from that of the other 16 regions. This was made clear by article 20 which stipulated that "the laws of the Romanian People's Republic and the decisions and directives of the central organs of state are compulsory in the territory of the Magyar Autonomous Region".[13] The State Council of the Autonomous Region, designated by article 57 as "the organ of state power", was merely a facade. In practice, the region did not enjoy self-government of any kind, and the only distinguishing features of its existence were that most of its officials were Hungarian, the Hungarian language could be used in administration and in the courts, and that bilingual Hungarian and Romanian signs were put up on public buildings.[14] Suspicions that the region was merely a sop to minority aspirations, and a pretext for not creating more cultural facilities for the Hungarians elsewhere, were reinforced by the abolition in 1953 of the specifically Hungarian wing of the Party but with its disappearance went any mechanism for defending the collective rights of the Hungarians; the extent to which the regime was prepared to tolerate the expression of individual rights became clear in 1956.[15]

The impact of the Hungarian uprising in Budapest upon Hungarian students and workers in Romania raised questions for the Party leadership about their loyalty to the state. Yet the repercussions of the revolt were also felt amongst the Romanians where the discontent with the regime was manifested in protests which had a largely economic basis.

Gheorghiu-Dej's concern over the reaction of the Hungarian minority in Transylvania to the uprising led him to pursue a policy of integration and his first step was to dilute the provision for Hungarian language teaching in schools, making it more difficult to receive a Hungarian language education up to university level in Romania. At the apex of the system of primary and secondary education in Hungarian stood the Hungarian language Bolyai University in Cluj, the Dr Petru Groza agricultural college in the same city, and the medical-pharmaceutical faculty at Târgu-Mureş. After 1956 this structure was whittled away. Hungarian language instruction began to be moved from single language schools to dual language ones.[16]

This effectively blurred the distinct status of the language and was carried to its logical conclusion with the merger of the Bolyai University in Cluj with the Romanian language Babeş University in the same city. At a meeting of the teaching staffs of both universities in June 1959 at which Ceauşescu, as Central Committee Secretary, is said to have presided, the merger was ratified[17] but the image of consensus was shattered by the suicide of a pro-rector of Bolyai University, László Szabedi. Despite the fact that special streams in each faculty in the merged Babeş-Bolyai University were reserved for Hungarian students, and classes and examinations were conducted in Hungarian, the closure of the separate university removed the distinct institutional identity which had ensured the provision of Hungarian language teaching and exposed it to erosion from within the new structure. And that erosion was not slow to take place.

A similar dilution took place in the administrative role played by Hungarians in the university. At the time of the merger the rector was Romanian but two of the three pro-rectors were Hungarian. By 1967, the number of pro-rectorships had been increased to five, of whom three were Romanian, seven of the eight deans were Romanian as was 61 per cent of the teaching staff.[18] In the Dr Petru Groza agricultural institute separate language instruction in Hungarian was dropped.

The policy of integration was extended in 1968 from education to local administration when two districts with a heavy Szekler population were transferred from the HAR to the Braşov region and three new ones with a majority Romanian population added. The proportion of Hungarians in the new region was reduced from 77 to 62 per cent, while that of Romanians increased from 20 to 35 per cent.[19] Concern about these changes spilt over from the Hungarian minority to Budapest. Within a month three senior members of the Hungarian politburo went to Romania and while there were no tangible results from their visit, they may have prevented the introduction of even further measures which would have affected the position of the Hungarian minority.

Gheorghiu-Dej's integrationist policy was concomitant with his assertion of autonomy from the Soviet Union. National Communism demanded national cohesion, hence the steps designed to obscure the distinct identity of the Hungarian Autonomous Region. They were paralleled by a series of anti-Russian measures in 1963, which involved closing the Russian Institute in Bucharest, eliminating Russian as a compulsory school subject, and replacing the Russian names of streets and public buildings with Romanian ones.

Gheorghiu-Dej's policy was continued by Ceauşescu. Some impartial observers detected an initial improvement in the position of the minorities, noting a wider use of the Hungarian language in Transylvania, but still pointing out restrictions on cultural exchanges.[20] Periodicals and newspapers from Hungary were only available in limited numbers although a publishing house in Bucharest specifically dedicated to the publication of literature in Hungarian and German continued to produce generous print runs of original works by Transylvanian Hungarian and German writers, as well as editions of novels and poetry written by national Hungarian and German authors. A measure of the prudence accorded by Ceauşescu to the minorities was the fact that his first domestic visits after becoming Party leader were to areas with large Hungarian populations and his speeches set the limits of his minority policies. On the one hand, he recognized the right of the Hungarians to their own culture and to use their own language, but on the other he was firm in his condemnation of "nationalism and national chauvinism".[21] Within a short time his preference for integration became clear in the proposals for administrative reform of 1967, but as his rule developed, integration turned into assimilation.

In 1967 and 1968, 'the Hungarian problem' for the regime was put into the context of administrative and territorial reform of the country as a whole.[22] To allay the concern of the Hungarian minority that the territorial reorganization would remove the little autonomy that it had Ceauşescu explained that "geographical and social-political conditions, the national composition of the population, traditional cultural connections... will have to be taken into consideration when forming the [new] counties", and emphasized that

> the local administrative bodies will see to it that
> the provisions of the country's constitution regarding the use of the
> mother tongue in the state administration, in schools and in cultural

> institutions are strictly observed in those localities where co-inhabiting nationalities live.[23]

The promotion of Mihai Gere and János Fazekas, the two most senior Hungarians in the Party leadership, to high office gave the minority some cosmetic reassurance.[24] Fazekas from the Politburo proposed that a 'strong county' comprising the most heavily populated Hungarian areas be created. His proposal was not, however, accepted by the Party commission charged with establishing the new administrative areas. Instead a compromise was worked out which still left a strong concentration of Hungarians but in two counties, not in a single one. The new form of organization into counties passed by the National Assembly in February 1968 left Hungarian speakers in a majority of more counties than previously in the old regions, but without the possibility of creating a single, clearly delineated, monolithic bloc of Hungarians, which could have presented a more convincing claim for autonomy. Some Hungarian counties were singled out for special investment under the development plan which aimed at equalizing the levels of industrialization to promote faster economic growth of the country. It is difficult to establish where administrative and economic reasons gave way to conscious population engineering. In one case, however, boundary changes turned a Hungarian majority into a minority.

In contrast to its reaction to the dissolution of the HAR in 1960, the Hungarian government made no move to suggest disapproval of this territorial reorganization. Hungary's relations with Romania were conditioned by Soviet attitudes towards the latter and the fidelity of the Romanian leadership to Moscow during the Hungarian uprising of 1956, and conversely, the revolt by Budapest, ensured that for a brief period until the end of the fifties, the treatment of the Hungarian minority was not an issue. However, as Gheorghiu-Dej developed his policy of autonomy from Moscow, a concomitant expression of Hungarian interest in Transylvania was heard. While never officially raising the minority question, senior Hungarian Party figures alluded to it on a number of occasions.

The Romanian leadership put this renewed Hungarian interest in their minority down to Moscow's irritation at the new course adopted by Bucharest in its domestic and foreign policy. In response, the RCP sponsored the publication of historical studies supporting Romania's rights to Bessarabia—most notably Karl Marx's *Notes on the Romanians* in December 1964, which broke the taboo of speaking openly about the Soviet annexation of Bessarabia and the Romanian identity of its population. This tit-for-tat response by Gheorghiu-Dej was the first in a series that was to punctuate Romanian-Soviet relations until the disintegration of the Soviet Union. So Transylvania was not just a Romanian-Hungarian issue, but a trigger for Romania to hint at reopening the question of Bessarabia, and even today, after Moldova's affirmation of its independence, Romania's legitimate interest in the new republic can be invoked by Budapest as a parallel for Hungarian interest in Transylvania.

The Soviet-led invasion of Czechoslovakia in 1968 presented Ceauşescu with his first major challenge concerning the Hungarian minority. The convergence of Soviet and Hungarian interest was once again mirrored in the strong criticism which both governments levelled at Ceauşescu for condemning the invasion. Fears that unrest among the minorities might be used as an excuse by the Soviet leaders to intervene in Romania led Ceauşescu to make a rapid tour of the major urban areas with significant Hungarian populations at the end of the month. His speeches in the two Hungarian counties of Covasna and Harghita were concessionary: ten major enterprises would be built there during the current five-year plan, for "there can be no true equality of rights, the national question cannot be considered solved, if material conditions are not ensured".[25] Two telegrams from groups of Hungarian and German intellectuals in support of the Party's attitude over Czechoslovakia were widely published.[26] In September Ceauşescu visited the counties bordering Hungary and Yugoslavia, obviously to nip any possible ethnic problems in the bud and to consolidate his position as a leader of all the peoples of Romania. Ceauşescu's fear of an outbreak of minority discontent was probably exaggerated: the Hungarian contribution of troops to the invasion of Czechoslovakia aroused as much disapproval amongst Hungarians in Hungary as it did amongst the Hungarian minority in Transylvania, and a common fear of the Soviet Union helped to improve relations between the ethnic groups in Transylvania. This improvement was reflected in increasing the number of radio and television programmes in Hungarian and German, and in extending the print runs of minority language publications. Greater representation of Hungarian and German interests was suggested by the establishment in 1969 of separate Hungarian and German Nationality Workers Councils.

An informed reader may well ask why Ceauşescu did not seek to exploit the dissatisfaction of the Hungarian minority by affording them the same conditions of emigration as those offered to Romania's Jewish and German minority. A cynical answer would be that there were no such similar hard currency spoils to be made from Hungarian emigration. The Hungarian currency was a soft one and presented little interest to Ceauşescu and the *Securitate*. Second, from the ideological point of view, emigration of an ethnic minority from one fraternal socialist state to another, could be construed as a failure to solve the 'minority problem' in the state of origin. For the Hungarian government there was certainly every reason to discourage large-scale emigration of the Transylvanian Hungarians to Hungary: it would pose enormous social and economic problems since a considerable proportion of a population some one-fifth the size of the total population of Hungary was involved.

For the time being the principal momentum for that leverage came from Soviet concern over Bucharest's foreign policy. Ceauşescu's state visit to China in June 1971, coupled with a warming of Yugoslavia's relations with Beijing, led Moscow to fear the development of a pro-Chinese camp in the Balkans which would challenge Soviet dominance of the area. Hungary took on the role of defender of the Soviet interest by criticizing both Yugoslavia and Romania while Soviet displeasure with Romania was manifested in the fact that Prime Minister Alexei Kosygin and not Party leader Brezhnev met Ceauşescu during his brief stopover at Moscow on his way back from the Far East. On the very day of Ceauşescu's return to Bucharest, 24 June, the degree of Soviet disapproval could be measured by

Hungary's dramatic resurrection of the minority question, on this occasion publicly for the first time since the imposition of Communist rule in Eastern Europe.[27] Zoltan Komocsin, a member of the Hungarian Politburo, declared in a statement to the Hungarian parliament: "We are fundamentally interested in having the inhabitants of both our country and Romania, including those of Hungarian nationality living there, come to understand that the fate and destiny of our peoples are inseparable from socialism". Komocsin's statement stung the Romanians and a long article by Paul Niculescu-Mizil, Central Committee Secretary in charge of relations with other Communist parties, appeared in *Scînteia* on 9 July accusing the Hungarians of 'flagrant' contradictions in their reporting of Ceauşescu's visit to China and advising them not to interfere in the internal affairs of Romania where all working people enjoyed equal rights, irrespective of their nationality.

On the same day, Ceauşescu himself alluded to the Hungarian intervention in a speech to Party representatives on political and cultural ideology in which he took the opportunity to broadly explain the regime's policies towards the minorities. They were, in his view, part of the new society which was being created under Communism in Romania:

> Widespread settlement over the course of centuries has led to Romanians, Magyars, Germans and other nationalities living side by side; everything that has been built in the circumstances of the past, and especially the present successes of socialist construction, is the joint work of the Romanian, Magyar and German working people and of those of other nationalities who... benefit today from the results of the building of our new society.[28]

This equated the new society with the Romanian nation and it followed from this conception that the minorities belonged not to other nations, but to the Romanian one. All citizens had equal rights, regardless of nationality. Ceauşescu warned that "Anybody trying to pursue a policy of national hatred pursues a policy against Socialism and Communism—and must be treated consequently as an enemy of our Socialist nation".[29]

Ceauşescu was careful to appeal to ideology in framing his scarcely veiled criticism of the Hungarians, an approach he consistently adopted in rebutting any attacks on his regime from within the socialist camp, but his use of 'enemies of the socialism' was applied equally to Western countries and appeared more frequently in his rhetoric after the signing of the Helsinki Summit Final Act in 1975. The Helsinki Agreement marked a watershed in the importance attached by the international community to the observance of human, and by extension, minority rights. It made respect for these rights a matter of legitimate concern for the international community and in practice linked economic credits and trade to a country's performance in this area. Romania's record on human rights since the imposition of Communist rule was once the worst in the socialist bloc. While the regime had ratified or signed a number of international instruments guaranteeing the rights of individuals and national minorities, its respect for them was totally arbitrary.

Safeguarding minority rights had always been hampered by problems of definition. The guiding principle behind the international agreements on human rights was the primacy of the individual rights of the citizen. Both the European Convention for the Protection of Human Rights (1950), to which Romania was not a signatory, and the Helsinki Final Act, to which it was, emphasize that rights are to be enjoyed and protected individually—hence the use of the "persons belonging to minorities" formula in them—and take the view that the individual, and not the minority group, is the possessor of rights. The practice of the United Nations followed this principle. After 1948, when the General Assembly of the UN adopted the Universal Declaration of Human Rights, the violation of individual human rights by governments was regularly condemned and was regarded as a matter for international interest. The same could not be said about minority rights. Whereas individual rights were no longer a strictly internal matter for the member governments of the UN, the issue of minority rights was, in most cases, kept as an internal preserve of the state by appeal to Article 2(7) of the UN Charter which precluded intervention in "matters which are essentially within the domestic jurisdiction of any state". Ceauşescu availed himself fully of this article in attempting to deflect criticism of his record on human rights' observance. In the absence of a legal definition of minority rights, and the consequent lack of treaty-based obligations covering them, measures in support of minority protection were largely limited to expressions of concern in the UN Commission of Human Rights in Geneva.

The absence of a legal concept for minority rights did not mean that minority protection in certain areas of human activity such as culture had not been legally established. In defining such protection international instruments had accepted that there was a collective dimension to individual rights. The UN Covenant on Civil and Political Rights (1966), to which Romania had adhered, stated (Article 27):

> In those states in which ethnic, religious or linguistic minorities exist, persons belonging to such minorities shall not be denied the right, in community with the other members of their group, to enjoy their own culture, to profess and to practice their own religion, or to use their own language.

By committing Romania to the Helsinki Agreement of 1975 Ceauşescu opened the door to international scrutiny of the regime's treatment of the Hungarian and German minorities in Transylvania and the Banat, and at the same time offered encouragement to those governments who wished to press the matter to do so. While the West German authorities were anxious not to prejudice the emigration of Germans from Romania, the Hungarian government was bound by no such consideration. Indeed, the latter was aware of the pressure it could exert on Bucharest by exploiting any publicity that was unfavourable for a state whose autonomous foreign policy was partly dependent on Western approval. Other facts converged to make the minority issue a more sensitive one and to aggravate relations between Hungary and Romania. One was the increasing disparity between the living standards of the two countries. Economic reform and Soviet subsidies had enabled the Hungarian government to provide its citizens with greater prosperity and a quality of life which outstripped that in Romania, causing at once admiration amongst the Hungarian minority, and envy amongst some Romanians. At a popular level the sight of Hungarians from Hungary bringing goods unavailable in Romania to their relatives in Transylvania was often mentioned with resentment to foreign visitors to the province.

A second development was the opportunity afforded by the Helsinki Agreement to the Hungarian minority to release its pent-up anger at what they regarded as discriminatory policies. This they did in *samizdat* publications produced illegally in Romania which increased considerably the amount of information about the Hungarian minority's position and as a result forced Bucharest to justify its policies. Hungarians in Transylvania began to speak out about their treatment at the same time as a small number of Romanian intellectuals, such as Paul Goma and Vlad Georgescu (discussed below), made their own general criticism of the regime. A string of protests began to be heard from Transylvanian Hungarians in the spring of 1977. One particular case was that of János Torok, a textile worker in Cluj, who publicly complained in March 1975 about the process for preselecting candidates for the Grand National Assembly whom he declared would not represent the best interests of the factory workers, in particular those of the Hungarian minority. He was detained whilst speaking, severely beaten by officers of the *Securitate* and then interned in the Dr Petru Groza psychiatric hospital where he was injected with large doses of drugs. He was freed in 1978 but still required to report regularly for checkups.[30]

Most of the Hungarians arrested for anti-regime protests were driven by their resentment over the erosion of provision for education in their native tongue. Some even died in mysterious circumstances. Lajos Kuthy, a Hungarian teacher from Braşov, was found shot dead in a forest near the city in 1976. Before his death he had collected signatures for a petition seeking the setting up of Hungarian classes in the Braşov region Jenő Szikzai, another teacher from Braşov, was picked up by the *Securitate* in the spring of 1977 and accused of persuading Hungarians to send their children to schools with Hungarian sections rather than to purely Romanian ones. He was beaten during interrogation and on his release from custody committed suicide.

The education issue dominated memoranda prepared in 1977 by two Hungarians from Transylvania, György Lazar (a pseudonym), and Lajos Takács.[31] Takács's memorandum was far more significant. Apart from the fact that the author was bold enough not to hide behind a pseudonym, the senior positions that Takács had held in the Romanian Communist Party gave particular weight and credence to his protest. As a former rector of the Bolyai University in Cluj and instrument of the regime in forcing its merger in 1959 with the Babeş university, and at the time of the memorandum vice president of the Hungarian Nationality Workers Council, Takács was well placed to furnish reliable data about the erosion of teaching in Hungarian in the education system, and to comment upon the effectiveness of the Workers Council. From references in the document it appeared that the memorandum was written in November 1977 but knowledge of it only reached the Western media in the spring of 1978 when *The Times, The Financial Times and The Guardian* referred to it on 25 April.

Addressing educational measures Takács argued that the merging of Romanian and Hungarian streams in a single school had led to a gradual reduction in the number of schools providing instruction in Hungarian. He pointed out that there were fewer opportunities for Hungarians to continue their education in their mother tongue, citing figures for the 1976–77 academic year which showed that of 34,738 Hungarian secondary school students, 15,591 attended technical secondary schools where the subjects were taught exclusively in Romanian. The explanation for this was not to be found in 'steering' Hungarian pupils towards Romanian schools, but in the lack of sufficient teachers for those pupils who wished to study in Hungarian. Without the possibility of study in their mother tongue, Hungarian pupils, Takács argued, ended up with a limited general education and little technical training and were unable to enter institutions of higher education. Quoting Ceauşescu's words that the language problem "must be solved in a manner which fulfils the conditions for students to learn in that language which they know best", he called upon the Ministry of Education to organize the school system in such a way that pupils could choose instruction in the language "which they know best".[32]

In support of his case he referred to Law no. 26 of 1974 which provided for the creation of Romanian language classes, regardless of the numbers of students, in those communities where there were Hungarian and German language schools. This law guaranteed Romanian children instruction in their own language, however small their number in a village, and Takács suggested that this provision be applied to Hungarian and German children as well. Here Takács was diplomatically attempting to turn the negative aspects of Law no. 278 of 1973 into positive ones for the minority communities. This law stipulated that at primary level, a minimum of 25 applicants in a given year was necessary before a class giving instruction in either Hungarian or German was opened; at the secondary level the minimum number rose to 36. By contrast, there were no such conditions imposed for Romanian classes.

Instruction in Hungarian required qualified teachers and their supply was linked to the provision of higher education in Hungarian. This had deteriorated considerably as a result of the merger of the Bolyai and Babeş universities in 1959. The basis for the merger was the establishment of two parallel sections in Romanian and Hungarian for all subjects but in practice this dual system was only operated in certain subjects, while the majority were taught only in Romanian. As a result, not only did the numbers of Hungarian teaching staff drop rapidly, but also the proportion of Hungarian students in the university population. Takács produced comparative figures for the academic year 1958–59 (the year of the merger) and 1976–77 to prove his point.[33] Furthermore the Petru Groza Agricultural College in Cluj agreed to teach classes in Hungarian in 1959. The effects of these measures was to reduce the proportion of Hungarian students entering higher education and the effect on the secondary school system in the technical schools, whose importance in a rapidly industrializing economy was obvious for job opportunities and advancement, was evident even over a period of three years.[34]

Takács also addressed cultural provision as a whole for the Hungarian minority. There had been a cutback in 1973 in the production of Hungarian language newspapers; some dailies were printed only three times per week or their size was reduced. Romanian newspapers suffered a similar fate, the explanation being a shortage of newsprint. However, the Romanian newspapers were restored to their original size a few months later whereas the Hungarian ones were not. The regime made much of the fact that 19 publishing houses in Romania produced material in Hungarian; Takács pointed out that in the period 1970 to 1977 twelve of them published fewer than ten works. He complained about the restrictions placed on subscribing to technical journals printed in Hungary, which compounded the difficulties facing young Hungarians who wanted to pursue a career in Romanian industry. It added to the obstacles faced by Hungarians who lived outside an area of minority concentration who, after being denied instruction in their own language, were put at a disadvantage in competition with native Romanians because of the need to learn a second language, and who thus ended up with a limited general education and little technical training.[35]

Ceauşescu's stance on these issues was clear from his speeches. In June 1973, he declared that "we cannot set up special institutes of physics, chemistry or other specialities for young people who do not know Romanian". Yet he also recognized that those who do not learn the language would be "in a position of inequality compared to Romanian young people" because they would not have "free access to all the forms of higher education". Entering his admonitory mode he insisted that "Romanian is not a foreign language to any youth living in Romania! It is the language of our socialist society and it must be learned by all Romanian citizens".[36]

From a Romanian standpoint, there was reason in Ceauşescu's words since the creation of what might be called a form of positive discrimination in favour of Hungarians, be it in education or in employment policy, was a luxury the developing state could not afford. Yet the Transylvanian Hungarians could respond that they had indeed enjoyed such a form of positive discrimination in the 1950s, when economic development was less advanced. This led the Hungarians to view the policy of equalization through modernization with suspicion; increasing investment in those Hungarian-dominated counties in order to level out development was regarded as a covert means of diluting the Hungarian concentration of population and of inducing assimilation.

Assimilation was encouraged in three ways: first, by the migration of Romanians into Transylvania and the movement away from the province of Hungarians and Germans (the latter through emigration); second, through the resultant decrease in the number of minority language schools by applying the quotas for minimum numbers of pupils; and third, by promoting the use of Romanian as the language of the majority and one essential for social mobility, even for the minorities. There was little doubt that equalization had produced assimilation; the question arose as to whether policies of equalization had been intended to produce assimilation. Supporters of Ceauşescu's policies answered 'No', and members of the Hungarian minority said 'Yes'. Migration of Romanians to the towns, including those in Transylvania, was a concomitant of urban development since until the application of Romania's development plan, most Romanians lived in rural areas. Conversely, a larger proportion of Hungarians, Germans and Jews lived in towns. On the one hand the emigration of Germans and Jews had reduced the cosmopolitan character of Transylvanian towns, releasing property for occupation by Romanians, and on the other the regime's strategy to expand industry and stimulate urban growth had ensured, according to one pro-Bucharest account, that since "Hungarians make up less than eight per cent of the population of Romania, it is inevitable that the proportion of Hungarians to Romanians in these cities will continue to shrink".[37] Economic needs, not ethnic affiliation, the regime's defence ran, determined labour distribution.

The three letters of Karoly Király suggested the contrary. Király was the vice president of the Hungarian Nationality Workers' Council who had resigned as candidate member of the RCP Executive Committee (Politburo) and as first secretary of Covasna County in 1972 for 'personal' reasons. The letters revealed that the real reason for his resignation had been his dissatisfaction with the discriminatory policies pursued against the Hungarians. The effects of these policies were catalogued in 1977 in three letters, respectively to Politburo member Ilie Verdeţ, responsible for ideological affairs and policies towards the nationalities, to János Fazekas, also a member of the Politburo, and the third to Central Committee member János Vincze.[38]

In his letter to Verdeţ, Király reiterated the criticism of the Hungarian Workers Council voiced by Takács. He complained that because it met irregularly, that its proceedings were not even conducted in Hungarian but in Romanian, and that statements made there were "prefabricated and censored by comrades in the county leadership", it had lost all prestige amongst the minority. Many Party officials, including those of Hungarian origin, used Romanian exclusively in their contacts with Hungarian workers, displaying thereby a lack of sensitivity and tact and giving the impression that the use of Hungarian was forbidden. Perhaps Király's most telling observation was that "national sentiment is a sensitive question which must be treated with special attention; it is a question which relates to the quality of nationality, and its solution cannot be measured in percentages as can industrial progress and results". A sense of discrimination is imparted as much by attitudes as by actions, as many members of a minority will testify, and the degree of sensitivity shown by the regime was evident from Verdeţ's failure to reply.

Király therefore sent the two further letters. Any suspicion that his objectivity might have been a victim of highly sensitive feelings and that his perception of discrimination was impressionistic was dispelled by his letter to Fazekas in which he detailed 'errors' in the handling of what he called 'the nationality question': opportunities were constantly being reduced for Hungarian children to study in their native tongue; restrictive quotas were being placed on the numbers of Hungarians who could be employed in certain institutions; and those who dared to speak out about minority matters were subjected to intimidation by the police. In the letter to Vincze he provided further examples of the problems encountered by Hungarians: the Hungarian State Theatre in Târgu Mureş had a Romanian director who did not speak Hungarian; the largely Hungarian towns of Târgu Mureş and Sovata had non-Hungarian speaking Romanian mayors, the bilingual Hungarian-Romanian signs erected in Covasna in 1971 were removed and by 1975 not a single locality was identified in Hungarian. Hungarian officials in factories were being replaced with Romanians who did not know Hungarian: at the '23 August' works and the chemical factory in Târgu Mureş not a single director or deputy director was Hungarian.

Király contended that this situation was in violation of Romania's constitution, the principles of Marxism-Leninism and of fundamental human rights. The fault lay, he boldly maintained, with the Party leadership and he called for a renunciation of policies based on "demagogy, the personality cult and the capricious application of Marxism".[39] Here were complaints that were not just the preserve of Hungarians, but were shared by fellow citizens such as Goma, and the unprecedented fact that they were as voiced by a leading Party figure at this time, some ten years before Silviu Brucan's admonitory statements, has not received the recognition that it deserves by the Romanian public.

After sending the August and September letters Király was finally summoned to Bucharest in October to discuss the first letter addressed to Verdeţ. During discussions with Verdeţ he was asked to reveal the names of others who had helped to draft it. He refused to do without asking their permission and after the meeting he secured the agreement of eight other members of the Hungarian minority to be identified with his letter. A week later he saw Verdeţ, again for discussions lasting eight hours. His proposals were ignored and he therefore consented to the publication of his letters in the West. In February 1978, Király was arrested in Târgu Mureş just days after his protests became known over Radio Free Europe and he and his family were banished to Caransebeş, a town in the south-west of the country. Hundreds of homes belonging to members of the Hungarian minority in Transylvania were searched by the *Securitate* for copies of Király's letters. In October, he was allowed to return to Târgu Mureş but he and his friends were placed under surveillance.

There were indications, nevertheless, that some of Király's criticisms elicited a response from Ceauşescu. The belief—held by many Hungarians in a hidden agenda to limit the number of managerial and skilled positions available in the Hungarian areas to members of the minority, while Romanians from other areas were given special incentives in housing to take up jobs in these areas—was, at least in public, if not in practice, partially addressed by the Romanian leader in a speech to the Nationality Councils in March 1978:

> Generally speaking, we must take action to direct graduates - especially educational cadres, but also medical and agricultural cadres - to their native localities, thus avoiding sending them from one part of the country to another.[40]

However, like many of Ceauşescu's declarations, this one ran counter to existing legislation and was merely window-dressing. Its impact, from the evidence available, was minimal, for two decrees issued in 1976, introduced to combat unemployment, or 'parasitism' as it was officially camouflaged, gave the authorities the power to direct labour to wherever was deemed necessary. Graduates continued to be assigned to jobs, where they had to remain several years after graduation, without regard for their ethnic background, so that Hungarian (and German) graduates were often sent to Romanian areas and, not unnaturally, settled down with a Romanian partner. Once more, the policy of equalization could be invoked for this process of ethnic dispersal, but for Hungarians it continued to smack of assimilation. There is no doubt that the resentment felt by the Hungarian and German minorities increased as living standards began to deteriorate.

The severe earthquake of 1977, followed by floods in 1980 and 1981, disrupted industrial production and reduced the exports of foodstuffs which Ceauşescu now looked to in order to pay off the foreign debt incurred through industrialization. In late 1981, the country's foreign debt rose to $10.2 billion and Ceauşescu requested its rescheduling. On the recommendation of the IMF, he cut imports. The implications of this cutback have not been fully appreciated for Romania had been a net importer of foodstuffs since the end of the 1970s.[41] More importantly, the very act of having to accept conditions from the Western banks dealt an enormous blow to Ceauşescu's inflated pride, generated xenophobic postures in him, and drove him into a self-imposed economic isolation after 1980. On its heels came political isolation which made him less dependent on the support of foreign governments that might have exercised some influence in persuading him to moderate his policies towards the minorities.

Equally dispiriting for the minorities was the sense of cultural isolation. This was fed by the legacy of the different historical experience of Romanians and Hungarians. The lack of what might be called 'synchronization' between the essentially Western cultural experience of the latter and Eastern Orthodox experience of the Romanians, and the resulting divergences in behavioural values, did little to foster convergence between the two peoples. Throughout the eighties, as Ceauşescu's personality cult and his cultivation of ultranationalist feeling intensified, so an intolerance towards the Hungarian minority in particular reared its ugly head in official circles. Banners proclaiming "we are masters in our own home" began to appear with increasing frequency at major rallies and reflected Ceauşescu's conception of the absolute sovereignty of the Romanians in their nation-state. Since Romanians were in their own home, they must therefore be masters in it. The implicit corollary was that the minorities were aliens. Insistence upon the 'national unitary' character of the Romanian state in regime-sponsored propaganda merely ignored the reality: the national unitary state did not exist; given the numerical strength and diversity of its minorities it merited rather the description of a multi-ethnic or multinational state. Those who claimed, and continue to claim, that it is a unitary state, are merely trying to make the reality fit their theory.

The official Romanian position that the country was not a multi-ethnic state but a unitary one debarred the minorities from claiming any allegiance to a second state. For the Hungarians of Transylvania to whom this author has spoken down the years, loyalty to the Romanian state, to have any meaning, must be one that is freely given and not coerced from them. They were hardly likely to give this loyalty freely if they were placed in the position of 'second class' citizens in the ancestral homeland which they shared with the Romanians. In the view of the Hungarians, the enjoyment of equal rights with the Romanians was equated with the granting of territorial autonomy for those of their number who lived in compact areas. Minority or group's rights could, according to the Hungarians, only be protected by according group autonomy, an argument rejected by Ceauşescu who consistently emphasized the individual rights enjoyed by each citizen in Romania, irrespective of nationality. Of course, the formal rights recognized by the Romanian constitution meant very little in practice under his rule.

There was no clearer indication of this than the arrest in January 1983 of the editors of *Ellenpontok* (Counterpoints), a clandestine Hungarian language journal which had been produced in Oradea since the end of 1981. Some of its contributors, among them pastor László Tökés, denounced the oppression of the Hungarian minority and interpreted it as an expression of traditional Romanian nationalism of which Ceauşescu was merely the latest exponent. Nine issues appeared before the editors were detained, beaten and finally expelled to Hungary. A second *samizdat* publication soon took its place. *Erdélyi magyar hírügynökség Erdelyi* (The Hungarian Press of Transylvania) first appeared on 20 May 1983 in the form of mimeographed reports chronicling the deteriorating economic and social conditions and was the main source of information about strikes in Transylvania in November 1986. One of its editors, Géza Szőcs, was forced to leave the country in 1986 after several of his statements on the situation of the Hungarian minority in Transylvania were passed on to the CSCE cultural forum in Budapest.[42]

Relations between Hungary and Romania deteriorated sharply when, in December 1986, the Hungarian Academy published a three-volume history of Transylvania. Its appearance elicited an angry response from a number of Romanian historians. On 12 March 1987 the Romanian daily *România liberă,*—after the Party newspaper the most authoritative and widely-read newspaper in the country—carried a lengthy article by three regime-sponsored historians, Ştefan Pascu, Mircea Muşat and Florin Constantiniu, condemning the 'conscious falsification' of the history of Transylvania presented in the work.[43] Romanian anger was especially aroused by the fact that the general editor of the history, Béla Köpeczi, was the Hungarian Minister of Education and the work was thus deemed to have government approval. The charge of 'conscious falsification' was based on the Hungarian denial of proof to the existence of a Romanian population in Transylvania before the beginning of the thirteenth century, the date at which Hungarian historians argue that the Romanians crossed from south of the Carpathians to settle in the province. This denial, the Romanians maintained, questioned the legitimacy of Romanian possession of the area, and this sedition led the Ministry of Education to prohibit distribution of the history in Romania. It was only in 1990, when the director of the 'Nicolae Iorga' Institute of History asked me to obtain the work for its library, that I realized that the country's premier institution of historical research did not possess a copy and that only a select group of historians called upon to do the regime's bidding had been favoured with access to the work.

The lengths to which the Romanians' ire carried them were demonstrated by the placing of a full-page advertisement in *The Times* on 7 April 1987 through a Greek intermediary. The advertisement repeated the charges levelled at the *History of Transylvania* in the article in *România liberă* but behind the mask of the Greek sponsor added others in a waspish language shorn of any diplomatic restraint. The authors of the history were

> interested less in the fate of the Magyar nationality in Romania and more in causing diversion and misleading public opinion. Their action is part of the attempts to create a false question of 'Minorities in Romania' which has no objective justification as in the years of socialism the Romanian state has completely and definitely solved the national question.

There is no doubt that these sentiments echoed the real feelings of Ceauşescu and his acolytes but their attempt to sway international opinion was seriously undermined by the final reference in the advertisement to the failure of the Hungarian uprising of 1956 in which the Romanians appeared to gloat:

> In their fight against socialism back in 1956 Hungarians have had no luck. They try now, with higher hopes, against socialists. There's still to be seen the way in which the Western world will support this manoeuvre, as recently Hungarians have requested in Vienna, and, also and more interesting, the way Russians will swallow it.

By bringing the Soviet Union into the dispute the advertisement, and Ceauşescu by extension, was implying that the Soviet leadership was once again using the Hungarians as a channel for interfering in Romanian affairs. Indeed Gorbachev, during his visit to Romania only a month later, referred to the minority question in his speech broadcast live to the Romanian public on 26 May. Underlining the need for friendship among peoples, the Soviet leader stated:

> It is known what great importance it [relations between the minorities] has for us and what great importance Lenin accorded to all aspects of national relations, asking that delicacy and special attention be given to solving these problems. I think that the Leninist precepts in this respect are still topical today.[44]

Ceauşescu turned a deaf ear to this counsel. Faced with this obduracy Karoly Király took up his pen once more. In a letter dated 16 August 1987 to Ceauşescu he described the economic situation as 'lamentable', the political atmosphere as 'oppressive', and derided "the triumph of official mendacity, which has become the basis of state policy". Blame for this state of affairs had to be shared equally between Ceauşescu and the Party *nomenklatura* which Király regarded as the leader's accomplice in misrule.[45] On the minorities issue, he characterized Ceauşescu's policy as one of forced assimilation which was bringing discredit to Romania internationally and which could "only sow the seeds of trouble". He linked the defence of the rights of the Transylvanian Hungarians with that of Romanians' rights in Soviet Moldavia, thus reasserting a common cause to which he had put his name in a statement in February 1985 alongside Géza Szőcs and two Romanian writers, Dorin Tudoran and Marius Tabacu.[46]

The Hungarian minority was also seriously affected by Ceauşescu's campaign of village redevelopment or 'systematization'. Originally outlined in 1972, the plan was given fresh impetus by the Romanian president in March 1988 when he proposed that the number of villages be reduced by more than half from 13,000 to five or six thousand by the year 2000; the displaced inhabitants would be re-housed in 558 'agro-industrial' towns.[47] Although the programme was not specifically aimed at Hungarian villages, and indeed most of the redevelopment took place in villages around Bucharest, the plan was bound to have a disproportionate effect upon the Hungarian minority because of the large number of small settlements in the predominantly Hungarian counties of Harghita and Covasna which were targeted for 'phasing out' (*dezafectare*), the planners' euphemism for either destruction or the cutting off of electricity and communications to produce atrophy.[48] Other information about the effects of systematization in the county of Mureş, 44 per cent of whose population was Hungarian, was passed on by officials in the county to Western embassies in Bucharest and asserted that 250 of the county's 480 settlements faced an uncertain future 'for economic reasons'. These settlements contained nearly 150 churches and 30 historical monuments, 35 of which were considered to be of prime importance. Almost half the churches were Roman Catholic, Reformed and Unitarian and some 60 were Romanian Orthodox. As the officials pointed out, the systematization plan "equally affected Hungarian, Romanian and Saxon settlements".

The impact of the programme upon a settlement pattern in Hungarian-inhabited parts of Transylvania which had a centuries-old history fuelled anxiety in Hungary which was tapped by an emerging opposition group, the Hungarian Democratic Forum (HDF) and a reforming minister Imre Pozsgay. The HDF organized a demonstration against systematization in Budapest on 27 June 1988 which attracted 40,000 participants, the largest protest on the streets of the capital since 1956.[49] Ceauşescu responded immediately by closing the Hungarian consulate in Cluj, a move unprecedented in relations between 'fraternal' states. In the text of a speech delivered on 28 June and released by the Romanian news agency *Agerpres* on the following day Ceauşescu gave details of a letter which he had sent to the Hungarian Prime Minister, Karoly Grosz, in which he called for an end to "nationalist and chauvinist activities", clearly inferring that the Hungarian government had been behind the Budapest demonstration. He stressed the value of the Romanian road to socialism and declared that the problems of Romanian citizens, irrespective of their ethnic origin, were the responsibility of the Romanian

Communist Party. Hungary's objections to Romania's minority policies, he continued, were only aimed at drawing attention from Hungary's own problems.

In a move to satisfy Hungarian public opinion Grosz told journalists on 30 June that he intended to visit Romania in order to discuss the problem of national minorities. The tension was maintained by a resolution of the Foreign Affairs Committee of the Hungarian parliament which, without mentioning the closure of the Cluj consulate, declared

> action unprecedented in the practice of socialist countries does serious harm to Hungarian-Romanian relations, and draws attention to the fact that all this is in flat contradiction to treaties concluded between the two countries, to the norms of European cooperation, as well as to the Helsinki Final Act of 1975.[50]

On 1 July, the Hungarian parliament passed a resolution calling on the Romanian government to review the systematization programme and to withdraw it. By doing so it would "remove a major obstacle hindering the coming together of the Hungarian and Romanian nations". The destruction of "all that is valuable in villages condemned to liquidation in the name of socialist progress would mean an irreplaceable loss not only to the Hungarian, German and other national minorities but to the Romanian people itself".[51]

Grosz was caught by surprise by Ceauşescu's invitation to meet him at short notice at the end of August in Arad near the border with Hungary. To avoid possible accusations of not wanting to negotiate with the Romanians Grosz decided to go but was clearly outmanoeuvred by Ceauşescu who implied that improvements in educational facilities for the Hungarian minority would be made. Grosz's favourable assessment of the meeting angered the Hungarian opposition and weakened both his own position and that of the Hungarian Socialist Workers' Party. The issue of Transylvania was proving as much an internal Hungarian political problem as one in bilateral relations with Romania. Those relations took another turn for the worse in November when Karolyi Gyorffy, Hungary's commercial counsellor in Bucharest, was detained after allegedly causing a traffic accident and then expelled for, the Romanians claimed, distributing leaflets hostile to Romania. Matyas Szuros, the Hungarian Party secretary responsible for foreign affairs, accused the Romanians of fabricating the story. "The facts, and even the Romanian statements prove without any doubt that this was a premeditated police action... which introduced a new element of tension into Hungarian-Romanian relations."[52] In retaliation the Hungarians expelled Pavel Platona, the political counsellor at the Romanian embassy in Budapest.

As his 28 June speech demonstrated, Ceauşescu adopted a new tack in trying to deflect the complaints of the Hungarian government over his treatment of the minorities. He suggested that they were inspired by the Hungarians own desire to use the minorities issue as a means of diverting the attention of Hungarian public opinion away from the hardships engendered by the economic reforms pursued by the Budapest authorities. This approach gave Ceauşescu the opportunity to display his credentials as an orthodox Communist who had remained more faithful to the tenets of Marxism-Leninism than the reformist Gorbachev and his ilk in other members of the socialist bloc. The tone set by Ceauşescu was followed by the Romanian media. On 4 September, the Party daily *Scînteia* accused the Hungarian press of distortion in its coverage of Romanian affairs and suggested that it should mind its own business.[53]

While ignoring the Hungarian political reforms the Romanian press throughout 1989 reproduced negative economic news from the country. On 5 February *Scînteia* quoted the Hungarian news agency MTI on failures to fulfil planned targets, and on 13 April it carried an item in the Hungarian Party daily on the heavy price increases of the previous three years. Transylvanian Hungarian sycophants of Ceauşescu were regularly trotted out to reinforce the implied link between Hungarian criticism of minority policies and the reform process in Hungary.[54]

Whatever the troubles experienced by the Hungarian economy, they paled into insignificance beside the scale of Romania's own difficulties; nevertheless, it was Hungary that felt the greatest impact of Ceauşescu's failed policies. The appalling economic hardship in the country drove thousands of Hungarians from Romania into Hungary. The numbers seeking asylum more than tripled from 6,500 in 1987 to 15,000 in 1988 (figures for 1985 and 1986 were 1,700 and 3,300 respectively). In 1988 13,400 refugees were granted temporary residence permits in Hungary, the vast majority being Hungarians from Transylvania and only eight per cent Romanians. By August 1989, the numbers had risen to 25,000, with more than 300 arriving each week, of whom some 25 per cent were Romanians (from January to May 1989, 5,000 refugees entered Yugoslavia). In 1988 1,650 refugees were returned to Romania but in March 1989 Hungary signed the United Nations 1951 Geneva Convention relating to refugees, the first Eastern bloc country to do so, and as a result only 29 asylum seeking were sent back by July 1989.[55] In an effort to stem the flow Ceauşescu approved the construction in late 1988 of a fence along those areas of the border with Hungary which lacked one, but the work was never completed, perhaps because as an accidental by-product of economic calamity emigration had the merit of reducing the numbers of the Hungarian minority. Romanian refugees, too, continued to make their way across, the most famous being the gymnast Nadia Comăneci in November 1989, and the most remarkable, two shepherds with a flock of 300 sheep. By the same month official Hungarian figures put the number of refugees from Romania at 24,000, one-sixth of whom were ethnic Romanians. This was an understatement of the true exodus, since many Romanians did not register with the Hungarian authorities but used the country for transit to Austria and the West.

The Soviet Union steered clear of the conflict between Hungary and Romania but its embarrassment at Ceauşescu's policies was clearly manifested by its decision to abstain from voting on a resolution adopted in March 1989 by the UN Human Rights Commission in Geneva to investigate human rights violations in Romania. Hungary joined the resolution's sponsors, thus provoking further Romanian anger. Another opportunity for Romanian wrath was provided by the reburial of the remains of Imre Nagy and his colleagues in Budapest on 16 June 1989. The Bucharest media presented the occasion not only as a huge demonstration of Hungarian irredentism directed against Romania, but also as an attack on socialism and the Warsaw Pact. The Romanian government protested to Hungary's ambassador in Bucharest about the "antisocialist, anti-Romanian, nationalist-chauvinistic, and revisionist demonstrations held in Budapest on 16 June".[56] On the same day the agency reported that meetings of working people had taken place throughout the country at which the participants had expressed their 'profound indignation' that Nagy's reburial had "turned into a political action that was clearly fascist, irredentist in nature, and aimed against the Hungarian Socialist Workers' Party, socialism and communism, and the Warsaw Treaty Organization".[57] In fact, neither Romania nor Hungarian-Romanian relations were mentioned in the speeches delivered at Nagy's funeral, despite the removal of the former Hungarian Prime Minister to Romania in 1956 for interrogation by the KGB. What clearly provoked the Romanian reaction was a declaration, published the day after the funeral, signed by representatives of Romanian *émigré* organizations and the HDF which accused the authorities in both Hungary and Romania, and the Ceauşescu regime in particular, of having created a crisis in Transylvania. To rectify this the signatories called for "autonomous political and cultural representation" of each nation in the province, as well as for "education for the minorities in their own language".

The charge of 'anti-socialist' contained in the protest note to the Hungarian ambassador echoed Ceauşescu's barely concealed disdain for the reforms in Hungary which the TASS correspondent at the reburial stressed had the support of Moscow. Ceauşescu had reiterated his commitment to rigid central economic planning and insisted that market forces were incompatible with Communist society in his address to the Romanian Party Conference on 14 December 1987. In dealing with the reforms advocated by Gorbachev Ceauşescu argued that he had already applied similar measures in Romania. Thus *Scînteia,* in its report of the nineteenth Soviet Party Conference in 1988 restricted coverage of Gorbachev's speech to those measures which had already been taken in Romania, thereby suggesting that the Soviet leader was following Ceauşescu's example. Furthermore, Gorbachev's admission that the Soviet Union had taken important decisions without "proper consultation with friends" gave Ceauşescu a justification for not applying *perestroika* (restructuring) and *glasnost* (openness).[58]

One effect of Ceauşescu's draconian economies was supremely ironical in view of the status of the Hungarian language in Romania. The reduction in Romanian TV coverage to two hours per evening in 1988 led Romanian children in western Transylvania to turn to Hungarian TV for entertainment. In the process, they picked up the language. Ceauşescu, the arch Romanian nationalist, can be credited with a measure whose direct result was to facilitate the spread of the Hungarian language amongst Romanian children. This sense of the absurd was coupled with one of growing desperation felt by the entire population of Romania. Amongst the Hungarians the need to restore self-confidence prompted the appearance of a new *samizdat* journal entitled *Kiáltó Szó* (Desperate Cry) in 1988. The editors renounced any claim to pursue a narrow group interest, pledging the journal to serve as a catalyst in bringing together "noble Hungarian and Romanian aspirations" and as a forum for "popularizing each other's artistic values". The target of their censure was not the Romanian people but "those majority forces that continue, both covertly and openly, to promote and assert discriminative and chauvinistic minority policies and fuel anti-Hungarian sentiments, thereby misleading and turning otherwise honest Romanians against us". There was a growing realization amongst Romanians that the minorities' quest for greater freedom was one which should be shared by them and, as if to encourage self-confidence, the first issue carried an article entitled 'Beyond the Ceauşescu era' which looked to a political system in which individuals and ethnic minorities would "enjoy the fruits of democracy".[59]

Kiáltó Szó printed an analysis of the life of the Reformed Church which acquired a prophetic dimension in the light of events leading to the Revolution. According to official statistics the Church had some 700,000 members, most of them drawn from the Hungarians in Transylvania. The traditional forms of church service, such as Sunday worship, did not attract the mass of faithful and therefore the pastors concentrated on bible classes, choir singing, and family visits to convey the Church's message. The report stated that there were no significant obstacles to organizing these activities; their success was dependent on the pastor's zeal, faith and willingness to make sacrifices.

Relations between the congregations and the church authorities, between pastors, deans and bishops, differed considerably in the two districts into which the Church was divided. László Papp, the bishop of Oradea, was opposed to the new forms of church activity and strictly forbade what he called 'pietist' deviations. Even services for the Week of Prayer for Christian Unity were forbidden by him, not to mention the organization of bible classes. The report described Papp's attitude as one "preferred by a communist state founded on atheist ideology". The situation in the Cluj district was considered to be less autocratic. Bishop Gyula Nagy neither encouraged active pastors nor punished them.[60] Yet even bishop Nagy's submissiveness attracted the criticism of a leading figure in the Reformed Church, Istvan Tökés. Formerly a lecturer at the Protestant Academy in Cluj and a deputy bishop, he was dismissed from the former post in 1983 and the latter in 1984 for his criticisms of the church leaders' cooperation with the regime. In a letter which reached the West in August 1988 he renewed his call for the church to follow its own constitution, suggesting that only in this way could state control be averted. After writing the letter the 72-year-old theologian was banned in spring 1988 from preaching in his native town of Cluj. Tökés complained about the lack of freedom in church elections, which were so rigged "that the will of the electors cannot be realized", and the failure to fill pastoral posts canonically, appointments being made according to "the despotism of the leadership or the bishops". His list of accusations also included the charge that church bodies "were the blind tools of the powers that be", and that the picture of the church's activity, the number of faithful, the number of pastors, was regularly distorted. He called for the convention of a new synod to work out a radical, new church order.[61]

Istvan Tökés's non-conformist spirit was shared by his son László. Born on 1 April 1952 in Cluj, he became a pastor in the Reformed Church and was appointed to a parish in the Transylvanian town of Dej. He was a contributor to *Ellenpontok* in 1982, writing an article on abuses of human rights in Romania, which led to his harassment by the *Securitate*. He and his friends were followed and eventually Tökés was dismissed from his parish in Dej by order of bishop Nagy and assigned to the village of Sânpietru de Câmpie some 40 kilometres from Cluj. Tökés refused to go and instead went to his parents' house in Cluj where he spent two years unemployed. He used part of this time to launch a letter-writing campaign in 1985 amongst the Hungarians of Transylvania to gather statistics about facilities for education in Hungarian.[62] His plight was brought to the attention of the Foreign Relations Committee of the US Senate and as a result Bishop Papp was instructed by the authorities in 1986 to appoint Tökés assistant pastor in the city of Timişoara, one of mixed Romanian, Hungarian and German population.[63]

If the subject of Transylvania and the Hungarian minority was and remains one of the most emotive in contemporary Romanian politics, the question of relations with the Romanian population east of the river Prut in the territory known formerly as Bessarabia, and today as the Republic of Moldova, elicits strong reactions. Just as the Hungarian government claims a justifiable interest in the fate of the Hungarian minority in Transylvania, so too does the Romanian state argue that it has a similar interest in the affairs of the Republic of Moldova. Yet Romania's interest was expressed far more subtly than the Hungarian one in Transylvania, despite the fact that Romanians represented more than 60 per cent of the Moldavian SSR's population, compared with the seven per cent which the Hungarians constituted in Romania. In the first place the Romanians in the Moldavian SSR represented in the Soviet Union the only minority of a fraternal socialist nation-state—the socialist Republic of Romania. Secondly, if Romania's claims to the republic's territory became too strident, the Soviet Union could use economic sanctions against her or even threaten invasion. An understanding of the Soviet-Romanian controversy over Bessarabia, which re-emerged in the final year of Gheorghiu-Dej's rule and simmered throughout the Ceauşescu period, demands an incursion into the province's past and the different interpretations given to that past by Romanian and Soviet historians. An examination of the politically inspired use of geographical, ethnic and linguistic labels by the Soviet authorities for the territory and its titular people is essential to an understanding of the true identity of Romanians in the territory between the rivers Prut and Dniester.

The problem begins with names. The principality of Moldavia emerged in the fourteenth century. It covered an area on both sides of the river Prut, extending in the east to the river Dniester. It is the designation of the area between the two rivers which gives rise to the problem. The southern area was originally called Bessarabia after its ruler Basarab I. So the area has acquired in the course of history two names which imply, however, fluctuating frontiers. It did not help, moreover, that both designations were adopted inconsistently by Western cartographers and chroniclers.

The modern form of the problem dates from 1812 when traditional Moldavia was partitioned, Russia acquiring the eastern half, between the rivers Prut and Dniester. This area was then renamed Bessarabia by Russian tsar Alexander I who thus applied to the whole area the name hitherto connoting its southern districts only. The western half of Moldavia became in 1859 one of the founding polities of modern Romania. After the Russian revolution Bessarabia rejoined (for the Romanians) the state of Romania in 1918, but continued to be called Bessarabia and was administered as a distinctive province. The Soviet government refused to recognize the new frontier and in 1924 created an Autonomous Moldavian Soviet Socialist Republic (AMSSR) in south-west Ukraine on the left bank of the Dniester. Of its half million population, only about 30 per cent were Romanians, the other major populations being Ukrainians (about 50 per cent) and Russians (ten per cent).[64] Thus a territory which had never before been called Moldavia, nor been part of the medieval principality of Moldavia, was created to give credibility to the Soviet government's claim to Bessarabia and to provide a nucleus for the 'reunification' of the Moldavians on the left bank of the Dniester (in the AMSSR) with those on the right bank (in Bessarabia). The first Soviet Moldavia had come into being.

Almost a month before the announcement of the creation of the AMSSR the Politburo of the Central Committee of the Communist Party of the Ukraine charged activists assigned to duties in the embryonic republic with the introduction of the Russian Cyrillic alphabet and with the "development of the national Moldavian language".[65] Here for the first time was a signal that the Soviet government intended to give to ethnic Romanians under its authority a distinct identity from their brothers and sisters in the Romanian national state. The imposition of the Cyrillic alphabet for writing Romanian was accompanied by the prescriptive use of the adjective 'Moldavian' to designate the Romanian language.

At face value, this programme accorded with the policies set by the Soviet authorities in the national republics in the 1920s, namely the cultivation throughout the Union of the native language for use in schools, the media and public life.[66] But in the AMSSR, it was different; applying the programme here meant fostering the language of the Ukrainian majority rather than that of the Romanian minority. That was scheduled for 'enrichment', in practice a euphemism for the 'Ukrainianization' of the Romanian language spoken by the minority. After decades of co-habitation with Ukrainian with no countervailing contacts with the main Romanian culture, the speech of the Moldavians on the left bank of the Dniester had already a pronounced Ukrainian character, both in script and vocabulary. It was the written forms which were manipulated, especially in dictionaries, to show that the Moldavian language was "independent and distinct from Romanian". In 1933, compulsory Cyrillic gave way to the use of the Latin alphabet, but five years later, Cyrillic was reintroduced, together with a purge of those who had earlier 'Romanianized' the language. Survivors of the political purges were themselves asked to conduct a linguistic purge,

> cleansing the Moldavian language of the Gallicized Roman words...which had been introduced by the enemies of the Moldavian people and endeavouring to use as many words as possible in Moldavian ....such as neologisms from the languages of the fraternal Russian and Ukrainian peoples.[67]

The cession of Bessarabia in late June 1940 allowed the Soviets to set up a Moldavian Soviet Socialist Republic, which was reinstated in 1944 after the temporary reoccupation of the territory by Romania which had given it the name of Transnistria.[68] The southern districts, however, went to the Ukrainian SSR. The MSSR was re-Communized and re-Russified; there was a mass deportation of ethnic Romanians to Kazakhstan on the one hand, and an influx of ethnic Russians and Ukrainians on the other. The ubiquity of Russian and Ukrainian activists in the bureaucracy provided the Soviet authorities with justification for the priority given to Russian in the official life of the Republic. At the same time, the influx of Russians and Ukrainians acted as a check against potential nationalist agitation among the Romanians, now officially Moldavians. Moldavians, the authorities maintained, were different from Romanians, as was their language and culture. This remained the case until the paths of socialist Romania and the Soviet Union began to diverge in the late 1950s. This development heralded a revival of the Bessarabian question.

In 1964, the Central Committee of the RCP put Marx into the arena. His *Notes on the Romanians* had been discovered in the Marx-Engels Archive of the International Institute for Social History (IISH) in Amsterdam in December 1957 by Stanislas Schwann, a Polish specialist on Marx. Since they related to Romania Schwann informed the Institute for the History of the RCP in Bucharest. The director of the IISH in Amsterdam turned down a request in 1958 from Ion Popescu-Puţuri, the head of the Party Institute, for a microfilm of the manuscripts on the grounds that he was preparing an edition of the texts but when Schwann discovered that they in fact contained notes taken by Marx from other publications on social and political conditions in Romania, the Dutch institution lost interest in publication. Popescu-Puţuri, a veteran Communist, was then authorized by the Romanian Party leadership to pay Schwann to continue his research on the texts and to try to persuade the Dutch to publish them. When Schwann failed to make progress, Andrei Oţetea, director of the 'N. Iorga' Institute of History in Bucharest, was despatched to Amsterdam in 1960 and signed an agreement with the IISS allowing the Romanians to publish excerpts from the manuscripts.[69]

Almost three years elapsed before the *Notes* were sent to the typesetter. Even allowing for the time necessary to translate Marx's text, the duration of the interval can only be explained by political considerations. Clearly Gheorghiu-Dej was holding the text up his sleeve until the occasion was ripe to produce it, and this he adjudged to be in the autumn of 1964, to be exact, 24 October, the day it was approved for printing.[70] The book went on sale in December and its print run of 20,500 copies was sold out almost immediately, testimony to the feverish interest of the Romanian public in this unprecedented event and the fertile ground of anti-Russian sentiment in which the Romanian regime could cultivate its popularity. By invoking the authority of Marx the Romanian regime could reconcile a national communist ideology with the anti-Russian sentiment of most of its subjects. The political motive for publication became evident from the content of the *Notes* themselves, and from the introduction to the book by A. Oţetea and G. Zane, a Romanian political economist. The *Notes* were not original writings of Marx but extracts from an unknown work in English and a study in French by Elias Régnault entitled *Histoire politique et sociale des Principautés Danubiennes* (a Political and Social History of the Principalities of the Danube Region), published in Paris in 1855, and Marx only referred marginally to Bessarabia. The editors were at pains to minimize the second-hand nature of Marx's observations and argued that his selection of material and his glosses on it demonstrated clearly his support for Romania's independence in the nineteenth century, underlining Marx's interpretation that neither the Turks nor the Russians had the right in international law to dispose of Romanian territory.[71]

Although incidental, Marx's notes on Bessarabia were forthright and clearly showed his sympathy for Romania's claim to the province. Their publication broke the taboo of speaking openly about Russia's annexation of Bessarabia in 1812 and the Romanian identity of its population. Soviet historiography replied in ideological terms. In the revised edition of the official history of the Moldavian SSR which appeared in 1965, emphasis was placed on the permanent nature of the Russian annexation of Bessarabia in 1812 as having "a progressive significance for the population of this region". It was an important turning point in the life of the Moldavian people, who as a result of this historic act, forever linked their future with the fate of their friends, the Great Russian people.[72]

In defence of their position Soviet officials drew on the attitude of the Romanian Communist Party towards Bessarabia during the interwar period, supporting the return of the province to the Soviet Union. The argument was echoed in Soviet Moldavia. In celebration of the twenty-fifth anniversary of the annexation of Bessarabia, the Party journal *Kommunist Moldavii* reproduced a series of articles from interwar Romanian Communist publications which advocated the return of Bessarabia to the Soviet Union.[73]

Soviet Moldavian reminders of this 'anti-Romanian' line of the RCP were a source of embarrassment to the nationalist credentials which Gheorghiu-Dej had given the Party and which Ceaușescu sought to strengthen. Their effect was to sting Ceaușescu into action. Without mentioning Bessarabia by name, Ceaușescu's speech of 7 May 1966 on the occasion of the forty-fifth anniversary of the foundation of the RCP constituted the strongest and most authoritative claim that Communist Romania made to Bessarabia:

> The indications given to the party to fight for the severance from Romania of some territories which were overwhelmingly inhabited by Romanians did not pay heed to the concrete conditions in Romania-a unitary state. They were deeply erroneous; they actually called for the dismemberment of the national state and the Romanian people's disintegration. The Marxist-Leninist teaching proclaims the right of the peoples to self-determination not with a view to the disintegration of the established national states, but, on the contrary, with a view to the liberation of the oppressed peoples and their constitution into sovereign national states in conformity with the will and decision of the mass of the people.[74]

For this he blamed the Comintern.

The sudden and unexpected journey of Leonid Brezhnev to Bucharest only three days after Ceauşescu's speech may have been an indication of how seriously the Soviet leader regarded the Romanian effrontery, especially as the Chinese Prime Minister Chou En-lai was due to visit Bucharest a week later. The Bessarabian issue was covered during the talks and Ceauşescu seems to have agreed to soften his language. While not abandoning his position, Ceauşescu did not express it again so explicitly until the Fourteenth Party Congress in November 1989. On the Soviet side, previous historical arguments underlining the Soviet claim to Bessarabia were repeated in propaganda issued to mark the twenty-sixth anniversary of the 1940 annexation but growing Soviet anxiety about the Moldavian SSR was reflected in a speech delivered by Ivan Bodiul, First Secretary of the Moldavian Communist Party, in February 1967 at a Central Committee plenum. He denounced propaganda which prevented the 'masses' from appreciating the justness of the Moldavian SSR's incorporation into the Soviet Union and attacked "bourgeois falsifiers of history" and their "attempts to deny the fact that Bessarabia was amputated from the Soviet Union". He called upon scholars in the Moldavian SSR

> to find ways to combat and unmask the foreign falsifiers who distort the truth about Bessarabia and to defend actively the interests of the Moldavian people and the unshakeable friendship that has existed for centuries between our people and the Soviet peoples.[75]

Bodiul's call was taken up by the Moldavian press and Party officials at a number of public occasions. Specific Romanian publications and historians were singled out for criticism by two historians from Kishinev University who attacked the Romanian historians Ion Oprea and Ion Popescu-Puţuri for their 'bourgeois' views.[76] This criticism was part of a campaign that reflected increased Soviet concern over nationalist feeling in the Moldavian SSR, expression of which had been voiced during the late 1960s at concerts given by artistic groups from Romania, the most notable being in 1970 at a performance in Kishinev when the visiting dance troupe was acclaimed with shouts of 'brothers.'[77]

The low point in the conflict between Soviet and Romanian historians over Bessarabia was reached with the publication in 1974 in Russian of a lengthy polemical work entitled *Moldavian Soviet Statehood and the Bessarabian Question* by A. M. Lazarev, a Russian from Bessarabia.[78] As rector of Kishinev University and chairman of the Supreme Soviet of the Moldavian SSR, Lazarev's political as well as academic credentials gave an authority to the book which aspired to be the final word on the history of Bessarabia. Lazarev's book was grotesque and inflammatory, redolent of the language of Stalinism. While concentrating on the period from 1918 to the present, Lazarev traced the birth of the Moldavian 'nation' to the emergence of the principality of Moldavia in the fourteenth century and in doing so made a crude attempt to argue that because the Moldavians speak a language 'independent' of Romanian, and have a historical tradition 'distinct' from that of the Romanians of Wallachia and Transylvania, they are therefore not Romanians. The corollary to this assertion, which was hinted at by Lazarev, was that the aspirations of the Moldavians had only been partially fulfilled since it was only the eastern half of the former Moldavian principality, Bessarabia, that had been incorporated into the Soviet Union. In other words, Moldavia on the west bank of the Prut River was considered by Lazarev as an irredenta of the Moldavian SSR.

In arguing that the Moldavians were not Romanians, Lazarev was forced to rewrite the history of the Romanians by distorting their ethnic origins. He supported his argument with semantic sophistry by claiming that the name 'Romania' and the concepts 'Romanian people' and 'Romanian language' had validity only after the union of 1859 of Moldavia and Wallachia as the United Principalities, without mentioning the fact that the early Moldavian chroniclers recognized the ethnic relationship of the Romanians of Wallachia, Transylvania and Moldavia by considering them to be "one and the same people, Romanians".[79] To support his claim of a separate identity for the Romanians in the Moldavian part of their history Lazarev asserted that their native tongue was not Romanian but Moldavian which was as distinct from Romanian as is Portuguese.[80] As one Western reviewer of the book commented, scholars are likely to remain sceptical about the existence of an independent Moldavian language until such time that a Romanian-Moldavian dictionary is produced.[81]

For Soviet-Romanian relations, it was not the clumsy artificiality of Lazarev's contentions but the vehemence of his attack on pre-Communist Romania and on Romanian historiography, including that of the post-1965 period that caused the greatest irritation. Here Lazarev surpassed himself:

> Bessarabia's seizure by bourgeois boyar Romania in 1918 is an indisputable fact. This is the most shameful page in the history of royalist Romania. Any other evaluation of this anti-Soviet action is incompatible with the historical truth.[82]

Romanian historians were warned that "no matter for how many years they should assert that Moldavians are Romanians, Moldavians will never and in no way become Romanians, while Soviet Moldavia will never become Romanian territory".[83]

Lazarev's position in presenting the history of Bessarabia since 1812 was summed up thus:

> Romania as a state (together with its official name, which reflects its international legal status), appeared on the map of Europe long after Bessarabia became part of Russia. The attempt by Romanian bourgeois historians to give retrospectively a wider meaning to the terms 'Romania' and 'the Romanian people,' and to use them to refer to foreign territories and foreign peoples,

> was not only a concrete example of historical falsification, but also the expression of the aggressive tendencies of the ruling classes in the Kingdom of Romania.[84]

No less a person than Ceauşescu took up the gauntlet thrown down by Lazarev. In a speech delivered on 28 March 1975 he referred obliquely to Lazarev's distortions by maintaining that

> the division of states and the arbitrary division of peoples are presented as expressions of certain historical needs, while the results of such artificially created situations are rationalized and interpreted as a natural process of forming distinct nations.[85]

Shortly afterwards a new museum of national history opened with prominently displayed maps of Romania showing Bessarabia and Northern Bukovina as part of the national territory. In the following year two members of the Party's Institute of Historical Studies produced a work on Romanian politics between 1918 and 1921 in which they referred to Bessarabia as this ancient Romanian territory.[86] However, the Romanian leader was careful to avoid criticizing the Soviet Moldavian historian directly and his caution set the tone for the muted response to the work in Romania. Instead, Ceauşescu authorized *Asociaţia România*, the government-sponsored association for relations with the émigré community, to distribute a complete Romanian translation of Lazarev's work with the request that it be reviewed as widely as possible in Western publications. It was also outside Romania that the propaganda section of the Central Committee arranged for the publication of the regime's official response to the book. Writing under the pseudonym of Petre Moldoveanu, Constantin Giurescu, the most distinguished Romanian historian, was asked to produce a polemical pamphlet refuting Lazarev's claims. Entitled *How to Falsify History*, it was printed in Milan by Constantin Drăgan, an Italian millionaire of Romanian origin, under the imprint of his publishing house Nagard (Drăgan spelt backwards) in 1975.

In Soviet Moldavia itself reviewers gave an uncritical validation of Lazarev's views, one sycophant even hailing the book as "a major contribution to Soviet historiography".[87] This sparring over Bessarabia continued throughout 1975, and was fuelled by the rehabilitation of Marshal Ion Antonescu, the wartime dictator who had led Romanian forces in the joint attack with Germany upon the Soviet Union in 1941 in the hope of regaining Bessarabia. Previously regarded as a taboo figure, Antonescu's success in reconquering Bessarabia and Northern Bukovina was adjudged by the propaganda section of the Romanian Central Committee to be too sensitive a subject to be treated in a work of history and therefore the Marshal's re-entry into the public domain was entrusted to a novelist, Marin Preda (1922–80). In *Delirul* (Delirium), Antonescu is presented as a tragic figure who sees Romania's only hope of retrieving Bessarabia in an alliance with Germany. For a Romanian public starved of all but Communist propaganda about Antonescu, the novel was like a breath of fresh air and its print run of 35,000 copies was sold out immediately. The partial vindication of the Marshal was roundly condemned in the Moscow *Literaturnaia gazeta* and as a result Preda was instructed by the Central Committee to produce a revised edition giving more emphasis to the struggle against Fascism in Romania during the war. The edition had a print run of 100,000 copies.[88]

Throughout the late 1970s and early 1980s the Romanian authorities refused to let the problem of Bessarabia fade into silence. In 1983, a historical atlas appeared with maps showing Bessarabia as part of Romania between 1918 and 1940, with one indicating the areas annexed by the Soviet Union "in autumn 1940".[89] But by this time the efficacy for Ceauşescu of playing the nationalist card had virtually vanished. In the face of the severe austerity measures which Ceauşescu had introduced in order to pay off the country's foreign debt which had risen to ten billion dollars at the end of 1981, most Romanians began to ask whether autonomy was worth the price. The question was put even more frequently after Mikhail Gorbachev became Soviet party leader in March 1985.

Ceauşescu's irritation with the policies of *glasnost* and *perestroika* soon left an echo in the pseudo-historical writings of his brother, Lt. Gen. Ilie Ceauşescu. An attack in an article by the general in the April 1989 issue of the military review *Lupta Intregului Popor* on ideological 'revisionism', that is, on *glasnost* and *perestroika*, was equated with the territorial 'revisionism' practised by Hungary and the Soviet Union in 1940 against Romania. The Soviet ultimatum of 26 June 1940 forced Romania to "surrender the territory between the Prut and the Dniester and the northern part of Bukovina, which were incorporated into the Soviet Union".[90] Nicolae Ceauşescu revived the parallel, although in a slightly different form, in his address to the Fourteenth Party Congress on 20 November 1989. In the process of reform, concessions had been made, he argued, to the "international class enemy" (capitalism) which had led to the 'de-ideologization' of international relations and the emergence of a new 'international imperialism'. These concessions were similar to those made by the Soviet Union to Germany in the Molotov-Ribbentrop Pact of August 1939 to which Ceauşescu alluded without mentioning it by name:

> One must never forget the lessons of history and the fact that Hitlerite Germany was encouraged to unleash World War II by the policy of concessions to Nazi Germany... We must never forget that the pact between Hitlerite Germany and the Soviet Union did not eliminate the threat [of war]... Romania believes, therefore, that one must move to to adopt [all] necessary measures for the solution of all the problems that are still pending. Primarily, it is necessary to adopt a clear and unequivocal position condemning and annulling all accords with Hitlerite Germany by drawing practical conclusions for cancelling the consequences of all these pacts and diktats.[91]

In calling for the reversal of the consequences of these pacts Ceauşescu was, in fact, arguing for the return of Bessarabia to Romania. The Soviet reaction was, in the words of a TASS commentator, that "no serious or responsible politician" could raise the issue of the post-war borders, "including the Soviet border with Romania".[92]

Yet behind Ceauşescu's obvious attempt to appeal once again to Romanian nationalist sentiment there lay an anxiety about possible Soviet intervention in Romania's internal affairs. In a speech to the heads of the North and South American delegations Ceauşescu referred to the Molotov-Ribbentrop Pact by name and expressed fear of a new agreement between the United States and the Soviet Union "to the detriment of other peoples". The forthcoming Malta summit between President Bush and General Secretary Gorbachev was seen, therefore, by Ceauşescu as a second Molotov-Ribbentrop Pact at the hands of which Romania would again suffer, for in his own self-centred view of international affairs, the two superpowers had nothing better to do than to plot his own downfall. As Michael Shafir concluded, Ceauşescu's remarks were meant as a warning to Gorbachev not to interfere in Romania and had been strengthened by the ending of a Romanian news blackout on the growth of the nationalist movement in the Moldavian SSR only a few days earlier.[93]

Barely a month after these words Ceauşescu fell, thus feeding the rumour mill in Romania that he had indeed been the victim of the American-Soviet plot which he had predicted. He was overthrown at the very height of the national revival in Moldavia which the nationalist in him could only have looked upon with joy, but which the Communist in him could not fail to regard with mixed feelings. The movement for national emancipation in Moldavia could not have emerged without the application of those very policies of *glasnost* and *perestroika* to which he was so resolutely opposed in his own country. In the exuberance generated by the Romanian revolution, calls for the union of Moldavia with Romania came from both sides of the river Prut but in Moldavia itself that newly-expressed nationalism, which initially was distinctly Romanian in character, has, since the declaration of independence in August 1991 of the renamed Moldova, assumed a Moldovan one. Acceptance of the latter proposition may, paradoxically, seem to be a validation of Soviet efforts to give a distinct identity to the Romanians of Moldova since their annexation of the republic in 1940, and those who attempt to develop a Moldovan self-consciousness may have to fall back on Soviet interpretations of the history and culture of the Moldovans.

Notes

1 This is a revised and updated version of chapters four and five of my *Ceauşescu and the Securitate. Coercion and Dissent in Romania, 1965–89* (London: Hurst; New York: M.E. Sharpe, 1995).

2 An original and stimulating analysis of Romanian national identity is given by Katherine Verdery, *National Ideology under Socialism* (Berkeley: University of California Press, 1991); see also Radu Cinpoies, *Nationalism and Identity in Romania. A History of Extreme Politics from The Birth of the State to EU accession* (London: I. B. Tauris, 2010).

3 *Metodica Predării Istoriei Patriei* [The Method for Teaching the History of the Homeland] (Bucharest: Editura Ştiinţifică şi Pedagogică, 1988).

4 The reverse also occurred, as in the case of the building of *Casa Republicii*, Ceauşescu's palace in Bucharest, when thousands of Hungarian construction workers were brought from Transylvania, although these were, in effect, migrant workers who received no right of residence in the capital.
5 Deletant, Ceauşescu and the *Securitate*, p.63.
6 R. King, Minorities under Communism. Nationalities as a Source of Tension among Balkan Communist States (Cambridge, Massachusetts: Harvard University Press, 1973), p.149.
7 E. Illyes, *National Minorities in Romania. Change in Transylvania* (Boulder, Colorado: East European Monographs, 1982), p.117.
8 King, *Minorities*, p.150.
9 Stefano Bottoni, 'The Creation of the Hungarian Autonomous Region in Romania (1952): Premises and Consequences' in *Regio Minorities, Politics, Society* (English edition), 2003, vol.1, pp.71–94 [80].
10 Bottoni, 'The Creation', p.86.
11 *Ibid.*
12 For an authoritative treatment of the national question in Transylvania under Communism see Stefano Bottoni *Transilvania rossa. Il comunismo romeno e la questione nazionale, 1944–1965* [Red Transylvania. The Romanian communism and the national question, 1944–1965] (Roma: Carocci Editore, 2007). A particular merit of Stefano Bottoni's study is his analysis of the genesis of the Hungarian Autonomous Region (HAR) and of what he terms its 'Stalinist eco-system', one which confronted questions of political ideology, national and cultural identity and economic backwardness.
13 Ghita Ionescu, *Communism in Rumania, 1948–1962* (London: Oxford University Press, 1964), pp.217–18.
14 King, *Minorities*, p.152.
15 See chapter six.
16 Whereas in the school year 1955–1956 there were 1,022 primary schools in which education was offered solely in Hungarian, by 1958–1959 this number had dropped to 915. In that same period the number of primary schools giving instruction in both Romanian and Hungarian increased from 38 to 124. In the sphere of secondary education a parallel decrease in Hungarian language provision took place: in the same interval of time the number of 493 schools had fallen to 469, whereas the number of dual language ones had risen from 10 to 77 (King, *Minorities*, p.153).
17 Michael Shafir, *Romania. Politics, Economics, Society* (London: Frances Pinter, 1985), p.160.
18 King, *Minorities*, p.154.
19 *Ibid.*, p.157.
20 *Ibid.*, p.158.
21 *Ibid.*
22 N. Ceauşescu, *Romania on the Way of Completing Socialist Construction*, vol.2 (Bucharest: Meridiane, 1969), p.543.
23 *Ibid.*, pp.547–48.
24 Mary-Ellen Fischer, *Nicolae Ceauşescu. A Study in Political Leadership* (Boulder, Colorado: Lynne Rienner, 1989), p.124.
25 Fischer, *Nicolae Ceauşescu*, p.148.
26 King, *Minorities*, p.165.
27 *Ibid.*, p.167.
28 Ceauşescu, *Romania*, vol.6 (Bucharest: Meridiane, 1972), p.190.
29 *Ibid.*
30 Romania: Forced Labor, Psychiatric Repression of Dissent, Persecution of Religious Believers. Ethnic Discrimination and Persecution, Law and the Suppression of Human Rights (New York: Amnesty International, 1987), p.40.

31 The existence of Lazar's text was first revealed on 17 April 1977 in the *Sunday Times*. Its 60 pages chronicled the experience of the Hungarian minority in Communist Romania and catalogued measures considered by the author to be highly discriminatory. Special attention was paid to the regime's educational policy which the author showed had resulted in a drastic fall in the availability of Hungarian language tuition at primary, secondary, and university level (*Witnesses to Cultural Genocide* (New York: American Transylvanian Federation, Committee for Human Rights in Rumania, 1979), pp.117–29).

32 *Witnesses*, p.150.

33 In 1958–59 there were 45 Romanian and 36 Hungarian teachers in the Faculty of Chemistry, and in 1976–77 63 Romanians and only 14 Hungarians. In the intervening 19 years 37 new Romanian staff were appointed, compared with only one Hungarian. Analogous figures for other faculties were:

		1958–59	1976–77
Law	Romanians	18	23
	Hungarians	15	4
Economics	Romanians	23	76
	Hungarians	15	19
Mathematics	Romanians	31	51
	Hungarians	19	14
History	Romanians	29	20
	Hungarians	14	7

Source: *Witnesses*, pp.152–53).

34 According to Takács, in the year 1957–58 there were 4,082 students attending Hungarian language institutions of higher education and 1,000–1,500 Hungarian students at Romanian language institutions out of an undergraduate population of 51,094. Hungarian students thus represented 10 per cent of all students. In 1974–75, this percentage had fallen to 5.7 (6,188 Hungarian students out of a total of 108,750). In the county of Cluj where the Hungarians made up 26 per cent of population (1966 census), there were 174 Romanian language classes for first year pupils of technical schools, and only two in Hungarian in the year 1973–74. By 1976–77 there were 192 Romanian language classes and nine Hungarian ones (one in agriculture, the remainder in engineering subjects). This development of technical schools followed from the education law of 1973 which aimed to make secondary education serve the needs of an industrializing economy; two-thirds of schools were to be devoted to technical subjects and only one-third to the humanities (G.Schopflin and H. Poulton, *Romania's Ethnic Hungarians* (London: Minority Rights Group, 1990), p.13).

35 *Witnesses*, pp.154–55.

36 Quoted from Fischer, *Nicolae Ceauşescu*, p.245.

37 Quoted from Shafir, *Romania*, pp.162–63.

38 The texts appeared in *Witnesses*, pp.163–78.

39 *Witnesses*, p.177.

40 Quoted from Schopflin and Poulton, *Romania's Ethnic Hungarians*, p.15.

41 A.H. Smith, 'The Romanian Enterprise', in I. Jeffries (ed.), *Industrial Reform in Socialist Countries* (London: Edward Elgar, 1992), p.204.

42 V. Socor, 'Dissent in Romania: the Diversity of Voices', *Radio Free Europe Research*, vol.12, no.22 (5 June 1987), p.5.

43 For an English translation see L. Peter (ed.), *Historians and the History of Transylvania* (Boulder, Colorado: East European Monographs, 1992), pp.174–96.

44 A.U. Gabanyi, 'Gorbachev Presents "Restructuring" to the Romanian Public', *RFE Research, Romanian SR/4* (29 May 1987), p.12.

45 *RFE Research, Romanian SR/1* (13 January 1988), pp.29–30.

46 Voices were also raised in protest at the restrictions on German cultural life. A group of ten young German writers from the Banat, known as *Aktionsgruppe Banat*, provided a critique of the Ceauşescu regime from the left, highlighting the nationalist bias in education and culture. Most of the group's members were arrested for interrogation and then dismissed from their jobs as journalists and teachers and forced to immigrate to West Germany. One of the most graphic accounts of life under Ceauşescu for a member of a minority was given by one of the writers Richard Wagner in his narrative *Ausreiseantrag* (Exit application) published in West Germany in 1988, English tr. *Exit: A Romanian Story* (London: Verso, 1990). The regime occupied everything, including language. Independent opinions could not be expressed: the regime decided what realistic literature was and what the writer considered realistic was then judged to be unrealistic. Nationalism in the classroom was exemplified by the fact that in English lessons a map of Romania and not of Britain hung on the wall. Wagner's terse, telegraphic and stark language matched perfectly the world he described. In a series of cameo portraits and situations people are pictured as leading a monotonous, monochromatic life, whispering in dark corners with expressionless faces. In this claustrophobic existence even the abnormal comes to be accepted as normal.

47 The Systematization plan is discussed in chapter eight of my *Ceauşescu and the Securitate. Coercion and Dissent in Romania, 1965–89* (London: Hurst, 1995).

48 A list of such villages in Harghita reached Britain in April 1989. They were, in alphabetical order of commune (in brackets), Cuşmed, Inlăceni, (Atid), Andreeni, Firtănuş, Laz-Firtănuş, Laz-Şoimuş, Medişoru Mic (Avrămeşti), Ciobăniş, Cotormani, Ghiurche (Ciucsângeorgiu), Atia, Calonda (Corund), Făncel, Valea Rotundă (Dealu), Ţengheler (Ditrău), Făgeţel (Frumoasa), Dealu Armanului, Nuţeni, Plopiş, Preluca, Toleşeni, Zăpodea (Gălăuţaş, Ghiduţ (Lazarea), Poiana Fagului, Puntea Lupului (Lunca de Jos), Bulgăreni, Firtuşu, Păltiniş, Păuleni, Satu Mic, Sâncel (Lupeni), Călugăreni, Chinuşu, Ghipeş, Locodeni, Petreni, Rareş (Mărtiniş), Aluniş, Dejuţiu, Mătişeni (Mugeni), Satu Nou (Ocland), Becaş, Bucin, Şaşvereş (Praid), Făgeţel, Martonca, Sineu (Remetea), Vilac (Săcel), Hosasău, Sântimbru Băi (Sâncrăieni), Valea Uzului (Sânmartin), Duda (Subcetate), Senetea (Suseni), Benţid, Cădaciu Mare, Cădaciu Mic, Chedia Mare, Chedia Mică, Nicoleni, Turdeni (Simoneşti), Pintic, Recea (Tulgheş), Iaşu, Ighiu, Nicoleşti, Obrănesçti, Vasileni (Ulieş), Desag, Poiana Târnavei (Zetea).

49 M. Rady, *Romania in Turmoil* (London: I.B. Tauris, 1992), p.73.

50 Untitled anonymous article in *The New Hungarian Quarterly*, no.3 (1988), p.59.

51 The New Hungarian Quarterly, pp.56–57.

52 *The Independent*, 23 November 1988.

53 M. Shafir, '"Revisionism" Under Romanian General's Fire: Ceauşescu's Brother Attacks Hungarian Positions', *RFE Research, Background Report/86* (17 May 1989), pp.2–3.

54 M. Shafir, "Revisionism", p.3.

55 Schopflin and Poulton, *Romania's Ethnic Hungarians*, pp.18–19.

56 M. Shafir, 'Romania and the Reburial of Imre Nagy', *RFE Research, Background Report/117* (30 June 1989), p.1.

57 *Ibid.*

58 M. Shafir, 'From Sofia to Beijing: Reactions to the 19th Soviet Party Conference', *RFE Research, Background Report/133* (13 July 1988), p.5.

59 S. Koppany, 'New Hungarian Minority Publication Appears in Transylvania', *RFE Research, Background Report/53* (21 March 1989), pp.1–3.

60 Anonymous article, 'Church Life in Romania', *Religion in Communist Lands*, vol.17, no.4 (Winter 1989), pp.356–59.

61 'Church Life', pp.359–60.

62 L. Tökés, *With God, For the People, as told to David Porter* (London: Hodder and Stoughton, 1990), pp.65, 79.

63 Rady, *Romania in Turmoil* (London: I.B. Tauris, 1992), p.86.

64 The population of the new republic is given in one Romanian source as 545,000 of whom 175,000 (32 per cent) were Moldavians and 250,000 Ukrainians (46 per cent); see E. Diaconescu, *Românii din Răsărit, Transnistria* (Iaşi, 1942), p.218. A Soviet Moldavian study gives the percentages of the AMSSR's population in 1940 as 28 per cent Moldavian and 51 per cent Ukrainian (A. Grecul, *Rastsvet Moldavskoi Sotsi Listicheskoi Natsii* (Kishinev, 1974), p.86).

65 M. Bruchis, One step back, two steps forward: on the language policy of the Communist Party of the Soviet Union in the National Republics (Boulder, Colorado: East European Monographs, 1982), p.52.

66 J. Pool, 'Soviet language planning: goals, results, options', in J.R. Azrael (ed.), *Soviet nationality policies and practices* (New York: Praeger, 1978), p.226.

67 Translated from the preface to *Cuvintelnic ortografic moldovenesc* (Tiraspol, 1939), as reproduced in Bruchis, p.61.

68 Not to be confused with the present-day breakaway republic of Trans-Dniester which covers only a segment of wartime Romanian Transnistria.

69 W.P. van Meurs, *Chestiunea Basarabiei în Istoriografiea comunistă* (Chişinău: Editura Arc, 1996), pp.270–77 and *id.*, 'The Bessarabian Question in Communist Historiography', unpubl. Ph.D thesis presented in Department of History, University of Utrecht, 1993, p.180.

70 This detail, together with the date the text was sent to the typesetter, can be found in the colophon of the book whose Romanian title is K. Marx, *Insemnări despre Români* (Bucharest: Editura Academiei Republicii Populare Române, 1964).

71 Marx, *Insemnări*, p.18.

72 Quoted from King, *Minorities*, p.229.

73 *Ibid.*

74 N. Ceauşescu, Romania on the Way of Completing Socialist Construction: Reports, Speeches, Articles, vol.1 (Bucharest: Meridiane, 1969), p.345.

75 King, *Minorities*, p.237.

76 S.K. Briaskin and M. Sitnik, *Triumful Adevărului Istoric* (Chişinău: Cartea Moldovenească, 1970), p.4.

77 N. Dima, *Bessarabia and Bukovina: The Soviet-Romanian Territorial Dispute,* (Boulder, Colorado: East European Monographs, 1982), p.53.

78 A.M. Lazarev, *Moldavskaya Sovetskaya Gosudarstvenost' i Bessarabskiy Vopros* (Kishinev: Izdatelstvo Kartya Moldovenyaske, 1974). It was reviewed in detail by J. Gold, 'Bessarabia: The Thorny "Non-Existent" Problem', in *East European Quarterly*, vo.13, no.1 (Spring 1979), pp.47–74.

79 Miron Costin (1633–1691) writes in the preface to his study of the Moldavians entitled *De Neamul Moldovenilor* that he had undertaken to show the origins of the "inhabitants of our land, Moldavia and so too of those of Wallachia, as mentioned above and of the Romanians of Transylvania, for they are all the same one people and settled in these lands at the same time" (M. Costin, *Opere alese*, ed. by L. Onu (Bucharest: Editura Ştiinţifică, 1967), p.133).

80 Lazarev, *Moldavskaya*, p.739.

81 Gold, 'Bessarabia', p.73.

82 There were echoes here of the language of a history of Northern Bukovina published in the Ukrainian SSR in 1969. The Romanian annexation of Northern Bukovina in 1918 is qualified as follows: "Having grabbed Bukovina, the Romanian occupiers instituted a savage regime of terror, economic and political oppression" (V. Kurylo et al., *Pivnichna Bukovyna, ii mynule i suchasne* (Uzhorod: Karpaty, 1969), p.92).

83 Lazarev, *Moldavskaya*, p.801.

84 *Ibid.*, p.531.

85 Quoted from R.R. King, 'The Escalation of Rumanian-Soviet Historical Polemics over Bessarabia', *RFE Research. Romania Background Report*, no.28 (12 February 1976), p.6.
86 M. Muşat and I. Ardeleanu, *Viaţa Politică în România, 1918–1921* (Bucharest: Editura Politică, 1976), p.10, note 4.
87 M. Sitnik, review in *Codri*, no.12 (1974), p.137.
88 Dennis Deletant, 'Cheating the Censor: Romanian Writers under Communism', *Central Europe*, vol.6, no.2 (November 2008), pp.144–45.
89 *Atlas pentru istoria României* (Bucharest: Editura didactică şi pedagogică, 1983), nos. 65–67, 73.
90 M. Shafir, '"Revisionism" under Romanian General's Fire: Ceauşescu's Brother Attacks Hungarian Positions', *RFE Research. Background Report*/86 (17 May 1989), p.4.
91 Quoted from M. Shafir, 'Highlights of the 14th Party Congress', *RFE Research. Romanian Situation Report*/9 (14 December 1989), p.30.
92 *Ibid.*
93 Shafir, 'Highlights', p.31.

14 Compliance towards the regime

A feature of public attitudes in Romania towards Ceauşescu was compliance.[1] His ability to garner support for his regime from intellectuals by using the 'nation' as his constant point of reference in defining his policies was equally efficacious when applied to creative writers and historians.[2] The corollary of Ceauşescu's achievement in this respect was a virtual absence of intellectual dissent or, expressed otherwise, a monotonous compliance by intellectuals with the regime.

Some Romanian *émigrés* and Western observers have sought an explanation for this compliance or acquiescence in the Romanians' past, in a long-entrenched Ottoman tradition of dissimulation, and in deep-rooted practices of corruption, nepotism and bribery.[3] They also point to the absence of a focal point of opposition in post-war Romania. The weakness of the pre-war Romanian Communist Party, which was proscribed between 1924 and 1944, may explain the few challenges to the Communist regime from within Marxist circles. Other analysts, and these include native Romanian writers themselves, ascribed this compliance to opportunism. The prospect of financial and material gain by accommodating oneself with the regime proved irresistible to many individuals and the resulting prevalence of opportunism amongst creative intellectuals was recognized by the poet Ana Blandiana as a blight on Romanian society and culture.[4]

However, the blandness of dissent amongst the creative intelligentsia is merely one aspect of the compliance which characterized the Ceauşescu era. The reasons for this docility on the part of intellectuals must be examined in the context of the relative absence of major challenges to the Ceauşescu regime from any group in society. That absence of challenge can be ascribed in part to the efficiency of the Communist Party machine and its insinuation into the public domain. Party membership was a passport to job security and advancement in professional life. Successful acceptance into the Union of Communist Youth *(Uniunea Tineretului Comunist)* for candidates under the age of 22, and promotion to membership of the RCP above that age, was a cause for celebration similar to that of a birthday or name day. Party membership signalled loyalty to the regime; without it professional advancement was virtually impossible.[5] Self-interest, therefore, dictated conformity and compliance.

The Ceauşescu period was marked not solely by the weakness of intellectual dissent, but of significant dissent from any quarter, with the exception of the Jiu valley strike of 1977 and the Braşov riot of 1987. The attitude of many Romanians was summed up by a young theatre director in 1988:

> What most people want to do under a dictatorship is to forget about it, get on with their lives, and enjoy themselves as best they can. Thus when Romanian TV was reduced to four hours of transmission per day in 1984 many citizens of Bucharest and the major cities acquired video recorders and cassettes with Western films. The import of these items was not banned, probably because amongst the users were Party and *Securitate* officials who did not alert Ceauşescu to the trend.[6]

The ambiguity of living in Ceauşescu's Romania was the subject of Paul Goma's novel *Bonifacia*, written in exile in France.[7] The novel portrays the ever-present duplicity of existence in a society in which the citizen must daily strike a balance between the demands of 'official' life and the attempt to lead an 'unofficial' one. The pressures of life and the fear of intrusion into it by the *Securitate* led many citizens to compartmentalize their existence into the public and private domains. Such a strategy of survival led to the blurring of distinctions with Western notions of morality. What might be termed 'amorality', translated by some outside observers as 'corruption', characterized the behaviour of many.

Any analysis of compliance under Ceauşescu must also consider the condition of the rural and urban workers, of the technical intelligentsia of engineers, economists and managers, and of the Church. Although the Romanian urban worker had a lower standard of living than his Hungarian or Polish counterpart, it was higher than that of a Romanian villager or peasant. Given the fact that in the early 1980s over 60 per cent of the urban workforce in Romania came originally from the village, the point of comparison for industrial workers was their birthplace. Wage differentials between the agricultural and urban sectors remained considerable throughout the Ceauşescu period. In 1965, the wages of a villager working on a cooperative or state farm were only half of the average income, and while they had risen by 1979 to 66 per cent of the average industrial wage, there was still obviously a marked discrepancy. As a result, a low status was associated with agricultural labour which in turn prompted migration to the towns and factories. At the same time, this low status generated low expectations.[8] The bulk of the peasantry had little knowledge of living standards in other parts of the Communist bloc.[9] With low expectations went a suspicion of authority, and a conviction of impotence.[10] These attitudes were inherited by those industrial workers who originated from the village. The significance of this peasant background in determining the outlook of industrial workers was highlighted by the calculation in 1982 that almost 30 per cent of Romania's urban workforce commuted from the village. Such a high proportion of commuting workers led to the creation of a semi-urban society in which the village and the ritual of the Orthodox Church remained very strong, and around which family reunions and feast days were celebrated.[11] Furthermore, the attitude of the prelates of the Orthodox Church, the largest religious denomination, has often been adduced as the prime example of not solely compliance but also sycophancy towards the Communist regime.[12]

The conviction of impotence which fieldwork by Western scholars on the Romanian peasantry revealed merits closer examination for an understanding of compliance towards the regime. The proverb *'capul plecat nici sabia nu-l taie'* ('the sword will not sever a bowed head') is often invoked as emblematic of Romanians' attitude to authority. This submissiveness can be derived from what the Romanian philosopher Mircea Vulcănescu called "the Romanian dimension of existence: which is characterised by its fatalism".[13] This acceptance of fate, which is determined by a belief in a spiritual eternity, can be equated in a political context with an acquiescence in temporal authority and recognition of the futility of resisting it. Such a conviction produced in some citizens a perverse pride in lamenting their personal plight: during the late 1980s, when austerity measures led to the introduction during the winter of heating restrictions in apartment complexes fuelled by a communal generator—common in those built in the 1960s in cities and towns—some citizens compared with a form of demonic pleasure the low temperatures in which they spent their 'leisure' hours.

A consequence of the massive drive to industrialize under Gheorghiu-Dej had been the creation of what might be termed a middle class of technicians, scientists and economic managers. The ability of this new class to articulate a group interest was linked to the degree to which the Party leadership was prepared to relax its monopoly of central planning and to introduce a measure of managerial autonomy, as the New Economic Mechanism in Hungary was to show in 1968. However, Ceauşescu abandoned in 1967 any such reformist ideas he may have had.[14] The Central Committee's rigid control over central planning was maintained, thereby suffocating any voice that the technocrats might have found in influencing policy. Ceauşescu's failure to reform therefore prevented any move towards market socialism and the development of any political constituency within the Party which a more pluralistic economic approach might have spawned.

Party membership itself increased steadily. By 1965, membership had reached 1,450,000—about eight per cent of the country's population.[15] After his accession to power in 1965, Ceauşescu sought to increase the Party's influence, broaden the base of popular support and bring in new members. His efforts to increase RCP membership were extremely effective. By February 1971, the Party claimed 2.1 million members. The Twelfth Party Congress in 1979 estimated membership at three million, and by March 1988, the RCP had grown to some 3.7 million members—more than twice as many as in 1965, when Ceauşescu came to power. Thus, in the late 1980s, some 23 per cent of Romania's adult population and 33 per cent of its working population belonged to the RCP.[16]

The stifling of the technocracy left the creative intelligentsia in the forefront of public life and it was to that body to which Ceauşescu turned in his appeals to national symbols. Ironically, it was the Warsaw Pact invasion of Czechoslovakia in August 1968 which allowed Ceauşescu to discover that appeals to national sentiment were an efficient mechanism of social control and personal dictatorship. The huge rally in Bucharest on 21 August and its acclamation of Ceauşescu's denunciation of the invasion proved to be his finest hour. It left an indelible mark upon him and whetted an appetite for the excesses of the personality cult. Significantly, Ceauşescu's defiance on that day also prompted several prominent writers to join the RCP. Their action shows how superficial it would be to dismiss all postures of writers as being dictated by opportunism or self-interest. Occasionally, creative intellectuals in Romania did act from deep conviction but the adulation of the Romanian leader expressed at various times by most writers, artists and journalists, shows that principled motivation was the exception.

In this sense there can be no doubt that during the period of Communist rule many creative intellectuals served the Party and the Ceauşescu dictatorship. Yet this is also true of the technical intellectuals or technocrats. Just as doctors could be found to conduct the psychiatric abuse of dissidents, and engineers and architects to implement the policies of systematization, so too did writers and artists picture the utopia rather than the dystopia of Communism. To have done otherwise would, of course, have invited immediate persecution by the regime and it is easy, when unflattering comparisons are made between the activities of intellectuals in Czechoslovakia, Hungary and Poland with those of their counterparts in Romania, to overlook the uniquely repressive nature of the Ceauşescu regime.

That said, the proclamation of the Romanian People's Republic on 30 December 1947 marked the beginning of an era in which the leadership of the Romanian Communist Party would seek, and succeed to a large degree, to exploiting literature for its own ends.[17] The measure of that success is reflected in the form and content of published literature between 1948 and 1989. Censorship provided the mechanism. The relationship of writers to the Party was largely one of acquiescence.[18] The activity of Miron Radu Paraschivescu (1911–71), Dumitru Ţepeneag (1937–) and Paul Goma (1935–) in the late 1960s and the 1970s, and the work of the novelists Augustin Buzura (1938–) and Marin Preda (1922–80), and of the poets Ana Blandiana (1942–), Mircea Dinescu (1950–), and Marin Sorescu (1936–96), constitute some notable exceptions.

Given the lack of sympathy for Marxism-Leninism amongst Romanians this conformity is striking.[19] It becomes remarkable when we consider that the young Communist regime in Romania identified itself so closely with the Soviet Union that some enthusiasts even sought to deny the ethnic character of the Romanians by accentuating the Slavonic element in their origins and language. While it is true that the supervision of such Soviet-inspired aberrations, including the method of Socialist Realism in literature and art, was entrusted to Russian-speaking Bessarabians on the Central Committee such as Iosif Chişinevski and Leonte Răutu, the practitioners were often native Romanians, examples being the historian Petre Constantinescu-Iaşi (1892–1977) and the poet Mihai Beniuc (1907–88).

Opportunism fuelled collaboration with the regime. The ranks of committed Communists among writers such as Geo Bogza (1908–93) and Saşa Pană (1902–81)[20] were swelled by those holding established left-wing views such as George Călinescu (1899–1965) and Mihail Sadoveanu (1880–1961).[21] Nevertheless, the alignment of accomplished writers with the new regime proved the exception rather than the rule. The symbol of resistance to the blandishments of the

Communists after the proclamation of the People's Republic was the poet and philosopher Lucian Blaga (1895–1961), who paid the price of his silence by being removed from his chair at Cluj University and excluded from public life for the rest of his days. Even Tudor Arghezi (1880–1967), an outstanding poet of the pre-war period with left-wing sympathies, found himself out of tune with the literary method imported from the Soviet Union in 1948 known as Socialist Realism. His poetry was the subject of an attack launched in the Party newspaper *Scînteia* by Sorin Toma who claimed that

> the ideological content of Arghezi's poetry—dissatisfaction with life, disgust and hatred towards man, pessimism, mysticism, the cultivation of everything morbid, the quest for death—has nothing original or national in it. In the period of the imperialist monopolies, this ideological content represents the standard goods on the world scale of decadent bourgeois art.[22]

By contrast, it was another accomplished writer who proved the most significant recruit to Socialist Realism. The qualities of *Mitrea Cocor* (Mitrea Cocor)[23] by Mihail Sadoveanu, a talented historical novelist, are best described by Jack Lindsay in his foreword to the English translation[24]:

> Mitrea Cocor was conceived and realized in the perspective opened [by] the revolutionary changes lived through by the author. Following the classic method of Socialist Realism, he moves from the particular to the essential, and gives to his character, the unfortunate orphan Mitrea, the inner qualities of the Rumanian peasant: ingenuity, love of work and of justice. Called to the colours and dispatched to the front, he discovers sincere friends among the soldiers compelled to go and shed their blood in a foreign land [the Soviet Union] and to attack people who have never troubled them or done them any harm. And so, in the soul of this peasant who is simple and illiterate, but honest and just, there awakens the revolutionary consciousness of the class-struggle, which previously did not enter into his scheme of things. Made prisoner, he becomes acquainted with the Soviet Union and gets to know collective farmers; he admires the organization of their farms, which he compares mentally with the poverty of his home village. Then it is that he at last understands the lies and baseness of the anti-Soviet propaganda with which he had been drenched in his own land. ...
>
> He enlists in the division of Rumanian volunteers to struggle at the side of the Soviet soldiers, to join them in the struggle for the overthrow of the oppressors who have stolen from them the right to human dignity enjoyed by the people of the Soviet Union. He will one day return free and triumphant to the village, marry the chosen of his heart, and continue the struggle beside other honest peasants of the village ....[25]

A new censorship body, the General Directorate of Press and Printing (*Direcţia generală a presei şi a tipăritorilor*), replaced the censorship department of the Ministry of Arts and Information which was deemed incapable of "assuring a proper activity in the fields of means of expression and public information".[26] The new body was established by decree in May 1949 and was made responsible to the Council of Ministers, thereby giving it an increased authority. It was charged with overseeing the publication of all printed matter and the distribution of films and works of art as well as all forms of literature. Its creation can be considered the beginning of the institutionalization of information control in Communist Romania.[27]

An idea of the impact of the Directorate can be gauged from the regular reports which it provided. An example is the report of the section monitoring the provincial press dated 10 May 1951, stamped 'secret'. The section was budgeted to have 93 censors, of whom 13 were allocated to the central, Bucharest, office and 80 to the provinces; in fact, the report stated, it had in 1951 67 censors, of whom 11 were assigned to Bucharest and the rest to the regions. In the period February–April 1951, 1,638 newspapers were verified, during which 1,517 errors of an ideological and printing nature were discovered. As a result, four editions of newspapers were withdrawn from sale with a print run of 61,700 copies.[28] A later report for 1951 identified the following errors in the press: in the edition of the newspaper *Luptătorul* (The Warrior) of 16 August 1951, published in the Moldavian town of Bacău, the sentence "the place of speculators has been taken by the state shops and cooperatives" was removed; in *Dobrogea nouă* (The new Dobrogea) of 9 September a bulletin of Voice of America was quoted. This reference was censored. In *Sportul popular* (People's Sport) of 20 December, instead of "CC (Central Committee) of the Romanian People's Republic" the words "Ca ca" (the shit) of the Romanian People's Republic" had been set as type.[29]

One of the strongest rebukes issued by the Directorate was to textbook authors over their failure to recognize the primacy of Soviet achievements in the arts, sciences and in the general field of human endeavour. A further report for 1951 criticizes the book *Chimia anorganică şi organică pentru clasa a VII-a elementară* (Organic and non-organic chemistry for the seventh elementary class) for not pointing out on page 159 that the Russian scientist Vizin had observed the explosive qualities of nitroglycerine before Alfred Nobel; in *Ştiinţele naturii şi igienă pentru clasa a IV-a* (Natural science and hygiene for the fourth class) "it is stated that the American scientist Franklin discovered electricity in 1752 when, in fact, the Russian Lomonosov had discovered it much earlier"; in *Fizica pentru clasa a III-a* (Physics for the third class) "there is no mention of the fact that Pozunov created the steam engine, twenty years before Watt".[30]

The mechanical application of Marxism to the presentation of history produced improbable assertions. In the grammar *Limba română* (The Romanian language) for the sixth class there appeared the sentence (on page 223) referring to the unsuccessful peasant uprising in Transylvania of 1784 that "if the peasantry had been led by the working class the outcome of the revolt would have been different". In a similar grammar book for the fourth class, Marx and Engels are said "to have loved each other very much and valued each other. Each enjoyed the joys and was proud of the successes of the other"(pp.193–94).[31] The same report went on to bemoan the fact that in the textbook *Limba română şi Istoria RPR* (The Romanian language and the History of the Romanian People's Republic) for the third class there is no mention of "the nefarious role played by the monarchy in the country's affairs" while "the story of the blue tit is inappropriate because the bird, once freed from its cage, returns to it, thereby showing that it does not appreciate freedom and is always in search of a master".[32]

Failure to conform to the method of Socialist Realism invited problems with the Directorate, even for those who enjoyed the favour of the regime. An example was George Călinescu, an eminent literary critic who was appointed director of the Institute of Literary History and Folklore in 1949: he was unable to publish his novel *Bietul Ioanide* (Poor Ioanide), which he had begun in 1947, until six years later. On publication it received a hostile press for what was regarded as excessive candidness in its portrayal of the different reactions from a number of intellectuals to the rise of right-wing movements in pre-war Romania. Yet the fact that the novel appeared in 1953 was indicative of an indulgence, manifest after Stalin's death, towards literature that did not wear the straitjacket of Socialist Realism.

The period from 1948 to 1953 had been characterized by the publication in Romanian translation of what may be considered Russian examples of the genre, such as Gor'kii's *Mother* and Sholokhov's *Virgin soil upturned*, leavened by native contributions of which *Mitrea Cocor* and the poetry of Mihai Beniuc, Dan Deşliu and Eugen Jebeleanu are indicative. The death of Stalin ushered in calls from Zaharia Stancu, the President of the Writers' Union, for the republication of the 'classics' of Romanian nineteenth-century literature, and even of works from the interwar years by Camil Petrescu, Cezar Petrescu, Liviu Rebreanu and Vasile Voiculescu.[33] In 1955, Tudor Arghezi was able to publish a collection of verse entitled *1907*, dedicated to the peasant uprisings of that year in Wallachia. Although this event was politically significant for the breach that it represented in the official attitude towards writers previously considered 'bourgeois' and 'decadent', that same year welcomed a new talent whose emergence was of greater artistic importance.

Marin Preda's (1922–80) *Moromeţii* (The Morometes) introduced one of the most convincing characters of post-war Romanian literature, the peasant farmer Ilie Moromete.[34] Set in the interwar period, the novel is centred on Ilie's relationship with his family and the village community. This relationship is conditioned by Ilie's authoritarian belief in his pivotal position in the family and village, one around which the fortunes of both must turn. Scornful of change, indifferent to innovation, Ilie is the champion of the old established order, one validated by time. "How can you live if you are not left in peace", he asks himself as he stubbornly, but vainly defends a stability that proves to be ephemeral in the face of time, a time which, to use one of the author's aphorisms, "no longer had patience". Ilie witnesses the breakup of the traditional village community as new economic forces come into play. The fragile family relationship is broken when Ilie's sons rebel against his authority by stealing his horses and fleeing to Bucharest. The end of the novel marks a watershed in Ilie's life. The destruction of its order and harmony anticipates the upheaval experienced by the village under Communist rule depicted in the second volume. The work is outstanding for its rich characterisation of individuals from the village community and it is hard to believe that it appeared at a time when Socialist Realist stereotypes still reigned supreme.[35]

A further indication that aesthetic qualities could triumph over ideological considerations was provided by *Groapa* (The Pit) by Eugen Barbu (1924–93), which appeared in 1957.[36] Its difficult nine-year gestation during which, according to the author, it was revised thirteen times, is explained more by its reception at the hands of some literary critics, than by the writer's search for a definitive version. With the vague terminology characteristic of literary criticism of the period, one reviewer opined that it contained "elements of human 'perilousness'",[37] but several of his colleagues were more specific in identifying the danger represented by the novel as a recrudescence of naturalism, a cardinal sin in the eyes of Socialist Realists. This charge was founded on Barbu's use of colourful slang in depicting the often insalubrious activities of a community of rogues that inhabited a seedy quarter on the fringes of Bucharest. The demolition in 1946 of this area, known as 'the pit of Ouatu', inspired Barbu to recall its world of vagabonds and swindlers. His eye for detail in the description of characters and their surroundings, coupled with their bawdy, humorous repartee, shows him at his most successful when handling figures from the lower rungs of society, a talent confirmed by his later novels.

Both *Moromeții* and *Groapa* were landmarks in the history of the post-war Romanian novel and stand out as such in the literature produced by what Preda termed "obsedantul deceniu" (the haunting decade) of the 1950s. The achievements of socialism are lauded by Petru Dumitriu (1924–2002) in his cosmeticized account of the construction of the Danube-Black Sea Canal *Drum fără pulbere* (Road without dust).[38] The reader is left ignorant of the fact that some 20,000 of the labourers were political prisoners, many of whom died during the course of the project.

The writers' principal role as "engineers of human souls" was reflected in Arghezi's *Cîntare omului* (Hymn to Mankind),[39] a collection of verse dedicated to man's gradual evolution towards self-discovery and his eventual self-realization in the new socialist order. Arghezi's rehabilitation was part of Gheorghiu-Dej's strategy to 'co-opt' major writers to the regime and avoid a genuine cultural 'liberalization'. This strategy was applied by Leonte Răutu, a close associate of Gheorghiu-Dej and head of the Propaganda and Culture section of the Central Committee between 1956 and 1965.[40] Under the new approach ideological constraints were relaxed and in 1959 Arghezi was able to publish a poem 'Psalm'. The poem continued a series with the same name which had been included in his prewar volume *Cuvinte Potrivite* (Fitting Words, 1927) and reflected the anguish of a spirit in search of God. The post-war generation would, perhaps, have only been able to appreciate the significance of the poem's publication later in that same year 1959 when Arghezi's complete *oeuvres* appeared for the first time, albeit with a cautionary preface written by the then President of the Writers' Union Mihai Beniuc. Beniuc tried to downplay, in true Marxist-Leninist spirit, the search for God, dismissing those verses in which the quest is expressed as "a search during which he [Arghezi] never found a trace or assignation, in the mystical sense I mean, with the person sought". He claimed to see in Arghezi's work of the 1950s

> a fairly rapid revolutionization of his position [caused] by those very revolutionary changes produced in the lives of our people, beginning with the armed insurrection of 23 August 1944 and our liberation from the Fascist yoke, then from the domination of the monarchy and the exploitation of the landowners and the bourgeoisie.[41]

Recognition of the regime's success in manipulating writers throughout the decade and its firm control over intellectuals can be perhaps seen in the Soviet choice of Romania as exile for the Hungarian Marxist critic György Lukács after the revolution of 1956. Yet this intellectual malleability masked a latent nationalism that the Party was to exploit fully in its clash with the Soviet Union over Comecon in the early 1960s. By drawing upon the inherent, nationalist anti-Russian sentiment of the population, the Romanian Workers' Party sought to move from reliance upon the Soviet Union to support from within Romania for its authority. Gheorghiu-Dej distanced himself further from his overlord by reversing the trend of Russianization in Romanian culture and education. The Russian Institute in Bucharest was closed, and Romanian names were restored to many of the city's streets which had been given Russian names.

These measures signalled a de-Stalinization of Romanian cultural policies that ushered in the rehabilitation of historical, political and literary figures who were prominent in the nineteenth-century movement for independence.[42] Contacts with the West were developed, exemplified by the visit of the Royal Shakespeare Company in 1964, and these had a leavening effect on cultural life. In literature the most significant act of rehabilitation was that of the critic and aesthetician Titu Maiorescu (1840–1917) in 1963. An advocate of art for art's sake and a repudiator of the social role of art, his readmittance into the public arena marked the abandonment by the Party of Socialist Realism as its aesthetic creed. This rejection paved the way for the restoration in 1964 of outstanding Romanian writers of the nineteenth century to their respected place in Romanian culture, and for the rehabilitation of a number of twentieth-century authors who had remained under a cloud because of their association either with 'undemocratic forces' or with 'decadent' literary movements, or because they had simply refused to compromise themselves by accepting the tenets of Socialist Realism.

George Călinescu's biographies of Mihail Eminescu (1850–89) and Ion Creangă (1839– 89), which had first appeared in 1944, were republished. The short stories of Ion Slavici (1848–1925), and poetry by Ion Barbu (1895–1961), Lucian Blaga (1895–1961), Octavian Goga (1881–1938), Adrian Maniu (1891–1968), Ion Minulescu (1881–1944), Ion Vinea (1895–1964), and Vasile Voiculescu (1884–1963) were reissued. In the theatre the comedy *Conu Leonida față cu reacțiunea*

(Mr Leonida faces the Opposition) and Năpasta (False Witness) by Ion Luca Caragiale (1852–1912) were staged for the first time since 1948.

Of greater importance for the future of Romanian literature was the emergence, permitted by this relaxation of rigid ideological control, of a clutch of writers, principally poets, from the post-war generation: Ioan Alexandru (1941–2000), Ana Blandiana (1942–), Marin Sorescu (1936–96) and Nichita Stănescu (1933–83). They were accompanied in their debuts by a number of older colleagues, 'the lost generation', who had written for the draw during the 1950s: Ion Caraion,[43] Geo Dumitrescu (1920–2004) and Ştefan Augustin Doinaş (1922–2002). Both groups injected a measure of refreshing nonconformism into contemporary literature by launching themselves into a revitalization of Romanian verse in which each poet sought to give his or her own vision of the world. In the confessional verse of Blandiana some critics detected an example offered by Nicolae Labiş (1935–56) with his credo "the struggle against inertia",[44] an attitude that can be explained as a desire to break free from the ideological clichés of the 1950s and which has led some observers to see a sinister hand behind his death under the wheels of a Bucharest tram in 1956.

The significance of the 'thaw' lies as much in its genesis as in its effect on Romanian literature. It resulted not from an attack on established ideological principles or from intellectual pressure, but from the changes in the political relationship between Romania and the Soviet Union that were triggered by the Comecon crisis. The concessions to writers were "granted by the regime rather than wrested from it"[45] and were awarded by Gheorghiu-Dej when his authority in the RWP was undisputed. It is myopic to see the 'thaw' as a sign of weakness on the part of the Party. The process of de-Stalinization was firmly controlled by the Party and never jeopardized its primacy in the country. Gheorghiu-Dej's supremacy was mirrored in the smoothness with which his designated successor, Nicolae Ceauşescu, took over the reins of power.

The compliance that had characterized relations between the intelligentsia and the RWP under Gheorghiu-Dej continued undisturbed after Ceauşescu's election as First Secretary in March 1965. This was largely due to the popularity of the anti-Soviet stance which the new leader developed into a national and nationalist brand of Marxism. A feature of this was the importance given to the nation in a socialist society, which found expression in Ceauşescu's report to the Ninth Congress of the Romanian Communist Party—to which title the Romanian Workers' Party reverted in June 1965—on 19 July 1965:

> For a long time to come, the nation and state will continue to be the basis of the development of socialist society. The development of the nation, the consolidation of the socialist state, comply with the objective requirements of social life.[46]

The role assigned to literature in society was to continue "shaping the new man's Socialist consciousness" by employing a new method: "deep-going Socialist humanism should pervade literary and artistic creation, which mirrors the Party's policy and activity devoted to the prosperity of our homeland, to the people's welfare and man's happiness".[47]

The RCP was depicted as leading the nation through socialism towards the fulfilment of its aspirations. By arguing that the Party represented the entire nation, Ceauşescu could claim for the Party and for himself legitimacy as the defender of the national interest. The corollary of this was that any criticism of the Party or its leader from Romanians, whether inside or outside the country, could be branded as treachery to the nation, a charge that was to be levelled in the early 1970s against dissenting voices, in particular Paul Goma. In a similar vein, pressure for internal change could be resisted by raising the spectre of threats to the nation from abroad, thus playing on the traditional dislike of the Soviet Union. Such tactics have the merit of diverting dissatisfaction with the Party's policies into support for the regime and were employed with success, particularly in the columns of the weeklies *Flacăra* (The Flame) and *Săptămâna* (The Week), edited respectively by Adrian Păunescu (from 1973) and Eugen Barbu (from 1970).

The stress placed on the nation in Ceauşescu's report was reflected in cultural developments by the search to identify the *'specificul național'* (the national characteristic) of Romanian culture.[48] Yet not all writers were mesmerized by the insistence upon the 'national identity' and 'the organic unity of the Romanians' in literary and historical publications. In 1966, an attempt was made by Miron Radu Paraschivescu (1911–71) to expand the aesthetic criteria admitted by the Party ideologists. On 15 May 1965, Paraschivescu took over the correspondence column of the literary monthly *Ramuri* (Branches), published in Craiova. Eleven months later to the day he succeeded in transforming the column into a four-page literary supplement with the title *Povestea Vorbii* (The Tale of Talk).[49] The supplement was host to a number of writers who, in most cases, found great difficulty in getting into print, an observation made at the time by the Bucharest weekly *Luceafărul* (The Evening Star).[50] Its second claim to nonconformity was Paraschivescu's assertion, in the first editorial, that he

> represented a group having precise values and intellectual affinities that differ from those of other journals. The essential point is that this group should not remain a closed shop, but should be enriched continually by new works and new authors without deviating at all from its general orientation and renouncing its characteristics.

The editor assumed the responsibility for the literature published in the supplement which would be "a veritable agora where the most conflicting of opinions could be openly exchanged, a sort of typographical Hyde Park where the spirit of spontaneity and not that of uniformity is abroad". A third feature of the supplement's existence was that Paraschivescu gave his services without remuneration, as did all the authors who he published. The bonds linking editor and contributor were thus spiritual and not commercial, and explain the continued solidarity of the group after *Povestea Vorbii*'s suppression. At the core of the group, apart from Paraschivescu himself, stood the poets Leonid Dimov (1926–87) and Virgil Mazilescu (1942–84), and the prose writer Dumitru Ţepeneag.

The emphasis placed by Paraschivescu upon aesthetic values to the exclusion of political dogma as criteria for publication exceeded the regime's limits of tolerance. Ironically, the principal charge levelled at the journal was its failure to reflect the *specificul naţional*. Adoption of this nationalist-inspired criterion thus became a litmus test of allegiance to the regime's cultural ideology. Refusal to accept it could constitute grounds for banishment from the literary establishment. The campaign of opposition to *Povestea Vorbii,* orchestrated by the Party and voiced in *Luceafărul* and *Contemporanul*, led to its suppression in December 1966, but the leavening experience of the journal's nine-month existence was to leave its mark. In the van of outspoken authors who raised their voices in 1968 were several of Paraschivescu's young protégés.

The events of Czechoslovakia during the 'Prague Spring' elicited a sympathetic response from the RCP since they conformed with Romanian advocacy of the view that each communist regime was entitled to determine its own policies without outside interference, explicit since the Comecon clash. In public statements and speeches, such as that made by Ceauşescu at the plenary session of the Central Committee of the RCP in March 1968, this view was reiterated: "No one can claim a monopoly of absolute truth as regards the development of social life; and no one can claim to have the last word in the realm of practice as well as in social and philosophical thought".[51]

However, one must be cautious not to draw too close a parallel between the Czech and Romanian experience of early 1968. None of the internal reforms emanating from the RCP, for example the return to the pre-Communist division of the country into counties and the restructuring of education, weakened to any degree the leading role of the Party. This is not to deny that a measure of 'liberalization' was admitted by the Party. Indeed, Ceauşescu in the same March speech invited intellectuals to participate in a discussion about political life in Romania in which they should not show "the slightest apprehension or reserve in public debates about internal politics".[52] The implications for literature of this invitation were spelt out by the journalist Paul Anghel in two articles from 28 March and 4 April which appeared in *Gazeta literară* (The Literary Gazette), the mouthpiece of the Writers' Union:

> Without departing from goals established *a priori*, the writer can, like the scientist, participate in the process of the search for the truth and prove the existence of a precise phenomenon; but more than that, he has the duty to tell us what exactly reality is and not how it ought to be or how he would like it to be.[53]

Of equal importance for writers and intellectuals was the plenary meeting of 25 April of the Central Committee at which Lucreţiu Pătrăşcanu, the Communist Minister of Justice in the Groza government who had been purged in 1948 and executed in 1954, was rehabilitated and the abuses of the Minister of the

Interior at the time, Alexandru Drăghici, condemned. Commenting on both decisions, Mihnea Gheorghiu recognised that "these abuses had been the cause of restraints which were harmful and dangerous for artistic creation and intellectual movements".[54]

The articles by Anghel and Gheorghiu were symptomatic of the vitality of literary debate engendered by Party pronouncements. A relaxation of censorship was evident from the thematic diversity of the literature which now surfaced. The drama *Iona* (Jonah) by Marin Sorescu was published in 1968[55] and performed to packed houses for a brief period in that year and in January 1969. Jonah, in the belly of a whale, cuts himself out only to find that the first whale had been swallowed by a second. Escaping from the second whale he finds himself in the belly of a third. The fisherman's predicament is the occasion for profound observations about human existence, expressed in a simple, colloquial language. Some critics interpreted the whale's belly as a symbol for the cosmos, others as intrauterine loneliness. Jonah may also be seen as a prisoner of convention. Clearly, his escape from captivity by committing suicide did not strike the optimistic note of socialist humanism by which "the people's welfare and man's happiness" were to be echoed. After 1969, the play was staged only once in Romania, in 1982 and then by a group of South American students working at the Bucharest Institute of Dramatic Art.

Marin Preda's *Intrusul* (The Intruder)[56] gave an exceptionally realistic portrayal of a young man unable to adapt to the new morality of contemporary urban society in which the novelist sees a corruption of traditional values. Notable for its metaphorical colour was Fănuş Neagu's (1932–) *Îngerul a strigat* (The Angel cried out),[57] an account of one man's vendetta to avenge the murder of his father, set against the background of the war, the drought of 1947 and the collectivization of agriculture in the early 1950s. The publication of two extracts from Paul Goma's *Ostinato*, in *Gazeta literară* in February and *România literară* in December 1968, extended the limits of censorship even further. The line was drawn at what Party spokesmen considered 'rightist tendencies', an accusation directed at the literary critic Ion Negoiţescu (1921–93) who had only re-emerged in print two years earlier. In February 1968, he published in the Oradea literary journal *Familia* (Family) an outline of a history of Romanian literature that he intended to write.

His proposal challenged the accepted values established by the official literary histories and reflected in school textbooks. Not only did he describe the years 1948–55 as a "historical void" but, more fatally, he proposed to omit such exponents of Socialist Realism as Eusebiu Camilar (1910–65) and Remus Luca (1923–2006). He ensured that he would become a target for the literary establishment by classifying the novels of Eugen Barbu, Marin Preda and Zaharia Stancu as "literature of transition". The Party newspaper *Scânteia*[58] cast doubt on the scholarly value of the intended history while *Luceafărul*,[59] whose editor was Eugen Barbu, expressed disappointment at Negoiţescu's underestimation of the literature of the 1950s and his overestimation of the young writers of the 1960s. Needless to say, Negoiţescu's history did not appear.[60]

The fate of a work similar to that of Negoiţescu's demonstrated that publication did not always represent safe passage over the hurdle of official sanction. The volume in question was an anthology of modern Romanian verse compiled by a young critic, Nicolae Manolescu, and entitled *Poezia română modernă* which adopted as its confines the poetry of George Bacovia and Emil Botta, both of whom were taboo figures. Although the anthology was given the censor's *imprimatur*, its contents clearly upset political sensibilities and orders were given for it to be seized in the bookshops.

Despite the fact that this attack on official literary values and on writers who embodied them was successfully fought off by the 'old guard' in the Manolescu case, the pressure for reform in the literary establishment, particularly among young writers, was mounting under the example of 'Prague spring'. While the RCP carefully dispensed the measures of concessions, as is shown by Ceauşescu's March speech, the effective administration of them called for sacrificial lambs. The green light given by the First Secretary to discuss internal policies produced a rapid response from younger writers. In their vanguard was Adrian Păunescu, the secretary of the *Uniunea Tineretului Communist* (Union of Communist Youth) section of the Writers' Union who, in April and May 1968, organized a series of meetings during which full rein was given to criticism of the editorial policy of *Luceafărul*, the editor-in-chief of which since 1962 had been Eugen Barbu. One of the May meetings was given a pronounced political character by Dumitru Ţepeneag, a writer closely identified with the *Povestea Vorbii* group. Ţepeneag accused Barbu of being the Party's cushion against pressure from the younger generation who wanted to see the implementation of a programme of reforms modelled on Czech lines instead of being asked to accept the sop of nationalism. The meeting ended with a call for Barbu's replacement with M.R. Paraschivescu and Nicolae Breban (1934–).[61]

Ţepeneag's outspokenness and the support it drew from his younger colleagues posed a threat to the Party's careful control of concessions. At a meeting of the bureau of the Writers' Union and representatives of the Central Committee, including the Party ideologist Paul Niculescu-Mizil, it was decided to sacrifice Barbu who was dismissed as editor of *Luceafărul* at the beginning of June. His successor was neither Paraschivescu nor Breban, but Ştefan Bănulescu (1926–98), a figure more acceptable to the Party, whose appointment was probably designed to head off a conflict between the two sides.

Whether that conflict would have occurred had the invasion of Czechoslovakia not taken place, can only be a matter of speculation. Ceauşescu's denunciation of Warsaw Pact allies in front of a huge crowd in Bucharest caught the public mood exactly and created a wave of support for the Party unequalled before or since. The rally to the Party colours, which were now those of the nation, was illustrated by a declaration in *Gazeta literară* signed by 23 young writers, among them Leonid Dimov, Alexandru Ivasiuc (1933–77), Petru Popescu (1944–), Adrian Păunescu and Dumitru Ţepeneag, which expressed their "complete agreement with the position of the Party and of the Romanian government, as defined by comrade Ceauşescu", and their undertaking to do "all in our power to defend our fundamental values, our country, and the peaceful construction of socialism in our country". The same day, 22 August 1968, Ivasiuc, Păunescu and Goma joined the Party.[62]

Despite the support given by writers to the Party in the wake of Ceauşescu's defiant stand over the invasion of Czechoslovakia, it was clear from the Writers' Conference of November 1968 that they were anxious not to lose the momentum for reform created by the June concession. The Party, for its part, stressed the need for caution in implementing radical changes too quickly and held up the example of Czechoslovakia as a warning of what might be the consequences. While the proceedings of the conference were organized on a more democratic basis—in the form for the first time of a general assembly in which all writers could participate instead of a meeting of 'mandated' delegates—the role that the Party expected its writers to play was carefully monitored. A statement published before the conference defined the constraints: "Marxism cannot accept the so-called independence or autonomy of art vis-à-vis society. It is the duty of literature to exercise a considerable influence on the intellectual, social and moral life of the individual".[63] Whilst it was admitted that each man possessed his own individual style and that "diversity of style signifies respect for the individuality of the artist, that does not mean that this individuality cannot be stimulated or pointed in a particular direction". The label to be attached to this method was not a new one, as emerged from the task assigned to literary critics who were to "require a literature that was committed, revolutionary, and founded on the principles of Socialist Humanism".

The Party's hopes of obtaining general support for the method were frustrated by the reaction of writers associated with *Povestea Vorbii* and others who sought to press home the advantage gained in the early summer. Concern that the debate should not degenerate into an attack on the Party's right to control literature led Marin Preda, as chairman of a session, to curtail certain of the speeches. More drastic measures were taken in the case of M.R. Paraschivescu who almost missed the conference because the Union of Writers' car that was to bring him from his country home failed to appear. He reached Bucharest by train just in time to deliver a speech that has been described by those present as politically the most outspoken since 1948. Paraschivescu insisted that every group of opinion in the Union had the right to publish its own journal at its own expense, a reference to his experience with *Povestea Vorbii*. He called for the establishment of an independent publishing house to print the work of those who did not belong to the Writers' Union, and for authors to be allowed to travel abroad and to visit the country of their choice.

The calls for institutional reform, of which Paraschivescu's discourse was the most extreme example, were insistent enough to persuade the conference to approve the introduction of a greater element of democracy in the organisation of the Union—which was splintered into a federation of regional associations—and to allow committees. Yet the Party was resolved to bring the Paraschivescu group into line, or failing that, to isolate them. Shortly after the review *Amfiteatru* published in its December issue, a round-table discussion in which several members of the group participated, its editor Ion Băieşu was dismissed. At the same time, strong attacks on the group appeared in *Scânteia* (15 January 1969) and *Contemporanul* (10 January 1969).[64]

The Party's success in exploiting the 'Prague spring' while repressing demands in autumn 1968 for a relaxation of its supervision of literature is illustrated by the 'regime-sponsored' novels that provided a reappraisal of the Gheorghiu-Dej era. This reappraisal appears to have been a consequence of the internal Party struggle for supremacy between Ceauşescu and Gheorghiu-Dej's old associates, Alexandru Drăghici, Chivu Stoica and Gheorghe Apostol, that developed late in 1967.

The denunciation of Gheorghiu-Dej and the rehabilitation of Pătrăşcanu paved the way for the publication of several novels which caused a stir at the time because of their apparently audacious presentation of repression during the late 1940s and the 1950s. Such novels as *Princepele* (The Prince)[65] by Eugen Barbu and *Păsările* (The Birds)[66] by Alexandru Ivasiuc were notable for their period detail and atmosphere. The former is a thinly disguised allegory of the Gheorghiu-Dej regime, set in the Romanian principalities during the Phanariot era (1711–1821). The prince (Gheorghiu-Dej) is portrayed as an instrument of a foreign will that has little sympathy for the interests of his subjects. The allusions to the Stalinist period are so thick as to include a project to build a canal which claims the lives of many of those involved in its construction. Dumitru Radu Popescu in his novel *F* seeks to apportion responsibility for the abuses committed in the name of Communism during the Stalinist era. A judicial enquiry exposes the violence employed in a village in the drive to forcibly collectivize peasant holdings. Reluctance to speak up about these crimes is equated with complicity in their perpetration.

The confines of the latitude allowed to novelists in their exposé of the recent past were indicated by the contrasting experience of Ivasiuc with his novel *Păsările* and Paul Goma with *Ostinato*. Both writers had been arrested as students in 1956 for involvement in actions connected with the Hungarian Revolution and had become friends in prison. Both novels describe similar experiences: the arrest of a man in the 1950s for political crimes and his efforts to readjust to society after his release. In his description of the methods used to enforce collectivisation, of prison life, and of the practices of the *Securitate* (security police), Goma went further than any other Romanian author had done and too far for the censor. After an extract from the novel appeared in *Viaţa românească* in June 1969, changes were demanded in the complete version when submitted for publication. Although Goma attempted to meet the censor's objections, he eventually lost patience and allowed publication in West Germany in 1971. Ivasiuc, on the other hand, made concessions in *Păsările* to enable it to pass the censor. His hero's arrest is justified on the grounds of his having denounced people innocent of any crime, and the security police officers are portrayed as veteran communists who are on friendly terms with those interrogated.

The events of the Gheorghiu-Dej regime play a less important role in what is aesthetically one of the most accomplished novels of the 1970s—*Absenţii* (The Absent Ones) by Augustin Buzura.[67] Constructed in the form of a monologue, the novel examines the spiritual crisis of a young doctor, Mihai Bogdan. This crisis is provoked by the corruption and opportunism which Bogdan encounters in the research institute where he works, and by his gradual estrangement from his friend and colleague who has been tainted by these vices. Bogdan's conscience is further troubled by memories of a tragic childhood which are accentuated by a grotesque perception of his immediate surroundings, his neighbours and his home. The interaction between the hero's past and present experience is skilfully manipulated and gives the novel much of its tension. In overcoming this burden on his conscience Bogdan represents the survival of the individual and the triumph of positive, one might say, Transylvanian values in a society corrupted by the psychosis of opportunism and deformed by its brutalization.

The critique of contemporary Romanian society in *Absenții*, and the reassessment of the immediate past represented by *F*, confirmed most writers in their optimism that the Party would tolerate a broader range of themes in creative literature. Despite some claims to the contrary,[68] there is little doubt that Ceaușescu's proposals for the "political-ideological activity, the Marxist-Leninist education of Party members and of all the working people", presented at a meeting of the Executive Committee of the RCP on 6 July 1971 were a bolt from the blue. Coming as they did in the wake of Ceaușescu's proposals, or 'theses' as they have popularly been dubbed, have been elevated to the status of a 'mini cultural revolution' by most observers. Although couched in the term 'Socialist Humanism', they in fact constituted a return to the method of Socialist Realism, and were therefore a reaffirmation of an ideological basis for literature that had, in theory, hardly been abandoned by the Party. The bland Socialist Humanism in literature, first advocated by Ceaușescu in July 1965, was little more than Socialist Realism fortified by a generous measure of nationalism: the Party leader defined it thus in July 1971:

> Similarly, it is necessary to make certain elucidations in connection with the notion of socialist humanism, which presupposes a more complex understanding of man in society, not taken as an isolated individual and exaggerating his individual features, but taken as a social being in close connection and interdependence with his fellows, with the interests of the mass of the people. Socialist humanism means the reflection of personal happiness in the context of the assertion of the personality of the entire people.[69]

The proposals called for "the continuous growth of the Party's leading role in all domains of political-educational activity", an emphasis on "the great achievements recorded by the Romanian people—builder of socialism", the improvement of ... "forms of political and ideological training of the Party cadres and members", "a more rigorous control... to avoid publication of literary works which do not meet the demands of the political-educational activity of our Party, [of] books which promote ideas and conceptions harmful to the interests of socialist construction".[70]

To underpin his 'theses' Ceaușescu revived 'traditionalist' arguments:

> A not very becoming practice has developed, comrades, to look only at what is being done elsewhere, abroad, to resort for everything to imports. This betrays also a certain concept of considering everything that is foreign to be better, a certain—let us say—prostration before what is foreign, and especially before Western makes. You well know that in the past

> Eminescu criticized and made fun of such mentalities in his poems. The more so we have to do it today. We are against bowing down.... [The] time has come for [emphasizing] the need to resort to [our] own forces in the first place and only afterwards to appeal to import.[71]

The artistic community was numbed by the proposals and shocked into displaying a temporarily united front against them. Such veterans of the regime as Zaharia Stancu (1902–74) and Eugen Jebeleanu (1911–91) joined a large number of younger colleagues, among them Augustin Buzura, Adrian Păunescu, Dumitru Radu Popescu (1935–) and Marin Sorescu, in sounding the death knell of Romanian literature. Leonid Dimov and Dumitru Ţepeneag, who were in Paris at the time, insisted upon a broadcast on Radio Free Europe on the need for creative freedom in literature. Nicolae Breban resigned as editor-in-chief of *România literară* while in West Germany and attacked the proposals in an interview given to *Le Monde*. Intimidation was used in an attempt to isolate these 'dissidents', in whose number was also included Paul Goma who had defied the regime by having *Ostinato* published in West Germany in the same year. In December 1971, a new law regarding state secrets prohibited the broadcasting or publication abroad of any written material that might prejudice the interest of the state. Furthermore, the law forbade Romanian citizens to have any contact with foreign radio stations or newspapers, the activity of which was considered hostile to Romania. It is clear against whom this new law was directed.

The solidarity of opposition to the proposals was not broken, however, by the authorities but by the writers themselves. The traditional friction and infighting between cliques re-emerged and fragmented the resistance. Adrian Păunescu and Fănuş Neagu argued over the editorship of *Luceafărul* after the resignation of Bănulescu. The position eventually went to a third party but, as a result Neagu left the opposition camp and aligned himself with Eugen Barbu, one of the few supporters of the proposals.[72] Moreover, resentment felt by many writers at Goma's success in West Germany allowed a wedge to be driven between opponents.[73] The Party was swift to exploit this split by persuading the Union of Writers to convene its 1972 conference with delegates elected by secret ballot in place of a general assembly.

By playing on writers' envy and offering increased pensions and royalties, the Party engineered the exclusion of Goma and Ţepeneag, who not only failed to be elected in the secret ballot but were jeered when they spoke at the Union delegate election meeting preceding the conference. Goma and Ţepeneag were thus 'outlawed' by the Party and their Union. It was not solely their refusal to accept conformity which marked them out. Several colleagues such as Blandiana, Buzura, Doinaş and Sorescu displayed similar artistic integrity. It was their readiness to challenge the Party's cultural dictates which made them a target of the regime. The intrepidness shown by both was deemed provocative by fellow writers who preferred subtle evasion of the regime's constraints and were therefore reluctant to support them.

The Writers' Union did manage to fight off the Party's attempts to foist its preferred candidates for the post of president upon it at the Writers' conference of 1977, but four years later it accepted the Party's nominee, Dumitru Radu Popescu. By this time the implications of the 'theses' had become increasingly evident, for they spawned a new ideology which some writers used as an opportune means of either reasserting a waning influence, in the case of Eugen Barbu, or of establishing one, in the case of Adrian Păunescu who, unlike Barbu, had originally criticized the 'theses'. That new ideology was protochronism. The espousal of protochronism, whose features were outlined in the previous chapter, introduced a third element into the conflict between the Party and the Union, namely the protochronists. The latter allied themselves with the Party leadership to establish a hold over publications and censorship and after being excluded from the Writers' conference of 1981 launched a campaign in retaliation to have the Union disbanded.[74]

As a result the Union's funds were partially frozen and it became impossible to grant members the loans which they sometimes needed to tide them over when they did not have an income from publication. The Party imposed new membership requirements, including approval by a local Party organization, and after 1981 no more national conferences were permitted. Few new members were admitted, partly because the Party leadership insisted that only those with the right political credentials should be considered, and partly because the Union executive blocked the very consideration of such nominees for fear that they might be eventually outnumbered. Meetings of the Union's sections of prose and poetry, and of its regional bodies, were forbidden with the result that its workings, including the award of literary prizes, was paralysed.

In these conditions of greater stringency, advocacy of protochronism offered a basis for advancement and influence within the literary establishment and it was eagerly seized by many critics and writers. At the same time the small number of writers who were willing to speak out against the Party's reimposition of a cultural ideology were picked off without difficulty. Nicolae Breban's return to Romania in May 1972 and his reinstatement as editor-in-chief of *România literară* demonstrated the reward for conformity. By contrast, Ţepeneag's isolation was officially confirmed when he was deprived of his citizenship in 1975 while in France on the false grounds that he had requested political asylum there. Goma, although dismissed from his position on the editorial board of *România literară* in 1973 and expelled from the Party, remained defiant and provided more embarrassment for the regime. Frustrated by the ban on his writings and encouraged by the initiative of Pavel Kohout in Czechoslovakia, Goma wrote a letter to Kohout and the other Charter 77 signatories in January 1977 expressing his solidarity with their movement. Shortly after sending this letter Goma persuaded seven others to sign with him an open letter to the 35 participating states at the Conference on Security and Cooperation in Europe (CSCE) in Belgrade which had signed the Helsinki Final Act in 1975, drawing attention to human rights abuses in Romania, and the government's failure to respect its international undertakings in this domain. The open letter was an unprecedented act. Goma's protest subsequently attracted the signatures of over 200 Romanian citizens, despite a campaign of intimidation against Goma and the other initial signatories carried out by the *Securitate*, and was the first publicly disseminated criticism of the regime within Romania since the imposition of Communist rule. However, only a handful of intellectuals signed the appeal, and the vast majority of the two hundred signatories actually wanted a passport to emigrate to the West. Goma was arrested on 1 April and only released from custody on 6 May 1977. After persistent official harassment he was allowed to leave Romania with his wife and child on 20 November 1977.[75]

The 'Goma affair' represented the sum of Western awareness of Romanian writers' activity during the late 1970s. His treatment by the regime for exposing human rights abuses in Romania caught the attention of the Western media, whereas the success of nonconformist writers in bypassing the ideological strictures of 1971 passed unrecognized. These writers were actively encouraged by a small number of directors of publishing houses who sanctioned an elastic interpretation of ideological tenets. Their number was further reduced with the death in 1980 of Marin Preda, director of *Cartea Românească*, who approved the publication of Buzura's *Fețele tăcerii* (The Faces of Silence) in 1974.[76]

In this novel a former Party activist, Radu Gheorghe and one of his political opponents, Carol Măgureanu, recall together the events that took place in a village during the early years of Communist power. Each tries to explain his own actions to a young reporter, Dan Toma, who is engaged to Gheorghe's daughter. The journalist is unwillingly drawn back into the period of the late 1940s, with its contradictions and personal suffering. The accounts, almost confessions, given by both men are coloured by their political beliefs. Gheorghe seeks to vindicate the results achieved by the regime while Măgureanu is much more reserved about its 'successes'. Toma, as the recipient of these two differing eyewitness accounts of revolutionary change, is gradually shaken out of his indifference to the past and becomes conscious of the nature of the revolution. The 'faces of silence' are 'faces' or 'aspects' of memory, represented by the two versions.

Among the writers for whom the nationalist posturing of Ceaușescu provided a channel for their own sympathies were Eugen Barbu and Marin Preda. Both reintroduced in novels published in 1975 the person of Marshal Ion Antonescu, Romanian dictator from 1940 to 1944, Barbu in *Incognito*[77]and Preda in *Delirul* (Delirium).[78] Their presentation of Antonescu is, however, quite different. Barbu's figure was the object of character assassination at the hands of an author who selectively uses official material to pass judgement on the dictator. There is little convincing development of action or character, the protagonist Vasile Dănacu, a member of the proscribed Communist Party, serving as the common bond between the events of the novel.[79] By infiltrating the Ministry of the Interior under a false identity on the orders of the Party, Dănacu takes part in an act of sabotage and an attempted rescue of a scientist from German hands, and witnesses the trial of Antonescu. The trial is fictitiously recreated and provides the author with an opportunity to attack the corruption of Romanian politics with an acerbity that exceeds the condemnation of it suggested by the official transcript of the trial.

This one-sided treatment of the Marshal contrasts with his sympathetic portrayal in *Delirul*. Preda's novel effectively rehabilitates the wartime leader and is said to have been validated by the ideological committee of the Central Committee.[80] The main character of the novel, Ştefan, a cousin of Niculae Moromete who is a principle figure in Preda's earlier success *Moromeţii*, is employed by a Bucharest newspaper to cover events on the Eastern Front. On his return to the capital, Ştefan discovers that his dispatches have been censored to disguise the heavy Romanian casualties. His condemnation of this censorship is contrasted with Antonescu's persistent deluding of the nation over the price of the campaign in the Soviet Union. Preda, unlike Barbu, does attempt to present a historically balanced view of Antonescu, on the one hand as saviour of the nation from the Iron Guard, the rebellion of which he crushed in January 1941, and on the other as leading the nation to disaster by invading Russian territory beyond Dniester.

While Preda does not contradict the official verdict on Antonescu as a public figure, he does challenge the authorised view of Antonescu the private man as presented in *Incognito*. The self-centred, conceited and unfeeling dictator of Barbu's novel is unrecognisable in the tragic figure of *Delirul*, driven by Romania's position between Germany and the Soviet Union to side with the former in the hope of regaining Bessarabia. In a lengthy conversation with his mother Antonescu explains that he came to power to save the country. Warned by his mother of the dangers of joining the Axis powers and of applying Nazi-inspired policies against the Jews, Antonescu reaffirms his determination to retrieve Bessarabia, and here Preda doubtless strikes a powerful note of sympathy with his readers.[81] Not surprisingly, the partial vindication of Antonescu provoked sharp criticism in the Moscow *Literaturnaia Gazeta*, which prompted the Romanian authorities to instruct Preda to produce a revised edition. The changes made were largely cosmetic.[82]

The sensational nature of *Incognito* and *Delirul*, with their introduction of figures and events that were previously taboo in the Communist period, assured their success with the public. This particular recipe was used by Ion Lăncrănjan, an avid exponent of protochronism, of whom it may be said that his output became progressively more subservient to the darker side of the Romanian mind. Whereas *Caloianul* (The Rain Talisman) attracted attention for its criticism of the part played by the Politburo members Ana Pauker and Iosif Chişinevski in the cultural life of the early 1950s, and for its suggestions of corruption and persecution,[83] *Fiul Secetei* (The Son of Drought) revealed the author's sympathies for the Iron Guard and his latent anti-Semitism.[84] Lăncrănjan went on to contribute to the officially encouraged chorus of rejoinders directed at what were regarded by the regime as Hungarian revisionist statements on the injustice of the Trianon award in 1920 of Transylvania to Romania. His *Cuvînt despre Transilvania* (Sermon on Transylvania) is a collection of lengthy anti-Hungarian diatribes that are distinguished by their vehemence and by their large print run of 50,000.[85]

The anti-Semitic language of Lăncrănjan's *Fiul Secetei* offered a foretaste of a revival of anti-Semitism in the Romanian media in the 1980s which the chauvinist postures of extreme protochronists nurtured. Anti-Semitic language reappeared in Romania for the first time since the Second World War in the Bucharest cultural weekly *Săptămâna*. In an unsigned editorial entitled 'Ideals', which appeared on 5 September 1980, the loyalty of indigenous Romanians to the Communist Party and the nation was contrasted with the cowardice of those who "run away in the face of hardships". The latter, the editorial explained, were

> visitors... avid for enrichment, teachers of the democratic tarantella clad in stinking mantles, Herods strangers to the interests of this nation... who occasionally succeed in making one dizzy with their display of traffiker patriotism. We have no need of lazy prophets, for Judas who lack the Romanian dimension of self-sacrifice in their easily purchaseable blood.[86]

Săptămâna"s editor was Eugen Barbu, an arch-protochronist, but the author of the editorial was later discovered to be a member of his staff, Corneliu Vadim Tudor, who after the overthrow of Ceauşescu resumed his partnership with Barbu to produce the ultranationalist and anti-Semitic weekly *România Mare*. The editorial alarmed the Jewish community in Romania, especially as the attack in *Săptămâna* echoed language used by Lăncrănjan in his *Fiul Secetei* where the hero is astonished that 'merchants and traffickers' were able to expel genuine workers from the Communist Party. While Rabbi Rosen, the leader of the Jewish community in Romania had demonstrated an aversion for direct confrontation with the regime, a number of Jewish intellectuals insisted that he take a stand on the issue.

At the end of September, Rosen sent a letter of protest to Gheorghe Pană, the mayor of Bucharest and nominally in charge of the Committee for Culture and Socialist Education in the capital, and on 8 October addressed a similar letter to *Săptămâna* which the magazine did not print.[87] It was only six weeks after the editorial's publication that a retraction appeared in the weekly on 24 October stating that the editorial board condemned any manifestation of nationalism, chauvinism and anti-Semitism. The retraction satisfied Rosen and there the matter might have rested had not a brochure containing material of a defamatory nature begun to circulate in significant numbers in Romania. The brochure included a copy of the *Săptămâna* 'Ideals' editorial as well as the text of Rosen's protest letter to the journal, the latter under the title "Chief Rabi [sic!] Trafficker Patriot". The hostile reaction in Israel and in Jewish circles abroad to the brochure's appearances led Romanian diplomats to explain that it had been printed abroad (ostensibly in Paris), and shipped into Romania by the Milan-based Iosif Constantin Drăgan, who was alleged to have close links with the *Săptămâna* editorial team.

This attempt to deflect a suspicion that the Romanian regime was itself the sponsor of anti-Semitic publications failed to convince anyone who knew how difficult it was to bring unauthorized publications into the country. The renewed international concern, and especially the power of the Jewish lobby in the US Senate to hold up the extension of Most Favoured Nation status, prompted Ceauşescu to take the unprecedented step for him of including a round condemnation of anti-Semitism in a speech delivered in Bucharest in April 1981.[88] And yet there were suggestions that the whole *Săptămâna* episode was sparked off by Ceauşescu's anger at the Jewish lobby's attempts to make the extension of Most Favoured Nation status conditional on Romania's goodwill over Jewish emigration. It would not have been the first time that a desire to ingratiate themselves with the president had spawned ill-considered actions by sycophants who took their leader at his word, however intemperate.

In the same year, 1980, there appeared what was politically the most notable novel of the post-war years in Romania: *Cel mai iubit dintre pământeni* (The Most Beloved of the Earth Dwellers).[89] This testimony of the first fifteen years of Communist power—that is, of the pre-Ceauşescu period—not only challenged the principles of some aspects of Marxist theory, such as the collectivization of agriculture and the nationalization of all means of production, but set up as its targets the subversion of the law for political ends and the abuses committed by the security forces.[90] Preda's graphic description of conditions in forced labour camps at a lead mine and on the Black Sea Canal conveys the torment and misery of a society at the mercy of the arbitrary use of power. Equally striking is Preda's assessment of the adverse moral effect that this totalitarian regime has upon its citizens. The perversion of traditional values in a society that has been taken over by 'troglodytes' is seen as a concomitant of Romania's political fate during what Preda's hero terms *era ticăloşilor* (the era of the villains).[91]

There was much speculation as to how the novel was able to appear, ranging from the claim that Preda, as the director of *Cartea Românească*, was able to publish the book on his own responsibility, thus bypassing the *Consiliul Culturii* (Council of Culture), to the assertion that he enjoyed the patronage of a powerful Party figure. The key to the publication of several outspoken works since 1980 lay in the boldness of the *redactor* (editor) assigned by the publishing house to vet each manuscript, for it was the editor who acted as initial censor and was responsible to the Council of Culture for the *imprimatur* he or she gave. Officials in the Council of Culture gave the final green light for publication.

Two editors at *Cartea Românească*, Gabriel Dimisianu and Georgeta Naidin, were relieved of their posts in early 1985 for failing to carry out their tasks in the manner expected of them. Naidin was responsible for 'editing' Augustin Buzura's novel *Refugii* (Places of Refuge) which offered a critique of socialist society but, unlike the novels of his contemporaries, was set in Ceauşescu's Romania.[92] Two newly married graduates are assigned posts in different towns, the husband as a teacher in a village called 'The Hump' (formerly named 'The Thieves Hideaway' and, before that, 'The Upper Hole'), the wife as a translator in a provincial town factory named 'Solidarity'. The satirical strain in these names is doubtless intentional, yet the novel itself is not satirical but realist. In the village the teacher uses paraffin lamps for light since 'electricity is on for only four hours a day',[93] the policeman is interested only in accumulating fines for petty infractions of the law, while the mayor concerns himself more with the labour potential of the children than with the quality of their education. In the town the factory managers drink real coffee and enjoy pheasant and boar, while the workers' canteen offers clear soup, beans with onion and semolina with sugar water. The greatest travesty of 'Socialist equity' is the local hospital's refusal to receive the old and gravely ill for fear of raising its mortality figures.[94]

Even the Party bosses are aware that economic chaos reigns. With the motto "the state pretends to pay us and we pretend to work" Romanian society had become brutalised, incapable of voicing a protest but passively accepting every ignominy that it was called upon to bear with monotonous regularity. Some of the passive achieved peace of mind by applying their creative talents at home, as is the case with an architect in the novel. The passiveness or indifference, often raised to the rank of a virtue by Romanians themselves, is interpreted by Buzura as cowardice. "After all", claims one of the characters,

> patience is our national weapon. And all those who have passed this way have been defeated by us through patience. They didn't have time, we had patience. We have made a virtue of it. We hide behind it, we defend ourselves with it, just as cowards hide in the shadow of children.[95]

Buzura sees in the postures of conformity and compliance an explanation for the degradation of Romanian society under Communism, a degradation marked by indifference, apathy and cowardice.

Buzura's portrayal of this degradation in *Refugii* was followed by the publication in January 1985 in his column in the Cluj cultural weekly *Tribuna* of some reflections on dictatorship. On the eve of Ceaușescu's birthday Buzura presented a portrait of a Party activist, simply referred to as R, in which many saw the Romanian leader:

> In those years of the haunting decade the teacher thought that R
> was the only illiterate person, but since R spoke all the time and
> asked about everything, he had no chance to prove it. Later,
> when he considered himself to know everything, R .... Turned
> into an arrogant, irritable person who lacked self-control...
> Little by little threats and curses took the place of questions.
> He threatened those who did not treat him properly... so that
> people began to blame him even for those sufferings that were
> not his fault.[96]

A fortnight later, in the same column, Buzura looked forward to the fortieth anniversary of the 'victory over Fascism' with reflections on Mussolini and the nature of dictatorship. He took up the idea that amongst the features of dictatorship was its power to make "one's life hell". "It is a sort of slow and obscure assassination, put into practice by a variety of invisible accomplices."[97] The pro-regime Bucharest weekly *Săptămâna* responded by criticising Buzura's two articles and after its publication on 14 February his column ceased to appear.

For statements on the realities of life in Romania poetry was the richest source. In a negative sense the activity of Adrian Păunescu is eloquent. The cap of opportunism fitted this poet well since, from being in the vanguard of critics of the July 1971 proposals, he ingratiated himself sufficiently with the Party under the banner of protochronism to be appointed editor-in-chief of the weekly literary journal *Flacăra* in 1973, and a member of the Central Committee until his displacement at the Thirteenth Party Congress in November 1984. Despite the punctuation of his accomplished verse by regular paeans in honour of the president during the 1980s, his fall from grace after the November Congress was rapid, attended by gratification from almost all fellow writers.[98] The pretext for his dismissal from *Flacăra* and an investigation into the source of his financial fortune was a concert of verse and music organized by him at Ploieşti in the late spring of 1985, in which his exhortation to perform the rites of the season during a temporary blackout was taken too literally. Reports of the ensuing dissipation reached the ears of the president who decided that his personal troubadour had gone too far. Although there was talk of his being sent for trial on corruption charges, Păunescu re-emerged in *Contemporanul* with a weekly column.

Among the few writers unwilling to bow the knee were Dorin Tudoran,[99] Ana Blandiana,[100] Ştefan Augustin Doinaş,[101] Marin Sorescu[102] and Ileana Mălănciou.[103] Their ranks were strengthened by a younger talent, Mircea Dinescu (1965–), whose poem 'Indulgenţă de iarnă' (Cold comfort) gave a response to the pressures of daily life:

God preserve me from those who want

what's best for me,
the nice guys
always ready to inform on me cheerfully.
From the priest with a tape-recorder under his vestment
and the blanket you can't get under without saying
Good evening.
From the dictator caught in the chords of the harp,
from those angry with their own people.
Now, when winter is drawing close,
we have neither high walls
nor geese on the Capitoline,
only great provisions of tolerance and fear.[104]

A less explicit but insidious challenge to the Party's claim to a monopoly of the truth emerged from the intellectual debate generated by two books published in the 1980s. One, *Jurnalul de la Păltiniş* (The Păltiniş Diary)[105], was written by the philosopher Gabriel Liiceanu; the other, *Epistolar* (Letters), was edited by him.[106] The inspiration for both was the philosopher Constantin Noica (1909–87), the most significant of the cultural figures to re-emerge into the cultural consciousness during the 'Bucharest spring' of 1968. Twenty years earlier he had been placed under arrest for writing a half-completed study of Goethe, the manuscript of which was confiscated and never returned. He was subsequently confined to the small provincial town of Câmpulung Muscel until December 1958, when he was sent to prison and held until August 1964. His experience was brought to the attention of Peter Benenson by the Romanian *émigré* Ion Raţiu and led to the founding of Amnesty International in 1961. Between 1949 and 1958, Noica supported himself by giving private lessons in mathematics and foreign languages, and this period of his life he describes as 'a delight', since it gave him a spiritual renewal and an opportunity for meditation. The fruits of those years have been offered to the public in a series of speculative works including *Rostirea filosofică românească* (Romanian Philosophical Speech, 1970) and *Sentimentul românesc al ființei* (The Romanian Sense of Being, 1978). Although Noica never held a teaching post he attracted a circle of followers from the younger generation of intellectuals, who regarded him as master, counsellor and friend.

Noica's objective was to produce a theory of the relationship between tradition and modernity, a project which naturally attracted the attention of both the *protocronişti* (protochronists) adherents of the theory that ethnic Romanians were the original inhabitants of their present homeland, and the modernists, advocates of the value of Romania's links with the West. Among the latter were his most enthusiastic disciples for whom the epithet 'Noicasian' was coined, but Noica's own position in the argument between the protochronists and modernists was ambiguous. This is not the place to dwell upon his hesitation.[107] What is more important for this assessment of intellectual compliance and dissidence is use made of Noica's work by both sides in an attempt to confer upon their case a greater authority. By underlining the nationalist aspects of Noica's philosophy, with its insistence upon the effort to identify a unique Romanian spirituality, the protochronists hoped to appropriate him and thereby gain greater political influence within Party circles.

Noica's propulsion from the realm of abstract philosophy into the arena of cultural politics resulted from the publication of the *Jurnalul* and the *Epistolar*. Despite their abstruse philosophical subject matter, many Romanian cultural intellectuals regarded both books as the most exciting publications of the decade. That view was not shared by all of their *émigré* colleagues, as shall be shown later. The two books produced a host of reviews in the Romanian literary press and added further fuel to the conflict between advocates of protochronism and their opponents. In *Jurnalul de la Păltiniş* Liiceanu gives us a record of Noica's conversation with his 'pupils', in this case principally the author and Andrei Pleşu, during visits of three to ten days to the philosopher's Transylvanian mountain retreat of Păltiniş between 1977 and 1981. In the sense that through his conversation Noica seeks the dialectal improvement of the learner, he is a Socratic figure. Such improvement is nurtured by a daily programme of reading, meditation and discussion, leavened by walks in the mountains near Păltiniş. Unlike Socrates, Noica has no enthusiasm for the life of the city streets, indeed the *Jurnalul* constantly echoes the relief expressed by the visitors at the brief escapes from the tension and 'hysteria' of Bucharest, or of what remained of its eighteenth-century centre. A further reason for avoiding Bucharest was the prevalence there of *protocronist* ideas: "Bucharest continues to lie under an offensive of *protocronism*, a cultural symptom that, by departing from an inferiority complex, almost always ends in a denial of Europe".[108]

It was as an alternative to these ideas that Liiceanu offered *Jurnalul*, as his choice for its subtitle, 'A paideutic model for humanist culture', showed. Noica's quest for 22 geniuses for whom he put himself forward as a trainer presented a challenge to the Party-backed attempt by the *protocronişti* to dominate cultural output. It was precisely Noica's importance as an agent of cultural transmission, and his search for geniuses rather than his writings, which his followers underlined and which attracted the ridicule of some of his critics who equated the search with the recruitment of football players.[109]

It was in the intellectual ferment generated by *Jurnalul* and captured in the sequel of letters entitled *Epistolar* that overt resistance to the regime was concentrated. Liiceanu's correspondence with both admirers and critics registered the debate, made public for the first time, about the need in Romania for living 'in truth' and for dispensing with ambiguity. The exercises in sincerity, self-criticism and the generosity of spirit displayed by all the correspondents in *Epistolar* were chords in the particular sense of harmony produced by the book, and provided a sign that the collective conscience of the forces of light in the country were stirring. The scale of the threat which the regime deemed to be posed by Liiceanu and his associates to its monopoly of control was evident from the selective serialization by the arch-protochronist Eugen Barbu of the *Epistolar* in the mass circulation cultural weekly *Săptămâna*. Over a period of almost a year the correspondents were ridiculed in Barbu's weekly column for their elitism and alleged hypocrisy by a man who had been collaborating for over a decade to promote a nationalist view of the Romanian past and its culture which by denying external influences, had deformed the Romanian's perception of themselves and their place in history. Whereas *Epistolarul* was, above all else, a plea for normality, and Noica, in the *Jurnalul* the symbol of that normality and a *purificatio spiritualis*, Barbu represented the complete antithesis, as his lauding of the Romanian Nero and his Poppaea amply demonstrated.

Barbu's assault on Liiceanu prompts the question of how the two books were published in the first place. As with Buzura's novels, the answer probably lies in the convergence of a number of factors, not least the boldness of the publisher's reader Sorin Mărculescu in both cases, and his desire to defend and promote certain cultural values. In the poverty of creative writing of the decade, the two books stood out with their artistic elegance. Liiceanu's profound intuition, his sensitivity to his surroundings, and his clarity of style enhanced the tensions explored in *Jurnalul* and ensured that it would be a bestseller. At the same time, the appearance of both books showed how hazardous it was to dismiss all cultural production in the 1980s as subservient to the regime. But how relevant were these two books to the public expression of dissent in Romania?

To return to the reception given to the books by some Romanian *émigrés* to which I alluded earlier, both were dismissed as 'abstract' and 'irrelevant'. Here is what Matei Călinescu, a respected literary critic resident in the United States, had to say:

> *Epistolarium* is a series of Socratic debates, and without a doubt, the exchange of letters of which the book consists is intellectually

very exciting. On the other hand, the debate could have occurred on the moon. There is absolutely nothing concrete in the book, none of the things we are discussing today. It could have been written 50 years ago or in another country.[110]

Călinescu commented on the divorce between intellectuals and politics and referred to a discussion the mathematician Mihai Botez had once had with Liiceanu:

> Liiceanu summarized his position as follows: 'We are here to deal with cultural matters. We cannot solve the problem of the meat supply'. In other words, intellectuals should focus on cultural matters, and as long as they can do it in an interesting fashion, its fine. Therefore, a fine book like *Epistolarium* is also a cultural confession of social irrelevancy.[111]

To the extent that Liiceanu's books had little manifest impact upon other social groups in Romanian society, such as the urban and peasant workers, Călinescu's assessment was correct. On numerous occasions Liiceanu and his associates emphasized that they saw their role as one of defending cultural values, and this they regarded as a means of protecting the people from the aberrations of *protocronism* and the personality cult. And here we should not overlook the identification of many of the arch *protocronişti*, such as Barbu, Corneliu Vadim Tudor, Artur Silvestri and Dan Zamfirescu, with the inanities of the cult. It is partly as a result of their activity that the generalized view of Romanian creative intellectuals as servants of the regime gained currency.

A crude assessment of the attitude of writers would be that as long as they could publish they did not question the regime and is pithily summed up in an anecdote of a person calling out to a newspaper vendor *'Aveţi România? Literară, da, liberă, nu'* (Have you got 'Romania'? 'Literary Romania', yes, 'Free Romania, no'). Those who expected writers to play the role of a surrogate opposition were disappointed; on the contrary they were used, by and large, to legitimize the regime. Yet in drawing this broad conclusion we run the risk of ignoring the moral choices and moral dilemmas which many people, not just creative intellectuals, have to face under a totalitarian system. Of course, those who criticized from outside the country ran far lesser risks than those who did it from inside, and a few writers, notably Augustin Buzura, did speak out, despite the risks, with the assistance of their friends in the publishing houses.

The phrase 'resistance through culture' has been appropriated by writers less deserving of the label than Liiceanu, Pleşu or other figures mentioned at the beginning of this chapter. It has been suggested that for Romanian intellectuals to do any more than they did under Ceauşescu would have been self-destruction, and the example of the suppression of Goma is cited in support of this contention. Yet the Goma protest was successfully isolated by the regime precisely because so few persons were prepared to support it. Despite this compliance a small number of writers, such as Blandiana and Dinescu, did consciously make a choice to speak out and run the risk of self-destruction. What other adjective than shameful is appropriate to describe the response to Dinescu's appeal for a general strike of writers in November 1989? Such reticence elicited a sense of guilt from the critic Octavian Paler after the revolution.[112]

For some literary critics, the degree of compromise with the regime offers a yardstick for a preliminary assessment of the aesthetic value of Romanian literature of the Communist period. A general classification of the literature which appeared between 1945 and 1989 was attempted by Ion Simuţ who broadly distinguished four parallel strands.[113] The first was what he termed 'opportunist literature', one virtually written to order according to the regime's dogmas and which embraced the work of Mihai Beniuc, Zaharia Stancu, Titus Popovici, Dumitru Popescu, Adrian Păunescu and Corneliu Vadim Tudor; the second 'subversive literature', which he regarded as a creation of the Ceauşescu era and which represented a deviation from the official line. Included in this category were the novelists Marin Preda and Augustin Buzura, the poet and playwright Marin Sorescu, the poets Ana Blandiana, Mircea Dinescu and Ileana Mălăncoiu, and the critics Nicu Steinhardt and Alexandru Paleologu. Simuţ placed within the category of 'dissident literature', which he defined as conveying "an attitude directly hostile to the Communist regime", the writings of Paul Goma, Dorin Tudoran, Ion Negoiţescu, Mircea Dinescu and Dan Petrescu. The first three were driven into exile where, of course, the bulk of this type of writing was produced, notably by Monica Lovinescu and Virgil Ierunca, with their regular literary reviews on Radio Free Europe. The final type of literature was 'apolitical or aesthetic literature', that which avoided the official dogmas and represented a form of internal exile. Simuţ considered the poetry of Ştefan Augustin Doinaş, Nichita Stănescu, Leonid Dimov and Mircea Cărtărescu, and the prose of Ştefan Bănulescu to be representative.

Simuţ was at pains to point out that his categorization had no claims to be exhaustive, and that it made no attempt to place the literature of the period on the scale of aesthetic values. A review of the creative literature of the post-war period shows that writing of value appeared, writing which ignored the official prescriptions, defied stereotype themes and rejected wooden language. In order to preserve a value such literature had to offer as authentic a view as possible of social reality. It did so without competition from the disciplines of history, sociology and political science, all of which were deliberately castrated under the Communist regime. It was only from Buzura's *Refugii*, for example, that readers could learn something about the miners' strike and its impact upon the mining community.

Another consideration of the literature of the period is linked to the means of expression. An Aesopian language characterized a major part of the prose and poetry. Novels developed more allusive formulae, such as the parable. Poetry had recourse to an entire symbolism stemming from the same strategy of circumlocution. The use of intertextual and the absurd were means of denying censors access to the main message. It was not surprising that in a country that announced record grain harvests but where bread was rationed, which produced petrol but that too was rationed, which built thousands of flats but could not heat them, where in order to buy underwear you had to buy two kilos of rotten fish, or in order to purchase a coffin you had to provide the wood,[114] a literature of the absurd, exemplified by the poetry of Sorescu, should flourish.

The length to which the absurd could be taken by writers was most evident in the propagation of the personality cult. This brings us back to the question of compliance amongst creative intellectuals. For if a small group of writers were prepared to ignore the official prescriptions in literature, an even larger body conspired in the concoction of the new truths demanded by the personality cult. New gods were created in the poems of Adrian Păunescu and the paintings of Sabin Bălaşa, and the insular society of Ceauşescu's Romania provided fertile ground for the development of a cult providing a focus for people's attention. Initially, the president was projected as that focus, but by the early 1980s it was extended to Elena.

As mentioned earlier, the seeds of the cult were sown in acclamation of Ceauşescu's denunciation of the Warsaw Pact invasion of Czechoslovakia in August 1968. From that date there can be detected a growing identification of Romania with a single figure in the editorials in the Party press, and in the statements of officials. At the same time the intellectual elite was called upon to add its voice to the appreciation of the leader.[115] Birthday anniversary volumes containing poetry and prose in honour of Ceauşescu and his wife were published annually in the 1980s.[116] An anthology of some of the titles conferred on Ceauşescu in the Romanian media in the 1980s, together with their authors, was compiled by Dan Ionescu and included 'architect', 'celestial body' (Mihai Beniuc), 'demiurge' (Corneliu Vadim Tudor), 'fir-tree' (Ion Manole), 'genius' (Eugen Barbu), 'god' (Corneliu Vadim Tudor), 'miracle' (Vasile Andronache), 'morning star' (Vasile Andronache), 'navigator' (Victor Nistea), 'Prince Charming' (Ion Manole), 'saint' (Eugen Barbu), 'saviour' (Niculae Stoian), 'sun' (Alexandru Andriţoiu), 'titan' (Ion Potopin), and 'visionary' (Viorel Cozma).[117]

Any discussion of the acquiescence and collusion of intellectuals under Ceauşescu should not ignore the role of the West in shoring up the regime. We are reminded of this by remarks made by Mihai Botez in 1989:

> People often ask me why the Romanians are not more courageous. I am not making apologies for the average Romanian, but I'd like to say that opposing the evil regime is often not a matter of mere courage but also of a cost-benefit analysis. A lot of my colleagues from the university often say: "let's suppose we'll speak out. We'll criticize. What will be the result? I will be expelled from the university, sent into internal exile or forced to leave the country. The consequences of my actions for the system will be nil. The system is very well organized to resist my challenge. And the West? It's practically not interested in us. For years, nobody in the West cared about the internal problems of Romania".[118]

Botez himself complained:

> For years, dissidents, people like me, were perceived as enemies of the West, because they were trying to distance President Ceauşescu, this

> golden boy of the West in the Soviet camp, from the U.S. When David Binder, probably one of the most influential Western journalists writing on Eastern Europe, came to Bucharest, I met him in the house of an American diplomat. He said some quite unpleasant things, such as "Who are you? What do you mean by Romanian dissidents? What do you mean by Romanian civil society? In the Balkans, such things never happen. We prefer to speak to people who represent 'real things' like Mr Ceauşescu. At least he has power.[119]

Binder's view was that of the pragmatist who recognized that foreign policy was also assessed on a cost-benefit analysis and the West's policy towards Romania was no different in that respect. "To tweak the nose of the Russians", one of the reasons suggested by Corneliu Bogdan, the former Romanian ambassador to Washington, for President Nixon's decision to visit Romania in August 1969, summed up American policy towards Ceauşescu for most of this period.[120] British policy was largely determined by considerations of trade. Ceauşescu's state visit to Britain in June 1978 was arranged in the hope that it "may act as a stimulus to British companies to grasp the growing opportunities for selling to Romania".[121]

In according no room to morality in its dealings with Ceauşescu the West had little right to expect much morality from Romanian intellectuals. As Botez was quick to point out, the success of Ceauşescu's foreign policy towards the West underpinned his absolute rule, and goes a long way to explain the compliance of intellectuals:

> The West, directly or indirectly, helped Ceauşescu and discouraged the opposition. Don't forget: three presidents of the United States, three presidents of France, the Emperor of Japan, the Queen of England and a lot of other important people expressed their admiration for Romanian policies and Romania's independent course. It is very difficult for the internal opposition to criticize and to fight a policy that is perceived as successful by practically everybody in the world.[122]

Notes

1 This is a revised version of chapter six in my *Ceauşescu and the Securitate. Coercion and Dissent in Romania, 1965–1989* (London: Hurst and Co., 1995).

2 The degree to which Ceauşescu succeeded in mobilizing support for his regime from cultural intellectuals and the reasons for that success are the subject of Katherine Verdery's path-breaking study of identity and cultural politics entitled *National Ideology under Socialism* (Berkeley: University of California Press, 1991).

3 Michael Shafir, *Romania: Politics, Economics, Society* (London: Francis Printer, 1985), p.146.

4 When asked what she despised the poet Ana Blandiana replied 'Opportunism'; see 'Un chestionar pentru Ana Blandiana', *Cartea Românească. Exemplar de Semnal*, no.2 (1984), p.11.

5 For example, appointment as a university lecturer was conditional upon Party membership. There were, however, exceptions. My own father-in-law, Andrei Caracostea, professor of constructions at Bucharest Polytechnic, was exempted from this requirement when appointed in 1952, shortly after his release from a two-year spell in a labour camp—on the charge, never brought before a court, that he was the son of a pre-war minister—since his expertise was needed by the regime for construction projects.
6 Author's conversation with Alexandru Darie, 2 October 1988.
7 Paris: Albin Michel, 1986.
8 Shafir, *Romania: Politics*, pp.140–41.
9 This situation was evident from this author's contacts with peasants throughout the 1970s and 1980s, with the exception of those Hungarian villagers in Transylvania who received visiting relatives from Hungary.
10 *Ibid.*
11 J. Cole, 'Family, farm and factory: rural workers in contemporary Romania', in D. Nelson (ed.), *Romania in the 1980s* (Boulder, Colorado: Westview Press, 1981), p.91.
12 See Chapter Three.
13 'The Romanian Dimension of Existence: A Phenomenological Sketch', *Romanian Sources*, vol.1, part 1 (1975), pp.5–34. This is an abridged version of the original Romanian text which was published in the author's *Izvoare de filosofie* (Bucharest, 1943). Vulcănescu was to become a victim of the Communist regime for he was arrested in 1948 and died in prison in October 1952.
14 Mary-Ellen Fischer, *Nicolae Ceauşescu. A Study in Political Leadership* (Boulder, Colorado: Lynne Rienner, 1989), pp.109–13.
15 Membership composition at that time was 44 per cent workers, 34 per cent peasants, 10 per cent intelligentsia and 12 per cent other categories. At the Thirteenth Party Congress in November 1984, it was announced that the nationality composition of the PCR was 90 per cent Romanian, seven per cent Hungarian (a drop of more than two per cent since the Twelfth Party Congress), less than one per cent German, and the remainder other nationalities. As of 1988, workers made up about 55 per cent of the Party membership, peasants 15 per cent, and intellectuals and other groups 30 per cent. Because of the PCR's special effort to recruit members from industry, construction and transportation, by late 1981 some 45.7 per cent of workers in these sectors belonged to the Party. In 1980, roughly 524,000 PCR members worked in agriculture. Figures on the educational level of the membership in 1980 indicated that 11 per cent held college diplomas, 15 per cent had diplomas from other institutions of higher learning, and 26 per cent had received technical or professional training (see: http://countrystudies.us/romania/70.htm).
16 http://countrystudies.us/romania/70.htm. Accessed on 30 December 2016. Compare the figures for Communist Party membership in Hungary in mid-1988—817,000 (10.3 per cent of the adult population). (http://www.photius.com/countries/hungary/government/hungary_government_social_composition_o~91.html. Accessed on 30 December 2016) and in Poland—2.1 million in 1986 (8.1 per cent of the adult population) (Paul G. Lewis, *Political Authority and Party Secretaries in Poland, 1975–1986* (Cambridge: Cambridge University Press, 1989), p.298).
17 The RCP became the Romanian Workers' Party on its amalgamation with the Social Democratic Party in February 1948.
18 For a descriptive approach to this relationship see Anneli Ute Gabanyi, *Partei und Literatur in Rumänien seit 1945* (Munich: R. Oldenbourg Verlag, 1975); for an analytical one see Michael Shafir's original and incisive Ph.D dissertation *The Intellectual and the Party: The Rumanian Communist Party and the Creative Intelligentsia in the Ceauşescu Period, 1965–1972* (Jerusalem, 1981), an outline of which he kindly allowed me to consult, and his 'Political Culture, Intellectual Dissent and Intellectual Consent: The Case of Romania', *Orbis*, vol.27 (Summer 1983), pp.393–420.

19 A document of 8 July 1940 signed by a certain Ilin gave the breakdown of RCP membership by districts as follows: Transylvania 780, Prahova 160, Oltenia 170, Dobrogea 260 (mostly Bulgarians), Lower Danube 90, Moldavia 250, Bukovina (end of March 1940) 380, Bessarabia (end of May 1940) 280, and Bucharest (including students) 440. An additional 1,200 members were listed as being in the army, and 200 in the Union of Communist Youth. The total number of RCP members was thus 4,210. With the loss of Bessarabia and Northern Bukovina the numbers dropped to 3,260, and the subsequent amputation of Northern Transylvania and the Dobrogea reduced them still further to about 1,000 (Moscow, RTsKhIDNI, fond 495, opis 180, dos. 482). I am grateful to Professor Ioan Chiper for this information.
20 Pseudonym of Alexandru Binder.
21 Călinescu stood in the elections of 1946 as a Popular Front candidate.
22 *Scînteia* 5, 7, 8, 10 January 1948. Quoted from D. Grăsoiu, *Bătălia Arghezi* (Cluj-Napoca: Editura Dacia, 1984), pp 154–5. Another casualty of the new literary norms was the young Nina Cassian whose volume of poetry *La scara 1/1* was criticised in *Scînteia* by Traian Şelmaru as 'unprincipled' that is, failing to reflect Marxist-Leninist principles. Cassian was forced to make a self-criticism in the weekly journal *Flacăra*, 7 March 1948.
23 Bucharest: Editura de Stat pentru Literatură şi Artă (ESPLA), 1949.
24 An item in *The London Magazine* in 1985 asserted that Jack Lindsay was "the most popular writer in Mongolia". Quoted from *Private Eye*, no. 606 (London: 8 March 1985), p.8.
25 M. Sadoveanu, *Mitrea Cocor* (London: Fore Publications, 1953), pp.XVII–XVIII.
26 Bogdan Ficeac, *Cenzura comunistă şi formarea 'Omului Nou'* (Bucharest: Nemira, 1999), p.34. For further reading on censorship during the period of Communist rule in Romania see Tiberiu Troncotă, *România comunistă. Propagandă şi cenzură* (Bucharest: Tritonic, 2006); Bujor Nedelcovici, *Scriitorul, Cenzura şi Securitatea* (Bucharest: Allfa, 2009); Emilia Şercan, *Cultul secretului. Mecanismele cenzurii în presa comunistă* Bucharest: Polirom, 2015).
27 Ficeac, *Cenzura*, p.34. The General Directorate's attributes were extended to include supervision of television broadcasts in resolution no.267 of 23 February 1954 issued by the Council of Ministers. Its head between 1951 and 1973 was Iosif Ardeleanu, a veteran Communist, who was notorious for his dogmatism and intolerance (Vladimir Tismăneanu, Dorin Dobrincu, and Cristian Vasile (eds.), *Comisia Prezidenţială pentru Analiza Dictaturii Comuniste din România. Raport Final* (Bucharest: Humanitas, 2007), p.786).
28 Ficeac, *Cenzura*, pp.52–53.
29 *Ibid.*, pp.56, 59. The latter misprint was not uncommon, suggesting a deliberate 'mistake' on the part of typesetters.
30 Ficeac, *Cenzura*, pp.64–65.
31 *Ibid.*, p.65.
32 *Ibid.*, p.67. An instructive case study of the application of censorship in the decade 1967–1977 is provided by *Tomis cenzurat/necenzurat* (Constanţa: Editura Tomis, 2007), a collection of documents from the Directorate of Press and Printing relating to the literary journal *Tomis* published in the port of Constanţa. A report dated 20 October 1967 on the contents of the review in the period 20 September to 20 October 1967 mentions a piece by the editor of the review, George Mihăescu, entitled 'Zoodidactica' about an ass who is given a particular Party-controlled position. But the ass is dim and ignorant, due to the fact that he never completed his secondary school studies. Concerned that he might lose his post to someone better educated, the ass summons the secondary school head teacher and, beating his hoof on the table, demands that he be given a secondary school certificate. All he needed then, the tale went, was to take a degree, and to this end he had enrolled in part-time study, where he literally devoured courses and books. In this way he had become an expert. "Since this tale", the report

claimed, "generalized the manner in which some persons in positions of responsibility, obtained their degrees, the regional Party organization has been informed and has ordered the offending material to be removed from the page" (pp.36–37).

33 Grăsoiu, *Bătălia Arghezi*, p.156.

34 Bucharest: ESPLA, 1955.

35 Preda's assured approach is missing from the second volume which appeared 12 years later, in 1967. See the comments of Eugen Simion, *Scriitori români de azi* (Bucharest: Cartea Românească, 1974) pp.275–76.

36 Bucharest: ESPLA, 1957.

37 Liviu Călin in his introduction to the 1966 ed. of the novel (Bucharest: Editura pentru Literatură) p. VI. Călin himself is tainted with the brush of Marxist criticism when he describes the clientele of an inn in the quarter as "the dark world of the lumpenproletariat, denied a social presence by the egotism of the parasitical classes". (p.VII).

38 Bucharest: ESPLA, 1954. The title is borrowed from the name given to the Danube by ancient Greek writers. Dumitriu, while director of ESPLA, fled Romania in 1960 and settled in West Germany. It is notable that in his post-1960 publications he omitted any mention of this work amongst his previously published novels.

39 Bucharest: ESPLA, 1956.

40 Comisia Prezidenţială, p.95, note 114.

41 Tudor Arghezi, *Versuri*, (Bucharest: Editura de Stat pentru Literatură şi Artă, 1959), p.8. Arghezi, in his foreword, had the decency to steer clear of this ideological claptrap.

42 For example, Nicolae Bălcescu (1819–52) and Mihail Kogălniceanu (1817–91).

43 Pseudonymn of Stelian Diaconescu who was born in the village of Palici in the commune of Rusăvăţ (today Vipereşti), Buzău county, on 24 May 1923 and died in Lausanne on 21 July 1986. He attended the 'B.P. Hasdeu' school in Buzău between 1935 and 1942 and then studied at the Faculty of Letters and Philosophy at the University of Bucharest. In 1945, he became the editorial secretary of the review *Lumea* and in 1947 was appointed press secretary at the Editura Fundaţiilor Regale (Royal Publishing House). He edited the poetry review *Agora* with Virgil Ierunca but was arrested in 1950 as an alleged enemy of the Communist regime and sentenced to hard labour for life (the punishment was commuted in 1955 when he was released). He spent the five years in labour camps on the Danube-Black Sea Canal and afterwards in the lead mines in Cavnic şi Baia Sprie. Between 1955 and March 1958 he worked as an editor on the review *Limbă şi literatură* but was rearrested and sentenced to 25 years jail. Pardoned in the general amnesty of 1964, Caraion signed, on his release, an undertaking to be a *Securitate* informer and wrote reports, under the code names, Nicolae Anatol' and 'Artur', on his friends—among them Ierunca, Monica Lovinescu and Marin Preda—until 1981 when he and his family received political asylum in Switzerland; see Delia Cornea and Dumitru Dobre (eds.), (*Cazul "Artur" şi exilul românesc. Ion Caraion în documente din Arhiva CNSAS* (Bucharest: Editura Pro Historia, 2006), pp.9–26.)

44 Ion Pop, *Poezia unei generaţii* (Cluj: Editura Dacia 1973), p.26.

45 Monica Lovinescu, 'The New Wave of Rumanian Writers', *East Europe*, vol.16, no.12 (December 1967), p.9.

46 Quoted from George Schöpflin, 'Rumanian Nationalism', *Survey*, nos.2–3 (Spring–Summer 1974), p.92. See also *Scînteia*, 20 July 1965.

47 Nicolae Ceauşescu, Romania in the Way of Completing Socialist Construction: Reports, Speeches, Articles, July 1965–September 1966 (Bucharest: Meridiane, 1969) p.89.

48 Anneli Ute Gabanyi, *Partei und Literatur, Partei und Literatur in Rumänien seit 1945* (Munich: R. Oldenbourg Verlag, 1975), p.148.

49 For my account of *Povestea Vorbii* I am indebted to Gabanyi, *Partei und Literatur.*, pp.145–47.

50 No. 20 (14 May 1965).

51 Gabanyi, *Partei und Literatur*, p.148.
52 *Ibid.*
53 *Ibid.*
54 *Luceafărul*, no. 17 (27 April 1968). See Gabanyi, *Partei und Literatur*, p.149.
55 Bucharest: Editura pentru Literatură. It was translated into English as one of a trilogy of Sorescu's plays in *The Thirst of the Salt Mountain*, translated by Andrea Deletant and Brenda Walker (London: Forest Books, 1985).
56 Bucharest: Editura pentru Literatură, 1968.
57 *Ibid.*
58 19 May 1968.
59 16 April 1968.
60 In 1971, his book *Lampa lui Aladin* (Aladdin's Lamp) was banned and the copies already printed were pulped. He was allowed to leave Romania in 1980 and settled in West Germany.
61 Gabanyi, *Partei und Literatur*, p.153.
62 *Gazeta literară*, 22 August 1968.
63 *România literară*, 17 October 1968.
64 Gabanyi, Partei und Literatur, p.162.
65 Bucharest: Editura Tineretului, 1969.
66 Bucharest; Cartea Românească, 1970.
67 Cluj: Editura Dacia, 1970.
68 Gabanyi, *Partei und Literatur*, p.176.
69 Nicolae Ceauşescu, Romania on the Way of Building Up the Multilaterally Developed Socialist Society, vol. 6. Reports, Speeches, Articles, May 1971–February 1972 (Bucharest: Meridiane, 1972), pp.174–80.
70 "Exposition on the Programme of the RCP for the improvement of ideological activity, for raising the general level of knowledge and the socialist education of the masses, for grounding the relations in our society on the principles of socialist and communist ethics and equity" (Ceauşescu, *Romania*, p.608).
71 Quoted from Verdery, *National Ideology*, p.176.
72 Others were Aurel Baranga and Mihnea Gheorghiu.
73 Monica Lovinescu, 'Sub zodia tezelor din iunie', *Ethos*, 1 (Paris, 1973) p.283.
74 Verdery, *National Ideology*, pp.186–87.
75 Michael Shafir, 'Who is Paul Goma?', *Index on Censorship*, no. 1 (1978), pp.33–36.
76 A. Buzura, *Feţele Tăcerii*, (Bucharest: Cartea Românească, 1974).
77 Bucharest: Editura Albatros, 1975.
78 Bucharest: Cartea Românească, 1975.
79 Parts of volume two of *Incognito* (1977) were shown by Marin Sorescu to have been plagiarised from the autobiography of the Soviet writer Konstantin Paustovskii (1892–1967) entitled *Povest' o zhizni* (1955). The publication of Sorescu's revelations needed the sanction of Dumitru Popescu, a senior Central Committee figure responsible for cultural affairs, since Barbu himself was a Central Committee member at the time. Popescu had long held Barbu in low esteem.
80 Michael Shafir, 'The Men of the Archangel Revisited: Anti-Semitic Formations among Communist Romania's Intellectuals', *Studies in Comparative Communism*, vol.XVI, no.3 (Autumn 1983), p.229.
81 *Delirul*, pp.152–53.
82 Bucharest: Cartea Românească, 1975, 2nd revised and enlarged edition.
83 I. Lăncrănjan, *Caloianul* (Bucharest: Editura Albatros, 1977).
84 I. Lăncrănjan, *Fiul Secetei* (Bucharest: Editura Albatros, 1979).
85 I. Lăncrănjan, *Cuvînt despre Transilvania* (Bucharest: Editura Sport-Turism, 1982).
86 Shafir, 'Men of the Archangel', p.224.
87 *Ibid.*, p.223.
88 *Ibid.*, p.225.

89 Bucharest: Cartea Românească, 3 vols, 1980; reprinted 1984.

90 At only one point does Preda seem to be making concessions when, in his account of interrogation by the *Securitate*, he makes his hero state, in contradiction with the general experience of political prisoners, that he was "tortured almost all the time, not physically, but by aggression and violence against my most intimate feelings". (vol. 2, p.21).

91 Vol.2, p.339.

92 Bucharest: Cartea Românească, 1984. Naidin at *Cartea Românească* had written what Bujor Nedelcovici considers to be "an objective, succinct and neutral" review of his book *Ereticul îmblânzit* (The Tamed Heretic), the manuscript of which he sent to the publishing house in May 1982. The report of Eugen Simion, the external reader, was, in the same author's view, "profound, subtle and objective" (both reports were found by Nedelcovici in his *Securitate* file). Their positive comments did not sway George Bălăiţă, the director of the publishing house, who forwarded the novel to the Council which asked for changes to be made. Nedelcovici refused and sent the text to France where it was published—contrary to Romanian law—under the title *Le Second Messager* (Paris: Albin Michel, 1985). See Nedelcovici, *Un tigru de hârtie*, pp.113–25.

93 *Refugii*, p.67.

94 *Ibid.*, p.435.

95 *Ibid.*, p.33.

96 *Tribuna*, no.3 (17 January 1985), p.5.

97 *Tribuna*, no. 5 (31 January 1985), p.2 quoted from *RFE-RL Research*, vol.10, no.9, part III (1 March 1985), p.15.

98 An example of his adulatory poetry was 'Priveşte, ţară!' (Look, country!) on the occasion of the Thirteenth Party Congress (*Scînteia*, 17 November 1984). The sun is said to rise through the president for Romanians.

99 The short story writer Dorin Tudoran (1945–) felt unable to accept the imposition from the Party in July 1981 of the new President of the Writers' Union Dumitru Radu Popescu. After resigning from the Council of the Union, Tudoran was dismissed as an editor of the cultural weekly *Luceafărul*. Consequently, he resigned from the Communist Party. Unable to find a publishing house willing to accept this work, he applied in April 1984 for a passport to emigrate with his family. His request was ignored and a year later he embarked on a hunger strike (on 15 April). On 26 April, a petition signed by, amongst others, Vladimir Bukovski, Eugene Ionescu and Eduard Kuznetsov, was published in the Paris press. Three months later, on the eve of consideration of the renewal of Romania's Most Favoured Nation status by the US Congress, both Tudoran and the dissident priest Gheorghe Calciu were granted exit visas by the Romanian authorities (see also Cristina Petrescu, *From Robin Hood to Don Quixote. Resistance and Dissent in Communist Romania* (Bucharest: Editura enciclopedică, 2013), pp.288–96).

100 Following the publication of four poems by Ana Blandiana in the December 1984 issue of the student review *Amfiteatru*, its poetry editor was demoted and the poet 'reprimanded'. One of the poems was 'The Children's Crusade', a comment on the Presidential decree outlawing abortion:

> An entire people, not yet born.
> But condemned to birth
> In columns before birth
> Foetus beside foetus,
> An entire people
> Which does not see, does not hear, does not understand,
> But moves forward.
> Through writhing bodies of women,
> Through the blood of mothers Unconsulted.

Since *Amfiteatru* appeared under the aegis of the Union of Communist Youth, whose head was Nicu Ceauşescu, the president's playboy son, no oversight of the review was exercised and the poems escaped censorship.

101 One remarkable example is 'Habeas Corpus Poeticum', *România literară,* 19 June 1978. I am grateful to the late Doreen Berry for drawing my attention to this poem. Doinaş was also a signatory, along with the philosophers Constantin Noica, Alexandru Paleologu and others, of a memorandum sent to the mayor of Bucharest in April 1985 showing how the monastery of Văcăreşti could be saved from its planned demolition to make way for the new presidential complex currently under construction.

102 A small selection of the verse of these poets in English translation can be found in *An anthology of Contemporary Romanian Poetry*, translated by Andrea Deletant and Brenda Walker (London: Forest Books, 1984). Sorescu's work has appeared in the following translations: *Selected poems*, translated by Michael Hamburger, *Newcastle upon Tyne* (Bloodaxe Books, 1983); *Let's Talk about the Weather*, translated by Andrea Deletant and Brenda Walker (London: Forest Books, 1985); *The Youth of Don Quixote*, translated by John F. Deane (Dublin: Daedalus Press, 1987); *The Biggest Egg in the World*, translated by D. J. Enright and others (Newcastle upon Tyne: Bloodaxe Books, 1987); *Vlad Dracula the Impaler*, translated by Dennis Deletant (London: Forest Books, 1987); *Hands behind my Back*, translated by Gabriela Dragnea, Stuart Friebert, and Adriana Varga (Ohio: Oberlin College Press, 1991). Marin Sorescu endured frequent battles with the censor, as his volume of censored poems published after the revolution shows, but a considerable body of his work publicly ironized the human condition in the period 1965 to 1989. A *Securitate* report of January 1986 reveals that among the writers placed under surveillance because of their contacts 'of a suspicious nature' with foreigners were: Mircea Dinescu, Ileana Mălănciou, Sorin Marculescu, Radu Cosaşu, Zsigmond Palocsay, Janos Szasz, Marin Sorescu, Emil Brumaru and Romulus Rusan (Arhiva Consiliului Naţional pentru Studierea Arhivelor Securităţii (ACNSAS) (The Archive of the National Council for the Study of the Archives of the *Securitate*), Fond 2629/4, 63r, 63v). I am grateful to Romulus Rusan for showing me this document.

103 Mălănciou's volume of verse *Urcarea muntelui* (The Scaling of the Mountain) was sold out within hours of publication in August 1985. It was criticized by the novelist Eugen Barbu for its 'negative' approach and the director of the publishing house responsible (Albatros) was dismissed. A selection of Mălănciou's poems in translation has been published in *Silent Voices: an Anthology of Contemporary Romanian Women Poets* (London: Forest Books, 1986).

104 From the volume *Democraţia naturii* (Nature's Democracy) (Bucharest: Cartea Românească, 1981) p.11. This poem and others by Dinescu appeared in Mircea Dinescu, *Exile on a Peppercorn*, translated by Andrea Deletant and Brenda Walker (London: Forest Books), 1985).

105 G. Liiceanu, *Jurnalul de la Păltiniş* (Bucharest: Cartea Românească, 1983).

106 G. Liiceanu, *Epistolar* (Bucharest: Cartea Românească, 1987).

107 It is discussed at length by Verdery, *National ideology*, pp.262–64.

108 Liiceanu, *Jurnalul*, p.137.

109 Verdery, *National ideology*, p.285.

110 M. Călinescu in *Romania: A Case of 'Dynastic' Communism* (New York: Freedom House, 1989), p.53.

111 *Ibid.*, p.75.

112 O. Paler, 'Care normalitate?', *România literară*, no.2 (11 January 1990), p.3.

113 I. Simuţ, 'Care patru literature?', *România literară*, no.29 (28 July-3 August 1993), p.10.

114 This author's experience in Cluj in the summer of 1987.

115 A host of examples from 1971 to 1973 are to be found in 'Antologia Ruşinii', *Ethos*, vol.1 (1973), Paris, pp.290–317; vol.2 (1975), pp.331–68.
116 See for example, the collections (no editors named) *Din fiecare inimă a ţării* (From every heart in the country) (Bucharest: Editura Eminescu, 1983); *Pentru cel ales* (For the chosen one), (Bucharest: Editura Eminescu, 1985); and *Prinos de sărbătoare* (Festival hommage) (Bucharest: Editura Eminescu, 1985).
117 'An A to Z of the Personality Cult in Romania', *Radio Free Europe*, SR/1 (2 February 1989), pp.9–14. A shortened version is reproduced by J. Sweeney, *The Life and Evil Times of Nicolae Ceauşescu* (London: Hutchinson, 1991), p.181.
118 Mihai Botez in *Romania: A Case of 'Dynastic' Communism* (New York: Freedom House, 1989), p.53.
119 Botez, *Romania*, pp.62–63.
120 J.F. Harrington and B.J. Courtney, *Tweaking the Nose of the Russians: Fifty Years of American-Romanian Relations, 1940–1990* (Boulder, Colorado: East European Monographs, 1991).
121 State Visit of the President of the Socialist Republic of Romania and Madame Ceauşescu 13–16 June 1978, Foreign and Commonwealth Office Background Note, June 1978.
122 *State Visit*, p.43.

15 Dissent

When asked by a Western diplomat in the mid-1980s about the incidence of dissent in Romania, a senior official of the Romanian Communist Party replied: "Corruption is our dissent".[1] Before discussing 'dissent' in the Romanian context, some clarification of the meaning of the term is advisable.[2] Several Romanian observers confuse dissent with non-conformism on the one hand, and with what they have called 'resistance through culture' on the other.[3] I take a dissident to be a person who operates outside the system, who poses a challenge to it, whereas a non-conformist operates from within. Both express opposition to a regime, but the degree of opposition is greater in a dissident than in a non-conformist. Moreover, dissidence involves a public act, such as a protest, whereas non-conformism is usually a discreet stance. Non-conformist attitudes manifested by writers in the Ceauşescu period have been presented since 1989 as 'resistance through culture'. If we take 'resistance' to imply a public *act*, the term 'resistance through culture' is an inappropriate term for those who sought through their literary work to extend the boundaries of official tolerance, either by adopting a line considered by the authorities as ideologically suspect, or by highlighting certain contemporary social problems, or both.[4] To pass judgement on such writers is difficult, for in their eyes their works were in themselves acts of resistance to the Ceauşescu regime, albeit that they often entered the public domain with the acquiescence or collusion of the censor. But there is a justifiable sense of culpability felt by the community of writers over their compliance with the Ceauşescu regime which led some of them after its overthrow to present their posture during the Ceauşescu era as they would like it to be seen, rather than as it was. The pages of the literary review *România literară* and the cultural journal *22* abounded with such views in 1990. These figures call to mind Brecht's hero in *Drums in the Night* (1922) who is the prototype of the armchair revolutionary.

How rare open dissent amongst intellectuals was during Ceauşescu's rule is suggested by an affirmation made to Michael Shafir in the early 1980s. "Romanian dissent", he was told, "lives in Paris and his name is Paul Goma".[5] This is, as Shafir recognises, an exaggeration, but it is symptomatic of the relative absence of challenge to the regime's authority in Romania until the 'Goma affair' broke out in the spring of 1977. It is important to stress here that outside Romania, a number of Romanian émigrés, most notably Ion Raţiu in London, led a campaign to highlight the human rights' abuses of the Communist regime through the publication in the late 1950s of a weekly newsletter *The Free Romanian Press* which he transformed in 1985 into a fortnightly newspaper in English and Romanian entitled *The Free Romanian/Românul liber.*[6]

The platform for Goma's exposure of human rights abuses in Romania came from the signing in 1975 of the Final Act of the Conference on Security and Cooperation in Europe (the Helsinki Agreement). Article VII of the 'Declaration on Principles Guiding Relations between Participating States' bound the signatories to "respect human rights and fundamental freedoms, including the freedom of thought, conscience, religion or belief, for all without distinction as to race, sex, language or religion". Ceauşescu's signature on this agreement, together with Romania's ratification a year earlier of the International Covenant on Civil and Political Rights, provided instruments in international law to which the Romanian regime could be held to account. But the direct stimulus for Goma's action came from the example of the Charter 77 movement in Czechoslovakia which itself took inspiration from the Helsinki process.

Goma was born in Bessarabia in 1935 to parents who were both schoolteachers. His father was arrested by the Soviet authorities after their annexation of the province in 1940 and upon his release two years later the family made their way to Romania and settled in Bucharest. Goma had been arrested in 1951 on suspicion of intending to join anti-Communist guerrillas based in the Carpathian foothills but was released after 11 days' detention and joined the Communist Youth Movement. In 1954, he was admitted to the School of Literature and Literary Criticism in Bucharest where in 1956, during a seminar, he read out part of a novel he had written in which the hero sets out to establish a students' movement similar to that in Hungary. He was promptly arrested on the charge of attempting to organize a strike at Bucharest University and sentenced to two years' imprisonment. On release he was exiled to a village east of Bucharest where he spent four years in compulsory confinement. Unable to resume his studies because he had been a political prisoner, he took a number of manual jobs until a decree of 1965 reopened the doors of universities to former detainees. He enrolled in the Faculty of Arts at Bucharest University but left within a year.

In the euphoria accompanying Ceauşescu's defiance of the Soviet Union in August 1968, Goma joined the Communist Party. Several months earlier he had submitted for publication the manuscript of his first novel *Ostinato*, based on his experiences at the hands of the *Securitate*, but the reader claimed to recognize Elena Ceauşescu in one of the characters and a ban was placed on further publication of Goma's writings. *Ostinato* appeared, nevertheless, in German translation in 1971 and as a result its author was dismissed from the Party. During the summer of 1972 he was allowed to visit France where he wrote *Gherla* which drew on the time he spent in the prison of that name in Transylvania. Denied publication in Romania, it appeared in French translation in 1976.

Frustrated by the ban on his writings and encouraged by the initiative of Pavel Kohout in Czechoslovakia, Goma wrote a letter to Kohout and the other Charter 77 signatories in January 1977 expressing his solidarity with their movement.[7]

Exasperated by his failure to attract support amongst his friends for this letter he wrote a few days later to Ceauşescu inviting him to sign it. This letter is one of the most revealing contemporary testimonies to the attitudes buttressing the acquiescence to authority and highlights the significance of the appeal to national sentiment in deflecting criticism, upon which Ceauşescu and his sycophants drew so often:

> Mr Ceauşescu,
> For a month now, since the publication of Charter 77 in Prague, I have been striving to persuade my acquaintances to show solidarity with the action of the Czechs and Slovaks. But without success. Some openly refused, honestly admitting that showing solidarity comes under article such and such of the Penal Code; others did not know the article, but knew the *Securitate*, from inside; yet others, somewhat more courageously, agreed to sign a letter of solidarity, but with an indecipherable signature; lastly, others suggested we wait a little, to see what happens in the meantime: if the Charter 77 action succeeds, then perhaps we will get a few crumbs of their success; if not, we have lost nothing, we have no gains, but we will not suffer the consequences that the Czechs will have to bear.
> Please believe me when I say that my fellow citizens' attitude upset me: all our neighbours are active, they are demanding the rights due to them, even the Russians (and we know who they are...) are screaming that they are not free and that their rights are being trampled upon. Only we Romanians stay silent. And we wait. For everything to be given to us on a plate. Our Romanians think only of what they will lose if the *Securitate* finds out, not of what they will gain, despite the *Securitate*. An acquaintance, a pure-blooded - Escu, insulted me profoundly, and not only me. Do you know what he said to me? He said: 'Look, you are getting worked up in a particular way, and you want to do certain things which are not characteristic of the Romanian, therefore you are not a Romanian!' 'What do you mean?', I asked, wounded to the red, yellow, and blue of our flag. 'It's true, my grandfather on my father's side was Macedonian (Goma), my grandmother on my mother's side was Greek (Cuza), it's true that I also have some Polish blood on my paternal grandmother's side, but what matter? What counts is that I feel Romanian. Because I was born in Romania (in the county of Orhei), because my mother tongue is Romanian, because my maternal grandfather was called Popescu, and because (and with this I shut him up!) I spent time in prison here, above and below my beloved homeland!' 'O.K., let's say that you are a Romanian', - Escu conceded, 'but you don't behave like a Romanian'. Well, I flew into a rage and asked him straight: 'Really? But what about Ceauşescu? Is he not a Romanian? On the contrary, he's very Romanian and in spite of this he went to Prague on 15 August to assure Dubcek of the Romanians' solidarity. And although he was a Romanian, he vehemently condemned

> the invasion of Czechoslovakia by Warsaw Pact troops from the balcony of the Central Committee building, saying that what they did was shameful!' That's what I said to him. To which he replied: 'Well just ask Ceauşescu what you asked me: for a signature on your letter of solidarity with the Czechs!'
> Mr Ceauşescu
> I realize that your august signature will never accept a place alongside the signature of a simple citizen, one who is, on top of that, an untalented writer. And even if this miracle occurred, what could be done with just two signatures? My wife could sign as well, but that wouldn't change anything; if thirty Hungarians could be found, then proportionately about ninety Romanian signatures would be necessary. Let's say fifty, or at least ten. But where are they going to come from? I already told you: the Romanians are afraid of the *Securitate*. It emerges that in Romania only two people are not afraid of the *Securitate*: you and me. But, as I already said, with only two signatures.... There is, however, a solution: individual solidarity. I have sent a letter with my own signature. Only my gesture will not dispel the fear of our fellow citizens of joining those who ask for rights which are ulitmately for ourselves. The situation would be completely different if you would send a similar letter, a declaration of support for Charter 77. I am firmly convinced that millions of Romanians will follow you, and will show solidarity with the Czechs and Slovaks. By doing this, you will show that you are consistent with your declarations of 1968, you will prove that you are fighting for socialism, democracy, and mankind. That's the first thing. The second is that Romania will be able to participate at the Belgrade Conference with its head held high.[8]

Shortly after sending this letter Goma persuaded seven others—Adalbert Feher, a worker, Emilia and Erwin Gesswein, instrumentalists in the Bucharest Philharmonic Orchestra, Carmen and Sergiu Manoliu, both painters, Ana Maria Năvodaru, a translator and wife of Goma, and Şerban Ştefaănescu, a draughtsman—to sign with him an open letter to the 35 participating states at the CSCE Belgrade Conference which had signed the Helsinki Final Act, drawing attention to human rights abuses in Romania, and the government's failure to respect its international undertakings in this domain. The open letter was an unprecedented act. Goma's protest, which subsequently attracted the signatures of over 200 Romanian citizens, despite a campaign of intimidation against Goma and the other initial signatories carried out by the *Securitate*,[9] was the first publicly disseminated criticism of the regime within Romania since the imposition of Communist rule. However, only a handful of intellectuals signed the appeal, and the vast majority of the two hundred signatories actually wanted a passport to emigrate to the West.[10]

This courageous move was immediately denounced by Ceauşescu. On 17 February, he delivered an ill-tempered speech, attacking "traitors of the country" which was clearly a reference to Goma's two letters; at ten o'clock that same evening the writer began to receive a string of threatening telephone calls. Every telephone call of support was interrupted whereas those containing insults and threats went undisturbed. On 18 February, a police cordon was thrown up around the apartment block where Goma lived and only residents were allowed through. Passports were given to the Gessweins and to Carmen and Sergiu Manoliu, but Goma and his wife refused this 'offer' to emigrate. On 22 February, Goma was invited to a meeting with Cornel Burtică, secretary for propaganda of the Central Committee. Burtică took him to task for saying that "Romania was under Romanian occupation", pointing out, rather illogically, that the standard of living had risen immeasurably since the Second World War. He tried to buy Goma off by promising to speed up the publication of a translation made by Goma's wife and to offer Goma work as a reporter. When tackled about the measures taken by the *Securitate*, Burtică replied that Ceauşescu had issued "specific orders that no action should be taken".[11]

This was clearly untrue and an attempt to distance the president from the punitive actions taken against Goma whilst at the same time portraying Ceauşescu as a moderate and reasonable man. It is true that on the following day the police cordon around Goma's block was relaxed and more people were able to get through to sign his letter, but at eight o'clock in the morning a worker named Vasile Paraschiv who had signed the letter and had returned to see Goma, was arrested by the police and taken to the *Securitate* headquarters and beaten. On 27 February, two other signatories, a Baptist pastor Pavel Nicolescu and a draughtsman Gheorghe Sandu, were arrested as they were leaving Goma's apartment.

On 1 March, Goma sent a second, more admonitory letter to the president which was profoundly prophetic. Goma urged Ceauşescu not to break that bond that his condemnation of the invasion of Czechoslovakia had created with his people. He was in danger of doing so because of the actions of the *Securitate*, who were

> ....'the traitors and enemies of Romania, who produce nothing and prevent those who produce from producing more... It is time for you, Mr President, to look at what is happening in our garden. It is time for you to remember that those leaders who have been concerned only with painting the fence and have left the garden to be overrun by weeds, have been excluded from the notion and reality of being leaders of a people. It is time for you to reconcile foreign policy with internal policy. It is time for you to return to us, among and with us'.[12]

On the same day Goma's telephone ceased to ring; however, when he lifted the receiver he could hear Radio Bucharest and the voices of eavesdroppers complaining that their connections were faulty. On the following day the psychiatrist Ion Vianu brought Goma a letter expressing his support. Vianu had published in the previous October an article in the Writers' Union journal *Viaţa Românească* pointing out the ways in which his discipline was being abused by the regime. On 3 March, the literary critic Ion Negoiţescu wrote to Goma expressing his support. By now 75 signatures had been gathered. On 12 March, Goma was summoned again to Burtică's office where he was offered the chance to publish; Goma declined, arguing that he would still be followed by the *Securitate*. Burtică again claimed that Ceauşescu had given orders that nothing should befall Goma, but still Goma refused. How shallow Burtică's guarantee was became evident a week later when Horst Stumpf, a former boxer, broke into Goma's flat and attacked him. The police, despite being summoned, did not appear. Stumpf repeated the attacks on two occasions just a few days later. Goma was interviewed on 28 March by French television network 'Antenne 2' reporter Henri Gallais as he was barricading himself in his flat with the help of some fellow signatories whose numbers had now risen to 180.

At the beginning of April a veritable campaign was launched in the Romanian press against capitalism, unemployment and the rise of fascism in the West. This followed closely on Goma's arrest on 1 April, news of which only percolated to the West ten days later. Goma's silence was attributed to the cutting of his telephone and his friends did not, therefore, investigate it further. On 2 April, Vianu was brought by *Securitate* officers to the amphitheatre of the Institute of Pharmacy in Bucharest where he was subjected to the anger and abuse of 200 persons, led by the rector, who dubbed him a "bandit", a "Fascist", and a "pig". He was dismissed from the Institute and from the hospital at which he worked. Goma was attacked in the literary weeklies which appeared on 8 April. Eugen Barbu called him "a nullity" in Săptămâna, Nicolae Dragoş accused him in *Luceafărul* of "trying to rouse reactionary elements, individuals ruled by an aversion to the successes of our order, elements which have nothing in common with literature". In *Contemporanul* Vasile Băran did not mention Goma by name but his target was equally obvious when he castigated "individuals calling themselves writers and journalists who sully with the dirtiest of dirt our noble profession". On the following day, Goma was expelled from the Writers' Union.

In the meantime, Ion Negoiţescu was detained for questioning by *Securitate* officers and under pain of a charge of 'homosexual practices' being brought against him, retracted his support of Goma, signing an article about patriotism in *România literară* on 14 April. Two other signatories, Ion Ladea and Gheorghe Sandu, were savagely beaten by *Securitate* interrogators. Within a few days international concern about Goma's arrest snowballed, with appeals for his release being made, amongst others, by Eugen Ionescu, Jean-Paul Sartre, Arthur Miller and Edward Albee. The growing chorus of protest threatened to overshadow the centenary celebrations of Romanian independence upon which Ceauşescu set great store; his image as the plucky defender of that independence against the great Russian bear to the north was losing some of its gilt as a result of the Goma affair and on 6 May 1977, four days before the fall of the anniversary, Goma was released from custody. After persistent official harassment Goma was allowed to leave Romania with his wife and child on 20 November 1977.

Their settlement in Paris did not, however, remove them from the long arm of the *Securitate*. Goma's successful defiance of the regime clearly rankled with the security police and its foreign intelligence arm, the CIE, assumed the task of silencing him and other critics. Goma was one of three Romanian *émigrés* to whom parcel bombs were addressed from Madrid in February 1981. On 13

January 1982, Matei Pavel Haiducu, a CIE agent based in France to carry out industrial espionage, received orders from the CIE head Lt. Gen. Nicolae Pleşiţă to murder both Paul Goma and another dissident writer, Virgil Tănase, by injecting them with a special poison designed to provoke cardiac arrest. Instead of obeying orders, Haiducu turned himself over to the French authorities. Haiducu's account of his mission reveals that the order to kill came not from Ceauşescu but from Pleşiţă in a desire to ingratiate himself with the president.[13] Pleşiţă's motive says much about the irritation felt by Ceauşescu at Goma's constant sniping at him from Paris and the plot was clearly designed to send a warning signal to other Romanian-born critics of the regime. At the same time it advertised, to the French public at least—Haiducu's revelations received little mention in the English language press—the fact that state-sponsored terrorism was an arm of Ceauşescu's policy. Goma, quite inadvertently this time, did as much to tarnish Ceauşescu as he had done through his courageous stand in 1977.

One of the notable signatories of Goma's first open letter was a Baptist pastor, Pavel Nicolescu. The Baptists were one of the Protestant denominations who had been increasingly subjected to official harassment after 1970, alongside the Penticostalists, the Adventists, the Reformed Adventists, and the Brethren (also known as Christians After the Gospels). Although no policy guidelines have been produced to explain this increase in persecution, it is probably no coincidence that an increase in the 1960s and early 1970s in Protestant membership, which was drawn mainly from amongst the Romanian population in Transylvania, was seen by the Ministry of Religious Faiths, and, of course, by the First Directorate of the *Securitate* to which the ministry reported, as a threat to the cohesion of the Romanian nation whose unity and indivisibility were essential features in the projection of Ceauşescu's expanding personality cult. A guarantor of that cohesion was the Romanian Orthodox Church which was deliberately promoted as virtually an established Church with a privileged position, and in this guise as a symbol of Romanian national identity.

The Baptist church had been recognized by the government in the August 1948 Law of Religious Faiths. However, the new statutes regulating their activity agreed with the Romanian Baptist Union in 1950 reduced the number of their communities and pastors. The Baptists were required to notify the Ministry of Religious Faiths of the candidates for baptism and gain their approval, but the leaders of the union were satisfied so long as churches remained open, even if only for services held at a time specified by the ministry. The period of 'relaxation' came to an end with the suppression of the Hungarian uprising in 1956. Large numbers of believers, mainly from Transylvania, were arrested and charged with conspiracy against the state, and some, such as the group known as the *Moisişti* from Arad who were identified with their alleged 'leader' minister Vasile Moisescu, were accused of 'pro-Hungarian nationalism'.[14] Despite these arrests the congregations clung to their faith and when ministers were released in the general amnesties of 1962–64 which liberated at least 12,000 'political' prisoners, they found an energetic flock, eager to reopen those churches which had been closed.

The strength of Baptist congregations grew rapidly throughout the late 1960s and prompted the government to take measures against the church. The Baptist seminary in Bucharest was closed by government order between 1968 and 1971, and at the end of 1973, only 12 of the 80 resident places were taken up. At the same time there were only 150 full-time ministers, and the majority of local churches depended on lay ministers.[15] One of those ministers, Iosif Ţon, a teacher at a Baptist seminary, decided in 1973 to press the Department of Religious Faiths, which had succeeded the Ministry of Religious Faiths in 1970, to relax the restrictions imposed upon his church. In a paper presented to the department he listed them: the Baptists could not appoint pastors without approval from the department; baptisms could only be performed with similar approval; and church finance, church leadership and church membership were also subject to government control.[16] In reply the department pointed to the Baptists' acceptance of the 1948 Law of Cults which regulated their activity, and claimed that it had to implement the law in order to prevent the proselytization of one faith by another. This was a clear reference to the growth of the Baptist community amongst Romanians at the expense of the Orthodox Church.

Ţon countered the last point by reminding the department that the law guaranteed a citizen's right to change from one denomination to another and expressed his view that the department was deliberately applying a policy to stop the spread of the Christian faith, a spread represented by the dramatic increase in Baptist membership. Following the presentation of Ţon's reply the department made some concessions in its practice of implementing the Law of Cults but did not formally announce these changes. To justify itself, the department argued that in consultation with the Baptist Union it had been in the process of addressing the issues raised by Ţon. Services were held more regularly, and the practice of referring appointments of pastors and notifying baptisms to the local inspector of cults was abandoned. Even the vindictive removal of Ţon in April 1974 from Bucharest to a small Baptist church in Ploieşti failed to puncture the Baptists' confidence.

Ţon's successful stand in 1973 encouraged a renewal of spirit among the Baptists. A growing number of pastors refused to be intimidated, probably, as Alan Scarfe indicates, discovering an inner freedom after accepting the cost of being a practising Christian.[17] The change of spirit was reflected in the joint protest of Baptist, Brethren and Pentecostal believers in May 1974 at the arrest and imprisonment of Vasile Rascol who was sentenced to two years in prison for distributing bibles. The authorities responded by ordering the detention of the leading signatories of the protest, Ţon, Aurel Popescu and Pavel Niculescu, who were interrogated and had their personal papers and books confiscated. The *Securitate* also questioned hundreds of other Baptists but no charges were brought and Ţon and his colleagues were released.

By 1975, Baptist numbers had grown to an estimated 160,000, with 10,000 of those being new recruits in the latter year alone, yet the dramatic increase in membership was not matched by a proportionate rise in the number of ministers or preaching halls. There is no doubt that the courageous stand taken by several ministers in defence of the right to worship in the early 1970s, in contrast to the acquiescence of most, although by no means all, of the Orthodox clergy, and the publicity abroad for it which was broadcast back to Romania by Radio Free Europe and the BBC, not only attracted new members to the Baptist church, but also encouraged Christians from other denominations to speak out about their own problems.

Further disclosures of the harassment to which Baptists and other Protestants had been subjected were made in March 1977 when a group of six prominent pastors and laity issued a 27-page report. It gave details on how decree No. 153, initially introduced in 1970 to cover hooliganism and juvenile delinquency, was invoked to justify the detention of Protestants for questioning and the imposition of fines. Under the provisions of paragraph one of the decree, which stated that "citizens who establish groups expressing through their activities parasitic, anarchistic attitudes contradictory to the elementary principles of socialist legality, as well as citizens who support such groups, are liable to be prosecuted, fined, or subjected to other forms of punishment".[18] In 1972, Baptists in the county of Alba and Penticostalists in the county of Cluj were charged under this law and fined. In 1975, approximately 200 members of the First Baptist church in Timişoara were fined a total of 30,000 *lei* under decree 153 for visiting the new premises of the church. In Răducăneşti, in the county of Vrancea, the local police raided the house of a Baptist where a meeting was in progress in January 1977 and removed the worshippers to the town hall. On 20 February, five of the worshippers, Gigel Filip, Vasile Crimana, Sterian Sava, Mihai Olteanu and Dumitru Mocana, were fined under the decree on the charge of being "members of the Baptist church and singing songs from Baptist books without authorization". The books in question had been printed officially in Romania.[19]

Among members of Protestant groups arrested in this period were Ghejan Titu, sentenced to six years imprisonment in 1975 for refusing to undergo combat training in the army on Saturdays, Ion Mocuţa, imprisoned for six years in 1968 for sending reports to foreign radio stations alleging that Seventh Day Adventists were being jailed and beaten, and Dumitru Blidaru from Topleţ in the county of Caraş-Severin, who was tried *in camera* in October 1975 for "spreading anti-state propaganda" after writing to Ceauşescu about the persecution of Protestants, and sent to the Dr Petru Groza psychiatric hospital in Bihor.

The six pastors and laymen who distributed the March 1977 report were arrested on 3 April 1977. They were the Baptist pastors Iosif Ţon and Pavel Nicolescu, Baptist teachers Aurel Popescu and Radu Dumitrescu, a Brethren layman Dr Silvia Ciotea, and a Pentecostalist minister Constantin Caraman. They were allegedly interrogated for 10 to 12 hours daily until 30 April, and Ţon and Nicolescu had their heads knocked against a wall by members of the *Securitate* and were repeatedly struck in the face, stomach and testicles, by boxers from the *Dinamo* sporting club, a club sponsored by the Ministry of the Interior. Ţon's wife said that she and her five-year-old daughter were questioned for 24 hours without a break by the *Securitate* and she was told that if her husband did not recant over the report, he would be killed.[20] The signatories were, nevertheless, released in May 1977, only to be rearrested in the autumn and threatened with charges of homosexuality and internment in psychiatric prisons. Dumitrescu was given a passport and emigrated, while the remainder were dismissed from their posts or had their preaching licences suspended. International attention to the plight of these Protestant believers was drawn by Bernard Levin in two articles in *The Times* (London) on 16 and 18 June 1978 which he wrote to coincide with Ceauşescu's state visit to the United Kingdom. As a result, the Başa family, who had suffered persecution for being members of the Pentecostal church, were granted their wish to emigrate in a cynical decision which was timed to give Ceauşescu a measure of international goodwill.

This was the only concession the regime made to public opinion abroad. In May 1978, a number of Protestants, including Pavel Nicolescu and Iosif Ţon, formed a movement called 'The Romanian Christian Committee for the Defence of Freedom, Religion, and Conscience'. In July, they sent an appeal signed by 27 members to the Department of Cults requesting recognition of a number of religious denominations declared illegal since 1948, notably the Greek-Catholic (Uniate) Church, the reformed Seventh Day Adventists and the Lord's Army. They called for freedom of worship and religious education in schools. A number of the signatories were shortly afterwards detained and beaten. In September 1978, nine of the Committee's members were expelled from the officially approved Baptist Union on the grounds that they had formed an 'illegal group', and in the following month a further three, Petru Ciocârteu, Ionel Prejban and Nicolae Rădoi from Caransebeş, were sentenced to several months imprisonment on charges of causing a public disturbance, even though witnesses stated that the three had been attacked by the police.[21] During the summer of 1979, eight Seventh Day Adventists were arrested for printing and distributing religious literature. The group had printed 10,000 copies each of 14 different titles, mainly on state printing presses according to police statements.[22]

A threat of psychiatric internment was made in 1978 to Traian Dors after he compiled and circulated a document among members of the Lord's Army community, estimated to number about 250,000 adherents, criticizing the treatment of religious believers and requesting recognition of the Army. The Lord's Army was an evangelical group set up in Sibiu by an Orthodox priest by the name of Iosif Trifa in 1923 and drew its support exclusively from Romanians, principally peasants from northern Moldavia. Trifa wanted to maintain the spirit of Orthodoxy, while at the same time creating a more personal faith among believers, and he and his associates, both priests and laymen, devoted themselves to a more intense spiritual activity. They met several times a week for prayer, Bible studies and preaching, but a struggle for control of the movement within the Orthodox Church led to the defrocking of Trifa. In 1948, the Lord's Army asked to be recognized as an independent denomination but was declared illegal and its priests arrested, among them Cornel Rusu from Simeria and Traian Dors from Beiuş. Both were released in 1952 but were rearrested a few months later, together with Ioan Opriş from Călan near Hunedoara, Serghei Paraschiv from Moldavia, Alexandru Codruţ from Nşmoloasa near Galaţi, Vasile Axinuţa from Lişna near Dorohoi and others.

They were released in 1954 but in 1958 there was a further wave of arrests following the internal clampdown which accompanied the withdrawal of Soviet troops.

The leaders of the Army were trapped by a typical ploy of the authorities. In furtherance of their request for legal recognition, Dors and Sergiu Grossu submitted a draft statute listing 22 regional group leaders. The arrest of all those named followed immediately and they were brought to trial in Cluj on a charge of belonging to 'an anti-state group' and sent to prison. Dors served a further six years in jail before being released in the general amnesty of 1964, but he was then confined to the town of Beiuş south of Oradea and remained under constant surveillance.[23]

Even after the amnesty persecution of the Army continued. In 1965, three members were arrested after a meeting held in the Banat and sentenced to two years' imprisonment, and fines were regularly imposed on members. Orthodox priests suspected of sympathizing with the Army received warnings from their bishops and one, Ştefan Gavrilă, was even suspended for having introduced in his parish the greeting 'Praise the Lord', commonly used by members of the Army.[24]

Harassment of Baptists also continued throughout the 1980s. One example concerned the closure on 15 October 1984 of the Baptist church in the village of Găujani in the county of Vâlcea. The lay pastor Petru Popescu, who built the church, was fined and denied his rations of fuel and food because his identity card was confiscated. On 26 April, he was arrested and imprisoned for two months.[25] Assertion of the right to freedom of religious worship was made most forcibly by the Baptists and other Protestant groups.

Despite being constantly watched and followed, the Baptist pastor Pavel Nicolescu visited the Orthodox priest Gheorghe Calciu in prison after his arrest in 1979. A year earlier Calciu had been expelled from his teaching post at the Orthodox seminary in Bucharest after preaching a series of sermons in the church of Radu Vodă calling on the young to reject atheism:

> Freedom means, at a social level, the contest of ideas, while in Christ it means liberation from sin and death. In our country atheism has a course which is imposed and is more and more limited. It rests on the authority of the state. Faith is in full flight, for it is a fact of life. Authoritarianism enslaves, life liberates.[26]

Calciu was arrested on 10 March 1979, sentenced to ten years' imprisonment for "propagating fascist ideology" and sent to Aiud prison. He was released on 20 August 1984 following widespread international pressure but was confined to a small village near the Bulgarian border. He was later allowed back to Bucharest but not permitted to leave it. In a letter which was made public outside Romania in June 1985 Father Calciu describe the restrictions imposed upon him:

> For months there have been three militiamen stationed day and night in the entrance-hall of the block where we live, another three at one end of the street, and another three at the other end. They check anyone who comes into the entrance-hall and accompany them to the flat they wish to visit;

> if [they say] they are coming to our home, their names are recorded in a register and, with the exception of relatives and very close friends, they are forbidden to come up. Three *Securitate* cars, each with two or three police in them, are stationed day and night near our building, and when we go out into town - even for bread or milk - at least six of them come with us, shoulder to shoulder, so that we don't exhange a word with anyone. People who innocently greet us have their identities checked, and are threatened and forbidden to have any contact with us.[27]

Other opponents of the regime were treated in an identical manner, among them Doina Cornea, the veteran Communist Silviu Brucan and the poet Mircea Dinescu. Such police pressure led Father Calciu to apply to emigrate and on 5 August 1985 he was allowed to leave the country with his family.

Father Calciu proved exceptional amongst Orthodox priests in his defence of Christian values. Although he was not the only priest of his denomination to speak out about problems of worship, examples of Orthodox protest were isolated and inevitably invite comparison with the defiance of the Protestant groups.[28] It is difficult to escape the conclusion that the Orthodox believers were not well served by their leaders under Ceauşescu; the leaders' compliance with the regime can of course be explained by the privileged position and the freedom to worship which they enjoyed, and they expressed their gratitude for that privilege in the ritual adulation of Ceauşescu. Sycophancy towards Ceauşescu became commonplace amongst the Orthodox hierarchy spawning declarations in which black was presented as white. Charity dictates that two examples suffice: one is the birthday telegram sent by Patriarch Teoctist to the Romanian president in January 1989 which gave thanks to him for creating "the climate of complete religious liberty for all confessions in our country".[29] The second is the congratulatory message sent by the Holy Synod to mark the fifteenth anniversary of Ceauşescu's 'election' on 28 March 1974 as president. The prelates expressed their thanks to the president for

> your personal and constant concern for the unending growth of the country's economic strength... for the ardent activity which you, as the greatest and most brilliant hero of peace... carry out for the victory of mankind's ideals of freedom and progress... for the atmosphere of complete religious freedom which you have ensured for the religious groups of our homeland.[30]

Whilst reprehensible in itself, this toadying to the regime was surpassed in its infamy by the silence of Orthodox prelates in the face of the destruction between 1984 and 1989 of eighteen churches as part of Ceauşescu's plan to rebuild the centre of Bucharest. There were, however, isolated protests from the Orthodox clergy. Dr Ion Dura, a priest appointed by the patriarchate in Bucharest to assist Romanian communities in the Benelux countries and based in Brussels, addressed an open letter dated 29 October 1987 to the Secretary General of the World Council of Churches in Geneva. Dura condemned the demolition of a large number of churches which had taken place since 1984 and warned that further destruction, including that of the cathedral of the Romanian Orthodox patriarchate in Bucharest, was planned. Dura ended his letter with this appeal:

> Do not allow, Mr Secretary General, the fear of some 18 million Romanian Orthodox believers that their patriarchal cathedral [will be razed]... turn into sad reality. Please, do everything within your powers in order that the faithful may render glory to God... in the confidence that their venerated churches will be safe forever from destruction.[31]

Quite understandably, Dura did not seek to return to Romania, and the very fact that his protest had come from outside the country is testimony to the fear stalking his superiors in Bucharest. But if this fear can be offered as an explanation for the silence amongst his fellow priests in Romania, it cannot excuse the failure of other Romanian Orthodox priests serving abroad to speak out.

If this silence was a hallmark of acquiescence to the regime, Patriarch Teoctist's telegram of support for Nicolae Ceauşescu, sent on 19 December 1989, just two days after the shootings in Timişoara, was an outrageous act of validation. The telegram congratulated Ceauşescu on his re-election as Party leader at the November Party Congress and praised his "outstanding activity" and "wise and far-seeing guidance". It hailed the "golden age which justifiably bears your name and its achievements which will endure for thousands of years".[32] Needless to say, there were retrospective efforts to erase the record of the telegram for in the December 1989 issue of the official bulletin of the Patriarchate, printed some months later, there was no mention of it; instead there appeared a message from the Holy Synod of the Church denouncing the destruction of churches by "the bulldozers of the tyrant Ceauşescu" expressing solidarity with the National Salvation Front![33] Old habits certainly die hard. Any grain of honour Teoctist might have gained on 18 January 1990 by bowing to public pressure and resigning was lost within two months when he was recalled, a sign that perhaps the Orthodox hierarchy was unable to find any prelate less compromised. Teoctist's reinstatement was proof of a poverty of morality and eloquent testimony to a church badly compromised by total servility to a despot.

It was only a few months after Goma's individual stand that Ceauşescu was faced with the first serious collective protest against his economic policies. The miners' strike of 1977 in the Jiu Valley was the most important challenge posed by a group of workers to Communist power in Romania since the spate of protests in Bucharest, Iaşi and Cluj triggered by the Hungarian uprising of 1956. The first eyewitness account of the strike was given by Istvan Hosszu, a miner from the Jiu Valley who left Romania in 1986, in an interview with Radio Free Europe on 17 July of that same year. This remains a more detailed account than the one given in a brief interview after the revolution by one of the strike leaders, Constantin (Costică) Dobre, a pit brigade chief from the Paroseni mine.[34]

The strike was sparked off by legislation introduced in July 1977 discontinuing disability pensions for miners and raising the retirement age from 50 to 55. Miners in the Lupeni mine decided to strike in protest at this decision and Hosszu, who worked in a neighbouring mine, decided to see for himself what was happening at Lupeni. He arrived on 1 August to find some 35,000 miners crammed into the grounds of the mine and straining to hear Dobre, an engineer from the Lupeni mine, G. Jurcă, and a woman whose name Hosszu did not recall, who was head of the Communist Youth in Lupeni. According to Hosszu these three persons attempted to calm the spirits of the miners who were demanding a meeting with Ceauşescu. The crowd then began to chant "Lupeni 29!" "Lupeni 29!", a reference to the miners' strike of 1929 at Lupeni, which had been used by Communist propaganda as a symbol of the labour struggle against capitalism. There was no sign of the mine manager or of the *Securitate* and it seemed to Hosszu that this was a deliberate ploy by the authorities to avoid inflaming the situation. Dobre and Jurcă agreed that the former, being a miner and therefore closer to his colleagues (Jurcă was an engineer) should draw up a list of the miners' demands, and present them to a mass meeting at the Lupeni mine. These were a reduction in the working day from eight to six hours, a restitution of retirement at 50, a reassessment of the criteria for sick leave, employment for miners' wives and daughters, the recruitment of competent medical personnel to work in the miners, and the objective presentation by the media of the strike.[35] Dobre put these points to the mass meeting on 3 August and they were approved unanimously.

Ceauşescu hastily convened a government commission to deal with the crisis and it was decided to send Ilie Verdeţ, the member of the Political Executive Committee responsible for the economy, Constantin Băbălău, the Minister of Mines, Clement Negruţ, the mayor of Petroşani, and Ghinea, the mayor of Lupeni, to talk to the miners. They no doubt intended to persuade them to call off their strike but they were not given the opportunity to do so. They were jostled by the miners and even punches were thrown as they tried to make their way to the mine manager's office. Verdeţ was told that the miners had no confidence in him since he had deceived the Central Committee as to the true situation in the Jiu Valley and was instructed to contact Ceauşescu with the demand that the Secretary General should come to Lupeni to discuss the miners' grievances directly with them. To this end Dobre, Jurcă and the anonymous woman from the Communist Youth decided to transfer Verdeţ to the Palace of Culture in Lupeni from where he could call Ceauşescu on a special line. There, under the supervision of a group of miners, Verdeţ repeated the words he had been told to say: "Please come immediately, the situation is serious!" To prevent any further details being passed on, and to make Ceauşescu realize that Verdeţ was effectively a prisoner, one of the miners in the escort hung up the receiver.

Ceauşescu arrived the same day in a convoy of black cars which tried to force a passage through the masses of miners. They failed and Ceauşescu was forced to get out of the car and make his way to the mine manager's office amidst chants of "Ceauşescu and the miners", "Ceauşescu and the people" which Dobre had persuaded the miners beforehand to utter as a sign of confidence in the Party leader. According to Hosszu, Ceauşescu was totally taken aback by the sight of so many protesters. His eyes darted from right to left and he was clearly shaken by the scene. When he reached the offices Dobre asked the crowd whether they should first let the Secretary General speak or whether the list of their grievances should be made known. The miners opted for the latter and these were read out in front of the strikers.

Ceauşescu then took the microphone from Dobre's hands and in a trembling voice declared: "Comrades, this is not the way... this is a disgrace for the entire nation, a disgrace! I have taken note of your grievances". He went straight to the point of the demand for a shorter working day. In an attempt to distort the reasoning behind the decision to extend it, he claimed that it had in fact been the Party leadership which had resolved to reduce working hours but that this decision had met with opposition from the miners. This insult to the miners' intelligence prompted the reply: "It is not us! Bandits, thieves!" Ceauşescu then proposed that the shorter progamme be introduced gradually at the Lupeni mines and extended to other pits. This suggestion was met with the chant: "a six hour day from tomorrow". Ceauşescu became visibly angered, surprised by the audacity of people who dared to express their point of view in his presence. He descended to the level of threats: "If you do not go back to work we'll have to stop pussyfooting around!" Prolonged booing and the cry of "Down with Ceauşescu" met these menaces and it was only when Dobre appealed for calm and urged the miners to let the Secretary General finish what he had to say that the atmosphere became less charged. Ceauşescu seized the opportunity to strike a more conciliatory note, conceding a reduction in the working day to six hours throughout the whole Jiu Valley, and agreeing to build factories which would offer work to miners' families. He promised that no retaliatory measures would be taken against those who had organized the strike, and that all of those who were to blame for the miners' discontent would be brought to account. After these promises were made the miners dispersed and some even returned to work on the evening shift of 3 August. But the next day, in spite of Ceauşescu's promises, the Jiu Valley was declared a 'restricted area', the army sent in and the *Securitate* began their work of repression. An investigation was launched to discover where the core of support for the strike lay and in the months following the strike many miners were moved to other mining areas, while some were said to have been sent to labour camps on the Danube-Black Sea Canal.

Father Gheorghe Calciu, the dissident priest who was imprisoned between 1979 and 1984, claimed in an interview in 1985 to have met miners in his various places of detention. Even the fate of the miners' leaders was unclear; two of their most prominent spokesmen, Dobre and Jurcă, were rumoured to have 'disappeared'. According to some of his friends Dobre died in a car accident stage-managed by the *Securitate* on 27 October 1977, and his colleague was the victim of a similar accident a month later. When tackled on this subject by the International Labour Organization, the Romanian authorities claimed that the two men never existed. However, immediately after the revolution of 1989

Dobre resurfaced and disclosed that he and his family had been picked up by the *Securitate* on 30 August 1977 and given forced domicile in the city of Craiova.[36] Most of Ceaușescu's other promises were not respected either: the eight-hour day was reinstated; only those miners who had worked underground for more than 20 years were allowed to retire at 50; and as for the media, they said nothing about the strike. The only concessions made were in the provision of improved medical care in the mines and in the creation of jobs for the miners' families.

The failure of the Romanian media to report the Jiu Valley strike characterized its total subservience as a tool to be manipulated by the regime and illustrated the blackout tactics used by the authorities throughout the postwar era to stifle the passage of potentially 'harmful' information to the populace. Access to information is just as essential for the individual to defend himself against authority as is manipulation of it for the government to protect itself. This control of the media and the 'sanitizing of news' was very effective in containing protest and in inculcating a sense of isolation and frustration amongst protesters, and played a self-fulfilling role: if no opposition to the regime was reported, then most of the public not only assumed that there was none, but, guided by this assumption, questioned the point in displaying any.

Alongside Goma, two other intellectuals presented a courageous symbol of dissent in Romania. They were Vlad Georgescu (1937–88), a historian, and Mihai Botez (1940–95) a mathematician.[37] Georgescu was arrested in spring 1977 and held in prison for three months after the *Securitate* discovered a manuscript of Georgescu challenging the Communist distortion of Romania's past. Upon his release, he took a bursary offered by the Woodrow Wilson International Center for Scholars in Washington DC, after which he decided to remain in the United States. In 1983, he was appointed director of the Romanian service of Radio Free Europe, in which capacity, until his death in November 1988 from a brain tumour, he gave prominence in broadcasts to letters critical of the Ceaușescu regime. It was Georgescu who in 1979 passed on Botez's first message—a memorandum on Romania's economic crisis—to the then director of RFE, Noel Bernard.

In a second memorandum on the same topic, broadcast in 1985, Botez renewed his criticism. The high profile given by RFE to Botez's text provided some insurance for him against the regime. This and other messages were passed on by journalists and diplomats based in Romania. After an interview published in the French weekly *L'Express* on 28 May 1987, in which he claimed that Romanians supported *glasnost* and *perestroika*, Botez was moved to a computer centre in the Danube port of Tulcea, well away from the attention of Western journalists. In the following year, he was given an exit visa for the US.[38]

There were also courageous yet spasmodic attempts by groups of manual workers to challenge authority. In January 1979, a group of 15 workers from the naval yards in the Danube port of Turnu Severin approached a Dr Ionel Cană, a general practitioner who had worked in Olt County among workers and had recently moved to Bucharest. Dr Cană had acquired a reputation for helping workers to draw up petitions complaining about labour conditions and he agreed to the men's proposal to set up SLOMR (Free Trade Union of the Working People of

Romania). The founding declaration was broadcast over Radio Free Europe on 4 March 1979 by Noel Bernard, the head of the Romanian section, and the union attracted more than 2,400 signatures of support from workers in towns such as Ploieşti and Constanţa, and Hungarian workers in Târgu Mureş and Timişoara. The dissident Orthodox priest Gheorghe Calciu offered to be a spiritual adviser. The group circulated a manifesto calling for the legalization of unofficial trade unions and observance of the right to free association. In April, the union, in an open letter to Ceauşescu, protested against the arrest of its members, among them Cană and an economist, Gheorghe Braşoveanu, the latter being confined to a psychiatric institution in March. Cană's successor as chairman, Nicolae Dascălu, was sentenced in June to 18 months in prison for allegedly passing state secrets to Amnesty International.[39]

The degree of paranoia about any opposition to Ceauşescu was illustrated most graphically in 1982 by the so-called 'Transcendental Meditation' affair. A number of questions remain unanswered about this episode, not least why the authorities, having permitted the practice of yoga whose techniques were introduced in Bucharest by an instructor based in Switzerland, should then have clamped down upon the practising group whose members included a number of promising writers and artists. Mystery also surrounds the part played by the instructor, named by a Romanian newspaper after the revolution as Nicolae Stoian, a Romanian *émigré* who later worked for the Romanian section of the BBC World Service.[40] According to the paper; Stoian visited Bucharest in the winter of 1977 in order to expound the virtues of transcendental meditation and was received by Elena Ceauşescu herself. He was given the opportunity, the newspaper alleged, to hold yoga classes in the Institute of Education and Psychology Research in Bucharest and over four years attracted a considerable audience amongst the cream of Romania's intellectuals.

All went well until early 1982 when the official publication of the Ministry of the Interior, *Pentru Patrie*, accused the meditation group of plotting to take Romania out of the Warsaw Pact. There followed a purge which was only surpassed in the Ceauşescu era by the shake-up following Pacepa's defection. Among the members of the group were Aneta Spornic, a protégé of Elena Ceauşescu, who was dismissed from her post as Minister of Education, senior Party members Marin Rădoi and Petre Gheorghe, who were censored, two Minister of the Interior generals, Vasile Maior and Gheorghe Zagoneanu, Marin Sorescu, the prominent poet and dramatist, and Andrei Pleşu, the future Minister of Culture in the first post-revolutionary government. Pleşu was vilified by the local Party secretary of the Union of Fine Artists and, like Sorescu, was hounded for months by the *Securitate*. Stoian was simply expelled from the country. Documents published after the revolution revealed that a list of several hundred members of the group was passed on 22 July 1982 by Ion Popa, secretary of the Bucharest Party Committee, to the then head of the *Securitate*, Tudor Postelnicu. Six days later, Postelnicu sent Popa several hundred files on the members, presumably as the basis for the attacks made on them in local Party meetings.

The unresolved questions about this curious affair prompted a rash of wild speculation. Some suggested after the revolution that it was all a plot by the *Securitate* to identify potential dissidents; if so, then why let the group practice yoga for four years? Others saw the hand of the KGB at work, suggesting to Ceauşescu that the meditation group was part of a plot to cement opposition to him and urging him to dissolve it.

In October 1981, workers went on strike in the open cast mines of Leurda, Lupoaia and Horăşti near the town of Motru in the south-west of the country. There were reports in the foreign press of attacks on public buildings in the town but no information was forthcoming about the aftermath of the strikes.[41] Miners in seven metal mines in the Maramureş region of northern Transylvania went on strike in September 1983 in protest at wage cuts introduced under a new wage law. Security police were sent in to break up the strike. The growing economic hardship imposed on the country by Ceauşescu sparked off more strikes in the Transylvanian cities of Cluj and Turda in November 1986. Following a reduction of the daily bread ration to 300 grams per person and pay cuts of up to 40 per cent for failure to fill output targets, Romanian and Hungarian workers went on strike at the Heavy Machine Plant and the Refrigeration Plant in Cluj, and at the glass factory in Turda. Leaflets in both languages demanding "meat and bread" and "milk for our children" circulated in Cluj, thus demonstrating inter-ethnic solidarity. Party officials rushed food to the factories and promised to meet the workers' grievances, whereupon the strikers returned to work, but just as in the Jiu Valley in 1977 the *Securitate* launched an investigation into the organization of the strike and several workers were moved to other areas.

The successive anti-regime protests prompted some Western intelligence agencies to question the stability of Ceauşescu's hold on power. In what proved to be a remarkably prescient memorandum of 17 December 1986, entitled 'Romania: Incipient Crisis', prepared by the Acting National Intelligence Officer for Europe for the US National Foreign Intelligence Board, the senior Intelligence Community advisory body to the Director of the CIA on the substantive aspects of national intelligence, the author argued that

> If a political crisis were to break out in Romania, it would most likely be precipated by:
> Ceauşescu's death or severe incapacitation;
> A palace *coup* engineered by a group or groups (as yet undefined) opposed to Ceauşescu's misrule;
> and/or
> a 'brush fire' of spontaneous but mutually reinforcing protest actions around the country.
> The intelligence and policy communities are fairly well attuned to at least the first two of these, as well as to the possible roles of the *Securitate,* the military and the Ceauşescu clan, and the USSR. There may be other crisis scenarios that we should consider, but the last, and the least well documented, scenario is my main concern.[42]

Within three months unrest had spread to the east of the country, encompassing for the first time in decades both workers and students. Once again, wage cuts imposed for failure to meet production targets and food supply problems were the trigger. On 16 February 1987 some 1,000 employees at the Nicolina rolling stock works in the Moldavian capital of Iaşi marched on the Party headquarters protesting at the pay cuts. Their demands were quickly met. On the following day, in what appears to have been an uncoordinated action, several thousand students from the university and polytechnic marched through the centre of the city in protest at the power and heating cuts imposed in student hostels, chanting "we want water to have a wash and light to be able to study". The authorities again gave in and no repressive action was taken against the students. At the Nicolina plant, however, 150 of the most prominent strikers were dismissed after the customary *Securitate*-directed post mortem.

Behind this string of protests against Ceauşescu's economic policies lay the introduction of draconian measures designed to reduce food and energy consumption, and wage reductions. Yet instead of heeding the warning signs of increasing labour unrest, Ceauşescu plunged blindly forward with the same measures, seemingly indifferent to their consequences. A sign that the cup of privations had filled to overflowing came on 15 November 1987 in Braşov, the country's second largest industrial centre. Here is an eyewitness account of events on that morning from a Hungarian visitor (the population is now over 80 per cent Romanian but formerly had significant German and Hungarian elements):

> It was about 11 as we were crossing the main square of Braşov, on
> our way to the bus-station. The shouting we heard was like that at a football
> match, but we realized this was no sports event when we could clearly make
> out the name of Ceauşescu being shouted over and over again. We stopped
> opposite Party Headquarters. Between 300 and 350 people were milling
> about in front of the building, watched by a steadily growing crowd of
> on-lookers. We joined this crowd and observed the events.
> Romanian-speaking friends translated the slogans being chanted:
> 'HOŢI' (thieves), 'JOS CU CEAUŞESCU' (down with Ceauşescu),
> 'LIBERTATE ŞI DREPTATE' (freedom and justice), and
> 'MUNCITORII LUPTĂTORI' (the fighting workers).
> The banner-waving crowd consisted mainly of middle-aged, poorly dressed
>
> people in working clothes and fur-hats; quite transparently they had come to negotiate. The workers standing before the gateway expected to be properly received, and wanted to send a delegation ahead. No one received them, though the apparatchiks were still in the building. On this day there were local elections in Braşov; voting is compulsory and the workers had gathered, in the first place, to cast their votes. Those inside the building, terrified by the slogans and the rising emotions of those in the square, fled through the back of the building.
>
> The first sign of the crowd's impatience was the tearing down of the sign 'Braşov Party Headquarters'. There was a moment's quiet. The building

remained silent. The workers attacked the ground-floor windows, smashing them in with stones and their flagpoles. Meanwhile, a group of 50 or so workers rammed the wooden gate until it broke open. Within minutes, the crowd was moving from floor to floor, smashing windows and throwing pictures, posters, radios, telephones, files and papers out into the crowd. A small group appeared by the gateway, bringing cheese, margarine and bread by the sackful, and began distributing them to the crowd. The crowd went wild. In theory, these foods are rationed, but they had, in fact, been quite unobtainable for months, even on ration cards. On the second floor a portrait of Ceauşescu could be seen in the bay of a window: a man was using his body to rip up the canvas and shatter the frame. Behind him a fur-hatted worker's sweeping gestures motioned the crowd to go in; many did so. Pictures, office equipment and furniture from inside were set alight. Everything was burnt, but there was no fire inside the building. Painted on its walls was the slogan '*LIBERTATE ŞI DREPTATE*'.

Finding no one to negotiate with, the crowd set off for the People's Council building opposite, the Romanian and the red Flags held high. By now there were some 5,000 people in the square. Here it was much the same story: the sign outside the building was torn down and its windows smashed in, its elaborate cornicing destroyed. The crowd met no resistance and it was all over in 15 minutes. Chairs and files were thrown out into the square and set on fire.

Now sirens could be heard. The crowd of onlookers drew back, the more active core of workers stayed where they were. Three fire engines appeared, and the firemen prepared to extinguish the pyres burning in front of the building. Hemmed in by the crowd, they could not get through and rapidly withdrew. Within five minutes two more fire engines appeared; when persuasion failed, they were beaten off with stones and chair-legs. Meanwhile, the building had emptied and the crowd would have gone back to the Party HQ. However, two armour-plated military vehicles carrying armed soldiers had entered the square. This was enough for the crowd to begin to disperse. In one corner of the square, trucks unloaded more armed soldiers with dogs.

The onlookers, ourselves included, tried to escape from the cordon thrown round the square. The soldiers let some through, but others were beaten up and dragged away. By now it was about one o'clock. Later it transpired that the majority of the more active workers were arrested on the spot, while the rest were carried off from their home in the middle of the night.

On Sunday night armed convoys patrolled the blacked-out city. There was no public transport. The army was on emergency standby; parts of the city centre were sealed off. The locals said that the protesters came from two Braşov factories. In the tractor factory the workers had received only 60 per cent or less of the wages due on the 10th of the month, while in the truck factory no one had been paid at all. The protest on the day of the local

> elections had begun as a demand for unpaid wages. On Monday, the factories had come to a standstill. On Tuesday, all outstanding wages were paid, and work resumed in the afternoon. By Tuesday, there was even food in the shops, as evidenced by queues up to 25 metres long for bread, milk and other essentials. Those in the queues were much amused by the sight of glaziers heading for the main square. Weeks later I heard that workers' meetings in the local factories had condemned the troublemakers and voted for the dismissal and prosecution of those who had taken part in the protest. It was this that prompted me to publish this account.[43]

This account provides the essential details of events that Sunday. The trouble started only five days after the implementation of a decree of Ceauşescu reducing heating quotas for domestic consumption by 30 per cent and instituting punitive charges for exceeding the quotas. Coming on top of the imposition of wage cuts for the second consecutive month for failure to meet production targets—they could not be met because of a shortage of orders since the internal market was stagnant and there had been a drop in exports—and chronic food shortages, particularly of potatoes which were an essential part of the diet of Braşov's inhabitants, the heating restrictions were the last straw for the working population. Several thousand workers at the Steagul Roşu plant—with a workforce of 22,000—came off the night shift and assembled, ostensibly to vote in the local elections taking place across the country that day. They marched off from the plant at about 9 a.m. in the direction of the Party headquarters in the centre of the city singing the anthem of the revolution of 1848 '*Deşteaptă-te, Române*' (Awake, Romanian) and chanting "'Down with the dictatorship" and "We want bread". They were joined by workers from the Braşov Tractor Plant (workforce 25,000) and by many townspeople as they made their way to the city centre where they forced their way into the Party headquarters as described above. A number of arrests were made after the disturbances.[44]

The Braşov protests are also a reminder of the inability of the Western media to penetrate the fog of obfuscation with which the regime covered the event. News of the disturbances barely trickled out of Brasov at the time, much less beyond Romania's borders. As in the case of the miners' strike a decade earlier in the Jiu Valley the Romanian media remained silent. It was left to foreign print and broadcast media to alert the world and—through the Romanian section of RFE and that of the BBC World Service—the Romanians themselves of this breach between the RCP and the Romanian working class.[45]

The fact that this protest took place in a major industrial centre whose production of lorries and tractors was largely for export, and whose workers were formerly among the best paid in Romania showed to what depths discontent with Ceauşescu's policies had sunk, a fact highlighted not only by a leading dissident, but, more startlingly, by Mihai Botez, a mathematician and erstwhile economic adviser of Ceauşescu. Botez was only one of three persons in Romania to speak out in support of the workers—the other two were Silviu Brucan and Doina Cornea. He issued a statement emphasizing that the protests signalled a "rejection of the leadership's economic and political strategies" and constituted "a severe warning to the leaders" from the working class. Botez warned that "repression would be the costliest option, with disastrous implications for the country".[46]

Even more significant, and unprecedented, was the intervention of Silviu Brucan (1916–2006), deputy editor of the party daily *Scînteia* from 1944 to 1956, and Romanian ambassador to the United States (1956–59) and to the United Nations (1959–62). In the evening of 26 November, Brucan invited two Western journalists, Nick Thorpe from the BBC and Particia Koza of UPI, to his house and handed them a statement to Western correspondents in Bucharest invoking the authority of the Party and alerting Ceaușescu to the fact that "a period of crisis has opened up in relations between the Romanian Communist Party and the working class". After a rise in the standard of living in the 1960s and 1970s, "the situation of the workers has deteriorated and the explosion in Brașov is a sign that the cup of anger is now full and the working class is no longer prepared to be treated like an obedient servant". He warned that "repression may result in total isolation, this time not only from the West, but also from the East".[47] Excerpts from Brucan's declaration were broadcast the following evening on BBC World Service News and the whole text in Romanian was transmitted on the BBC Romanian Service, Radio Free Europe and Voice of America, thus enabling millions of Romanians to hear for the first time a warning to Ceaușescu delivered from a significant Party figure.

One collective manifestation of support for the Brașov workers was reported in the Western press: on 22 November several hundred students at the city's polytechnic held a meeting of solidarity with the workers. The Romanian media, by contrast, kept quiet about the demonstrations of 15 November and the concomitant arrests, but this blanket of silence was lifted by foreign journalists who revealed that the city was being patrolled by troops with dogs and that cordons had been thrown up around the Party headquarters. The first official acknowledgement, albeit an indirect one, of the disturbances came on 2 December when Radio Bucharest reported that an extraordinary meeting of workers' representatives at the Red Flag lorry factory had 'unanimously' resolved to dismiss the management. The communiqué ascribed to the meeting stated that those workers "who engaged in acts that are alien to our society" were to be moved or "brought to account in accordance with the law".[48] In a cynical attempt to deflect responsibility for the protests—although these were not directly mentioned—from Ceaușescu, the management was accused of "unlawful" wage reductions and a telegram was addressed by the meeting to the president expressing its "complete attachment to the internal and foreign policies of the Party and state".[49] At the time the telegram was published, the investigations which the *Securitate* had begun on the day after the protests at the two factories had already led to the detention of some 200 workers. An underground 'Committee to Support the Detainees', set up in December 1987, claimed to have compiled a list of 425 workers, among them several women, who were being held, and in the middle of the month a group trial was held in Brașov at which 61 persons were sentenced for periods ranging from 18 months to three years in prison on charges of 'hooliganism'.[50]

Signs that Ceauşescu was severely shaken by the Braşov disturbances were evident in his decisions to postpone the National Party Conference by a week and not to attend Mikhail Gorbachev's briefing for Warsaw Pact leaders in East Berlin but to send his foreign minister instead. At the same time, in order to prevent further criticism of the regime at a time of unrest, prominent dissidents were detained or placed under house arrest in early December. They included Doina Cornea, the university lecturer from Cluj who was dismissed from her post in September 1983 for having used Western philosophical texts in her lectures, and her son Leontin Juhas, who together with Cornea distributed a leaflet outside Cluj factories expressing support for the Braşov workers. Others, who were either confined to their homes or arrested, were Mihai Botez's wife Mariana Celac, an urban planner who was a critic of the urban and rural resettlement programme; Ion Puiu, a veteran National Peasant Party politician and critic of the regime; Florian Russu, the leader of the outlawed National Peasant Party youth group; Radu Filipescu, a young electronics engineer who had been sentenced in September 1983 to ten years imprisonment for printing and distributing anti-Ceauşescu leaflets but was released in April 1986; Nicolae Stăncescu and Ion Fistioc, both Party members, who had submitted proposals for reform to the leadership and to the Soviet Embassy in Bucharest with the request that they be forwarded to Gorbachev; Nelu Prodan, a young Baptist; and Gabriel Andreescu, a 36-year old geophysicist, who sent an open letter to a human rights conference sponsored by Solidarity in Cracow at the end of August 1988 calling on Romanian citizens to adopt a policy of non-cooperation with the regime and to "refuse to go along with harmful decisions by the authorities".

Steps were also taken to silence Brucan. After his declaration was broadcast he was effectively placed under house arrest. Two policemen were posted outside his house and another two at the end of his street to stop diplomats and reporters from approaching his home. His telephone was cut off and he was told by a senior officer that he could only leave the house once a day, in the morning, to go shopping. When he did leave he was accompanied by four plain-clothes *Securitate* officers who discouraged anyone from talking to Brucan. After two weeks he was summoned by the head of the Party Control Commission, Ion Constantin, who reprimanded him for making a declaration "hostile to the Party and to the country" and for choosing "the worst imperialist news agencies to make it to". Brucan replied by saying that the two agencies were those to whom Ceauşescu had granted interviews on numerous occasions and that he considered it his duty to defend the workers every time that their demands were legitimate. Accused of being a traitor to the Party and the country by another official present called Catrinescu, Brucan countered by asking him about his background. "I worked at a metal factory during the war", replied Catrinescu. "Then you served the German war machine", retorted Brucan. "And you dare to call me a traitor!" With this exchange Constantinescu brought the meeting to a close, accusing Brucan of being unreasonable.[51]

The restrictions on Brucan remained in place but it was an illustration of the ambivalence of their application that Brucan managed to pass a second statement to the American press agency UPI on 11 December. In a conversation with me on 13 November 1988 during a visit to London, Brucan told me that one of the *Securitate* officers engaged in his supervision had been a student of his at Bucharest University and had agreed to facilitate the delivery of this statement in which he said that the Party was "wrestling with the grave problem of worker unrest" and that "the response will be made public at next week's Party Conference".[52] Romanian Communists "are now aware of the dire consequences which repression against the brave workers of Braşov would entail" and for this reason Brucan would "refrain from further statements on Romanian affairs".[53] Information on the close surveillance under which he was forced to live were revealed in a letter from a close friend of Brucan, dated 8 January 1988, the contents of which were disclosed by Nick Thorpe, the BBC World Service correspondent in Budapest, in a despatch broadcast one week later. Brucan's villa

> is under tight surveillance, 24 hours a day by four militiamen in three shifts. No visitors are allowed, not even relatives. No mail whatsoever reached him over the recent period, including Christmas and the New Year, and the only newspaper to arrive has been the Communist Party daily *Scînteia*. The single stroll he is allowed each morning takes place with two militiamen in front of him, two behind and one on either side...The disconnection of the phone meant that his wife was unable to call a doctor when she was ill. All for the sake of watching a Marxist and a Party veteran, writes the author. This is the Romanian version of Socialism with a human face, he concludes.[54]

Restrictions on Brucan were lifted on 8 February after the visit of John Whitehead, the US Deputy Secretary of State to Bucharest. Brucan was invited to a reception hosted by Whitehead at the American Embassy on 5 February but was told he could not leave his home by the *Securitate* major guarding him. On the following morning, Thomas Simons, US Deputy Assistant Secretary of State who had served at the American Embassy in Bucharest in the 1970s and spoke Romanian, tried to visit Brucan but in spite of showing his passport was denied entry by the *Securitate* officers. Two days later, Brucan's telephone was reconnected, the post began to arrive and he was allowed to come and go as he pleased, although he was still shadowed at a distance by *Securitate* officers. His freedom of movement was extended to allow him to accept an official invitation to visit the United States and Britain in November 1988 where he presented papers on the "Crisis of Communism". At a conference in the US he was invited to give the same paper in Moscow and at the completion of his visit to London, during which he revealed his intention to visit Moscow,[55] he flew to the Soviet capital where he was received by Anatoli Dobrynin, the former Soviet ambassador to Washington.[56] The status of his reception in all three countries gave a clear signal to Ceauşescu of the favour which Brucan enjoyed, one which was all the more powerful because it spanned the ideological divide of West and East. Here was proof of the isolation of Ceauşescu of which Brucan had warned in his first statement after Braşov, and of the Romanian president's perverse success in uniting West and East against him.

A realization of the need to improve Ceauşescu's poor image abroad had led to the advance notice given by the State Council in October 1987 of a decree granting an amnesty and pardon for some convicted offenders which would come into effect two months later on 30 December, the fortieth anniversary of the Romanian Republic. A pardon was given to those prisoners serving sentences of up to five years, and those with longer sentences had them reduced. More serious crimes, such as murder, abortion, assault and robbery, were not covered by the decree. Included in the amnesty were those who attempted to leave the country illegally without a passport. Although tens of thousands of Romanian citizens emigrated legally between 1975 and 1986, thousands of others attempted to do so illegally and were arrested. Others less fortunate were shot by Romanian border guards while trying to cross the frontiers into Hungary and Yugoslavia, while an unknown number died while attempting to swim the Danube. Unmarked gravestones on the Yugoslav side of the river testify to their efforts.

Clearly, the decree was introduced to influence the US Congress in its decision of whether to suspend for six months Most Favoured Nation status for Romania, yet there were also practical considerations. Overcrowding in Romania's jails, produced by the large numbers of offenders, put pressure on Ceauşescu to take some form of action, and the decree of October 1987 was the sixteenth such amnesty since he had become Romania's leader.[57] What proportion of these offenders had tried to escape the country was impossible to assess but it is hard to avoid the conclusion that many of the 25,000 young people who were reported to have committed penal offences in 1981 alone, were detained for trying to do just that.[58]

There was no reference to political prisoners in the decree. This was no surprise since the Romanian authorities denied there were any, but Amnesty International named some 15 people held for political offences in a report published in July 1987. Among them were Francisc Barabas, aged 40, a member of the Hungarian minority, who was sentenced to six years jail in November 1983 (raised to seven years on appeal), for distributing leaflets denigrating Ceauşescu in Miercurea Ciuc; Ion Bugan, aged about 50, an electrician from Tecuci, who was sentenced to ten years imprisonment in 1983 for having driven through the centre of Bucharest with a picture of Ceauşescu bearing the caption "We don't want you, hangman"; Dumitru Iuga, aged 40, an electrician from Bucharest, who planned an anti-Ceauşescu protest with a small group of students and workers and was sentenced with seven others to terms ranging from five to ten years; and Gheorghe Năstăsescu, a 56-year-old building worker from Iaşi, who denounced Ceauşescu on a Bucharest street and was sent to jail for nine years.[59]

Human rights violations were brought into the very chamber of the relevant UN agency by the case of Dumitru Mazilu, a Romanian official who, after being commissioned in 1985 by the United Nations to compile a report on "human rights and youth in Romania", was prevented from presenting it to the Subcommission on the Prevention of Discrimination and the Protection of the Minorities in Geneva in June 1987. At that time the subcommission was told by Romanian representatives that Mazilu, who had been appointed by the Romanian government to the subcommission in 1983, had suffered a heart attack and was in hospital, but his failure to appear at the subcommittee's session on 8 August 1988 aroused suspicions among his colleagues. The Swedish UN Under Secretary General stated that Mazilu had expressed a willingness to continue work on the report and to come to Geneva but that since the authorities in Bucharest would not let him travel the UN had decided to ask the Romanian government to receive a UN member to work with Mazilu in Bucharest. The Romanians ignored the request.[60]

There followed the disclosure by the Reuter news agency of the contents of a letter which Mazilu had written in April 1988 to the chairman of the UN subcommission in which he catalogued the "arsenal of repressive measures" which had been taken against him since he refused to abandon work on his report in the autumn of 1987. In December of that year, he had been forced to retire from his position as head of the Foreign Ministry's legal department after having spent two periods in hospital, and since February 1988 more than 20 policemen had followed him and his family "day and night".

Mazilu's assertion that the "frequent violations of the rights and freedoms of young people in different countries, including my own" made his study absolutely necessary, doubtless sounded somewhat hollow to close observers of Romanian affairs in view of Mazilu's record as a servant not merely of the Ceauşescu regime,[61] but, allegedly, also of the security apparatus. Born in Bacău in 1934, he was reported to have been recruited into the *Securitate* in 1952 and trained as an interrogator. In 1956, when he enrolled at the University of Bucharest for a law degree he held the rank of Lieutenant Major.[62] He completed his studies in 1960 and rose to the rank of colonel, studied law and obtained a doctorate at Cluj University. According to *România liberă* he was appointed commandant of the Ministry of the Interior cadet school at Băneasa and later a professor at the Ştefan Gheorghiu Party Academy.[63] In the early 1970s, he was named Deputy Director of the Institute of Political Science and the Studying of the National Question, and in 1974 he became Secretary General of the Romanian Association for the United Nations. In 1981, he represented Romania at the UN session of the General Assembly's Juridical Committee.[64]

The UN showed no misgivings about Mazilu's belated metamorphosis and treated his case as a genuine human rights problem in itself but what proved to be a more realistic, if cynical view, was expressed by the Soviet representative on the subcommission who declared that there was "no point" in its approving a resolution asking the Secretary General Javier Perez de Cuellar to establish "personal contact" with Mazilu, in view of the official Romanian observer's statement that his country would reject any moves implying "inspection or control". There could be no greater exposure of the UN's lack of teeth in enforcing respect of its own charter on human rights' observance than this failure to rectify the abuse by a signatory state of the human rights of one of its own committee members![65]

It was little wonder, then, that Ceauşescu felt that he could act with impunity against the most courageous and honourable of Romania's dissidents, Doina Cornea, a lecturer at Cluj University who was dismissed from her post on 15 September 1983. Doina Cornea was born in Braşov in 1929. In 1948, she enrolled at

Cluj University to study French and Italian and after completing her degree was given a position as a teacher of French at the secondary school in Zalău where she married a local lawyer. In 1958, she moved back to Cluj where she was taken on as an assistant lecturer at the university. Her misgivings about the impact of the Communist regime on Romanian society were first given a public airing in 1982.

At first sight we might interpret Doina Cornea's string of protests as purely political acts, containing as they did programmes for democratic reform, denunciations of the demolition of villages and expressions of solidarity with fellow dissenters. Yet they also had a deep moral content whose hallmark provides a continuity with the letters she wrote after the revolution.[66] At the heart of Cornea's messages stood the belief that every individual should feel responsible for his actions and should recognize that any failure to act responsibly had repercussions for society at large. Spiritual and moral regeneration implied a renunciation of a materialist conception of life and in a series of reflections addressed to the young in 1985 Doina Cornea analysed the part played by materialism in disorientating Romanian society.

It was clear from the very first letter that Cornea sent to Radio Free Europe in 1982 that she was not solely preoccupied with the material problems confronted by Romanians but with the spiritual problems of Romanian society. The crisis facing Romania was in her view as much a spiritual as a material one. In the letter, addressed "To those who have not ceased to think", she reflected on the deeper reasons for the crisis:

> The difficulties which have befallen us have made me think about the deeper causes which have engendered them. In your broadcasts you invoke most often the immediate causes, for example an economic policy which is erroneously conceived, the excessive centralization of power, finally our extremely rigid economic and social system. Living here as a teacher I glimpse a deeper and more general reason behind this catastrophe; it is the cultural and spiritual devaluation of our society resulting from the imposition of a reductionist and sterilizing ideology. I ask myself how we could have reached this state, and especially whether each one of us, small and insignificant individuals, does not bear some blame for all of this. If we examine ourselves thoroughly, down to the depths of our soul, will we not find that we have made so many compromises, have accepted and disseminated so many lies?[67]

In accepting these lies the Romanians had become "a people without a scale of moral and spiritual values, a people fed solely on slogans", and this process of "spiritual draining" lay behind all the inadequacies of life. Cornea depicted herself and her fellow intellectuals as "passive onlookers at a regrettable perversion of consciences" which had led to the replacement of moral values by material ones. This situation could only be reversed by a return to the 'spiritual' which she defined as "the highest value, one which generated intelligence, ethics, culture, liberty and responsibility". She called upon her fellow teachers to cease teaching things which neither they nor their students and pupils believed in: "accustom them to thinking more freely, more courageously, more conscientiously and more generously".

At the end of her letter Doina Cornea apologized for not revealing her name, on the grounds that she considered it more important to be able to maintain her contact with students. It was due to a misunderstanding that she was named as the signatory when it was broadcast in August 1982 on Radio Free Europe: she had signed the letter simply to show that it was authentic. The revelation of her name had the expected consequences. She was interrogated by officers of the *Securitate* and denounced in a meeting of teaching staff at the University of Cluj. On 15 September 1983, after 25 years as a lecturer in French, Cornea's contract of employment at the university was rescinded by the rector on the grounds that she had given the students the diary of Mircea Eliade to read, and that she had said in her classes that Romanian culture ran the risk of being discredited because of the compromises made by the majority of intellectuals.

These details were made public in a second letter sent to the BBC and RFE in January 1984 in which she protested at the severe restrictions placed upon academic freedom and expressed her sadness that her university authorities had not had the curiosity to find out directly from her what ideals she was attempting to defend in her classes, let alone the courage to defend its employees.[68] There followed a steady trickle of texts from Cornea in the form of meditations which were read out on RFE in 1984, 1985 and 1986.[69] The question implicit in each of them was: "how can we Romanians find the path towards that authentic state of inner purity without which life loses all its quality?" Her answer was that in order to gain that inner purity a moral and spiritual regeneration must take place and this was dependent upon the removal of fear and the abandonment of cowardice. It was cowardice which paved the way to daily duplicity and to collective paranoia. As long as this moral and spiritual regeneration failed to take place, public life in Romania would continue to be contaminated by 40 years of perversity. This theme was to be repeated in the message of her post-revolutionary letters: even if the political and economic situation changed, the moral perversity would not without a conscious recognition on the part of the individual of the need to change his or her behaviour and to act accordingly.[70]

In August 1987, Cornea addressed her first open letter to Ceauşescu. It advocated the need for reform in Romania's educational system which was subservient to political interests. She called for greater autonomy for universities, more academic exchanges with foreign universities, the exemption of teachers and students from extra-curricular duties such as harvesting in the last two weeks of September, the introduction of religious education and the creation of schools for the handicapped. She supported her argument that the purpose of education was to teach pupils how to think rather than cram their heads full of facts by advocating the inclusion in school textbooks of extracts from the writings of distinguished Romanian writers such as Mircea Eliade, Constantin Noica, Emil Cioran and Eugen Ionesco. Whether Ceauşescu was actually made aware of the contents of the letter is open to doubt. No reply was received and no particular further sanction was applied to Cornea by the authorities. They did act three months later.

On learning of the workers' riot in Braşov on 15 November 1987, Cornea made some leaflets which she distributed on 18 November with her son Leontin Iuhas outside the university and factories in Cluj, calling on workers to show solidarity with those in Braşov. They were arrested the following day and held by the *Securitate* until the end of December when, as a result of the public outcry reported in the Western media, and in particular of a documentary about Romania under Ceauşescu by Christian Duplan, transmitted on French TV on 10 December, containing a previously recorded interview with Cornea, they were released. She accompanied her acknowledgement of the part played by the media in her release and her expression of thanks to all those who demonstrated on her behalf in Paris, Geneva and London, with a protest against the Romanian authorities' interception of her correspondence, their interruption of her telephone calls, and their shadowing of visitors to her house. In short, she concluded, they were doing everything to isolate her and all those who were trying to speak out in the midst of the disaster surrounding them.[71]

In the summer of 1988, Cornea heard on RFE that she had been invited to a human rights conference in Cracow; the letter of invitation never reached her. Her application for a passport to travel was turned down and this rejection prompted her to write a letter of thanks to the conference organizers, offering, at the same time, a contribution to the possible theme of discussion "Why does the opposition movement in the Socialist countries not succeed?" The answer, she wrote, was to be found in the writings of the Romanian philosopher Constantin Noica (1909–87) who suggested that the individual had been robbed of spiritual fulfilment by the imposition of a totalitarian materialist ideology. This ideology had spawned a social system which crushed the individual, thereby causing the social system to become effete and inefficient, for without pluralism and spiritual diversification society was condemned to stagnation, mediocrity and uniformity. The members of such societies had, with a few exceptions, been 'contaminated' by materialistic considerations and lacked the courage to challenge the political order.

Both this letter and the following one, known as the 23 August letter—the date of its transmission in 1988 on RFE and deliberately timed to coincide with Romania's national day—were smuggled out of the country by Josy Dubie, the director of the programme *Red Disaster* about Doina Cornea and Romania, which was shown on Belgian TV on 8 December 1988 and later on French and Canadian networks. The 23 August letter was addressed to Ceauşescu and was written by Cornea at the request of two workers, Iulius Filip and Dumitru Alexandru Pop, who had founded a free trade union called *Libertatea* (Freedom) and who intended to sign it—they in fact had already signed a previously written letter composed by Cornea in July as a protest against village systematization but this only reached RFE in early September (see below). It represented Cornea's political programme and was an outspoken indictment of Ceauşescu whom she held personally responsible for the spiritual and economic disaster hanging over the country. The opening lines presage the blasts of criticism which were to follow:

Mr President of the State Council,
While abuses, repression, corruption, injustice, falsehood and disinformation multiply, the concern, distress, and uncertainty of the population grow. Since your internal and present foreign policy, together with your economic and social policies, put at risk the country's future, its security, its international good name, as well as the physical, moral, and spiritual integrity, we dare to address the following plea to you which offers as an alternative, two possible solutions to avoid an imminent and irreparable disaster:

(a) Either you should give up, together with the *nomenklatura* which supports you, the running of the country if you are unwilling to change your policies to avoid admitting that they are the wrong ones; such a gesture would indeed be proof of responsibility and abnegation, and the Romanian people would be grateful to you, just as it was grateful when, in the 1960s, you gave it a kind of breathing space and hope;
(b) Or you should introduce some reforms, starting with the principle of democratic pluralism, of separating the administration and judiciary from the Party, of using competence and morality in choosing figures for responsible positions, irrespective of their political affiliation, and of liberalizing society, the economy, institutions and culture.

The great majority of the population shares this view. Braşov is proof.[72]

Cornea went on to charge Ceauşescu with "damaging and exhausting the most important resources of the people", with "the spiritual draining of the individual", the "suppression of individual responsibility, of creativity and of inventivity". She offered her own programme of political and economic reform, calling upon the Romanian leader to respect the Orthodox Church's autonomy from the state, to re-establish the Greek-Catholic (Uniate) Church, to make all trials public, to free political prisoners, to guarantee freedom of expression, freedom of the press, freedom of assembly and freedom of travel. In the economic sphere her proposals (they may have been drafted by some of the other signatories) included the closing down of loss-making factories, the re-tooling of others to make them internationally competitive, the hiring of foreign managers, the abolition of unprofitable collective farms and the recreation of private land ownership. Finally, she called for an end to the destruction of villages under the 'systematization' plan which had driven "hundreds of thousands of peasants" from their ancestral lands and homes.

Ceauşescu's plan, accelerated to reduce the number of the country's villages by half by the year 2000, represented a spectacular own-goal by the Romanian leader for it managed to draw international attention to the excesses of the regime and brought Doina Cornea her largest measure of domestic support.[73] Twenty-seven teachers, writers and workers from the towns of Cluj, Sibiu, Făgăraş, and Zărneşti in Transylvania, including Iulius Filip and Dumitru Alexandru Pop, put their names to Doina Cornea's third open letter to Ceauşescu.[74] This letter marked an example rare in Romania of collective dissident protest from intellectuals and workers. Written in July 1988 but broadcast by RFE only at the beginning of September and published by *The Spectator* and *Le Monde*, it was devoted entirely to the plan and presented a ringing condemnation of it. Cornea's arguments were presented in the language of Romanian traditionalists who placed village life at the core of national identity: "a village is a spiritual community which has been pieced together over the centuries... it is the cemetery... the church. By striking the peasant's house, you are striking at the nation's soul".

If Ceauşescu wanted to raise the peasants' standard of living they could be helped by returning their land to them. The whole systematization plan should be put to the people:

> We consider that you do not have the right, without committing a grave abuse of power, to demolish villages without the agreement of the people affected and without even the agreement of the whole nation.[75]

In a move that represented the height of irony for the Romanian leader a group of Hungarians in Cluj announced their support for Cornea's appeal.[76] Systematization thus succeeded in forging a unity between Romanians and Hungarians where all the regime's other measures had failed; but it was a unity in opposition to Ceauşescu.

Following the publication of this letter Cornea was placed under house arrest, a restriction which was only lifted on 21 December 1989. Before house arrest was imposed she managed to have smuggled out a letter addressed to Pope John Paul II and signed by herself and six other members of the Greek-Catholic Church including her son and four of the signatories of the systematization protest,[77] appealing for his help in restoring the rights of their Church in Romania:

> In spite of the official declarations from the Romanian authorities that there are no longer any Greek Catholics in this country, we wish to reaffirm our existence before the Holy See and the whole world and request at the same time your support in maintaining it and restoring its rights to it.[78]

Their appeal had been prompted by a proposal from the Romanian authorities that former Greek Catholics, who are exclusively Transylvanian Romanians, join the Roman Catholic Church, most of whose faithful are Hungarians, and that the services of the Roman Catholics should be in Romanian. Acceptance of the proposal would have two consequences: former Greek Catholics in rural areas would, the signatories claimed, be assimilated into the Orthodox Church simply because there was no other faith represented in the Romanian village—in fact, this had already happened following the suppression of the Greek-Catholic Church in 1948, although there was no acknowledgement of it in the letter; and second, Roman Catholic Hungarians would see the position of their language eroded.

Cornea's struggle against the regime now took on an overtly religious dimension which meant that the Vatican could not remain indifferent to her fate.

Indeed, a campaign to secure her release from house arrest gathered momentum in the winter of 1988, fired by the transmission of the *Red Disaster* documentary on Belgian TV. The European Parliament and the International Confederation of Free Trade Unions passed resolutions in support of Cornea, and Laurent Fabius, president of the French National Assembly, Valery Giscard d'Estaing, former president of France, and Leo Tindemans, Belgian foreign minister, intervened personally with the Romanian government.[79] In January 1989, the British ambassador to Romania, Hugh Arbuthnott, was manhandled by Romanian policemen as he attempted to approach Mrs Cornea's home in Cluj and was turned back. Several other European Community ambassadors took a lead from Arbuthnott, most notably the Dutch ambassador Coen Stork, in making overt enquiries about the fate of Mrs Cornea but the regime gave no ground.[80] Nevertheless, international pressure continued to mount.

In March, the United Nations Human Rights Commission in Geneva voted to investigate alleged violations by Romania. In April 1989, the BBC received the texts of two more open letters written by Cornea to Ceauşescu. The first, dated 9 April 1989 and signed by six others,[81] carried her most blistering attack yet on the president:

> This suffocating regime which you imposed against our very being, moral and biological, has become ever more difficult to bear. You have razed to the ground our oldest and most beloved churches. You have dug up the graves of our past rulers. You have started to destroy the the country's villages, some of them hundreds of years old, in order to destroy their natural life. You have crushed the inner souls of people, humiliating them in their hopes and legitimate aspirations, humbling their consciences, forcing them, through pressure and terror, to accept lies as truth and truth as lies, and to thus acquiesce in their own moral crippling...
> Put an end to this repressive policy which is even more destructive than the economic disaster you have caused. Ana Blandiana, Dan Deşliu, Mircea Dinescu, are our poets, the poets of the entire nation, not your personal property... Stop the oppression of the righteous! Stop the infamous court cases with their trumped-up charges!... Set free the journalists and printers whose only guilt is that they cannot live a lie... Stop persecuting the former leading Communists who rightly reproach you for ruining the economic and social fabric of the country...[82]

Less than a week later the second letter was sent.[83] It catalogued the measures taken against Cornea and her family and showed that they had no basis in Romanian law. Nowhere will we find a more succinct indictment of the regime's disregard for the rule of law and of the arbitrary nature of the exercise of power. The purpose of these arbitrary and illegal practices was, as Cornea pointed out, to crush the people's will and had made the country "a gigantic prison in which the citizen is permanently attacked and humiliated". But she ended on a defiant note with the certainty that "fragile life will overcome".[84]

The international notoriety which Mrs Cornea's detention attracted was confirmed by the invitation extended to her by Mrs Mitterrand, the wife of the French president, to attend a human rights conference in Paris between 22 and 24 June to mark the bicentenary of the French Revolution. Once again the Romanian authorities refused to grant Cornea an exit visa. Another invitation, extended this time by the Commission for Relations with non-member European countries of the Council of Europe, to address a meeting in Strasbourg in July, failed to reach her because it was handed to the Romanian ambassador in Paris.

By this time Doina Cornea's treatment by the Romanian authorities had ceased to be unique; she shared her predicament with writers and political figures such as Mircea Dinescu and Silviu Brucan, but she had taken her stance long before the changes in the Soviet Union offered a political umbrella, however pervious, to those whose professional or family ties linked them to the home of Communism. Cornea remained for almost seven years a largely isolated figure and yet because her views were formed from her own experience of daily life, one shared by her audience, her message gained in power. The gravest crimes committed by the Ceauşescu regime were, in her eyes, to strip people of their human dignity, to reduce them to an animal state where their major daily concern was to struggle to find food, to institutionalize misery and to atomize and homogenize the peoples of Romania. That few of her fellow citizens responded to this message should not be regarded as a failure on her part, but confirmation at once of the enormity of the task she set herself and of Ceauşescu's success in brutalizing his people. Her lonely challenge to the dictator, her refusal to abandon her own dignity and to fall silent in the face of persecution and intimidation, bear testimony to the inner strength of a remarkable lady who for the better part of a decade represented the conscience of Romanians.

It is no exaggeration to say that no single case drew more attention to Romania's abuse of human rights and to the country's consequent, but belated, quarantining by the international community. Amidst an avalanche of criticism from both West and East the UN Human Rights Commission in Geneva adopted on 9 March 1989, by 21 votes for, to 7 against, a resolution calling for an inquiry into alleged human rights abuses in Romania, the first such investigation to be authorized in any country for five years. A mark of the country's growing isolation was the abstention from voting of her Eastern bloc allies, the Soviet Union, Bulgaria and East Germany, while Hungary went even further and joined the resolution's sponsors. The resolution highlighted the rural resettlement (systematization) plan and the country's treatment of its ethnic minorities, drawing attention to the many thousands of Hungarian refugees who had fled Transylvania in the preceding months.[85]

The Romanian delegation made desperate attempts to influence the vote; its chief delegate Gheorghe Dolgu accused Hungary of conducting a revisionist campaign in a desire to divert its people's attention from internal economic problems.

He sought support from Third World countries, which had a majority on the 43 nation UN panel, but the sheer weight of evidence against Romania undermined his case. On 3 March, the International Confederation of Free Trade Unions lodged a formal complaint with the UN Commission that Romania was gravely abusing workers' rights. On 6 March, US Ambassador Vernon Walters criticized Romania for placing itself "well outside the established European consensus on human rights" by refusing to accept certain provisions of the final document of the CSCE meeting in Vienna, and on the eve of the UN vote, the West German-based League for the Defence of Human Rights in Romania issued a plea for three journalists on the government newspaper *România Liberă*, Petre Mihai Băcanu, Mihai Creangă and Anton Uncu, who had been arrested two months earlier for preparing a clandestine newspaper entitled *România.* The paper, printed on a makeshift press assembled by Alexandru Chivoiu, Nicolae Neacşu and Elena Gheorghe, reproduced an article on tyranny and demagogy by the national poet Mihai Eminescu, a condemnation of Ceauşescu's rule by Uncu, a plea from Creangă to the public to read the paper, an editorial by Băcanu outlining the paper's programme, and an article in the spirit of the editorial by a fourth journalist Ştefan Niculescu Maier. Băcanu's editorial embraced wholeheartedly the spirit of *glasnost,* proclaiming that the newspaper would

> promote honest, open, and even polemical reporting, without claiming that it possessed a monopoly of truth, but we will try to find it... we want a change of direction in our lives, a reinvigoration, the removal of all constraints on the activity of an individual which wound his dignity, and reform in place of bureaucratic and cynical rule.[86]

The paper's appearance was timed to coincide with the extravagant celebration of Ceauşescu's birthday on 21 January but a contact of one of the journalists informed the *Securitate* and all of those involved in the production were arrested.[87]

Confirmation of Romania's pariah status quickly followed. On 8 March, the European Community lodged a protest with Romania about the harassment of Doina Cornea, and on the same day the Council of the Standing Conference of Communities and Regions of Europe adopted a resolution recommending that support be given to Romanian villages threatened with demolition under the rural resettlement programme. On 15 March, a group of 35 countries participating in the Inter-Parliamentary Union Congress held in Budapest decided to cancel an Inter-Parliamentary Union (IPU) conference due to be held in Bucharest in May On the following day, the European Parliament adopted a resolution condemning the suppression of "even basic human rights in Romania", "the brutal suppression of minorities", and the "deliberate neglect of handicapped and old people". The European Community's External Affairs Commissioner Frans Andriessen announced that the EC had suspended talks on a new trade agreement with Romania because of the country's poor record on respect for human rights.

These moves taken by the international community coincided with the growing disaffection with Ceauşescu within senior political circles. On 10 March, an open letter to the president was made public by the BBC bearing the signatures of six veteran figures in the Party. Three of them were former members of the Political Executive Committee (Politburo): Gheorghe Apostol (1913–2010), First Secretary of the Party from April 1954 to October 1955[88]; Alexandru Bîrlădeanu (1911–97), the Party's leading economist who played a key role in charting Romania's autonomy from the Soviet Union; and Constantin Pîrvulescu (1895–1992) who was a founding member of the RCP in 1921 and its secretary for a brief period from April 1944 until 1945. The other signatories were Silviu Brucan,[89] Corneliu Mănescu (1916–2000), Minister of Foreign Affairs from 1961 to 1972 and president of the UN General Assembly from 1967 to 1968, and Grigore Ion Răceanu (1906–1996), a veteran member of the Party.[90]

As has been pointed out, this was not the first time that Pîrvulescu and Brucan had protested against Ceauşescu's policies. At the Twelfth Party Congress in 1979, Pîrvulescu, then aged 84, accused the Secretary General of putting personal interests above those of his country and declared that he would not vote for Ceauşescu's re-election. Brucan, in the wake of the Braşov riot of November 1987, broke the official silence in Romania to speak in support of the demonstration against the regime by referring to the legitimate grievances of the workers. But the 'Letter of the Six', as it became known, was completely without precedent in three respects: first, it was a protest against Ceauşescu's policies from within the senior ranks of the Communist Party itself; second, it was a collective protest; and finally, by sending their letter abroad the signatories showed that there was no Party mechanism which they could use to discuss internal Party affairs. The letter was at once an admittance of Ceauşescu's complete emasculation of the RCP, and of his dictatorship over the country. Yet unlike Doina Cornea's letters, the 'Letter of the Six' was not written in the spirit of respect for a pluralist democracy; it advocated Party pluralism rather than democratic pluralism by casting its criticisms from a mould of allegiance to the one-party state. Using the model of Gorbachev's policy of *glasnost* the signatories declared that their reason for speaking out was because "the very idea of socialism, for which we have fought, is discredited by your policy" and because "our country is being isolated in Europe". In doing so they realized that they were "risking our liberty and even our lives". This was no shallow fear: Brucan had twice been warned by the head of the Party's control commission for ignoring Communist discipline by discussing Party affairs outside its organization following his statement in support of the Braşov workers in November 1987.

The letter made five principal points. The first addressed the condemnation which Ceauşescu's policies had attracted from both within and without Romania: "the international community is reproaching you for your failure to observe the Helsinki Final Act which you have signed yourself. Romanian citizens are reproaching you for your failure to respect the constitution on which you have sworn". In support of their argument 'the Six' cited:

(a) the Systematization, or rural resettlement, plan which involved 'the forced removal of peasants to three-storey apartment blocks';

(b) the decree forbidding Romanian citizens to have contact with foreigners which 'has never been voted by the legislative body and never published';
(c) the civic centre, otherwise known as the House of the People or House of the Republic, which 'had no public budget' and was being built 'against all existing laws regulating constructions and their financing';
(d) the use of the *Securitate* against workers 'demanding their rights';
(e) the requirement that employees work on Sundays which contravened Article 19 of the constitution; and
(f) the opening of mail and the cutting off of telephone conversations.

As an interim balance the authors concluded: "the constitution is virtually suspended and there is no legal system in force". Without respect for the law from the very top "society cannot function". The second and third points of the letter addressed the economy and the problems caused by planning and mismanagement in industry and agriculture: "Planning no longer works... an increasing number of factories lack raw materials, energy or markets... and agricultural policy is in disarray". The rural resettlement plan was irrational: "Why urbanize villages when you cannot ensure decent conditions of human life in the cities, namely, heating, lighting, transport, not to mention food?" Facetiously, the letter argued that "a government which for five winters in a row is unable to solve such vital problems for the population proves that it is incompetent and unsuitable for government. Therefore, we are not pressing on you any demand in this respect".

The final points in the letter singled out the policies which had led to an erosion of Romania's international prestige. The mass emigration of the country's ethnic minorities showed that "the policy of forced assimilation should be renounced", some countries, such as Denmark and Portugal, had closed their embassies in Bucharest, Most Favoured Nation status with the United States had been surrendered, and the EEC was unwilling to extend its trade agreement with Romania. The blame for this increasing isolation rested with Ceauşescu for his policies had attracted so much international criticism that Romania had effectively been placed in quarantine: "How are you going to improve Romania's external relations when all the leaders of the non-Communist nations of Europe refuse to meet you?" A constructive note was struck at the end of the letter. The signatories expressed their willingness "to participate in a dialogue with the government on the ways and means to overcome the present impasse". The six were thus careful not to lay themselves open to the charge of subversion by openly calling for the president's removal, and could similarly defend themselves against the accusation of treachery by claiming advocacy of an internal solution to the country's problems in keeping with Ceauşescu's oft-quoted principle of "master of our destiny".

Experience has shown that a necessary condition for a challenge to Communist rigidity in Eastern Europe was criticism by senior Party activists who became disillusioned with the Communist system. Milovan Djilas in Yugoslavia, Imre Nagy in Hungary, Alexander Dubcek in Czechoslovakia and Rudolf Bahro in the

German Democratic Republic all advocated change from within the Party.[91] In Romania, by contrast, there had been no such figure of comparable stature. Apart from Pîrvulescu's outburst in 1979, there had been no public dissent from within Party circles until Brucan's protest in the wake of the Braşov riots in 1987, and even then, as in the Letter of the Six, there was no self-questioning of the validity of Marxism. There was no recognition of the failure of socialist planning, which was merely said to be no longer working in the Romanian economy. The six openly accepted the need for the *Securitate*, admitting that they created it "in order to defend the socialist order against the classes of exploitation", and implied that only Ceauşescu's abusive use of it against the workers had contributed to the crisis. Here lay the fundamental flaw in the credibility of their appeal: failure to recognize their own prominent role in the abuses committed in the name of Stalinism in Romania in the late 1940s and 1950s and to admit the error of their ways gave them no moral authority upon which to base their protest. On the contrary, apologists for Ceauşescu could merely dismiss it as the desperate action of a group of largely pro-Soviet activists who were ousted from their prominent positions in the mid-1960s as Ceauşescu consolidated his position by appointing 'national' Communists. There was also the problem of a generation gap which had to be bridged if the dissent voiced by the six was to attract public support from the younger echelon of the Party. Not only was the average age of the signatories 80 (Pîrvulescu was 94), but they were identified with the Stalinist period of Romanian history, one which the younger *nomenklaturists* of the Party's Ştefan Gheorghiu Academy looked upon with distaste. But by the same token, the very fact that Brucan had been able to travel freely to the Soviet Union, the United States and the United Kingdom in the autumn of 1988, that is, after lodging his protest at the treatment of the Braşov workers in the previous year, showed that Ceauşescu was wary of subjecting him to the same treatment that lesser mortals had endured at the hands of the *Securitate*. That caution stemmed from the close interest shown by both the US and British embassies in Brucan's fate—Brucan had been the official guest of the US, UK and Soviet governments during his visits to these countries. However, the relative immunity he enjoyed did not exempt him from the wrath of Ceauşescu. The order went out for Brucan to be moved from his house in the exclusive residential district of Bucharest to rooms in the suburb of Dămăroaia, while Mănescu was deposited in a two-roomed dwelling with an earth floor in the Bucharest district of Chitila, and his daughter Alexandra moved to Piatra Neamţ. Pîrvulescu was taken to a village near Vaslui and Bîrlădeanu placed in a house in the Vatra Luminoasa district of Bucharest.

How seriously Ceauşescu took the letter became apparent only three days after its contents became known in the West. In a move designed to draw some of the sting out of the letter's criticism of the president, Bucharest radio disclosed on 14 March 1989 that Mircea Răceanu, a deputy director in the Foreign Ministry and adopted son of Grigore Ion Răceanu, one of the signatories, had been arrested on 31 January for "consorting with foreign elements" and that he would be "tried for espionage following investigations *which have yet to be completed*" (my italics).[92] The timing of the announcement of Mircea Răceanu's indictment was clearly an attempt by the authorities to link the six signatories to the protest letter with treason and espionage and seemed to foreshadow a show trial reminiscent of the Stalinist period. In an elaboration of the charge against Răceanu an official press statement said that the *Securitate* had "uncovered a grave action of betrayal... by Mircea Răceanu, formerly employed in the diplomatic service, who had placed himself at the service of a foreign power".[93] An editorial in the Party newspaper *Scînteia* on 17 March underlined the association between reform and treachery by claiming that attempts to undermine national independence had been "preceded by [the appearance of] perfidious, treacherous watchwords... adopted with distressing naivety by some people" or used in "ill faith by treacherous people".[94]

The regime's obsession with security was confirmed by the dismissal, also on 17 March 1989, of the young Romanian poet Mircea Dinescu from the editorial staff of the Writers' Union weekly *România literară*. In August 1988, Dinescu went to the Soviet Union as a guest of the USSR Union of Writers and in an interview with Radio Moscow's Romanian service broadcast on 25 August he gave the most emphatic expression of support for *glasnost* and *perestroika* given by a Romanian writer. He described the reform process in the Soviet Union as "a great turning point", one with implications for the writer and his duty to society, and these duties contrasted with the role assigned to Dinescu and his colleagues by the Romanian Communist Party:

> Under Socialism writers should not be mere instruments, mere fellows who travel on this road... Each one must develop freely and express his own perceptions of life and the world. The polity can only gain by this [freedom]. The writer is his own conscience. Some time ago it used to be said that writers were the trustworthy helpers of the Party. One should better understand the precise sense of these words; one ought to understand how the writer can be a trustworthy helper. The writer is an extraordinarily keen observer of life, and it is in this way that he can help the Party comprehend reality better... Generally, the mission of literature is not to provide solutions, but to point out the problems.[95]

The fact that this interview was rebroadcast suggested that Moscow welcomed Dinescu's views about reform and, taken together with his wife's half-Russian parentage, may well have given him a sense of insulation from Ceauşescu's wrath. Upon his return to Bucharest in September, Dinescu invited a number of friends, among them Gabriel Liiceanu, Alexandru Paleologu and Andrei Pleşu, to his home to draft a collective protest against Ceauşescu's destruction of Romanian culture and the country's villages. The group could not agree on a text and Dinescu decided to make his own protest. After the meeting members of the group were visited by officers from the *Securitate* who argued that Dinescu's action was prompted by the KGB and that it was directed against Romania and not just against Ceauşescu; if they gave an undertaking not to attend another meeting, the officers would make sure that their activities did not reach the ears of Ceauşescu. Dinescu was placed under close surveillance, as indeed were his friends. A clear sign of the authorities' displeasure was a refusal by the censorship officials in the Council of Culture to give the *imprimatur* for his volume of poetry *Death reads the Newspaper*. Pressure was placed on him to apologize for what Mihai Dulea, the regime's literary 'commissar', considered to be the 'slanderous' nature of some of the poems, but the poet declined. When this author met Dinescu at a private party on 1 October 1988—having been friends since 1984 when helping to select the poems for an English translation of his verse—he convinced me of his determination to resist this pressure and, if need be, to make a public stand against the regime. My support was offered by promising to do what was possible by drawing attention of the British press to any stand that he took.

In March 1989, Dinescu's private feelings about the abuses of the regime were made public in an interview published in the Parisian daily *Libération* on 17 March. He was summoned at lunchtime on that day by the president of the Writers' Union, Dumitru Radu Popescu—also director of *România literară*—who, flanked by the novelist Constantin Ţoiu, informed him that he had been sacked for attending embassy receptions and meeting foreigners without permission. An hour later he was called to his local Communist Party headquarters and told that his membership had been revoked. Clearly, the catalyst for these strictures had been the publication of the interview which Dinescu had given three months earlier at his home in December 1988 to a correspondent of the Parisian daily in which he attacked the regime's spiritually degrading treatment of its people. Its publication on 17 March coincided with the Letter of the Six RCP dignitaries and the letter of Dan Deşliu,[96] and repeated several of the points made in these two protests:

> Personal opinion has been abolished. Any attempt to utter unpleasant truths is classified as heresy and promptly punished. Today when you read the Constitution it seems like a fairy tale from *A Thousand and One Nights*. Not only do fundamental human rights have no residence permit in Romania, but those related organs which should be defending them, not to mention the police and the security service, have become instruments of intimidation and terror of the population...
> You ask why artists are silent? In our part of the world you won't find many fanatics or kamikazis. Even our poets were staid heads of families who were able, at the height of the king's power, to write antimonarchal articles and poems. When times are somewhat kind to us, some of us are courageous and express reality. But we become cowardly and base again as soon as times get harsh. People have got used to watching, waiting for statues to be knocked down, for what do you think Socialism is other than the knocking down of statues.[97]

Dinescu reserved some of his most facetious comments for the president and his wife. In an obvious reference to the Ceauşescus' efforts to mask their lack of education by courting academic awards abroad, he declared:

> Some people collect English hats as they collect PhDs and academic titles... and are probably more versed in the history of football than in the history of Marxism, which they advocate... They imagine that the *Communist Manifesto* is a leaflet that Marx used to paste on walls at night... They teach peasants how to grip a hoe, explain to workers which end of the nail to hit... and teach writers to write from left to right.

However, unlike the six Party veterans, Dinescu did not shy from mentioning the reform process applied elsewhere in Eastern Europe on the initiative of Gorbachev:

> I do not know whether Gorbachev is considered a 'good Tsar' or not... but millions who had been forced into silence, in Poland, Hungary, Bulgaria, Czechoslovakia, the GDR, and Romania perceive him as the Messiah of socialism with a human face.[98]

On 17 March, the day of publication, Dinescu was placed under partial house arrest. For four days, Romanians were allowed to visit his home on Strada Bitolia but not foreigners, and then on 21 March all visits were prohibited. Food parcels for Dinescu's family, some of them provided by the British, Dutch and Soviet embassies, were taken by friends, among them the historian Ludovic Demeny, to the house of Dinescu's parents-in-law who lived just a few doors down and who were allowed to visit. Demeny was prevented from delivering food in September when three *Securitate* officers from the surveillance team stopped him and warned him not to make further visits.[99] From 17 March to 22 December 1989, Dinescu's house was kept under 24-hour hour surveillance by three six-man teams each working eight-hour shifts.[100] Dinescu and his wife Maşa were allowed to go out shopping, always flanked by two *Securitate* officers, but they were not allowed to receive visitors. In April, the British ambassador tried to pass a letter to Maşa outside her home as she was returning from shopping one day but the *Securitate* men stepped in quickly to prevent delivery. Like Doina Cornea, Dinescu received 'black spot' letters, threatening unsigned letters with black edges in the form of obituary notices, during this period of partial house arrest which lasted until the morning of 22 December 1989. Claims that he received visits from Stanislav Petouhov, the Bucharest correspondent of *Pravda*, are dismissed by Dinescu as untrue.[101] His only visitor, apart from close members of his family, during the nine months' deprivation of freedom was an official from the Writers' Union who was allowed in to tell him that his request to go to the Black Sea for a family holiday had been rejected.

Dinescu attacked the president of the Writers' Union immediately after his dismissal for failing to protect writers in an open letter sent on 17 March: "Perhaps you have somehow forgotten, Mr President, but you too are a writer and together we ought to eat the bread of that liberty which you have refused me by throwing me into unemployment". According to the poet, the grounds for his dismissal were "for receiving visits from diplomats and journalists from socialist and capitalist countries without permission".[102] The inclusion of 'Socialist countries' was a measure of the complete isolation which Ceauşescu now placed the country in and of his determination to restrict Romanians' contacts with outsiders of all nationalities. This was first indicated by the issue of presidential decree No. 408 in December 1985, which made failure to report a conversation with a foreigner a criminal offence. The legality of this decree, which had never been published, was challenged by the Brucan group. On 17 March 1989, *Scînteia* carried an editorial underlining the need to safeguard state secrets, especially since "reactionary circles have not given up the attempts to promote hostile, anti-socialist and anti-Romanian attitudes". In an apparent attempt to justify the continuing need for the presidential decree the paper pointed out that

> some people's undignified behaviour with representatives of other states sometimes arises from apparently harmless foibles and deficiencies, such as boasting and verbosity, which are used to advantage, sought and even entertained by traitors, spies, enemies of the country, [and] adversaries of Socialism.

Support for Dinescu came from seven writers: Geo Bogza (1908–93), a short story writer and veteran socialist; the poet Stefan Augustin Doinaş (1922–2002); Dan Hăulică, editor of the cultural monthly *Secolul 20*; Octavian Paler (1926–2007), a critic; and Andrei Pleşu (1948–), Alexandru Paleologu (1919–2005) and Mihai Şora (1916–), all essayists. In a letter to the president of the Writers' Union the seven expressed regret "that contemporary Romanian literature should be called into question in the person of one of its foremost representatives", and asked that "everything possible be done in order to make good an injustice and a mistake whose moral, professional and human consequences are extremely damaging."[103] Although the signatories of this letter made a point of not disseminating it abroad in order to avoid provocation of the Romanian authorities, they were all prohibited from publishing except Bogza, a veteran Communist, who continued his column in *România literară*. Pleşu, a close friend of Dinescu, was dismissed from his post as an art historian on the grounds that it had been 'abolished' and was presented with the choice of either going to work as a museum curator at Tescani, a locality in the vicinity of Bacău some 300 km north-west of Bucharest, or remaining unemployed and thus running the risk of prosecution as a 'parasite'. Under Romanian law there was no basis for this action. On 5 April, Pleşu left for Tescani without any explanation from the authorities as to why he was forced into 'internal exile' while the post he was given barely allowed him to support himself, not to mention his family in Bucharest. His wife was placed under surveillance and told not to receive any visitors but at the end of May it was reported that these restrictions had been lifted. Pleşu was advised not to communicate with his friend Dinescu.

The poets Ana Blandiana and Dan Deşliu (1927–96) were also victims of the regime's repression. Following publication in the student review *Amfiteatru* in December 1984 of the four poems by her condemning the regime's brutalization of Romanians, Blandiana was forbidden to publish verse for a while.[104] In the spring of 1985, she was allowed a regular half-column of comment in the weekly *România literară* but in August 1988 her right to publish was withdrawn after the attention of Mihai Dulea, the effective head of the Council of Culture and Socialist Education, was drawn by a saleslady at a bookshop in Suceava to Blandiana's poem entitled 'A star on my street' which had appeared the previous month in her volume of children's verse entitled 'Events on my street'.[105] The subject of the poem, a tomcat named Arpagic, was identified with Ceauşescu and deemed to be a parody of him. A *Securitate* report of 30 August 1988 stated that the Council of Culture and Socialist Education had

> analysed the problem and found the publishing house guilty alongside Doina Mandaj, a former instructor [censor] at the Council of Culture and Socialist Education, who had admitted that she had only given a superficial reading to the volume, since it was a children's book. It should be mentioned that Ana Blandiana has tried on previous occasions to publish inappropriate poems. As a consequence, it has been resolved that Viniciu Gafiţa, the director of the Ion Creangă publishing house, who had exceeded the age-limit, should be pensioned off while Doina Mandaj removed from the Council of Culture and Socialist Education. At the same time, measures were taken to withdraw the book from bookshops.[106]

Constantin Olteanu, the Central Committee Secretary in charge of propaganda, gave orders that Blandiana should be forbidden to publish.[107] While an anthology of her poetry appeared in April 1989, it did not include any verse written after the interdiction. The publication of the anthology followed a letter to Ceauşescu on 3 March in which Blandiana pointed out that

> in these six months since I have been unable to publish in Romania, a book of mine has appeared in the German Democratic Republic, two others are at press in the Soviet Union, one is in the course of publication in England, and another in preparation in Italy, but I am a Romanian writer whose natural and inalienable right is to publish in her own country and language, and to contribute in this way, through her writings, to their flourishing.[108]

As for Deşliu, he had been a poet of Socialist Realism during the 1950s but in 1971 protested at Ceauşescu's mini cultural revolution and became a defender of non-conformist writers in the Writers' Union. He was reported to have resigned from the Party in 1981 in protest at infringements of the Writers' Union statutes when Dumitru Radu Popescu was imposed as its president. He appeared for a while on television as a variety show host until an unscripted critical allusion to the style of presidential rule led to his removal from the programme in 1984. On 3 March 1989, he wrote an open letter to Ceauşescu opining that Romania's problems "lie in you and your aberrant view of reality: you think you are the owner of all Romania and all Romanians, and for all your atheism you are an out-and-out mystic".[109] He told Voice of America in a telephone interview on 14 March that was interrupted that he had been attacked in Bucharest and beaten. Two days later the police searched his flat on the grounds that he was suspected of black market dealings in coffee beans. Three days later he was arrested and apparently accused of stealing a plate from the Writers' Union.[110] After being allowed home, his flat was placed under permanent guard and he went on hunger strike. At the beginning of May he was taken to hospital number 9 in Bucharest where he was force-fed. On learning of Deşliu's letter of protest Doina Cornea declared her wholehearted support for it:

> I am entirely behind his courageous deed and I express my total admiration for him. I also extend my support to Aurel Dragoş Munteanu and Mircea Dinescu and I declare my solidarity with their actions. I note that at last certain former leading figures in the Romanian Communist Party have courageously denounced the personality cult in Romania in the name of truth and equity, as well as the failure to respect human rights and the constitution. As a consequence I declare my solidarity with their position, but I would like to insist upon the fact that I am not a communist, and that I cannot, under any form, adhere to their political ideology, in spite of the admiration which I have for their courage. Justice for Răceanu![111]

Once again Doina Cornea showed her remarkable courage by speaking out against the regime's abuses. In emphasizing this, it is worthy of note that both she and six of the seven signatories of the 20 March letter from Bogza and others were all in their sixties (the exception being Pleşu who was in his early forties). The only other writer of a younger generation to add his voice in support of Dinescu, Deşliu and Blandiana was Aurel Dragoş Munteanu. In an open letter to the President of the Writers' Union dated 8 April 1989, he said that he had been "brutally dismissed" from the staff of the literary weekly *Luceafărul* for political reasons and that his telephone had been cut off. He appealed to the president to initiate a public debate on the case of the persecuted writers and to defend their rights of free speech.[112] More than six months would pass before any writer of either Pleşu's generation or of a younger one would speak out.

Dinescu himself drew attention to the same abuse of the law mentioned by Cornea in a second open letter dated 22 June to the President of the Writers' Union.[113] He revealed that his mail, telephone calls and friends were under constant surveillance, and that his only contact with the outside world had been an anonymous death threat. Fear for his life doubtless prompted his cry that "I still want to live" and his defiant statement that "suicide is an inefficient form of protest". Added to this catalogue of persecution was the halting of the publication of his wife's translation of Pasternak, thus denying the Dinescu family—the couple had two young children—their sole remaining source of income. Dinescu accused the regime of "suffering a relapse by honouring its initial vocation for ideological and state terrorism" and charged the president of the Writers' Union and other members of its leadership with "impudence" for writing about "the abuses, atrocities, and crimes of the 1950s" while being "directly responsible for the censorship, intimidation, isolation, and elimination from cultural and social life of certain fellow members".[114]

As if any were needed, further ammunition for the international community's attacks on the gross abuses of human rights perpetrated by the Ceauşescu regime was supplied by Dumitru Mazilu's long overdue *Report on Human Rights and Youth* for the Commission on Human Rights of the Economic and Social Council of the United Nations. Despite being held under close surveillance since February 1988, Mazilu managed to get a copy of his report to Geneva where it was presented to the forty-first session of the Subcommission on Prevention of Discrimination and Protection of Minorities on 10 July 1989. Although presented as a catalogue of injustices directed against Romanian youth, it was in fact a damming indictment of the regime's treatment of all Romanian citizens. Its searing attack on Ceauşescu's policies was magnified by the colourful intemperance of its language which must have made riveting reading for the UN delegates. The report's opening paragraphs set the tone while at the same time avoiding any mention of Ceauşescu by name:

> How can it be, the young Romanians ask us, that in our century, in which civilization has attained unimagined heights, whole peoples should be terrorized in the world's plain sight, while criminal tyrants, instead of being removed and punished as they should be, are glorified by a cult of disgusting vulgarity?

Mazilu asked what kind of civil society it was that would tolerate the transformation of the individual

> into a beast of burden useful only to put into practice the tyrants' plans of aggrandisement, so as to assure their immortality?' Not even in a nightmare world does it seem possible to hear that - as is happening in Romania, newborn babies are denied registration for the first three to four weeks [to hide the true infant mortality rate – *author's note*], while old people are refused aid in case of need if they have reached the age of sixty, and while medicine is out of the question altogether.[115]

Mazilu's report elicited an almost hysterical response from the Romanian nominee to Geneva, Ion Diaconu. He described it as

> a political pamphlet, a collection of slogans... too fantastic and too crazy to comment on... It contains a list of defamatory affirmations and accusations directed at one country, at its internal policy, its political and social system... I doubt that everything in this paper has been written by its author. He was either ill or acting for personal political purposes.[116]

How seriously some members of the UN subcommission took Mazilu's plight and that of Romania's citizens is shown by their recommendation that the panel defer discussion of the report until the following year in the hope that he would then be able to attend!

While the pillorying of Ceauşescu continued in the international arena, more writers summoned up the courage to rally to the symbols of resistance. The literary critic Alexandru Călinescu (1945–), a university professor at Iaşi, added his name to the list of those who wrote to D.R. Popescu in protest at Dinescu's persecution. As a consequence he too was banned from publishing. On the 28 September, yet another critic, Radu Enescu (1925–94), the driving force behind the literary review *Familia* published in the western Transylvanian town of Oradea, raised his voice in support of Dinescu. He described Popescu as "an undertaker who zealously dispenses his energies worthy of a better cause in silently burying, without a church service, contemporary Romanian literature". He admonished the president of the Writers' Union for the measures taken against Dinescu, Ana Blandiana, Ştefan Augustin Doinaş and Andrei Pleşu, and suggested that if the national poet Eminescu were still alive, he would also be placed on the list of banned writers.[117]

Călinescu and Enescu were not the only new names to show that they were not afraid of interdiction or persecution. To the small but growing pile of protest letters on D.R. Popescu's desk—all of which went unanswered—was added in late November a collective protest signed by 18 young academics and writers, a sign that Dinescu's courage had finally spurred the younger generation of intellectuals into attempting a public display of dissent. The 18, among whom was the writer Stelian Tănase (1952–), condemned the banning of those writers and critics who had expressed their support for Dinescu and in doing so salvaged something of the reputation of Romanian intelligentsia who, apart from the notable examples chronicled above, had remained embarrassingly silent over the fate of one of their fellows.[118] The protest, marshalled by Tănase, only crystallized a month before the dictator's downfall, and reached the Western media shortly before the revolution of December 1989.[119] Stelian Tănase's opposition to the Ceauşescu regime did not enter the public domain. That does not make it any less courageous.[120]

Indeed, this failure by writers to close ranks against the regime's oppression did not pass unobserved by Dinescu, despite his isolation. In a long statement signed on 11 November, he delivered a blistering attack on Romania's educated classes whom he held responsible for the country's predicament through their acquiescence in the regime and their sycophancy. The Orthodox Church was full of "trade unionists in religious vestments", its icons those of the president, journalists were "apostles of the personality cult", and most writers "trusted handmaidens of the Party". Dinescu argued that the only salvation for the nation's dignity lay in organised defiance by those "who have not knelt before the tyrant".[121] On the same day, 11 November, Alexandru Paleologu wrote to D.R. Popescu to challenge the legality of the ban placed on his writing and to appeal to his conscience over the treatment meted out to Dinescu and his family.[122] One week later, Mihai Şora wrote in a similar vein.[123]

In the view of Mircea Iorgulescu, an editor of the weekly *România literară* who requested asylum in France in August 1989 Dinescu's stand had indeed caused a crisis of conscience amongst Romanian intellectuals, writers now had to choose between adopting an "unreserved, frank attitude of protest" and carrying on their "seemingly normal activity in order to leave the impression that Romanian literature and culture have not vanished".[124]

Şora's letter was sent only two days before the opening of the Fourteenth Party Congress which took place on 20 November. Several weeks earlier the protest against Ceauşescu had received significant momentum from the clandestine circulation of two letters, one in the form of an appeal to the congress delegates not to re-elect Ceauşescu, the other putting a number of questions to him about his mismanagement of the economy and human rights violations. Both letters were issued in the name of 'The National Salvation Front' (*Frontul Salvării Naţionale*) and were sent to the West in the summer of 1989, being broadcast by Radio Free Europe respectively on 27 August and 8 November.[125] The composition of this 'Front' remained a mystery until a short while after the revolution and naturally invited claims that the National Salvation Front, which assumed power after Ceauşescu's overthrow, was this same clandestine group. However, the two letters sent six months earlier under the name of the NSF were said by Silviu Brucan to have been written by Alexandru Melian, a professor at Bucharest University, who had no connection with any of the leading members of the post-revolutionary NSF.[126] This view is challenged by General Nicolae Militaru who claimed that he and Ion Iliescu were leading members of the clandestine NSF and that "Iliescu agreed with the name NSF from the very beginning. He was the one who had the idea to write the appeal [to the November Congress], which was then composed by a professor, Alexandru Melian".[127]

Another protest at the proposed re-election of Ceauşescu at the congress was made by Dan Petrescu, a writer living in Iaşi, who in a telephone interview with Radio Free Europe on 8 October denounced "the network of corruption" within Romania and the "formidable discrepancy between appearance and reality". What was remarkable about the interview, apart from Petrescu's courage in speaking out, was the fact that, untypically, Petrescu was not cut off. Nevertheless, normality returned the following day when he was placed under house arrest.

Petrescu had begun a hunger strike on 8 October to protest against his dismissal as a librarian at the University of Iaşi and the authorities' refusal to grant him a passport to travel to the West for medical treatment. This was not the first of his protests. After the Braşov riots of November 1987, he gave an interview to the French daily *Libération* (27 January 1988) calling for a moral regeneration in Romania based on an alliance between workers and intellectuals. He had been allowed to travel to France by the authorities in the hope that he would not return to Romania but "he could not leave his country in the scoundrels' hands". It was an illusion to believe that the situation in Romania could be changed by simply removing Ceauşescu; only by changing the system that produced Ceauşescu could reform come to the country, and an indispensable condition of reform was the elimination of the pervasive corruption which was paralysing the country. In his

Radio Free Europe interview Petrescu confirmed reports of a petition he, Doina Cornea, and ten other dissidents had circulated earlier in October 1989 condemning the proposal to re-elect Ceauşescu as Party leader at the Fourteenth Congress. The other signatories were Gina and Dan Sâmpălean, Mariana Marin, Eugen Amarandei, Alexandru Tacu, Liviu Antonesei, Gabriela Iavolschi and Filip Raduţ. In his telephone interview, Petrescu announced that his friend, Luca Pitu, who had been dismissed from his post as lecturer in French at Iaşi University for associating with Petrescu, had joined the protest. Others who the authorities had threatened with dismissal were a university colleague Alexandru Călinescu, Alexandru Tacu, a librarian and poet, the philosophers Gabriel Liiceanu and Andrei Pleşu, the poets Mariana Marin, Nicolae Ionel and Aurel Dumitraşcu, the literary critics Liviu Antonesei and Sorin Antohi, and Gabriela Antonesei and Eugen Amarandei, Petrescu's neighbours.[128]

The letters had no impact whatsoever on the congress proceedings, for immediately after the opening national anthem applause broke out amongst the 3,308 delegates, and to the accompaniment of rhythmic clapping chants of "Ceauşescu re-elected at the Fourteenth Congress!", "Ceauşescu, RCP!", "Ceauşescu and the people!", "Ceauşescu, Romania!" and "Ceauşescu, Peace!" went up. The very first resolution put to the congress by Manea Mănescu, a member of the Politburo, was to have Ceauşescu proclaimed chairman of the congress and it met with universal acclamation. This set the pattern of mechanical voting for proposals from the chair which was repeated throughout the congress proceedings.[129]

It was as though the Party leadership and the delegates had buried their heads in the sand, oblivious to the warnings set out in the letter issued in the name of the National Salvation Front. Yet another 'Front' signalled its existence in the Moldavian capital of Iaşi on 10 December when handwritten leaflets issued in the name of the Romanian Popular Front (*Frontul Popular Român*) were displayed in the history faculty of the university calling on students to join a protest meeting at 2 p.m. on 14 December in Piaţa Unirii against "the policies of the madman and his madwoman". To prevent the meeting taking place the militia and fire-tenders were brought in to cordon off the square and even a tram stop was removed to prevent people alighting from it. At the same time a party meeting of university teachers was hastily arranged for 2 p.m. in the university to distract staff from joining the students. As an extra precautionary measure a national judo meeting was arranged in Iaşi on the same day and many of the rooms in the Unirea hotel overlooking the square were occupied by members of the *Dinamo* team, the club of the Ministry of the Interior. These measures succeeded, for the students were reduced to standing around in groups on the fringes of the cordon. The local state security office managed to identify some of the members of this Front, one of whom was a worker named Cassian, and they were arrested but released on 22 December.[130]

The most significant act of personal defiance of the Ceauşescu regime proved to be that of a Transylvanian Hungarian. Among the persistent critics of the Communist Party's interference in the affairs of the Hungarian Reformed Church in Transylvania were Istvan Tőkés, a former deputy bishop, and his son László, a pastor, who had initially been appointed to a parish in the Transylvanian town of Dej. László was a contributor to *Ellenpontok* (Counterpoints), a clandestine Hungarian language journal produced in Oradea in 1981 and 1982 and the only major *samizdat* printed in Romania. Amongst his articles was one on abuses of human rights in Romania and this led to his harassment by the *Securitate*. He and his friends were placed under surveillance and eventually Tőkés was dismissed from his parish in Dej by order of Bishop Nagy and assigned to the village of Sânpietru de Câmpie some 40 kilometres from Cluj. Tőkés refused to go and instead went to his parents' house in Cluj where he spent two years unemployed. He used part of this time to launch a letter-writing campaign in 1985 amongst the Hungarians of Transylvania to gather statistics about facilities for education in Hungarian.[131] His plight was brought to the attention of the Foreign Relations Committee of the US Senate and as a result Bishop Papp was instructed by the authorities in 1986 to appoint Tőkés assistant pastor in the city of Timişoara, one of mixed Romanian, Hungarian and German population.[132]

As Ceauşescu's village systematization programme gathered momentum, so Tőkés used his sermons to encourage resistance to it. He called for solidarity between Hungarians and Romanians who were both suffering at the hands of the regime and made no special pleading for Hungarian villages. In the summer of 1988 he talked with representatives in all 13 deaneries of the Reformed Church to organize resistance to proposals to destroy villages, and at his own deanery meeting in Arad in September he and three other Hungarian pastors spoke in favour of a statement which attracted the support of 15 of the 26 pastors present. It read:

> We, the deaneries of the Reformed Church, propose to resist these programmes [of destruction] and make contact with other denominations and fight alongside them. There may be economic and political reasons for them, but we believe the moral consequences are so incalculable that the churches must fight to gain a compromise.[133]

The statement was sent to Bishop Papp and within 24 hours every signatory had been visited by *Securitate* officers and cross-examined about the meeting. Tőkés's own file was handled by the head of the Timişoara *Securitate*, Colonel Traian Sima, who authorized visits to Tőkés's church flat by anonymous visitors who would hurl insults and threats. A cultural festival organized with the Catholic Church in Timişoara on 31 October led to threats of expulsion being made against those students who had participated. Bishop Papp sent a letter to Tőkés banning all youth activities in the Oradea diocese, which included Timişoara, but undeterred, Tőkés decided to hold another festival in the spring of 1989 with the Orthodox Church whose metropolitan agreed. On 31 March, at the instigation of the Department of Cults and the *Securitate*, Bishop Papp ordered Tőkés to stop preaching in Timişoara and ordered him to move to Mineu, an isolated parish in northern Transylvania. Tőkés refused to comply with the order and his congregation expressed its support for him. The bishop then began civil proceedings to evict him from his church flat. Since he was no longer deemed by the Timişoara authorities to be a resident of the city, his ration book was withdrawn and power supplies to his flat were cut off. Tőkés's parishioners rallied round, bringing him and his wife and young child food and fuel. Their action contrasted with that of his fellow pastors. Fear of incurring Bishop Papp's displeasure—70 per cent of the two hundred pastors in the diocese had never been promoted from probationary status and were still directly answerable to Papp—coupled with a feeling that Tőkés's defiance was pointless, meant that the authors of an open letter appealing to the bishop to put an end to the harassment of Tőkés could not find one pastor who was prepared to add his signature.[134]

However, there was one quarter from which Tőkés could rely on support; that was Hungary. The ability and willingness of the Hungarian media and authorities to publicize Tőkés's plight marked him out from ethnic Romanian dissidents who had no ready-made champions waiting in the wings to take up their cause and ensured that Tőkés would remain a running sore for the Ceauşescu regime. Tőkés's wife was among the first to acknowledge this. After the revolution, she declared: "The international publicity held them off. If he had been an unknown and nameless figure, they would have killed him sooner or later".

On the other hand, it was probably the publicity that caused the authorities to use the cover of the law, as well as physical intimidation, in order to remove Tőkés from Timişoara.[135] On 24 July 1989, an interview with Tőkés was shown on Hungarian television in which he spoke out against the systematization plan, describing it as an attempt to eradicate Hungarian culture in Transylvania. On 6 August, he was detained for questioning by the *Securitate* and then released. On 25 August, Bishop Papp dismissed Tőkés from the ministry, an action which violated church law. Elod Kincses, Tőkés's lawyer, pointed out that according to the Reformed Church's statutes only the disciplinary body of the church had the right to dismiss clergy. On 14 October, eight members of the Reformed Church Council were brought to a meeting under conditions of arrest and voted to expel Tőkés; the other 23 members had gone into hiding.[136]

In the meantime members of Tőkés's congregation was arrested and beaten. One parishioner, Erno Ujvarossy, who in May had petitioned Bishop Papp in support of Tőkés, was found murdered in woods outside Timişoara on 14 September. Istvan Tőkés was arrested briefly in October when he arrived in Timişoara to visit his son. A court order was made for Tőkés's eviction on 20 October. Tőkés lodged an appeal. Tudor Postelnicu, the Minister of the Interior, ordered Sima to enforce the order. On 2 November, four attackers armed with knives broke into the flat while *Securitate* agents looked on but fled after Tőkés and friends managed to fight them off. After this incident, in which Tőkés was cut on the forehead, the Romanian ambassador was summoned to the Hungarian Foreign Ministry and told of the Hungarian government's concern for the pastor's safety.

Parishioners continued to smuggle in food and firewood for Tőkés to the sacristy of the church, despite the attention of *Securitate* agents. On 28 November, Tőkés was informed that his appeal had been turned down and that his eviction would be enforced on 15 December. As Christmas approached parishioners brought gifts of food to the sacristy in groups and afterwards gathered outside Tőkés's flat next to the church to show their support. The two guards were unable to move them along and this gave hope to his supporters. On the day of the eviction a human chain was formed around the block in which he lived and the militia were unable to gain access. Tőkés leaned out of his window and thanked the crowd but advised them to leave. His advice was met with cries of "We won't leave" and several hundred stayed in groups close to the apartment.

The victimization of Tőkés and his family took its toll of his pregnant wife Edit who, depressed and exhausted with the strain of harassment and a sleepless night awaiting eviction, fell ill. Tőkés asked his neighbour to get word to the family doctor on the morning of 16 December and she duly appeared. Within half an hour the mayor of Timişoara himself appeared with three doctors. Desperate to defuse the situation, the mayor tried to persuade Mrs Tőkés to go into hospital, but the family doctor encouraged her to resist. The mayor relented. Shortly afterwards workmen arrived and began to repair the windows to the flat, shattered a month earlier as an act of intimidation. The door broken down by the four attackers was also restored to the amazement of his supporters who maintained their vigil outside. Throughout the morning their numbers grew, swelled by young Romanians who were attracted by the sight of such a large crowd and the rumour that the *Securitate* were unable to disperse it.[137]

Tőkés acknowledged to the mayor that "the situation was improving" and the latter seized upon this to ask him to tell the crowd to disperse. Tőkés agreed and went to the window. Thanking them for their support, he advised them to leave, saying that their gathering was illegal. The crowd roared its disapproval, chanting in chorus "Don't believe him!" Furiously the mayor stormed out of the flat, to the jeers of the crowd. At noon he returned, complaining angrily to Tőkés that the protesters had not left. Tőkés took the mayor to the window and invited him to address the people. The mayor gave an assurance that Tőkés would not be evicted but to no avail. Some in the crowd accused the pastor of collaborating with the authorities. "We want it in writing", they cried, and added to their demand a retraction of the decision to transfer Tőkés to Mineu, and confirmation of his appointment as pastor in Timişoara.

Rashly, the mayor promised to produce such a document in one hour, but being a Saturday this was unrealistic. The ministries closed at lunchtime on that day and after an hour the excuses were trotted out; no one was available in the legal department. At 2 p.m. the deputy mayor arrived. He warned that unless the demonstrators went away, Tőkés would be held responsible for the consequences. Tőkés suggested that the leaders of the different churches in the city be brought to the flat to witness the mayor's promise, and the deputy mayor telephoned the mayor with the idea. It was rejected. The pastor then proposed that a delegation from the street be brought in. The deputy mayor agreed. Six Romanians and four Hungarians sat down in the church office and discussed the situation with him. Progress was reported to the mayor who, strangely, now promised that a document would be sent from Bucharest in an hour. Representatives of the congregation would be able to collect it from the town hall. The representatives duly went to the town hall after an hour but there was no document. Instead, the mayor sent back an ultimatum with them that if the crowd had not dispersed by 5 p.m. the fire brigade would be sent in to scatter them with water cannons.

The demonstrators' defiance had been fuelled by the conviction that members of the *Securitate* were in Tőkés's flat and were either holding him against his will, or preparing to evict him. This fear was incited by provocateurs in the crowd, who could be clearly seen shouting. While the core of the crowd was made up of people who had joined the vigil against eviction, most of the newcomers had been drawn by the sight of the original protest, or by news of it. As Tőkés himself related:

> Some had no idea what had started the demonstration. All day people came and went; as some left to go to their homes or to queue for food, others arrived to take their place. Consequently I had to go to the windows frequently to assure new arrivals that I was still alive and had not been evicted.[138]

After the mayor's warning Tőkés pleaded with the crowd to go home, but they were convinced that he was acting under threats from the *Securitate* and refused. Some called upon him to come down into the street and lead them but Tőkés realized that this might play into the hands of the regime who could put the blame for the protests on the Hungarian minority.

By 7 p.m. the crowds now filled several streets extending from the church. It contained many students from the local polytechnic and university. Around the church Romanians linked hands with Hungarians in a human chain and hymns were sung. About 30 minutes later the first bars of *Deşteaptă-te Române* ('Romanians awake!'), a Romanian national song which had been sung in the Braşov protests of November 1987, were falteringly taken up. Little known in the Hungarian community, the song was an anthem of resistance to oppression and a sign that a Hungarian protest had now become a Romanian revolt. As Tőkés himself put it:

> A demonstration of solidarity became a revolt in solidarity. I could not have imagined this. Hungarians and Romanians had always been opposed to each other. The regime had fostered real hatred between the two peoples. The support I received from the ethnic Romanians during those days was an overwhelming experience. How moving to see the Romanian crowd under my windows chanting their national hymn. Until that day, the hymn had separated us. From that day on it united us.[139]

After the anthem came the first, bold cries of "Down with Ceauşescu!", "Down with the regime!", and "Down with Communism!" The crowd then began to move off from the church and cross the bridge towards the city centre and the Party headquarters. They stoned its windows before militia reinforcements, brought up just before 10 p.m., managed to drive the demonstrators back to Tőkés's church where they turned water cannons on them. The crowd seized the cannons, broke them up and threw the parts into the river Bega. They then marched on shops, smashing the windows and broke into a bookstore where they burned copies of books on Ceauşescu in ceremonial piles. By midnight the street outside Tőkés's flat and the church was relatively quiet as the violence continued elsewhere in the city.

Three hours later, Tőkés's torment resumed. The door to his flat was broken down by plain-clothes *Securitate* agents as he, his wife and two friends scampered out to another exit into the courtyard and climbed a ladder to the church upstairs. They barricaded themselves in the sacristy but the door was broken down and they were all seized. The male friend was punched and kicked by the agents, while a uniformed officer by the name of Veverka buried his white-gloved fist repeatedly into Tőkés's face and stomach and swore at him. With his face covered in blood, Tőkés, wearing a clerical robe and yellow slippers, was dragged into his office below to find the head of the Department of Cults, Cumpănaşu. The beating continued until Cumpănaşu ordered a halt. He told Tőkés to sign a blank piece of paper on which would be entered the pastor's acceptance of his eviction and dismissal. Tőkés refused, was punched again and then complied. He and his wife were then hustled into separate cars and driven to the *Securitate* headquarters in Timişoara. Once there, only the driver left Tőkés's car, and after ten minutes he returned and both cars sped off to the village of Mineu. Two days later, on 19 December, their interrogation began in the town of Zalău.[140]

László Tőkés was questioned in the army HQ and Edit in a hospital. There were several interrogation teams who used a mixture of abuse and sympathy in an attempt to extract from them confessions that they were foreign agents. Their interrogation continued over the next two days but on the morning of 22 December the *Securitate* failed to appear to take them to Zalău. The militia remained posted outside the house in Mineu until army jeeps appeared and ordered them away. Tőkés's parents-in-law arrived soon afterwards and together they heard the news of Ceauşescu's flight on the radio. A reflex of obedience still led the couple to report to the *Securitate* offices in Zalău where they were told they were free to go. Only 24 hours earlier a statement by Bishop Papp had been issued, accusing the pastor of "indiscipline", of "grossly violating the statute of organization and functioning of the Reformed Church in Romania and the laws of the Romanian state", and of "denigrating and making a tendentious presentation of the realities in our country".[141] A week later the bishop fled the country to Hungary, and from there travelled to Metz to join his son.

Fate has its own way of rewarding the courageous and of punishing tyrants. Despite the divisiveness of Ceauşescu's policies towards the peoples of Romania, their shared experience of suffering under his rule brought them together. It was the defiance of Tőkés which provided the catalyst for the display of ethnic solidarity which sparked off the overthrow of the dictator. This convergence of circumstance started the series of events which led to the revolution.

The vigil held in support of Tőkés turned into major demonstrations in the city on the 16 and 17 December. They were brought to a halt by the intervention of the army which opened fire on the crowd. The number of casualties was initially estimated at several thousand, but subsequent investigations put the figure at 122.[142] On Elena Ceauşescu's orders, 40 of the dead were transported by lorry to Bucharest and cremated to make identification impossible. Here was a clear sign of her cruelty and ruthlessness. On 18 December, industrial workers in Timişoara staged peaceful protests in their tens of thousands within the factory gates but on 20 December these overflowed into the streets and effectively brought an end to Communist rule in the city. The crowds proclaimed Timişoara a free city, this two days before Ceauşescu fled from Bucharest. On the streets of Timişoara there were chants of "Today in Timişoara, tomorrow throughout the whole land", and the fervour there was gradually transmitted to all those who had been waiting for years for the end of the dictatorship. The Romanian revolution had begun.

One may argue that it was only a matter of time before Ceauşescu fell, given his isolation in the international arena, and the growing dissent at home. But it was the merit of Tőkés and of his parishioners that they pressed on with their protest against a bishop's abuse of power which was characteristic of a denial of human rights which typified the Ceauşescu regime. Tőkés's stand, based on the right of his church to defend the interests of its faithful, transcended the narrowness of a sectarian claim and acquired the symbol of a common cause of peoples united against oppression. While the experience of the Hungarian minority in Transylvania under Ceauşescu left a legacy of mistrust among both Hungarians and Romanians, their common membership of NATO and of the European Union, secured since the collapse of Communism in Eastern Europe, has done much to allay this.

Speaking only five days after the Ceauşescus' execution on Christmas Day 1989, the literary critic Dan Hăulică attributed Romania's torment under the dictator directly to passivity and a lack of resistance. Paraphrasing the words of the painter Goya, Hăulică declared that "the sleep of a nation brings forth monsters".[143] After 25 years of shame, he argued, Romania had recovered its self-esteem. Dignity and freedom, words whose meaning had become so debased under Ceauşescu, had been given back their true value by the revolution.[144] What Romania would find more difficult to shake off was the legacy of compliance towards a dictatorship.

APPENDICES: LETTERS OF DISSENT

The letters presented here were all written in 1989.[145] As Nicolae Ceauşescu's despotic excesses increased in the 1980s, so a small number of intellectuals raised their voices against the abuses of the regime. The most prominent was Doina Cornea. These letters show that the cup of privations was filled to overflowing.[146] They have been translated by this author.

MD 1

Open letter to the President of the Writers' Union, Dumitru Radu Popescu, from Mircea Dinescu

Mr President

I begin with a short story whose unsuspecting author you are. A few years ago you sent two Romanian poets to a communist country in the Far East in order to make contact with writers there. During their two-week stay they were unable to meet any native authors since in that country the writers, being extremely well brought up, gave up the vanity of signing [works] personally and renounced individual initiative, being organized in a sort of cooperative which delivers goods anonymously or collectively. The two Romanians saw instead a capital with gigantic statues, with trees encased in glass and declared monuments of nature because the Father of the Nation had, as a child, leaned on their trunks, fascinating museums in which they were able to admire an ash-tray with the stub of a cigarette smoked by the same Father as a youth, and a sacred stone on which the Venerable figure, in his old age, had stopped to rest. They walked along streets on which passers-by offered foreigners the smile of their ideology, as though that mysterious organ which produces human sadness had been removed from their bodies, and where little children came out of school in the step of a march-past, happy in their turn to be, every one of them, the children of that same father. However, the principal character in this true story which takes place in the Far East is an innocent 'goose soup with noodles'.

Having returned from a working visit to a model factory, where they were able to admire the mechanical ballet of the workers who, in harmony with their tools, put the lathes to shame with the agility and precision of their movements, the two Transylvanians (for I forgot to tell you, the poets were both from Transylvania) were sitting on the terrace of the international hotel at a lonely little table in front of some tea cups. As they were talking of this and that in a dreamy prelude to the meal for which they would have two hours to wait, one of the poets, unaccustomed to the local dishes, said: 'I could just do with some goose soup with noodles, like we have at home in Transylvania'. Sipping from the little translucent porcelain cups which seemed even to vibrate in the monsoon wind, the two poets alone on that terrace were to remain stupefied two hours later when the *maitre d'hotel*, together with the waiter, triumphantly placed on their table a golden tureen in which the poor goose was steaming in the company of some Transylvanian noodles. Neither the pleasant aroma of the soup, nor the ceremonial smiles of its bearers, could wipe the fear from the faces of the poets who had sipped tea from two superb porcelain microphones.

Mr President, I shall stray a little from the moral of this story to return to Bucharest of 1989. For several months I have been followed step by step by some men in plain clothes who trail me in my journeys around the capital of the Socialist Republic of Romania. Their principal base is a blue minibus which is usually parked at the end of my street where the respective gentlemen toy with a pack of playing cards to kill the boredom until the other game, that of following me, begins when I make my appearance. Recently these four gentlemen have been joined by two ladies who have the strange habit of whispering mysteriously into some plastic bags, while the men take from under their jackets some small gadgets and also whisper something which I cannot catch. Here is the scenario: if I get on a bus one of the lads who is hanging around at the bus stop gets on as well, while the rest of the team follows in a Dacia car. If I go on foot, one of them gets out and step by step we are able to admire the new architecture of Bucharest as a group. No matter what building I enter, a private house or institution, no matter how long

I stay, these lads patiently wait for me. I have got used to their faces and have almost developed a liking for them. Can they possibly be timid admirers of my as yet unfinished works of poetry, and are unable to overcome their shyness to ask me for my autograph? Can they be part of the team of my future biographers who do not want to miss a second of the movements and private life of the poet? Or are they possibly extraterrestrials, in which case I ought not to be writing to you but to your union colleague, Ion Hobana, secretary for foreign relations, the greatest expert in flying saucers and extraterrestrials in our Party? Another odd thing is that whenever a friend, be he Romanian, Saxon, Hungarian, Jew or someone else, telephones to say that he is coming to see me, the six mysterious persons appear at the corner of the street mumbling into the plastic bags and continuing to work on my fictional biography.

I first noticed these gentlemen last summer after my return from the Baltic countries where I had spent my holiday at the invitation of the Soviet Writers' Union. I shall not remind you of the fact that I had been invited officially in a letter handed personally to you by the secretary of the Soviet Writers' Union, and that it was only with difficulty that I eventually managed to leave in a private capacity after nerve-racking and tiring entreaties. The interview given by me to Radio Moscow in which I expressed my enthusiasm for the magic effect of the words *perestroika* and *glasnost* which I had observed in the Soviet press and television, as well as in the social life in the republics, this accursed interview, then, did not go down well with certain people, nor did my speech 'Bread and Circuses', given two months later to a literary colloquium at the West Berlin Academy of Arts. Added to this was the fact that, although we live in a country without censorship, the manuscript of my book of verse *Death reads the Newspaper*, after being accepted by the *Cartea Romanească* Publishing House, was censored at the Council of Culture and Socialist Education. As a consequence I felt justified as the sole owner of this manuscript in exporting it. May my author's vanity be forgiven, but after having eight books of poetry published in Romanian, and several others in foreign languages, after four prizes of the Writers' Union and one offered by the Romanian Academy, I had begun naively to believe that I was a professional writer. I had begun to believe that I was a free man, that I was born free and that I would die free, that liberty is the raw material of my trade and that without it I cannot exist.

Since I still consider the Writers' Union a writers' trade union which ought to defend its members, I wish to alert you, Mr President, that on 14 March it was you, as director of the review *România literară,* who informed me officially that I had been removed from the position of an editor of the review on the grounds that I attended without permission receptions given by foreign embassies, and that I was visited by journalists, writers and diplomats from both socialist and capitalist countries. I shall remind you of what I told you on other occasions, that a writer is primarily a public person and that everything I write and conceive is addressed to the public at large, without any ideological bias, that I am not in possession of state secrets, and that the very essence of tragic existential and professional secrets gives substance to a putative work, and that from their revelation, from direct contact with people irrespective of their colour and nationality, a writer's destiny is adumbrated. Perhaps you have somehow forgotten, Mr President, that you too are a writer and together we ought to eat our bread from that same freedom which you deny me by punishing me and casting me into the role of an unemployed person. It probably did not occur to you that a couple with two children cannot live on unpublished verses and a signature on the black list, just as it probably did not occur to you that at the same time as you insinuate that I broke an unpublished official decree, the basic clauses in the statutes of the institution which you head have been flagrantly contravened, since for more than four years the Writers' Union has been paralysed because its governing council, of which I myself am a member, has not received permission to meet. Before hearing my sentence I thought that you had called me to put our signatures to a protest at the arrest of the dramatist Vaclav Havel, our Czech colleague, and at the death sentence imposed on Salman Rushdie. But it was not to be, Mr President. Pity.

Let us return to more pleasant things, Mr President, to our Transylvanian soup. A week ago at the canteen of the Writers' House, I lingered at a table with the poet Dan Deşliu. After our departure a colleague witnessed a grotesque scene in which three characters, certainly extraterrestrials, were searching frantically in the kitchen for a certain plate with several slices of bread which had been on our table, and which the waiter had cleared away together with other harmless plates. The troublesome plate was recovered. This event was related to me in a whisper—one whispers, Mr President, everywhere—and so I returned on 14 March with the wicked thought of stealing the plate. As we sat at a table with several colleagues Dan Deşliu and I, the only ones to know about the story of the plate, were surprised when the waitress substituted for the plate with rolls on our table a different plate with slices of bread, under the pretext that they were fresher. Dan Deşliu sensed the telegraphic qualities of this piece of crockery and put it in his bag with the intention of studying it at home at leisure. To be candid, I doubted that in a writers' restaurant in the Socialist Republic of Romania plates with ears could be placed on the tables of the hungry authors. And yet, Mr President, the Transylvanian soup with noodles undermined my scepticism. What remained to be confirmed was proved sooner than we expected. In broad daylight, in the courtyard of the Writers' Union, the poet Dan Deşliu was attacked by a man as he was getting into a taxi. His bag was snatched from under his arm and the culprit ran off down *Calea Victoriei* with the wretched vinyl bag containing a ballpoint pen, a pretzel and a precious plate. Deşliu's desperate shouts and chase were to no avail, for the policemen in abundant numbers on the street merely followed the event as timid observers.

After all these merry pranks which seem illusions I can only wish you, Mr President, a healthy appetite.

Mircea Dinescu Bucharest,
17 March 1989

MD 2

Open Letter to the President of the Writers' Union of the Socialist Republic of Romania

Mr President

When leading representatives of the Romanian clergy give a blessing from official pulpits to the destruction of villages, and therefore also of the churches therein, it is no wonder that a president of the Writers' Union blesses in his turn the 'demolition' of members of his own guild. But what bare-faced impudence and what authority do you and your other colleagues in the leadership of the Writers' Union have today to write about the abuses, atrocities and crimes of the 1950s when you are directly responsible for taking the right to sign from your fellow writers, for their intimidation, isolation and their removal from social and cultural life?!

A regime which kept Vasile Voiculescu in chains, which pushed Nicolae Labiş under the wheels of a tram, which forced Blaga and Arghezi to eat their words, is now suffering a relapse by honouring its initial vocation for ideological and state terrorism.

The elimination of some contemporary Romanian writers from contemporary Romanian literature by an authority however elevated, and given with the same nonchalance as an order for removing potatoes from the yards of a cooperative farm, is tantamount to a veritable cultural tragedy whose proportions you will only realize in the future. It was not enough that the names of Constantin Noica, Mircea Eliade, Eugen Ionescu and Emil Cioran had become undesirable again, there had to be added to the black list the names of Andrei Pleşu, Ştefan Augustin Doinaş, Ana Blandiana, Alexandru Paleologu, Dan Hăulică, Octavian Paler, Mihai Şora, Dan Deşliu, Aurel Dragoş Munteanu, Dan Petrescu and Alexandru Călinescu! And did the noble purity of an intellectual such as Doina Cornea have to be so humiliatingly debased? While in neighbouring Socialist states the victims of Stalinism are being exhumed, while millions of hostages to fear are being freed from the terror of totalitarianism and are rediscovering the human right of no longer being afraid to say out loud what they are thinking, here in Romania the situation is the reverse, as in the curse of the prophet Caragiale.

To dispel any confusion about my present situation let me offer you, Mr President, a short biographical note: For almost 100 days I have been held under house arrest for having been interviewed by a journalist from the left-wing Parisian daily *Libération*. Since I do not have the mentality of a cannibal and do not consider that a foreigner should be eaten or at least beaten when he crosses the threshold of your house, I admit that I thought that I was free man in that interview. But from the 17 April [17 March?] my house has been kept under 24 hours surveillance by plain-clothes agents and not only foreigners, but also Romanian colleagues have been prevented from visiting me. In my turn I have been banned from visiting any private home. Since this same date my telephone has been cut off and my mail stopped, with a single exception—a vulgar and anonymous letter containing a death threat. As if my illegal dismissal from the Party and from the editorial offices of *România literară* was not enough, my wife, who is a translator by profession, has been banned from publishing and her translation of Pasternak, which has been submitted to the Univers Publishing House, has been held over, thus cutting off my sole means of subsistence.

In what country in the world could a single interview about the unease in one's own profession and the social situation around you change your destiny so violently?

Under what articles in the Romanian constitution am I being punished?

What secret tribunal decided that I no longer have the right to speak even to my best friends?

And why are writers more and more closely guarded while villains and common law criminals are given an amnesty by virtue of a truly original Socialist Humanism?

When a regime responds with real weapons to the paper arsenal of the poet it can guarantee itself now a commensurate posthumous glory.

Since I consider for the time being suicide to be an inefficient form of protest (the gesture of the young anonymous martyr who set fire to himself on the ski slope in Braşov last winter has sadly been forgotten, probably because we lack the necessary dimension of understanding the significance of such a tragic voluntary act),[147] I inform you, Mr President, that I want to go on living.

Mircea Dinescu

Bucharest,
22 June 1989

RE 1

Letter from Radu Enescu

Mr Dumitru Radu Popescu

President of the Writers' Union

I hereby bring to your attention my unreserved solidarity with the letter sent to you at the end of April by my illustrious colleagues Geo Bogza,, Ştefan Augustin Doinaş, Dan Hăulică, Octavian Paler, Andrei Pleşu, Alexandru Paleologu and Mihai Şora, to which my distinguished colleague from Iaşi Alexandru Călinescu added his support. The signatories to this letter considered the illegal dismissal of the poet Mircea Dinescu from his post at *România literară*, the harassment, persecution of him and his family, to be actions not only in flagrant breach of the statutory norms applicable to the writers' guild, but also measures designed to attack his human dignity. They also represent a sad recrudescence of an attitude which we all thought was dead and buried alongside the consignment to the darkness of shame and oblivion of the years of dogmatism and other mental malformations which had been officially condemned in Romania. The letter also describes the withdrawal of Ana Blandiana's right to publish as 'grave'. The return to what we thought impossible has nevertheless taken place. The acting leadership of the Union, presided over by yourself, has responded brutally by forbidding the signatories, together with other writers, from publishing. You have passed sentence on some of the most meritorious contemporary writers by heaping them onto the list of the banned because they asked for the restoration of legality in the affairs of the Union.

As President of the Union you ought to have been a *primus inter pares* who defends his colleagues, just as the whole writers' guild defended you unanimously during that scandalous meeting in which you were pinned to the pillar of infamy because of your short story *The Blue Lion*. It seems that the blue lion has been overcome by a strange amnesia and has evaporated, but not into legend but into a strange desire to cleanse you of the glory of an honourable past as though it was a stain. Today you have become a *primus contra pares*, a sort of undertaker who zealously expends energies worthy of a better cause on silently burying, rather like a thief at the dead of night contemporary Romanian literature without a funeral service.

You have cast Mircea Dinescu into the street! It's true that you did it by telephone. A long time ago the infamous minister Chiţu sacked Eminescu from his post as school inspector by telegraph. But you have the benefit of the achievements of the technical and scientific revolution! Your telephone works, unlike number 79 67 23 at 25 Intrarea Bitoliei where one of the greatest Romanian poets lies crucified.[148] I repeat what I have written on several occasions: Mircea Dinescu represents a turning point in our lyric poetry, a mutation in the poetic sensibility of the age, a creative writer of whom Romania can be proud in the face of the world and of posterity. Instead of taking draconian measures against him, your duty was to propose him on Romania's behalf for the Nobel Prize for literature for the current year.

Why isn't Ana Blandiana, this worthy lady with a genuine international reputation and not one forged and paid for behind the scenes, why isn't she allowed to put her name to her writing? Are you by some chance waiting for her to come to you on her knees to beg you to give back to her popular column in *România literară*? You should know that my knowledge of this lady of Romanian letters does not lead me to beg! On the contrary, Ana Blandiana deserves apologies!

You have banned Ştefan Augustin Doinaş! You seem to have forgotten that at a time when you weren't able to say your ABC Doinaş had written 'The boar with the silver teeth, a poem which entered Romanian literature anthologies long ago'. Do you imagine that offering a monumental translation of Goethe's *Faust* is a sort of *hors d'oeuvres*, like your offering a bottle of beer to your horse? This great poet and outstanding cultural figure would be honoured anywhere as a monument of national pride. Here in his homeland he is stigmatized like an outlaw. No wonder! Two substantial studies about his work have been laying for years with publishers. On the other hand, three books have appeared about you, with the usual publicity for them guaranteed beforehand.

In a book with associations with astronomy you branded the ignorant priest Grama. If Eminescu were alive today you would put him on the list of the pernicious. He would annoy you, he would injure your insatiable pride. In the D.R. Popescu galaxy Romanian poetry is bereft of Doinaş, Dinescu and Blandiana, essay-writing by figures of the first rank like Andrei Pleşu for example, a sparkling profound spirit of European stature whom few countries could match from amongst their intellectuals. It is possible that soon a literary history will appear which is expurgated and amputated, full of huge black areas of a desert from the neo-galaxy of D.R. Popescu.

Put me on the list of banned writers as well! I consider it dishonourable to publish when writers of the first order have had their pens wrenched from their hands. I declare that I do not retract anything which I have written above. Any retraction or contrary declaration is a sham, obtained under pressure, false and designed to compromise me.

Before I forget: I urge you kindly to display the decision to dismiss Mircea Dinescu with your signature in the Museum of Romanian Literature. For the knowledge of future generations and your posthumous glory!

Radu Enescu
28 September 1989

MD 3
The Mammoth and Literature[149]

Not long ago in the frozen wastes of Siberia several mammoths were found who were completely frozen. To the amazement of scientists camomile flowers were found in the mammoths' stomachs. I am not going to discuss here the hypocrisy of nature, nor the tragic destiny of these gentle herbivores, but rather an insult contained in a comparison made in the title of a Western newspaper article 'In Romania - the last Stalinist Mammoth'. Stalinist -certainly, but why mammoth? Because I strongly fear that after a possible change in the social climate we shall find in the capacious belly of our Stalinist not camomile but several dozens of corpses. Little known or even anonymous people who had the courage to shout their exasperation, even within the four walls of their home, have been, or are still being 'put out to graze'. The merry, robust, facetious folklore of the Romanians has been transformed into a whispered lamentation, into a folklore of fear, of macabre rumours capable of paralysing the will and speech. The fear of death, FEAR, has become the national product which is on offer in abundance, without rationing cards, on any street corner in Romania.

Who can intervene? 'Can the apolitical hands of a musician?' - forgive my vanity in quoting myself, but I mean that up till now our daily prayers have not been heeded. The priests, on the other hand, have been forced to become like trade unionists in cassocks, because on religious festivals the most devout transmission belts of the Party bring forth incense and prayers for the health of The National Bulldozer[150] without fear of the Lord on high. The 'accidental death' of several inconvenient prelates, as well as the lay treatment applied by the employees of the Secu monastery[151] to more outspoken priests, has instilled a permanent fear under the vestments. In our country we do not have the Polish Catholic factory, nor the militant church, nor the miracle making ikon of Czestochowa. We have the ikon of the president, militarized factories and churches with the greatest productivity in the world in performing burial services, when winter falls inside people's homes.

Where can you run to when the Berlin wall was imported brick by brick and reconstructed at Romania's frontiers? Europe has become for the providential

Leader a diabolical Atlantis which is sinking in the mire of democracy and it is only through his personal genius that the Romanians will escape this disaster.

Who is there to defend you? Blind justice? Well, those gentlemen who at university studied the force and superiority of the 'Romanian left' over 'Roman law' have become brutalized in the impotence and obedience specific to the system so that to avoid losing their jobs they themselves have come to consider the sweet Constitution of the Socialist Republic of Romania simple propaganda material, a tool of the devil which you cannot take advantage of when facing the courts. A former schoolfriend, who in a moment of despair and disgust pasted up a few leaflets attacking the president in the North Station, was sentenced in 1970 to five years in prison and, would you believe it, it was the defence lawyer himself who denounced him the most fiercely during the trial, held of course behind closed doors.

Who can you turn to? To our popular militia? Those sturdy, rosy-cheeked lads who left the cooperative farms untended, in the care of old men and women, and who were planted in their fine uniforms every ten metres on the streets of Bucharest and who look at the population as though they were a docile flock of sheep. In their short period of training they have learned that everything which moves after 8 pm, when the lights go out and restaurants, cinemas, theatres close, that is, when Romania's towns die, all the pedestrians are suspect criminals or at least arsonists ready to set fire to the statue of comrade Lenin, which as a matter of fact was set alight last year.

Where can you find some support? From the press? From the apostles of the personality cult, who write with the spoon with which they eat? For the last 20 years the same crudely touched-up photographs have been appearing in our newspapers, the same lame phrases bandied around, and the only columns with any life in them have been those announcing deaths. In fact the great journalists seemed to have all perished in the Second World War.

What about *glasnost*? Is something filtering through the Soviet transparence? I do not know why but the window through which the Moscow press sees the situation in Romania is pretty dirty, as though there is an eclipse. That is, you cannot see anything. I have the impression that Mr Gorbachev is looking at Romania through the dark glasses of General Jaruzelski.

And the dissidents? They seem from time to time to let out a cry or two. The strange feeling I have recently is that the extremely few dissidents there are kept alive by the regime paradoxically for propaganda purposes. It is too late to make them disappear after the Western press and the human rights agencies have noted their existence. Do you think, however, that the Romanians are by nature more silent than the Germans, Hungarians or Poles because up to now they have only produced one dissident for every two million inhabitants? Not at all. In fact in Romania there are 20 million protesters, unpublicised dissidents who carry on with their lives with a gag in their mouths. I haven't heard of anti-fascist demonstrations taking place on the streets of Berlin in the 1940s. Clearly there were whispers in many houses, but in the street there was order and discipline, the black terror acted mechanically, the people fed themselves on the optimism of the party and the state, the so-called traitors were shot before they were brought to trial.

In our country there cannot be political trials for the simple reason that the Constitution says clearly that any citizen has the right to express his opinions freely, even more than that, in the Party statutes it says that any Party member can criticise the Secretary General himself. The tactics of the organs of repression are to act in a clandestine manner, as though they were in opposition. 'The Sons of Avram Iancu', those who sent death threats to German writers who had emigrated from Romania to West Germany, also sent their 'kisses' to many Hungarian and Romanian intellectuals in Romania. We would have reported these delicate letter writers to the Central Committee, but we were afraid of coming across their 'father' there. By contrast, dangerous workers are not sent any kind of letter. They are delivered to their own homes in a wooden box and only their terrified families understand the message, because officially their death are recorded as being accidents at work, or a road accident, or suicide, or apoplexy etc. If you are harnessed to the cart of protesters you must be careful not to go into town on your own, not to let your children play outside, not to sit for too long in an armchair with radioactive upholstery in a certain institution, to wipe your door handle clean to make sure it is not poisoned. The situation in our country cannot be compared to anything in the world. When I heard that Vaclav Havel was able to watch television in jail in Prague and had in his cell a word processor, I thought it was a good joke. As a writer in Romania you are not allowed to keep a typewriter in your home without a police permit, while as regards prison, a former Romanian dissident poet, in a 'friendly' discussion with the procurator, was given the choice of only three months in prison, in the company of some common law criminals who fancied young men, or exile. The poet thanked the procurator for his sincerity and chose exile.

In this encouraging atmosphere where are Romanian writers, those 'reliable handmaidens of the Party', pampered as they have been until recently? In the 1950s, those who made a pact with the devil joined the category of the privileged. For example, from the royalties on a single poem published on the front page of the Party newspaper you could buy an overcoat of English cloth and you could eat for a month at the finest restaurant in Bucharest. What glorious times! You sang the praises of Uncle Joe [Stalin] but uncle paid, he didn't play. In fact he also paid those who refused to sell their talent handsomely. Many were sent to be retrained, their pens wrenched from their hands, and they were given instead the hammer and sickle from the Party's panoply in order to cut reeds in the Danube Delta and in order to knock the nails into their own coffins on the Danube-Black Sea Canal. In the meantime the ball continued. *Pelişor*, the former residence of King Carol, was given the title of House of Creativity for those who had come out on the conveyor belt of the new writers' factory. History was lifting its skirts right over its head: the Socialist Realist poets sprawled in the bed of Queen Marie, composing ungrammatical and enthusiastic 'revolutionary' poems. On the basis of a 'praise to Stalin' or 'green leaf'[152] luxury villas were awarded and many a fortune amassed. And so the first Party millionaires from amongst the writers entered the arena and since then this type of 'activist of the pen', hunchbacked with so many privileges, has been elected to lead the writers' guild and to be its spokesman.

The wind of freedom in the 1960s gathered up from the ground many artists who seemed to have been buried under the haughty rubbish of mediocrity. The Party—which never errs—threw to the furious crowd its former probationers, took censorship off to the chiropodist's to have its long nails trimmed, deigned to accept that Socialist Realism was suffering from diabetes and that therefore there was no longer any need to sprinkle so much sugar over reality. This miracle, however, was not to last very long.

In the 1970s, when writers failed to show enthusiasm for the new cultural revolution imported from China, the confiscations and reprisals began: *Pelişor* became once more a summer residence for the new princes; the price of a poem regained its symbolic value, that is, the equivalent of a steak at the restaurant, but with bread brought from home; authors' photographs were removed from the covers of their own books to prevent, God forbid, a personality cult emerging. At the same time the red herring that the Union of Writers must be abolished because it was an old style, Soviet-type organization, was produced. In any case, each year brought with it a new gift: the placing of new epaulettes on the shoulders of censorship, the locust-like invasion by amateurs of the 'Song to Romania' festival,[153] a well-orchestrated confusion of values, the marginalization of those unwilling to compromise, and the prominence given to the official dulcimer players.

The Union of Writers' last throb of dignity expired in 1981 when, at the national conference of writers many voices were not at all in tune with the melody required by the centre. Yet the insufficient passive resistance of some of the important writers, the fact that we didn't take our demands to the limit and accepted the imposition from above of an obedient leadership, the void left by the mass emigration of disillusioned artists, all these undermined the Union of Writers which was transformed into a cooperative for producing alienation. The spectre of misery hovers over the majority of writers while month by month the mountain of homages to the beloved Demolitioners grows.[154] It is an irony of fate which we probably deserve, if only for the veiled collaborationism of agreeing to publish a neutral article alongside the chauvinistic and lyrical dung of those who stand on all fours in front of the tyrant.

A general strike of true writers would be the most apposite solution for saving the name of Romanian culture. Although if they all put their heads together, the present mammoths will leave the history books and enter the botany ones, under the heading of grazing on camomile.

Mircea Dinescu
11 November 1989

AP 1

Letter from Alexandru Paleologu[155]

Mr Dumitru Radu Popescu
President of the Writers' Union
Mr President

The undersigned, a Romanian writer, member of the legally-constituted executive committee of the Writers' Union, wrote you a letter in April signed by six colleagues in which we made known to you our profound disapproval of the arbitrary measures taken against the poet Mircea Dinescu. You did not reply colleague to colleague to our letter.

On the other hand we have learned from rumours circulating publicly—no one has notified us—that 'our right to sign' has been withdrawn. Then we discovered that, indeed, with the exception of one of our number, that we had been banned from literary life. Since no one has openly assumed responsibility for taking this decision, and since you were the sole addressee of our letter, one can only conclude that, at least formally, the decision belongs to you. It is illegal. Besides that, it is also ridiculous.

Illegal, first of all, since such a sanction does not appear in any law or statute, and secondly, because you do not have the authority to take measures against us since you are nothing more than our representative, mandated by us by vote—you no doubt remember the circumstances; I assure you that I certainly cannot forget them.

Ridiculous, since it ought to be obvious, at least from relatively recent historical experience, that no administrative or political measure can remove a poet, writer, or artist from the public consciousness in which they have entered. They can be persecuted, in extreme cases, even be liquidated,—but that is all. This, however, always produces an effect contrary to that desired, in the words of Tacitus, *punitis ingeniis, gliscit auctoritas*,[156] while those who carry out these deeds cover themselves irremediably in shame. I shall not ask you when this illegal and ridiculous sanction will cease. But I do ask what your feelings are as the slow physical suppression of Mircea Dinescu and his family goes ahead.

Alexandru Paleologu
11 November 1989

PS I have sent a copy of this letter to each of the co-signatories of the letter of 9 April, with the exception of Geo Bogza.

MS 1
Letter from Mihai Şora

Mr Dumitru Radu Popescu
President of the Writers' Union
Mr President

A year ago, together with another six of my colleagues, I signed a letter addressed exclusively to you in which I protested against the treatment to which the poet Micea Dinescu had been subjected, referring at the end of the letter to the fate of the poet Ana Blandiana. The former was a former editor, the latter a former regular contributor, of a literary weekly directed by you, therefore both had been deprived of an elementary material means of a decent existence on your orders. Of course, not one of the signatories of that letter expected to receive a reply which would offer even the slightest plausible justification, even if it was after the event, for the measures taken against Mircea Dinescu and Ana Blandiana. Since it was in line with a mode of behaviour to which we have long become accustomed, your silence did not surprise any of us, any more than did the rumour which immediately appeared of the existence of a black list containing the names of six of the seven signatories of the protest addressed to you. What did surprise us, however, was the fact that the rumour in question eventually proved not to be a rumour at all, and that our protest, which was totally legitimate, even totally legal against the unlawful expulsion from literary life of two of its eminent representatives, had as a direct result—one of amazing rapidity on this occasion—the expulsion of a further six of us; a seventh was not slow to join us, even though he knew the risk of his action. There are upstanding men to be found in Moldavia as well,[157] as the chronicler says.

As far as I personally am concerned, I do not want to repeat the protest which I made, and which henceforth I shall always make every time that it is a question of the fate of literature and culture in this country, but I am anxious to inform you that a manuscript of mine has been laying around unread for over a year at the *Cartea Românească* publishing house. It is titled 'I, you, he, her' or 'The Generalized Dialogue' which under the title 'The Moment and Time' figured in the approved plan of publication when I submitted it. It is a continuation of reflections in my previous books, this time in the realm of ethics and politics. More precisely it is about widening dialogue and communal life at the base of civil society in such a way as to permit it to adapt, obviously from the bottom upwards, the state to the continually-changing needs of its own polymorphous development. Since I am unable to wait forever for a reply from the publisher in question, I am warning you that if I do not receive a promise of publication of my work in 1990, I shall feel free to proceed as I think fit.

Mihai Şora
17 November 1989

Notes

1 Both figures wish to remain anonymous.
2 A fundamental study of dissent in Ceauşescu's Romania is Cristina Petrescu, *From Robin Hood to Don Quixote. Resistance and Dissent in Communist Romania* (Bucharest: Editura enciclopedică, 2013).
3 I take as my starting point Sorin Alexandrescu's essay 'A gândi altfel, a fi disident, a acţiona în rezistenţă', *Identitate în ruptură* (Bucharest: Univers, 2000), pp.227–40.
4 Alexandrescu, 'A gândi altfel', p.231.
5 Michael Shafir, *Romania. Politics, Economics and Society* (London: Pinter Pub Ltd., 1985), p.168.
6 Ion Raţiu, *Jurnal. Vol 1. Începuturile unui exil îndelungat (1940–1954)*, ed. by Stejărel Olaru (Bucharest: Corint, 2016).
7 For the original text see *Limite*, nos 24–25 (September 1977), p.9.
8 *Limite*, pp.9–10. This author's translation.
9 *Ibid.*
10 Dragoş Petrescu, '"Rebellious" vs. "Non-Rebellious" Nations. British Perceptions of Romanian Anti-Communist Dissidence in the 1980s', *Romania and Britain: Rela-*

tions and Perspectives from 1930 to the Present, proceedings of the British-Romanian Symposium, New Europe College, Bucharest, convenors, Dennis Deletant, Anca Oroveanu, British Council, Romania, 2005, p.153.

11 *Limite*, p.4.
12 *Ibid.*
13 M.P. Haiducu, *J'ai Refusé de Tuer* (Paris: Plon, 1984).
14 A. Scarfe, 'Romanian Baptists and the State', *Religion in Communist Lands*, vol.4, no.2 (Summer 1976), p.15.
15 T. Beeson, *Discretion and Valour. Religious Conditions in Russia and Eastern Europe* (London: Fontana, 1974), p.305.
16 A. Scarfe, 'Romanian Baptists', p.16.
17 *Ibid.*, p.18.
18 *Romania. Forced Labor, Psychiatric Repression of Dissent, Persecution of Religious Believers, Ethnic Discrimination and Persecution, Law and the Suppression of Human Rights in Romania* (New York: Amnesty International USA, 1978), p.30.
19 *Ibid.*, p.31.
20 *Ibid.*, p.33.
21 *Romania. Human Rights Violations in the Eighties* (London: Amnesty International, 1987), p.6.
22 In *Religion in Communist Lands*, vol.8 (1980), p.61.
23 Alan Scarfe, 'The Evangelical Wing of the Orthodox Church in Romania', *Religion in Communist Lands*, vol.3, no.6 (Nov.–Dec. 1975), pp.15–188.
24 'The "Lord's Army" Movement in the Romanian Orthodox Church', *Religion in Communist Lands*, vol.8, no.4 (1980), p.316. A fate similar to that of Traian Dors had been shared by Pastor Richard Wurmbrand before his release from Romania in 1964 by an evangelical group in Norway. Born to Jewish parents, Wurmbrand converted to Christianity as a young man and was ordained as a Lutheran pastor in Bucharest in 1940. His defiance of Iron Guard attempts to close his church led to his arrest on three occasions and to beatings by the police and prepared him for what was to come under the communists. After the war, he renewed his connections with the Western church missions in Bucharest and for this reason was arrested in February 1948. He spent more than eight years in various prisons before being released in the amnesty of 1956 but was rearrested in 1959 and served a further five years in custody until the general amnesty of 1964. After Wurmbrand's release a Christian group in Norway negotiated with the Romanian authorities for him to be allowed to leave the country and raised £2,500 for his 'ransom'. In May 1966 he testified before a Senate Committee in Washington to his experiences in prison and stripped to the waist to show 18 torture wounds on his body (R. Wurmbrand, *In God's Underground* (London: W.H. Allen, 1968)).
25 In *Religion in Communist Lands*, vol.14 (1986), p.88.
26 G. Calciu, *Şapte cuvinte către tineri* (Munich: Ion Dumitru, 1979), p.25.
27 *Romania. Human Rights Violations in the Eighties*, p.25.
28 Lesser known but forthright expressions of concern about the restrictions imposed upon Orthodox clergy were made by Father Ştefan Gavrila and Father Costică Maftei in Bucharest. The latter was brought from a rural parish to the Bucharest parish of Titan, a newly developed area on the outskirts of the capital. In spite of having 300,000 parishioners, Maftei was unable to obtain permission for a new church to be built and was forced to conduct his ministry from his flat. In 1978, Maftei wrote to the West drawing attention to his plight. For details see 'Notes' in *Religion in Communist Lands*, vol.7 (1979), p.60.
29 'Telegramă,'*Biserica Ortodoxă Română*, Year CVII, nos 1–2 (January–February 1989), p.4.
30 *Religion in Communist Lands*, vol.17, no.4 (Winter 1989), p.365.
31 *Radio Free Europe Research*, Romanian SR/1 (13 January 1988), p.43.
32 'Telegramă', *România liberă*, 20 December 1989.

33 *Biserica Ortodoxă Română*, Year CVII, nos 11–12 (November–December 1989), p.4.
34 *România liberă*, 13 January 1990.
35 'La Grève des Mineurs Roumains en 1977: Un Temoignage', *L'Autre Europe*, 11–12 (1986), p.156).
36 *România liberă*, 13 January 1990. In an interesting twist to Dobre's fate he was posted to the Romanian Embassy in London in the spring of 1990 and shortly afterwards requested political asylum of the British authorities. How he managed to secure the posting at that particular time begs a number of questions about his relationship with the Romanian authorities. In a book based on Istvan Hosszu's revelations Dobre is mentioned not as Ioan but as Constantin (Z. Csalog, *Borton volt a hazam, Hosszu Istvan Beszel* (Budapest: Europa Konyvkiado, 1989)).
37 Georgescu's death at the age of 51, prompted allegations that his tumour had been induced by the *Securitate* but no credible evidence has been produced to support such a claim.
38 *O viză de plecare definitivă,* one which would not allow him to return to Romania.
39 Dennis Deletant, 'Romania', in G. Arnold et al. (eds.), *Revolutionary and Dissident Movements of the World* (Harlow: Longman Current Affairs, 1991), p.280.
40 *România liberă*, 20 March 1992, p.3.
41 For these and the following details of labour unrest see Vladimir Socor, 'Recurring Workers' Protests', *Romanian SR/13, Radio Free Europe Research*, vol.12, no.47 (27 November 1987), pp.5–9.
42 https://www.cia.gov/library/readingroom/docs/CIA-RDP87R00529R000100080006-0 .pdf. Accessed on 19 January 2017.
43 I am grateful to my colleague Peter Sherwood at The School of Slavonic and East European Studies, University College, London, for drawing my attention to this account and for translating it from Hungarian.
44 Marius Oprea, Stejărel Olaru, *Ziua care nu se uită: 15 noiembrie 1987, Braşov* (*The Day We Won't Forget, 15 November 1987*), (Bucharest: Polirom, 2002).
45 I was interviewed at the time by BBC TV. My knowledge of the disturbances came from the BBC, and their information came from second-hand accounts. There were no BBC correspondents based in Bucharest—not to mention Braşov—and the town had been virtually sealed off after 16 November. The scale of the protests and its repercussions were a mystery to me, as was the fate of protesters. Since the BBC interviewer, from our pre-discussion off camera, realized that I could not bring information on these points, he questioned me about the possible consequences for the regime.
46 Vladimir Socor, 'The Workers' Protest in Braşov: Assessment and Aftermath', *Romania Background Report /231, Radio Free Europe Research* (4 December 1987), p.3.
47 S. Brucan, *Generaţia Irosită* (Bucharest: Editurile Universul & Calistrat Hogaş, 1992), pp.168–69.
48 V. Socor, 'The Workers' Protest', p.4.
49 *România liberă*, 3 December 1987, p.1.
50 For details, see Marius Oprea and Stejărel Olaru, *Ziua care nu se uită.*
51 Brucan, *Generaţia irosită*, p.172.
52 Brucan recognized his contact with me during this visit in his interrogation by the *Securitate* on 4 April 1989; see Radu Ioanid (ed.), *Dosarul Brucan. Documente ale Direcţiei a III-a Contraspionaj a Departamentului Securităţii Statului (1987–1989),*ediţia a II-a, Institutul de Investigare a Crimelor Comunismului şi Memoria Exilului Românesc (Bucharest: Polirom, 2013), p.551.
53 Despatch from Vienna by David Blow, BBC World Service, SSP, XN76, 11 December 1987.
54 BBC World Service, CAP, XN36.
55 *The Independent*, 14 November 1988.
56 Doubts about Brucan's claim in a post-revolution article ('Intîlnirea secretă Brucan-Gorbaciov', *Evenimentul Zilei*, 19 November 1992) to have been received by

Mikhail Gorbachev during this visit were expressed to this author by Ceslav Ciobanu, one of Gorbachev's translators from Romanian into Russian (Paris, 4 December, 2009). Ciobanu explained that as a matter of protocol, he or one of the other relevant translators, would have been present at such a meeting, even if Brucan's knowledge of Russian would have obviated the need for translation, but neither he nor any of his colleagues were called upon to attend.

57 P. Gafton, 'Amnesty and pardon', *RFE Research. Romanian SR/13* (27 November 1987), p.13.

58 *Ibid.*

59 *Human Rights Violations in the Eighties* (London: Amnesty International, 1987), p.12.

60 Michael Shafir, 'The Mazilu Riddle: Romanian Official Fails to Appear before UN Body', *Radio Free Europe Research, Romanian SR/10* (23 August 1988), pp.23–23.

61 *Ibid.*

62 *România liberă*, 24 January 1990.

63 *România liberă*, 13 January 1990.

64 Details taken from Shafir, 'The Mazilu Riddle', p.23.

65 Mazilu was by no means the first Romanian official, charged with carrying out UN duties, to be recalled to Bucharest and then refused permission to continue their work abroad. In 1977 Sorin Dumitrescu, a member of UNESCO's hydrology department, failed to return to his post after home leave and was forced to sign a letter of resignation. He was allowed to leave Romania in 1978. Liviu Bota, the director of the UN Institute for Disarmament and Research in Geneva, was summoned to Bucharest in late 1985 and not allowed to return. In the wake of strong international protests he was allowed to resume his post in February 1988 (see Shafir, 'The Mazilu Riddle...' p.25).

66 See the observations of her daughter Ariadna Combes in the preface to Doina Cornea, *Scrisori deschise şi alte texte* (Bucharest: Humanitas, 1991), p.7.

67 Cornea, *Scrisori deschise*, pp.13–14.

68 *Ibid.*, p.19.

69 *Ibid.*, pp.27–57.

70 *Ibid.*, pp.143–201.

71 *Ibid.*, pp.63–64.

72 *Ibid.*, pp.74–75.

73 Details of the plan and its application are to be found in Dennis Deletant, *Ceauşescu and the Securitate. Coercion and Dissent in Romania, 1965–89* (London: Hurst, 1995), chapter eight.

74 The others were George Vasilescu, a lawyer from Cluj; Haralambie Circa and Samoilă Popa, both teachers from Sibiu; Puiu Neamţu an electrician from Făgăraş; Teohar Mihadas, a writer from Cluj; Isaia Vatca a painter from Cluj; Dan and Gina Sâmpăleanu, both teachers from Blaj; Crucita Mariana, a housewife from Turda; Peter Ivan Chelu, a theatre director; Melinda Chelu, an architect from Cluj; Zoltan and Judith Wrabel, Eniko Tabacu, Rachel Szocs, and Viorica Hecia, all teachers from Cluj; Marius Tabacu, a musician from Cluj; Marin Lupeu, Ioan Voicu, Mihai Torja, Marin Brâncoveanu, Bogdan and Monica Şerban, all workers from Zărneşti; and Mihai Hurezeanu and Ion Rostas, both workers from Cluj. Iulius Filip, one of the founder members of the independent trade union *Libertatea* had been arrested in 1982 after writing a letter of support to the Polish trade union Solidarity. After five years in prison, during which time he was beaten, he was released but forced to choose from three places of work, none of which was close to his home and family in Cluj. He chose the town of Zlatna, some 150 km from Cluj and commuted to work. He and his wife were placed under constant surveillance and they applied to emigrate. In June 1988, pressure was brought to bear on the couple to withdraw their application but they refused. In July, Filip went to Bîrlad in Moldavia to meet fellow workers who were sympathetic to the aims of *Libertatea* but he was arrested upon arrival and accused of a robbery committed in Cluj. He was badly beaten and detained for four

days before being freed. On his return to Cluj he was rearrested, this time for a robbery carried out in Bîrlad; he was beaten again by Major Jurcut of the *Securitate*. *East European Reporter* (Spring–Summer 1989), p.24.

75 D. Cornea, *Scrisori deschise*, pp.84–85.

76 V. Socor, 'Recent texts by Doina Cornea', *Radio Free Europe, RAD Background report/246 (Romania)* (30 December, 1988), p.3.

77 They were Viorica Hecia, Puiu Neamţu Dan and Gina Sâmpăleanu.

78 D. Cornea, *Scrisori deschise*, p.86.

79 V. Socor, 'Recent texts', p.1.

80 Stork, who was appointed Dutch ambassador in January 1988, was a constant source of moral support for Doina Cornea and other critics of the regime such as Andrei Pleşu and the architect Mariana Celac, the wife of Mihai Botez. Hence, he was placed under 24 hour surveillance; see Cătălin Strat (ed.), *Dosarul de Securitate al lui Ambasador Coen Stork, cu o prefaţă de Dennis Deletant* (Bucharest: Humanitas, 2013).

81 They were George Vasilescu from Cluj; Bogdan and Monica Şerban, Ioan Voicu and Mihai Torja, all from Zărneşti; and Marin Brâncoveanu from Poiana in Gorj County.

82 The full text was published in *The Spectator* on 29 April 1989, pp.13–14. It contains slight differences from the Romanian text published in Doina Cornea, *Scrisori deschise*, pp.121–22 (in the English version the name of Andrei Pleşu follows that of Mircea Dinescu).

83 An English translation is to be found in Dennis Deletant, 'Crimes against the Spirit', *Index on Censorship*, no.8 (1989), pp.26–27.

84 For the full text see Doina Cornea, *Scrisori Deschise*, pp.97–100. Here the letter is dated 'March 1989'. The text which reached the BBC carried the date '15 April 1989'.

85 Dan Ionescu, 'Romania's Growing International Isolation', *Romania/3, Radio Free Europe Research*, 29 March 1989, p.31.

86 'Cuvinte Arestate', *România liberă*, 7 January 1990, p.3.

87 The initiative for the clandestine newspaper had come from Băcanu and Niculescu Maier whose friendship had developed since the latter was giving private lessons to Băcanu's son (author's conversation with Ştefan Niculescu Maier, 17 September, 2016). Those arrested were never brought to trial. After being held in the *Securitate* headquarters in Rahova for three months, each of the detainees, except Băcanu, was sent to a different provincial town under house arrest. In Niculescu Maier's case the town was Craiova. Băcanu remained in Rahova prison. All were released after 22 December 1989 (author's conversation with Ştefan Niculescu Maier, 17 September, 2016).

88 Apostol considered himself the natural successor to Gheorghiu-Dej but did not enjoy the favour of his Politburo colleagues who opted for Ceauşescu in March 1965. Following this rejection, Apostol's star waned rapidly and he failed to be elected to the Politburo at the Tenth Party Congress in August 1969. In retaliation he sent an irate letter to *Scînteia,* castigating Ceauşescu for ignoring Gheorghiu-Dej's achievements. Not surprisingly, the letter was not published. A translation can be found in Dennis Deletant, *Communist Terror in Romania. Gheorghiu-Dej and the Police State, 1948–1965* (London: Hurst, 1999), pp.292–95.

89 Silviu Brucan (1916- 2006). Born Saul Bruckner into a Jewish family in Bucharest, he joined the Party in the 1930s. After the *coup* of August 23, 1944, he became editor of the Party newspaper *Scânteia.*

90 For biographical details of Răceanu see the selected biographies. For the full text of the letter see Michael Shafir, 'Former Senior RCP Officials Protest Ceauşescu's Policies', *Radio Free Europe Research, Romania/3* (29 March 1989), pp.8–11. A good deal of misinformation and perhaps disinformation has circulated concerning the manner in which the letter reached the West. There seems little doubt that Silviu Brucan sent at least two copies of the letter on 1 March through the open post, one to the offices of Associated Press in Vienna, the second to a friend in London. The friend

in London informed the BBC World Service who sent a messenger to collect the letter. It was broadcast by the Romanian service of the BBC on 10 March and on the same evening a despatch from London by Misha Glenny containing details of a telephone conversation with Brucan on the subject of the letter was transmitted in English (I am grateful to the Caris Information Service of the BBC World Service for providing me with a copy of the despatch). That same evening this author was interviewed by the BBC English language service on the significance of the letter and shown a translation of it. In an alleged declaration made by Silviu Brucan to the *Securitate* on 23 March 1989, Brucan said that he had sent a copy of the letter to me in London (*Dosarul Brucan.*, p.529. I have no reason to disbelieve this. However, the only text of the letter that I saw was that shown to me in English translation on 10 March at the BBC. The name of the American correspondent William Pfaff has also been invoked in connection with the transmission of the letter to the West. Here is what Pfaff has to say about the matter: "I have been credited by Radio Free Europe (and elsewhere) with having brought the text of the dissident communist leaders' letter of March 1989 to the West. This is not true. I seem to have provided a useful diversion in these events, but the text of the letter was simply mailed by Mr Brucan to addresses in Vienna and London, for transmission to The Associated Press and the BBC. When after several days the BBC had broadcast nothing, Mr Brucan concluded that the letter had not got through (actually it had) and made another handwritten copy that he gave to the American Embassy, asking that it be immediately typed on an embassy machine and his version destroyed. His arrest promptly followed. According to him, the embassy had been penetrated by the Romanian security service, the *Securitate*, and an American officer had been turned". Pfaff also revealed that Brucan had shown him a draft proposal for reform of the Romanian Communist Party during a visit to Bucharest "in the late winter of 1988–89" (International Herald Tribune, 6 June 1991, p.10).

91 Shafir, 'Former Senior RCP Officials', p.6.

92 *Summary of World Broadcasts, BBC Monitoring*, EE/0547 (14 March 1989), p.5.

93 *Scânteia*, 14 March 1989, p.3. Mircea Răceanu was arrested on the evening of 31 January *en route* by car with his wife to attend a reception at the US embassy in Bucharest. He was searched by *Securitate* officers and found to be carrying materials regarding a meeting of Warsaw Pact experts on 17 and 18 January 1989, on the back of which Răceanu had noted details about the arrest of journalists from *România liberă* who were preparing a *samizdat* edition of the daily, and of the role played by Elena Ceauşescu in blocking cultural exchanges between Romania and the US and the possible replacement of Constantin Dăscălescu as prime minister; see Mircea Răceanu, *Infern '89. Povestea unui condamnat la moarte*, 2nd rev.ed. (Bucharest: Curtea Veche, 2009), pp.59–60; see also ACNSAS, Dosar penal P011564, vol.5, Rechizitoriu, p.3.

94 See Selected Biographies.

95 This is a translation by this author of the Romanian text given to him on 6 January 1990 by Dinescu.

96 See below.

97 *Libération*, 17 March 1989.

98 *Ibid.*

99 Author's interview with L. Demeny 14 January 1990.

100 Author's interview with M. Dinescu, 8 January 1990.

101 For example, Radu Portocala, *Autopsie du coup d'état Roumain* (Paris: Calmann-Levy, 1990), p.31.

102 An extract from this letter appears in Dennis Deletant, 'An Island of Stalinism', *The Independent*, 28 November 1989, p.25.

103 For the full text see Dennis Deletant, 'Crimes against the Spirit', *Index on Censorship*, no.8, 1989, p.33.

104 ACNSAS, Fond D 120, vol.2, p.255. I am grateful to the late Romulus Rusan for a sight of this note of the *Securitate*.

105 *Întâmplări de pe strada mea* (Bucharest: Ion Creangă, 1988).
106 Archive of the National Council for the Study of the *Securitate* Archives (ACNSAS), D 118, vol.15, ff.498r, 498v. A second *Securitate* note of the following day adds that the manuscript was read at the publishing house by Gheorghe Vasile and that the illustrator was Doina Botez. No action was taken against these persons. Doina Mandaj was transferred to the Albatros publishing house (ACNSAS, D 10966, vol.15). I am grateful to the late Romulus Rusan for showing me both documents.
107 ACNSAS, D 118, vol.15, f 498v.
108 Ana Blandiana, 'The Most Famous Tomcat in Town', *Index on Censorship*, no.8 (1989), p.34.
109 For the text of the letter see Deletant, *'Crimes'*, p.28.
110 For this incident see the appendix letter of dissent MD 1.
111 Private communication.
112 C. Ştefănescu, 'The Writer Aurel Dragoş Munteanu Protests against the Harassment of Writers', *RFE Research, SR/5* (16 June 1989), p.33.
113 For the full text see appendix MD 2.
114 Extracts from the letter were quoted in Crisula Ştefănescu, 'The Poet Mircea Dinescu Complains about Romania's Cultural Tragedy', *Radio Free Europe Research, Romania/6* (4 August 1989), pp.29–30.
115 *Report on Human Rights and Youth*, prepared by Dumitru Mazilu, Special Rapporteur and submitted to the Commission on Human Rights, UN Economic and Social Council, on 10 July 1989, p.3.
116 Reuter, Geneva, 30 August 1989.
117 For the full text see appendix letter RE 1.
118 An example of how the will to protest was overcome by fear is shown by a note sent to this author by the poet Marin Sorescu from Bucharest and dated 26 October 1989. Entitled 'Eminescu: grounds for concern for the Romanian authorities' it read: "They [the authorities] have not allowed a single Romanian writer to take part in the commemorative conference organized by the Italian Encyclopedia in Rome at the beginning of October to mark the hundredth anniversary of the poet's death. Zoe Dumitrescu-Buşulenga and Marin Sorescu were not given a Romanian exit visa. Had Eminescu's spirit needed such a visa it certainly would not have received one. The poet Marin Sorescu was also refused a visa to participate in a writers' conference in Canada (at the very time when Romania signed a trade agreement with Canada to which country Romania gave an assurance that she would respect human rights). Life has been reduced in this country to the level of humiliation and shortages of basic goods, and has become ever more difficult to support". When confirmation was sought from the poet of his desire that the note should be published, he had second thoughts.
119 The signatories of 'the letter of the 18' were Anca Oroveanu, Anca Vasiliu, Andrei Cornea, Radu Bercea, Magdalena Ghica, Ioan Buduca, Carmen Banciu, Gheorghe Iova, Dan Ciachir, Doru Mareş, Bogdan Ghiu, Alin Teodorescu, Dan Oprescu, Mariana Marin, Angela Marinescu, Dana Arsene, Liviu Ioan Stoiciu and Stelian Tănase.
120 The genesis of that protest forms one axis of his diary. And it is his diary which constitutes one of the 'voices', as Tănase puts it, of his book *At Home There's Only Speaking in a Whisper. File and Diary Recording the Late Years of the Romanian Dictatorship*. Translated from the Romanian by Sorana Corneanu (Boulder, Colorado: East European Monographs, 2007). The other is his *Securitate* file, dating from March 1989 until December 1989, to which he sought and gained access in 2001. Documents from it are placed collage-like alongside the diary, to allow—the note to the Romanian edition translated and rather confusingly reproduced here, says—'to allow an uninterrupted reading of both File and Diary'.
121 For the full text see appendix letter of dissent MD 3.
122 For the full text see appendix letter of dissent AP 1.

123 For the full text see appendix letter of dissent MS 1.
124 C. Ştefănescu, 'Exiled Literary Critic Mircea Iorgulescu Speaks Out', *Radio Free Europe Research, SR/8* (10 November 1989), p.24.
125 M. Shafir, 'Ceauşescu's Overthrow: Popular Uprising or Moscow-Guided Conspiracy?', *RFE. Report on Eastern Europe*, vol.1, no.3 (19 January 1990), p.15.
126 S. Brucan, *Generaţia Irosită* (Bucharest: Editurile Universul & Calistrat Hogaş, 1992), p.218.
127 Author's interview with General Nicolae Militaru, 7 January 1995.
128 C. Ştefănescu, 'The Writer Dan Petrescu Criticizes Regime in Telephone Interview with RFE', Radio Free Europe Research, SR/8 (10 November 1989), pp.17–20.
129 D. Ionescu, 'The Fourteenth RCP Congress', *RFE Research. SR/9* (14 December 1989), p.21.
130 Cassian Maria Spiridon, *Iaşi, 14 decembrie 1989: Începutul Revoluţiei Române* (Iaşi: Timpul, 1994).
131 Laszlo Tőkés, *With God, For the People*, as told to David Porter (London, 1990), pp.65, 79.
132 Martin Rady, *Romania in Turmoil* (London: IB Tauris, 1992), p.86.
133 Tőkés, *With God*, p.108.
134 Rady, *Romania in Turmoil*, p.88.
135 *Ibid.*
136 F. Tupper-Carey, 'Romania', *Religion in Communist Lands*, vol.18, no.2 (Summer 1990), p.181.
137 Tőkés, *With God*, pp.147–48.
138 Tőkés, *With God*, p.154.
139 V. Socor, 'Pastor Tőkés and the Outbreak of the Revolution in Timişoara', *RFE Research*, vol.1, no.5 (2 February 1990), p.24.
140 Tőkés, *With God*, pp.162–75.
141 Rady, *Romania in Turmoil*, p.90.
142 *Adevărul*, 21 December 1991, pp.2–3.
143 Goya's original words were: "The sleep of reason brings forth monsters".
144 Round-table discussion, Romanian TV, 30 December 1989.
145 The letters in the appendices in this were all written in Romanian in 1989 and transmitted via the BBC to me at that time in *samizdat* form. I translated them and extracts were broadcast by the World Service before the overthrow of Ceausescu on 22 December 1989. Only extracts from them were published in Romanian after 1990. I published the texts that I had translated, with the permission of those authors who were alive at the time, in an article entitled 'Cheating the Censor: Romanian Writers under Communism', *Central Europe*, vol.6, no.2 (November 2008), pp.122–71.
146 For a discussion of opposition to the communist regime see my 'Romania, 1945–89: Resistance, Protest and Dissent' in Kevin McDermott and Matthew Stibbe (eds.), *Revolution and Resistance in Eastern Europe. Challenges to Communist Rule* (Oxford: Berg, 2006), pp.81–99.
147 Liviu Babeş set himself on fire in Poiana Brasov on 2 March 1989, on Bradu slope, as a protest against the regime. He died from his burns.
148 The house of Dinescu's parents-in-law.
149 Copy sent to this author via the BBC in November 1989.
150 A reference to Ceauşescu and his plans for 'systematizing' Bucharest.
151 A monastery by that name but also a play on *Securitate*.
152 *Foaie verde*, the traditional opening invocation in a folk-song.
153 The national festival conceived and planned by the propaganda department of the Central Committee in 1975, and designed to provide "the widest framework for the intensification of cultural and educational activities, for the participation of the mass of the people in the development of the homeland's new spiritual assets, a new form

for the assertion of the talent, sensitivity and creative genius of our people". (Nicolae Ceauşescu, *Romania on the Way of Building Up the Multilaterally Developed Socialist Society*, vol.13 (Bucharest: Meridiane, 1978), p.316). The festival was given the name *Cântarea României* (Song to Romania). One facet of the 'new form' of the festival was its permanence. For over a decade a series of spectacles with mass participation was staged under the umbrella of *Cântarea României*; in 1985 there were 3,593,316 active participants in the 153,000 artistic groups which performed. As for the spiritual assets developed by the spectacles, these were submerged by the emphasis given to national liberty, independence and unity, the guardian of which was Ceauşescu as head of state and party leader.

154 The Ceauşescus.

155 Paleologu (1919–2005), literary critic and close friend of Constantin Noica, was arrested in September 1959 for alleged anti-regime 'activities' and sentenced to several years' imprisonment. His trial is described and discussed in Stelian Tănase, *Anatomia Mistificării, 1944–1989* (Bucharest: Humanitas, 1997). He was released in June 1964 under an amnesty. He was one of the few intellectuals to admit, after 1989, to have been an informer of the *Securitate* in the years 1963 to 1984 (Cristina Petrescu, *From Robin Hood to Don Quixote*, p.379, note 159).

156 "When men of genius are punished their standing grows", wrote Tacitus of the doomed republican historian Cremutius Cordus in Annals 4.35.

157 A reference to Alexandru Călinescu.

16 Repression, degeneration and isolation

Ceauşescu's shortsighted economic policies and their negative impact upon the living standards of Romanians at the end of the 1970s fuelled increasing internal discontent. In order to contain it, Ceauşescu turned to the *Securitate*.[1] Whilst not relying on the extremes of repression pursued during the early years of Communist rule in Romania, Ceauşescu showed that his rule was capable of resorting to the practices of the past in order to maintain his dominance of Romanian society. The institutions and legal codification of coercion remained unchanged. Some provisions of the penal code remained dormant until he found it convenient to resuscitate them; such was the case with the decree requiring the registration of typewriters with the police which was revived in a decree which came into force in April 1983, and with a provision of Gheorghiu-Dej, introduced in 1958, which made failing to report a conversation with a foreigner a criminal offence (decree no. 408 of December 1985). Photocopying machines were a rarity, and the few that were available in national libraries were closely supervised and special permission was required for their use. The materials and number of copies made were carefully recorded by a librarian. The secret police's abuses of human rights undermined any legitimacy that Ceauşescu could claim for his regime and served only to draw the attention of the international community to its excesses. Indeed, the defection of Ion Mihai Pacepa to the United States in late July 1978 was one of the greatest blows in this sense ever delivered to an East European intelligence agency.

As deputy head of the DIE (*Departamentul de Informaţii Externe*) (UM 0920), the foreign intelligence agency of the *Securitate*, and a deputy minister of the Interior, Pacepa was one of the highest-ranking intelligence and security officials ever to defect from the Soviet bloc. Pacepa tells us that he was born in Bucharest in 1928. His father came from what is today Slovakia and had moved to Transylvania while the province was under Hungarian rule, before settling in Bucharest in 1920. Ion Pacepa studied at the Bucharest Polytechnic from 1947 until 3 January 1951 when he was recruited into the DGSP. In his book *Moştenirea Kremlinului*[2] Pacepa revealed that he was assigned to the Directorate of Counter-sabotage of the *Securitate*. In either March 1954 or 1955[3] Pacepa was transferred to the Directorate of Foreign Intelligence (Directorate I), headed at that time by Maj. Gen. Vasile Vâlcu, a Bulgarian who had worked in the Foreign Intelligence Directorate of the NKGB, and had been made chief of the Romanian Intelligence Directorate in 1954.

In 1957, Pacepa was sent to work under cover as the deputy head of the Romanian commercial mission at Frankfurt in West Germany. He returned the following year after his cover was blown by two other Romanian intelligence officers who were arrested in West Germany in the act of receiving secret documents from the Romanian-born wife of an American officer.[4] In October 1959, Pacepa was appointed by Alexandru Drăghici, minister of the Interior, head of the technical department of Directorate I, that is, head of Romanian industrial espionage. Such espionage, like all Romanian foreign intelligence activity, was coordinated by the KGB's Foreign Intelligence Directorate, and Pacepa was given his instructions by the Soviet technical adviser to Drăghici whom he named as Colonel Boris Alexeivici Kotov.[5] When Kotov, together with the other KGB counsellors, was withdrawn at Gheorghiu-Dej's request at the end of 1964, the way was clear for priority to be given to Romanian needs in the realm of industrial espionage, needs which were dictated by Ceauşescu. In April 1972, the existing directorate was rechristened *Departamentul de Informaţii Externe* (DIE) and its head, Col. Gen. Gheorghe Nicolae Doicaru, became Ceauşescu's national security adviser.[6] Pacepa was appointed Doicaru's deputy in 1973 and in this capacity oversaw most of Romanian foreign intelligence activity, some of which he described in his book *Red Horizons*[7] but carefully avoided mention of his own part in them.

As a result of Pacepa's defection, the DIE network was totally destroyed and Ceauşescu himself was severely embarrassed internationally, for Pacepa's information damaged Romania's partners in clandestine activities. Pacepa also proved a time bomb for Ceauşescu since his public revelations almost ten years later in his book *Red Horizons* dispelled any remaining traces of the international respectability which the Romanian leader had attempted to preserve for himself as the potential successor to Tito as a spokesman for the non-aligned countries by exposing his alleged direct involvement in murder, blackmail, drug-smuggling and kidnapping. At the same time, the serialization of the book on Radio Free Europe in 1989 served only to confirm for Romanians their suspicions of the criminal behaviour of Ceauşescu and his family, and completely punctured the inflated myths of the personality cult.

Speculation surrounds the reason for Pacepa's flight.[8] The general himself gives the following explanation:

> It was more an accumulation—than a combination—of factors that made me reach that decision [to defect, author's note]. Let me explain. I became a *Securitate* officer in January 1951, when the first generation of Romania's engineers and economists trained under the Communist rule were about to graduate. At that time I was 22 years old and, as many young Romanian intellectuals who had grown up under the influence of the postwar patriotic fervor, I was willing to try anything to help rebuild my homeland. Once the second largest oil and grain exporter in Europe, Romania was starving in those days. Four years of war on Germany's side had squeezed the country

> like a sponge, and what little remained had been shipped off to the Soviet Union—the "liberating" Red Army had laid waste to the land worse than a plague of locusts. I spent my first three years as *Securitate* officer (lieutenant) in the domestic directorate for counter sabotage, where I had the task to protect Romania's chemical industry. The next three years I was chief of Romania's intelligence station in West Germany, whose main task was scientific and technological intelligence.
>
> In 1960, I became head of Romania's industrial espionage service, called S&T from Science and Technology. At that time, the country's gross national product ($43.9 billion) was ridiculous when placed alongside that of Poland ($116.9 billion) or even that of East Germany ($96.5 billion)—which had half of Romania's population. In chapter 26 of "Red Horizons" (pp 392–408), published when Ceaușescu was still in full glory, I described a Politburo meeting that analyzed my S&T activity. I suggest you take a look at that chapter. It is relevant. In 1972 I became deputy chief of the DIE, and I had gradually realized that sooner or later I would have to screw up my courage and break with that evil society. The physical move proved to be more difficult for me than the mental one, though.
>
> For one thing, I felt sorry for my future self: Ceaușescu would sentence me to death and would then erase anything that might remind people that there had ever been a General Pacepa. *Defector*, that word used by the US government for a Soviet bloc official who chose freedom in the West, also acted as a chain around my ankles, for the word lay in frighteningly close proximity to the word *traitor*. Finally, there was my privileged life at the top of Romanian society: my Bucharest villa with its swimming pool and sauna, my tennis court, my cars and drivers, my summer house at the Black Sea, my hunting lodge in the Carpathian mountains.
>
> The prospect of being directly involved in political killings was the drop that finally burst the dam of my indecision. On July 23, 1978, one day after Ceaușescu ordered my DIE to secretly assassinate Noel Bernard [the director of the Romanian section of Radio Free Europe, author's note], I flew to Bonn, where I had to deliver a secret message from Ceaușescu to the West German chancellor, Helmut Schmidt. That Sunday the music suddenly went dead on my TAROM flight to Vienna, where I was to pick up an Austrian plane for the rest of my trip. A woman's voice cut in fuzzily with an announcement in Romanian and German: "Ladies and Gentlemen, our plane will land at Schwechat airport in a few minutes. Captain Georgescu and his crew wish you a pleasant sojourn in Vienna and hope you will fly TAROM soon again." As I was leaving for the airport's VIP salon, I cast one final glance over my shoulder at the white BAC 1-11 plane with the Romanian flag painted on its tail. I knew that I had flown TAROM for the last time.[9]

Other explanations for Pacepa's flight have been suggested. One theory has it that Pacepa feared being held responsible for his failure to negotiate the purchase of Fokker aircraft from West Germany and demotion,[10] another that he was about to be arrested as a KGB agent, a third that he was in the crosshairs of the counter-intelligence department of the *Securitate* as one of a number of senior officers allegedly involved in contraband smuggling of Western goods such as video and cassette recorders, alcohol and cigarettes into Romania using Romanian international transport lorries (*Tir-uri*). The latter investigation was triggered by, according to one source, information supplied by the counter-intelligence unit of the DIE which monitored the officers' movements.[11] According to another account, it was an anonymous letter from an official in the Ministry of Finance that prompted Ceaușescu to order an enquiry, one conducted by a team working under the supervision of General Constantin Olteanu, one of the Romanian leader's military counsellors.[12] Fearing that the net was closing in on him, Pacepa is said to have asked Gheorghe Oprea (1927–89), a Politburo member, for permission to go to Cologne in connection with the Fokker negotiations and it was granted. Pacepa allegedly arranged with General Teodor Sârbu, a friend, to alert him if his house was on list of those to be searched.[13] Pacepa, having reached Vienna, was said to have telephoned Sârbu at the agreed time of 10 p.m. in Bucharest. However, Sârbu did not return home until 10.30 and therefore missed the call. Pacepa interpreted this as a sign that his house had been searched and decided to defect.[14] Pacepa describes the circumstances of his defection thus:

> My whole defection process in West Germany took four days, not weeks as Wippl claims.[15] I arrived in West Germany on July 23, 1978. The next morning I requested political asylum at the US Embassy. On July 27, 1978, I boarded a US military plane at the US Rhein-Main Air Force Base in Germany, and on July 28, 1978, I landed at the US Presidential Airport near Washington D.C.[16] Between July 24, 1978 (when I asked for political asylum) and July 27, 1978 (when I left for the US), I was NOT debriefed by either German or US intelligence, contrary to what Wippl alleges. I met only twice [Pacepa's emphasis] with the same CIA officer (I'll use only his code name "Pete") – and never in a bar. The first meeting took place on July 24, when I asked for political asylum at the US Embassy in Bonn. There I talked only with "Pete" in the super secret CIA area. After a couple of hours, "Pete," who went in and out of the secure area to discuss with his chief of station and the US Ambassador, told me that only President Carter could approve my request because of my very high positions in Romania. "Pete" also informed me that the process might take a couple of days, and we established another meeting for July 27, at 10 PM in the Hotel Dom in Cologne.
>
> There were four long days of waiting, during which I had several official meetings as Ceaușescu's representative. On that same Monday I met Hans-Jürgen Wischnewski (the number two member of Germany's government) to give him a secret message from Ceaușescu, and I spent the rest of the day in the acoustically protected "bubble" at the Romanian embassy, in the company of the DIE chief of station, Gen. Ștefan Constantin. Tuesday I flew to Bremen with the head of the Romanian Commercial Agency for discussions with

> Fokker. Wednesday I met Frederick W. Smith, the chairman/owner of Federal Express, who wanted to buy 100 commercial planes that would be produced in Romania in cooperation with Fokker. On July 27, I had another meeting with Hans-Jürgen Wischnewski, and in the evening I attended the dinner given for me by the Romanian ambassador, Ion Morega, in the salons of the embassy. On that same July 27, at 10 PM, I had my second meeting with "Pete" at Hotel Dom in Cologne. He gave me a highly classified cable signed by Admiral Stansfield Turner, the director of central intelligence, stating that President Carter had granted me political asylum, security protection, and help for starting a new life in America. It also said that a US military airplane was waiting at the U.S. Rhein-Main Air Force Base to take me to Washington D.C. A four-car motorcade took Pete and me to the Rhein-Main Air Force Base. I was pleasantly surprised to find a pile of cloths engraved with the White House seal waiting for me on the plane, as all I had with me were the shirt and pants I was wearing. I wanted to start my new life without any encumbrances from my past. That was why the only things I took with me were my passport, a camera containing a couple of snapshots of my daughter, Dana, and a wristwatch I had gotten from King Hussein of Jordan for saving his life from a plot organized by Yasser Arafat. Everything else I left in my room at Intercontinental Hotel in Cologne.[17]

News of Pacepa's disappearance was published in *Die Welt* on 8 August and confirmation that he had defected came two days later from Washington.[18]

One thing, however, seems clear. Pacepa was not engaged in espionage for the United States before his defection.[19] To become a naturalized citizen of the United States, a foreign national must meet several legal standards: the applicant must lawfully enter the country and gain legal permanent resident status. After becoming a legal resident, a foreign national must reside in the United States continuously for five years (or three years for spouses of US citizens).[20] Under the provisions of Public Law 110, commonly known as the Central Intelligence Agency Act of 1949, expedited naturalization is given to those foreign citizens who are deemed to have served the security interests of the country.[21] It is in this context that we should interpret the award of naturalization after only two years to the Polish defector Colonel Ryszard Kuklinski (1930–2004) who, over the course of nine years, passed vital information regarding Soviet and Polish military plans, as well as Warsaw Pact intelligence, to the CIA and was extracted from Poland in 1981.[22] Similarly, Mircea Răceanu, a senior Romanian diplomat, who passed on information to the CIA for more than a decade, but who, unlike Kuklinski, was caught in January 1989, received naturalization in a little over two years from the time of his arrival in the United States in May 1990.[23] Pacepa, on the other hand, was regarded by the US authorities as a member of the Romanian *nomenklatura* and government and had to wait ten years for his naturalization to be granted.[24]

There followed the greatest purge amongst the intelligence and security services in Communist Romania. According to Pacepa a third of the Council of Ministers was demoted, 22 ambassadors replaced and more than a dozen high-ranking security officers arrested.[25] Feverish efforts were made to withdraw DIE officers abroad, some of whom chose to defect once uncovered. In 1978, the DIE was said by Pacepa to have 560 legal and clandestine officers, and 1,100 'associates' in the Ministry of Foreign Trade. Their numbers had been boosted as a result of secret decree signed by Ceauşescu in 1973 which empowered the DIE to recruit anyone working in the Foreign Ministry or in the Ministry for Foreign Trade and to pay them an extra salary. Some 70 per cent of the personnel in trade legations in the West and in the Third World were undercover DIE officers while the rest, with the exception of Marin Ceauşescu, head of the commercial office in Vienna, were collaborators of the DIE. In the Ministry of Foreign Trade five deputy ministers and 11 directors were undercover DIE officers. The catalogue of infiltration continued: the General Directorate of Customs was headed by an undercover DIE officer, and 38 of the 41 directors of foreign trade companies were officers or collaborators of the DIE.[26]

A major casualty of Pacepa's flight was the Interior Minister Teodor Coman. On 5 September, it was reported that he had been 'released' from his office by presidential decree and replaced by George Homoştean, First Secretary of the Alba County Party.[27] Personnel changes in the DIE were also to be expected. Pacepa's boss, Lt. Gen. Alexandru Dănescu, appointed by Ceauşescu as recently as March 1978, was removed in October. Lt. Gen. Nicolae Pleşiţă, a first deputy minister of the Interior, was sacked and transferred to be commandant of the Ministry's Officers School at Băneasa just outside Bucharest.[28] The DIE was reorganized and styled the CIE (*Centrul de Informaţii Externe*). Romus Dima was appointed its chief. Doicaru, too, was a Pacepa victim; he was dismissed as Minister of Tourism on 15 August, a sign that Ceauşescu anger against his intelligence officers went extremely deep.

This upheaval in the Romanian intelligence and security services compounded a series of earlier organizational changes affecting the Ministry of the Interior, the first of which had resulted from the miners' strike in the Jiu valley in August 1977. Some officials had been replaced: structural changes had been introduced into the ministry which were embodied in a State Council decree published on 8 April 1978. The most significant of these was the recreation of a Department of State Security *Departamentul Securităţii Statului* (DSS) within the Ministry of the Interior. Tudor Postelnicu, the Party secretary of Buzău County and a friend of Ceauşescu's son Nicu, was appointed minister state secretary in the Ministry of the Interior and head of the DSS in March 1978.

This restoration of the department to its position of authority prior to the 1968 reform was one signal of an end to the period of 'socialist legality' trumpeted by Ceauşescu a decade earlier; the second was the extension of the ministry's remit to include "defence of the independence, national sovereignty and territorial integrity of the state". This expansion of the ministry's duties also required it to be responsible for security matters not just to the Party's Central Committee, where there was a secretary charged with responsibility for the armed forces and security—at the time of the 1989 revolution this was Col. Gen. Ion Coman—but also to the Supreme Command of the Romanian Armed Forces of which Ceauşescu was chairman. In practice, both the minister and the head of the DSS reported directly to Ceauşescu himself. The increased importance assigned to the DSS, and the control over it with which Ceauşescu invested himself, invites parallels with the prescriptive control exercised by the *Securitate* of the 1950s. The promotion of one of the president's brothers, Nicolae Andruţă Ceauşescu, to the rank of Lieutenant General and to the post of commandant of the officer training school for the *Securitate* troops at Băneasa on the outskirts of Bucharest emphasized that control.

Promoting the cult in the wake of Ceauşescu's 'election' to the new post of President of the Republic in March 1974, and its extension to his wife Elena—the second most important figure in the Party and state after her appointment as first deputy prime minister in March 1980—absorbed a significant amount of the DSS's resources. Disbursements were made from special hard currency accounts controlled by an agency within the CIE known as *Departamentul Operaţiuni Valutare Speciale* (OVS)[29] (The Department of Special Hard Currency Operations). Sums from this department were used to pay foreign publishers to publish hagiographies of Ceauşescu and the ghostwritten studies on chemistry attributed to his wife, "the scholar of world-renown". Bucharest sources allege that the occasion for a CIE officer's defection in Vienna in January 1989 was his assignment to pay a Western publisher the reputed sum of $30,000 for publication of one of Elena's 'studies'.

Furtherance of the cult was assumed by Elena who, from 1985, took especial interest in it and regularly browbeat the successive Central Committee propaganda secretaries to ensure that public meetings were festooned with photographs of the happy couple.[30] In the words of J.F. Brown, Elena

> played her own dominating role in the Romanian tragedy, exercising an influence on her husband that some considered to be decisive at times... In the last few years of their rule and of their lives, as they grew more isolated, they fed each other's sense of unreality, more so than all the pomp and paraphernalia of the personality cult.[31]

She became increasingly protective of her husband as his diabetes seemed to be accelerating both his ageing and his irascibility, and it was for this reason that she frustrated the attempts of Major General Emil Macri, the head of the Second Directorate, to discuss with the president the true state of the country's disastrous economic plight.[32] That said, Romanian statistics suffered from the reputation of being grossly massaged and soon "began surpassing even themselves in fantasy".[33] It is clear that Nicolae Ceauşescu was party to this deception from the disclosure on Romanian TV after the revolution of documents from his summer residence at Neptun on the Black Sea which contained two columns of harvest figures, one true and the other false. It was the latter set which he had communicated to the Politburo in the autumn of 1989.[34]

It is the height of irony that a special anti-terrorist unit, known by its acronym of USLA (*Unitate Specială de Luptă Antiteroristă*),[35] was set up within the DSS in 1978. Its first commander was Colonel Ştefan Blaga.[36] Charged with "the activity of preventing, detecting, neutralizing, and liquidating terrorist actions on

Romania's territory", USLA was established at the very same time that it and another body within the DSS, the Foreign Intelligence Department (DIE/CIE), was actively planning terrorist acts outside the country.[37] The CIE sought to silence critics abroad of Ceauşescu. The case of Monica Lovinescu, the daughter of a distinguished literary critic, who had taken refuge in France after the war, was offered by Pacepa as further evidence of Ceauşescu's direct involvement in such actions. Her regular cultural broadcasts on Radio Free Europe, in which she criticized with bitter sarcasm Ceauşescu's attempts to subordinate Romanian literature to his own ends, so infuriated the Romanian leader that it was he himself who gave orders for her to be silenced. Pacepa alleged that a DIE/CIE officer, Major Gheorghe Şerbănescu, who was a specialist in Arabic and liaison officer with the Palestine Liberation Organization, received instructions in 1977 from Ceauşescu to beat up Lovinescu so savagely "as to prevent her writing and talking for the rest of her days". Şerbănescu engaged three PLO members and instructed them as to how to carry out the operation. One of the men, disguised as a postman, rang the doorbell of Lovinescu's Paris flat and when she answered the other two rushed in and punched her repeatedly in the face and about the body.[38]

A second target of the DIE/CIE was a Romanian engineer, Constantin Răuţă, who on the evening of November 24, 1973 arrived at Kennedy Airport in New York with a diplomatic visa issued by the American Embassy in Bucharest. He was listed as an attaché to a delegation to prepare for the visit of Ceauşescu to the White House at the invitation of President Richard Nixon. After he managed to lose the team assigned to monitor him in the United States at a transfer airport (La Guardia), he took a taxi to a police station and informed the officers there that he wanted to request political asylum. The two FBI agents who arrived at the police station informed him that the Bureau of Immigration office, where he had to file the request, was closed for the day and that he would have to wait until the next morning to fill out the paperwork.

Răuţă informed the FBI agents that he wanted to use the documents and the probes, which were in his briefcase, to reveal Ceauşescu's "true face and intentions". He also wanted to use them to negotiate with the Ceauşescu regime for the release of his wife and son, who had been left behind as hostages in Bucharest, to ensure that he would return home. As the chief engineer for the electronic alarm systems abroad in all Romanian embassies, and also the Romanian Intelligence Service (DIE/CIE) locations in Romania, he had in his briefcase not only proof of numerous violations by the Ceauşescu regime of basic human rights in Romania, but also "proof of the duplicity of that regime in its dealings with the United States in the planned visit to the White House of Ceauşescu" who was scheduled to arrive in Washington, DC, the following week.[39]

According to Răuţă, a CIA officer visited Răuţă in his hotel room later that evening and informed him that President Nixon had decided to grant him political asylum, but that his briefcase and the accompanying material, would have to be returned to Romanian officials as constituting a diplomatic pouch. Ceauşescu's visit went ahead. After a persistent campaign by Dr Răuţă in the US, his family was finally able to join him after five years and nine months.[40]

Emil Georgescu, who had been working as a programme editor for Radio Free Europe since January 1974, was a third target. Ceauşescu himself allegedly gave the order to CIE head General Nicolae Pleşiţă for Georgescu to be silenced because of his barbed critiques of the personality cult.[41] A DIE/CIE disinformation operation was launched in 1980 to compromise him. Signed and anonymous letters sent to Radio Free Europe at the behest of the DIE/CIE insinuated that Georgescu had been in receipt of payments to secure exit visas for Romanians wishing to emigrate. An unsuccessful blackmail operation run by Maj. Gen. Eugen Luchian, head of the Visa and Passport Office, was mounted to persuade Georgescu to leave his post at RFE in return for an exit visa for his mother in Bucharest. Georgescu continued his acerbic broadcasts until 28 July 1981 when he was stabbed 22 times by two French citizens while leaving his Munich home. Georgescu, despite being severely wounded, survived this attempt on his life and his attackers were arrested. They refused to give any information about who had hired them and on 21 July 1982 were sentenced to 11 years, and four and a half years respectively for attempted murder.[42] In their report on the crime the West German security service concluded that "other persons from the Romanian Intelligence Service are said to have been given the assignment of liquidating the Romanian *émigré* once and for all".[43]

Such was Pleşiţă's zeal in satisfying Ceauşescu's obsession with stifling criticism of his rule that the DSS became the state sponsor and accomplice of international terrorism. On the orders of Tudor Postelnicu, the head of the DSS, and with the apparent approval of Ceauşescu, DSS units gave support to Ilici Ramirez Sanchez, alias Carlos the Jackal, and his associates, in their effort to eradicate opponents of the Romanian dictator.[44] The principal target was General Pacepa. In August 1979, Lt. Col. Sergiu Nica of USLA (UM 0620) and Lt. Col. Ion Diaconescu, a DIE/CIE officer (U.M. 0544) contacted Carlos in Prague with the aim of murdering Pacepa and offered him $10,000 to carry out the deed.[45] According to a report written by Nica in February 1990, Carlos was unwilling to carry out the mission since he did not have the necessary resources in the United States.[46]

A string of embarrassments for Pleşiţă began in October 1980 when the West German Federal Prosecutor's Office reported the arrest of a Romanian citizen for spying on emigrants to West Germany for the CIE. In the following month Florian Rotaru, a code clerk at the Romanian embassy in Vienna, defected to West Germany with a fifty-kilogram postbag contained classified information. He was flown from there to the United States.

Postelnicu, in the meantime, authorized contact to be maintained with Carlos and to this end he and his partner Magdalena Kopp[47] were given a safe house in Bucharest where they stayed during visits made in 1980 and 1981. Carlos's deputy, Johannes Weinrich (code name 'Steve'), the principal architect of the Carlos group's attacks, had the habit of keeping a record of their contacts with foreign agencies and searches of one of the group's bases, in Budapest, allowed the Hungarian Security Service, to discover a plan to murder a number of Romanian contributors to Radio Free Europe and to carry out an attack on the Romanian section of the broadcaster in Munich. In return, the group requested 34 passports of varying citizenships and three Romanian diplomatic passports for Carlos, Kopp and Weinrich.[48] In early February 1981, parcel bombs were addressed from Madrid to three Romanian émigrés, Paul Goma, a novelist, Nicolae Penescu, a member of the Romanian National Committee in exile, and Şerban Orescu, a journalist working for Radio Free Europe.[49]

On 21 February 1981, Swiss terrorist Bruno Bréguet a member of the Carlos group, detonated a bomb at RFE/Radio Liberty headquarters in Munich. The bomb was a sophisticated device weighing approximately 20 kilos of plastic explosives affixed to the wall at ground level near the Czechoslovak service. Two persons in the neighbourhood and four RFE/RL employees were injured, one seriously.[50] The involvement of the DIE/CIE in the planning of the attack was confirmed by Magdalena Kopp in a deposition made to German prosecutors after her voluntary return to Germany over Christmas 1995.[51] Although significant damage was caused to the Czechoslovak service, the Romanian service was able to resume broadcasting shortly afterwards.

This failure on the part of the DIE/CIE was compounded in the following year. On 13 January 1982, Matei Pavel Haiducu (real name Major Hirsch), a DIE/CIE agent based in France to carry out industrial espionage, received orders from Pleşiţă to murder both Paul Goma and another dissident writer, Virgil Tănase, by injecting them with a special poison designed to provoke cardiac arrest.[52] Pleşiţă's plans backfired with Haiducu's defection in July 1982. It proved the most serious in a series of setbacks for the DIE/CIE under Pleşiţă's direction. In March 1981, an Austrian police chief had been arrested in Vienna on charges of spying for Romania.[53] In the summer of 1982 came Haiducu's defection. He told the French secret service of Pleşiţă's instructions to him to kill Goma and Tănase, and as a direct result President Mitterrand cancelled a visit to Romania in July. In January 1983, a French court sentenced Traian Munteanu, a Romanian computer technician, to two years in jail for espionage, and six months later Mihai Manole, a 37-year-old Romanian-born engineer who was a naturalized French citizen working for a shipbuilding firm in Dieppe, was arrested by the French police and charged with industrial espionage on behalf of Romania. In August, three Romanian diplomats and one employee of the Romanian embassy were expelled from Belgium on charges of spying against NATO.[54]

A presidential decree issued on 26 November 1984 released Pleşiţă from the position of first deputy minister, meaning implicitly his removal as head of the DIE/CIE. He was relegated to the position of commandant of the *Securitate* training school at Gradiştea, some 40 kilometres south of Bucharest, and replaced as DIE/CIE chief by Lt. Gen. Aristotel Stamatoiu. The attempts by Pleşiţă to make good some of the damage caused by Pacepa's defection were compromised by a succession of failures which served to erode still further Ceauşescu's crumbling image abroad.[55]

This catalogue of disaster continued into 1984. A Romanian embassy employee, Nicolae Iosif, was found dead outside the Embassy in Paris in April with a dagger beside his body. In September, Ion Constantinescu, a CIE cipher officer (UM 0525) from the Romanian embassy in Bonn asked for asylum. It was later reported that five Romanian diplomats, named as Counsellor Constantin Ciobanu, First Secretary Ioan Lupu, Second Secretaries Dan Mihoc and Ion Grecu, and Third Secretary Ion Constantin, had been expelled from West Germany.[56] Shortly afterwards Haiducu appeared on French television and declared that the Romanian ambassador to France, Dumitru Aninoiu and his press attaché Ion Badea, were DIE/CIE agents.[57]

Ceauşescu's ability to translate his anger at his critics abroad into violence against their persons put Western security services on the alert. Early in 1989, Ion Raţiu, a prominent *émigré* critic of Ceauşescu, received word from West German sources that two women agents had been sent to assassinate him, and he was offered protection; even the author of this book was considered significant enough to warrant the ambiguous warning from an official in the Romanian Foreign Ministry, transmitted via a British visitor in July 1989, that he was "number seven on the *Securitate's* list".

At home, the brutality of some of the beatings administered to opponents of the regime was evident from the fate of Gheorghe Ursu, an engineer from Bucharest who was arrested on 21 September 1985 for keeping a diary and correspondence critical of the Ceauşescus. He was held at the *Securitate* headquarters on Calea Rahovei where he was beaten by two prisoners at the instigation of his interrogators and moved, as a result of his injuries, to the hospital of Jilava jail where he died on 17 November. An enquiry in March 1990 revealed that Ursu had died as a result of repeated blows with a heavy object to his abdomen.[58] In July 2003, former *Securitate* officers Tudor Stănică and Mihail Creangă were each sentenced to 12 years' imprisonment for having instigated the murder of Ursu. The two were found guilty of deliberately assigning Ursu to a cell where two violent common criminals were serving time, and of having prevented their subordinates from intervening when the prisoner was being beaten. Stănică was released on health grounds in 2004. Marian Clită, one of the criminals, was tried in 2000 for Ursu's murder and sentenced to 20 years' jail (commuted later to eight) of which he served two. In May 2017, Tudor Postelnicu, the head of the *Securitate* between March 1978 and October 1987, and two of Ursu's alleged *Securitate* interrogators, Marin Pîrvulescu and Vasile Hodiş, were charged in connection with Ursu's death. Their trial had yet to be concluded at the time of writing.[59]

A notable target of the *Securitate* was the Nobel prize-winning author Herta Müller.[60] In her Nobel Prize Lecture, delivered on 7 December 2009, Müller described how a *Securitate* officer attempted to recruit her as an informer in her office.

> He yelled at me: *Write*. Without sitting down, I wrote what he dictated—my name, date of birth and address. Next, that I would tell no one, no matter how close a friend or relative, that I... and then came the terrible word: *colaborez—I am collaborating*. At that point I stopped writing. I put down the pen and went to the window and looked out onto the dusty street, unpaved and full of potholes, and at all the humpbacked houses....I said: *N-am caracterul—I don't have the character for this*. I said it to the street outside. The word

> CHARACTER made the *Securitate* man hysterical. He tore up the sheet of paper and threw the pieces on the floor. Then he probably realized he would have to show his boss that he had tried to recruit me, because he bent over, picked up the scraps and tossed them into his briefcase. ...With his briefcase under his arm he said quietly: *You'll be sorry, we'll drown you in the river.* I said as if to myself: *If I sign that, I won't be able to live with myself anymore, and I'll have to do it on my own. So it's better if you do it.*[61]

Nothing illustrates more graphically how the *Securitate* attempted to use fear as a weapon against the citizen, and how some found the internal strength to overcome it.

Foreign observers and analysts deemed to be adversaries of the regime also attracted the attention of the *Securitate.* As Katherine Verdery, a distinguished anthropologist has perceptively written, she was "a target and assumed enemy, and the *Securitate* set itself the task of producing evidence to determine what kind of enemy" she was.[62] In analyzing the work practices of the *Securitate,* based on the reading of her file, Verdery is aware, as others are when consulting theirs, of an extraordinary expenditure of time, money and effort. The need for "conspirativity" (*conspirativitate*) required compartmentation that kept each officer's activity and his or her informers a secret both from colleagues as well as from the public. But such compartmentation led to duplication of officers' efforts, inefficiency and often incoherence. In this regard, conspirativity was carried to an extreme by the *Securitate,* compared with the practice of the political police in other communist regimes in East Central Europe.

Sycophancy played a major part in the support given to Ceauşescu, by the *nomenklatura* and as General Pleşiţă's instructions to Haiducu demonstrated, it was a motive behind actions in the CIE. Yet within the army there appears to have been disillusionment among some senior officers with Ceauşescu's inflexibility. In February 1990, the first revelation about a plot to remove Ceauşescu emerged. Major General Ştefan Kostyal, who had served as a deputy of the Higher Political Directorate of the Army, in a statement published in the weekly *Cuvântul* on 28 February 1990, claimed that he had received orders from Ceauşescu in 1970 to dismiss from the army all officers of the national minorities. Kostyal complained that Ceauşescu was using the invasion of Czechoslovakia as "an excuse to remove from the head of the army specialists trained in the Soviet Union" and apparently protested, an action which led to his demotion to the rank of private. In a later interview with the author Edward Behr, Kostyal said that his opposition to Ceauşescu was motivated by his growing personality cult and that he therefore decided, in concert with the former commander of the Romanian navy Rear Admiral Nicolae Mihai, to address a letter to the Central Committee, protesting about it. As a result Mihai was demoted and Kostyal sent into internal exile. He also stated that he was one of a number of senior officers who were retired from the army in 1970 because he had a Russian wife.[63] Kostyal demanded a hearing before an army commission in 1971 and attacked Ceauşescu's 'erratic', that is, anti-Soviet, foreign policy. Kostyal's behaviour was written off in Party circles as the work of a Soviet agent and failed to rally any support. He was promptly taken off the army reserve, his pension stopped and sent to work as a labourer outside Bucharest. The protest of Kostyal and Mihai seems to have formed the substance of this 'conspiracy' of 1970.

Another conspiracy emerged, Kostyal recalled, in 1984. Two groups which had been plotting independently to overthrow Ceauşescu, merged. Once again, the Soviet connections of some of their members should not be overlooked. One group was formed by General Ion Ioniţă, Minister of Defence between 1966 and 1976, who, like Kostyal, was married to a Russian, and who had been a colleague of Kostyal at the Voroshilov Military Academy in Moscow from 1956 to 1958. In 1976, Ioniţă was appointed a deputy prime minister and became a member of the Political Executive Committee, the Politburo. In March 1979, he lost his seat on the Defence Council and in the following November was demoted to alternate membership in the Politburo. He was dropped from the government and the Politburo in May 1982, and from the Central Committee in November 1984.[64] Ioniţă's demotion embittered him towards Ceauşescu and he drew up plans for his military overthrow. He attracted to his group Janos Fazekas, a leading Hungarian member of the Party, who was a Central Committee secretary from 1954 to 1961, a member of the Politburo from 1967 to 1974, and Minister of Domestic trade from 1974 to 1982. Kostyal also joined this group. The second group had been formed around Colonel General Nicolae Militaru, the alleged Soviet spy who had been removed from his position as head of the Bucharest military garrison in 1978 and was to become minister of defence for a brief period after Ceauşescu's overthrow. It included, Kostyal said, Ion Iliescu, the future president and at the time an established member of the Communist Party *nomenklatura*.

The two groups merged in 1984 and a *coup* was planned for the autumn when Ceauşescu was due to visit West Germany (15–17 October). A senior Party official, Vasile Patilineţ, was allegedly recruited while serving as ambassador to Turkey. Patilineţ had strong connections with the *Securitate*, having been Central Committee secretary for military and security affairs from 1965 to 1972, and a member of the Defence Council from 1969 to 1972. Two of the plotters, General Gheorghe Gomoiu and General Dimitrie Popa, betrayed the plan, which would involve units from the Bucharest garrison, to Ceauşescu and the units concerned were sent in September to help with the harvest.[65] The *coup* was thus called off.[66] In 1986, an unsuccessful attempt was made to obtain pistols from a military unit in the port of Constanţa and shortly afterwards Patilineţ was killed in a car accident with his son in Turkey on 9 October. One conspirator alleged that the accident was staged by the *Securitate* acting on Ceauşescu's orders,[67] although he produced no supporting evidence for his claim, and it was also to the *Securitate* that he attributed Ioniţă's death from cancer on 24 July 1987.[68]

Ceauşescu was astute enough to realize that his own position of personal dominance was ultimately dependent on the loyalty of the *Securitate*. He therefore paid them well, giving them higher salaries than those received by their colleagues of the same rank in the armed forces. A lieutenant colonel in the *Securitate* received a monthly salary of 7,800 lei in December 1989, a thousand *lei* more than his counterpart in the army and more than double the average. *Securitate* officers had access to the special shops and facilities reserved for senior Party members, whereas their army counterparts did not. Moreover, instead of ensuring the country's defence, the role of the army was relegated to that of providing a cheap labour force for the megalomaniacal building projects that Ceauşescu initiated. As draconian economic measures fuelled even greater and more widespread disaffection with his policies in the mid-1980s, Ceauşescu became even more dependent on coercion for the maintenance of his rule, and this dependence necessitated closer supervision of the Ministry of the Interior. These considerations led him to promote the family friend Postelnicu to the position of minister of the Interior on 3 October 1987. His successor as minister state secretary in the Ministry of the Interior and head of the DSS was Colonel General Iulian Vlad.[69]

In the face of an increasing restiveness on the part of the population, amply demonstrated by the Braşov disturbances in November 1987, Ceauşescu ordered Postelnicu to improve the effectiveness of security forces and to this end the minister issued order no. 02600 on 5 July 1988 approving "Measures which must be taken by units of the Ministry of the Interior for increasing its combat and intervention effectiveness".[70] It appears that in the wake of this order new special security units were set up in the major provincial cities under the authority of the *Securitate* to work alongside the USLA forces. The order was accompanied by a ban, issued by the ministry, on the holding of wedding receptions and parties in restaurants to prevent the gathering of people in groups. In an interview given by Silviu Brucan and Nicolae Militaru on 23 August 1990 it was revealed that the special security force for Bucharest numbered 600 men and was placed under the command of Col. Gheorghe Goran, the head of the Bucharest DSS.[71] To these elite forces must be added the 484 men, commanded by Maj. Gen. Marin Neagoe, who constituted the Presidential Protection Group (Fifth Directorate). There were small units of USLA troops based at the provincial airports. The men of the Presidential Protection Group, the Bucharest security force and USLA were all trained in the techniques of urban warfare and were equipped with modern automatic weapons with infrared sights. It was they who, Brucan alleged, took up positions in accordance with a contingency plan drawn up in 1985 to combat a popular rising around strategic buildings such as the TV and radio stations, the Ministry of Defence and the Central Committee building, and on the evening of 22 December1989 made a concerted sniper attack on the army and the population in the centre of Bucharest and at the TV station which began at 7 p.m. Some of these officers held two identity cards and passports, and keys to two flats stocked with food in freezers and civilian and military clothes. These specialist security units supplemented the Ministry of the Interior troops, known as *trupele de securitate*, who at the time of the revolution numbered 23,370 officers and men. Among the latter were the 2,000 officer cadets of Ministry of the Interior Military Academy at Băneasa on the outskirts of Bucharest, commanded by Lt. Gen. Nicolae Andruţă Ceauşescu.

One final aspect of the Securitate's activity deserves mention—its control of Romanian exports. Light was shed upon this by the Romanian press after the Romanian revolution, with the focus being placed on the activity of the foreign trade company Dunărea which was in direct subordination to the Centre for Foreign Intelligence (CIE) of the *Securitate*.[72] The relationship of the *Dunărea* sales to those of arms made through the intermediary of Marin Ceauşescu, one of the president's brothers, who was head of the Romanian Foreign Trade Mission in Vienna, has not been satisfactorily established (Marin committed suicide on 28 December 1989). The proceeds of these sales are reported to have been placed in a secret Swiss account.[73] Ceauşescu saw arms sales as a means of paying off Romania's debts to Western banks. His best customer was Egypt. After Cairo's decision to break its close military links with the Soviet Union in the mid-1970s, Ceauşescu stepped in to supply spare parts for Egypt's Soviet-made tanks and artillery. Romania also supplied reconditioned equipment to Iraq during the Iran-Iraq war, thus offsetting the poor performance of its civilian industrial exports by earning hard currency through the export of cheap, unsophisticated weapons. The success of this strategy made Romania in 1987 the second largest exporter of arms in the Warsaw Pact after the Soviet Union. Using his links with Cairo Ceauşescu was alleged by the West German weekly *Der Spiegel* in an issue published at the beginning of May 1989 to have obtained the technology for the production of a medium-range missile system which a firm in Munich had supplied to Argentina. It was passed from Argentina to Egypt and Iraq and on payment of $200 million to Cairo it was transferred to Romania.

Equally intriguing was the allegation, made in an article in the *Washington Post*, that Marin Ceauşescu and his brother Ilie, first deputy defence minister, supplied the United States with advanced Soviet military technology during the 1980s. As part of a wider intelligence drive directed by the CIA into the upper echelons of East European defence ministries, the US government is said to have paid more than $40 million to Romania through foreign intermediaries in the decade since the relationship with the two Ceauşescu brothers began in 1979. According to CIA sources, about 20 per cent of the money was deposited in Swiss bank accounts controlled by the Ceauşescu family. Although Nicolae Ceauşescu does not appear to have been personally involved, it is inconceivable that he did not know about the operation. Among the weapons obtained by the CIA in this way through Romania were the latest version of the *Shilka*, a sophisticated Soviet anti-aircraft mobile rocket launcher that had been modified by the Romanians, and radar systems used in identifying targets and directing the fire of Soviet anti-aircraft weapons.[74]

A further source of hard currency for the *Securitate* was the commission charged by the directors of various Romanian-controlled companies such as *Crescent, Terra, Delta, Trawe* and *Carpaţi* from foreign companies for the conclusion of contracts. These payments were handled by a special agency within the DIE/CIE known as *Departamentul Operaţiuni Speciale Valutare* (OVS) 'special hard currency actions') which was staffed by between 15 and 20 officers. A company called *Argus* was used as a screen for the OVS and paid the salaries of the employees of these foreign trade companies.[75] The *Carpaţi* company was an exception; it was part of the *Carpaţi* enterprise which included the National Tourist Office with the same name and was controlled by the political and administrative section of the Romanian Communist Party. All Romanian 'special hard currency dealings' with socialist bloc countries were channelled through *Carpaţi* to the coffers of the Party and in this respect such a procedure followed a practice inherited from the Soviets. But similar payments of a Western provenance were handled by the *Securitate*.[76]

The degree of Ceauşescu's intrusion into the lives of individuals was most potently illustrated by measures of family planning.[77] Abortion on demand had been legalized in 1957 and became the principal means of family planning. When the 1966 birth rate dropped to 14 per thousand people (much the same as in Britain), thereby heralding a decline in the workforce and a threat to the pace of the country's industrialization, the law was adjusted to allow abortion only to women over 40, mothers of four or more children, victims of rape and incest, and in cases of possible foetal abnormality. After the 1966 law went into effect, the abortion-related mortality rate among Romanian women increased to a level ten times that of any other European country. Since contraceptives, while not illegal, were virtually unobtainable, many women used abortion as the principal method of birth control and were forced to obtain it illegally. An indication of Ceauşescu's insensitivity over the issue was his insistence that coercive measures against doctors and others who carried out clandestine abortions be enforced. Not only were those who carried out illegal abortions jailed but, in the case of doctors, their licence to practise their licence was withdrawn.[78]

From a peak in 1969 of twenty-one per 1,000 people, the birth rate showed an annual decline thereafter, due both to the increase in the number of illegal abortions and the fall in living standards in the late 1970s. Figures for 1981 showing the birth rate at six per 1,000 people led Ceauşescu to insist that steps be taken to reverse this trend. Prime Minister Constantin Dăscalescu took up this theme in a speech in September 1983. In March 1984, Ceauşescu issued a summons before a gathering of National Women's Councils in Bucharest to "breed, comrade women, it is your patriotic duty".[79] At the same time, he issued one of his notorious unpublished orders that women of childbearing age were to be subjected to compulsory gynaecological examination to check that they were not breaking the law by using contraceptive devices. A lady doctor told this author that she was required to conduct monthly examinations of factory women in Bucharest, to ask each one of them if she was pregnant and if not, why not. In fact, she consistently falsified records in the patients' favour and sold contraceptive pills to them which she had obtained from other East European countries.

To bolster the drive to increase the birth rate, Ceauşescu introduced punitive additional taxation for all childless couples over 25. In 1986, he raised the minimum age for women to be allowed an abortion from 40 to 45 and lowered the age at which women could marry from 16 to 15. Although the birth rate did rise between 1986 and 1988, it fell again in 1989 to 16 per 1,000. But the measures led to tragedy. There was a dramatic increase in backstreet and self-induced abortions, especially among young working women, despite the harsh penalties given to those involved in them. Doctors risked fines and imprisonment if they gave medical help without legal authorization when self-induced abortions went wrong and the delays in securing this often led to deaths. *Securitate* officers were assigned to every maternity hospital to ensure that the provisions of the abortion law were strictly observed, although in some cases they turned a blind eye. One of this author's most harrowing experiences of Romania was the sight in the bathroom of a Bucharest hospital in December 1989 of a pile of dead foetuses. The figures for deaths among Romanian women resulting from the anti-abortion law are the single most powerful indictment of the inhumanity of Ceauşescu's regime. In the 23 years of its enforcement, the law is estimated to have caused the death of over 10,000 women from unsafe abortions. The majority died from post-abortion haemorrhage and blood poisoning.[80] The black irony of this tragedy is that it took place in a country whose 'First Lady', Elena Ceauşescu, was lauded in its media as the 'Woman-Mother' in a land with a "wondrous cult of Women-Mothers".[81]

Of the thousands of exhortations made by Ceauşescu to the Romanian people none was seized upon with more alacrity by the international media than his call that "we must radically reduce the number of villages from about 13,000 at present to 5,000 to 6,000 at most", made in an address to the National Conference of the Presidents of People's Councils on 3 March 1988.[82] His 'systematization plan', as it was dubbed, was interpreted by the Western media as a project to physically demolish seven to eight thousand villages. Coming at a time when conservation and concern for the environment had been promoted to the top of the Western political agenda, Ceauşescu's plan sent shock waves around the capitals of Europe and North America. Public awareness in the West of Ceauşescu's disregard for Romania's architectural heritage had been aroused by reports which trickled out in the early 1980s of his razing of the centre of Bucharest to make way for a new administrative complex of gargantuan proportions. The centrepiece of this project was a presidential palace, whose original name 'The House of the People' assumed Orwellian overtones since some 40,000 hapless citizens were forcibly evicted from their homes to make way for its construction. As the project proceeded, the palace was rechristened 'The House of the Republic' since around it were to be concentrated new ministry and other public buildings.[83]

The impetus for this redevelopment came from the earthquake of March 1977. Ceauşescu was shaken by the collapse of several buildings in the centre of Bucharest and urged his planners to look for an area of the city that would be more resistant to tremors where a new administrative centre could be built. "The idea of constructing a centre for the capital of course belongs to Comrade Ceauşescu", stated Petre Vraciu, an architect at the planning department in Bucharest.[84] Ceauşescu's conception of the centre was as the core of a vast redevelopment of the capital which was to be symbolic of his political achievements as a whole. "I am looking for a symbolic representation of the two decades of enlightenment we have just lived through; I need something grand, something very grand, which reflects what we have already achieved", he was reported to have said.[85] Just as centralization was the hallmark of Ceauşescu's rule, so the instruments of his power were to be concentrated in one area: alongside the House of the Republic was to be erected a House of Science and Technology, the brainwave of the pseudo-qualified "scientist of world renown" Elena, the Ministry of the Interior, the State Archives and a National Library.

Because of their proximity to the city centre and their location on higher ground—thus making them safer from the effects of an earthquake—the Uranus, Antim and Rahova quarters of the city were the districts chosen for the site of the administrative centre, but at the same time they were the oldest areas of the city with a concentration of historical monuments, principally monastic buildings and churches, some of them more than three hundred years old. The residential parts of these districts contained some of the capital's most elegant houses, ranging from single and two-storey family houses with large courtyards to three or four-storey buildings designed by celebrated architects such as Ion Mincu and Horia Creangă. For the design of the House of the People Ceauşescu held a competition which was won by Anca Petrescu, a 25-year-old straight out of architecture school. It was she who conceived the second largest public building in the world after the Pentagon, one 86 metres high with facades 276 metres long covering an area of 6.3 hectares. Its principal facade would look out over a wide, straight, triumphal boulevard, flanked by massive apartment blocks for the favoured of the regime, which exceeded the length of the Champs-Élysées. Adjacent to the boulevard, christened the Victory of Socialism, and to the House of the Republic, were the sites of the various ministries and public buildings. Petrescu's design required the destruction of the entire district of Uranus and much of the Rahova and Antim quarters.

Little attempt was made by Petrescu to achieve a balance between these buildings of historical interest in the area and the new development. Ceauşescu simply took the plan, added a few embellishments of his own, and presented it to the various Party and state bodies under the title of *indicaţii* (suggestions), the usual euphemism for the president's dictates. The funding for the plan, known officially as *Ansamblul Bulevardul Victoria Socialismului* (The Boulevard of the Victory of Socialism Complex), was granted by a presidential decree issued on 29 December 1981, and as the programme for development expanded to include new areas adjacent to the Uranus district, a second decree was enacted on 5 September 1984 for further monies to be provided. As Petrescu herself confided after Ceauşescu's overthrow, the president was obsessed with the project and his appetite for reconstruction grew with its progression. Nicolae and Elena visited the site every Saturday morning, "very formal, very businesslike, never praising anyone. He had more regard for the workers than for the architects, shaking hands with craftsmen, talking informally to the foremen".[86] But he had difficulty in making up his mind about matters of detail; first Petrescu had to build to full-scale *papier-maché* models of columns or window for Ceauşescu to appreciate the effect of changes he was recommending, and even then he constantly changed his mind. Since the president was unable to master problems of perspective and scale, the project grew and the area around it expanded. As a consequence, the House of the People "began to look smaller, so now he wanted it bigger".[87]

This entailed even further demolition. Thousands of family dwellings and a number of churches were completely razed to the ground before the international outcry forced Ceauşescu to agree to the relocation of one or two churches by moving them on huge wooden rollers. Initial reaction in Romania to the Bucharest and other urban redevelopment plans was confined to expressions of concern in professional circles about their impact in several cities upon buildings of historical interest. A special meeting was held from 25 to 27 May 1979 at the Transylvanian Museum of History in Cluj on 'Urban Renovation and Contemporary Problems' at which 24 architects and historians from Bucharest, Cluj, Piteşti, Sibiu and Timişoara stressed the need for an inventory of historical buildings to be drawn up so that they could be protected. In December of the same year a similar event was held in Bucharest whose proceedings were published.[88] A series of similar events, designed to generate discussion about the plans for Bucharest's redevelopment, followed. Photographic exhibitions of Bucharest in the interwar period were held in the summer of 1982 and when the large-scale demolition of the Uranus quarter began in 1984, a special edition of the review *Arhitectura* devoted to the architectural heritage of the area was published.[89] With one exception all the buildings in the district were demolished: villas, one and two-storey houses, small blocks of flats and public buildings. Only the sixteenth-century Mihai Vodă church and bell tower survived, being moved 225 metres in 1985 to be hemmed in by new tall blocks of flats. In 1984, five Orthodox churches were razed, in the following year three others, in 1986 three more and a synagogue, and in 1986 six churches were demolished. Several more were moved and screened off entirely by new buildings.[90] The most notorious target for demolition was the Văcăreşti monastery, built in the eighteenth century and situated on the outskirts of the capital. It was to make way for the construction of a new Palace of Justice!

No protest was heard from the senior Orthodox clergy. By contrast, on 14 December 1984 a letter signed by three members of the Central State Commission for National Cultural Patrimony, Professor Grigore Ionescu, an architect, Dr Răzvan Theodorescu, an art historian, and Professor Dinu Giurescu, a historian of Romanian culture, was sent to the press and propaganda section of the Party Central Committee calling for a halt to the demolition of the Văcăreşti monastery. Although the monastery and its associated buildings had been used as a prison between 1864 and 1970, restoration work on its internal decoration, which included paintings of saints in the Byzantine style, had begun in 1974. The same letter was sent a month later with the addition of four other signatures, those of archaeologists Professor Dionisie Pippidi and Dr Radu Popa, the art historian Dr Vasile Drăguţ, and the architect Dr Aurelian Triscu. A third letter, signed by Grigore Ionescu, Dinu Giurescu, R. Theodorescu, V. Drăguţ and Virgil Cândea, head of the *România* association, the propaganda body directed at émigrés, was sent on 22 October 1985.[91] All were to no avail. Other historical monuments destroyed were the nineteenth century Brâncovenesc hospital, the Sfânta Vineri church (which had a large congregation) and, on a smaller scale, the house of Nicolae Iorga (1871–1940), the distinguished Romanian historian and former prime minister, located at 6 Boulevard Ilie Pintilie. The demolition had taken place on 2 July 1986, despite the fact that the mayor's office in Bucharest and the Institute of History bearing Iorga's name had completed formalities to have the house moved some 50 metres to avoid demolition. Andrei Pippidi, Iorga's grandson, sent a letter of protest to several prominent cultural journals, including *România Literară, Luceafărul* and *Contemporanul,* but the text was never published. So that his voice could be heard, Pippidi entrusted the letter to this author who was visiting Bucharest to be passed on to Vlad Georgescu, director of the Romanian section of Radio Free Europe, and it was duly broadcast in October 1986. "The time comes when one learns to express aloud a protest thought out for a long time but never before uttered. The blind mutilation of our city has to be halted", Pippidi wrote.[92] In a sad dereliction of moral leadership, the Orthodox Church not only failed to give its support to these initiatives, but even tried to stifle protest. A memorandum submitted by Dinu Giurescu to the Council of the Archbishopric of Bucharest on 8 December 1985 calling upon it to support his request for a cessation of church demolition was rejected.[93]

If internal protest went unheeded, a few Romanian architects tried to arouse international concern. One, Ştefan Gane, set up an International Association for the Protection of Historical Monuments and Sites in Romania on 1 March 1985 in Paris with the aim of enlisting the support of government and non-government agencies about the demolition of central Bucharest. Its attempt to get UNESCO to intervene with the Romanian government initially fell on deaf ears although the new director general did react positively in the summer of 1987. Some scholars have argued that only after Gorbachev's policies highlighted Ceauşescu's 'old-fashioned Stalinism' did the Western media put the Romanian president's dictates, and the human suffering they entailed, under the microscope. Rural systematization and the destruction of Bucharest were seen as two examples of a catalogue of aberrations which included a ban on birth control and reductions in domestic heating and food supplies. This is only partially true. As far as the major demolition in Bucharest was concerned, it only began a few months before Gorbachev's accession to power in March 1985 and therefore it was inevitable that more extensive press coverage should be commensurate with the pace of destruction. An analysis of press coverage of Romanian affairs in Britain, West Germany, France, and the United States records a surge in articles on the demolition in 1985 which one suspects was prompted by the striking visual impact which this graphic illustration of Ceauşescu's megalomania offered.[94] The spotlight of media attention was redirected on Romania at the time of the workers' demonstrations in Braşov in November 1987 and it was in this ambience of heightened interest in the internal situation in the country that Ceauşescu announced in March 1988 his renewal of the drive for systematization. Coupled with revelations about the demolition in Bucharest of churches engulfed by an ever-expanding drive to extend the area of the presidential complex, the systematization plan led environmental groups in the West to coordinate both national and international actions of protests. The most effective in terms of attracting media attention, and in providing moral support to the Romanian people, was *Opération Villages Roumains.*

This movement recommended that European villages 'adopt' Romanian ones. Tens of thousands of letters addressed to the mayors of Romanian villages proposing 'adoption' were sent from European communities to Romania as the numbers of adoptive villages grew: by the beginning of May 1989, 231 communes in Belgium, 95 in France and 42 in Switzerland had adopted Romanian villages. The British campaign, mounted in June with the backing of HRH The Prince of Wales, who in an unprecedented political intervention by a member of the royal family had condemned the systematization programme in a speech delivered on 27 April 1989, had secured 52 adoptions by September.[95] As soon as a village in the West adopted a Romanian one the news was broadcast by the Romanian services of the BBC and Radio Free Europe and visitors returning from Romania reported the gratitude expressed to them by Romanians for the outside support. In the autumn of 1989, children throughout Belgium built 250,000 small paper houses as a symbolical present to the children of Romania and exhibited them in the village of Floreffe. One year later the exhibition occupied the vast floor of the 'House of the Republic', Ceauşescu's former 'House of the People'.

Through his plans for systematization Ceauşescu succeeded in imprinting Romania upon the consciousness of Europe for only the second time in his career. The first occasion had been his denunciation on 21 August 1968 of the Warsaw Pact invasion of Czechoslovakia. But whereas then he won the admiration of Europe and the rest of the world for his courageous defiance of the Soviet Union, his claim in 1989 was one of notoriety. Ceauşescu became the ogre of Europe. The international media probed deeper into the character of his repressive regime and the Romanian Foreign Ministry was instructed in May 1989 to counter the *Opération Villages Roumains* campaign with the claim that the policy of systematization was to be applied more slowly. In fact, Ceauşescu's plans continued to be carried out to the letter. On 24 May, a large number of private houses were demolished in the villages of Otopeni, Dimieni and Odăile to the north of Bucharest and their rubble taken in 200 dump trucks and deposited in two large pits.[96] The dislodged population of the three villages were rehoused in four-storey apartment blocks in Otopeni. In the case of Buda and Odoreanu, in the county of Giurgiu, these were evacuated to make way for a large reservoir being constructed as part of the Bucharest-Danube Canal.

Whether the international campaign eventually led Ceauşescu to temper his policy of bulldozing homes in the summer and autumn of 1989, as some foreign diplomats alleged, is an open question, but at least we have no evidence that it was accelerated, as was the case with the works to complete the presidential complex in the centre of Bucharest. What the campaign did achieve was to let the Romanian people know that their villages would not, as one campaigner has written, borrowing a line from the poet Dylan Thomas, "go silent into that dark night", forgotten by the rest of Europe.[97] What no one associated with the campaign could have foreseen was that the links established between communities throughout Europe and the villages in Romania provided the perfect springboard for humanitarian aid to be channelled to an identifiable destination after Ceauşescu's overthrow. The full enormity of the dictator's rule and the suffering it caused prompted adoptive communities in Europe to target their own Romanian villages as recipients of food, clothing, medicines and practical aid. Hospitals and children's homes in the area became the special focus of attention. Thousands of ordinary European citizens travelled overland in convoys to their own adopted village with aid supplies and having assessed the needs of the Romanian community, made return visits.[98]

Systematization under Ceauşescu was not just a planning process; it was an attempt at social engineering. It threatened to destroy traditional skills, a way of life linked with the land, and the individuality of the village and its inhabitants. Ceauşescu's obstinacy procured a success, in his terms, for his plan but its execution trampled on the moral being of his citizens. The plan, like so many of his other infamous edicts, such as the abortion decree, eventually provoked a reaction in that moral being which led to the dictator's downfall. Few localities in Romania do not show the mark of systematization; the suffering that the plan caused is less easy to identify.

It is tempting, against this background of the regime's degeneration to overlook Ceauşescu's efforts to reduce Cold War tensions. In this regard, he was consistent in his search for attenuating the arms race, offering his own proposals for dialogue on disarmament between the Warsaw Pact and NATO. In the pursuit of this strategy, Ceauşescu found himself once again, at the end of 1978, at variance with the other members of the pact, this time at the Moscow meeting of the Political Consultative Committee held on 22–23 November, and over a proposal, amongst other things, to increase military expenditure.[99] Only a few days before the Moscow meeting, Marshal Kulikov, the Commander-in-Chief of the Warsaw Pact Armed Forces (WPAF), travelled to Bucharest with drafts of the documents to be discussed and agreed to during the meeting. Included in the documents was a resolution approving the report of the Commander-in-Chief and a memorandum of principles to be inserted in the WPAF War Statute. The draft resolution on the report of the Commander-in-Chief claimed that the preparations for defending Western Europe by NATO at that time were "increasing the risks posed for the peace and security of all countries within the socialist community". In light of this, the resolution called for an acceleration of the military preparedness of the armed forces of the member states, increased procurement and the target of between 70 and 100 per cent interoperability of the main categories of weaponry for all the allied armies.

Ceauşescu rejected this analysis of the situation in Europe at the Politburo meeting of 20 November 1978 and the proposal to increase military expenditure. He argued for a minimum five per cent reduction in troops and expenditure, and for the withdrawal of "some military units deployed on the territories of other states". In respect of the WPAF War Statute, Ceauşescu stated that "the principles governing this document must be negotiated, and not established beforehand".[100] Ceauşescu deployed these same arguments at the Moscow meeting of the PCC. Romanian opposition was summed up in the Polish assessment of the meeting. "Overall", the Polish memorandum stated,

> the Moscow meeting confirmed that Romania's stance regarding many international questions has undergone a further, negative evolution; the existing divisions are deepening. Romania is conducting ever more clearly a foreign

> policy contrary to the principles of socialist internationalism. [...] Comrade Ceaușescu's refusal to sign the resolution on military matters [...] will lead to the further weakening of Romania's ties to the Warsaw Treaty's military structure.[101]

Other parts of the Final Declaration were also contested by the Romanian delegation, including a condemnation of the Camp David accords, and support for Vietnam and China's foreign policy.[102] In 1980, the WPAF War Statute was agreed by all members of the pact—except Romania.

Ceaușescu's insistence on "no external involvement in the domestic affairs of others", a constant slogan displayed on banners at his public engagements in Romania, was repeated during the Polish crisis of 1980. At the meeting of the pact's Political Consultative Committee in Moscow on 5 December, Leonid Brezhnev declared that the gathering demonstrated that "we all back the Polish leadership in its efforts to overcome the crisis which appeared in this country". But, he warned, "if the situation in Poland does not stabilize... much to our regret all of the measures taken to help Poland of which we spoke about before [i.e. economic assistance] will not yield the desired results".[103] Ceaușescu was more guarded. He spoke of the delicate problems facing the Polish government and argued that they should be addressed by the Poles themselves. In his view, the most important requirement before the Polish Party

> should be to regain the trust of the working class, of the popular masses, to organize them and, together with the working class, to act against the antisocialist and counterrevolutionary forces, using all of the means at the disposal of the socialist state'.[104]

The Polish crisis was a major item on the agenda of the meeting of the Committee of Defence Ministers of the Warsaw Pact, held in Warsaw on 2–4 December 1981. The majority of ministers argued that the problem had only one solution: military intervention. The Romanian defence minister, Constantin Olteanu, with the backing of his Hungarian counterpart, Lajos Czinege, was opposed to such action: "What is happening in Poland is a strictly a domestic problem of this state... Romania is not in favour of military intervention there".[105] The Romanian position on foreign military intervention in Poland was discussed at the meeting of the Romanian Politburo of 13 December 1981. Ceaușescu reported that:

> The Soviets wanted to introduce, in the general communiqué of this Meeting [of the Committee of Warsaw Pact Defence Ministers] an appreciation [of the situation in] Poland, asserting that, since the security of socialist countries was in fact endangered, it was necessary to intervene [in Poland] so that security could be guaranteed. In fact, they wanted the intervention to be approved. Naturally, the other delegates agreed.
> We were against [the intervention], and the Hungarians said they had to ask what the opinion of their authorities at home was on that score.

> It goes without saying that we told them we did not accept [the introduction of this clause] in the communiqué, and it was not accepted. They wanted then to issue a separate communiqué. The Hungarians then said that if the Romanian comrades did not sign as well, they would not sign.[106]

In the face of the severe austerity measures that Ceauşescu introduced in the early 1980s in order to pay off the country's foreign debt, many Romanians began to ask whether autonomy was worth the price. The question was put even more frequently after Mikhail Gorbachev's accession to the Soviet leadership in March 1985.[107]

Gorbachev's summit meeting with President Ronald Reagan in Reykjavik on 11–12 October 1986 and their attempt to agree on the complete elimination of nuclear weapons vindicated Ceauşescu's calls in this regard and for the mutual reduction of conventional forces and military spending within NATO and the Warsaw Pact. On the heels of the summit seven Warsaw Pact foreign ministers met in Bucharest on 16 October. Despite Ceauşescu's efforts to build on the summit, he was reported by the Romanian media as having failed to convince Warsaw Pact countries to unilaterally reduce their stockpiles of weapons. The Party newspaper *Scânteia* quoted the Romanian leader as telling representatives of the Soviet bloc countries, "I think it would be very important that our countries... should pass, even unilaterally each of them, a certain reduction of arms".[108] According to the *Agerpres* news agency, Ceauşescu told the seven Warsaw Pact foreign ministers that reducing their stockpiles of arms would not affect their security, "but it will exert a powerful influence on all states in Europe and the world over". "I know that an agreement was not reached in the talks you had here", he was quoted as saying. "However, I hope that the party and state leadership of every country will analyze again the problems and will reach adequate decisions." The Romanian proposal was apparently submitted during the conference but rejected. In his speech, Ceauşescu said that he favoured a separate agreement on reducing missiles in Europe, irrespective of whether the two superpowers come to terms on the US space-based missile defence system (or 'Star Wars'). Romania was "fully backing all the Soviet Union's proposals... but not necessarily conditioned on the global settlement of all the (arms) issues simultaneously". He went on to state, "In our opinion we must act for the settlement... of all problems in stages—and one of these stages would be the solving of the problem of removing missiles from Europe".[109]

By the time Gorbachev visited Romania in May 1987, a remarkable 180-degree turn had occurred in Romanians' perception of the Soviet Union and its relationship to Romania.[110] This change in attitude hinged on the evolution of Ceauşescu himself: if in 1965 Ceauşescu presented a young, dynamic face of Communism compared with the ageing, reactionary Brezhnev, now, 22 years later, it was Gorbachev who had assumed Ceauşescu's mantle and the latter that of Brezhnev. In a speech broadcast live during his visit to Bucharest on 26 May, Gorbachev presented to the Romanian public his concepts of *glasnost* ('openness') and *perestroika* ('restructuring')—and in so doing offered implicit criticism of Ceauşescu's resistance to reform.

Ceauşescu's barely concealed irritation with Gorbachev's policies was evident in his speech at the Meeting of Warsaw Pact leaders of 29 May:

> I am now trying to raise, in a nutshell, the following matter. I discussed it with Comrade Gorbachev, but I would like to raise it before you as well. This matter concerns the relationships or, more to the point, the situation in the Communist and workers' movement. It goes without saying that we do not have the time to discuss this matter here, but we are of the opinion that we shall have to discuss it at a special meeting.[111]

Ceauşescu reiterated his commitment to rigid central economic planning and insisted that market forces were incompatible with Communist society. In his address to the Romanian Party Conference on 14 December, Ceauşescu argued that he had already applied similar measures in Romania to those advocated by the reformist Gorbachev. Thus *Scânteia*, in its report of the Nineteenth Soviet Party Conference in 1988, restricted coverage of Gorbachev's speech there to those measures which had already been taken in Romania, thereby suggesting that the Soviet leader was following Ceauşescu's example. Furthermore, Gorbachev's admission that the Soviet Union had taken important decisions without "proper consultation with friends" gave Ceauşescu a justification for neither applying *perestroika* nor *glasnost*.[112]

The enthusiasm for reform amongst Romanians could be seen in the queues that formed in July 1988 in front of the *Aeroflot* offices in Bucharest as Romanians were admitted five at a time not to purchase airline tickets, but to pick up free copies in Romanian of the Soviet leader's report to the nineteenth conference of the Soviet Communist Party, coverage of which had been restricted in the Romanian media to those measures which had already been taken in Romania. Ceauşescu, the arch-nationalist, had succeeded in making Romanians look to the Soviet Union for hope.

Soviet concerns over the rapidly changing situation in the Soviet bloc were reflected in a February 1989 report by the Bogomolov Commission for Alexander Yakovlev, key foreign policy advisor to Gorbachev. It predicted the following scenarios for Romania:

1. Favourable scenario: Changes take place in the leadership of the country. As a result, N. Ceauşescu is replaced by reasonable politicians capable of understanding and putting into practice the ideas of radical reforms and a renewal of socialism. There are favourable preconditions in Romania for the use of market relations, a relatively dynamic restructuring and modernization of the economy with a real liberation of economic initiative and the creation of a multi-sector competitive economy.
2. Middle-deadlock scenario: The present leadership of the country or continuity of policy remains. If the resources that are freed as the external debt gets paid off are used to reduce social tension, then it is possible to maintain general political stability for quite a while, while maintaining the political prob-

> lems of the country and its further lagging behind in scientific and technical progress. If, however, the leadership chooses to ignore the task of improving the living standards of the population and diverts the liberated resources for the realization of new ambitious projects, then one cannot exclude a social explosion. In case the processes of renewal in other socialist countries by that time have not proven the feasibility of the policy of reform, there could be the danger of a decisive shift of the country in the direction of the West (including its exit from the Warsaw Pact) [as the] population has become disenchanted with socialist values and was traditionally brought up in the spirit of community with the Latin [*romanskiy*] world. Financial and material support from the West, highly probable if there are real changes, may prove to be very effective for a country possessing a good deal of natural and economic resources.
>
> Since the regime still has not exhausted its resources and has recently been accumulating the experience of combined repressive measures and social manoeuvring to maintain social stability, the second scenario seems to be more likely. In its favour is a relatively low level of national self-consciousness and the absence of organized opposition in Romania. At the same time, an obvious irrationality of the policy of the current leadership produces growing dissatisfaction not only on the grass-roots level, but even among the ruling elite [*verkhushka*]. Therefore, a possibility of some kind of changes "from the top" cannot be excluded.[113]

How fossilized Ceauşescu had become is highlighted by his distrust of technical innovation. Apart from the limited development and production of Romanian computers, the technological revolution of the 1980s bypassed the country. Romanians were denied access to information while the personal computer, the fax machine and the photocopier were considered subversive and kept under tight control. Use of a photocopier required the registration of the user's ID and the permission of the host institution. In a meeting of the Defence Council of 31 May 1989, Ceauşescu criticized the 'misguided' use of electronics in the Romanian defence industry, claiming that old technology was more reliable:

> There is no point in our equipping [the army] and spending money on materials which deteriorate. The second thing in this respect is the issue of electronics. It seems to me that here, too, we exaggerate the introduction of electronics...Let us leave the equipment that we have alone!...
> The classical equipment we have is better, more reliable, and gives better results.[114]

Ceauşescu, the champion of Czechoslovak independence in 1968, had come full circle by 1989.[115] His conversion to the 'Brezhnev doctrine', and his aversion to *perestroika* and *glasnost* widened the gulf between him and Gorbachev. In private, Gorbachev made no secret of his distaste for Ceauşescu, who he called "the Romanian dictator", and when the two men met for drinks at Ceauşescu's residence during a Warsaw Pact gathering in Bucharest in July 1989, the atmosphere was icy. According to Gorbachev's translator, Ceslav Ciobanu, the two leaders traded barbs and Raisa Gorbachev had to intervene to calm spirits.[116] Gorbachev, at the meeting of the Consultative Political Committee of the pact held in Bucharest on 7–8 July, spoke of reforming the alliance; he underlined the need "to respect the independence of fraternal parties" and ruled out "the use of force or the threat of force". For his part, Ceauşescu expressed his concern about events in Poland and about the fact that the Polish Party was losing its grip on the situation.[117] At the same meeting of the CPC he called upon

> the socialist state members of the Warsaw Pact and all socialist countries to analyse and solve together the present problems of socialist construction, the means to better collaborate in preparation for crisis and ensuring the economic and social development of all peoples on the path of socialism.[118]

His worries increased when representatives of Solidarity entered the government. On 19 August, what the Romanian embassy in Warsaw termed

> the considerations of the party and state leadership of the Socialist Republic of Romania, respectively those of comrade Nicolae Ceauşescu, general secretary of the Romanian Communist Party and president of the Socialist Republic of Romania ....in connection with the present situation in Poland and the formation of the government of the Polish People's Republic

were relayed to the Polish ambassador in Bucharest and a similar message sent to the Hungarian Party.[119] The replies received from both Warsaw and Budapest suggest that Ceauşescu had proposed joint action by the Warsaw Pact "using all means to prevent the elimination of socialism in Poland".[120] Both governments disputed Ceauşescu's reading of events in Poland and firmly rejected his alleged proposal of Pact intervention.

The Polish reply pointed to the common position adopted at the Warsaw Pact meeting in Bucharest in July, one agreed in the final communiqué by Romania, in which it was stated that "there is no universal model of socialism and no one has a monopoly of the truth".[121] There was consternation in both Warsaw and Budapest at the new position taken by Bucharest, one which contradicted Romania's traditional stance within the Pact. In the Hungarian reply this about-turn was emphasized:

> The Romanian point of view cannot be understood if we bear in mind, in particular, the systematic public promotion by Romania of the principles of non-interference in the internal affairs, the sovereignty, [and] the relations between the socialist countries. The present Romanian position is in total contradiction to the view expressed by the above principles, which provided the basis upon which, for example, Romania established her policy in 1968 regarding the events in Czechoslovakia.[122]

What form this 'intervention' should take was not made clear, but on the basis of the evidence currently available it is hazardous to suggest that Ceauşescu was calling for military intervention.[123] The recently published report of the meeting between Ceauşescu and the Soviet ambassador to Bucharest Evghenie Mihailovic Tjazelnikov sheds some light. Invited by the Romanian leader to his villa at Snagov, some 20 miles north of Bucharest, at 11 p.m. on 19 August 1989, and in the presence of Romanian Foreign Minister Ioan Totu, Tjazelnikov was asked by Ceauşescu to transmit to Gorbachev his appeal for 'urgent measures' to be taken to prevent "he liquidation of socialism" in Poland. Ceauşescu claimed that the entry of Solidarity into the Polish government "played into the hands of the United States and NATO" and that therefore he requested Gorbachev to see his way to meeting him on the following day. The reply came from the Soviet Politburo, transmitted by Eduard Shevardnadze to his counterpart Totu, in which it considered the best course to be to allow the Polish Workers' Party to resolve the situation itself.[124] The diary entry of Tjazhelnikov on his meeting with Ceauşescu[125] and the Soviet Politburo resolution regarding the appeal of the Romanian leader[126] refer not to military intervention, but to the convocation of an urgent meeting of the pact leaders to discuss common action over Poland.[127]

Ceauşescu's irritation with the policies of *glasnost* and *perestroika* can be detected in a report by A. Iakovlev dated 2 October 1989 for the Central Committee of the CPSU on the meeting in Varna on 26–28 September 1989 of the Party Secretaries of the Socialist countries in which he noted that "the Romanians left their formulation until the last minute, omitting mention of *perestroika*". He commented: "All of this brings into question the necessity of continuing the practice of issuing communiqués on this type of meeting".[128] The Romanian leader's disapproval with Gorbachev's reforms left an echo in his address to the Fourteenth RCP Congress on 20 November 1989.[129] In the process of reform concessions had been made, he argued, to the 'international class enemy' (capitalism) which had led to the 'de-ideologization' of international relations and the emergence of a new 'international imperialism.' These concessions were similar to those made by the Soviet Union to Germany in the Molotov-Ribbentrop Pact of August 1939 to which Ceauşescu alluded without mentioning it by name:

> One must never forget the lessons of history and the fact that Hitlerite Germany was encouraged to unleash World War II by the policy of concessions to Nazi Germany...We must never forget that the pact between Hitlerite Germany and the Soviet Union did not eliminate the threat [of war]... Romania believes, therefore, that one must move to adopt [all] necessary measures for the solution of all the problems that are still pending. Primarily, it is necessary to adopt a clear and unequivocal position condemning and annulling all accords with Hitlerite Germany by drawing practical conclusions for cancelling the consequences of all these pacts and diktats.[130]

In calling for the reversal of the consequences of these pacts Ceauşescu was, in fact, arguing for the return of Bessarabia to Romania. The Soviet reaction was, in the words of a TASS commentator, that "no serious or responsible politician" could raise the issue of the postwar borders, "including the Soviet border with Romania".[131]

Yet behind Ceauşescu's obvious attempt to appeal once again to Romanian nationalist sentiment there lay an anxiety about possible Soviet intervention in Romania's internal affairs. In a speech to the heads of the North and South American delegations Ceauşescu referred to the Molotov-Ribbentrop Pact by name and expressed fear of a new agreement between the United States and the Soviet Union "to the detriment of other peoples". The forthcoming Malta summit between President Bush and General Secretary Gorbachev was seen, therefore, by Ceauşescu as a second Molotov-Ribbentrop Pact at the hands of which Romania would again suffer for, in his own self-centred view of international affairs, the two superpowers had nothing better to do than to plot his own downfall. As Michael Shafir concluded, Ceauşescu's remarks were meant as a warning to Gorbachev not to interfere in Romania and had been strengthened by the ending of a Romanian news blackout on the growth of the nationalist movement in the Moldavian SSR only a few days earlier.[132]

The same tension was evident from the minutes of the meeting between the two leaders in the Kremlin on 4 December 1989. The economic penalties exacted by the Soviet Union upon Ceauşescu for his autonomous policies were recognized by the Romanian leader, in particular the reduction in oil and gas deliveries:

> *Ceauşescu*:
> - As early as 1968 we said: we need to develop our economy because no one will help us otherwise. We have taken steps in that direction.
> *Gorbachev*:
> - You have done a lot.
> *Ceauşescu*:
> - Until 1984, we did not import even one liter of gasoline from the Soviet Union.
> *Gorbachev*:
> - You had no need for it. You had your own gasoline. This is already clear now.
> *Ceauşescu*:
> - I just wanted to remind you.
> *Gorbachev*:
> - In any case, you have done a lot.
> *Ceauşescu*:
> - We have worked on and succeeded in bringing about the development of society and the economy. What you are doing now we have tried in the past. We created then the so-called private-holders and after a year we saw they are getting rich and we put a stop to the entire

situation.

Gorbachev:

- Is this the future you see for us?

Ceauşescu:

- If some get rich by playing the market, that is not a future, you know that I'm sure. We have introduced the idea of economic self-rule, the new economic mechanism, and leadership councils.

Gorbachev:

- As I listen to you I cannot help but think that in a year you have time to visit every administrative region in your country.

Ceauşescu:

- Maybe not quite all the regions.

Gorbachev:

- Tell me, though, in a country as big as ours, how could we rule in the same manner as you? We need to think of different methods.

Ceauşescu:

- We, too, have autonomy, but there is a difference between the autonomy of republics or even regions and the autonomy of factories. In any case, general direction and control from the center are necessary, even for the Soviet Union.

Gorbachev:

- Comrade Ceauşescu, we too desire a powerful center, but we think of it in a somewhat different manner.[133]

......

Ceauşescu:

- The problem of natural gas is not one for the future, it regards the situation at this time.

Dăscălescu [Romanian prime minister]:

- For the past few days, something must have happened on your side, we are receiving 7 million cubic meters less a day. We were told that this will only last a few days. Could you please analyze this problem?

Gorbachev:

- This happens every year. Always something more.

Dăscălescu:

- It is not more, it is less.

Following the collapse of the Communist regimes in Poland, Hungary and Czechoslovakia, the fall of the Berlin Wall, and the overthrow of the Bulgarian leader Todor Zhivkov, the writing was on the wall for Ceauşescu but he was blind to the message. He was so out of step with the rapid changes in Central Europe that he believed it possible to reverse the 'velvet revolutions' that had taken place. But any military intervention by the Soviet Union was out of the question. Both Gorbachev's refusal to use force to maintain Communist regimes, signalled to Erich Honecker, the East German leader in October 1989, and the

Malta summit of 2–3 December, showed that the Brezhnev doctrine was dead. For his part, Ceauşescu seemed confident that he could buck the trend of revolution and remain in power.[134]

His rapid overthrow caught the Soviet Union off guard. Foreign Minister Edward Shevardnadze, in a note to Gorbachev of 20 December, five days after the protests against the attempted eviction of pastor Laszlo Tőkés from Timişoara which sparked off anti-Ceauşescu demonstrations, reported:

> On the events in Romania in the last few days we can still only judge on the basis of information that comes from news agencies, primarily Western ones. This information is often contradictory and does not allow one to construct a true picture. Our attempts to obtain the official version via Bucharest produced no results. Today, 20 December the Romanian ambassador will be invited to the MFA USSR [Ministry of Foreign Affairs of the Union of Soviet Socialist Republics] in order to obtain from him information on this issue.[135]

A more detailed picture was provided by the Yugoslav ambassador to Moscow, Milan Veres, to I.P. Aboimov, Soviet deputy foreign minister, on 22 December.[136] The Romanian Foreign Ministry relayed to Moscow the Romanian government's "deep indignation in regards with the inaccurate and tendentious way in which the Soviet mass media is presenting the alleged events taking place in Timişoara"[137] while Ceauşescu even went so far as to blame Moscow for the disturbances. In a memorandum of a conversation with Ion Bucur, Romanian ambassador to Moscow on 21 December, Aboimov told Bucur that during Ceauşescu's meeting with the Soviet chargé d'affaires in Bucharest the Romanian leader claimed that he had information that "the action in Timişoara was allegedly prepared and organized with the consent of the member-states of the Warsaw Treaty Organization".[138]

Following Ceauşescu's flight from Bucharest on 22 December, and the provisional government's appeals for international aid in quelling the violence in the capital, the US Secretary of State James Baker, in anticipation of his appearance on a major American television show on 24 December and expectation of questions on Romania, instructed his ambassador in Moscow to question the Soviet authorities about the situation there.[139] As Thomas Blanton points out, 'the key exchange between Matlock and Aboimov comes when the US ambassador "hinted at an idea, apparently on instructions from Washington", that "the military involvement of the Soviet Union in Romanian affairs might not be regarded in the context of the Brezhnev doctrine"'. Aboimov rejected the invitation, declaring, "We stand against any interference in the domestic affairs of other states....Thus, the American side may consider that 'the Brezhnev doctrine' is now theirs as our gift". The last phrase refers to the US invasion of Panama to oust the dictator Manuel Noriega.[140] The exchange stands, in Thomas Blanton's words, "as perhaps the most dramatic American expression of changed attitudes marking the end of the Cold War".[141]

At the same time as the Matlock-Aboimov meeting, the Soviet Politburo issued a statement on 'The Situation in Eastern Europe and the Position of the USSR.'[142] The first steps in connexion with the situation in Romania were listed as follows:

1. To publish a TASS statement in relation to military action in Bucharest, presenting the threat to lives of Soviet citizens.
2. Re: future developments in Romania, to publish the statement of the Soviet government in support of the National Salvation Front and their program.
3. To address the leaders of Bulgaria, Czechoslovakia, Hungary, the German Democratic Republic, Poland and Yugoslavia with an offer to arrange regular contacts and exchange of information about the situation in and around Romania. To offer to these governments to hold regular consultations of the Ministers of Foreign Affairs in Warsaw.
4. To take measures to set up direct contacts with the leadership of the National Salvation Front, principally with Ion Iliescu.
5. To create a working group (comrades E.A. Shevardnadze, V.A. Kriuchkov, M.A. Moiseev) to consider the possible variations of the development of the situation in the Moldovan SSR, in particular the possible attempt by extremist groups of Soviet citizens to go to the border [with Romania] and cross it in order to support the National Salvation Front.
6. Bring attention to the fact that the Council of Ministers of the USSR is preparing an offer of humanitarian and other support to Romania.[143]

   The Council of Ministers of the Soviet Union prepared messages of congratulation to the new leaders of Romania, Ion Iliescu, head of the National Salvation Front, and Petre Roman, the Prime Minister.[144]

Notes

1 For comprehensive details of the organization of the *Securitate* see Dennis Deletant, *Ceauşescu and the Securitate. Coercion and Dissent in Romania, 1965–89* (London: Hurst, 1995).

2 Bucharest: Editura Venus, 1993, p.44. Pacepa classified this directorate as Directorate IVa but in fact this directorate in March 1951 was known, according to *Securitate* records, as Directorate C and only received the designation IV sometime later.

3 Pacepa gives both years, pp.152–54.

4 Ion Mihai Pacepa, *Moştenirea Kremlinului* (Bucharest: Venus, 1993), p.179.

5 *Ibid.*, p.183.

6 The DIE was renamed *Direcţia Generală de Informaţii Externe* (DGIE) in March 1978, and in October of the same year rechristened *Centrul de Informaţii Externe* (CIE): see Deletant, *Ceauşescu and the Securitate*, p.381.

7 London: Heinemann, 1988. An unflattering assessment of the book is given in a review by Francis E. Sturwold dated 27 October 1988, a copy of which, dated 27 October 1988, was sent to Tom Smeeton on the Permanent Select Committee on Intelligence of the US House of Representatives. The reviewer offers the caveat: "This reader would advise against accepting many of Pacepa's statements at face value". See the blog of Victor Roncea at http://roncea.ro/2017/02/22/cia-despre-aberatiile-scrise-de-pacepa-daca-ar-putea-plange-copacii-ar-face-o-pentru-ca-au-furnizat-hartia-pentru-aceasta-carte-cia-confirma-ceausescu-dusmanul-nr-1-al-urss-in/. Accessed 14 April 2017.

8 See Larry Watts's discussion in http://larrylwatts.blogspot.com/2013/08/the-mysterious-mr-pacepa-04012013.html. Accessed 14 October 2016.

9 E-mail communication to this author from Ion Mihai Pacepa. 4 November 2016 and quoted with his permission.

10 Liviu Ţăranu (ed.), *Ion Mihai Pacepa în Dosarele Securităţii. 1978–1980* (Bucharest: Consiliul Naţional pentru Studierea Arhivelor Securităţii, 2009), p.36.

11 Private source. Counter-intelligence officers, being restricted in their opportunities to travel, were jealous of their colleagues in the DIE who were involved in the transports abroad. With Ceauşescu's permission, counter-intelligence officers mounted surveillance.

12 Liviu Ţăranu (ed.), Ion Mihai Pacepa în Dosarele Securităţii, p.46.

13 Sârbu headed the 'SD brigade', a specialist unit of the DIE charged with gathering technological intelligence with both civil and military applications. Almost 300 of the SD's staff were assigned abroad, the principal targets being the major industrial nations of the West. Organized geographically and by category of industry, the brigade's activity was based on the acquisition of intelligence with military, including nuclear, applications. Sârbu's fate was bound up with Pacepa's. After the latter's defection in summer 1978, Sârbu was arrested on suspicion of being himself a spy and then released and transferred to the Ministry of the Interior Academy at Băneasa in Bucharest. He died in an explosion in a garage in a small town called Voila north of Bucharest on 20 July, 1984 (P.M. Băcanu, 'Moartea unui general', *România liberă,* 20 July 1990).

14 Private information.

15 Pacepa is referring to an interview given by Joe Wippl, a former CIA officer, concerning Pacepa's defection; see http://www.news.ro/social/exclusiv-ofiterul-cia-care-a-supravegheat-fuga-lui-mihai-pacepa. Accessed 31 October 2016.

16 Andrews Air Force base.

17 E-mail communication to this author from Ion Mihai Pacepa, 28 October 2016 and quoted with his permission.

18 Radio Free Europe Research. Romanian Situation Report/22 (8 September 1978), p.13.

19 Matthew Nimetz, a State Department counsellor, during a visit to Bucharest (6–8 September 1978), told Romanian Foreign Minister Ştefan Andrei that Pacepa's defection was as much a surprise to the US as it was to the Romanians (author's interview with Mircea Răceanu, 12 February 2017).

20 During that period, he or she must be physically present in the country for at least 50 per cent of the time.

21 SECTION 8 of the Act, enacted by Congress on 20 June 1949, reads: "Whenever the Director, the Attorney General, and the Commissioner of Immigration shall determine that the entry of a particular alien into the United States for permanent residence is in the interest of national security or essential to the furtherance of the national intelligence mission, such alien and his immediate family shall be given entry into the United States for permanent residence without regard to their inadmissibility under the immigration or any other laws and regulations, or to the failure to comply with such laws and regulations pertaining to admissibility : Provided, That the number of aliens and members of their immediate families entering the United States under the authority of this section shall in no case exceed one hundred persons in any one fiscal year" (http://www.legisworks.org/congress/81/publaw-110.pdf. Accessed 31 October 2016).

22 https://www.cia.gov/news-information/featured-story-archive/2010-featured-story-archive/colonel-ryszard-kuklinski.html. Accessed 31 October 2016.

23 Personal communication to this author by Mircea Răceanu and cited with his permission; for details of Răceanu's fate after his arrest in January 1989 see chapter 15, footnote 93 and selected biographies.

24 Pacepa received his naturalization on 28 July 1988, ten years to the day that he was granted political asylum in the United States; see Sorin Roşca Stănescu, Cornel Dumitrescu, *Autopsia: demontarea unei înscenări securiste împotriva generalului Pacepa* (Bucharest: Omega Ziua, 1999), p.228.
25 Pacepa, *Red Horizons* (London: Heinemann, 1988), p.425.
26 Pacepa, Moştenirea Kremlinului, p.285.
27 *Scînteia*, 5 December 1978. Coman's deputy, Ion Savu, was also replaced.
28 Nicolae Pleşiţă (1929–2009) was a manual labourer who left school at the age of 16. He joined the Union of Communist Youth in 1945 and the *Securitate* in 1948. After training in the Soviet Union in 1958–1959, he rose to the rank of major in 1961, colonel in 1966, major general in 1967, becoming adjutant to Ceauşescu and head of the First Directorate of the *Securitate* (Internal Security) in 1972. He was demoted from this position following the suicide of Ceauşescu's doctor, Abraham Schachter, in March 1973 (see chapter 12), but was soon back in what proved to be short-lived favour in 1978 as first deputy minister of the Interior for after Pacepa's flight in August he was moved to the position of commandant of the officers' school in Băneasa. He bounced back again in 1980 when he was appointed head of the CIE (Mihnea Berindei, Dorin Dobrincu, and Armand Goşu (eds.), *Istoria Comunismului din România.* Vol.III. *Documente Nicolae Ceauşescu (1972–1975)* (Iaşi: Polirom, 2016), p.52, footnote 16).
29 Unitate Militară (UM 0107), known until October 1978 as *Aport Valutar Special* (AVS).
30 Manuela Marin, Originea şi evoluţia cultului personalităţii lui Nicolae Ceauşescu 1965–1989 (Alba Iulia: Altip, 2008), pp.108–85.
31 J.F. Brown, Surge to Freedom: The End of Communist Rule in Eastern Europe (London: Adamantine Press, 1991), pp.207–8.
32 Author's interview with Lt. Col. Cornel Dohotaru, deputy to Macri, 13 August 1994.
33 Brown, *Surge to Freedom*, p.209.
34 The regime claimed a grain harvest of 32 million tonnes for 1987 when weather conditions were unfavourable. "In 1989, the figures soared. Ceauşescu put the grain harvest figure at 60 million tonnes when it was something like 16 million. All this at a time when many foodstuffs were severely rationed or totally unobtainable". (*Ibid.*).
35 UM 0620 (UM meant *unitate militară* (military unit), 0 signified a classified unit, and 620 was the code number of USLA).
36 Blaga headed the unit until 1984. Its commander in 1989 was Colonel Gheorghe Ardeleanu and its strength 795 officers and men (Dennis Deletant, *Ceauşescu and the Securitate. Coercion and Dissent in Romania, 1965–89* (London: Hurst, 1995), p.326). The creation of USLA was driven by the presence of large numbers of Arab students in Romanian universities which raised fears that the internecine struggles within the various factions of the Palestinian Liberation Movement would spill over into Romania. These fears were borne out on 4 December 1984 when the Second Secretary at the Jordanian Embassy was shot dead outside the Bucharest hotel in the capital. On 12 August 1985, Ahmed Mohammed Ali Al Hersch, a 27-year-old Palestinian studying in Bucharest, was arrested with the assistance of *USLA* for the murder and sentenced to 20 years' imprisonment. In 1988, in the wake of decree no. 11 issued by Ceauşescu, his sentence was reduced by half, and in September 1991, under article 60 of the penal code, it was cut by another four years, with the result that on 3 September 1991 he was released from Galaţi jail and left the country (*România liberă*, 16 June 1993, p.16).
37 Richard Cummings, *Cold War Radio. The Dangerous History of American Broadcasting in Europe, 1950–1989* (Jefferson, North Carolina; London: McFarland & Company, 2010), p.97.
38 Pacepa, Moştenirea Kremlinului, p.493.
39 Personal communication from Constantin Răuţă to this author, 2 December 2016 and used with his permission.

40 During the campaign plans were allegedly drawn up by CIE General Gheorghe Maxim (Manea) to murder Răuţă in the US (personal communication to this author from Ion Mihai Pacepa). Răuţă went on to work on major US aerospace projects such as Hubble, EOS and Landsat. He was also involved in the development of various space defence systems for the United States.

41 Pacepa, *Red Horizons*, p.163.

42 They were named in the trial documents as Gerard Freddy Layani, born in Paris on 15 May 1956, sentenced to 11 years for attempted murder, and Jean-Claude Cottenceau, born in Paris on 27 March 1948, sentenced to four years and six months for aggravated assault; see Richard Cummings, *Cold War Radio. The Dangerous History of American Broadcasting in Europe*, p.161 and Liviu Tofan, *Şacalul Securităţii. Teroristul Carlos în solda spionajului românesc* (Bucharest: Polirom, 2013), p.20.

43 Pacepa, *Red Horizons,* p.164.

44 For a study of Carlos and his terrorist network see Oliver Schröm, *Im Schatten des Schakals. Carlos und die Wegbereiter des internationalen Terrorismus* (Berlin: Christoph Links Verlag, 2002).

45 The CIE made the initial contact with Carlos through the brother of Palestine Liberation Organization leader Yasser Arafat in August 1979; see Cummings, *Cold War Radio*, p.97.

46 *Ibid.*, p.28. In 1990, the Romanian foreign intelligence service, renamed SIE (*Serviciul de Informaţii Externe*) declassified two documents connected with the weapons given in Bucharest to Carlos's network. The first document, entitled 'Operatiunea 207' (Operation 207), the planned assassination of Pacepa, dated June 22, 1981 and registered under No. 0010748, was issued by the CIE (U.M. 0544) and was addressed to U.M. 0297, a subordinate unit. This document officially removed from the inventory of U.M. 0297 the weapons and the ammunition given to Carlos for 'Operation 207' (assassination of Pacepa). Among them were: three grenade launchers, five Walther revolvers and two silencers. The second declassified document, entitled 'Operatiunea 363' (Operation 363) and issued by U.M. 0544, was dated December 9, 1981. This document removed from the inventory of U.M. 0297 the weapons and the ammunition given to Carlos's team for demolishing the RFE headquarters with plastic explosive (personal communication to this author from Ion Mihai Pacepa and used with his permission).

47 Born in Neu-Ulm Germany in 1948, died in Frankfurt in 2015.

48 These documents were issued by the *Securitate;* see Tofan, *Şacalul Securităţii*, annexes 9 and 10, pp.170–75.

49 Goma and Penescu were living in Paris, and Orescu in Cologne. Goma regarded the package as suspicious and did not fully open it. Penescu was less fortunate and was badly injured, while Orescu saw the bomb inside his parcel which exploded and wounded him in the foot (Tofan, *Şacalul Securităţii*, pp.54–55).

50 For a detailed account of the background to the bombing, the role of Carlos and Weinrich, and the involvement of the *Securitate*, see Cummings, *Cold War Radio*, pp.92–170 and id., 'The 1981 Bombing of RFE/RL'. *Radio Free Europe, Radio Liberty Archive*, 9 February 1996. http://www.rferl.org/a/1080043.html. Accessed 16 October 2016.

51 German prosecutor Detlev Mehlis mentions this deposition in April 1997 and it is cited by Tofan, *Şacalul Securităţii*, p.120. On 16 February 1982, Magdalena Kopp was arrested in Paris by the French authorities together with Bruno Bréguet, a Swiss citizen who had served a prison sentence in Israel for possession of explosives. The French police found in their car five kilograms of plastic explosive, false passports and sketch plans for various terrorist operations. She was sentenced to four years in jail on 24 May 1982. Kopp was released on May 4, 1985, with a reduction of seven months for good behaviour, but she was deported to West Germany, where she was detained again and questioned by the German authorities. When she was released,

Magdalena moved to Syria, where she was reunited with Carlos. On 17 August, 1986 she gave birth to their daughter Elba Rosa Ramirez Kopp. In 1990, Kopp and Carlos decided to separate. She went to Venezuela together with Carlos's mother, while Carlos travelled to Sudan with a diplomatic passport. Her association with Carlos was made public in the Venezuelan press and as a result she moved to Germany with her daughter. She lived in her hometown of Neu-Ulm until her death on 15 June 2015.

52 Matei Pavel Haiducu, *J'ai refusé de tuer* (Paris: Plon, 1984).

53 R. de Fleurs, 'Are there Problems in the Secret Service?', *Radio Free Europe Research*, vol.10, no.9, Romania SR/4 (22 February 1985), p.25.

54 *Ibid.*

55 Pleşiţă himself had briefly been a casualty of Pacepa's flight. A career officer in the *Securitate*, his name first appeared in the Romanian press in May 1958 when he was reported to have been awarded the Romanian People's Republic Star, fourth class, as a captain in the Ministry of the Interior. In the 1970s, he was given rapid promotion within the Party and at the Eleventh Party Congress in 1974 was elected a member of the Auditing Commission. In December 1976, he was listed as Major General and first deputy minister of the Interior at a ceremony at the Interior Ministry's officers' school at Băneasa.

56 The five were the subject of an article linking them with the bomb attack on the Romanian office of Radio Free Europe in Munich on 21 February 1981 although no proof of their involvement in this act has been produced (Laurenţiu Mihu, 'Ei sunt terorişti de la Europa liberă', *Evenimentul Zilei*, 28 November 2007).

57 *Ibid.* Ceauşescu's increasing reliance upon the *Securitate* is illustrated by his secret decree no. 408, issued under the aegis of the State Council on 26 December 1985 which, under article 10, stipulated that heads of protocol in all ministries, with the exception of the Ministry of Defence, should be 'active *Securitate* officers'. Unconfirmed information about the presence of *Securitate* officers in the Ministry of Foreign Affairs during the period 1964–1971 puts their figure at 40% in 1964, 30% in 1968, and 80% in 1971. In practice, after the issue of decree 408, all freshly appointed Romanian diplomats posted abroad had to be *Securitate* officers.

58 Gheorghe Ursu, *Europa Mea* (Cluj-Napoca: Dacia, 1991), p.356.

59 Dimitrie Lăcătuş, 'Relatare de la procesul Gheorghe Ursu. Spinoasa problema a continuitatii intre institutiile statului roman de azi cu cel comunist'. http://www.contributors.ro/reactie-rapida/relatare-de-la-procesul-gheorghe-ursu-spinoasa-problema-a-continuitatii-intre-institutiile-statului-roman-de-azi-cu-cel-comunist. Accessed 11 May 2017.

60 Cristina Petrescu provides a fascinating comparative analysis of Müller's own traumatic experiences at the hands of the *Securitate* as reflected in her novels and in the writer's own file in 'Eine Zeugin gegen die Securitate: Herta Müller', Joachim von Puttkamer, Ştefan Sienerth and Ulrich A. Wien (eds.), *Die Securitate in Siebenbürgen* (Köln, Weimar, Wien: Böhlau Verlag, 2014), pp.342–73.

61 http://www.nobelprize.org/nobel_prizes/literature/laureates/2009/muller-lecture_en.html. Accessed 13 October 2016. The case of the Romanian German writer Rolf Bossert, who was attacked by *Securitate*-instigated hooligans outside the Goethe Institute in central Bucharest, has attracted little attention; see Gerhardt Csejka and Ştefan Sienerth (eds.), *Vexierspiegel Securitate. Rumäniendeutsche Autoren im Visier des kommunistischen Geheimdienstes.* Veröffentlichungen des Instituts für deutsche Kultur und Geschichte Südosteuropas an der LMU München (Regensburg: Verlag Friedrich Pustet, 2015), vol.129, passim.

62 *Secrets and Truths. Ethnography in the Archive of Romania's Secret Police.* The Natalie Zemon Davis Annual Lectures (Budapest-New York: Central European University Press, 2014), p.162.

63 E. Behr, Kiss the Hand You Cannot Bite. The Rise and Fall of the Ceauşescus (London: Hamish Hamilton, 1991), pp.220–21.

64 M. Shafir, 'Preparing for the Future by Revising the Past', *Radio Free Europe. Report on Eastern Europe*, vol.1, no.41 (12 October 1990), p.32, note 10.
65 *Cuvântul*, no.5, 28 February, 1990.
66 Deletant, *Ceauşescu and the Securitate*, pp.343–48; see also Adam Burakowski, *Dictatura lui Nicolae Ceauşescu, 1965–1989, Geniul Carpaţilor* (Iaşi: Polirom, 2011), pp.293–94.
67 Nicolae Radu, 'Nicolae Radu', *NU*, no.13, 1990.
68 *NU*, no.20, 4–11 August 1990.
69 Vlad was, unlike Postelnicu, a career officer in the *Securitate*. He served as a captain in the cadres' directorate in the late 1950s and gradually rose through the ranks, becoming Major General in 1977. On 9 May 1980, he was promoted state secretary in the Ministry of the Interior with the rank of Lieutenant General. On 15 April 1983, he became a deputy minister and on 21 August 1984 Colonel General.
70 S. Brucan, *Generaţia irosită* (Bucharest: Universul/Calistrat Hogaş, 1992), p.232.
71 'Adevărul, numai adevărul' in *Adevărul*, 23 August 1990, p.3.
72 It bore the military designation UM 0107.
73 'Activitatea Comisiei guvernamentale pentru recuperarea fondurilor deturnate din patrimoniul statului', *NU*, 86 (2–9 September 1992).
74 'Ceauşescu's brothers "sold secrets to US"', *Daily Telegraph*, 7 May 1990 quoting report in *The Washington Post* of 6 May.
75 *Evenimentul Zilei*, 4 September 1992, p.3.
76 L. Turcu, 'Cum pot fi găsite conturile lui Ceauşescu', *Evenimentul Zilei*, 8 September 1992.
77 Gail Kligman, The Politics of Duplicity. Controlling Reproduction in Ceauşescu's Romania (Berkeley: The University of California Press, 1998): see also Daniela Drăghici, A Personal View of Women's Sexual and Reproductive Lives in Romania (1), paper presented at the 32nd Annual Psychosocial Workshop on March 30, 2004 in Boston, Massachusetts, USA and A. Baban, 'Romania', in H. P. David (ed.), From abortion to contraception: A resource to public policies and reproductive behavior in Central and Eastern Europe from 1917 to the present (Westport, Connecticut: Greenwood Press, 1999), pp.191–221.
78 See the transcript of the meeting of the Permanent Bureau of the RCP Politburo held on 13 January 1975 in Mihnea Berindei, Dorin Dobrincu, Armand Goşu (eds.), *Istoria Comunismului din România.* Vol.III. *Documente Nicolae Ceauşescu (1972–1975)* (Iaşi: Polirom, 2016), doc.71, pp.458–62.
79 David Aspinall (D. Deletant), 'Romania: Queues and Personality Cults', *Soviet Analyst*, vol.13 (10 May 1984), p.4.
80 P. Stephenson et al., 'The Public Health Consequences of Restricted Abortion Lessons from Romania', *American Journal of Public Health* vol.82 (October 1992), pp.1328–31.
81 *Orizont*, 6 January, 1984.
82 *Scânteia*, 4 March 1988.
83 David Aspinall, 'Romania: Queues and personality cults', pp.4–5.
84 Quoted from M. Cavalcanti, 'Totalitarian States and their Influence on City-Form: The Case of Bucharest', *Journal of Architectural and Planning Research*, vol.9, no.4 (Winter 1992), p.278.
85 *Ibid.*
86 Quoted from E. Behr, 'Kiss the Hand You Cannot Bite'. The Rise and Fall of the Ceauşescus (London: Hamish Hamilton, 1991), p.194.
87 *Ibid.* Some comic on-site incidents involving Ceauşescu are related by J. Sweeney, *The Life and Evil Times of Nicolae Ceauşescu* (London: Hutchinson, 1991), pp.169–70.
88 D.C. Giurescu, *The Razing of Romania's Past* (Washington, DC: US/ICOMOS, 1989), p.42. Giurescu's work is the most comprehensive account of the effects of urban redevelopment in the 1980s on Romanian city centres.

89 Giurescu, *The Razing*, p.44.
90 *Ibid.*, p.50.
91 *Ibid.*, p.62.
92 D. Ionescu, 'More Protests Against Demolition in Bucharest', *RFE Research*, vol.11, no.41 (10 October 1986), pp.35–36.
93 Giurescu, *The Razing*, p.52.
94 *Ibid.*, p.65.
95 The speech, printed in *The Times* on 28 April 1989, made no concession to diplomacy: "We in this country are painfully aware of the trauma caused by uprooting traditional communities at the behest of 'benevolent', know-all planners... That process should have made us, therefore, all the more sensitive to the awful spectre of an entire society—not just certain districts—losing its roots and its ancient communities, which is what is happening today in a corner of Eastern Europe, in Romania. There President Ceauşescu has embarked on the wholesale destruction of his country's cultural and human heritage. What happened here in the 1960s is, of course, not comparable with the policy known as 'systematization', which aims to transform Romania's rural environment into over 500 urban collectives designated as 'agro-industrial complexes'. The object is to reshape the nation's identity, to create a new type of person, utterly subordinate to its dreams. To achieve this, President Ceauşescu has set about destroying the cities and villages of his country and replacing them with blocks of flats which are a repetition of failed 1960s social engineering, mixed with the atmosphere of George Orwell's '1984'." The Chairman of the British Campaign was Sir Bernard Braine. Members of the Sub-Committee were Victoria Clark, Jessica Douglas-Home, Simon George, John Laughland, Charmian Marshall, Maria Nalder, Iolanda Stranescu, Malcolm Taylor, Dr Eugene Varallja, Mary Walsh and Dennis Deletant. The Prince instructed his Civic Trust to place rooms in its headquarters in Carlton Gardens at the disposal of the campaign.
96 A. Gavrilescu, 'Otopeni: agonia unui oraş rămas sat', *Adevărul*, 1 August 1991, p.1.
97 Loraine, Joan, (1990), *Operation Ursoaia: Porlock's Village in Romania,* privately printed; see note 64.
98 A moving, but by no means unique, example of the determination and generosity of spirit of many such volunteers is provided by Joan Loraine from the village of Porlock in Somerset, England. She wrote an account of her visit to her adopted village of Ursoaia in the county of Vrancea under the title '*Operation Ursoaia': Porlock's Village in Romania*, which was privately printed in 1990. In gauging the impact of her visit this letter of thanks speaks for itself:

Dear Villagers of Porlock,
In the name of the 260 inhabitants of Ursoaia we convey the best wishes for the health of the English people and yourselves. We never imagined that someone from England would come to our village so remote and hidden in the hills. The children were amazed for they had never seen things of the kind that you brought them. Maybe things would have been different for them had not the tyrant Ceauşescu been a dictator for 25 years. We had no one to complain to because Ceauşescu ignored the constitution.

On behalf of the inhabitants of Ursoaia we thank you again wholeheartedly for the help you have given us and for a gesture we did not think that we would experience. It would give us great pleasure to welcome you in the summer of 1990. Please keep in touch by writing to me. We will never forget you. (Quoted with the author's permission).

Ion Bouros, Ursoaia.

99 Two provocative yet valuable studies on Romania's relations with its Warsaw Pact partners, principally with the Soviet Union, are Larry L. Watts, *With Friends Like These. The Soviet Bloc's Clandestine War against Romania* (Bucharest: RAO, 2010)

and the same author's *Extorting Peace: Romania and the End of the Cold War, 1978–1989* (Bucharest: RAO, 2013).

100 Dennis Deletant and Mihail E. Ionescu (eds.), *Romania and the Warsaw Pact, 1955–1989* (Bucharest: Politeia-SNSPA, 2004), pp.271–76.

101 Mircea Munteanu, The Beginning of the End for Détente: The Warsaw Pact Political Consultative Committee, e-dossier no. 24, Cold War International History Project (CWIHP), 2011, https://www.wilsoncenter.org/publication/the-beginning-the-end-for-detente-the-warsaw-pact-political-consultative-committee. Accessed 15 April 2015.

102 Munteanu, *The Beginning.*

103 *Ibid.*, p.305.

104 *Ibid.*, p.315.

105 Dumitru Preda and Mihai Retegan, *1989. Principiul Dominoului* (Bucharest: Editura Fundaţiei Culturale Române, 2000), p.16.

106 Deletant and Ionescu, *Romania and the Warsaw Pact*, pp.332–34.

107 See Simon Gheorghiu, Independenţă versus reformă. România în contextul relaţiilor sovieto-americane în perioada 'perestroika' (1985–1989) (Brăila: Editura Istros, 2015), pp.145–222.

108 *Scânteia*, 17 October, 1986.

109 *Associated Press News Archive*, http://www.apnewsarchive.com/1986/Romanian-Fails-to-Win-Unilateral- Disarmament-Pledge. Accessed 1 December 2016.

110 Gorbachev's visit took place between 25–27 May.

111 Deletant and Ionescu, *Romania and the Warsaw Pact*, pp.349–50.

112 Michael Shafir, 'From Sofia to Beijing: Reactions to the 19th Soviet Party Conference.' *Radio Free Europe Research, Background Report*, no.133 (13 July 1988), pp.1–5 [5].

113 'Memorandum to Alexander Yakovlev from the Bogomolov Commission (Marina Sylvanskaya),' February, 1989, History and Public Policy Program Digital Archive, Donation of Professor Jacques Levesque; copy on file at the National Security Archive. Translated by Vladislav Zubok and Gary Goldberg. http://digitalarchive.wilsoncenter.org/document/112484. Accessed 17 April 2017.

114 Deletant and Ionescu, *Romania and the Warsaw Pact*, p.394.

115 Mircea Munteanu, 'The Last Days of a Dictator', *Cold War International History Project Bulletin*, no.12/13 (Fall/Winter 2001), pp.215–17 [217].

116 Ceslav Ciobanu in conversation with this author, Paris, 4 December, 2009.

117 Preda and Retegan, *1989. Principiul Dominoului*, p.26.

118 Larry Watts, *Cei dintâi vor fi cei din urmă. România şi sfârşitul războiului rece* [The First will be the Last. Romania and the End of the Cold War] (Bucharest: RAO, 2013), p.652, my translation.

119 Preda and Retegan, *1989. Principiul Dominoului*, pp.164–65.

120 *Ibid.*, p.170 (my translation).

121 *Ibid.*, p.167.

122 *Ibid.*, p.171.

123 Larry Watts argues that "the documentary evidence provides little support for taking Soviet, Polish and Hungarian affirmations of Romania's advocacy of military intervention at face value". A rebuttal of Watts's argument was offered by Mark Kramer (Mark Kramer, Larry Watts, Continuing Debate: Ceauşescu's Appeal for Joint Warsaw Pact Action on 19 August 1989), Cold War International History Project e-dossier no.61, http://www.wilsoncenter.org/publication/continuing-debate-ceauşescu. Accessed 24 May 2016. See also Watts, *Cei dintăi*, p.652, note 3.

124 Ştefan Karner, Mark Kramer, Peter Ruggenthaler, and Manfred Wilke (eds.), *Der Kreml unde die Wende 1989. Interne Analysen der sowjetischen Führung zum Fall der kommunistischen Regime* (Innsbruck, Wien, Bozen: StudienVerlag, 2014), docs 71, 72.

125 See Soviet Ambassador Evghenni Mikhaillovich Tiazhelnikov's journal entry in Ştefan Karner, Efim Iosifovich Pivovar, Natalya Georgievna Tomilina, and Alexander Oganovich Chubarian (eds.), *Konec épohi: SSSR i revolûcii v stranah Vostočnoj Evropy v 1989–1991 gg.: Dokumenty* [The End of An Epoch: The USSR and the Revolutions in the Eastern European Countries in 1981–1991. Documents], (Moscow: Rosspen, 2015), document 241 (cited from Larry Watts, 'The Eve of the Romanian Revolution. Some Considerations'). https://www.academia.edu/22363045, pp.46–47. Accessed 1 December 2017.

126 Resolution of the CPSU CC Politburo No. 132, 'Regarding the Appeal of Cde. Ceauşescu', 21 August 1989, *History and Public Policy Program Digital Archive*, RGANI, F. 3, Op. 103, D. 180, L. 63, and RGANI, F. 3, Op. 103, D. 181, Ll. 140–41. Translated for Cold War International History Project (CWIHP) by Mark Kramer. RGANI is the acronym for the Russian State Archive of Contemporary History (*Rossiiskii Gosudarstvennyi Arkhiv Noveishei Istorii.)*

127 Larry Watts, 'The Eve of the Romanian Revolution'. Accessed 1 December 2016. It is also worth bearing in mind the judicious interpretation of Ceauşescu's intent at this time that he was "seeking the convening of a congress of communist parties, rather than military intervention" (Peter Siani-Davies, *The Romanian Revolution of December 1989* (Ithaca: Cornell University Press, 2005), p.49). See also Dennis Deletant, Larry Watts, and Adam Burakowski, 'Did Nicolae Ceauşescu Call for Military Intervention against Poland in August 1989?', *Cold War International History Project*, e-dossier no.60, http://www.wilsoncenter.org/publication/did-nicolae-ceau%C8%99escu-call-for-military-intervention-against-poland-august-1989. Accessed 30 September 2016.

128 RGANI, fond 3, opis 103, delo 183, S 43–47.

129 The Communist Party of the Soviet Union sent a small delegation; see 'Minutes of conversation of A. Iakovlev with the Romanian ambassador to Moscow, Ion Bucur. 2 October, 1989. Note of acceptance by Mikhail Gorbachev to Nicolae Ceauşescu's invitation to the delegation of the CPSU to attend the 14th Party Conference of the Romanian Communist Party.' (RGANI, fond 5, opis 102, delo 778, S 86–87).

130 Quoted from M. Shafir, 'Highlights of the 14th Party Congress', *RFE Research. Romanian Situation Report/9* (14 December 1989), p.30.

131 *Ibid.*

132 Shafir, 'Highlights', p.31. Ceauşescu had signalled his intention to refer at the Party Congress to the recent nationalist agitation in the Moldovan Soviet Socialist Republic in a meeting of the Politburo on 13 November 1989; see 'Sedinţa Comitetului Politic Executiv de la 13 noiembrie 1989', ANIC, Fond CC al PCR – Secţia Cancelarie, dos. no.63/1989 (I am grateful to Larry Watts for drawing my attention to this document.)

133 Mircea Munteanu, 'The Last Days of a Dictator', *Cold War International History Project Bulletin*, no.12/13 (Fall/Winter 2001), pp.217–25 [217].

134 See the speech delivered by Ceauşescu at the opening of the 14th Congress of the Romanian Communist Party on 20 November 1989 (Michael Shafir, 'From Sofia to Beijing: Reactions to the 19th Soviet Party Conference.' *Radio Free Europe Research, Background Report*, no. 133 (13 July 1988), p.5).

135 Svetlana Savranskaya, Thomas Blanton, and Vladislav Zubok (eds.), *Masterpieces of History. The Peaceful End of the Cold War in Europe, 1989* (Budapest, New York: Central European University Press, 2010), p.662.

136 Savranskaya, Blanton and Zubok, *Masterpieces of History*, pp.663–65.

137 'Telegram from the Romanian Embassy in Moscow to the Ministry of Foreign Affairs,' December 21, 1989, History and Public Policy Program Digital Archive, Arhivele Ministerului Afacerilor Externe, Moscow/1989, vol.10, pp.297–98 http://digitalarchive.wilsoncenter.org/document/111564. Accessed 17 April 2017.

138 Savranskaya, Blanton and Zubok, *Masterpieces of History*, p.663.

139 I am indebted here to Thomas Blanton's commentary on the record of the conversation between Ambassador Jack Matlock and Aboimov; see Savranskaya, Blanton and Zubok, *Masterpieces of History*, pp.661–62.

140 Savranskaya, Blanton and Zubok, *Masterpieces of History*, p.662. Blanton writes that Matlock's (and subsequently Baker's own) invitation to the Soviets is deemed "stupid" (Shevardnadze's later characterization) and possibly "a provocation to put the Soviet Union on a par with the United States in Panama".

141 *Ibid.*

142 RGANI, fond 3, opis 103, delo 192, ll.43 (undated).

143 RGANI, fond 3, opis 103, delo 192, S 24.

144 "Please accept our sincere congratulations on being named Prime Minister of Romania. We hope that Soviet-Romanian relations will fully develop in the interests of the realization of the deep democratic transformation in our countries, the strengthening of our friendship, and the full cooperation between the people of the Soviet Union and Romania. We wish you successful activity in your high office." (RGANI, fond 3, opis 103, delo 192, S 27, 145–46.)

17 Revolution

Barely a week spanned the demonstrations outside the home of Laszlo Tőkés in Timişoara and the flight of Nicolae Ceauşescu from the Central Committee building in the capital. The vigil held in support of Tőkés on 15 December turned into a major demonstration on the following day.[1] Some of the protesters attempted to enter the Party county headquarters but the building was deserted and the doors locked, so they turned their attention to nearby shops and set fire to volumes of Ceauşescu's speeches looted from a bookshop. Eventually, the security forces dispersed them with water cannons. Fresh crowds gathered on the morning of 17 December in the centre of the city and moved towards the local Party headquarters which they found protected by a double cordon of troops and fire engines. As the crowd advanced, one of the engines came to meet it and sprayed it with water, thus infuriating the protesters who pushed the troops back, thereby allowing some young demonstrators to break into the building. The youths ransacked the lower floors before the security forces forced them out. Most of the crowd streamed back towards the Hotel Continental to join hundreds of other protests throwing stones and petrol bombs. The army garrison was also attacked and furniture from it seized and set on fire. It was amidst this chaos that in the late afternoon the first gunshots were heard and the first victims of the revolution fell.[2]

The gunshots were the result of an order given to troops to use live ammunition on the demonstrators. That order was given, according to First Deputy Defence Minister Lieutenant General Victor Atanasie Stănculescu, by the Minister of Defence, Colonel General Vasile Milea, doubtless on the command of Ceauşescu himself.[3] The latter was in constant touch by telephone with Tudor Postelnicu, the Minister of the Interior, to keep himself informed of the disturbances, and ordered firm measures to be taken against the protesters.[4] After the ransacking of the local Party headquarters in Timişoara on 17 December, Radu Bălan, the county Party secretary and Ilie Matei, the secretary of the Party Central Committee who was a native of the city, rang Ceauşescu to tell him of events. A full meeting of the Party Political Executive Committee was convened just after 5 p.m. Ceauşescu blamed the disturbances on "revisionist circles and agents both from the East and West. Their aim was to destabilize Romania, to act to destroy Romania's independence and her territorial integrity". He chided Milea and Postelnicu:

> Instead of doing what I told you, you sent in the army with blank bullets. ... Not one of the soldiers was equipped with live ammunition. Do you know how you behaved? Pure and simple, you displayed a defeatist attitude. If I had known that you were not capable of stopping these hooligans, these wayward elements, I would have called upon 500 workers, armed them, and then we would have solved the problem.
>
> ...
>
> I told you what you had to do. But you did not do it. You should have fired! You should have fired warning shots and if they did not stop, you should have fired at them. In the first place, you should have fired at their legs...[5]

An hour later, Ceauşescu gave a teleconference from the basement of the Central Committee building in Bucharest in which he addressed country Party chiefs and senior officials. They must have been dismayed to see a tired, fossilized Ceauşescu flanked by his stone-faced wife and surrounded by a dinosaur-like group of Politburo members. The sight hardly evinced authority, rather the weakening of a grip on power. Ceauşescu blamed the violence on a few 'hooligan' elements and claimed that behind Tőkés lay,

> foreign spy agencies, principally Budapest because he [Tőkés] also gave an interview. Actually the facts are well-known. Moreover, it is known that both in the East as well as in the West everyone is saying that things ought to change in Romania. Both East and West have decided to change things and they are using any means possible.[6]

The teleconference was followed by a broadcast to the nation in the same vein by Ceauşescu. The broadcast had a profoundly negative effect upon many viewers, especially the young. Protesters in Timişoara were infuriated to be described as stooges of a foreign power.

A stream of senior army and *Securitate* officers were sent from the capital to put down the protests. Major General Emil Macri, head of the economic counter-espionage directorate of the *Securitate* was joined by Lieutenant General Constantin Nuţă and Major General Mihalea Velicu, the heads of the militia on the morning of 17 December. That same afternoon Colonel General Ion Coman, secretary of the Central Committee responsible for military and security affairs, Major General Ştefan Guşă, First Deputy Defence Minister and Chief of the General Staff, Lieutenant General Victor Stănculescu, first deputy defence minister responsible for procurement, and Lieutenant General Mihai Chiţac, head of the chemical troops and commander of the Bucharest garrison, arrived.[7] Live ammunition was distributed to the troops as the security forces moved to the offensive. Demonstrators were shot dead in the city centre, near the cathedral and in *Piaţa Operei* (Opera Square), as well as in the suburbs (Calea Lipovei and Piaţa Traian). Tanks abandoned by the army in Calea Girocului were withdrawn after the army fired upon protesters. The violent repression left more than 60 civilians dead and more than two hundred wounded. About seven hundred persons had been arrested.[8]

Despite the crisis facing his regime Ceauşescu flew to Iran on the morning of 18 December for a three-day state visit. He was probably persuaded to go ahead with the visit by the promise of signing contracts for the sale of arms to the Iranians estimated to be worth more than $2 billion.[9] His wife Elena was left in charge of the situation at home, to be assisted by Politburo members Manea Mănescu and Emil Bobu. Yet Ceauşescu's absence undermined any authority which his regime had maintained and even ignited rumours that he had taken substantial gold reserves to Iran as insurance against possible flight. In an effort to hide evidence of those murdered by the army, the bodies of 40 civilians were taken from the Timişoara mortuary, on Elena Ceauşescu's orders—as rumour had it—and heaped into a refrigerated lorry which took them first to the local militia headquarters and then to Bucharest where they were cremated and the ashes scattered at the entrance to a canal in a village called Popeşti-Leordeni, on the southern outskirts of Bucharest.[10] Such treatment of the bodies was regarded as un-Christian by the largely devout Orthodox population and certainly fuelled hostility to the regime, at the same time adding confusion to calculations of the exact numbers of dead from 17 and 18 December.

More demonstrators died on 19 December as thousands of factory workers reported for work but joined in sympathy strikes with colleagues who had gone on strike elsewhere in the city. On 20 December, tens of thousands of workers decided to come out of the factory gates and joined forces in a mass march to the *Piaţa Operei* in the city centre. There, although confronted by lines of troops and armoured vehicles, they surged forward and with shouts of *'Noi suntem poporul!'* ('We are the people!'), *'Armata e cu noi!'* ('The army is on our side!') and *'Nu vă fie frică, Ceauşescu pică)'* ('Have no fear, Ceauşescu will fall') they embraced the soldiers, stuffing flags in the turrets of the armoured personnel carriers and tanks, and handing flowers, cigarettes and bread to the young soldiers. From that moment the regime could no longer count on the army to defend it.[11] Timişoara was, some in the crowd claimed, '*un oraş liber*'('a free city'). The crowd moved towards the Opera House and as troops withdrew to a side street, entry was made through a back door. At this point some eyewitnesses report that a certain Claudiu Iordache made an emotional appeal for the army to withdraw.[12] Others state that the first person to address the crowd from the Opera House balcony, where a loudspeaker system already set up on the balcony in anticipation that the Prime Minister Constantin Dăscălescu would address the crowd, was Lorin Fortuna, a professor at Timişoara Polytechnic.[13] His speech, delivered at around 2 p.m., was followed by a succession of others from factory representatives urging the crowd, estimated at about 40,000 persons, to remain united.[14]

A few streets away, outside the Party county headquarters, another large crowd had gathered, calling upon the prime minister, Constantin Dăscălescu and senior Political Executive Committee (Politburo) member, Emil Bobu, who had arrived earlier in the day from Bucharest, to speak to the crowd from the balcony. When they did, they were booed and quickly withdrew. It was then agreed that a delegation drawn from the crowd should join the two officials in the building for negotiations. Several of the senior army commanders were present at the talks which culminated in a demand for the resignation of Ceauşescu and the government, and free elections.[15] Dăscălescu stonewalled, pleading the need to consult with Bucharest, and gave little ground, conceding merely the return of the bodies of the dead, the release of arrested demonstrators, and immunity for the delegation. After Ceauşescu's defiant broadcast that evening, the talks were suspended and the crowds dispersed. This proved to be a felicitous development for during the night, on Ceauşescu's orders, between ten and twenty thousand workers from Oltenia were given patriotic guard uniforms and dragooned into boarding special trains for Timişoara, with orders to drive from the streets of the city the 'hooligans' and 'drunks' who were acting at the behest of foreign intelligence agencies,. When the workers arrived the next morning, they found no one to target and spent the day aimlessly until, with Ceauşescu's approval, they returned home.[16]

Instead, the spokesperson of citizens of Timişoara, Lorin Fortuna, had established that same morning the Romanian Democratic Front with himself at the head. Its composition was enlarged with the inclusion of some of those who had taken part in the negotiations with Dăscălescu, but with pressure from others that it should be expanded even further it soon became clear—and this was evident in the immediate aftermath of Ceauşescu's overthrow—that while the opponents of Ceauşescu knew what they were against, there was no agreement as to what they were for. A programme was eventually issued by Fortuna which called for the resignation of Ceauşescu, the organization of free elections, the creation of a democratic media, respect for human rights and economic reforms. According to one source, troops intervened to stop the publication of the programme on 21 December and it was only after Ceauşescu's flight that it appeared on 22 December as a leaflet with the title 'The Tyranny has Fallen' and was broadcast on Romanian radio.[17] Nevertheless, the protesters in Timişoara had effectively brought an end to Ceauşescu's dictatorship two days before Ceauşescu fled from Bucharest. Thus for two days there were dual centres of power in Romania, one established by the anti-Ceauşescu Romanian Democratic Front in Timişoara, the other in the Central Committee building in Bucharest.

The hostility to Ceauşescu unleashed in Timişoara quickly spread to neighbouring towns and then into Transylvania. Protesters took to the streets on 20 December in Jimbolia, Sânnicolau Mare, Deta and Lugoj, and on the following day came out in Buziaş, Reşiţa, Caransebeş, Oradea, Arad, Cluj, Sibiu, Târgu-Mureş, Braşov and Bucharest. On the morning of 22 December demonstrations took place in Alba Iulia, Bistriţa, Miercurea-Ciuc, Sfântu-Gheorghe and Turda.[18] Only in Oltenia and Moldavia did towns remain largely quiet, with bemused citizens in Piteşti—for example—aimlessly milling around and limply dangling pro-Ceauşescu banners when the address of Ceauşescu, due to be relayed that morning to the main square from the capital, was abruptly abandoned. In Cluj, 26 demonstrators were shot dead by army units on 21 December.[19] In Sibiu, where Nicu Ceauşescu, the dictator's son, was the county Party secretary, demonstrators took to the streets chanting anti-Ceauşescu slogans on the morning of 21 December, and an assortment of armed militia, *Securitate* troops and cadets from three army academies in the cities were sent onto the streets to maintain public order. Eyewitnesses stated that the *Securitate* troops opened fire on the demonstrators at midday. The protesters eventually made their way to the *Securitate* and militia headquarters, which were in the same complex and opposite one of the military academies, and demanded the release of those demonstrators who had been arrested. After getting no response from the head of the *Securitate*, Lieutenant Colonel Petrişor, some in the crowd of around 3,000 began to stone the headquarters late in the evening. They then set fire to the trees around the militia HQ, an act which led to shots being fired from inside the building. Four demonstrators were killed and 11 wounded. The *Securitate* and militia chiefs asked the commander of the Sibiu military garrison, Lt. Col. Dragomir, for reinforcements and three armoured personnel carriers (APCs) were sent to guard the militia headquarters.

The protesters remained outside the *Securitate* and militia throughout the night and around midday on 22 December tried to force the gates of the *Securitate* building. At that point automatic fire resumed, first from the *Securitate* headquarters and then from those of the militia. Shortly afterwards, the fire was directed at the military academy opposite and at the cadets who were guarding the militia buildings. There followed a veritable gun battle between the army cadets, led by their officers and the militia and *Securitate* officers. A group of militia, dressed in khaki jackets, tried to gain entry to the academy but were captured by the defenders. Other cadets took an APC and opened fire on the militia and *Securitate* buildings. In the course of the afternoon militia and *Securitate* officers also tried to take the two other military academies, and regular soldiers and civilians were fired upon by snipers at other points in the town. As a result of these attacks more than 50 people were killed, eight of whom were soldiers, 23 from the *Securitate* and militia, and more than 30 civilians.[20]

Judged in retrospect Ceauşescu made three fatal errors. In his broadcast of 20 December he completely misjudged the mood of the people by displaying no hint of compassion for the victims of Timişoara and by dismissing the demonstrations as the work of 'fascists' and 'hooligan elements', inspired by Hungarian irredentism. With echoes in his ears of the people's acclamation of his speech of 21 August 1968 denouncing the Warsaw Pact invasion, he made his second mistake. He convened a public meeting of support on 21 December in Bucharest, in an atmosphere, this time, of public disgust at his lack of humanity. After the broadcast of 20 December, meetings were convened at factories and military barracks to mobilize support for Ceauşescu and were addressed by local Party officials. At the same time, the Political Executive Committee took the decision to organize a mass meeting the following morning in Bucharest's *Piaţa Palatului* to demonstrate unstinting approval for the regime and therefore implicit backing for the repression in Timişoara. It was to be televised and broadcast nationally. Selected by factory, workers were taken by bus to the square the following morning, equipped with the usual banners for Party-orchestrated meetings proclaiming 'Peace', 'Ceauşescu and the People', 'Ceauşescu—R(omanian) C(ommunist) P(arty).' Ceauşescu began to speak at 12.31 p.m.[21] Scarcely had he began with a few introductory remarks than, to his bewilderment, a disturbance in the crowd—off camera—and high-pitched screams caused him to break off his speech. The live television and radio coverage was cut, but not before Ceauşescu's confusion had been captured by the cameras and transmitted to the thousands watching on television. For the first time in the history of the Communist regime in Romania, a stage-managed address by its leader had been interrupted in full view of the public. It proved to be a fatal blow, first to Ceauşescu, and second, to his entire regime.

The origin of the commotion in the crowd has never been clearly established. Correspondents of the BBC interviewed several members of the crowd, standing in different places in the square, in the early days of January 1990, and a number of explanations were given.[22] One of them, Leon Nica, said that the loud, crackling noise caught by Ceauşescu's microphone, was the sound of banners being trampled underfoot as they were discarded by their bearers, concerned that a group of young men chanting 'Timişoara' standing close to them, would be arrested by the *Securitate* and they too detained.[23] Another, a cameraman of Romanian television, said that it was the noise of short-circuiting loudspeakers, a third person claimed that the sound came from a firework let off in the crowd, a fourth that it was caused by tear gas grenades fired at the public by the security forces. The sound may have resulted from a combination of any of these incidents but the result was that when Ceauşescu was able to resume his speech, he did so from a position of fragility. He attempted to placate the crowd by announcing salary and pension increases, but this stratagem only angered them further. At the end of his speech large groups of young people remained in the city centre and, encouraged by the mild, unseasonal weather, lingered into the evening. It was at this point that they were fired upon by the army and security troops, and many were shot dead.[24]

On the following morning of 22 December, Ceauşescu committed his third error. He summoned yet another public meeting of support and attempted to make an address at 11.30 a.m. Boos and stones were directed at the balcony of the Central Committee building and Ceauşescu was ushered inside by the head of his personal bodyguard, Major General Marin Neagoe.[25] He fled from the rooftop in a helicopter accompanied by his wife and two of his closest allies, Manea Mănescu and Emil Bobu, and two bodyguards, Major Florian Raţ and Captain Marian Constantin Rusu. Ceauşescu ordered the helicopter pilot to land at Snagov, some 30 km to the north of Bucharest, where he had a country mansion, and it was from here that he and his wife collected a suitcase of clothing. Mănescu and Bobu remained behind as the helicopter took off once more with the Ceauşescus and the bodyguards, first, according to the pilot Major Vasile Maluţan, in the direction of the helicopter base at Otopeni, and then, on Ceauşescu's instructions, to the parachutists' base at Boteni, but the pilot was told by the commandant there that he could not land. The pilot received orders to tell Ceauşescu that he was short of fuel and fearful of being spotted by radar, and so Ceauşescu ordered him to put down on a main road just outside Titu, near the village of Serdanu, some 35 km to the south of the town of Târgovişte.[26] The bodyguards flagged down a car driven by a doctor named Nicolae Decă, who took them as far as the village of Văcăreşti, just outside Târgovişte, where his car ran out of fuel, forcing the bodyguards to commandeer a second car, this one belonging to an engineer named Nicolae Petrişor who took them to the steelworks at Târgovişte where a bodyguard got out to seek local Party assistance but did not return.[27] Petrişor, uncertain what to do with the presidential couple, decided to drive to a nearby agricultural experimental station where the manager, bewildered and frightened, shut them away in a room and summoned the local police.[28] The two policemen (*miliţieni*) took them to the Târgovişte police headquarters where the *Securitate* was also based but crowds blocking the entrance prevented them from entering.[29] The policemen then drove the couple to a nearby village called Răţoaia where they tried to remain out of sight in some reeds by a lake until the commotion in Târgovişte died down. On being informed that relative calm had been restored by an army unit around the police station, the policemen returned to headquarters in the early evening and the Ceauşescus were then taken to the army garrison in the town.[30]

In Bucharest, following the flight of the Ceauşescus, crowds began to gather at the television centre in the north of the city. A delegation of protesters was permitted to enter to negotiate a resumption of broadcasting to convey the news of the morning's events in the city.[31]The TV management was evasive until a number of armoured cars carrying, among others, the well-known actor Ion Caramitru and the dissident poet Mircea Dinescu, arrived. It was Caramitru who was the first person to appear on Romanian television after the interruption of service. In a voice quivering with emotion he declared: "Brothers, thanks to God we are in the television studios, we managed here on the back of tanks, with the army and with students and with the people whom you see and with thousands and thousands of Romanians".[32] A stream of speakers followed. They included senior Party members who had fallen out with Ceauşescu—Ion Iliescu and Silviu Brucan—and figures unknown to the public but who were to rise to prominence later—Petre Roman and Gelu Voican Voiculescu. Iliescu, judging from eyewitness accounts, entered the TV studios with an air of authority.[33]

Iliescu, a former Party head in Iaşi county who had been marginalized by Ceauşescu, was rumoured in the West to enjoy the favour of Mikhail Gorbachev, a view which gained credence following the former's enigmatic call for reform in the literary journal *România literară* in September 1987.[34] He issued a call to all 'responsible' persons, in particular the authors of the 'Letter of the Six', to go the Central Committee building at 5 p.m. to form a Committee of National Salvation. He himself appeared there, before television cameras, flanked by a number of figures including General Nicolae Militaru, Petre Roman and Voiculescu. After declaring that the *Securitate* no longer existed, having been absorbed into the army, he appealed for support for the new provisional authority which was to be established. He then withdrew to an office in the Central Committee where, in concert with a dozen or so others, including Silviu Brucan, General Militaru, Colonel Gheorghe Ardeleanu, head of the anti-terrorist brigade, *Unitate Specială de Luptă Antiteroristă* (USLA), and Petre Roman, a provisional government, styled 'The Council of the National Salvation Front', was formed.[35] Despite Iliescu's invitation, two of the signatories of the 'Letter of the Six', Gheorghe Apostol and Grigore Răceanu, were refused entry.[36]

The decision to place the Ceauşescus on trial, according to Brucan, was taken on the evening of 24 December by Iliescu, Roman, Brucan, Voiculescu and Militaru, who had all moved to the Ministry of Defence for security reasons.[37] Stănculescu was tasked with making the logistical arrangements.[38] To give a fig-leaf of legality to the proceedings an 'Exceptional Military Tribunal' was constituted. It was before this kangaroo court that the unsubstantiated charge of genocide was brought as well as the accusation, among others, that Ceauşescu had undermined the national economy. Ceauşescu challenged the constitutionality of the court and argued that, as president, he was responsible only to the Grand National Assembly. The CNSF was the product of a foreign plot, he claimed. But to no avail since the verdict had been preordained. The trial lasted little under an hour and after a short period of deliberation military prosecutor Colonel Gică Popa, the head of the tribunal, sentenced the two accused to death.[39] The Ceauşescus, hands bound, were led outside and summarily shot by a firing squad.

The army itself revealed details of the part played by some of its units in events in Bucharest on 21 and 22 December. This was the subject of an investigation made by the military procurator's office in March 1990. The report, drawn up by Captain Cornel Iordache, provided an interim assessment of the army's role and recommended an extension of the investigation, but according to Mirel Curea, a journalist on the staff of *Evenimentul Zilei* no follow-up action was taken and it was only in July 1993 that the report's conclusion were made public.[40] The details that emerged showed an army command that remained faithful to Ceauşescu until the moment of Defence Minister Vasile Milea's death about 10.40 a.m. on 22 December. Iordache began his investigations with the 1st Armoured Division since this provided the bulk of the army forces which took part in the quelling of the demonstrations on 21 December. This division was part of the First Army under the command of Major General Gheorghe Voinea and was made up of two regiments, the 1st Mechanized based in the *Antiaeriană* district of the capital, the 2nd Mechanized garrisoned on the Olteniţa road. The orders received by the regiment were transmitted by the First Army Command, which in turn received them from the Ministry of Defence, with the exception of those orders given directly to forces in the field by the Minister of Defence, Colonel General Vasile Milea.

At 1525 hours on 17 December the First Army Command ordered the 1st Armoured Division to implement the plan *'Radu Cel Frumos'* (Radu the Handsome), the code word for actions of a limited nature.[41] According to the Defence Ministry's general order no. 0048 of 13 October 1988, actions of a limited nature "were designed to crush foreign aggression and to defend the country's revolutionary achievements and territorial integrity". There was no mention in them of a role to be played by the army in maintaining public order in peacetime. Moreover, Captain Iordache established in discussions with a number of officers that there had never been concerted actions with Ministry of Interior forces in order to put down anti-government demonstrations. One might question this statement since army units were certainly used alongside the militia during the riots in Braşov in November 1987 in order to patrol the streets. In the period 17–20 December no information was given to the troops about the reasons behind the orders to implement the 'Radu Cel Frumos' plan. On the other hand, rumours abounded that in Timişoara bands of hooligans had ransacked shops and attacked soldiers, killing a number of tank crews. This latter rumour must have had a considerable psychological impact on troops from an armoured regiment. On 18 December, an order came from the Army Upper Political Council for personal radios to be removed from the troops, while at 0900 hours on 20 December the order went out for wives and relatives not to come to the barracks. At 0330 hours on 21 December, the Political Council of the First Army gave the order for political assemblies to be held in its units and at such a meeting of the1st Mechanized regiment its commander, Colonel Florea-Marin Oană, railed against the 'hooligans' in Timişoara. At midday, the officers and men went to the TV room to watch the meeting organized by Ceauşescu in front of the Central Committee building.

Fifty minutes later Major General Gheorghe Voinea ordered all units of the First Army to form into columns and ammunition to be distributed. At 1338 and 1345 hours orders were received for the 1st and 2nd regiments respectively to take up positions close to the Central Committee. The first columns went into the city centre under the command of Colonel Oană and Major Ionel Marin. They consisted of armoured cars but not tanks, and by 1945 hours 24 cars from the 1st regiment and 13 from the 2nd had taken up positions. From the statements made by the two regimental commanders to Captain Iordache their mission was to block off the roads leading to the Central Committee and, if necessary, to fire warning shots into the air, but under no circumstances to fire on the population. However, according to another witness, Constantin Dobre, who was a counter-espionage officer with the 1st Mechanized regiment, Defence Minister Milea in his presence gave orders to Colonel Oană to fire if necessary at demonstrators' legs. But such an order was not given to the troops and in any case, Iordache added, if the troops had fired on the population, there would have been a veritable massacre. As it was, according to a Major Ion Guzu, "only about 30 people were shot dead".

The 2nd Mechanized regiment took up positions on Bulevardul Magheru with one column at the *Scala* cinema and another drawn across the road from the Sala Dalles to the intersection with 13 December Street. The 1st Mechanized regiment stationed itself outside the Central Committee and in the streets that fanned out from the square in front of it, such as Oneşti Street and Calea Victoriei. Cordons of troops and armoured cars were set up on several streets, a typical one being that in the area of *Sala Dallas* and the Intercontinental hotel, where in fact several protesters were shot dead. The cordon was made up of two lines of Ministry of Interior troops (*trupele de Securitate*) carrying shields, a third line of militia troops and a row of armoured cars between which were placed Ministry of Interior troops and cadets from the Ministry of the Interior Academy at Băneasa. Behind the cars were infantry troops from the 98th guard battalion under the command of Colonel Amariucăi which formed part of the Infantry and Tank Command of General Ion Hortopan. In addition, many witnesses reported the presence of groups of men in plain clothes who were probably from sections of the *Securitate*.

After 2000 hours, a barricade, made up of tables and chairs from the *Dunărea* restaurant was erected in front of the Intercontinental Hotel by the demonstrators. It is ironic to think that many of these young demonstrators would not have been present but for the impact of Ceauşescu's decree of 1966 outlawing abortion, and that, in a sense, he was to be overthrown by the generation he himself created. Later in the evening, lorries were brought up to reinforce the barricade and were set on fire. Armoured cars from the 2nd Mechanized regiment were used to break down the barricade but without success. Moreover, about 2300 hours an armoured car (no.3 E-225) under the command of Lieutenant Nicu Şerban was set on fire. Its crew managed to get out. At 2250 hours Colonel Pârcălăbescu conveyed Defence Minister Milea's order to the First Army Command that a company of eight tanks from the 1st Mechanized regiment should go to the Intercontinental Hotel. The order was passed on to Major Valentin Roşca, the tank battalion commander of the 1st regiment. The latter took five tanks up to the barricade by the hotel in front of traffic island in University Square. It was burning and the demonstrators had retreated from it after tear gas had been used against them. A tipper truck had in the meantime been moved up behind the barricade and four of the tanks moved slowly forward to demolish it. At the same time the various troops who had taken up position by *Sala Dalles* (*trupe de Securitate*, cadets from the Băneasa Academy, soldiers from the 98th guard battalion) fired warning shots and advanced behind the tanks. The demonstrators fled down *Bulevardul 1848* to *Piaţa Unirii* (Union Square) while the tanks regrouped, two of them under Major Roşca's command turning into *Bulevardul Republicii* and stopping outside the Ministry of Agriculture (they were joined later by two other tanks together with men from the 98th battalion).

Another three tanks under Colonel Marin Oană carried on down past Union Square to the Budapest restaurant on *Bulevardul Dimitrie Cantemir* where they dislodged another barricade made up of metal containers and a lorry. One of the tanks directed machine-gun fire on the lorry to extinguish its lights and when checked, no one was found inside it. About 0200 hours on 22 December three armoured cars and an artillery unit under Captain Cristian Călinescu were brought up on Colonel Oană's orders but, according to Captain Iordache's report, there were no further incidents that night. At 0900 hours, however, huge columns of well-organized workers converged on the city centre and stopped at the cordons of troops where they tried to persuade them not to suppress the anti-Ceauşescu protests. It was, however, news of Defence Minister Milea's suicide which became public about 1100 hours that led to a spontaneous decision, according to Iordache, by units of the 1st Armoured Division to return to their barracks. By 1103 hours Colonel Oană's men were thus back at their regimental base.[42] At the same time and quite independently, Colonel Gheorghe Carp, the division's commander, had decided in concert with fellow officers to pull back his men without orders from above. At this point Captain Iordache was at pains to stress the following details entered in the operational record. At 0954 hours, General Eftimescu at the

Defence Ministry had sent an order to the First Army Command instructing "all units to obey only the commander-in chief's [i.e. Ceauşescu's] orders". But at 1007 hours, a radio message bearing the Defence Minister's codename 'Rondo' was sent to the First Army and to the 1st Armoured Division ordering them not to fire at anyone. This second message effectively negated the first and reinforced the resolve of the commanders of the 1st Armoured Division to take their men back to barracks. This unilateral decision of the divisional officers was confirmed by the receipt later of orders calling for the return of the armour to its previous positions, orders which were not obeyed. Thus at 1124 hours, Colonel Buliga of the First Army Command conveyed General Voinea's order that all armoured cars should withdraw to the front of the Central Committee building; the order was repeated six minutes later. At 1138 hours, General Constantinescu also gave an order that armoured cars should regroup in this same place. They did not. In fact, the withdrawal of armoured cars and troops from in front of the Central Committee building just minutes before Ceauşescu's flight from it was the signal for the demonstrators to enter the building.

A sketch outlining the position of forces deployed that evening in the centre of the city was published in the daily *Evenimentul Zilei* on 5 July 1993. It revealed that these forces were composed of an assortment of units drawn from the army, the Ministry of Interior troops (*trupele de Securitate*), the troops of the militia (*Forţele de Ordine Internă*), and the Patriotic Guards, a part-time workers' militia whose formation had been proclaimed by Ceauşescu on 21 August 1968, the day of the Soviet invasion of Czechoslovakia, and officially decreed two weeks later. The army component was made up of several tanks and armoured cars from the First and Second armoured regiments of the First Army, based in Bucharest. The armour was used to back up platoons of MI troops, cadets from the MI academy at Băneasa, cadets from the Army Military Academy in Bucharest, shield-bearing troops from the militia (*scutieri*), soldiers from the 98th guard battalion, as well as USLA troops in plain clothes.[43]

The importance of securing the cooperation of Colonel Gheorghe Ardeleanu and the USLA anti-terrorist brigade under his command was highlighted by his presence alongside Ion Iliescu, Silviu Brucan, Colonel General Nicolae Militaru and Petre Roman in the Central Committee building in the late afternoon of 22 December when the National Salvation Front was established. Indeed, doubts about Ardeleanu's allegiance to the new order seemed to account for his dismissal from his command in early January 1990 under suspicion of having ordered his deputy, Lt. Col. Gheorghe Trosca, to mount an attack on the Ministry of Defence on the morning of 24 December 1989 when the key figures in the NSF and army were gathered there. Evidence produced later suggested otherwise: in an attempt to cover up an attempted pro-Ceauşescu counter-revolution by some army commanders the story was put about that morning that a group of 'terrorists' using armoured vehicles had attacked the Ministry of Defence. A host of reporters made their way to the scene and relayed television pictures showing two armoured cars riddled with bullets and seven bodies, one of which had been partially burned. The new authorities confirmed that the bodies were those of USLA soldiers and for five days they were left in the street.

Later further details emerged. There were, in fact, five survivors among the USLA unit who stated that it had been ordered by General Nicolae Militaru, the post-Ceauşescu defence minister appointed on 23 December, through Colonel Ardeleanu, to help the army remove some 'terrorists' who were attacking the ministry. Their declarations were confirmed in January 1993 with the publication of the radio conversation between the USLA command and Trosca which showed that far from being ordered to attack the Ministry of Defence, the USLA unit had been called in to "neutralize terrorists who had wormed their way into the buildings surrounding the Ministry".[44] Trosca selected the men for the mission and led them in three armoured personnel carriers. En route one of the vehicles broke down but the other two continued. Over the radio Lt. Col. Ion Bliorţ, Ardeleanu's second deputy, passed on the order to Trosca to pick up the representative of the National Salvation Front, Constantin Isac, who had been delegated by the NSF to coordinate the USLA mission with the army units surrounding the ministry. The two USLA Armoured Personnel Carriers were to wait behind the last tank and to wait for details from the army command as to the positions of the 'terrorists'.[45]

When Trosca took up this position he informed Bliorţ and added what was to prove a very significant detail: his two USLA APCs were parked with the rear towards the ministry and facing the buildings from where the terrorists were believed to have fired. After a few minutes one of the army tanks fired a burst of machine-gun fire at Trosca's APC. Two of the USLA men, sergeant majors Teodor Neagoe and Ion Costache, were wounded. Trosca asked Bliorţ to tell the army not to fire on them and that he had two wounded. A minute later he was told that an ambulance would come and that the tank would flash its lights three times, while he should return the signal in order to identify himself. The tank signalled and Trosca's APC responded. The tank then opened fire with its heavy machine gun, first on Trosca's APC, and then on the second one commanded by Captain Eugen Cotună. At the same time the tank moved forward and struck the first APC, crushing senior warrant officer Ion Muicaru who was trying to take shelter, under its tracks. Three of the other men managed to gain the refuge of a block of flats where they were picked up by soldiers the following day, having telephoned their HQ to say where they were. Despite this, they were placed under arrest as 'terrorists'. Another survivor remained gravely wounded in the first APC, together with two dead colleagues.

Constantin Isac, although wounded in both legs, managed to get away. He returned to the scene the next day at first light and was astonished to find the two personnel carriers now facing the ministry, suggesting that they were in an attacking position, while the dead men, including those who perished inside the APCs, were strewn on the pavement. Seven USLA men were killed.[46] The only thing certain about this incident is that the army command at the Ministry of Defence was in contact with the USLA command and the USLA unit was fired upon after it had identified itself and not as a result of confusion and misunderstanding. Ardeleanu's other deputy, Lt. Col. Ion Bliorţ, was retired after this incident. But because of the unanswered questions about it some were inclined to believe a suspicious hand lay behind Ardeleanu's death at the age of 55 on 15 June 1993. Death resulted, according to doctors, from inhalation of toxic fumes from an anti-Colorado beetle repellant which Ardeleanu was spraying in his garden in the town of Ştei (formerly Dr Petru Groza) near Oradea.[47]

Colonel General Iulian Vlad, the head of the *Securitate*, had, like Ardeleanu, also adopted an ambiguous stance towards the revolution.[48] He made a radio broadcast on the afternoon of 23 December from the Ministry of Defence in which he pointed out that Ministry of the Interior troops were "fighting shoulder to shoulder with the Romanian army for the survival of the national being of the Romanian people".[49] He did not, however, call upon them to cease fighting and to lay down their arms, as he had been requested to do so by Silviu Brucan. Brucan, suspecting Vlad's loyalty, secured the agreement of Iliescu and Militaru for a meeting that evening to test Vlad. At the meeting Brucan challenged the *Securitate* chief about his failure to order his men to lay down their arms. Vlad gave an indignant reply that this was the first time that his loyalty to the revolution had been questioned. Brucan then asked him about the *Securitate*'s contingency plans in case of a revolt against the regime. Why had not these been revealed to the army? Vlad denied the existence of such a plan. Pressed further, he claimed that even if such a plan existed, he knew nothing of it. Vlad pointed out that some Ministry of the Interior units (the so-called *Forţele de Ordine Internă* 'Forces for Internal Order') were under the direct command of Tudor Postelnicu, the Minister of the Interior and asked that he be given 24 hours to draw up a plan for the capture of *Securitate* forces. When Vlad failed to deliver, he was arrested the following day.[50]

A third key commander upon whom the NSF could not count was Major General Ştefan Guşă, Ceauşescu's Chief of the General Staff and a deputy defence minister. Although he was named a member of the NSF Council when it was set up on 22 December, Brucan doubted his commitment to the revolution. On 28 December, Guşă was dismissed by the council for, Iliescu told a news conference the following day, "mistakes impermissible for a military commander" which were made in the defence of the Central Committee building against pro-Ceauşescu forces.[51]

Fear of snipers kept the inhabitants of Bucharest off the streets at nightfall. The ubiquity of snipers in Bucharest spawned a host of rumours about their aims and allegiance. Indeed, rumour factories were the only institutions which, alongside the *Securitate*, had worked overtime during Ceauşescu's rule. On the streets and in the press the snipers were generally dubbed 'terrorists'. Some Romanians regarded them as *securişti,* members of the *Securitate*, while informed commentators described them more specifically as rogue elements of USLA, the anti-terrorist unit of the *Securitate*, who, until Ceauşescu's execution on Christmas Day, fought to restore the dictator to power, but who, after his death, gradually faded into the shadows. A team of three or four men who broke into the residence of the British Ambassador opposite the Romanian TV studios on *Strada Emil Pangratti* and installed a machine gun on the roof fitted the description of all the above categories. They sprayed the studios for more than an hour before tank-fire reduced the residence to a burned-out shell.[52] The gunmen were never caught.

Paranoia, mistrust, uncertainty about the future, a glut of firearms in circulation, some in the hands of young men fired by *machismo*, who had little idea of how to use a rifle or an automatic weapon, characterized the atmosphere in the city.[53]

Indeed, many of the conscripts whom this author witnessed exchanging fire with snipers, returned fire over the heads of civilians, placing the latter in a direct line of fire from the adversary. Such basic failures in training resulted in many friendly-fire casualties in Bucharest. The danger posed by snipers was vividly brought home to this author. On the evening of 7 January 1990, I was making my way along a lugubrious street in the centre of the city to visit a family friend when, stepping into the light of a street lamp, I heard a sudden crack and then ping from a low wall fronting a house which I was passing. On the pavement just in front of me lay the head of a bullet. As I bent down to examine it, a militiaman, rifle in hand, came running out of the shadows and shouted to me to get out of the light. I left the bullet, moved to the shadow of a car and crouched down beside it. After a few minutes the militiaman, who had taken cover behind another vehicle, crept forward, picked up the bullet and handed it to me. It was still warm. "There", he said, "you were a foot away from death. There is a sniper in the block of flats opposite and we are trying to take him out." He asked me what I was doing on the street at that particular hour and I explained that I had come to visit a friend. He asked the name of the friend and the number of his house and from my accent realized that I was not Romanian. When I told him that I was British, he made the sign of the cross and exclaimed, "God was watching over you tonight". Fortunately, I was only a few steps away from my destination. He accompanied me to the gate and then retreated into the gloom. I shouted my thanks to him.[54]

From the evidence available it is likely that the USLA troops and some *Securitate* Fifth Directorate officers were the 'terrorists' about whom so much was written in the Romanian and foreign media after 22 December. Many of them, Brucan stated, had been captured by the army or by civilians, and others simply went home after seeing the film of the Ceauşescus' execution on the TV. Those who were captured were all released within a few days. Some of them then fled abroad, together with *Securitate* officers. When asked about the involvement of foreign terrorists, Brucan alleged that "some 30 foreigners, most of them Palestinians who were being trained at the Băneasa military academy and other *Securitate* centres", had assisted the Romanian 'terrorists'. A number of them had been killed or wounded and their bodies had disappeared from the morgues or, after being treated for their wounds in hospital, they had been flown out of the country.[55] No credible evidence was ever produced of foreign terrorist participation in the revolution and the photographed bodies of 'Arab' terrorists shown to foreign press correspondents at the time could equally well have been of swarthy Romanians. Nevertheless, "unconfirmed but very reliable military and governmental sources" interviewed by Radio Free Europe said that "shortly after the capture of Palestinians, Libyans and other Arabs who had fought on the side of the pro-Ceauşescu forces, [the Libyan leader] Quadhafi had threatened to kill all Romanian specialists in Libya if the Arabs were not allowed to leave Romania".[56]

Mystery still surrounds the sudden explosion of gunfire which erupted in the main square facing the Central Committee building on the evening of 22 December, just as the crowd was about to be addressed by a series of speakers led by Ion Iliescu. The crowd in the square panicked and the army returned the fire.

The gunfire in the square led people to believe in the existence of pro-Ceauşescu counter-revolutionary forces and since the forces most likely to have remained loyal to the dictator were those of the *Securitate*, most Romanians attributed this gunfire to them. Who carried out the attack, which left the building pockmarked with bullet-holes and set the adjacent university library on fire, has never been established. It left several people dead and some argue that it was a 'diversion', staged in order to give credibility to the existence of 'counter-revolutionary' forces who were attempting to restore the dictator to power, and therefore to give legitimation to the creation of the 'National Salvation Front', proclaimed barely hours earlier by Ion Iliescu. This view sat comfortably with the argument that a popular revolt, begun in Timişoara, was hijacked by second-echelon Communists led by Iliescu and turned into a 'revolution'. Others went further and claimed that the events in Timişoara were the first step in a conspiracy, led by anti-Ceauşescu Communists fronted by Iliescu, to overthrow Ceauşescu but to maintain Communists, if not the Party, in power. Many Romanians felt that they had been duped, and that the sacrifice made in December 1989 had been to no avail. Their view may be summed up in the verdict that while the Communist Party was declared dead in January 1990, no one ever produced a death certificate. They pointed to the presence of Lieutenant General Victor Stănculescu, First Deputy Minister of Defence under Ceauşescu, in the CNSF. Stănculescu, who had played, it was proved later, a prominent role in the repression by the army of demonstrations in Timişoara on 17 and 18 December, was appointed Minister of the National Economy on 28 December 1989 and held the position until 16 February 1990, when he became Minister of Defence.

This author, who at the time was working as a consultant to the BBC with chief foreign affairs correspondent John Simpson, was asked by General Stănculescu to meet him on 6 January 1990.[57] I seized the opportunity to ask him about his actions on 22 December, the day of Ceauşescu's flight. His account, reproduced below, is based upon my notes from that and several subsequent interviews with him. He told me that he had been informed on 22 December by army telephone, which he had at home, that he should go to the Central Committee. General Vasile Milea, the Minister of Defence, was still alive.[58] Stănculescu had come home from hospital at 9.30 a.m. The officer on the phone told him that the minister (of Defence) wanted to see him at the Central Committee. Shortly afterwards the officer phoned again to say that something had happened at the Central Committee, without saying what, and that Stănculescu should go there straightaway. Then a car came, sent by Silviu Curticeanu, head of Ceauşescu's office, with two or three men from the Fifth Directorate (personal bodyguard) of the *Securitate* who told Stănculescu that Curticeanu had sent them to pick him up immediately and take him to the Central Committee. They told Stănculescu on the way that Milea had committed suicide.

Stănculescu went up to the first floor and was met by Curticeanu who told him that "the comrades", that is, the two Ceauşescus, were waiting for him. The latter were waiting for him, not in Ceauşescu's office, but in the anteroom, and asked him, "What's wrong with you, what kept you?" Stănculescu replied that he had injured his leg in an accident and that it was in a cast. "Milea has betrayed us and has committed suicide", they exclaimed. "Here's the situation. There are some army units which are to come to the square (in front of the Central Committee). Find out where they are and when they are coming." On the same floor there was a room full of generals—the operational command of the army—among them General Gheorghe Voinea, the head of the Bucharest garrison, and General Eftimescu, head of the operational section of the General Staff. In a second room a communications centre for the army had been set up. The generals told Stănculescu that two regiments, one of tanks, the other of other armoured vehicles, had set out from *Şoseaua Olteniţei* for the square on the orders of Milea. Stănculescu left the room and in the communications centre found a captain, Marius Tufan, and asked him whether he was in contact with the two units. At his reply that he was, Stănculescu told him to pass on his order that they should return to barracks. Stănculescu went back to report to the Ceauşescus. He believed that given their state of agitation they had come into the corridor. He told them that the two units were on the way.

Ceauşescu ordered him to go back and tell the units to get to the Central Committee more quickly. Stănculescu went back and considered what to do next. He decided to repeat his order. He found Tufan and told him to transmit a general message saying that he had given the order that the two units should return to barracks. Stănculescu, by way of a parenthesis, said that Milea had emerged from Ceauşescu's office in an agitated state and ordered Tufan to hand over his pistol. Tufan did so and followed Milea up to the sixth floor where Milea went into his office. A shot was heard, several officers went in and they found the minister dead.

Stănculescu returned to the Ceauşescus and reported that the two units were on the way but the pressure in the square was growing. He advised them to leave the building by helicopter without knowing that there was not enough open space on the roof because of the aerials which the *Securitate* had to dismantle to allow a helicopter to land; a second helicopter had nowhere to land. The Ceauşescus went back to their office, spoke with Curticeanu, and, Stănculescu believed, with Manea Mănescu.[59] None of the other generals and officers came out of their offices, not one asked Stănculescu what they should do. He claimed that they avoided him because since he had been caught up in events in Timişoara he did not know what role each one had played in the violence in Bucharest. He learned later that General Hortopan was alongside Milea, and that Eftimescu transmitted Milea's order for the regiments to come from Olteniţei. Ceauşescu asked him how long it would take for the helicopter to come and Stănculescu replied, in half an hour. Ceauşescu agreed that Stănculescu should make the call. He then telephoned General Rus, the head of the air force, to ask him how long it would take him to send two helicopters.

The idea of the helicopters had come, Stănculescu recounted, around 11 or 11.15 a.m. The Ceauşescus had gone into the president's office, but Stănculescu could see that they were frightened. They were already panicking, they had, he said, turned yellow, they were fearful, perspiring and agitated. It was then that the idea [of the helicopters] occurred to him. He telephoned General Rus from the communications centre and the latter told him that the helicopters would arrive but General Marin Neagoe, the head of the Fifth Directorate of the *Securitate* had to give his order as well—that was the procedure—the order had to come from two channels. Rus asked Stănculescu to check that the roof could take the helicopters and Stănculescu told Neagoe to verify this. Neagoe's men were equipped with automatic weapons, grenades and cartridge belts and they patrolled the corridors. There were not more than 50 or 60 of them in the building. Not one of them was in military uniform. It was only after the news spread of Ceauşescu's departure by helicopter that Neagoe's men disappeared and arms were found in various rooms, when the building was stormed by demonstrators and others who helped themselves to weapons. Neagoe went off to check whether the helicopters could land and sent a colonel, a deputy of his, to do this. Stănculescu escorted the two Ceauşescus to the lift, accompanied by three bodyguards and, he thought, Mănescu, although he could not be sure.

Stănculescu stayed below and told the adjutant Mateiciuc to go up to see where the Ceauşescus could get out to the helicopter. The adjutant went up in the second lift which arrived after the Ceauşescus, who got onto the roof—Stănculescu was told—through a window on the sixth floor to reach the roof terrace. Probably they were given a chair to climb on to get out through the window onto the terrace. The *Securitate* had already taken down several aerials. The second helicopter was unable to land. The adjutant told Stănculescu that the first helicopter had already landed when the Ceauşescus got to the roof. When Mateiciuc told Stănculescu that the Ceauşescus had got into the helicopter Stănculescu too took the lift to the sixth floor so that he could get rid of his pistol and leave the building. Mateiciuc was also in civilian clothes and he and Stănculescu went into an office, opened a desk drawer and deposited their pistols. They then went down the stairs and left the Central Committee building by the main door, which was being besieged by revolutionaries.[60]

Mateiciuc stayed behind. He wanted to get to the ministry as quickly as possible to find out what was happening to the Ceauşescus. When Stănculescu got to the main entrance the building had not yet been invaded at this point, but he did pass some people—he did not recognize them—as he went out of the door and limped down the steps into the streets. Someone in the crowd asked him if he was on their side and he said 'yes'. Then Stănculescu took a flag with a long pole from someone and carrying it horizontally, said to those on his right and left: "Clear the way so that I can get to the car." People were asking: "What did you do to your leg?" "It's in plaster", he replied and then he was congratulated "for having the courage and strength" to be with them there.

Stănculescu withdrew through the crowd to entrance D of the Central Committee building and then on to the Ministry of Food Production which was in the old Ministry of Defence building, in the hope of finding a car. His aim was to get to the Ministry of Defence in *Drumul Taberei*, to take control of the army. It was only when he reached the Ministry of Food Production that he asked General Rus, on a government phone, to follow Ceauşescu's helicopter. When he got to the Ministry of Defence he received the first news from Rus about the helicopter landing at Snagov and its departure from there. While at the Ministry of Food Production he told people there that he needed a car to get to the Ministry of Defence but was informed that there was none available. He then phoned his own office and got the same reply. He instructed them to send an officer in his own private car to collect him. When he reached the Ministry of Defence he asked them to get a doctor to cut the plaster cast from his leg.

The decision to put his leg in plaster was, Stănculescu related, a family ploy. After he got back at about 4 a.m. (22 December) from Timişoara his driver told him about events in the centre of Bucharest. He took a shower and told his wife he was leaving for the ministry. His wife objected and suggested that "it would be better if you went to the hospital and get a doctor to admit you".[61] He followed her advice. When he got to the hospital he asked for the duty doctor and was told it was General Niculescu. He explained his situation to him and said that he did not want to go to the Ministry of Defence at that particular time. Niculescu decided to put Stănculescu's leg in plaster; if anyone should ask what was wrong with his leg he should reply that he had a problem with his meniscus cartilage. Niculescu never let on to anyone. Stănculescu went home and rang the duty officer to tell him to report that he had hurt his leg and that it was now in plaster and that he could not move. However, after a while, a car turned up at the door with two or three men who told Stănculescu that Curticeanu had summoned him, on the order of Ceauşescu, and he had no option but to go.

Later in the afternoon of 22 December Ion Iliescu arrived at the Ministry of Defence. Stănculescu advised him not to leave the ministry since it was only there that he could guarantee his security. He gave Iliescu and his companions meals, folding beds and blankets, and brought in armoured units to protect the ministry. Stănculescu maintained contact with the head of the air force, General Rus, who kept him informed of the flight of the helicopter carrying Ceauşescu and his wife from Snagov towards Târgovişte. It was Colonel Kemenici, commander of the Târgovişte garrison, who telephoned Stănculescu with news of the Ceauşescu's capture. Stănculescu passed the information on to Iliescu but did not tell him where Ceauşescu was being held.

Around 6 p.m. on 23 December, Iliescu came to Stănculescu—he was in the minister's office while Iliescu and company were in the minister's council room but they went into the minister's bathroom to discuss important matters for fear of microphones—and told Stănculescu that they had appointed General Nicolae Militaru Minister of Defence. Stănculescu got up to vacate the minister's chair but Iliescu told him to stay put for the time being since he was familiar with all the problems. Shortly afterwards, Stănculescu moved office to the procurement department and Militaru took his place.

On the morning of 25 December, Stănculescu was told to organize the departure of a group of magistrates to the place where Ceauşescu was being held. He ordered General Rus to send five helicopters to the Ghencea stadium [62] together with several parachutists from Boteni. He then told General Dafinescu, the head of Logistics, to bring him four metres of yellow flag silk who asked Stănculescu what it was for. He replied simply that he needed it. A few years later, Petre Roman claimed that it was his idea to use this yellow 'scarf' but it was the recognition signal that Stănculescu used with Kemenici on his approach to Târgovişte where Ceauşescu was being held under an armed guard formed, on Stănculescu's orders, of a company of mountain rangers and a unit of tanks.[63] Stănculescu, in his own words, took up the narrative:

> Iliescu said to me in the Minister [Minister of Defence]'s office—I think that Brucan was there as well—that they had arranged for a group of people to go to Târgovişte, drawn from the Military Prosecutor's Office, and from the courts. I told Iliescu to send them to open ground by the *Steaua* Football Club stadium where the club wanted to build an athletics track and I ordered the helicopters to land there. I said to Iliescu we should get to Târgovişte about 10 am and therefore we should be away from Bucharest around 9 am. Iliescu said that there should be a trial and that the Ceauşescus 'should disappear', those were the words, 'they should disappear so that we can crush the resistance being offered at that time'.[64]
>
> ....
>
> We now get to Gelu Voican and the question of him saying that he had arranged things and all that was needed was for me to name the place.[65] It was he who instructed me to go to Târgovişte and already when I was in the helicopter I learned from prosecutor [Dan]Voinea what the final outcome would be, execution.
>
> I found out on landing at Târgovişte that Colonel Popa, who was in a different helicopter, would be the head of the military tribunal. We stopped on the way at the military base at Boteni to pick up seven parachutists but I only told them their mission—in fact only Boeru their senior officer—to execute the Ceauşescus after we had landed.[66]......
>
> We told the parachutists that we needed three volunteers for an execution and it was only after we took the Ceauşescus out of the Armoured Personnel Carrier that they realized who their victims would be. We showed the Ceauşescus into a room to be examined by a doctor while I, Voican and Popa arranged the room for the trial, where the judges and the lawyers were to sit. I then ordered Kemenici to provide officers from his garrison required by Popa for the tribunal and it was only then that he realized that there was to be a trial. Up to then he regarded Ceauşescu as the commander-in-chief and a person to be protected.
>
> ....
>
> At the end of the trial I went outside and I didn't see the scuffle involving the soldiers who bound the Ceauşescus hands together. I think that the soldiers bound them on their own initiative.
>
> ....
>
> There was no order given to 'fire'. The parachutists opened fire without the order being given. The officer commanding the parachutists should have given the order but he too fired. I went towards the helicopters and saw that terrible spectacle of them being taken to the wall. The three parachutists then stepped back and emptied their magazines—about 20 bullets

each—into them. Asked to comment on the claim that the Ceauşescus sang the 'International' Stănculescu said that he heard nothing.

.....

It was 2.30 in the afternoon. I was in my general's uniform, standing in front of the helicopters.....I ordered the doctor to check that they were dead and then gave the order that tarpaulins should be brought to wrap the bodies in. The bodies were placed in the second helicopter and I got into the first, the one that I had come in, and in half an hour we were away.

....

Kemenici was left on his own in front of the building, no one shook his hand, I didn't even thank him. We landed at Boteni to refuel.

....

It was only when we landed and I went to Ghencea [the football stadium of the Steaua army club] and the lads from Ghencea came, and I asked them for something to eat and drink because we were frozen, that I had a feeling of dissatisfaction, of uncertainty about the future. We left the helicopters on the ground [by the stadium] and went to eat in the club canteen. Not a word was heard, only the sound of spoons as we ate.

......

We left an officer to make sure that the two bodies wrapped in tarpaulins were taken out of the helicopter to await the arrival of ambulances to take them to the morgue. They took some time to arrive and so the club commander invited us into the stadium as we were frozen and drained from the helicopter flight. It was then that the commander proposed that we should eat something, before we left to accompany the ambulances in a convoy.

....

Măgureanu was there, Voiculescu, Colonel Popa, Major Florescu Mugurel, the lawyers Teodorescu and Lucescu, the cameraman [the cameraman was a person whom I had taken on in the procurement department of the army to make film presentations of equipment that we made at various military fairs] and several officials from the club. I phoned the Ministry of Defence from the club director's office, his name was Colonel Gavrilă, and got hold of General Militaru. I told him simply that we had returned and that all the matters agreed upon in the plan drawn up in Bucharest had been resolved. Militaru had nothing to say.

After the meal I went to Ministry and handed over to the film cassettes from the execution.

I said just one thing: 'Don't broadcast the whole cassette because we're on it and I don't want people to find out who was present. Just show a few scenes.' In fact, the very end of the film, with the execution, was cut short. There was a big argument at the TV between Sergiu Nicolaescu and the people there and eventually Nicolaescu and Iliescu decided that the entire cassette should be shown but the first screening was the truncated version in which the Ceauşescus are shown lying on the ground.

.....

> I enquired at the *Steaua* club and they said that the ambulances had not arrived.
>
> I took an APC with my adjutant, the driver, an NCO and some other men and drove from the Ministry in search of the bodies. We reached the *Steaua* club and they told me there that the bodies were not there. I telephoned the helicopter crew and they said that they had left the bodies on the ground at the club because night was falling and they didn't have the necessary equipment to do a night flight to their base in Boteni. We drove around looking for the bodies in the lights of the APC and when we got close to the Ministry of Defence our tyres were shot out.
>
> Then we took heavy machine-gun fire from in front and behind. One of the 14.5 mm bullets hit our gunner in the neck and as he fell his hand set off our machine-gun, as though we were returning fire, but that was not our intention. My adjutant, Mateiciuc, an exceptional man, lifted the hatch-cover of the APC and shouted; 'You fuckers, you're firing on a general of the Romanian army'. The firing stopped and we got out of the APC. I gave orders for the badly wounded officer to be lifted out of the APC and stopped a car. I asked the driver to take him to the military hospital, gave him my ID card, and told him to show it to the doctors and tell them to do all they could to save the man.
>
> This 'ambush' was organized, it was not the result of confusion. We didn't find the bodies. It was important to be able to show them to the public.
>
> I couldn't sleep a wink. Then I remembered, the military unit behind the *Steaua* club was the mechanized regiment, and so the next morning I went there with a military ambulance. I got out and a lieutenant presented himself to me. I asked him if he had seen what had happened the previous evening and he replied that he had seen the helicopters which had flown off after leaving two bundles on the ground.
>
> A captain had ordered the lieutenant to have them taken away and he and six or seven soldiers had done so without even looking inside the bundles. I asked him if he knew what the bundles were and he said no. I then ordered him to put them in the ambulance which drove off with them to the morgue. When I returned to the Ministry I told them that I had found the bodies.[67]

Under a decree signed by Iliescu on 26 December 1989 the Department of State Security was removed from the control of the Ministry of the Interior and placed under the Ministry of National Defence. Iliescu tasked the deputy prime minister in the provisional government, Gelu Voican Voiculescu, with the responsibility for assembling a new security structure. On the very same evening that the decree disbanding the DSS had been issued, Voiculescu convened an extraordinary meeting of all the heads of *Securitate* units who had not been arrested. He assured them that while the new government planned to dismember the former Communist police structures, it would not take action against individual *Securitate* officers. In effect, the *Securitate* was integrated into the system and legitimized, thus enabling its officers to organize the release of all their colleagues held on suspicion of firing on demonstrators during the revolution. It is true that on 30 December a further decree was issued under which the *Securitate* was dismantled and its directorate chiefs placed under arrest or in the reserve, but this was merely window-dressing. By then most of the suspected 'terrorists' had been given their freedom. The unreliability of witnesses, bureaucratic inertia, and the desire to protect vested interests involving President Iliescu's bodyguard, the SPP *(Serviciul de Pază şi de Protocol),* which contained officers from the former Fifth Directorate and the anti-terrorist brigade of the SRI, whose numbers include former USLA men, explains why the investigations into the deaths of the officially recognized 1,000 or so victims of the revolution were not completed and why relatively few charges were brought.[68]

Stănculescu's revelations highlight the ambiguity of the situation in which senior figures in the army found themselves. The events of December 1989 showed that the forces of the *Securitate*, militia and army were only as efficient as their weaknesses allowed them to be. They were not trained in dealing with crowd control, and the heavy-handed actions of the army resulted in the deaths of many of the 1,104 official victims of the revolution.[69] Of these almost 300 of the dead were soldiers as were some 700 of the 3,300 wounded. Most of the soldiers were killed in exchanges with snipers, the so-called 'terrorists'. About 800 suspected 'terrorists' were arrested by the army but were later freed in the course of 1990. Major General Mugurel Florescu, the deputy prosecutor general, said that many had been released through lack of witnesses since the people who had brought them in left and did not return. A partial list of those detained as 'terrorists' was published in the weekly *Tinerama* in September 1993, but we cannot be sure that all those named actually fired on soldiers and civilians. Still less do we know under whose authority they might have been acting.

The forces deployed against the demonstrators were drawn from the army, the Ministry of Interior troops, the troops of the militia, the Patriotic Guards and USLA. It is quite likely that the 'terrorists' were an assortment of renegade elements from all these forces, and the use of the term 'terrorist' by the populace and the media was an attempt to rationalize opposition to the fledging authority of the revolutionary government. This same assortment made it difficult for the authorities to clearly implicate, in the case of the *Securitate*, and exonerate, in the case of the army, particular forces in their resistance to the new order and therefore to avoid the embarrassment of admitting that soldiers, militia, and *Securitate* officers were equally involved in shedding innocent blood after Ceauşescu's execution, the military procurator was given the order to release all 'terrorist' suspects. By whom is not yet clear.

Nevertheless, some senior *Securitate* officers were tried on charges of shooting of demonstrators during the revolution. The first was Iulian Vlad, the last DSS head, who was arrested on 31 December 1989 on a charge of complicity to genocide, which carried a maximum penalty of life imprisonment. The charge was later reduced by a military court to 'favouring genocide', and his sentence was subsequently reduced to nine years, which was to run concurrently with two other lesser terms. The first was for three and a half years, which Vlad received in March 1991 for illegally detaining the number two man in the National Salvation Front (FSN), Dumitru Mazilu, in December 1989. The second was for four years, which he received in May 1991 for the "abusive detention" of more than 1,000 demonstrators in late December 1989. On 4 January 1994, Vlad was released on parole, after having served a three and a half year term.

Other senior *Securitate* officers were sentenced in May 1991 to terms of two to five years of imprisonment each for 'illegally detaining' and 'abusively interrogating' an unspecified number of protesters during the revolution. On 10 May, Major General Gianu Bucurescu received a prison term of four years, while Lieutenant General Gheorghe Dănescu received a term of three and a half years. Colonel Marin Bărbulescu, head of the Bucharest militia, received a term of five years. Lieutenant General Gheorghe Vasile, the military counter-intelligence chief and Colonel Gheorghe Goran, head of the Bucharest DSS, were both acquitted of these charges. In a separate trial, Major General Marin Neagoe, head of the Fifth Directorate of the *Securitate*, was sentenced on 28 May 1991 to seven years in prison for "abusing his office". General Aristotel Stamatoiu, head of the Foreign Intelligence Service, and General Morţoiu were also sent to prison, but were released in November 1992. Nicolae Andruţa Ceauşescu, the commandant of the Ministry of the Interior military academy and a brother of Nicolae Ceauşescu, was sentenced in June 1990 to fifteen years' imprisonment for leading some 2,000 officer cadets in the shooting of demonstrators in University Square on 21 December 1989. He died in hospital of cancer on 14 December 2000. The former Minister of the Interior, Tudor Postelnicu, was also tried on the charge of genocide at the end of January 1990, and was sentenced on 2 February to life imprisonment. He was released on medical grounds on 4 February 1994.

While details of the *Securitate*'s composition were made public by Virgil Măgureanu, the director of the successor body, *Serviciul Român de Informaţii*, in a report to a joint session of the Romanian parliament on 22 November 1990, little was revealed about the numbers of informers.[70] The motives for collaboration with the *Securitate* were multiple. Connection through family or friendship with an officer in the *Securitate* could be a guarantee of preferment in all state institutions, irrespective of personal merit and the *Securitate* used this system of patronage to great effect. The advantages were reciprocal, for in return for the support of an officer, the employee was expected to pass back information. The second form involved branch officials of the Communist Party. In every institution there was a local Party organization whose secretary *Securitate* officers would regularly interview, although they were required to obtain permission for the local Party secretary.

There were other, more basic, motives for collaboration with the *Securitate* which we can ascribe simply to human weakness; blackmail by the *Securitate*, a personal grudge or jealously against an individual; the desire to feel part of a privileged group; insurance in times of difficulty. The institutionalization of police control itself made forms of collaboration a legal requirement. Every block of flats was required to nominate from among its residents a 'caretaker' who would not only be responsible for the upkeep of the building but also for keeping a register of all tenants and visitors who spent more than 24 hours in a flat. Every fortnight the register would be inspected by the local *Securitate* officer in whose 'beat' the block fell. After the 1989 revolution some 'caretakers' were unfairly vilified as collaborators by their fellow tenants. Similarly, some figures were vilified as *Securitate* officers in cases where the position they occupied was designated by Ceauşescu *post facto* as one that could only be held by a *Securitate* officer, and hence the incumbent was recruited into the agency.

As has already been stated, fear is a great labour-saving device and it is a mark of the success of the *Securitate* in instilling that fear that Romanians came to hold the widespread belief that the visible presence of so many engaged in 'collaboration' with the secret police represented but a drop in the ocean of a ubiquitous network of officers and informers. The *Securitate* were as much a state of mind as the instrument of state terror. Figures ranging from one in ten to one in three of the population (i.e. 2.3 to 8 million) have been frequently picked from the air as an estimate of the *Securitate*'s strength, but none of these figures have any solid basis of evidence to support them and such numbers would have to include all the casual informants and busybodies which, as has been pointed out, all totalitarian systems produce in parasitic abundance.[71]

Some of the speculative media estimates were boosted by the inclusion of all those who had contact with agencies of the Ministry of the Interior, irrespective of whether they came under the control of the *Securitate*. Thus all those who were granted passports were adjudged to have made concessions to the *Securitate*, either in the form of accepting a *misiune* ('a mission') in the form of reporting on the activities of Romanian relatives and friends abroad, or of informing on them at home, for which the favour of a passport was the reward. This is certainly the case with many Romanians who were allowed to travel in the Communist era, but it is unlikely to be true of all. The *Securitate* and the DIE were selective in their interest in Romanians wanting to travel abroad and it is doubtful whether they had the resources to charge every traveller with a mission. Even if they did, we cannot be sure that everyone so ordered actually complied.

Silviu Brucan presented as fact the figure of "almost 700,000 informers.... and about 10,000 agents for street surveillance, just in Bucharest" at the time of Ceauşescu's overthrow[72] while Virgil Măgureanu, head of the SRI, offered a more authoritative national figure of 400,000.[73] A reliable network of informers is crucial to the success of any security service and the *Securitate* had no qualms about squeezing as much information as possible from its resource. The numbers of informers grew steadily over the years and although a nationwide figure has yet to be revealed, the publication of details from the Sibiu county inspectorate of the *Securitate* gave some idea of the scale of informing. The number of informers in the records of the latter in 1989 was 10,500, of whom more than half were active during the days of the revolution. In relation to the adult population of the county (325,000) the figure represents roughly one in 30. However, if we add the informers working for the militia, whose numbers have not been released, the percentage would rise considerably.[74]

In 1972 Maj. Gen. Costandache, the coordinator of the Centre for Information and Documentation of the then Council for State Security, sent all the county inspectorates of the CSS standard forms on which details of the sources of information of the Securitate were to be entered. This information remained stored in the computer banks of the CID. The informers were classified in four categories: hosts (*gazde*), collaborators (*colaboratori*), informers *(informatori*) and residents (*rezidenţi*). The first category comprised those who, willingly or not, placed their homes at the disposal of the *Securitate* officer to enable him to meet his source in secret. The proportion of hosts to the other types of informer was one in 20. The second group, the collaborators, represented almost half the informers. These met officers from time to time and provided them with information which they signed. Those who agreed to give information on a regular basis signed an undertaking to this effect (*angajament*). They were then given a cover name. The last group, the residents, was made up of people whose social position gave them the possibility of building up their own small network of informers. Many of them were retired *Securitate* officers.

Party members who served as informers formed a separate group. They could only be used with the permission of the local Party and their collaboration had to be requested by the head of the *Securitate* inspectorate. A list of such informers was kept by the municipal Party secretary or by the deputy county secretary. All information, except that obtained by Directorate VI for penal investigation, was paid for after its value was assessed by the bureau for analysis. The reasons for collaboration have been outlined above but during the period 1968–73, that is, after the Soviet invasion of Czechoslovakia, the numbers who did so from conviction increased. After that date, such altruism waned and by 1988 some *Securitate* officers stooped to the most abject form of blackmail in order to meet their target of recruits. They were to be found everywhere, even in old people's homes and schools: in the *Securitate* records in Sibiu, the names of 98 children between the ages of 9 and 16 were found.[75]

Several questions about the revolution remain unanswered. It is difficult to obtain a clear picture of a number of events since they have been clouded by the rumour factories which, alongside the *Securitate*, were the only institutions which worked overtime during Ceauşescu's rule. Matters have also been confused by a series of writers who invented conspiracy theories which have no convincing evidence to support them. The feeling that many had of being misled, or that the sacrifice made in December 1989 was to no avail, was aggravated by the suspicion that the fighting in Bucharest after Ceauşescu's flight was a diversion, carried out to give the impression of the revolution, and therefore to give legitimacy to the National Salvation Front which emerged after the dictator's downfall.

The questions are encapsulated in the report of the *Serviciul Român de Informaţii* (SRI), the post-Communist security service,[76] into the events of the revolution:

> The beginning of the Romanian revolution at Timişoara has not been regarded by everybody as merely the expression of spontaneous revolt of a population which, over the years, had become profoundly dissatisfied both materially and spiritually. On the contrary, numerous scenarios have been attributed to

> the revolution, placing its origins either outside Romania, or within in various plots which had long been hatched.[77]

These scenarios were invoked because the events of late December 1989 were marked by certain deeds which, in the opinion of the SRI, "point to the premeditated acts of certain individuals who are to be distinguished from the crowds who came out spontaneously onto the streets". Among such acts cited by the report were those of a group of youths who, on the afternoon of 16 December, at a point when the number of people gathered around the home of pastor Tőkés had fallen considerably, broke the windows of several shops and blocked the buses.[78]

Question marks were also raised in the report about certain acts of provocation against the army in Timişoara. These required, it was claimed, an "expert hand" and consisted of blocking the tracks of tanks by placing strips of wire in them, using special keys to open the spare diesel tanks and setting fire to the oil, and throwing Molotov cocktails and ball bearings at the troops.

> It should be pointed out in reply to these claims of 'premeditated acts' that exactly the same measures have often been taken by demonstrators against security forces in other parts of the world during periods of civil unrest without there being any accusations of 'conspiracy' or 'foreign intervention' levelled to explain them.[79]

However, there was concrete evidence of foreign involvement in the revolution, according to the SRI report, more specifically of Soviet interference:

> The data and existing information led to the conclusion that the Soviet apparatus of intelligence and diversion was involved in all phases of the events. Beginning on 9 December 1989, the number of Soviet tourists in 'private' cars grew considerably from about 80 per day to 1,000. The occupants—two or three to a car—were mostly men of athletic build aged between 25 and 40. They avoided hotels, sleeping in their cars, and in the rare cases when they required hotel services they paid in hard currency...... Most of these cars were en route to Yugoslavia but some of them were forbidden entry to that country because weapons were found in the vehicles. One thing is certain, that during the events in Timişoara there were a large number of 'Soviet tourists'.[80]

This same report states:

> A short while after the revolution, there was an accident involving a car in which a Soviet citizen Alexandr Lout and another man were travelling. While repairs were being carried out on the car at a garage, 12 Romanian army camouflage uniforms were found together with a Soviet tunic with the pips of a major. The two men claimed that they were officers in the reserve and that they had previously fought in Afghanistan.[81].....

> Direct Soviet involvement in the violent events during the Revolution has been the subject of speculation amongst historians and commentators. The issue is not so much one of the presence of Soviet 'tourists' in Romania in late December 1989, but of the scale of that presence. Convincing evidence to support the contention that 25,000 of the 37,000 Soviet tourists who allegedly visited or transited Romania in the two weeks before the flight of Ceauşescu stayed in the country for several months has yet to be produced.[82]

The SRI report goes on to state:

> Invisible and silent, anonymous and impeccably trained, merciless and well-armed, the 'terrorists' constituted in the minds of the public the most obsessive presence of the last days of December 1989....
>
> If we add to the above catalogue of considerations stray bullets which caused death and wounding, personal vendettas, the use of weapons by people untrained in their use, panic reactions and bravura deeds, the reasons behind so many human sacrifices and material losses become less mysterious.[83]

The controversy about the revolution—and whether, in fact, there was a revolution—is reflected in its historiography. Here is a sample of views:

> Someone asked: But should we call this a revolution? After all, a revolution involves violence.....In fact, we always have to qualify it; we call it "velvet", we call it "peaceful", we call it "evolutionary"....I call it "refolution" – a mixture of revolution and reform. Curiously enough, the moment when people in the West finally thought there was a revolution was when they saw television pictures of Romania: crowds, tanks, shooting, blood in the streets. They said: 'That—we know *that* is a revolution', and of course the joke is that it was the only one that wasn't.[84]
>
> The Romanian revolution of December 1989 is a controversial moment in our history. The disputes involve both the synthetic definition of the event (was it a revolution, a people's revolt, or a *coup d'état*?), as well as the reconstruction of some of its particular aspects and, especially, the role played by the participants, whether individuals or institutions.....This derives from the uncertainty which hovers over the *agents provocateurs*, over the causes and the political effects of the principal events of December 1989. Ruxandra Cesereanu [in her study *Decembrie 89. Deconstrucţia unei revoluţii* [85]] tried to place the various accounts of the revolution in three categories: the first—of those who believe in a straightforward successful mass uprising against a dictatorship; the second—of those who believe in a *coup d'état* carried by either internal or external forces; the third—of those who believe in a combination of these two explanations.[86]
>
> The revolution of 1989 had a marked anti-Communist character, exemplified by the following: the chanting of anti-Communist slogans,

> the destruction of Communist flags (red flags with the hammer and sickle), the symbolic flying of the national flag from which had been cut out the Communist emblem of the country (in the overwhelming majority of places in Romania), the removal of the adjectives 'Communist'/'Socialist' from public signs, the removal from public places of Romanian and Soviet Communist statues and monuments, the removal of the names of Communist activists or of Communist slogans from public buildings etc…In the period which immediately followed 22 December 1989, the group which seized power hijacked the pronounced anti-Communist character of the revolution by undermining the spontaneous anti-Communist demonstrations of the people, by censoring the anti-Communist messages broadcast on the television network which had become the 'headquarters' of the first 'telerevolution' in history. The television was used to create the majority of the 'diversions', the most effective being the permanent 'danger of death' embodied by the 'terrorists faithful to the dictator Ceauşescu'…..The danger seemed entirely credible given that in the period 22–27 December there were 942 deaths recorded and thousands of wounded… Afterwards, not a single terrorist was arrested and tried.[87]

Were, then, the events of December 1989 in Romania 'a revolution'? Following Peter Siani-Davies's analysis the word 'revolution' is associated with two popular metaphors.[88] "The first is that it is a relatively quick and violent single incident … conventionally distinguished by a time-related epithet, such as 'The October Revolution' in Russia or the 'February Revolution' of 1848 in Paris", and his analysis

> would argue that 'The Romanian Revolution of December 1989' might be added to this list. Secondly, the idea of revolution can embrace a longer process of social change often spanning many decades, in which case it is usually referred to in more general terms, as in the Russian, French, or Chinese Revolution.[89]

The claim can be made that there was a rupture in sovereignty in Romania represented by the transfer of power from the Romanian Communist Party to the National Salvation Front. There were competing centres of power in Timişoara after the establishment of the Romanian Democratic Front on 20 December in opposition to the remnants of the Communist Party organization in the county council building; indeed, such a duality of power can be extrapolated to distinguish Timişoara from the rest of the country in the period 20–25 December.[90] Are we to disqualify the use of the term 'revolution' in the Romanian context not because a rupture took place in sovereignty but because there was no rupture in continuity, that is, Communists took over power? Or is it that some see the authenticity of a revolution defined not only in policy change, but also in a change of mentality?

We can dismiss the notion that Nicolae Ceauşescu's overthrow was a *coup d'état.* As has been pointed out, Erich Honecker in East Germany, Todor Zhivkov in Bulgaria and Milos Jakes in Czechoslovakia were all victims of palace *coups* and had Ceauşescu been removed after the December 17 Political Executive Committee meeting and replaced by a fellow member, he could have been placed in that category, but his retreat from the centre of Bucharest in the face of vociferous protest bears the mark of revolution, as does

> the mass mobilization, widespread violence, spontaneous creation of revolutionary institutions, breakdown of the revolutionary coalition, and subsequent fierce struggle between the revolutionary contenders on the streets of Romania's cities.[91] That multiple sovereignty did not last longer can be explained by two, at first sight, rather contradictory conditions; firstly, high levels of coercion prevented the appearance of an effective opposition prior to the revolution and, secondly, at the same time, such was the advanced level of state breakdown in Romania that in the end the regime needed only a limited challenge before it collapsed.[92]

Fate has its own way of rewarding the courageous and of punishing tyrants. Despite the divisiveness of Ceauşescu's policies towards the peoples of Romania, their shared experience of suffering under his rule brought them together. It was the defiance of Tőkés which provided the catalyst for the display of ethnic solidarity which sparked off the overthrow of the dictator. This convergence of circumstance started the series of events which led to the revolution. One may argue that it was only a matter of time before Ceauşescu fell, given his isolation in the international arena, and the growing dissent at home. But it was the merit of Tőkés and of his parishioners that they pressed on with their protest against a bishop's abuse of power which was characteristic of a denial of human rights which typified the Ceauşescu regime. Tőkés's stand, based on the right of his church to defend the interests of its faithful, transcended the narrowness of a sectarian claim and acquired the symbol of a common cause of peoples united against oppression. What the Romanian revolution does demonstrate is that the heroes die, the fighters go home and opportunists make their way to the fore.

Notes

1 See chapter 15.
2 Peter Siani-Davies, *The Romanian Revolution* (Ithaca and London: Cornell University Press, 2005), pp.61–62. Siani-Davies's study is the most comprehensive and judicious account of the revolution of which I am aware.
3 Dinu Săraru în dialog cu Victor Atanasie Stănculescu, *Generalul Revoluţiei cu piciorul în ghips* (Bucharest: RAO, 2005), p.104.
4 Sergiu Nicolaescu, *Revoluţia, începutul adevărului: un raport personal* (Bucharest: Editura Topaz, 1995), p.277.
5 Quoted from the transcript of the Politburo meeting published by Mihnea Berindei, '20 de ani de la revoluţie. Ceauşescu, decembrie 1989', *Revista 22*, 22 December, 2009 (my translation).
6 Quoted from Peter Siani-Davies, *The Romanian Revolution*, pp.64–65.

7 Stănculescu and Chiţac were charged in January 1998 with "incitement to commit murder" for their part in events in Timişoara when they served respectively as First Deputy Minister of Defence and Head of the Chemical Corps and Commander of the Bucharest garrison. They were each sentenced by the Romanian Supreme Court on 15 July 1999 to 15 years' jail for the murder of 72 people and the wounding of 253 others during the uprising in Timişoara on 17 and 18 December 1989. Both generals lodged an appeal against their conviction. Their sentences were upheld by the Supreme Court on 25 February 2000 but further appeals delayed their application. Eventually, on 15 October 2008, the Supreme Court upheld the sentence once again. Chiţac's health deteriorated rapidly and on 16 September 2010 he was transferred from Jilava prison hospital to the Bucharest military hospital where he died of heart failure on 1 November. After serving five years of his sentence Stănculescu was released from Jilava prison on 20 May 2014. He died in Bucharest on 19 June 2016. Guşă died in 1994 at the age of 54. Coman (1926–2016) was arrested on 22 December 1989, tried and sentenced on 9 December 1991 to jail terms of 25 years for his actions in Timişoara. These sentences were reduced on appeal in 1997 to 20 years, while on 11 December 2000 President Emil Constantinescu granted him a pardon for the rest of the sentence so that Coman only actually spent little more than three years in jail (from 1997).

8 Siani-Davies, *The Romanian Revolution*, p.68.

9 *Ibid.*, p.69.

10 Filip Teodorescu, *Un risc asumat* (Bucharest: Viitorul Românesc, 1992), pp.294–99.

11 Miodrag Milin, *Timişoara: 15–21 Decembrie '89* (Timişoara, 1990), pp.117–18.

12 *Ibid.*, pp.124–25.

13 Constantin Dăscălescu (1923–2003). A lathe operator by trade, he left school at the age of 16. He joined the Party in 1945 and studied at various Party schools from 1949 to 1962. From 1968 to 1975 he was party secretary for Galaţi County and in 1979 became a member of the Permanent Bureau of the Politburo. In 1982, he was appointed prime minister; see Mihnea Berindei, Dorin Dobrincu, and Armand Goşu (eds.), *Istoria Comunismului din România.* Vol.III. *Documente Nicolae Ceauşescu (1972–1975)* (Iaşi: Polirom), 2016, p.186, footnote 1.

14 Teodorescu, *Un risc asumat*, p.106.

15 Titus Suciu, *Reportaj cu sufletul la gură: traseele revoluţiei* (Timişoara: Facla, 1990), p.274.

16 Milin, *Timişoara*, pp.170–71; see also Siani-Davies, *The Romanian Revolution*, p.77.

17 Siani-Davies, *The Romanian Revolution*, pp.77–78.

18 *Ibid.*, pp.78–79.

19 A report in the newspaper *Ziua* claimed that the Cluj military prosecutor, Titus-Liviu Domsa, had prepared the ground in March 1990 for a number of army officers to be prosecuted, but had climbed down after local commanders had threatened to occupy Cluj city centre with armoured vehicles if charges were brought (Foreign Broadcast Information Service (henceforth FBIS) -EEU-98-071, "Romania: army chief accused of involvement in 1989 "massacre", 12 March 1998.) It was only in 1997 that the decision was taken to reopen the Cluj dossiers and Gheorghe Surdescu was appointed as prosecutor. The army's role in Cluj was especially sensitive because the name of General Constantin Degeratu, the then Army Chief of Staff, was linked to it. Degeratu was a colonel in the Fourth Army in that city in December 1989 and he was alleged to have transmitted orders from General Ilie Ceauşescu, a brother of Nicolae, to put down the demonstrations in Cluj. Degeratu strongly denied these claims in an interview given in April 1998 to the daily *Adevărul*. In his defence he argued that as an officer in the operational section of the Fourth Army in charge of research and analysis he was only charged with drawing up regional defence plans but his accusers have argued that these duties included the tactics used by the army in crushing the demonstrations in Cluj. A further twist to the story came when Constantin Darna, head of UM

0215, came to Degeratu's support. He disclosed that the accusations were concocted by 0215 officers in Cluj, a significant proportion of whom were probably *Securitate* officers, since Darna himself announced that up to 50% of the 0215 officers in the counties were recruited from this source (FBIS-EEU-98-153, "Romania: officer admits plot to discredit chief of staff", 2 June 1998). Darna's intervention, together with the announcement several days earlier that the military prosecutor had decided to press charges against six persons who occupied key positions in the Communist Party and army in Cluj in December 1989, took the spotlight off Degeratu. The persons in question were Ioachim Moga, former first secretary of the Cluj Party Committee, Nicolae Constantin, former Political Executive Committee member, General Iulian Topliceanu, former commander of the Fourth Army, Colonel Valeriu Burdea, former commander of military unit 01215 based in Floreşti, Lt Col Laurenţiu Cocan, former divisional commander of the above unit, and Major Ilie Dicu, former company commander with unit 01278 Someşeni. According to the prosecutor's charges, the first two accused ordered the peaceful anti-Ceauşescu protests to be put down, and the army, in carrying out this order, resorted to a totally unjustified use of force on the direct orders of Burdea, Cocan and Dicu. As a consequence, 26 people were killed and another 52 were wounded. (FBIS-EEU-98-141, "Romania: Former Cluj Party, Military heads charged for '89 role", 21 May 1998). The charges against the army officers were adjudged to be proscribed but Moga (b. 14 March 1926) was sentenced on 23 May 2005 on two charges of murder to eight and five years' imprisonment, to be served concurrently. His lawyers successfully petitioned the court for a stay of imprisonment on medical grounds and Moga died of heart problems on 2 December 2007 in a Cluj hospital.

20 I base this account on Paul Abrudan, *Sibiul în revoluţia din Decembrie 1989* (Sibiu: Casa Armatei, 1990), pp.24–27.

21 Siani-Davies, *The Romanian Revolution*, p.84.

22 I was present at and translated these interviews for the BBC "Panorama" documentary, broadcast on 8 January 1990.

23 For more on Nica see Siani-Davies, *The Romanian Revolution*, p.85, note 99.

24 For details see Siani-Davies, *The Romanian Revolution*, pp.86–87.

25 Personal protection of Ceauşescu and his wife was the responsibility of the Fifth Directorate of the *Securitate*.

26 Author's interview with Vasile Maluţan, 5 January, 1990. Lieutenant General Victor Atanasie Stănculescu, Deputy Minister of Defence, told me in an interview on 6 January 1990 that he had issued these orders. Both interviews were for the BBC "Panorama" documentary, broadcast on 8 January 1990.

27 As Peter Siani-Davies writes, "the other bodyguard had already been lost somewhere en route" (*The Romanian Revolution*, p.95). According to Gelu Voican Voiculescu Ceauşescu wanted Decă to take him to Voinesti because there was a national radio transmitter there under the command of a distant relative of Elena Ceauşescu. Ceauşescu hoped that the workers at the steel works in Târgovişte would support him but the car carrying him was turned away (Gelu Voican Voiculescu, interview with Radu Moraru for the programme *Naşul*, re-transmitted Televiziunea B1, 27 June 2008).

28 BBC interview with Nicolae Petrişor, 3 January 1990 (for the BBC "Panoroma" documentary, broadcast on 8 January 1990.)

29 According to one account, cited by Siani-Davies, a car from the presidential fleet also appeared at the agricultural station and accompanied the militiamen's car to Târgovişte but then became detached as both vehicles tried to approach the police headquarters (*The Romanian Revolution*, p.96).

30 Author's interview with Lieutenant General Victor Atanasie Stănculescu, Deputy Minister of Defence, 6 January 1990.

31 Siani-Davies, *The Romanian Revolution*, p.104.

32 *Ibid.*

33 Author's interview with Mircea Dinescu, 8 January 1990.

34 One of the earliest mentions of the rumour was an article in *Der Spiegel* in November 1986; see Siani-Davies, *The Romanian Revolution*, p.107, footnote 40. For Ilescu's background see Biographies.
35 The names of the 39 members of the CNSF are listed in Siani-Davies, *The Romanian Revolution*, p.116, footnote 61.
36 Brucan claimed that Apostol had collaborated with the *Securitate* after their detention but did not elaborate on the reasons for Răceanu's exclusion; author's interview with Brucan, 8 January 1990.
37 This was confirmed by Brucan to this author (interview on 8 January 1990). According to Stănculescu, the decision was taken on the night of 23/24 December; see his account below of these events.
38 Details below.
39 Popa committed suicide on 1 March 1990; see Richard Hall, "Rewriting the Revolution: Authoritarian Regime-State Relations and the Triumphs of *Securitate Revisionism in Post-Ceauşescu Romania*." PhD thesis, Indiana University, 1997, pp.343–44.
40 *Evenimentul Zilei*, 6 July 1993, p.3. The details for 17–21 December are taken from Iordache's report.
41 The choice of the name was significant since Radu was the Turkish-backed prince who drove the 'independent' Vlad the Impaler (a Ceauşescu favourite) from the seat of Wallachia in 1462.
42 There is clearly some inconsistency here since if the news of Milea's suicide only became public at 1100 the troops could not have been back in their barracks by 1103!
43 *Evenimentul Zilei*, 16 June 1993, p.3, and 5 July 1993, p.3.
44 Ion Itu, "Armata Trage în Propriul Minister", *Tinerama*, no.110 (8–14 January 1993), p.5.
45 *Ibid.*
46 Lieutenant Colonel Trosca, Captain Eugen Cotună, senior warrant officer Ion Muicaru, warrant officer Emil Oprea and sergeant majors Teodor Neagoe, Ion Costache and Constantin Surpăţeanu.
47 Militaru himself, when asked for his reaction to the death, declared that "Gheorghe Ardeleanu and Iulian Vlad are the only people who could reply to everything that happened in December 1989. I regret that with his departing, very many replies about those December events have gone to the grave with him. Someone, probably, was counting on this because at some stage Colonel Ardeleanu might have spoken. I knew Ardeleanu and I do not think he was so stupid as not to realize that that substance was poisonous. In 1990, I met him by chance with his family and he told me that he was under permanent surveillance and that at some future date we would meet to discuss a number of things in more detail. Ardeleanu's death ought to be a warning signal for Iulian Vlad" (*Evenimentul Zilei*, 16 June 1993).
48 Iulian Vlad (23 February 1931–30 September 2017) was a career officer in the *Securitate*. He joined in 1951, spent six months in the Soviet Union in 1956 at a KGB academy, became head of training in the *Securitate* in the late 1950s with the rank of Lieutenant Colonel and was promoted to Major General in 1971. On 3 October 1987, he was appointed Minister State Secretary in the Ministry of the Interior and head of the *Securitate* (Mihnea Berindei, Dorin Dobrincu, and Armand Goşu (eds.), *Istoria Comunismului din România*. Vol.III. *Documente Nicolae Ceauşescu (1972–1975)* (Iaşi: Polirom, 2016), p.53, footnote 18).
49 Radio Bucharest, 23 December 1989, 4.35 p.m.
50 Siviu Brucan, *Generaţia Irosită* (Bucharest: Universul & Calistrat Hogaş, 1992), pp.224–25.
51 M. Shafir, "The Revolution: An Initial Assessment", *Radio Free Europe. Report on Eastern Europe*, vol.1, no.4 (26 January 1990), p.40.
52 The ambassador was not at home at the time, but his wife and three daughters were. On the intrusion of the gunmen they took shelter in the basement and spent a couple of

terrifying hours there before the shooting ceased. They survived unharmed physically, but were so traumatized that the ambassador withdrew with them to Sofia.

53 Richard A. Hall, in a series of articles and blogs, has painstakingly examined the small-arms and munitions used by various Romanian forces during the revolution and argues convincingly that members of the *Securitate* injured, maimed, and killed Romanian citizens during the revolution using *dum-dum* bullets that were outlawed by international conventions to which Romania was a party; see, *inter alia*, "Ce demonstrează probele balistice dupa 7 ani?", *22*, 17–23 December, 1996 and "The *Securitate* roots of a modern Romanian fairy tale: The Press, the former *Securitate* and the historiography of December 1989", *RFE/RL reports*, vol.4, no.7 (3 April 2002), vol.4, no.8 (17 April 2002), vol.4, no.9 (1 May 2002) and his blog *The Archive of the Romanian Revolution of December 1989* https://romanianrevolutionofdecember1989.com/. Accessed on multiple occasions.

54 Dennis Deletant, "Revisiting the 1989 Romanian Revolution: Some Personal Reflections", *Archiva Moldaviae*, Iaşi, vol.IV, 2014, pp.227–52 [p.230].

55 Silviu Brucan, *The Wasted Generation* (Boulder, Colorado: Westview, 1993), p.185.

56 Shafir, "The Revolution", p.37, note 35.

57 The background to this meeting is given in Deletant, "Revisiting the 1989 Romanian Revolution", pp.227–52. Subsequently, General Stănculescu, having met me at his request in January 1990, gave me several more interviews in the period 1991–1995 about his role in the overthrow and execution of Ceauşescu.

58 Milea committed suicide that morning.

59 Manea Mănescu (1916–2009) was a brother-in-law of Ceauşescu and a member of his inner circle.

60 Through his actions Stănculescu could claim if necessary to Ceauşescu, that he was helping him to escape the building, and to the revolutionaries, that he was removing Ceauşescu from the seat of power, thereby facilitating his overthrow.

61 Dinu Săraru, *Generalul revoluţiei*, p.45.

62 The grounds of the army football team *Steaua*.

63 Kemenici had been warned that a commando would come by helicopter to save Ceauşescu, hence Stănculescu told Kemenici that he would identify himself with a yellow "scarf".

64 Săraru, Generalul revoluţiei, p.62.

65 Gelu Voiculescu Voican (1941–) was an engineer who, according to his official biography, was arrested in July 1985 and sentenced to 18 months' imprisonment for "possession of anti-regime propaganda". It is not clear how he came to be in the entourage of Ion Iliescu. Kemenici, uncertain about the situation and his own position in Târgovişte suggested to Voiculescu Voican that he give him and the Ceauşescus an armed escort to Bucharest but the latter refused, fearing that if the situation changed, Kemenici might receive orders that the members of the tribunal should be taken captive during their return to the capital. (Gelu Voiculescu Voican, interview with Radu Moraru for programme *Nasul*, re-transmitted Televiziunea B1, 27 June 2008).

66 Săraru, Generalul Revoluţiei, p.65.

67 An abridgement of Stănculescu's interviews with me and the similar one given in Săraru, *Generalul Revoluţiei*, pp.66–96.

68 The composition of the *Securitate* on 22 December is given in Appendix 10.

69 Of the 1,104 dead, 543 were killed in Bucharest; across the country 162 died before 22 December, 942 after 22 December. 3,352 persons were wounded of whom 1,879 in Bucharest; through the whole of Romania 1,107 were wounded before 22 December and 2,245 after that date. In the ranks of the army there were 260 dead and 545 wounded and in the ranks of the *Securitate* and militia 65 dead and 73 wounded (Ruxandra Cesereanu, *Decembrie '89. Deconstrucţia unei revoluţii*, Iaşi: Polirom, 2004, p.61.)

70 Dennis Deletant, Communist Terror in Romania. Gheorghiu-Dej and the Police State, 1948–1965 (London: Hurst and Co., 1999), p.392.
71 Walter Bacon, "Romanian Secret Police", in J.R. Adelman (ed.), *Terror and Communist Politics:The Role of the Secret Police in Communist States* (Boulder, Colorado and London: Westview, 1984), p.135.
72 Brucan, *Generaţia irosită*, p.198.
73 *Cuvântul*, 18–24 August 1992. In conversation with this author (16 August 1993), Dr Măgureanu told me that he believed about 170,000 of this figure were active at the time of the Revolution.
74 *Ibid.*
75 *Ibid.*
76 Its Director was Virgil Măgureanu. Măgureanu came from a humble background and details of his career, published in 1992, cast an interesting light on the workings of the *Securitate*. Born Virgil Asztalos in March 1941 in the county of Satu Mare at a time when it was under Hungarian rule, his secondary schooling was pursued in a textile apprentice school where he was appointed Communist Youth secretary. In 1964, he enrolled at the Faculty of Philosophy at Bucharest University and after graduating in 1969 he was appointed assistant lecturer in political science at the Party Academy "Ştefan Gheorghiu" in Bucharest. It was at this time that he adopted his mother's maiden name, Măgureanu, to avoid the suspicion that he might be of Hungarian background. In the summer of 1971, he transferred to the department of scientific socialism at the university and it was from here that he was recruited to work undercover in the DIE on 1 September 1972 with the rank of captain. He was given the conspiratorial name of Mihai Mihăilă and underwent three months of training before moving on to the documentation section. On 31 March 1973, he was placed on the reserve on the grounds of having been "appointed to a civilian job". He returned to the "Ştefan Gheorghiu" Academy, presumably working undercover since he signed an official secrets document on 27 March 1973 pledging himself not to reveal anything about the DIE or his work there ("Dosarul de Securitate al domnului Măgureanu", *Tinerama*, no.70 (27 March–2 April 1992). Măgureanu shared friends with Silviu Brucan. After the latter's involvement with "The Letter of the Six" Măgureanu was sent on Ceausescu's orders to the provincial town of Focşani in 1989. Măgureanu was selected by Iliescu as a member of the tribunal to judge Ceauşescu and was contacted by Voiculescu Voican to attend the trial (Round-table discussion with Măgureanu, Ion Talpeş and Victor Roncea, *Realitatea TV*, 21 Aug 2008).
77 Punct de vedere preliminar al Serviciului Român de Informaţii privind evenimentele din Decembrie 1989 (Bucharest: SRI, 1993), p.3.
78 *Ibid.*
79 Punct de vedere preliminar, p.8.
80 *Ibid.*, p.20.
81 Ibid., p.22.
82 See Marius Mioc's blog *"Răstălmăcirile lui Larry Watts şi răstălmăcirile altora despre Larry Watts,"* ianuarie 24, 2013. https://mariusmioc.wordpress.com; see also, Richard Andrew Hall, "All the 'Soviet Tourists', where do they all come from?", *The Archive of the Romanian Revolution of December 1989* https://romanianrevolutionofdecember1989.com/, accessed on multiple occasions.
83 Punct de vedere preliminar, p.23.
84 Timothy Garton-Ash, "Conclusions", in Sorin Antohi and Vladimir Tismăneanu (eds.), *Between the Past and Future. The Revolutions of 1989 and their Aftermath* (Budapest: Central European University Press, 2000), p.395.
85 Ruxandra Cesereanu, *Decembrie '89. Deconstrucţia unei revoluţii* (Iaşi: Polirom, 2009).
86 Bogdan Murgescu, 'Reprezentarea Revoluţiei din 1989. Câteva consideraţii' in *Revoluţia Română din Decembrie 1989. Istorie şi memorie* (Iaşi: Polirom, 2007), pp.11–12.

87 Vladimir Tismăneanu, Dorin Dobrincu, and Cristian Vasile (eds.), *Comisia Prezidențială pentru Analiza Dictaturii Comuniste din România. Raport Final* (Bucharest: Humanitas, 2007), p.454.
88 Peter Siani-Davies, "Romanian Revolution or *Coup d'état*? A Theoretical View of the Events of December 1989", *Communist and Post-Communist Studies*, vol.29, no.4 (1996), pp.453–65, (p.457).
89 *Ibid.*
90 *Ibid.*, p.458. The analysis of contradiction forms the subject of Jolan Bogdan, *Performative Contradiction and the Romanian Revolution* (Lanham, Maryland: Rowman and Littlefield International, 2017).
91 Siani-Davies, "Romanian Revolution or *Coup d'état*?", p.459.
92 *Ibid.*

18 Epilogue

Since the overthrow of Ceauşescu, Romania's progress along the road to political and economic reform has been hesitant. Given the chequered achievements of successive governments since the revolution it is difficult to escape the conclusion that the political will to reform has been lukewarm. Events have shown that the impetus for reform has come from outside rather than from within. The International Monetary Fund, the Council of Europe, the European Union and NATO have been the major catalysts of reform and the need to satisfy the requirements of these institutions in order to achieve integration into the so-called 'Euro-Atlantic structures' spurred and guided the reform process in Romania.

Whereas Ceauşescu succeeded in uniting Romanians in opposition to him, his fall threw them into confusion. In what at the time seemed to be the only revolution to live up to its name the reasoning in the West was that because Romania had cast aside a communist dictator it would become democratic and peaceful. The Romanians whom I met in Bucharest in the closing days of December—and they were largely young men and women in their late teens and early twenties who were helping to guard the Central Committee building and the TV headquarters—were exuberant at Ceauşescu's overthrow but that exuberance was tinged with apprehension about the future. That apprehension proved prophetic. At Christmas 1989, the Western and Romanian media were interpreting the overthrow as the 'people's revolution', rightly praising the predominant role of the young, and yet within a month many Romanians had become disillusioned, complaining bitterly about the 'theft' of their revolution.[1]

The legacy of totalitarian rule in Romania was therefore markedly different from that elsewhere. In the words of one of the young 'revolutionaries' wearing the tricolour armband of red, yellow and blue whom I met guarding the entrance to a metro station shortly after my arrival in Bucharest with the BBC in late December 1989, "we want real democracy, not Romanian democracy". That they should do so is not surprising. Although the Romanian Communist Party was declared dead in January 1990, no one produced a death certificate—members of the Party merely swopped their cards for those of the ruling National Salvation Front and most of them carried on as if nothing had changed in Romanian political life. The NSF tried to blend into the present and bury the past. Its successors, the Democratic Front for National Salvation (*Frontul Democrat al Salvării Naţionale,*

FDSN) and the Social Democratic Party of Romania (*Partidul Social Democrat din România PDSR*) showed a similar reluctance to question the past. Only some of those responsible for the bloodshed in December 1989 were brought to trial. They included 25 members of the politburo and the Central Committee, and 11 generals in the *Securitate* and the militia. For the events in Timişoara 29 leading figures in the Communist Party, the *Securitate* and the militia were convicted of "incitement to murder". Yet these convictions relate to the events between 16 and 22 December. The 800 suspected 'terrorists' who were arrested by the army between 22 and 28 December were freed early in 1990. Many senior army, *Securitate* and militia officers whose own subordinates have publicly identified as giving orders for demonstrators to be fired upon in Bucharest and in Cluj-Napoca on 21 December, remained at liberty and some of them were even promoted to even more senior positions within the army and police. The anti-democratic instincts of those who grasped power in late December 1989 brought the miners to Bucharest in June 1990. Their incursions then and in the following year bore the hallmarks of the tactics used by the communists in Romania in 1945 and elsewhere in Central Europe to subvert democratic order.

3.12–3.13: B.B. mirrored NV.

Yet the overthrow of Ceauşescu did lead to a political revolution: the single-party monopoly was removed, multiparty elections—albeit flawed in May 1990—were held, the command economy was dismantled, and censorship abolished. There was a democratic transfer of power in 1996 when the neo-communists suffered their first defeat at the ballot box since 1990. At the personal level, possession of a passport became a right, not a privilege, in early 1990 and therefore restrictions on travel abroad by the state were removed. The reviled abortion decree, introduced by Ceauşescu, was immediately rescinded. Yet the rule of law was fragile, and reform of the judicial system was sorely needed. The political will to bring senior politicians to court to face credible charges of corruption was wanting. For Romanians, in the words attributed to Honoré de Balzac, "Laws are spider webs through which the big flies pass and the little ones get caught", ran particularly true.[2]

One analyst of Romania had this to say about the country in 1990: "Political life in Romania is again being vitiated by malevolence, calumny, fantastic rumour, paranoia, and irresponsibility. Things are indeed getting back to normal".[3] Much of this is still true today.[4] Indeed, Prime Minister Dacian Ciolos complained in October 2016 that he was upset that "in Romania no one no longer trusts anyone and everyone proceeds from the assumption that everything is a lie".[5]

Communism in Romania, as elsewhere in the communist bloc, robbed societies of their trust in institutions beyond the family or other highly personalized networks. A concomitant post-communist problem was the failure to reform the politicized bureaucracy which was woefully inefficient. The lack of efficient administrative capacity has hindered Romania's ability to use the EU funding it is given. The high degree of centralization and the unchallenged 'wisdom' of rapid industrialization under Ceauşescu denied the country the flexibility of response required to promote economic and political reform after his removal from power. It could be argued that

> a higher degree of rebelliousness under Communism made the difference between the countries in East-Central Europe that experienced a more rapid transition to democracy, i.e. the Czech Republic, Hungary and Poland and those where the process was more tortuous and painful, as in the case of Bulgaria and Romania.[6]

Romania suffered from a chronic shortage of hard currency in the period 1980–89 and indeed in the early years of the following decade. Romanian exports fell from $10 billion in 1989 to under $5.8 billion in 1990 and $4.3 billion in 1991. In 1994, they rose to $6.1 billion and in the following year to $7.9 billion.[7] Romania's hard currency reserves at the end of 1989 had, according to one source, fallen to $1.8 billion, to which we should add the Romanian National Bank's reserves in gold which stood at almost $1 billion.[8] An additional issue that the Romanian state had to deal with by the early 1990s were the consequences of the fact that a substantial part of its foreign currency reserves had 'disappeared' in the Ceauşescu years.

In this regard, some consideration of the role of the *Securitate* in the Romanian economy under Ceauşescu is important. For example, the export of Romanian arms was reported to have been managed by *Dunărea*, a *Securitate* controlled company. The proceeds of these sales were alleged to have been placed in a secret Swiss account.[9] Another source of hard currency for the *Securitate* was the commission charged by the directors of various *Securitate* controlled foreign trade companies such as *Crescent, Metalimportexport, Vitrocim, Terra, Delta, Trawe* and *Carpaţi* from foreign companies for the conclusion of contracts. All of these companies had accounts at the Romanian Bank for Foreign Trade (BRCE, Bancorex).[10] The monies generated by the above-mentioned *Securitate* controlled companies could not be traced by the post-Ceauşescu authorities. On 12 March 1990, the forensic accountancy company Peat Marwick Thorne and the law firm Gowling, Strathy and Henderson in Toronto were contracted by the Romanian Ministry of Justice, on behalf of the Romanian government, to track down the *Securitate* accounts and those allegedly held by Nicolae and Elena Ceauşescu in which more than $400 million dollars were believed to have been held. The Canadians' enquiries ran into the sand regarding the *Crescent* company whose director was a prominent politician, Dan Voiculescu. The Romanian authorities refused to cooperate further in the investigation. The Canadian accountants discovered that *Crescent* had an account at the Romanian Bank for Foreign Trade (BRCE, Bancorex) several of whose directors were alleged to be former *Securitate* officers.[11]

In 1996, after the PSD (former Communist Party) fell from power, an audit carried out under the new Centre-Right government by the Romanian Audit Office concluded that

> a documented account of what happened to the state's hard currency reserves, which stood at 1.1 billion dollars in January 1990, could not be established since the hard currency account was closed illegally and without justification by the Romanian Bank for Foreign Trade (BRCE). In 1991, the BRCE

> opened an account at the Romanian National Bank under the title 'Romanian National Bank-State Hard Currency Fund' from which it made on four occasions, payments without supporting documents totalling $906 million, claiming that these were payments made towards the foreign debt of the Romanian state.[12]

The 'disappearance' of the above-mentioned hard currency funds after 1990 added to the shortage of hard currency at the disposal of successive Romanian governments after 1990.

A major legacy of communist rule in Romania was legal confusion. After 1990, the five-year economic plan was abandoned and a 'jungle' economy emerged in which the principal elements were the accumulation of capital and the formation of new economic and political elites. The latter often had their roots in the ranks of old Communist Party activists and members of the *Securitate*.[13] The slow rate of privatization in 1990–96 can be explained by the former communist elites' desire to control change in Romania. To control change in the economy they required time to accumulate capital. Such privatizations were often by management buy-outs in the absence of a credible legal framework. They could be termed 'a-legal' rather than 'illegal'. A numerous class of profiteers took advantage of this climate. Most of them were managers of state-owned enterprises who perfected the art of buying and selling under the table, but this black economy extended to the heads of the *Securitate* controlled trade companies involved in dealing in precious metals and arms. Many of these company heads siphoned off their commission for sales to private accounts abroad and used these funds after 1990 to fund new import-export companies based on the contacts they had made with foreign partners under Ceauşescu.

The transition from the state-controlled command economy to a market economy was hesitant, with laws being introduced while communist-era laws, not being annulled, were still on the statute book. This situation led to duplication of legislation and judicial inconsistency in the early 1990s. It is thus hardly surprising that foreign investors shied away from Romania. Foreign direct investment in Romania between 1990 and 2003 totalled 10 billion USD, whereas by comparison Poland received almost the same amount in 2000 alone.[14]

A report by an influential Washington think-tank on Romania's progress towards respecting the rule of law concluded "Despite considerable progress, rule of law in Romania continues to be a major area of concern".[15] Speaking at the launch of the report in Cluj-Napoca on 6 October 2014, former US ambassador to Romania Mark Gitenstein recognized the benefits that had accrued to Romania by advancing along the path to reform:

> This report and my support for its conclusions are based on a very elemental syllogism, a so-called 'virtuous cycle': Transparency, application of the rule of law, fighting corruption, building independent empowering institutions (the opposite of what is happening in Russia for example) creates greater prosperity. That in turn creates greater social and economic stability which in

> turn fosters greater internal investment (through equity markets) and external investment (through foreign direct investment) which in turn creates greater prosperity and stability and so on.[16]

These observations should not blind us to the achievements of the last 27 years. That said, it was only after the 2012 constitutional crisis that observers of Romania felt able to believe that an aspiration for the rule of law could be translated into a respect for it. Only through such respect can a country be accepted as an equal partner in the Euro-Atlantic structures. Yet good government still eludes Romania. Here the dictum that 'we should never make the perfect the enemy of the good' comes to mind but this does not justify the cognitive dissonance exhibited by many in government in Romania over the last quarter-century which is reflected in denials that a problem exists. Perhaps, in analyses of Romania, a logic to a situation where no logic exists is applied, yet the fact remains that failure to respect the rule of law and widespread corruption pose a danger to the internal cohesion and stability of the state. The contempt of the electorate shown by the Social Democratic Party government of Liviu Dragnea by its furtive issue of an executive order—it did not go through parliament—on the night of 31 January 2017 to decriminalize misconduct by public officials causing damage worth less than about $48,000 opened the SDP to the charge that it was not a party that represented the interests of disadvantaged social groups and the working class but one for corrupt oligarchs and bureaucrats. In effect, the SPD government, it can be argued, was seeking to legalize corruption, transforming its *de facto* status into a *de jure* one. The order met with the largest continuous street protests seen in Romania since the revolution, with more than 150,000 persons estimated to have gathered on five successive evenings in front of the government's headquarters in Bucharest's *Piaţa Victoriei* and tens of thousands more rallying on the streets of around 20 other cities calling for the measure to be withdrawn. It provoked a swift reaction from the embassies of Belgium, Canada, France, Germany, Netherlands and the United States. In a joint statement, the embassies declared that the ordinance "can only undermine Romania's standing in the international community and risks damaging partnerships that are based on common values, inherent in the guiding principles of the EU and NATO".[17]

Western values rest implicitly on an idea of human kind which seeks to cultivate the inherent dignity of the individual. The West enshrines that aim in institutions which it has formed and which are based on freedom, government by consent and the rule of law. Some Romanian politicians now respect the application of the law, and the vigilance of the press. Many do not. Honesty is a more important attribute than the capacity to charm; character trumps personality. Corruption, autocratic impulses, widespread incompetence and a lack of professionalism have characterized the attitudes and actions of successive governments and the bureaucracy since the revolution. Over the last three years, major progress has been made in the drive against corruption in the ranks of the political and business elite. Addressing the other flaws in the public domain will require not only a continued concerted effort from the judicial institutions and from Romanian society, but especially a commitment from the Romanian government and parliament to respect and protect the will of the people.

Notes

1 For an incisive analysis of the six months following the revolution see William McPherson, 'In Romania', *Granta*, vol.33 (January 1991), pp.9–58.
2 Plutarch has Anacharsis laughing at Solon the Lawgiver for "imagining that the dishonesty and covetousness of his countrymen could be restrained by written laws, which were like spiders' webs, and would catch, it is true, the weak and poor, but would easily be broken by the mighty and the rich". Plutarch, *The Lives of the Noble Grecians and Romans*, The Dryden Translation 66, 1952.
3 J.F. Brown, *Surge to Freedom: The End of Communist Rule in Eastern Europe* (London: Adamantine Press, 1991), p.220.
4 A broader treatment of the progress towards a culture of democracy in present-day Romania is to be found in my 'Romania's Commitment to the Rule of Law?', in Lavinia Stan and Diane Vancea (eds.), *Post-Communist Romania at Twenty-Five. Linking, Past, Present and Future* (Lanham, Boulder, New York, London: Lexington Books, 2016), pp.219–40.
5 *Evenimentul Zilei,* 6 October 2016.
6 Dragoş Petrescu, '"Rebellious" vs. "Non-Rebellious" Nations. British Perceptions of Romanian Anti-Communist Dissidence in the 1980s', *Romania and Britain: Relations and Perspectives from 1930 to the Present,* proceedings of the British-Romanian Symposium, New Europe College, Bucharest, convenors, Dennis Deletant, Anca Oroveanu, British Council, Romania, 2005, p.163.
7 Bogdan Murgescu, *România şi Europa. Acumularea decalajelor economice (1500–2010)* (Iaşi: Polirom, 2010), pp.466–67.
8 Murgescu, *România şi Europa*, p.466, footnote 3.
9 'Activitatea Comisiei guvernamentale pentru recuperarea fondurilor deturnate din patrimoniul statului', *NU*, 86 (2–9 September 1992).
10 *Evenimentul Zilei*, 4 September 1992, p.3. Liviu Turcu, 'Cum pot fi găsite conturile lui Ceauşescu', *Evenimentul Zilei*, 8 September 1992.
11 http://aleximreh.wordpress.com/2011/02/05/crescent-dan-voiculescu-autorii-loviturii-de-stat-l-au-asasinat-pe-ceausescu-pentru-a-deturna-averea-diavolului-in-stil-mafiot/. Accessed 6 February 2011. See also Dan Badea, *Evenimentul Zilei*, 28 May 1998.
12 http://aleximreh.wordpress.com/2011/02/05/crescent-dan-voiculescu-autorii-loviturii-de-stat-l-au-asasinat-pe-ceausescu-pentru-a-deturna-averea-diavolului-in-stil-mafiot/. Accessed 6 February 2011.
13 Bogdan Murgescu, *România şi Europa*, p.467.
14 http://www.inblickosteuropa.se/?p=/2articles/12/marinescu.html. Accessed 7 December 2014.
15 CEPA, *Romania's "Tipping Point". Advancing the Rule of Law, Governance and Public Leadership. Findings of the U.S.-Romania Initiative Working Group* (Washington, DC: CEPA), July 2014, p.10.
16 My thanks to ambassador Gitenstein for passing on to me a copy of his speech.
17 https://ro.usembassy.gov/category/press-releases/?_ga=1.111403716.1301586139.1472573002. Accessed 3 February 2017. US Senator John McCain (R-AZ), Chairman of the Senate Armed Services Committee, released the following statement on 3 February 2017 on the protests taking place in Romania: "I am deeply concerned by the decree of the Romanian government to decriminalize certain graft offenses. This decree undermines the significant progress Romania has made in its fight against corruption, and it could stall further anti-corruption efforts. Romania's President, Klaus Iohannis and the judicial community have warned that such a decree could undermine the rule of law

and Romania's international standing. The Romanian people clearly understand the implications as more than 200,000 protesters poured into the streets yesterday and continue their demonstrations today. I hope the Government of Romania will heed these concerns and prevent backsliding on its reform efforts. Romania is a stalwart NATO ally with almost 600 troops fighting in Afghanistan and is home to one of our critical missile defence sites. The integrity of rule of law, including critical anti-corruption legislation, is a cornerstone of Romania's vibrant democracy and is an integral component of what makes Romania a more capable and reliable ally. With ever-increasing threats to democracy in Europe today from Russia and its proxies, Romania cannot afford to retreat in the fight against corruption". http://www.mccain.senate.gov/public/index.cfm/2017/2/statement-by-sasc-chairman-john-mccain-on-protests-in-romania. Accessed 4 February 2017.

19 Conclusion

The violent manner of Ceauşescu's demise set Romania's experience of political change apart from that of the other Central and East European states and was itself an indication that in Romania the peaceful overthrow of dictatorship was impossible. The obvious question arises: Why was this so? One analyst has eloquently and concisely observed that Ceauşescu's "once sturdy patriotism had become a deranged nationalism".[1] His successful appeal to nationalism allowed him to tyrannize his people and allowed the people themselves to be tyrannized. There is some merit in the argument that this was matched by a predilection on the part of Romanians for authoritative rule, as evidenced by the royal dictatorship of King Carol II and the regime of Ion Antonescu. But both the latter were a response to perceived threats to Romania's territorial integrity.

Overt challenges to Communist rule in Romania were uncommon and none threatened to overthrow the regime.[2] As Nicolae Ceauşescu's despotic excesses increased in the 1980s, so too did people ask, not only in the West, but in parts of the Soviet bloc: why don't the Romanians resist or rebel? Four explanations were usually given. One was that there was no focal point for opposition. A second was that Romanians were by nature timorous and passive, conditioned by their history under the foreign imperial rule of the Ottoman Turks, the Habsburgs, the Romanovs and the Soviet Communists, to adopt a defensive stance rather than come out in open revolt. Such a stance involved apathy, duplicity and a reliance upon the individual rather than the group. The third explanation was that passiveness was engendered by the Orthodox faith, to which more than 80 per cent of Romanians belong. This life, necessarily, is a tale of tears, a judgement of God upon the people. Justice would come in the afterlife. The fourth explanation was that the secret police, the *Securitate*, was extremely efficient. This should not be underestimated. The *Securitate* knew that it could reckon on 'passivity', especially if the regime espoused at least one popular cause, for example, an anti-Russian stance. All four explanations have some cogency in them, but they are not entirely valid in themselves nor do they offer a complete answer to the question.

Let us take the first explanation. The absence of a focal point of opposition was a feature of post-war Romania. The traditional elites had been destroyed by the Communism. At the time of its imposition, Romania was a predominantly agricultural country with little industry and only a small working class. Organized labour did not represent a significant force in Romanian politics before the Second World War and there were no traditional links between the intellectuals and industrial workers. The weakness of the pre-war Romanian Communist Party, which was proscribed between 1924 and 1944, explains the few challenges to the Communist regime from within Marxist circles. Although Romania's intelligentsia was one of the most sophisticated in Central Europe, and one of the most powerfully influenced by French literary currents, it remained untouched by the French passion for leftist values. Without a tradition of working-class activism, and a social group that espoused egalitarian principles, there was no drive for revisionist initiatives.[3] The notable exception was Lucreţiu Pătrăşcanu, a leading figure in the Party, who was purged for 'nationalist deviation' in 1948 and executed in April 1954. Ironically, that 'nationalist deviation' was to be embodied precisely by Ceauşescu and used to deflect any influence the reformist Gorbachev attempted to bring to bear upon the fossilized Stalinist.

Sycophancy and participation in Ceauşescu's pervasive personality cult within all strata of Romanian society fed his megalomania.[4] Ceauşescu's protest at the Warsaw Pact invasion of Czechoslovakia in August 1968 led him to discover that appeals to national sentiment could be an efficient mechanism of social control and personal dictatorship. It persuaded him of the rewards to be gained by lending emphasis to national symbols and to his own position in Romania. The huge rally in Bucharest on 21 August and its acclamation of Ceauşescu's denunciation of the occupation proved to be his finest hour, which whetted his appetite and that of his wife Elena, for the establishment of a personality cult. Stridently nationalist slogans were gradually incorporated into this cult and into the permanent festival introduced known as *Cântarea României* (Song to Romania) which became an extension of it. This national festival, conceived and planned by the propaganda department of the Central Committee in 1975, was designed to provide

> the widest framework for the intensification of cultural and educational activities, for the participation of the mass of the people in the development of the homeland's new spiritual assets, a new form for the assertion of the talent, sensitivity and creative genius of our people.[5]

One facet of the 'new form' of the festival was its permanence. For over a decade a series of spectacles with mass participation was staged under the umbrella of *Cântarea României*; in 1985 there were 3,593,316 active participants in the 153,000 artistic groups which performed. As for the spiritual assets developed by the spectacles, these were submerged by the emphasis given to national liberty, independence and unity, the guardian of which was Ceauşescu as head of state and party leader.[6]

The accusation of timidity was largely based on what *appeared* to be a complete absence of challenge to the Communist regime in Romania; unfavourable comparisons were made with the popular unrest in East Germany in June 1953 and in Poland in summer 1956, the uprising in Hungary in 1956, the Prague Spring in 1968, and the Solidarity movement of the early 1980s in Poland. The unchallenged acceptance of this charge was itself confirmation of the validity of the explanation regarding the efficiency of the *Securitate*, for it provided a measure of the secret police's success in preventing information about resistance to the regime from leaking to the outside world. The first major collective protests against the regime in Romania were prompted by the example of the Hungarian uprising in October 1956, but there was a news blackout in Romania and little information about them reached the West where the Suez crisis and the events in Hungary dominated the headlines. The failure of the Romanian media to report the strike of miners in the Jiu valley in south-western Romania in August 1977 characterized its role of a tool to be manipulated by the regime. There were a number of isolated, small-scale workers' protests in provincial towns in Romania in the 1980s about which nothing was generally known until almost a decade later. Even today, little has appeared in print about them.

Access to information was as essential for the individual to defend him/herself against authority as was manipulation of it for the government to protect itself. This control of the media and the sanitizing of news was very effective in containing protest and in inculcating a sense of isolation and frustration amongst protesters, and played a self-fulfilling role: if no opposition to the regime was reported, then most of the public not only assumed that there was none, but, guided by this assumption, questioned the point in displaying any.

It is not enough to ascribe the lack of resistance to Communism in Romania solely to the efficiency of the *Securitate*; other factors such as the linkage between formal and informal systems in Romanian society and duplicity played a major part.[7] The regime institutionalized the lie and therefore it was not surprising that citizens developed coping strategies to address this perversion. Life in a country where the abnormal became normal, where, despite an oil production that was the largest in Eastern Europe after the Soviet Union, petrol was rationed and where, despite the trumpeting of record harvests of grain, bread was rationed, led Romanians to cultivate dual *personae,* in a private and a public form, to 'muddle through', and to get on with their lives. Networks of relatives or friends were forged in order to cope with the labyrinthine bureaucracy of the state and the unpredictable turns in Ceauşescu's policies.

There was no solace to be found in Romanian television. Its transmissions were reduced in the 1980s to four hours per evening, with programming dominated by reports on Ceauşescu's omnipresence in regions throughout the country and propaganda on economic 'achievements'. Faced with such an austere diet, it is not surprising that those who could afford to do so turned to video players, acquired on the black market, to watch Western films. In western Transylvania inhabitants tuned their TV sets to watch Hungarian television while in eastern Romania Soviet channels were accessible and viewed. In Bucharest, there was a run in the late 1980s on Bulgarian-Romanian dictionaries, such was the popularity of Bulgarian programmes of popular entertainment.

Many in the population looked to their Christian faith for spiritual sustenance. In maintaining this they drew upon inexhaustible reserves of patience. Standing in queues for basic foodstuffs became a daily ritual. In tolerating the debasement of their dignity they received little guidance from the Orthodox Church whose prelates, with very few exceptions, failed them. Following the suppression in 1948 of the Uniate (Greek Catholic) Church, which derived its authority from Rome, the Orthodox Church could claim to represent the spiritual needs of the great majority of Romanians, but its direction was entirely subordinated to the interests of the Communist Party. Despite this, it was commonplace to see churches, filled to capacity on Sundays, notably by women of all ages.

Finally, it is important to bear in mind that the peasantry represented 80 per cent of the country's population in 1945 and that it was politically emasculated, first through the arrest of the leaders of the National Peasant Party and their imprisonment after trial in the autumn of 1947, and then through the detention of thousands—80,000 on the admission of Gheorghiu-Dej in 1962—who resisted the programme of forced collectivization initiated in 1949.

The most remarkable Romanian dissident was Doina Cornea. At the heart of Cornea's messages stood the belief that every individual should feel responsible for his actions and should recognize that any failure to act responsibly had repercussions for society at large. Spiritual and moral regeneration implied a renunciation of a materialist conception of life and in a series of reflections addressed to the young in 1985, Cornea analysed the part played by materialism in disorientating Romanian society. The crisis facing Romania was, in her view, as much a spiritual as a material one. In the letter sent to Radio Free Europe, addressed 'To those who have not ceased to think', she reflected on the deeper reasons for the crisis:

> The difficulties which have befallen us have made me think about the deeper causes which have engendered them. In your broadcasts you invoke most often the immediate causes, for example an economic policy which is erroneously conceived, the excessive centralization of power, finally our extremely rigid economic and social system. Living here as a teacher I glimpse a deeper and more general reason behind this catastrophe; it is the cultural and spiritual devaluation of our society resulting from the imposition of a reductionist and sterilizing ideology. I ask myself how we could have reached this state, and especially whether each one of us, small and insignificant individuals, does not bear some blame for all of this. If we examine ourselves thoroughly, down to the depths of our soul, will we not find that we have made so many compromises, have accepted and disseminated so many lies?[8]

In accepting these lies the Romanians had become "a people without a scale of moral and spiritual values, a people fed solely on slogans", and this process of 'spiritual draining' lay behind all the inadequacies of life. Cornea depicted herself and her fellow intellectuals as "passive onlookers at a regrettable perversion of consciences" which had led to the replacement of moral values by material ones. This situation could only be reversed by a return to the 'spiritual' which she defined as "the highest value, one which generated intelligence, ethics, culture, liberty and responsibility". She called upon her fellow teachers to cease teaching things which neither they nor their students and pupils believed in: "accustom them to thinking more freely, more courageously, more conscientiously, and more generously".[9] The downfall of Ceauşescu allowed the younger generation to do just that.

Notes

1 J.F. Brown, *Surge to Freedom: The End of Communist Rule in Eastern Europe* (London: Adamantine Press, 1991), p.209.
2 For a broader presentation and analysis of resistance, protest and dissent in Romania, see Dennis Deletant, *Ceauşescu and the Securitate: Coercion and Dissent in Romania, 1965–89* (London: Hurst; New York: M.E. Sharpe, 1995).
3 Vladimir Tismaneanu, *Stalinism for All Seasons. A Political History of Romanian Communism* (Berkeley and London: University of California Press, 2003), p.35.
4 See chapter 14.
5 Nicolae Ceauşescu, *Romania on the Way of Building Up the Multilaterally Developed Socialist Society*, vol.13 (Bucharest: Meridiane, 1978), p.316.
6 The insistence with which the cult was driven is exemplified by the fact that in early 1989, instructions were issued to editors of academic journals that Ceauşescu's speeches should be quoted extensively in their publications. Cristian Popişteanu, the editor of the popular historical monthly *Magazin Istoric*, revealed to me in January 1990, that he had been instructed by the propaganda section of the Party to mention Ceauşescu's name at least seven times on each printed page of his editorials.
7 Steven L. Sampson, 'Muddling Through in Rumania (or: Why the Mamaliga Doesn't Explode)', *International Journal of Rumanian Studies*, vol.3 (1981–83), pp.165–85.
8 Doina Cornea, *Scrisori deschise şi alte texte* (Bucharest: Humanitas, 1991), pp.13–14.
9 *Ibid.*

Appendix 1 The Report of V. Lesakov

Top Secret
Annexe No.6
For Comrade L.S. Baranov

During the period of my stay in Bucharest, between 7–20 August, I had meetings with leading activists of the RCP's Central Committee, including secretaries Gheorghiu-Dej, Ana Puaker and Vasile Luca, and also with the deputy head of the Allied Control Commission, comrade Susaikov. Besides helping me to resolve the problems connected with my mission (gathering materials for articles and information about the Party), Susaikov, Ana Pauker and Luca raised the matter of serious differences of opinions between the CC secretaries, namely between Dej on the one hand, and Pauker and Luca on the other, in the course of their discussions with me. In this respect I consider it necessary to report to you the content of those discussions.

In the discussion which I had on 8 August, comrade Susaikov told me of the existence of two groups in the leadership of the Party's Central Committee: one group consists of Gheorghiu-Dej and 'his men': Maurer, the Deputy Minister of Industry, Zeiger, Gheorghiu-Dej's private secretary, and Gaston [Marin]; the other group is made up of Vasile Luca and Ana Pauker, although the latter has fewer disputes with Gheorghiu-Dej than Luca. The principal cause of these divergences lay, in Susaikov's view, in Gheorghiu-Dej's unwillingness to discuss the major issues in the Politburo and to take decisions on them alone. Gheorghiu-Dej virtually ignores the Party and is very sensitive in his reactions to proposals made by Pauker and Luca since he fears that their authority in the Party may grow.

Comrade Susaikov believes that Gheorghiu-Dej is striving to remove Pauker and Luca from the Party leadership. As an example, he mentions the occasion when Gheorghiu-Dej, during the parliamentary election campaign, proposed that Pauker and Luca should not be included on the list of candidates on the grounds that they were not Romanian and had come from the Soviet Union. When the International Federation of Women was set up, Gheorghiu-Dej proposed that Pauker be elected to the Federation's leadership and sent on a permanent posting to Paris.

Comrade Susaikov noted that independent actions, which are not discussed in the Politburo, produce gross political errors. Thus, for example, Gheorghiu-Dej prepared two laws on finance which were in essence correct, but did not inform any of the Communists about them and presented them to the Minister of Finance, the liberal Alexandrini, who brought them before the budget commission. At the commission, Luca and other members who backed the Communists, declared themselves against the laws, particularly because they had been proposed by Alexandrini. The latter declared that he was personally against these laws, but that they had been proposed by the Communists. Only the wise behaviour of Ana Pauker allows this chapter to be closed.

In July and August, trade union elections were held. Pauker suggested to Gheorghiu-Dej over the phone that they meet and discuss a series of measures related to this matter, but Gheorghiu-Dej replied that he did not have time and that at the same time he was meeting the Social Democrats Voitec and Rădăceanu to discuss the elections. At Pauker's suggestion that Luca be invited to this meeting as a knowledgeable person regarding the organizing of elections—Luca as a Central Committee secretary dealt with the unions—Gheorghiu-Dej replied that he would meet the Social Democrats alone.

Comrade Susaikov considers that all these actions of Gheorghiu-Dej can be ascribed, in large measure, to the influence of Maurer and Zeiger who are cautious members of the Party. Pauker and Luca are trying to weaken Maurer's influence on Gheorghiu-Dej. To this end, they have proposed that Miron Constantinescu, a Politburo member, be named general secretary of the Higher Economic Council in place of Maurer, but Gheorghiu-Dej has not been willing to accept this for some time. The Politburo took the decision to appoint Constantinescu to this position at the meeting which took place during Gheorghiu-Dej's visit to Moscow. Maurer, who was present at this meeting, did not dare to vote against. When Luca telephoned Gheorghiu-Dej in Moscow with news of this decision, Gheorghiu-Dej said: "if Maurer agrees, then I agree".

On 15 August, I had a meeting with Vasile Luca. Regarding the situation in the Party leadership, Luca declared that we (referring to himself and to Pauker) want the Party to run the country and the ministries—where there are Communist ministers—and not the ministries to run the Party as is happening at present. Luca repeated what comrade Susaikov had told me. Luca considers that Pauker and Teohari Georgescu are largely in agreement with him, although the latter is trying to keep at arm's length from these disputes.

Luca said that when tasks were being assigned to the Central Committee secretaries, Gheorghiu-Dej tried to remove him (Luca) and Pauker from the Party leadership. Gheorghiu-Dej proposed that Pauker should head the administrative and women's sections, Luca the unions, and the organization and Agitprop sections Gheorghiu-Dej reserved for himself, that is, as Luca put it, "for his own people".

Luca reported that there were many bourgeois economists in the Ministry of Industry who, by working with Maurer, influence the Ministry's work. There are also many old hands in the Ministry of Justice (the Minister is the Communist Pătrăşcanu) who are sabotaging the Ministry's work. "Honest people can be expelled more quickly than Fascists from this ministry", said Luca. The Ministry drags its feet when looking into the cases of various criminals or even supports them. Even though he is aware of this situation in the Ministry of Justice, Gheorghiu-Dej has not taken a single step against Pătrăşcanu.

According to Luca, Maurer is the man who at present is aiming at establishing economic ties with the West. It was at his insistence that last year the greatest Romanian capitalists, Auschnit and Malaxa, were sent last year to set up economic links with the United States; they are there at this moment and are spreading reactionary propaganda. Maurer in his work consults with the General Union of Romanian Industrialists instead of relying on and taking advice from the unions. Luca is of the view that Maurer is consciously trying to discredit trade with the Soviet Union by taking measures so that machinery acquired from the Soviet Union is sold under price in Romania. In Luca's opinion, Gheorghiu-Dej allows himself to be influenced by such people as Maurer and also commits political errors because Gheorghiu-Dej does not have sufficient political training and has difficulty handling economic problems.

Luca believes that without the involvement of the Central Committee of the Soviet Communist Party he and Pauker cannot get positive results since they do not carry authority in Gheorghiu-Dej's eyes and the latter will resolve all problems on his own. At the same time, Luca stated that this discord was not known to anyone outside the Politburo and that they are not reflected in the Party's activity. Luca said that all the Politburo members tried to uphold and to strengthen Gheorghiu-Dej's authority as general secretary of the Party in their speeches. He emphasized that no one aspired to this position and that they were no other candidatures in the Party for the post, but we [Luca and Pauker] want the Party and not the ministries to solve all the major problems.

In conclusion, Luca requested that the CC of the Soviet Communist Party be informed about these differences of opinions and asked for help in removing them.

On 19 August I had my second meeting with Ana Pauker. At the first meeting, which took place on 8 August, Pauker did not raise the problem of differences of opinion in the leadership of the Party. At the second meeting, she did express her opinion, which was in essence similar to those of comrade Susaikov and Luca.

With regard to the sending of Auşnit and Malaxa to the United States, she declared that Gheorghiu-Dej's approval of Maurer's initiative was prompted by the fact that they, 'the national Communists', had to show concern for the country's economy, whereas 'the Muscovite group' thought more of the Soviet Union.

Pauker said that when fixed prices were set after the introduction of the monetary reform on 16 August, Gheorghiu-Dej ordered Apostol, the unions' leader and a member of the Politburo, as well as the leaders of the Party organization in Bucharest, to organize working groups and to 'lynch' all those who were going to put up the prices of goods. This decision of Gheorghiu-Dej was adopted at the Politburo meeting of 18 August.

Following a proposal by Tătărescu, Gheorghiu-Dej agreed to hold weekly meetings with Groza, Rădaăceanu and Tătărescu in order to discuss current major problems. In Pauker's opinion, the Communists, who were in a majority in the government, not to speak of parliament where they had an absolute majority, should not have taken part in these meetings. Nevertheless, Gheorghiu-Dej agreed with Tătărescu's proposal and took part.

Pauker considers that all of Gheorghiu-Dej's errors can be ascribed to his lack of political and general training. He does not apply his knowledge to the problems which he has at present to resolve. He is very preoccupied with his work in the Ministry and barely deals with Party matters. Similarly, he does nothing to improve his ideological and political level.

On the evening of 19 August I had a discussion with Gheorghiu-Dej. At my request, he addressed the current political problems facing the country. With regard to the role of the Party, he emphasized that the principal problem facing him was the poor political training of the Party members and, in this respect, of its leadership. Gheorghiu-Dej believes that as a result many mistakes are made but at the same time, the fundamental political line is correct.

He did not refer to the problem of differences of opinion in the Party leadership but, when speaking about the struggle with the Social Democrats and the discord among the latter, Gheorghiu-Dej remarked that "we, too, have our differences in the Party and we are at each other's throats sometimes".

V. Lesakov.

RGASPI (Russian State Archive of Social and Political History) (Rossiiski Gosudarstvennyi Arkhiv Sotsial'noi I Politicheskoi Istorii) Fond 575 Opis 1 dosar 33 Signed by V. Lesakov on 26 August 1947

I am grateful to Prof Ioan Chiper of the 'N.Iorga' Institute of History for providing me with this source reference.

Appendix 2 The organization of the Romanian Security Service 1948–1965

All information presented below on the organization of the Romanian security services down to 1965 is taken from *Organizarea şi funcţionarea Organelor Ministerului de Interne de la Infiinţare pînă în prezent* (Bucharest: Ministry of the Interior, 1978, 144 pp.). I am grateful to the relevant authorities in Romania for allowing me to consult this document.

1) The organization of the DGSP (*Direcţia Generală a Securităţii Poporului*) as established by decree on 30 August 1948:
   Directorate I Domestic Intelligence
   Directorate II Counter-sabotage
   Directorate III Counter-espionage in the Prisons and Police
   Directorate IV Counter-espionage in the Armed Forces
   Directorate V Penal Investigation
   Directorate VI Protection of Ministers
   Directorate VII Technical
   Directorate VIII Cadres
   Directorate IX Political (responsible for Party purity)
   Directorate X Administration
   Auxiliary departments dealt with interception of mail, surveillance and eavesdropping, and further included a cipher section and a secretariat.
   Thirteen regional directorates, including that for the city of Bucharest, were established.
2) On 30 March 1951, by decree no. 50, the DGSP (*Direcţia Generală a Securităţii Poporului*) is referred to by the new name of the DGSS (*Direcţia Generală a Securităţii Statului*) which was structured as follows:
   Directorate A Foreign Intelligence
   Directorate B Counter-espionage
   Directorate C Counter-sabotage
   Directorate D Transport
   Directorate E Counter-espionage in the Militia
   Directorate F Surveillance
   Directorate G Penal Investigation
   Directorate H Counter-espionage in the Armed Forces
   Directorate I Protection of Party leadership

Directorate J Cadres and Schools
Directorate K Administration
Directorate L Political
There were also departments for accounts, records, interception of mail, transport of secret documents and a secretariat. To reflect the local government reorganization of September 1950 when the counties (*județe*) were combined to form 28 regions, the number of regional directorates was increased to match this figure.

3) The Ministry of State Security (*Ministerul Securității Statului*) was set up as a distinct body from the Ministry of the Interior on 20 September 1952. It incorporated the DGSS.
4) On 7 September 1953, the Ministry of State Security was amalgamated with the Ministry of the Interior.
5) The Ministry of the Interior was reorganized on 11 July 1956 and divided into two departments: the Department of Security (*Departamentul Securității*) and the Department of the Interior (*Departamentul Internelor*). The latter was given responsibility for the militia and prisons while the former inherited the structure of the DGSS with the following modifications:
Directorate I Foreign Intelligence
Directorate II Counter-espionage
Directorate III Domestic Intelligence
Directorate IV Counter-sabotage
Directorate V Counter-espionage in the Armed Forces
Directorate VI Transport
Directorate VII Surveillance
Directorate VIII Penal Investigation
Directorate IX Protection of Party leadership
Directorate of Cadres and Schools
Directorate of Administration
Secretariat
Department B Radio counter-intelligence
Department C Records
Department D Transport of prisoners
Department F Interception of mail
Department H Cipher
Department K Counter-espionage in the prisons and militia
Department T Technical
A school for training officers and one for learning foreign languages was also placed under the control of the DS as were the security troops and the frontier guards.
6) On 30 May 1963, the control of the security troops was removed from the DS (*Departamentul Securității*) and placed under a separate department within the Ministry of the Interior. By the same decree of the 30 May Directorate I (Foreign Intelligence) of the DS was redesignated UM (*Unitate militară*) 0123/1 and given the name *Direcția Generală de Informații Externe* (DGIE).

Appendix 3 The statement of Gheorghe Pintilie, former head of the *Securitate*, dated 15 May 1967 and presented to the Party Commission charged with investigating the death of Ştefan Foriş.

'The undersigned Gheorghe Pintilie, being questioned by Vasile Patilineţ at the Central Committee about what I know about Ştefan Foriş, and my views in connection with this matter, have the following to say. Personally, I did not see a single document from the period of the bourgeois regime which showed any trace of contact between Foriş and the bourgeois *Siguranţa*, nor do I have any knowledge that such a document might exist. We interrogated former police and agents of the bourgeois *Siguranţa* for years on end without finding any sign of such a link. As regards what happened to Foriş I know the following:

In 1941, some of the comrades who were in jail, including me, began to feel that something was not right with the Party leadership. It was a very vague feeling. We were concerned about the large number of arrests of Communists at that time.

In 1941 or 1942, the Party leadership sent a leather jacket to the prison to be given to Dej. The jacket was accompanied by a letter from the Party leadership which, among other things, used the form of address to Dej as "you, as a future commissar". It was I who received the jacket and I took it to Dej. On learning that it came from the Party leadership, he refused to accept it with the words: "Screw him, he wants to buy me. You can do what you want with it, tear it up, throw it away, whatever."

Later, on another occasion, Dej spoke to me of Foriş as someone whom he didn't trust or about whom he was unhappy. At the same time, he told me to keep my mouth shut about his views of Foriş. I thus realized that the other Communist prisoners did not know of Dej's attitude. All of this took place in Caransebeş jail. It was known in the jail that 'fractionist' sentiments had appeared in the Party and that these had made themselves felt in the prison as well. Sometime in 1942, this 'fractionism' grew and each group sought to establish links with those in jail to persuade them that they were right. Dej gave orders that none of the jailed Communists should get in touch with any of the groups on the grounds that we didn't know what was going on outside and who was in the right. In insisting that no contacts were to be made with any group, Dej made a point of stressing that this applied to Foriş's group in particular. No one was to respond to any communication, and although messages came from the Central Committee, no replies were given.

It was against this background that a document came from the Central Committee asking us for the names of all the Communists belonging to the Party in jail. Dej handed me this document with the words: "There, there's your proof!" My view about this document was that if it wasn't an act of betrayal, it was in any case a grave error and a gross lack of vigilence. It was at this very same time that the number of Party members arrested increased.

From this point onwards word got around amongst other Party leaders in jail such as Teohari [Georgescu], Vinţe and Chişinevski that Foriş was a traitor. At the same time, the secretaries of Party groups began saying that something was amiss in the Party leadership. At this time, Dej was concerned about the whereabouts of Costică Pîrvulescu since he had been sought in several places and could not be found. It was in this atmosphere that a number of comrades were primed in prison to 'sort out' the Party leadership, starting with Foriş.

After 23 August 1944, I was given the task of keeping Foriş under guard. After Foriş was released at the beginning of 1945, it was also I who was instructed in June 1945 to re-arrest him and detain him. The order was given by Dej. Ana Pauker might have been present as well when this order was given. I kept Foriş in the following places: in a room in the headquarters of the Central Committee, in a basement in the building where I lived, and in a house on Popa Şapcă street. As Foriş's guard I used two or three comrades, yet they didn't know the identity of their prisoner. During the whole period of his detention, Foriş was very obedient and disciplined, doing everything he was asked. For example, he was told not to go near the window, so as not to be seen from outside, told not to shout or to speak to anyone, not to give his name. He followed all these instructions.

Each day, sometimes every other day, I was summoned by Dej and asked about Foriş, how he looked, what his attitude was. During Foriş's detention, Dej visited him several times and talked to him. What they discussed I do not know. I never saw Dej emerge from their meetings with anything on paper. Sometimes their discussions were very animated, with them shouting at each other. Sometimes Dej was accompanied by another comrade from the Party leadership when he went to talk to Foriş. Among those who went with Dej were, I remember, Ana Pauker and Teohari Georgescu. No one, however, contacted Foriş without Dej being present. In summer 1946, I received instructions from Dej and, separately from Teohari Georgescu that I should do away with Foriş.

When Dej gave me these instructions, I asked how I should proceed, he replied: "Haven't you got a brain? You sort it out!" Over the following days I was continually asked by Dej if I had dealt with Foriş. Eventually, when I kept saying "not yet", he chided me with "why do you keep pussy-footing around with him, as though you were about to give up?" When I told him that Foriş had been liquidated, Dej said, "Thank goodness we've finished with that wretch."

In getting rid of Foriş I was assisted by Bulgaru and my former chauffeur, who later left for the Soviet Union. It was also they who helped me to get rid of Pîrgariu, who was buried in the same place as Foriş. I was the only person among us who knew the identities of the murdered persons. Foriş and Pîrgariu were buried in a house on Aleea Alexandru which I have indicated on the spot'. (Cristian Troncotă, 'Ghiţă Ordonă, Pantiuşa execută', *Dosarele Istoriei*, no.3, 1997, pp.33-34).

The report of the Party Commission, drawn up by Gheorghe Stoica, Vasile Patilineţ, Ion Popescu-Puţuri and Nicolae Guină, concluded that 'Foriş's execution was carried out by Gheorghe Pintilie, aided by his chauffeur Dumitru Necin, through blows administered with an iron bar. The body was thrown into a specially prepared pit in the grounds of the building in which he was killed. A few days after Foriş's murder, two other persons were killed in the same place and in the same way, only one of whom was identified as N. Pîrgariu. All three were thrown into the same pit and their bodies covered with earth and rubble (stenogram of Gheorghe Pintilie's deposition before the Commission, *ibid.,* p.35)).

Regarding the disappearance of Foriş's mother, it has been established that since she came to the Central Committee headquarters on repeated occasions in tears, shouting from the street for the return of her son, she was arrested in the summer of 1946 and sent to Oradea under the supervision of the local Party committee. According to the declaration of Zoltan Eidlitz, former secretary for the cadres in the Bihor county, and Adolf Vogel, in whose house Foriş's mother was held, it emerges that the latter died at the beginning of 1947. Since she had been brought in exceptional circumstances to Oradea—as the two witnesses declare—her disappearance had to be engineered in the same way. In order to remove any trace of her, her body was thrown into the river Crişul Repede, with a stone attached to her neck ('Declarations of Laurentiu Cziko, Zoltan Eidlitz, Dumitru Cernicica, former Party secretary of Bihor county, and Adolf Vogel' (*Ibid.*).

Pintilie gave a similar account to Lt Gen Grigore Răduică, a senior *Securitate* officer, who had also been ordered by Nicolae Ceauşescu to investigate Foriş's fate in 1967 (P. Stefănescu, *Istoria Serviciilor Secrete Româneşti*, Bucharest: Divers Press, 1994, p.251). A Party obituary of Foriş dates his arrest to 9 June 1945 and his murder to the summer of 1946 (N.I. Florea, 'Ştefan Foriş', *Analele de Istorie*, vol.18 (1972), no.3, p.153). This chronology is corroborated by George Fotino, a private secretary to the Minister of the Interior, Teohari Georgescu. Georgescu himself described under interrogation in May 1953 how the decision was taken to get rid of Foriş: 'In spring 1946 General Nicolski came to me and asked me "What are we going to do with Foriş? He has been under arrest for some time. I told him that I would make enquiries and let him know. A few days later, I went to the Party General Secretary and asked him, "What are we going to do with Foriş. We've held him for a long time, shall we get rid of him?" Comrade Gheorghiu told me that he agreed with my proposal. After that I looked for Vasile Luca and Ana Pauker. I found them together in a room of Pauker's on the first floor. I asked them, “What are we going to do with Foriş?” in the sense that we should get rid of him. Both were in agreement (ASRI, Fond P, file 40009, vol.1, pp.230–40. Marius Oprea was kind enough to show me this document). Fotino recalled an attempt made by Foriş’s mother to seek an unscheduled audience with Georgescu in the early summer of 1945 to ascertain the whereabouts of her son. When Fotino, who had never heard of Foriş, went into the Minister’s office to tell him that a certain ‘Mrs Foriş’ was in the ante-room and would like to see him, Georgescu went bright red and told him to tell her that he had been called away to a meeting, adding an instruction to Fotino that ‘the woman was not to be allowed into the Ministry again’ (author’s interview with G. Fotino, 9 April 1994). Pintilie was co-opted as a member of the RCP Central Committee at a plenary meeting on 10–11 June 1948 (*Scânteia*, 13 June 1948, p.1). Despite being attacked in the April 1968 Central Committee plenary meeting for his role in Foriş’s murder, Pintilie was decorated by Ceauşescu in May 1971 on the 50th anniversary of the Party. Pintilie’s chauffeur, Dimitrie Necin (Dumitru Mitea), had originally been sent to Romania as one of three-man NKGB group parachuted in May 1944 into the area of Predeal with a radio transmitter to communicate to the Red Army information on German military activity (M. Mircu, Dosar *Ana Pauker*, Bucharest: Gutenberg, 1991, p.130, note 21). Pintilie consistently denied to Eduard Mezincescu that he had wielded the iron bar, claiming that the chauffeur Mitea struck the mortal blows (E. Mezincescu interview with this author, 16 June 1994), but his sadistic impulses were revealed in a drunken confession he once made at a party to Tatiana Brătescu, Ana Pauker’s daughter, in the early 1950s. He told her that as a member of the Komsomol in the Ukraine he had discovered a priest holding a service on the edge of his village in a hollow. He gathered other youths and together they pinned down the priest and buried him alive by piling earth over him with tractors (interview with T. Brătescu, 30 July 1994).

Appendix 4 The Romanian Foreign Ministry

On 23 August 1944, there were 279 diplomats and consuls (out of a total of 957 employees) working in the Ministry. A characteristic feature of the diplomatic service was its core of high quality personnel who had gained their experience in the inter-war period. They were marked by their professionalism and patriotism, and displayed both in the difficult period after 23 August 1944, and after the imposition of the Groza government. As a result of the increasing number of states with which Romania established diplomatic relations, a new law on the organization of the Foreign Ministry was adopted in March 1946 which led to an increase of about one hundred in the number of diplomats. On 30 April 1946, there were still 91 posts vacant in the Ministry, among them 15 heads of mission and 31 counsellors. The parties supporting the Groza government were quick to profit from this situation and used the new law to place their own members or supporters in diplomatic posts. Of the 45 persons taken on, the main beneficiary was the Liberal Party whose leader, Gheorghe Tătărescu, was Foreign Minister. The Communists occupied second place, with 11 posts, followed by the Ploughmen's Front with ten. Up to January 1947, there was a continuous rise in the number of diplomatic personnel taken on but after that date economy measures began to bite. On 1 June 1947, 9 diplomats and six consuls were dismissed, and on 1 September the numbers were reduced further by 36. None of those dismissed were members of the Communist Party.

The 'Communization' of the diplomatic corps began only after the removal of Tătărescu from the Foreign Ministry and his replacement by Ana Pauker on 7 November 1947. After this date, the Romanian Foreign Ministry was literally occupied by communists. Those employees who were not members of the Communist Party were denied access to the Ministry. But when the communists realized that they did not have the experience to deal with certain matters, they appealed briefly to some of the older diplomats. However, these, too, were dismissed on 20 November. At the same time new recruits were taken on, using the criteria of their social background and political persuasion. 268 new staff were recruited between November 1947 and March 1948, the prime consideration for employment being the extent of their activity on behalf of the Communist Party.

A detail which sheds light on the way in which Pauker ran the Ministry of Foreign Affairs is her sponsorship of Ana Toma. On 1 December 1947, Toma was appointed to the Foreign Ministry with the rank of First Secretary (head of chancery). On 8 May 1948, under a decree signed by the President of the Praesidium of the Romanian People's Republic, Professor C. Parhon, and countersigned by Pauker, Toma became secretary general of the Foreign Ministry. Even before that date, Toma had been granted exceptional powers within the Ministry. An example is the authorization for Toma, signed by Pauker on 29 January 1948, to approve expenditure "in the major interest of the state" within the budget agreed by the Ministry of Finance for any sum for which receipts could be shown, and up to a maximum of 20% of the budget when receipts could not be shown. In the latter case, a written order of Toma, specifying that payment was to be made without receipts, would suffice. How much money passed through Toma's hands on the basis of the authorization will probably never be known. These funds could have been used for espionage or propaganda exercises on behalf of the regime. The diplomatic historian Ion Calafeteanu does not rule out the theory that Pauker used the money to support the Zionist movement and to facilitate Jewish emigration from Romania, actions which would have discredited her in Stalin's eyes and contributed to Gheorghiu-Dej's victory in the struggle for power (Ion Calafeteanu, 'Schimbări în aparatul diplomatic românesc după 6 martie 1945', *6 Martie 1945. Inceputurile Comunizării României* (Bucharest: Editura Enciclopedica, 1995), pp.164–71).

Appendix 5 The formation of the Groza government

Gheorghiu-Dej confirmed in a meeting of the Romanian Politburo on 29 November 1961 that the idea to remove Pauker was planted in his mind in January 1946 by Vyshinsky; see 'Stenograma Şedinţei Biroului Politic al CC al PMR din ziua 29 noiembrie 1961' pp.12–13, reproduced in *Sfera Politicii*, no. 48, 1997, p.36. At the Moscow Conference in December 1945, the United States proposed that the Groza government should be reorganized to include members of the opposition parties. Stalin made a limited concession in this respect in the agreement signed on 26 December, in which the three Allies recommended that the Groza government should include one member each of the National Peasant and Liberal parties. Vyshinsky, Harriman and Clark-Kerr arrived in Bucharest from Moscow in 31 December to oversee the implementation of the agreement. The opposition parties nominated Ion Mihalache and Dinu Brătianu. The Groza government rejected these nominations, and finally Emil Haţieganu and Mihail Romniceanu were included in the cabinet to represent the National Peasants and Liberals respectively. The relevant passage in the Politburo minutes reads as follows. Gheorghiu-Dej is speaking:

"Vishinsky arrived on behalf of the Soviet Union, Harriman for the Americans and Clark for the British. Vyshinsky got in touch with us, explained the whole business and we consulted with Groza and Tătărescu and those responsible for these matters. We agreed to accept a representative from each of these parties, as well as the date proposed by them for the elections. We agreed amongst ourselves not to accept leading figures from these two parties but only second-rate people. We then settled upon Romniceanu and Haţieganu, if you recall. Then Groza, who was in constant touch with Vyshinsky, told him of our position... In the evening we went to the theatre. I, Groza and Ana were there. There were many of us. Vyshinsky was there as well, if I'm not mistaken."

Comrade E. Bodnăraş: "No, Vyskinsky wasn't there."

Comrade Gh. Gheorghiu-Dej: "Towards the finale Ana got up and called me. She continued to play the role of leader, although I was the general secretary. She still pulled all the strings and summoned me and said: 'My dear Ghiţă, look, there's a problem. You've got to go to Groza and inform him that we have to substitute Bebe [Dinu] Brătianu for Romniceanu'. I asked, 'Why?'. I think she gave the following reason: 'It will be easier, things will be understood more easily'.

It seemed that this proposal was supposed to help Vyshinsky. From the way she spoke to me, I took it to be a suggestion. This was her way of doing things, these things emerged from somewhere. She was never precise about it, but the suggestion was that they came from the highest Soviet circles."

Comrade E. Bodnăraş: "All the more because we knew that Susaikov was leaning towards Brătianu."

Comrade Gh. Gheorghiu-Dej: "We didn't know that then. We found out afterwards. So I went to Groza after the theatre and told him: 'Look, here's the problem. You remember that we settled on Romniceanu and Haţieganu, but now there's a proposal that we change Romniceanu for Bebe Brătianu'. He gazed in surprise at me. Then I told him the same story that there would be heated discussions and that a solution must be found, and we should give Vyshinsky a helping hand. When he heard this he said: 'O.K.'

The next day, Groza told Vyskinsky what I had told him. Vyshinsky hit the roof when he heard. Vyskinsky, Susaikov and their translator went to Groza's house. When Vyshinsky heard the whole story he got very angry. Groza said afterwards that Vyshinsky was almost shouting: 'What is the meaning of this? Have I come here, sent by my government, with an easy task? Am I one to run away from problems? I don't understand you'. In other words, a pretty heated discussion. 'Why did you make this last-minute change?' Groza did not say at the outset that Gheorghiu-Dej had come to see him. Then he related how Gheorghiu-Dej had come to see him and what I had said.

And so Vyshinsky sent for me and I went to Groza's house. I realized that the atmosphere was glacial. There was me, Groza, Vyshinsky, Susaikov and the translator. Vysinsky then asked me: 'Comrade Dej, you came by last night. Listen to what Mr Groza has to say. Well, then? What happened? Why?' Again the temperature rose. I said: 'Look here, Comrade Vyshinsky, Ana went to the theatre last night and made a concrete proposal to ease the discussions with the two representatives of the US and Britain in terms that suggested that it came from the Soviets. I then came and informed Groza in the exact words used by Ana to me'.

Vyshinsky calmed down, but it was now the turn of Susaikov. The penny dropped later. I wondered why Ana had raised the matter of Romniceanu's replacement by Bebe Brătianu. Susaikov then put the question: 'But who is the general secretary?' In other words he was asking: 'Why have you come here with this story involving Ana when you are the general secretary'. I then asked him: 'But who really is the general secretary?' I knew that he and Ana were close, they visited each other and talked. This happened less frequently with me.

Susaikov said nothing and Vyshinsky took me to one side and said: 'Comrade Dej'—the others heard, perhaps, because he wasn't speaking softly, but fairly loudly—'how is Ana of help to you?' I said, 'You can see for yourself what help she gives me, and if this was not the only example'. He thought for a little and said, 'Wouldn't it be better if she was removed?' Removed could be understood in the sense that she should be removed from the leadership or removed from Romania.

I then said to Vyshinsky: 'Comrade Vyshinsky, such a thought never crossed my mind, but I shall think about it and reflect on what you have said'. And with that it was over.

On a later occasion, Vyshinsky criticised Ana and Teohari Georgescu very harshly over the question of the Iron Guardists."

Appendix 6 Conditions in the Aiud Central Penitentiary

The Aiud Central Penitentiary has the following staff:

DIRECTOR: ALEXANDRU GUTAN, a communist from Cetatea Albă (in Bessarabia).
DEPUTY DIRECTOR: Mareş, an ex-inmate of the prison, whether as political or common-law offender I do not know.
WARDERS: These have in their care the cells of the prison where only political prisoners are kept.

1. Head Warder: I. Urdărianu
2. Warder: Furda
3. Warder: Filimon
4. Warder: Onica

The cells contained (30 March 1947) about 400 political offenders. I have now been informed that the *Sumanele Negre*[1] have also been brought here.

Types of prisoner:

- War criminals (Romanian and Hungarian)
- National Peasant Party members
- Iron Guard members

Accommodation

The prisoners are kept in four-by-two metre cells, containing one iron bed each. The necessary linen is supposed to be brought from their respective homes. Prisoners have the right to keep a suitcase each in their cells. All cells, without exception, are densely inhabited by bed bugs. The central heating is almost non-existent—about 6 metres of tubing and no radiators, through which, during the last winter, circulated small quantities of warm water for two or three hours daily.

On entry in the prison each detained person is subjected to a search. I will here recount what happened to the former Antonescu cabinet ministers, of which I was one.

We arrived on 6 March 1947 and were taken under escort to the prison. We were put six each in a cell without any search having been made and with all our luggage. The cells were quite empty and contained no beds. At about 1900 hours, the director came, asking us each our names, and left in a very civilized manner.

At about 24.30 hours, we were awakened by bangings on the door and obscene language. Lacking any sort of sleeping space, we had put our baggage next to the doors. We got up, took away the baggage and the following persons burst through the door, the deputy director Mareş and an Iron Guardist, whose name I do not know. Two of us (General Sichiţiu, a 70-year old man, and Colonel Cristea Manea) were unable to get up. Both had arrived ill, especially Colonel Manea, who has a perianal fistula with 12 craters, which had just formed an abscess.

They were kicked by Mareş for their inaction, General Sichiţiu receiving a blow on the right eye-socket and several on his back. Colonel Manea was also severely kicked. After having got up, they were again hit with the butt end of a 'Schmeisser' sub-machine gun, with which the deputy director was armed. After having asked us our names, Mareş left.

The second evening, we were subjected to a search under the supervision of Mareş... Clothes were torn, personal belongings messed up, medicines spilt. They stole everything they found and took a liking to. I can give one example. General Arbore had his gold pencil stolen. On 27 March, he told this to his wife in the presence of the head warden, Urdărianu, in the parlour. The latter immediately reported this conversation to the deputy director and on 12 April, just before Easter, he was not allowed to receive any food parcels...

Treatment

The food consists of a lump of about 300 grams of maize meal, together with a cloudy water called soup, morning and night, or five slices of unskinned potatoes in perfectly crystalline water. Most of the time, the prisoners eat the potatoes, keeping the water in order to wash their more intimate parts, as this is the only warm water which they receive. Those who were on a diet received plenty of soup......

All prisoners, excepting those condemned to hard labour, have the right to receive 3 kg of food parcels from home. For Christmas, they were approved 5 or 6 kg each, but immediately after Christmas, the deputy director made a midnight search, confiscating all the remaining food.

The prison has a canteen from which political prisoners are forbidden to buy anything, except those who are ill, who receive a little booklet where the man in charge of the canteen writes the quantities and sums to pay, and the prison cashier pays these sums from the money sent to the prisoners by their families...

Water is distributed normally through a pump system, which draws it to the highest storey and then distributes it to the respective washbasins. The pumps broke down in the autumn of 1946 and were not repaired. Today, water is distributed to the prisoners in buckets, about 2 litres daily, because apart from a plate, a spoon and a bottle of water, all other recipients were confiscated from the cells. This water must suffice for washing both body and clothes and for drinking.

The WC is a real calamity. Every floor has 90 cells. On some floors there are two and even three political prisoners in each cell. All these have to use six drain holes without water, which fill up after being used three times. They are only cleaned once every 24 hours.

Rats circulate in legions through the prison drain system.

The prisoners are taken out of their cells for five to ten minutes morning and night in order for the cells to be cleaned, and half an hour morning and afternoon to take exercise in the quad. The rest of the time they stay in their cells...

The Aiud prisoners have lived and probably still live days and nights of real terror. The deputy director Mareş used to search the cells five nights a week. The technique was as follows:

The door opened and Mareş, accompanied by one or two Iron Guardists, of whom one was usually Boian-Moisescu, the former chief of Iron Guard police, came in. They stripped you to the skin and started searching. They tore the mattress open, strewing all its contents on the floor, and then threw the inmates' salt, food, medicine, clothing, etc. on top. They confiscated everything they liked and the Iron Guardists cut suitcases and shoes or boots open with a knife if these seemed suspicious. Woe befell he who protested.

I will now quote two cases, that of Romulus Daianu and of Reinhardt.

The first was a journalist and the second a police officer, formerly in the Bucharest Prefecture of Police. Daianu worked for two days to tidy up his cell after such a visit and Reinhardt was put in 36 lb chains for nine days for having concealed a small ikon on which was written a sentence from a sermon preached in prison and censored by the administration—ikons were completely banned, as well as family photographs...

Family visits are allowed in the parlours twice a month only, on [the] 12th and 27th of each month. The families are received at the train station by the police, escorted from there to the police station, hotel and prison and immediately after, taken out of town. They are forbidden to contact anyone in Aiud, even if they have relatives or friends in this town...

Written in English by an anonymous former member of Antonescu's cabinet in 1947.

Notes

1 See Chapter 3.

Appendix 7 The arrest and interrogation of Herbert (Belu) Zilber

We have to thank Herbert Zilber for shedding further light on how his own arrest and interrogation was used to implicate Pătrăşcanu in the charge of being an agent of the *Siguranţa*. This he did in an autobiographical memoir written in the early 1970s but published only in 1991 (published under the pseudonym of Andrei Şerbulescu, *Monarhia de Drept Dialectic*, Bucharest; Humanitas, 1991). Zilber had been Pătrăşcanu's number two in the talks conducted in 1944 with the opposition parties to plan Romania's volte-face but in May 1947 he was expelled from the Communist Party for failing to follow the 'Party line' and on suspicion of being 'an Anglo-American spy'. His expulsion should have been a warning to Pătrăşcanu who had attracted the enmity of Gheorghiu-Dej. Being ostracized by his friends prompted Zilber to write to Ana Pauker in November 1947 with a request that his innocence be established through a full investigation of his activities (Şerbulescu, *Monarhia*, p.46). In a letter to Ceauşescu, dated 6 September 1966, Zilber outlined the ordeal that followed:

> I was arrested by order of the Central Committee on 6 February 1948. A long and detailed interrogation carried out by the organs of the Ministry of the Interior (February 1948–December 1951) on the initiative and under the direction of the Party proved without any doubt my total innocence. This conclusion was communicated to me during the interrogation and after the completion of the investigations (Şerbulescu, *Monarhia*, p.182).

Zilber's interrogation began on 2 April 1948 at the hands of Marin Jianu, secretary general of the Ministry of the Interior, and Alexandru Nicolski, the chief interrogator of the Ministry of the Interior, who sought to extract a declaration from him that he had been an agent of the *Siguranţa*. A 'confession' by Zilber would have been enough to implicate his friend Pătrăşcanu. In the evenings he was brought before Rangheţ and Drăghici who were responsible for the Party investigation. Zilber's interrogation ceased in December 1951 when he thought that he might be released, but it was resumed in September 1952 with a new team of interrogators amongst whom I only know the names of the Minister Alexandru Drăghici, Colonel Şoltuţiu, Captain Moraru and Captain David. On the night of 17/18 September 1952 I was beaten for the first time, while on the night of 24/25 September 1952 I was beaten three times on the soles of my feet. Comrade Colonel Şoltuţiu, said to me, these are his very words:' Your protectors have gone. The Party is now in strong hands. You must declare all the crimes you committed with Pătrăşcanu and others'. Since I did not know what crimes I had committed nor who the 'others' were, I asked the young officer who was supervising that evening my beating in the cellar of Malmaison prison, tearing the hair from my head. The latter enlightened me: 'You should declare all the crimes you have committed with Lucreţiu Pătrăşcanu, Ana Pauker, Vasile Luca, Teohari Georgescu, Ion Gheorghe Maurer, Ştefan Voitec, Aurel Vijoli, Petre Năvodaru, Mihnea Gheorghiu, Ilie Zaharia, Carol Neuman and others. It is the order of the Secretariat [of the Party]'... Later Colonel Şoltuţiu added to the list Emil Calmanovici, Jack Berman, Remus Koffler, Alexandru Ştefănescu, Luiza Năvodaru, Vera Călin, Petea Petrescu (Gancev) and others. I realized that a trial on the model of those in Moscow, Sofia, Budapest, Prague and Warsaw was being organized in which I had to play the role of the criminal spy. With my swollen feet I reflected upon the alternative which was placed before me and I concluded that any resistance was futile. I had to declare all the crimes that were usual in such interrogations... I declared that I was an agent of the *Siguranţa*, an Anglo-American spy, a conspirator, an assassin, and a traitor. I did not hesitate to declare that I intended to spread the plague in working-class districts, that I organized inflation and sabotaged the stabilization programme, that I handed over the Banat to Yugoslavia in a deal with Mosha Piajde, etc. Everything, of course, in complicity with Pătrăşcanu, Vijoli, Maurer, Voitec and all the other conspirators suggested by the interrogators. I admitted the final plot at the express demand of Alexandru Drăghici on 5 May 1953, a demand which he made in his very office in the presence of Colonel Şoltuţiu. It was a question of a 'plot' which was the imagination of Radu Buzeşti (convicted in the Maniu trial), a person of whom I had never heard and whom I met for the first time at a so-called 'confrontation' in July 1953. Naturally this Radu Buzeşti not only declared that he knew me, but he even dictated my whole life story, exactly as I had written it down [for the interrogators]. I specifically mention this plot because it was on the basis of this fiction that Pătrăşcanu was condemned to death and executed, while I and others spent many terrible years in prison (Şerbulescu, *Monarhia*, pp.182–83).

Appendix 8 UM 0920/A, redesignated UM 0110 in August 1978

The new unit was divided into four departments. All elements of the UM 0920/A were guarded around the clock and equipped with alarm systems and closed circuit television systems, connected via special telephone and courier systems.

a. *UM 0920/A* – Operations Sector had 250 personnel. It consisted of eight operational services, supported by three administrative bureaus (secretariat and couriers; administration and finance; personnel). The headquarters was in a large apartment building located next door to the West German Consulate in Bucharest, on Rabat Street, in an area designated for foreign embassies and the Romanian elite (within walking distance of Ceauşescu's residence). As cover, the building was identified as the Institute for Marketing (*Institutul de Marketing*), an organization created by the DIE and used as cover for some of its headquarters buildings (geographical brigades, the Illegal brigade and the Technical Operations brigade) and for most of the DIE officers. The building had several entrances from three separate streets, in order to make it difficult for an observer to determine the number of people actually working in it. The designations for the operational services and their sections were based on a decimal system. For instance, the first (USSR) service had the designation UM 0920/A100. Its third section (visitors) was UM 0920/A130, and the second bureau of this section was UM 0920/A132.

1. USSR, with three sections (official representatives; Romanians with studies and relatives in the USSR; Soviet visitors to Romania).
2. Hungary, with three sections (official representatives; Romanians with relatives in Hungary; Hungarian visitors).
3. Bulgaria, with the same three sections as Hungary.
4. East Germany, with the same three sections as Hungary.
5. Other socialist countries (Czechoslovakia, Poland, Cuba), with the same three sections.
6. Yugoslavia, with two sections (pro-Soviet Yugoslav émigrés who came as refugees to Romania after Tito's 1948 break with Moscow; western Yugoslav émigrés visiting Romania). This service was a later addition. It was created in 1974, following a secret agreement of cooperation between

the Romanian and Yugoslav ministries of interior, signed in May 1974 during a visit to Romania of Luca Banovic, the Yugoslav federal secretary for internal affairs. Through Pacepa and Lieutenant Colonel Constantin Iosif, this service was in indirect contact with the Yugoslav security service (SDB) whose chief, Silvio Gorenc, made frequent visits to Romania.

7. Comintern, a service without subdivisions, covering basically Romanian Communist Party members who had joined the Party before August 1944, when it became legal.
8. Antiterrorism, with two sections (intelligence; operations).

b. *UM 0920/AT* – Technical Operations Sector had 500 personnel, distributed across six services. As of 1978, the designated capacity of this sector was 600 targets for telephone intercept and 400 targets for microphone monitoring. The transcripts were handwritten only, containing most of the recorded conversations; political discussions, sexual activity and extramarital affairs were transcribed verbatim. The tapes were automatically kept for ten days, longer or indefinitely upon special request. Tapes on extramarital affairs were routinely kept for the life of the target or indefinitely. Personal tapes were made for each target, containing the most characteristic facts recorded. For the most important targets (such as the prime minister), these personal tapes were kept in two copies, one at the unit headquarters and one in a secret underground archive in the Carpathian Mountains. In 1972, the UM 0920/AT was located inside the Central Committee headquarters, the only security unit secretly quartered there. As cover the building was identified as the 'Presidential Archives'. In 1975, Ceauşescu ordered that the UM 0920/AT be removed from the Party headquarters to avoid political embarrassment in case of leaks or compromise. He personally ordered that a nearby seven-floor office building occupied by various state organizations be evacuated and used as headquarters for the UM 0920/AT and for the Technical Operations Sector of the DIE's Service VS, in charge of counter-intelligence within the DIE. The new location was situated approximately half a block west of the main monitoring centre of the *Securitate*, on the next street south-east of the headquarters (13 December Street). As cover, the building was identified as the Institute for Marketing. (The building was severely damaged during the 1977 earthquake, but repairs were completed in less than three months.)

1. UM 0920/AT100 – technical penetrations, with three sections (telephone installations and repairs, under cover as telephone company employees; surreptitious entry; connections, for running private telephone lines into the monitoring centre).
2. UM 0920/AT200 – monitoring, with two sections (telephone intercepts; microphones and transmitters), both organized into four shifts working around the clock.
3. UM 0920/AT300 – transcribing, divided into several bureaus, based on languages (Russian and Bulgarian; Hungarian; German; Polish and

Czechoslovak; Yugoslav; Romanian), most of them organized into two six-hour shifts.

4. UM 0920/AT400 – telex, monitoring all telex communications made by Warsaw Pact country representatives in Romania.
5. UM 0920/AT500 – radio, monitoring all encoded radio communications made by Warsaw Pact country representatives in Romania. Complete copies of the encoded traffic were kept in a special archive.
6. UM 0920/AT600 – technical maintenance.

c. *UM 0920/AF* – Surveillance Section had about 250 personnel and was divided into four services. The section was located on Maria Rosetti Street (across from the DIE Cipher Centre) and used as cover 'Institute of Marketing – Garage'. It had an entirely independent radio surveillance network, using a Telefunken radio telephone and encoding system imported through West Berlin and a fleet of around thirty Romanian cars. For special cases the section had around ten additional West German and Italian built cars and a relatively large collection of foreign licence plates and documents. For cover reasons, women officers and disguises were widely used. Secret photographs and movies were common. Although it was small compared to other Romanian surveillance services, the UM 0902/AF proved to be quite efficient. The major consideration in the work of this section was the secrecy of its operations, because of its ultra-sensitive targets.

1. UM 0920/AF100 – investigations, identifications.
2. UM 0920/AF200 – surveillance, organized into thirty independent teams of three officers, and a disguise section.
3. UM 0920/AF300 – surveillance of embassies, organized into three sections (militiamen at the embassies; secret photography of embassy visitors; identification of visitors).
4. UM 0920/AF400 – technical, with four sections (radio communications; photo lab; mechanics; car maintenance).

d. *UM 0920/AC* – Mail Censorship Sector had 150 personnel and worked in three shifts around the clock to monitor correspondence received from Warsaw Pact countries. It had sections for translation, analysis and archives, as well as photographic and chemical laboratories. It had no connection with the Romanian postal service, receiving the mail rather from the *Securitate*'s Mail Censorship Directorate. Its *modus operandi* was to make photocopies of every censored item and immediately return the original, except for items suspected of containing secret writing or microdots. Besides its individual targets, photocopies of whose correspondence was sent to the UM 0920/A, the AC Sector conducted total censorship for all Warsaw Pact countries. The analysis section was in charge of deciding the final destination of each item contained in the general censorship (send to the UM 0920/A, or keep in UM

0920/AC archives, organized by country, name and address). The UM 0902/AC, located on Izvor Street, had no formal cover.

Operational objectives of UM 0920/A

1. The UM 0920/A unit, as conceived by Ceauşescu in 1972, had as its major objectives the prevention and neutralization of Warsaw Pact country actions against Romania, such as: attempts on Ceauşescu's life and threats to his personal security; attempts at a *coup d'etat*; the use of individuals or groups living in Romania as initiators of pretexts for foreign military intervention; intelligence operations, especially within the CC of the RCP and the armed and security forces. The main operational methods approved for the UM 0920/A were:

    a. Limited monitoring of all Warsaw Pact country embassies and all other official representations and their employees by such means as interception of official and private telephone conversations, including the governmental (TO) line, mail, telex and encoded traffic; and identification and monitoring of people connected with these representations. Any offensive methods that might eventually be compromised and used as evidence, such as attempts to recruit official representatives from Warsaw Pact countries, to install microphones in their offices or apartments, or to make surreptitious entries were strictly forbidden. The only exceptions, approved in 1977, were the use of intelligence officers under cover as militiamen to guard the embassies and of deep cover officers as Romanian employees working in the embassies and other representations.
    b. Selective monitoring of visitors from the Soviet Union, Hungary, Bulgaria, East Germany and, rarely, from Czechoslovakia and other socialist countries. A computerized system for recording the visitors from Warsaw Pact countries was initiated in 1977.
    c. Complete data on all persons living in Romania who had been born in a Warsaw Pact country, had relatives there or had studied or travelled there. Such persons were selectively and periodically monitored.

2. Although the structure and funding for the UM 0920/A were approved by Ceauşescu in the first half of 1972, it took more than a year for the personnel slots to be filled almost completely with officers, most of whom were transferred from *Securitate* and DIE units in various regional areas of Romania, for security reasons. Up until the defection of Ion Pacepa, the UM 0920/A had very few spectacular results leading to public trials. According to Ceauşescu's directions, none of the agents discovered to have connections with Soviet bloc intelligence services was interrogated about this connection or convicted of espionage on behalf of a Warsaw Pact country. The firm order was that

> each case be 'neutralized', and Ceauşescu considered that the best way to do that was to arrest and sentence the agent for some entirely innocuous, mostly invented reason. Among the 'neutralized' cases was an alleged Soviet illegal resident under cover as a Romanian citizen (engineer), married to a Soviet woman, who committed suicide when a *Securitate* team came to arrest him; a Bulgarian living in Romania (without any access to classified information or political decisions) whose connection with Bulgarian intelligence was proved, and he was arrested and sentenced at a staged trial to ten years for embezzlement; and two Hungarian citizens connected with the Hungarian government, who were convicted of embezzlement.[1]

General Victor Neculicioiu was appointed head of UM 0110 in 1983 and was removed from his command on 23 December 1989.[2] Born in 1932, he studied accountancy at high school in Braşov and joined the *Securitate* in 1951. His early career was spent in Braşov where he rose to become deputy head of counter-intelligence in 1965. In 1972, he was appointed head of the Braşov *Securitate* county directorate and two years later, chief of the Inspectorate of the Ministry of the Interior in the same city. In retirement he was promoted in May 2000 to the rank of Major General by presidential decree.[3] He died on 16 December 2013 in Cristian, Transylvania.

Notes

1 Private information.
2 Author's interview with General Nicolae Militaru, 7 January 1995.
3 Mihnea Berindei, Dorin Dobrincu, and Armand Goşu (eds.), *Istoria Comunismului din România*. Vol.III. *Documente Nicolae Ceauşescu (1972–1975)* (Iaşi: Polirom, 2016), p.234, footnote 8.

Appendix 9 The organization of the *Securitate* at 22 December 1989

In March 1978, the Department of State Security—*Departamentul Securității Statului (DSS)*—was created within the Ministry of the Interior. Its head was given the rank of Minister-Secretary of State within the Ministry of the Interior, and some directorate chiefs held the position of Deputy Minister. The DSS inherited the structure of the DS, as constituted in June 1973, with a few modifications and preserved it until its abolition on 30 December 1989.

The composition of the DSS as at 22 December 1989
Minister-Secretary of State and Head of the DSS: Col. Gen. Iulian Vlad
Deputy Minister and Head of the CIE: Lt. Gen. Aristotel Stamatoiu
Deputy Minister: Maj. Gen. Gianu Bucurescu
State Secretary: Maj. Gen. Ştefan Alexie
The political council of the DSS
10 officers, 2 NCOs and 1 civilian = 13
Head of the Political Council: Maj. Gen. Ioan Marcu
U.M. 0544 CIE (Centre for Foreign Intelligence)
715 officers, 36 technical warrant officers, 197 NCOs and 111 civilians = 1,059
Head: Lt. Gen. Aristotel Stamatoiu
UM 0195 CIE counter-intelligence (control of Romanian embassies abroad and monitoring the activities of Romanian émigrés)
386 officers, 5 technical warrant officers, 42 NCOs and 18 civilians = 451
Head: Maj. Gen. Ioan Moţ
UM 0110 CIE counter-intelligence (monitoring the activity of Soviet agents in Romania)
264 officers, 8 technical warrant officers, 15 NCOs and 17 civilians = 304
Head: Maj. Gen. Victor Neculicioiu
UM 0525 CIE Cipher
412 officers, 15 technical warrant officers, 32 NCOs and 16 civilians = 475
Head: Maj. Gen. Gheorghe Radu
ICE Dunărea (subordinated to the CIE)
115 officers, 10 NCOs and 12 civilians = 137
Head: Col. Constantin Gavril

The national directorates
Directorate I Domestic Intelligence
98 officers, 8 NCOs and 8 civilians = 114
Head: Col. Gheorghe Raţiu
Deputy Heads: Col. Ilie Merce
Lt. Col. Gabriel Anastasiu
Lt. Col. Elena Moca
Directorate II Economic counter-espionage (UM 0630)
150 officers, 6 NCOs and 11 civilians = 167
Head: Maj. Gen. Emil Macri
Deputy Heads: Lt. Col. Constantin Stan
Lt. Col. Claudiu Bucur
Directorate III Counter-espionage
215 officers, 4 technical warrant officers, 22 NCOs and 1 civilian = 242
Head: Maj. Gen. Aurelian Mortoiu
Deputy Heads: Col. Filip Teodorescu
Lt. Col. Emil Radulescu
Lt. Col. Gheorghe Diaconescu
Directorate IV Military counter-espionage
926 officers, 17 technical warrant officers, 160 NCOs and 30 civilians = 1,133
Head: Lt. Gen. Gheorghe Vasile
Deputy Heads: Col. Radu Bălăsoiu
Lt. Col. Mihai Uţă
Lt. Col. Dumitru Petanca
Directorate V Protection of the Party leadership (UM 0666)
306 officers, 14 technical warrant officers, 144 NCOs and 20 civilians = 484
Head: Maj. Gen. Marin Neagoe
Directorate VI Penal investigation
36 officers, 1 technical warrant officers, 26 NCOs and 9 civilians = 72
Head: Col. Gheorghe Vasile
Deputy Head: Patru Murariu
Special units
Special Anti-Terrorist Unit (Unitate specială de luptă antiteroristă, USLA) UM 0620
184 officers, 21 technical warrant officers, 580 NCOs and 10 civilians = 795
Head: Col. Gheorghe Ardeleanu
Deputy Head: Lt. Col. Gheorghe Trosca
Lt. Col. Ion Bliorţ
Special surveillance unit 'F' (Unitate specială de filaj F)
447 officers, 13 technical warrant officers, 252 NCOs and 65 civilians = 777
Head: Col. Ion Băjenaru
Deputy Head: Lt. Col. Paula Stanciu
Special service for protecting state secrets UM 0500
43 officers, 8 NCOs and 6 civilians = 57
Independent Service for Foreign Trade

41 officers, 2 NCOs and 2 civilians = 45
Head: Col. Ştefan Alexandru
Centre for Information and Documentation
174 officers, 32 technical warrant officers, 50 NCOs and 16 civilians = 272
Head: Lt. Col. Dan Nicolici
Service 'D' Disinformation (Tasks included the launching of false rumours and discrediting the activities of 'reactionary' groups abroad.)
20 officers and 2 NCOs = 22
Head: Col. Dumitru Tatu
Independent Law Secretariat
19 officers and 9 NCOs = 28
Head Col. Florica Dobre
Deputy Head Lt. Col. Aurel Rogojan
Independent Service for Cadre Education and Mobilization
28 officers and 7 NCOs = 35
Head: Col. Maria Petrescu
Deputy Head: Eugen Jeledintan
Technical and transmission command (known as Comandamentul pentru Tehnica Operativă şi Transmisiuni)
20 officers, 3 technical warrant officers, 10 NCOS and 9 civilians = 42
Head: Maj. Gen. Ovidiu Diaconescu
This can be described as a technical directorate and comprised
1) Service 'C' (transport of secret documents)
5 officers, 1 technical warrant officer, and 71 NCOs = 77
Head: Col. Mircea Ştefănescu
2) Special unit 'P' (technical research and planning)
171 officers, 257 technical warrant officer, 9 NCOs and 28 civilians = 465
Head: Lt. Col. Teodor Hristea
3) Special unit 'R' for ensuring radio communication between the DSS and the militia and Ministry of Interior troops, as well as intercepting foreign radio transmissions.
230 officers, 100 technical warrant officers, 20 NCOs and 99 civilians = 449
Head: Col. Remus Radu
Deputy Head: Lt. Col. Tiberiu Lopatită
4) Special unit 'S' for intercepting correspondence.
300 officers, 7 technical warrant officers, 67 NCOs and 14 civilians = 388
Head: Col. Constantin Marinescu
Deputy Head: Lt. Col. Eugen Grigorescu
Lt. Col. Aurora Negoiţă
5) Special technical installation unit 'T' for surveillance of telephones and video monitoring, also known as 'Tonola' (Tehnica operativă).
404 officers, 35 technical warrant officers, 19 NCOs and 19 civilians = 477
Head: Maj. Gen. Alexandru Ţencu
Deputy Head: Lt. Col. Gheorghe Busu
Lt. Col. Ştefan Toader

6) Special air unit for transporting the Party leader.
22 officers, 19 technical warrant officers and 3 NCOs = 44
Training centres for DSS personnel
1) A school for cadres at Grădiştea near Bucharest with a staff of 61 officers, 12 technical warrant officers, 18 NCOs and 79 civilians = 170
2) A small centre at Bran near Braşov with 8 officers, 5 technical warrant officers, 4 NCOs and 13 civilians = 30
3) A special instruction centre in Bucharest with 12 officers, 8 NCOs and 5 civilians = 25
The county and Bucharest DSS offices
4,017 officers, 182 technical warrant officers, 1,297 NCOs and 563 civilians = 6,059

The Command of the Security Troops (Comandamentul Trupelor de Securitate)
1,387 officers, 136 technical warrant officers, 924 NCOs, 536 civilians and 20,387 troops = 23,370
Head: Maj. Gen. Dumitru Ghiţă

The total number of personnel in the DSS in December 1989 was 38,682 of whom 23,370 were in the security troops command. Of the remaining figure of 15,312 there were 6,602 in the national directorates and special units, 2,426 in the CIE, 6,059 in the county offices, and 225 in the schools.

In addition to the security troops the regime could call upon the Inspectorate General of the Militia, referred to in the DSS as the Forces of Internal Order (*Forţele de Ordine Internă*), for maintaining public order. The head of the militia was Major General Constantin Nuţă and his deputy Major General Mihalea Velicu.[1]

Notes

1 Dennis Deletant, *Communist Terror in Romania. Gheorghiu-Dej and the Police State, 1948–1965* (London: Hurst and Co., 1999), pp.377–80.

Select bibliography

Primary sources

Great Britain

The National Archives, Kew, London (TNA)

Romania

Arhiva Consiliul National pentru Studierea Arhivelor fostei Securităţi (Archive of the National Council for the Study of the Archives of the former *Securitate*) (ACNSAS)

Arhiva Ministerului Afacerilor Externe (Archive of the Ministry for Foreign Affairs, Bucharest)

Arhivele Naţionale Istorice Centrale (The Central Historical National Archives, Bucharest)

Russia

Arkhiv Veshnii Politiki Rossiskoi Federatsii (The Foreign Policy Archive of the Russian Federation) (AVPRF)

Rossiiski Gosudarstvennyi Arkhiv Sotsial'noi I Politicheskoi Istorii) (Russian State Archive of Social and Political History) (RGASPI)

The United States

The National Archives and Records Administration, College Park, Maryland, USA (NARA)

Unpublished Studies

Brett, Dan (2010), *Peasants and Politics: Agrarianism and Rural Transformation in Romania, 1918–1947*. Thesis submitted to the School of Slavonic and East European Studies, University College, London, December, 2010, 414pp.

Chiriac, Bogdan (2017), *The Trial of the Antonescu Group (May 6–17, 1946) and the Communist Takeover in Romania. A Historical Interpretation*. Thesis submitted to the History Department of the Central European University, Budapest, February, 2017, 390pp.

Dobrincu, Dorin (2006), *Rezistenţa armată anticomunistă din România (1944-începutul anilor 60)*. Thesis submitted to the Faculty of History, Iaşi University for the Degree of Doctor of Philosophy, Iaşi, April, 2006. 2 vols.

Mavrodin, Corina (2017), *A Maverick in the Making: Romania's de-Satellization Process and the Global Cold War (1953–1963)*. Thesis submitted to the Department of International History of the London School of Economics for the Degree of Doctor of Philosophy, London, February, 2017, 287pp.
Muraru, Andrei (2011), *Procesele criminalilor de război din Transnistria*, Thesis submitted to the Faculty of History, Iaşi University for the Degree of Doctor of Philosophy, Iaşi, August, 2011, 287pp.

Published collections of documents and monographs etc.

Ardeleanu, Ion, Vasile Arimia, and Mircea Muşat (eds.), (1984), *23 August 1944. Documente*, 4 vols (Bucharest: Editura Ştiinţifică şi Enciclopedică).
Berindei, Mihnea, Dorin Dobrincu, and Armand Goşu (eds.), (2009), *Istoria Comunismului din România. Documente Perioada Gheorghe Gheorghiu-Dej (1945–1965)* (Bucharest: Humanitas).
Berindei, Mihnea, Dorin Dobrincu, and Armand Goşu (eds.), (2012), *Istoria Comunismului din România*. Vol.II. *Documente Nicolae Ceauşescu (1965–1971)* (Iaşi: Polirom).
Berindei, Mihnea, Dorin Dobrincu, and Armand Goşu (eds.), (2016), *Istoria Comunismului din România*. Vol.III. *Documente Nicolae Ceauşescu (1972–1975)* (Iaşi: Polirom).
Brătescu, G. (ed.), (1995) *Lichidarea lui Marcel Pauker* (Bucharest: Univers Enciclopedic).
Budura, Romulus Ioan (ed.), (2008), *Relatiile Romano-Chineze, 1954–1975* (Bucharest: Ministerul Afacerilor Externe, Arhivele Naţionale).
Burcea, Mihai; Marius Stan, and Mihail Bumbeş (eds.), (2009), *Dictionarul ofiterilor si angajatilor civili ai Directiei Generale a Penitenciarelor*. Vol. I. *Aparatul central (1948–1989)* (Bucharest: Polirom).
Buzatu, Gheorghe and Mircea Chiriţoiu (1998), *Agresiunea Comunismului în România. Documente din arhivele secrete, 1944–1989*, 2 vols (Bucharest: Paideia).
Cartea Albă a Securităţii, (1994–96), 6 vols (Bucharest: SRI).
Cătănuş, Dan (ed.), (2004), *Între Beijing şi Moscova. România şi conflictul sovieto-chinez* (Bucharest: Institutul pentru Studiul Totalitarismului).
Cătănuş, Dan and Vasile Buga (eds.), (2012), *Gh. Gheorghiu-Dej la Stalin. Stenograme, Note de Convorbire, Memorii, 1944–1952* (Bucharest: Institutul Naţional pentru Studiul Totalitarismului).
Ceauşescu, Nicolae (1969), *Romania on the Way of Completing Socialist Construction*, vols 1–3 (Bucharest: Meridiane).
Ceauşescu, Nicolae (1970–1989), *Romania on the Way of Building-Up the Multilaterally Developed Socialist Society*, vols. 4–28 (Bucharest: Meridiane).
Ciucă, Marcel-Dumitru (ed.), (1995), *Procesul Mareşalului Antonescu. Documente*, 4 vols (Bucharest: Editura Saeculum, Editura Europa Nova, 1995).
Ciuceanu, Radu, Ioan Chiper, Florin Constantiniu, and Vitalie Văratec (1997), *Misiunile lui A.I. Vişinski în România. Din istoria relaţiilor româno-sovietice 1944–1946. Documente secrete* (Bucharest: Institutul Naţional pentru Studiul Totalitarismului).
Conditions of an Armistice with Roumania (1945), Miscellaneous No.1 (1945), (London: HMSO), (Cmd. 6585).
Demetriade, Oana Ionel and Alexandru Şerbănescu (2015), *Generalul Nicolae Rădescu. Profilul unui Om de Stat în Imagine şi Documente* (Bucharest: Editura Oscar Print).
Dobre, Florica, Banu Florian, Camelia Duică, Silviu B. Moldovan, and Liviu Ţăranu (2004), *Trupele de Securitate (1949–1989)* (Bucharest: Nemira).

Documente diplomatice române. *Seria a III-a. România şi Tratatul de la Varşovia. Conferinţele Miniştrilor de Afaceri Externe, with an introduction by Mioara Anton* (2009), Ministerul Afacerilor Externe, Institutul Diplomatic Român (Buzău: Alpha).

Documents on the Expulsion of the Germans from Eastern-Central-Europe, vol.III. *The Fate of the Germans in Rumania* (1961) (Bonn: Federal Ministry for Expellees, Refugees, and War Victims).

Foreign Relations of the United States (FRUS), 1944, (1966), vol.IV (Washington, DC: Department of State).

Foreign Relations of the United States, 1977–1980, (2015). Vol. XX. *Eastern Europe*, Ashley, Carl and Munteanu, Mircea (eds.) (Washington, DC: Department of State).

Gheorghiu-Dej, Gheorghe (1952), *Articole şi cuvîntări* (Bucharest: Editura pentru literatura politică).

Gheorghiu-Dej, Gheorghe (1963), *Articole şi cuvîntări* (Bucharest: Editura politică).

Ioanid, Radu (ed.), (2013), *Dosarul Brucan. Documente ale Direcţiei a III-a Contraspionaj a Departmentului Securităţii Statului (1987–1989)*, 2nd ed. (Iaşi: Polirom).

Ioanid, Radu (ed.), (2015), *Securitatea şi vânzarea evreilor. Istoria acordurilor secrete dintre România şi Israel* (Iaşi: Polirom).

Memorialul Ororii. *Documente ale Procesului Reeducării din închisorile Piteşti, Gherla* (1995) (Bucharest: Editura Vremea).

Nastasă-Kovacs, Lucian (ed.), (2002), *Maghiarii din România. Mărturii documentare* (1945–1955) (Cluj: Centrul pentru Resurse şi Diversitate Etnoculturală).

Nastasă-Kovacs, Lucian (ed.), (2003), *Maghiarii din România. Mărturii documentare* (1956–1968) (Cluj: Centrul pentru Resurse şi Diversitate Etnoculturală).

Nastasă-Kovacs, Lucian (ed.), (2003), *Evreii din România. Mărturii documentare* (1945–1965) (Cluj: Centrul pentru Resurse şi Diversitate Etnoculturală).

Oprea, Marius (2002), *Banalitatea răului. 0 istorie a Securităţii în documente 1949–1989* (Iaşi: Polirom).

Partidul Muncitoresc Romîn. *Congresul al II-lea al PMR, 23–28 Dec. 1955* (1956) (Bucharest: Editura Politică).

Partidul Muncitoresc Romîn. *Congresul al III-lea al PMR, 20–25 Iunie 1960* (1960) (Bucharest: Editura Politică).

Prigoana. *Documente ale Procesului C. Noica, C. Pillat, N. Steinhardt, Al. Palelologu, A. Acterian, S. Al-George, Al.O. Teodoreanu* (1996) (Bucharest: Editura Vremea).

Preda, Dumitru and Mihai Retegan (2000), *1989. Principiul dominoului. Prăbusirea regimurilor comuniste europene* (Bucharest: Editura Fundaţiei Culturale Române).

Principiul Bumerangului. *Documente ale Procesului Lucreţiu Pătrăşcanu* (1996) (Bucharest: Editura Vremea).

Procesul unui grup de spioni, *trădători şi complotişti în slujba Vaticanului şi a centrului de spionaj italian, Bucureşti, 10–17 septembrie 1951* (1952) (Bucharest: Editura de stat pentru literatura ştiinţifică).

Refugiaţii polonezi în România 1939–1947. *Documente din Arhivele Naţionale ale României. Polscy uchodżcy w Rumunii 1939–1947. Dokumenty z Narodowych archiwów Rumunii* (2013), 2 vols (Warsaw and Bucharest: Arhivele Naţionale ale României, Institutul Memoriei Naţionale – Comisia pentru Condamnarea Crimelor Împotriva Naţiunii Poloneze).

Retegan, Mihai (ed.), (2002), *Război politic în blocul comunist. Relaţii româno-sovietice în anii şaizeci. Documente* (Bucharest: Editura RAO).

România în anii celui de-al doilea război mondial (1989), 3 vols (Bucharest: Editura Militară).

Ross, G., (ed.), (1984), *The Foreign Office and the Kremlin. British Documents on Anglo-Soviet Relations, 1941–45* (Cambridge: Cambridge University Press).
Rusalii *'51 Fragmente din deportarea în Bărăgan* (1994) (Timişoara: Editura Marineasa).
Scurtu, Ion et al. (eds.), (1994), *Viaţa politică în Documente* (Bucharest: Arhivele Statului).
Tudor, Alina and Dan Cătănuş (eds.), (2000), *Amurgul ilegaliştilor. Plenara CC al PMR din 9–13 iunie 1958* (Bucharest: Editura Vremea).
Tudor, Alina and Dan Cătănuş (2001), *O destalinizare ratată. Culisele cazului Miron Constantinescu - Iosif Chişinevschi* (1956–1961) (Bucharest: Editura Elion).
Volokitina, T.V., G.P. Murashko, and A.F. Noskova (eds.), (2002), *Sovietskiy faktor v Vostochnoy Evrope 1944–1953.* [The Soviet factor in Eastern Europe 1944–1953. Documents.], 2 vols (Moscow: Rosspen).
Volokitina, T.V, G.P. Murashko, A.F. Noskova, and T.A. Pokivailova (eds.), (2002), *Moskva i Vostochnaya Evropa. Stanovlenie politicheskih sovetskogo tipa. 1949–1953.* [Moscow and Eastern Europe: The establishment of Soviet political systems in 1949–1953] (Moscow: Rosspen).

Monographs, memoir and creative literature

6 martie 1945. *Începuturile Comunizării României* (1995), (Bucharest: Editura Enciclopedică) (no author or editor).
Abraham, Florin (2017), *Romania since the Second World War. A Political, Social and Economic History* (London: Bloomsbury).
Abrudan, Paul (1990), *Sibiul în revoluţia din decembrie 1989* (Sibiu: Casa Armatei).
Accoce, Pierre and Pouget Daniel (1972), *Le Réseau Caraman –Treize Roumains ont fait trembler l'OTAN* (Paris: Fayard).
Adorian, Gheorghe (ed.), (1971), *Voluntari români în Spania, 1936–1936* (Bucharest: Editura Politică).
Alexandrescu, Sorin (2000), *Identitate în ruptură* (Bucharest: Humanitas).
Alexe, Vladimir (2004), *România secretă* (Bucharest: Editura Elit).
Almond, Mark (1992), *The Rise and Fall of Nicolae and Elena Ceauşescu* (London: Chapmans).
An Anthology of Contemporary Romanian Poetry (1984), translated by Andrea Deletant and Brenda Walker (London: Forest Books).
Andrew, Christopher and Oleg Gordievsky (1991), KGB. *The Inside Story of Its Foreign Operations from Lenin to Gorbachev* (London: Sceptre).
Antohi, Sorin and Vladimir Tismăneanu (eds.), (2000), *Between the Past and Future. The Revolutions of 1989 and their Aftermath* (Budapest: Central European University Press).
Anton, Mioara (2007), *Ieşirea din cerc. Politica externă a regimului Gheorghiu-Dej* (Bucharest: Institutul Naţional pentru Studiul Totalitarismului).
Anuarul Statistic al Republicii Socialiste România, 1988 (1989) (Bucharest: Direcţia Centrală de Statistică).
Aparaschivei, Sorin (2013), *Spionajul american în România, 1944–1948* (Bucharest: Editura Militară).
Apostol, Gheorghe (1998), *Eu şi Gheorghiu-Dej* (Bucharest: privately printed).
Arnăţoiu, Ioana Raluca (1997), *Luptătorii din munţi. Toma Arnăţoiu. Grupul de la Nucşoara. Documente ale anchetei, procesului, detenţiei* (Bucharest: Vremea).
Aspinall, David (pseudonymn of Dennis Deletant) (1984), 'Romania: Queues and Personality Cults', in *Soviet Analyst*, vol.13, no.10, 16 May.

Axworthy, Mark, Cornel Scafeş, and Cristian Craciunoiu (1995), *Third Axis, Fourth Ally. Romanian Armed Forces in the European War, 1941–1945* (London: Arms and Armour).
Baciu, Nicholas (1984), *Sell-Out to Stalin. The Tragic Errors of Churchill and Roosevelt* (New York: Vantage Press).
Bacu, D. (1977), *The Anti-Humans* (Monticello, IL: TLC).
Balas, Egon (2000), *Will to Freedom* (Syracuse: Syracuse University Press).
Banu, Florian (2016), *De la SSI la SIE. O istorie a spionajului românesc în timpul regimului comunist (1948–1989)* (Bucharest: Corint).
Banu, Florian and Liviu Ţăranu (2004), Aprilie 1964 – *"Primăvara de la Bucureşti": Cum a fost adoptată "Declaraţia de independenţă a Romaniei?* (Bucharest: Editura Enciclopedică).
Barker, Elisabeth (1976), *British Policy in South-East Europe in the Second World War* (London: Macmillan).
Beeson, Trevor (1974), *Discretion and Valour, Religious Conditions in Russia and Eastern Europe* (London: Fontana).
Behr, Edward (1991), *Kiss the Hand You Cannot Bite. The Rise and Fall of the Ceauşescu* (London: Hamish Hamilton).
Bellu, Ştefan (1993), *Pădurea răzvrătită. Marturii ale rezistenţei anticomuniste* (Baia Mare: Editura Gutinul).
Betea, Lavinia (1995), *Maurer şi lumea de ieri* (Arad: Fundaţia Culturală Ion Slavici).
Betea, Lavinia (1997), *Alexandru Bârlădeanu despre Dej, Ceauşescu şi Iliescu* (Bucharest: Editura Evenimentul Românesc).
Betea, Lavinia (2001), *Convorbiri neterminate. Corneliu Mănescu în dialog cu Lavinia Betea* (Iaşi: Editura Polirom).
Betea, Lavinia (2006), *Lucreţiu Pătrăşcanu. Moartea unui lider comunist*, 2nd rev.ed. (Bucharest: Editura Curtea Veche).
Bishop, Robert and E.S. Crayfield (1949), *Russia astride the Balkans* (London: Evans).
Blandiana, Ana (1982), *Proiecte de trecut* (Bucharest: Cartea Românească).
Blandiana, Ana (1988), *Întâmplări de pe strada mea* (Bucharest: Editura Ion Creangă).
Boca, Ioana (2001), *1956. Un an de ruptură* (Bucharest: Fundaţia Academia Civică).
Bogdan, Jolan (2017), *Performative Contradiction and the Romanian Revolution* (Lanham, MD: Rowman and Littlefield International).
Boia, Lucian (1998), *Miturile comunismului românesc* (Bucharest: Editura Nemira).
Borsody, S.(ed.), (1988), *The Hungarians: A Divided Nation* (New Haven: Yale Center for International and Area Studies).
Bosomitu, Ştefan, (2014), *Miron Constantinescu. O biografie* (Bucharest: Humanitas).
Bosomitu, Ştefan and Mihai Burcea (2012), *Spectrele lui Dej. Incursiuni în biografia şi regimul unui dictator* (Iaşi: Polirom).
Botez, Mihai (1992), *Românii despre ei înşişi* (Bucharest: Litera).
Bottoni, S. (2007) *Transilvania rossa. Il comunismo romeno e la questione nazionale* (1944–1965) (Rome: Carocci editore).
Brătianu, Dan M. (1996), *Martor dintr-o ţară încătuşată* (Bucharest: Fundaţia Academia Civică).
Briaskin, S.K. and M. Sitnik (1970), *Triumful Adevărului Istoric* (Chişinău: Cartea Moldovenească).
Brisca, Adrian and Radu Ciuceanu (1998), *Rezistenţa armată din Bucovina, 1944–1950*, (Bucharest: INST).
Brown, J.F. (1988), *Eastern Europe and Communist Rule* (Durham and London: Duke University Press).

Brown, J.F. (1991), *Surge to Freedom: The End of Communist Rule in Eastern Europe* (London: Adamantine Press).

Brucan, Silviu (1993), *The Wasted Generation* (Boulder, San Francisco, and Oxford: Westview Press).

Bruchis, M. (1982), *One Step Back, Two Steps Forward: On the Language Policy of the Communist Party of the Soviet Union in the National Republics* (Boulder, CO: East European Monographs).

Bucur, Ioan-Marius (2003), *Din istoria Bisericii Greco-Catolice Române, 1918–1953* (Cluj-Napoca: Editura Accent).

Bucur, Ioan Marius (2015), *Culpa de a fi Greco-catolic. Procesul episcopului Alexandru Rusu* (1957) (Cluj-Napoca: Argonaut).

Bucur, Maria (2002), *Eugenics and Modernization in interwar Romania* (Pittsburgh: University of Pittsburgh Press).

Budeancă, Cosmin (ed.), (2007–2010), *Experienţe carcerale în România comunistă*, 4 vols, *Institutul de Investigare a Crimelor Comunismului şi Memoria Exilului Românesc* (Bucharest: Polirom).

Budeancă, Cosmin and Florentin Olteanu (eds.), (2008), *Forme de represiune în regimurile comuniste*, Institutul de Investigare a Crimelor Comunismului şi Memoria Exilului Românesc (Bucharest: Polirom).

Burakowski, Adam (2011), *Dictatura lui Nicolae Ceauşescu, 1965–1989. Geniul Carpaţilor*, translated by Vasile Moga (Iaşi: Polirom).

Burger, Ulrich (2003), *Zwischen Konfrontation und Kooperation. Die historischen Parteien Rumäniens in der Politischen Auseneinandersetyung mit der Sowjetunion in den Jahren 1955 unde 1945* (Sankt Augustin: Gardez Verlag).

Buzatu, Gheorghe (1996), *Românii în arhivele Kremlinului* (Bucharest: Univers Enciclopedic).

Buzatu, Gheorghe (2011), *Nicolae Ceauşescu. Biografii Paralele* (Iaşi: Tipo Moldova).

Buzura, Augustin (1988), *Drumul cenuşii* (Bucharest: Cartea Românească).

Calafeteanu, Ion and Alexandru Cornescu-Coren (2002), *România şi criza din Orientul Mijlociu (1965–1971)* (Bucharest: Editura Sempre).

Calciu, Gheorghe (1979), *Şapte cuvinte către tineri* (München: Ion Dumitru).

Câmpeanu, Pavel (2002), *Anii numărătorii inverse* (Iaşi: Polirom).

Cancicov, M. (1990), *Le cachot des marionnettes: quinze ans de prison en Roumanie, 1949–1964* (Paris: Criterion).

Case, Holly (2009), *The Transylvanian Question and the European Idea During World War II* (Stanford, CA: Stanford University Press).

Cătănus, Dan (2011), *Tot mai departe de Moscova. Politica externă a României 1956–1965* (Bucharest: Institutul Naţional pentru Studiul Totalitarismului).

Cătănuş, Dan and Vasile Buga (eds.), (2012), *Gh. Gheorghiu-Dej la Stalin. Stenograme, Note de Convorbire, Memorii, 1944–1952* (Bucharest: Institutul Naţional pentru Studiul Totalitarismului).

Cătănuş, Dan and Chiper Ioan (1999), *Cazul Ştefan Foriş. Lupta pentru Putere în PCR de la Gheorghiu-Dej la Ceauşescu* (Bucharest: Editura Vremea).

Ceauşescu, Ilie (1988), *Romanian Military Doctrine Past and Present* (Boulder, CO: East European Monographs).

Cernat, Paul, Ion Manolescu, Mitchievici Angelo, and Ioan Stanomir (2004–2008), *Explorări în comunismul românesc*, 3 vols (Iaşi: Polirom).

Cesereanu, Ruxandra (2009), *Decembrie '89. Deconstrucţia unei revoluţii* (Iaşi: Polirom).

Chelaru, Rodica (2001), *Culpe care nu se uită. Convorbiri cu Cornel Burtică* (Bucharest: Curtea Veche).

Chimet, Iordan (1996), *Momentul Adevărului* (Cluj-Napoca: Editura Dacia).

Chiper, Ioan, Florin Constantiniu, and Adrian Pop (eds.), (1993), *Sovietizarea României. Percepţii anglo-americane* (Bucharest: Iconica).

Cinpoeş, Radu (2010), *Nationalism and Identity in Romania: A History of Extreme Politics from the Birth of the State to EU Accession* (London: I.B. Tauris).

Ciobanu, Mircea (1991), *Convorbiri cu Mihai I al României* (Bucharest: Humanitas).

Cioroianu, Adrian (2005), *Pe umerii lui Marx. O introducere în comunismul românesc* (Bucharest: Curtea Veche).

Cipăianu, George (2014), *Catholicisme et Communisme en Roumanie, 1946–1955. Une Perspective Diplomatique Française* (Cluj-Napoca: Editura Fundaţiei pentru Studii Europene).

Clark, Roland (2015), *Holy Legionary Youth. Fascist Activism in Interwar Romania* (Ithaca, NY: Cornell University Press).

Constante, E. (1995), *The Silent Escape* (Berkeley: University of California Press).

Constantinescu, Emil (2004), *Adevărul despre România* (Bucharest: Editura Universalia).

Constantiniu, Florin (1997), *O istorie sinceră a poporului român* (Bucharest: Univers Enciclopedic).

Constantiniu, Florin (2002), *1941. Hitler, Stalin şi România* (Bucharest: Univers Enciclopedic).

Constantiniu, Florin, A. Duţu, and M. Retegan (1995), *România în război, 1941–1945* (Bucharest: Editura Militară).

Coposu, Corneliu (1990), *Armistiţiul din 1944 şi implicaţiile lui* (Bucharest: Editura Gândirea românească).

Coposu, Corneliu (1992), *Dialoguri cu Vartan Arachelian* (Bucharest: Editura Anastasia).

Coposu, Corneliu (1996), *Confesiuni – dialoguri cu Doina Alexandru* (Bucharest: Editura Anastasia)

Cornea, Delia and Dumitru Dobre (eds.), (2006), *Cazul "Artur" şi exilul românesc. Ion Caraion în documente din Arhiva CNSAS* (Bucharest: Editura Pro Historia).

Cornea, Doina (1991), *Scrisori deschise şi alte texte* (Bucureşti, Humanitas).

Cornea, Doina (1999), *Faţa Nevăzută a Lucrurilor (1990–1999). Dialoguri cu Rodica Palade* (Cluj: Editura Dacia).

Corut, Pavel (2004), *N-a fost triumful minciunii. Pavel Coruţ în dialog cu generalul Ştefan Guşă* (Iaşi: Editura Canova).

Cosmovici, E., M. Cosmovici, and Marie-Joelle Desserre (eds.), (2000), *La voix de l'effroi. La Roumanie sous le communisme. Récits et témoignages* (Bucharest: Association Europe Chrétienne).

Crişan, Gheorghe (2004), *Piramida puterii*, vol.1, *Oameni politici şi de stat, generali şi ierarhi din România* (23 august-22 decembrie 1989) (Bucharest: Editura Pro Historia).

Croitor, Mihai (2012), *În Umbra Kremlinului. Gheorghe Gheorghiu-Dej şi Geneza Declaraţiei din Aprilie 1964* (Cluj-Napoca: Editura Mega).

Croitor, Mihai and Sanda Borşa (2014), *Triunghiul Suspiciunii*, vol.1. *Gheorghiu-Dej, Hruşciov şi Tito (1954–1964)* (Cluj-Napoca: Editura Mega).

Crump, Laurien (2015), *The Warsaw Pact Reconsidered: International Relations in Eastern Europe, 1955–69* (London: Routledge).

Cummings, Richard (2010), *The Dangerous History of American Broadcasting in Europe, 1950–1989* (Jefferson, NC; London: McFarland & Company).

Curticeanu, Silviu (2000), *Mărturia unei istorii trăite. Imagini suprapuse* (Bucharest: Editura Albatros).
Deakin, F.W., E. Barker, and J. Chadwick (eds.), (1988), *British Political and Military Strategy in Central, Eastern and Southern Europe in 1944* (London: Macmillan).
Deletant, Dennis (1995), *Ceausescu and the Securitate: Coercion and Dissent in Romania, 1965–89* (London: Hurst & Co.; New York: M.E. Sharpe).
Deletant, Dennis (1999), *Communist Terror in Romania: Gheorghiu-Dej and the Police State* (London: Hurst).
Deletant, Dennis (2000), *Good Wine Needs a Bush: The British Council and Romania. 1937 to the Present* (London and Bucharest: The British Council).
Deletant, Dennis (ed.), (2005), *In and Out of Focus. Romania and Britain. Relations and Perspectives from 1930 to the Present* (Bucharest: British Council).
Deletant, Dennis (2006), *Hitler's Forgotten Ally. Ion Antonescu and his Regime, Romania 1940–1944* (Basingstoke: Palgrave Macmillan).
Deletant, Dennis (2016), *British Clandestine Activities in Romania during the Second World War* (Basingstoke: Palgrave Macmillan, 2016).
Deletant, Dennis (ed.), (2017), *Witnessing Romania's Century of Turmoil. Memoirs of a Political Prisoner. Nicolae Mărgineanu* (Rochester, NY: University of Rochester Press).
Deletant, Dennis and Mihail E. Ionescu (2002), *Romania and the Warsaw Pact, 1955–1989*, Cold War International History Project, Working Paper No. 43, Washington, DC, July.
Deletant, Dennis and Mihail E. Ionescu (eds.), (2004), *Romania and the Warsaw Pact, 1955–1989* (Bucharest: Politeia-SNSPA).
Deletant, Dennis and Maurice Pearton (1998), *Romania Observed* (Bucharest: Editura Enciclopedică).
Dima, N. (1982), *Bessarabia and Bukovina: The Soviet-Romanian Territorial Dispute* (Boulder, CO: East European Monographs).
Dimitrov, Gheorghi (1997), *Dnevnik (9 marta 1933–6 februari 1949)* (Sofia: Universitetsko izdatelstvo 'Sv. Kliment Ohridski').
Dinescu, Mircea (1985), *Exile on a Peppercorn*, translated by Andrea Deletant and Brenda Walker (London: Forest Books).
Dobeş, Andrea (2010), *Reprimarea elitelor interbelice Colonia 'Dunărea' Sighet (1950–1955)* (Sighetu Marmaţiei: Editura Valea Verde).
Dobincu, Dorin and Constantin Iordachi (eds.), (2005), *Ţărănimea şi puterea. Procesul de colectivizare a agriculturii în România (1949–1962)* (Iaşi: Polirom).
Dobre, Florica (2006), *Securitatea. Structuri-cadre, Obiective si Metode*, 2 vols, *Consiliul National pentru Studierea Arhivelor Securitatii* (Bucharest: Editura Enciclopedică).
Dobre, Florica et al. (eds.), (2003), *Bande, Bandiţi şi Eroi* (Bucharest: Editura enciclopedică).
Dobre, Florica, Luminiţa Banu, Florian Banu, and Laura Stancu (2011), *Acţiunea "Recuperarea". Securitatea şi Emigrarea Germanilor din România (1962–1989)* (Bucharest: Editura Enciclopedică).
Dobrincu, Dorin, (ed.), (2008), *Listele Morţii. Deţinuţii Politici Decedaţi în Sistemul Carceral din România Potrivit Documentelor Securităţii, 1945–1958* (Iaşi: Polirom).
Domenico, Viorel (1999), *Ceauşescu la Târgovişte, 22–25 decembrie 1989* (Bucharest: Editura 'Ion Cristoiu').
Drace-Francis, Alex (2013), *The Traditions of Invention. Romanian ethnic and social stereotypes in historical context* (Leiden and Boston: Brill Publishers).
Dragomir, Elena (2014), *Cold War Perceptions. Romania's Policy Change Towards the Soviet Union, 1960–1964*, Academic Dissertation, Department of Economic and Political Studies, Faculty of Social Sciences (University of Helsinki).

Dragomir, Elena (2015), *Cold War Perceptions: Romania's Policy Change towards the Soviet Union, 1960–1964* (Cambridge: Cambridge Scholars Publishing).

Dura, Ioan (1994), *Monahismul românesc în anii 1948–1989* (Bucharest: Harisma).

Ember, Judit (1989), *Menedekjok-1956* (Budapest: Szabad Ter Kiadö).

Eşan, Ioan (1993), *Vulturii Carpaţilor. Rezistenţa anticomunistă din Munţii Făgăraş. 1948–1958* (Bucharest: Editura RAR).

Ficeac, Bogdan (2009), *Cenzura comunistă şi formarea 'Omului Nou'* (Bucharest: Nemira).

Fischer, Mary Ellen (1989), *Nicolae Ceauşescu. A Study in Political Leadership* (Boulder, CO: Lynne Rienner).

Fischer-Galaţi, Stephen (1991), *Twentieth Century Rumania*, 2nd ed. (New York: Columbia University Press).

Florian, Claudiu, Dumitru Preda, and Ottmar Traşcă (2009), *România-Republica Federală Germania, vol.1. Începutul Relaţiilor Diplomatice, 1966–1967* (Bucharest: Editura Enciclopedică).

Funderburk, David B. (1987), *Pinstripes and Reds. An American Ambassador Caught Between the State Department and Romanian Communists, 1981–1985* (Washington, DC: Selous Foundation Press).

Gabanyi, Anneli Ute (1975). *Partei und Literatur in Rumänien seit 1945* (Munich: R. Oldenbourg Verlag).

Gabanyi, Anneli Ute (2000), *The Ceauşescu Cult. Propaganda and Power Policy in Communist Romania* (Bucharest: Editura Fundaţiei Culturale Române).

Gallagher, Tom (2005), *Theft of a Nation. Romania since Communism* (London: Hurst).

Galloway, G. and B. Wylie (1991), *Downfall. The Ceauşescu and the Romanian Revolution* (London: Futura).

Gavrilă-Ogoranu, Ion (1993–2004), *Brazii se frâng, dar nu se îndoiesc. Rezistenta anticomunista în Muntii Fagarasului*, 4 vols (Timişoara: Editura Marineasa, 1993, 1995, 1999; vol.4, Făgarăş: Mesagerul de Făgăraş).

Georgescu, Adriana (1996), *La început a fost sfirşitul. Dictatura roşie la Bucureşti* (Bucharest: Editura Anastasia).

Georgescu, Vlad (1983), *Politica şi istorie. Cazul comuniştilor români* (1944–1977) (Munich: Ion Dumitru Verlag).

Georgescu, Vlad (1991), *The Romanians: A History* (Columbus: Ohio State University Press).

Gheorghiu, Simion (2015), *Independenţă versus reformă. România în contextul relaţiilor sovieto-americane în perioada 'Perestroika'* (1985–1989) (Brăila: Editura Istros).

Gilberg, Trond (1975), *Modernization in Romania since World War II* (New York: Praeger).

Gillet, Olivier (1997), *Religion et Nationalisme. L'idéologie de l'Eglise Orthodoxe Roumaine sous le régime comministe* (Bruxelles: Editions de l'Université de Bruxelles).

Giurescu, Constantin (1994), *Five Years and Two Months in the Sighet Penitentiary* (Boulder, CO: East European Monographs).

Giurescu, Dinu C. (1989), *The Razing of Romania's Past* (Washington, DC: US/ICOMOS).

Giurescu, Dinu C. (1994), *Five Years and Two Months in the Sighet Penitentiary* (May 7, 1950-July 5, 1955 (Boulder, CO: East European Monographs).

Giurescu, Dinu C. (1994), *Romania's Communist Takeover: The Rădescu Government* (Boulder, CO: East European Monographs).

Glantz, David M. (2007), *Red Storm over the Balkans* (Lawrence: University Press of Kansas).

Govrin, Yosef (2002), *Israeli-Romanian Relations at the End of the Ceauşescu Era. As Observed by Israel's Ambassador to Romania 1985–1989* (London: Frank Cass).

Grăsoiu, D (1984), *Bătălia Arghezi* (Cluj-Napoca: Editura Dacia).

Hall, Richard A., *The Archive of the Romanian Revolution of December* 1989 https://romanianrevolutionofdecember1989.com/. Accessed 10 May 2017.

Harrington, Joseph F and Bruce J. Courtney (1991), *Tweaking the Nose of the Russians. Fifty Years of American-Romanian Relations, 1940–1990* (Boulder, CO: East European Monographs).

Hazard, Elizabeth W. (1996), *Cold War Crucible. United States Foreign Policy and the Conflict in Romania, 1943–1953* (Boulder, CO: East European Monographs).

Heinen, Armin (1986), *Die Legion 'Erzengel Michael' in Rumänien Soziale Bewegung und Politische Organisation* (Munich: R. Oldenbourg Verlag).

Hentea, Călin (2016), *Memorii în papuci. Despre o tinereţe obişnuită* (Bucharest: Editura Eikon).

Hintikka, Kaisamari (2000), *The Romanian Orthodox Church and the World Council of Churches, 1961–1977* (Helsinki: Luther Agricola Society).

Hitchins, Keith (1994), *Rumania 1866–1947* (Oxford: Oxford University Press).

Hitchins, Keith (2014), *A Concise History of Romania* (Cambridge: Cambridge University Press).

Hlihor, Constantin and Ioan Scurtu (2000), *The Red Army in Romania* (Iaşi, Oxford, and Portland: The Center for Romanian Studies).

Hodoş, G. (1987), *Show Trials. Stalinist Purges in Eastern Europe*, 1948–1954 (New York: Praeger).

Iliescu, Ion (1994), *Romania at the Moment of Truth* (Paris: Henri Berger).

Illyes, E. (1982), *National Minorities in Romania. Change in Transylvania* (Boulder, CO: East European Monographs).

Ioanid, Ion (1991–1996), *Închisoarea noastră cea de toate zilele* (Bucharest: Editura Albatros vol.I–II, 1991, vol.III, 1992, vol.IV, 1994, vol.V, 1996).

Ioanid, Radu (2000), *The Holocaust in Romania: The Destruction of the Jews and Gypsies under the Antonescu Regime, 1940–1944* (Chicago: Ivan R. Dee. Published in association with the United States Holocaust Memorial Museum).

Ioanid, Radu (2005), *The Ransom of the Jews. The Extraordinary Secret Bargain between Romania and Israel* (Chicago: Ivan R. Dee).

Ionescu, Aristide (1992), *Dacă vine ora H pe cine putem conta* (Piteşti, n.p.).

Ionescu, Ghita (1964), *Communism in Rumania, 1944–1962* (London: Oxford University Press).

Iordachi, Constantin (2004), *Charisma, Politics and Violence: The Legion of the "Archangel Michael" in Inter-war Romania* (Trondheim: Trondheim Studies on East European Cultures and Societies, no.15).

Jela, Doina (1995), *Cazul Nichita Dumitru. Incercare de reconstituire a unui proces comunist, 29 august-1 septembrie 1952* (Bucharest: Humanitas).

Jela, Doina (2001), *Lexiconul negru. Unelte ale represiunii comuniste* (Bucharest: Humanitas).

Jela, Doina, Cătălin Strat, and Albu Mihaela (2004), *Afacerea Meditaţia Transcententală* (Bucharest: Humanitas).

Jianu, Ion (2008), *Scrisoarea celor şase* (Bucharest: Editura Curtea Veche).

Joo, Rudolf (1994), *The Hungarian Minority's Situation in Ceauşescu's Romania* (New York: Columbia University Press).

Jowitt, Kenneth (1971), *Revolutionary Breakthroughs and National Development: The Case of Romania, 1944–1965* (Berkeley; Los Angeles: University of California Press).

Kaplan, Robert (2016), *In Europe's Shadow. Two Cold Wars and a Thirty-Year Journey Through Romania and Beyond* (New York: Random House).

Karner, Stefan, Mark Kramer, Peter Ruggenthaler, and Manfred Wilke (eds.), (2014), *Der Kreml unde die Wende 1989. Interne Analysen der sowjetischen Führung zum Fall der kommunistischen Regime* (Innsbruck, Wien, and Bozen: StudienVerlag).

Karner, Stefan, Efim Iosifovich Pivovar, Natalya Georgievna Tomilina, and Alexander Oganovich Chubarian (eds.), (2015), *Конец эпохи. СССР и революции в странах Восточной Европы в 1989–1991 гг. Документы* [The End of An Epoch: The USSR and The Revolutions in the Eastern European Countries in 1981–1991. Documents] (Moscow: Rosspen).

Kirk, Roger; Mircea Răceanu (1994), *Romania versus the United States. Diplomacy of the Absurd, 1985–1989* (New York: St Martin's Press).

Kligman, Gail (1998), *The Politics of Duplicity. Controlling Reproduction in Ceauşescu's Romania* (Berkeley: The University of California Press).

Kligman, Gail and Katherine Verdery (2011), *Peasants under Siege. The Collectivization of Romanian Agriculture, 1949–1962* (Princeton: Princeton University Press).

Kopeczi, Bela (ed.), (1986), *Erdely Törtenete*, 3 vols (Budapest: Akadémiai Kiadö).

Lazăr, Traian D. (2006), *Iuliu Maniu şi Serviciile Secrete* (Bucharest: Editura Mica Valachie).

Lazarev, A.M. (1974), *Moldavskaya Sovetskaya Gosudarstvenost' i Bessarabskiy Vopros* (Kishinev: Izdatelstvo Kartya Moldovenyaske).

Lee, Arthur Gould (1950), *Crown against Sickle* (London: Hutchinson).

Leuştean, Lucian (2003), *România şi Ungaria în cadrul Noii Europe* (Iaşi: Polirom).

Leuştean, Lucian N. (2009), *Orthodoxy and the Cold War: Religion and Political Power in Romania, 1947–1965* (Basingstoke, England, and New York: Palgrave Macmillan).

Levy, Robert (2001), *Ana Pauker. The Rise and Fall of a Jewish Communist* (Berkeley: The University of California Press).

Light, Duncan; David Phinnemore (eds.), (2001), *Post-Communist Romania. Coming to Terms with Transition* (Basingstoke and England: Palgrave Macmillan).

Liiceanu, Gabriel (1983), *Jurnalul de la Păltiniş* (Bucharest:Cartea Românească).

Liiceanu, Gabriel (1987), *Epistolar* (Bucharest: Cartea Românească).

Loraine, Joan, (1990), *Operation Ursoaia: Porlock's Village in Romania*, privately printed.

Lungu, Dov (1989), *Romania and the Great Powers, 1933–1940* (Durham and London: Duke University Press).

Lupu, M., C. Nicoară, and G. Onişor (1997), *Cu unanimitate de voturi* (Bucharest: Fundaţia Academia Civică).

Maitland, Patrick (1946), *European Dateline* (London: Quality Press).

Manea, Nornan (1997), *Despre clovni: dictatorul şi artistul* (Cluj-Napoca: Biblioteca Apostrof).

Marin, Irina (2012), *Contested Frontiers in the Balkans: Ottoman and Habsburg Rivalries in Eastern Europe* (London: I.B. Tauris).

Marin, Manuela (2008), *Originea şi evoluţia cultului personalităţii lui Nicolae Ceauşescu 1965–1989* (Alba Iulia: Editura Altip).

Marineasa, Viorel and Daniel Vighi (1994), *Rusalii '51. Fragmente din deportarea în Bărăgan* (Timişoara: Editura Marineasa).

Markham, Reuben H. (1949), *Rumania under the Soviet Yoke* (Boston: Meador Publishing).

Marx, Karl (1964), *Insemnări despre Români* [Notes on the Romanians] (Bucharest: Editura Academiei Republicii Populare Române).

Mărgineanu, Nicolae (1991), *Amfiteatre şi închisori* (Cluj: Editura Dacia).

Mastny, Vojtech (2001), *Learning from the Enemy: NATO as a Model for the Warsaw Pact, Zürcher Beiträge zur Sicherheitspolitik und Konfliktforschung Nr. 58* (Zürich: Forschungsstelle für Sicherheitspolitik und Konfliktanalyse der ETH Zürich).

McDermott, Kevin and Matthew Stibbe (eds.), (2006), *Revolution and Resistance in Eastern Europe. Challenges to Communist Rule* (Oxford: Berg).
Milin, Miodrag (1997), *Timişoara în revoluţie şi după* (Timişoara: Editura Marineasa).
Mioc, Marius (1997), *Revoluţia din Timişoara aşa cum a fost* (Timişoara: Editura Brumar).
Mioc, Marius (2002), *Revoluţia fără mistere* (Timişoara: Editura Almanahul Banatului).
Mircu, Mircu (1991), *Dosar Ana Pauker* (Bucharest: Editura Gutenberg).
Mungiu-Pippidi and Gérard Althabe Alina (2002), *Secera şi buldozerul. Scorniceşti şi Nucsoara. Mecanisme de aservire a ţăranului român* (Iaşi: Editura Polirom).
Munteanu, Mircea (2011), *The Beginning of the End for Détente: The Warsaw Pact Political Consultative Committee*, e-dossier no. 24, CWIHP, http://legacy.wilsoncenter.org/va2/index.cfm. Accessed 10 May 2017.
Murgescu, Bogdan (2007), *Revoluţia română din decembrie 1989. Istorie şi memorie* (Iaşi: Polirom).
Murgescu, Bogdan (2010), *România şi Europa. Acumularea decalajelor economice (1500–2010)* (Iaşi: Polirom).
Muşat, Mircea. and I. Ardeleanu (1982), *Political Life in Romania, 1918–1921* (Bucharest: Editura Academiei Republicii Socialiste România).
Neculau, Adrian (ed.), (2004), *Viaţa cotidiană în comunism* (Iaşi: Polirom).
Nedelcovici, Bujor (2009), *Scriitorul, Cenzura şi Securitatea* (Bucharest: Allfa).
Nelson, Daniel N. (ed.), (1981), *Romania in the 1980s* (Boulder, CO: Westview Press).
Nicolaescu, Sergiu (1995), *Revoluţia, începutul adevărului: un raport personal* (Bucharest: Editura Topaz).
Niculescu-Mizil, Paul (2002), *O istorie trăită. Memorii*, vol.I (Bucharest: Editura Enciclopedică).
Niculescu-Mizil, Paul (2003), *O istorie trăită. Memorii*, vol.II (Bucharest: Editura Enciclopedică).
Olaru, Stejărel and Herbstritt Georg (2005), *Stasi şi Securitatea* (Bucharest: Humanitas).
Oprea, Marius (2002), *Banalitatea Răului. O Istorie a Securităţii în Documente, 1949–1989* (Iaşi: Polirom).
Oprea, Marius (2003), *The Day We Won't Forget* (Iaşi: Polirom).
Oprea, Marius (2004), *Moştenitorii Securităţii* (Bucharest: Humanitas).
Oprea, Marius (2009), *Şase feluri de a muri*(Bucharest: Polirom).
Organizarea şi funcţionarea Ministerului de Interne de la înfiinţare până în prezent (1978) (Bucharest: Ministerul de Interne).
Osca, Alexandru and Vasile Popa (1997), *România. O fereastră deschisă în Cortina de Fier* (Focsani, n.p.).
Pacepa, Ion (1988), *Red Horizons* (London: Heinemann).
Pacepa, Ion (1993), *Moştenirea Kremlinului* (Bucharest: Editura Venus).
Paiuşan, Cristina; Radu Ciuceanu (2001), *Biserica Ortodoxă Română sub regimul comunist (1945–1958)*, vol.1 (Bucharest: Institutul Naţional pentru Studiul Totalitarismului).
Paraschiv, Vasile (2005), *Lupta mea pentru sindicate libere în România* (Iaşi: Polirom).
Paraschiv, Vasile (2007), *Aşa nu se mai poate, tovarăşe Nicolae Ceauşescu* (Bucharest: Curtea Veche).
Pătrăşcanu, Lucreţiu (1970), *Sub trei dictaturi*, 2nd ed. (Bucharest: Editura Politică).
Pearton, Maurice (1971), *Oil and the Romanian State* (London: Oxford University Press).
Pearton, Maurice and Dennis Deletant (1996), 'The Soviet Takeover in Romania, 1944–48', in Gill Bennett (ed.), *The End of War in Europe, 1945* (London: HMSO), pp.204–20.
Pelin, Mihai (1997), *Culisele Spionajului Românesc. DIE 1955–1980* (Bucharest: Editura Evenimentul Românesc).

Peter, Lászlo (ed.), (1992), *Historians and the History of Transylvania* (Boulder, CO: East European Monographs).

Petrescu, Cristina (2013), *From Robin Hood to Don Quixote. Resistance and Dissent in Communist Romania* (Bucharest: Editura enciclopedică).

Petrescu, Dragoş (2014), *Entangled Revolutions. The Breakdown of the Communist Regimes in East-Central Europe* (Bucharest: Editura enciclopedică).

Petrov, Nikita (2010), *Kto rukovodil organami gosbezopasnosti 1941–1954. Spravochnik.* [Who directed the State Security Organs? 1941–1954. Manual], "Memorial" international organization (Moscow: Zvenia Publishing House).

Petrov, Nikita (2011), *Po scenariu Stalina: Rol organov NKVD-MGB SSSR v sovietizacii stran Centralnoy i Vostochnoy Evropi 1945–1953.* [Following the script of Stalin: The Role of Organs of the Soviet Union's People's Commissariat for State Security-Ministry for State Security in the Sovietization of East Central Europe, 1945–1953] (Moscow: Rosspen).

Pintilie, Florin (2003), *Serviciul Special de Informaţii din România. 1939–1947* (Bucharest, n.p.).

Pleşu, Andrei (1988), *Minima Moralia* (Bucharest: Cartea Românească).

Pop, Ion (1973), *Poezia unei generaţii* (Cluj: Editura Dacia).

Popa, Ilie (2016), *Antologia liricii de detenţie anticomunistă din spaţiul românesc* (Bucharest: Fundaţia Culturală Memoria).

Popescu, Dumitru (1993), *Un fost lider comunist se destăinuie* (Bucharest: Editura Expres).

Porter, Ivor (1989), *Operation Autonomous. With S.O.E. in Wartime Romania* (London: Chatto and Windus).

Porter, Ivor (2005), *Michael of Romania. The King and the Country* (London: Sutton Publishing).

Portocala, Radu (1990), *Autopsie du coup d'état Roumain* (Paris: Calmann-Levy).

Povestea Elisabetei Rizea din Nucşoara (1993), (Bucharest: Humanitas).

Preda, Dumitru and Mihai Retegan (2000), *1989. Principiul Dominoului* (Bucharest: Editura Fundaţiei Culturale Române).

Prunduş, S.A. and C. Plăianu (1992), *Cardinalul Alexandru Todea* (Cluj: Ordinul Sfântul Vasile cel Mare).

Punct de vedere preliminar al Serviciului Român de Informaţii privind evenimentele din decembrie 1989 (1993) (Bucharest: SRI).

von Puttkamer, Joachim, Stefan Sienerth, and Ulrich A. Wien (eds.), (2014), *Die Securitate in Siebenbürgen* (Köln, Weimar, and Wien: Böhlau Verlag).

Quinlan, Paul D. (1977), *Clash Over Romania. British and American Policies towards Romania: 1938–1947* (Los Angeles: American Romanian Academy).

Răceanu, Mircea (2005), *Cronologie comentată a relaţiilor româno-americane. De la începutul cunoaşterii reciproce până la prăbuşirea regimului comunist în România* (Bucharest: Silex).

Răceanu, Mircea (2005), *Istoria Naţiunii Celei mai Favorizate în relaţiile româno-americane* (Bucharest: Institutul Naţional pentru Memoria Exilului).

Răceanu, Mircea (2009), *Infern '89. Povestea unui condamnat la moarte*, 2nd rev. ed. (Bucharest: Curtea Veche).

Rady, Martyn (1992), *Romania in Turmoil: A Contemporary History* (London: IB Tauris, 1992).

Ratesh, Nestor (1991), *Romania: The Entangled Revolution* (New York: Praeger).

Raţiu, A. and W. Virtue (1978), *Stolen Church: Martyrdom in Communist Romania* (Huntington, IN: Our Sunday Visitor).

Raţiu, Ion (2016), *Jurnal. Vol 1. Începuturile unui exil îndelungat (1940–1954)*, Stejărel Olaru (ed.) (Bucharest: Corint).

Retegan, Mihai (2000), *In the Shadow of the Prague Spring. Romanian Foreign Policy and the Crisis in Czechoslovakia, 1968* (Iaşi, Portland, and Oxford: The Center for Romanian Studies).

Retegan, Mihai (2002), *Război politic în blocul communist* (Bucharest: RAO).

Retegan, Mihai (2014), *1968. Din Primăvară până în Toamnă* (Bucharest: Editura RAO).

Ritual of Liquidation. The Case of the Moscow Trials (1954) (Glencoe, IL: The Free Press).

Roberts, Henry L. (1951), *Rumania: Political Problems of an Agrarian State* (New Haven: Yale University Press, 1951).

Romania: A Case of "Dynastic" Communism (1989) (New York: Freedom House).

Romania: Forced Labor, Psychiatric Repression of Dissent, Persecution of Religious Believers. Ethnic Discrimination and Persecution, Law and the Suppression of Human Rights (1987) (New York: Amnesty International).

Romania's "Tipping Point". Advancing the Rule of Law, Governance and Public Leadership. Findings of the U.S.-Romania Initiative Working Group (2014) (Washington, DC: CEPA).

Ronnas, P. (1984), *Urbanization in Romania, A Geography of Social and Economic Change since Independence* (Stockholm: Stockholm School of Economics).

Roşca Stănescu, Sorin and Cornel Dumitrescu (1999), *Autopsia: demontarea unei înscenări securiste împotriva generalului Pacepa* (Bucharest: Omega Ziua).

Rusan, Romulus (1994), *Memoria ca formă de justiţie* (Bucharest: Fundaţia Academia Civică, 1994).

Rusan, Romulus (1997), *O enigmă care împlineşte şapte ani. Timişoara, 1989–1996* (Bucharest: Fundaţia Academia Civică).

Sampson, Steven (1984), *National Integration through Socialist Planning. An Anthropological Study of a Romanian New Town* (Boulder, CO: East European, Monographs).

Samuelli, Annie (1967), *The Wall Between* (Washington, DC: Robert B. Luce).

Săndulescu, Şerban (1996), *Decembrie '89. Lovitura de stat a confiscate Revoluţia Română*, 2nd ed. (Bucharest: Omega Press).

Săraru, Dinu and Victor Atanasie Stănculescu (2005), *Dinu Săraru în dialog cu Victor Atanasie Stănculescu. Generalul revoluţiei cu piciorul în ghips* (Bucharest: RAO).

Sava, Constantin and Constantin Monac (2001), *Revoluţia română din decembrie 1989, retrăită prin documente şi mărturii* (Bucharest: Editura Axioma).

Savranskaya, Svetlana, Thomas Blanton, and Vladislav Zubok (eds.), (2010), *Masterpieces of History. The Peaceful End of the Cold War in Europe, 1989* (Budapest and New York: Central European University Press).

Schecter, J.L. and V.V. Luchkov (eds.), (1990), *Khrushchev Remembers. The Glasnost Tapes* (Boston: Little, Brown and Co.).

Schopflin, G. and H. Poulton (1990), *Romania's Ethnic Hungarians* (London: Minority Rights Group).

Schröm, Oliver (2002), *Im Schatten des Schakals. Carlos und die Wegbereiter des internationalen Terrorismus* (Berlin: Christoph Links Verlag).

Scurtu, Ioan (ed.), (1996), *România. Retragerea Trupelor Sovietice, 1958* (Bucharest: Editura Didactică şi Pedagogică).

Sebastian, Mihail (2000), *Journal. 1935–1944*. Translated by Patrick Camiller. Introduction and notes by Radu Ioanid (Chicago: Ivan R. Dee in association with the United States Holocaust Memorial Museum).

Sejna, J. (1982), *We Will Bury You* (London: Sidgwick and Jackson).

Selejan, Ana (1992), *Trădarea intelectualilor* (Sibiu: Editura Transpres).

Selejan, Ana (1993), *Reeducare şi prigoană* (Sibiu: Editura Thausib).

Selejan, Ana (1994), *Literatura în totalitarism. 1949–1951*. Vol.1 (Sibiu: Editura Thausib).

Selejan, Ana (1995), *Literatura în totalitarism. 1952–1953*. Vol.2 (Sibiu: Editura Thausib).

Selejan, Ana (1996), *Literatura în totalitarism. Anul 1954*. Vol.3 (Sibiu: Editura Fronde).

Selejan, Ana (1998), *Literatura în totalitarism. 1955–1956*. Vol.4 (Bucharest: Cartea românească).

Selejan, Ana (1999), *Literatura în totalitarism. 1957–1958*. Vol.5 (Bucharest: Cartea românească).

Selejan, Ana (2000), *Literatura în totalitarism. 1959–1960*. Vol.6 (Bucharest: Cartea românească).

Şerbulescu, Andrei [Belu Zilber] (1991), *Monarhia de Drept Dialectic* (Bucharest: Humanitas).

Şercan, Emlia (2015), *Cultul secretului. Mecanismele cenzurii în presa comunistă* (Bucharest: Polirom).

Seton-Watson, Hugh (1962), *Eastern Europe Between the Wars 1918–1941*, 3rd ed. (New York and London: Harper Row).

Seton-Watson, R.W. (1934), *A History of the Roumanians* (Cambridge: Cambridge University Press).

Sfetcu, Paul (2000), *13 ani în anticamera lui Dej* (Bucharest: Editura Fundaţiei Culturale Române).

Shafir, Michael (1985), *Romania. Politics, Economics and Society* (London: Frances Pinter).

Shevchenko, Arkady N. (1985), *Breaking with Moscow* (New York: Alfred A. Knopf).

Shevyakov, A.A. (1985), *Otnosheniya mezhdu Sovetskim Soyuzom I Rumyniey 1944–1949* (Moscow: Nauka).

Siani-Davies, Peter (2005), *The Romanian Revolution* (Ithaca and London: Cornell University Press).

Şiperco, Andrei (ed.), (2015), *Confesiunile elitei comuniste. România 1944–1965. Arhiva Alexandru Şiperco*, 2 vols (Bucharest: Institutul Naţional pentru Studiul Totalitarismului).

Sitariu, Mihaela (1998), *Rezistenţa anticomunistă. Timişoara 1956* (Bucharest: Editura Sophia).

Sorescu, Marin (1985), *Let's Talk about the Weather*, translated by Andrea Deletant and Brenda Walker (London: Forest Books).

Sorescu, Marin (1985), *The Thirst of the Salt Mountain*, translated by Andrea Deletant and Brenda Walker (London: Forest Books).

Sorescu, Marin (1987), *Vlad Dracula the Impaler*, translated by Dennis Deletant (London: Forest Books).

Sorescu, Marin (1991), *Hands behind my Back*, translated by Gabriela Dragnea, Stuart Friebert, and Adriana Varga (Oberlin, OH: Oberlin College Press).

Şperlea, Florin (2003), *La Armata Populară. Sovietizarea Armatei Române* (1948–1955) (Bucharest: Ziua).

Spiridon, Cassian Maria (1994), *Iaşi, 14 decembrie 1989: Începutul Revoluţiei Române* (Iaşi: Timpul).

Stan, Florin (2016), *România-Israel. Relaţii bilaterale* (1948–1991) (Cluj-Napoca: Argonaut).

Stan, Lavinia and Lucian Turcescu (2007), *Religion and Politics in Post-Communist Romania* (Oxford: Oxford University Press).

Stan, Lavinia and Diane Vancea (eds.), (2016), *Post-Communist Romania at Twenty-Five. Linking, Past, Present and Future* (Lanham, Boulder, New York, and London: Lexington Books).
Stănescu, Flori and Dragoş Zamfirescu (1998), *Ocupaţia Sovietică în România. Documente 1944–1946* (Bucharest: Vremea).
Ştefănescu, Paul (1994), *Istoria Serviciilor Secrete Româneşti* (Bucharest: Divers Press).
Stehle, Hansjakob (1981), *Eastern Politics of the Vatican, 1917–1979*, translated by Sandra Smith, (Athens: Ohio University Press).
Steinhardt, N. (2008), *Jurnalul fericirii* (Iaşi: Polirom).
Stoenescu, Alex Mihai (2004), *Interviuri despre revoluţie* (Bucharest: RAO).
Stoenescu, Alex Mihai (2004–2005), *Istoria loviturilor de stat în România*, vol.4, parts 1+2: *Revoluţia din decembrie 1989* (Bucharest: RAO).
Strat, Cătălin (ed.), (2013), *Dosarul de Securitate al lui Ambasador Coen Stork, cu o prefaţă de Dennis Deletant* (Bucharest: Humanitas).
Suciu, Titus (1990), *Reportaj cu sufletul la gură: traseele revoluţiei* (Timişoara: Facla).
Sweeney, John (1991), *The Life and Evil Times of Nicolae Ceauşescu* (London: Hutchinson).
Tănase, Stelian (1998), *Elite şi societate. Guvernarea Gheorghiu-Dej, 1948–1965* (Bucharest: Humanitas).
Tănase, Stelian (2003), *Anatomia Mistificării* (Bucharest: Humanitas).
Tănase, Stelian (2005), *Clienţii lu'tanti Varvara. Istorii clandestine* (Bucharest: Humanitas).
Tănase, Stelian (2007), *At Home There's Only Speaking in a Whisper. File and Diary Recording the Late Years of the Romanian Dictatorship*. Translated from the Romanian by Sorana Corneanu (Boulder, CO: East European Monographs).
Tănase, Stelian (2010), *Auntie Varvara's Clients*, translated by Alistair Ian Blyth (Plymouth: University of Plymouth Press).
Tănăsescu, Florian and Nicolae Tănăsescu (2005), *Constantin (Bebe) I.C. Brătianu – Istoria P.N.L. la interogatoriu* (Bucharest: Editura Paralela 45).
Ţăranu, Liviu (ed.), (2009), *Ion Mihai Pacepa în Dosarele Securităţii. 1978–1980* (Bucharest: Consiliul Naţional pentru Studierea Arhivelor Securităţii).
Teodorescu, Filip (1992), *Un risc asumat. Timişoara, decembrie 1989* (Bucharest: Editura Viitorul Românesc).
Thomas, Evan (1995), *The Very Best Men: Four Who Dared: The Early Years of the CIA* (New York: Simon and Shuster).
Ţîrău, Liviu (2005), *Între Washington şi Moscova: România 1945–1965* (Cluj-Napoca: Tribuna).
Tismăneanu, Vladimir (1992), *Arheologia terorii* (Bucharest: Editura Eminescu).
Tismăneanu, Vladimir (1995), *Fantoma lui Gheorghiu-Dej* (Bucharest: Editura Univers).
Tismăneanu, Vladimir (2003), *Stalinism for All Seasons. A Political History of Romanian Communism* (Berkeley and Los Angeles: University of California Press).
Tismăneanu, Vladimir, Dorin Dobrincu, Cristian Vasile et al. (eds.), (2007), *Raportul Final al Comisiei Prezidenţiale pentru Analiza Dictaturii Comuniste din România* (Bucharest: Humanitas).
Tismăneanu, Vladimir and Cristian Vasile (2008), *Perfectul acrobat. Leonte Răuntu, Măştile Răului* (Bucharest: Humanitas).
Tofan, Liviu (2013), *Şacalul Securităţii. Teroristul Carlos în solda spionajului românesc* (Bucharest: Polirom).
Tökés, László (1990), *With God, For the People, as told to David Porter* (London: Hodder and Stoughton).
Tomaziu, George (1995), *Jurnalul unui figurant* (Bucharest: Editura Univers).

Tomaziu, George (2015), *The Witness*, edited and translated by Janet Reid (London: Theed Street Publishing).

Tomis cenzurat/necenzurat (2007) (Constanţa: Editura Tomis).

Totok, William and Elena-Irina Macovei (2016), *Între mit şi bagatelizare. Despre reconsiderarea critică a trecutului. Ion Gavrilă-Ogoreanu şi rezistenţa armată anticomunistă din România* (Iaşi: Polirom).

Trial of the Group of Spies and Traitors in the Service of the Espionage of Tito's Fascist Clique (1950) (Bucharest: Romania's Ministry of Foreign Affairs).

Troncotă, Cristian (1997), *Mihai Moruzov şi Serviciul Secret de Informaţii al Armatei Române* (Bucharest: Editura Evenimentul Românesc).

Troncotă, Cristian (2003), *Duplicitarii. O istorie a Serviciilor de Informaţii şi Securitate ale regimului comunist din România* (Bucharest: Elion).

Troncotă, Cristian (2006), *Tortionarii. Istoria instituţiei Securităţii regimului comunist din România (1948–1964)* (Bucharest: Elion).

Troncotă, Tiberiu (2006), *România comunistă. Propagandă şi cenzură* (Bucharest: Tritonic).

Tudorancea, Radu (2014), *Ipostazele "ajutorului frăţesc". RPR şi războiul din Coreea* (1950–1953) (Cluj-Napoca: Eikon).

Ţugui, Pavel (1999), *Istoria şi limba română în vremea lui Gheorghiu-Dej* (Bucharest: Editura Ion Cristoiu).

Ursu, Gheorghe (1991), *Europa Mea* (Cluj-Napoca: Dacia).

van der Grift, Liesbeth (2012), *Securing the Communist State: The Reconstructions of Coercive Institutions in the Soviet Zone of Germany and Romania (1944–1948)* (Lanham, MD: Lexington Books).

van Meurs, Wim P. (1994), *The Bessarabian Question in Communist Historiography. Nationalist and Communist Politics and History-Writing* (Boulder, CO: East European Monographs.

Vasile, Cristian (2003), *Între Vatican si Kremlin. Biserica Greco-Catolică în timpul regimului comunist* (Bucharest: Curtea Veche Publishing).

Vasile, Cristian (2005), *Biserica Ortodoxă Română în Primul Deceniu Comunist* (Bucharest: Curtea Veche).

Veiga, Francisco (1989), *La Mistica del Ultranacionalismo. Historia de la Guardia de Hierro* (Barcelona: Universitat Autonoma de Barcelona, Bellaterra).

Verca, Filon (1993), *Paraşutaţi în România vândută. Mişcarea de rezistenţă 1944–1948* (Timişoara: Editura Gordian).

Verdery, Katherine (1991), *National Ideology under Socialism. Identity and Cultural Politics in Ceauşescu's Romania* (Berkeley: Los Angeles).

Verdery, Katherine (1996), *What was Socialism and What Comes Next?* (Princeton: Princeton University Press).

Verdery, Katherine (2014), *Secrets and Truths. Ethnography in the Archive of Romania's Secret Police.* The Natalie Zemon Davis Annual Lectures (Budapest and New York: Central European University Press).

Verona, Sergiu (1992), *Military Occupation and Diplomacy. Soviet Troops in Romania 1944–1958* (Durham and London: Duke University Press).

Vianu, Lidia (1998), *Censorship in Romania* (Budapest: Central European University Press).

Vişa, Augustin (1997), *Din închisorile fasciste în cele comuniste din URSS şi România* (Bucharest: Institutul pentru Analiză şi Politică Iuliu Maniu).

Vulcănescu, Mircea (1992), *Ultimul Cuvânt* (Bucharest: Humanitas).

Vuza, George Pavel (2008), *Însemnările unui procurator* (Bucharest: Vremea).
Wagner, Richard (1990), *Exit: A Romanian Story* (London: Verso).
Watts, Larry L. (2010), *With Friends Like These. The Soviet Bloc's Clandestine War Against Romania* (Bucharest: Military Publishing House).
Watts, Larry L. (2013), *Cei dintâi vor fi cei din urmă* (The First will be the Last) (Bucharest: RAO).
Watts, Larry L. (2013), *Extorting Peace: Romania and the End of the Cold War, 1978–1989* (Bucharest: RAO).
Weiner, Robert (1984), *Romanian Foreign Policy and the United Nations* (New York: Praeger).
Wickert, Erwin (2001), *Die Glücklichen Augen. Geschichten aus meinem Leben* (Stuttgart-München: Deutsche Verlagsanstalt).
Witnesses to Cultural Genocide (1979) (New York: American Transylvanian Federation, Committee for Human Rights in Rumania).
Wurmbrand, Richard (1968), *In God's Underground* (London: W.H. Allen).
Zarojanu, Tudor Călin (2005), *Viaţa lui Corneliu Coposu: cu documente din arhiva fostei Securităţi* (Bucharest: Editura Maşinii de Scris).
Zavatti, Francesco (2014), *Comunisti per Caso* (Milano: Mimesis).
Zidaru, Marian (2005), *Relaţii politice şi economice româno-britanice, 1939–1947* (Bucharest: Univers Ştiinţific).
Zwass, Adam (1989), *The Council for Mutual Economic Assistance*. The Thorny Path from Political to Economic Integration (New York: M.E. Sharpe).

Selected Articles

Achim, Viorel (2003), 'Deportarea ţiganilor în Transnistria', *Anuarul IRIR 2002*, Bucharest, pp.129–45.
Analele Sighet (1994–2003), Rusan, Romulus (ed.), 10 vols (Bucharest: Fundaţia Academia Civică).
Ban, Cornel (2012), 'Sovereign Debt, Austerity and Regime Change', *East European Politics and Societies and Cultures*, vol.26, no.4 (November), pp.743–76.
Boca, Ioana (2006), '1956 în Romania', in Doina Jela and Vladimir Tismăneanu (eds.), *Ungaria 1956: Revolta minţilor şi sfârşitul mitului communist* (Bucharest: Curtea Veche), pp.169–95.
Brett, Dan (2015), 'Romania: New Problems and Old Challenges', in Sharon L. Wolchik and Jane L. Curry (eds.), *Central and East European Politics: From Communism to Democracy*, 3rd ed. (Lanham, MD: Rowman & Littlefield), pp.373–405.
Broun, Janice (1984), 'The Latin-Rite Roman Catholic Church of Romania', *Religion in Communist Lands*, vol.12, no.2, pp.168–84.
Burakowski, Adam (2006), 'Un eveniment important aproape necunoscut: Demonstraţia studenţilor din Bucureşti , 24 decembrie 1968', *Arhivele Totalitarismului*, nos.1–2, pp.238–47.
Burcea, Mihai (2014), 'Judecarea comuniştilor în timpul războiului. Procesul lui Petre Gheorghe', in Adrian Cioroianu (ed.), *Comuniştii înainte de Comunism. Procese şi Condamnări* (Bucharest: Editura Universităţii din Bucureşti), pp.307–88.
Cârstocea, Raul (2009), *'Uneasy Twins? The Entangled Histories of Jewish Emancipation and Anti-Semitism in Romania and Hungary*, 1866–1913,' *Slovo*, vol.21, pp.64–85.
Cavalcanti, Maria (1992), 'Totalitarian States and Their Influence on City-Form: The Case of Bucharest', *Journal of Architectural Planning Research*, vol.9, no.4, pp.275–86.

Coposu, Corneliu (1994), 'Exilul Românesc: Identitate şi Conştiinţă istorică', *Lupta*, no.232 (7 octombrie), p.5.

Croitoru, Mihai (2011), 'An Episode of the Romanian-Soviet Differences. "The Medium Body-Weight of Slaughtered Pigs in Romania"', *Studia Universitatis Babeş-Bolyai. Historia*, vol.56 (December), pp.105–15.

Deletant, Dennis (1989), 'Crimes Against the Spirit', in *Index on Censorship*, no.8, pp.26–27.

Deletant, Dennis (1989), 'An Island of Stalinism', *The Independent*, 28 November 1989, p.25.

Deletant, Dennis (2005), 'Romania', in Persak, Krzysztof and Kaminski, Lukasz (eds.), *A Handbook of the Communist Security Apparatus in East-Central Europe 1944–1989* (Warsaw: Institute of National Remembrance), pp.285–328.

Deletant, Dennis (2008), 'Cheating the Censor: Romanian Writers under Communism', *Central Europe*, vol.6, no.2 (November), pp.122–71.

Deletant, Dennis (2014), 'Revisiting the 1989 Romanian Revolution: Some Personal Reflections', *Archiva Moldaviae*, Iaşi, vol.IV, pp.227–52 [p.230].

Eyal, Jonathan (1990), 'Why Romania Could Not Avoid Bloodshed', in G. Prins (ed.), *Spring in Winter. The 1989 Revolutions* (Manchester and New York: Manchester University Press), pp.139–62.

Falls, Donald R. (1993), 'Soviet Decision-Making and the Withdrawal of Soviet Troops from Romania', *East European Quarterly*, vol.27, no.4 (Winter), pp.489-502.

Gheorghe, Eliza (2013), 'Atomic Maverick: Romania's Negotiations for Nuclear Technology, 1964–1970', *Cold War History*, vol.13, no.3 (August 2013), pp.373–92.

Ghibianski, Leonid (1995), 'URSS şi câteva aspecte ale formării blocului sovietic în Europa Orientală', in *6 Martie 1945. Inceputurile Comunizării României* (Bucharest: Editura Enciclopedică), pp.254–61.

Granville, Johanna (2008), 'Temporary Triumph in Timişoara: Unrest among Romanian Students in 1956', *History*, vol.93, no.1 (1 January), pp.69–93.

Hanak, H. (1988), 'The Politics of Impotence: The British Observe Romania, 6 March 1945 to 30 December 1947', in I. Agrigoroaie, Gh. Buzatu, and V. Cristian (eds.), *Românii în istoria universală*, vol.III/1 (Iaşi), pp.429–50.

Hitchins, Keith (1975), 'The Romanian Orthodox Church and the State', in B.R. Bociurkiw and J.W. Strong (eds.), assisted by J.K. Laux, *Religion and Atheism in the USSR and Eastern Europe* (Toronto: University of Toronto Press; London: Macmillan), pp.314–27.

Ionniţiu, Mircea (1991), '23 August 1944. Amintiri şi reflecţiuni', *Revista istorică*, vol.2, nos.9–10, pp.557–75.

Klein, G. (1995), 'Începuturile rezistenţei antisovietice în România (23 august 1944–6 martie 1945)', in *6 martie 1945. Începuturile Comunizării României* (Bucharest: Editura Enciclopedică), pp.295–311.

Lăcătuş, Dimitrie (2017) 'Relatare de la procesul Gheorghe Ursu. Spinoasa problema a continuitatii intre institutiile statului roman de azi cu cel comunist'. http://www.contributors.ro/reactie-rapida/relatare-de-la-procesul-gheorghe-ursu-spinoasa-problema-a-continuitatii-intre-institutiile-statului-roman-de-azi-cu-cel-comunist. Accessed 10 May 2017.

Latham Jr., Ernest H. (2012a), 'All Thankful: Reports by Neutral Observers of American Prisoner War Held in Romania 1943–1944', in *Timeless and Transitory: 20th Century Relations between Romania and the English-Speaking World* (Bucharest: Vremea), pp.270–98.

Latham Jr., Ernest H. (2012b), *'Efficient and Rapid: The Letters of Major Walter Ross of OSS to his Commanding Officer*, Lieutenant Commander Edward Green, during the Evacuation of Allied Airmen from Romania, 30 August–2 September 1944', in *Timeless and Transitory: 20th Century Relations between Romania and the English-Speaking World* (Bucharest: Vremea), pp.299–345.

Latham Jr., Ernest H. (2012c), 'Useful Service Rendered: The Romanian Life of Dimitri Demetrius Dimancescu', in *Timeless and Transitory: 20th Century Relations between Romania and the English-Speaking World* (Bucharest: Vremea), pp.397–445.

Levy, Robert (1995), 'Did Ana Pauker prevent a "Rajk Trial" in Romania?', *East European Politics and Societies*, vol.9, no.1 (Winter), pp.143–78.

Levy, Robert (1995), 'Power Struggles in the Romanian Communist Party during the Formation of the Groza regime', in *6 Martie 1945. Inceputurile Comunizării României* (Bucharest: Editura Enciclopedică, 1995), pp.70–90.

Mark, Eduard (1994), 'The OSS in Romania, 1944–45: An intelligence operation of the early Cold War', *Intelligence and National Security*, vol.9, no.2, pp.320–44.

McPherson, William (1991), 'In Romania', *Granta*, vol.33 (January), pp.9–58.

Michelson, Paul and J.T. Michelson (2001), 'Amintiri despre 'mini-revoluţie' din România', *Analele Sighet*, no.9, pp.863–70.

Miroiu, Andrei (2010), 'Wiping Out "The Bandits": Romanian Counterinsurgency Strategies in the Early Communist Period', *The Journal of Slavic Military Studies*, vol.23, no.4, pp.666–691, DOI: 10.1080/13518046.2010.526021.

Naimark, Norman and Leonard Gibianskii (1999), 'Introduction' in N.M. Naimark and L. Gibianskii (eds.), *The Establishment of Communist Regimes, 1944–1949* (Boulder, CO: Westview Press).

Papacostea, Şerban (1996), 'Captive Clio: Romanian Historiography under Communist Rule', *European History Quarterly*, vol.26, no.2, pp.181–208.

Pearton, Maurice (1995), 'Puzzles about Percentages', in Dennis Deletant (ed.), *Occasional Papers in Romanian Studies*, no.1 (London: School of Slavonic and East European Studies, University of London). pp.7–13.

Pearton, Maurice (1998), 'The Romanian Leadership and its Problems, 1956–1957–1958', in Maurice Pearton and Dennis Deletant (eds.), *Romania Observed* (Bucharest: Editura Enciclopedică), pp.217–75.

Pechlivanis, Paschalis (2017), 'Between Détente and Differentiation: Nixon's visit to Bucharest in August 1969', *Cold War History*, DOI: 10.1080/14682745.2016.1267144.

Percival, Mark (1995), 'British Attitudes towards the Romanian Historic Parties and the Monarchy, 1944–47', in Dennis Deletant (ed.), *Occasional Papers in Romanian Studies*, No.1 (London: School of Slavonic and East European Studies, University of London).

Petrescu, Dragoş (2015), 'Closely Watched Tourism: The Securitate as Warden of Transnational Encounters, 1967–1989', *Journal of Contemporary History*, vol.50, no.2, pp.337–53.

Pokivailova, T.A. (1995), 'A.Y. Vyshinski, first deputy Commissar for Foreign Affairs of the USSR and the Establishment of the Groza Government', in *6 martie 1945. Începuturile Comunizării României* (Bucharest: Editura Enciclopedică), pp.53–54.

Roşianu, M. (1964), 'Cum a fost organizata· evadarea tovarăşului Gheorghe Gheorghiu-Dej din lagărul de la Târgu-Jiu în august 1944', *Scînteia*, 18 August, pp.2–3.

Sampson, Steven L. (1981–83), 'Muddling Through in Rumania (or: Why the Mamaliga Doesn't Explode)', *International Journal of Rumanian Studies*, vol.3, pp.165–85.

Şandru, D. (1995), 'Detinuţii politici de la Gherla în 1947', *Anuarul Institutului de Istorie Cluj-Napoca*, vol.34, pp.271–82.

Scarfe, Alan (1975), 'The Evangelical Wing of the Orthodox Church in Romania', *Religion in Communist Lands*, vol.3, no.6, pp.15–19.

Scarfe, Alan (1976), 'Romanian Baptists and the State', *Religion in Communist Lands*, vol.4, no.2, pp.14–20.

Scarfe, Alan (1977), 'Patriarch Justinian of Romania: His Early Social Thought', *Religion in Communist Lands*, vol.5, no.3, pp.164–69.

Schöpflin, George (1974), 'Rumanian Nationalism', *Survey*, nos.2–3, pp.77–104.

Secaşiu, Claudiu (1991), 'Regele Mihai şi executarea Mareşalului Antonescu. Adevăr şi Legendă', *Cotidianul. Supliment Cultural*, 8 July, p.5.

Shafir, Michael (1978), 'Who is Paul Goma?', *Index on Censorship*, vol.7, no.1, pp.33–36.

Shafir, Michael (1983), 'Former Senior RCP Officials Protest Ceauşescu's Policies', *Radio Free Europe Research, Romania/3* (29 March 1989), pp.8–11.

Shafir, Michael (1983), 'The Men of the Archangel Revisited: Anti-Semitic Formations among Communist Romania's Intellectuals', *Studies in Comparative Communism*, vol. XVI, no.3 (Autumn), pp.228–48.

Shafir, Michael (1989), 'Highlights of the 14th Party Congress', *RFE Research. Romanian Situation Report*/9 (14 December 1989), pp.4–8.

Shafir, Michael (1989), '"Revisionism" under Romanian General's Fire: Ceausçescu's Brother Attacks Hungarian Positions', *RFE Research. Background Report*/86 (17 May 1989), pp.4–7.

Smith, Alan H (1992), 'The Romanian Enterprise', in I. Jeffries (ed.), *Industrial Reform in Socialist Countries* (London: Edward Elgar).

Socor, Vladimir (1987), 'The Workers' Protest in Braşov: Assessment and Aftermath', *Romania Background Report/231, Radio Free Europe Research*, 4 December.

Stanciu, Cezar (2013), 'A Rebirth of Diplomacy: The Foreign Policy of Communist Romania between Subordination and Autonomy, 1948–1962', *Diplomacy and Statecraft*, vol.24, no.2, pp.253–72.

Tampa, N. (1995), 'Starea de spirit din România la începutul anului 1945 [The Atmosphere in Romania at the Beginning of 1945],' *6 martie 1945. Începuturile Comunizării României*, (Bucharest: Editura Enciclopedică), pp.312–18.

Ţârău, V. (1994), 'Campania electorală şi rezultatul real al alegerilor din 19 noiembrie 1946 în judeţele Cluj, Someş şi Turda', in Sorin Mitu and Florin Gogâltan (eds.), *Studii de Istorie a Transilvaniei* (Cluj: Asociaţia Istoricilor din Transilvania şi Banat), pp.204–12.

Turcu, Liviu, (1992), 'Cum pot fi găsite conturile lui Ceauşescu', *Evenimentul Zilei*, 8 September.

Valev, E.B. (1964), 'Problemele dezvoltării economice a raioanelor dunărene din România, Bulgaria şi URSS', in *Viaţa economică*, Anul II, nr. 24 (43), pp.7–43.

Watts, Larry (2013), 'Romania Security Policy and the Cuban Missile Crisis', *Cold War International History Project, e-dossier no.38* (April 17).

Zhihua, Shen and Yafeng Xia (2009), 'New Evidence for China's Role in the Hungarian Crisis of October 1956: A Note', *The International History Review*, vol.31, no.3 (September), pp.558–75.

Index